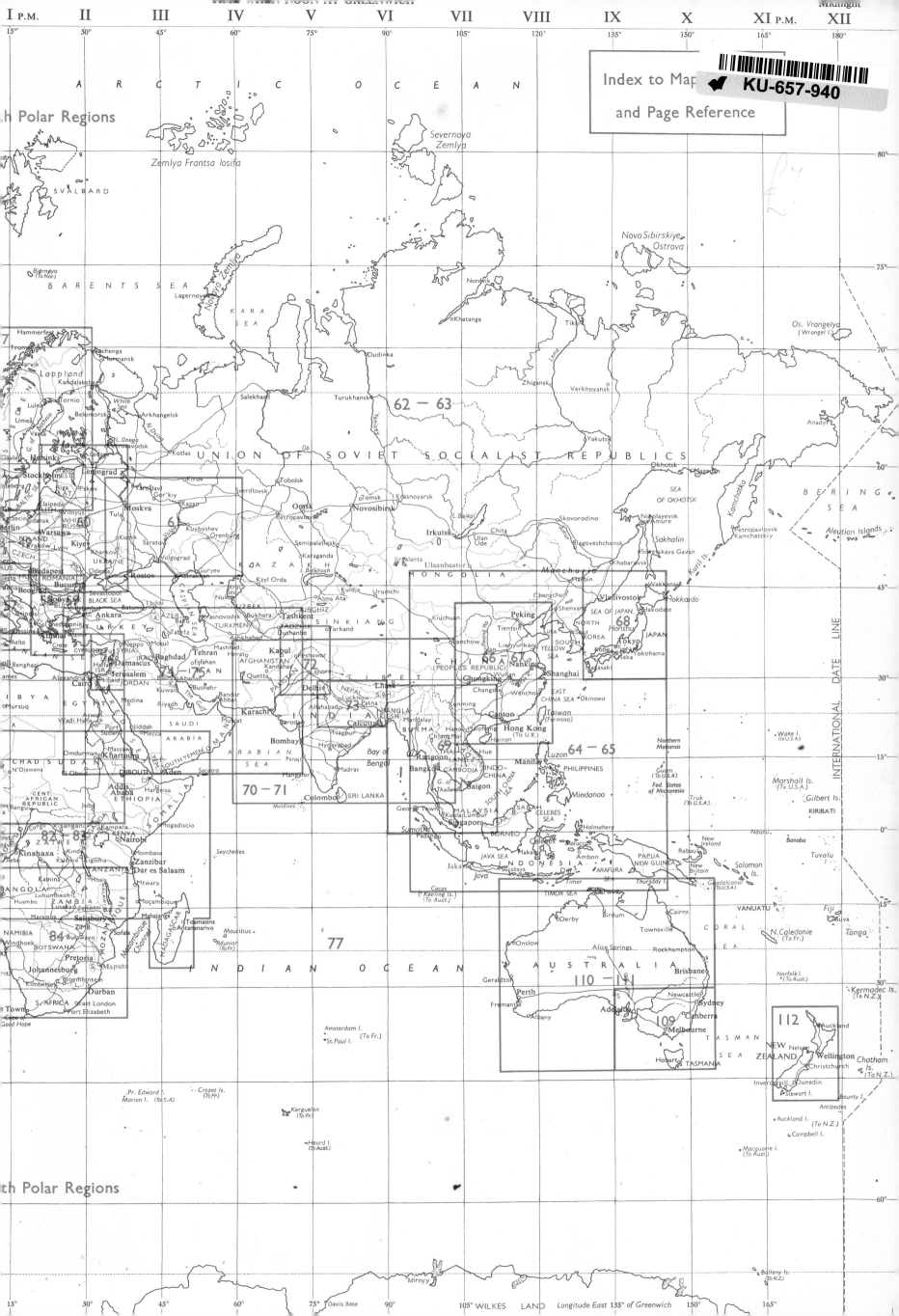

WORLD ATLAS

JOHN C. BARTHOLOMEW, M.A., F.·R.S.E.
DIRECTOR, THE GEOGRAPHICAL INSTITUTE, EDINBURGH

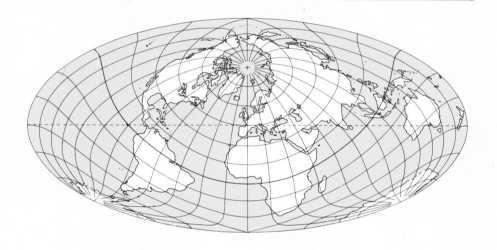

BOOK CLUB ASSOCIATES
LONDON

As Edinburgh World Atlas
First Edition – 1954
Eighth Edition – 1973

As The World Atlas
Ninth Edition – 1974
Tenth Edition – 1975
Eleventh Edition - 1977
Reprinted - 1979
Twelfth Edition - 1982

THIS EDITION PUBLISHED 1982 BY
BOOK CLUB ASSOCIATES
BY ARRANGEMENT WITH
JOHN BARTHOLOMEW & SON LTD
© 1982 JOHN BARTHOLOMEW & SON LTD
PRINTED IN GREAT BRITAIN
AT THE GEOGRAPHICAL INSTITUTE, EDINBURGH

FOREWORD

THIS Atlas, planned originally for academic purposes, has become so popular among general readers throughout the world, on account of its fresh scientific approach to many world problems, that it is now issued as a library and general reference atlas under the present modified title.

A humanistic viewpoint is given to all continental areas by showing density of population along with its vegetational, climatic and physical backgrounds. Special introductory maps show racial distinctions along with mineral and agricultural resources of the world.

Students of cartography will find matter of interest in the new projections employed. These to the number of four are designed to show more realistic relations of the inhabited land masses, as in the *Nordic* Projection on pages 22-23, which reveals the proximity of the Soviet Union to the United States; another, the *Regional* on pages 14-15, claims to show conformal properties (truth to shape) in the best manner possible; while another, the *Atlantis* on page 11, is ideal for displaying world air communications centred on the Atlantic Ocean.

Place-names are spelt on the most rational system possible, *viz.*, to conform with the local usage of the country in question; traditional or English forms are given in brackets where these are of sufficient importance.

A new form of co-ordinate system for the ready location of positions has been introduced and is explained on page 1; being related to time, it is known as the "Hour System".

THE GEOGRAPHICAL INSTITUTE,
EDINBURGH, July 1954.

JOHN BARTHOLOMEW.

PREFACE TO SEVENTH EDITION

Recent strides in the advancement of our knowledge of the earth and its resources are reflected in a series of new world maps illustrating structure, seismology, relief, continental drift, minerals, energy, food and soils. The British Isles likewise have a comparable series of new maps.

In conformity with the metrication of units of measurement, all temperature maps have been redrawn in degrees Celsius (°C) and spot heights have been altered from feet to metres.

JOHN C. BARTHOLOMEW

EDINBURGH, September 1970.

CONTENTS

The contraction " M " is used to denote scale of map in millionths.

PAGE

1 GEOGRAPHICAL CO-ORDINATES
2–3 GEOGRAPHICAL TERMS
4 CLIMATIC TABLES
5 STATES AND POPULATION
6 WORLD EXPLORATION (Old World)
7 WORLD EXPLORATION (New World)
8–9 MAP PROJECTIONS
10 MAP PROJECTIONS (modern)
11 WORLD AIRWAYS
12 ASTRONOMICAL CHARTS

THE WORLD

13 (a) STRUCTURE   1 : 130 M.
     (b) SEISMOLOGY   1 : 130 M.
14–15 PHYSIOGRAPHY   1 : 90 M.
     Drainage Regions, Continental Drift
16–17 TEMPERATURE AND AIR MOVEMENTS
     Air Pressure and Winds, January, July
     Temperature, January, July
     Air Masses and Fronts
     Storm Tracks
     Temperature Extremes
     Amount of Cloud
18–19 RAINFALL AND OCEANOGRAPHY
     Climatic Regions
     Length of Growing Seasons
20–21 ECONOMIC RESOURCES
     Minerals   Food
     Energy   Soils
22–23 ETHNOLOGY   1:140 M.
     Cephalic Index, Religions
24–25 STATES OF THE WORLD
     Changes of Sovereignty
     Time Zones
26 NORTH POLAR REGIONS   1 : 30 M.
     Temperature, January, July
27 SOUTH POLAR REGIONS   1 : 30 M.
     Temperature, January, July

EURASIA

28 VEGETATION   1 : 45 M.
     Rainfall, January, July
29 POPULATION   1 : 45 M.
     Temperature, January, July
30–31 EURASIA   1 : 30 M.
     Races

EUROPE

32–33 EUROPE   1 : 15 M.
34 NORTH–WEST EUROPE   1 : 10 M.
35 BRITISH ISLES   1 : 6 M.
     Geology
     Structure and
     Land Use
36   Climate
     Population
     Energy
     Industry   1 : 8 M.
37 NORTH ENGLAND   1 : 1¼ M.
     Isle of Man
38–39 SOUTH ENGLAND AND WALES   1 : 1¼ M.
     Channel Islands
40–41 SCOTLAND   1 : 1¼ M.
     Shetland, Fair Isle, St Kilda
42–43 IRELAND   1 : 1¼ M.
     Population
44 THE LOW COUNTRIES   1 : 1¼ M.
45 SWITZERLAND   1 : 1¼ M.
46–47 SCANDINAVIA AND THE BALTIC   1 : 4½ M.
     Iceland, The Faeroes
48–49 GERMANY, POLAND & CZECHOSLOVAKIA   1·3 M.
50–51 CENTRAL EUROPE & MEDITERRANEAN   1 : 10 M.
52–53 IBERIAN PENINSULA   1 : 3 M.
54–55 FRANCE AND NORTH ALGERIA   1 : 3 M.
     Corsica

PAGE

EUROPE—*continued*

56–57 ITALY AND THE ADRIATIC   1 : 3 M.
58–59 THE BALKANS AND LOWER DANUBE   1 : 3 M.
60 EUROPEAN RUSSIA   1 : 6 M.
61 VOLGA BASIN   1 : 6 M.

ASIA

62–63 SOVIET UNION   1 : 17½ M.
64–65 THE FAR EAST   1 : 15 M.
66–67 EAST CHINA   1 : 6 M.
68 JAPAN   1 : 6 M.
69 INDO-CHINA   1 : 10 M.
     Singapore
70–71 INDIA, PAKISTAN AND SRI LANKA   1 : 10 M.
     Races, Population, Religions
72 PUNJAB AND KASHMIR   1 : 4 M·
73 PLAIN OF THE GANGES   1 : 4 M.
74–75 THE MIDDLE EAST   1 : 10 M.
76 THE LEVANT COAST   1 : 2½ M.
77 INDIAN OCEAN   1 : 40 M.
     Islands

AFRICA

78 VEGETATION   1 : 35 M.
     Rainfall, January, July
79 POPULATION   1 : 35 M.
     Temperature, January, July
80–81 NORTH-WEST AFRICA   1 : 12½ M.
     Azores, Cape Verde
82–83 CENTRAL AND EAST AFRICA   1 : 12½ M.
     Ascension, St Helena, Madagascar
84 SOUTH AFRICA   1 : 12½ M.
     The Cape, Witwatersrand

NORTH AMERICA

85 ATLANTIC OCEAN   1 : 48 M.
86 VEGETATION   1 : 34 M.
     Rainfall, January, July
87 POPULATION   1 : 34 M.
     Temperature, January, July
88–89 CANADA   1 : 12½ M.
90 GULF OF ST LAWRENCE   1 : 5 M.
91 GREAT LAKES   1 : 5 M.
92 PACIFIC COAST   1 : 5 M.
93 NORTH CENTRAL STATES   1 : 5 M.
94–95 MIDDLE WEST STATES   1 : 5 M.
96 MIDDLE ATLANTIC STATES   1 : 2½ M.
97 SOUTHERN STATES   1 : 5 M.
98–99 UNITED STATES OF AMERICA   1 : 12½ M.
     Hawaiian Is., San Francisco,
     Alaska, New York
100 MEXICO   1 : 10 M.
101 THE CARIBBEAN   1 : 10 M.
     The Panama Canal

SOUTH AMERICA

102 VEGETATION   1 : 32 M.
     Rainfall, January, July
103 ARGENTINA AND CHILE   1 : 12½ M.
     South America Population
104–105 BRAZIL & NORTH ANDEAN STATES   1 : 12½ M.
     South America Temperature, Jan., July

AUSTRALASIA

106–107 PACIFIC OCEAN   1 : 45 M.
     Islands
108 VEGETATION   1 : 28 M.
     Temperature, January, July
     Rainfall, January, July
109 SOUTH-EAST AUSTRALIA   1 : 5 M.
     Tasmania
110–111 AUSTRALIA   1 : 12½ M.
     Population
112 NEW ZEALAND   1 : 5 M.
     Population

INDEX OF GEOGRAPHICAL NAMES

GEOGRAPHICAL CO-ORDINATES

THE most ancient function of geography has probably been to describe the location of places on the earth's surface. Thus it came about that early Greek philosophers, absorbed in conjectures as to the size and shape of the world they lived in, hit on the method of measuring its estimated circumference by 360 degrees to the circle. Any locality could then be determined by reference to a prime meridian and the number of degrees from the Equator. This method was adopted by Claudius Ptolemy of Alexandria in his tables and maps; and with modifications is much the same as the system of latitude and longitude in use to-day. That it should have survived so long is testimony of its efficiency, especially for navigational purposes. For more ordinary use, however, it is surprising that a simpler and more easily quoted system has not been adopted. True, there have been attempts in that direction. The circle has been divided into 100, which would help if all maps were so printed. More noteworthy are the systems of Military and National Grids, which served an

essential purpose during both World Wars. For civilian and international use, however, these grids stand at great disadvantage. Being imposed in right-angled pattern on a particular projection of limited area, they are not suitable for extending to other areas. For instance, a grid planned for Great Britain on Transverse Mercator's Projection would not at the same time be suitable for Germany. Moreover, unless the grid were printed on all maps in common use it would be of little service to the man-in-the-street.

To avoid these disadvantages, therefore, the system used in this atlas has been devised. It has the merit of being international. It is related to the World Grid, based on Greenwich, and can thus be used on any map, if necessary without being specially so printed. It avoids the confusing factor of reading east and west of a prime meridian. Its formula is compact and simple to understand. Finally, it is capable of infinite precision by the use of decimal subdivision.

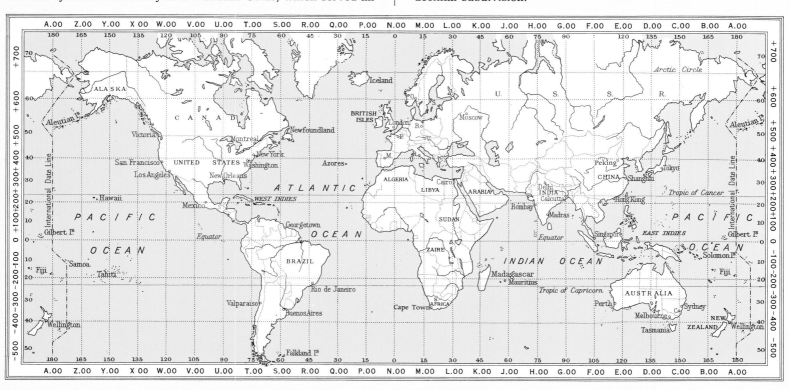

RULES FOR USE OF "HOUR" CO-ORDINATES

1. The World is divided into twenty-four *hour* zones, each of 15° longitude and denoted by a letter of the alphabet, omitting I and O which may be confused with numerals. Starting point of the **A** zone is the meridian 180° E. of Greenwich, associated with the International Date Line. All readings are made East to West, *i.e.*, with transit of the Sun, Greenwich being **N**.

2. Every *hour* zone of 15° is subdivided longitudinally, *i.e.*, by *Westings* into 90 units, reading likewise East to West. For greater precision these may be divided into further decimal parts. The units are marked in the top and bottom borders of each map.

   It will be found that 60 units *Westing* = 10° of longitude

06	,,	= 1°	,,
01	,,	= 10′	,,
001	,,	= 1′	,,
0001	,,	= 6″	,,

3. In the co-ordinate of latitude the quadrant from Equator to Pole is divided into 90 parts, each of which is then subdivided into 10 units.

   Thus 100 units *Northing* = 10° of latitude

010	,,	= 1°	,,
001	,,	= 6′	,,
0001	,,	= 36″	,,

   The coupling sign + or − marks this co-ordinate, meaning North or South respectively from the Equator. These *Northing* or *Southing* units are marked on the East and West sides of the Atlas maps. Further decimal subdivisions may also be used.

4. The complete co-ordinate is given by the *hour* figure or *Westing*, followed by the latitude figure or *Northing*,

   thus **M 89 + 522** = Cambridge, England
   and **T 12 + 389** = Washington, D.C.

   As the *hour* letter and the + or − are both treated as if they were decimal points, it is important to include the initial 0's so that all readings less than 10 should be written 05, 001, or as the case may be.

5. Readings apply to the space between the last digit given and the next digit; but, where greater precision on a larger scale is required, as in the case of the annexed One-Inch section of the English Lake District readings may be made to several places of decimals. Here the Church at Grasmere becomes **N 1813 + 54456**.

6. The above system, as used in this Atlas, is intended to assist travellers, writers, or scientific and commercial interests in their work. Free permission is accordingly given by the author for its use anywhere without restriction. It may be described as Bartholomew's Hour System of Geographical Co-ordinates.

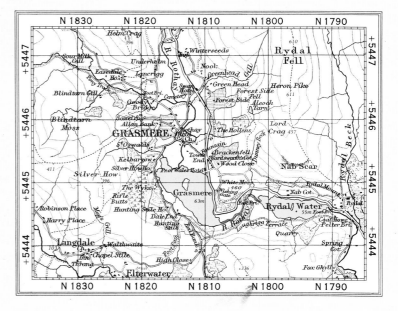

GEOGRAPHICAL TERMS

Abad *(Persian)*, town.
Aborigines, the earliest inhabitants of a country.
Ada *(Turkish)*, island.
Aiguille *(French)*, needle; applied to certain pinnacle-shaped mountain peaks.
Ain, Bir *(Arabic)*, a well or spring.
Ainu, a race inhabiting N. Hokkaido and S. Sakhalin.
Air Mass, an extensive body of air, moving or stationary, having throughout similar characteristics of temperature and humidity.
Akaba *(Arabic)*, pass.
Alf, älv, elf, elv *(Swedish* and *Norse)*, river.
Alluvium, fine sand or silt deposited, largely during flood periods, by streams and rivers.
Anticline, an arch of strata on both sides of which the rocks dip downwards.
Anticyclone, a high pressure system occurring in the zone of the "Westerlies", usually accompanied by fine weather. Wind tends to move outwards in clockwise direction in the Northern Hemisphere, anticlockwise in the Southern.
Antipodes, that part of the earth diametrically opposite to our feet, on the same meridian, but with latitude and seasons reversed, *e.g.* New Zealand is the antipodes of Great Britain.
Arctic Circle, constituted by the parallel 66°32′ N., separating North Temperate and North Frigid Zones. North of this at mid-summer the sun does not set during the 24 hours, while at mid-winter it does not rise. In the Southern Hemisphere the same conditions apply S. of the **Antarctic Circle,** 66°32′ S.
Artesian Well, a water supply obtained by tapping porous rock strata from which the water rises by natural pressure. Derived from Artois in France.
Atolls, circular coral reefs enclosing a central lagoon connected with the outside sea by an opening. Found mostly in the Pacific Ocean.
Avalanches, masses of loosened snow and ice mixed with earth and stone, precipitated with destructive force down mountain sides.
Axis, the imaginary line running from pole to pole through the centre of and on which the earth revolves.
Aztecs, the highly civilised dominant race in Mexico at the time of the Spanish invasion in 1519.
Bahia *(Portuguese* and *Spanish)*, bay.
Bahr *(Arabic)*, sea, lake, river.
Bal, Bally, Baile *(Celtic)*, town, village.
Ban *(Siamese)*, village.
Bandar, Nagar, Pura *(Indian)*, town.
Bantu, *i.e.*, "people"; correlated races of Africa between lat. 5° N. and 25° S. They include Xhosas and Zulus.
Bar, gravel, sand or mud deposited across the mouth of a river by currents or wave action; often impedes navigation.
Bas *(French)*, low, low-lying.
Basin, area of land drained by a river, and its tributaries.
Basin of Inland Drainage, an area of land which has no surface drainage outlet to the sea.
Basques, an ancient race with a distinct language inhabiting N.E. Spain and S.W. France, on the shores of the Bay of Biscay.
Basutos, a branch of the Bantu race occupying Lesotho.
Batang *(Malay)*, river.
Beaches, Raised, small platforms of land, formerly sea shore, now left dry through a rise of the land level.
Beaufort Scale, a scale of 13 symbols used in weather maps to portray the force of the wind from calm to more than 120 kilometres per hour.
Bedouins, nomadic tribes of Arabia and North Africa.
Beled *(Arabic)*, country, village.
Ben, Beinn *(Celtic)*, mountain.
Bender *(Persian)*, harbour, landing-place.
Black Earth, fertile soil in S. Russia and parts of Romania and Hungary on which heavy grain crops are grown.
Boers, descendants of the early Dutch colonists in South Africa.
Bora, a cold, dry, northerly wind, blowing in winter and spring along the Dalmatian coast of the Adriatic Sea.
Bore or **Eagre,** a tidal wave arising in the estuaries of certain rivers.
Boulder Clay, a glacial deposit, consisting of boulders of various sizes embedded in finer material, laid down under a glacier or ice cap and often found to great depths in glaciated valleys.
Brdo *(Czech.)*, a hill.
Brunn *(German)*, a spring, well.
Bugt, Bukt *(Danish* and *Swedish)*, a bay.
Buran, snow blizzards of winter occuring in Russia and Siberia.
Burun *(Turkish)*, a headland, promontory.
Bush, The, interior uncultivated scrubland.
Bushmen, or in Afrikaans **Boesmanne** an aboriginal Negrito nomadic race of south central Africa, now mostly in the Kalahari desert.
Butte *(French* and *Amer.)*, an isolated hill or peak.
Cabo *(Portuguese* and *Spanish)*, a cape.
Campo *(Italian* and *Spanish)*, a plain.
Campos, grasslands of S.E. Brazil.
Cañan or Canyon *(Spanish)*, a deep gorge or ravine with lofty sides. Formed by rapid erosion of the softer strata in a dry region, *e.g.*, Colorado Canon.
Catingas, open forest lands on the plateaux of Eastern Brazil, north of 15° S. Drier and warmer than the adjoining **Cerrados**; they contain cactus, mimosa and other types of dry vegetation.
Cephalic Index, the shape of the head expressed by a number which is obtained by giving the breadth of the head as a percentage of its length.
Cerrados, semi-dry plateaux of S.E. Brazil covered with grass and trees of stunted growth.
Chart, map of the sea for use of navigators.
Chinook, a warm, dry west wind blowing down the east slopes of the Rocky Mountains.
Chotts, *see* Shotts.
Chow *(Chinese)*, town of the second rank.
Chrebet *(Russian)*, a chain; mountain range.
Cidade *(Portuguese)*, town.
Cima, Pizzo *(Italian)*, mountain peak.
Cirrus Clouds, very lofty (eight to ten kilometres high) fibrous looking clouds, associated with fine weather.
Città *(Italian)*, town, city.
Ciudad *(Spanish)*, city, town.
Climate, the generalisation of day to day weather conditions.
Col *(French)*, **Colle** *(Italian)*, a pass or neck.
Cold Front, the sloping boundary between an advancing mass of cold air and warmer air under which the cold air forms a wedge.
Continental Shelf, a sea-covered platform extending from the coast-line of all continents. It varies in width and the edge is usually marked by the isobath for 200 metres.
Contour, a line on a map joining all points which are situated at the same height above sea-level.
Cordillera *(Spanish)*, mountain range.
Crater, the cup-shaped cavity forming the mouth of a volcano.
Creek *(Amer.)*, a stream or small river.
Crevasse, rent or fissure in a glacier or ice sheet.
Cumulus Clouds, massive rounded clouds (approx. 1500 metres high), associated with hot weather and rising air-currents.
Cycle of Erosion, the development of the landscape by the various processes of denudation from the youthful stage, after a period of instability and mountain building, through maturity till the surface is reduced to a peneplane.
Cyclone, a low pressure system, or **depression,** generally associated with stormy or wet weather. Winds tend to blow inwards in anti-clockwise direction in N. Hemisphere; clockwise in South.
Daban *(Mongolian)*, a pass.
Dagh *(Turkish)*, mountain.
Dake, Take *(Japanese)*, mountain.
Dal *(Norwegian, Swedish)*, valley.
Darya *(Persian)*, sea, stream, river.
Date Line, this follows approximately the 180° meridian from Greenwich, and marks the point where according to international convention the day begins. A ship crossing this line eastwards goes back a day, while westward it goes forward a day.
Declination, the deviation of the compass needle from True North.
Delta, a triangular or finger-shaped tract of mud and detritus deposited by a river at its mouth when it no longer has sufficient speed to keep them in suspension.
Denudation, the slow process of laying bare and levelling down the physical features of the earth's surface by natural forces.
Depression, a localised and mobile low pressure system occuring in the zone of the "Westerlies" associated with rain and stormy weather.
Derbend *(Persian, Turkish)*, pass.
Desert, a barren area of land, practically devoid of rainfall or vegetation.
Dip, the angle between the downward slope of a stratum of rock and the horizontal.
Dogger Bank, important fishing ground in North Sea, depth varies from 11 to 36 metres.
Doldrums, nautical term for a region of calms and baffling winds near the equator between the N.E. and S.E. Trade Winds.
Dolina *(Slav.)*, a large hollow or basin caused by the dissolving of limestone. Cultivated if not occupied by a pond.
Donga *(Afrikaans)*, ravine, gulley.
Dorp *(Dutch)*, **Dorf** *(German)*, village.
Dunes, mounds formed by wind-blown sand; capable of considerable advances over level ground unless arrested by the planting of suitable vegetation.
Earthquake, disturbance of the earth's surface generally occuring along faults or lines of weakness in the earth's crust. Sometimes cause great destruction, especially on alluvial ground.
Eiland *(Dutch)*' island.
Ennis *(Irish)*, island.
Equator, imaginary line circumscribing the globe midway between the poles and at its greatest circumference (40 074.72 km). It constitutes the zero from which latitudes N. and S. are calculated.
Equinox, one of the two periods of the year when day and night are of equal duration owing to the sun's crossing the Equator. 20th March and 22nd September.
Erosion, the wearing away of surface features of the earth by the action of wind, water or ice.
Escarpment, the steep face of a hill or range which on the other side slopes gently downwards *e.g.*, Cotswold and Chiltern escarpments.
Eskimos or **Esquimaux,** an aboriginal race inhabiting the Arctic coasts of America, especially of Greenland and Alaska. They live chiefly by fishing.
Estuary, the lower reaches of a river affected by the tides.
Falu *(Hungarian)*, village.
Fault, a break or crack in the earth's surface.
Fell *(Norwegian*, **Fjeld**; *Swedish*, **Fjäll**), mountain.
Fen *(Anglo-Saxon)*, swampy or boggy land.
Fiume *(Italian)*, river.
Fjord, old glacial valley filled by the sea. Sides often steepened by faulting.
Flood Plain, the generally flat area in the bottom of a valley which is covered by water when the river draining it is in flood.
Föhn, a dry warm wind in the valleys of the Alps, blowing in winter from the south.
Fork, the junction of two streams or rivers of approximately the same size.
Fu *(Chinese)*, town of importance.
Ganga *(Indian)*, river.
Gap, *see* **Pass.**
Gawa, Kawa *(Japanese)*, river.
Gebel, Jebel *(Arabic)*, rock, mountain.
Geysers, intermittent spouting hot springs associated with volcanic activity as in Iceland.
Glaciers, rivers of ice originating in snowfields, and moving slowly down valleys until they melt, or on reaching the sea break off as icebergs.
Gol, Song *(Mongolian)*, river.
Gora *(Slav.)*, mountain.
Gorod, Grad *(Slav.)*, town.
Gran Chaco, "the great hunting place", is an extensive area between Argentina, Bolivia and Paraguay consisting for the most part of swampy plains with varied vegetation; rich in animal and bird life.
Grand Banks, submarine banks situated south-east of Newfoundland. One of the best cod fishing grounds in the world.
Great Circle, a circle on the earth's surface whose plane passes through the centre of the earth.
Great Circle Route, shortest distance between two points on the earth, hence used for preference by shipping and air services.
Growing Season, that part of the year during which plant growth is possible. The main factors limiting the length of the period are the occurrence of killing frosts and drought.
Guba *(Russian)*, bay.
Gulch *(Amer.)*, a narrow, deep ravine.
Gulf Stream, great warm water current originating in the Gulf of Mexico and flowing across the Atlantic to North-West Europe.
Gunung *(Malay)*, mountain.
Hachures, closely drawn lines sometimes used on maps to denote ground relief. They should follow the direction of slope and vary in intensity with the gradient.
Haf *(Swedish)*, sea.
Hai, Hu *(Chinese)*, sea or lake.
Hamn *(Swedish)*, harbour.
Harmattan, a hot dry wind laden with clouds of reddish dust from the desert blowing over the Guinea Lands in December, January and February. It is an extension of the N.E. Trade wind.
Havn *(Danish)*, harbour.
Havre *(French)*, harbour, port.
Hegy *(Hungarian)*, mountain.
Height of Land *(Amer.)*, a watershed or divide.
Hinterland, region inland from a coast. Often deciding factor in location or growth of a port.
Ho *(Chinese)*, river.
Hoek *(Dutch)*, cape.
Höhe *(German)*, height, hill.
Horse Latitudes, regions of calms and variable winds between 25° and 40° N. and S. on the polar margins of the Trade Winds.
Horst, a block of rock left upstanding by the down faulting of rocks on either side. Exact opposite of rift valley.
Hottentots, an indigenous race in western South Africa.
Hsi *(Chinese)*, west.
Hsien *(Chinese)*, town of the third class.
Humidity, the amount of water vapour in the air. Relative Humidity is percentage of moisture contained as compared with that contained in air completely saturated at the given temperature.
Hurricane or **Typhoon,** a violent and destructive tropical cyclone which occasionally blows in the Gulf of Mexico and the China Seas (where it is known as Typhoon) in August, September or October.
Icebergs, detached masses of ice floating in the Polar Seas, carried along by ocean currents. Originate from glaciers, terminating in the sea. Danger to navigation in Atlantic.
Inch, Innis *(Celtic)*, island.

Irmak *(Turkish)*, river.

Isla *(Spanish)*, **Isola** *(Italian)*, island.

Isobars, lines connecting points having the same barometric pressure at a given time.

Isobaths, lines connecting points of the ocean of equal depths.

Isohyets, lines connecting points with equal rainfall over given period.

Isotherms, lines connecting points of equal temperature at a given time.

Jaur, Javr, Järvi *(Finnish)*, lake.

Jesero *(Serbian)*, lake.

Joch *(German)*, mountain ridge; pass.

Joki *(Finnish)*, river.

Jug *(Serbian)*, **Yug** *(Russian)*, south.

Kahli *(Arabic)*, desert.

Kampong *(Malay)*, village.

Karroos, terraced plains between the mountains in South Africa. Desert in dry season, but develop vegetation in wet season and are used as sheep pasture.

Karst, the porous limestone region of the Dinaric Alps north-east of Adriatic Sea. Also applied to similar types of country in other lands where the river system disappears underground.

Kato *(Greek)*, under.

Khamsin *(Arabic)*, "Fifty"), name given to Sirocco in Lower Egypt where it blows for fifty days between April and June.

Kiang *(Chinese)*, river.

Koppie *(S. African)*, a small hill.

Kraal, a native dwelling in South Africa.

Kuh *(Persian)*, mountain.

Kul *(Turkish)*, lake.

Kum or **Qum** *(Turkish)*, sand.

La *(Tibetan)*, pass.

Lac *(French)*, **Lacul** *(Romanian)*, lake.

Lago *(Italian, Portuguese, Spanish)*, lake.

Lande *(French)*, heath or waste land.

Latitude, the angular distance of a place N. or S. of the equator measured on its meridian. Each degree represents sixty geographical or nautical miles equal to 69.172 statute miles (111.319 km).

Levante *(Italian)*, east.

Levees, embankments, natural or artificial, erected along the banks of rivers and built, as on the Mississippi, to prevent flooding.

Llanos, grasslands of the N.W. Orinoco Basin.

Loch, Lough *(Celtic)*, lake.

Loess, a post glacial wind-blown soil of great fertility; found in N. European Plain and in the Hwang Ho Valley of China.

Long Forties, a portion of the North Sea, so known to fishermen because the depth of water approximates 40 fathoms (73 metres).

Longitude, the angular distance of any place on the globe eastward or westward from a standard meridian, as in Great Britain that of Greenwich. Each degree of longitude represents 4 minutes of time, so that 15° of longitude represent an hour.

Magyars, native name of Hungarians.

Mallee, type of Australian scrub growing in the Murray-Darling and other areas. It is characterised by low-growing eucalyptus and other gum trees.

Maoris, the aboriginal inhabitants of New Zealand.

Marais *(French)*, marsh.

Mean Annual Rainfall, the average amount of rain which falls in a year. The average is deduced from observations taken over a considerable period.

Meander, the winding about of a river in its flood plain when it has reached its base line of erosion but still has energy for further erosion.

Medine *(Arabic)*, town.

Mer *(French)*, **Meer** *(German)*, sea.

Meridian, an imaginary line represented by a portion of a circle passing through the earth's two poles and on which all places have noon at the same time.

Miasto *(Polish)*, village.

Mile (geographical) = 1 minute of latitude, or 6080 feet (1.15 statute miles)(1.9 kilometres).

Millibar, a standard unit of barometric pressure. Average pressure is approximately 1013 millibars or 76 cms of mercury.

Mistral, a violent, dry, cold wind blowing in winter down the Rhône Valley which acts as a funnel when a depression lies over the Mediterranean.

Monsoon, seasonal winds blowing over the S.E. half of Asia. General direction October to March from N.E., April to September from S.W.

Mont *(French)*, **Monte** *(Italian)*, mount.

Monte, a type of deciduous hardwood forest situated in the higher portions of the **Gran Chaco**, moister than **Cerrados**.

Montagna *(Italian)*, mountain range.

Moraine, the waste material deposited by a glacier.

More *(Russian)*, sea.

Muang *(Siamese)*, town.

Myo *(Burmese)*, town.

Nagar *(Indian)*, town.

Nahr *(Arabic)*, river.

Nam *(Siamese)*, river.

Nan *(Chinese)*, south.

Näs *(Scandinavian)*, cape.

Natural Scale, *see* Representative Fraction.

Neap-Tides, period of lowest tide-range, when sun and moon are at right angles, as seen from the earth.

Negeri *(Malay)*, town.

Nejd *(Arabic)*, high plain.

Nimbus, dark water-laden rain cloud.

Nor *(Mongol.)*, lake.

Nos *(Russian)*, cape.

Oasis, fertile spot in a desert owing its existence to a spring or well.

Occluded Front, a line along which warm air of the atmosphere has been raised from the earth's surface by the junction of cold and warm fronts.

Ola *(Mongolian)*, mountain range.

Oxbow Lake, remains of a pronounced meander which has been short circuited by the river cutting through its neck. They occur on a river like the Mississippi.

Ozero *(Russian)*, lake.

Pack Ice, sea ice which has drifted from its original position. It takes the form of floes of various sizes and can be either loosely or tightly packed together.

Pampa *(Argentina)*, dreary expanse of treeless grass plain, and salt steppe, lat. 30° to 40° S., between the Andes and the Atlantic Ocean.

Pampero, a cold south-westerly wind that sweeps over the pampas in Central South America.

Pass, a depression or **Gap** in a mountain range which serves as way for communication between the lands on either side.

Peneplane, the almost level surface which, if the normal course of denudation is undisturbed, results from the erosion of a landscape by running water. The gradient of a river draining a peneplane is just great enough for the flow of water to be maintained.

Pizzo *(Italian)*, peak.

Plain, an area of flat or undulating ground usually at low level.

Planina *(Bulg., Serb.)*, mountain range.

Plateau, an area of relatively flat ground at considerable attitude, sometimes called a Tableland.

Polder, land recovered from the sea in Holland, and protected by dykes from being again flooded.

Ponente *(Italian)*, evening, west.

Pont, Ponte *(French, Span., Italian)*, bridge.

Potomos *(Greek)*, river.

Prairie, a series of grassy plains stretching eastwards from the Rocky Mountains in Canada and U.S.A.

Primeval Forest, a forest which has not been interfered with by man and is allowed to remain in its natural state.

Pristan *(Russian)*, port, harbour.

Projection, is the process of transferring the outline of the features on the earth's spherical surface on to a flat surface, thus constituting a map.

Pueblo *(Spanish)*, village.

Pulau *(Malay)*, island.

Puna, a high plateau between the E. and W. Andes in Bolivia and Peru.

Pur, Pura *(Indian)*, town.

Ras *(Arabic)*, cape.

Reef, a ridge of rock or coral generally covered by sea, but exposed at low tide.

Representative Fraction, a fraction representing a distance of unit lengths on a map over its corresponding length on the earth's surface.

Ria, river valley drowned by the sea owing to a fall in the land level.

Rieka *(Slav.)*, river.

Rift Valley, valley with steep walls caused by the sinking of land between two parallel geological faults.

Rio *(Portuguese, Spanish)*, river.

River Capture, process by which one river having more rapid powers of erosion than another cuts into the head waters of the latter and steals certain of its tributaries.

Riviera, narrow strip of sea coast between Toulon and Spezia, noted for mild climate in winter.

Roaring Forties, nautical name of steady northwesterly winds between lat. 40° and 60° S. Equivalent to Westerlies of N. Hemisphere.

Ross *(Celtic)*, promontory.

Saki *(Japanese)*, cape.

Sargasso Sea, an area of calms and floating seaweed in the N. Atlantic, east of the Bahamas and the Antilles Current.

Savannas, grasslands of the sub-tropics.

Sea Level, the mean level of the sea between high and low tide.

Selo *(Russian)*, village.

Selva *(Portuguese)*, forest. The name of Selvas is given to the vast rain forests of the Amazon basin.

Shan *(Chinese)*, mountain range.

Shotts *(Arabic)*, salt marshy lakes of N. Algeria and Tunisia.

Sierra *(Spanish)*, **Serra** *(Portuguese)*, mountain range.

Silt, material, finer than sand, which is often carried in suspension by rivers and deposited by them, on flood plains and deltas, when the river has lost the force required to hold the load.

Sirocco, a hot southerly wind blowing off Africa in Southern Mediterranean Countries.

Sjö *(Swedish)*, lake.

Slieve *(Irish)*, mountain.

Snow Line, the lower limit in altitude of the region which is never free from snow.

Spring Tides, period of highest tides at new or at full moon time, *i.e.* when sun and moon are pulling in line with the earth.

Stad, Stadt *(Dutch, Swedish, German)*, town.

Steppe, large expanses of grassland as in European Russia and S.W. Siberia.

Strath *(Celtic)*, broad valley of a river.

Stratus, cloud in the form of a level or horizontal sheet.

Sudd, large floating islands of vegetable matter which impede navigation on the Upper White Nile.

Syd *(Danish-Norwegian)*, south.

Sziget *(Hungarian)*, island.

Taiga, coniferous forest belt south of the Tundra, chiefly used for hunting.

Tanjong *(Malay)*, cape.

Tind *(Norwegian)*, peak.

Trade Winds, regular steady winds in the tropics, between latitudes 30° N. and 30° S. blowing to the equator, from N.E. in N. Hemisphere and S.E. in Southern.

Tributary, a river or stream which flows into and thus becomes part of a larger river.

Tropics, the parallels 23½° N., **Tropic of Cancer**, and 23½° S., **Tropic of Capricorn**, are "turning points" in the apparent seasonal movements of the sun. On June 22nd at noon it is vertically over all points on the Northern Tropic, on December 22nd at noon it is vertically over all points on the Southern Tropic.

Tundra, treeless plains along Arctic and Antarctic coasts; hard frozen in winter, and only partly thawed in summer; scanty vegetation of lichens and mosses.

Tung *(Chinese)*, east.

Ula *(Mongol.)*, mountain.

Vatn *(Norwegian)*, lake.

Veld, grassy plain in South Africa.

Volcano, a vent in the earth's crust through which molten rock, ashes and steam are ejected from the hot interior.

Wadi, Oued *(Arabic)*, a water-course.

Wallace's Line, an imaginary line dividing the characteristic flora and fauna of Asia from that of Australasia. It passes between the islands of Bali and Lombok, thence through the Strait of Macassar between Borneo and Celebes and south of the Philippine Islands. Named after Alfred Russel Wallace the noted scientist.

Warm Front, the sloping boundary in the atmosphere between an advancing mass of warm air and colder air over which the warm air rises.

Watershed, the land-form separating head streams of two river systems. Also known as **waterparting** or **divide**.

Westerlies, predominantly westerly winds in the northern and southern hemispheres N. of 30° N. and S. of 30° S.

Zee *(Dutch)*, sea.

CLIMATIC TABLES

A selection of characteristic stations in different parts of the world, giving Mean Temperature in degrees Celsius (°C),
and Mean Rainfall in millimetres for each month of the year.

Climatic Type	Station	Lat.	Alt in m.		Jan.	Feb.	Mar.	April	May	June	July	Aug.	Sept.	Oct.	Nov.	Dec.	Year
SUB-POLAR	Nome, Alaska	64.30N	7	°C	−17.1	−14.6	−13.2	−8.2	1.3	7.1	10.1	9.7	5.1	−1.7	−9.8	−14.3	−3.8
				mm	25	28	23	15	23	30	74	76	58	38	25	28	445
	North Cape, Norway	71.6 N	6	°C	−3.6	−4.2	−3.4	−0.3	2.8	6.8	9.9	10.0	6.6	2.1	−1.1	−2.9	1.9
				mm	58	61	58	46	48	46	66	58	84	76	74	66	747
WEST MARITIME	Stanley Harbour, Falkland Is.	51.41s	2	°C	9.7	9.8	8.6	6.7	4.7	3.1	2.6	3.0	4.1	5.3	6.8	8.3	6.1
				mm	71	58	56	61	76	61	56	53	33	38	53	71	686
	Ben Nevis, Scotland	56.48N	1344	°C	−4.4	−4.6	−4.5	−2.3	0.7	4.2	4.7	4.4	3.3	−0.8	−2.0	−3.9	−0.5
				mm	480	340	391	221	196	193	279	348	394	386	399	478	4105
	Christchurch, N.Z.	43.31s	6	°C	16.3	15.9	14.5	11.9	8.8	6.4	5.9	6.8	9.4	11.7	13.6	15.7	11.4
				mm	56	46	53	51	66	71	46	46	41	41	46	51	640
	Edinburgh, Scotland	55.55N	80	°C	3.9	4.2	5.2	7.4	10.1	13.2	14.8	14.6	12.6	9.2	6.3	4.4	8.8
				mm	43	41	48	36	51	48	69	79	51	66	53	53	635
	Paris, France	48.50N	50	°C	2.5	3.9	6.2	10.3	13.4	16.9	18.6	18.0	15.0	10.3	6.0	2.9	10.3
				mm	36	28	36	38	48	53	51	48	53	48	41		528
	Valdivia, Chile	39.46s	43	°C	15.3	14.9	13.7	11.9	10.8	9.2	7.8	7.9	9.6	10.6	11.8	13.7	11.4
				mm	74	81	163	236	389	445	391	343	185	127	112	122	2667
	Valentia, Ireland	51.56N	9	°C	6.9	6.8	7.2	8.9	11.1	13.7	14.9	14.9	13.7	10.8	8.6	7.5	10.4
				mm	140	132	114	94	79	81	97	122	104	142	140	165	1415
	Victoria, B.C.	48.24N	26	°C	3.8	4.6	6.3	8.8	11.6	13.9	15.7	15.4	13.3	10.2	6.9	5.1	9.6
				mm	117	81	64	41	30	23	10	15	46	64	147	147	787
SEMI-CONTINENTAL	Chicago, Illinois	41.53N	251	°C	−3.6	−2.8	2.6	8.6	14.7	20.0	23.3	22.7	19.1	12.7	5.3	−0.9	10.1
				mm	53	53	66	74	91	84	86	76	79	66	61	53	841
	Nashville, Tennessee	36.10N	175	°C	3.8	4.9	9.7	14.9	20.2	24.4	26.1	25.3	22.2	15.8	9.4	5.1	15.2
				mm	119	107	130	112	97	107	104	89	89	61	89	99	1204
	Warsaw, Poland	52.13N	119	°C	−3.1	−1.9	1.8	7.9	14.1	17.2	18.8	17.5	13.5	7.9	2.2	−1.2	7.9
				mm	33	25	33	41	51	61	86	66	46	41	36	36	478
COLD CONTINENTAL	Moscow, U.S.S.R.	55.50N	146	°C	−10.8	−9.0	−4.3	3.4	11.8	15.6	18.0	15.8	9.7	3.7	−2.8	−7.9	3.6
				mm	33	30	36	36	46	66	81	79	53	53	46	41	599
	Verkhoyansk, U.S.S.R.	67.33N	101	°C	−50.5	−44.0	−31.0	−13.3	1.6	13.1	15.6	10.0	1.9	−15.0	−36.5	−46.4	−16.2
				mm	5	3	0	3	5	13	30	23	5	5	5	5	99
	Winnipeg, Manitoba	49.53N	232	°C	−15.6	−17.7	−9.4	3.2	11.1	16.8	19.1	17.7	12.1	4.8	−5.9	−14.5	1.4
				mm	23	18	30	36	51	79	79	56	56	36	28	23	513
EAST MARITIME	Miyako, Japan	39.38N	30	°C	−0.6	−0.3	2.6	8.2	12.3	16.0	19.9	22.1	18.5	12.6	7.2	2.2	10.0
				mm	69	66	89	99	119	127	135	178	216	170	81	64	1412
	St John's, Newfoundland	47.34N	38	°C	−4.7	−5.3	−2.4	1.6	6.1	10.6	15.2	15.4	12.1	7.4	2.8	−1.7	4.8
				mm	137	127	117	109	91	91	97	94	97	137	152	137	1382
PRAIRIE STEPPE	Bahia Blanca, Argentina	38.43s	15	°C	23.2	22.2	19.4	15.3	11.5	8.4	8.1	9.4	12.2	14.9	18.6	21.7	15.4
				mm	51	56	66	56	30	23	25	41	58	51	53		533
	Calgary, Alberta	51.2 N	1033	°C	−10.9	−9.2	−3.7	4.6	9.5	13.5	16.2	15.2	10.4	5.4	−2.4	−7.0	3.4
				mm	13	15	18	20	58	74	66	64	33	18	18	13	401
	Semipalatinsk, U.S.S.R.	50.26N	180	°C	−17.5	−16.8	−9.8	3.5	14.0	20.0	22.2	19.6	12.7	3.4	−6.6	−14.4	2.5
				mm	13	5	10	10	20	23	28	10	15	15	15	20	185
MANCHURIAN	Peking, China	39.55N	40	°C	−4.7	−1.5	5.0	13.7	19.9	24.5	26.0	24.7	19.8	12.5	3.6	−2.6	11.7
				mm	3	5	5	15	36	76	239	160	66	15	8	3	632
HUMID TEMPERATE	Brisbane, Australia	27.28s	42	°C	25.1	24.7	23.5	21.3	18.1	15.7	14.7	15.8	18.5	21.0	23.1	24.7	20.5
				mm	160	157	142	91	71	66	58	53	53	66	94	122	1135
	Charleston, S. Carolina	32.47N	15	°C	9.9	10.7	14.2	17.7	22.3	25.6	27.0	26.7	24.6	19.4	14.3	10.6	18.6
				mm	79	84	86	74	86	122	180	168	127	91	61	74	1229
	Wuhan, China	30.35N	36	°C	3.8	4.5	9.6	16.2	21.7	25.7	28.6	28.5	24.4	18.2	12.1	6.3	16.6
				mm	53	28	71	122	127	178	218	117	56	99	28	15	1113
MEDITERRANEAN	Adelaide, Australia	34.55s	43	°C	23.4	23.3	21.1	17.8	14.3	11.9	10.8	12.1	13.9	16.6	19.4	21.7	17.2
				mm	20	15	28	46	71	76	66	61	46	46	25	20	521
	Athens, Greece	37.58N	107	°C	9.1	9.7	11.3	14.8	19.1	23.5	26.7	26.4	22.9	18.9	14.1	11.2	17.4
				mm	53	43	30	23	20	18	8	13	18	41	66	66	394
	Gibraltar	36.6 N	15	°C	12.8	13.3	14.1	15.9	18.2	20.8	23.0	23.8	22.2	18.7	15.8	13.4	17.6
				mm	130	107	122	69	43	13	0	3	36	84	163	140	897
	Marseilles, France	43.18N	75	°C	6.9	7.9	10.0	12.8	16.3	19.7	22.2	21.3	19.4	14.8	10.6	7.6	14.1
				mm	41	38	48	56	43	28	18	20	61	97	71	53	574
	Sacramento, California	38.35N	22	°C	8.1	10.2	12.6	14.7	18.0	21.6	22.9	22.3	20.6	16.0	11.6	8.4	15.6
				mm	97	71	71	38	18	3	0	0	8	20	48	97	472
SEMI-ARID	Alice Springs, Australia	23.38s	587	°C	28.5	27.8	24.8	20.1	15.4	12.4	11.4	14.7	18.6	22.9	26.1	27.9	20.9
				mm	46	43	30	20	18	15	10	10	10	18	25	41	284
	Denver, Colorado	39.45N	1613	°C	−1.2	−0.2	3.8	8.6	13.7	19.6	22.3	21.6	16.9	10.3	4.0	−0.2	9.9
				mm	10	13	25	53	61	36	46	36	25	25	15	18	363
	Kabul, Afghanistan	34.35N	1905	°C	−0.7	2.1	8.2	14.9	20.0	22.9	24.8	24.2	20.4	14.6	10.4	4.7	13.9
				mm	25	20	119	56	15	5	5	0	3	25	5		284
	Karachi, Pakistan	24.51N	4	°C	18.5	20.2	23.9	27.0	29.3	30.4	29.1	28.0	27.8	26.7	23.3	19.7	25.3
				mm	15	10	8	3	8	18	71	43	15	0	3	3	188
	Madrid, Spain	40.24N	655	°C	4.6	6.5	8.7	12.2	16.1	20.8	25.1	24.8	19.6	13.4	8.4	5.0	13.7
				mm	33	33	41	41	43	33	10	38	46	51	41		422
	Tombouctou, Mali	16.37N	250	°C	21.7	23.1	28.4	33.1	34.7	34.3	31.8	30.3	31.8	31.6	27.1	21.7	29.1
				mm	0	0	3	0	8	23	89	71	28	10	0	0	229
DESERT	Esfahān, Iran	32.40N	1773	°C	1.2	5.3	9.4	15.6	20.7	25.2	27.8	25.6	22.4	16.1	9.1	4.4	15.2
				mm	18	13	23	15	5	0	0	0	0	3	15	23	114
	Swakopmund, Namibia	22.40s	6	°C	17.0	17.3	17.4	15.5	15.9	14.7	13.6	12.7	13.4	14.5	14.8	16.4	15.2
				mm	0	3	5	0	0	0	0	0	0	3	0	5	18
	Yuma, Arizona	32.45N	43	°C	12.6	15.1	18.1	21.2	24.9	29.3	32.7	32.3	28.8	22.4	16.1	13.2	22.3
				mm	13	10	8	3	0	0	5	15	8	5	8	10	84
DRY TROPICAL	Bombay, India	18.55N	11	°C	24.2	24.3	26.4	28.4	29.9	28.9	27.4	27.1	27.2	28.0	27.0	25.2	27.0
				mm	3	0	3	0	18	523	693	406	300	61	10	0	2017
	Cuyaba, Brazil	15.36s	165	°C	27.2	27.1	27.1	26.8	25.3	24.1	24.4	25.7	27.8	27.6	27.8	28.4	26.4
				mm	251	211	211	102	53	5	5	30	51	114	152	206	1389
	Darwin, N. Australia	12.28s	30	°C	28.8	28.6	28.9	28.9	27.7	26.1	25.2	26.3	28.1	29.6	29.9	29.5	28.1
				mm	404	330	257	104	18	3	3	3	13	56	122	262	1570
	Manila, Philippines	14.35N	14	°C	24.8	25.3	26.6	28.1	28.6	27.8	27.1	27.1	26.8	26.6	25.8	25.1	26.5
				mm	20	10	20	33	114	234	439	406	363	170	132	76	2032
	Veracruz, Mexico	19.10N	15	°C	21.9	22.9	23.8	26.1	27.2	27.5	27.6	27.7	26.9	24.7	23.8	21.6	25.2
				mm	10	15	15	3	109	318	376	226	295	229	81	51	1727
WET TROPICAL	Georgetown, Guyana	6.50N	23	°C	25.8	25.8	26.1	26.4	26.3	26.0	26.1	26.5	27.2	27.3	26.9	26.1	26.4
				mm	201	117	183	152	282	297	251	165	79	79	170	282	2253
	Lagos, Nigeria	6.27N	8	°C	27.2	27.9	28.5	28.1	27.7	26.3	25.6	25.4	25.8	26.4	27.4	27.5	26.9
				mm	28	46	94	147	267	472	279	71	135	196	66	20	1819
	Singapore	1.24N	3	°C	25.7	26.1	26.8	27.1	27.5	27.3	27.2	27.0	26.9	26.7	26.3	25.9	26.7
				mm	216	155	165	175	183	170	173	216	180	208	254	264	2360
MOUNTAIN	Bogota, Colombia	4.36N	2661	°C	14.2	14.4	14.8	14.8	14.7	14.5	14.0	13.9	13.9	14.4	14.6	14.5	14.4
				mm	58	61	104	145	114	61	51	56	61	163	117	66	1057
	Darjeeling, India	27.3 N	2248	°C	4.5	5.3	9.8	13.4	14.6	15.5	16.4	16.1	15.2	12.9	8.8	5.4	11.5
				mm	20	28	51	104	198	615	805	660	465	135	5	5	3094
	Johannesburg, S. Africa	26.11s	1806	°C	19.2	18.6	17.4	15.4	12.4	10.4	10.3	12.4	15.2	17.0	17.5	18.4	15.3
				mm	157	132	112	43	20	3	13	13	25	66	137	137	843
	Mexico City, Mexico	19.26N	2278	°C	12.2	13.8	15.8	17.9	18.3	17.7	16.9	16.7	16.2	14.8	13.6	11.9	15.5
				mm	5	5	15	15	48	99	104	119	104	46	13	5	587

STATES AND POPULATIONS

	area (sq. km)	POPULATION
AFGHANISTAN	657 500	17 600 000
ALBANIA	28 748	2 170 000
ALGERIA	2 381 730	14 600 000
ANDORRA	453	20 000
ANGOLA	1 246 700	5 673 000
ARGENTINA	2 778 412	24 000 000
AUSTRALIA	7 686 900	12 959 000
Australian Capital Terr.	2 432	158 000
New South Wales	801 432	4 663 000
Northern Territory	1 347 515	93 000
Queensland	1 727 520	1 869 000
South Australia	984 381	1 186 000
Tasmania	68 332	392 200
Victoria	227 620	3 546 000
Western Australia	2 527 623	1 053 000
AUSTRIA	83 849	7 456 000
BAHAMAS, THE	11 400	171 000
BAHRAIN	598	216 000
BANGLADESH	142 776	75 000 000
BARBADOS	430	238 141
BELGIUM	30 513	9 676 000
BELIZE	22 963	126 000
BENIN	112 600	2 800 000
BERMUDA	53	55 000
BHUTAN	46 600	1 000 000
BOLIVIA	1 098 580	5 100 000
BOTSWANA	600 000	700 000
BRAZIL	8 511 965	98 000 000
BRUNEI	5 765	142 000
BULGARIA	110 912	8 490 000
BURMA	678 034	28 870 000
BURUNDI	27 834	3 800 000
CAMBODIA	181 305	7 200 000
CAMEROON	475 500	6 200 000
CANADA	9 976 169	21 568 000
Alberta	661 188	1 627 900
British Columbia	948 600	2 184 600
Manitoba	650 090	988 200
New Brunswick	73 437	634 600
Newfoundland	404 519	522 100
Northwest Territories	3 379 689	34 800
Nova Scotia	55 490	789 000
Ontario	1 068 587	7 703 000
Prince Edward Island	5 657	111 600
Quebec	1 549 677	6 027 800
Saskatchewan	651 903	926 200
Yukon	536 327	18 400
CAPE VERDE	4 033	272 000
CENT. AFRICAN REP.	623 018	1 520 000
CHAD	1 284 000	3 710 000
CHILE	756 945	10 000 000
CHINA	9 560 975	750 000 000
Inner Mongolia	450 000	9 000 000
Sinkiang	1 646 790	8 000 000
Tibet	1 221 600	1 250 000
COLOMBIA	1 138 914	22 500 000
CONGO	342 000	1 000 000
COSTA RICA	50 900	1 800 000
CUBA	114 524	8 553 395
CYPRUS	9 255	600 000
CZECHOSLOVAKIA	127 870	14 362 000
DENMARK	43 069	4 976 000
DJIBOUTI	23 000	81 000
DOMINICAN REP.	48 442	4 200 000
ECUADOR	281 341	6 500 000
EGYPT	1 000 253	34 700 000
EL SALVADOR	21 393	3 700 000
EQUATORIAL GUINEA	28 051	290 000
ETHIOPIA	1 221 900	26 400 000
FAEROES	1 373	38 000
FALKLAND ISLANDS	11 961	2 105
FIJI	18 272	533 000
FINLAND	337 032	4 706 000
FRANCE	549 430	51 600 000
FRENCH GUIANA	91 000	51 000
GABON	267 000	500 000
GAMBIA, THE	11 295	364 000
EAST GERMANY	108 173	17 042 000
WEST GERMANY	248 533	61 682 000
GHANA	238 539	9 600 000
GIBRALTAR	6	26 833
GREECE	131 944	9 000 000
GREENLAND	2 175 600	47 000
GUATEMALA	108 889	5 500 000
GUINEA	245 857	3 920 000
GUINEA-BISSAU	36 125	560 000
GUYANA	214 970	700 000
HAITI	27 750	5 000 000
HONDURAS	112 088	2 700 000
HONG KONG	1 032	4 078 000
HUNGARY	93 030	10 415 000
ICELAND	103 000	200 000
INDIA	3 287 593	638 388 000
INDONESIA	1 904 334	129 000 000
IRAN	1 648 180	30 550 000
IRAQ	438 446	9 800 000
IRELAND, Rep. of	68 893	3 000 000
ISRAEL	20 700	3 080 000
ITALY	301 224	55 000 000
IVORY COAST	322 463	4 500 000
JAMAICA	11 525	2 040 000
JAPAN	372 077	106 958 000
JORDAN	97 740	2 467 000
KENYA	582 600	11 800 000
KIRIBATI	655	70 000
KOREA, NORTH	127 158	14 500 000
KOREA, SOUTH	98 431	33 400 000
KUWAIT	16 000	800 000
LAOS	236 800	2 962 000
LEBANON	10 400	2 855 000
LESOTHO	30 340	1 200 000
LIBERIA	111 000	1 300 000
LIBYA	1 759 540	2 100 000
LIECHTENSTEIN	160	21 350
LUXEMBOURG	2 586	345 000
MADAGASCAR	594 180	7 655 000
MALAWI	126 338	4 530 000
MALAYSIA	333 507	10 800 000
MALI	1 240 000	5 300 000
MALTA	316	326 000
MAURITANIA	1 030 700	1 400 000
MAURITIUS	1 865	836 000
MEXICO	1 967 183	52 500 000
MONACO	15	23 000
MONGOLIA	1 565 000	1 290 000
MOROCCO	458 730	15 700 000
MOZAMBIQUE	784 961	8 234 000
NAMIBIA (S.W. Africa)	824 293	852 000
NEPAL	141 400	11 500 000
NETHERLANDS	40 893	13 270 000
NETHERLANDS ANTILLES	1 019	225 000
NEW HEBRIDES	14 760	84 000
NEW ZEALAND	268 680	2 900 000
NICARAGUA	148 000	2 210 000
NIGER	1 267 000	4 200 000
NIGERIA	923 773	58 000 000
NORWAY	324 219	3 918 000
OMAN	212 000	660 000
PAKISTAN	803 994	58 000 000
PANAMA	75 650	1 826 000
PAPUA-NEW GUINEA	461 700	2 467 000
PARAGUAY	406 752	2 500 000
PERU	1 285 215	14 400 000
PHILIPPINES	299 400	40 600 000
POLAND	312 700	32 900 000
PORTUGAL	92 082	9 700 000
PUERTO RICO	8 891	2 770 000
QATAR	22 000	80 000
ROMANIA	237 500	20 600 000
RWANDA	26 330	3 800 000
SAN MARINO	61	19 000
SAUDI ARABIA	2 263 600	7 200 000
SENEGAL	197 161	3 925 000
SIERRA LEONE	73 326	2 550 000
SOLOMON IS.	29 785	163 000
SOMALIA	637 660	2 790 000
SOUTH AFRICA	1 221 042	22 700 000
Cape of Good Hope	721 004	5 363 000
Natal	86 967	2 980 000
Orange Free State	129 153	1 387 000
Transvaal	283 918	6 273 000
SPAIN	504 748	34 600 000
SRI LANKA	65 610	13 033 000
SUDAN	2 505 813	16 700 000
SURINAM	17 400	385 000
SWAZILAND	173 400	408 000
SWEDEN	449 793	8 127 000
SWITZERLAND	41 288	6 270 000
SYRIA	185 680	6 600 000
TAIWAN	35 961	14 990 000
TANZANIA	939 700	14 000 000
THAILAND	514 000	38 000 000
TOGO	56 000	2 004 711
TRINIDAD & TOBAGO	5 128	1 070 000
TUNISIA	164 150	5 300 000
TURKEY	780 576	37 010 000
TUVALU	24.6	10 000
UGANDA	236 037	9 764 000
UNION OF SOVIET SOCIALIST REPS.	22 400 000	246 300 000
Armenian S.S.R.	29 759	2 600 000
Azerbaijan S.S.R.	86 853	5 300 000
Byelorussian S.S.R.	207 588	9 100 000
Estonian S.S.R.	45 092	1 357 000
Georgian S.S.R.	69 670	4 800 000
Kazakh S.S.R.	2 717 000	13 500 000
Kirghiz S.S.R.	198 652	3 100 000
Latvian S.S.R.	64 000	2 365 000
Lithuanian S.S.R.	65 190	3 129 000
Moldavian S.S.R.	33 800	3 700 000
Russian S.F.S.R.	17 077 962	130 090 000
Tadzhik S.S.R.	143 072	3 100 000
Turkmen S.S.R.	487 956	2 300 000
Ukrainian S.S.R.	604 000	47 900 000
Uzbek S.S.R.	447 000	12 500 000
UNITED ARAB EMIRATES	83 660	180 000
UNITED KINGDOM OF GT. BRITAIN & N. IRELAND	230 608	55 356 000
England and Wales	130 362	48 604 000
Scotland	78749	5 224 000
Northern Ireland	14147	1 528 000
Channel Islands	195	125 240
Isle of Man	588	49 743
UNITED STATES OF AMERICA	9 363 353	209 000 000
Alabama	133 167	3 444 165
Alaska	1 518 800	302 173
Arizona	295 022	1 772 482
Arkansas	137 539	1 923 295
California	411 012	19 953 134
Colorado	269 998	2 207 259
Connecticut	12 973	3 032 217
Delaware	5 328	548 104
District of Columbia	174	756 510
Florida	151 670	6 789 443
Georgia	152 488	4 589 575
Hawaii	16 705	769 913
Idaho	216 412	713 008
Illinois	146 075	11 113 976
Indiana	93 993	5 193 669
Iowa	145 791	2 825 041
Kansas	213 063	2 249 071
Kentucky	104 623	3 219 311
Louisiana	125 674	3 643 180
Maine	86 027	993 663
Maryland	27 394	3 922 399
Massachusetts	21 386	5 689 170
Michigan	150 779	8 875 083
Minnesota	217 735	3 805 069
Mississippi	123 584	2 216 912
Missouri	180 486	4 677 399
Montana	381 084	694 409
Nebraska	200 017	1 483 791
Nevada	286 296	488 738
New Hampshire	24 097	737 681
New Jersey	20 295	7 168 164
New Mexico	315 113	1 016 000
New York	128 401	18 241 266
North Carolina	136 197	5 082 059
North Dakota	183 022	617 716
Ohio	106 765	10 652 017
Oklahoma	181 090	2 559 253
Oregon	251 180	2 091 385
Pennsylvania	117 412	11 793 909
Rhode Island	3 144	949 723
South Carolina	80 432	2 590 516
South Dakota	199 551	666 257
Tennessee	109 412	3 924 164
Texas	692 403	11 196 730
Utah	219 932	1 059 273
Vermont	24 887	444 732
Virginia	105 816	4 648 494
Washington	176 617	3 409 169
West Virginia	62 629	1 744 237
Wisconsin	145 438	4 417 933
Wyoming	253 597	332 416
UPPER VOLTA	274 122	5 600 000
URUGUAY	186 926	3 000 000
VATICAN CITY	0.44	1 000
VENEZUELA	912 050	11 000 000
VIETNAM	329 650	41 000 000
YEMEN	195 000	5 750 000
YEMEN, SOUTH	160 300	1 280 000
YUGOSLAVIA	255 804	20 800 000
ZAIRE	2 345 409	22 800 000
ZAMBIA	752 262	4 500 000
ZIMBABWE	389 361	6 930 000

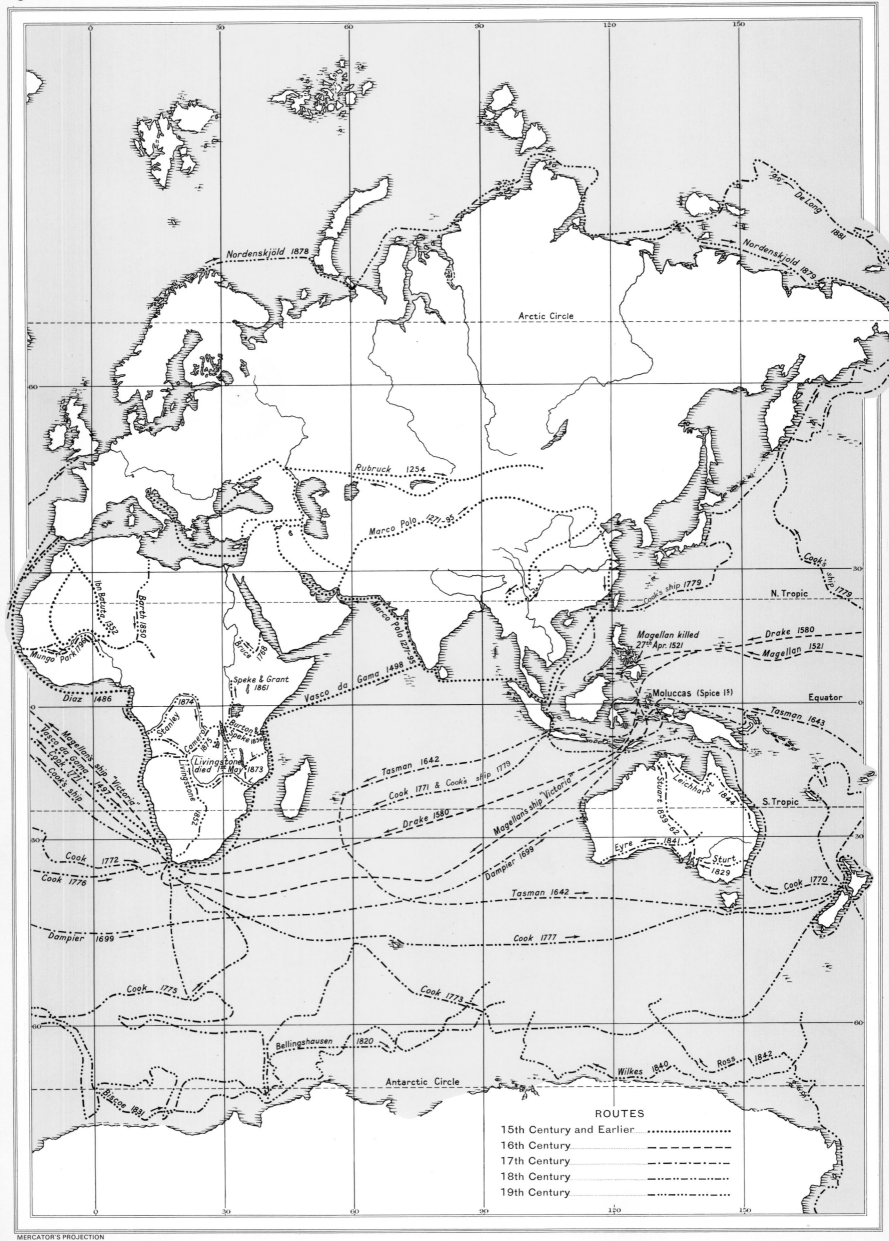

ROUTES

15th Century and Earlier	••••••••••••••
16th Century	– – – – – –
17th Century	–·–·–·–·
18th Century	–··–··–··
19th Century	–···–···–

MERCATOR'S PROJECTION

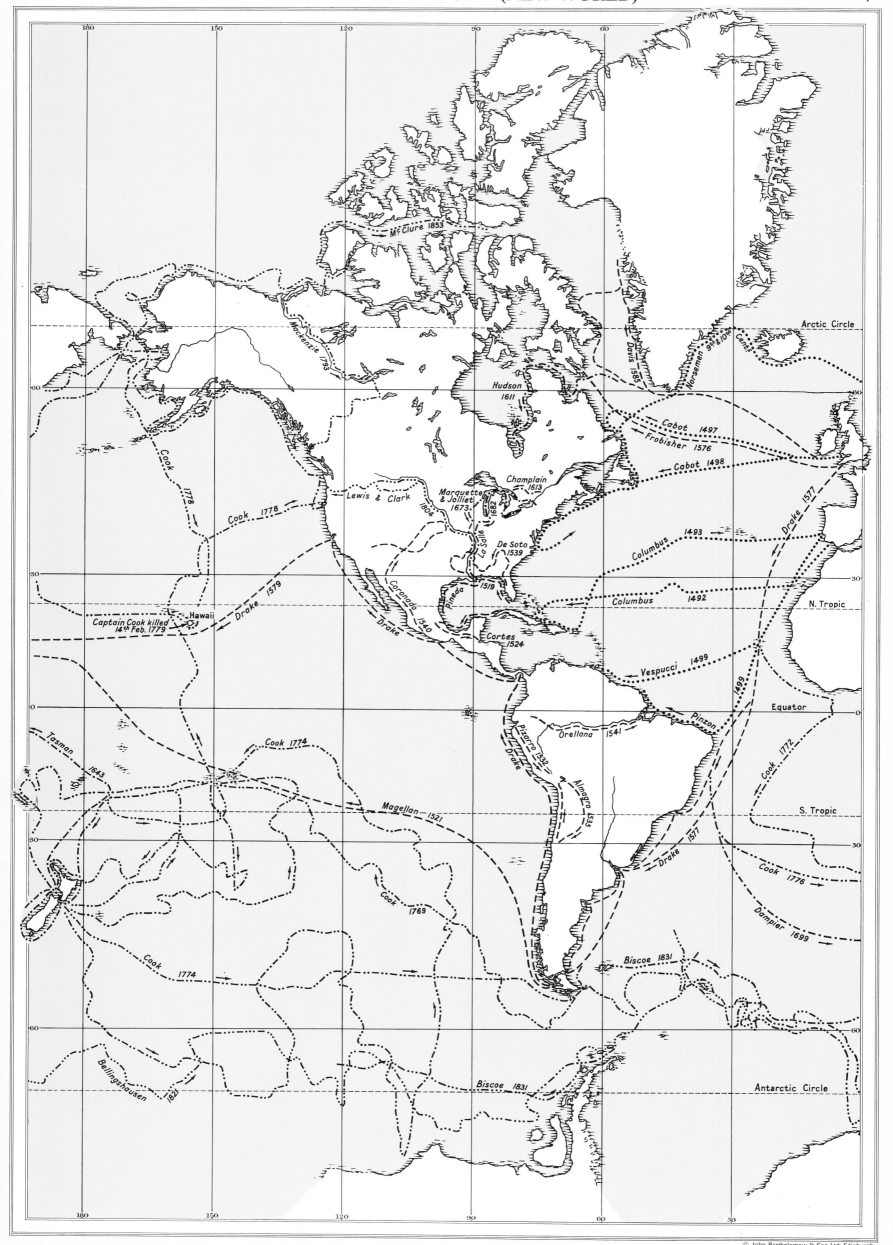

STEREOGRAPHIC PROJECTION

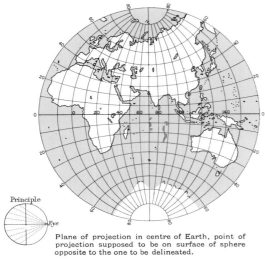

Plane of projection in centre of Earth, point of projection supposed to be on surface of sphere opposite to the one to be delineated.

ORTHOGRAPHIC PROJECTION

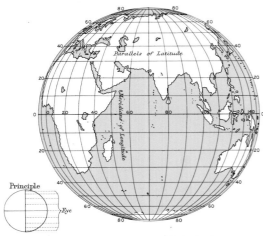

Plane of projection in centre of Earth, the eye or point of projection supposed to be at infinite distance so that lines of projection are all parallel.

EQUIDISTANT OR GLOBULAR PROJECTION

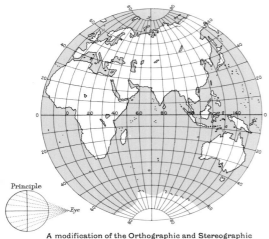

A modification of the Orthographic and Stereographic in which the point of projection is supposed to be removed to a point outside of the opposite surface of the sphere.

POLAR PROJECTIONS

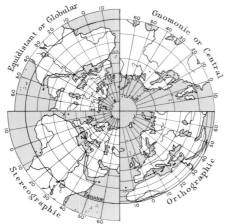

The Gnomonic Projection cannot be made to include the whole hemisphere. The Stereographic and Globular Projections can be extended to include more than the hemisphere.

MERCATOR'S PROJECTION

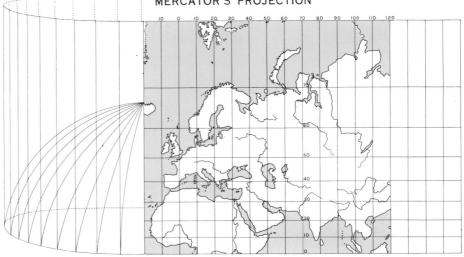

The plane of projection is the surface of an imaginary cylinder surrounding the globe and touching its surface at the Equator. At the Equator its scale agrees with the globe, but as each parallel of latitude becomes a great circle equal to the Equator, the scale increases as we go North and South. The latitude is, however, increased in same proportion as the longitude. Mercator's projection is the only one which gives the true direction of one point in relation to another, and is therefore most used for the purposes of navigation.

GALL'S STEREOGRAPHIC PROJECTION

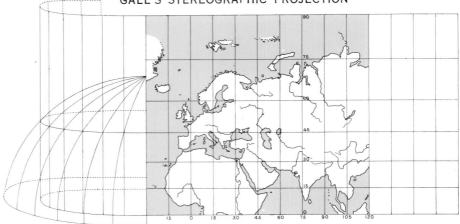

This is another Cylindrical Projection, but the cylinder, instead of touching the sphere only at the Equator as in Mercator's, is supposed to be sunk into its surface so that it cuts its surface half way between the Equator and the poles, and thus coincides with the two parallels of 45° N. and S. Lat. The parallels are projected stereographically.

SANSON'S (SINUSOIDAL) PROJECTION

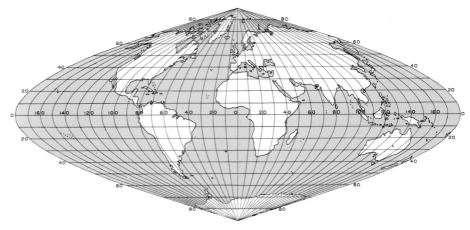

The parallels are drawn at their true distances from the Equator and along each of these. correct distances are measured through which the meridians are drawn. The projection is obviously equal-area.

MOLLWEIDE'S HOMOLOGRAPHIC PROJECTION

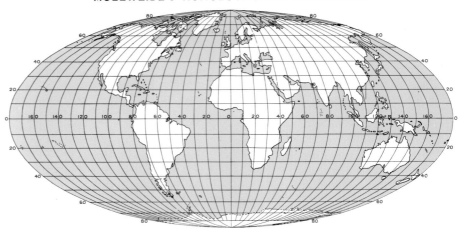

This is an equal area projection. The complete circle on the map is made to equal the world hemisphere. Parallels are so drawn that the zone enclosed by them bears the same relation to the area of the circle as the similar zone on the Earth bears to the hemisphere. The meridians are ellipses cutting the parallels at equal distances.

CONIC PROJECTION WITH ONE STANDARD PARALLEL

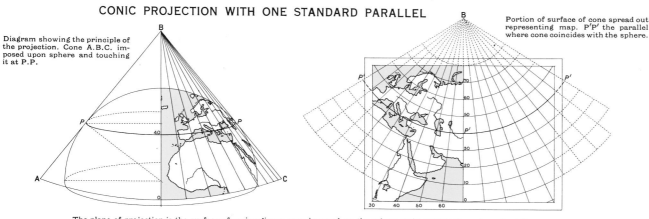

Diagram showing the principle of the projection. Cone A.B.C. imposed upon sphere and touching it at P.P.

Portion of surface of cone spread out representing map. P'P' the parallel where cone coincides with the sphere.

The plane of projection is the surface of an imaginary cone imposed on the sphere and touching its surface along the parallel of 40° P.P. Distances measured along that parallel on the map are absolutely correct as they exactly coincide with the globe. But the scale is distorted to the North and South of tangential parallel according to distance away from it.

CONIC PROJECTION WITH TWO STANDARD PARALLELS

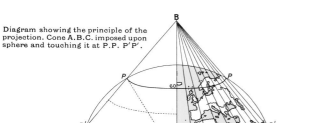

Diagram showing the principle of the projection. Cone A.B.C. imposed upon sphere and touching it at P.P. P'P'.

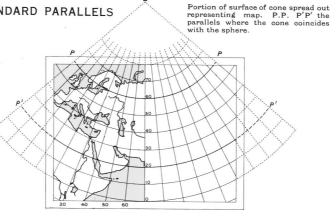

Portion of surface of cone spread out representing map. P.P. P'P' the parallels where the cone coincides with the sphere.

In this case the cone is supposed to cut the sphere along two parallels PP. and P'P', which, however, are plotted their true distance apart (i.e. the distance along the arc PP', not the chord). The map has therefore the advantage of coinciding with the globe along two parallels instead of one as in the Simple Conic.

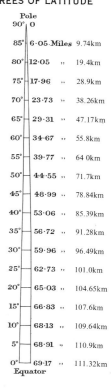

LENGTH OF DEGREES OF LONGITUDE AT VARIOUS DEGREES OF LATITUDE

Pole 90°	0	
85°	6·05 Miles	9.74km
80°	12·05 ,,	19.4km
75°	17·96 ,,	28.9km
70°	23·73 ,,	38.26km
65°	29·31 ,,	47.17km
60°	34·67 ,,	55.8km
55°	39·77 ,,	64 0km
50°	44·55 ,,	71.7km
45°	48·99 ,,	78.84km
40°	53·06 ,,	85.39km
35°	56·72 ,,	91.28km
30°	59·96 ,,	96.49km
25°	62·73 ,,	101.0km
20°	65·03 ,,	104.65km
15°	66·83 ,,	107.6km
10°	68·13 ,,	109.64km
5°	68·91 ,,	110.9km
0°	69·17 ,,	111.32km
Equator		

BONNE'S PROJECTION

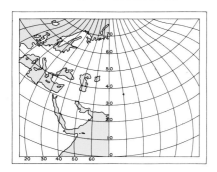

This is a development of the Conic Projection and differs from the pure Conic in that instead of distances being correctly measured along one parallel, true distances are measured along each parallel.

VAN DER GRINTEN'S PROJECTION

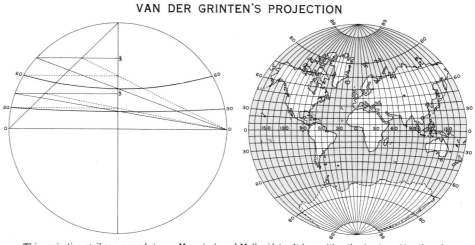

This projection strikes a mean between Mercator's and Mollweide's. It has neither the great exaggeration of land areas towards the Pole, of the former, nor the excessive angular distortion of the latter.

COVERING OF A 2½ INCH WORLD GLOBE IN GORES

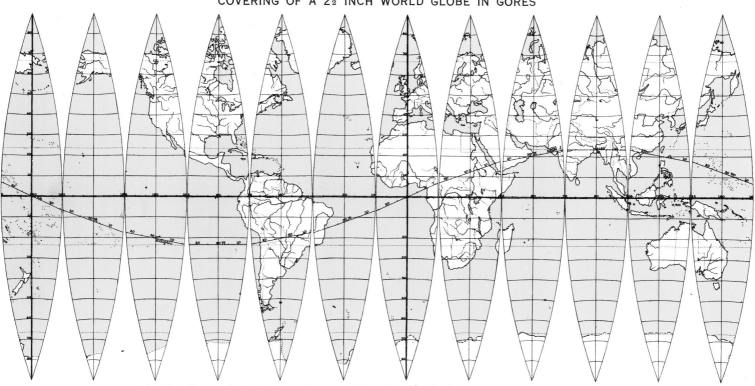

Note—These Gores are designed to be cut out and mounted on a Globe 2½ inches in diameter, which they will exactly cover.

LAMBERT'S AZIMUTHAL PROJECTION

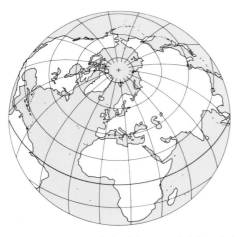

This projection is calculated from a selected central point as in a Polar, the crossing of degree lines being calculated to retain equal-area properties. It gives excellent treatment of large continental masses, but necessarily leads to some distension in circumferential areas.

BARTHOLOMEW'S ATLANTIS PROJECTION

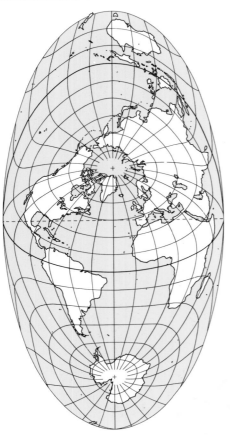

A novel application of Mollweide's Homolographic, the main axis being taken as a transverse great circle running through the poles. The minor axis lies on an oblique great circle touching 45°N. It is equal-area and shows the land masses in unbroken formation with regard to the N. Atlantic Ocean.

TETRAHEDRAL PROJECTION

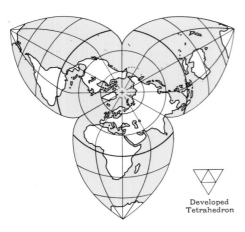

Developed
Tetrahedron

One of the simplest yet most natural developments of the Globe. Prof. J. W. Gregory was first to point out the Earth's affinity to a tetrahedron, whose edges represented the main lines of mountain folding.

AITOFF'S PROJECTION

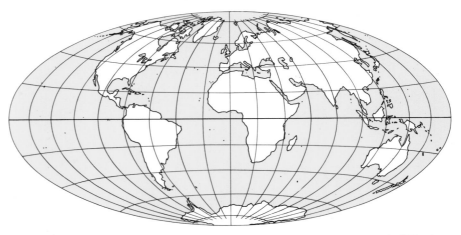

This is developed from Lambert's equal-area treatment of the hemisphere. Co-ordinates on the "X" axis are doubled while those on the "Y" remain as they were. The result is an ellipse containing an equal-area grid which may be subdivided for the whole world.

BARTHOLOMEW'S NORDIC PROJECTION

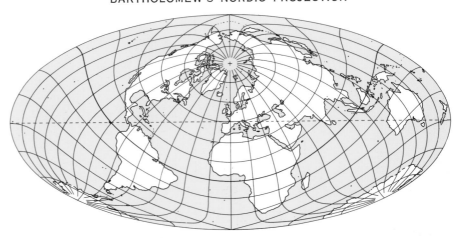

Like Aitoff's, this is a development of Lambert's Azimuthal. The main axis, however, instead of following the Equator becomes an oblique great circle, in this case touching 45° N. and 45° S. It is equal-area and gives a good basis for distributional maps, particularly in the north temperate and circum-polar areas.

BARTHOLOMEW'S RE-CENTRED SINUSOIDAL PROJECTION

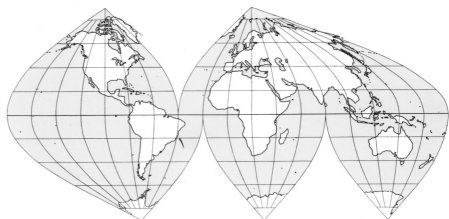

The equal-area properties and simple construction of the Sinusoidal are here applied to each continental mass separately so as to preserve optimum conformity. It was developed from Prof. Paul Goode's idea of the "Interrupted Homolographic" over which it claims certain advantages for purposes of land distribution.

BARTHOLOMEW'S REGIONAL PROJECTION

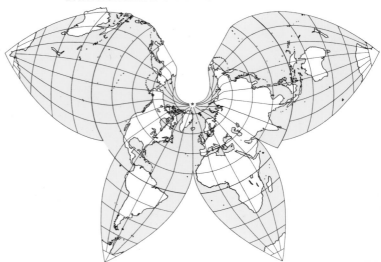

This arrangement claims to combine the best conformal properties with those as near equal-area as possible. It recognises that the chief field of man's development is in the North Temperate Zone and from a cone cutting the globe along two selected parallels it is continued on interrupted lines to complete the Earth.

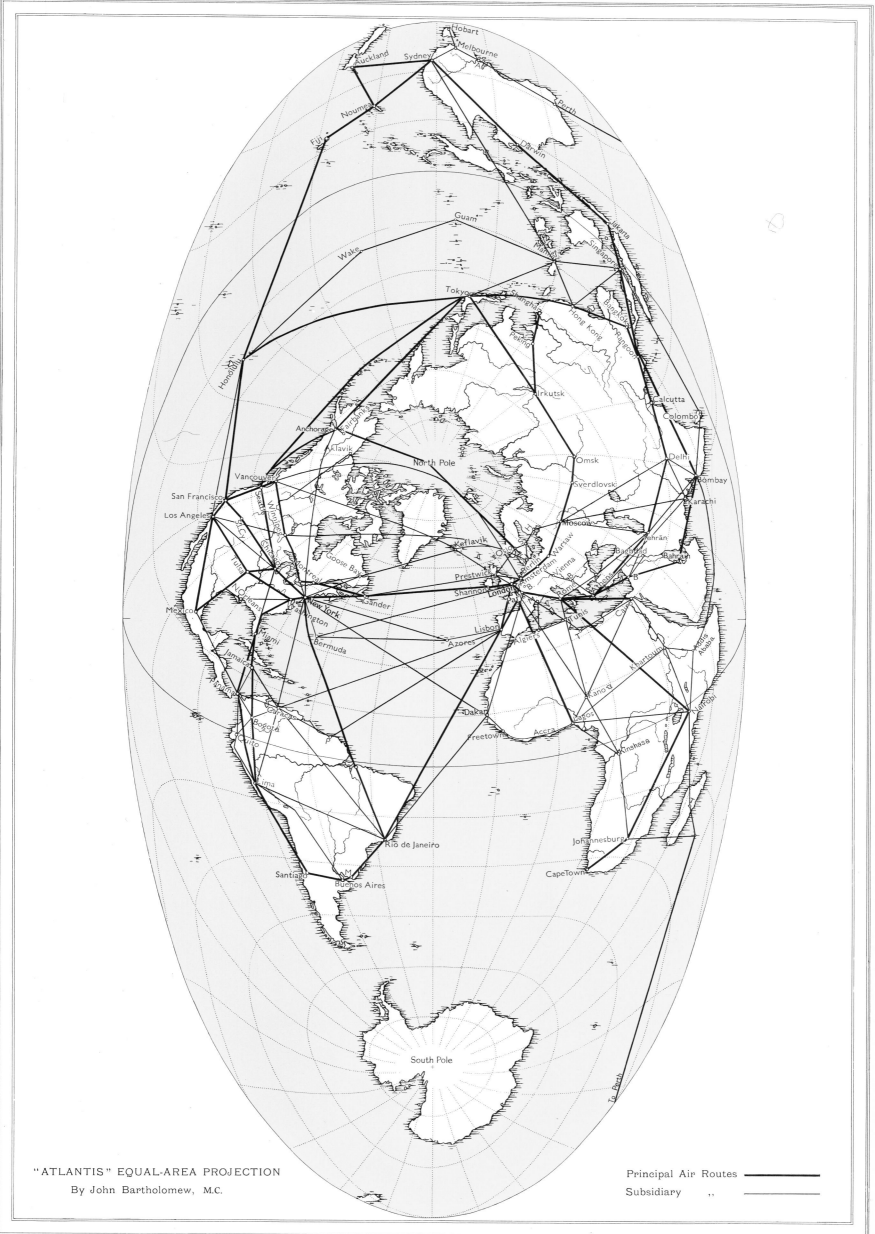

"ATLANTIS" EQUAL-AREA PROJECTION

By John Bartholomew, M.C.

Principal Air Routes ━━━━━

Subsidiary   ,, ─────

1:120M

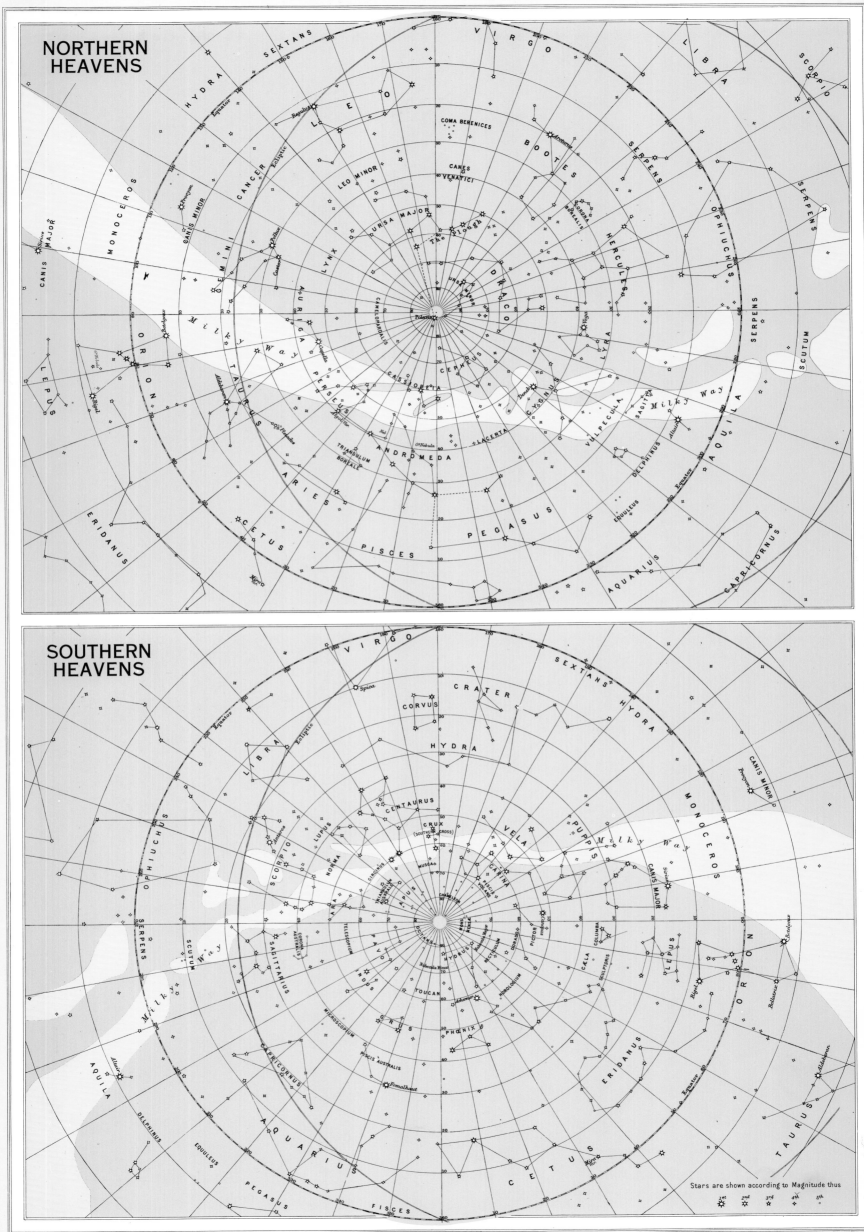

NORTHERN
HEAVENS

SOUTHERN
HEAVENS

Stars are shown according to Magnitude thus

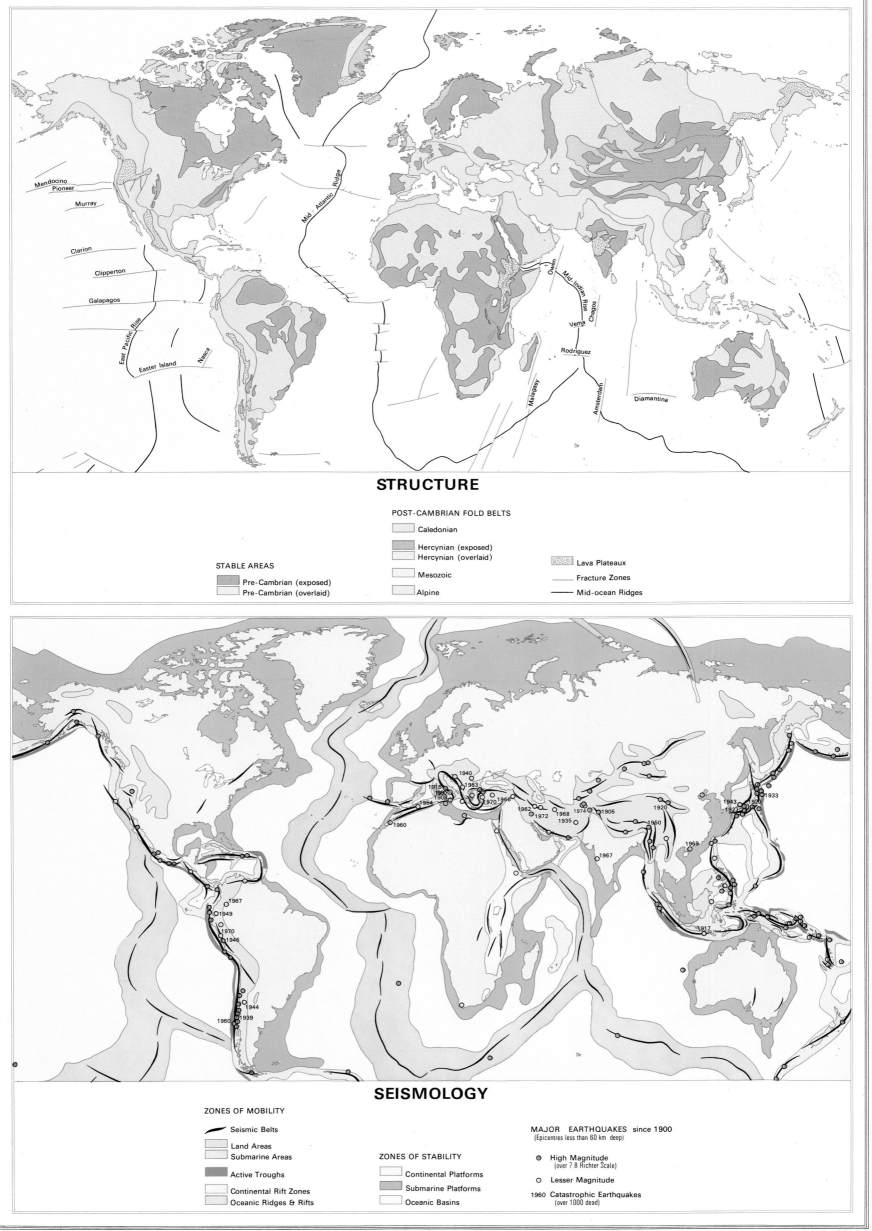

STRUCTURE

POST-CAMBRIAN FOLD BELTS

- Caledonian
- Hercynian (exposed)
- Hercynian (overlaid)
- Mesozoic
- Alpine

- Lava Plateaux
- Fracture Zones
- Mid-ocean Ridges

STABLE AREAS

- Pre-Cambrian (exposed)
- Pre-Cambrian (overlaid)

Mendocino
Pioneer
Murray
Clarion
Clipperton
Galapagos
East Pacific Rise
Easter Island
Nasca
Mid - Atlantic Ridge
Owen
Mid Indian Rise
Chagos
Vema
Rodriguez
Malagasy
Amsterdam
Diamantina

SEISMOLOGY

ZONES OF MOBILITY

- Seismic Belts
- Land Areas
- Submarine Areas
- Active Troughs
- Continental Rift Zones
- Oceanic Ridges & Rifts

ZONES OF STABILITY

- Continental Platforms
- Submarine Platforms
- Oceanic Basins

MAJOR EARTHQUAKES since 1900
(Epicentres less than 60 km deep)

- High Magnitude
  (over 7.8 Richter Scale)
- Lesser Magnitude

1960 Catastrophic Earthquakes
(over 1000 dead)

© John Bartholomew & Son Ltd, Edinburgh

1:140M

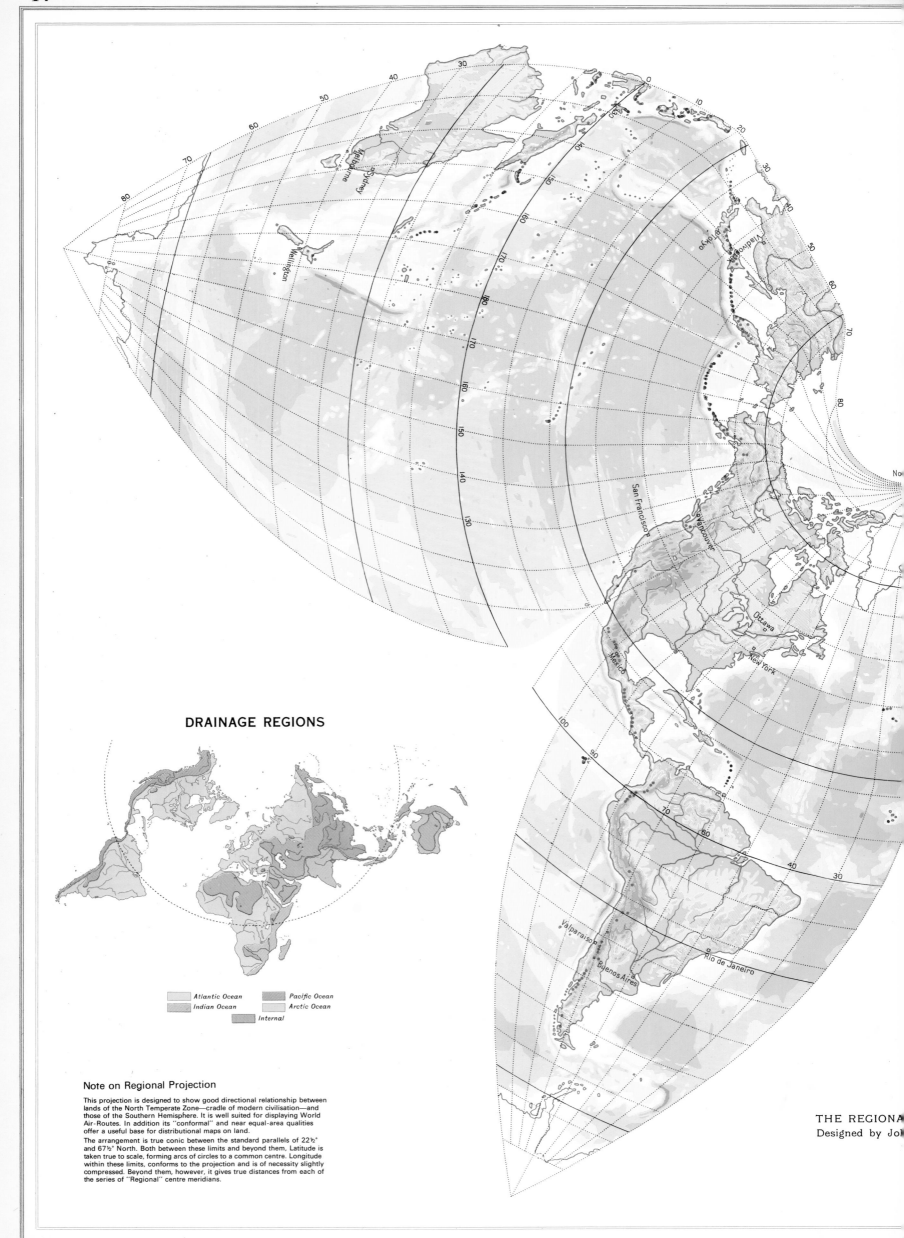

DRAINAGE REGIONS

Atlantic Ocean | Pacific Ocean
Indian Ocean | Arctic Ocean
Internal

Note on Regional Projection

This projection is designed to show good directional relationship between lands of the North Temperate Zone—cradle of modern civilisation—and those of the Southern Hemisphere. It is well suited for displaying World Air-Routes. In addition its "conformal" and near equal-area qualities offer a useful base for distributional maps on land.

The arrangement is true conic between the standard parallels of 22½° and 67½° North. Both between these limits and beyond them, Latitude is taken true to scale, forming arcs of circles to a common centre. Longitude within these limits, conforms to the projection and is of necessity slightly compressed. Beyond them, however, it gives true distances from each of the series of "Regional" centre meridians.

THE REGIONA
Designed by Jo

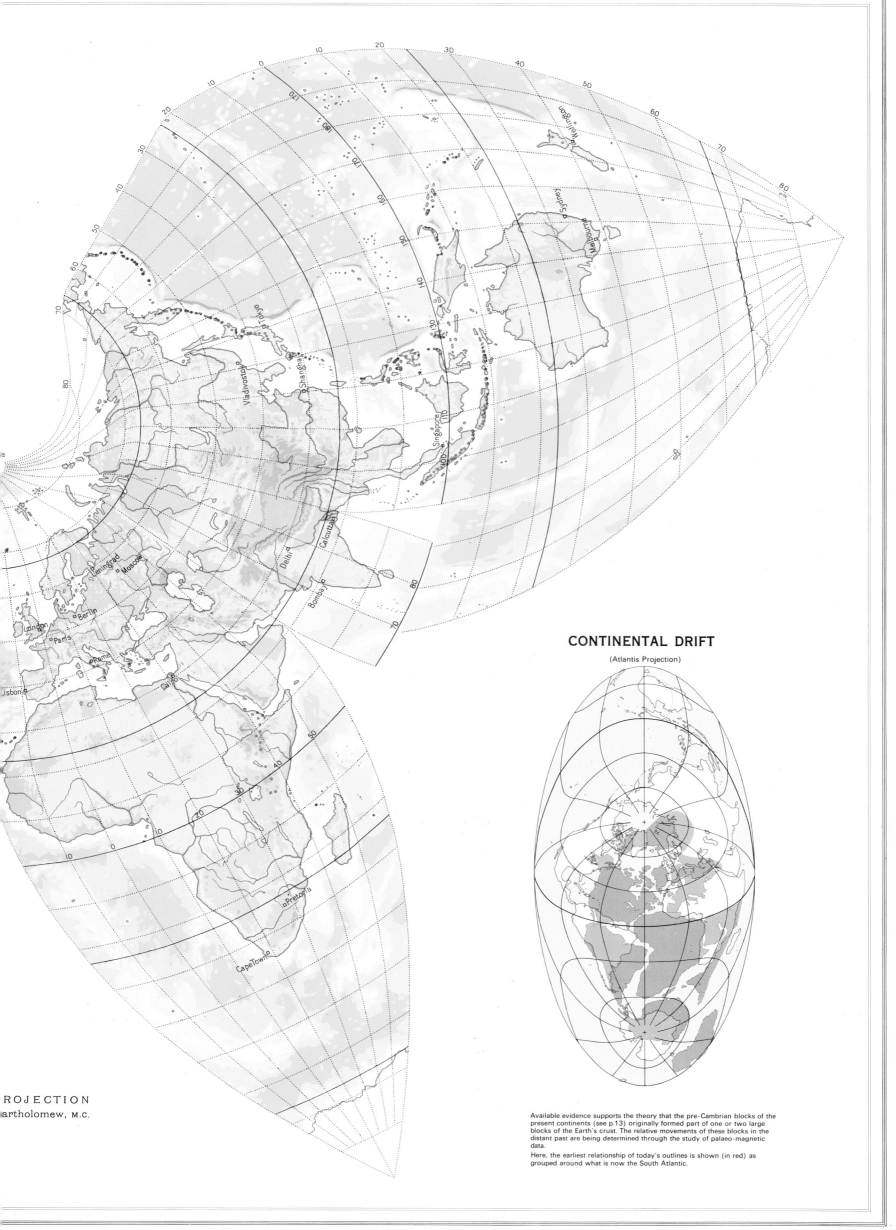

CONTINENTAL DRIFT

(Atlantis Projection)

Available evidence supports the theory that the pre-Cambrian blocks of the present continents (see p.13) originally formed part of one or two large blocks of the Earth's crust. The relative movements of these blocks in the distant past are being determined through the study of palaeo-magnetic data.

Here, the earliest relationship of today's outlines is shown (in red) as grouped around what is now the South Atlantic.

ROJECTION

artholomew, M.C.

0	200	500	1000	2000	4000	Metres
0	660	1640	3280	6560	13120	Feet.

• Active Volcanoes

M

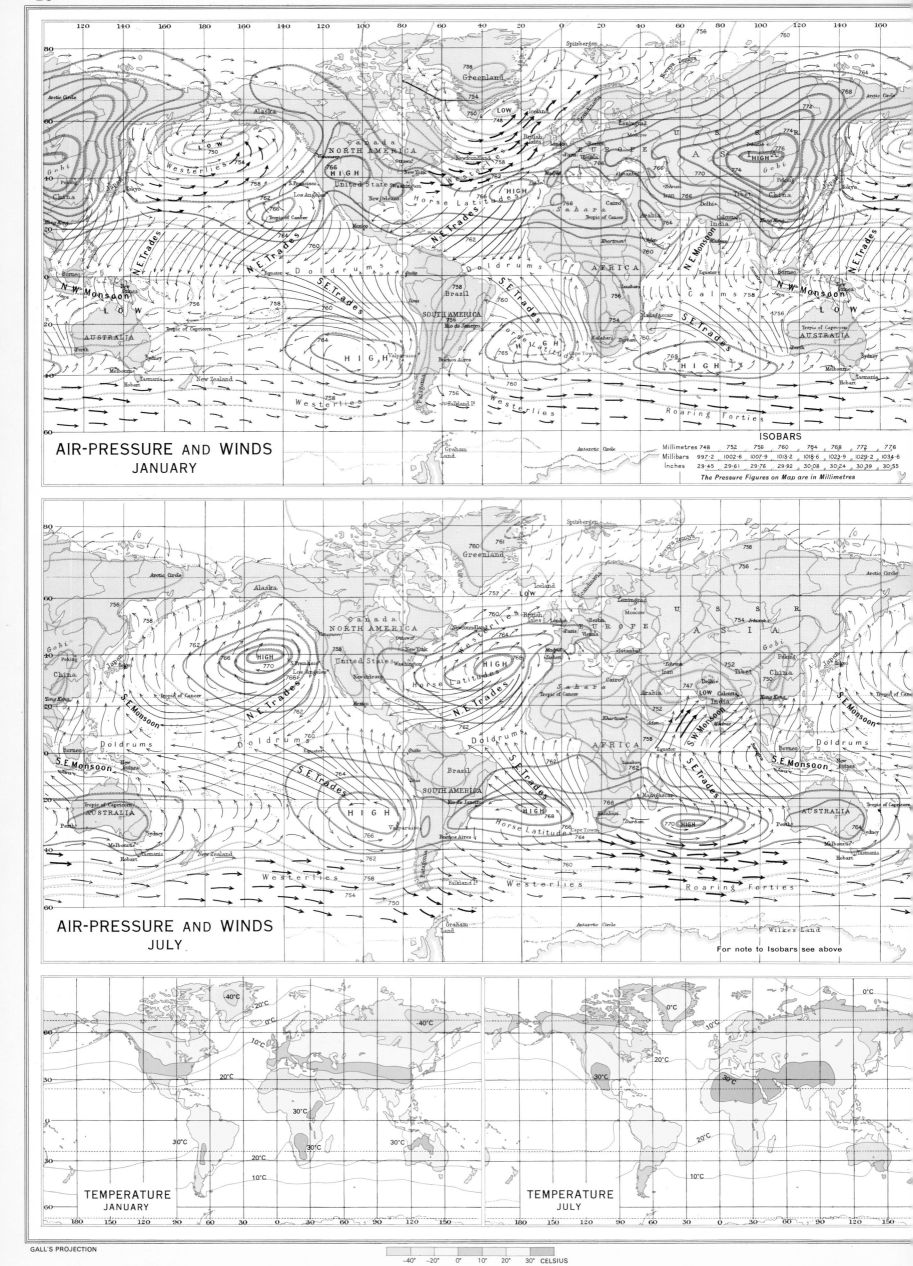

AIR-PRESSURE AND WINDS
JANUARY

ISOBARS
Millimetres	748	752	756	760	764	768	772	776
Millibars	997·2	1002·6	1007·9	1013·2	1018·6	1023·9	1029·2	1034·6
Inches	29·45	29·61	29·76	29·92	30·08	30·24	30·39	30·55

The Pressure Figures on Map are in Millimetres

AIR-PRESSURE AND WINDS
JULY

For note to Isobars see above

TEMPERATURE
JANUARY

TEMPERATURE
JULY

GALL'S PROJECTION

−40° −20°   0°   10°   20°   30° CELSIUS

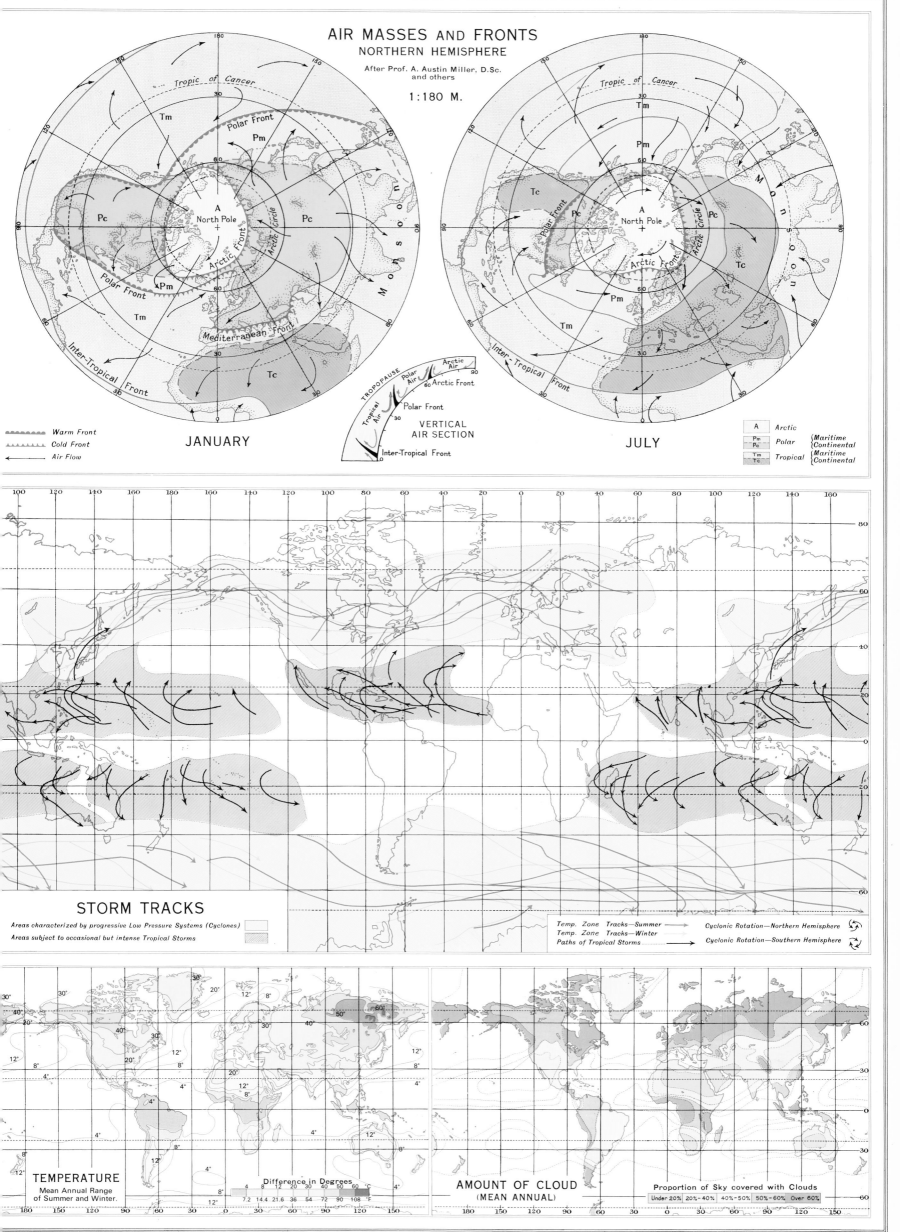

AIR MASSES AND FRONTS
NORTHERN HEMISPHERE
After Prof. A. Austin Miller, D.Sc.
and others

1:180 M.

JANUARY

JULY

VERTICAL
AIR SECTION

- Warm Front
- Cold Front
- Air Flow

A	Arctic	
Pm	Polar	Maritime
Pc		Continental
Tm	Tropical	Maritime
Tc		Continental

STORM TRACKS

Areas characterized by progressive Low Pressure Systems (Cyclones)
Areas subject to occasional but intense Tropical Storms

Temp. Zone Tracks—Summer
Temp. Zone Tracks—Winter
Paths of Tropical Storms

Cyclonic Rotation—Northern Hemisphere
Cyclonic Rotation—Southern Hemisphere

TEMPERATURE
Mean Annual Range
of Summer and Winter.

Difference in Degrees
°C
7.2 14.4 21.6 36 54 72 90 108 °F

AMOUNT OF CLOUD
(MEAN ANNUAL)

Proportion of Sky covered with Clouds
Under 20% 20%-40% 40%-50% 50%-60% Over 60%

© John Bartholomew & Son Ltd, Edinburgh

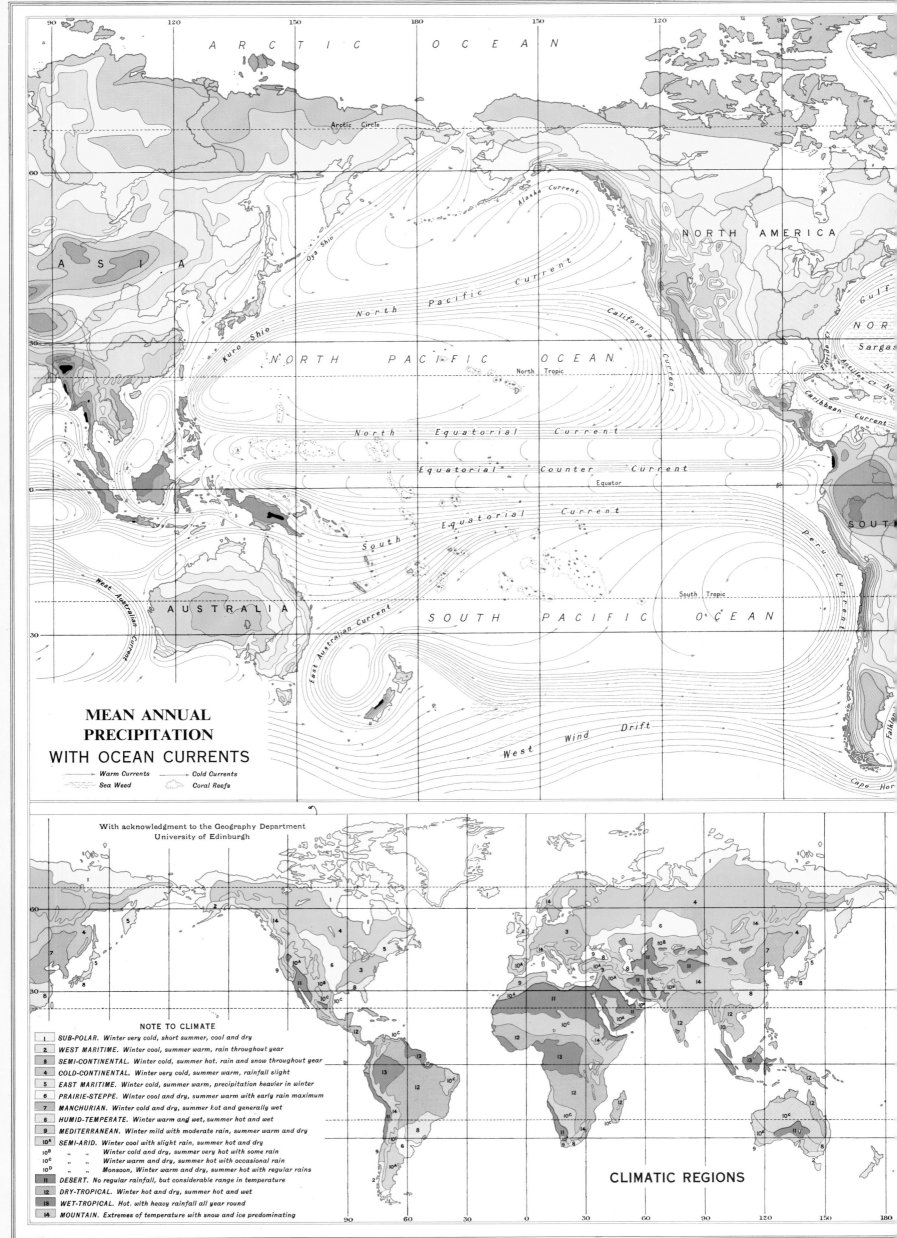

MEAN ANNUAL PRECIPITATION
WITH OCEAN CURRENTS

⟶ Warm Currents   ⟶ Cold Currents
〰 Sea Weed   Coral Reefs

With acknowledgment to the Geography Department
University of Edinburgh

NOTE TO CLIMATE

1	SUB-POLAR.	Winter very cold, short summer, cool and dry
2	WEST MARITIME.	Winter cool, summer warm, rain throughout year
3	SEMI-CONTINENTAL.	Winter cold, summer hot, rain and snow throughout year
4	COLD-CONTINENTAL.	Winter very cold, summer warm, rainfall slight
5	EAST MARITIME.	Winter cold, summer warm, precipitation heavier in winter
6	PRAIRIE-STEPPE.	Winter cool and dry, summer warm with early rain maximum
7	MANCHURIAN.	Winter cold and dry, summer hot and generally wet
8	HUMID-TEMPERATE.	Winter warm and wet, summer hot and wet
9	MEDITERRANEAN.	Winter mild with moderate rain, summer warm and dry
10A	SEMI-ARID.	Winter cool with slight rain, summer hot and dry
10B	" "	Winter cold and dry, summer very hot with some rain
10C	" "	Winter warm and dry, summer hot with occasional rain
10D	" "	Monsoon, Winter warm and dry, summer hot with regular rains
11	DESERT.	No regular rainfall, but considerable range in temperature
12	DRY-TROPICAL.	Winter hot and dry, summer hot and wet
13	WET-TROPICAL.	Hot, with heavy rainfall all year round
14	MOUNTAIN.	Extremes of temperature with snow and ice predominating

CLIMATIC REGIONS

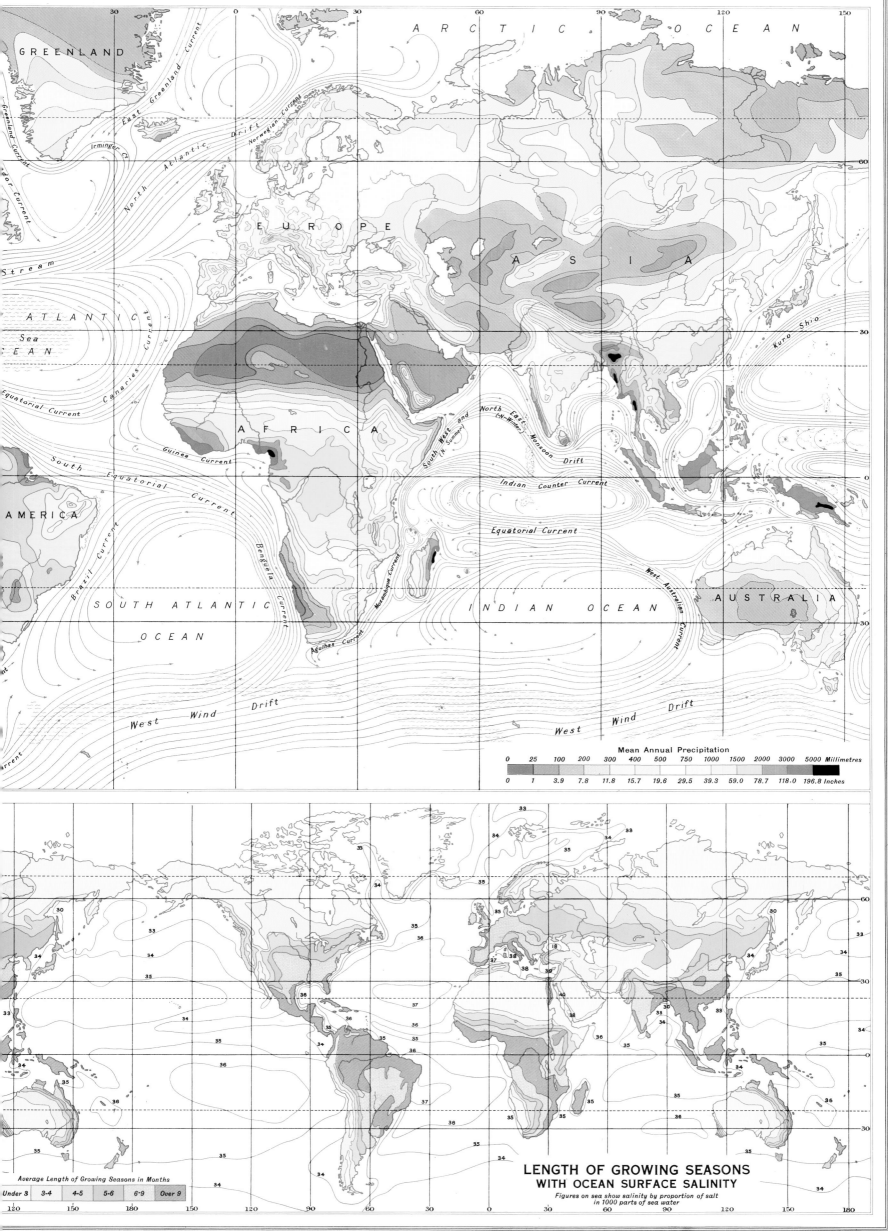

ARCTIC OCEAN

GREENLAND

East Greenland Drift

Irminger Ct.

Labrador Current

North Atlantic Drift

Norwegian Current

EUROPE

ASIA

Gulf Stream

ATLANTIC

Sea

OCEAN

Canaries Current

Equatorial Current

South Equatorial Current

Guinea Current

AFRICA

Kuro Shio

South West and North East (N-Winter) Monsoon Drift

(N. Summer)

Indian Counter Current

AMERICA

Brazil Current

Equatorial Current

Benguela Current

Mozambique Current

INDIAN OCEAN

West Australian Current

AUSTRALIA

SOUTH ATLANTIC

OCEAN

Agulhas Current

West Wind Drift

West Wind Drift

Mean Annual Precipitation
0 25 100 200 300 400 500 750 1000 1500 2000 3000 5000 Millimetres
0 1 3.9 7.8 11.8 15.7 19.6 29.5 39.3 59.0 78.7 118.0 196.8 Inches

33

34

35

33

34

35

30

33

16

35

36

37

38

38

40

38

34

33

35

36

36

37

34

35

36

36

34

35

34

35

34

35

36

35

37

35

36

35

34

35

35

34

34

35

34

Average Length of Growing Seasons in Months					
Under 3	3-4	4-5	5-6	6-9	Over 9

LENGTH OF GROWING SEASONS
WITH OCEAN SURFACE SALINITY

Figures on sea show salinity by proportion of salt in 1000 parts of sea water

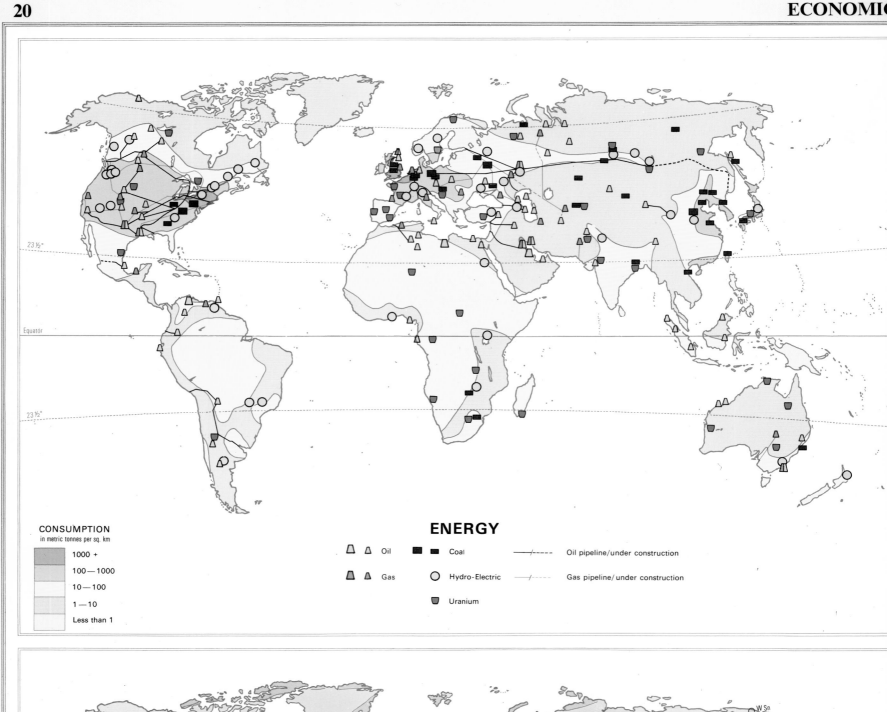

ENERGY

CONSUMPTION
in metric tonnes per sq. km

1000 +
100 — 1000
10 — 100
1 — 10
Less than 1

△ △ Oil   ■ ■ Coal   ————/----- Oil pipeline/under construction

△ △ Gas   ○ Hydro-Electric   ——/---- Gas pipeline/under construction

▢ Uranium

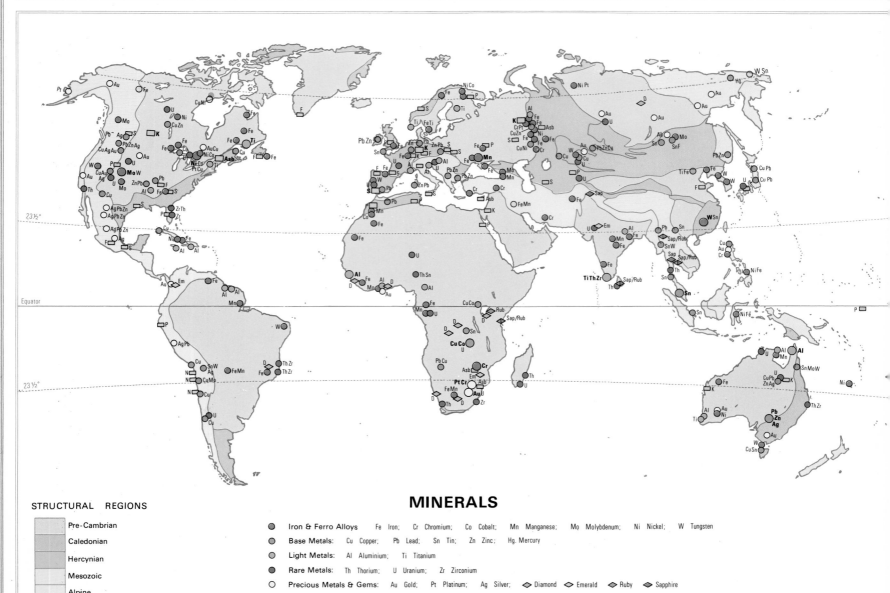

MINERALS

STRUCTURAL REGIONS

Pre-Cambrian
Caledonian
Hercynian
Mesozoic
Alpine

● Iron & Ferro Alloys   Fe Iron; Cr Chromium; Co Cobalt; Mn Manganese; Mo Molybdenum; Ni Nickel; W Tungsten

● Base Metals: Cu Copper; Pb Lead; Sn Tin; Zn Zinc; Hg. Mercury

● Light Metals: Al Aluminium; Ti Titanium

● Rare Metals: Th Thorium; U Uranium; Zr Zirconium

○ Precious Metals & Gems: Au Gold; Pt Platinum; Ag Silver;   ◇ Diamond ◇ Emerald ◆ Ruby ◇ Sapphire

▢ Chemical, Fertiliser & Industrial Minerals   F Fluorite; N Nitrates; P Phosphate (Rock) K Potash S Sulphur; Asb Asbestos

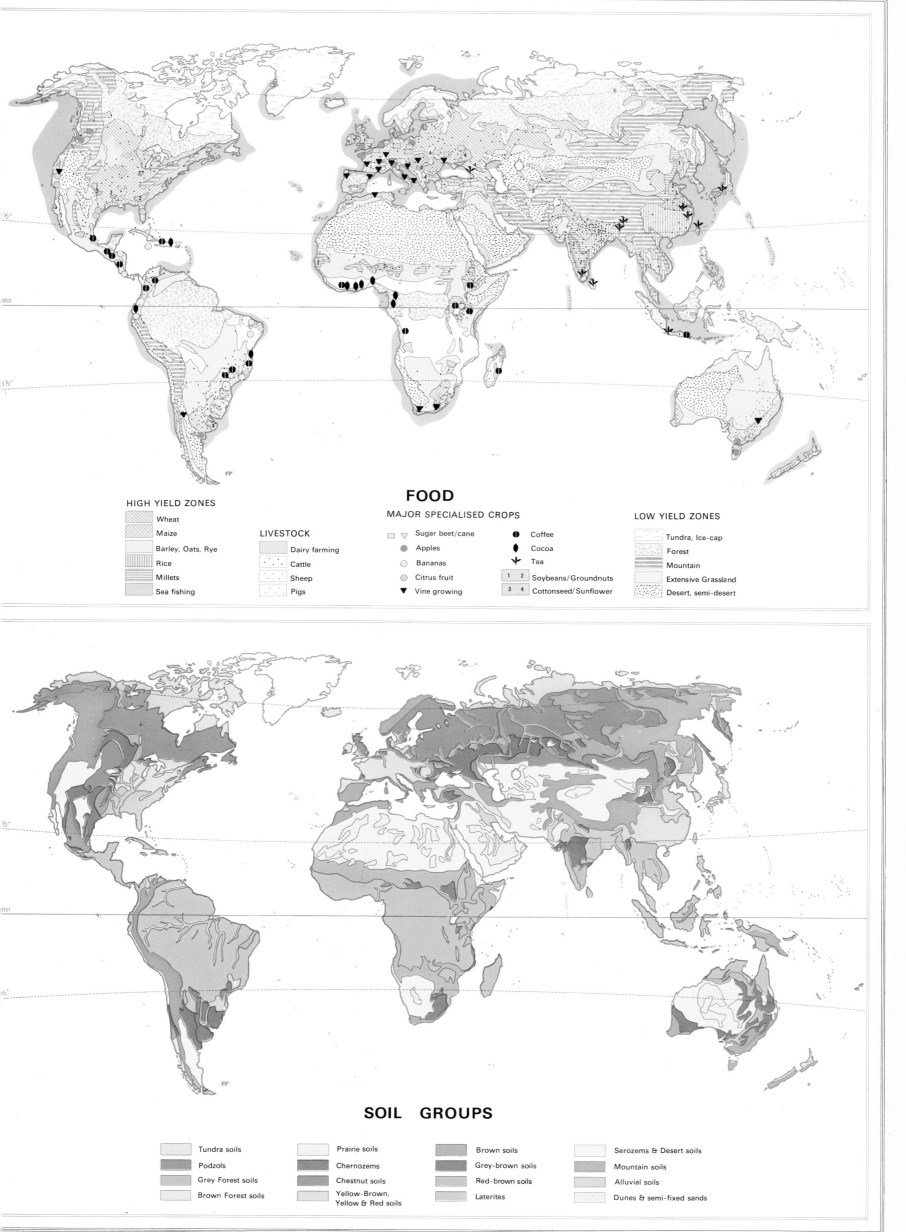

FOOD

HIGH YIELD ZONES

- Wheat
- Maize
- Barley, Oats, Rye
- Rice
- Millets
- Sea fishing

LIVESTOCK

- Dairy farming
- Cattle
- Sheep
- Pigs

MAJOR SPECIALISED CROPS

- Sugar beet/cane
- Apples
- Bananas
- Citrus fruit
- Vine growing
- Coffee
- Cocoa
- Tea
- Soybeans/Groundnuts 1 2
- Cottonseed/Sunflower 3 4

LOW YIELD ZONES

- Tundra, Ice-cap
- Forest
- Mountain
- Extensive Grassland
- Desert, semi-desert

SOIL GROUPS

- Tundra soils
- Podzols
- Grey Forest soils
- Brown Forest soils
- Prairie soils
- Chernozems
- Chestnut soils
- Yellow-Brown, Yellow & Red soils
- Brown soils
- Grey-brown soils
- Red-brown soils
- Laterites
- Serozems & Desert soils
- Mountain soils
- Alluvial soils
- Dunes & semi-fixed sands

1:135M

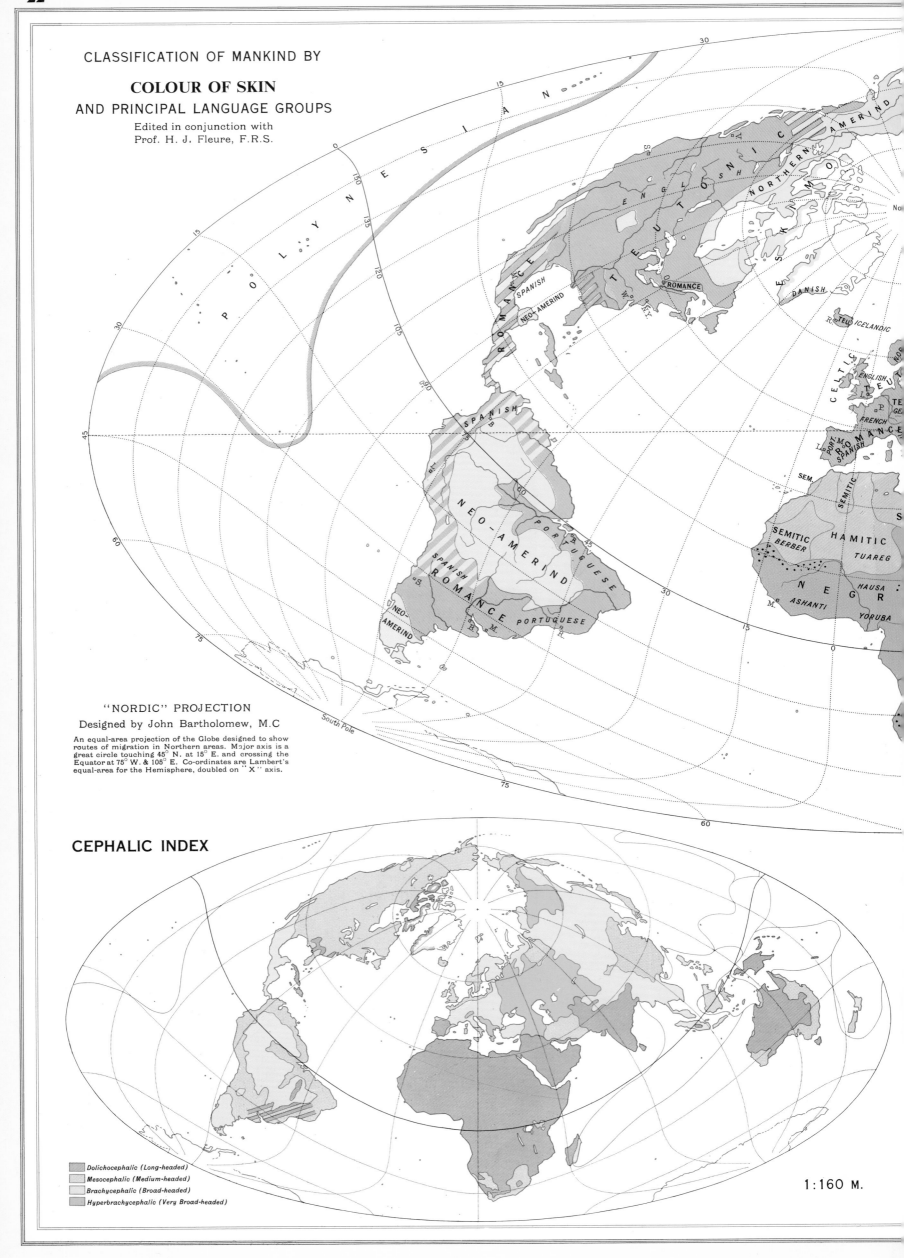

CLASSIFICATION OF MANKIND BY

COLOUR OF SKIN

AND PRINCIPAL LANGUAGE GROUPS

Edited in conjunction with
Prof. H. J. Fleure, F.R.S.

"NORDIC" PROJECTION

Designed by John Bartholomew, M.C

An equal-area projection of the Globe designed to show
routes of migration in Northern areas. Major axis is a
great circle touching 45° N. at 15° E. and crossing the
Equator at 75° W. & 105° E. Co-ordinates are Lambert's
equal-area for the Hemisphere, doubled on "X" axis.

CEPHALIC INDEX

Dolichocephalic (Long-headed)
Mesocephalic (Medium-headed)
Brachycephalic (Broad-headed)
Hyperbrachycephalic (Very Broad-headed)

1:160 M.

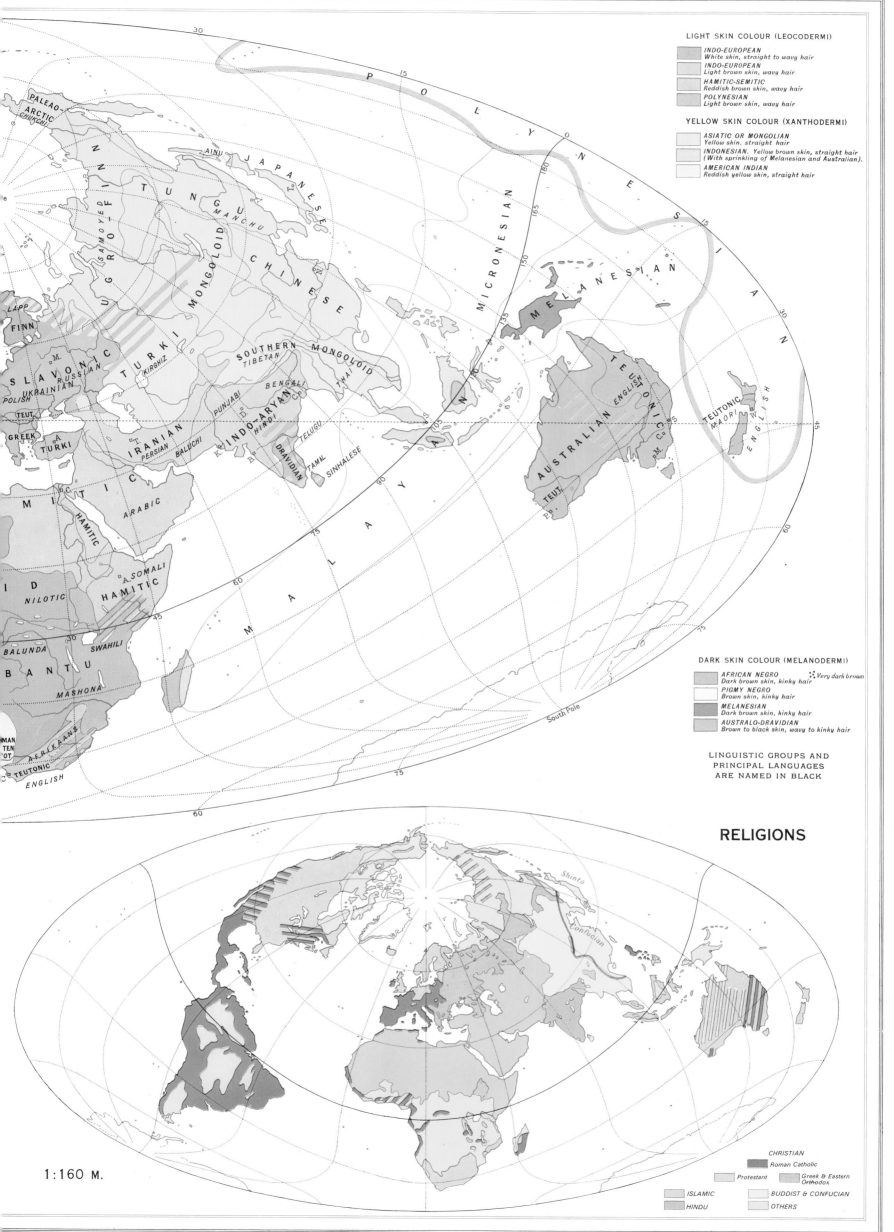

LIGHT SKIN COLOUR (LEOCODERMI)

INDO-EUROPEAN
White skin, straight to wavy hair
INDO-EUROPEAN
Light brown skin, wavy hair
HAMITIC-SEMITIC
Reddish brown skin, wavy hair
POLYNESIAN
Light brown skin, wavy hair

YELLOW SKIN COLOUR (XANTHODERMI)

ASIATIC OR MONGOLIAN
Yellow skin, straight hair
INDONESIAN. Yellow brown skin, straight hair
(With sprinkling of Melanesian and Australian).
AMERICAN INDIAN
Reddish yellow skin, straight hair

DARK SKIN COLOUR (MELANODERMI)

AFRICAN NEGRO ∷ Very dark brown
Dark brown skin, kinky hair
PIGMY NEGRO
Brown skin, kinky hair
MELANESIAN
Dark brown skin, kinky hair
AUSTRALO-DRAVIDIAN
Brown to black skin, wavy to kinky hair

LINGUISTIC GROUPS AND
PRINCIPAL LANGUAGES
ARE NAMED IN BLACK

RELIGIONS

1:160 M.

CHRISTIAN
Roman Catholic
Protestant   Greek & Eastern
                 Orthodox
ISLAMIC   BUDDIST & CONFUCIAN
HINDU   OTHERS

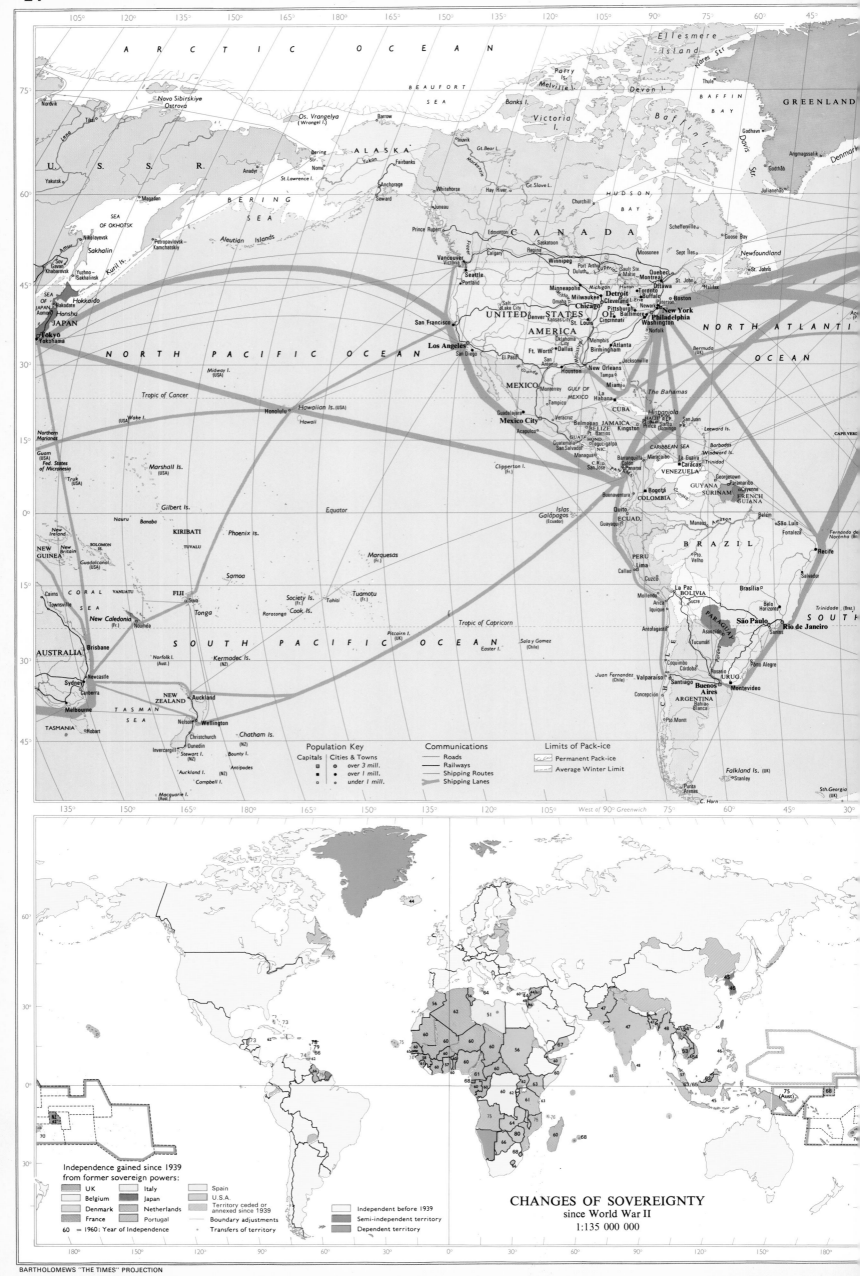

Population Key

Capitals | Cities & Towns
■ over 3 mill. | ● over 1 mill.
■ over 1 mill. | ● under 1 mill.

Communications

Roads
Railways
Shipping Routes
Shipping Lanes

Limits of Pack-ice

Permanent Pack-ice
Average Winter Limit

CHANGES OF SOVEREIGNTY
since World War II
1:135 000 000

Independence gained since 1939 from former sovereign powers:

UK | Italy | Spain
Belgium | Japan | U.S.A.
Denmark | Netherlands | Territory ceded or annexed since 1939
France | Portugal | Boundary adjustments
60 = 1960: Year of Independence | Transfers of territory

Independent before 1939
Semi-independent territory
Dependent territory

BARTHOLOMEWS "THE TIMES" PROJECTION

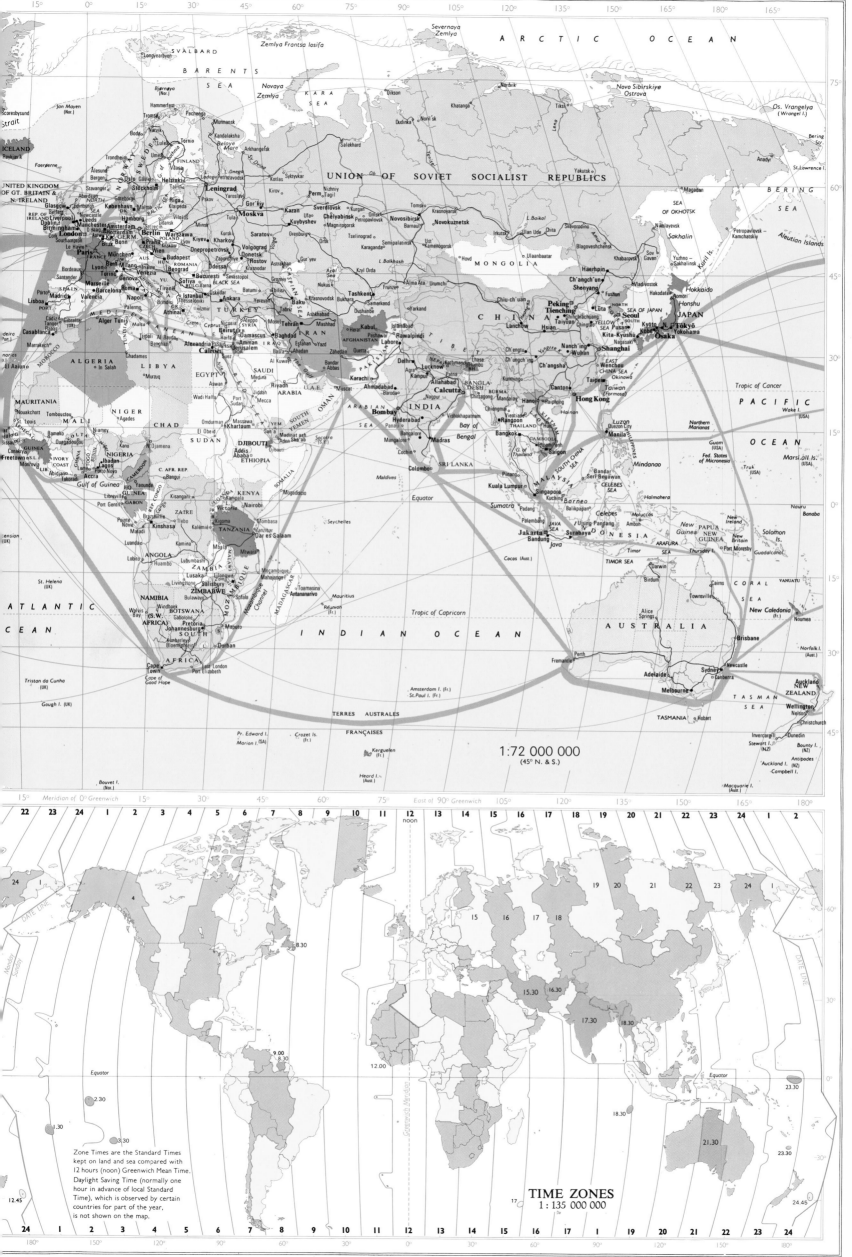

TIME ZONES
1 : 135 000 000

1:72 000 000
(45° N. & S.)

Zone Times are the Standard Times kept on land and sea compared with 12 hours (noon) Greenwich Mean Time. Daylight Saving Time (normally one hour in advance of local Standard Time), which is observed by certain countries for part of the year, is not shown on the map.

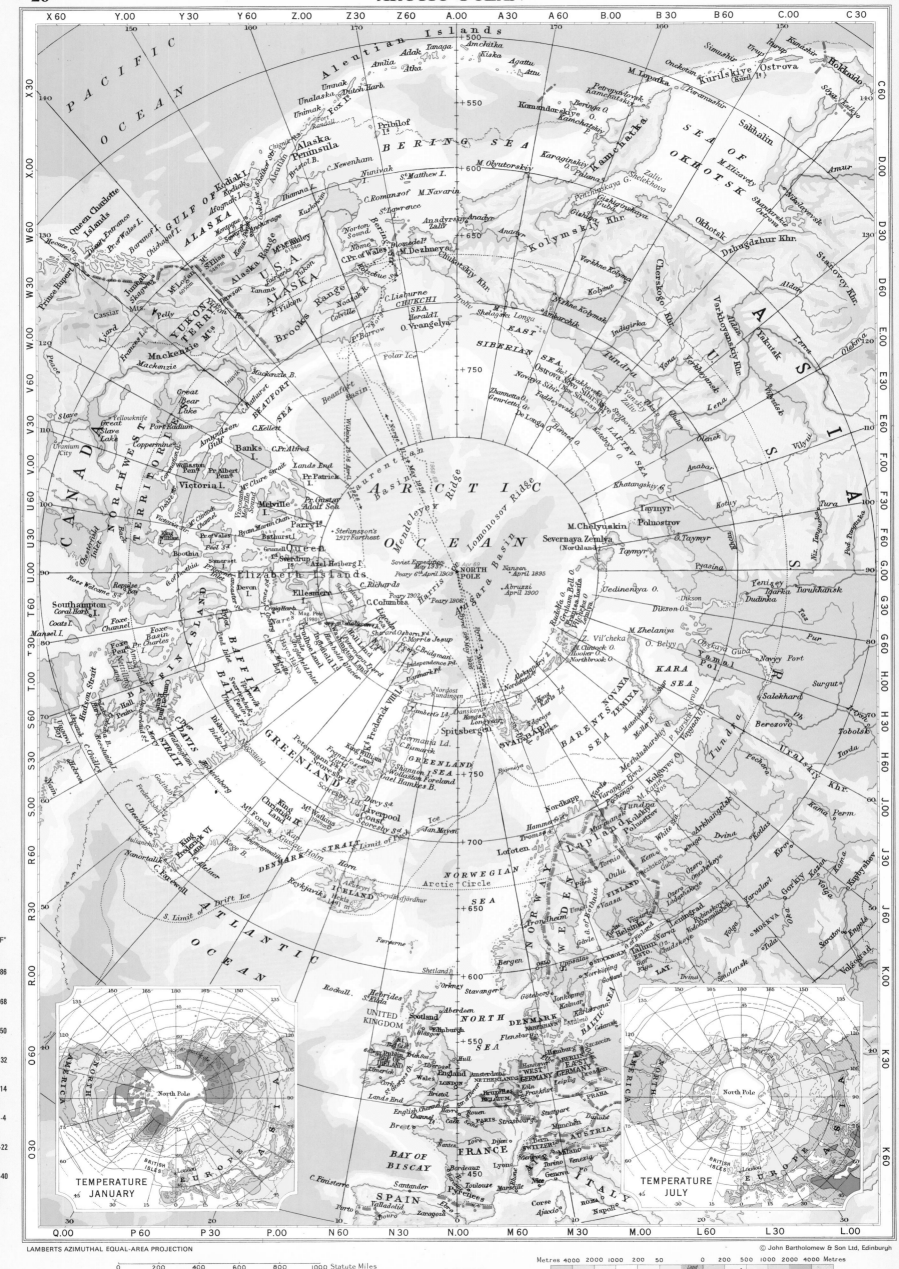

TEMPERATURE
JANUARY

TEMPERATURE
JULY

LAMBERTS AZIMUTHAL EQUAL-AREA PROJECTION

© John Bartholomew & Son Ltd, Edinburgh

1:30M

Statute Miles

Kilometres

Metres 4000 2000 1000 200 50   0   200 1000 2000 4000 Metres

Feet 13120 6560 3280 660 160   0   660 1640 3280 6560 13120 Feet

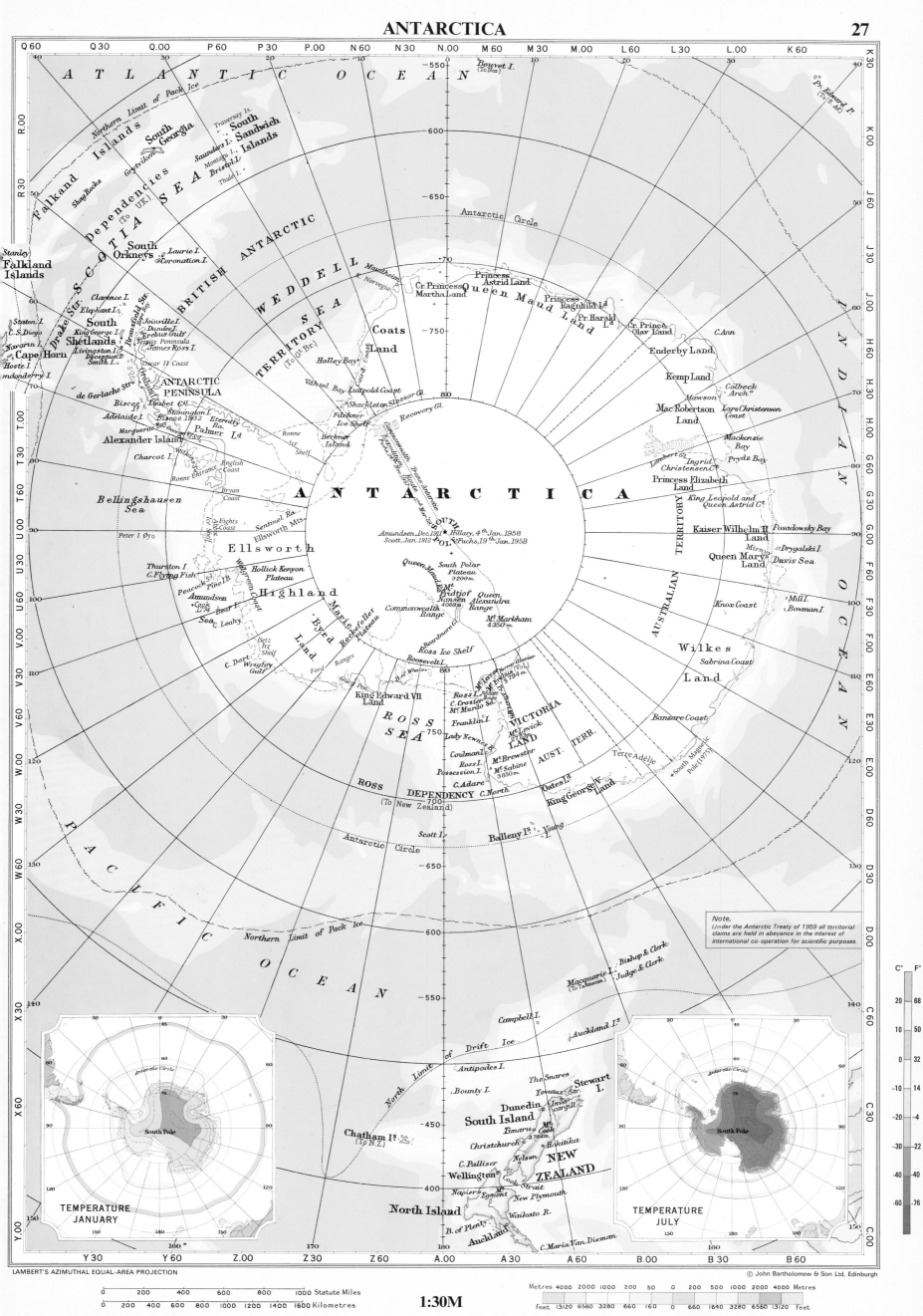

LAMBERT'S AZIMUTHAL EQUAL-AREA PROJECTION

1:30M

© John Bartholomew & Son Ltd, Edinburgh

Antarctic Bases (1970-71) are shown by a red dot.

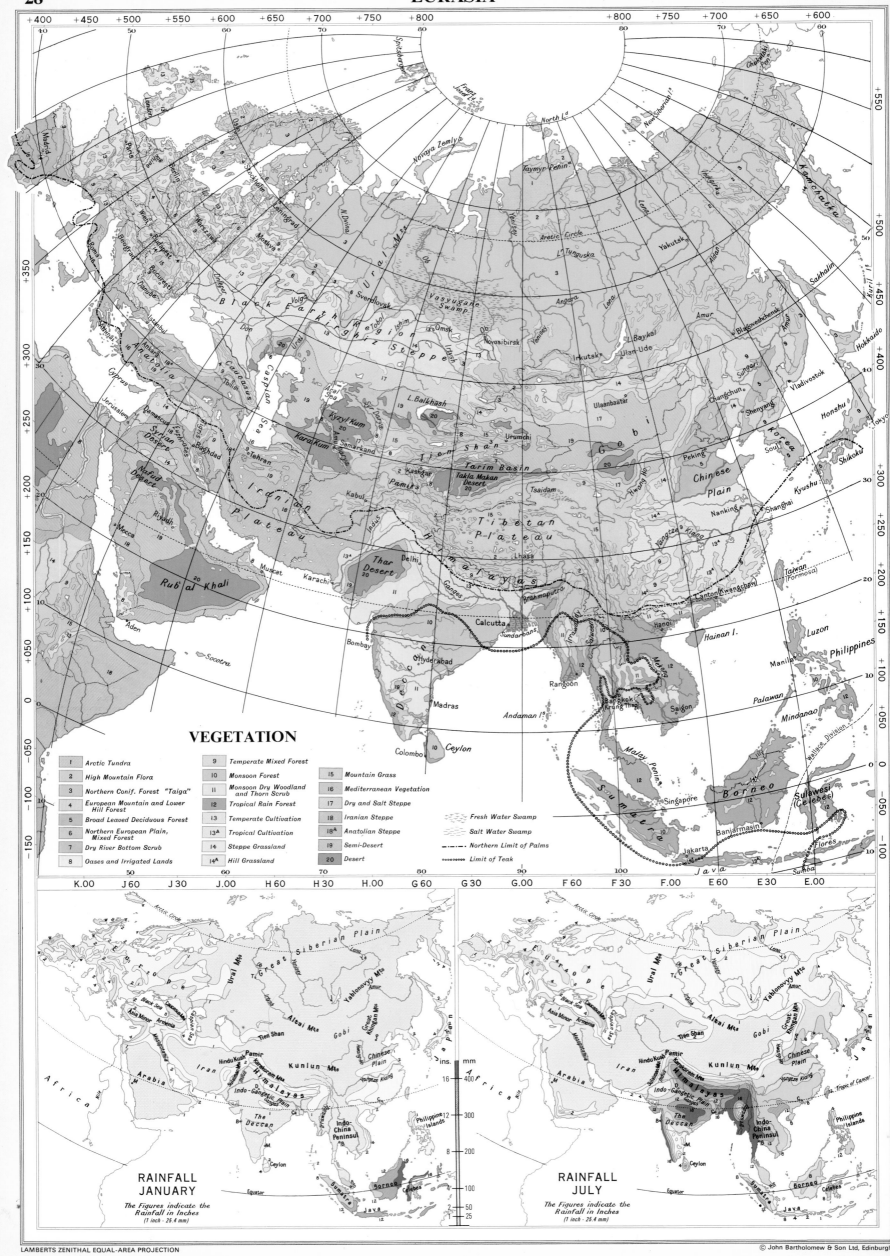

VEGETATION

1 Arctic Tundra	9 Temperate Mixed Forest	15 Mountain Grass
2 High Mountain Flora	10 Monsoon Forest	16 Mediterranean Vegetation
3 Northern Conif. Forest "Taiga"	11 Monsoon Dry Woodland and Thorn Scrub	17 Dry and Salt Steppe
4 European Mountain and Lower Hill Forest	12 Tropical Rain Forest	18 Iranian Steppe
5 Broad Leaved Deciduous Forest	13 Temperate Cultivation	18A Anatolian Steppe
6 Northern European Plain, Mixed Forest	13A Tropical Cultivation	19 Semi-Desert
7 Dry River Bottom Scrub	14 Steppe Grassland	20 Desert
8 Oases and Irrigated Lands	14A Hill Grassland	Fresh Water Swamp
		Salt Water Swamp
		Northern Limit of Palms
		Limit of Teak

RAINFALL
JANUARY

*The Figures indicate the
Rainfall in Inches*
(1 inch = 25.4 mm)

RAINFALL
JULY

*The Figures indicate the
Rainfall in Inches*
(1 inch = 25.4 mm)

LAMBERTS ZENITHAL EQUAL-AREA PROJECTION

© John Bartholomew & Son Ltd, Edinburgh

1:45M

0   200   400   600   800   1000 Statute Miles

0   200 400 600 800 1000 1200 1400 1600 Kilometres

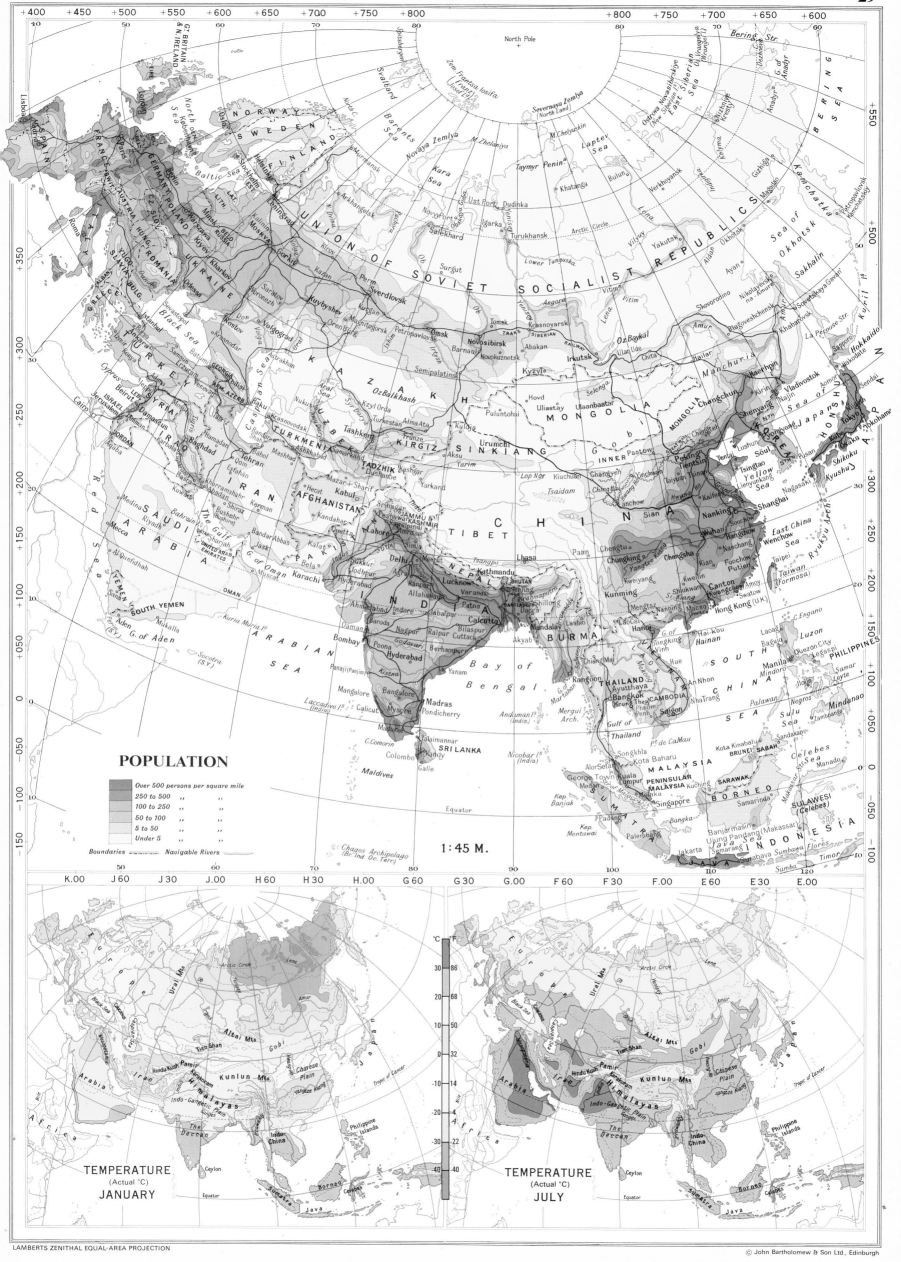

POPULATION

	Over 500 persons per square mile
	250 to 500 " "
	100 to 250 " "
	50 to 100 " "
	5 to 50 " "
	Under 5 " "

Boundaries .... Navigable Rivers

1:45 M.

TEMPERATURE
(Actual °C)
JANUARY

TEMPERATURE
(Actual °C)
JULY

LAMBERTS ZENITHAL EQUAL-AREA PROJECTION

© John Bartholomew & Son Ltd., Edinburgh

0 200 400 600 800 1000 Statute Miles

1:45M

0 200 400 600 800 1000 1200 1400 1600 Kilometres

ARCTIC OCEAN

Severnaya Zemlya (North Land)

Laptev Sea

East Siberian Sea

BERING SEA

Aleutian Islands

Arctic Circle

Tropic of Cancer

SEA OF OKHOTSK

SAKHALIN

Kuril'skiye Ostrova

U S S R

SIBERIA

REPUBLICS

MONGOLIA

INNER MONGOLIA

The Gobi

MANCHURIA

SEA OF JAPAN

JAPAN

NORTH KOREA

SOUTH KOREA

Honshu

Hokkaido

Kyushu

Shikoku

TOKYO

PEKING (PEI-CHING)

YELLOW SEA

Cheju Do (Quelpart)

C H I N A

Nan Shan

Chin Ling Shan

EAST CHINA SEA

NANKING

Shanghai

TAIWAN (FORMOSA) (China Nat. Rep.)

Hong Kong (U.K.)

Macao (Port.)

Hainan

BURMA

THAILAND

LAOS

CAMBODIA

INDO CHINA

HANOI

Bangkok

Phnom Penh

Saigon

Gulf of Tongking

Gulf of Thailand

SOUTH CHINA SEA

PHILIPPINES

Manila

Quezon City

Luzon

Mindanao

Samar

Leyte

Panay

Negros

Palawan

SULU SEA

CELEBES SEA

MALAYSIA

SARAWAK

SABAH

Kuala Lumpur

Singapore

BORNEO (KALIMANTAN)

SUMATRA

I N D O N E S I A

JAVA SEA

Jakarta

MOLUCCA SEA

BANDA SEA

CELEBES (SULAWESI)

ARAFURA SEA

NEW GUINEA

IRIAN JAYA

PAPUA NEW GUINEA

CORAL SEA

Equator

Cape York Peninsula

NORTH PACIFIC OCEAN

Fed. States of Micronesia

Northern Marianas

Guam (USA)

Ogasawara Gunto (Bonin Is.)

Kazan Retto (Volcano Is.)

CEASE FIRE LINE 1953

Ryukyu Retto

Okinawa Gunto

International Boundaries

State Boundaries

© John Bartholomew & Son Ltd, Edinburgh

BONNE'S PROJECTION

1:1

0 100 200 300 400 500 600 700 800 Kilometres

BONNE'S PROJECTION

1:10M

© John Bartholomew & Son Ltd , Edinburgh

| 0 | 100 | 200 | 300 | 400 Statute Miles |

| 0 | 100 | 200 | 300 | 400 | 500 | 600 Kilometres |

Metres 3000 2000 1000 500 200 100 50   Land Depression   0 200 500 1000 2000 Metres

Feet 9840 6560 3280 1640 660 330 160   0 660 1640 3280 6560 Feet

BARENTS SEA

NORWEGIAN SEA

ATLANTIC OCEAN

NORTH SEA

IRISH SEA

ENGLISH CHANNEL

Denmark Strait

Arctic Circle

ICELAND

NORWAY

SWEDEN

FINLAND

LAPLAND

U.S.S.R.

BELO RUSSIA

POLAND

EAST GERMANY

WEST GERMANY

NETHERLANDS

BELGIUM

DENMARK

ESTONIA

LATVIA

LITHUANIA

UNITED KINGDOM OF GT. BRITAIN AND N. IRELAND

SCOTLAND

ENGLAND

WALES

REP. OF IRELAND

NORTHERN IRELAND

Moskva (Moscow), Leningrad, Helsinki, Stockholm, Oslo, Bergen, Berlin, Warszawa (Warsaw), Łódź, Copenhagen, Reykjavik, London, Dublin, Belfast, Edinburgh, Glasgow

LAND USE

1:6M

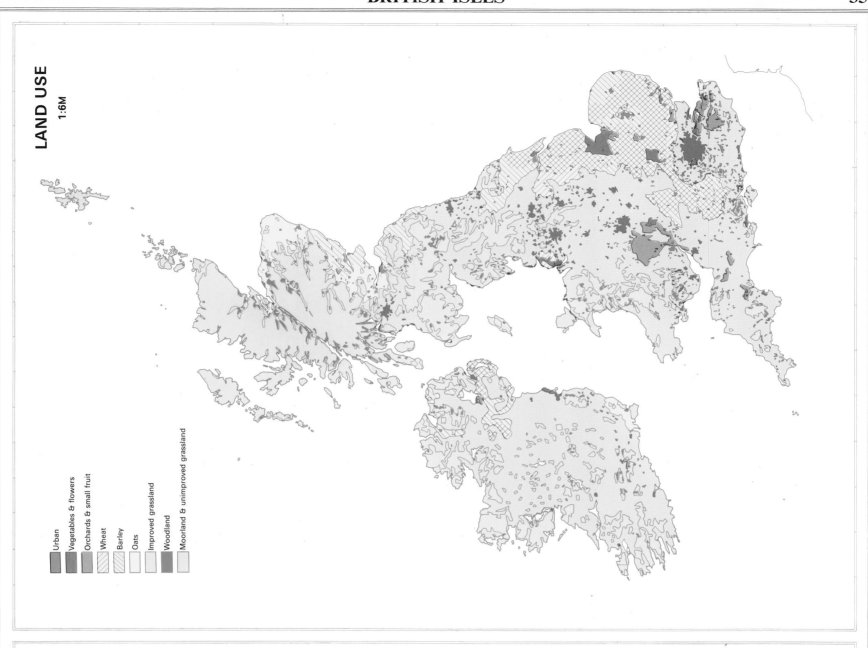

Legend:
- Urban
- Vegetables & flowers
- Orchards & small fruit
- Wheat
- Barley
- Oats
- Improved grassland
- Woodland
- Moorland & unimproved grassland

STRUCTURE

1:6M

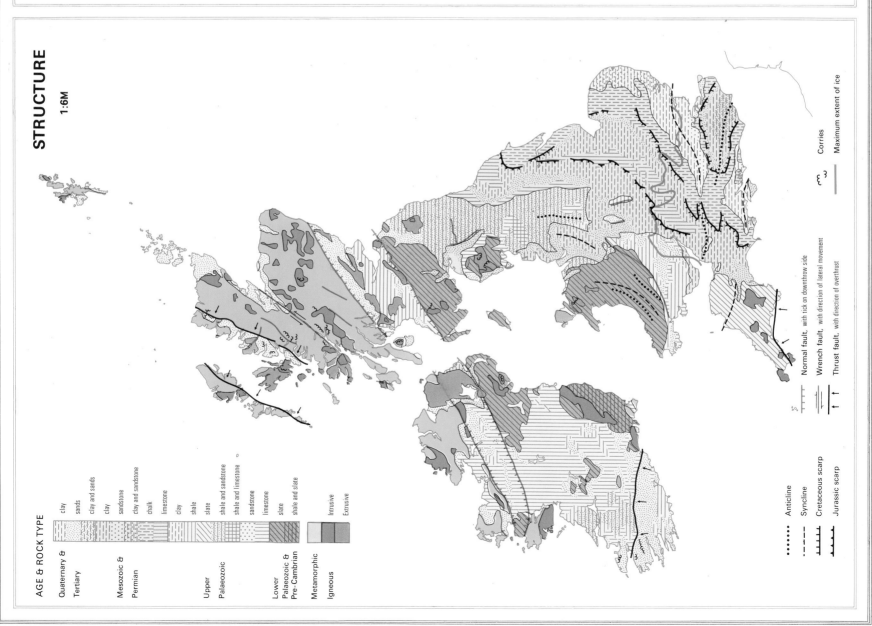

AGE & ROCK TYPE

Quaternary &
- clay
- sands
- clay and sands

Tertiary
- clay
- sandstone
- clay and sandstone

Mesozoic &
- chalk
- limestone
- clay
- shale
- slate

Permian

Upper
- shale and sandstone
- sandstone
- limestone

Palaeozoic

Lower
- slate
- shale and slate

Palaeozoic &
Pre-Cambrian

Metamorphic

Igneous
- Intrusive
- Extrusive

- Anticline
- Syncline
- Cretaceous scarp
- Jurassic scarp

- Normal fault, with tick on downthrow side
- Wrench fault, with direction of lateral movement
- Thrust fault, with direction of overthrust

- Corries
- Maximum extent of ice

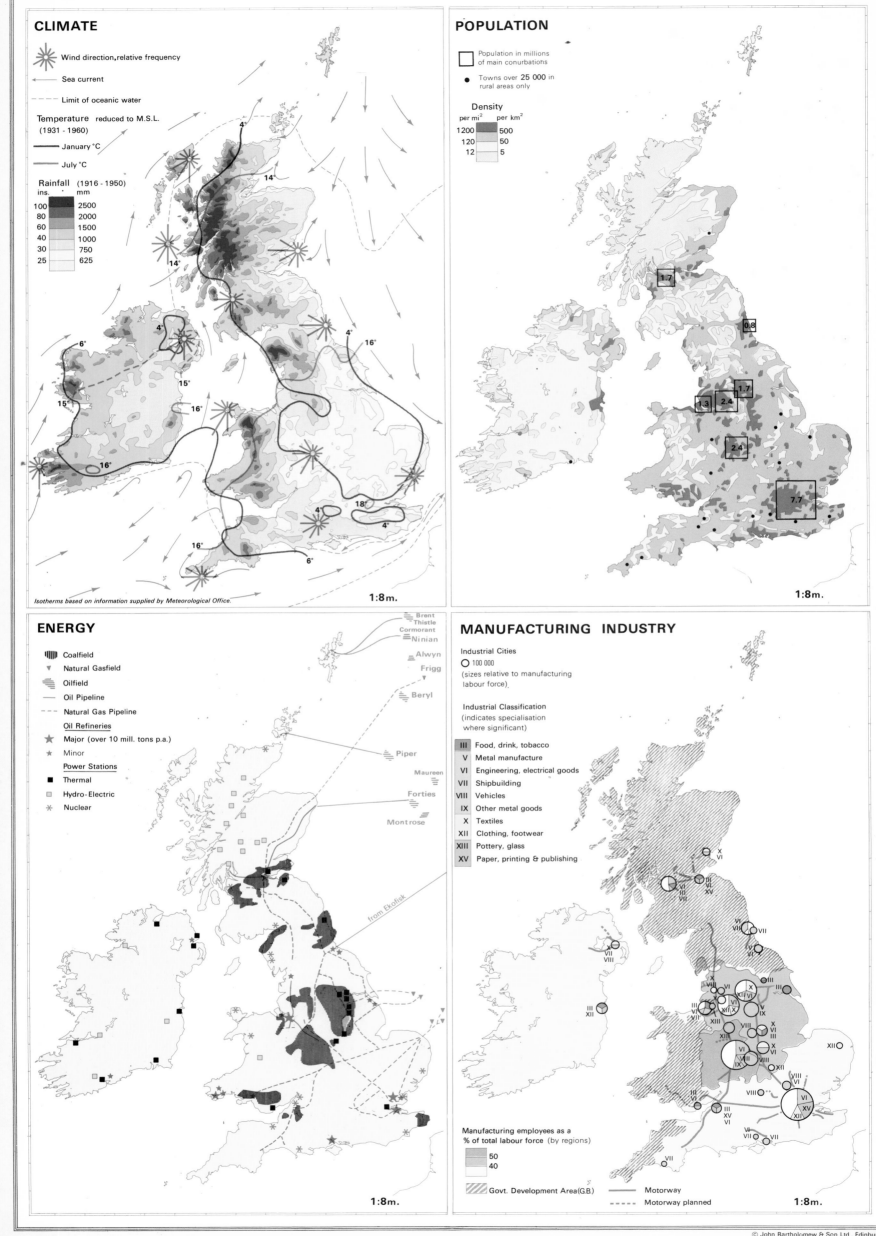

CLIMATE

Wind direction, relative frequency

Sea current

Limit of oceanic water

Temperature reduced to M.S.L.
(1931 - 1960)

January °C

July °C

Rainfall (1916 - 1950)

ins.	mm
100	2500
80	2000
60	1500
40	1000
30	750
25	625

Isotherms based on information supplied by Meteorological Office.

1:8m.

POPULATION

Population in millions of main conurbations

Towns over 25 000 in rural areas only

Density

per mi²	per km²
1200	500
120	50
12	5

1:8m.

ENERGY

Coalfield

Natural Gasfield

Oilfield

Oil Pipeline

Natural Gas Pipeline

Oil Refineries

★ Major (over 10 mill. tons p.a.)

★ Minor

Power Stations

■ Thermal

□ Hydro-Electric

✳ Nuclear

Brent
Thistle
Cormorant
Ninian
Alwyn
Frigg
Beryl
Piper
Maureen
Forties
Montrose

from Ekofisk

1:8m.

MANUFACTURING INDUSTRY

Industrial Cities

◯ 100 000

(sizes relative to manufacturing labour force).

Industrial Classification
(indicates specialisation where significant)

III Food, drink, tobacco

V Metal manufacture

VI Engineering, electrical goods

VII Shipbuilding

VIII Vehicles

IX Other metal goods

X Textiles

XII Clothing, footwear

XIII Pottery, glass

XV Paper, printing & publishing

Manufacturing employees as a % of total labour force (by regions)

50

40

Govt. Development Area (G.B.)

Motorway

Motorway planned

1:8m.

© John Bartholomew & Son Ltd , Edinburgh

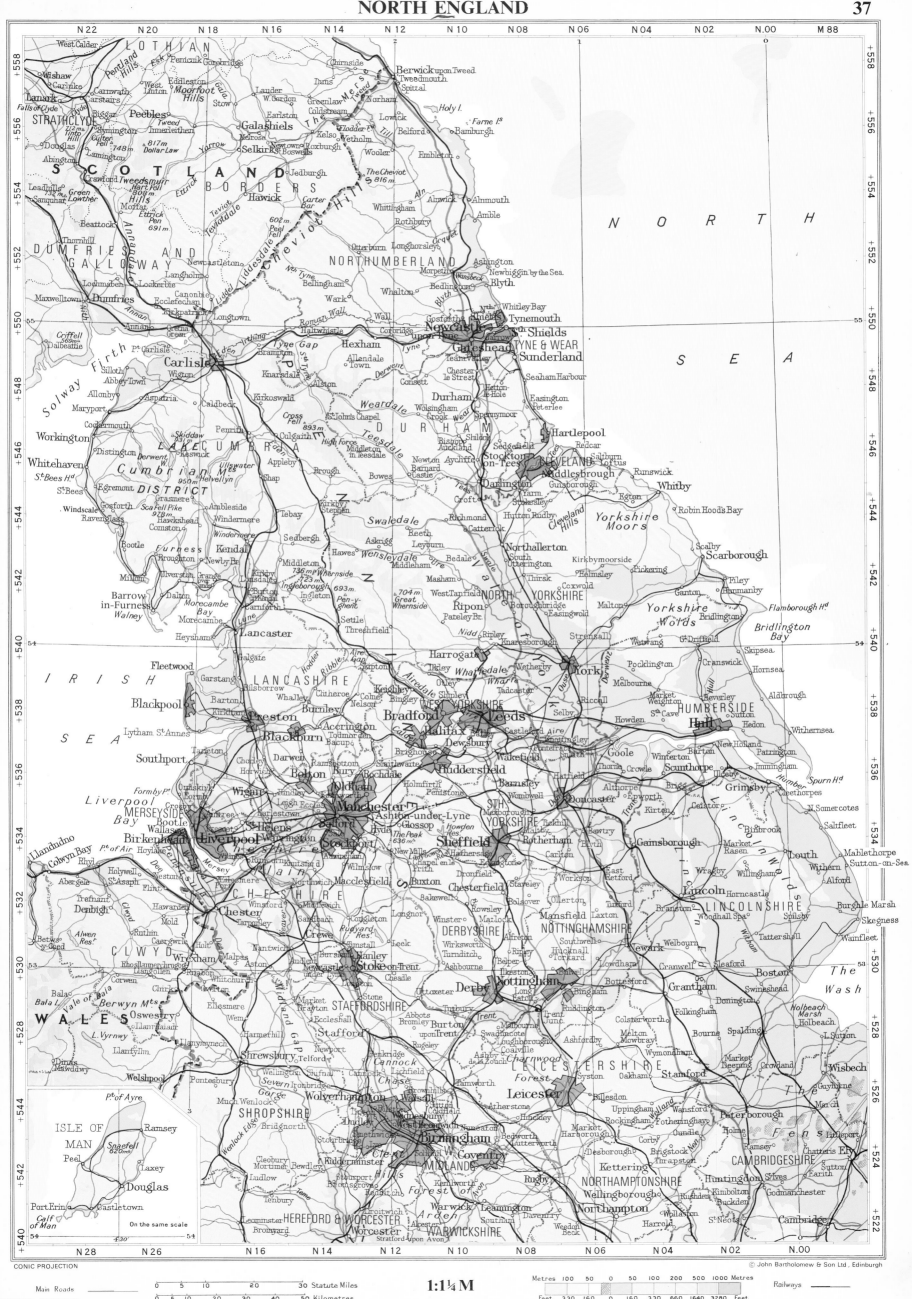

LOTHIAN
West Calder Penicuik Gorebridge
Wishaw Carluke West Linton Eddleston Stow
Lanark Carnwath Moorfoot Hills Lauder W. Gordon
Falls of Clyde Biggar Peebles Innerleithen Earlston
STRATHCLYDE Tweeddale Tweed Galashiels Melrose Kelso
Douglas Symington 817m Dollar Law Selkirk St Boswells Roxburgh Coldstream
Dumfries Lamington 748m Yarrow BORDERS Jedburgh
Leadhills Green Lowther Ettrick Hawick Carter Flodden Fd
Sanquhar Moffat Teviot teviotdale Bar The Cheviot 816m
DUMFRIES Beattock 602m Peel Fell Byrness
AND Thornhill Annandale Newcastleton Wooler
GALLOWAY Lockerbie Langholm No. Tyne Bellingham NORTHUMBERLAND
Maxwelltown Dumfries Ecclefechan Canonbie Wark Whalton
Kirkpatrick Longtown Roman Wall Wall
Criffel Gretna Green Haltwhistle Corbridge Newcastle upon Tyne
Dalbeattie Pt. Carlisle Tyne Gap Hexham Gateshead TYNE & WEAR
Silloth CARLISLE Brampton Tyne Allendale Sunderland
Abbey Town Wigton Knarsdale Town Consett Chester le Street
Allonby Aspatria Caldbeck Alston Derwent Durham
Maryport Cockermouth Skiddaw Penrith Cross Fell DURHAM Peterlee
Workington Keswick 931m 893m St. John's Chapel Weardale Bishop HARTLEPOOL
Whitehaven Distington LAKE Ullswater Culgaith High Force Auckland Stockton Redcar
St Bees Hd CUMBRIA 950m Middleton Newton on-Tees CLEVELAND Saltburn
Egremont Grasmere Helvellyn in teesdale Barnard Castle Darlington Middlesbrough Loftus
Windscale Gosforth Scafell Pike 978m Shap Bowes Croft Yarm Guisborough Runswick
Ravenglass Hawkshead Appleby Teesdale Stokesley Egton Whitby
Bootle Coniston Windermere Kirkby Brough Swaledale Reeth Richmond Hutton Rudby Cleveland Hills Robin Hood's Bay
Millom Furness Kendal Stephen Askrigg Catterick Yorkshire Moors
Barrow Ulverston Grange 736m Whernside Hawes Wensleydale Leyburn Bedale Northallerton Scalby
in-Furness Dalton Morecambe 723m Ingleborough Middleham South Scarborough
Walney Bay Burton Ingleton 693m Masham Otterington Thirsk Kirkbymoorside Pickering Filey
Morecambe Kirkby Pen-y-ghent West Tanfield Helmsley Coxwold Ganton Hunmanby
Lonsdale Settle 704m Ripon NORTH Boroughbridge Easingwold Malton Yorkshire Flamborough Hd
Heysham Lancaster Threshfield Great Whernside Pateley Br. YORKSHIRE Wolds Bridlington
Fleetwood Galgate Nidd Ripley Strensall Wetwang Gt. Driffield Bridlington Bay
Garstang Skipton Knaresborough York Pocklington Cranswick
Blackpool Pilsborrow Hodder Ribble Aire Harrogate Market Skipsea
Barton Whalley gap Ilkley Wharfedale Wetherby Melbourne Weighton Hornsea
Lytham St Annes LANCASHIRE Clitheroe Keighley Shipley Wharfe Tadcaster Sth. Cave Aldbrough
Preston Burnley Colne Bingley Selby Howden Beverley HUMBERSIDE
Southport Blackburn Accrington Nelson Bradford Leeds Castleford Goole Hull Hedon Withernsea
Darwen Todmorden Halifax Aire Pontefract Winterton Barton New Holland Patrington
Formby Pt. Chorley Ramsbottom Bacup Dewsbury Wakefield Thorne Scunthorpe Immingham Spurn Hd
Ormskirk Horwich Bury Rochdale Brighouse Crowle Brigg Grimsby
Liverpool Wigan Bolton Oldham Holmfirth Barnsley Epworth Cleethorpes
Bay MERSEYSIDE Leigh Eccles Ashton-under-Lyne Penistone Wombwell Caistor N. Somercotes
Bootle St Helens Manchester Glossop Mexborough SOUTH Kirton Market
Wallasey Warrington Salford Hyde The Peak Penkhull YORKSHIRE Rasen Louth
Birkenhead Liverpool Stockport 636m Doncaster Gainsborough Wragby Withern
Hoylake Widnes CHESHIRE New Mills Sheffield Maltby Tuxford Sutton-on-Sea
Pt. of Air Northwich Wilmslow Chapel en le Hathersage Rotherham Bawtry Mablethorpe
Colwyn Bay Neston Frith Dronfield Worksop East Retford Alford
Rhyl Chester Knutsford Buxton Coalville Carlton LINCOLNSHIRE
Abergele St. Asaph Macclesfield Bakewell Chesterfield Bolsover Ollerton Lincoln Horncastle
Denbigh Holywell Winsford Sandbach Leek Matlock Staveley Mansfield Laxton Wragby Burgh le Marsh
Betws-y-Coed Flint Tarporley Congleton Longnor Wirksworth Rowsley Woodhall Spa Spilsby
CLWYD Mold Crewe Rudyard Res. Winster Ripley Branston Skegness
Alwen Res. Ruthin Nantwich Burslem DERBYSHIRE Turnditch Belper Newark Tattershall Wainfleet
Ruabon Caergwrle Holt Malpas Audlem Hanley Ashbourne Alfreton Hucknall Lowdham
Llangollen Wrexham Whitchurch Newcastle Stoke-on-Trent Cheadle Torkard Sleaford Boston
Corwen Llanarmon Aston under Lyme Uttoxeter NOTTINGHAMSHIRE Cranwell The
Bala Chirk Ellesmere Market Stone Nottingham Bingham Bottesford Folkingham Wash
Vale of Bala Berwyn Mts Oswestry Drayton STAFFORDSHIRE Derby Long Grantham Donington Holbeach
Dinas Llanfyllin Wem Eccleshall Abbots Bromley Eaton Huddington Swineshead Holbeach Marsh
Mawddwy Llanymynech Harmer Hill Stafford Burton Trent Trent Junc. Colsterworth Spalding
L. Vyrnwy Shrewsbury Newport Rugeley upon Trent Melbourne Ashford by Melton Bourne L. Sutton
Welshpool Telford Cannock Lichfield Swadlincote Loughborough Mowbray Market Deeping Crowland
Pontesbury Wellington Shifnal Chase Tamworth Ashby Charnwood Oakham Stamford Wisbech
SHROPSHIRE Ironbridge Cannock Walsall de la Zouch Forest Syston Wansford March
Much Wenlock Gorge Wolverhampton Sutton LEICESTERSHIRE Uppingham Rockingham Wansford The
Wenlock Edge Bridgnorth Dudley Coldfield Atherstone Leicester Billesdon Fotheringhay Thrapston Oundle Holme Guyhirn Fens
Bewdley West Bromwich Nuneaton Hinckley Market Corby Peterborough
Cleobury Kidderminster Birmingham Bedworth Harborough Desborough Brigstock Ramsey St. Ives CAMBRIDGESHIRE
Mortimer Ludlow Stourbridge Clent Coventry Lutterworth Kettering Thrapston Chatteris Ely
Tenbury Bromsgrove MIDLANDS Rugby NORTHAMPTONSHIRE Huntingdon Godmanchester
HEREFORD & WORCESTER Redditch Warwick Leamington Daventry Wellingborough Kimbolton Buckden St. Neots
Leominster Droitwich Arden Kenilworth Southam Harrold Cambridge
Bromyard Worcester Stratford upon Avon Alcester Weedon Northampton Harrold

SCOTLAND

NORTH SEA

IRISH SEA

WALES

ISLE OF MAN
Pt. of Ayre
Ramsey
Snaefell 620m
Peel
Laxey
Douglas
Port Erin
Castletown
Calf of Man

CONIC PROJECTION

Main Roads 0 5 10 20 30 Statute Miles
0 5 10 20 30 40 50 Kilometres

1 : 1¼ M

Metres 100 50 0 50 100 200 500 1000 Metres
Feet 330 160 0 160 330 660 1640 3280 Feet

Railways

© John Bartholomew & Son Ltd., Edinburgh

NATIONAL BOUNDARY
New County/Regional Names are shown thus ------ SHROPSHIRE

Main Roads ———
Railways ————

0   5   10   20   30   40   50 Statute Miles
0 5 10   20   30   40   50   60   70   80 Kilometres

1:1

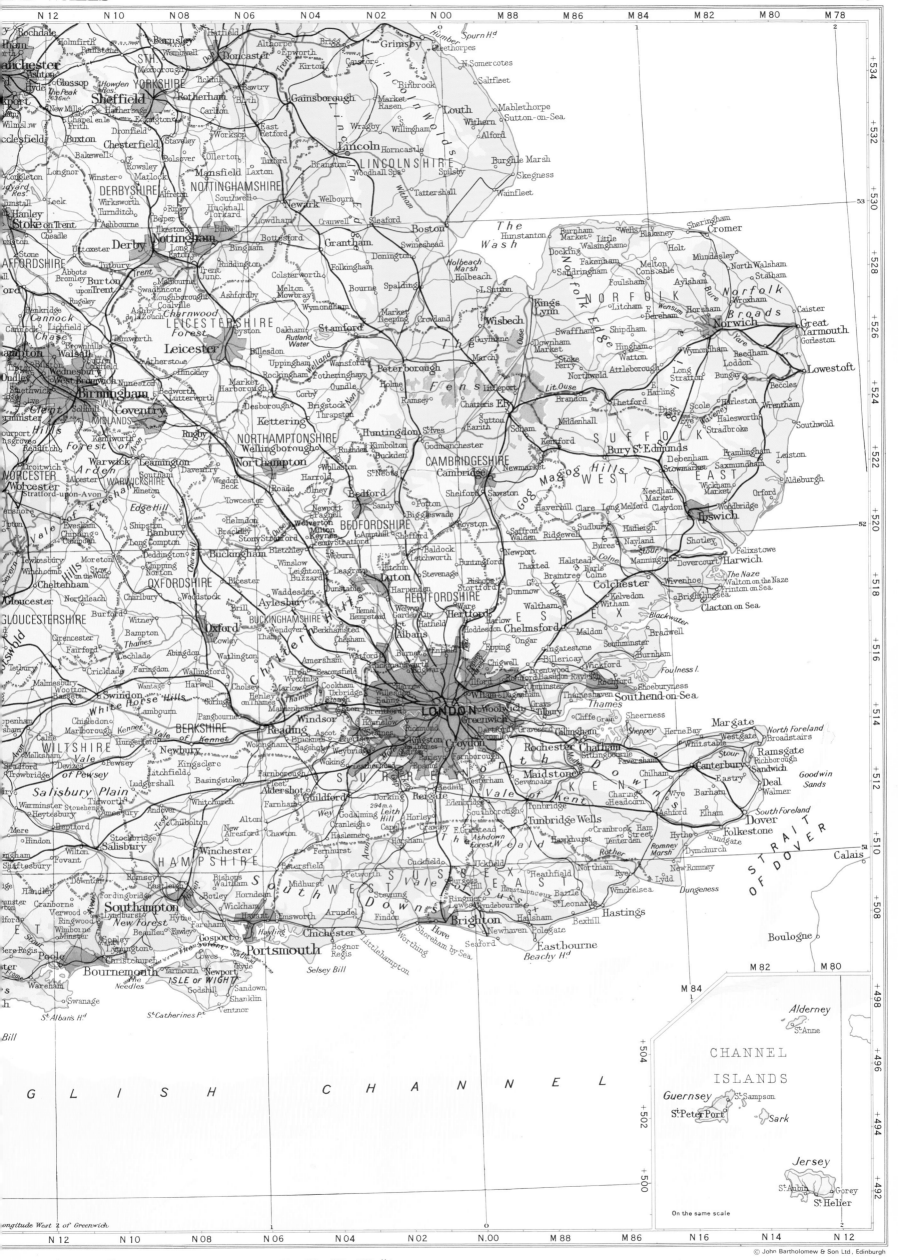

N 12 N 10 N 08 N 06 N 04 N 02 N 00 M 88 M 86 M 84 M 82 M 80 M 78

+534
+532
+530
+528
+526
+524
+522
+520
+518
+516
+514
+512
+510
+508
+506
+504
+502
+500
+498
+496
+494
+492

Rochdale Holmfirth Barnsley Hatfield Althorpe Brigg Grimsby Humber Spurn H?
Manchester Ashton STH Mexborough Wombwell Doncaster Trent Epworth N Somercotes Saltfleet
Glossop The Peak 636m Howden Res YORKSHIRE Tickhill Kirton Cleethorpes
Hyde New Mills Sheffield Rotherham Bawtry Gainsborough Market Rasen Louth Mablethorpe Sutton-on-Sea
Wilmslow Chapel en le Frith Hathersage Dronfield Worksop East Retford Wragby Willingham Alford
Macclesfield Buxton Chesterfield Staveley Ollerton LINCOLNSHIRE Horncastle Skegness
Bakewell Rowsley Bolsover Tuxford Lincoln Burghle Marsh Spilsby
Longnor Winster Matlock Mansfield Laxton Branston Woodhall Spa Wainfleet
STAFFORDSHIRE DERBYSHIRE Alfreton NOTTINGHAMSHIRE Welbourn Tattershall
Leek Wirksworth Turnditch Ripley Hucknall Southwell Newark Sleaford Boston The Wash Hunstanton Wells Blakeney Sheringham Cromer
Hanley Ashbourne Torkard Bilhell Lowdham Granwell Swineshead Burnham Market Walsingham Little Walsingham Holt Mundesley
Stoke on Trent Cheadle Ilkeston Nottingham Bingham Grantham Donington Docking Fakenham Melton Constable North Walsham Stalham
Uttoxeter Burton Trent Long Eaton Bottesford Folkingham Spalding Holbeach Marsh Sandringham Foulsham Aylsham
upon Trent Swadlincote Melbourne Trent Junc Melton Bourne L Sutton Downham NORFOLK Litcham Dereham Wroxham Norfolk Caister
Abbots Bromley Rugeley Coalville Ashfordby Mowbray Holbeach Kings Swaffham Shipdham Hingham Broads Great Yarmouth
Penkridge Cannock Ashby de la Zouch Charnwood Oakham Colsterworth Crowland Wisbech Lynn Stoke Ferry Watton Attleborough Loddon Norwich Gorleston
Lichfield Chase Loughborough Forest Rutland Stamford Market Deeping Guyhirne Northwold Long Stratton Reedham Lowestoft
Brownhills Tamworth LEICESTERSHIRE Water Uppingham Welland March Littleport Brandon Thetford Diss Harleston Bungay Beccles
Walsall Atherstone Leicester Billesdon Rockingham Fotheringhay Peterborough Holme Ramsey Ely Mildenhall Scole Waveney Wrentham Southwold
Birmingham Nuneaton Hinckley Market Corby Oundle Chatteris Sutton Earith Soham Kenford SUFFOLK Eye Harling Halesworth Stradbroke
West Bromwich Bedworth Harborough Desborough Brigstock Nene Thrapston Huntingdon St Ives Godmanchester Newmarket Bury St Edmunds Diss Stowmarket Framlingham Leiston
Smethwick Coventry MIDLANDS Lutterworth Kettering Wellingborough CAMBRIDGESHIRE Needham Debenham Saxmundham Aldeburgh
Solihull Rugby Northampton Kimbolton St Neots Cambridge Newport Gog Magog Hills Market Wickham Woodbridge Orford
WORCESTER Kenilworth Warwick Daventry Wollaston Harrold Olney Sheford Sandy Potton Royston WEST Haverhill Clare Long Melford Sudbury Hadleigh Claydon Ipswich
Worcester Alcester Leamington Southam NORTHAMPTONSHIRE Weedon Beck Roade Biggleswade Saffron Sawston EAST Needham Shotley
Stratford-upon-Avon Kineton Towcester Bedford Shefford Walden Ridgewell Nayland Stour Dovercourt Harwich
Evesham Vale of Evesham Edge Hill Arden Warwick BEDFORDSHIRE Ampthill Fenny Letchworth Newport Thaxted Halstead Colne Wivenhoe The Naze Walton on the Naze
Droitwich Shipston Banbury Wolverton Milton Keynes Stratford Woburn Baldock Hitchin Stevenage Bishops Braintree Earls Colne Frinton-on-Sea
Hills Tewkesbury Moreton Long Compton Buckingham Bletchley Leighton Dunstable Hemel Harpenden Stortford Dunmow Witham Brightlingsea
Winchcomb Stow on the Wold Deddington Chipping Norton Buzzard Leagrave Luton Hempstead Welwyn Harlow Waltham Chelmsford Maldon Clacton on Sea
Cheltenham Northleach Charlbury Woodstock Brill Aylesbury HERTFORDSHIRE Hatfield Garden City Hoddesdon Ongar Southminster
GLOUCESTERSHIRE Burford Witney OXFORDSHIRE Thame Wendover Berkhamsted Chesham St Albans Hertford Epping Ingatestone Bradwell
Gloucester Bampton Oxford Cowley Wallington Amersham Beaconsfield Watford Barnet Enfield ESSEX Billericay Brentwood Wickford Foulness I
Cirencester Fairford BUCKINGHAMSHIRE High Wycombe Marlow Cookham Rickmansworth Edgware Romford Upminster Rochford Shoeburyness
Malmesbury Wootton Lechlade Faringdon Cholsey Henley on Thames Maidenhead Uxbridge Ealing Ilford Dagenham Grays Thameshaven Southend-on-Sea
Cricklade Marlborough Wantage Pangbourne Reading Windsor Bracknell Staines Kingston LONDON Woolwich Tilbury Thames
Chiseldon Swindon White Horse Hills Lambourn Goring Ascot Bagshot Hounslow Croydon Greenwich Cliffe Grain Sheerness Margate North Foreland
WILTSHIRE Calne Newbury Vale of Kennet Wokingham Weybridge Epsom Bromley Dartford Gravesend Gillingham Sheppey Herne Bay Westgate Broadstairs
Devizes Kingsclere BERKSHIRE Woking Leatherhead Barnes Farnborough Chatham Whitstable Ramsgate
Bradford Trowbridge Vale of Pewsey Hungerford Basingstoke Fleet Aldershot Guildford SURREY Redhill Reigate Sevenoaks Rochester Maidstone Faversham Canterbury Sandwich
Warminster Stonehenge Ludgershall Andover Whitchurch Farnham Godalming Dorking Leith Hill 294m Edenbridge Vale of Kent KENT Charing Chilham Barham Deal Walmer
Heytesbury Amesbury Tidworth Alton New Alresford Chawton Haslemere Cranleigh Horley Tonbridge Headcorn Ashford Wye Eastry Goodwin Sands
Mere Hindon Deptford Salisbury Plain Stockbridge Chilbolton Winchester Farnhurst Crawley E Grinstead Tunbridge Wells Cranbrook Ham Street Tenterden Hythe Dover South Foreland
Salisbury Wilton Fovant Romsey Bishops Waltham Petersfield Midhurst Ashdown Forest Weald Hawkhurst Rother Romney Marsh Dymchurch STRAIT OF DOVER Calais
Shaftesbury HAMPSHIRE Cuckfield SUSSEX Uckfield Northiam New Romney Lydd Folkestone Sandgate
Handley Downton Eastleigh SOUTH WEST Steyning Heathfield Battle Rye Winchelsea Dungeness Boulogne
Cranborne Verwood Botley Horndean DOWNS Vale Ringmer St Leonards Hastings
Fordingbridge Romsey Southampton Havant Emsworth Arundel Findon Lewes Herstmonceux Bexhill
DORSET Wimborne Ringwood New Forest Hythe Fareham Chichester Bognor Worthing Brighton Newhaven Polegate Eastbourne
Poole Beaulieu Gosport Hayling Littlehampton Hove Shoreham by Sea Seaford Beachy H?
Bournemouth Christchurch Lymington Portsmouth Bognor Regis EAST
Wareham Swanage Yarmouth Newport Cowes The Solent Selsey Bill
St Albans H? ISLE OF WIGHT Sandown
Bill St Catherines P? Godshill Shanklin
Ventnor

GLISH CHANNEL

M 82 M 80
M 84
CHANNEL
ISLANDS
Alderney St Anne
Guernsey St Sampson
St Peter Port Sark
Jersey
St Aubin Gorey
St Helier
On the same scale

+504
+502
+500
+498
+496
+494
+492

longitude West of Greenwich

N 12 N 10 N 08 N 06 N 04 N 02 N.00 M 88 M 86 N 16 N 14 N 12

© John Bartholomew & Son Ltd, Edinburgh

M

Metres 200 100 50 0 50 100 200 500 1000 Metres
Feet 660 330 160 0 160 330 660 1640 3280 Feet

NATIONAL BOUNDARY
COUNTY/REGION BOUNDARY ..... CUMBRIA

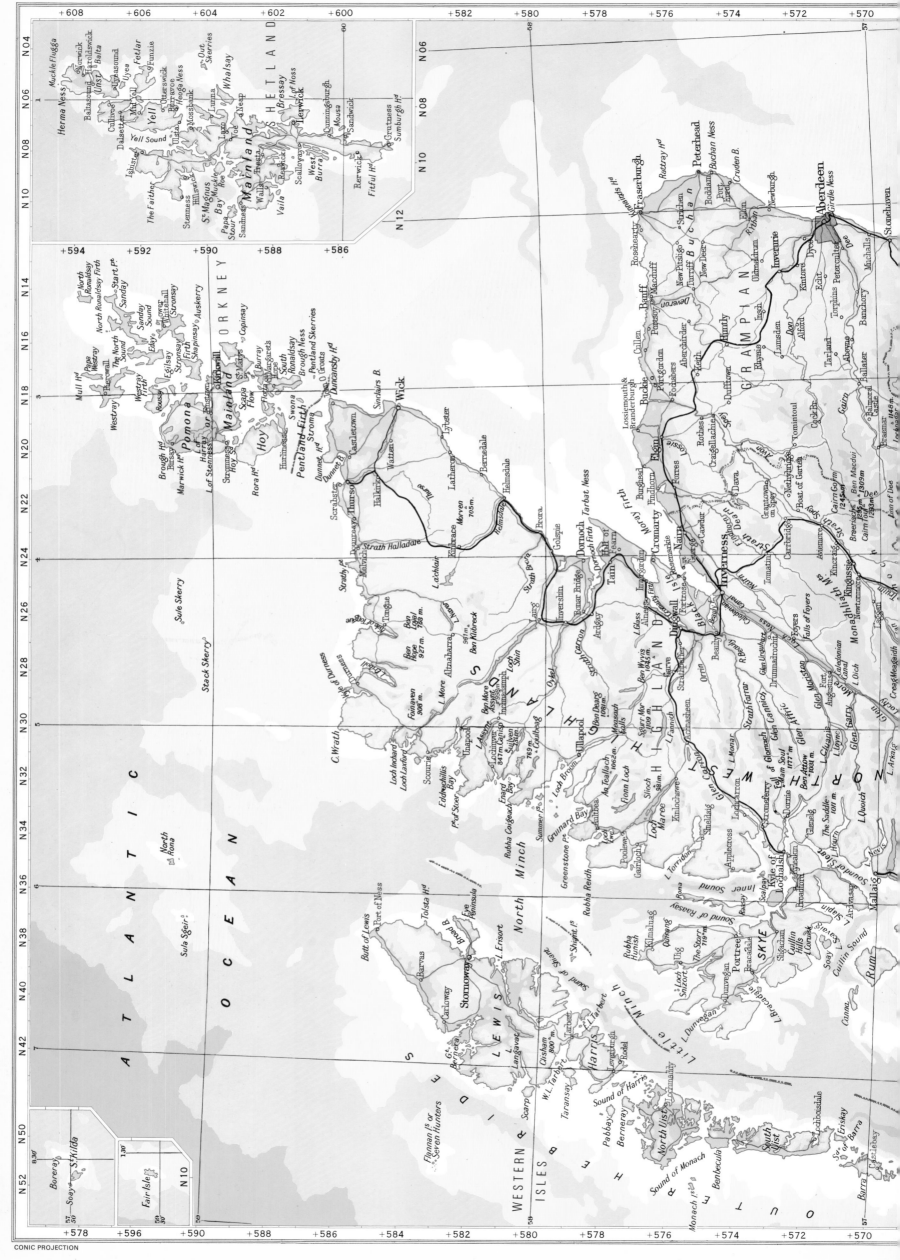

CONIC PROJECTION

Main Roads ————
Railways ————

| 0 | 5 | 10 | 20 | 30 | 40 | 50 Statute Miles |
| 0 | 5 | 10 | 20 | 30 | 40 | 50 | 60 | 70 | 80 Kilometres |

1:1

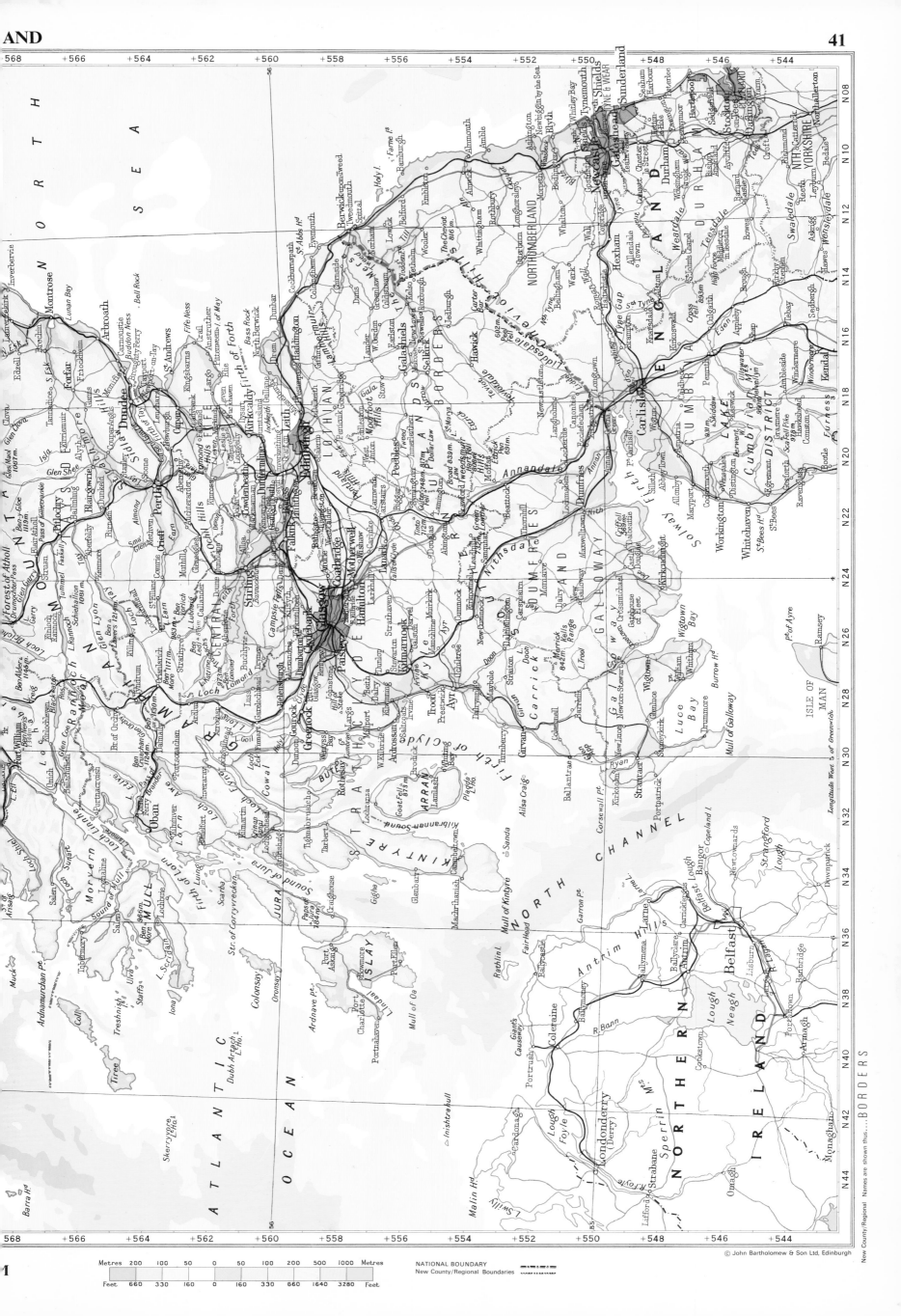

NORTH SEA

ATLANTIC OCEAN

NORTH CHANNEL

NORTHUMBERLAND

ENGLAND

CUMBRIA
LAKE DISTRICT

DUMFRIES AND GALLOWAY

BORDERS

LOTHIAN

CENTRAL

STRATHCLYDE

FIFE

TAYSIDE

GRAMPIAN

NORTHERN IRELAND

Belfast
Londonderry (Derry)
Armagh
Coleraine
Ballymena
Antrim
Lisburn
Bangor
Newtownards
Downpatrick
Lurgan
Portadown
Omagh
Strabane
Cookstown
Magherafelt

ISLE OF MAN
Ramsey

Glasgow
Edinburgh
Dundee
Perth
Stirling
Falkirk
Motherwell
Hamilton
Paisley
Greenock
Ayr
Kilmarnock
Carlisle
Newcastle upon Tyne
Sunderland
Durham
Hartlepool
Stockton
Darlington
Middlesbrough
Berwick upon Tweed
Galashiels
Hawick
Peebles
Dumfries
Stranraer
Oban
Fort William
Montrose
Arbroath
St Andrews
Kirkcaldy
Leith

NTH YORKSHIRE

Firth of Forth
Firth of Clyde
Firth of Tay
Solway Firth
Luce Bay
Wigtown Bay

MULL
ISLAY
JURA
ARRAN
KINTYRE
BUTE

Isle of May
Bass Rock
Farne Is.
Holy I.
Lindisfarne
Rathlin I.
Ailsa Craig

The Cheviot 816m
Merrick 842m
Goatfell 873m

MORVERN
COWAL
KYLE
CARRICK
ANNANDALE
NITHSDALE

Lough Neagh
Lough Foyle
Belfast Lough
Strangford Lough
Carlingford Lough

Antrim Hills
Sperrin Mts.

Giant's Causeway
Fair Head
Malin Hd.
Mull of Galloway
Mull of Kintyre
Mull of Oa

Metres 200 100 50 0 50 100 200 500 1000 Metres
Feet 660 330 160 0 160 330 660 1640 3280 Feet

NATIONAL BOUNDARY
New County/Regional Boundaries

© John Bartholomew & Son Ltd, Edinburgh

New County/Regional Names are shown thus....BORDERS

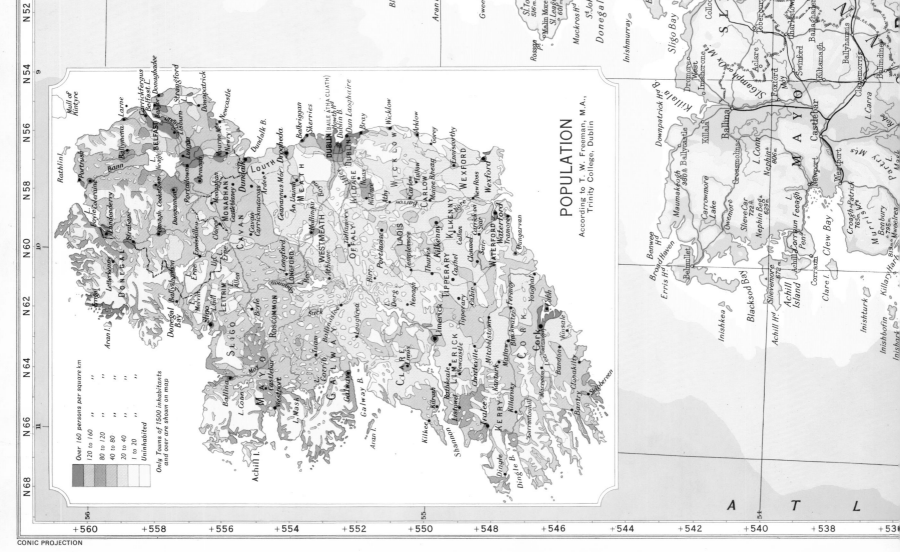

POPULATION

According to T. W. Freeman, M.A.,
Trinity College, Dublin

Over 160 persons per square km
120 to 160 ,, ,, ,, ,,
80 to 120 ,, ,, ,, ,,
40 to 80 ,, ,, ,, ,,
20 to 40 ,, ,, ,, ,,
1 to 20 ,, ,, ,, ,,
Uninhabited

Only Towns of 1500 inhabitants
and over are shown on map

CONIC PROJECTION

Main Roads ———
Railways ———

0   5   10   20   30   40   50 Statute Miles
0   5   10   20   30   40   50   60   70   80 Kilometres

1:1

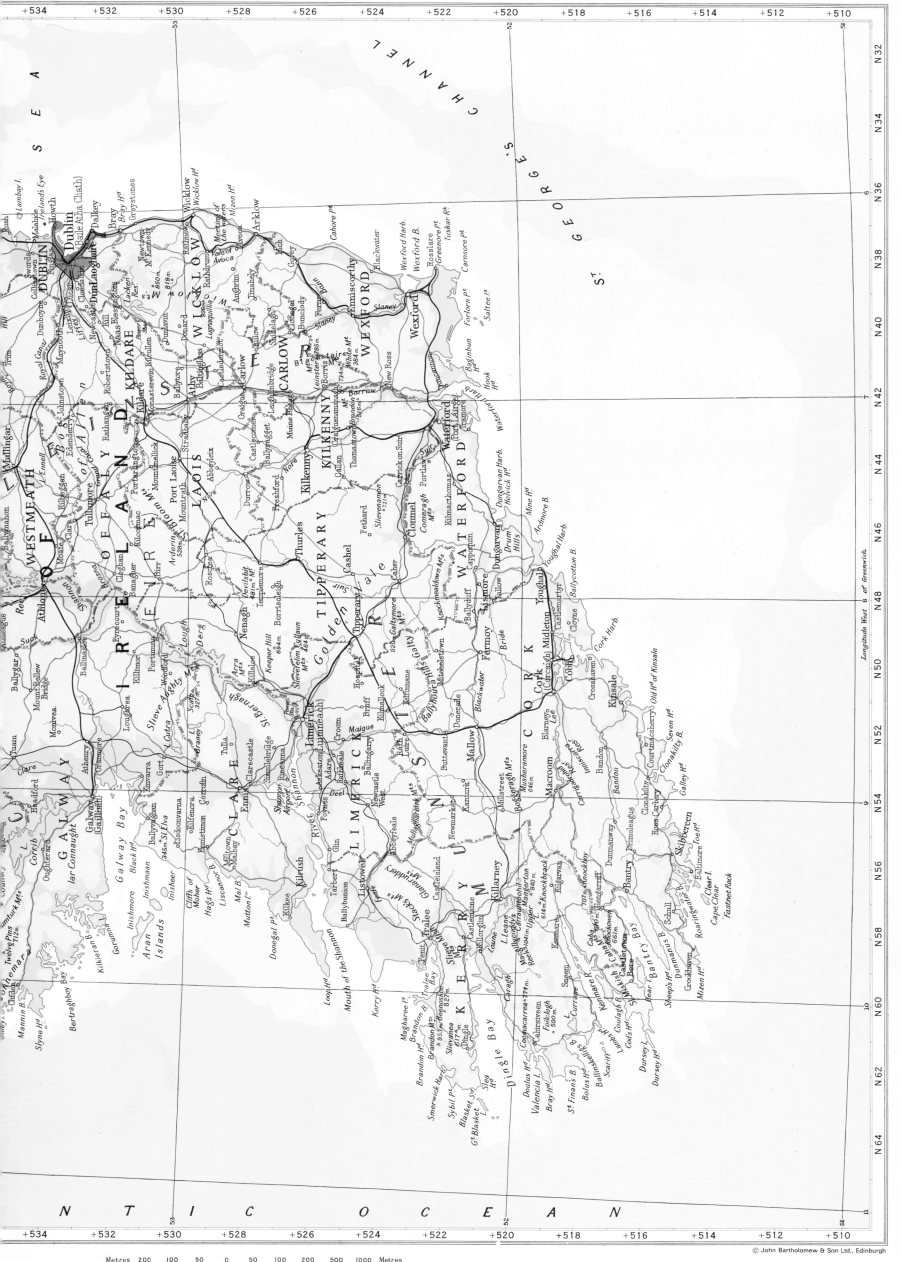

Metres 200 100   50   0   50   100   200   500 1000 Metres

Feet   660 330 160   0   160 330 660 1640 3280 Feet

State Boundary

County Boundaries

M

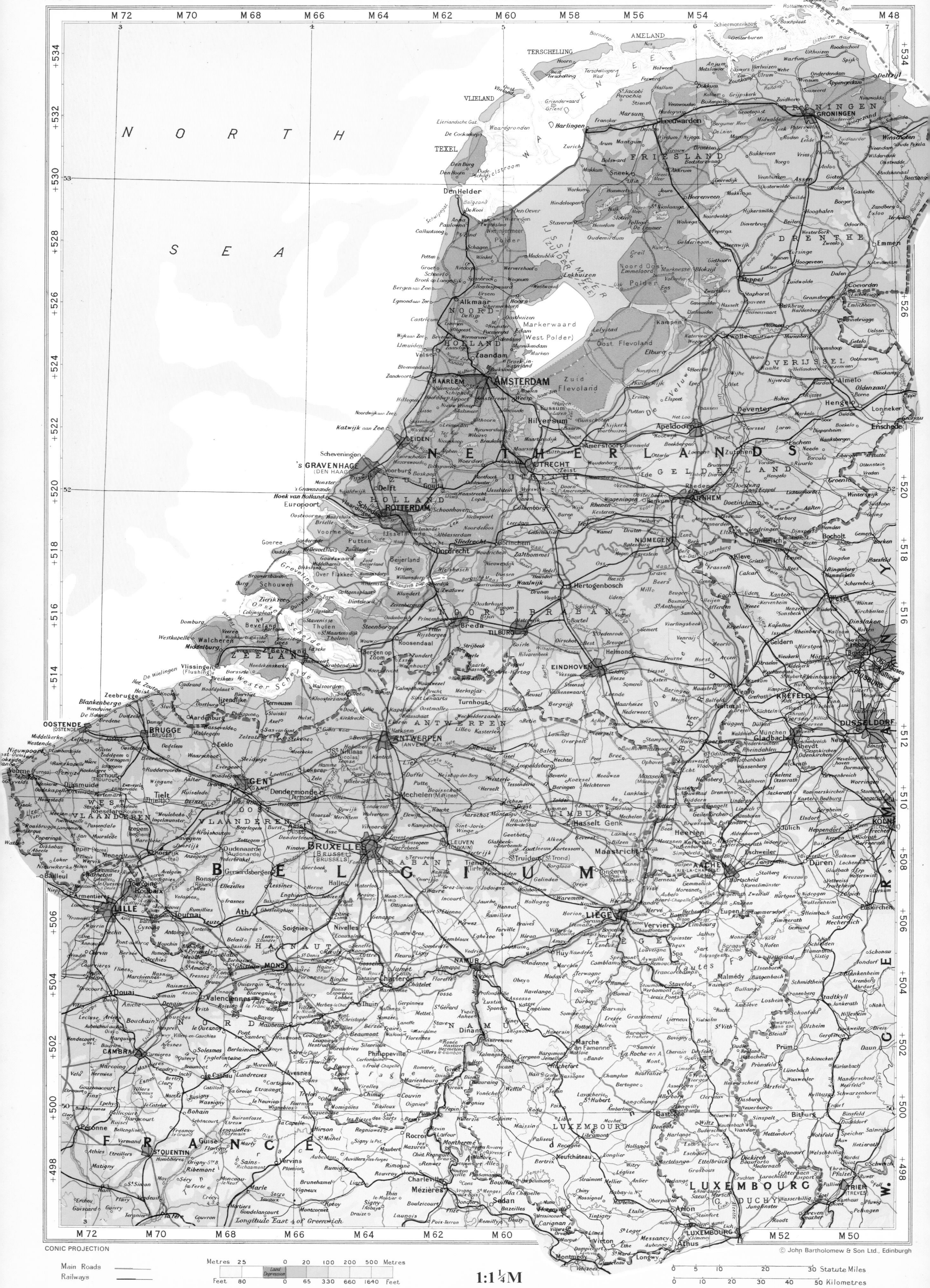

NORTH SEA

NETHERLANDS

BELGIUM

FRANCE

LUXEMBOURG

CONIC PROJECTION

Main Roads ———
Railways ———

Metres 25   0   20   100   200   500 Metres
Feet   80   0   65   330   660   1640 Feet
Land Depression

1:1¼M

0   5   10   20   30 Statute Miles
0   10   20   30   40   50 Kilometres

© John Bartholomew & Son Ltd., Edinburgh

Longitude East of Greenwich

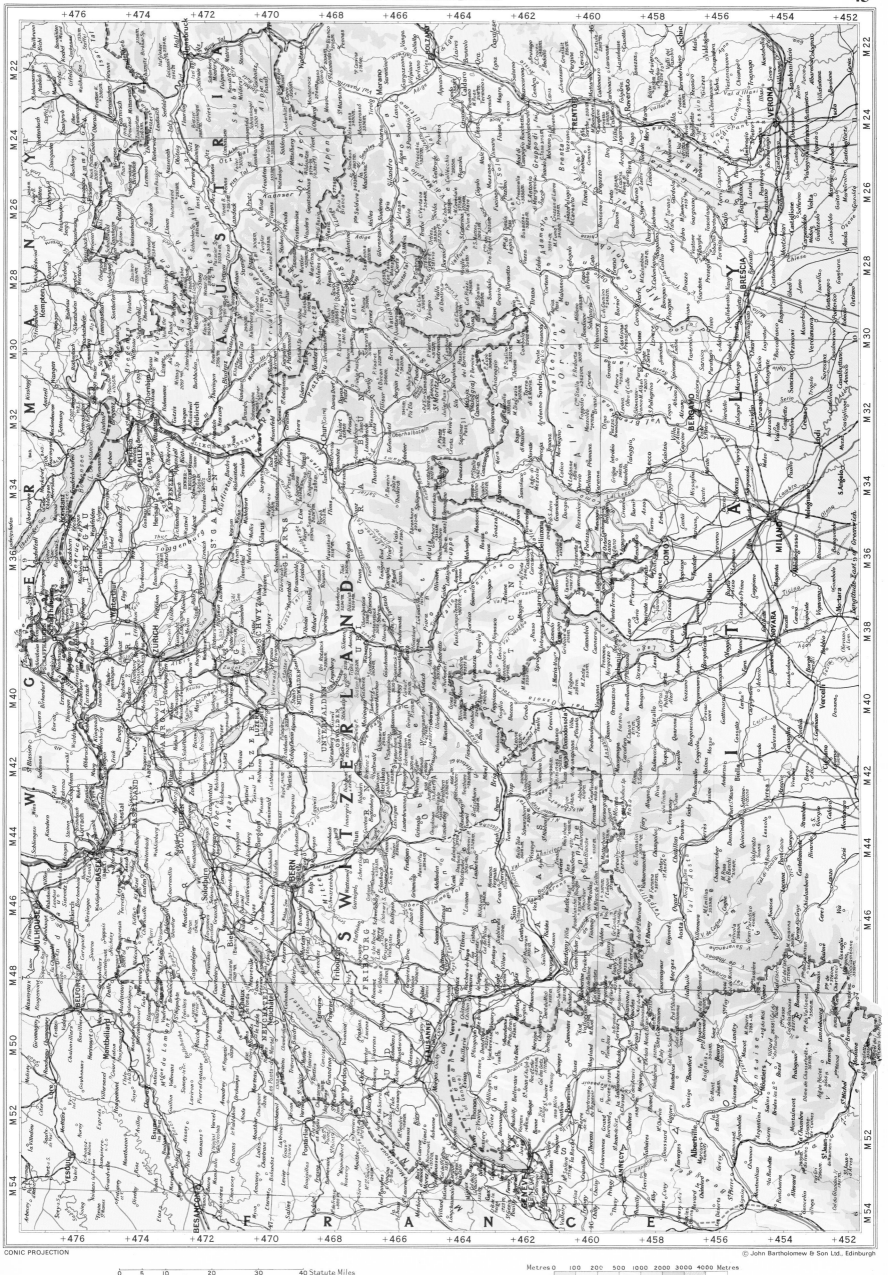

CONIC PROJECTION

1:1¼M

© John Bartholomew & Son Ltd. Edinburgh

0 5 10 20 30 40 Statute Miles
0 10 20 30 40 50 60 Kilometres

Metres 0 100 200 500 1000 2000 3000 4000 Metres
Feet 0 330 660 1640 3280 6560 9840 13120 Feet

3

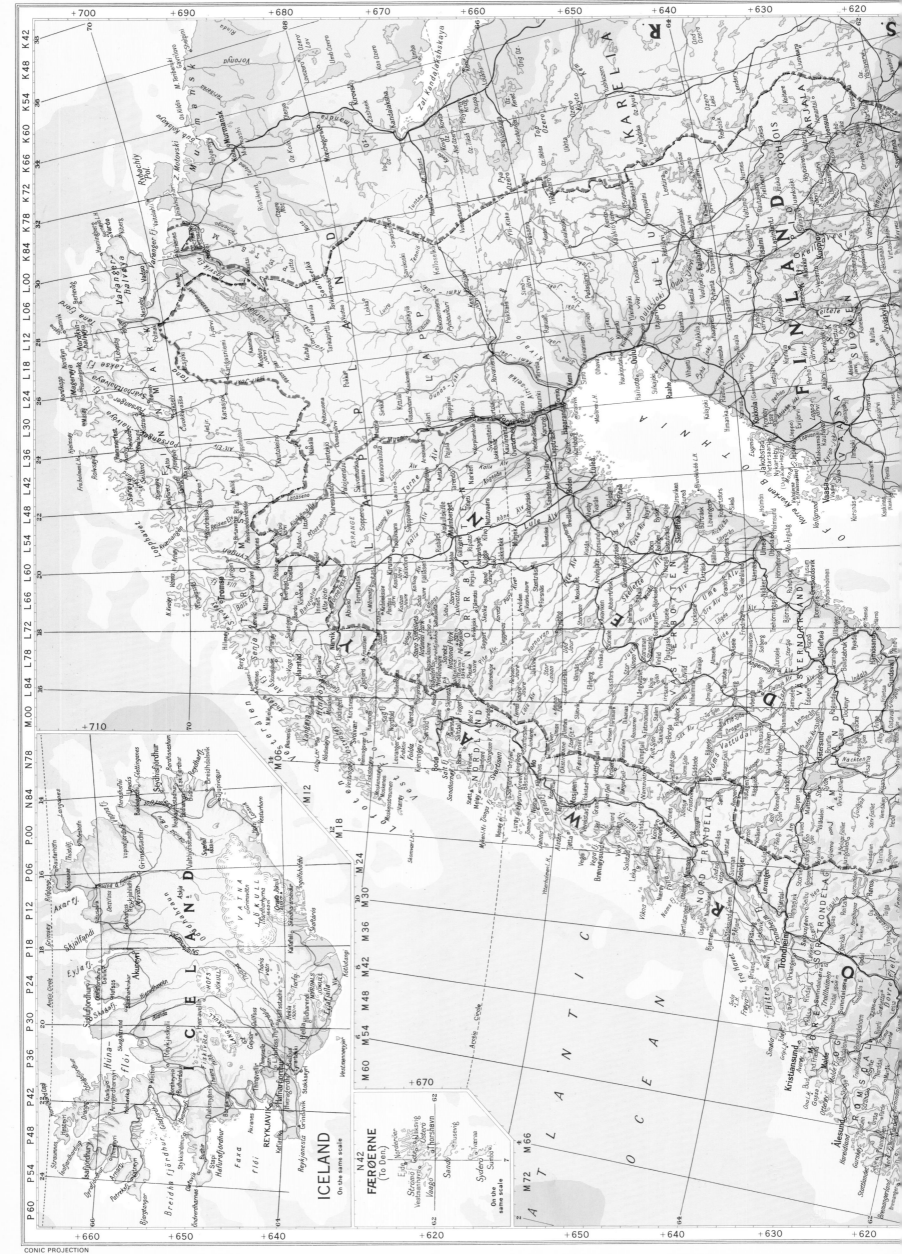

ICELAND
On the same scale

FÆRØERNE
(To Den.)
On the same scale

Main Roads
Railways

0 20 40 60 80 100 120 140 160 180 Statute Miles
0 20 40 80 120 160 200 240 280 Kilometres

1:4

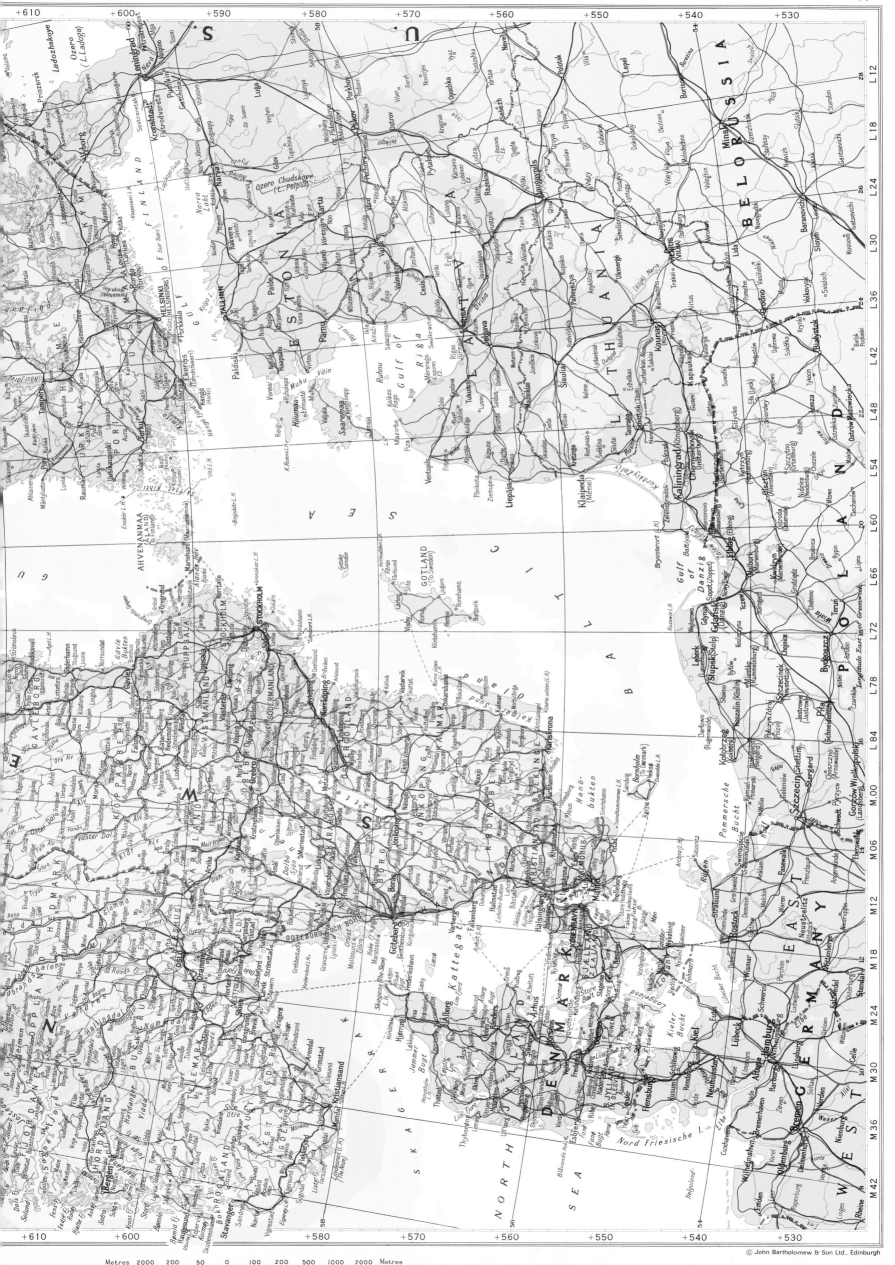

Metres	2000	200	50	0	100	200	500	1000	2000	Metres
Feet	6560	660	160	0	330	660	1640	3280	6560	Feet

International Boundaries

State Boundaries

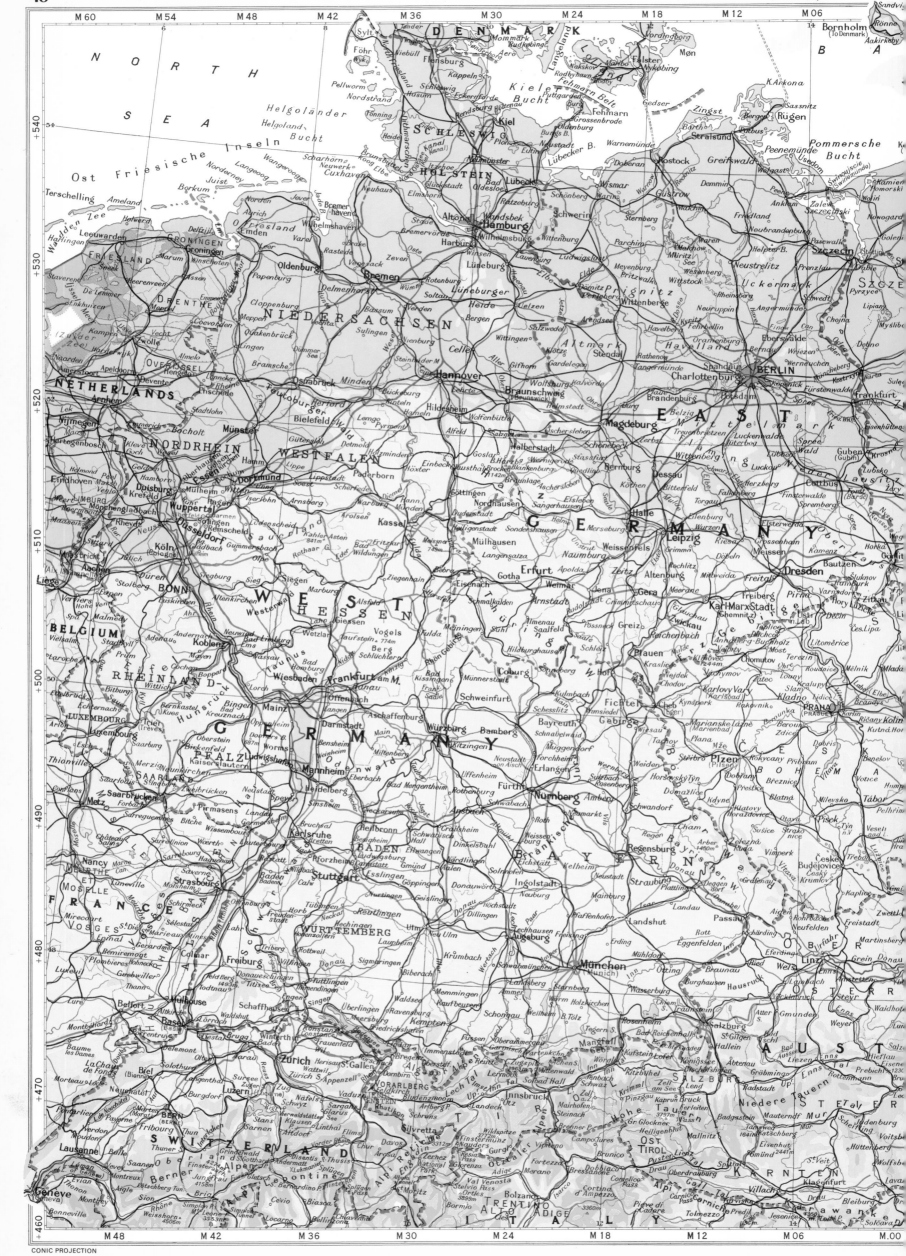

Main Roads _____
Railways _____

CONIC PROJECTION

0 10 20 30 40 50 60 70 80 90 100 110 120 Statute Miles
0 10 20 30 40 60 80 100 120 140 160 180 Kilometres

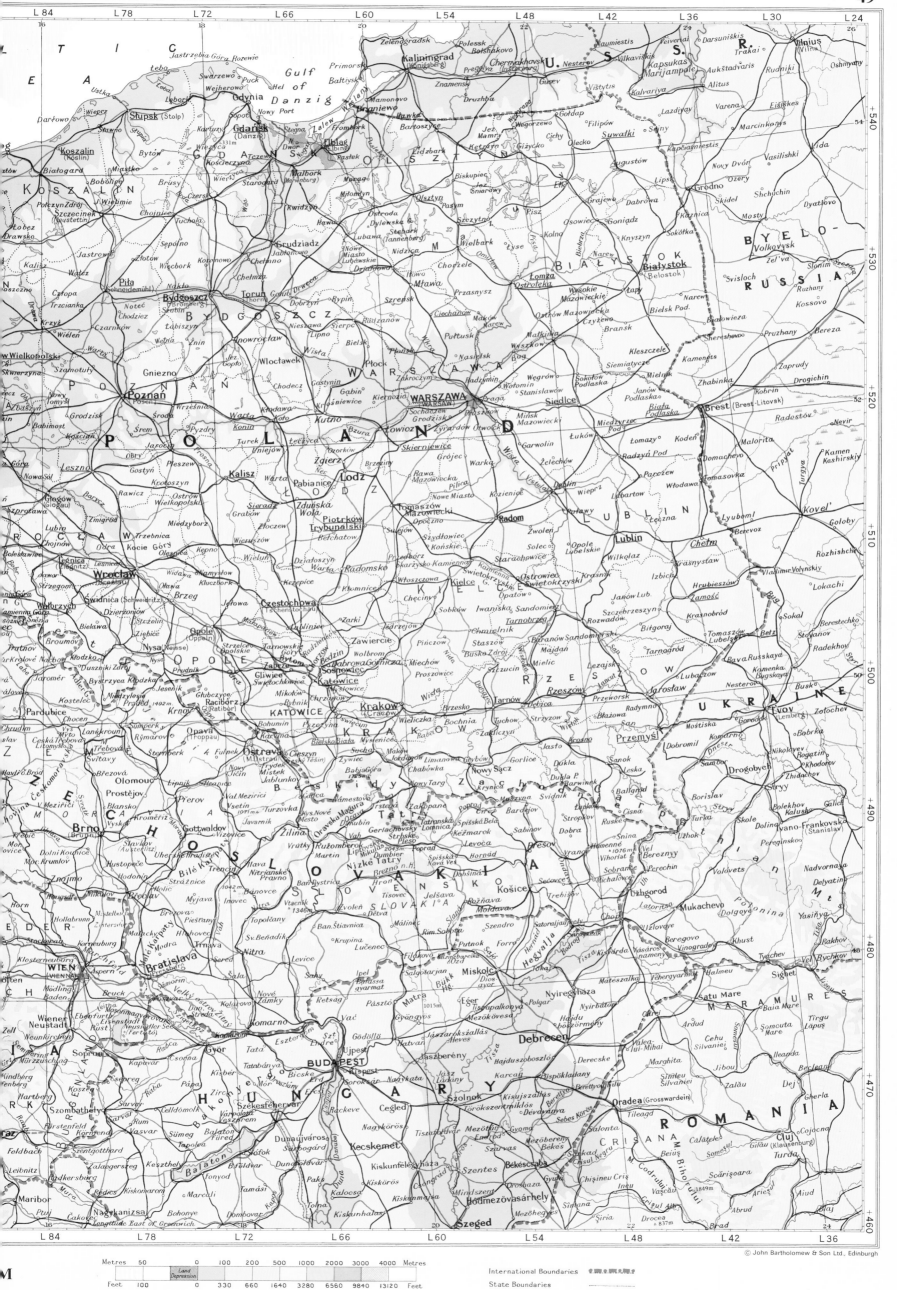

International Boundaries ▪▪▪▪▪   Main Roads ━━━
State Boundaries ▪▪▪▪▪   Railways ━━━

0   100   200   300   400 Statute Miles
0   100   200   300   400   500   600 Kilometres

1:

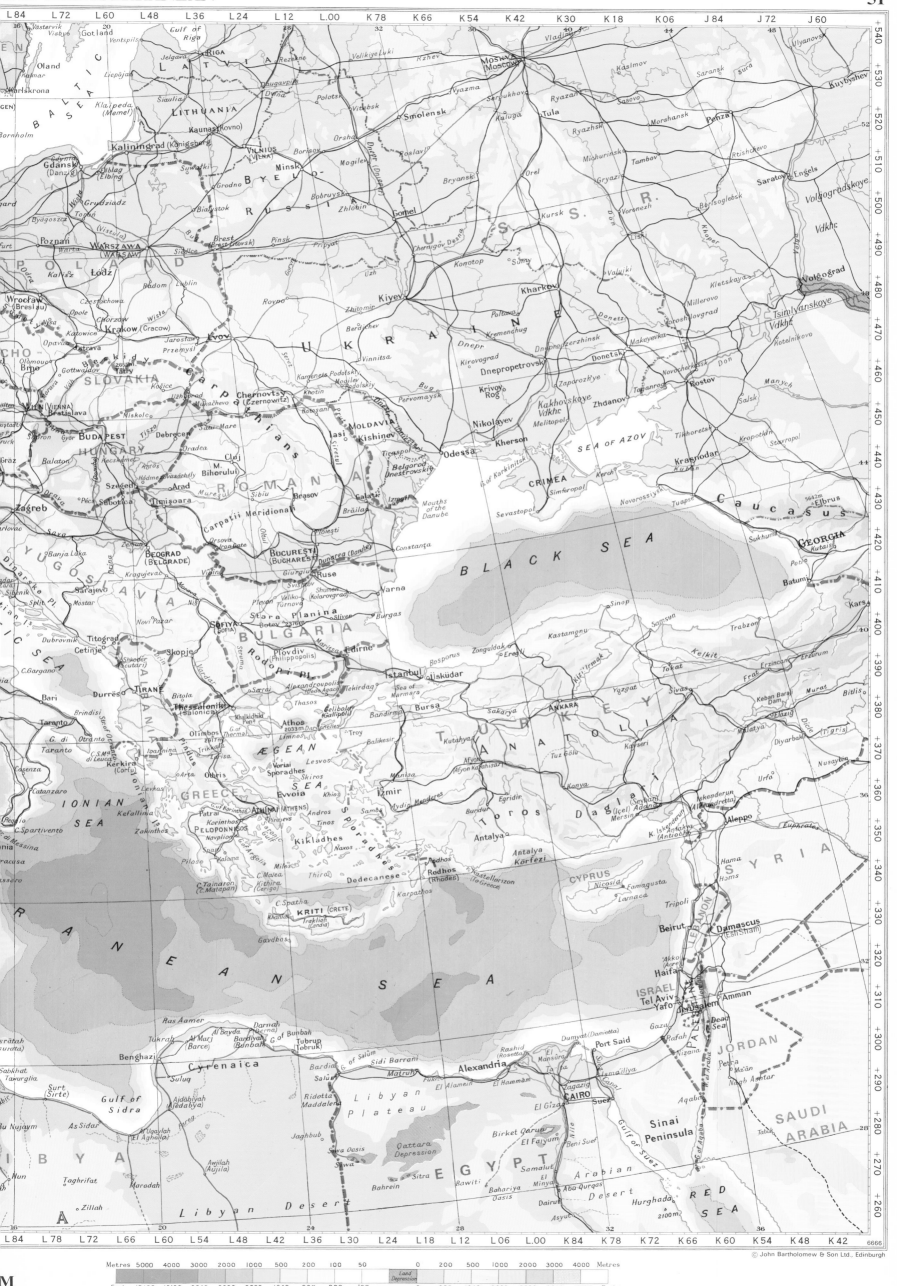

© John Bartholomew & Son Ltd., Edinburgh

Metres 5000 4000 3000 2000 1000 500 200 100 50 | Land Depression | 0 200 500 1000 2000 3000 4000 Metres

Feet 16400 13120 9840 6560 3280 1640 660 330 160 | 0 660 1640 3280 6560 9840 13120 Feet

Main Roads ————
Railways ————

0 10 20 30 40 50 60 70 80 90 100 110 120 Statute Miles
0 10 20 40 60 80 100 120 140 160 180 Kilometres

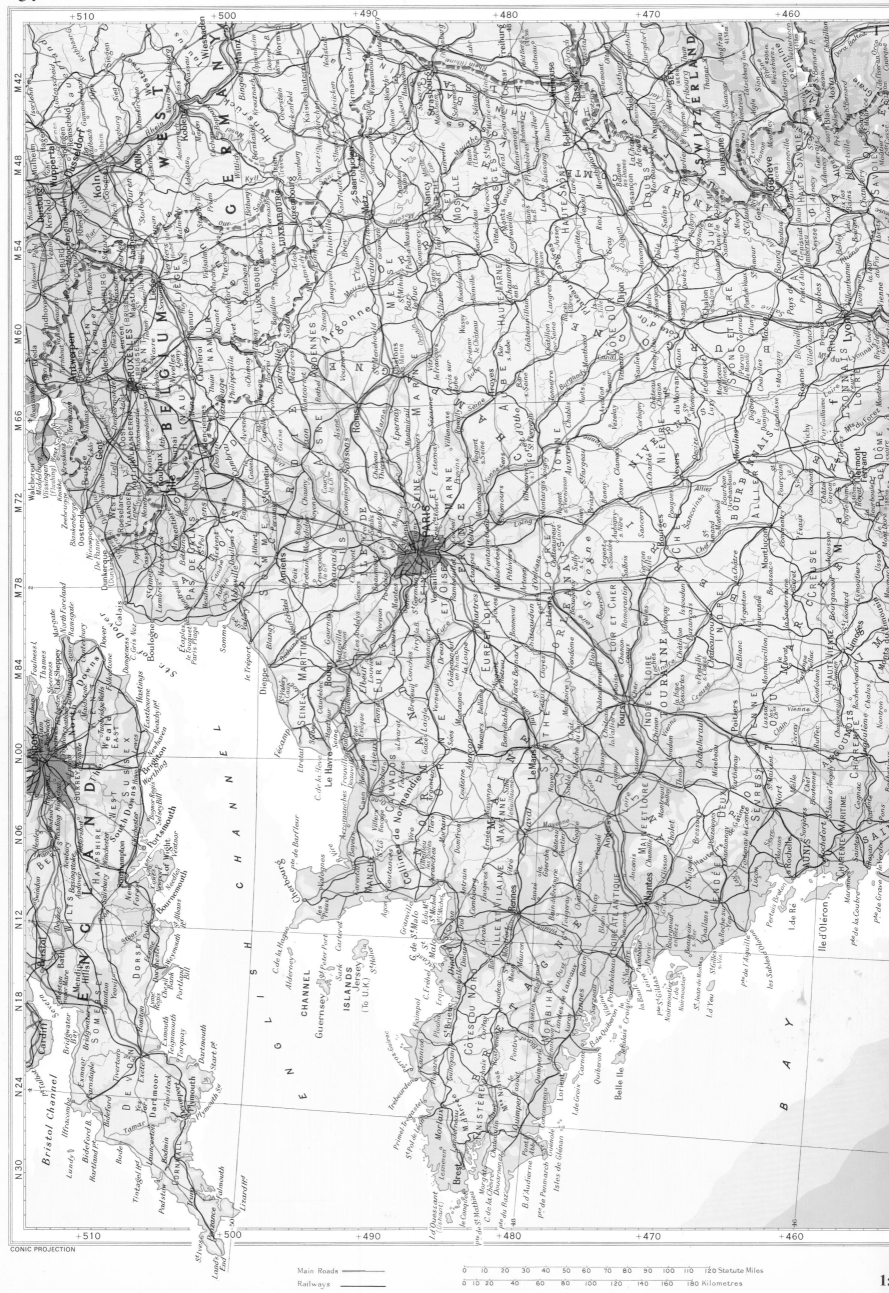

Main Roads

Railways

0 10 20 30 40 50 60 70 80 90 100 110 120 Statute Miles

0 10 20 40 60 80 100 120 140 160 180 Kilometres

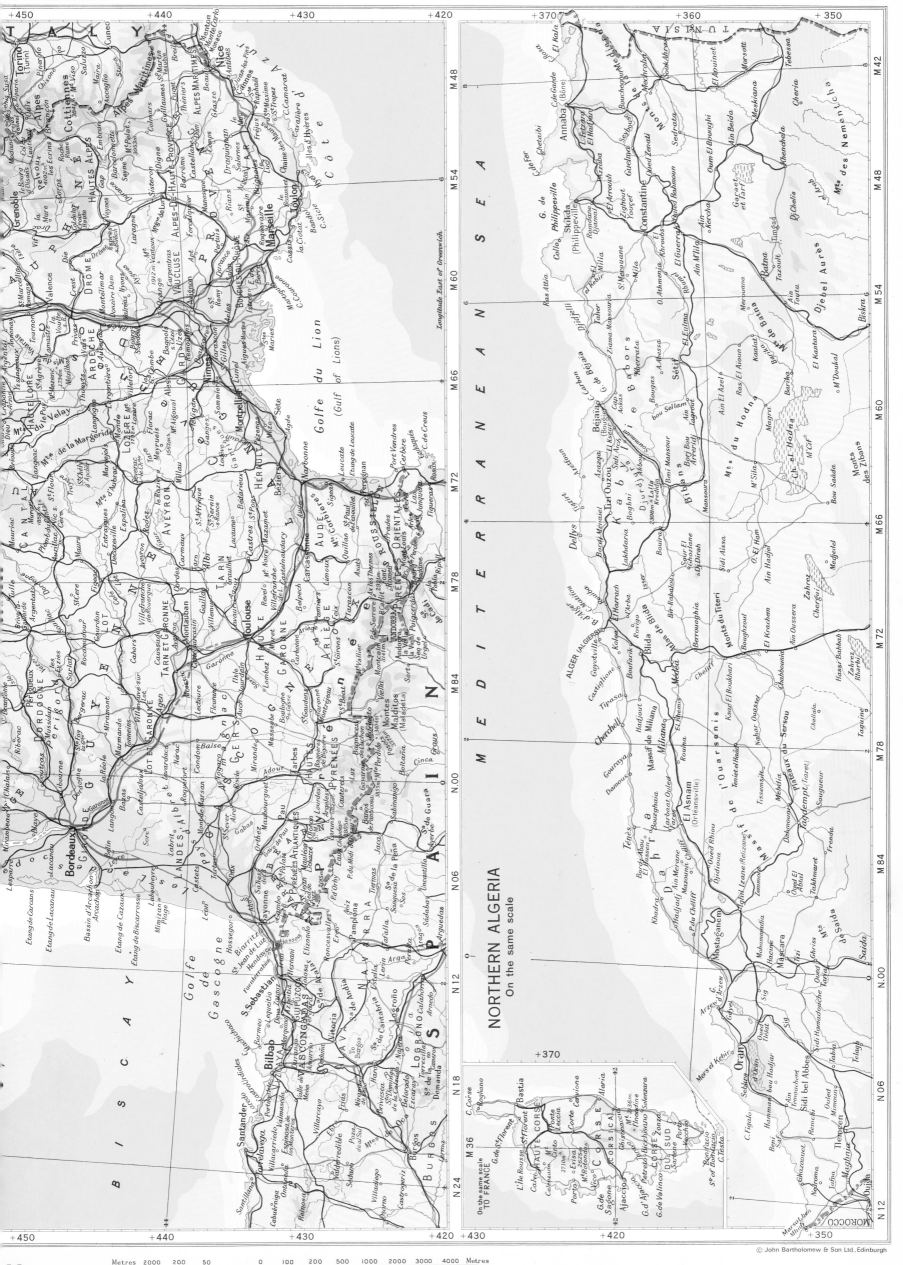

NORTHERN ALGERIA
On the same scale

On the same scale
TO FRANCE

M

Metres 2000 200 50   Land Depression   0 100 200 500 1000 2000 3000 4000 Metres

Feet 6560 660 160   0 330 660 1640 3280 6560 9840 13120 Feet

International Boundaries
State Boundaries

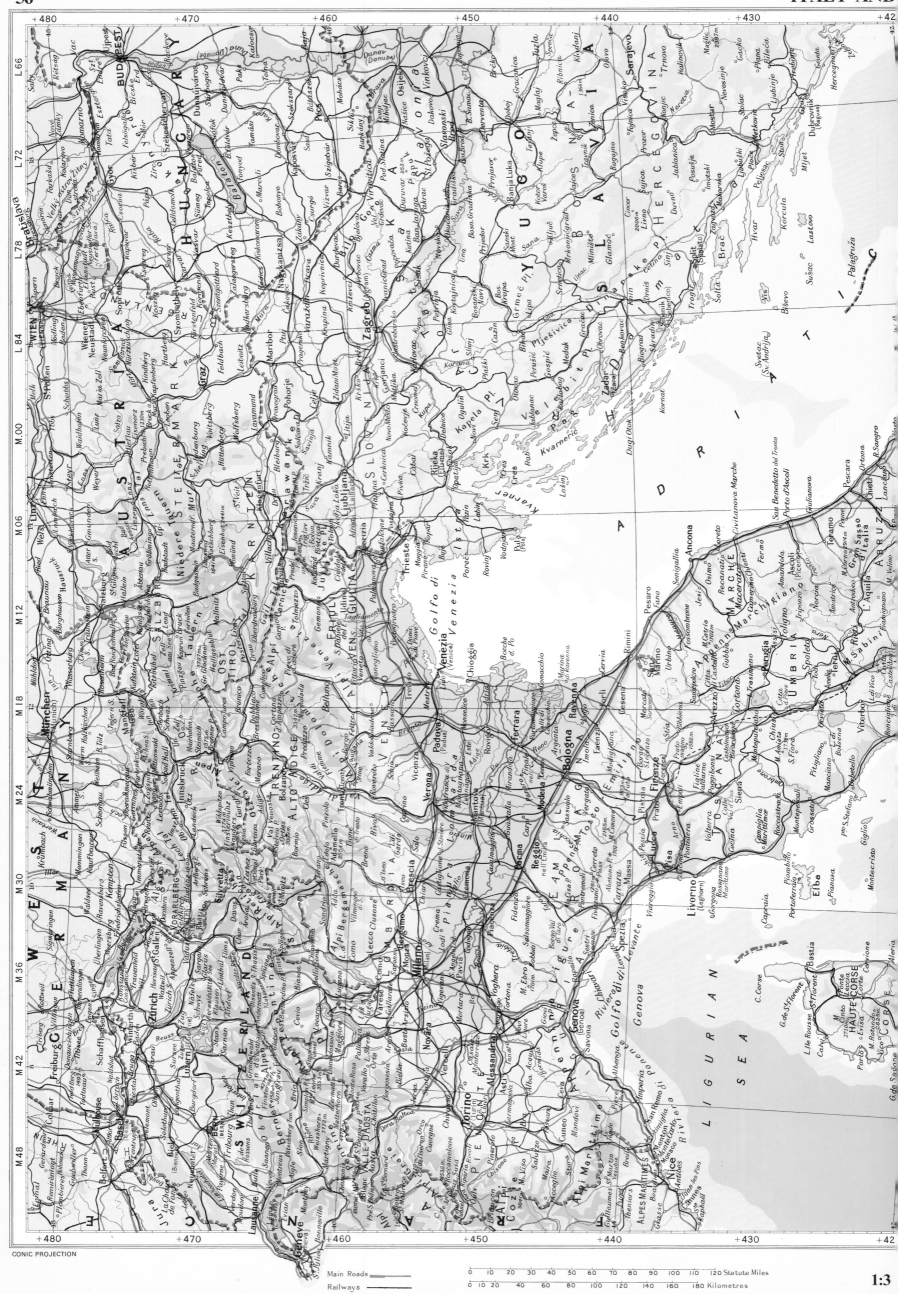

Main Roads
Railways

0 10 20 30 40 50 60 70 80 90 100 110 120 Statute Miles
0 10 20   40   60   80   100   120   140   160   180 Kilometres

1:3

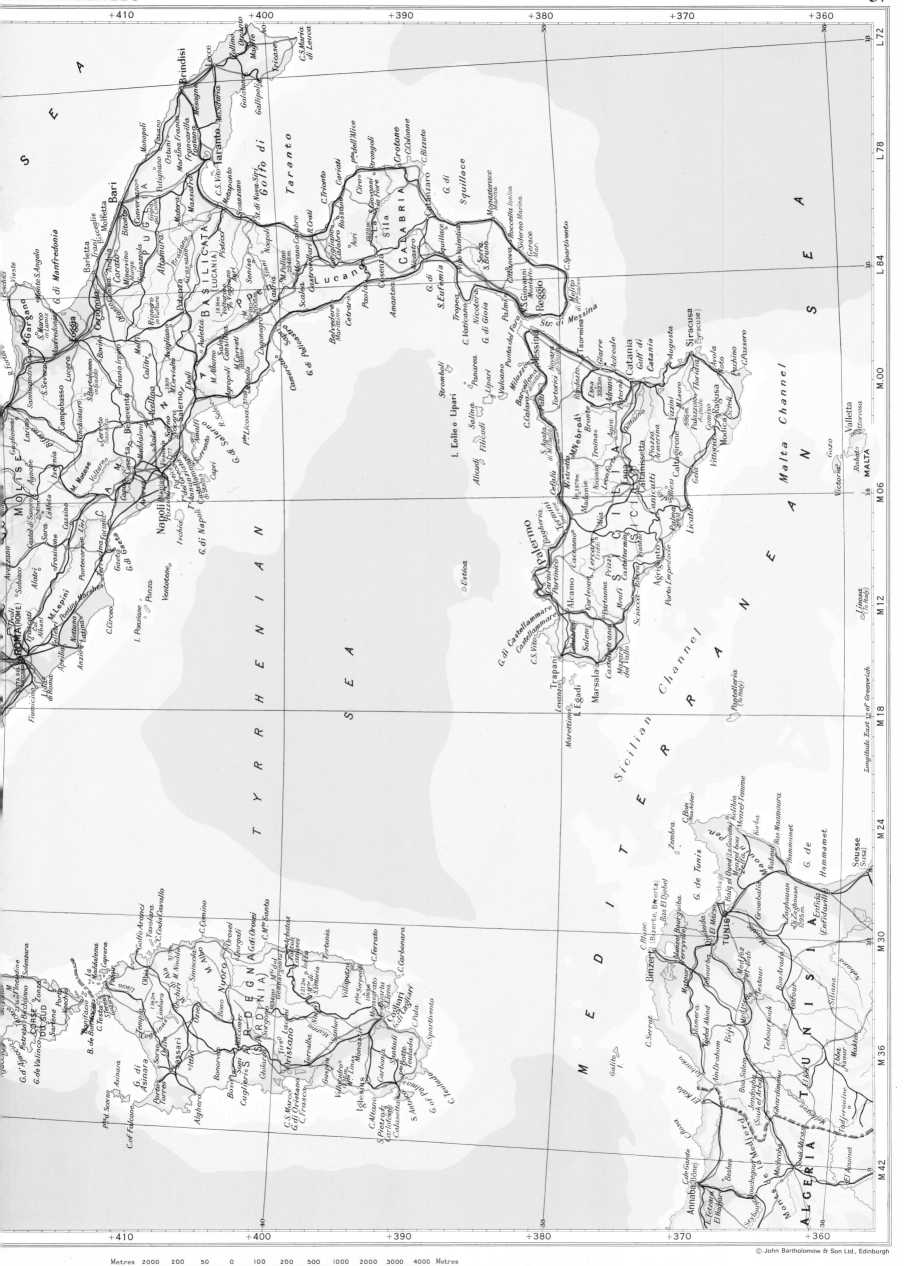

© John Bartholomew & Son Ltd., Edinburgh

Metres 2000 200 50 0 100 200 500 1000 2000 3000 4000 Metres
Feet 6560 660 160 0 330 660 1640 3280 6560 9840 13120 Feet

International Boundaries
State Boundaries

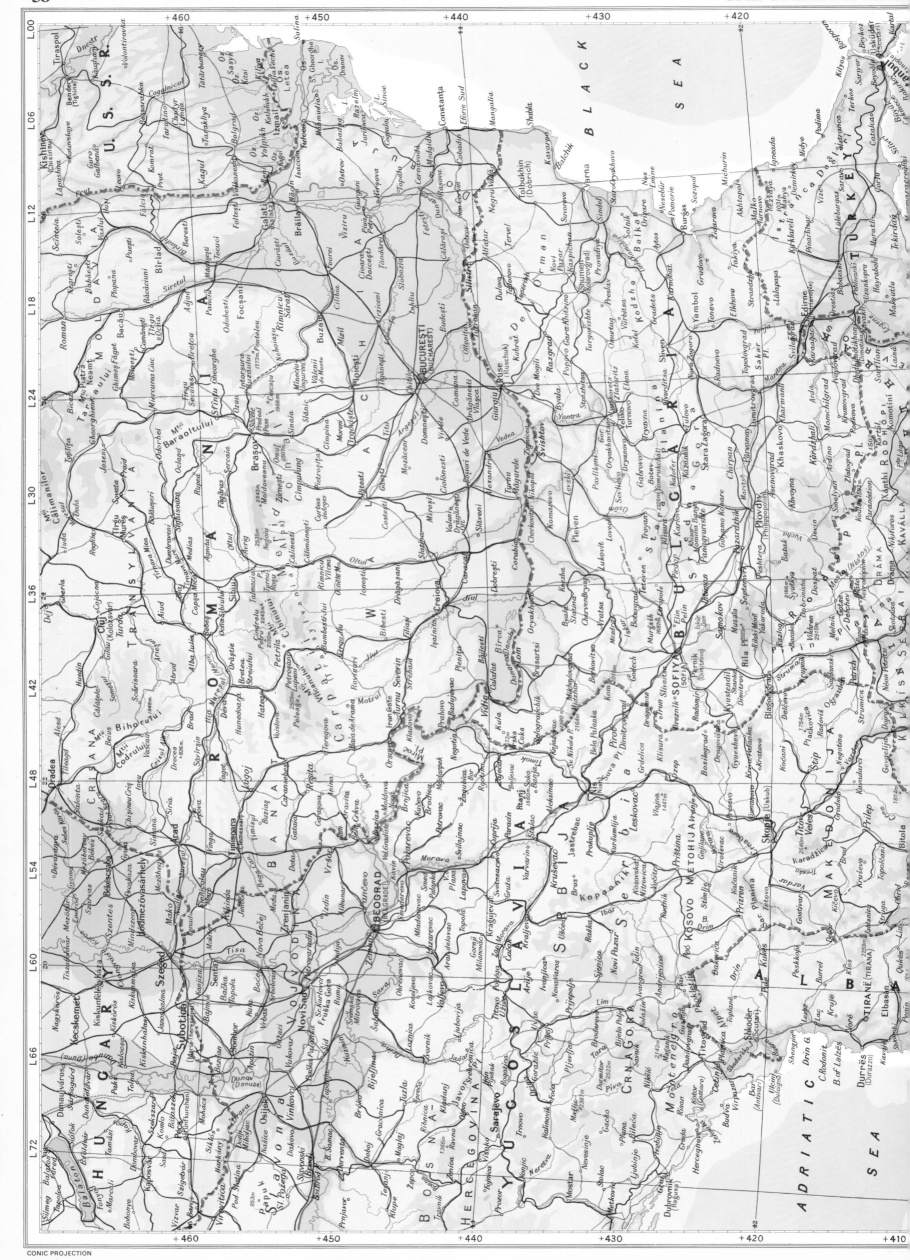

Main Roads ——————
Railways ————————

0 10 20 30 40 50 60 70 80 90 100 110 120 Statute Miles
0 10 20 40   60   80   100   120   140   160   180 Kilometres

1:3

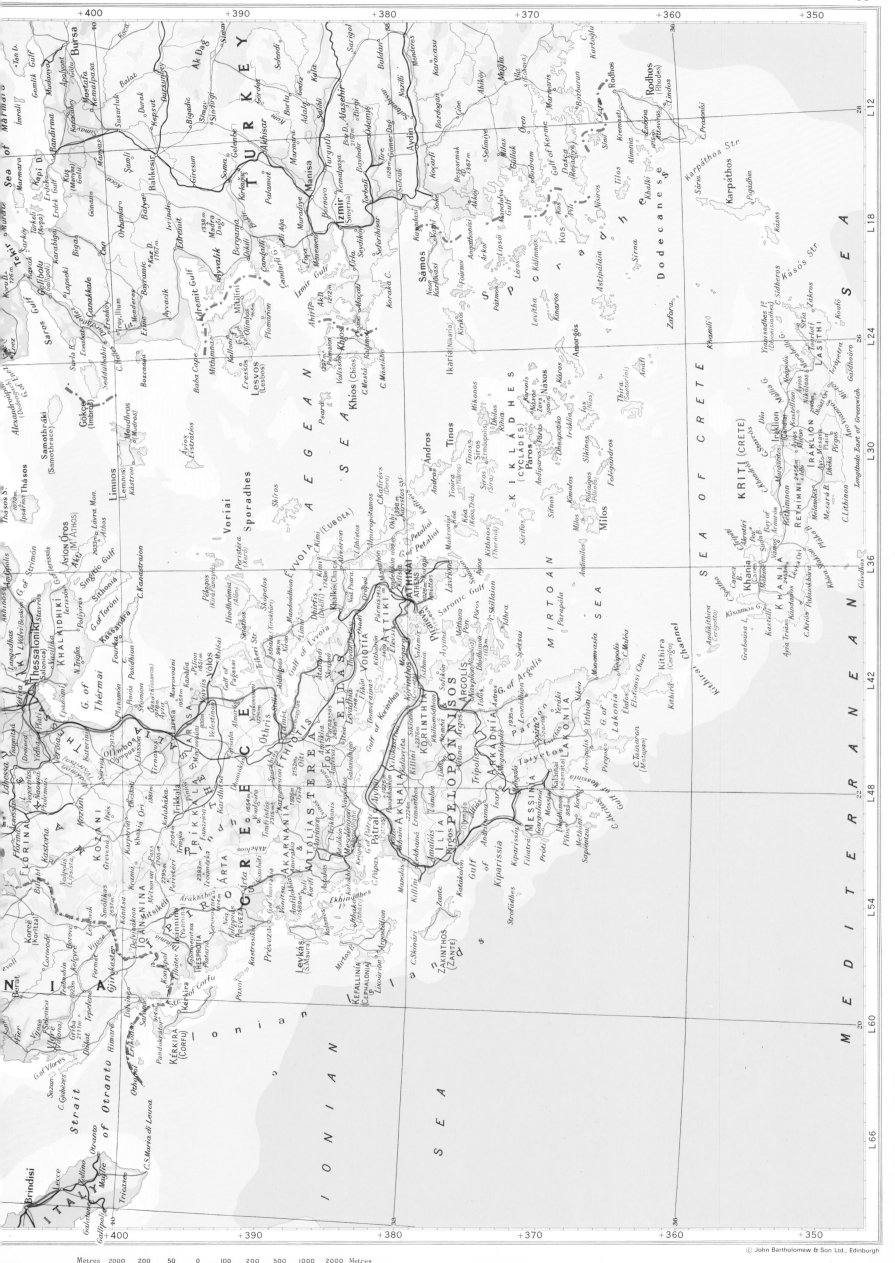

© John Bartholomew & Son Ltd., Edinburgh

| Metres | 2000 | 200 | 50 | 0 | 100 | 200 | 500 | 1000 | 2000 | Metres |
| Feet | 6560 | 660 | 160 | 0 | 330 | 660 | 1640 | 3280 | 6560 | Feet |

International Boundaries
State Boundaries

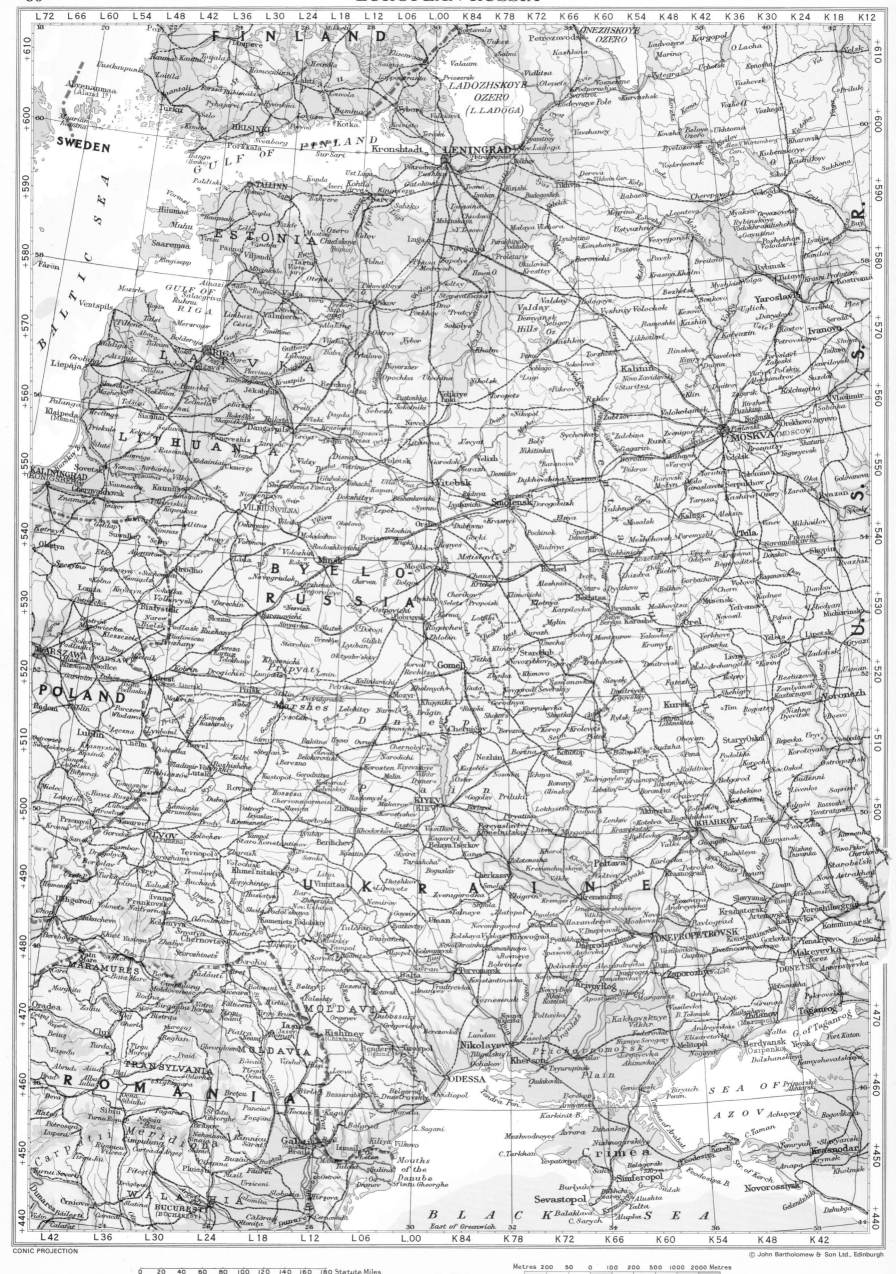

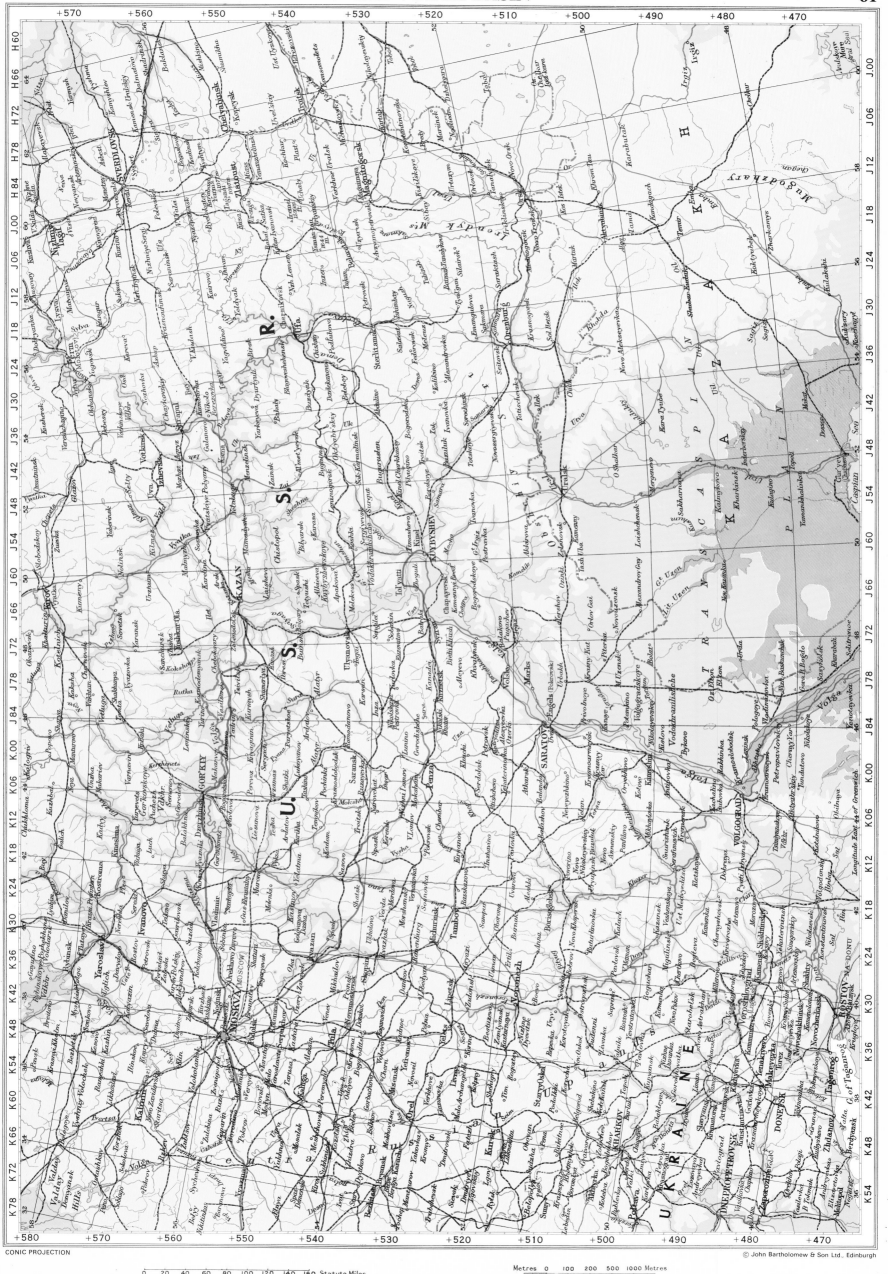

CONIC PROJECTION

© John Bartholomew & Son Ltd., Edinburgh

| 0 | 20 | 40 | 60 | 80 | 100 | 120 | 140 | 160 | Statute Miles |

| 0 | 20 | 40 | 60 | 80 | 100 | 120 | 160 | 200 | 240 | Kilometres |

Metres 0   100   200   500   1000 Metres

Feet 0   330   660   1640   3280   Feet

Land Depression

1:6M

CONIC PROJECTION

Main Roads _____
Railways _____

0   100   200   300   400   500   600 Statute Miles

0   100 200 300 400 500 600 700 800 900 1000 Kilometres

1:17

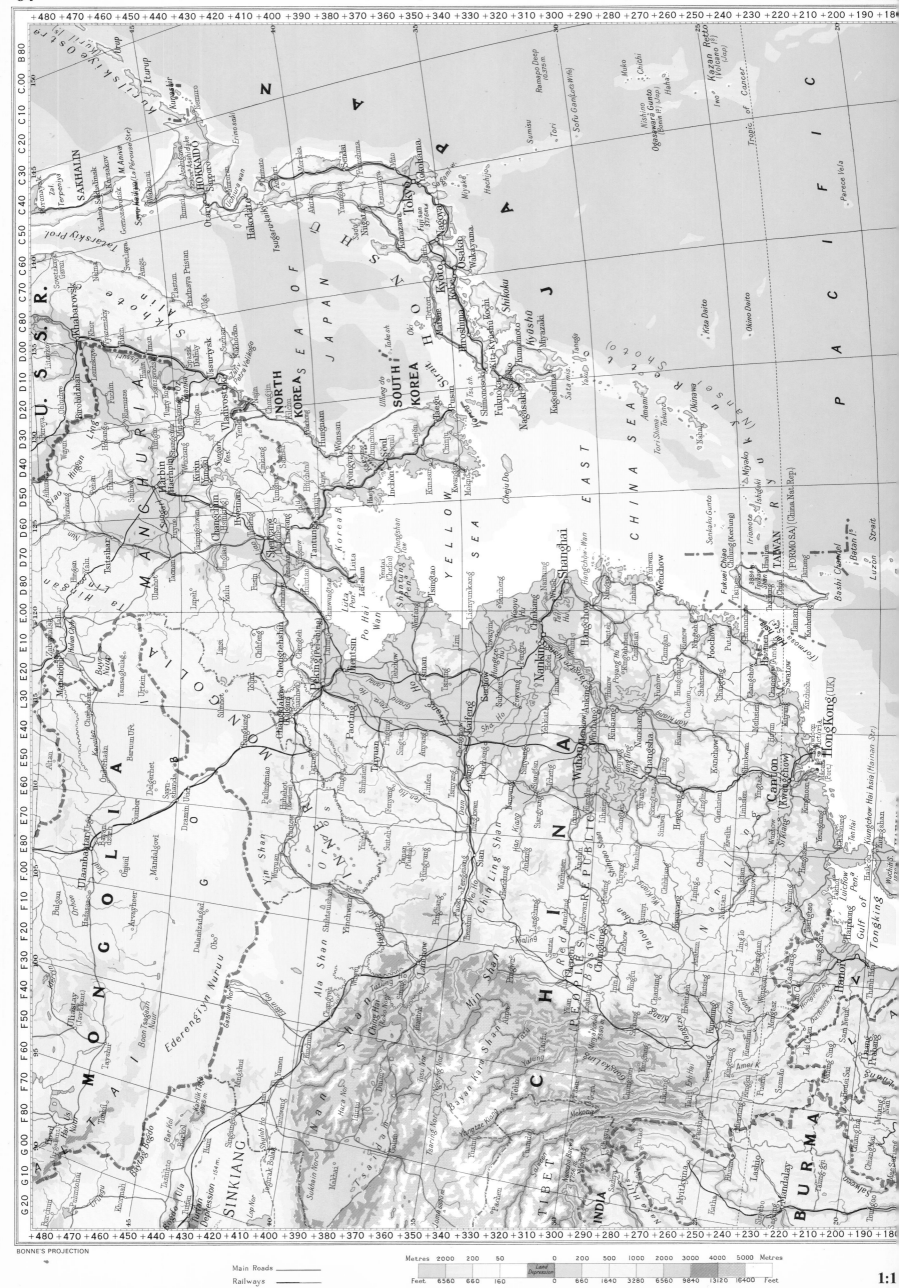

Main Roads _____
Railways _____

Metres	2000	200	50		0	200	500	1000	2000	3000	4000	5000	Metres
				Land Depression									
Feet	6560	660	160	0	660	1640	3280	6560	9840	13120	16400		Feet

1:1

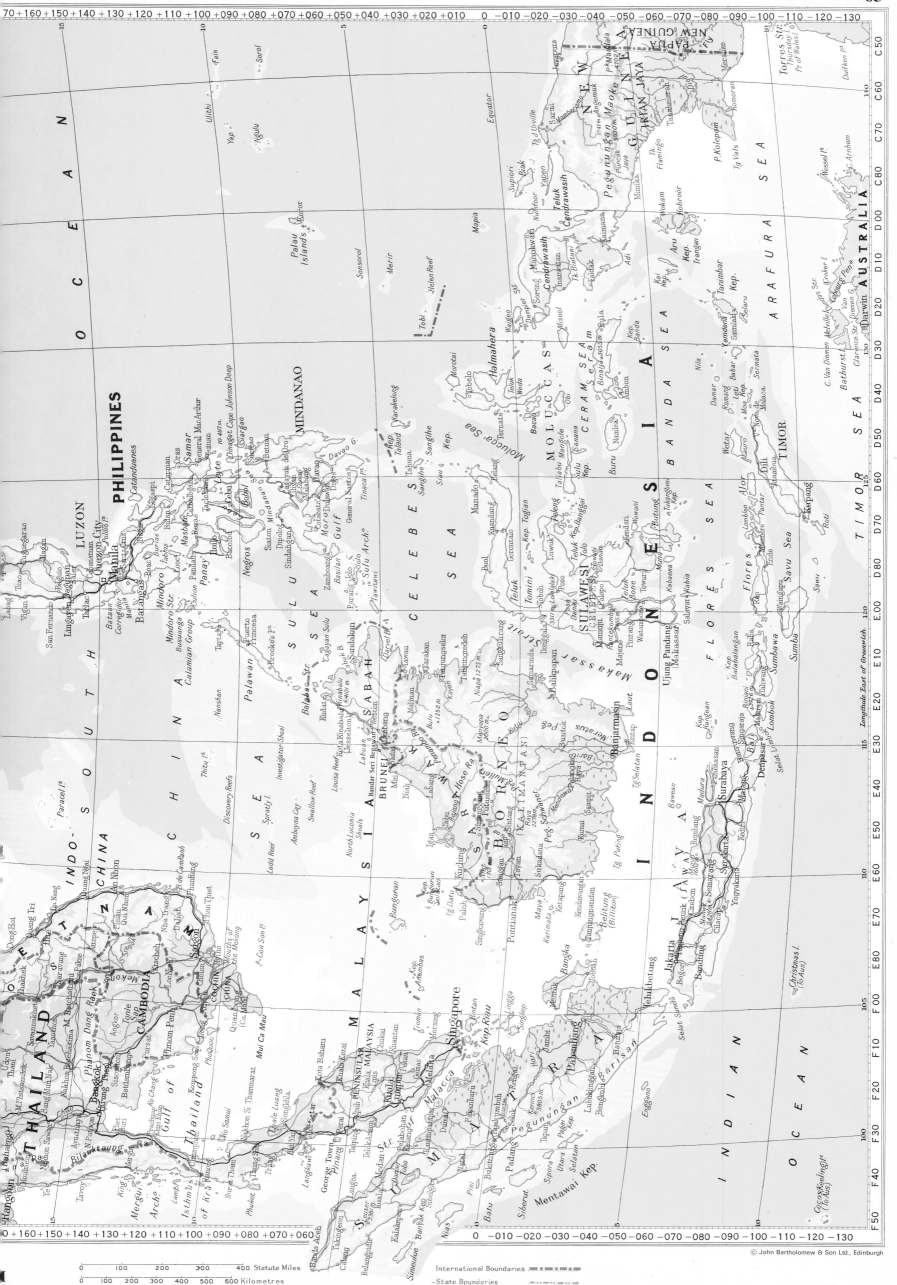

| 0 | 100 | 200 | 300 | 400 Statute Miles |
| 0 | 100 | 200 | 300 | 400 | 500 | 600 Kilometres |

International Boundaries
State Boundaries

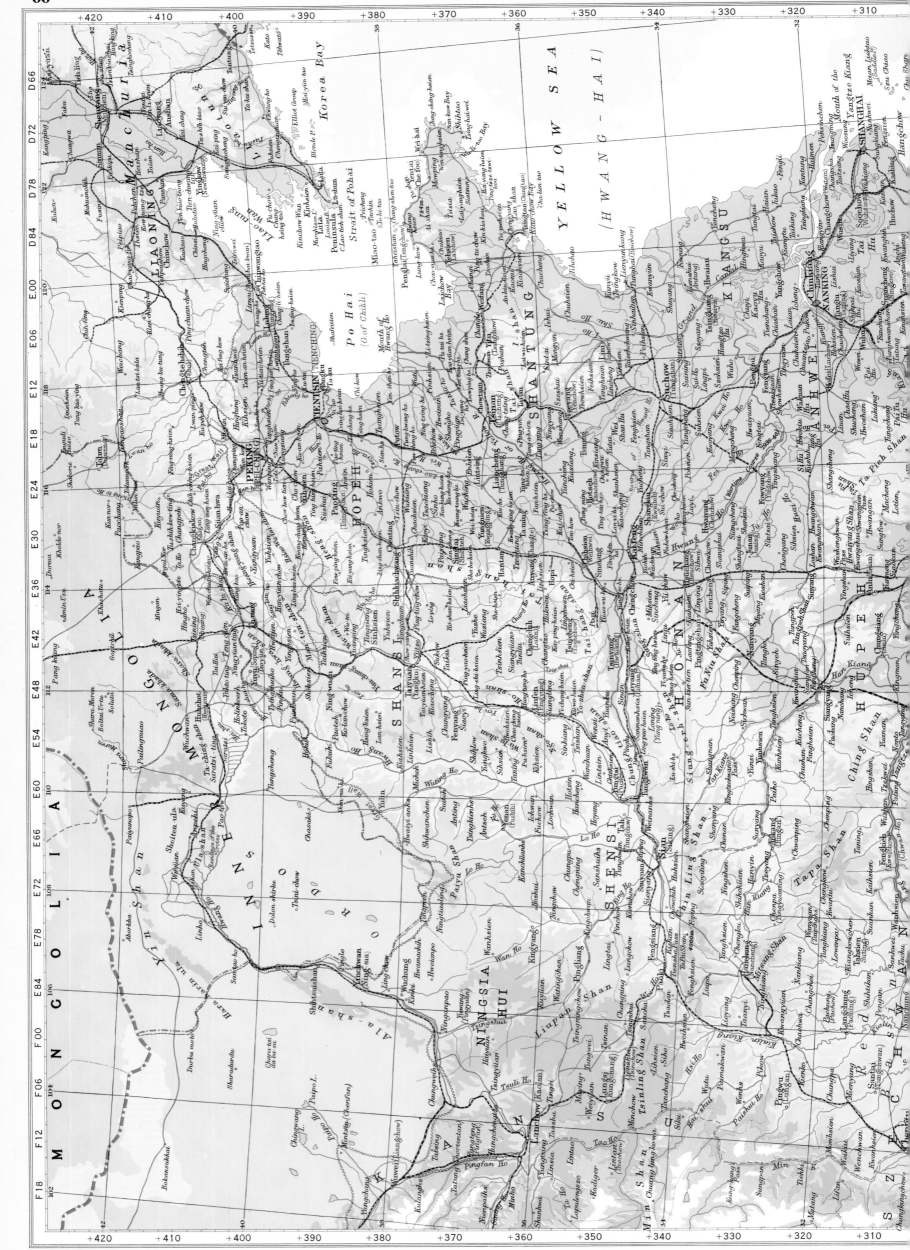

CONIC PROJECTION

Main Roads ————
Railways ————

0 20 40 60 80 100 120 140 160 180 200 220 240 Statute Miles
0 20 40 80 120 160 200 240 280 320 360 Kilometres

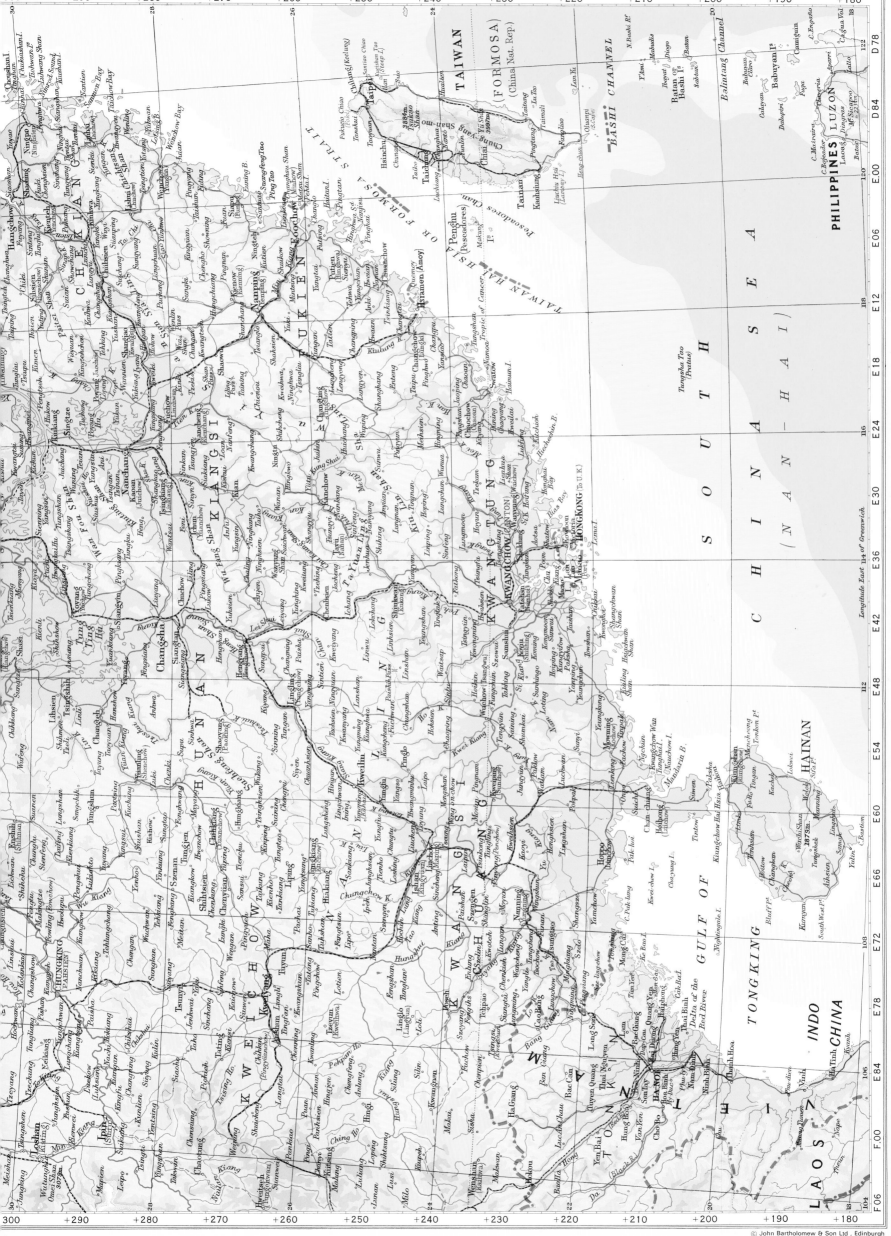

Metres 2000 200 50 0 200 500 1000 2000 3000 4000 Metres

Feet 6560 660 160 0 660 1640 3280 6560 9840 13120 Feet

© John Bartholomew & Son Ltd , Edinburgh

International Boundaries

State Boundaries

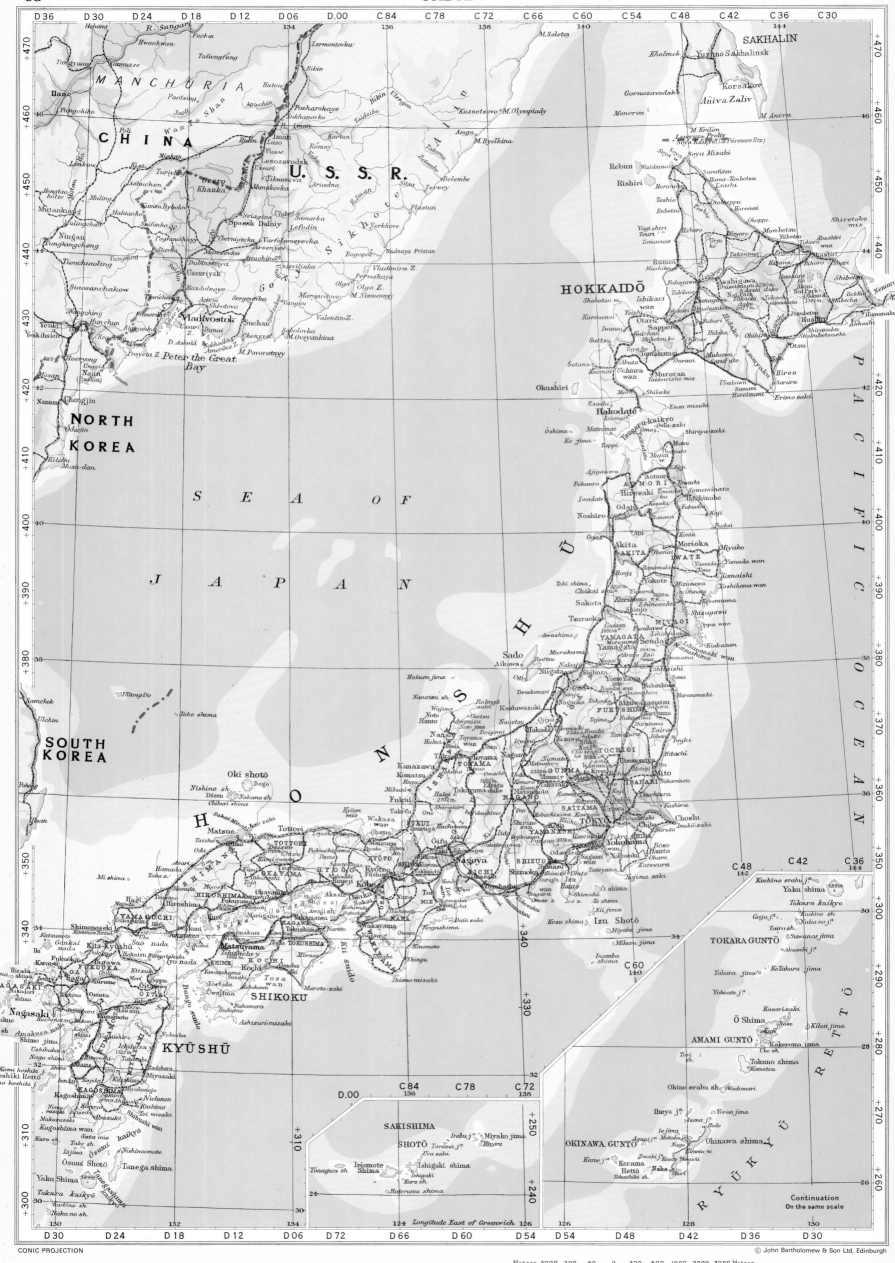

CONIC PROJECTION

1:6M

© John Bartholomew & Son Ltd, Edinburgh

AFGHANISTAN

IRAN

Hindu Kush

KABUL

Kandahar

PAKISTAN

BALUCHISTAN

Kalat

Karachi

Mouths of the Indus

SIND

Tropic of Cancer

Muscat

Ras al Hadd

ARABIAN SEA

PUNJAB

Lahore

Amritsar

ISLAMABAD

Rawalpindi

Srinagar

JAMMU & KASHMIR

Ladakh

HIMACHAL PRADESH

DELHI

HARYANA

RAJASTHAN

Bikaner

Jodhpur

Jaipur

UTTAR PRADESH

Lucknow

Kanpur

Allahabad

KUTCH

GUJARAT

Ahmadabad

Baroda

Indore

MADHYA PRADESH

Bhopal

Jabalpur

Kathiawar

Surat

Khandesh

Nagpur

Berar

INDIA

BOMBAY

Poona

MAHARASHTRA

Hyderabad

ANDHRA

PRADESH

KARNATAKA

Bangalore

Mysore

Mangalore

Calicut

KERALA

Cochin

TAMIL NADU

Salem

MADRAS

Pondicherry

Trivandrum

Cape Comorin

SRI LANKA

Colombo

Amindivi Islands

Laccadive Islands

LAKSHADWEEP

Minicoy

Nine Degree Channel

Eight Degree Channel

Gulf of Mannar

Jaffna

RELIGIONS

	Hindu
	Sikh
	Muhammadan
	Buddhist
	Christian
	Animist

PAKISTAN

NEPAL

BHUTAN

BURMA

INDIA

Sri Lanka

CONIC PROJECTION

Main Roads

Railways

0   100   200   300   400 Statute Miles

0   100   200   300   400   500 Kilometres

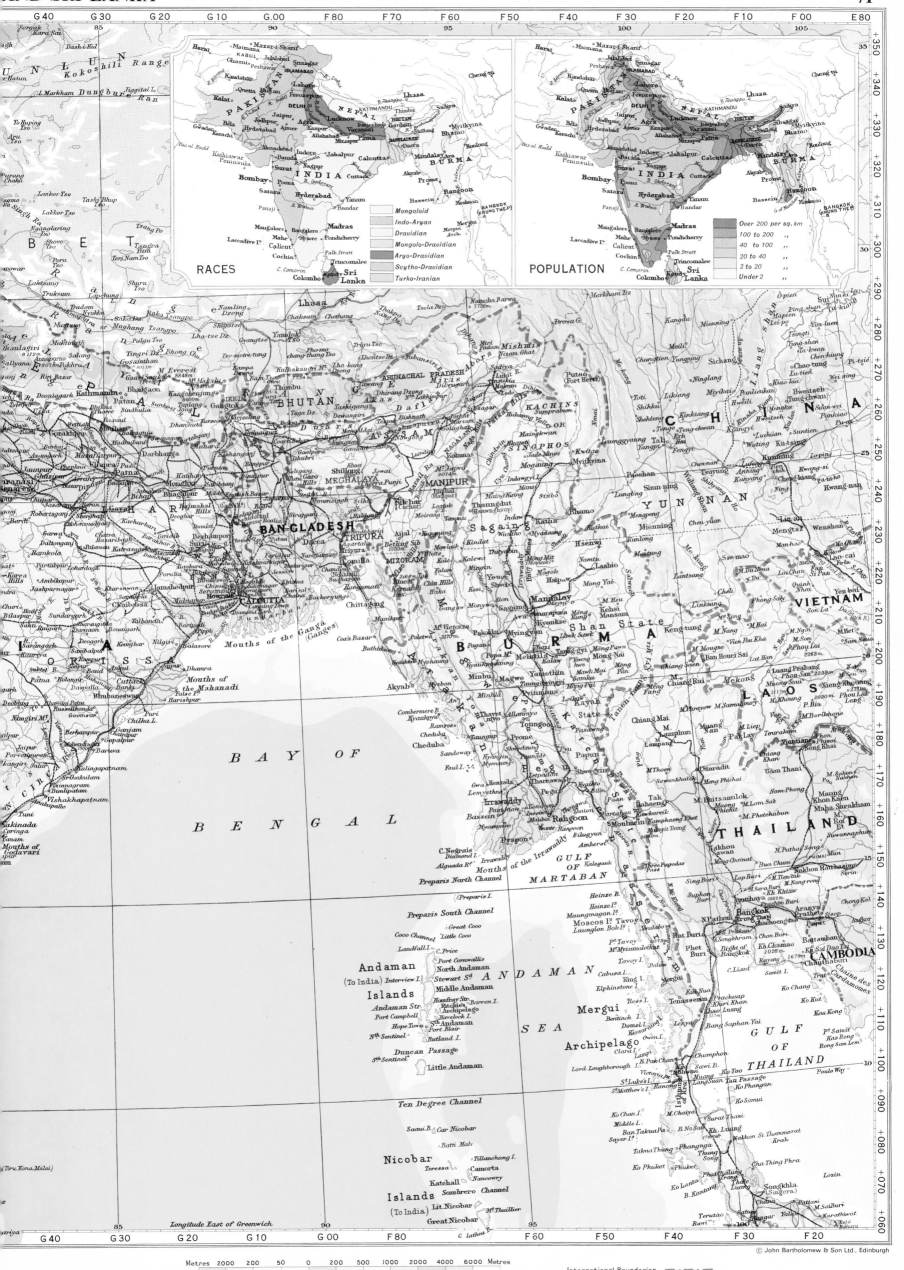

RACES

Mongoloid
Indo-Aryan
Dravidian
Mongolo-Dravidian
Aryo-Dravidian
Scytho-Dravidian
Turko-Iranian

POPULATION

Over 200 per sq. km
100 to 200 ,,
40 to 100 ,,
20 to 40 ,,
2 to 20 ,,
Under 2 ,,

BAY OF BENGAL

Mouths of the Ganga (Ganges)

Andaman Islands (To India)

ANDAMAN SEA

Mergui Archipelago

Nicobar Islands (To India)

Ten Degree Channel

Longitude East of Greenwich

© John Bartholomew & Son Ltd., Edinburgh

1:10M

Metres	2000	200	50	0	200	500	1000	2000	4000	6000	Metres
Feet	6560	660	160	0	660	1640	3280	6560	13120	19690	Feet

International Boundaries
State Boundaries

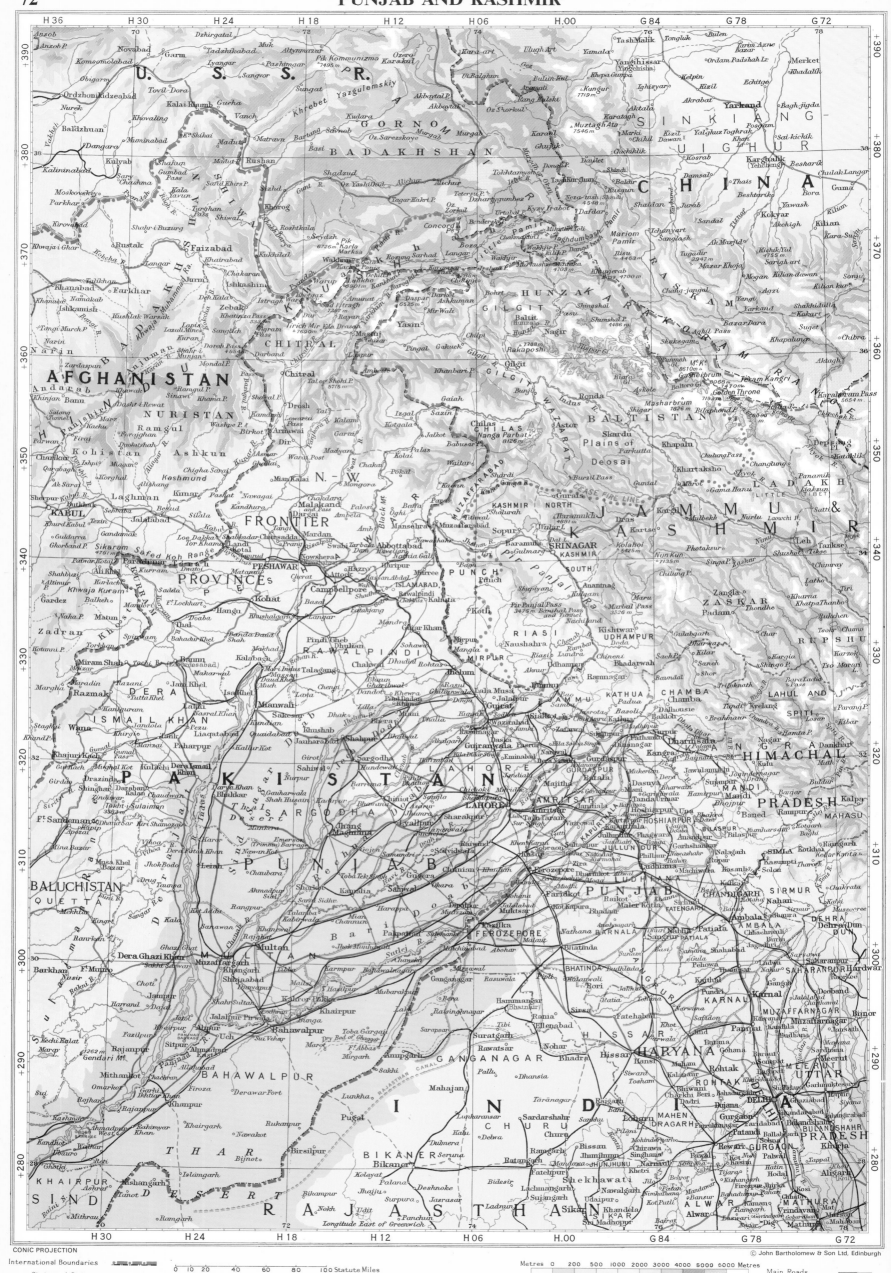

International Boundaries

State and Division
Boundaries

0 10 20   40   60   80   100 Statute Miles

0 10 20 40   60   80   100 120 140 160 Kilometres

1:4M

Metres 0   200   500 1000 2000 3000 4000 5000 6000 Metres

Feet 0   660 1640 3280 6560 9840 13120 16400 19690 Feet

© John Bartholomew & Son Ltd, Edinburgh

Main Roads

Irrigation Canals

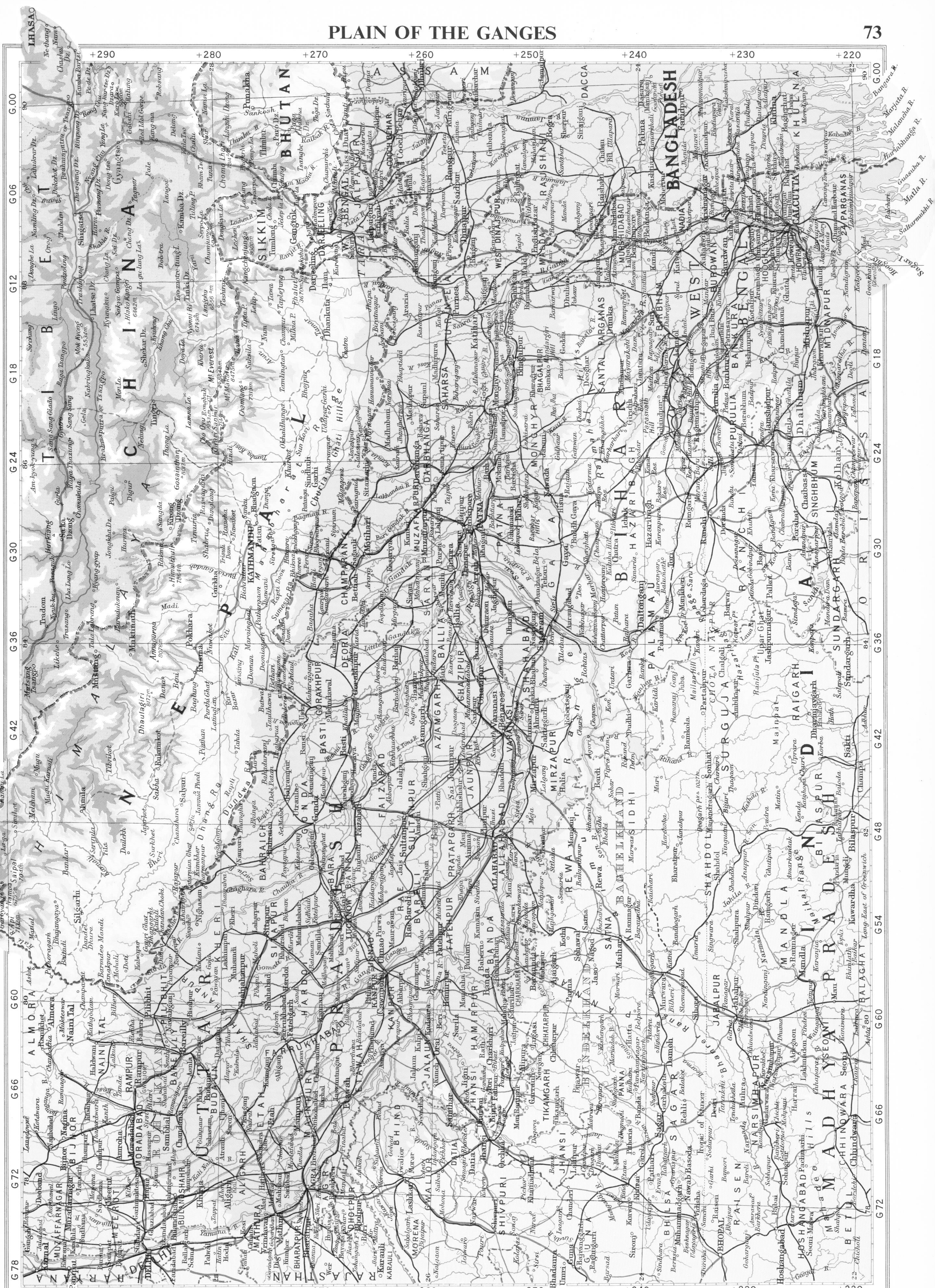

CHINA

TIBET

NEPAL

BHUTAN

SIKKIM

ASSAM

BANGLADESH

WEST BENGAL

BIHAR

UTTAR PRADESH

MADHYA PRADESH

ORISSA

HARYANA

RAJASTHAN

HIMALAYA

LHASA

DACCA

CALCUTTA

24 PARGANAS

CONIC PROJECTION

International Boundaries

State and Division Boundaries

1:4M

0 10 20 40 60 80 100 Statute Miles

0 10 20 40 60 80 100 120 140 160 Kilometres

Metres 0 200 500 1000 2000 3000 4000 5000 6000 Metres

Feet 0 660 1640 3280 6560 9840 13120 16400 19690 Feet

© John Bartholomew & Son Ltd, Edinburgh

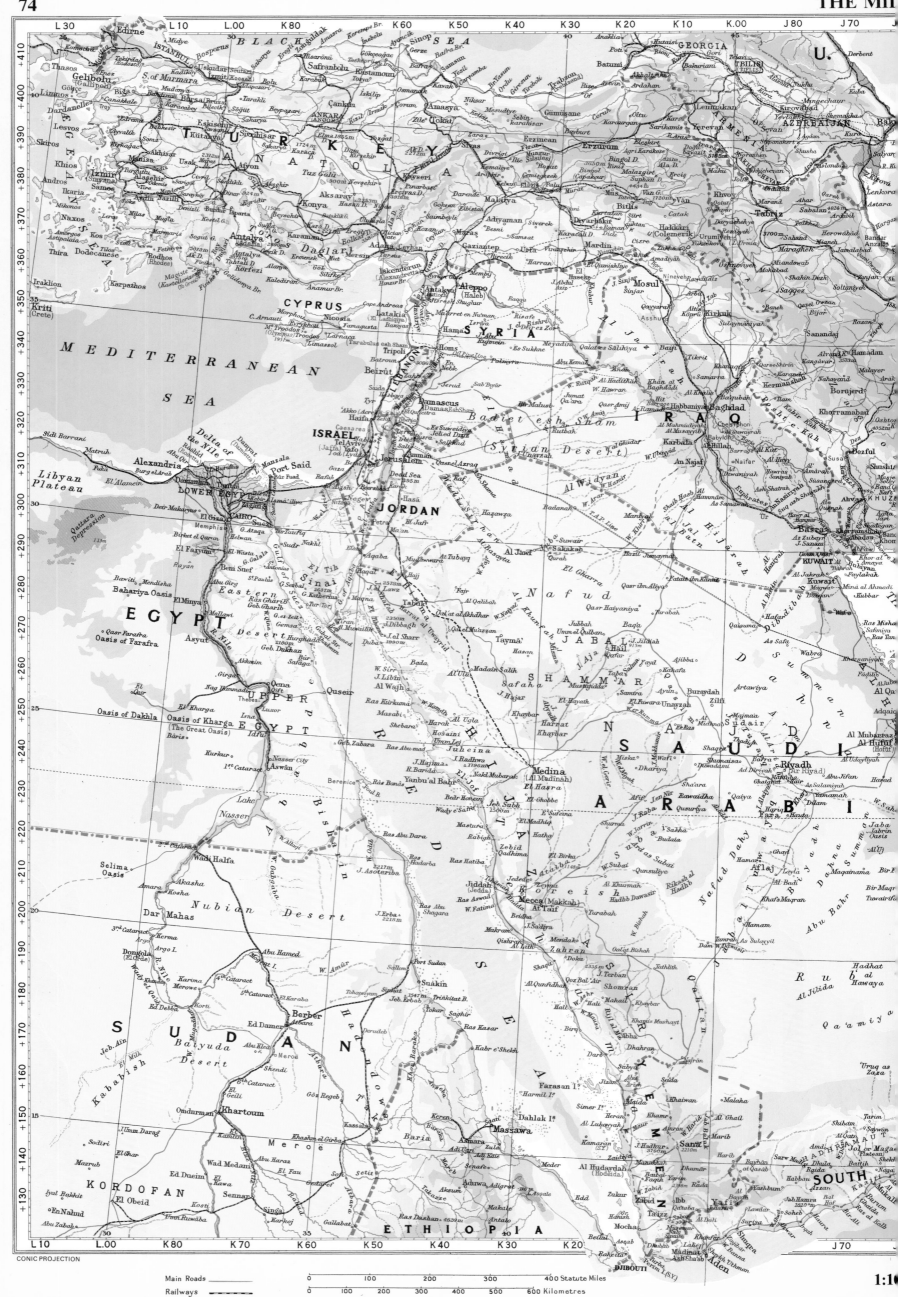

74

THE MIL

CONIC PROJECTION

Main Roads

Railways

0   100   200   300   400 Statute Miles

0 100 200 300 400 500 600 Kilometres

1:10

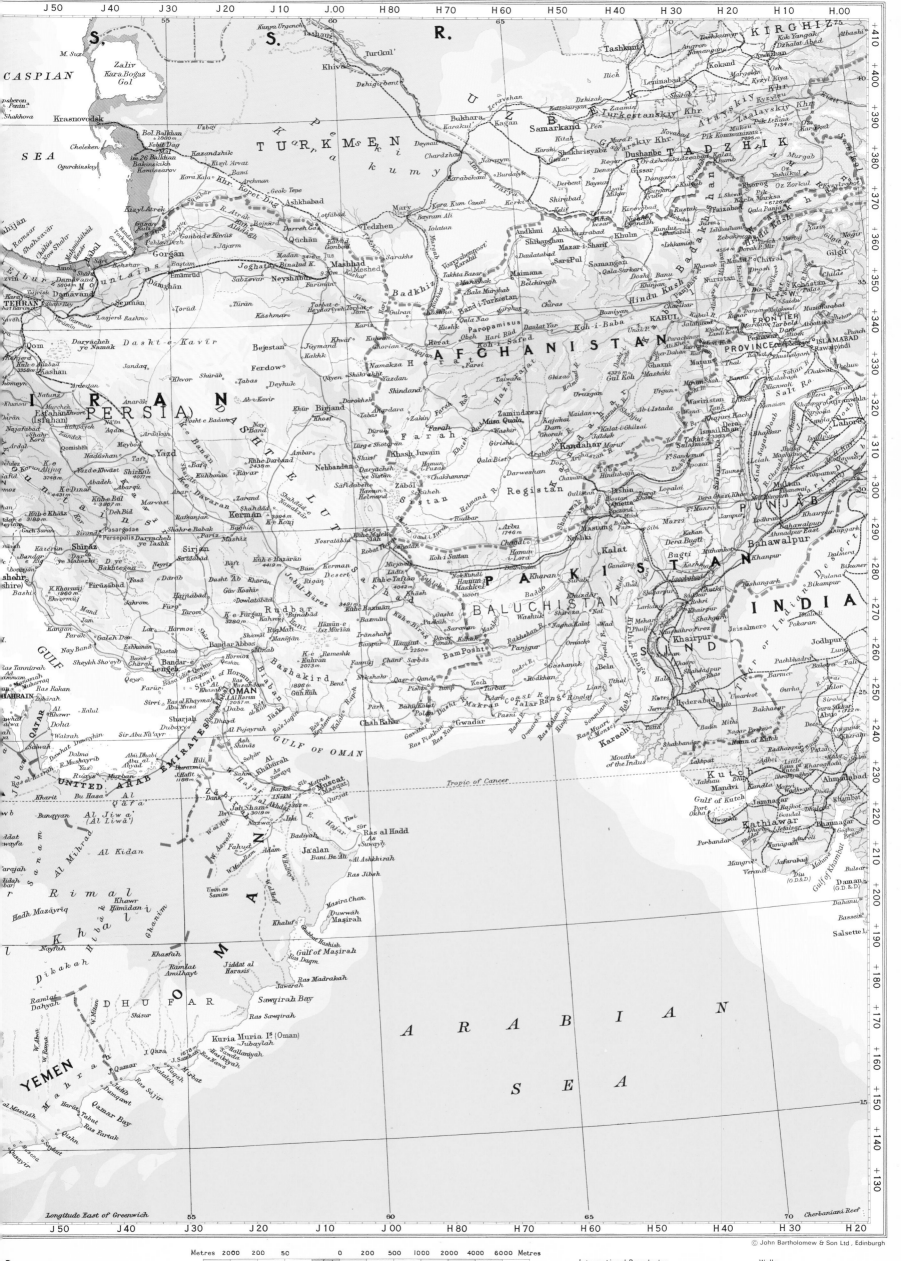

Metres	2000	200	50		0	200	500	1000	2000	4000	6000 Metres
				Land Depression							
Feet	6560	660	160		0	660	1640	3280	6560	13120	19690 Feet

International Boundaries

State Boundaries

Wells

CONIC PROJECTION

0 10 20 30 40 50 60 70 80 Statute Miles

0 10 20 30 40 50 60 70 80 90 100 110 120 Kilometres

1:2½M

Metres 2000 200 50 0 100 200 500 1000 2000 3000 Metres

Feet 6560 660 160 0 330 660 1640 3280 6560 9840 Feet

© John Bartholomew & Son Ltd., Edinburgh

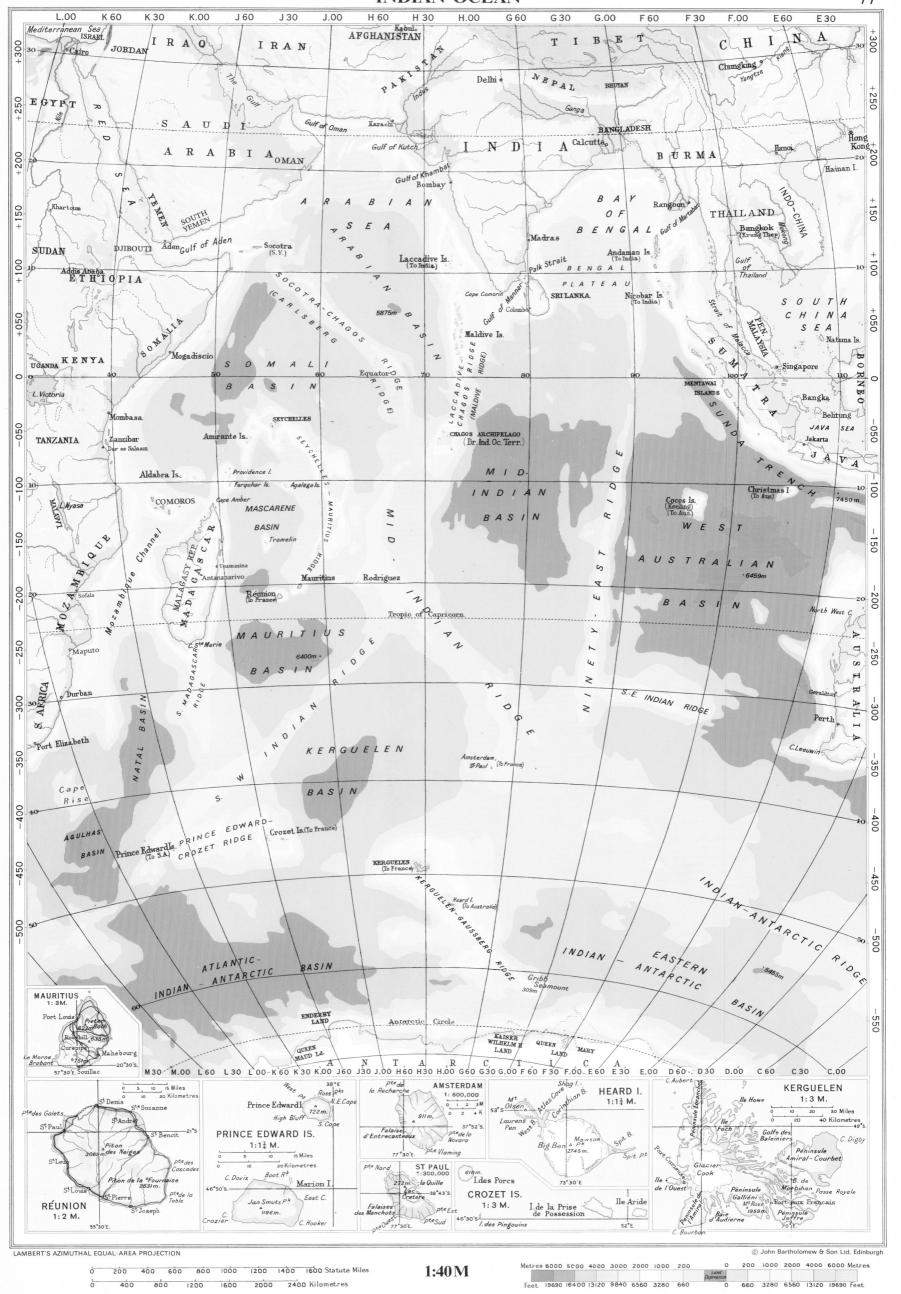

LAMBERT'S AZIMUTHAL EQUAL-AREA PROJECTION

© John Bartholomew & Son Ltd, Edinburgh

1:40M

5

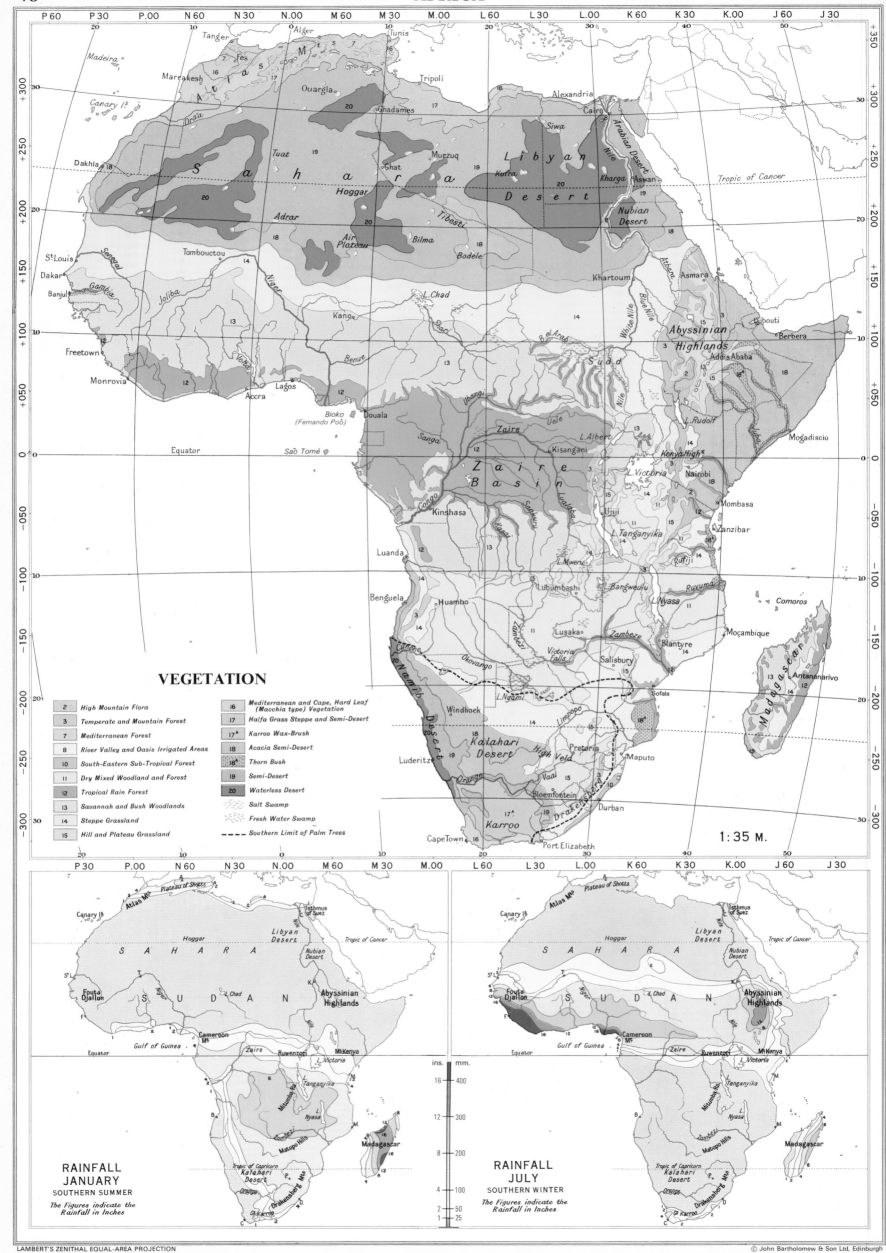

VEGETATION

2	High Mountain Flora
3	Temperate and Mountain Forest
7	Mediterranean Forest
8	River Valley and Oasis Irrigated Areas
10	South-Eastern Sub-Tropical Forest
11	Dry Mixed Woodland and Forest
12	Tropical Rain Forest
13	Savannah and Bush Woodlands
14	Steppe Grassland
15	Hill and Plateau Grassland
16	Mediterranean and Cape, Hard Leaf (Macchia type) Vegetation
17	Halfa Grass Steppe and Semi-Desert
17*	Karroo Wax-Brush
18	Acacia Semi-Desert
18*	Thorn Bush
19	Semi-Desert
20	Waterless Desert
	Salt Swamp
	Fresh Water Swamp
---	Southern Limit of Palm Trees

1:35 M.

RAINFALL
JANUARY
SOUTHERN SUMMER
The Figures indicate the
Rainfall in Inches

RAINFALL
JULY
SOUTHERN WINTER
The Figures indicate the
Rainfall in Inches

ins. mm.
16 — 400
12 — 300
8 — 200
4 — 100
2 — 50
1 — 25

LAMBERT'S ZENITHAL EQUAL-AREA PROJECTION

© John Bartholomew & Son Ltd, Edinburgh

1:35M

0 200 400 600 800 1000 Statute Miles

0 200 400 600 800 1000 1200 1400 1600 Kilometres

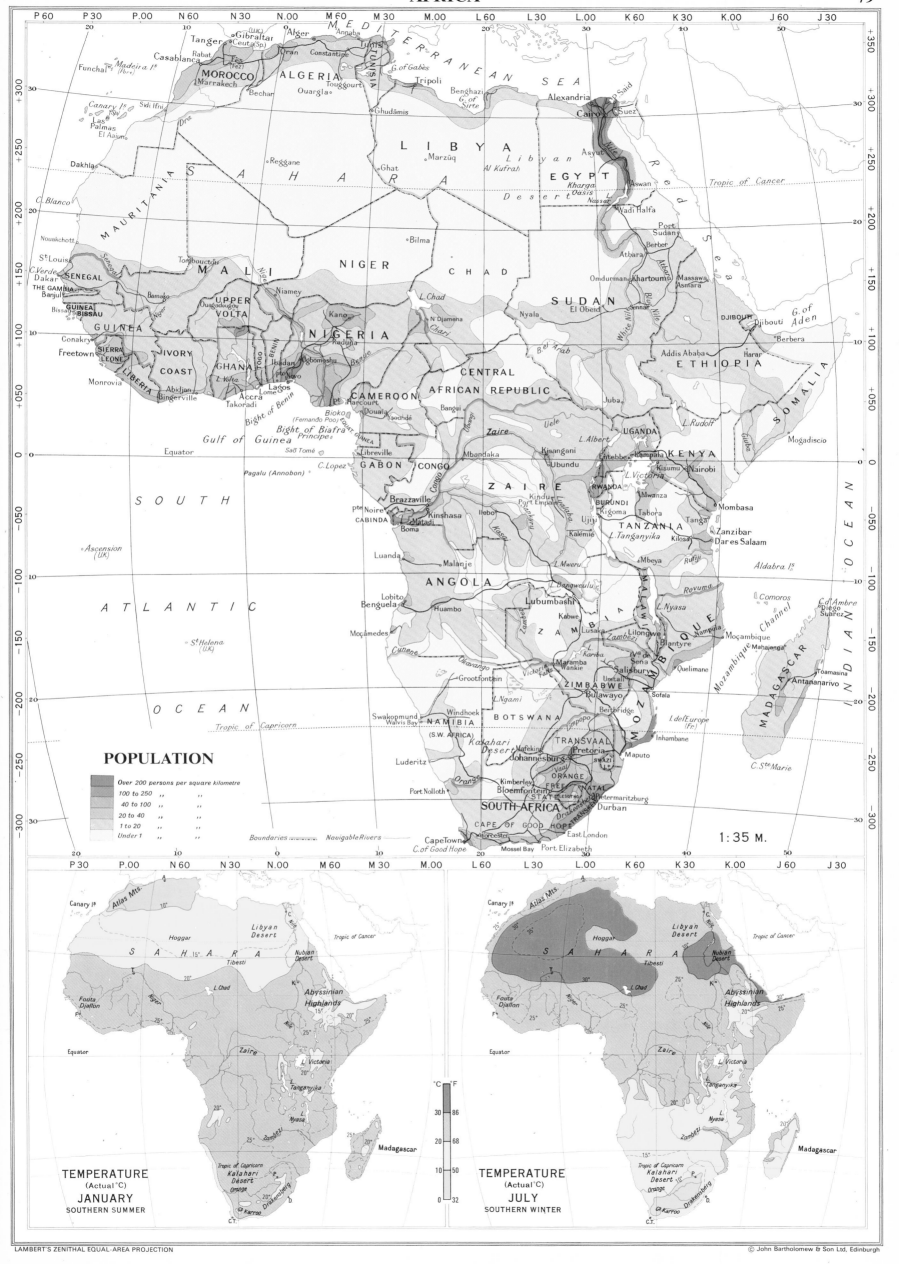

POPULATION

	Over 200 persons per square kilometre
	100 to 250 „ „ „
	40 to 100 „ „ „
	20 to 40 „ „ „
	1 to 20 „ „ „
	Under 1 „ „ „

Boundaries .... Navigable Rivers ——

1 : 35 M.

TEMPERATURE
(Actual °C)
JANUARY
SOUTHERN SUMMER

TEMPERATURE
(Actual °C)
JULY
SOUTHERN WINTER

LAMBERT'S ZENITHAL EQUAL-AREA PROJECTION

© John Bartholomew & Son Ltd, Edinburgh

1:35M

0 200 400 600 800 1000 Statute Miles

0 200 400 600 800 1000 1200 1400 1600 Kilometres

Main Roads ——————
Railways ——————

| 0 | 50 | 100 | 200 | 300 | 400 | 500 Statute Miles |
| 0 | 50 100 | 200 | 300 | 400 | 500 | 600 | 700 | 800 Kilometres |

1:12

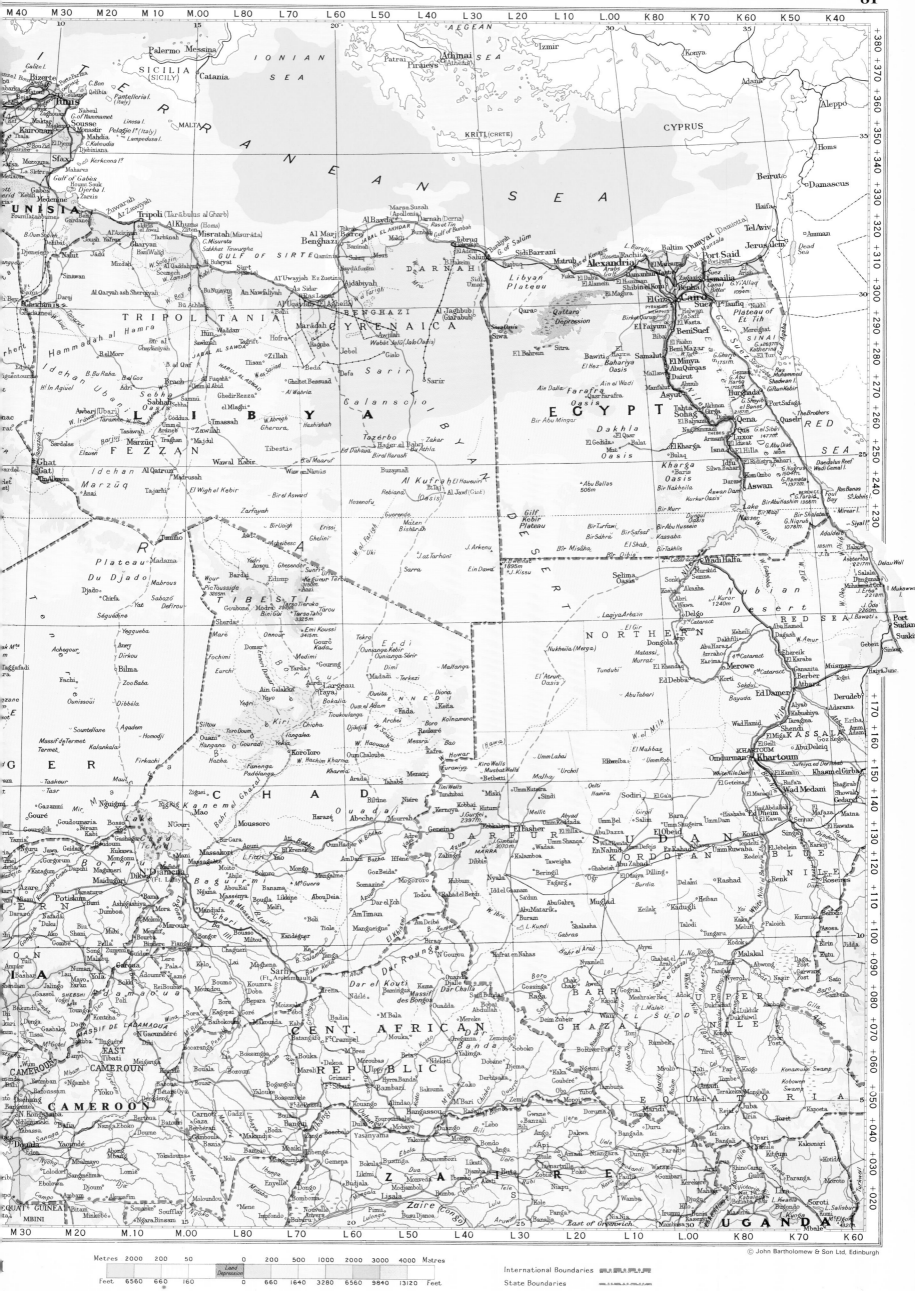

Metres 2000 200 50 0 200 500 1000 2000 3000 4000 Metres
Feet 6560 660 160 0 660 1640 3280 6560 9840 13120 Feet

Land Depression

International Boundaries
State Boundaries

© John Bartholomew & Son Ltd, Edinburgh

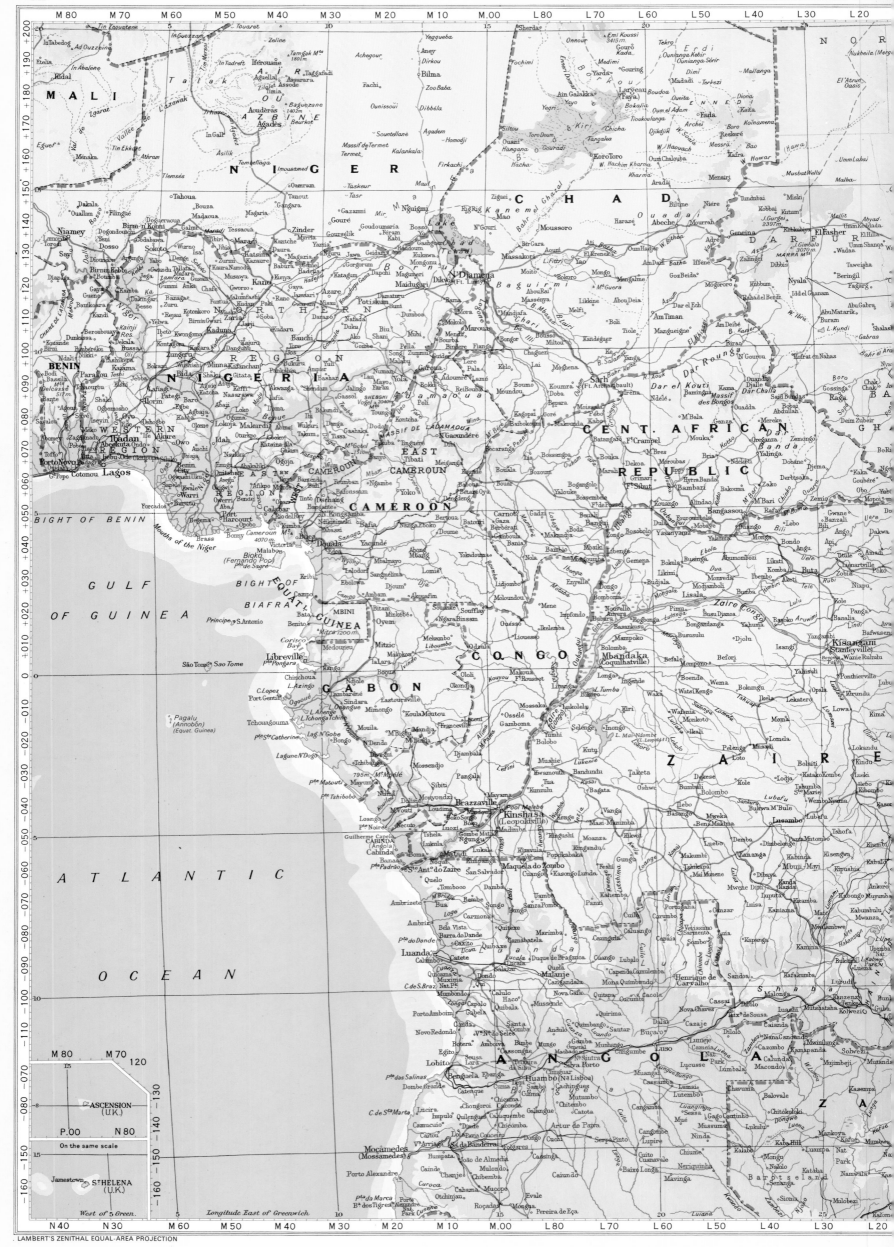

Main Roads _____
Railways _____

0 50 100   200   300   400   500 Statute Miles
0 50 100 200 300 400 500 600 700 800 Kilometres

1:1

Metres	2000	200	50		Land Depression	0	200	500	1000	2000	3000	4000	Metres
Feet	6560	660	160				660	1640	3280	6560	9840	13120	Feet

International Boundaries
State Boundaries

MADAGASCAR
(MALAGASY REP.)
On the same scale

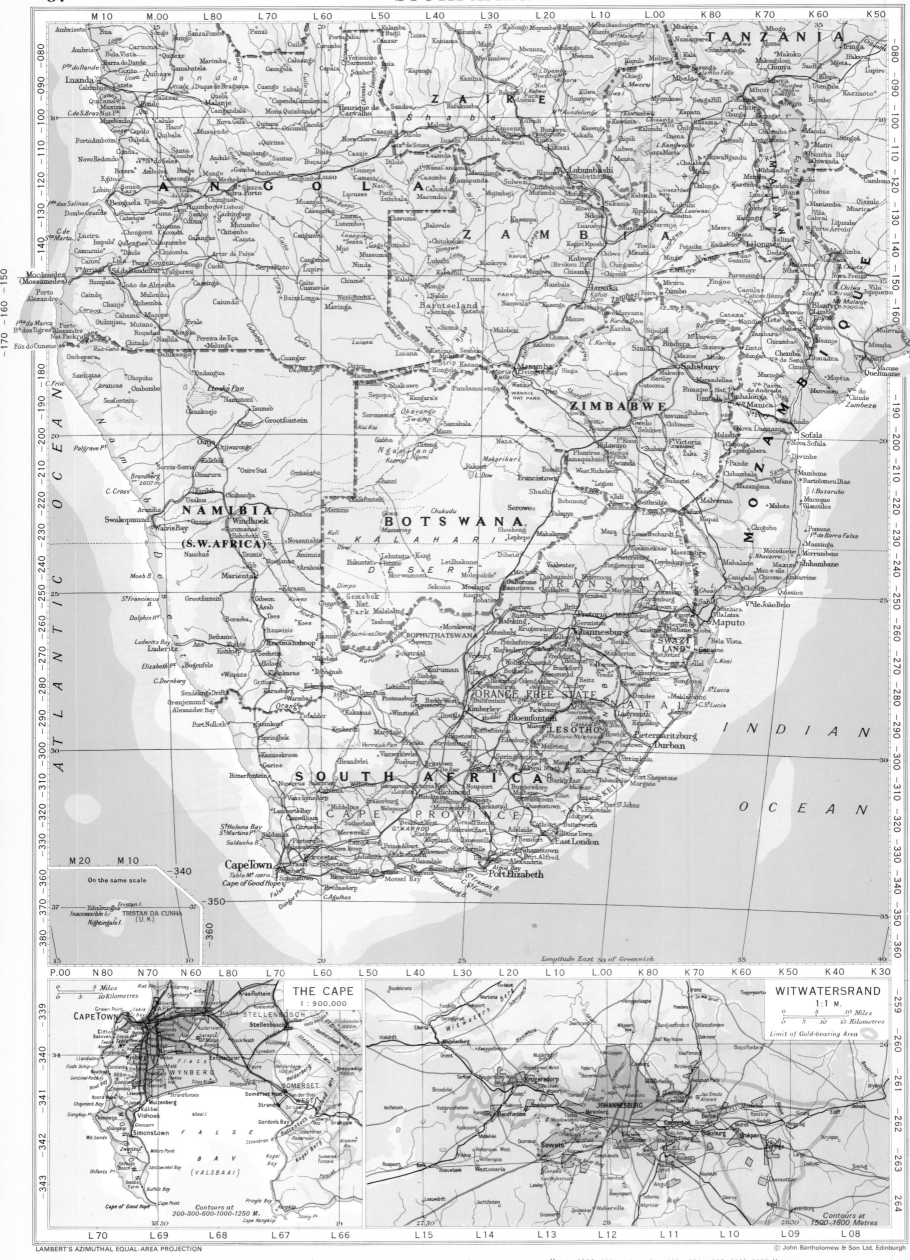

© John Bartholomew & Son Ltd, Edinburgh

1:12½ M

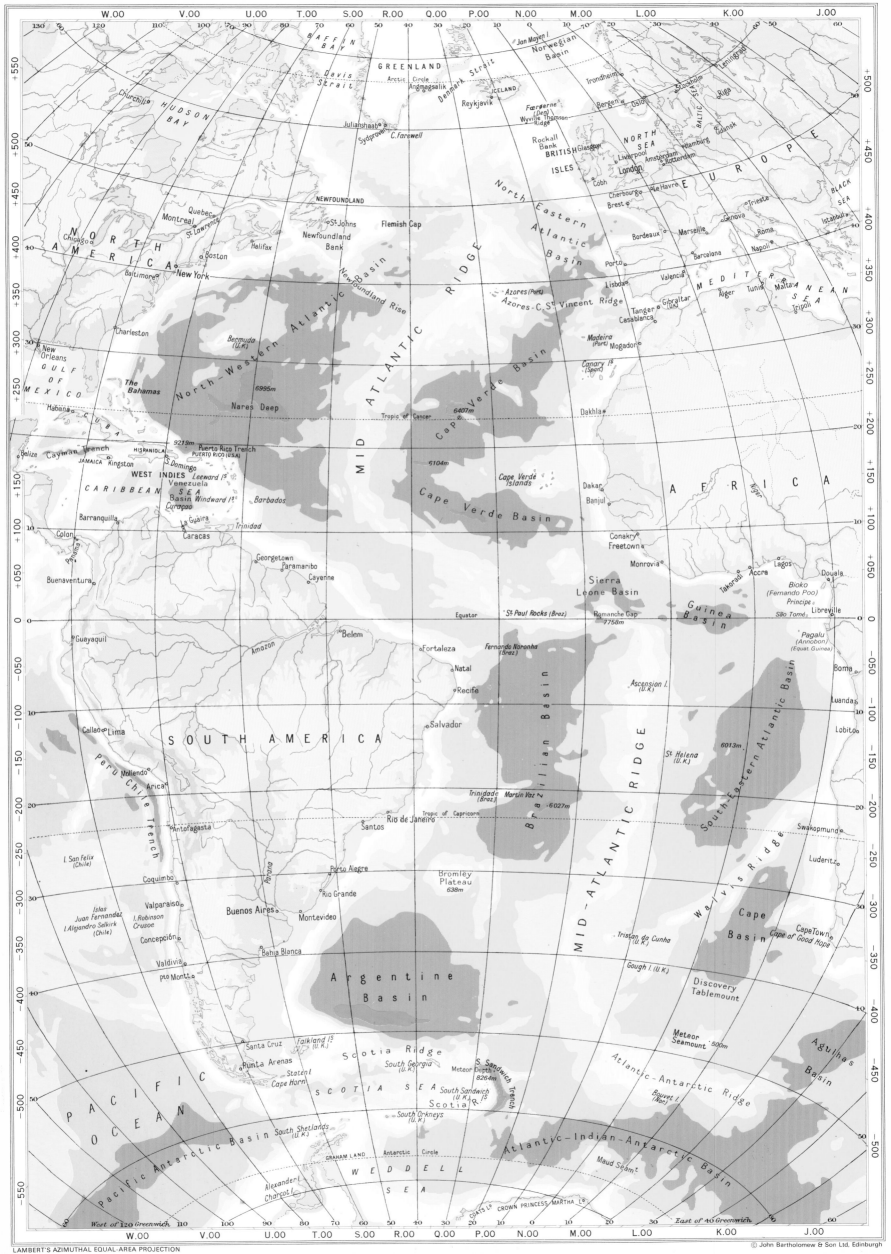

LAMBERT'S AZIMUTHAL EQUAL-AREA PROJECTION

© John Bartholomew & Son Ltd, Edinburgh

1:48M

0 200 400 600 800 1000 Statute Miles
0 400 800 1200 1600 Kilometres

Metres 6000 5000 4000 2000 200 0 200 1000 2000 4000 Metres
Feet 19690 16400 13120 6560 660 0 660 3280 6560 13120 Feet

VEGETATION

1	Northern Treeless Zone (Tundra)
2	Mountain Top Flora
3	Northern and Mountain Conif. Forest
4	South-Eastern Conif. Forest
5	North-Eastern Conif. Forest
6	British Columbian (dry) Coniferous
7	Cent. American Pine-Cedar Forest
9	Northern and Central Deciduous Mixed Forest
10	Appalachian Piedmont Forest
12	Tropical Rain Forest
13	"Prairie" Wheat Lands (Long Grass)
13ᴬ	Californian Valley Agriculture
13ᴮ	Savannah (Largely Cultivated)
14	"Plains" Wheat Lands (Short Grass)
15	Sage Brush
16	River Bottom Vegetation
17	Creosote Bush
18	Chaparral
19	Semi-Desert
20	Waterless Desert

Fresh Water Swamp
Northern Limit of Humid Sub-Tropical Fruits
Limit of Cotton
Northern Limit of Maize (American Corn)

1:34 M.

Longitude West 100° of Greenwich

RAINFALL JANUARY

The Figures indicate the Rainfall in Inches

RAINFALL JULY

The Figures indicate the Rainfall in Inches

ins.	mm.
16	400
12	300
8	200
4	100
2	50
1	25

1:34M

0   200   400   600   800 Statute Miles

0   200   400   600   800   1000   1200 Kilometres

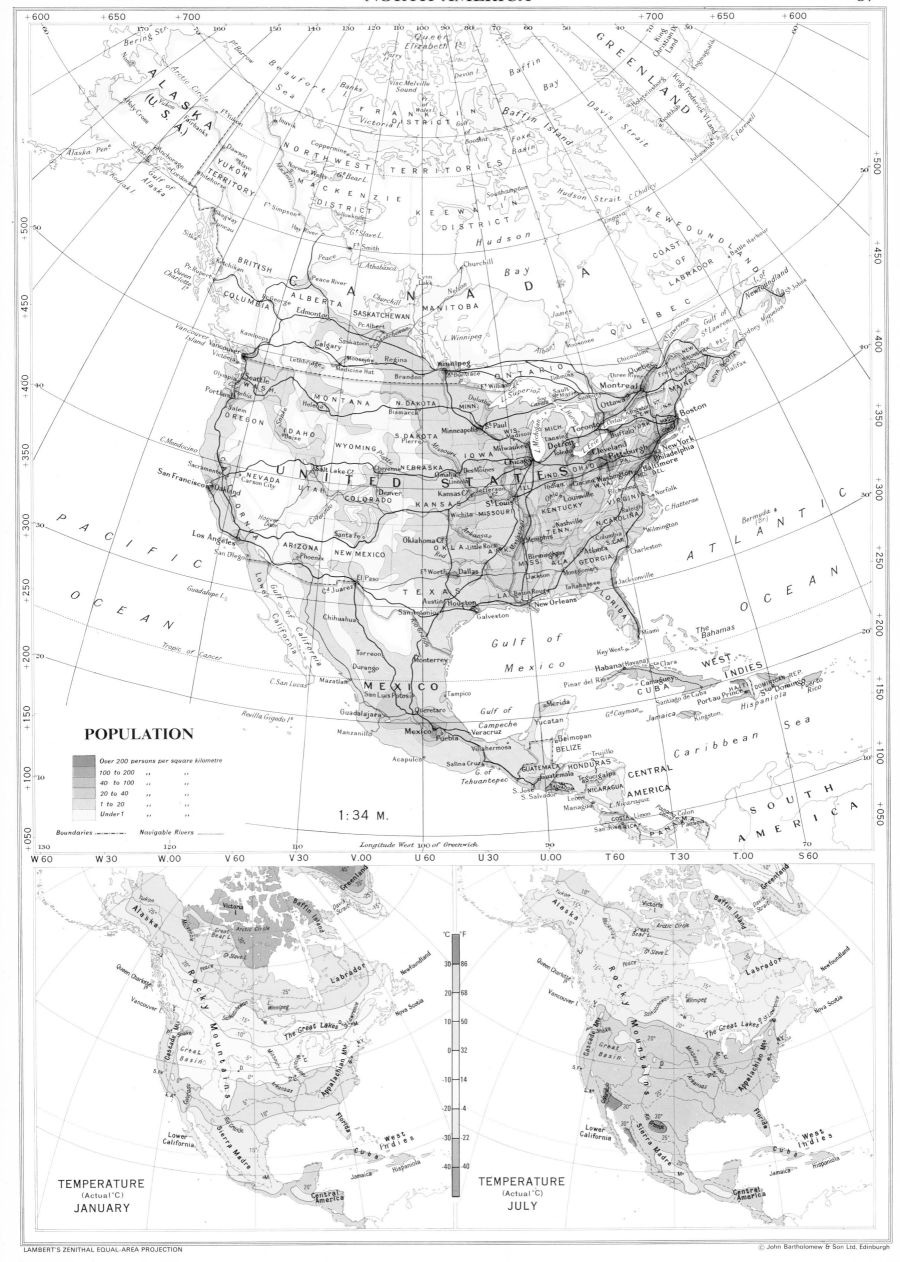

POPULATION

Over 200 persons per square kilometre
100 to 200 ,, ,, ,,
40 to 100 ,, ,, ,,
20 to 40 ,, ,, ,,
1 to 20 ,, ,, ,,
Under 1 ,, ,, ,,

Boundaries .... Navigable Rivers ~~~~~

1:34 M.

TEMPERATURE
(Actual °C)
JANUARY

TEMPERATURE
(Actual °C)
JULY

LAMBERT'S ZENITHAL EQUAL-AREA PROJECTION

© John Bartholomew & Son Ltd, Edinburgh

1:34M

0   200   400   600   800 Statute Miles

0   200   400   600   800   1000   1200 Kilometres

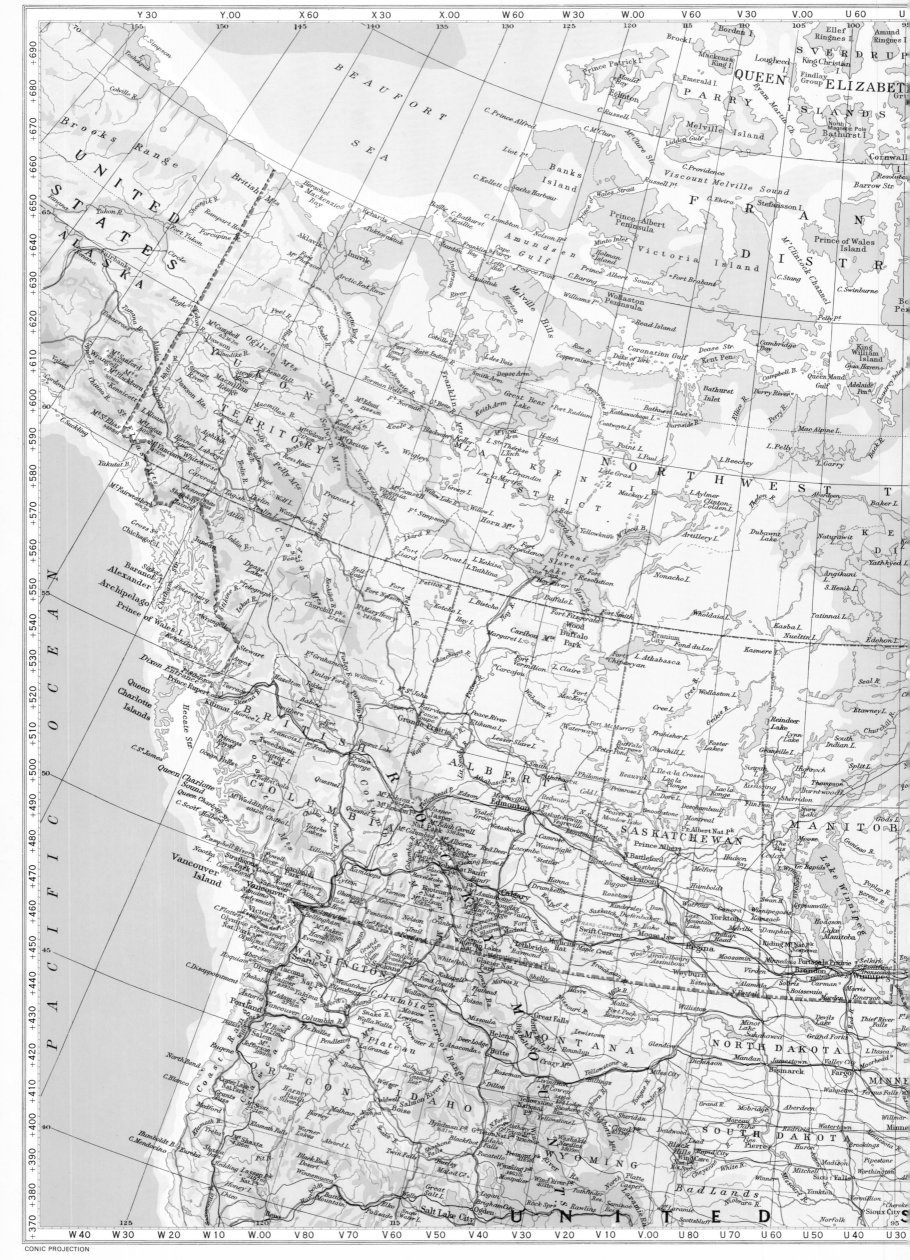

Main Roads ————
Railways ————

0   50 100   200   300   400   500 Statute Miles
0 50 100 200 300 400 500 600 700 800 Kilometres

1:12

+690
+680
+670
+660
+650
+640
+630
+620
+610
60
+590
+580
+570
+560
55
+550
+540
+530
+520
+510
50
+500
+490
+480
+470
+460
45
+450
+440
+430
+420
+410
40
+400
+390
+380
+370

ICA

ISLANDS
Ellesmere
Heiberg
Island
Island
85

Smith Bay
Grise Fiord
Clarence Hd.
C. Atholl
C. York
Dundas
(Thule Air Base)
Thule
Melville Bay
Holms I.

Devon Island
Coburg I.
C. Fitz Roy
C. Parker

Lancaster Sound
Prince
Regent
Inlet
Brodeur
Pen.
Bylot I.
C. Byam Martin
C. Graham Moore
C. Maccalloch
Pond
Inlet
C. Adair
Scott Inlet
C. Eglinton
Clyde Inlet
C. Aston
Clyde

Upernavik

GREENLAND

Svarten Huk
Pen.
Umanak
Nägssaq Pen.
Disko

Sondre Stromfjord

65

Angmagssalik

C. Scoresby

Gulf
of
Boothia
Creswell
Bay
Quartz L.
Erichsen L.
Steensby
Inlet
Koch I.
Gillian L.
Igloolik
Rowley I.
Bray I.
Spicer I.
Foley I.
Air
Force I.

BAFFIN

ISLAND

Home Bay

C. Henry Kater
Padloping Island
C. Dyer

DAVIS

STRAIT

Holsteinsborg

Godhavn
Godthaab
Disko

Christianshaab

Melville
Peninsula
Foxe
Basin
Prince
Charles
Island
Nettilling Lake
Cumberland Pen.
C. Walsingham

Cumberland Sound
C. Mercy

Holsteinsborg

60

Narssarssuaq
Frederikshåb
Ivigtut
Julianehåb
C. Farewell
Nanortalik

Rae
Isthmus
Repulse
Arctic Circle
Wager B.
Vansittart I.
Committee
Bay
Foxe
Peninsula
Cape Dorset
Mill I.
Bowman B.
Amadjuak
Lake
Frobisher Bay
C. Murchison

Kogerlussuaq

TERRITORIES
Southampton
Island
South B.
Seahorse Pt.
Salisbury I.
Lake Harb.
Loks I.
Frobisher Bay
Resolution I.
Hatton Headland

ATLANTIC

C. Kendall
Daly
B.
Chesterfield Inlet
C. Southampton
Coats I.
Mansel I.
Nottingham I.
C. Pembroke
C. Low
Ivugivik
C. Wolstenholme
Saglouc
(Sugluk)
Big I.

Button Is.
C. Chidley
C. Killinek

Rankin Inlet

KEEWATIN
DISTRICT
Smith I.
New Quebec Crater
Maricourt
(Wakeham Bay)
Koartac
Payne R.
Payne B.
(Bellin
Payne Bay)
Akpatok I.
C. Hopes Advance

Nachvak Fd.
Cirque Mt. Ramah
Saglek B.
Hebron
C. Mugford

55

Eskimo Point
Eskimo
Povungnituk
Povungnituk
Payne L.
Ungava
Bay
Fort
Chimo
Fort
Nouveau Quebec
(George
River)

Nutak

Povungnituk
Ottawa
Islands
Koksoak R.
Fort
McKenzie
Leaf R.
George R.
Quebec R.

Nain

NEWFOUNDLAND

Adlavik Is.
C. Harrison

+530

C. Churchill
HUDSON
Kogaluk R.
Inoucdjouac
(Port Harrison)
Whale R.
Indian
House L.
Hopedale
Hamilton Inlet
Rigolet

Carwright

C. St. Lewis
Battle Harbour
CapeCharles
Belle Isle
C. Bauld

C. Tatnam
BAY
The Sleepers
Fort McKenzie
Michikamau
Naskaupi R.
Lake
Melville
L A B R A D O R

North West River
Goose Bay

C. Henrietta
Maria
York Factory
Belcher Is.
Lit. Whale R.
Upper Seal
L.
Eaton
Canyon
Bienville
L.
Schefferville
Burnt Creek
Churchill
Falls
Churchill
(Hamilton) R.

Hare B.
Bell I.
White Bay

50

Fort
Severn
Shamattawa
(abandoned)
Poste
de-la-Baleine
Gt. Whale R.
Kaniapiskau
L.
Labrador
City
Bowdoin
Canyon
Churchill
(Hamilton) R.
Atikonak L.
Romaine R.
Natashquan R.

St. Anthony

Mushuau
L. Michikamau

ISLAND OF
NEWFOUNDLAND

Twillingate
Fogo
Freels
Gander
Bonavista B.
Bonavista

Sandy L.
Severn R.
Winisk R.
Bear L.
Fort George
JAMES
Ft. George
Ashuanipi
Gagnon
Gull L.
Seven Is.
Sept Iles
Moisie
Mingan
Natashquan
Havre-St. Pierre
Kegaska
B. of Islands
Corner Brook
C. St. George's
Channel
Port aux Basques
Fortune B.

Bonne Bay
Grand Falls
Gambo
Clarenville
Trinity B.
Harbour Grace
Conception B.
Avalon
Pen.
St. John's
Placentia B.
St. Mary's
Cape Race

BAY
Akimiski
I.
Nouveau
Comptoir
Eastmain R.
Mistassini
L.
L. Evans
Mistassini
Chibougamau
Peribonka R.
Bersimis R.
QUEBEC
Betsiamites
B. St. Lawrence
Baie Comeau
Anticosti I.
Cartier
Gulf of
Magdalen Is.
North Pt.
Prince
Edward I.

Cabot Str.
C. Ray
North Str.
St. Paul I.
C. North
Cape Breton I.
Sydney Mines
Glace Bay
C. Breton
Louisburg
Miquelon
(Fr.)
St. Pierre
(Fr.)

Sachigo R.
Winisk R.
Attawapiskat R.
Kapiskau
R.
Ft. Albany
Albany R.
Charlton I.
Rupert R.
I. Rupert
Albanel
Gouin
Reservoir
Père
La Tuque
Roberval
L. St. John
Chicoutimi
Tadoussac
Rimouski
Matane
Gaspé
Gaspésie Pk.
Chaleur B.
Bathurst
Chatham
Northumberland Str.
Charlottetown
Amherst
Pictou
Strait of Canso
Canso
New Glasgow
Mulgrave
Antigonish

45

Trout L.
Big Trout L.
Attawapiskat
Kapiskau
Fort Albany
Moosonee
Moose R.
Kesagami
L.
Grant
Harricanaw R.
Amos
Val d'Or
Senneterre
Parent
St. Maurice R.
Shawinigan
Trois Rivières
Joliette
Sorel
Drummondville
Victoriaville
Thetford
Mines
Mégantic
Edmundston
Campbellton
NEW
BRUNSWICK
Moncton
Sackville
NOVA
Truro

Lac
Seul
L. St. Joseph
Osnaburgh
Armstrong Sta.
Waboose Dam
Ogoki R.
Lake
Nipigon
Geraldton
Long L.
Hearst
Kapuskasing
Smooth Rock Falls
Cochrane
Matheson
Noranda
Rouyn
Belleterre
Ville-Marie
Mont Laurier
Maniwaki
Gracefield
Buckingham
Montebello
Hawkesbury
L'Original
Grenville
Lachute
St. Jérôme
Ste. Agathe
Joliette
St. Hyacinthe
Granby
Sherbrooke
Coaticook
Sherbrooke
MAINE
Presque Isle
Caribou
Houlton
Woodstock
Fredericton
SCOTIA
Windsor
Dartmouth
Halifax

Sioux Lookout
Sandy L.
Savant L.
Ignace
Dryden
Vermilion Bay
Kenora
Rainy L.
Fort Frances
Atikokan
Quetico
Park
Thunder Bay
Nipigon
TRANS-CANADA HIGHWAY
White River
Marathon
Schreiber
Nipigon
Terrace Bay

MINNESOTA
Duluth
Two Harbors
Superior
ONTARIO
Chapleau
Missanabie
Foleyet
Timmins
Haileybury
New Liskeard
Cobalt
Timiskaming
Mattawa
North Bay
Sturgeon Falls
Pembroke
Renfrew
Arnprior
Ottawa
Smiths Falls
Perth
Brockville
Prescott
Cornwall
Massena
Ogdensburg
Lancaster
Alexandria
Plattsburg
VERMONT
Montpelier
Burlington
NEW
HAMPSHIRE
Concord
Augusta
Waterville
Bangor
Rockland
Bath
Portland
Biddeford
Portsmouth

Eau Claire
Apostle Is.
Superior
Bayfield
Ashland
Ironwood
Hibbing
Virginia
St. Croix
Stillwater
St. Paul
Minneapolis
Menomonie
Chippewa
Wausau
Rhinelander
Houghton
MICHIGAN
Marquette
Munising
Newberry
Sault
Ste. Marie
Blind River
Elliot Lake
Sudbury
Espanola
Little Current
Manitoulin I.
Georgian
Bay
Parry Sound
Huntsville
Algonquin
Park
Bracebridge
Orillia
Barrie
Peterborough
Lindsay
Belleville
Kingston
Watertown
Adirondack
Mts.
Glens Falls
Saratoga
Schenectady
Troy
Albany
Pittsfield
MASSACHUSETTS
Springfield
Worcester
Lowell
Boston
Gloucester
Cape Cod
C. Sable

LaCrosse
Winona
Austin
Rochester
Red Wing
WISCONSIN
Eau Claire
Wisconsin
Rapids
Oshkosh
Appleton
Green Bay
Manitowoc
Sheboygan
Milwaukee
Racine
Kenosha
Waukegan
Evanston
Chicago
90
Muskegon
Grand
Rapids
Holland
Lansing
Flint
Saginaw
Bay City
Owosso
MICHIGAN
Huron
Port Huron
Sarnia
London
St. Thomas
Chatham
Windsor
Detroit
Lake Erie
Cleveland
80
Owen Sound
Collingwood
Goderich
Stratford
Kitchener
Guelph
Hamilton
Toronto
Oakville
St. Catharines
Lake Ontario
Rochester
Oswego
Syracuse
Utica
Rome
N E W   Y O R K
Binghamton
Elmira
Ithaca
Auburn
Geneva
Buffalo
Niagara Falls
Jamestown
Olean
Warren
Scranton
Wilkes-Barre
CONNECTICUT
Hartford
New Haven
Bridgeport
Providence
RHODE ISLAND
New Bedford
Taunton
Brockton
Nantucket
Martha's Vineyard
Fall River
Newport

40

Madison
Janesville
Beloit
Rockford
Freeport
Waukegan
Chicago
Poughkeepsie
Kingston
Catskill
Newburgh
Paterson
Newark
New York
70
Long I.
Long Branch
New Haven

STATES

Longitude West 65° of Greenwich

Metres	2000	200	50	0	200	500	1000	2000	3000	4000	Metres
Feet	6560	660	160	0	660	1640	3280	6560	9840	13120	Feet

International Boundaries
Province Boundaries

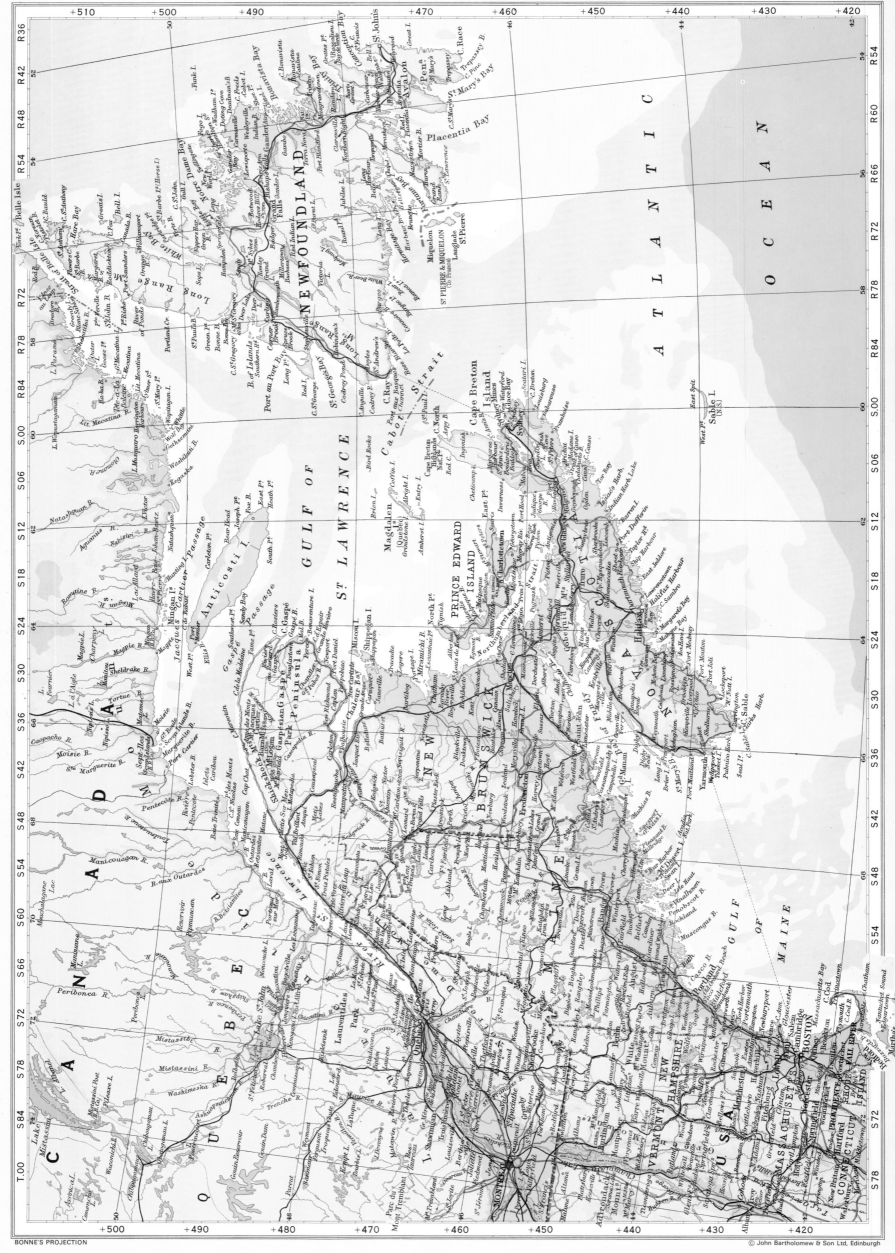

BONNE'S PROJECTION

1:5M

Statute Miles
0   50   100

Kilometres
0   50   100   150

Metres 2000 200 50 0 100 200 500 1000 Metres
Feet 6560 660 160 0 330 660 1640 3280 Feet

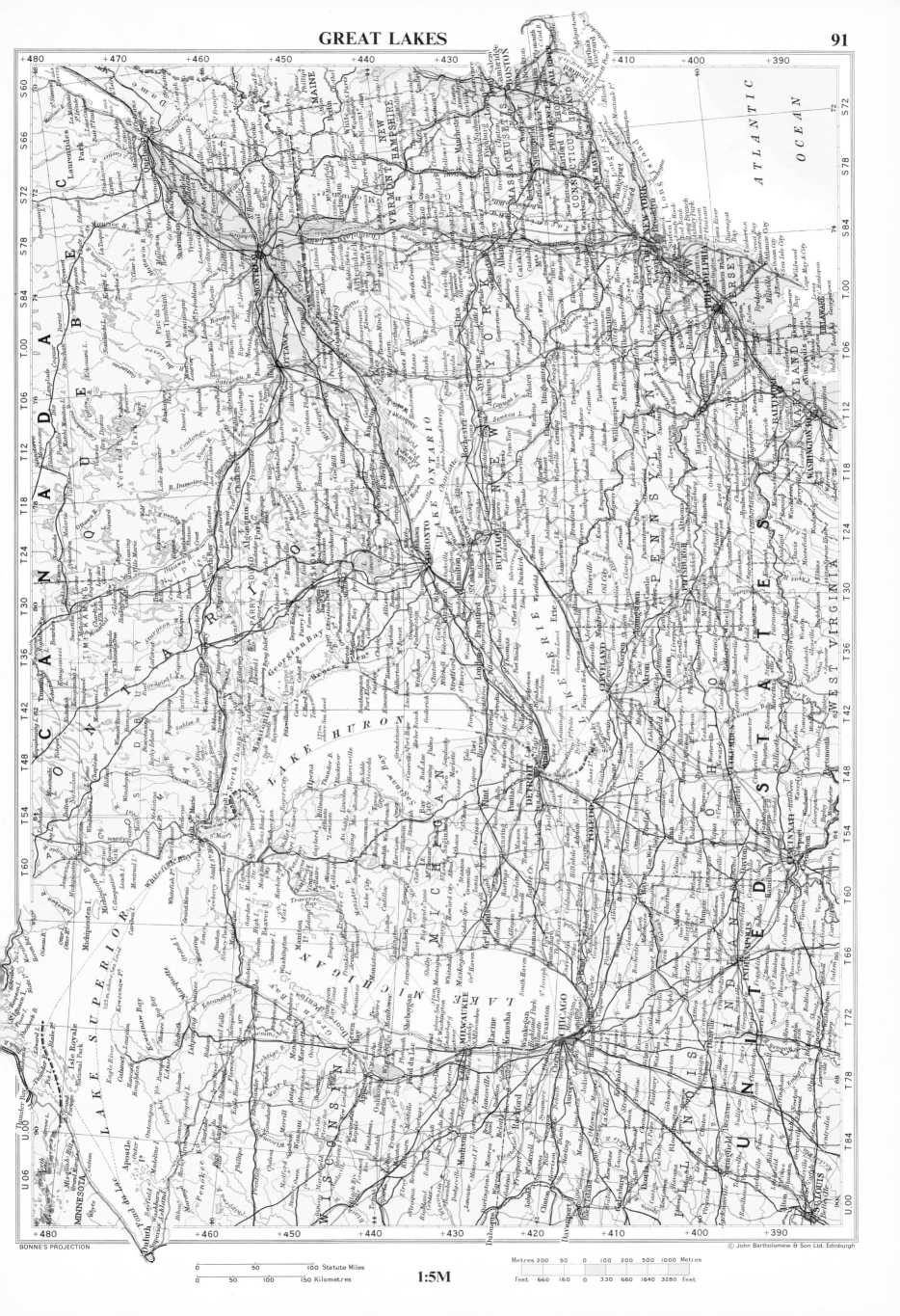

1:5M

© John Bartholomew & Son Ltd, Edinburgh

Statute Miles			
0	50	100	
0	50	100	150 Kilometres

Metres	200	50	0	100	200	500	1000 Metres
Feet	660	160	0	330	660	1640	3280 Feet

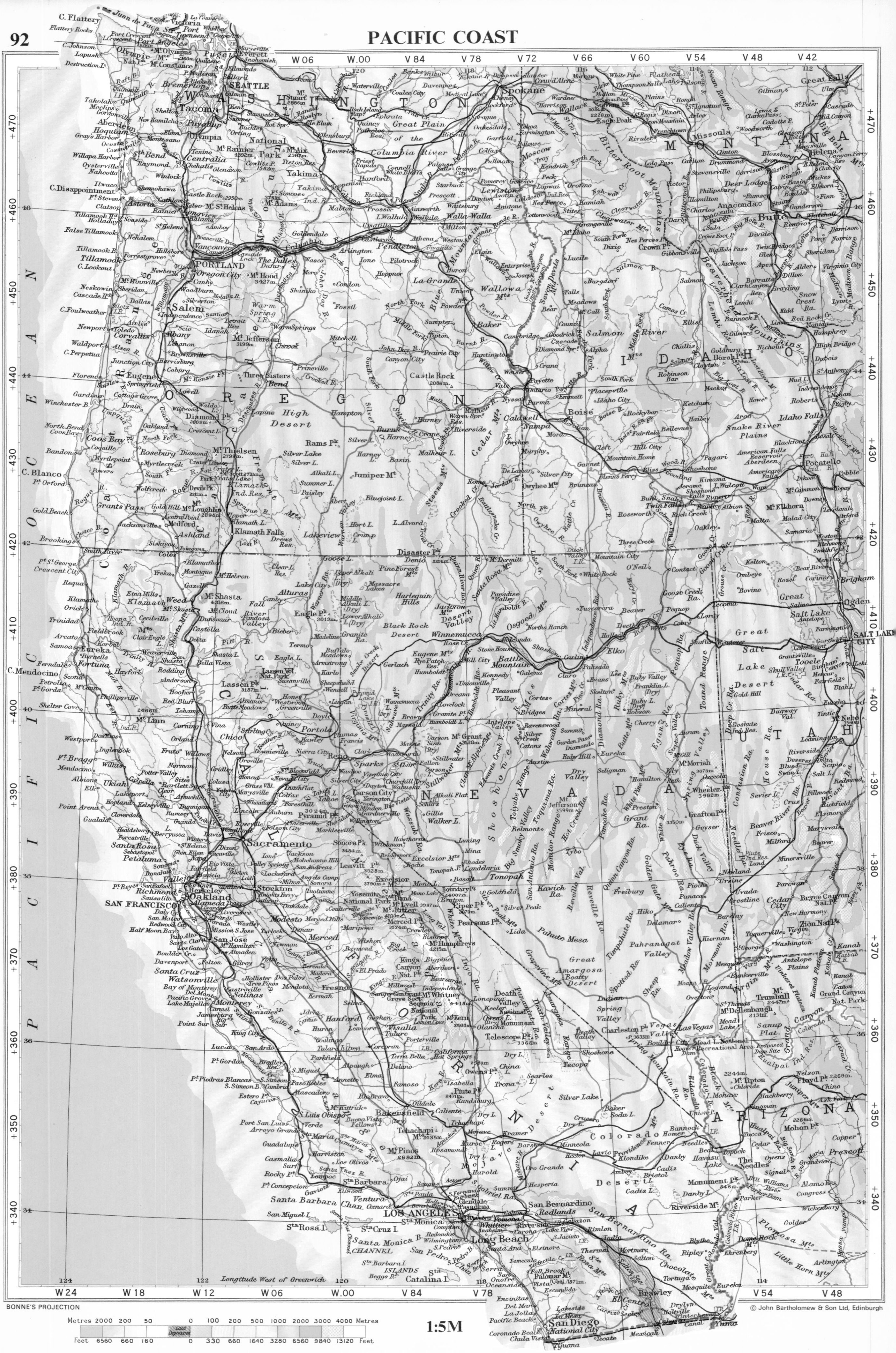

WASHINGTON

OREGON

IDAHO

MONTANA

NEVADA

UTAH

CALIFORNIA

ARIZONA

PACIFIC OCEAN

BONNE'S PROJECTION

1:5M

© John Bartholomew & Son Ltd, Edinburgh

Metres 2000 200 50 0 100 200 500 1000 2000 3000 4000 Metres

Feet 6560 660 160 0 330 660 1640 3280 6560 9840 13120 Feet

Land Depression

Longitude West of Greenwich

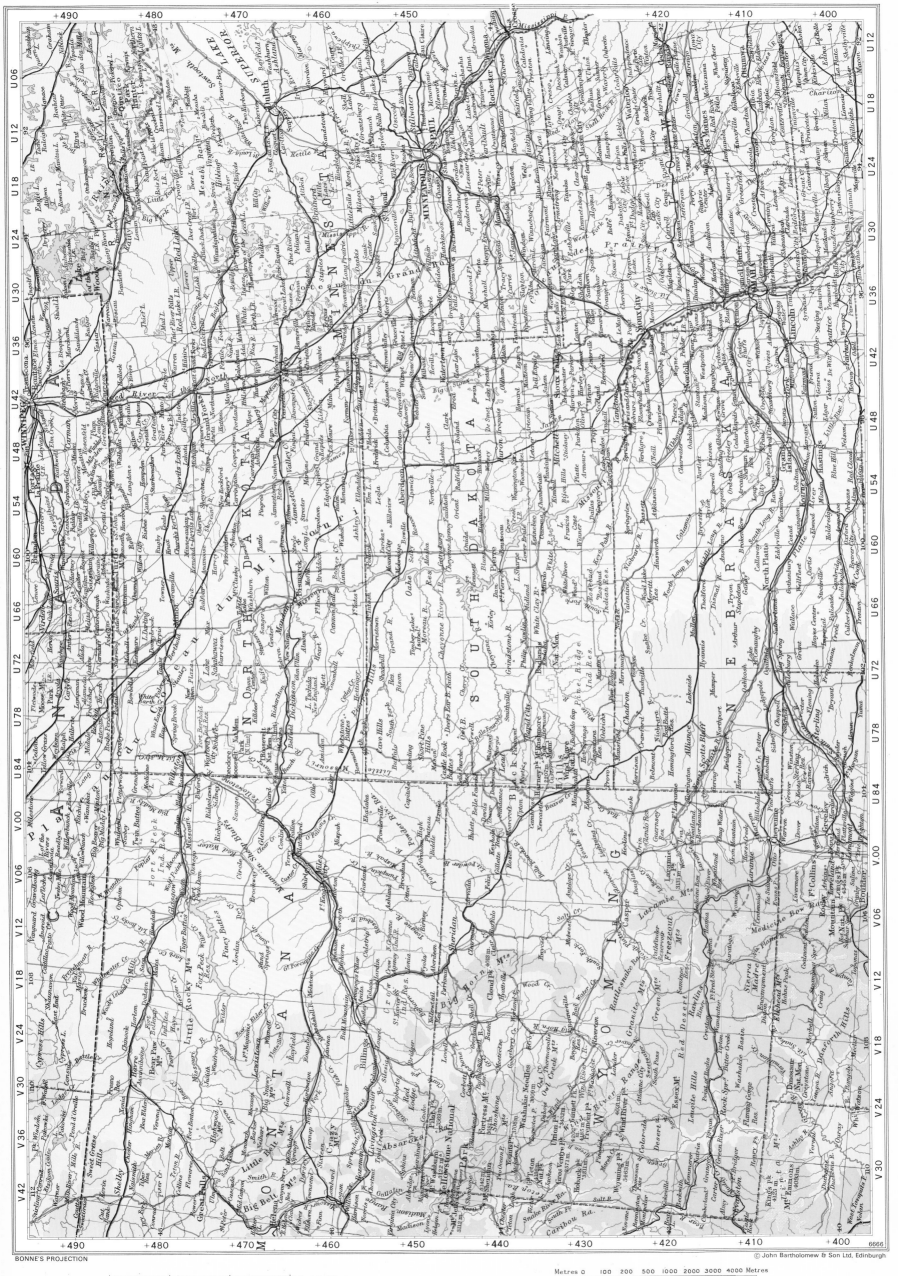

BONNE'S PROJECTION

1:5M

© John Bartholomew & Son Ltd, Edinburgh

| Statute Miles | 0 | 50 | 100 | 150 |
| Kilometres | 0 | 50 | 100 | 150 | 200 | 250 |

| Metres | 0 | 100 | 200 | 500 | 1000 | 2000 | 3000 | 4000 Metres |
| Feet | 0 | 330 | 660 | 1640 | 3280 | 6560 | 9840 | 13120 Feet |

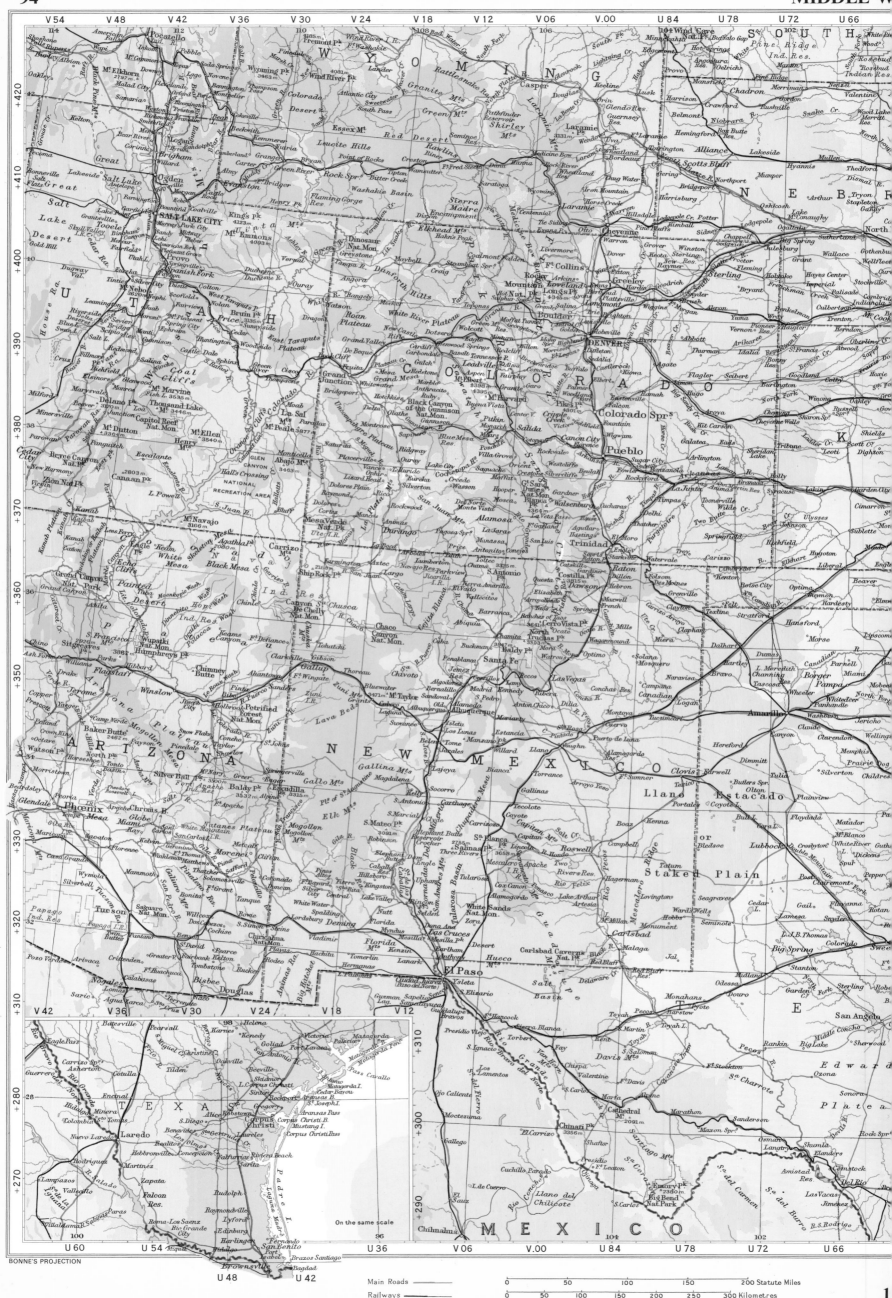

Main Roads ⸺
Railways ⸺

0	50	100	150	200 Statute Miles

| 0 | 50 | 100 | 150 | 200 | 250 | 300 Kilometres |

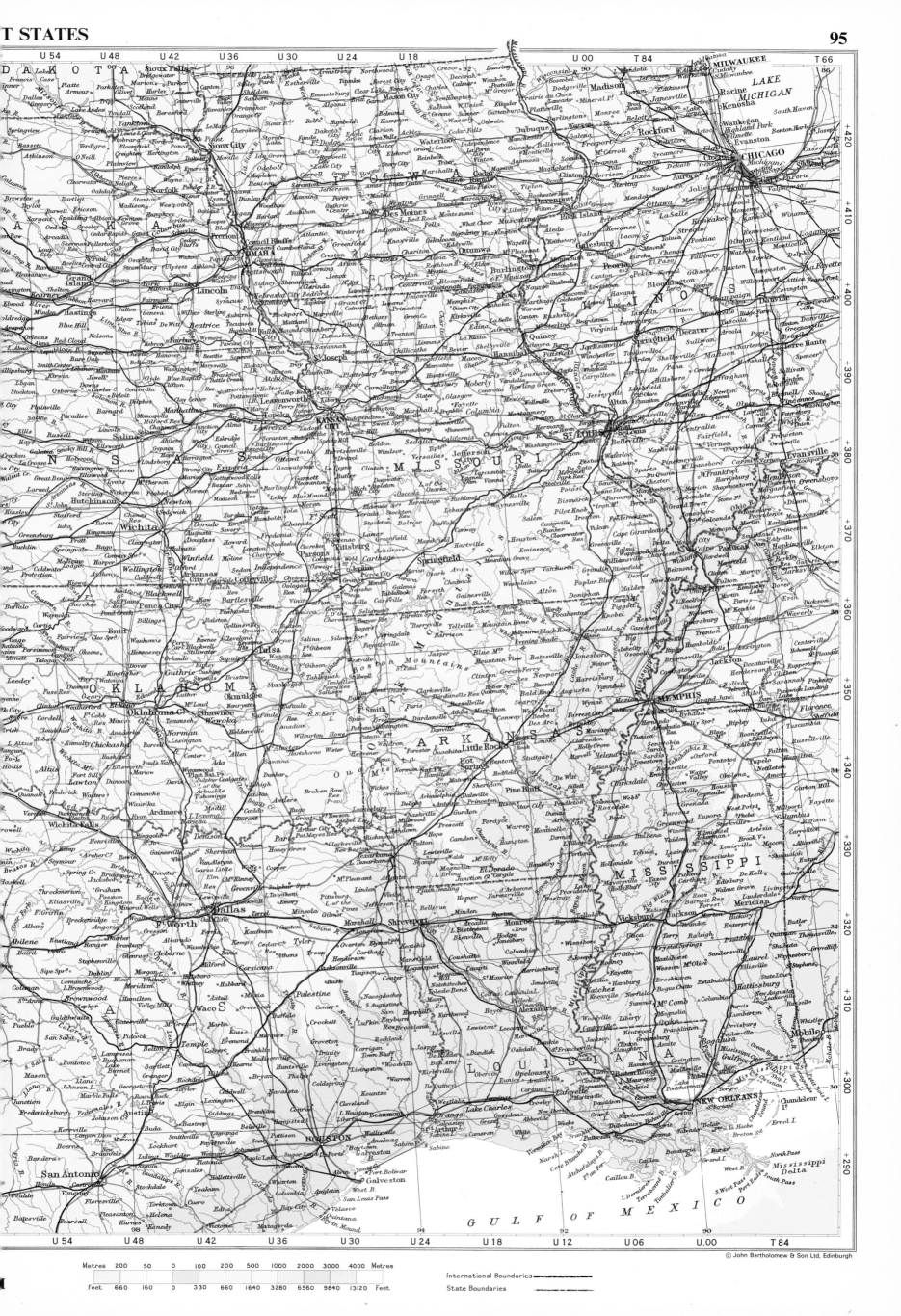

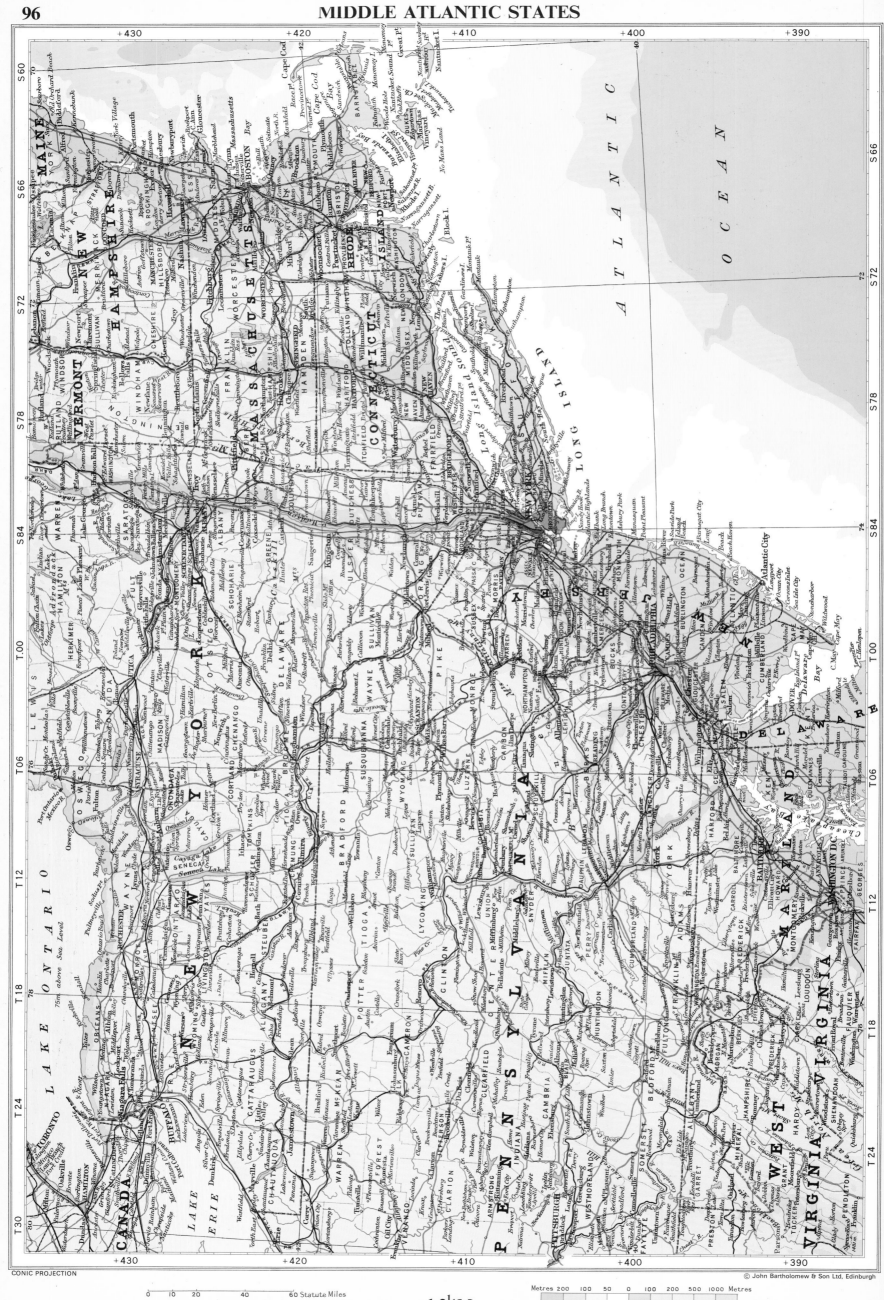

CONIC PROJECTION

1:2½ M

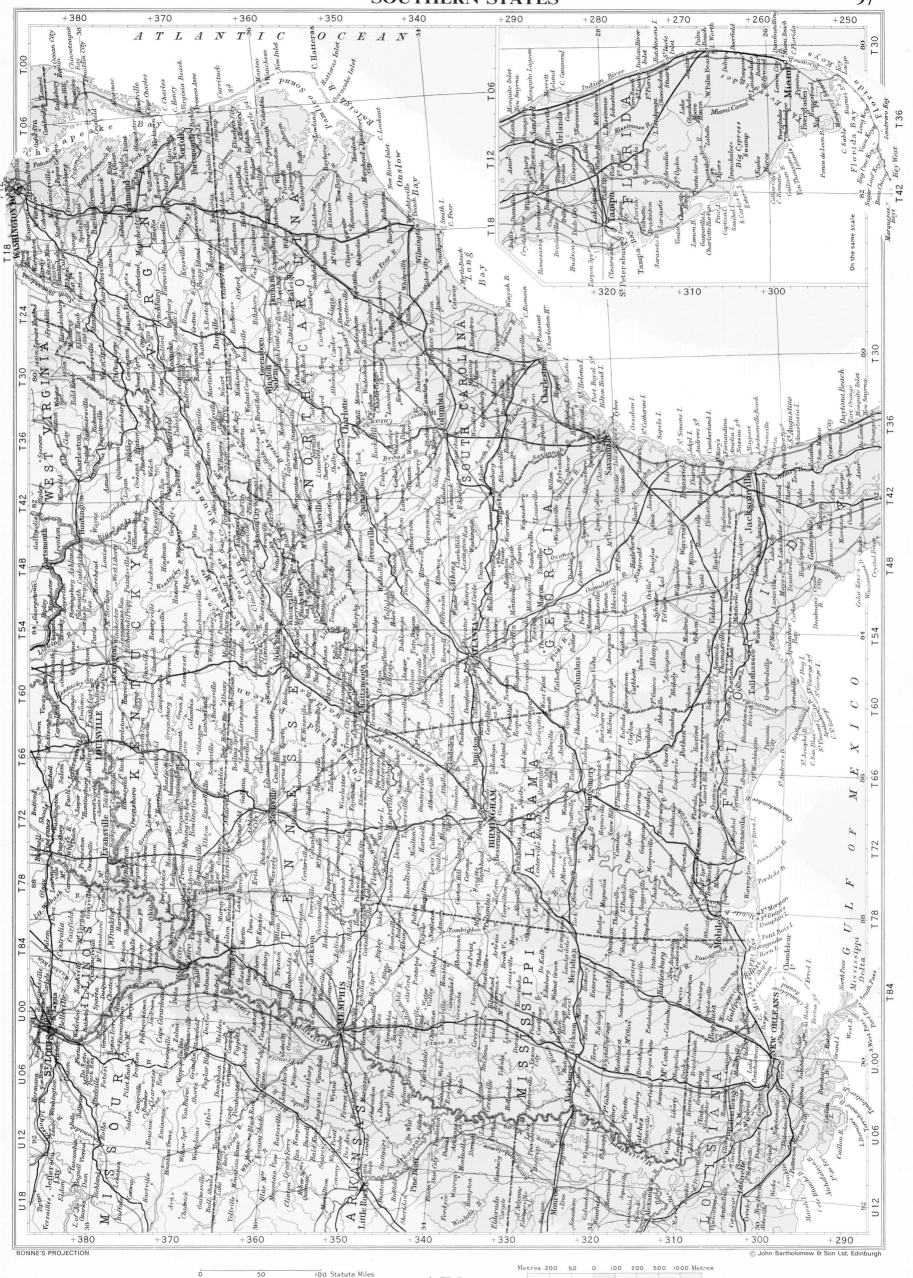

BONNE'S PROJECTION

1:5M

© John Bartholomew & Son Ltd, Edinburgh

HAWAII
1:6¼ M.

0   50   100 Miles
0   50   100   150 Kilometres

SAN FRANCISCO

0   2   4 km
0   1   2

CONIC PROJECTION

Main Roads _____
Railways _____

0   50   100   200   300   400   500 Statute Miles
0   50 100   200   300   400   500   600   700   800 Kilometres

1:12

NEW YORK

Miles
0   1   2   4 km
0   1   2

ALASKA
1:25 M
0 50 100 200 300 Miles
0 100 200 300 400 Kilometres

© John Bartholomew & Son Ltd, Edinburgh

Metres 2000 200 50   0   200 500 1000 2000 3000 4000 Metres
                          Land
                       Depression
Feet 6560 660 160   0   560 1640 3280 6560 9840 13120 Feet

International Boundaries
State Boundaries

G U L F   O F   M E X I C O

P A C I F I C   O C E A N

UNITED STATES

MEXICO

TEXAS

LOUISIANA

MISSISSIPPI

CHIHUAHUA

SONORA

COAHUILA

NUEVO LEON

TAMAULIPAS

DURANGO

SINALOA

ZACATECAS

S. LUIS POTOSI

NAYARIT

JALISCO

GUANAJUATO

HIDALGO

MICHOACAN

GUERRERO

OAXACA

VERACRUZ

PUEBLA

CHIAPAS

TABASCO

CAMPECHE

YUCATAN

QUINTANA ROO

GUATEMALA

HONDURAS

SALVADOR

BELIZE

Gulf of Campeche

Gulf of Tehuantepec

Gulf of California

Gulf of Honduras

Yucatan Channel

Tropic of Cancer

Baja California (Norte)

Baja California (Sur)

Revilla Gigedo Is.

BONNE'S PROJECTION

© John Bartholomew & Son Ltd, Edinburgh

1:10M

0   100   200   300 Statute Miles
0   100   200   300   400   500 Kilometres

Metres 2000 200 50 0 200 500 1000 2000 3000 4000 Metres
Feet 6560 660 160 0 660 1640 3280 6560 9840 13120 Feet

PANAMA CANAL
1:1000000

Contours are drawn at 100 and 200 Metres

Canal ——— Railway ······

ATLANTIC OCEAN

GULF OF MEXICO

THE BAHAMAS

WEST INDIES

Great Bahama Bank

CUBA

GREATER ANTILLES

JAMAICA

HAITI

DOMINICAN REP.

HISPANIOLA

PUERTO RICO

San Juan

LESSER ANTILLES

LEEWARD ISLANDS

WINDWARD ISLANDS

ANTIGUA

GUADELOUPE

DOMINICA

MARTINIQUE

ST. LUCIA

ST. VINCENT

BARBADOS

GRENADA

TOBAGO

TRINIDAD

CARIBBEAN SEA

YUCATAN

MEXICO

CAMPECHE

QUINTANA ROO

BRITISH HONDURAS

GUATEMALA

EL SALVADOR

HONDURAS

NICARAGUA

COSTA RICA

PANAMA

CENTRAL AMERICA

PACIFIC OCEAN

COLOMBIA

VENEZUELA

GUYANA

Mouths of the Orinoco

Gulf of Mexico

Tropic of Cancer

Florida Str.

Yucatan Channel

Gulf of Honduras

Gulf of Darien

Gulf of Panama

HABANA (HAVANA)

Kingston

Port au Prince

Santo Domingo

CARACAS

Maracaibo

Cartagena

Panama

Colón

Bonne's Projection

1:10M

0   100   200   300 Statute Miles

0   100   200   300   400   500 Kilometres

Metres 2000 200 50 0 200 500 1000 2000 3000 4000 Metres

Feet 6560 660 160 0 660 1640 3280 6560 9840 13120 Feet

© John Bartholomew & Son Ltd. Edinburgh

VEGETATION

1	Antarctic Tundra
2^A	Andean Mountain Zone, Paramos (wet)
2^B	,, ,, ,, Punas (dry)
2^C	,, ,, ,, Tola (arid)
3	Hill Tropical Forest
5	Catingas
6	Chaco
7	Inter-Andean Basin Cultivation
9	Park Land
10	Temperate Forest
11	Mixed Tropical Forest
12	Tropical Rain Forest

13	Pampas (Rich Grass)
14	Llanos (Plateau Grass)
15	Campos Cerrados and Savannah
16	Mediterranean Type Vegetation
17	"Monte," Xerophil Bush
17^A	Salt Swamp
18	Patagonian Steppe
19	Semi-Desert
20	Waterless Desert
	Fresh Water Swamp
– – –	Southern Limit of Hevea (Wild Rubber)
–·–·–	Southern Limit of Quebracho
ooooooo	Extent of Yerba Maté

1:32 M.

RAINFALL
JANUARY
SOUTHERN SUMMER
The Figures indicate the
Rainfall in Inches

ins.   mm.
16 — 400
12 — 300
8 — 200
4 — 100
2 — 50
1 — 25

RAINFALL
JULY
SOUTHERN WINTER
The Figures indicate the
Rainfall in Inches

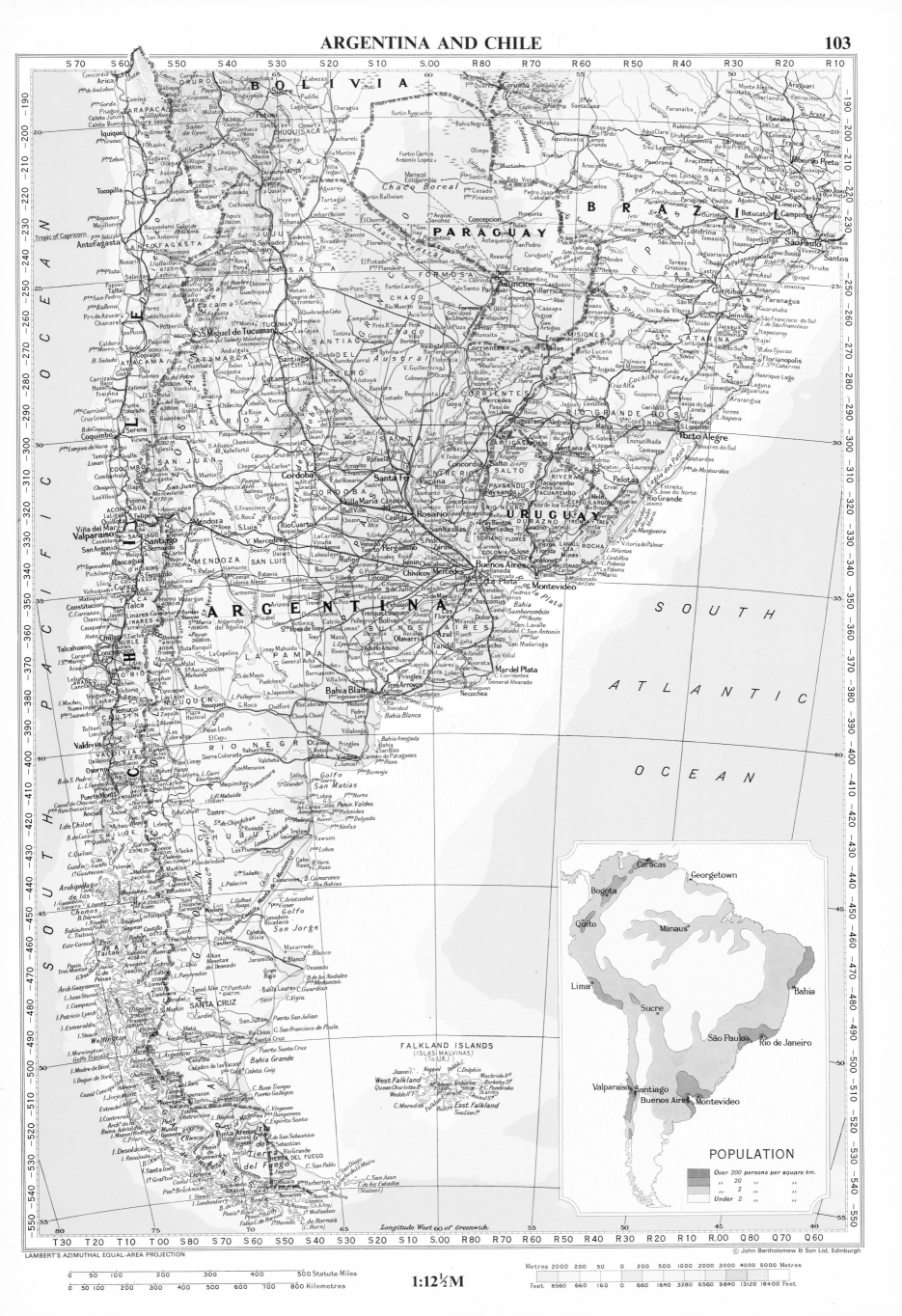

FALKLAND ISLANDS
(ISLAS MALVINAS)
(To U.K.)

POPULATION

Over 200 persons per square km.
" 20 " " " "
" 2 " " " "
Under 2 " " " "

LAMBERT'S AZIMUTHAL EQUAL-AREA PROJECTION

© John Bartholomew & Son Ltd., Edinburgh

1:12½M

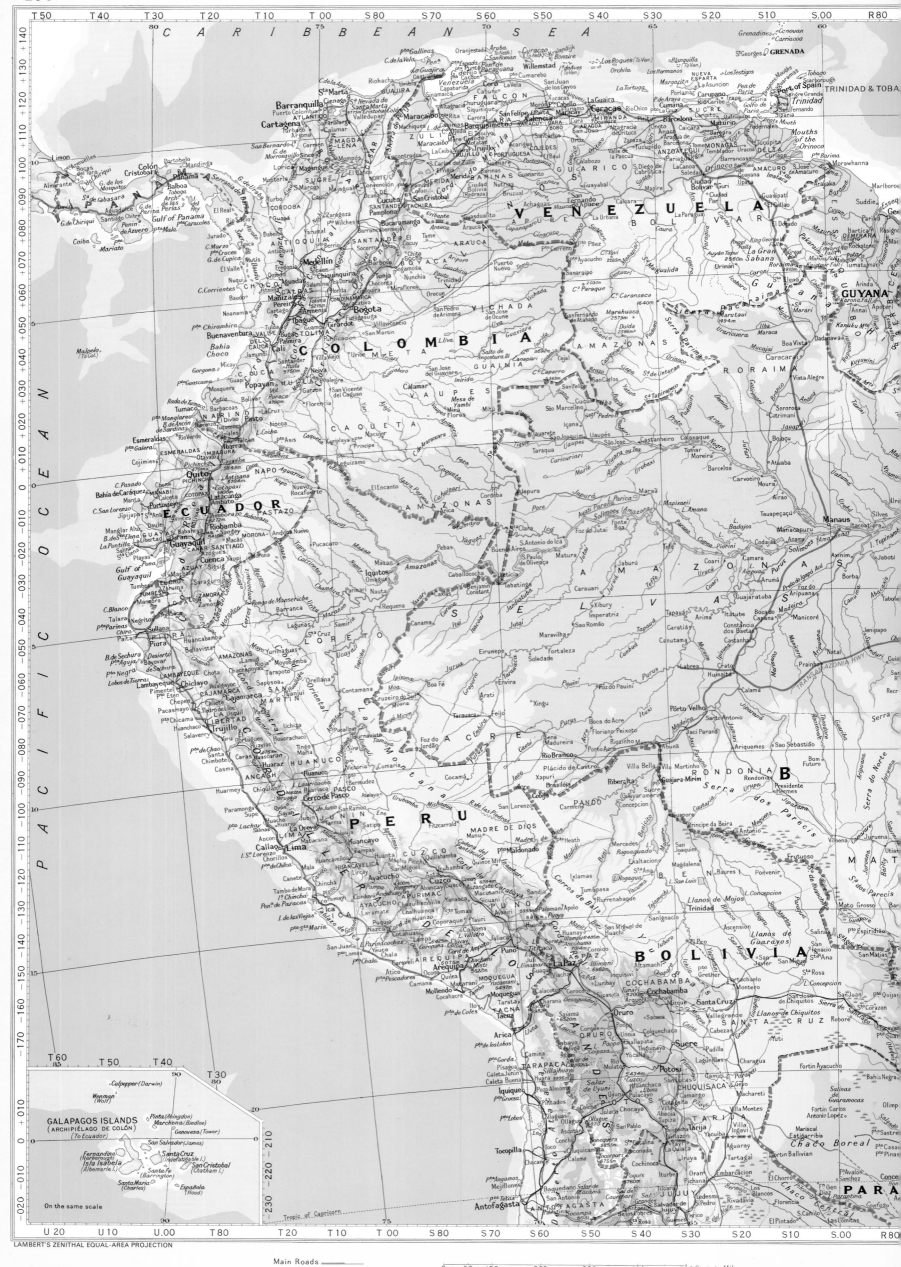

GALAPAGOS ISLANDS
(ARCHIPIÉLAGO DE COLÓN)
(To Ecuador)

On the same scale

LAMBERT'S ZENITHAL EQUAL-AREA PROJECTION

Main Roads ———
Railways ———

0   50 100   200   300   400   500 Statute Miles
0 50 100   200   300   400   500   600   700 800 Kilometres

1:12½

LAMBERT'S AZIMUTHAL EQUAL-AREA PROJECTION

1:45

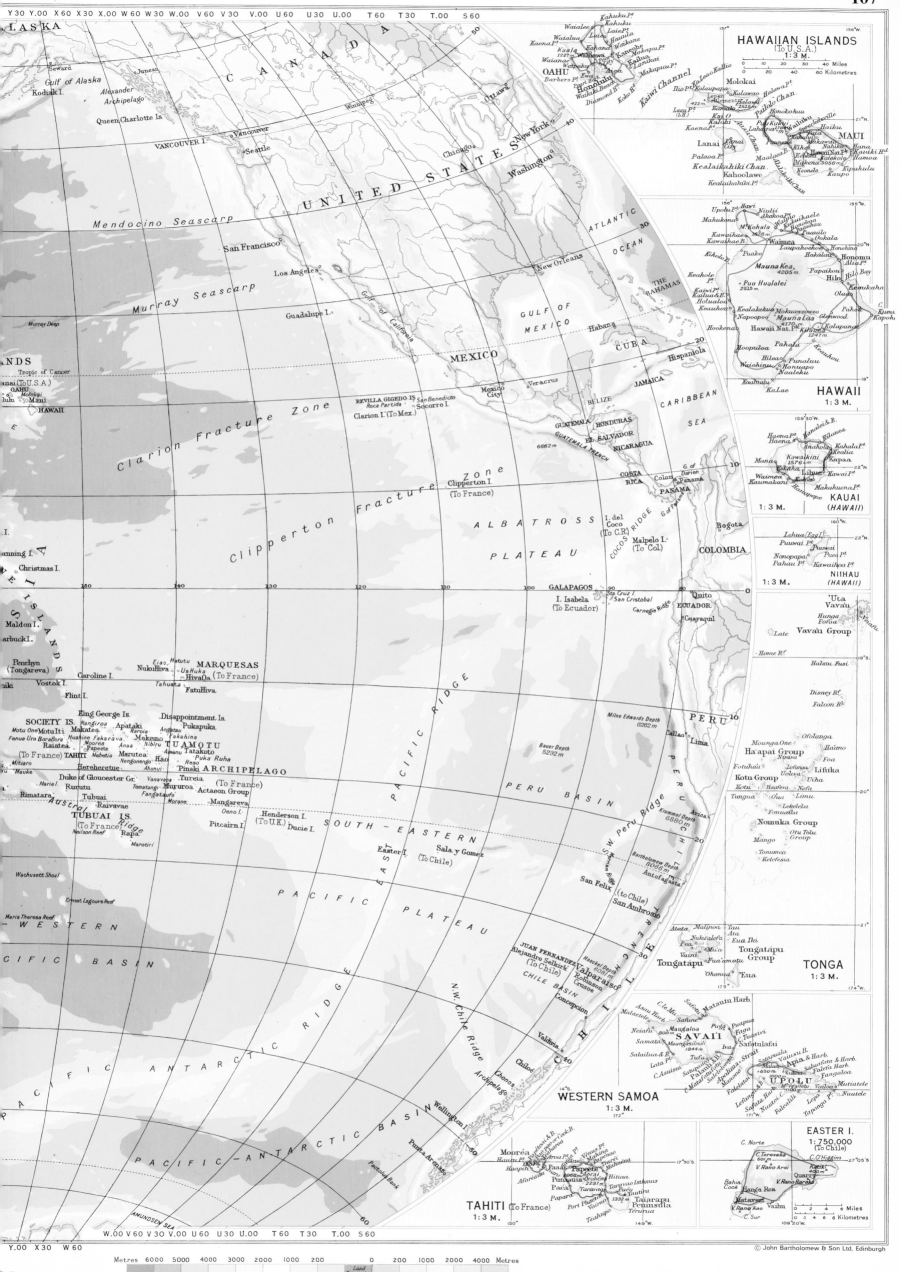

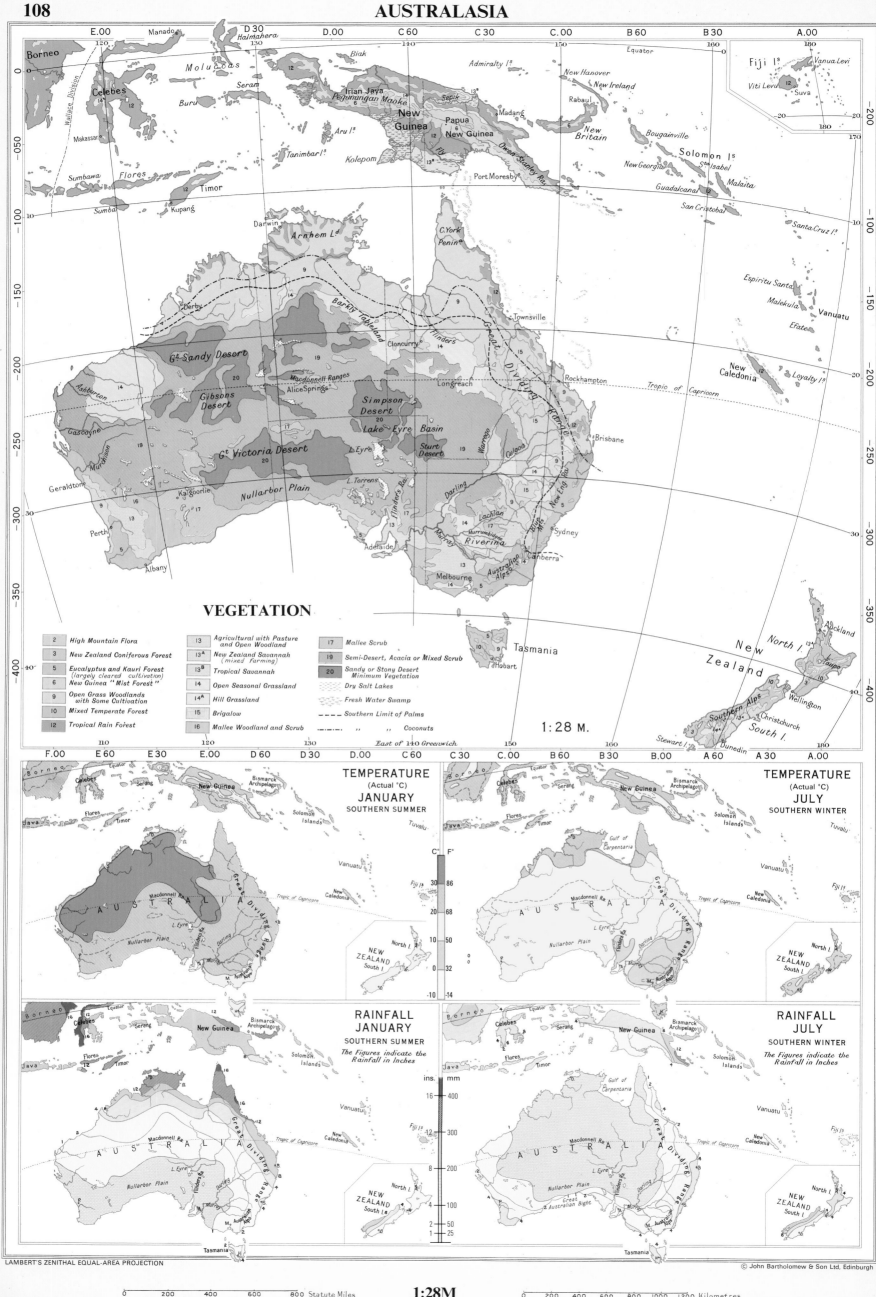

VEGETATION

2	High Mountain Flora	13	Agricultural with Pasture and Open Woodland	17	Mallee Scrub
3	New Zealand Coniferous Forest	13A	New Zealand Savannah (mixed farming)	19	Semi-Desert, Acacia or Mixed Scrub
5	Eucalyptus and Kauri Forest (largely cleared cultivation)	13B	Tropical Savannah	20	Sandy or Stony Desert Minimum Vegetation
6	New Guinea "Mist Forest"	14	Open Seasonal Grassland		Dry Salt Lakes
9	Open Grass Woodlands with Some Cultivation	14A	Hill Grassland		Fresh Water Swamp
10	Mixed Temperate Forest	15	Brigalow		Southern Limit of Palms
12	Tropical Rain Forest	16	Mallee Woodland and Scrub		" " Coconuts

East of 140 Greenwich

1:28 M.

TEMPERATURE (Actual °C) JANUARY SOUTHERN SUMMER

TEMPERATURE (Actual °C) JULY SOUTHERN WINTER

C° F°
30 — 86
20 — 68
10 — 50
0 — 32
-10 — -14

RAINFALL JANUARY SOUTHERN SUMMER
The Figures indicate the Rainfall in Inches

RAINFALL JULY SOUTHERN WINTER
The Figures indicate the Rainfall in Inches

ins. mm
16 — 400
12 — 300
8 — 200
4 — 100
2 — 50
1 — 25

LAMBERT'S ZENITHAL EQUAL-AREA PROJECTION

© John Bartholomew & Son Ltd, Edinburgh

0   200   400   600   800 Statute Miles

1:28M

0   200   400   600   800   1000   1200 Kilometres

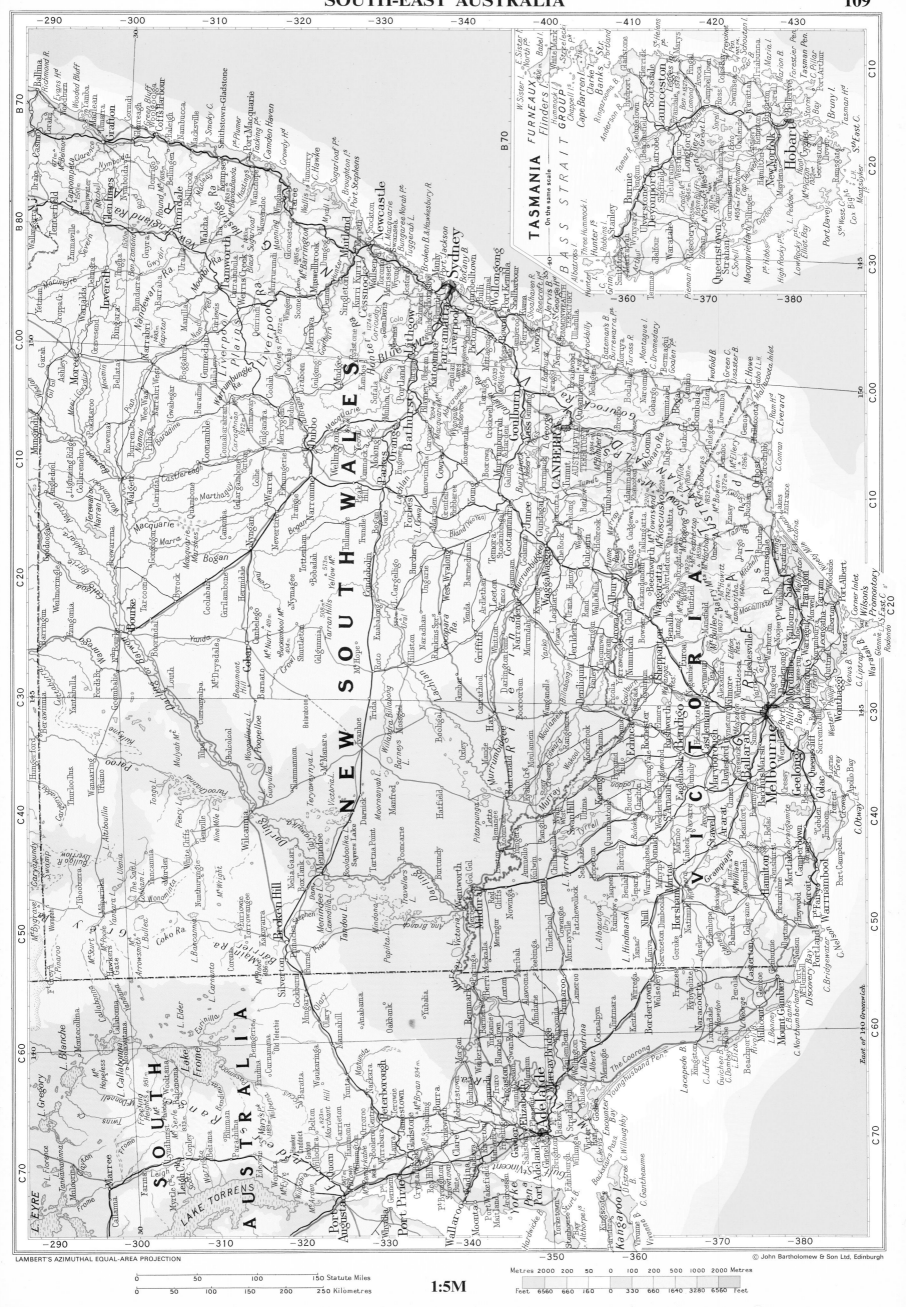

TASMANIA On the same scale

LAMBERT'S AZIMUTHAL EQUAL-AREA PROJECTION

1:5M

© John Bartholomew & Son Ltd, Edinburgh

	50	100	150 Statute Miles
	50	100	150	200	250 Kilometres

Metres 2000	200	50	0	100	200	500	1000	2000 Metres
Feet 6560	660	160	0	330	660	1640	3280	6560 Feet

FLORES SEA

Karimunjawa Is. · Bawean · Postilyon Is. · Tanáhjampea · Kalaotoa · Gunungapi · Damar · Nila · Molu · Tanimbar I⁵ · Jamdena

Madura · Kangean I⁵ · Kalao · Wetar · Roma · Babari I · Selaru

Cirebon · Semarang · Pamekasan · Madura Str. · Singaraja · Lombok · Sangeang · Komodo · Flores · Lomblen · Alor · Wetar Str. · Leti I⁵ · Moa · Sermata

Bandung · Slamet 3428m · Surakarta · Semeru 3676m · Banyuwang · Bali · Rinjani 3726m · Sumbawa · Sumba Str. · Ende · Atambua · Pantar · Dili

ARA

JAVA · Barung · Denpasar · Lombok Str. · Sumba · Waingapu · Savu Sea · Kupang · TIMOR

Sumba · Sawu I⁵ · Roti

C. Van Diemen · Melville I · Dundas Str. · Co

TIMOR SEA · Cartier I. · Bathurst I. · Van Diemen G. · Clarence Str.

Darwin · Humpty Doo

Joseph Bonaparte · Buff Jungle · Batchelor

Scott Reef · Browse I. · Admiralty G. · C. Londonderry · Cambridge G. · Queen's Chan. · Anson B. · Adelaide River · Arn

Bonaparte Archipelago · York Sd. · Pago Mission · Pine Cree

Brunswick B. · Collier B. · Karunjie · GULF BASIN · Wyndham · Katherine · Victoria

Yampi Sound · Black Rocks · King Leopold Ra. · M⁵Ord 936m · Gibb River · Ord River · Victoria River Downs · Matarank · Birdu

C. Lévêque · King Sound · Kimberley Plateau · Halls Creek · Ord River · M⁵ Wollastor

Dampier Land · Derby · Fitzroy · NOR · Wave Hill · L. Wood

Rowley Shoals · Broome · Noonkanbah · Fitzroy · Powell · C

Tanami · Tenn

La Grange · TERR

Goldsworthy · Wallal · Great Sandy Desert · DESERT BASIN · Sturt Cc.

De Grey · Shay Gap · L. Dora · Stansmore Ra. · Truer Ra.

Port Hedland · Marble Bar · L. Mackay · M⁵Heu 1468m

Dampier Arch. · Roebourne · Nullagine · Throssel Ra. · Macdonn

Monte Bello I⁵ · Dampier · Wittenoom · Hermannsburg · James Ra.

Barrow I. · Preston · Fortescue · M⁵ Enid · Ethel Creek · L. Macdonald

North West C. · Onslow · Hamersley Range · Mt. Bruce 1235m · Newman · Gibson Desert · L. Amadeus

Exmouth · Minderoo · M⁵1129m · Tom Price · Mt. Whaleback · Giles · Petermann Ra. · Musgrave Ra.

Learmonth · Ashburton · Brockman · Paraburdoo · L. Disappointment · Tonkinson Ra. · M⁵Aloysius 1085m · M⁵Woodroffe 1515m

Winning Pool · Mt Vernon · Mundiwindi · WESTERN

Tropic of Capricorn · Wilhambury · Lyons · Teano Ra. · Milgun

Minilya · McLeod · Barlee Ra. · M⁵Augustus 1105m · AUSTRALIA

Geographe Chan. · Carnarvon · Gascoyne · Horse Shoe · L. Nabberu · L. Carnegie · L. Maurice

Shark B. · Wooramel · Robinson Ranges · Peak Hill · Great Victoria Desert

Dirk Hartogs I. · Murchison · Meekatharra · Wiluna · L. Wells

Gantheaume B. · Meeberrie · Big Bell · Cue · L. Maitland · Salt Lakes

Yalgoo · Nannine · Sandstone · Lawlers · L. Rason

Northampton · Mullewa · M⁵Magnet · Leonora · L. Carey · Laverton · Maralinga · AU

Houtman Abrolhos · Geraldton · Yuna · Senew · L. Monger · Payne's Find · L. Barlee · Menzies · L. Raeside · Nullarbor Plain · Ooldea

Dongara · Carnamah · L. Moore · Nullarbor Plain · Forrest · EUCL · Nullarbor

Walbri · Kalannie · Bonnie Rock · Kalgoorlie · Rawlinna · Haig · BASIN · Mundrabilla · Eucla

Moora · Bencubbin · Ballfinch · Coolgardie · Zanthus · Eyre · Fowler's B.

Goomalling · Southern Cross · Boulder · L. Lefroy

Perth · Merredin · Norseman · Balladonia · Great Australian Bight

York · Corrigin · L. Cowan · Salmon Gums

Fremantle · Hyden · C. Pasley

Kwinana · Pingelli · Lake Grace · Newdegate · Esperance · Recherche Arch.

Pinjarra · Dwerda · Lake King · Pingrup · King George S⁵

Geographe B. · Collie · Narrogin · Wagin · Hopetoun

C. Naturaliste · Bunbury · Katanning · Stirling Ra. · C. Knob

Busselton · Kojonup · Bluff Knoll 1109m

Augusta · Manjimup · Albany

C. Leeuwin · Northcliffe · Denmark

D'Entrecasteaux Pt. · Nornalup

INDIAN OCEAN

NORTH WEST BASIN · COASTAL PLAIN · PERTH BASIN

POPULATION

Darwin

Cloncurry · Townsville

Alice Springs

Kalgoorlie · Brisbane

Perth · Sydney

Adelaide · Canberra

Melbourne

Hobart

Over 500 persons per square mile
,,   50   ,,   ,,   ,,
,,   5   ,,   ,,   ,,
Under 5   ,,   ,,   ,,

BONNE'S PROJECTION

Main Roads ———
Railways ———
Artesian Basins – – –

0 50 100 200 300 400 500 Statute Miles
0 50 100 200 300 400 500 600 700 800 Kilometres

Longitude East 130 of Greenwich

1:12

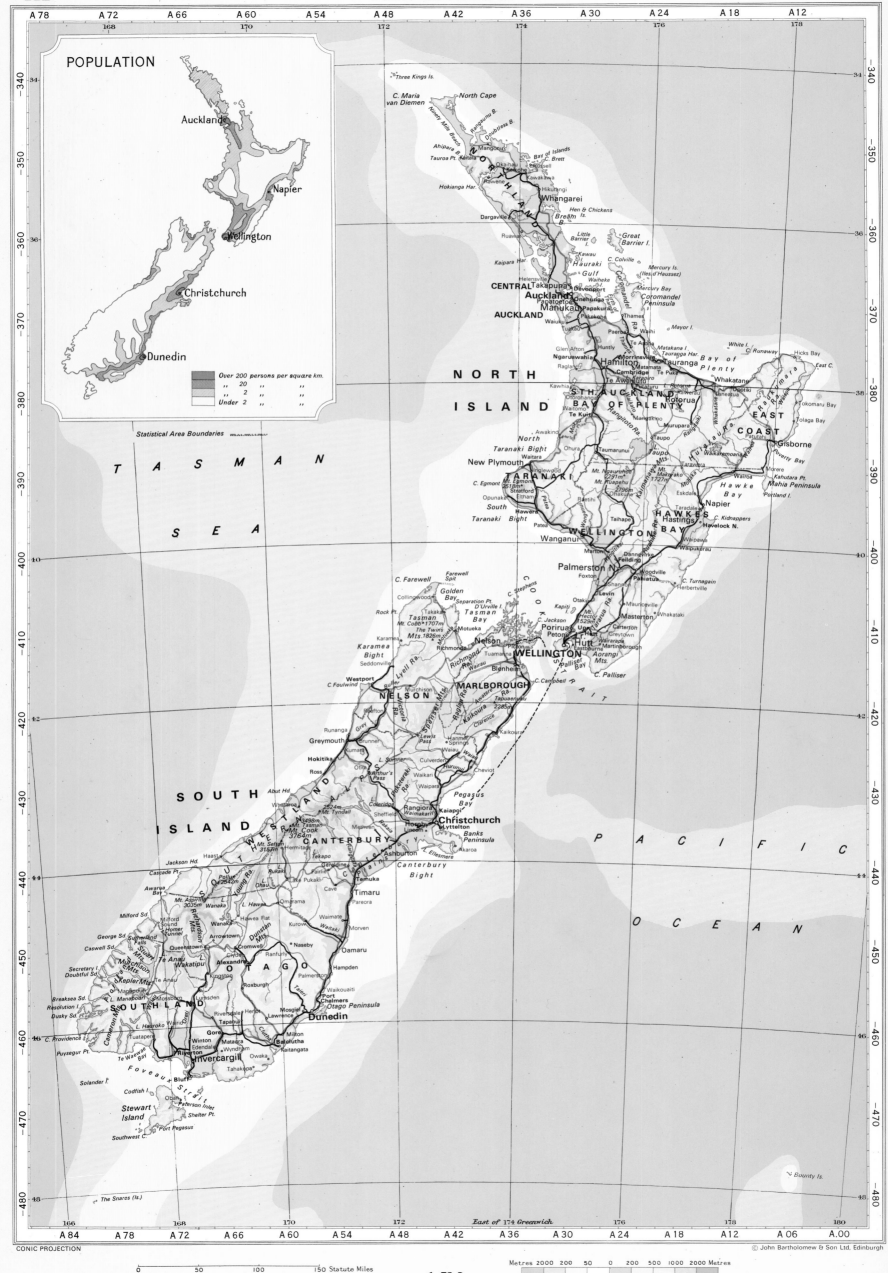

POPULATION

Auckland

Napier

Wellington

Christchurch

Dunedin

Over 200 persons per square km.
,, 20 ,, ,, ,,
,,   2 ,, ,, ,,
Under 2 ,, ,, ,,

Statistical Area Boundaries

GENERAL INDEX

For explanatory notes on the use of Index see page 1 of Atlas.

LIST OF ABBREVIATIONS

Afghan., Afghanistan.
Afr., Africa.
Ala., Alabama.
Alta., Alberta.
Alg., Algeria.
Antarc., Antarctica.
Arch., Archipelago.
Argent., Argentina.
Ariz., Arizona.
Ark., Arkansas.
Aust., Australia.
B, Bay, Bahia.
B.C., British Columbia.
Belg., Belgium, Belgian.
Bol., Bolivia.
Bots., Botswana.
Bulg., Bulgaria.
C., Cape, Cabo.
Cal., California.
Can., Canal.
Car., Carolina.
Cel., Celebes.
Cent., Central.
Chan., Channel.
Co., County.
Col., Colony.
Colo., Colorado.
Colomb., Colombia.
Conn., Connecticut.
Cord., Cordillera.
Cr., Creek.
Czech., Czechoslovakia.
Del., Delaware.
Den., Denmark.
Dep., Department.
Des., Desert.
Dist., District.
Div., Division.

Dom., Dominican, Dominion.
E., East, Eastern.
Ecua., Ecuador.
Eiln., Eilanden.
Eng., England.
Equat., Equatorial.
Ethio., Ethiopia.
Fd., Fjord.
Fla., Florida.
Fr., French, France.
G., Gulf.
Ga., Georgia.
Geb., Gebirge.
Ger., Germany.
G.F., Goldfield.
Gt., Great.
Guat., Guatemala.
Harb., Harbour.
Hd., Head.
Hisp., Hispaniola.
Hond., Honduras.
Hung., Hungary.
I., Is., Island, Islands.
Ia., Iowa.
Ida., Idaho.
Ill., Illinois.
Ind., Indiana.
Indon., Indonesia.
It., Italian, Italy.
Iv. Cst., Ivory Coast.
Jap., Japan.
Kan., Kansas.
Ky., Kentucky.
L., Lake, Loch, Lough, Lago
La., Louisiana.
Lab., Labrador.

Ld., Land.
Leb., Lebanon.
Lit., Little.
Lith., Lithuania.
Lr., Lower.
Madag., Madagascar.
Man., Manitoba.
Mass., Massachusetts.
Maur., Mauritania.
Md., Maryland.
Me., Maine.
Mex., Mexico.
Mich., Michigan.
Minn., Minnesota.
Miss., Mississippi.
Mo., Missouri.
Mong., Mongolia.
Mont., Montana.
Mozamb., Mozambique.
Mt., Mte., Mount, Mont, Monte.
N., North, Northern, New.
N.B., New Brunswick.
N.C., North Carolina.
N. Dak., North Dakota.
Neb., Nebraska.
Nev., Nevada.
Nfd., Newfoundland.
N.H., New Hampshire.
N.I., Netherlands Indies.
Nic., Nicaragua.
N. Ire., Northern Ireland.
N.J., New Jersey.
N. Mex., New Mexico.
N.S., Nova Scotia.
N.S.W., New South Wales.
N.-W. Terr., North-West
Territories.
N.Y., New York.

N.Z., New Zealand.
O., Ohio.
Oc., Ocean.
O.F.S., Orange Free State.
Okla., Oklahoma.
Ont., Ontario.
Ore., Oregon.
Oz., Ozero.
Pa., Pennsylvania.
Pac., Pacific.
Pak., Pakistan.
Pan., Panama.
Para., Paraguay.
P.E.I., Prince Edward Island.
Pen., Peninsula.
Phil., Philippines.
Pk., Peak, Park.
Plat., Plateau.
Port., Portuguese, Portugal.
Prot., Protectorate.
Prov., Province.
Pt., Point.
Pto., Puerto.
Qnsld., Queensland.
Que., Quebec.
R., River, Rio.
Ra., Range.
Reg., Region.
Rep., Republic.
Res., Reservoir.
Rhod., Rhodesia.
R.I., Rhode Island.
Rom., Romania.
Russ., Russia.
S., South, Southern.
Sa., Serra, Sierra.
Sard., Sardinia.
Sask., Saskatchewan.

S.C., South Carolina.
Scot., Scotland.
Sd., Sound.
S. Dak., South Dakota.
Set., Settlement.
Sol., Solomon.
Som., Somaliland.
Sp., Spanish, Spain.
St., Ste., Sta., Saint, Sainte,
Santa.
Str., Strait.
Swed., Sweden.
Switz., Switzerland.
Tanz., Tanzania.
Tenn., Tennessee.
Terr., Territory.
Tex., Texas.
Trans., Transvaal.
U.A.E., United Arab Emirates.
Ukr., Ukraine.
Up., Upper.
U.S.A., United State of
America.
U.S.S.R., Union of Soviet
Socialist Reps.
Ut., Utah.
Va., Virginia.
Val., Valley.
Venez., Venezuela.
Vict., Victoria.
Vol., Volcano.
Vt., Vermont.
W., West, Western.
Wash., Washington.
W.I., West Indies.
Wis., Wisconsin.
Wyo., Wyoming.
Yugosl., Yugoslavia.

Aachen

Aachen, *W. Germany* M53+507 **48**
Aagerbate, *Syria* K45+350 **76**
Aalen, *W. Germany* M30+488 **48**
Aalsmeer, *Netherlands* M62+523 **44**
Aalst (Alost), *Belgium* M66+509 **44**
Aalten, *Netherlands* M51+519 **44**
Aarau, *Switzerland* M42+474 **45**
Aarberg, *Switzerland* M46+470 **45**
Aarburg, *Switzerland* M43+473 **45**
Aardenburg, *Netherlands* M69+513 **44**
Aare, R., *Switzerland* M44+472 **45**
Aargau, canton, *Switzerland* M41+474 **45**
Aba, *Zaire* K88+036 **83**
Abacaxis, *Brazil* R82-040 **104**
Abaco I., Gt., *Bahamas, The* T13+263 **101**
Abaco I., Lit., *Bahamas, The* T17+268 **101**
Abadan, *Iran* J70+303 **74**
Abadeh, *Iran* J44+312 **75**
Abaete, *Brazil* R23-016 **105**
Abajo Mts., *Utah* V27+378 **94**
Abajo Pk., *Utah* V27+376 **98**
Abakan, *U.S.S.R.* F83+537 **63**
Abancay, *Peru* S78-137 **104**
Abarqu, *Iran* J40+311 **75**
Abashiri, *Japan* C34+440 **68**
Abashiri Bay, *Japan* C32+442 **68**
Abau, *Papua New Guinea* C09-102 **111**
Abaya L., *Ethiopia* K42+062 **83**
Abbasabad, *Iran* J52+366 **75**
Abbeville, *France* M79+501 **54**
Abbeville, *Georgia* T50+320 **97**
Abbeville, *Louisiana* U12+300 **95**
Abbeyfeale, *Ireland, Rep.* N56+524 **43**
Abbeyleix, *Ireland, Rep.* N44+529 **43**
Abbot Ice Shelf, *Antarctica* T80-730 **27**
Abbottabad, *Pakistan* H11+342 **72**
Abdul Aziz, Jebel, *Syria* K30+365 **74**
Abdulino, *U.S.S.R.* J35+537 **61**
Abeche, *Chad* L56+138 **81**
Abeele, *Belgium* M74+508 **44**
Abelessa, *Algeria* M62+226 **80**
Abengourou, *Ivory Coast* N22+068 **80**
Abeokuta, *Nigeria* M70+072 **80**
Aberaeron, *Wales* N26+522 **38**
Aberdare, *Wales* N21+517 **38**
Aberdeen, *Mississippi* T81+338 **97**
Aberdeen, *Montana* V14+450 **93**
Aberdeen, *S. Dakota* U51+455 **93**
Aberdeen, *Washington* W23+470 **92**
Aberdeen, *Scotland* N12+571 **40**
Aberdeen L., *N.-W. Terr.* U55+645 **88**
Aberfeldy, *Scotland* N23+566 **41**
Aberfoyle, *Scotland* N26+562 **41**
Abergavenny, *Wales* N18+518 **38**
Aberystwyth, *Wales* N24+524 **38**
Abha, *Saudi Arabia* K12+181 **74**
Abidjan, *Benin* N24+054 **80**
Ab-i-Istada L., *Afghanistan* H42+325 **75**
Abilene, *Kansas* U44+389 **95**
Abilene, *Texas* U58+324 **95**
Abingdon, *Virginia* T42+367 **97**
Abington, *Massachusetts* S65+421 **96**
Abisko, *Sweden* L66+683 **46**
Abitibi L., *Ontario* T28+488 **89**
Abitibi R., *Ontario* T40+500 **89**
Abomey, *Benin* M78+072 **80**
Aboyne, *Scotland* N17+571 **40**
Abqaiq, *Saudi Arabia* J61+262 **74**
Abrantes, *Portugal* N49+395 **52**
Abrets, les, *France* M57+456 **54**
Abrud, *Romania* L42+469 **58**
Abruzzi, dep., *Italy* M07+420 **56**
Abtenau, *Austria* M10+475 **48**
Abu, *India* H14+246 **70**

Abu Deleiq, *Sudan* K68+158 **81**
Abu Dhabi, *U.A.E.* J33+245 **75**
Abu ed Duhur, *Syria* K48+357 **76**
Abu el Jirdhan, *Jordan* K55+303 **76**
Abu Jifan, *Saudi Arabia* J73+246 **74**
Abu Kemal, *Syria* K24+345 **74**
Abul Abyadh I., *U.A.E.* J38+243 **75**
Abu Mombasi, *Zaire* L46+034 **82**
Abuna, *Brazil* S32-098 **104**
Abu Qurqas, *Egypt* K86+278 **81**
Abuya Myeda, mt., *Ethiopia* K30+106 **83**
Abu Zabad, *Sudan* L04+122 **81**
Abyei, *Sudan* L08+096 **81**
Abyy, *U.S.S.R.* C30+685 **63**
Abyn, *Sweden* L52+650 **46**
Acajutla, *El Salvador* T88+136 **101**
Acambaro, *Mexico* U64+200 **100**
Acaponeta, *Mexico* V02+225 **100**
Acapulco, *Mexico* U59+168 **100**
Acara & R., *Brazil* R20-022 **105**
Acarigua, *Venezuela* S55+095 **104**
Acatlan, *Mexico* U49+182 **100**
Accomac, *Virginia* T04+377 **97**
Accra, *Ghana* N02+056 **80**
Accrington, *England* N14+538 **37**
Achaguas, *Venezuela* S49+075 **104**
Achao, *Chile* S81-424 **103**
Achill & I., *Ireland, Rep.* N60+539 **42**
Achinsk, *U.S.S.R.* F86+564 **63**
Achray, *Ontario* T17+459 **91**
Acklins, I., *Bahamas, The* S84+225 **101**
Aconcagua, mt., *Argentina* S60-325 **103**
Acores, Is., *Atlantic Ocean* P70+390 **80**
Acoyapa, *Nicaragua* T61+120 **101**
Acre & B., *Israel* K60+329 **76**
Actaeon Group, Tuamotu
Archipelago X05-228 **107**
Acton Vale, *Quebec* S75+457 **91**
Ada, *Minnesota* U39+473 **93**
Ada, *Oklahoma* U40+348 **95**
Adair, C., *N.-W. Territories* S68+713 **89**
Adairville, *Kentucky* T71+367 **97**
Adak, I., *Aleutian Is.* Z70+514 **99**
Adalia. *See* Antalya
Adam, *Oman* J15+223 **75**
Adama, *Ethiopia* K34+084 **83**
Adamello, mt., *Italy* M27+462 **56**
Adammaby, *New S. Wales* C08-360 **109**
Adams, *New York* T06+438 **91**
Adam's Bridge, India–
Sri Lanka G63+091 **70**
Adams, Mt., *Washington* W09+462 **92**
Adams, Pk., *Sri Lanka* G58+069 **70**
Adana, *Turkey* K58+370 **74**
Ada-Pazari, *Turkey* K88+408 **74**
Adare, *Ireland, Rep.* N53+525 **43**
Adare, C., *Antarctica* A55-710 **27**
Addis Ababa, *Ethiopia* K38+090 **83**
Addis Derra, *Ethiopia* K38+102 **83**
Addison, *New York* T13+421 **96**
Adelaer, C., *Greenland* Q65+610 **26**
Adelaide, *Cape Province* L22-328 **84**
Adelaide, *S. Australia* C69-350 **109**
Adelaide, I., *Antarctica* S50-670 **27**
Adelaide Pen., *N.-W. Terr.* U45+674 **88**
Adelboden, *Switzerland* M45+465 **45**
Adelie Ld., *Antarctica* C60-680 **27**
Adelong, *New South Wales* C12-354 **109**
Ademuz, *Spain* N08+401 **53**
Aden, *Yemen, South* K00+127 **74**
Adh Dhahiriya, *Jordan* K60+314 **76**
Adhoi, *India* H27+234 **70**
Adhra, *Syria* K51+336 **76**

Adi, I., *New Guinea* D08-042 **65**
Adi Kaie, *Ethiopia* K34+146 **83**
Adilabad, *India* G67+197 **70**
Adirondack Mts., *New York* S84+444 **91**
Adi Ugri, *Ethiopia* K38+148 **83**
Adoni, *India* G76+156 **70**
Adoumre, *Cameroon* M08+092 **81**
Adour R., *France* N08+434 **55**
Adra, *Spain* N19+367 **52**
Adraj, *Saudi Arabia* J55+201 **75**
Adrano, *Sicily* M01+376 **57**
Adrar, *Algeria* N02+276 **80**
Adria, *Italy* M18+451 **56**
Adrian, *Michigan* T55+419 **91**
Adriatic Sea, *Italy* L84+425 **56**
Aduwa, *Ethiopia* K36+140 **83**
Aegean Sea, *Greece* L30+385 **59**
Aegina, I., *Greece* L39+377 **59**
Aeltre, *Belgium* M69+511 **44**
Ærøskøbing, *Denmark* M27+549 **47**
Aerschot, *Belgium* M61+510 **44**
Aesch, *Switzerland* M44+475 **45**
Afferden, *Netherlands* M54+516 **44**
Affua, *Brazil* R31-004 **105**
Afghanistan, *Asia* H60+340 **75**
Afif, *Saudi Arabia* K12+239 **74**
Afogados de Ingazeira,
Brazil Q46-078 **105**
Afognak I., *Alaska* Y20+582 **99**
Afrin, *Syria* K49+365 **76**
Afula, *Israel* K58+326 **76**
Afyon, *Turkey* K87+387 **74**
Agab Workei, *Ethiopia* K48+136 **83**
Agadès, *Niger* M42+168 **80**
Agadir, *Morocco* N58+304 **80**
Agartala, *India* F82+239 **71**
Agathla Pk., *Arizona* V32+368 **94**
Agattu, I., *Aleutian Is.* A40+518 **99**
Agawa, *Ontario* T57+476 **91**
Agde, *France* M69+433 **55**
Agen, *France* M86+442 **55**
Aghda, *Iran* J38+325 **75**
Agiabampo, *Mexico* V25+264 **100**
Agira, *Sicily* M03+376 **57**
Agno, *Switzerland* M37+460 **45**
Agordat, *Ethiopia* K42+154 **83**
Agra, *India* G72+272 **73**
Agram. *See* Zagreb
Agrigento, *Sicily* M08+373 **57**
Agrihan, I., *Mariana Is.* C25+180 **106**
Agrinion, *Greece* L52+387 **59**
Agropoli, *Italy* M00+404 **57**
Agua Clara, *Brazil* R47-204 **105**
Aguadas, *Colombia* T03+056 **104**
Aguadilla, *Puerto Rico* S42+185 **101**
Aguadulce, *Panama* T33+082 **101**
Agua Limpa, *Brazil* R26-042 **105**
Agua Prieta, *Mexico* V27+312 **100**
Aguaray, *Argentina* S22-222 **103**
Aguascalientes, *Mexico* U74+218 **100**
Agudo, *Spain* N29+390 **52**
Agudos, *Brazil* R24-224 **105**
Aguilar, *Spain* N28+375 **52**
Aguilar de Campós, *Spain* N26+428 **52**
Aguilas, *Spain* N10+374 **53**
Aguirre, B., *Argentina* S35-550 **103**
Agulhas C., *Cape Province* L60-348 **84**
Agusta, *W. Australia* E29-340 **110**
Ahar, *Iran* J77+385 **74**
Ahmadnagar, *India* H01+191 **70**
Ahmadpur East, *Pakistan* H23+291 **72**

Ahmadabad, *India* H14+230 **70**
Ahraura, *India* G42+250 **73**
Ahtopol, *Bulgaria* L13+421 **58**
Ahuachapan, *El Salvador* T89+140 **101**
Ahualulco, *Mexico* U85+207 **100**
Ahus, *Sweden* M04+559 **47**
Ahvaz, *Iran* J67+313 **74**
Ahvenanmaa, *Finland* L60+603 **47**
Ahwar, *Yemen, South* J80+135 **74**
Aigle, *Switzerland* M48+463 **45**
Aihunkiu, *China* D45+489 **64**
Aijal, *India* F73+239 **71**
Aikawa, *Japan* C71+380 **68**
Ailsa Craig, I., *Scotland* N31+552 **41**
Aim, *U.S.S.R.* D06+588 **63**
Ain, dep., *France* M56+461 **54**
Ain Galaka, *Chad* L70+180 **81**
Ain Safra, *Mauritania* N72+194 **80**
Ainsworth, *Nebraska* U60+426 **95**
Aintree, *England* N18+535 **37**
Aira, *Ethiopia* K58+090 **83**
Airdrie, *Scotland* N24+558 **41**
Aire, *France* N02+437 **55**
Aire R., *England* N07+537 **37**
Airolo, *Switzerland* M38+465 **45**
Aishihik L., *Yukon* X12+612 **88**
Aisne, dep., *France* M68+495 **54**
Aitkin, *Minnesota* U22+465 **93**
Aiun, El, *Morocco* N80+270 **80**
Aix, *France* M57+435 **55**
Aix, Mt., *Washington* W07+469 **92**
Aix-la-Chapelle. *See* Aachen
Aiyina, I., *Greece* L39+377 **59**
Aiyion, *Greece* L48+383 **59**
Aizpute, *Latvia* L50+567 **47**
Aizuwakamatsu, *Japan* C60+375 **68**
Ajaccio & G. d', *Corsica* M38+419 **57**
Ajaigarh, *India* G58+249 **73**
Ajanta, *India* G85+205 **70**
Ajanta Ra. *See* Sahiadriparvat
Ajibba, *Saudi Arabia* K04+273 **74**
Ajigasawa, *Japan* C58+408 **68**
Ajlun, *Jordan* K56+323 **76**
Ajmer, *India* H02+263 **70**
Ajodhya, (Ayodhya), *India* G46+267 **73**
Ajoewa, *Surinam* R72+026 **105**
Akalkot, *India* G83+176 **70**
Akan Nat. Park, *Japan* C36+435 **68**
Akanthou, *Cyprus* K67+354 **76**
Akaoka, *Japan* D08+335 **68**
Akarnania and Aitolia,
Greece L51+388 **59**
Akaroa, *New Zealand* A42-437 **112**
Akashi, *Japan* D00+347 **68**
Akbarpur, *India* G60+263 **73**
Akcha, *Afghanistan* H53+369 **75**
Akhdhar, Jebel, *Oman* J14+232 **75**
Akhisar, *Turkey* L13+389 **74**
Akhterine, *Syria* K46+365 **76**
Akhtyrka, *Ukraine* K61+504 **60**
Akimiski I., *N.-W. Terr.* T38+532 **89**
Akita, *Japan* C59+397 **68**
Akkrum, *Netherlands* M55+530 **44**
Aklavik, *N.-W. Territories* W86+689 **88**
Ako, *Nigeria* M26+104 **82**
Akola, *India* G77+207 **70**
Akpatok I., *North-West
Territories* S49+603 **89**
Akra, Jebel el, *Turkey* K54+359 **74**
Akron, *Colorado* U80+402 **94**
Akron, *Ohio* T39+411 **91**
Akrotiri Pen., *Crete* L35+356 **59**
Aksaray, *Turkey* K66+383 **74**
Aksehir, *Turkey* K82+383 **74**

Aksehir

1

Aksha, *U.S.S.R.* E40+503 63
Aksi, *Estonia* L20+585 47
Akti, *Greece* L35+403 59
Aktyubinsk, *Kazakh.* J17+504 62
Akure, *Nigeria* M58+072 80
Akureyri, *Iceland* P19+657 46
Akyab, *Burma* F73+202 71
Alabama, state, *U.S.A.* T70+326 99
Alabama R., *Alabama* T74+313 99
Alaejos, *Spain* N31+413 52
Alagoa de Baixo, *Brazil* Q44-082 105
Alagoas, *Brazil* Q35-096 105
Alagoinhas, *Brazil* Q50-122 105
Alagon, *Spain* N07+417 53
Alaja, *Syria* K55+358 76
Alajuela, *Costa Rica* T55+100 101
Alakurtii, *U.S.S.R.* K85+672 62
Alakpa, *Nigeria* M64+086 82
Al' Ala, *Saudi Arabia* K41+267 74
Alameda, *California* W14+377 92
Alameda, *Saskatchewan* U74+496 88
Alamogordo, *New Mexico* V06+330 94
Alamogorda Res., *New Mex.* U87+346 94
Alamos, *Mexico* V24+271 100
Alamosa, *Colorado* V06+374 94
Åland, *See* Ahvenanmeri
Ålands Hav. *Sweden-Finland* L64+600 47
Alapaevsk, *U.S.S.R.* H80+578 61
Alasehir, *Turkey* L09+384 74
Ala Shan, *China* F10+394 64
Al Ashkharah, *Oman* J03+219 75
Alaska, state, *U.S.A.* Y00+630 99
Alaska, G. of, *Alaska* X60+586 99
Alaska Pen., *Alaska* Y60+560 99
Alaska Ra., *Alaska* Y25+610 99
Alaska Highway, *Alaska-Can.* X38+632 88
Alatyr, *U.S.S.R.* J80+548 61
Alavus, *Finland* L38+626 46
Alawoona, *S. Australia* C57-348 109
Al 'Ayn, *Oman* J31+196 75
Alaysky Khrebet, *Kirgiz* H20+400 62
Alazeiskoye Plat., *U.S.S.R.* C10+680 63
Albacete, *Spain* N11+390 53
Alba de Tormes, *Spain* N33+408 52
Albaida, *Spain* N03+389 53
Alba Iulia, *Romania* L39+461 58
Albanel L., *Quebec* S78+511 90
Albania, *S. Europe* L60+410 51
Albany, *Alabama* T70+342 99
Albany, *Georgia* T55+315 97
Albany, *Kentucky* T61+367 97
Albany, *Missouri* U26+403 95
Albany, *New York* S83+426 91
Albany, *Oregon* W19+446 92
Albany, *W. Australia* E13-350 110
Albany R., *Ontario* T52+514 89
Albarracin, *Spain* N09+405 53
Al Bayda', *Libya* L49+326 81
Albemarle Sd., *N. Carolina* T08+360 97
Albergaria a-Velha, *Portugal* N50+407 52
Alberique, *Spain* N03+391 53
Albert, *New Brunswick* S28+457 90
Albert L., *Zaire* K86+014 83
Albert, Mt., *Quebec* S37+489 90
Alberta, prov., *Canada* - 88
Alberta Mt., *Alberta* V75+526 88
Albert Edward, Mt., *Papua New Guinea* C18-084 111
Albert Lea, *Minnesota* U20+437 93
Alberton, *Prince Edward I.* S24+468 90
Alberton, *Victoria* C20-386 109
Albertville, *France* M52+457 54
Albi, *France* M77+439 55
Albia, *Iowa* U17+410 95
Albina, *Surinam* R56+054 105
Albion, *Michigan* T59+423 91
Albion, *New York* T19+432 91
Albocácer, *Spain* N00+403 53
Alborg, *Denmark* M30+570 47
Albufeira, *Portugal* N49+371 52
Albufera de Mexcaltitlan, *Mex.* V04+220 100
Albuñol, *Spain* N19+368 52
Albuquerque, *New Mexico* V10+350 94
Alburquerque, *Spain* N42+392 52
Albury, *New South Wales* C19-360 109
Alcacer do Sal, *Portugal* N51+384 52
Alcala de Chisvert, *Spain* M99+403 53
Alcala de Henares, *Spain* N20+405 52
Alcamo, *Sicily* M12+380 57
Alcañices, *Spain* N38+417 52
Alcañiz, *Spain* N01+410 53
Alcantara, *Brazil* Q87-024 105
Alcantara, *Spain* N41+397 52
Alcantarilla, *Spain* N15+387 53
Alcaraz, *Spain* N15+387 53
Alcázar de San Juan, *Spain* N19+394 52
Alcazarquivir, (Ksar-el-Kebir,) *Morocco* N36+350 80
Alcira, *Spain* N03+391 53
Alcobaca, *Portugal* N54+395 52
Alcolea del Pinar, *Spain* N15+410 53
Alcoutim, *Portugal* N45+375 52
Alcoy, *Spain* N03+387 53
Aldabra Is., *Indian Ocean* J76-093 77
Aldama, *Chihuahua, Mexico* V06+288 100
Aldama, *Tamaulipas, Mexico* U69+229 100
Aldan & R., *U.S.S.R.* D58+588 63
Aldeburgh, *England* M80+522 39
Aldeia Cumare, *Brazil* R34-109 105
Alderney, I., *Channel Is.* N13+497 54
Aldershot, *England* N05+512 39
Al Dola, *Yemen, South* J85 + 146 74
Aledo, *Illinois* U04+412 95
Alegrete, *Brazil* R65-298 103
Aleih, *Lebanon* K56+338 76
Alejandro Selkirk, I., *Chile* T35-338 107
Aleksandrov, *U.S.S.R.* K38+564 60
Aleksandrovsk Sakhalinskiy, *U.S.S.R.* C46+510 63
Aleksandry Zemlya, *Arctic Oc.* K00+808 62
Alekseyeka, *Kazakh.* H25+520 62
Alemquer, *Brazil* R59-019 105
Alencon, *France* M89+484 54
Alenquer, *Portugal* N54+390 52
Aleppo, *Syria* K47+362 76
Ales, *France* M65+441 55
Aleshki, *U.S.S.R.* K19+516 61
Alessandria, *Italy* M38+449 56
Ålesund, *Norway* M53+625 46
Aletschhorn, mt., *Switzerland* M42+465 45

Aleutian Is., *Bering Sea* A00+512 99
Aleutian Ra., *Alaska* Y40+580 26
Alexander Arch., *Alaska* X05+575 99
Alexander I., *Antarctica* S60-700 27
Alexandra, *New Zealand* A63-452 112
Alexandra, *Victoria* C26-372 109
Alexandretta. *See* Iskenderun
Alexandria, *Egypt* L00+310 81
Alexandria, *Louisiana* U14+312 95
Alexandria, *Minnesota* U32+459 93
Alexandria, *Ontario* S88+453 91
Alexandria, *Virginia* T13+388 96
Alexandrina, L., *S. Aust.* C65-355 109
Alexandroúpolis, *Greece* L25+408 59
Alexveeka, *U.S.S.R.* J82+522 61
Aleysk, *U.S.S.R.* G44+525 62
Al Falluja, *Iraq* K07+334 74
Alfaro, *Spain* N11+422 53
Alfred, *Maine* S64+435 96
Alfredo Chaves, *Brazil* R40-290 103
Alga, *Kazakh* J16+498 62
Ålgård, *Norway* M55+588 47
Algauer Alpen, *Austria, etc.* M29+474 48
Algeciras, *Spain* N33+361 52
Algeria, *N.-W. Africa* M70+280 80
Al Ghail, *Yemen* K00+161 74
Alghero, *Sardinia* M40+405 57
Algiers (El Djezair), *Algeria* M72+366 55
Algoa B., *Cape Province* L24-338 84
Algoma, *Ontario* T47+462 91
Algoma, *Wisconsin* T75+446 91
Algona, *Iowa* U26+430 95
Algonquin Park, *Ontario* T22+456 91
Alguada Reef, *Burma* F65+158 71
Alhama de Granada, *Spain* N24+370 52
Al Harsha, *Saudi Arabia* J52+196 75
Al Hauta, *Yemen, South* J70 + 159 74
Al Hillah, *Iraq* K03+325 74
Alia, *Sicily* M08+358 57
Aliabad, *Iran* J50+366 75
Aliaga, *Spain* N04+407 53
Alibag, *India* H13+187 70
Alicante, *Spain* N03+384 53
Alice, *Texas* U48+278 94
Alice Springs, *N. Terr., Aust.* D06-237 111
Aliceville, *Alabama* T80+331 95
Alicudi, I., *Italy* M04+386 57
Aliganj, *India* G65+275 73
Aligarh, *India* G73+278 72
Ali Khel, *Afghanistan* H32+340 75
Alimnia, I., *Greece* L13+363 59
Aling Kangri, *Tibet* G55+328 70
Alingsås, *Sweden* M15+579 47
Alipur Duar, *India* G02+265 73
Alipur, *Pakistan* H24+294 72
Alipura, *India* G64+257 73
Alirajpur, *India* H03+222 70
Alivérion, *Greece* L36+385 59
Al Jesab, *Saudi Arabia* J86+150 74
Aljustrel, *Portugal* N49+379 52
Alken, *Belgium* M58+509 44
Al Khubba, *Saudi Arabia* J45+222 75
Alkmar, *Netherlands* M61+526 44
Allahabad, *India* G49+254 73
Allanmyo, *Burma* F58+194 71
Allard, *Montana* U88+470 93
Allariz, *Spain* N47+422 52
Allata, *Ethiopia* K38+066 83
Allaykha, *U.S.S.R.* C15+708 63
Alle, *Belgium* M60+498 44
Allegan, *Michigan* T65+426 91
Alleghany Mts., *U.S.A.* T41+370 99
Allegheny R., *Penn., etc.* T23+420 96
Allen, Bog of, *Ireland, Rep.* N43+534 43
Allen L., *Ireland, Rep.* N48+541 42
Allenby Bridge, *Jordan* K57+319 76
Allende, *Mexico* V03+268 100
Allentown, *Pennsylvania* T03+406 96
Alleppey, *India* G82+096 70
Alliance, *Nebraska* U77+422 94
Alliance, *Ohio* T37+409 91
Allier, dep. *France* M73+464 54
Allier, R., *France* M69+453 54
Alliston, *Ontario* T29+442 91
Alloa, *Scotland* N23+561 41
All Pines, *Belize* T80+168 101
Allumette I., *Quebec* T12+458 91
Alma, *Michigan* T58+434 91
Alma, *New Brunswick* S29+456 90
Alma Ata, *Kazakh.* G78+431 62
Almaden, *Spain* N29+388 52
Almagro, *Spain* N22+389 52
Almansa, *Spain* N07+389 53
Al Mat, *Iraq.* K28+330 74
Almazán, *Spain* N15+415 53
Almeirim, *Brazil* R45-015 105
Almeirim, *Portugal* N52+392 52
Almelo, *Netherlands* M50+524 44
Almeria & Gulf, *Spain* N09+369 53
Al'met'yevsk, *U.S.S.R.* J60+547 61
Almirante, *Panama* T44+094 101
Almiropótamos, *Greece* L35+383 59
Almiros, *Greece* L43+392 59
Almodôvar, *Portugal* N48+375 52
Almodóvar, *Spain* N25+388 52
Almond R., *Scotland* N21+564 41
Almont, *N. Dakota* U69+467 93
Almonte, *Ontario* T07+452 91
Almora, *India* G62+296 73
Almorox, *Spain* N26+402 52
Almudebar, *Spain* N04+421 53
Almunia de Doña Godina, la, *Spain* N08+414 53
Al Musayyib, *Iraq* K04+329 74
Al Muwaila, *Saudi Arabia* K57+277 74
Alness, *Scotland* N26+577 40
Alnwick, *England* N10+554 37
Alocén, *Spain* N17+405 53
Aloja, *Latvia* L31+578 47
Alon, *Burma* F59+221 71
Alór. *See* Iliodhrómia, I.
Alor, I., *Indonesia* D60-084 65
Alora, *Spain* N28+368 52
Alor Setar, *Malaysia* F28+062 69
Alost, *Belgium* M66+509 44
Aloysius, Mt., *W. Australia* D43-260 110
Alpena, *Michigan* T51+451 91
Alpes-Maritimes, dep., *Fr.* M48+438 55
Alphen, *Netherlands* M62+521 44
Alpine, *Texas* U83+304 98
Alps, mts., *Cent. Europe* M42+460 50

Al Qatrun, *Libya* M02+250 81
Al Qayyara, *Iraq* K11+359 74
Al Qunfidhah, *Saudi Arabia* K23+192 74
Al Qurnah, *Iraq* J75+310 74
Als, I., *Denmark* M30+549 47
Al Selaïl, *Saudi Arabia* K00+194 74
Alsten, *Norway* M15+660 46
Alston, *England* N15+548 37
Alsunga, *Latvia* L51+570 47
Alta Gracia, *Argentina* S26-316 103
Altagracia, *Venezuela* S69+107 104
Altagracia de Orituco, *Venez.* S38+099 104
Altai, Mts., *Central Asia* G20+505 62
Altamachi, *Bolivia* S38-167 104
Altamaha R., *Georgia* T43+318 99
Altamira, *Brazil* R44-032 105
Altamura, *Italy* L80+408 57
Altan Bulag, *Mongolia* E81+503 63
Altar, *Mexico* V40+307 100
Altata, *Mexico* V18+246 100
Altdorf, *Switzerland* M38+469 45
Altea, *Spain* N00+386 53
Altenburg, *E. Germany* M16+510 48
Altin Kopru, *Iraq* K05+358 74
Altmark, *E. Germany* M21+527 48
Alto Molocue, *Mozambique* K44-156 83
Alton, *Illinois* U01+390 95
Alton, *Missouri* U09+367 97
Altona, *Germany* M30+535 48
Altona, *New York* S82+449 91
Altoona, *Pennsylvania* T21+405 96
Altrincham, *England* N14+534 37
Alstätten, *Switzerland* M33+474 45
Aluras, *California* W03+415 92
Altus, *Oklahoma* U56+346 95
Altyn Tagh, *China* G30+380 30
Al Ugla, *Saudi Arabia* K43+258 74
Al 'Uj, *Saudi Arabia* J66+228 74
Alûksne, *Latvia* L18+574 47
Alula, *Somalia* J56+118 83
Alumine, *Argentina* S66-392 103
Alupka, *U.S.S.R.* K65+444 60
Alushta, *U.S.S.R.* K65+444 60
Alva, *Oklahoma* U52+368 95
Alvarado, *Mexico* U35+188 100
Alvear, *Argentina* S22-352 103
Älvesta, *Sweden* M03+569 47
Alvho, *Sweden* M01+615 47
Alvin, *Texas* U32+294 95
Alvito, *Portugal* N48+383 52
Alvord, L., *Oregon* V82+424 92
Alwar, *India* G81+275 72
Alward, *New Brunswick* S33+462 90
Alyab, *Sudan* K68+172 81
Alyth, *Scotland* N19+566 41
Alytus, *Lithuania* L36+544 47
Amadeus L., *N. Terr., Aust.* D25-246 110
Amadi, *Sudan* K88+056 81
Amadiyah, *Iraq* K10+371 74
Amadjuak, *N.-W. Territories* S75+641 89
Amadjuak L., *N.-W. Terr.* S65+648 89
Amakusa Nada, *Japan* D32+325 68
Amål, *Sweden* M14+591 47
Amalfi, *Italy* M03+407 57
Amalias, *Greece* L52+378 59
Amami Gunto, *Japan* D34+283 68
Amanalco, *Mexico* U60+192 100
Amantea, *Italy* L84+392 57
Amapa, *Brazil* R34+020 105
Amapala, *Honduras* T76+133 101
Amarah, *Iraq* J77+320 74
Amarante, *Brazil* Q77-063 105
Amarapura, *Burma* F53+218 71
Amaravti, *India* G73+210 70
Amargosa, *Brazil* Q59-130 105
Amarillo, *Texas* U68+352 94
Amarracão, *Brazil* Q70-030 105
Amasra, *Turkey* K74+418 74
Amasya, *Turkey* K55+406 74
Amatique, G. de, *Guatemala* T82+160 100
Amatitlan, *Guatemala* U04+145 100
Amazon, Mths. of the, *Brazil* R30+006 105
Amazonas, R., *Brazil* R53-020 105
Amb, *Pakistan* H12+343 72
Ambala, *India* G79+304 72
Ambam, *Cameroon* M22+024 82
Ambar, *Iran* J06+318 75
Ambarchik, *U.S.S.R.* B15+697 63
Ambato, *Ecuador* T22-013 104
Ambato Boéni, *Madagascar* J80-164 83
Amberg, *Germany* M18+494 48
Ambergris Cay, *Bahamas, The* S70 + 212 101
Ambergris Cay, *Belize* T78+180 101
Ambérieu, *France* M58+460 54
Ambert, *France* M68+455 54
Ambikapur, *India* G41+231 73
Ambilobe, *Madagascar* J66-132 83
Ambleside, *England* N18+544 37
Amblève, *Belgium* M53+504 44
Ambohimahasoa, *Madagascar* J78-212 83
Ambon, I., *Indonesia* D41-037 65
Ambositra, *Madagascar* J76-206 83
Ambrim, I., *Vanuatu* A67+169 106
Ambriz, *Angola* M10-080 82
Ambrizete, *Angola* M12-074 82
Amchitka, I., *Aleutian Is.* A05+508 99
Amd, *Yemen, South* J72 + 154 74
Amderma, *U.S.S.R.* H82+698 62
Ameca, *Mexico* U85+205 100
Ameland I., *Netherlands* M55+534 44
American Falls, *Utah* V47+428 94
American Fork, *Utah* V41+404 94
Americus, *Georgia* T56+320 99
Amerongen, *Netherlands* M57+520 44
Amersfoort, *Netherlands* M58+522 44
Amersham, *England* N04+517 39
Ames, *Iowa* U22+420 95
Amesbury, *Massachusetts* S65+429 96
Amethi, *India* G49+262 73
Amfiklia, *Greece* L44+387 59
Amfilokhia, *Greece* L53+389 59
Amga & R., *U.S.S.R.* D18+610 63
Amgu, *U.S.S.R.* C74+457 63
Amherst, *Burma* F45+160 71
Amherst, *Massachusetts* S75+424 96
Amherst, *Nova Scotia* S25+458 90
Amherst I., *Ontario* T10+441 91
Amherstburg, *Ontario* T49+422 91
Amiens, *France* M76+499 54

Amik Lake, *Ontario* T28+456 91
Amindivi I., *Indian Oc.* H14+110 70
Amingaon, *India* F79+263 71
Aminuis, *Namibia* L64+236 84
Amirante Is., *Indian Ocean* J40-060 77
Amla, *Saudi Arabia* K11+206 74
Amlah, *Saudi Arabia* J89+173 74
Amlwch, *Wales* N26+534 38
Amm Adam, *Sudan* K54+164 81
Amman, *Jordan* K54+319 76
Ammanford, *Wales* N24+518 38
Amol, *Iran* J46+364 75
Amorgós, I., *Greece* L24+372 59
Amos, *Quebec* T18+488 89
Amoy. *See* Hsiamen
Amparo, *Brazil* R10-225 105
Amqui, *Quebec* S44+485 90
Amraho, *Sudan* K78+186 81
Amran, *Yemen* K06+157 74
Amreli, *India* H23+214 70
Amriswil, *Switzerland* M34+475 45
Amritsar, *India* H01+316 72
Amroha, *India* G69+289 73
Amstelveen, *Netherlands* M61+523 44
Amsterdam, *Netherlands* M60+524 44
Amsterdam, *New York* S85+429 96
Amsterdam, I., *Indian Ocean* G75-380 77
Am Timan, *Chad* L60+110 81
Amu Darya, *Turkmen* H75+400 62
Amund Ringnes I., *North-West Territories* U45+782 88
Amundsen G., *N.-W. Terr.* W10+706 88
Amundsen Sea, *Antarctica* V20-720 27
Amur, R., *U.S.S.R. - China* D60+528 63
Amyun, *Lebanon* K55+343 76
An, *Burma* F66+198 71
Anabama, *S. Australia* C59-328 109
Anabta, *Jordan* K59+323 76
Anaconda, *Montana* V48+461 92
Anadarko, *Oklahoma* U48+350 95
Anadyr & R., *U.S.S.R.* A15+645 63
Anadyrskiy Zaliv, *U.S.S.R.* Z80+640 63
Anáfi. I., *Greece* L25+364 59
Anah, *Iraq* K18+345 74
Anai, *Libya* M20+240 81
Anaimalai Hills, *India* G80+106 70
Anaiza, *Saudi Arabia* K05+262 74
Anakapalle, *India* G42+177 71
Analalava, *Madagascar* J74-148 83
Anama. *Brazil* S08-035 104
Anamizu, *Japan* C78+372 68
Anamosa, *Iowa* U08+422 95
Anandpur, *India* G81+312 72
Anantapur, *India* G74+146 70
Anar, *Iran* J28+309 75
Anarak, *Iran* J38+333 75
Anardarra, *Afghanistan* H80+328 75
Añatolia, *Turkey* K80+390 74
Anatuya, *Argentina* S17-284 103
Anchorage, *Alaska* Y00+612 99
Anchuras, *Spain* N29+395 52
Ancohuma, mt., *Bolivia* S51-160 104
Ancon, *Peru* T14-118 104
Ancona, *Italy* M09+435 56
Ancud, *Chile* S82-418 103
And Fd., *Norway* L83+692 46
Andacolla, *Argentina* S64-371 103
Andalgala, *Argentina* S38-275 103
Andalsnes, *Norway* M44+626 46
Andaman Is. and Sea, *Bay of Bengal* F65+124 71
Andeer, *Switzerland* M33+466 45
Andelfingen, *Switzerland* M38+476 45
Andenne, *Belgium* M59+505 44
Andermatt, *Switzerland* M38+466 45
Anderson, *Indiana* T64+401 91
Anderson, S. *Carolina* T46+345 97
Anderson R., *N.-W. Terr.* W40+684 88
Andes, Cord. de los, *South America* S70-429 103
Andevoranto, *Madagascar* J66-189 83
Andhra Pradesh, *India* G70+167 70
Andikithira, I., *Greece* L40+358 59
Andimilos, I., *Greece* L35+368 59
Andiparos, I., *Greece* L30+370 59
Andizhan, *Uzbek* H15+409 62
Andkhui, *Afghanistan* H59+369 75
Andoas Nuevo, *Ecuador* T11-023 104
Andorra & rep., *Pyrenees* M81+425 53
Andover, *England* N09+512 39
Andover, *Massachusetts* S67+427 96
Andover, S. *Dakota* U47+454 93
Andøya, *Norway* L86+691 46
Andrade, *Mozambique* K60-186 84
Andreanof Is., *Aleutian Is.* Z73+513 99
Andreas, C., *Cyprus* K62+357 76
Andreyevka, *Ukraine* K57+488 60
Andria, *Italy* L83+412 57
Andriba, *Madagascar* J78-176 83
Andritsaina, *Greece* L49+375 59
Andros I., *Bahamas, The* T18 + 244 101
Andros, I., *Greece* L31+378 59
Androscoggin R., *Maine* S66+444 90
Anegada, B., *Argentina* S10-402 103
Anegada, I., *Virgin Is.* S26+188 101
Aneiza, Jebel, *Iraq* K34+322 74
Anelo, *Argentina* S53-383 103
Aneta, *N. Dakota* U48+477 93
Aney, *Niger* M14+192 81
Angalé, *Cent. Afr. Rep.* L54+098 81
Anganguéo, *Mexico* U62+195 100
Angaston, S. *Australia* C66-345 109
Angel Fall, *Venezuela* S15+056 104
Angel de la Guarda, I., *Mex.* V50+292 100
Angelholm, *Sweden* M13+562 47
Angemuk, mt., *New Guinea* C70+036 65
Angers, *France* N04+475 54
Angikuni L., *N.-W. Terr.* U60+628 88
Angkor, *Cambodia* F06+134 69
Angledool, *New S. Wales* C12-291 109
Anglesey, I., *Wales* N27+533 38
Angliers, *Quebec* T25+475 91
Angmagssalik, *Greenland* Q55+660 26
Angol, *Chile* S76-379 103
Angola, *New York* T24+426 96
Angola, *W. Africa* L76-100 82
Angora. *See* Ankara
Angoulême, *France* M89+456 54
Angoumois, prov., *France* M89+459 54
Angra, *Brazil* Q86-229 105

Anguilla, I., *Leeward Is.* S18+183 **101**
Angul, *India* G30+208 **71**

Anhalt, *Germany* M18+517 **48**
Anholt, I., *Denmark* M20+567 **47**
Anhwei, prov., *China* E18+320 **66**
Animas Ra., *New Mexico* V22+316 **94**
Anina, *Romania* L49+451 **58**
Anita, *Montana* V18+459 **93**
Anjengo, *India* G80+087 **70**
Anjou, prov., *France* N03+473 **54**
Anjouan I., *Comoro Is.* K04-122 **83**
Anjozorobe, *Madagascar* J74-184 **83**
Ankacho, *U.S.S.R.* E72+632 **63**
Ankang, *China* E65+327 **66**
Ankara, *Turkey* K73+399 **74**
Anking (Hwaining), *China* E17+305 **67**
Ankober, *Ethiopia* K30+094 **83**
Ankwo, *China* E28+384 **66**
Anlier, *Belgium* M56+498 **44**
Anlu, *China* E37+313 **66**
Anlu. *See* Chungsiang
Ann C., *Antarctica* J55-660 **27**
Ann, C., *Massachusetts* S63+427 **96**
Anna, *Illinois* T85+374 **97**
Anna, *U.S.S.R.* K27+514 **61**
Annai, *Guyana* R85+039 **104**
An Najaf, *Iraq* K04+320 **74**
Annam, *Vietnam* E80+174 **69**
Annan & R., *Scotland* N20+550 **41**
Annapolis, *Brazil* R24-164 **105**
Annapolis, *Maryland* T09+390 **96**
Annapolis, *Nova Scotia* S33+447 **90**
Annapurna, Mt., *Nepal* G38+285 **71**
Ann Arbor, *Michigan* T52+423 **91**
An Nasiriyah, *Iraq* J84+311 **74**
Annecy & L. d', *France* M53+459 **54**
Anniston, *Alabama* T65+336 **97**
Annobon I., *See* Pagalu
Annonay, *France* M62+452 **55**
Annuello, *Victoria* C43-348 **109**
An Numas, *Saudi Arabia* K16+193 **74**
Anoka, *Minnesota* U22+452 **93**
Anole, *Somalia* K18-008 **83**
Ano Viannos, *Crete* L27+350 **59**
Anpehi, *China* E65+410 **66**
Ansariya, Jebel el, *Syria* K53+356 **76**
Ansbach, *W. Germany* M27+493 **48**
Anshan, *China* D75+412 **64**
Anshun, *China* E84+263 **67**
Ansi, *China* F54+407 **64**
Ansin, *China* E25+389 **66**
Anson B., *N. Terr., Aust.* D29-134 **110**
Ansongo, *Mali* M88+156 **80**
Ansonia, *Connecticut* S78+413 **96**
Anstruther, *Scotland* N16+562 **41**
Anta, *Peru* S74-134 **104**
Antakya (Antioch), *Turkey* K53+362 **76**
Antalo, *Ethiopia* K32+132 **83**
Antalya, *Turkey* K86+369 **74**
Antalya, G. of, *Turkey* K84+367 **74**
Antarctic Peninsula, S25-660 **27**
Antelope I., *Utah* V43+410 **94**
Antequera, *Paraguay* R73-240 **103**
Antequera, *Spain* N27+370 **52**
Anthony, *Kansas* U48+371 **95**
Anthony Lagoon, *N.T., Aust.* C87-178 **111**
Antibes, *France* M47+486 **55**
Anticosti I., *Quebec* S18+495 **90**
Antigo, *Wisconsin* T85+451 **91**
Antigonish, *Nova Scotia* S12+456 **90**
Antigua, I., *Leeward Is.* S10+170 **101**
Antilhue, *Chile* S78-398 **103**
Antilla, *Cuba* T05+209 **101**
Antilles, Greater, *West Indies* - **101**
Antilles, Lesser, *West Indies* - **101**
Antioquia, *Colombia* T05+064 **104**
Antipodes Is., *Pacific Ocean* A04-500 **106**
Antivari. *See* Bar
Antlers, *Oklahoma* U34+343 **95**
Antofagasta, *Chile* S62-235 **103**
Antofagasta de la S., *Arg.* S44-261 **103**
Antofalla, mt., *Argentina* S48-256 **103**
Antoing, *Belgium* M69+506 **44**
Antongil, B. d', *Madagascar* J60-158 **83**
Antonito, *Colorado* V06+370 **94**
Antrain, *France* N09+485 **54**
Antrim & co., *N. Ireland* N37+547 **42**
Antrim Hills, *N. Ireland* N36+550 **42**
Antsirabe, *Madagascar* J78-198 **83**
Antsirana, *Madagascar* J64-124 **83**
Antsla, *Estonia* L20+578 **47**
Antung, *China* See Tantung
Antwerp. *See* Antwerpen
Antwerpen, & prov., *Belg.* M63+512 **44**
Anupgarh, *India* H11+292 **72**
Anupshahr, *India* G71+283 **73**
Anuradhapura, *Sri Lanka* G58+084 **70**
Anvers. *See* Antwerpen
Anyang, *China* E33+361 **66**
Anyi, *China* E54+351 **66**
Anykščiai, *Lithuania* L29+556 **47**
Anzhero Sudzhensk, *U.S.S.R.* G21+560 **62**
Aomori, *Japan* C56+408 **68**
Aonla, *India* G65+283 **73**
Aosta, *Italy* M46+457 **56**
Aoudèras, *Niger* M40+176 **80**
Aouni, *Chad* L80+130 **81**
Apakova, *U.S.S.R.* J61+545 **61**
Apalachee B., *Florida* T54+300 **97**
Apalachicola & B., *Florida* T60+297 **97**
Aparri, *Philippines* D80+183 **65**
Apataki, I., *Tuamotu Arch.* X70-150 **107**
Apatin, *Yugoslavia* L66+457 **58**
Ape, *Latvia* L19+575 **47**
Apeldoorn, *Netherlands* M54+522 **44**
Apennines, mts., *Italy* M18+440 **50**
Api, mt., *Nepal* G54+300 **73**
Apiaí, *Brazil* R23-244 **103**
Apodi, *Brazil* Q47-055 **105**
Apollo Bay, *Victoria* C38-388 **109**
Apolo, *Bolivia* S51-146 **104**
Apostle Is., *Wisconsin* U02+470 **91**
Apostoles, *Argentina* R65-278 **103**
Apoteri, *Guyana* R82+040 **104**
Apozai, *Pakistan* H34+312 **70**
Appalachian Mts., *U.S.A.* T54+346 **99**
Appenzell & canton, *Switz.* M34+473 **45**
Appleby, *England* N15+546 **37**
Applecross, *Scotland* N35+574 **40**
Appleton, *Wisconsin* T81+443 **91**

Appleton City, *Missouri* U24+382 **95**
Approuague, *Fr. Guiana* R41+042 **105**
Apsley, *Tasmania* C17-424 **109**
Apsley, *Victoria* C53-370 **109**
Apt, *France* M58+439 **55**
Apuhi, *Brazil* R88-052 **104**
Aqaba, *Jordan* K60+295 **76**
Aqiq, *Sudan* K40+180 **83**
Aqraba, *Jordan* K58+321 **76**
Aqua, *Mexico* V06+296 **100**
Aquidauana, *Brazil* R65-205 **105**
Aquila, L', *Italy* M10+424 **56**
Aquin, *Haiti* S80+182 **101**
Arabia, pen., *S.W. Asia* **74**
Arabian Sea, *S. Asia* H60+150 **30**
Aracaju, *Brazil* Q43-109 **105**
Aracati, *Brazil* Q47-046 **105**
Arad, *Romania* L52+462 **58**
Arada, *Chad* L56+150 **81**
Arafura Sea, *Indonesia* D00-094 **65**
Aragua de Barcelona, *Venez.* S29+094 **104**
Araguaia, R., *Brazil* R24-070 **105**
Araguari, *Brazil* R19-187 **105**
Arak, *Iran* J62+341 **74**
Arakaka, *Guyana* S00+078 **104**
Arakan, *Burma* F60+200 **71**
Arakan Yoma, *Burma* F66+205 **71**
Araks, R., *Iran* J78+390 **62**
Aralsk, *Kazakh* H80+468 **62**
Aralskoye More (Aral Sea),
   Kazakh-Uzbek J00+450 **62**
Aramac, *Queensland* C28-225 **111**
Arambagh, *India* G13+229 **73**
Aran I., *Ireland, Rep.* N51+550 **42**
Aran Is., *Ireland, Rep.* N58+531 **43**
Aranda de Duero, *Spain* N22+417 **52**
Arani, *Bolivia* S34-175 **104**
Aranjuez, *Spain* N22+400 **52**
Aran Mawddwy, *Wales* N22+528 **38**
Aransas B., *Texas* U42+280 **94**
Araouane, *Mali* N22+186 **80**
Arapiraca, *Brazil* Q41-048 **105**
Arapey, *Uruguay* R75-309 **103**
Arapkir, *Turkey* K40+390 **74**
Arapuni, *New Zealand* A28-380 **112**
Ararangua, *Brazil* R27-289 **103**
Ararat, *Victoria* C42-373 **109**
Ararat, mt., *Turkey* K04+398 **74**
Araria, *India* G15+262 **73**
Arassuahy, *Brazil* Q72-169 **105**
Araty, *Brazil* S64-079 **104**
Arauca, *Colombia* S64+070 **104**
Arauco, *Chile* S80-372 **103**
Aravalli Ra., *India* H10+254 **70**
Araxa, *Brazil* R12-196 **105**
Arbatax, *Sardinia* M31+399 **57**
Arbil, *Iraq* K06+363 **74**
Arboga, *Sweden* L85+594 **47**
Arbois, *France* M56+469 **54**
Arbon, *Switzerland* M33+475 **45**
Arbroath, *Scotland* N16+566 **41**
Arcade, *New York* T21+425 **91**
Arcadia, *Michigan* T67+445 **91**
Arcadia, *Wisconsin* U07+442 **93**
Arcen, *Netherlands* M53+515 **44**
Archbald, *Pennsylvania* T04+415 **96**
Archidona, *Spain* N26+371 **52**
Arcot, *India* G64+129 **70**
Arctic Ocean - **26**
Arctic Red River, *N.-W. Terr.* W80+672 **88**
Ardabil, *Iran* J71+383 **74**
Ardahan, *Turkey* K14+412 **74**
Ardakan, *Iran* J35+324 **75**
Årdal, *Norway* M43+612 **47**
Ardal, *Iran* J55+321 **75**
Ardara, *Ireland, Rep.* N51+548 **42**
Ardatov, *U.S.S.R.* K11+552 **61**
Ardèche, dep., *France* M64+446 **55**
Ardee, *Ireland, Rep.* N39+539 **42**
Arden, Forest of, *England* N11+523 **37**
Ardennes, dep., *France* M61+496 **54**
Ardennes Mts., *Belg., etc.* M57+499 **44**
Arderin, *Ireland, Rep.* N46+530 **43**
Ardez, *Switzerland* M29+468 **45**
Ardgay, *Scotland* N26+579 **40**
Ardglass, *N. Ireland* N34+543 **42**
Ardino, *Bulgaria* L29+416 **58**
Ardlethan, *New S. Wales* C19-344 **109**
Ardmore, *Oklahoma* U41+342 **95**
Ardmore B., *Ireland, Rep.* N46+519 **43**
Ardrishaig, *Scotland* N33+560 **41**
Ardrossan, *Scotland* N29+556 **41**
Ardrossan, *S. Australia* C73-344 **109**
Ardud, *Romania* L43+476 **49**
Arecibo, *Puerto Rico* S40+185 **101**
Areia, *Brazil* Q58-133 **105**
Areia Branco, *Brazil* Q43-050 **105**
Areião, *Brazil* R26-044 **105**
Arenales, *Argentina* S09-343 **103**
Arenales, mt., *Chile* S80-471 **103**
Arenas de San Pedro, *Spain* N31+402 **52**
Arendal, *Norway* M37+584 **47**
Arenys de Mar, *Spain* M75+416 **53**
Arequipa, *Peru* S70-163 **104**
Arèvalo, *Spain* N28+410 **52**
Arezzo, *Italy* M19+434 **56**
Argentan, *France* N00+487 **54**
Argentat, *France* M78+451 **55**
Argentina, rep., *S. America* - **103**
Argentino, L., *Argentina* S75-503 **103**
Argent-sur-Sauldre, *France* M75+475 **54**
Argo, *Sudan* K88+192 **81**
Argolis, G of, *Greece* L42+372 **59**
Argonne, *France* M60+493 **54**
Argos, *Greece* L44+376 **59**
Arguedas, *Spain* N10+424 **53**
Argun, R., *U.S.S.R.-China* E04+510 **63**
Argungu, *Nigeria* M62+128 **80**
Argyll, co., *See* Strathclyde
Århus, *Denmark* M29+561 **47**
Ariake Wan, *Japan* D23+313 **68**
Ariano Irpino, *Italy* M00+412 **57**
Arica, *Chile* S62-186 **103**
Arica, *Colombia* S70-021 **104**
Ariège, dep., *France* M80+430 **55**
Arikemes, *Brazil* S19-099 **104**
Arilje, *Yugoslavia* L59+437 **58**
Arima, *Brazil* S22-057 **104**
Arinda, *Guyana* R82+047 **104**
Aripuana, *Brazil* S02-052 **104**

Arisaig & Sd. of, *Scotland* N35+568 **41**
Arivechi, *Mexico* V24+290 **100**
Ariza, *Spain* N13+413 **53**
Arizona, *Argentina* S32-356 **103**
Arizona, state, *U.S.A.* V50+347 **98**
Arizona Plat., *Arizona* V36+446 **94**
Arizpe, *Mexico* V30+304 **100**
Arka, *Yemen, South* J76 + 136 **74**
Arka, *U.S.S.R.* C48+601 **63**
Arkabutla Res., *Mississippi* U01+348 **95**
Arkadelphia, *Arkansas* U18+342 **95**
Arkadhia, *Greece* L46+374 **59**
Arkaig L., *Scotland* N31+570 **40**
Arkansas, state, *U.S.A.* U20+350 **99**
Arkansas R., *Arkansas, etc.* U20+354 **99**
Arkansas City, *Arkansas* U07+336 **97**
Arkansas City, *Kansas* U42+370 **95**
Arkhangelsk, *U.S.S.R.* K25+647 **62**
Arklow, *Ireland, Rep.* N37+528 **43**
Arkoi, I., *Greece* L19+374 **59**
Arles, *France* M62+437 **55**
Arlon, *Belgium* M55+497 **44**
Arltunga, *N. Terr., Aust.* D02-232 **111**
Armagh & co., *N. Ireland* N40+543 **42**
Armenia, *Colombia* T04+048 **104**
Armenia, *U.S.S.R.* K05+405 **74**
Armentieres, *France* M73+507 **54**
Armidale, *New S. Wales* B81-305 **109**
Arminna, *Egypt* K80+222 **81**
Armirós, B of, *Crete* L34+354 **59**
Armisticio, *Paraguay* R57-249 **103**
Armori, *India* G60+205 **70**
Armstrong, *Ontario* T83+502 **89**
Armyanskaya, rep., *U.S.S.R.* K00+400 **62**
Arnaudville, *Louisiana* U11+304 **97**
Arnauti, C., *Cyprus* K76+351 **76**
Arnawai, *Pakistan* H20+353 **72**
Arnhem, *Netherlands* M55+520 **44**
Arnhem, C., *N. Terr., Aust.* C78-122 **111**
Arnhem Ld., *N. Terr., Aust.* D10-130 **110**
Arnissa, *Greece* L49+408 **59**
Arnöy, *Norway* L56+701 **46**
Arnprior, *Ontario* T08+454 **91**
Arnsberg, *W. Germany* M42+514 **48**
Arnstadt, *E. Germany* M24+508 **48**
Arolla, *Switzerland* M45+460 **45**
Aroostook, *New Brunswick* S46+468 **90**
Arorae, I., *Kiribati* A20-030 **106**
Arosa, *Switzerland* M32+468 **45**
Arouelli, *Chad* L44+186 **81**
Aroya, *Colorado* U79+338 **94**
Arrah, *India* G32+255 **73**
Arran I., *Scotland* N31+556 **41**
Arras, *France* M73+503 **54**
Arrayas, *Brazil* R11-131 **105**
Arroba, *Spain* N27+391 **52**
Arromanches, *France* N05+493 **54**
Arronches, *Portugal* N44+391 **52**
Arrow L., *Ireland, Rep.* N50+541 **42**
Arrowsmith, Mt., *N.S.W.* C51-301 **109**
Arrowtown, *New Zealand* A67-449 **112**
Arroyo, *Puerto Rico* S35+180 **101**
Års, *Denmark* M33+568 **47**
Arsk, *U.S.S.R.* J60+561 **61**
Arta, *Greece* L54+392 **59**
Artawiya, *Saudi Arabia* J88+266 **74**
Artemovsk, *U.S.S.R.* F68+545 **63**
Artemovsk, *Ukraine* K42+486 **60**
Artemovski, *U.S.S.R.* E3C+582 **63**
Artemovski, *U.S.S.R.* H79+573 **61**
Artenay, *France* M79+481 **54**
Artesia, *New Mexico* U86+328 **94**
Artibonite, R., *Haiti* S74+190 **101**
Artigas, *Uruguay* R69-304 **103**
Artillery L., *N.-W. Terr.* V17+636 **88**
Artois, prov., *France* M76+503 **54**
Artvin, *Turkey* K20+412 **74**
Aru, *Zaire* K84+028 **83**
Aruanã, *Brazil* R36-148 **105**
Aru Kep., *Indonesia* D04-063 **65**
Arumá, *Brazil* S13-046 **104**
Arundel, *England* N04+508 **39**
Arundel, *Quebec* S88+460 **91**
Aruppukkottai, *India* G72+095 **70**
Arusha, *Tanzania* K50-034 **83**
Aru Tso, *Tibet* G46+339 **71**
Arvada, *Wyoming* V47+446 **93**
Arvida, *Quebec* S67+484 **90**
Arvika, *Sweden* M14+597 **47**
Arvilla, *N. Dakota* U45+479 **93**
Arzamas, *U.S.S.R.* K07+554 **61**
Arzeu, *Algeria* N02+358 **80**
Arzua, *Spain* N49+429 **52**
As, *Belgium* M57+510 **44**
Aš, *Czechoslovakia* M17+502 **48**
Asahigawa, *Japan* C46+437 **68**
Asansol, *India* G18+237 **73**
Åsarna, *Sweden* M04+627 **46**
Asbestos, *Quebec* S70+458 **91**
Asbury Park, *New Jersey* S84+402 **96**
Ascension, *Bolivia* S19-156 **104**
Ascension, B. de la, *Mexico* T74+196 **100**
Ascension I., *Atlantic Ocean* N87-080 **85**
Aschaffenburg, *W. Germany* M35+499 **48**
Ascoli, *Italy* M09+428 **56**
Ascona, *Switzerland* M37+462 **45**
Ascot, *England* N04+514 **39**
Ascotan, *Chile* S50-215 **103**
Aseda, *Sweden* L88+572 **47**
Åsele, *Sweden* L76+641 **46**
Åsen, *Sweden* M07+613 **47**
Asenovgrad, *Bulgaria* L31+420 **58**
Asgata, *Cyprus* **76**
Ashanti, reg., *Ghana* **80**
Ashbourne, *England* N12+531 **37**
Ashburton, *England* N23+505 **38**
Ashburton, *New Zealand* A49-439 **112**
Ashburton, R., *W. Aust.* E20-230 **110**
Ashdod, *Israel* K62+318 **76**
Asheboro, *N. Carolina* T29+357 **97**
Asheville, *N. Carolina* T45+356 **97**
Ash Fork, *Arizona* V45+352 **94**
Ashkhabad, *Turkmen* J10+380 **62**
Ashland, *Kansas* U58+372 **95**
Ashland, *Kentucky* T46+385 **97**
Ashland, *Maine* S51+466 **90**
Ashland, *Montana* V08+456 **93**
Ashland, *Ohio* T44+409 **91**
Ashland, *Oregon* W16+422 **92**
Ashland, *Pennsylvania* T08+408 **96**
Ashland, *Virginia* T15+376 **97**
Ashland, *Wisconsin* U09+466 **93**
Ashland City, *Tennessee* T72+363 **97**
Ashley, *New S. Wales* C01-292 **109**

Ashley, *N. Dakota* U56+461 **93**
Ashraf, *Iran* J39+367 **75**
Ash Shihr, *Yemen, South* J62 + 148 **74**
Ashtabula, *Ohio* T35+418 **91**
Ashton-under-Lyne, *England* N12+535 **37**
Ashton, *Idaho* V40+441 **93**
Ashuanipi L., *Labrador* S37+528 **89**
Ashuradeh, *Iran* J37+369 **75**
Ashville, *Alabama* T67+338 **97**
Asinara, I. & G. di, *Sardinia* M39+409 **57**
Asino, *U.S.S.R.* G24+570 **62**
Asir, *Saudi Arabia* K20+203 **74**
Askeaton, *Ireland, Rep.* N54+526 **43**
Åskersund, *Sweden* M01+589 **47**
Askvoll, *Norway* M59+614 **47**
Aslandus, *Iran* J76+394 **74**
Asmara, *Ethiopia* K36+152 **83**
Aspern, *Austria* L81+483 **49**
Aspiring, Mt., *New Zealand* A68-444 **112**
Aspres-sur-Buech, *France* M56+445 **55**
Assab, *Ethiopia* K14+130 **83**
As Sabya, *Yemen* K14+172 **74**
As Safa, *Saudi Arabia* J80+277 **74**
Assam, *India* F70+255 **71**
As Sauda, *Yemen* K07+160 **74**
Assaye, *India* G84+203 **70**
Asse, *Belgium* M65+509 **44**
Assen, *Netherlands* M52+530 **44**
Asshur, *Iraq* K14+356 **74**
Assiniboia, *Saskatchewan* V05+496 **88**
Assiniboine, Mt., *Alberta* V63+507 **88**
Assiniboine R., *Manitoba* U50+498 **88**
Assinica L., *Quebec* T01+504 **90**
Assu & R., *Brazil* Q41-056 **105**
Assumar, *Portugal* N44+391 **52**
Assynt L., *Scotland* N30+582 **40**
Asti, *Italy* M41+449 **56**
Astipálaia, I., *Greece* L22+366 **59**
Aston, C., *N.-W. Territories* S44+700 **89**
Astor, *Kashmir* H01+353 **72**
Astorga, *Spain* N36+425 **52**
Astoria, *Oregon* W23+462 **92**
Astrakhan, *U.S.S.R.* J73+463 **62**
Åsträsk, *Sweden* L60+646 **46**
Astros, *Greece* L44+374 **59**
Astudillo, *Spain* N26+422 **52**
Asuncion, *Paraguay* R76-252 **103**
Aswân, *Egypt* K72+238 **81**
Asyût, *Egypt* K82+270 **81**
Atacama, Des., *Chile* S56-200 **103**
Atakpame, *Togo* M84+076 **80**
Atalaia, *Brazil* Q36-094 **105**
Ataländi, *Greece* L42+387 **59**
Atambua, *Timor I., Indon.* D62-090 **65**
Atar, *Mauritania* N78+206 **80**
Atara, *Yemen* J89+145 **74**
Ataran, R., *Burma* F42+160 **71**
Atbara, *Sudan* K66+178 **81**
Atbasar, *Kazakh.* H39+518 **62**
Atchafalaya B., *Louisiana* U08+294 **95**
Atchison, *Kansas* U31+396 **95**
Ateca, *Spain* N11+413 **53**
Ath, *Belgium* M67+506 **44**
Athabasca, *Alberta* V49+549 **88**
Athabasca, L., *Alta.-Sask.* V30+592 **88**
Athabasca R., *Alberta* V65+544 **88**
Athboy, *Ireland, Rep.* N41+536 **42**
Athenry, *Ireland, Rep.* N52+533 **43**
Athens. *See* Athinai
Athens, *Georgia* T51+339 **97**
Athens, *Tennessee* T57+354 **97**
Atherton Plat., *Queensland* C30-176 **111**
Athinai, *Greece* L38+380 **59**
Athleague, *Ireland, Rep.* N49+535 **43**
Athlone, *Ireland, Rep.* N48+534 **43**
Athna, *Cyprus* K67+350 **76**
Athol, *Massachusetts* S73+426 **96**
Athol, *New Zealand* A68-455 **112**
Atholl, Forest of, *Scotland* N24+568 **41**
Athy, *Ireland, Rep.* N42+530 **43**
Atico, *Peru* S82-162 **104**
Atienza, *Spain* N18+412 **52**
Atikonak L., *Labrador* S27+528 **89**
Atka, *U.S.S.R.* B80+607 **63**
Atka, I., *Aleutian Is.* Z55+519 **99**
Atkarsk, *U.S.S.R.* K00+518 **61**
Atlanta, *Georgia* T56+337 **97**
Atlanta, *Michigan* T55+450 **91**
Atlantic, *Iowa* U30+414 **95**
Atlantic City, *New Jersey* S86+394 **96**
Atlin, *British Columbia* W81+597 **88**
Atlit, *Israel* K60+327 **76**
Atoka, *Oklahoma* U36+344 **95**
Atrauli, *India* G70+280 **73**
At Ta'if, *Saudi Arabia* K28+211 **74**
Attalla, *Alabama* T66+340 **97**
Attawapiskat, L. & R., *Ont.* T78+520 **89**
Attica, *Indiana* T73+403 **95**
Attica, *New York* T20+428 **96**
Attiki, *Greece* L41+382 **59**
Attleboro, *Massachusetts* S68+419 **96**
Attleborough, *England* M84+525 **39**
Attock, *Pakistan* H16+339 **72**
Attu, I., *Aleutian Is.* A40+524 **99**
Atukesi, *Japan* C31+430 **68**
Atupi, *Brazil* R55+014 **105**
Auburn, *Iowa* U30+416 **95**
Aughnacloy, *N. Ireland* N42+544 **42**
Aughrim, Ireland, Rep. N38+528 **43**
Augsburg, *W. Germany* M25+484 **48**
Augusta, *Arkansas* U08+353 **97**

Augusta, *Georgia* T42+334 **97**
Augusta, *Kansas* U42+377 **95**
Augusta, *Kentucky* T54+387 **97**
Augusta, *Maine* S59+444 **90**
Augusta, *Sicily* L89+372 **57**
Augusta, *Wisconsin* U07+447 **91**
Augustów, *Poland* L43+538 **49**
Augustus, Mt., *W. Australia* E12–246 **110**
Auletta, *Italy* L87+406 **57**
Aumale, *Algeria* M68+360 **80**
Aunis, prov., *France* N08+461 **54**
Aura, *Finland* L44+606 **47**
Auraiya, *India* G63+264 **73**
Aurangabad, *India* G33+247 **73**
Aurangabad, *India* G88+199 **70**
Auray, *France* N18+477 **54**
Aurillac, *France* M76+449 **55**
Aurora, *Illinois* T80+418 **91**
Aurora, *Ontario* T27+440 **91**
Aus, *Namibia* L82-266 **84**
Au Sable, *Michigan* T50+445 **91**
Au Sable Forks, *New York* S82+445 **91**
Austin, *Minnesota* U18+437 **93**
Austin, *Nevada* V73+395 **92**
Austin, *Texas* U46+303 **95**
Austin, L., *W. Australia* E12–276 **110**
Austral Is., *Pacific Oc.* Y00–250 **107**
Australia, *Australasia* **110-111**
Australian Alps, *Vic.-N.S.W.* C10–368 **109**
Australian Capital Terr.
   Australia C06–355 **109**
Austria, *Central Europe* M06+474 **50**
Autlan, *Mexico* U87+197 **100**
Autun, *France* M64+470 **54**
Auvergne, prov., *France* M72+454 **55**
Auxerre, *France* M69+478 **54**
Aux Sources, Mt.,
   Lesotho L06–288 **84**
Ava, *Burma* F54+218 **71**
Avallon, *France* M66+475 **54**
Avalon Pen., *Newfoundland* R52+473 **90**
Avanoas, *Namibia* M12-184 **84**
Avare, *Brazil* R24–231 **105**
Avaviken, *Sweden* L68+656 **46**
Aveiro, *Brazil* R60–034 **105**
Aveiro, *Portugal* N52+406 **52**
Avelgem, *Belgium* M69+508 **44**
Avellanada, *Argentina* R80–347 **103**
Avellino, *Italy* M01+409 **57**
Avenir, *French Guiana* R53+048 **105**
Averoy, *Norway* M45+630 **46**
Aversa, *Italy* M05+410 **57**
Avesnes, *France* M66+501 **54**
Avesta, *Sweden* L83+601 **47**
Aveyron, dep., *France* M73+441 **55**
Avezzano, *Italy* M09+419 **57**
Avia Teria, *Argentina* S04–266 **103**
Aviemore, *Scotland* N23+572 **40**
Avigliano, *Italy* L86+408 **57**
Avignon, *France* M61+440 **55**
Avila, *Spain* N28+406 **52**
Aviz, *Portugal* N47+391 **52**
Avoca, *Iowa* U32+414 **95**
Avoca, *Tasmania* C14–418 **109**
Avoca, *Victoria* C39–371 **109**
Avola, *Sicily* L89+369 **57**
Avon, co., *England* N15+515 **38**
Avon R., *England* N10+523 **37**
Avon R., *Scotland* N20+574 **40**
Avranches, *France* N08+487 **54**
Awaji Shima, *Japan* D00+344 **68**
Awakino, *New Zealand* A32–387 **112**
Awe L., *Scotland* N32+563 **41**
Awjilah, *Libya* L52+292 **81**
Awusa L., *Ethiopia* K40+070 **83**
Axat, *France* M77+428 **55**
Axel, *Netherlands* M67+513 **44**
Axel Heiberg, *North-West*
   Territories U15+790 **89**
Axminster, *England* N18+508 **38**
Ayabaca, *Peru* T28–046 **104**
Ayacucho, *Argentina* R82–371 **103**
Ayacucho, *Peru* S85–132 **104**
Ayaguz, *Kazakh* G59+480 **62**
Ayakhta, *U.S.S.R.* F66+593 **63**
Ayamonte, *Spain* N44+372 **52**
Ayan, *U.S.S.R.* C70+563 **63**
Ayancik, *Turkey* K61+419 **74**
Ayaviri, *Peru* S64–147 **104**
Aydin, *Turkey* L13+379 **74**
Ayerbe, *Spain* N04+423 **53**
Ayia, *Greece* L43+397 **59**
Ayion Óros, *Greece* L35+403 **59**
Ayios Evstratios, *Greece* L30+395 **59**
Aylesbury, *England* N05+518 **39**
Aylmer, *Ontario* T36+428 **91**
Aylmer, L., *N.-W. Territories* V20+643 **88**
Aylsham, *England* M82+528 **39**
Aylwin, *Quebec* T06+460 **91**
Aymores, *Brazil* Q67–196 **105**
Ayon Ostrov, *U.S.S.R.* A65+700 **63**
Ayora, *Spain* N06+390 **53**
Ayr, *Queensland* C15–195 **111**
Ayr & R., *Scotland* N28+555 **41**
Ayun, *Saudi Arabia* K08+265 **74**
Ayutla, *Guatemala* U13+147 **100**
Ayutla, *Mexico* U55+169 **100**
Ayutthaya, *Thailand* F27+144 **69**
Ayvalik, *Turkey* L20+394 **74**
Aywaille, *Belgium* M56+505 **44**
Azaila, *Spain* N03+413 **53**
Azamgarh, *India* G41+261 **73**
Azare, *Nigeria* M28+116 **81**
Azaz, *Syria* K48+366 **76**
Azerbaydzhanskaya, rep.,
   U.S.S.R. J80+410 **62**
Azi, *Latvia* L27+563 **47**
Azogues, *Ecuador* T23+026 **104**
Azores Is. *See* Açores Is.
Azov, Sea of, *U.S.S.R.* K48+460 **60**
Azpeitia, *Spain* N14+432 **53**
Aztec, *New Mexico* V15+367 **98**
Azua, *Dominican Rep.* S64+184 **101**
Azuaga, *Spain* N34+382 **52**
Azul, *Argentina* R89–367 **103**
Azzan, *South Yemen* J74+144 **74**
Az Zubayr, *Iraq* J74+304 **74**
Baabda, *Lebanon* K57+338 **76**
Baalbek, *Lebanon* K53+340 **76**
Baarle Nassau, *Netherlands* M60+514 **44**
Baarn, *Netherlands* M58+522 **44**

Babahoya, *Ecuador* T26–018 **104**
Babar, I., *Indonesia* D32–080 **65**
Babati, *Tanzania* K56–042 **83**
Babel I., *Tasmania* C11–399 **109**
Bab el Mandeb, *Red Sea* K10+120 **30**
Babenna, *Syria* K54+356 **76**
Babine L., *Brit. Columbia* W38+550 **88**
Babispe, *Mexico* V23+305 **100**
Babol, *Iran* J44+366 **75**
Babura, *Nigeria* M40+126 **82**
Babuyan Is., *Philippines* D80+192 **64**
Babylon, *Iraq* K03+326 **74**
Bacabal, *Brazil* R69–053 **105**
Bacadehuachi, *Mexico* V24+298 **100**
Bacalar, *Mexico* T81+187 **100**
Bacan, I., *Indonesia* D45+006 **65**
Bacău, *Romania* L18+465 **58**
Bacchus Marsh, *Victoria* C33–377 **109**
Bacerac, *Mexico* V23+303 **100**
Bach long Vi, I., *Vietnam* E74+202 **69**
Back R., *N.-W. Territories* U40+660 **88**
Bäckefors, *Sweden* M17+588 **47**
Backergunge, *Bangladesh* F88+224 **71**
Backstairs Pass., *S. Aust.* C72–357 **109**
Bac-Ninh, *Vietnam* E83+212 **69**
Bacoachi, *Mexico* V40+296 **100**
Bacoachic, *Mexico* V28+309 **100**
Bacolod, *Philippines* D72+106 **65**
Bacup, *England* N13+537 **37**
Bada, *Saudi Arabia* K48+269 **74**
Badajoz, *Brazil* R17–026 **105**
Badajoz, *Spain* N41+389 **52**
Badalona, *Spain* M77+415 **53**
Badarma, *U.S.S.R.* F15+578 **63**
Badas, *Brunei* E33+046 **65**
Bad Axe, *Michigan* T48+438 **91**
Bad Ems, *W. Germany* M44+503 **48**
Baden, *W. Germany* M43+480 **48**
Baden, *Switzerland* M40+475 **45**
Baden-Baden, *W.Germany* M40+487 **48**
Badin, *Pakistan* H36+246 **70**
Badiya, *Oman* J09+225 **75**
Bad Kissingen, *W. Germany* M29+502 **48**
Bad Lands, *Nebraska, etc.* U80+426 **98**
Badnur, *India* G72+218 **70**
Badon, *Senegal* N74+128 **80**
Badrinath, *India* G63+308 **70**
Baduen, *Somalia* J74+070 **83**
Badulla, *Sri Lanka* G53+070 **70**
Baena, *Spain* N26+376 **52**
Baerle-Duc, *Belgium* M60+514 **44**
Baetas, *Brazil* S14–061 **104**
Baffin B., *N.-W. Territories* S30+714 **89**
Baffin I., *N.-W. Territories* S60+680 **89**
Bafia, *Cameroon* M24+046 **81**
Bafoulabe, *Mali* N64+136 **80**
Baf'q, *Iran* J28+316 **75**
Bafra, *Turkey* K54+415 **74**
Baft, *Iran* J21+291 **75**
Bagata, *Zaire* L72–038 **82**
Bage, *Brazil* R54–312 **103**
Bagenalstown. *See* Muine Bheag
Baghdad, *Iraq* K04+334 **74**
Bagherhat, *Bangladesh* G01+227 **73**
Baghin, *Iran* J19+302 **75**
Baghpat, *India* G76+290 **72**
Baginbum Hd., *Ireland, Rep.* N41+522 **43**
Bagley, *Minnesota* U32+475 **93**
Bagnell, *Missouri* U16+382 **97**
Bagnols-sur-Ceze, *France* M62+442 **55**
Bagotville, *Quebec* S65+484 **90**
Baguio, *Philippines* D86+165 **65**
Bahaar-i-Gaz, *Iran* J37+368 **75**
Bahadurgarh, *India* G79+287 **72**
Bahama I., Grand, *Bahamas, The* T20+266 **101**
Bahamas, The, *West Indies* T10+250 **101**
Bahawalpur, *Pakistan* H19+294 **72**
Baheri, *India* G63+287 **73**
Bahia. *See* Salvador
Bahia Blanca, *Argentina* S13–386 **103**
Bahia de Caráquez, *Ecuador* T33–007 **104**
Bahia Laura, *Argentina* S39–483 **103**
Bahia Negra, *Paraguay* R79–202 **103**
Bahia Solano, *Colombia* T14+063 **104**
Bahra, *Saudi Arabia* K33+214 **74**
Bahraich, *India* G50+276 **73**
Bahrain, *The Gulf* J57+261 **75**
Bahret el Ateibe, *Syria* K50+335 **76**
Bahret el Hijane, *Syria* K50+333 **76**
Bahret Homs, *Syria* K51+346 **76**
Bahu Kalat, *Iran* H81+257 **75**
Bahus, *Brazil* R48–184 **105**
Baiao, *Brazil* R26–028 **105**
Baibokoum, *Chad* L86+078 **81**
Baiburt, *Turkey* K30+403 **74**
Baidaratskaya B., *U.S.S.R.* H60+700 **62**
Baie St Paul, *Quebec* S63+474 **91**
Baie Verte, *New Brunswick* S25+460 **90**
Baiji, *Iraq* K09+350 **74**
Baikit, *U.S.S.R.* F51+617 **63**
Baikonur, *Kazakh* H55+478 **62**
Baile-Atha-Cliath. *See* Dublin
Bailen, *Spain* N21+381 **52**
Baillie, *N.-W. Territories* W50+706 **88**
Baimak Tanalykovo, *U.S.S.R.* J14+526 **61**
Bainbridge, *Georgia* T57+309 **97**
Bairnsdale, *Victoria* C14–378 **109**
Baital Faqih, *Yemen* K10+146 **74**
Baitik Bogdo, *China* F80+450 **64**
Baixo Longa, *Angola* L66–164 **84**
Baja, *Hungary* L66+462 **58**
Baja California, state, *Mexico* V60+300 **100**
Baján, *Mexico* U68+265 **100**
Bajmok, *Yugoslavia* L64+460 **58**
Bakaly, *U.S.S.R.* J37+552 **61**
Bakel, *Senegal* N74+148 **80**
Baker, *Montana* U86+463 **93**
Baker, *Oregon* V77+448 **92**
Baker I., *Pacific Ocean* Z70+004 **106**
Baker L., *N.-W. Territories* U40+644 **88**
Baker, Mt., *Washington* W10+483 **98**
Baker Butte, *Arizona* V38+344 **94**
Bakersfield, *California* V84+354 **92**
Bakhasar, *India* H23+247 **70**
Baklansk, *U.S.S.R.* H64+558 **61**
Bakloh, *India* G85+325 **72**
Bako, *Ethiopia* K50+058 **83**
Bakonyerdo, *Hungary* L72+473 **49**
Bala, *Wales* N22+529 **38**

Balabac Str., *Philippines* E20+076 **65**
Balagnat, *India* G58+220 **70**
Balakhta, *U.S.S.R.* F79+552 **63**
Balaklava, *S. Australia* C70–342 **109**
Bala Murghab, *Afghanistan* H70+356 **75**
Balancan, *Mexico* U10+178 **100**
Balaquer, *Spain* M83+418 **53**
Balashov, *U.S.S.R.* K11+515 **61**
Balasore, *India* G18+215 **71**
Balat, *Egypt* L04+256 **81**
Balaton, L., *Hungary* L74+469 **49**
Balazote, *Spain* N13+389 **53**
Balboa, *Panama* T27+090 **101**
Balcarce, *Argentina* R80–379 **103**
Balchik, *Bulgaria* L11+434 **58**
Balclutha, *New Zealand* A62–463 **112**
Bald Knob, *Arkansas* U10+353 **95**
Bald Knob, *W. Virginia* T30+384 **97**
Baldwin, *Illinois* U02+382 **97**
Baldwin, *Michigan* T65+439 **91**
Baldwinsville, *New York* S08+431 **96**
Baldy Pk., *Arizona* V28+340 **98**
Baldy Pk., *New Mexico* V04+358 **94**
Baleares, Is., *Medit. Sea* M72+395 **53**
Balearic Is. *See* Baleares
Balen, *Belgium* M59+512 **44**
Baler, *Philippines* D81+158 **65**
Balestrand, *Norway* M51+612 **47**
Baley, *U.S.S.R.* E20+517 **63**
Balfour, *N. Dakota* U63+479 **93**
Balfour, *Tasmania* C30–413 **109**
Bali, I., *Indonesia* E30–084 **65**
Balikesir, *Turkey* L13+397 **74**
Balikpapan, *Borneo* E19–012 **65**
Balk, *Netherlands* M57+529 **44**
Balkh, *Afghanistan* H49+368 **75**
Balkhash & Oz., *Kazakh* H00+469 **62**
Ballabgarh, *India* G76+283 **72**
Ballachulish, *Scotland* N31+567 **41**
Ballaghaderreen, *Ireland, Rep.* N51+539 **42**
Ballantrae, *Scotland* N30+551 **41**
Ballara, *Queensland* C60–210 **111**
Ballarat, *Victoria* C37–376 **109**
Ballater, *Scotland* N18+570 **40**
Ballé, *Mali* N52+154 **80**
Ballenas, B. de, *Mexico* V50+268 **100**
Ballenas Channel, *Mexico* V52+292 **100**
Balleny Is., *Antarctica* B10–670 **27**
Ballia, *India* G35+257 **73**
Ballina, *Ireland, Rep.* N55+541 **42**
Ballina, *New S. Wales* B69–289 **109**
Ballinasloe, *Ireland, Rep.* N49+533 **43**
Ballindine, *Ireland, Rep.* N54+537 **42**
Ballingarry, *Ireland, Rep.* N53+525 **43**
Ballinluig, *Scotland* N22+566 **41**
Ballinrobe, *Ireland, Rep.* N55+536 **42**
Ballinskelligs B., *Ireland, Rep.* N62+518 **43**
Ballston Spa, *New York* S83+430 **96**
Ballybay, *Ireland, Rep.* N41+541 **42**
Ballybofey, *Ireland, Rep.* N47+548 **42**
Ballybunion, *Ireland, Rep.* N56+525 **43**
Ballycastle, *Ireland, Rep.* N56+543 **42**
Ballycastle, *N. Ireland* N37+552 **42**
Ballyclare, *N. Ireland* N36+547 **42**
Ballyconnell, *Ireland, Rep.* N45+541 **42**
Ballycotton B., *Ireland, Rep.* N47+518 **43**
Ballyduff, *Ireland, Rep.* N48+521 **43**
Ballygar, *Ireland, Rep.* N50+535 **43**
Ballygawley, *N. Ireland* N42+545 **42**
Ballyhaise, *Ireland, Rep.* N44+540 **42**
Ballyhaunis, *Ireland, Rep.* N53+538 **42**
Ballyhoura Hills, *Ireland, Rep.* N51+523 **43**
Ballyjamesduff, *Ireland, Rep.* N43+539 **42**
Ballymahon, *Ireland, Rep.* N47+534 **43**
Ballymena, *N. Ireland* N37+549 **42**
Ballymoney, *N. Ireland* N39+551 **42**
Ballymote, *Ireland, Rep.* N51+541 **42**
Ballynahinch, *N. Ireland* N35+544 **42**
Ballyquintin Pt., *N. Ireland* N33+543 **42**
Ballyragget, *Ireland, Rep.* N44+528 **43**
Ballyshannon, *Ireland, Rep.* N49+545 **42**
Ballyvaghan, *Ireland, Rep.* N55+53i **43**
Balmoral, *Victoria* C49–372 **109**
Balombo, *Angola* M00–124 **82**
Balotra, *India* H16+258 **70**
Balrampur, *India* G47+274 **73**
Balranald, *New S. Wales* C39–346 **109**
Balsam L., *Ontario* T23+446 **91**
Balta, *Ukraine* L02+479 **60**
Baltanas, *Spain* N26+419 **52**
Baltic Sea, *N.-W. Europe* **47**
Baltim, *Egypt* K84+316 **81**
Baltimore, *Ireland, Rep.* N56+515 **43**
Baltimore, *Maryland* T10+393 **91**
Baltinglass, *Ireland, Rep.* N40+529 **43**
Baltistan, *Kashmir* G84+354 **72**
Baltiysk, *U.S.S.R.* L60+547 **47**
Baluchistan, *Pakistan* H60+275 **70**
Balurghat, *India* G07+252 **73**
Bam, *Iran* J10+290 **75**
Bama, *Nigeria* M08+116 **81**
Bamako, *Mali* N48+126 **80**
Bambari, *Cent. Afr. Rep.* L56+056 **81**
Bamberg, *W. Germany* M25+499 **48**
Bamenda, *Cameroon* M30+058 **81**
Bamfield, *Michigan* T53+446 **91**
Bamian, *Afghanistan* H43+348 **75**
Bampton, *England* N21+510 **38**
Bampur, *Iran* H87+272 **75**
Bam Tso, *Tibet* G04+281 **71**
Banaras, *India* G42+254 **73**
Banat, *Romania* L50+455 **58**
Banayyan, *Saudi Arabia* J53+232 **75**
Banbridge, *N. Ireland* N38+544 **42**
Banbury, *England* N08+521 **39**
Ban Chamai, *Thailand* F32+082 **69**
Banchory, *Scotland* N15+570 **40**
Bancroft, *Ontario* T17+450 **91**
Banda, *India* G58+255 **73**
Banda Atjeh, *Sumatra* F59+056 **65**
Banda Sea, *Indonesia* D50–055 **65**
Banda Banda, Mt., *N.S.W.* B76–312 **109**
Bandar. *See* Machilipatnam
Bandar Abbas, *Iran* J22+272 **75**
Bandarawela, *Sri Lanka* G54+068 **70**
Bandar e Deylam, *Iran* J59+302 **75**
Bandar e Lengeh, *Iran* J31+266 **75**
Bandar e Rig, *Iran* J56+295 **75**
Bandar e Shapur, *Iran* J64+304 **74**

Bandar Jissah, *Oman* J08+235 **75**
Bandar Shah, *Iran* J36+370 **75**
Bandera, *Argentina* S13–289 **103**
Banderas, B., *Mexico* V03+206 **100**
Bandiagara, *Mali* N22+140 **80**
Bandikui, *India* G81+269 **70**
Bandin Tologoi, *China* F07+412 **64**
Band-i-Qir, *Iran* J66+316 **74**
Bandirma, *Turkey* L12+404 **74**
Bandol, *France* M56+431 **55**
Bandon & R., *Ireland, Rep.* N52+517 **43**
Bandundu, *Zaire* L76–034 **82**
Bandung, *Java* E75–068 **65**
Baned, *India* G78+315 **72**
Banes, *Cuba* T05+210 **101**
Bañeza, la, *Spain* N35+422 **52**
Banff, *Scotland* N15+577 **40**
Banff & Park, *Alberta* V63+510 **88**
Bangada, *Congo* L12+040 **83**
Bangalore, *India* G74+131 **70**
Bangassou, *Cent. Afr. Rep.* L42+048 **81**
Bangka, I., *Indonesia* E84–022 **65**
Bangkok, (Krung Thep),
   Thailand G27+138 **69**
Bangkok, Bight of, *Thailand* F28+131 **69**
Bangladesh, *S. Asia* G05+246 **71**
Bang Mun Nak, *Thailand* F28+160 **65**
Bangor, *Maine* S53+448 **90**
Bangor, *N. Ireland* N34+546 **42**
Bangor, *Pennsylvania* T02+408 **96**
Bangor, *Wales* N25+532 **38**
Bang Saphan Yai, *Thailand* F33+113 **69**
Bangui, *Cent. Afr. Rep.* L68+044 **81**
Bangweulu L., *Zambia* L02–112 **83**
Ban Houei Sai, *Laos* F27+203 **69**
Bania, *Cent. Afr. Rep.* L84+040 **82**
Bani Bu 'Ali, *Oman* J05+221 **75**
Banica, *Dominican Rep.* S69+190 **101**
Baniyas, *Syria* K54+352 **76**
Baniyas, *Syria* K56+332 **76**
Banja Luka, *Yugoslavia* L77+448 **56**
Banjarmasin, *Indonesia* E32-034 **65**
Ban Jaruga, *Yugoslavia* L79+454 **56**
Banjul, *The Gambia* P10+134 **80**
Banka, *India* G18+249 **73**
Banki, *India* G26+203 **71**
Bankipore, *India* G29+256 **73**
Banks I., *N.-W. Territories* W00+730 **88**
Banks I., *Queensland* C46–120 **111**
Banks Is., *Pacific Ocean* A72–145 **106**
Banks Pen., *New Zealand* A40–437 **112**
Banks Str., *Tasmania* C12–406 **109**
Bankura, *India* G17+232 **73**
Bann R., *Ireland, Rep.* N39+525 **43**
Bann R., *N. Ireland* N37+544 **42**
Banningville. *See* Bandundu
Bannockburn, *Scotland* N24+561 **41**
Bannu, *Pakistan* H26+330 **72**
Bañolas, *Spain* M73+421 **53**
Baños de Montemayor, *Spain* N35+403 **52**
Ban-pot, *Thailand* F31+160 **69**
Bansda, *India* H09+208 **70**
Bansi, *India* G43+272 **73**
Banswara, *India* H03+236 **70**
Bantalor, *New Brunswick* S38+463 **90**
Ban Thakham, *Thailand* F34+089 **69**
Bantry & B., *Ireland, Rep.* N57+517 **43**
Banu, *Afghanistan* H34+356 **75**
Banur, *India* G80+305 **72**
Banyak Kep., *Indonesia* F46+022 **65**
Banyo, *Cameroon* M20+068 **81**
Banyuwang, *Java* E34-082 **65**
Banzare Coast, *Antarctica* D65-660 **27**
Banzyville. *See* Yasanyama
Bapaume, *France* M73+501 **54**
Baquedano, *Chile* S58–230 **103**
Ba'quba, *Iraq* K02+337 **74**
Bar, *Yugoslavia* L65+421 **58**
Bara, *Sudan* K88+138 **81**
Barabanki, *India* G53+270 **73**
Barabinsk, *U.S.S.R.* G70+553 **62**
Baraboo, *Wisconsin* T89+435 **91**
Baracoa, *Cuba* S87+203 **101**
Barada, *Syria* K47+359 **76**
Baradine & R., *N.S.W.* C06–309 **109**
Barahona, *Dominican Rep.* S66+182 **101**
Barahona, *Spain* N16+413 **53**
Barail Ra., *India* F70+252 **71**
Baraimi, *U.A.E.* J26+243 **75**
Barak R., *India* F70+250 **71**
Baramula, *Kashmir* H04+342 **72**
Baranagar, *India* G09+227 **73**
Baranof I., *Alaska* X00+570 **99**
Baranovichi, *U.S.S.R.* L23+532 **60**
Baranów, *Poland* L51+505 **49**
Baraque Michel, *Belgium* M53+505 **44**
Barataria I., *Louisiana* U00+292 **95**
Baratta, *S. Australia* C65–320 **109**
Baraunda, *India* G57+250 **73**
Baraut, *India* G76+291 **72**
Barbacena, *Brazil* Q83–212 **105**
Barbacoas, *Colombia* T19+016 **104**
Barbadillo del Mercado, *Spain* N20+421 **52**
Barbados, I., *Windward Is.* R88+132 **101**
Barbastro, *Spain* M89+420 **53**
Barbezieux, *France* N01+455 **54**
Barbuda, I., *Leeward Is.* S10+177 **101**
Barca d'Alva, *Portugal* N41+410 **52**
Barcaldine, *Queensland* C28–234 **111**
Barcarrota, *Spain* N41+385 **52**
Barce. *See* Marj, el
Barcelona Pozza di Gotto,
   Sicily L89+382 **57**
Barcellos, *Brazil* S18–010 **104**
Barcelona, *Spain* M76+414 **53**
Barcelona, *Venezuela* S27+101 **104**
Barcelonnette, *France* M50+444 **55**
Barcelos, *Portugal* N52+415 **52**
Barco de Avila, el, *Spain* N33+404 **52**
Barcoo, R., *Queensland* C34–242 **111**
Bardera, *Somalia* K15+022 **83**
Bardi, *India* G45+245 **73**
Bardia, *Libya* L30+318 **81**
Bardsey, I., *Wales* N29+528 **38**
Bardstown, *Kentucky* T63+378 **97**
Bareilly, *India* G63+284 **73**
Barents Sea, *Arctic Ocean* K30+750 **62**
Barentsøya, I., *Arctic Ocean* L50+785 **62**
Barfurush. *See* Babol
Bargal, *Somalia* J54+112 **83**
Barh, *India* G26+255 **73**

Barhaj, *India* G37+263 73
Bar Harbor, *Maine* S49+444 90
Bari, *India* G74+267 73
Bari, *Italy* L79+411 57
Bari Doab, *Pakistan* H12+304 72
Barinas, *Venezuela* S61+086 104
Baring, C. *N.-W. Territories* V72+700 88
Baringa, *Zaire* L56+008 82
Barisal, *Bangladesh* F88+227 71
Barisan, Pegunungar, *Sum.* F25-014 65
Barito, R., *Indonesia* E32-028 65
Barkah, *Oman* J12+238 75
Barkald, *Norway* M24+620 47
Barkhan, *Pakistan* H33+299 72
Barkly Tableland, *Australia* C70-192 111
Bârlad, *Romania* L14+462 58
Bar le Duc, *France* M60+488 54
Barlee, L., *W. Australia* E03-290 110
Barlee Ra., *W. Australia* E20-236 110
Barletta, *Italy* L83+413 57
Barmedman, *New S. Wales* C15-341 109
Barmer, *India* H21+257 70
Barmera, *S. Australia* C57-342 109
Barmouth, *Wales* N24+527 38
Barnaby River, *N.B.* S33+469 90
Barnard Castle, *England* N11+545 37
Barnato, *New S. Wales* C30-316 109
Barnaul, *U.S.S.R.* G33+535 62
Barn Bluff, *Tasmania* C25-417 109
Barne Inlet, *Antarctica* B30-800 27
Barnegat B., *New Jersey* S85+398 91
Barnesville, *Minnesota* U39+466 93
Barneveld, *Netherlands* M56+521 44
Barnsley, *England* N09+536 37
Barnstable, *Massachusetts* S62+417 96
Barnstaple, *England* N24+511 38
Baroda, *India* H10+222 70
Barotseland, *Zambia* L41-160 84
Baroyeca, *Mexico* V24+279 100
Barpeta, *India* F84+263 71
Barquinha, *Portugal* N51+394 52
Barquisimeto, *Venezuela* S56+100 104
Barra, *Saudi Arabia* J85+249 74
Barra Hd., *Scotland* N45+568 41
Barra, I., *Scotland* N45+570 40
Barra, Sd. of, *Scotland* N44+571 40
Barraba, *New S. Wales* B87-304 109
Barrackpore, *India* G10+228 73
Barracon, *Argentina* R52-263 103
Barra de Tonala, *Mexico* U23+160 100
Barra do Corda, *Brazil* R01-055 105
Barra do Pirai, *Brazil* Q83-224 105
Barra do Rio Doce, *Brazil* Q59-196 105
Barra do Rio Grande, *Brazil* Q80-111 105
Barra dos Bugres, *Brazil* R73-150 104
Barra Mansa, *Brazil* Q85-224 105
Barran, *Somalia* J68+102 83
Barranca, *Peru* T10-048 104
Barranca Bermeja, *Colombia* S83+071 104
Barrancas, *Venezuela* S13+088 104
Barrancos, *Portugal* N42+382 52
Barranqueras, *Argentina* R84-276 103
Barranquilla, *Colombia* S89+109 104
Barre, *Vermont* S75+442 91
Barreiras, *Brazil* R00-122 105
Barreirinha, *Brazil* R72-029 105
Barreirinhas, *Brazil* Q77-026 105
Barreiro, *Portugal* N54+387 52
Barreiros, *Brazil* Q31-087 105
Barreme, *France* M52+440 55
Barrie, *Ontario* T28+444 91
Barrier I., Great, *N.Z.* A27-360 112
Barrier I., Little, *N.Z.* A29-362 112
Barrington, Mt., *N.S.W.* B82-321 109
Barringun, *New S. Wales* C26-290 109
Barron, *Wisconsin* U11+454 93
Barrow, *Argentina* S02-382 103
Barrow-in-Furness, *England* N19+541 37
Barrow R., *Ireland, Rep.* N42+524 43
Barrow Str., *N.-W. Terr.* U45+736 88
Barrow Creek, *N. T., Aust.* D08-214 111
Barry, *Wales* N20+514 38
Barry Mts., *Victoria* C20-372 109
Barsi, *India* G85+182 70
Bar-sur-Aube, *France* M62+482 54
Bar-sur-Seine, *France* M64+481 54
Bartibog, *New Brunswick* S34+473 90
Bartica, *Guyana* R82+063 104
Bartle Frere Mt., *Queensland* C35-176 111
Bartlesville, *Oklahoma* U36+367 95
Baruva, *India* G32+190 71
Barvaux, *Belgium* M57+503 44
Barwa, *India* G34+232 73
Barwani, *India* H01+220 70
Barwon, R., *New S. Wales* C26-302 109
Basel (Basle), *Switzerland* M44+476 45
Baselland, canton, *Switz.* M43+474 45
Bashi, *Iran* J53+286 75
Bashi Chan., *Phil.-Taiwan* D80+215 67
Bashkirskaya, aut. rep., *U.S.S.R.* J30+550 62
Basia, *India* G30+229 73
Basilan, I., *Philippines* D77+066 65
Basilicata, reg., *Italy* L83+405 57
Basingstoke, *England* N07+513 39
Baskatong L., *Quebec* T05+468 91
Bàsmo, *Norway* M06+663 46
Basongo, *Zaire* L58-044 82
Basra, *Iraq* J73+305 74
Bas-Rhin, dep., *France* M42+486 54
Bass Str., *Vict.-Tasm.* C30-395 111
Bassac, *Laos* E85+149 69
Bassein, *Burma* F61+168 71
Bassein, *India* H13+196 70
Basses, Gt. & Lit., *Sri Lanka* G50+061 70
Basses-Alpes. *See* Alpes-de-Haute Provence
Basses-Pyrénées. *See* Pyrénées Atlantiques.
Basse Terre, *Leeward Is.* S09+160 101
Bassevelde, *Belgium* M68+512 44
Bàstad, *Sweden* M13+564 47
Bastak, *Iran* J33+272 75
Basti, *India* G43+268 73
Bastia, *Corsica* M33+427 56
Bastogne, *Belgium* M56+500 44
Bastrop, *Louisiana* U11+328 95
Basura, *Mexico* V43+311 100
Basutoland. *See* Lesotho
Bata, *Equatorial Guinea* M32+018 82
Bataan, *Philippines* D88+147 65
Batabano, *Cuba* T43+227 101
Batacosa, *Mexico* V24+278 100

Batala, *India* G89+318 72
Batalha, *Portugal* N53+397 52
Batan Is., *Philippines* D78+210 64
Batangas, *Philippines* D84+137 65
Batavia, *Argentina* S35-348 103
Batavia, *See* Jakarta
Batavia, *New York* T19+430 96
Bataysk, *U.S.S.R.* K31+471 61
Batchawana, *Ontario* T55+472 91
Batchelor, *N. Terr., Aust.* D24-131 110
Batdambang, *Cambodia* F11+130 69
Bateman's B., *New S. Wales* B89-358 109
Batenburg, *Netherlands* M56+518 44
Batesburg, *S. Carolina* T39+339 97
Batesville, *Arkansas* U10+358 95
Batesville, *Mississippi* U00+344 97
Bath, *England* N14+514 38
Bath, *Maine* S59+439 90
Bath, *New York* T14+423 96
Bathgate, *Scotland* N22+559 41
Bathurst. *See* Banjul
Bathurst, *New Brunswick* S34+476 90
Bathurst, *New S. Wales* C03-334 109
Bathurst Inl., *N.-W. Terr.* V15+670 88
Bathurst I., *N. Terr., Aust.* D28-116 110
Bathurst I., *N.-W. Terr.* U60+756 88
Batie, *Upper Volta* N18+098 80
Batiscan, *Quebec* S74+465 91
Batlow, *New South Wales* C12-355 109
Batna, *Algeria* M52+356 80
Baton Rouge, *Louisiana* U07+304 95
Batopilas, *Mexico* V14+270 100
Batraki, *U.S.S.R.* J68+532 61
Batroun, *Lebanon* K56+342 76
Batticaloa, *Sri Lanka* G50+077 70
Battice, *Belgium* M55+506 44
Battih, *Saudi Arabia* J67+150 74
Battle Creek, *Michigan* T61+424 91
Battleford, *Saskatchewan* V20+529 88
Battleford, N., *Saskatchewan* V20+530 88
Battle Harbour, *Labrador* R65+526 89
Battle Mountain, *Nevada* V72+406 92
Batu, *Indonesia* F40-005 65
Batumi, *U.S.S.R.* K20+418 62
Baturaja, *Sumatra* F05-040 65
Baturi, *Mexico* V23+258 100
Baturite, *Brazil* Q54-044 105
Bauchi, *Nigeria* M32+104 81
Baud, *India* G34+208 71
Baudette, *Minnesota* U28+488 93
Baudo, *Colombia* T13+052 104
Baudouinville. *See* Moba
Bauge, *France* M88+475 54
Baunt, *U.S.S.R.* E40+553 63
Baures, *Bolivia* S22-137 104
Bauru, *Brazil* R24-221 105
Bauska, *Latvia* L35+564 47
Bautzen, *E. Germany* M03+512 48
Bawal, *India* H08+281 72
Bawean, I., *Indonesia* E44-058 65
Bawiti, *Egypt* L08+282 81
Bawku, *Ghana* N00+110 80
Bawtry, *England* N06+534 37
Bay Is., *Honduras* T68+164 101
Bayamo, *Cuba* T11+204 101
Bayana, *India* G77+269 73
Bayan Aul, *Kazakh* G86+507 62
Bayan Dzurikhe, *Mongolia* E76+477 64
Bayanga, *Cent. Afr. Rep.* L84+054 81
Bayan Kara Shan, *China* F30+335 64
Bayan Tumen, *Mongolia* E34+480 64
Bayazit, *Turkey* K08+396 74
Bay City, *Michigan* T53+436 91
Bay City, *Texas* U36+290 95
Bayern, *W. Germany* M18+490 48
Bayeux, *France* N05+493 54
Bayir, *Jordan* K50+308 76
Baykal, Oz, *Russia* E80+533 63
Bay Minette, *Alabama* T77+308 97
Bayona, *Spain* N53+421 52
Bayonne, *France* N09+435 55
Bayou Bodcau Res., *La.-Ark.* U20+329 95
Bayovar, *Peru* T36-058 104
Bayram Ali, *Turkmen* H77+375 62
Bayreuth, *W. Germany* M21+499 48
Bayrischer Wald, *W. Germany* M12+490 48
Bays, L. of, *Ontario* T24+453 91
Baza, Sa. de, *Spain* N08+375 53
Bazar Musa Khel, *Pakistan* H31+309 72
Bazaruto, I., *Mozambique* K58-218 84
Bazas, *France* N01+444 55
Bazias, *Romania* L52+448 58
Bazman, *Iran* J00+278 75
Beach, *N. Dakota* U84+470 93
Beachport, *S. Australia* C60-374 109
Beachy Hd., *England* M89+508 39
Beacon, *New York* S84+415 96
Beaconsfield, *Tasmania* C20-412 109
Beal Ra., *Queensland* C52-250 111
Beaminster, *England* N17+508 38
Bear Is. *See* Medvezhi Osa.
Bear L. & R., *Ida.-Ut.* V38+420 94
Beardmore Gl., *Antarctica* A70-850 27
Bearn, prov., *France* N03+432 55
Bear Paw Mts., *Montana* V26+483 93
Beata, I., *Dominican Rep.* S69+175 101
Beatenberg, *Switzerland* M43+467 45
Beatrice, *Nebraska* U40+403 95
Beattock, *Scotland* N21+553 41
Beattyville, *Kentucky* T52+376 97
Beauceville, *Quebec* S64+462 91
Beaufort, *S. Carolina* T34+325 97
Beaufort, *Victoria* C40-374 109
Beaufort Basin, *Arctic Oc.* Y30+750 26
Beaufort Sea, *Arctic Ocean* W60+720 26
Beaufort West, *Cape Prov.* L44-324 84
Beaugency, *France* M80+478 54
Beauly & Firth, *Scotland* N27+575 41
Beaumaris, *Wales* N25+533 38
Beaumont, *Belgium* M65+502 44
Beaumont, *France* M76+491 54
Beaumont, *New Zealand* A62-458 112
Beaumont, *Texas* U25+302 95
Beaune, *France* M61+470 54
Beauport, *Quebec* S67+469 91
Beaurainng, *Belgium* M60+501 44
Beauvais, *France* M78+494 54
Beauvoir-sur-Mer, *France* N12+469 54
Beaver, *Oklahoma* U64+368 94
Beaver, *Utah* V46+383 94

Beaver I., *Michigan* T63+457 91
Beaver R., *Saskatchewan* V25+542 88
Beaver Dam, *Wisconsin* T83+435 91
Beaver Falls, *Pennsylvania* T32+408 91
Beaverhead Mts., *Idaho* V53+454 92
Beawar, *India* H04+261 70
Beazley, *Argentina* S40-337 103
Bebedouro, *Brazil* R21-209 105
Becerrea, *Spain* N43+429 52
Bechuanaland. *See* Botswana
Becleau, *Romania* L35+472 49
Beda, *Yemen* J84+142 74
Bedak, *Afghanistan* H44+345 75
Bedar, *Spain* N12+372 53
Beddgelert, *Wales* N25+530 38
Bedford, *Pennsylvania* T21+400 96
Bedford, *Quebec* S78+451 91
Bedford, *Virginia* T27+373 97
Bedford & co., *England* N03+521 39
Bedretto, *Switzerland* M39+465 45
Bedr Honein, *Saudi Arabia* K38+237 74
Beduval, *Saskatchewan* V16+552 88
Bedzin, *Poland* L66+504 49
Beeac, *Victoria* C48-382 109
Beebe, *Arkansas* U11+351 97
Beechey, L., *N.-W. Terr.* V10+653 88
Beechworth, *Victoria* C20-364 109
Beecroft Hd., *N.S.W.* B85-350 109
Beek, *Netherlands* M54+518 44
Beek, *Netherlands* M55+509 44
Beekbergen, *Netherlands* M54+522 44
Beenoskee, *Ireland, Rep.* N60+522 43
Beerlegem, *Belgium* M68+509 44
Beernem, *Belgium* M70+511 44
Beers, *Netherlands* M55+517 44
Beersheba, *Israel* K61+312 76
Beeville, *Texas* U46+284 94
Befale, *Zaire* L54+004 82
Befandriana, *Madagascar* J68-154 83
Bega, *New South Wales* C01-367 109
Behbehan, *Iran* J57+306 75
Beho, *Belgium* M54+502 44
Beidha, *Saudi Arabia* K30+208 74
Beilen, *Netherlands* M51+529 44
Beilul, *Ethiopia* K16+130 83
Beinwil, *Switzerland* M41+473 45
Beira, *Mozambique* K60-198 84
Beirût (Beyrouth), *Lebanon* K57+339 76
Beisan, *Israel* K57+325 76
Beitbridge, *Zimbabwe* L00-222 84
Beit-et-Din, *Lebanon* K56+337 76
Beit Guvrin, *Israel* K60+316 76
Beius, *Romania* L46+467 58
Beja, *Portugal* N47+380 52
Béjar, *Spain* N35+404 52
Bejestan, *Iran* J11+346 75
Bejucal, *Cuba* T44+230 101
Békéscsaba, *Hungary* L54+467 49
Bela, *Pakistan* H52+261 70
Bela, *India* G47+259 73
Belair, *Louisiana* T89+298 97
Belang, *Celebes* D61+010 65
Belangpidie, *Sumatra* F50+038 65
Belaya Tserkov, *Ukraine* K89+498 60
Belcher Is., *N.-W. Terr.* T25+560 89
Belchirag, *Afghanistan* H58+358 75
Belchite, *Spain* N04+413 53
Belcoo, *Ireland, Rep.* N47+543 42
Beldanga, *India* G10+240 73
Belebey, *U.S.S.R.* J35+541 61
Belem, *Mexico* V32+278 96
Belém (Pará), *Brazil* R21-014 105
Belen, *Argentina* S42-278 103
Belen, *New Mexico* V11+346 94
Belen, *Panama* T35+090 101
Belfast, *Maine* S54+444 90
Belfast & L., *N. Ireland* N35+546 42
Belfeld, *Netherlands* M53+513 44
Belfield, *N. Dakota* U79+469 93
Belford, *England* N11+556 37
Belfort, *France* M49+476 54
Belgaum, *India* H02+159 70
Belgium, *Europe* M63+507 50
Belgorod, *U.S.S.R.* K51+507 60
Belgorod Onestrovskiy, *Ukr.* K88+462 60
Belgrade. *See* Beograd
Belgrano, *Argentina* R82-358 103
Belin, *France* N05+445 55
Belitung, I., *Indonesia* E72-029 65
Belize, *Belize* T80+161 101
Belize, *Central America* T84+170 101
Bell I., *Newfoundland* R63+507 90
Bellac, *France* M84+461 54
Bella Coola, *Brit. Columbia* W40+521 88
Bellaire, *Michigan* T61+450 91
Bellaire, *Ohio* T35+400 91
Bellary, *India* G78+152 70
Bellavista, *Peru* T22-056 104
Bellbrook, *New S. Wales* B75-308 109
Belledune, *New Brunswick* S35+478 90
Bellefontaine, *Ohio* T53+404 91
Bellefonte, *Pennsylvania* T17+409 96
Belle Fourche, *S. Dakota* U83+447 93
Belle Ile, *France* N19+473 54
Belle Isle, *New Brunswick* S34+457 90
Belle Isle, *Newfoundland* R62+518 90
Belle Isle, Str. of, *Nfd., etc.* R72+513 90
Belleme, *France* M87+484 54
Belle Plain, *Iowa* U14+418 95
Bellerive, *Tasmania* C16-429 109
Belleville, *France* M62+461 54
Belleville, *Kansas* U46+398 95
Belleville, *Illinois* U00+386 95
Belleville, *Ontario* T14+422 91
Bellevue, *Iowa* U03+423 95
Bellevue, *Ohio* T55+467 91
Belley, *France* M56+458 54
Belle Yella, *Liberia* N60+076 80
Bellinger, *New S. Wales* B74-304 109
Bellingham, *England* N13+551 37
Bellingham, *Washington* W14+485 98
Bellingshausen Sea, *Antarc.* T60-670 27
Bellinzona, *Switzerland* M36+462 45
Bellows Falls, *Vermont* S75+431 96
Belluno, *Italy* M16+462 56
Bell Ville, *Argentina* S16-325 103
Belmez, *Spain* N32+383 52
Belmond, *Iowa* U22+429 95
Belmont, *Missouri* T85+367 97
Belmont, *New York* T18+422 96

Belmont L., *Pennsylvania* T03+418 96
Belmonte, *Brazil* S47-058 104
Belmonte, *Brazil* Q54-158 105
Belmonte, *Portugal* N44+404 52
Belmullet, *Ireland, Rep.* N60+542 42
Belo Horizonte, *Brazil* Q84-200 105
Beloit, *Kansas* U48+394 95
Beloit, *Wisconsin* T84+425 95
Belomorsk, *Karelskaya* K61+645 62
Belorado, *Spain* N19+424 52
Beloretsk, *U.S.S.R.* J10+540 61
Belorusskaya S.S.R. *See* Byelorussia
Belostok. *See* Bialystok
Beloye Oz., *U.S.S.R.* K44+602 60
Beloyo More, *U.S.S.R.* K30+658 62
Belp, *Switzerland* M45+469 45
Belt, Lille, *Denmark* M31+553 47
Belt, Store, *Denmark* M24+555 47
Beltana, *S. Australia* C70-308 109
Belterra, *Brazil* R60-026 105
Belton, *S. Carolina* C68-322 109
Belturbet, *Ireland, Rep.* N45+541 42
Belvedere Marittimo, *Italy* L85+396 57
Belver, *Portugal* N48+395 52
Belvidere, *Illinois* T83+422 95
Belvidere, *New Jersey* T01+408 96
Belyy, Os., *U.S.S.R.* H30+730 62
Bemidji, *Minnesota* U30+474 93
Benagerie, *S. Australia* C58-315 109
Ben Alder, *Scotland* N27+568 41
Benalla, *Victoria* C24-365 109
Benapol, *India* G07+230 73
Benares. *See* Varanasi
Benavente, *Spain* N34+420 52
Benbecula, I., *Scotland* N44+574 40
Benbury, *Ireland, Rep.* N59+536 42
Ben Cruachan, *Scotland* N31+564 41
Bencubbin, *W. Australia* E11-308 110
Bend, *Oregon* W08+441 92
Bendery, *Moldavia* L03+469 60
Bendigo, *Victoria* C34-368 109
Bendoc, *Victoria* C07-371 109
Benevento, *Italy* M01+412 57
Bengal, B. of, *India, etc.* G00+180 71
Bengal, East, *Bangladesh* G03+240 73
Bengal, West, *India* G14+235 73
Ben Gardane, *Tunisia* M24+330 81
Benghazi, *Libya* L60+320 81
Benguela, *Angola* M10-126 82
Benha, *Egypt* K82+304 81
Ben Hope, *Scotland* N28+584 40
Beni, R., *Bolivia* S43-130 104
Beni-Abbès, *Algeria* N14+302 80
Benicarlo, *Spain* M88+404 53
Benin, rep., *W. Africa* M80+098 80
Benin, Bight of, *W. Africa* M80+050 80
Benin City, *Nigeria* M56+064 80
Beni Saf, *Algeria* N08+354 80
Beni Suef, *Egypt* K84+290 81
Benito, *Rio Muni* M32+014 82
Benjamin Constant, *Brazil* S61-044 104
Benkelman, *Nebraska* U70-400 95
Benkovac, *Yugoslavia* L87+441 56
Ben Lawers, *Scotland* N25+565 41
Ben Ledi, *Scotland* N26+563 41
Ben Lomond, *N.S.W.* B80-301 109
Ben Lomond, *Scotland* N28+562 41
Ben Lomond, *Tasmania* C15-416 109
Ben Macdhui, *Scotland* N22+571 40
Ben More, *Scotland* N27+564 41
Ben More Assynt, *Scotland* N29+581 40
Bennett, *Brit. Columbia* X00+599 88
Bennettsville, *S. Carolina* T28+346 97
Ben Nevis, *Scotland* N30+568 41
Bennington, *Vermont* S79+429 96
Benson, *Arizona* V32+320 94
Benson, *Minnesota* U34+453 93
Benson Mines, *New York* T00+442 91
Bentinck's I., *Burma* F42+117 71
Benton, *Arkansas* U16+345 97
Benton Harbor, *Michigan* T69+421 91
Benue R., *Nigeria* M40+080 80
Ben Vorlich, *Scotland* N25+563 41
Benwee Hd., *Ireland, Rep.* N59+543 42
Ben Wyvis, *Scotland* N27+577 40
Beograd, *Yugoslavia* L57+448 58
Beppu, *Japan* D21+332 68
Berar, *India* G74+205 70
Berat, *Albania* L60+407 59
Berawinnia, *New S. Wales* C33-290 109
Berber, *Sudan* K66+180 81
Berbera, *Somalia* K00+104 83
Berberati, *Cent. Afr. Rep.* L86+044 81
Berdichev, *Ukraine* L09+498 60
Berdigyastyakh, *U.S.S.R.* D46+623 63
Berdyansk, *Ukraine* K50+468 60
Bere Regis, *England* N13+507 39
Beresford, *S. Dakota* U42+430 93
Beresti, *Romania* L13+461 58
Berezniki, *U.S.S.R.* J20+594 62
Berezovo, *U.S.S.R.* H60+641 62
Berg, *Norway* L77+695 46
Berga, *Spain* M79+421 53
Bergamo, *Italy* M32+457 56
Bergen, E. *Germany* M10+544 48
Bergen, *Norway* M58+604 47
Bergen, *W. Germany* M31+528 48
Bergen-op-Zoom, *Neth.* M64+515 44
Bergerac, *France* M87+449 55
Bergisch Gladbach, *W. Germany* M46+510 48
Bergün, *Switzerland* M32+466 45
Berhampur, *India* G10+241 73
Berhampur, *India* G31+192 71
Beri, *India* G80+287 72
Bering, *U.S.S.R.* Z62+648 63
Beringen, *Belgium* M59+510 44
Bering Sea, *Asia-America* A00+590 99
Bering Str., *Asia-America* Z30+652 99
Berislavl, *Ukraine* K69+468 60
Berjeik, *Netherlands* M58+513 44
Berkâk, *Norway* M30+629 46
Berkeley, *California* W14+379 92
Berkley, *Virginia* T08+368 97
Berkovitsa, *Bulgaria* L42+433 58
Berkshire (Berks), co., *Eng.* N08+515 39
Berkshire Hills, *Massachusetts* S79+423 96
Berlin, *Germany* M10+525 48
Berlin, *New Hampshire* S67+445 91
Berlin, *Wisconsin* T83+440 91
Bermagui, *N.S.W.* C00-364 109

Bermillo de Savago, *Spain* N37+414 **52**
Bermudas, Is., *Atlantic Oc.* S30+320 **99**
Bern & canton, *Switzerland* M45+469 **45**
Bernalillo, *New Mexico* V10+353 **94**
Bernasconi, *Argentina* S23–379 **103**
Bernay, *France* M86+492 **54**
Bernburg, *E. Germany* M20+518 **48**
Berne. *See Bern*
Berneau, *Belgium* M56+507 **44**
Berneck, *Switzerland* M32+474 **45**
Berner Alpen, *Switzerland* M46+463 **45**
Bernina, Passo del, *Switz.* M30+464 **45**
Beromunster. *See Munster*
Berri, *S. Australia* C57–343 **109**
Berri, prov., *France* M76+471 **54**
Berriedale, *Scotland* N21+582 **40**
Berrigan, *New S. Wales* C25–357 **109**
Berry, *New South Wales* B86–348 **109**
Berry Is., *Bahamas, The* T18 + 256 **101**
Berryville, *Virginia* T18+391 **96**
Bersillies, *Belgium* M65+503 **44**
Berthierville, *Quebec* S79+461 **91**
Berthold, *N. Dakota* U71+483 **93**
Bertoua, *Cameroon* M08+046 **81**
Bertraghboy B., *Ireland, Rep.* N59+534 **43**
Bertrix, *Belgium* M59+499 **44**
Beru, I., *Kiribati* A23–018 **106**
Berwick, *Pennsylvania* T08+411 **96**

Berwick-upon-Tweed, *Eng.* N12+558 **37**
Berwyn Mts., *Wales* N20+529 **38**
Berzee, *Belgium* M64+503 **44**
Bescançon, *France* M54+473 **54**
Beskidy Zachodnie, mts.,
  Central Europe L54+495 **49**
Besni, *Turkey* K43+378 **74**
Bessala, *Congo* L86–026 **82**
Bessemer, *Alabama* T72+334 **97**
Best, *Netherlands* M58+515 **44**
Betanzos, *Spain* N49+434 **52**
Betbetti, *Sudan* L34+152 **81**
Bethanie, *Namibia* L76–264 **84**
Bethany, *Missouri* U24+403 **95**
Bethel, *Alaska* S65+444 **90**
Bethlehem, *O.F.S.* L10–284 **84**
Bethlehem, *Israel* K59+317 **76**
Bethlehem, *Pennsylvania* T02+406 **96**
Betling Sib., *India* F75+238 **71**
Betsiamites, *Quebec* S52+490 **90**
Betsiamites R., *Quebec* S58+493 **90**
Bettiah, *India* G32+268 **73**
Beugen, *Netherlands* M54+517 **44**
Beulah, *Victoria* C46–360 **109**
Beveland, Noord, I.,
  Netherlands M67+516 **44**
Beveland, Zuid, I.,
  Netherlands M66+515 **44**
Beveren, *Belgium* M65+512 **44**
Beverley, *England* N02+538 **37**
Beverlo, *Belgium* M59+511 **44**
Beverly, *Massachusetts* S65+426 **96**
Beverst, *Belgium* M57+509 **44**
Bewdley, *England* N14+524 **38**
Bex, *Switzerland* M48+463 **45**
Beyla, *Guinea* N52+088 **80**
Beypazari, *Turkey* K79+402 **74**
Beypore, *India* G85+113 **70**
Beysehir, *Turkey* K80+376 **74**
Bezdán, *Yugoslavia* L67+458 **58**
Bezhitsa, *U.S.S.R.* K64+533 **60**
Beziers, *France* M71+434 **55**
Bezwada, *India* G56+165 **70**
Bhabua, *India* G38+250 **73**
Bhadarwah, *Kashmir* G85+329 **72**
Bhadaur, *India* G88+305 **72**
Bhadaura, *India* G76+248 **73**
Bhadohi, *India* G44+254 **73**
Bhadra, *India* G89+291 **72**
Bhadreswar, *India* G10+228 **73**
Bhagalpur, *India* G18+252 **73**
Bhakkar, *Pakistan* H23+317 **72**
Bhamo, *Burma* F46+242 **71**
Bhandara, *India* G62+211 **70**
Bhannis, *Lebanon* K56+339 **76**
Bhanrer Ra., *India* G63+234 **73**
Bharatpur, *India* G75+272 **73**
Bhatgaon, *Nepal* G27+276 **73**
Bhatinda, *India* H00+302 **72**
Bhatnair, *India* H04+295 **72**
Bhatpara, *India* G09+229 **73**
Bhavnagar, *India* H17+216 **70**
Bhawani Patna, *India* G40+200 **71**
Bhera, *Pakistan* H12+325 **72**
Bhilwara, *India* H02+254 **70**
Bhima R., *India* G82+172 **70**
Bhind, *India* G67+265 **73**
Bhir (Bir), *India* G85+190 **70**
Bhiwani, *India* G83+288 **72**
Bhojpur, *India* G35+255 **73**
Bhong Chu, R., *Tibet* G17+286 **71**
Bhopal, *India* G75+233 **73**
Bhuj, *India* H32+232 **70**
Bhusawal, *India* G85+210 **70**
Bhutan, *S. Asia* G00+270 **71**
Biafra, Bight of, *W. Africa* M38+026 **80**
Biak, I., *New Guinea* C84+010 **65**
Białogard, *Poland* L84+540 **49**
Białowieza, *Poland* L37+527 **49**
Białystok, *Poland* L41+531 **49**
Biarritz, *France* N09+435 **55**
Biasca, *Switzerland* M36+464 **45**
Biderach, *Germany* M32+481 **48**
Bibon, *Wisconsin* U07+464 **91**
Bic, *Quebec* S52+484 **90**
Bicknell, *Indiana* T74+388 **91**
Bida, *Nigeria* M54+092 **80**
Bidar, *India* G74+179 **70**
Biddeford, *Maine* S63+435 **90**
Bideford & B., *England* N25+510 **38**
Bidon, *Algeria* M84+222 **80**
Biel, *Switzerland* M47+471 **45**
Bielefeld, *Germany* M39+520 **48**
Bieler See, *Switzerland* M47+471 **45**
Bielopole, *Ukraine* K64+512 **60**
Bielsk, *Poland* L41+528 **49**
Bienne. *See Biel*
Bière, *Switzerland* M52+466 **45**
Bietschhorn, mt., *Switz.* M43+464 **45**
Big I., *N.-W. Territories* S63+620 **89**
Big L., *Arkansas* U01+357 **95**
Biga, *Turkey* L16+404 **74**

Big Bell, *W. Australia* E13–272 **110**
Big Belt Mts., *Montana* V40+468 **93**
Big Bend Nat. Pk., *Texas* U80+292 **94**
Big Blue R., *Kan.-Neb.* U40+400 **95**
Bigelow, *Maine* S63+451 **90**
Biggar, *Saskatchewan* V18+518 **88**
Biggar, *Scotland* N21+556 **41**
Biggleswade, *England* N02+521 **39**
Big Hatchet Mts., *New Mex.* V20+316 **94**
Bighorn Mts., *Wyoming* V15+444 **98**
Bighorn R., *Montana, etc.* V19+450 **98**
Bignona, *Senegal* P08+128 **80**
Big Rapids, *Michigan* T63+437 **91**
Big Salmon R., *Yukon* W80+612 **88**
Big Sandy R., *Kentucky, etc.* T45+380 **93**
Big Spring, *Texas* U68+322 **94**
Bigtimber, *Montana* V30+458 **93**
Big Trout L., *Ontario* T88+540 **89**
Bihac, *Yugoslavia* L85+448 **56**
Bihar, *India* G26+252 **73**
Bihar, *India* G30+248 **71**
Biharamulo, *Tanzania* K82–026 **83**
Bihorului, Mti, *Romania* L45+464 **58**
Bijagos, Arqui. Dos.,
  Guinea-Bissau P04+114 **80**
Bijapur, *India* G85+168 **70**
Bijar, *Iran* J74+359 **74**
Bijawar, *India* G63+246 **73**
Bijnabad, *Iran* J12+280 **75**
Bijnor, *India* G71+294 **72**
Bikaner, *India* H10+280 **72**
Bikin, *U.S.S.R.* D04+467 **63**
Bikini, I., *Marshall Is.* A85+120 **106**
Bilaspur, *India* G79+312 **72**
Bilaspur, *India* G47+220 **73**
Bilauktaung Ra.,
  Burma-Thailand F38+145 **65**
Bilbao, *Spain* N18+433 **52**
Bileća, *Yugoslavia* L70+429 **58**
Bilecik, *Turkey* L00+402 **74**
Bilé Karpaty, *Czechoslovakia* L74+490 **49**
Bilimbaevski, *U.S.S.R.* J02+568 **61**
Bilin, *Burma* F47+173 **71**
Bilisht, *Albania* L54+406 **59**
Bilkis, *Iran* J15+371 **75**
Billabong, R. *See Moulamein*
Billeroo, *S. Australia* C60–312 **109**
Billings, *Montana* V21+458 **93**
Billiton, I. *See Belitung.*
Bilma, *Niger* m12+184 **81**
Bilo Goro, *Yugoslavia* L78+458 **56**
Biloxi, *Mississippi* T84+304 **95**
Bilsi, *India* G67+282 **73**
Bilta, *Norway* L50+693 **46**
Bilthoven, *Netherlands* M59+t21 **44**
Bilugyun, I., *Burma* F45+164 **71**
Bilyarsk, *U.S.S.R.* J58+550 **61**
Bilzen, *Belgium* M55+509 **44**
Bimbe, *Angola* L84–120 **82**
Bimberi, Mt., *New S. Wales* C08–356 **109**
Bimlipatam, *India* G39+178 **71**
Binaiya, mt., *Ceram I., Indon.* D34-032 **65**
Binche, *Belgium* M65+504 **44**
Bindki, *India* G56+261 **73**
Bindura, *Zimbabwe* K82–172 **84**
Binefar, *Spain* M88+418 **53**
Bingara, *New South Wales* B86–299 **109**
Bingen, *W. Germany* M43+500 **48**
Bingerville, *Ivory Coast* N24+054 **80**
Bingham, *England* N06+529 **37**
Bingham, *Maine* S59+451 **90**
Bingham Canyon, *Utah* V43+406 **94**
Binghamton, *New York* T06+422 **96**
Bingiri, *Zaire* L28–054 **82**
Bingol, *Turkey* K28+390 **74**
Binh Dinh (An Nhon),
  Vietnam E65+139 **69**
Binn, *Switzerland* M41+464 **45**
Binnaway, *New S. Wales* C06–315 **109**
Bint, *Iran* J03+263 **75**
Bintan, I.,
  Riau Arch., Indonesia F02+011 **65**
Bintuni, Tk., *New Guinea* D12–024 **65**
Bir Ali, *Yemen, South* K70 + 140 **74**
Birao, *Japan* C40+423 **68**
Birchip, *Victoria* C43–360 **109**
Birchwood, *New Zealand* A73–459 **112**
Birdsboro, *Pennsylvania* T05+403 **96**
Birdsville, *Queensland* C64–278 **111**
Birdum,
  N. Terr., Australia D11–156 **110**
Birecik, *Turkey* K42+371 **74**
Birein, *Syria* K50+350 **76**
Bir Fadhil, *Saudi Arabia* J61+222 **74**
Bir Gara, *Chad* L84+132 **81**
Birhan, mt., *Ethiopia* K42+108 **83**
Birjand, *Iran* J04+328 **75**
Birkao, *Somalia* K20–012 **83**
Birkenhead, *England* N18+534 **37**
Bir Malusi, *Iraq* K30+335 **74**
Bir Maqran, *Saudi Arabia* J61+217 **74**
Birmingham, *Alabama* T71+335 **93**
Birmingham, *England* N11+525 **37**
Birmingham, *Michigan* T49+426 **91**
Birney, *Montana* V10+452 **93**
Birni-n-Kebbi, *Nigeria* M64+122 **80**
Birni-n' Konni, *Niger* M58+136 **80**
Birobidzhan, *U.S.S.R.* D12+488 **63**
Birq, *Saudi Arabia* K21+181 **74**
Birr, *Ireland, Rep.* N47+531 **43**
Birrie, R., *New South Wales* C18–294 **109**
Birsilpur, *India* H16+282 **72**
Birsk, *U.S.S.R.* J28+554 **61**
Birzhay, *Lithuania* L31+562 **47**
Bisalpur, *India* G61+283 **73**
Bisauli, *India* G66+283 **73**
Bisbee, *Arizona* V29+314 **94**
Bisbee, *N. Dakota* U56+486 **93**
Biscay, B. of, *France-Spain* N24+460 **50**
Bischofszell, *Switzerland* M34+475 **45**
Biscoe B. *Antartica* Y00–770 **27**
Biscoe, I., *Antartica* A40–660 **27**
Biscotasing, *Ontario* T43+472 **91**
Bisha, *Saudi Arabia* K09+201 **74**
Bishnath, *India* F71+266 **71**
Bishnupur, *India* G16+230 **73**
Bishop Mt., *Wyoming* V24+410 **93**
Bishop Auckland, *England* N10+547 **37**
Bishop's Falls, *Nfd.* R63+490 **90**
Bishops Stortford, *England* M89+519 **39**

Bishri, Jebel el, *Syria* K36+354 **74**
Bisisthal, *Switzerland* M37+469 **45**
Biskia, *Ethiopia* K46+154 **83**
Bismarck, *N. Dakota* U65+468 **93**
Bismarck Arch., *Pacific Oc.* C00–050 **106**
Bismarck C., *Greenland* P25+770 **26**
Bison, *S. Dakota* U75+455 **93**
Bissau, *India* G89+282 **72**
Bissau, *Guinea-Bissau* P04+118 **80**
Bissett, *Ontario* T18+462 **91**
Bistcho, L., *Alberta* V85+598 **88**
Bithur, *India* G58+266 **73**
Bitlis, *Turkey* K18+385 **74**
Bitola, *Yugoslavia* L52+411 **58**
Bitterfeld, *E. Germany* M16+516 **48**
Bitter Root Mts., *Idaho* V44+469 **92**
Bivio, *Switzerland* M32+465 **45**
Biwa Ko, *Japan* C84+352 **68**
Biysk, *U.S.S.R.* G27+526 **62**
Bizerte, *Tunisia* M32+372 **81**
Bjelóvar, *Yugoslavia* L79+459 **56**
Björkö, *Sweden* L66+599 **47**
Bjorli, *Norway* M41+623 **46**
Björna, *Sweden* L68+636 **46**
Bjørnør, *Norway* M29+642 **46**
Bjørnøya, I., *Barents Sea* L63+743 **62**
Black Hd., *Ireland, Rep.* N55+532 **43**
Black Hills, *S. Dakota* U85+442 **98**
Black Isle, *Scotland* N25+576 **40**
Black Mt., *Pakistan* H13+345 **72**
Black Mts., *Arizona* V57+358 **92**
Black Mts., *Wales* N19+519 **38**
Black Ra., *New Mexico* V17+330 **94**
Black R., *Arkansas, etc.* U08+360 **95**
Black Sea, *Europe-Asia* K60+440 **30**
Blackall, *Queensland* C27–242 **111**
Blackburn, *England* N15+537 **37**
Blackdown Hills, *England* N19+509 **38**
Blackfoot, *Idaho* V44+432 **92**
Blackpool, *England* N18+538 **37**
Blackriver, *Michigan* T50+448 **91**
Black River Falls, *Wisconsin* U05+443 **91**
Black Rock, *Arkansas* U07+361 **97**
Black Rock Des., *Nevada* V84+412 **92**
Blacksod B., *Ireland, Rep.* N61+541 **42**
Black Sugar Loaf, mt.,
  New South Wales B81–314 **109**
Blackville, *New Brunswick* S35+467 **90**
Blackville, *S. Carolina* T38+333 **97**
Black Volta R., *Ghana* N14+094 **80**
Blackwater, *Ireland, Rep.* N38+524 **43**
Blackwater I., *N.-W. Terr.* W28+644 **88**
Blackwater Res., *Scotland* N29+567 **41**
Blackwater R.,
  Cork, etc. Ireland, Rep. N47+520 **43**
Blackwater R.,
  Meath, etc. Ireland, Rep. N40+537 **42**
Blackwater R., *N. Ireland* N40+545 **42**
Blackwell, *Oklahoma* U44+368 **95**
Blaenavon, *Wales* N19+518 **38**
Blagoveshchensk, *U.S.S.R.* D44+504 **63**
Blagoveshchensk, *U.S.S.R.* J24+550 **61**
Blagoevgrad, *Bulgaria* L42+420 **58**
Blair, *Nebraska* U37+416 **95**
Blair Atholl, *Scotland* N23+568 **41**
Blairgowrie, *Scotland* N20+566 **41**
Blairmore, *Alberta* V56+496 **88**
Blaj, *Romania* L36+462 **58**
Blanc, C., *Mauritania* P12+208 **80**
Blanc, le, *France* M83+466 **54**
Blanc, Mt., *France-Italy* M48+458 **54**
Blanca, B., *Argentina* S10–394 **103**
Blanca Pk., *Colorado* V03+378 **98**
Blanca, Sierra, *New Mexico* V05+332 **94**
Blanche, L., *S. Australia* C62–292 **109**
Blanche Town, *S. Australia* C62–343 **109**
Blanchewater, *S. Australia* C63–295 **109**
Blanco, C., *Oregon* W28+428 **92**
Blanco Pico, *Costa Rica* T50+095 **101**
Bland, *Virginia* T37+371 **97**
Blandford, *England* N13+509 **39**
Blanes, *Spain* M73+417 **53**
Blaney Park, *Michigan* T65+462 **91**
Blangy, *France* M80+499 **54**
Blankenberge, *Belgium* M71+513 **44**
Blantyre-Limbe, *Malawi* K60–158 **83**
Blaregnies, *Belgium* M67+504 **44**
Blasket Sd., *Ireland, Rep.* N63+521 **43**
Blaton, *Belgium* M68+505 **44**
Blaye, *France* N04+451 **55**
Blayney, *New South Wales* C04–336 **109**
Błazowa, *Poland* L47+499 **49**
Blenheim, *New Zealand* A36–415 **112**
Blenheim, *Ontario* T42+424 **91**
Blessington, *Ireland, Rep.* N39=532 **43**
Blida, *Algeria* M72+364 **80**
Blind River, *Ontario* T48+462 **91**
Blinman, *S. Australia* C28–311 **109**
Blitta, *Togo* M84+084 **80**
Blitzen, Mt., *Nevada* V68+414 **92**
Block I., *Rhode Island* S70+412 **96**
Bloemfontein, *O.F.S.* L22–290 **84**
Blois, *France* M82+476 **54**
Blokzijl, *Netherlands* M54+527 **44**
Bloody Foreland,
  Ireland, Rep. N50+552 **42**
Bloomfield, *Iowa* U14+408 **95**
Bloomington, *Illinois* T84+407 **95**
Bloomsburg, *Pennsylvania* T09+410 **96**
Blossburg, *Pennsylvania* T12+417 **96**
Blount Springs, *Alabama* T70+340 **97**
Blue Mt., *India* F72+227 **71**
Blue Mts., *Jamaica* T10+180 **101**
Blue Mts., *New S. Wales* B88–334 **109**
Blue Mts., *Oregon* V81+450 **92**
Blue Mts., *Pennsylvania* T04+407 **96**
Blue Earth, *Minnesota* U25+437 **93**
Bluefield, *W. Virginia* T37+373 **97**
Bluefields, *Nicaragua* T53+120 **101**
Blue Lake, *Michigan* T60+448 **91**
Blue Ridge, mts., *U.S.A.* T48+350 **99**
Blue Stack Mts.,
  Ireland, Rep. N49+547 **42**
Bluff, *New Zealand* A70–466 **112**
Bluff, *Utah* V28+371 **98**
Bluff Knoll, *W. Australia* E15–344 **110**
Blumenau, *Brazil* R25–270 **103**
Blyth, *England* N09+551 **37**
Blytheville, *Arkansas* U00+359 **95**
Blyukherovsk, *U.S.S.R.* D70+552 **63**
Bo, *Sierra Leone* N70+082 **80**

Boac, *Philippines* D79+134 **65**
Boaco, *Nicaragua* T65+124 **101**
Boafé, *Brazil* S71–072 **104**
Boardman, *N. Carolina* T24+345 **97**
Boat of Garten, *Scotland* N22+572 **40**
Boa Vista, *Brazil* Q59–088 **105**
Boa Vista, *Brazil* S03+027 **104**
Boa Vista Tocantins, *Brazil* R15–064 **105**
Bobadah, *New S. Wales* C20–323 **109**
Bobi, *Paraguay* R67–269 **103**
Bobo Dioulasso, *Upper Volta* N26+112 **80**
Bobolice, *Poland* L81+589 **49**
Bobrov, *U.S.S.R.* K30+510 **61**
Bobruysk, *Byelorussia* L05+532 **60**
Bocas del Toro, *Panama* T43+094 **101**
Bocca do Curua, *Brazil* R56–054 **105**
Bocca do Tauary, *Brazil* S69–082 **104**
Bochnia, *Poland* L57+512 **44**
Bocholt, *Belgium* M57+512 **44**
Bocholt, *W. Germany* M50+519 **48**
Bochum, *W. Germany* M47+515 **48**
Bocota, *Mozambique* K70–228 **84**
Bodola, *Zaire* L48+018 **82**
Bodalla, *New South Wales* C00–361 **109**
Bodaybo, *U.S.S.R.* E34+578 **63**
Boden, *Sweden* L50+658 **46**
Boden See, *Switzerland-*
  Germany M33+476 **45**
Boderg L., *Ireland, Rep.* N48+539 **42**
Bodmin & Moors, *England* N28+505 **38**
Bodø, *Norway* M04+672 **46**
Boela, *Ceram I., Indonesia* D27–032 **65**
Boende, *Congo* L56–004 **82**
Boentok, *Borneo* E31–016 **65**
Boeol, *Celebes* D82+011 **65**
Boertange, *Netherlands* M47+530 **44**
Bofin L., *Ireland, Rep.* N48+538 **42**
Bogalusa, *Louisiana* T89+308 **95**
Bogan, R., *New S. Wales* C18–312 **109**
Bogandé, *Upper Volta* N00+128 **80**
Bogan Gate, *New S. Wales* C14–331 **109**
Bogbonga, *Zaire* L64+014 **82**
Bogdarin, *U.S.S.R.* E39+544 **63**
Bogdo Ula, *China* G02+434 **64**
Boggabri, *New South Wales* C00–307 **109**
Boggeragh Mts.,
  Ireland, Rep. N54+520 **43**
Boghari. *See Ksar El Boukhari*
Bognor Regis, *England* N04+508 **39**
Bogong, Mt., *Victoria* C16–367 **109**
Bogor, *Java, Indonesia* E80–065 **65**
Bogorodskoye, *U.S.S.R.* J67+524 **61**
Bogorodskoye, *U.S.S.R.* C57+525 **63**
Bogota, *Colombia* S83+046 **104**
Bogotol, *U.S.S.R.* G03+561 **62**
Bogra, *Bangladesh* G04+249 **73**
Bohemia, *Czechoslovakia* M06+496 **48**
Böhmer Wald, *Germany-*
  Czechoslovakia M12+492 **48**
Bohol, I., *Philippines* D64+100 **65**
Boiestown, *New Brunswick* S38+465 **90**
Boigu, I., *Papua*
  New Guinea C47–093 **111**
Boim, *Brazil* R61–027 **105**
Bois, L. des, *N.-W. Terr.* W17+668 **88**
Bois Blanc I., *Michigan* T57+458 **91**
Boisé, *Idaho* V68+436 **92**
Boise City, *Oklahoma* U75+368 **94**
Bois-le-Duc. *See 'sHertogenbosch*
Boissevain, *Manitoba* U60+493 **88**
Boké, *Guinea* N86+110 **80**
Bokhara, R., *New S. Wales* C16–294 **109**
Bokki, *Cameroon* M10+088 **81**
Bokn Fd., *Norway* M58+591 **47**
Bokoro, *Chad* L76+122 **81**
Bolan, *Pakistan* H42+295 **70**
Bolan Pass, *Pakistan* H46+296 **70**
Bolangir, *India* G38+206 **71**
Bolbec, *France* M87+496 **54**
Bole, *Ghana* N14+090 **80**
Bölebyn, *Sweden* L52+654 **46**
Bolgrad, *Ukraine* L08+457 **60**
Bolintin, *Romania* L25+444 **58**
Bolivar, *Argentina* S07–362 **105**
Bolivar, *Colombia* T11+018 **104**
Bolivar, *Missouri* U20+376 **95**
Bolivia, rep., *S. America* — **104**
Bollstabruk, *Sweden* L74+630 **46**
Bolmen, L., *Sweden* M08+569 **47**
Bolobo, *Zaire* L82–022 **82**
Bologna, *Italy* M22+445 **56**
Bologoye, *U.S.S.R.* K66+578 **60**
Bolotnoye, *U.S.S.R.* G34+554 **62**
Bolsena, L. di, *Italy* M19+426 **56**
Bolshevik, Ostrov, *U.S.S.R.* F10+787 **63**
Bolshoy Lyakhovskiy, Ostrov,
  U.S.S.R. C45+735 **63**
Boltaña, *Spain* N00+425 **53**
Bolton, *England* N15+536 **37**
Bolu, *Turkey* K82+408 **74**
Bolus Hd., *Ireland, Rep.* N62+518 **43**
Bolzano, *Italy* M22+465 **56**
Bomal, *Belgium* M57+504 **44**
Bomba, Gulf of, *Libya* L40+322 **81**
Bombala, *New S. Wales* C04–369 **109**
Bombarral, *Portugal* N55+393 **52**
Bombay, *India* H13+190 **70**
Bomfim, *Brazil* Q61–104 **105**
Bomfim, *Brazil* R22–166 **105**
Bomhus, *Sweden* L77+606 **47**
Bom Jardin, *Brazil* S63–067 **104**
Bom Jesus do Gurgueia,
  Brazil Q86–092 **105**
Bømlo, I., *Norway* M59+597 **47**
Bomnak, *U.S.S.R.* D36+547 **63**
Bomoseen, L., *Vermont* S79+437 **96**
Bonaduz, *Switzerland* M33+468 **45**
Bonaire, I., *Neth. Antilles* S49+122 **94**
Bonar Bridge, *Scotland* N26+579 **40**
Bonaventure I.., *Quebec* S25+485 **90**
Bonavista, *Newfoundland* R49+482 **90**
Bonavista B., *Newfoundland* R48+489 **90**
Bondo, *Zaire* L36+038 **82**
Bône ('Annaba), *Algeria* M44+368 **81**
Bone, G. of, *Celebes* D86–035 **65**
Bo'ness, *Scotland* N21+560 **41**
Bongor, *Chad* L88+104 **81**
Bonham, *Texas* U37+336 **95**
Bonifacio & B. de, *Corsica* M35+414 **57**
Bonn, *W. Germany* M48+507 **48**
Bonne Bay, *Newfoundland* R78+496 **90**

Bonne Terre, *Missouri* U04+379 **97**
Bonneval, *France* M82+482 **54**
Bonneville Salt Flats, *Utah* V54+410 **94**
Bonney, L., *S. Aust.* C58-376 **109**
Bonnie Rock, *W. Australia* E09-304 **110**
Bonny, *France* M73+475 **54**
Bonny, *Nigeria* M46+044 **80**
Book Plat., *Colorado* V20+397 **94**
Boolaboolka L., *N.S.W.* C40-326 **109**
Booleroo Centre, *S. Australia* C70-329 **109**
Booligal, *New S. Wales* C31-339 **109**
Boom, *Belgium* M64+511 **44**
Boone, *Iowa* U23+422 **95**
Boone, *N. Carolina* T40+362 **97**
Booneville, *Mississippi* T82+346 **97**
Boon Tsagan Nur, *Mongolia* F36+456 **64**
Boonville, *Missouri* U16+390 **95**
Boonville, *New York* T02+435 **96**
Boorindal, *New S. Wales* C23-304 **109**
Booroorban, *New S. Wales* C32-348 **109**
Boorowa, *New S. Wales* C08-344 **109**
Boort, *Victoria* C38-360 **109**
Boothia, G. of, *N.-W. Terr.* T70+700 **89**
Boothia Pen., *N.-W. Terr.* U20+706 **89**
Bootle, *England* N20+543 **37**
Bootle, *England* N18+534 **37**
Boqueron, *Cuba* T01+200 **101**
Boquete, *Panama* T45+088 **101**
Boramo, *Somalia* K10+100 **83**
Borås, *Sweden* M12+577 **47**
Borazjan, *Iran* J53+292 **75**
Borba, *Brazil* R88-044 **104**
Bordeaux, *France* N04+448 **55**
Borders, reg., *Scotland* N16+555 **41**
Bordertown, *S. Australia* C55-363 **109**
Borga, *Sweden* M00+648 **46**
Borge Fjell, *Norway* M08+653 **46**
Borger, *Netherlands* M49+529 **44**
Borger, *Texas* U68+357 **94**
Borgholm, *Sweden* L80+569 **47**
Borgne, *Haiti* S75+198 **101**
Borisoglebsk, *U. S. S. R.* K17+514 **61**
Borisov, *Byelorussia* L09+551 **60**
Bo River Post, *Sudan* L12+068 **81**
Borja, *Spain* N09+418 **53**
Borjas Blancas, *Spain* M83+415 **53**
Borkum I., *W. Germany* M49+536 **48**
Borlänge, *Sweden* L88+605 **47**
Borneo, *Indonesia* — **65**
Bornholm, I., *Denmark* M00+551 **47**
Bor Nor, *China* E14+476 **64**
Borodino, *U.S.S.R.* K56+554 **60**
Borogontsy, *U.S.S.R.* D20+626 **63**
Borovë, *Albania* L57+397 **59**
Borovichi, *U.S.S.R.* K67+586 **60**
Borris, *Ireland, Rep.* N41+526 **43**
Borrisoleigh, *Ireland, Rep.* N48+527 **43**
Borroloola, *N. Terr., Aust.* C81-161 **111**
Borskoe, *U.S.S.R.* J50+530 **61**
Borūjerd, *Iran* J67+339 **74**
Borzya, *U.S.S.R.* E21+506 **63**
Bosco, *Switzerland* M39+463 **45**
Boscobel, *Wisconsin* U04+431 **91**
Bosiljgrad, *Yugoslavia* L45+425 **58**
Boskoop, *Netherlands* M62+521 **44**
Bosna-Hercegovina, *Yugosl.* L72+443 **58**
Boso Pen, *Japan* C57+353 **68**
Bosobolo, *Zaire* L60+040 **82**
Bosoli, *Botswana* L14-210 **84**
Bosporus, *Turkey* L06+413 **74**
Bossier City, *Louisiana* U22+325 **95**
Bosso, *Niger* M10+136 **81**
Bostan, *Pakistan* H48+304 **70**
Boston, *England* N00+530 **37**
Boston, *Massachusetts* S66+424 **91**
Boston Mts., *Arkansas* U24+358 **95**
Botany B., *New S. Wales* B84-340 **109**
Botera, *Angola* M04-118 **82**
Bothaville, *O.F.S.* L20-274 **84**
Bothnia, G. of, *N.-W. Europe* — **46-47**
Botswana (Bechuanaland) L30-216 **84**
Bouake, *Ivory Coast* N30+078 **80**
Bour, *Cent. Afr. Rep.* L86+060 **81**
Bou Arfa, *Morocco* N12+326 **80**
Bouches-du-Rhône, dep., *Fr.* M59+436 **55**
Bou Djébéha, *Mali* N16+184 **80**
Boudoukou, *Ivory Coast* N18+082 **80**
Boudry, *Switzerland* M49+470 **45**
Bougainville, I., *Solomon Is.* B60-060 **106**
Bougaroun C., *Algeria* M48+368 **80**
Bougie (Begaia), *Algeria* M60+366 **80**
Bougouni, *Mali* N46+114 **80**
Bouillon, *Belgium* M60+498 **44**
Boularderie I., *Nova Scotia* S03+463 **90**
Boulder, *Colorado* V02+400 **94**
Boulder, *W. Australia* D81-309 **110**
Boulder Mt., *Idaho* V56+440 **98**
Boulia, *Queensland* C61-227 **111**
Boulogne, *France* M80+508 **54**
Bouna, *Ivory Coast* N18+092 **80**
Boundary, *Brit. Columbia* W71+564 **88**
Bountiful, *Utah* V42+408 **94**
Bounty Is., *Pacific Ocean* A05-475 **106**
Bourbonnais, prov., *France* M71+465 **54**
Bourem, *Mali* N02+168 **80**
Bourg, *France* M59+462 **54**
Bourg Argental, *France* M63+453 **55**
Bourges, *France* M76+471 **54**
Bourget, L. du, *France* M55+457 **54**
Bourgogne, prov., *France* M61+471 **54**
Bourg St Pierre, *Switz.* M47+460 **45**
Bourke, *New S. Wales* C24-302 **109**
Bourkes, *Ontario* T31+483 **91**
Bournemouth, *England* N11+507 **38**
Bouvet I., *Atlantic Ocean* M70-540 **27**
Bovigny, *Belgium* M55+502 **44**
Bovino, *Italy* L88+413 **57**
Bow R., *Alberta* V44+502 **88**
Bowbells, *N. Dakota* U74+488 **93**
Bowen, *Queensland* C10-200 **111**
Bowen, C., *N.-W. Terr.* S88+720 **89**
Bowie, *Texas* U47+336 **95**
Bowling Green, *Kentucky* T68+370 **97**
Bowling Green, *Missouri* U08+394 **95**
Bowling Green, *Ohio* T52+414 **91**
Bowling Green, *Virginia* T14+380 **97**
Bowman, *N. Dakota* U81+462 **93**
Bowman I., *Antarctica* F20-650 **27**
Bowmanville, *Ontario* T22+439 **91**
Bowral, *New South Wales* B88-345 **109**

Bowser, *Victoria* C22-363 **109**
Box Elder, *Montana* V30+483 **93**
Boxholm, *Sweden* M00+582 **47**
Boxmeer, *Netherlands* M54+516 **44**
Box Tank, *New S. Wales* C47-322 **109**
Boxtel, *Netherlands* M58+516 **44**
Boydton, *Virginia* T20+367 **97**
Boyle, *Ireland, Rep.* N50+540 **42**
Boyne, R., *Ireland, Rep.* N38+537 **42**
Boyne City, *Michigan* T60+453 **91**
Boyoma Falls, *Zaire* L26+002 **82**
Bozeman, *Montana* V36+457 **93**
Bozoum, *Cent. Afr. Rep.* L82+062 **81**
Bra, *Italy* M43+447 **56**
Brabant, prov. *Belgium* M62+508 **44**
Brabant, Noord, prov., *Neth.* M60+516 **44**
Brac, I., *Yugoslavia* L80+433 **56**
Bracadale L., *Scotland* N39+573 **40**
Bracebridge, *Ontario* T26+450 **91**
Bräcke, *Sweden* L88+628 **46**
Bracknell, *England* N05+514 **39**
Brad, *Romania* L43+461 **58**
Braddock, *N. Dakota* U60+465 **93**
Braddock, *Pennsylvania* T29+404 **96**
Bradford, *England* N10+538 **37**
Bradford, *Pennsylvania* T22+419 **96**
Braemar, *Scotland* N20+570 **40**
Braeriach, *Scotland* N22+571 **40**
Braga, *Portugal* N51+416 **52**
Bragado, *Argentina* S03-352 **103**
Bragança, *Brazil* R11-011 **105**
Bragança, *Portugal* N41+418 **52**
Bragança Paulista, *Brazil* R10-228 **105**
Brahmanbaria, *Bangladesh* F83+240 **71**
Brahmaputra R., *India* F70+265 **71**
Braidwood, *Illinois* T79+413 **91**
Braidwood, *New S. Wales* C01-354 **109**
Brail, *Switzerland* M30+466 **45**
Brăila, *Romania* L12+452 **58**
Braine l'Alleud, *Belgium* M64+507 **44**
Braine le Comte, *Belgium* M65+506 **44**
Brainerd, *Minnesota* U25+463 **93**
Braintree, *England* M87+519 **39**
Brak, *Libya* M04+276 **81**
Brampton, *Ontario* T29+437 **91**
Branchville, *S. Carolina* T35+333 **97**
Brandenburg, *E. Germany* M15+524 **48**
Brandon, *England* M86+524 **39**
Brandon, *Manitoba* U59+498 **88**
Brandon B. and Head,
  Ireland, Rep. N61+523 **43**
Brandon Mt., *Ireland, Rep.* N42+525 **43**
Brandsen, *Argentina* R80-352 **103**
Brandvlei, *Cape Province* L56-304 **84**
Branford, *Florida* T48+300 **97**
Braniewa, *Poland* L61+544 **49**
Bransfield Str., *Antarctica* R60-620 **27**
Bransk, *Poland* L43+527 **49**
Brantford, *Ontario* T32+431 **91**
Brantôme, *France* M86+453 **55**
Branxholme, *Victoria* C49-379 **109**
Bras d'or L., *Nova Scotia* S05+459 **90**
Brasilia, *Brazil* R23-160 **105**
Brasov, *Romania* L27+456 **58**
Brassus, le, *Switzerland* M53+466 **45**
Bratislava, *Czechoslovakia* L78+482 **49**
Bratsk, *U.S.S.R.* F19+561 **63**
Brattleboro, *Vermont* S76+428 **96**
Braunau, *Austria* M12+482 **48**
Braunlage, *W. Germany* M26+517 **48**
Braunschweig, *W. Germany* M27+523 **48**
Braunwald, *Switzerland* M36+469 **45**
Brava, *Somalia* K06+012 **83**
Brawley, *California* V63+330 **92**
Bray & Hd., *Ireland, Rep.* N36+532 **43**
Bray Hd., *Ireland, Rep.* N63+519 **43**
Brazil, *Indiana* T73+395 **95**
Brazil, rep., *S. America* — **104-105**
Brazos R., *Texas* U34+294 **95**
Brazos Santiago, *Texas* U43+260 **96**
Brazzaville, *Congo* L88-042 **82**
Brčko, *Yugoslavia* L67+449 **58**
Bream B., *New Zealand* A33-358 **112**
Brechin, *Scotland* N16+567 **41**
Breckenridge, *Minnesota* U40+463 **93**
Brecknock, Pen., *Chile* S70-546 **103**
Brecknock, *See Powys*
Břeclav, *Czechoslovakia* L79+488 **49**
Brecon, *Wales* N20+520 **38**
Brecon Beacons, *Wales* N20+519 **38**
Breda, *Netherlands* M61+516 **44**
Bredasdorp, *Cape Province* L60+346 **84**
Bredene, *Belgium* M72+512 **44**
Bredoo, *New South Wales* C06-360 **109**
Bredy, *U.S.S.R.* H89+525 **61**
Bree, *Belgium* M56+511 **44**
Breidha fjördhur, *Iceland* P54+652 **46**
Breil, *France* M45+439 **55**
Breithorn, mt., *Switzerland* M43+465 **45**
Brejo, *Brazil* Q77-036 **105**
Bremangerland, *Norway* M60+618 **46**
Bremen, *W. Germany* M37+531 **48**
Bremerhaven, *W. Germany* M39+536 **48**
Bremerton, *Washington* W16+475 **92**
Bremgarten, *Switzerland* M40+474 **45**
Brenham, *Texas* U38+302 **95**
Brenner Pass, *Austria-Italy* M21+470 **56**
Breno, *Italy* M28+459 **56**
Brent, *Ontario* T21+461 **91**
Brentford, *England* N02+515 **39**
Brentwood, *England* M88+516 **39**
Brescia, *Italy* M29+455 **56**
Breskens, *Netherlands* M69+514 **44**
Breslau. *See Wroclaw*
Bressay I., *Scotland* N06+601 **40**
Bressuire, *France* N03+468 **54**
Brest, *France* N27+484 **54**
Brest, *Byelorussia* L38+521 **60**
Brest-Litovsk. *See Brest*
Bretagne, prov., *France* N17+480 **54**
Bretcu, *Romania* L22+460 **58**
Breton Sd., *Louisiana* T74+295 **95**
Breugel, *Netherlands* M57+515 **44**
Brevard, *N. Carolina* T46+352 **97**
Breves, *Brazil* R33-116 **105**
Brevik, *Norway* M32+590 **47**
Brewarrina, *New S. Wales* C19-300 **109**
Brewer, *Maine* S52+448 **90**
Brewster Mt., *Antarctica* A75-730 **27**
Brewton, *Alabama* T72+311 **97**
Brežice, *Yugoslavia* L86+459 **56**

Březová, *Czechoslovakia* L75+486 **49**
Brezova, *Czechoslovakia* L81+496 **49**
Bria, *Cent. Afr. Rep.* L48+066 **81**
Briançon. *France* M50+449 **55**
Briare, *France* M73+476 **54**
Bribbaree, *New S. Wales* C12-341 **109**
Bridgehampton, *New York* S74+409 **96**
Bridgend, *Wales* N21+515 **38**
Bridgeport, *Connecticut* S79+412 **91**
Bridgeport, *Nebraska* U79+418 **94**
Bridgeport L., *Texas* U48+332 **95**
Bridgeton, *New Jersey* T01+395 **96**
Bridgetown, *Nova Scotia* S31+449 **90**
Bridgman C., *Arctic Ocean* Q00+840 **26**
Bridgnorth, *England* N15+525 **38**
Bridgton, *Maine* S64+440 **90**
Bridgwater & B., *England* N18+511 **38**
Bridlington & B., *England* N01+541 **37**
Bridport, *Tasmania* C16-410 **109**
Brielle, *Netherlands* M65+519 **44**
Brienz, *Switzerland* M42+468 **45**
Brienzer See, *Switzerland* M42+467 **45**
Brier I., *Nova Scotia* S38+443 **90**
Brig, *Switzerland* M42+463 **45**
Brigels, *Switzerland* M36+468 **45**
Brigham, *Utah* V42+415 **94**
Bright, *Victoria* C18-367 **109**
Brightlingsea, *England* M84+518 **39**
Brighton, *Colorado* U89+400 **94**
Brighton, *England* N01+508 **39**
Brighton, *S. Australia* C69-351 **109**
Brighton, *Tasmania* C16-427 **109**
Brignoles, *France* M54+434 **55**
Brindaban, *India* G74+275 **72**
Brindisi, *Italy* L72+406 **57**
Brinkley, *Arkansas* U08+349 **97**
Brinkworth, *S. Australia* C70-337 **109**
Brione, *Switzerland* M37+463 **45**
Brioude, *France* M70+453 **55**
Brisbane, *Queensland* B71-274 **111**
Brissago, *Switzerland* M38+461 **45**
Bristol, *England* N15+515 **38**
Bristol, *New Brunswick* S45+465 **90**
Bristol, *Pennsylvania* T00+401 **96**
Bristol, *Rhode Island* S68+417 **96**
Bristol, *Tennessee* T43+366 **97**
Bristol B., *Alaska* Y60+580 **99**
Bristol Channel, *England* N23+513 **38**
Bristol I., *South Sandwich Is.* P80-580 **27**
British Columbia, prov. *Canada* — **88**
British Guiana, *See Guyana*
British Honduras, *See Belize*
British Isles, *N.-W. Europe* — **34**
Brito, *Nicaragua* T65+114 **101**
Britonto, *Italy* L79+411 **57**
Britstown, *Cape Province* L38-306 **84**
Brive-la-Gaillarde, *France* M81+452 **55**
Briviesca, *Spain* N20+425 **52**
Brno, *Czechoslovakia* L80+492 **49**
Broach, *India* H12+216 **70**
Broad B., *Scotland* N37+582 **40**
Broadalbin, *New York* S85+431 **91**
Broadford, *Pennsylvania* T27+401 **96**
Broadford, *Scotland* N36+572 **40**
Broadhaven, *Ireland, Rep.* N60+543 **42**
Broadus, *Montana* V02+455 **93**
Brock I., *N.-W. Territories* V50+776 **88**
Brockton, *Massachusetts* S66+421 **96**
Brockville, *Ontario* T04+446 **91**
Brod, *Yugoslavia* L53+415 **58**
Brodeur Pen., *N.-W. Terr.* T75+723 **89**
Brodhead, *Wisconsin* T86+427 **91**
Brodick, *Scotland* N31+556 **41**
Brodribb, *Victoria* C08-377 **109**
Broek-in-Waterland,
  Netherlands M60+524 **44**
Broglio, *Switzerland* M38+464 **45**
Broken B., *New S. Wales* B83-336 **109**
Broken Bow, *Nebraska* U58+414 **95**
Broken Hill, *Zambia* L10-144 **83**
Broken Hill, *New S. Wales* C51-319 **109**
Bromberg. *See Bydgoszcz*
Bromley, *England* N00+514 **39**
Bromptonville, *Quebec* S72+455 **91**
Brønnøysund, *Norway* M16+655 **46**
Bronte, *Sicily* M01+378 **57**
Brookfield, *Missouri* U18+498 **95**
Brookhaven, *Mississippi* U02+316 **95**
Brookings, *Oregon* W26+421 **92**
Brookings, *S. Dakota* U40+444 **93**
Brooklyn, *Iowa* U14+417 **95**
Brooklyn, *New York* S84+406 **96**
Brooklyn, *Nova Scotia* S28+441 **90**
Brooks Ra., *Alaska* Y50+674 **99**
Brook's Point, *Philippines* E13+089 **65**
Brookville, *Pennsylvania* T25+411 **96**
Broom L., *Scotland* N31+579 **40**
Broome, *W. Australia* D76-178 **110**
Brora, *Scotland* N23+580 **40**
Brosna R., *Ireland, Rep.* N48+532 **43**
Brough Hd., *Orkney, Scot.* N20+592 **40**
Broughton, *England* N19+543 **37**
Broughty Ferry, *Scotland* N17+565 **41**
Broumov, *Czechoslovakia* L82+506 **49**
Brouwershaven, *Netherlands* M67+517 **44**
Brown, Mt., *S. Australia* C72-325 **109**
Brown's Valley, *Minnesota* U41+456 **93**
Brownsville, *Kentucky* T68+372 **97**
Brownsville, *Tennessee* T86+356 **97**
Brownsville, *Texas* U45+259 **94**
Brownville, *Maine* S54+453 **90**
Brownwood, *Texas* U54+316 **95**
Brownwood, L., *Texas* U55+318 **95**
Broxburn, *Scotland* N21+559 **41**
Brozas, *Spain* N41+396 **52**
Bruce Coast, *Antarctica* P25-730 **27**
Bruce Mt., *W. Australia* E08-226 **110**
Bruce Mines, *Ontario* T53+463 **91**
Bruck an der Mur, *Austria* M13+473 **48**
Bruff, *Ireland, Rep.* N51+525 **43**
Bruges, *Belgium* M71+512 **44**
Brugg, *Switzerland* M41+475 **45**
Brugge, *See Bruges*
Bruin Pk., *Utah* V32+396 **94**
Bruly, *Belgium* M63+500 **44**
Brummen, *Netherlands* M53+521 **44**
Brunei & state, *Borneo* E31+050 **65**
Brunette Downs, *N.T., Aust.* C85-184 **111**
Brunflo, *Sweden* M01+631 **46**
Brunn. *See Brno*
Brunner, *New Zealand* A52-425 **112**

Brunssum, *Netherlands* M54+509 **44**
Brunswick. *See Braunschweig*
Brunswick, *Georgia* T39+312 **97**
Brunswick, *Maine* S60+439 **90**
Brunswick, *Maryland* T15+393 **96**
Brunswick B., *W. Australia* D61-152 **110**
Brunswick, Pen. de, *Chile* S70-535 **103**
Bruny I., *Tasmania* C16-434 **109**
Brusa. *See Bursa*
Brusartsi, *Bulgaria* L42+437 **58**
Brush, *Colorado* U82+402 **94**
Brusio, *Switzerland* M29+463 **45**
Brussel (Brussels). *See Bruxelles*
Bruthen, *Victoria* C13-377 **109**
Bruxelles (Brussels),
  Belgium M64+508 **44**
Bruzual, *Venezuela* S56+079 **104**
Bryan Coast, *Antarctica* T30-750 **27**
Bryansk, *U.S.S.R.* K64+533 **60**
Bryce Canyon Nat. Park, *Ut.* V47+377 **92**
Brynmawr, *Wales* N19+518 **38**
Bryson, *Quebec* T10+457 **91**
Bryson City, *N. Carolina* T51+354 **97**
Brzeg, *Poland* L75+509 **49**
Brzesko, *Poland* L56+500 **49**
Bsharri, *Lebanon* K54+343 **76**
Bua, *Angola* M10-072 **82**
Buayan, *Philippines* D59+061 **65**
Bubasa, *Ethiopia* K16+088 **83**
Bubiyan I., *The Gulf* J71 + 298 **74**
Bubulu, *Uganda* K64+008 **83**
Bucaramanga, *Colombia* S79+072 **104**
Buchach, *Ukraine* L27+491 **60**
Buchan, *Victoria* C11-374 **109**
Buchan Ness, *Scotland* N11+575 **40**
Buchanan, L., *Queensland* C25-216 **111**
Buchanan L., *Texas* U51+308 **95**
Buchardo, *Argentina* S21-347 **103**
Bucharest. *See Bucuresti*
Buchs, *Switzerland* M33+472 **45**
Buckhannon, *West Virginia* T31+389 **91**
Buckie, *Scotland* N18+577 **40**
Buckingham, *Quebec* T03+456 **91**
Buckingham & co., *England* N06+520 **39**
Buckley, *New Zealand* A10-384 **112**
Bucksport, *Maine* S53+446 **90**
Buctouche, *New Brunswick* S28+465 **90**
Bucuresti, *Romania* L23+444 **58**
Bud, *Norway* M48+630 **46**
Buda, *Texas* U47+301 **95**
Budaia, *Saudi Arabia* K10+230 **74**
Budapest, *Hungary* L66+475 **49**
Budaun, *India* G65+282 **73**
Bud Bud, *India* G14+233 **73**
Buddh Gaya, *India* G30+247 **73**
Bude, *England* N27+508 **38**
Budesti, *Romania* L21+442 **58**
Budhana, *India* G76+293 **72**
Budleigh Salterton, *England* N20+506 **38**
Budva, *Yugoslavia* L67+423 **58**
Buea, *Cameroon* M36+042 **81**
Buenaventura, *Colombia* T12+040 **104**
Buena Vista, *Georgia* T57+323 **97**
Buena Vista, *Virginia* T26+377 **97**
Buenos Aires, *Argentina* R81-346 **103**
Buenos Aires, *Colombia* S60-032 **104**
Buenos Aires, L.,
  Chile-Argentina S76-465 **103**
Bufa, mt., *Mexico* U89+207 **100**
Buffalo, *Minnesota* U23+452 **93**
Buffalo, *Missouri* U19+377 **97**
Buffalo, *New York* T23+429 **91**
Buffalo L., *N.-W. Terr.* V63+602 **88**
Buffalo, *S. Dakota* U82+456 **93**
Buffalo, *Wyoming* V10+444 **93**
Buff City, *Tennessee* T41+365 **97**
Bufumine, *Chad* L84+150 **81**
Bug. R., *Poland, etc.* L51+525 **49**
Buga, *Colombia* T08+038 **104**
Bugulma, *U.S.S.R.* J43+545 **61**
Buguruslan, *U.S.S.R.* J46+536 **61**
Builth Wells, *Wales* N20+521 **38**
Buinsk, *U.S.S.R.* J70+550 **61**
Buique, *Brazil* Q43-086 **105**
Buitenpost, *Netherlands* M53+532 **44**
Bujumbura, *Burundi* L04-034 **83**
Buka, I., *Solomon Is.* B60-050 **106**
Bukama, *Zaire* L24-092 **82**
Bukavu, *Zaire* L06-026 **83**
Bukene, *Tanzania* K74-042 **83**
Bukhara, *Uzbek* H64+398 **62**
Bukoba, *Tanzania* K78-014 **83**
Bukwimba, *Tanzania* K70-028 **83**
Bülach, *Switzerland* M39+475 **45**
Bulagan, *Mongolia* F09+488 **64**
Bulan, *Philippines* D67+125 **65**
Bulandshahr, *India* G73+284 **72**
Bulawayo, *Zimbabwe* L08-202 **84**
Bulgaria, *Europe* L30+425 **51**
Bulinski, *U.S.S.R.* D70+680 **63**
Bullange, *Belgium* M52+504 **44**
Buller, Mt., *Victoria* C21-371 **109**
Buller R., *New Zealand* A48-418 **112**
Bulli, *New S. Wales* B84-343 **109**
Bulloo Cr., *Queensland* C40-280 **111**
Bull Shoals Res., *Arkansas* U17+365 **95**
Bulnes, *Chile* S74-366 **103**
Bulo Burti, *Somalia* J86+038 **83**
Bulsar, *India* H12+206 **70**
Bulu, mt., *Borneo* E25+028 **65**
Bulun, *U.S.S.R.* D46+709 **63**
Bulun Tokhor, *China* G15+470 **64**
Bumba, *Zaire* L44+020 **82**
Buna, *Kenya* K30-012 **83**
Buna, *Papua New Guinea* C10-087 **111**
Bunbury, *W. Australia* E26-332 **110**
Bunclody, *Ireland, Rep.* N40+526 **43**
Buncrana, *Ireland, Rep.* N45+551 **42**
Bundaberg, *Queensland* B76-248 **111**
Bundarra, *New S. Wales* B84-302 **109**
Bundi, *India* G86+254 **70**
Bundoran, *Ireland, Rep.* N50+545 **42**
Bungay, *England* M81+525 **39**
Bungo, *Angola* L86-074 **82**
Bungo Str., *Japan* D16+330 **68**
Buninyong, *Victoria* C37-377 **109**
Bunker, *Missouri* U18+377 **97**
Bunkie, *Louisiana* U13+309 **95**
Bunschoten, *Netherlands* M58+522 **44**
Buochs, *Switzerland* M39+470 **45**
Buolkalakh, *U.S.S.R.* E02+731 **63**

Buorkhaya, Guba, U.S.S.R. D20+720 63
Buq, Iran H81+286 75
Buraida, Saudi Arabia K05+265 74
Bur Akaba, Somalia K06+026 83
Buram, Sudan L30+108 81
Burao, Somalia J86+094 83
Buraq, Syria K51+332 76
Burazjun, Iran J35+299 75
Burchun, China G19+477 64
Burd, Jebel, Saudi Arabia K35+272 74
Burdekin, R., Queensland C20-200 111
Burdur, Turkey K88+377 74
Burdwan, India G12+232 73
Bureå, Sweden L53+646 46
Bureinskiy Khrebet, U.S.S.R. D10+500 63
Bureir, Israel K62+316 76
Büren, Switzerland M46+471 45
Bureya, U.S.S.R. D31+496 63
Burg, Den, Netherlands M68+517 44
Burgas, Bulgaria L15+425 58
Burgaw, N. Carolina T18+346 97
Burgdorf, Switzerland M44+471 45
Burgenland, prov., Austria L82+473 49
Burgess Hill, England N01+509 39
Burghersdorp, Cape Province L22-310 84
Burgos, Spain N22+423 52
Burhanpur, India G82+213 70
Buria, India G76+302 72
Burity, Brazil Q78-039 105
Burkesville, Kentucky T62+368 97
Burketown, Queensland C63-176 111
Burkeville, Virginia T19+372 97
Burks Falls, Ontario T26+457 91
Burley, Idaho V54+426 94
Burlington, Colorado U74+392 94
Burlington, Iowa U07+408 95
Burlington, New Jersey S89+402 96
Burlington, Ontario T29+434 91
Burlington, Vermont S79+445 91
Burlington, Wisconsin T80+427 95
Burlyuk, U.S.S.R. K68+448 80
Burma, S. Asia F50+210 31
Burnak, U.S.S.R. K21+518 61
Burnham, England N18+512 38
Burnham-on-Crouch, Eng. M85+516 39
Burnie, Tasmania C25-411 109
Burnley, England N14+538 37
Burns, New South Wales C54-321 10ʋ
Burns, Oregon V85+436 92
Burnside R., N.-W. Terr. V25+661 88
Burntisland, Scotland N19+561 41
Burra, S. Australia C66-336 109
Burren Junction, N.S.W. C06-301 109
Burriana, Spain N01+399 53
Burrinjuck & Res., N.S.W. C09-350 109
Burrow Hd., Scotland N26+547 41
Burrundie, N. Terr., Aust. D19-134 110
Burry Port & Inlet, Wales N26+517 38
Bursa, Turkey L06+402 74
Burt L., Michigan T58+455 91
Burton-in-Kendal, England N16+542 37
Burtonport, Ireland, Rep. N50+549 42
Burton-upon-Trent, England N10+528 37
Burträsk, Sweden L56+645 46
Burtundy, New S. Wales C47-337 109
Buru I., Indonesia D50-034 65
Burullus L., Egypt K86+314 81
Burum, Yemen, South J66 + 143 74
Burundi, Cent. Africa L00-035 83
Burunurt, Mongolia E39+467 64
Bury, England N14+536 37
Buryatskaya A.S.S.R.,
    U.S.S.R. E60+527 63
Bury St Edmunds,
    England M86+522 39
Busembatia, Uganda K68+006 83
Bushehr (Bushire), Iran J54+289 75
Bushmills, N. Ireland N39+552 42
Bushnell, Florida T43+286 97
Busra, Syria K51+325 76
Bussa, Nigeria M62+102 80
Bussaco, Portugal N50+404 52
Busselton, W. Australia E28-338 110
Bussum, Netherlands M59+523 44
Bustam, Iran J30+365 75
Buta, Zaire L30+028 82
Butana, India G80+292 72
Buta Ranquil, Argentina S59-370 103
Butaritari, I., Kiribati A40+040 106
Bute, S. Australia C72-339 109
Bute I., Scotland N31+558 41
Bütgenbach, Belgium M53+504 44
Buthidaung, Burma F74+210 71
Butler, Missouri U26+382 95
Butler, Pennsylvania T29+409 91
Butschwil, Switzerland M35+474 45
Butte, Montana V45+460 92
Buttes, Switzerland M51+469 45
Buttevant, Ireland, Rep. N52+522 43
Button Is., Quebec S27+606 89
Butuan, Philippines D57+090 65
Butung I., Indonesia D73-050 65
Buturlinovka, U.S.S.R. K26+508 61
Buxar, India G36+255 73
Buxton, England N11+533 37
Buy, U.S.S.R. K21+586 60
Buyaga, U.S.S.R. D47+597 63
Buyr Nuur, lake, Mongolia E15+475 63
Buzancais, France M82+469 54
Buzău, Romania L19+451 58
Buzuluk, U.S.S.R. J46+528 61
Buzzards B., Massachusetts S65+416 96
Bwahit, mt., Ethiopia K40+132 83
Byam Martin Channel
    North-West Territories V00+762 88
Bydgoszcz, Poland L72+531 49
Byelaya, R., U.S.S.R. J36+558 61
Byelokatay, U.S.S.R. J06+557 61
Byelorussia (White Russia)
    U.S.S.R. L12+540 60
Byelyy, Os., U.S.S.R. H30+730 62
Bygland, Norway M43+588 47
Byglandsfjord, Norway M43+586 47
Bylot, I., N.-W. Territories T20+728 89
Byng Inlet, Ontario T34+457 91
Byrock, New S. Wales C22-306 109
Byron, C., New S. Wales B68-286 111
Byske, Sweden L53+649 46
Bytom, Poland L66+504 49
Bytow, Poland L75+542 49

Caaguazu, Paraguay R66-254 103

Caballo Res., New Mexico V14+330 94
Caballo Cocha, Peru S63-038 104
Caballos, Sierra de los,
    New Mexico V13+329 94
Cabañas, Cuba T47+229 101
Cabanatuan, Philippines D84+155 65
Cabar, Yugoslavia M02+456 56
Cabedello, Brazil Q28-070 105
Cabellos, Uruguay R74-307 103
Cabezas, Bolivia S20-188 104
Cabezo del Buey, Spain N31+387 52
Cabo Blanco, Argentina S35-472 103
Cabo Frio, Brazil Q75-226 105
Cabosa I., Burma F43+128 71
Cabo Verde, Arquipelago de,
    See Cape Verde Is.
Cabra, Spain N27+375 52
Cabrera I., Balearic Is., Spain M72+391 53
Cabrobo, Brazil Q56-086 105
Cabuérniga, Spain N26+432 52
Cabure, Venezuela S58+112 104
Čačak, Yugoslavia L58+439 58
Cacapon R., W. Virginia T21+394 96
Cacequy, Brazil R58-299 103
Cáceres, Spain N38+394 52
Cachinal, Chile S57-250 103
Cachipoque, Angola L64-120 82
Cachoeira, Brazil Q54-127 105
Cachoeira do Iguacu, Arg. R58-257 103
Cachoeira do Sul, Brazil R47-300 103
Caconda, Angola M00-138 82
Cacouna, Quebec S57+479 90
Cadaqués, Spain M71+423 53
Caddo L., Louisiana U24+328 95
Cadereyta, Mexico U60+256 100
Cader Idris, Wales N24+527 38
Cadillac, Michigan T63+443 91
Cadiz, Spain N38+365 52
Cadiz, Gulf of, Spain N43+368 52
Caen, France N02+492 54
Caerleon, Wales N18+516 38
Caernarvon B., Wales N27+525 38
Caernarvon, Wales N26+531 38
Caerphilly, Wales N19+516 38
Cagayan de Oro, Philippines D62+084 65
Cagayan Sulu, I., Phil. E09+071 65
Cagliari & G. di, Sardinia M35+183 101
Caguas, Puerto Rico S36+183 101
Caha Mts., Ireland, Rep. N59+517 43
Cahir, Ireland, Rep. N48+524 43
Cahirsiveen, Ireland, Rep. N61+519 43
Cahore Pt., Ireland, Rep. N37+526 43
Cahors, France M81+444 55
Caibarien, Cuba T27+226 101
Caicara, Bolivar, Venezuela S37+074 104
Caicara, Brazil S31-032 104
Caicara, Monagas, Venezuela S22+098 104
Caicos Is., Bahama Is. S70+216 101
Caihaique, Chile S70-454 103
Cailloma, Peru S70-152 104
Caillou B., Louisiana U06+291 95
Caimanera, Cuba T02+200 101
Caird Coast, Antarctica P40-750 27
Cairn Gorm, Scotland N22+571 40
Cairns, Queensland C25-168 111
Cairn Toul, Scotland N22+570 40
Cairo, Egypt K82+300 81
Cairo, Georgia T55+308 97
Cairo, Illinois T85+370 95
Caister, England M80+527 39
Caistor, England N02+535 37
Caiza, Bolivia S21-217 104
Cajamarca, Peru T21-072 104
Čakovec, Yugoslavia L82+464 56
Cala, Spain N38+380 52
Calabar, Nigeria M40+050 80
Calabozo, Venezuela S44+089 104
Calabria, dep., Italy L80+391 57
Calacoto, Bolivia S53-172 104
Calafat, Romania L42+440 58
Calafate, Argentina S70-503 103
Calais, France M79+510 54
Calais, Maine S44+452 90
Calama, Brazil S17-079 104
Calama, Chile S53-224 103
Calamar, Colombia S89+102 104
Calamar, Colombia S71+019 104
Calamian Group, Phil. E00+120 65
Calamocha, Spain N08+409 53
Calang, Sumatra F57+047 65
Calaoria. See Reggio
Calatayud, Spain N10+414 53
Calava C., Sicily M00+382 57
Calbuco, Chile S79-417 103
Calcasieu L., Louisiana U20+296 95
Calceta, Ecuador T31-008 104
Calchaqui, Argentina S02-299 103
Calcutta, India G09+226 73
Caldas da Rainha, Portugal N55+394 52
Calder R., England N10+537 37
Caldera, Chile S65-271 103
Caldwell, Idaho V70+437 92
Caldwell, Texas U40+305 95
Caledonia, Minnesota U09+436 93
Calella, Spain M73+416 53
Calenzana, Corsica M38+369 55
Caleta Buena, Chile S61-199 103
Caleta Olivia, Argentina S45-464 103
Calgary, Alberta V54+510 88
Cali, Colombia S76+036 104
Calicut, India G86+114 70
California, G. of, Mexico V40+280 100
California, state, U.S.A. V17+404 98
Calimali, Mexico V50+282 100
Calingasta, Argentina S57-313 103
Calla, Spain N08+405 53
Callabonna & L., S. Aust. C59-298 109
Callan, Ireland, Rep. N44+525 43
Callander, Ontario T26+462 91
Callander, Scotland N25+562 41
Callanna, S. Australia C73-296 109
Callao, Peru T13-120 104
Calmon, Brazil R36-267 103
Calmpthout, Belgium M63+514 44
Calpulalpam, Mexico U74+221 100
Caltagirone, Sicily M03+372 57

Caltanissetta, Sicily M06+375 57
Calulo, Angola M00-100 82
Calumet I., Quebec T10+458 91
Calunda, Angola L40-122 82
Calvados, dep., France N03+490 54
Calverton, Virginia T16+386 97
Calvillo, Mexico U77+218 100
Calvinia, Cape Province L60-316 84
Camabatela, Angola L88-084 82
Camaguey, Cuba T18+212 101
Camaguey, Is. de, Cuba T18+223 101
Camana, Peru S77-166 104
Camara, Brazil S16-038 104
Camarat C., France M50+432 55
Camargo, Bolivia S31-206 104
Camargo, Mexico U52+262 100
Camargo, Mexico V01+277 100
Camarones & B., Argentina S35-448 103
Camataqui, Bolivia S32-210 104
Ca-Mau, Vietnam E89+092 69
Ca-Mau, Vietnam F01+086 69
Camaxilo, Angola L66-084 82
Cambados, Spain N53+425 52
Cambay, India H14+223 70
Cambay, G. of, See Khambat
Cambell River, B.C. W32+500 88
Cambodia, S. E. Asia F00+120 69
Cambodia, C. See Ca-mau, Pt.
Cambrai, France M71+502 54
Cambrian Mts., Wales N22+525 38
Cambridge, Massachusetts S67+424 96
Cambridge, New Zealand A27-379 112
Cambridge and Isle of Ely, co.
    England N00+524 37
Camden, Arkansas U17+336 95
Camden, Maine S54+443 90
Camden, New Jersey T01+399 96
Camden, New South Wales B86-340 109
Camden, New York T04+433 91
Camden, S. Carolina T34+343 97
Camden Haven, N.S.W. B74-317 109
Camedo, Switzerland M38+462 45
Cameron, Missouri U29+398 95
Cameron, Texas U42+308 95
Cameron Mts., New Zealand A78-460 112
Camerota, Italy L88+400 57
Cameroon, W. Africa M16+050 82
Cameta, Brazil R27-022 105
Camilla, Georgia T55+312 97
Camina, Chile S57-194 103
Caminha, Portugal N53+418 52
Caminreal, Spain N08+408 53
Camoa, Mexico V25+276 100
Camocim, Brazil Q65-030 105
Camooweal, Queensland C71-200 111
Camorta I., Nicobar Is. F69+081 71
Campana, Argentina R84-341 103
Campana, I., Chile T02-482 103
Campania, dep., Italy M01+411 57
Campas, Mexico V28+300 100
Campbell, Missouri U00+365 97
Campbell B., N.-W. Terr. U85+676 88
Campbell I., Pacific Ocean A62-528 106
Campbell Mt., Yukon X21+646 88
Campbellford, Ontario T17+443 91
Campbellpore, Pakistan H16+338 72
Campbellton, N.B. S40+480 90
Campbelltown, N.S.W. B85-341 109
Campbeltown, Scotland N33+554 41
Campbell Town, Tasmania C15-419 109
Campeche & state, Mexico U03+198 100
Campeche, G. of, Mexico U24+190 100
Camperdown, Victoria C41-383 109
Campiglia Marittima, Italy M27+431 56
Campillos, Spain N28+370 52
Campina Grande, Brazil Q35-074 105
Campinas, Brazil R12-228 105
Campobasso, Italy M02+416 57
Campo Belo, Brazil T02-210 105
Campobello I., N.B S42+449 90
Campo Formosa, Brazil Q62-104 105
Campo Formoso, Brazil R20-170 105
Campo Gallo, Argentina S18-266 103
Campo Grande, Brazil R59-206 105
Campo Largo, Brazil Q87-116 105
Campo Maior, Brazil Q73-048 105
Campo Maior, Portugal N42+390 52
Campos, Brazil Q67-217 105
Campo Sales, Brazil Q63-070 105
Campos Novos, Brazil R78-273 103
Campsie Fells, Scotland N25+560 41
Campulung, Romania L30+453 58
Camrose, Alberta V46+532 88
Camsell Mt., N.-W. Terr. W21+617 88
Canaan, New Brunswick S30+463 90
Canaan, New Hampshire S72+436 91
Canada, North America 88-89
Cañada de Gomez, Argent. S09-327 103
Canadian, Texas U62+359 94
Canadian Channel, Quebec S18+499 90
Canadian R., Oklahoma, etc U67+359 98
Cañadon de las Vacas Arg. S56-506 103
Canakkale, Turkey L22+401 74
Canama, Brazil S72-056 104
Canandaigua, New York T14+429 96
Canandaigua L., New York T14+428 96
Cananea, Mexico V33+310 100
Cananeia, Brazil R18-250 103
Canarias, Islas, Atlantic Oc. P00+280 80
Canarreos, Arch. de los,
    Cuba T44+220 101
Canary Is. See Canarias, Islas
Canas, Portugal N47+405 52
Canaseraga, New York T17+425 96
Canatlan, Mexico U89+244 100
Cañaveral, Spain N38+398 52
Canaveral, C., Florida T34+284 99
Cañaveras, Spain N15+404 53
Canavieiras, Brazil Q54-156 105
Canbelego,·N. South Wales C22-316 109
Canberra, Cap. Terr., Aust. C06-353 109
Canby, Minnesota U38+447 93
Candasnos, Spain N00+415 53
Candelo, New South Wales C02-368 109
Candia. See Iráklion
Canea. See Khania
Canella, Brazil R35-294 103
Canelones, Uruguay R67-345 103
Canete, Chile S80-378 103
Canete, Peru T09-131 104
Cañete, Spain N10+400 53

Cangamba, Angola L60-136 82
Cangandala, Angola L81-098 82
Cangas, Spain N39+431 52
Canguaretama, Brazil Q31-064 105
Canha, Portugal N52+388 52
Canicatti, Sicily M07+373 57
Cankiri, Turkey K68+406 74
Canna, I., Scotland N40+571 40
Cannanore, India G88+120 70
Cannelton, Indiana T71+379 97
Cannes, France M48+435 55
Cannock, England N12+527 38
Canonba, New South Wales C16-313 109
Canon City, Colorado V02+384 94
Canora, Saskatchewan U74+514 88
Canosa, Italy L84+412 57
Canowindra, New S. Wales C08-336 109
Canso & C., Nova Scotia S06+454 90
Canso, Str. of, Nova Scotia S07+455 90
Cantabrica, Cord., Spain N24+429 52
Cantal, dep., France M73+452 55
Cantanhede, Portugal N52+403 52
Canterbury, England M84+513 39
Canterbury, New Brunswick S45+459 90
Canterbury Bight, N.Z. A46-440 112
Canterbury Plains, N.Z. A50-440 112
Can Tho, Vietnam E85+100 69
Canton (Kwangchow), China E40+232 67
Canton, Mississippi U00+326 95
Canton, New York T01+446 91
Canton, Ohio T38+408 91
Canton, S. Dakota U40+432 93
Canton I., Phoenix Is. Z42-030 106
Canton Res., Oklahoma U52+362 95
Canuelas, Argentina R83-351 103
Canutama, Brazil S27-066 104
Canyon de Chelly Nat. Mon.,
    Arizona V26+362 94
Capabarida, Venezuela S63+112 104
Capakcur. See Bingol.
Capana, Brazil S10-058 104
Capao Bonito, Brazil R21-240 103
Cap Chat, Quebec S40+491 90
Cap de la Madeleine, Quebec S75+464 91
Cape Barren I., Tasmania C12-404 109
Cape Breton I., Nova Scotia S06+460 90
Cape Breton Highlands Nat.
    Park, Nova Scotia S04+470 90
Cape Charles, Virginia T06+372 97
Cape Clear, Ireland, Rep. N57+514 43
Cape Coast, Ghana N08+052 80
Cape Cod B., Massachusetts S61+419 96
Cape Fear R., N. Carolina T22+346 97
Cape Girardeau, Missouri T88+373 95
Cape Haitien, Haiti S73+198 101
Cape May, New Jersey T00+389 96
Cape May Court House,
    New Jersey S89+391 96
Cape Province, South Africa L40-300 84
Cape Tormentine, N.B. S23+461 90
Cape Town, Cape Province L70-340 84
Cape Verde Is., Atlantic Ocean P60 + 160 80
Cape York Pen., Queensland C45-132 111
Capelle, la, France M67+500 54
Capilla, Argentina R85-343 103
Capilla del Monte, Argentina S28-309 103
Capitan Mts., New Mexico V02+336 94
Caplan, Quebec S34+481 90
Capoompeta, mt., N.S.W. B78-294 109
Capote Mt., Texas U86+300 94
Cappoquin, Ireland, Rep. N47+521 43
Capraia, I., Italy M31+430 56
Capreol, Ontario T35+467 91
Caprera, I., Sardinia M33+413 57
Capri, I., Italy M04+404 57
Capricorn Chan., Queensland B75-226 111
Caprivi Strip, Namibia ,L40-180 84
Carabaya, Cord. de, Peru S62-140 104
Caracarai, Brazil S05+023 104
Caracas, Venezuela S42+105 104
Caracol, Brazil Q79-093 105
Caragh L., Ireland, Rep. N59+521 43
Caraguatay. Paraguay R71-250 103
Caransebes, Romania L47+454 58
Caraomer, Romania L11+438 58
Carapegua, Paraguay R73-257 103
Caraquet, New Brunswick S30+478 90
Caras, Peru T17-092 104
Caratasca Lag., Honduras T54+154 101
Caratiá, Brazil S26-060 104
Carauari, Brazil S42-048 104
Caravaca, Spain N13+381 53
Caravelas, Brazil Q56-178 105
Caraveli, Peru S81-158 104
Carballino, Spain N48+424 52
Carballo, Spain N52+432 52
Carbonara C., Sardinia M33+391 57
Carbondale, Illinois T86+377 95
Carbondale, Pennsylvania T03+415 96
Carbon Hill, Alabama T75+339 97
Carcajou, Alberta V72+580 88
Carcassone, France M76+432 55
Carcoar, New South Wales C05-337 109
Carcross, Yukon W89+601 88
Carcura, Libya L60-132 81
Cardamom Hills, India G77+100 70
Cardenas, Cuba T37+230 101
Cardiel, L., Argentina S68-490 103
Cardiff, Wales N19+515 38
Cardigan, Wales N28+521 38
Cardigan B., Wales N27+525 38
Cardona, Spain M76+419 53
Cardston, Alberta V50+492 88
Cardwell, Queensland C24-180 111
Carey, L., W. Australia D76-288 110
Carhaix, France N21+483 54
Carhue. See Adolfo Alsina
Caribbean Sea, S. & Cent. America 101
Caribou, Maine S48+469 90
Caribou, Newfoundland R69+490 90
Caribou Mts., Alberta V65+591 88
Caribrod. See Dimitrovgrad
Carichic, Mexico V11+278 100
Carinda, New South Wales C14-305 109
Cariñena, Spain N07+413 53
Carinhanha, Brazil Q83-142 105
Caripito, Venezuela S19+100 104
Carius, Brazil Q57-062 105
Carl, L., Oklahoma U44+362 95

Carlet, *Spain* N03+392 **53**
Carleton, *Quebec* S36+481 **90**
Carleton, Mt., *N.B.* S42+473 **90**
Carleton Place, *Ontario* T07+451 **91**
Carlingford & L.
  Ireland, Rep. N37+540 **42**
Carlinville, *Illinois* U00+392 **95**
Carlisle, *England* N18+549 **37**
Carlisle, *Kentucky* T54+383 **97**
Carlisle, *Pennsylvania* T14+402 **96**
Carlisle, *S. Carolina* T39+346 **97**
Carlos Casares, *Argentina* S08−356 **103**
Carlow & co., *Ireland, Rep.* N42+528 **43**
Carlsbad, *New Mexico* U86+324 **94**
Carlsbad Caverns Nat. Park,
  New Mexico U87+320 **98**
Carlton, *Minnesota* U15+467 **93**
Carmacks, *Yukon* X10+617 **88**
Carman, *Manitoba* U46+496 **88**
Carmarthen, *Wales* N26+518 **38**
Carmarthen B., *Wales* N27+516 **38**
Carmaux, *France* M77+440 **55**
Carmel, *New York* S82+414 **96**
Carmel, Mt., *Israel* K60+327 **76**
Carmelo, *Uruguay* R80−340 **99**
Carmen, *Bolivia* S47−115 **104**
Carmen, *Colombia* T01+097 **104**
Carmen, *Mexico* U11+186 **100**
Carmen I., *Mexico* V36+259 **100**
Carmen de Patagones,
  Argentina S17−407 **103**
Carmensa, *Argentina* S46−352 **103**
Carmi, *Illinois* T79+382 **97**
Carmona, *Spain* N34+375 **52**
Carnarvon, *Cape Province* L48−312 **84**
Carnarvon, *W. Australia* E37−249 **110**
Carndonagh, *Ireland, Rep.* N44+552 **42**
Carnegie, L., *W. Australia* D74−260 **110**
Carnot, *Cent. Afr. Rep.* L84+050 **81**
Carnoustie, *Scotland* N16+565 **41**
Carnsore Pt., *Ireland, Rep.* N38+522 **43**
Caro, *Michigan* T50+435 **91**
Carolina, *Brazil* R15−072 **105**
Carolina, *Transvaal* K88−262 **84**
Caroline I., *Pacific Ocean* Y00−100 **107**
Caroline Is., *Pacific Ocean* C00+050 **106**
Carora, *Venezuela* S60+102 **104**
Carpathian Mts., *Cent. Europe* L42+490 **49**
Carpatii Meridionali, *Rom.* L42+450 **58**
Carpentaria, G. of, *Aust.* C66−140 **111**
Carrantuohill, *Ireland, Rep.* N59+520 **43**
Carrara, *Italy* M29+441 **56**
Carrathool, *New S. Wales* C28−344 **109**
Carrbridge, *Scotland* N23+573 **40**
Carreño, *Spain* N35+434 **52**
Carrickfergus, *N. Ireland* N35+547 **42**
Carrickmacross, *Ireland, Rep.* N40+540 **42**
Carrick-on-Shannon,
  Ireland, Rep. N49+539 **42**
Carrick-on-Suir, *Ireland, Rep.* N45+523 **43**
Carrieton, *S. Australia* C69−324 **109**
Carrington, *N. Dakota* U55+474 **93**
Carrión-de-los-Condes, *Sp.* N28+424 **52**
Carrizo Mts., *Arizona* V26+368 **94**
Carrizo Springs, *Texas* U59+286 **94**
Carrizozo, *New Mexico* V05+336 **94**
Carroll, *Iowa* U30+422 **95**
Carrollton, *Alabama* T79+332 **97**
Carrollton, *Kentucky* T61+387 **91**
Carrollton, *Missouri* U22+394 **95**
Carrowmore L., *Ireland, Rep.* N59+542 **42**
Carroz, le, *Switzerland* M53+466 **45**
Carsamba, *Turkey* K50+411 **74**
Carse of Gowrie, *Scotland* N19+564 **41**
Carson City, *Nevada* V89+392 **92**
Carson Sink, *Nevada* V82+397 **92**
Carstairs, *Scotland* N22+557 **41**
Carstensz G., mt., (Pk. Sukarno)
  Irian Jaya, Indon. C76−040 **65**
Cartagena, *Colombia* T03+105 **104**
Cartagena, *Spain* N06+377 **53**
Cartago, *Colombia* T05+047 **104**
Cartago, *Costa Rica* T53+099 **101**
Cartaxo, *Portugal* N53+391 **52**
Cartaya, *Spain* N43+373 **52**
Carter, *Wyoming* V32+414 **93**
Carter Bar, *Scot.-Eng.* N15+553 **41**
Carteret, *France* N11+494 **54**
Cartersville, *Georgia* T59+342 **97**
Carterton, *New Zealand* A27−410 **112**
Carthage, *Illinois* U07+404 **95**
Carthage, *Missouri* U26+372 **95**
Carthage, *New York* T03+440 **91**
Carthage, *N. Carolin* T27+354 **97**
Carthage, *Tennessee* T66+363 **97**
Cartier, *Ontario* T39+467 **91**
Cartwright, *Labrador* R72+530 **89**
Carumbay, *Bolivia* S13−190 **104**
Carupano, *Venezuela* S19+106 **104**
Carutaperá, *Brazil* R06−012 **105**
Caruthersville, *Missouri* T88+362 **95**
Carvoeiro, *Brazil* S12−014 **104**
Casablanca, *Chile* S69−333 **103**
Casablanca, *Morocco* N46+336 **80**
Casaccia, *Switzerland* M32+464 **45**
Casa Grande, *Arizona* V40+328 **99**
Casas Ibañez, *Spain* N09+393 **53**
Cascade, *Montana* V40+473 **93**
Cascade Ra., *Oregon, etc.* W14+426 **98**
Cascais, *Portugal* N56+387 **52**
Casco B., *Maine* S60+437 **90**
Caserta, *Italy* M04+411 **57**
Caseville, *Michigan* T49+439 **91**
Cashel, *Ireland, Rep.* N47+525 **43**
Casilda, *Argentina* S07−331 **103**
Casilda, *Cuba* T30+217 **101**
Casino, *New South Wales* B72−288 **109**
Casma, *Peru* T20−096 **104**
Casmalia, *California* W04+347 **92**
Caspe, *Spain* N00+413 **53**
Casper, *Wyoming* V08+428 **93**
Caspian Sea, *Europe-Asia* J60+400 **30**
Cassai, *Angola* L48−108 **82**
Cassamba, *Angola* L58−132 **82**
Cassel, *France* M75+508 **54**
Casselton, *N. Dakota* U42+470 **93**
Cassiar Mts., *Brit. Columbia* W55+592 **88**
Cassilis, *New South Wales* C00−320 **109**
Cassinga, *Angola* L84−152 **84**
Cassino, *Brazil* R44−323 **99**
Cassino, *Italy* M07+415 **57**

Cassipore, *Brazil* R37+034 **104**
Cassis, *France* M57+432 **55**
Cassopolis, *Michigan* T66+419 **91**
Cassou, *Upper Volta* N12+116 **80**
Cassville, *Missouri* U23+368 **95**
Castanhal, *Brazil* S14−064 **104**
Castanheiro, *Brazil* S34−002 **104**
Castaño, *Argentina* S58−310 **103**
Castasegna, *Switzerland* M33+463 **45**
Castejaloux, *France* N00+443 **55**
Castellammare & G. di, *Sic.* M13+380 **57**
Castellammare di Stabia,
  Italy M03+407 **57**
Castellane, *France* M51+439 **55**
Castellar de Santiago, *Spain* N19+386 **52**
Castelli, *Argentina* R77−360 **103**
Castello, *Brazil* Q69−053 **105**
Castellón de la Plana. *Spain* N00+400 **53**
Castellote, *Spain* N16+404 **53**
Castelnaudary, *France* M78+433 **55**
Castelo Branco, *Portugal* N45+398 **52**
Castelo de Vide, *Portugal* N44+394 **52**
Castelsarrasin, *France* M83+440 **55**
Castelvetrano, *Sicily* M13+377 **57**
Casterton, *Victoria* C52−376 **109**
Castets, *France* N07+439 **55**
Castillo, mt., *Chile* S74−460 **103**
Castine, *Maine* S53+444 **90**
Castlebar, *Ireland, Rep.* N56+539 **42**
Castlebellingham, *Ireland, Rep.* N38+539 **42**
Castleblayney, *Ireland, Rep.* N40+541 **42**
Castlecomer, *Ireland, Rep.* N43+528 **43**
Castlederg, *N. Ireland* N46+547 **42**
Castledermot, *Ireland, Rep.* N41+529 **43**
Castle Douglas, *Scotland* N24+549 **41**
Castleisland, *Ireland, Rep.* N57+522 **43**
Castlemaine, *Ireland, Rep.* N58+522 **43**
Castlemaine, *Victoria* C35−371 **109**
Castlemartyr, *Ireland, Rep.* N48+519 **43**
Castlepollard, *Ireland, Rep.* N44+537 **42**
Castlerea, *Ireland, Rep.* N51+538 **42**
Castlereagh, R., *N.S.W.* C10−308 **109**
Castle Rock, *Utah* V37+412 **94**
Castle Rock, mt., *Oregon* V79+440 **92**
Castle Rock Buttes, *S. Dak.* U81+450 **93**
Castletown, *Scotland* N20+586 **40**
Castletown Bere, *Ireland, Rep.* N60+517 **43**
Castlewellan, *N. Ireland* N35+542 **42**
Castres, *France* M77+436 **55**
Castro, *Brazil* R30−248 **103**
Castro, *Chile* S83−424 **103**
Castro Marin, *Portugal* N44+372 **52**
Castropol, *Spain* N42+435 **52**
Castrovillari, *Italy* L83+398 **57**
Castuera, *Spain* N33+388 **52**
Cat I., *Bahamas, The* T04+243 **101**
Catabola, *Angola* L76−122 **82**
Catak, *Turkey* K14+382 **74**
Catamarca, *Argentina* S35−285 **103**
Catanduanes, I., *Philippines* D64+137 **65**
Catania & G. di, *Sicily* M00+375 **57**
Catanzaro, *Italy* L80+389 **57**
Catarina la Grande, *Mexico* U19+163 **100**
Cataraman, *Philippines* D62+124 **65**
Catastrophe, C., *S. Australia* C84−350 **111**
Catabalogan, *Philippines* D60+116 **65**
Catahoula L., *Louisiana* U13+315 **95**
Cateau, le, *France* M69+501 **54**
Cathcart, *New S. Wales* C04−368 **109**
Cathedral Mt., *Texas* U82+302 **94**
Catingueiro, *Brazil* R20−113 **105**
Catlettsburg, *Kentucky* T46+384 **97**
Catonsville, *Maryland* T10+393 **96**
Catorce, *Mexico* U66+237 **100**
Catrilo, *Argentina* S21−363 **103**
Catskill, *New York* S83+422 **96**
Catskill Mts., *New York* S86+422 **96**
Cattaraugus, *New York* T23+424 **96**
Cauquenes, *Chile* S74−359 **103**
Causapscal, *Quebec* S43+484 **90**
Cauto, R., *Cuba* T13+206 **101**
Cauvery R., *India* G72+113 **70**
Caux, *French Guiana* R42+043 **105**
Cavalcante, *Brazil* R15−139 **105**
Cavallo Pass, *Texas* U38+283 **94**
Cavan & co., *Ireland, Rep.* N44+540 **42**
Cave, *New Zealand* A54−443 **112**
Cavendish, *Victoria* C48−375 **109**
Cavergno, *Switzerland* M38+463 **45**
Caviana, I., *Brazil* R31+002 **105**
Cawnpore. See Kanpur
Caxias, *Brazil* Q76−004 **104**
Caxias, *Brazil* Q80−048 **105**
Caxias do Sul, *Brazil* R37−293 **103**
Cayambe, *Ecuador* T19+011 **104**
Cayenne, *French Guiana* R44+048 **105**
Cayes, Les, *Haiti* S83+182 **101**
Cayo, *Belize* T80+172 **101**
Cayuga, *Ontario* T29+430 **91**
Cayuga, L., *New York* T10+427 **96**
Cazage, *Angola* L56−112 **82**
Cazalla de la Sierra, *Spain* N35+379 **52**
Cazenovia, *New York* S05+429 **96**
Cazin, *Yugoslavia* L85+450 **56**
Cazorla, *Spain* N18+379 **52**
Ceará. See Fortaleza
Ceanannus Mór, *see* Kells
Ceara Mirim, *Brazil* Q32−056 **105**
Cebaco, I., *Panama* T37+075 **101**
Cebollar, *Argentina* S39−291 **103**
Cebollera, *Spain* N16+420 **53**
Cebu, *Brazil* D66+104 **65**
Cecil, *Georgia* T50+310 **97**
Ceclavin, *Spain* N41+398 **52**
Cedar, *Utah* V34+394 **94**
Cedar L., *Texas* U74+328 **94**
Cedar Mts., *Oregon* V77+432 **92**
Cedar Ra., *Utah* V47+404 **92**
Cedarburg, *Wisconsin* T78+433 **91**
Cedar City, *Utah* V48+376 **94**
Cedar Falls, *Iowa* U14+426 **95**
Cedar Key, *Florida* T49+293 **99**
Cedar Rapids, *Iowa* U10+420 **95**
Cedar Springs, *Michigan* T63+433 **91**
Cedral, *Mexico* U64+238 **100**
Cedros, I., *Mexico* V62+281 **100**
Ceduna, *S. Australia* D08−320 **111**
Cefalu, *Sicily* M06+380 **57**
Cegled, *Hungary* L61+472 **49**
Cehegin, *Spain* N11+381 **53**
Ceiba, la, *Honduras* T72+157 **101**

Cejita Blanca, *New Mexico* V12+363 **94**
Celanova, *Spain* N48+422 **52**
Celaya, *Mexico* U65+206 **100**
Celebes (Sulawesi), *Indonesia* E00−023 **65**
Celebes Sea, *Indonesia* E00+038 **65**
Celje, *Yugoslavia* L88+462 **56**
Celle, *W. Germany* M30+526 **48**
Celles, *Belgium* M69+507 **44**
Cemisgezek, *Turkey* K36+391 **74**
Cenis, Mte., *France* M49+452 **56**
Center, *Texas* U25+318 **95**
Centerville, *Alabama* T73+329 **97**
Centerville, *Iowa* U17+407 **95**
Centerville, *Missouri* U06+373 **97**
Centerville, *Tennessee* T75+357 **97**
Central. reg.. *Scotland* N26+562 **41**
Central, Cord., *Peru* T14−078 **104**
Central African Rep., *Afr.* L60+070 **81**
Central America T66+140 **101**
Central City, *Nebraska* U48+410 **95**
Centralia, *Illinois* T85+386 **95**
Centralia, *Washington* W18+467 **92**
Central Lake, *Michigan* T62+452 **91**
Centreville, *New Brunswick* S46+465 **90**
Cephalonia. See Kefallinia
Ceram Sea, *Indonesia* D40−030 **65**
Cerignola, *Italy* L85+413 **57**
Cerigo. See Kithira I.
Cerigotto. See Andikithira I.
Cerknica, *Yugoslavia* M04+458 **56**
Cermik, *Turkey* K33+382 **74**
Cernauti. See Chernovtsy
Cerralvo, *Mexico* U59+261 **100**
Cerralvo, I., *Mexico* V29+243 **100**
Cerreto Sannita, *Italy* M03+413 **57**
Cerro de Pasco, *Peru* T08−107 **104**
Cervera de Pisuerga, *Spain* N27+429 **52**
Cesena, *Italy* M17+441 **56**
Cesis, *Latvia* L29+573 **47**
Ceská Lipa, *Czechoslovakia* M03+507 **48**
Ceské Budějovice, *Czech.* M03+489 **48**
Cessnock, *New S. Wales* B82−329 **109**
Cetinje, *Yugoslavia* L66+424 **58**
Cetraro, *Italy* L84+395 **57**
Cette. See Sete
Ceuta, *N. Africa* N32+358 **80**
Ceuta, B. de, *Mexico* V13+241 **100**
Cevennes, *France* M68+445 **55**
Ceyhan, *Turkey* K58+370 **74**
Ceylon I., & rep. See Sri Lanka
Chabatok, *Quebec* S83+504 **90**
Chablis, *France* M67+478 **54**
Chacabuco, *Argentina* S03−346 **103**
Chacance, *Chile* S58−223 **103**
Chachapoyas, *Peru* T17−064 **104**
Chachoengsao, *Thailand* F24+136 **69**
Chaco, R., *New Mexico* V18+360 **94**
Chad, rep., *Cent. Africa* L70+150 **81**
Chad (Tchad), L., *Chad* M04+134 **81**
Chadron, *Nebraska* U78+428 **94**
Chadwick, *Missouri* U18+369 **97**
Chagai, *Pakistan* H62+293 **70**
Chagda, *U.S.S.R.* D26+568 **63**
Chagny, *France* M61+469 **54**
Chagos Arch., *Indian Ocean* H13−057 **77**
Chah Bahâr, *Iran* H86+253 **75**
Chaibassa, *India* G25+225 **73**
Chaise Dieu, *France* M68+453 **55**
Chakansur, *Afghanistan* H77+311 **75**
Chakia, *India* G40+251 **73**
Chaksam, *Tibet* F85+293 **71**
Chakwal, *Pakistan* H13+329 **72**
Chala, *Peru* S86−158 **104**
Chalchihuites, *Mexico* U84+236 **100**
Chalcis. See Khalkis
Chaleur B., *Quebec-N.B.* S34+479 **90**
Chalham, I., *Chile* S86−507 **103**
Chalhuanca, *Peru* S81−143 **104**
Chaling, *China* E38+269 **67**
Chalisgaon, *India* H00+205 **70**
Chalk River, *Ontario* T14+460 **91**
Challapata, *Bolivia* S41−189 **104**
Chalons-sur-Marne, *France* M64+489 **54**
Chalon-sur-Saône, *France* M61+468 **54**
Chalus, *France* M84+456 **54**
Cham, *W. Germany* M14+492 **48**
Chama, *New Mexico* V08+368 **94**
Chaman, *Pakistan* H51+309 **70**
Chamba, *India* G83+326 **72**
Chamberlain L., *Maine* S56+462 **90**
Chamberlain, *S. Dakota* U58+438 **93**
Chambersburg, *Pennsylvania* T17+399 **96**
Chambéry, *France* M54+456 **54**
Chambivas, *Brazil* R22−066 **105**
Chambord, *Quebec* S72+484 **90**
Chamcal, *Argentina* S37−304 **103**
Chamo, L., *Ethiopia* K44+058 **83**
Chamonix, *France* M49+459 **54**
Champa, *India* G44+220 **73**
Champagne, prov., *France* M65+489 **54**
Champaign, *Illinois* T80+402 **95**
Champerico, *Guatemala* U11+142 **100**
Champlain L., *N.Y.-Vermont* S80+442 **91**
Champlitte, *France* M57+476 **54**
Champlon, *Belgium* M67+501 **44**
Chamusca, *Portugal* N51+393 **52**
Chanco, *Chile* S75−356 **103**
Chancy, *Switzerland* M54+462 **45**
Chanda, *India* G60+200 **70**
Chandausi, *India* G68+284 **73**
Chandeleur Is & Sd., *La.* T84+298 **95**
Chanderi, *India* G71+247 **73**
Chandernagore, *India* G10+228 **73**
Chandigarh, *India* G79+307 **72**
Chandod, *India* H08+220 **70**
Chandpur, *Bangladesh* F86+233 **71**
Chandpur, *India* G70+292 **73**
Chanduria, *Bangladesh* G06+229 **73**
Changchih, *China* E42+361 **66**
Changchow, *China* E14+244 **67**
Changchow, *China* E01+318 **66**
Changchun, *China* D57+438 **64**
Ch'angkang, *China* E68+192 **64**
Changkiakow, *China* E31+408 **66**
Changlo, *China* E07+367 **66**
Changpeh, *China* E31+411 **66**
Changping, *China* E22+403 **66**
Changpu, *China* E13+242 **67**
Changsha, *China* E42+282 **67**
Changshan, *China* E09+289 **67**

Changte. See Anyang
Changteh, *China* E51+290 **67**
Changting, *China* E22+257 **67**
Changyeh, *China* F26+389 **64**
Channel Is., *English Chan.* N15+494 **54**
Chantada, *Spain* N47+426 **52**
Chanthaburi, *Thailand* F17+126 **69**
Chantilly, *France* M75+492 **54**
Chanute, *Kansas* U33+376 **95**
Chany, Oz., *U.S.S.R.* G75+550 **62**
Chao, R., *Thailand* F150 **65**
Chaoan, *China* E20+237 **67**
Chaochow, *China* E20+237 **67**
Chao Hu, *China* F08+273 **66**
Chapala, L., *Mexico* U78+202 **100**
Chapayevsk, *U.S.S.R.* J62+530 **61**
Chapleau, *Ontario* T50+478 **91**
Chapell Is., *Tasmania* C14−403 **109**
Chapra, *India* G31+258 **73**
Char, *Mauritania* N78+216 **80**
Chara, *U.S.S.R.* E10+570 **63**
Charagua, *Bolivia* S19−197 **104**
Charana, *Bolivia* S57−175 **104**
Charcot, I., *Antarctica* S85−700 **27**
Chard, *England* N18+509 **38**
Chardzhou, *Turkmen* H70+390 **62**
Charente, dep., *France* M89+458 **54**
Charente, R., *France* N04+457 **54**
Charente-Maritime, dep.,
  France N06+458 **54**
Chari R., *Chad* L80+108 **81**
Charikar, *Afghanistan* H35+350 **75**
Charité, la, *France* M72+472 **54**
Chariton, *Iowa* U20+410 **95**
Charkhari, *India* G62+254 **73**
Charleroi, *Belgium* M63+504 **44**
Charles R., *Massachusetts* S68+424 **96**
Charles City, *Iowa* U16+430 **95**
Charleston, *Illinois* T80+394 **95**
Charleston, *Mississippi* U00+340 **97**
Charleston, *Missouri* T86+370 **95**
Charleston, *Queensland* C38−186 **111**
Charleston, S., *Carolina* T30+328 **97**
Charleston, W. *Virginia* T40+384 **97**
Charleston Pk., *Nevada* V64+362 **92**
Charlestown, *Ireland, Rep.* N52+539 **42**
Charles Town, W. *Virginia* T17+393 **96**
Charlestown (Rath Luire),
  Ireland. Rep. N52+523 **43**
Charleville, *France* M62+498 **54**
Charleville, *Queensland* C23−264 **111**
Charlevoix, *Michigan* T62+453 **91**
Charlotte, *Michigan* T59+426 **91**
Charlotte, *N. Carolina* T35+352 **97**
Charlotte, *New York* T16+433 **91**
Charlotte Amalie, *Virgin Is.* S29+184 **101**
Charlotte Harbor, *Florida* T43+270 **97**
Charlottenburg, *Germany* M10+525 **48**
Charlottesville, *Virginia* T21+381 **97**
Charlottetown, *P.E.I.* S19+463 **90**
Charlton, *Victoria* C40−363 **109**
Charlton I., *N.-W. Terr.* T26+517 **89**
Charmey, *Switzerland* M47+466 **45**
Charnwood Forest, *England* N08+527 **37**
Charolles, *France* M64+464 **54**
Charrote, Sierra, *Texas* U72+308 **94**
Charsadda, *Pakistan* H19+342 **72**
Charters Towers, *Queensland* C23−200 **111**
Chartres, *France* M81+485 **54**
Charvonnex, *France* M53+460 **45**
Chascomus, *Argentina* R78−356 **103**
Chaska, *Minnesota* U22+448 **93**
Chasseneuil, *France* M87+458 **54**
Châteaubriant, *France* N08+477 **54**
Château Chinon, *France* M67+471 **54**
Château-du-Loir, *France* M87+477 **54**
Châteaudun, *France* M82+481 **54**
Château Gontier, *France* N04+478 **54**
Château-la-Valliere, *France* M88+475 **54**
Chateaulin, *France* N25+482 **54**
Châteauneuf-en-Thymerais,
  France M82+486 **54**
Châteaurenault. *France* M85+476 **54**
Châteauroux, *France* M81+468 **54**
Château Salins, *France* M51+488 **54**
Château Thierry. *France* M70+491 **54**
Châteauvillain, *France* M60+480 **54**
Châtelet, *Belgium* M63+504 **44**
Châtellerault, *France* M87+468 **54**
Châtel-St Denis, *Switzerland* M49+465 **45**
Chatfield, *Minnesota* U13+438 **93**
Chatham, *England* M87+514 **39**
Chatham, *New Brunswick* S33+471 **90**
Chatham, *New York* S82+424 **91**
Chatham, *Ontario* T43+424 **91**
Chatham, *Virginia* T27+368 **97**
Chatham Is., *Pacific Ocean* Z70−442 **106**
Chatillon-sur-Seine, *France* M63+478 **54**
Chatra, *India* G31+242 **73**
Chatrapur, *India* G30+194 **71**
Châtre, la, *France* M78+466 **54**
Chattahoochee R., *Georgia* T59+309 **99**
Chattanooga, *Tennessee* T62+350 **97**
Chaudiere R., *Quebec* S67+467 **91**
Chau-doc, *Vietnam* E89+108 **69**
Chauka R., *India* G52+274 **73**
Chaumont-en-Bassigny, *Fr.* M59+481 **54**
Chaunskaya Guba, *U.S.S.R.* A60+695 **63**
Chausa, *India* G36+255 **73**
Chautauqua L., *New York* T26+422 **96**
Chaux de Fonds, la, *Switz.* M49+471 **45**
Chaves, *Brazil* R29−003 **105**
Chaves, *Portugal* N45+418 **52**
Chayu, *Tibet* F47+284 **64**
Chazon, *Argentina* S20−332 **103**
Cheadle, *England* N12+530 **37**
Cheb, *Czechoslovakia* M16+501 **48**
Cheboksary, *U.S.S.R.* J76+562 **61**
Cheboygan, *Michigan* T57+456 **91**
Checmu, *Mexico* T70+213 **100**
Cheduba I., *Burma* F68+189 **71**
Che foo. See Yentai
Chehalis, *Washington* W18+466 **92**
Chekiang, prov., *China* E00+292 **67**
Chekunda, *U.S.S.R.* D16+508 **63**
Chelforó, *Argentina* S39−391 **103**
Chelkar, *Kazakh* J04+479 **62**
Chelm, *Poland* L39+511 **49**
Chelmsford, *England* M87+517 **39**
Chelsea, *Vermont* S75+440 **91**

Chelsea, *Wisconsin* U02+453 **91**
Cheltenham, *England* N12+519 **39**
Chelva, *Spain* N06+397 **53**
Chelyabinsk, *U.S.S.R.* H81+551 **61**
Chemba, *Mozambique* K62-172 **84**
Chembar, *U.S.S.R.* K10+529 **61**
Chemnitz. *See* Karl Marx
    Stadt
Chenab R., *Pakistan* H22+303 **72**
Chenchow. *See* Hwaiyang
Chengchow, *China* E37+346 **66**
Chengho, *China* E07+274 **67**
Chênghsien, *China* E37+348 **66**
Chengshan Tow, *China* D74+373 **64**
Chêng-têhshih. *China* E12+410 **66**
Chengtu, *China* F06+306 **66**
Chenhsien, *China* E42+258 **67**
Chennan. *See* Tehpao
Chenoa, *Illinois* T83+408 **91**
Chenting, *China* E32+381 **66**
Chenyüan, *China* E69+271 **67**
Chepen, *Peru* T27-072 **104**
Chepes, *Argentina* S40-313 **103**
Cher, R. & dep., *France* M85+473 **54**
Cherbourg, *France* N10+497 **54**
Cherchell, *Algeria* M76+364 **80**
Cheremkhovo, *U.S.S.R.* F11+532 **63**
Cherepovets, *U.S.S.R.* K39+592 **60**
Cherkassy, *Ukraine* K78+494 **60**
Chermoz, *U.S.S.R.* J24+587 **62**
Chernigov, *Ukraine* K82+515 **60**
Chernikovsk, *U.S.S.R.* J25+548 **61**
Chernovsk, *U.S.S.R.* J71+580 **61**
Chernovtsy, *Ukraine* L24+483 **60**
Chernyakhovsk, *U.S.S.R.* L49+546 **47**
Cherokee, *Iowa* U34+427 **95**
Cherokees, L. o' the, *Okla.* U29+367 **95**
Cherra Pungi, *India* F79+252 **71**
Cherryfield, *Maine* S47+446 **90**
Cherskogo, Khrebet, *U.S.S.R.* C20+640 **63**
Chertkovo, *Ukraine* K29+494 **60**
Chervenbyreg, *Bulgaria* L35+433 **58**
Cherwell R., *England* N08+517 **39**
Chesapeake B., *Maryland* T08+388 **99**
Cheshire, co., *England* N15+532 **37**
Cheshskaya Guba, *U.S.S.R.* J80+675 **62**
Chesley, *Ontario* T36+443 **91**
Chester, *England* N17+532 **37**
Chester, *Illinois* T89+379 **97**
Chester, *Pennsylvania* T03+398 **96**
Chester, *S. Carolina* T38+347 **97**
Chesterfield, *England* N09+532 **37**
Chesterfield, *S. Carolina* T31+348 **97**
Chesterfield Inlet, *North-West*
    Territories U10+639 **89**
Chesterfield Is., *Pacific Oc.* B40+190 **106**
Chester-le-Street, *England* N09+549 **37**
Chestertown, *Maryland* T07+392 **96**
Chesuncook L., *Maine* S56+460 **90**
Chethang, *Tibet* F79+293 **71**
Chetumal & B., *Mexico* T77+184 **100**
Cheviot, *New Zealand* A40-429 **112**
Cheviot, The, *England* N13+555 **37**
Cheviot Hills, *Eng.-Scot.* N14+553 **37**
Cheyenne, *Wyoming* U88+412 **93**
Cheyenne R., *S. Dakota* U70+445 **93**
Chhachrauli, *India* G75+303 **72**
Chhata, *India* G75+277 **72**
Chhatarpur, *India* G62+249 **73**
Chhibramau, *India* G63+271 **73**
Chhindwara, *India* G66+221 **73**
Chiai, *Taiwan* D87+235 **67**
Chiang Mai, *Thailand* F36+188 **69**
Chiang Rai, *Thailand* F31+199 **69**
Chiapa, *Mexico* U18+167 **100**
Chiapas R. & state, *Mexico* U16+170 **100**
Chiasso, *Switzerland* M36+458 **45**
Chiavari, *Italy* M34+443 **56**
Chiba, *Japan* C59+356 **68**
Chibia, *Angola* M08-154 **84**
Chibougamau L., *Quebec* S86+498 **90**
Chicago, *Illinois* T76+418 **95**
Chichagof I., *Alaska* X05+578 **99**
Chichester, *England* N03+508 **39**
Chickasha, *Oklahoma* U48+350 **95**
Chiclayo, *Peru* T29-068 **104**
Chico, *California* W11+397 **92**
Chicoana, *Argentina* S33-252 **103**
Chicopee & R., *Massachusetts* S76+422 **96**
Chicoutimi, *Quebec* S66+484 **90**
Chicundo, *Transvaal* K86-228 **84**
Chidambaram, *India* G62+115 **70**
Chidley, C., *Quebec* S27+603 **89**
Chiang-kan, *Thailand* F20+179 **69**
Chiengue, *Angola* L82-116 **82**
Chienou, *China* E19+268 **67**
Chieti, *Italy* M05+424 **56**
Chièvres, *Belgium* M67+506 **44**
Chigha Khur, *Iran* J54+320 **75**
Chignecto B., *New Brunswick-*
    Nova Scotia S31+454 **90**
Chignik, *Alaska* Y42+555 **26**
Chichow. *See* Kweichih
Chih-fêng, *China* E06+423 **66**
Chihi, *Tanzania* K50-094 **83**
Chikiang, *China* E62+274 **67**
Chihsien, *China* E34+354 **66**
Chihuahua & state, *Mexico* V06+286 **100**
Chik-Ballapur, *India* G74+135 **70**
Chikien, *China* D85+522 **63**
Chikmagalur, *India* G84+133 **70**
Chikwawa, *Malawi* K60-160 **83**
Chilas, *Kashmir* H05+354 **72**
Childress, *Texas* U62+346 **94**
Chile, rep., *S. America* **104**
Chilecito, *Argentina* S45-292 **103**
Chilete, *Peru* T23-073 **104**
Chilia Veche, *Romania* L04+454 **58**
Chilka L., *India* G27+196 **71**
Chilko L., *Brit. Columbia* W25+512 **88**
Chilko R., *Brit. Columbia* W20+518 **88**
Chillan, *Chile* S73-364 **103**
Chillicothe, *Missouri* U22+398 **95**
Chillicothe, *Ohio* T48+394 **91**
Chillingollah, *Victoria* C42-353 **109**
Chilliwack, *Brit. Columbia* W10+493 **88**
Chiloe, I. de, *Chile* S84-426 **103**
Chilonga, *Zambia* K82-122 **83**
Chilpancingo, *Mexico* U56+174 **100**
Chiltern, *Victoria* C20-362 **109**
Chiltern Hills, *England* N04+518 **39**

Chilton, *Wisconsin* T79+441 **91**
Chiluane, *Mozambique* K60-206 **84**
Chilubula, *Zambia* K86-102 **83**
Chilung, *Taiwan* D80+251 **67**
Chilwa L., *Malawi* K56-154 **83**
Chimay, *Belgium* M64+501 **44**
Chimbai, *Uzbek* J01+430 **62**
Chimbote, *Peru* T21-091 **104**
Chimkent, *Kazakh* H33+423 **62**
Chimpek, *Kazakh* H06+450 **62**
China, rep., *Asia* E60+330 **31**
Chinandega, *Nicaragua* T73+126 **101**
Chincha, *Peru* T07-135 **104**
Chinchaga R., *Alberta* V85+580 **88**
Chinchon, *Spain* N21+402 **52**
Chinchow, *China* D82+412 **64**
Chindwin R., *Burma* F60+225 **71**
Ching Hai, *China* F28+64
Chingleput, *India* G59+128 **70**
Ching Shan, *China* E54+314 **66**
Chingtao, *China* D88+361 **66**
Chinhai, *China* D79+300 **67**
Chin Hill, *Burma* F68+227 **71**
Chini, *India* G70+315 **72**
Chiniot, *Pakistan* H12+316 **72**
Chinishk, *Iran* J06+322 **75**
Chinju, *Korea* D42+353 **64**
Chinkiang, *China* E03+322 **66**
Chin Ling Shan, *China* E80+345 **64**
Chinook, *Montana* V25+486 **93**
Chinsura, *India* G10+229 **73**
Chinwangtao, *China* E02+399 **66**
Chioggia, *Italy* M16+452 **56**
Chios, I. *See* Khios, I.
Chipchiahue, *Argentina* S51–421 **103**
Chipili, *Zambia* L06–110 **83**
Chipman, *New Brunswick* S35+462 **90**
Chippewa Falls, *Wisconsin* U09+449 **93**
Chippewa, R., *Wisconsin* U06+456 **99**
Chipping Norton, *England* N09+519 **39**
Chipping Sodbury, *England* N14+515 **38**
Chiputneticook Ls.,
    Maine-New Brunswick S47+457 **90**
Chiquian, *Peru* T12-102 **104**
Chiquimula, *Guatemala* T87+147 **100**
Chiquinquira, *Colombia* S83+056 **104**
Chiras, *Afghanistan* H55+353 **75**
Chirawa, *India* G86+282 **72**
Chi-ri-cahua Mts., *Arizona* V27+320 **93**
Chiriqui, Lag. de, *Panama* T42+093 **101**
Chiriqui Grande, *Panama* T43+090 **101**
Chirpan, *Bulgaria* L28+422 **58**
Chirripo Grande, mt.,
    Costa Rica T52+097 **101**
Chisamba Falls, *Zambia* K86–101 **83**
Chishmy, *U.S.S.R.* J28+545 **61**
Chisimaio, *Somalia* K14–002 **83**
Chisinau. *See* Kishinev
Chistopol, *U.S.S.R.* J56+554 **61**
Chita, *U.S.S.R.* E39+520 **63**
Chitipa, *Malawi* K70+098 **83**
Chitorgarh, *India* H01+248 **70**
Chitradurga, *India* G81+142 **70**
Chitral & R., *Pakistan* H19+358 **72**
Chitre, *Panama* T33+080 **101**
Chittagong, *Bangladesh* F79+223 **71**
Chittoor, *India* G65+133 **70**
Chiusi, *Italy* M18+430 **56**
Chiuta L., *Malawi* K56-146 **83**
Chiva, *Spain* N04+395 **53**
Chivasso, *Italy* M43+452 **56**
Chivay, *Peru* S69-156 **104**
Chivilcoy, *Argentina* S00–349 **103**
Chivota, Sierra, *New Mexico* V14+354 **93**
Chivyu, *U.S.S.R.* J36+635 **62**
Chiwanda, *Tanzania* K60–114 **83**
Chmielnik, *Poland* L55+506 **49**
Choapam, *Mexico* U35+174 **100**
Choban Bey, *Syria* K45+366 **76**
Chocaya, *Bolivia* S38–209 **104**
Chocen, *Czechoslovakia* L83+500 **49**
Cho-chow, *China* E24+395 **66**
Choco, Cord. de, *Colombia* T13+070 **104**
Choconta, *Colombia* S82+052 **104**
Choele Choel, *Argentina* S34–393 **103**
Choiseul, I., *Solomon Is.* B48–070 **106**
Choix, *Mexico* V17+272 **100**
Chojna, *Poland* M03+529 **48**
Choke Mts., *Ethiopia* K44+106 **83**
Cholet, *France* N05+471 **54**
Cholon, *Vietnam* E80+108 **69**
Choluteca, *Honduras* T74+133 **101**
Choma, *Zambia* L18–168 **84**
Chomutov, *Czechoslavakia* M10+505 **48**
Chone, *Ecuador* T31–006 **104**
Chongjin, *Korea* D32+418 **64**
Chong Kal, *Cambodia* F09+139 **69**
Chonos, Arch. de los, *Chile* T00-450 **103**
Chorillos, *Peru* T12–124 **104**
Chorley, *England* N16+537 **37**
Chorrera, *Panama* T28+089 **101**
Chorzele, *Poland* L54+533 **49**
Chorzow, *Poland* L66+503 **49**
Chosi, *Japan* C55+357 **68**
Chos Malal, *Argentina* S62–373 **103**
Chota, *Peru* T22–066 **104**
Choushan I., *China* D77+300 **67**
Christchurch, *England* N11+508 **39**
Christchurch, *New Zealand* A44-435 **112**
Christiansborg, *Virginia* T32+371 **97**
Christianshaab, *Greenland* R40+690 **89**
Christie, Mt., *Yukon* W58+634 **88**
Christmas I., *Indian Ocean* E86–104 **65**
Christmas I., *Pacific Ocean* Y45+020 **107**
Chrudim, *Czechoslovakia* L85+499 **49**
Chrzanów, *Poland* L64+502 **49**
Chuale I., *Mozambique* K72-250 **84**
Chuambara, *Mozambique* K68-154 **84**
Chuanchow, *China* E09+249 **67**
Chuanhsien, *China* E54+260 **67**
Chubut & R., *Argentina* S40-435 **103**
Chuchow, *China* E40+278 **67**
Chuchow. *See* Lishui
Chucul, *Argentina* S25–330 **103**
Chudovo, *U.S.S.R.* K81+591 **60**
Chudskoye, Oz., *Eston.-U.S.S.R.* L16+58 **47**
Chuho, *China* D42+451 **64**
Chuhsien, *China* E07+355 **66**
Chuhsien, *China* E07+289 **67**
Chukai, *Malaysia* F09+042 **65**

Chukhloma, *U.S.S.R.* K14+588 **61**
Chukotskiy Khrebet, *U.S.S.R.* A30+682 **63**
Chulman, *U.S.S.R.* D61+567 **63**
Chulym, *U.S.S.R.* G55+551 **62**
Chumbi, *Tibet* G06+274 **71**
Chumikan, *U.S.S.R.* C88+547 **63**
Chuna, R., *U.S.S.R.* F40+572 **63**
Chunar, *India* G43+250 **73**
Chunchôn, *Korea* D43+380 **64**
Chungan, *China* E12+277 **67**
Chunghsien, *China* E72+303 **67**
Chungking, *China* E81+295 **67**
Chungshan, *China* E53+246 **67**
Chungsiang, *China* E44+312 **66**
Chungtien, *China* F32+277 **64**
Chunian, *Pakistan* H06+309 **72**
Chunya, *Tanzania* K70–086 **83**
Chuquibambilla, *Peru* S77–140 **104**
Chuquicamata, *Chile* S53–222 **103**
Chur, *Switzerland* M33+469 **45**
Churapcha, *U.S.S.R.* D16+621 **63**
Churchill, *Manitoba* U25+588 **88**
Churchill C., *Manitoba* U21+590 **89**
Churchill L., *Saskatchewan* V20+560 **88**
Churchill, R. & Falls, *Lab.* S10+530 **89**
Churchill R., *Manitoba* U35+570 **88**
Church's Ferry, *N. Dakota* U55+483 **93**
Churia Ghati Hills, *Nepal* G24+269 **73**
Churu, *India* H00+283 **72**
Chusca, Sierra, *New Mexico* V20+362 **94**
Chusovoi, *U.S.S.R.* J12+582 **62**
Chuvashskaya. aut. rep.,*U.S.S.R.* J80+560 **62**
Chwan Ho. *See* Yangtze Kiang
Cibao, Cord. de, *Dom. Rep.* S62+190 **101**
Cicero, *Illinois* T77+418 **95**
Cidones, *Spain* N16+418 **53**
Ciechanow, *Poland* L56+529 **49**
Ciego de Avila, *Cuba* T22+218 **101**
Cienaga, *Colombia* S85+110 **104**
Cienfuegos, *Cuba* T33+222 **101**
Cierfs, *Switzerland* M28+466 **45**
Cieszyn, *Poland* L67+498 **49**
Cieza, *Spain* N08+383 **53**
Cifuentes, *Spain* N16+408 **53**
Cilacap, *Java* E67+077 **65**
Cimaltepec, *Mexico* U39+163 **100**
Cimarron R., *Oklahoma, etc.* U60+370 **98**
Cincinnati, *Ohio* T57+391 **91**
Cioara, *Romania* L15+448 **58**
Ciotat, *France* M57+432 **55**
Circeo C., *Italy* M12+412 **57**
Circle, *Alaska* X56+568 **99**
Circle, *Montana* V04+474 **93**
Circleville, *Ohio* T48+396 **91**
Cirebon, *Java* E49+066 **65**
Cirencester, *England* N12+517 **39**
Ciro, *Italy* L78+394 **57**
Cirque Mt., *Labrador* S22+591 **89**
Citlaltepetl, mt., *Mexico* U44+190 **100**
Citrusdal, *Cape Province* L66–326 **84**
Cittanova, *Italy* L83+384 **57**
Ciudad Bolivar, *Venezuela* S21+082 **104**
Ciudad Chetumal, *Mexico* T79+183 **100**
Ciudad Juarez, *Mexico* V09+316 **100**
Ciudad Madero, *Mexico* U48+223 **100**
Ciudad Real, *Spain* N23+390 **52**
Ciudad Rodrigo, *Spain* N39+406 **52**
Ciudad Victoria, *Mexico* U54+238 **100**
Civray, *France* M88+461 **54**
Civril, *Turkey* L02+383 **74**
Cizre, *Turkey* K17+374 **74**
Clackmannan, *Scotland* N22+561 **41**
Clacton-on-Sea, *England* M83+518 **39**
Claire, L., *Alberta* V42+587 **88**
Clamecy, *France* M69+474 **54**
Clara, *Ireland, Rep.* N46+533 **43**
Clara I., *Burma* F43+108 **71**
Clare, *Michigan* T59+438 **91**
Clare, *S. Australia* C69–338 **109**
Clare, co., *Ireland, Rep.* N53+528 **43**
Clare I., *Ireland, Rep.* N60+538 **42**
Clarecastle, *Ireland, Rep.* N54+528 **43**
Claremont, *New Hampshire* S74+434 **96**
Claremore, *Oklahoma* U34+364 **95**
Claremorris, *Ireland, Rep.* N54+537 **42**
Clarence, *Yukon* X36+658 **88**
Clarence Hd., *N.-W. Terr.* T27+766 **89**
Clarence I., *Antarctica* R54–610 **27**
Clarence, I., *Chile* S72–541 **103**
Clarence, R., *New S. Wales* B74–294 **109**
Clarence, R., *New Zealand* A40-423 **112**
Clarence Str., *N. Terr., Aust.* D24–120 **110**
Clarendon, *Arkansas* U08+347 **97**
Clarinda, *Iowa* U30+406 **95**
Clarion, *Iowa* U22+428 **95**
Clarion, *Pennsylvania* T26+412 **96**
Clarion R., *Pennsylvania* T24+413 **96**
Clark, S. Dakota* U44+449 **93**
Clarke I., *Tasmania* C12–405 **109**
Clarkesville, *Texas* U30+336 **95**
Clarksburg, *West Virginia* T32+393 **91**
Clarksdale, *Mississippi* U04+342 **97**
Clarksville, *Tennessee* T74+365 **95**
Claro, *Switzerland* M36+463 **45**
Clausthal, *W. Germany* M28+517 **48**
Clay Center, *Kansas* U43+394 **95**
Claydon, *England* M83+521 **39**
Clayton, *Alabama* T63+319 **97**
Clayton, *New Jersey* T01+397 **91**
Clayton, *New Mexico* U80+365 **94**
Clear I., *Ireland, Rep.* N57+514 **43**
Clear L., *California* W17+390 **92**
Clear Lake, *Iowa* U18+432 **95**
Clearfield, *Pennsylvania* T21+410 **96**
Clearmont, *Wyoming* V08+446 **93**
Clearwater L., *Quebec* T00+558 **89**
Clearwater R., *Idaho* V63+461 **92**
Cleburne, *Texas* U44+324 **95**
Clent Hills, *England* N12+524 **37**
Clermont, *Queensland* C15–226 **111**
Clermont, *Transvaal* L12–236 **84**
Clermont-Ferrand, *France* M71+458 **54**
Cleveland, *Ohio* T40+415 **91**
Cleveland, *Tennessee* T59+351 **97**
Cleveland, *Texas* U30+302 **95**
Cleveland Hills, *England* N07+544 **37**
Clew Bay, *Ireland, Rep.* N59+538 **42**
Clifden, *Ireland, Rep.* N60+535 **43**
Clifton, *Arizona* V57+330 **93**
Clifton, *Tennesse* T78+354 **97**
Clifton Forge, *Virginia* T29+378 **97**

Clifton Ville, *Wisconsin* T83+447 **91**
Clinch Mts., *Tenn.-Va.* T48+364 **97**
Clinton, *Arkansas* U16+356 **97**
Clinton, *Illinois* T84+402 **95**
Clinton, *Iowa* U02+418 **95**
Clinton, *Massachusetts* S70+424 **96**
Clinton, *Missouri* U22+384 **95**
Clinton, *Oklahoma* U54+354 **95**
Clinton, *Ontario* T39+436 **91**
Clinton Colden L., *N.W.T.* V18+632 **88**
Clinton Dam, *Tennessee* T55+362 **97**
Clipperton I., *Pacific Ocean* V25+100 **107**
Clisson, *France* N08+471 **54**
Clitheroe, *England* N13+539 **37**
Clogham, *Ireland, Rep.* N47+532 **43**
Clogher, *N. Ireland* N43+544 **42**
Clonakilty & B., *Ireland, Rep.* N53+516 **43**
Cloncurry, *Queensland* C57–207 **111**
Clones, *Ireland, Rep.* N43+542 **42**
Clonmel, *Ireland, Rep.* N46+524 **43**
Clonegal, *Ireland, Rep.* N40+527 **43**
Cloquet, *Minnesota* U15+467 **93**
Clorinda, *Argentina* R77–252 **103**
Cloud Pk., *Wyoming* V12+446 **98**
Clover, *Virginia* T22+369 **97**
Clovis, *New Mexico* U80+344 **94**
Cloyne, *Ireland, Rep.* N49+519 **43**
Cluj, *Romania* L38+468 **58**
Clun Forest, *Wales* N20+524 **38**
Clunes, *Victoria* C37–373 **109**
Clusone, *Italy* M30+458 **56**
Clyde, *New Zealand* A64–451 **112**
Clyde, Firth of, *Scotland* N30+555 **41**
Clyde, Inlet, *N.-W. Terr.* S50+704 **89**
Clyde R., *Scotland* N26+559 **41**
Clydebank, *Scotland* N26+559 **41**
Coahuila, state, *Mexico* U74+270 **100**
Coalcoman, *Mexico* U78+188 **100**
Coamo, *Puerto Rico* S38+180 **101**
Coari, *Brazil* S19–040 **104**
Coast Mts., *Brit. Columbia* W30+510 **88**
Coast Ra., *Oregon, etc.* W23+418 **92**
Coatbridge, *Scotland* N24+558 **41**
Coatepeque, *Guatemala* U11+147 **100**
Coatesville, *Pennsylvania* T05+399 **96**
Coaticook, *Quebec* S71+451 **91**
Coats I., *N.-W. Terr.* T45+620 **89**
Coats Ld., *Antarctica* N75–750 **27**
Cobalt, *Ontario* T28+474 **91**
Coban, *Guatemala* U02+155 **100**
Cobar, *New S. Wales* C25–316 **109**
Cobargo, *New S. Wales* C01–364 **109**
Cobb, Mt., *New Zealand* A45–410 **112**
Cobden, *Victoria* C42–384 **109**
Cobequid Mts., *Nova Scotia* S26+455 **90**
Cobh, *Ireland, Rep.* N50+518 **43**
Cobija, *Bolivia* S53–110 **104**
Cobleskill, *New York* S87+427 **91**
Coboconk, *Ontario* T23+447 **91**
Cobourg, *Ontario* T19+440 **91**
Cobourg Pen., *N. Terr., Aust.* D15–114 **110**
Cobram, *Victoria* C26–359 **109**
Cobre, El, *Cuba* T06+201 **101**
Coburg, *W. Germany* M24+502 **48**
Coburg I., *N.-W. Terr.* T20+760 **89**
Cocachacra, *Peru* S71–170 **104**
Cocamá, *Peru* S68–105 **104**
Cochabamba, *Bolivia* S36–174 **104**
Cochin, *India* G82+100 **70**
Cochin China, *Vietnam* F00+102 **69**
Cochinoca, *Argentina* S35–227 **103**
Cochran, *Georgia* T50+324 **97**
Cochrane, L., *Chile-Argent.* S72–472 **103**
Cochrane, *Ontario* T36+492 **89**
Cockburn, S. *Australia* C54–321 **109**
Cockburn I., *Ontario* T50+459 **91**
Cockburn, Mt., *W. Australia* D45–157 **110**
Cockburnspath, *Scotland* N14+559 **41**
Cockermouth, *England* N20+547 **37**
Cockscomb Mts., *Belize* T84+166 **101**
Coco, I. del, *Pacific Ocean* T70+045 **107**
Cocos Is. (Keeling), *Indian Oc.* F45–120 **77**
Cocula, *Mexico* U83+203 **100**
Cocuy, *Columbia* S75+064 **104**
Cod C., *Massachusetts* S60+421 **96**
Codajas, *Brazil* S12–036 **104**
Codfish I., *New Zealand* A74–467 **112**
Codó *Brazil* Q83–044 **105**
Cod's Hd., *Ireland, Rep.* N61+517 **43**
Cody, *Wyoming* V24+445 **93**
Coe Hill, *Ontario* T17+448 **91**
Coeur d'Alene, *Idaho* V71+477 **92**
Coevorden, *Netherlands* M49+527 **44**
Coeymans, *New York* S83+425 **96**
Coffeyville, *Kansas* U34+370 **95**
Coff's Harbour, *N.S.W.* B71–303 **109**
Cognac, *France* N02+457 **54**
Cogolludo, *Spain* N19+410 **52**
Cohoes, *New York* S82+428 **96**
Cohuna, *Victoria* C35–358 **109**
Coiba, I., *Panama* T40+075 **101**
Coimbatore, *India* G78+110 **70**
Coimbra, *Portugal* N50+402 **52**
Coin, *Spain* N28+366 **52**
Coire. *See* Chur
Cojimies, *Ecuador* T30+003 **104**
Coko Ra., *New S. Wales* C51–305 **109**
Colac, *Victoria* C39–384 **109**
Colair L., *India* G52+166 **70**
Colbeck Arch, *Antarctica* H85–680 **27**
Colby, *Kansas* U66+394 **94**
Colcha, *Bolivia* S47–208 **104**
Colchester, *England* M85+519 **39**
Coldingham, *Scotland* N13+559 **41**
Coldstream, *Scotland* N13+557 **41**
Coldwater, *Mississippi* U00+347 **97**
Colebrook, *New Hampshire* S69+449 **91**
Coleman, *Alberta* V57+496 **88**
Coleman, *Texas* U56+318 **95**
Colemerik. *See* Hakkâri
Coleraine, *N. Ireland* N40+551 **42**
Coleraine, *Victoria* C50–375 **109**
Coleridge, L., *New Zealand* A51–433 **112**
Colgong, *India* G16+252 **73**
Colhué Huapi, L., *Argentina* S53–455 **103**
Colima & state, *Mexico* U82+192 **100**
Colinas, *Honduras* T80+150 **101**
Coll, I., *Scotland* N39+566 **41**
Collahuasi, *Chile* S52–210 **103**
Collarenebri, *New S. Wales* C09–296 **109**
Collie, *New South Wales* C10–317 **109**

Collie, W. Australia E21-333 **110**
Collier B., W. Australia D65-160 **110**
Collines-de-Normandie,
  France N06+490 **54**
Collingwood, Ontario T31+445 **91**
Collingwood, Queensland C45-222 **111**
Collo, Algeria M50+368 **80**
Collooney, Ireland, Rep. N51+542 **42**
Colmar, France M46+481 **54**
Colmars, France M50+442 **55**
Colmena, Argentina S01-286 **103**
Colmenar de Oreja, Spain N21+401 **52**
Colmenar Viejo, Spain N23+406 **52**
Colmi, Honduras T64+150 **101**
Colmonell, Scotland N29+551 **41**
Colne, England N13+539 **37**
Colne R., England M85+519 **39**
Cologne. See Köln
Colomb-Bechar (Bechar),
  Algeria N12+314 **80**
Colombia, Brazil R23-202 **105**
Colombia, rep., S. America **104**
Colombier, Switzerland M49+470 **45**
Colombo, Sri Lanka G62+070 **70**
Colon, Argentina R79-321 **103**
Colon, Argentina S07-338 **103**
Colon, Cuba T34+227 **111**
Colon, Panama T28+093 **111**
Colon, Venezuela S74+080 **104**
Colonel Fer. Gomez, Brazil R36+008 **105**
Colonelganj, India G49+271 **73**
Colonia, Uruguay R77-344 **103**
Colonia Alvear, Argentina S46-350 **103**
Colonia Sarmiento, Argent. S55-457 **103**
Colonsay, I., Scotland N37+561 **41**
Colorado, Texas U65+323 **94**
Colorado, state, U.S.A. V17+391 **98**
Colorado Des., California V66+349 **92**
Colorado Des., Wyoming V28+424 **93**
Colorado Plat., Arizona V30+360 **94**
Colorado, R., Argentina S22-393 **103**
Colorado R., Texas U36+292 **95**
Colorado R., U.S.A. V57+333 **98**
Colorado R., Utah, etc. V30+380 **94**
Colorado R., Little, Arizona V38+358 **94**
Colorados, Arch. de los, Cuba T56+224 **101**
Colorado Springs, Colorado U89+388 **94**
Colotlan, Mexico U80+223 **100**
Colpoy B., Ontario T36+449 **91**
Colquechaca, Bolivia S37-190 **104**
Colton, California V74+341 **92**
Columbia, Alabama T61+313 **97**
Columbia, Indiana T63+412 **91**
Columbia, Kentucky T62+371 **97**
Columbia, Louisiana U13+321 **97**
Columbia, Mississippi T89+312 **99**
Columbia, Missouri U14+390 **95**
Columbia, Pennsylvania T09+400 **96**
Columbia, S. Carolina T36+340 **97**
Columbia, Tennessee T72+356 **97**
Columbia C., Canada S60+820 **26**
Columbia, Dist. of, U.S.A. T12+386 **91**
Columbia, Mt., Alberta V75+524 **88**
Colombia Plat., Wash., etc. V80+469 **98**
Colombia R., Canada-
  U.S.A. W06+457 **92**
Columbiana, Alabama T70+332 **97**
Columbus, Georgia T60+325 **97**
Columbus, Indiana T65+392 **91**
Columbus, Kansas U30+372 **95**
Columbus, Mississippi T80+336 **95**
Columbus, Montana V26+456 **93**
Columbus, Nebraska U42+414 **95**
Columbus, Ohio T48+400 **91**
Columbus, Texas U39+297 **95**
Colville L., N.-W. Terr. W25+678 **88**
Colville Ra., New Zealand A26-370 **112**
Colwyn Bay, Wales N22+533 **38**
Comacchio, Valli di, Italy M18+447 **56**
Comana, Romania L23+442 **58**
Comayagua, Honduras I76+144 **101**
Combarbala, Chile S66-311 **103**
Comber, N. Ireland N34+545 **42**
Comblain, Belgium M57+505 **44**
Comeragh Mts., Ireland, Rep. N45+522 **43**
Comino C., Sardinia M31+405 **57**
Comiso, Sicily M02+369 **57**
Comitan, Mexico U12+162 **100**
Commissioners L., Quebec S73+482 **90**
Commonwealth Ra., Antarc. Z80-850 **27**
Como, Italy M36+458 **56**
Como, L. di, Italy M35+460 **56**
Comores, Arch. des, See Comoro Is.
Comorin C., India G74+081 **70**
Comoro Is., Ind. Oc. K06-122 **83**
Compiègne, France M73+494 **54**
Comporta, Portugal N53+384 **52**
Compostela, Mexico U89+213 **100**
Comrie, Scotland N24+564 **41**
Conakry, Guinea N82+096 **80**
Conceicao do Araguaya,
  Brazil R27-086 **105**
Conceicao do Arroio, Brazil R33-299 **103**
Concepcion, Argentina S17-312 **103**
Concepcion, Argentina R78-284 **103**
Concepcion, Bolivia S40-114 **104**
Concepcion, Chile S78-368 **103**
Concepcion, Paraguay R75-234 **103**
Concepcion del Oro, Mexico U68+245 **100**
Concepcion del Uruguay,
  Argentina R80-325 **103**
Conception B., Nfd. R48+478 **90**
Conception I., Bahamas, The T01+239 **101**
Conception, Pt., California W03+346 **98**
Conchas Res., New Mexico U86+354 **94**
Conchi, Chile S52-219 **103**
Concord, Massachusetts S68+425 **96**
Concord, New Hampshire S69+432 **91**
Concord, N. Carolina T34+354 **97**
Concordia, Argentina R79-313 **103**
Concordia, Kansas U46+395 **95**
Concordia, Mexico V06+232 **100**
Concordia, Peru S63-185 **104**
Condobolin, New S. Wales C18-331 **109**
Condom, France M88+440 **55**
Condor, Cord. del, Peru T20-040 **104**
Conemaugh, Pennsylvania S28-401 **103**
Conesa, Argentina S28-401 **103**
Confolens, France M86+460 **54**
Congo, rep., Cent. Africa. See Zaire.
Congo, rep., Cent Africa M00+002 **82**

Congo R. (Zaire) Cent. Afr. L76-016 **82**
Coniston Water, England N19+543 **37**
Coney I., New York S83+405 **96**
Conlin, Montana V00+469 **93**
Conn L., Ireland, Rep. N56+540 **42**
Connacht, prov.,
  Ireland, Rep. N51+538 **42**
Connecticut R., Conn., etc. S74+413 **96**
Connecticut R., Vermont S75+428 **91**
Connecticut, state, U.S.A. S80+415 **99**
Connellsville, Pennsylvania T28+400 **96**
Connemara, Ireland, Rep. N58+535 **43**
Connors, New Brunswick S53+472 **90**
Conrad, Montana V42+482 **93**
Conroe, Texas U33+302 **95**
Conshohocken, New Jersey T02+401 **96**
Conselheiro Lafaiete, Brazil Q80-204 **105**
Constance. See Konstanz
Constance, L. See Boden See
Constanta, Romania L08+442 **58**
Constantine, Algeria M50+362 **80**
Constitucion, Chile S75-354 **103**
Consuegra, Spain N22+394 **52**
Contamana, Peru T00-073 **104**
Conthey, Switzerland M46+462 **45**
Contreras, I., Chile T00-519 **103**
Contwoyto L., N.-W. Terr. V42+657 **88**
Conway, Arkansas U14+351 **95**
Conway, Missouri U18+376 **95**
Conway, New Hampshire S67+440 **91**
Conway, S. Carolina T 24+339 **97**
Conwy, Wales N23+533 **38**
Coober Pedy, S. Australia D03-287 **111**
Cooch Behar, India G03+263 **73**
Cook, B. de, Chile S60-552 **103**
Cook Inl., Alaska Y15+590 **99**
Cook Is., Pacific Ocean Y60-200 **106**
Cook, Mt., New Zealand A59-436 **112**
Cook Str., New Zealand A32-414 **112**
Cook's Passage, Queensland C29-147 **111**
Cookshire, Quebec S70+454 **91**
Cookstown, N. Ireland N40+546 **42**
Cooktown, Queensland C28-154 **111**
Coolabah, New S. Wales C20-311 **109**
Coolah, New S. Wales C02-318 **109**
Coolamon, New S. Wales C17-348 **109**
Coolgardie, W. Australia D83-309 **110**
Cooma, New South Wales C06-362 **109**
Coomacarrea,
  Ireland, Rep. N60+520 **43**
Coonabarabran, N.S.W. C04-313 **109**
Coonalpyn, S. Australia C61-357 **109**
Coonamble, New S. Wales C09-309 **109**
Coondiwindi, Queensland B88-283 **111**
Cooper Cr., S. Australia C66-278 **111**
Cooperstown, New York T00+427 **96**
Coorg, India G83+122 **70**
Coorong, The, S. Australia C62-355 **109**
Cootamundra, New S. Wales C12-347 **109**
Cootehill, Ireland, Rep. N42+541 **42**
Copenhagen. See Köbenhavn.
Copetonas, Argentina S03-386 **103**
Copiapo, Chile S62-273 **103**
Copley, S. Australia C69-306 **109**
Coporaque, Peru S70-148 **104**
Copper Cliff, Ontario T37+465 **91**
Coppermine, North-West
  Territories V65+672 **88**
Coppermine R., N.-W. Terr. V60+664 **88**
Coppet, Switzerland M53+463 **45**
Coquar, Quebec T02+481 **91**
Coquilhatville (Mbandaka),
  Zaire L70+001 **82**
Coquimbo & B. de, Chile S68-299 **103**
Corabia, Romania L33+438 **58**
Coracoes, Brazil R02-217 **105**
Coraki, New S. Wales B71-288 **109**
Corangamite, L., Victoria C40-382 **109**
Corato, Italy L82+411 **57**
Corazon, Sierra, Texas U82+295 **94**
Corcaigh. See Cork
Corcovado, G. del, Chile S80-434 **103**
Corcovado, mt. Chile S76-432 **103**
Corcubion, Spain N55+429 **52**
Cordell, Oklahoma U54+352 **95**
Cordoba, Mexico U42+190 **100**
Cordoba, Peru T00-139 **104**
Córdoba, Spain N29+379 **52**
Cordoba and Sa. de,
  Argentina S26-314 **103**
Cordova, Alaska X70+605 **99**
Corfu. See Kérkira, I.
Corfu, Str. of Greece L60+395 **59**
Coria, Spain N39+400 **52**
Corigliano Calabro, Italy L81+396 **57**
Corindi, New S. Wales B71-300 **109**
Coringa, India G47+168 **71**
Corinth. See Korinthos
Corinth, Mississippi T81+349 **95**
Corinto, Brazil Q87-184 **105**
Corinto, Nicaragua T73+126 **101**
Coristine, Ontario T24+461 **91**
Cork & co., Ireland, Rep. N51+519 **43**
Cork Harb., Ireland, Rep. N49+518 **43**
Corleone, Sicily M10+378 **57**
Corner Inl., Victoria C22-387 **109**
Corner Brook, Nfd. R78+490 **90**
Corning, Iowa U28+410 **95**
Corning, New York T13+421 **96**
Cornwall, New York S84+414 **96**
Cornwall, Ontario S88+450 **91**
Cornwall, co., England N28+504 **38**
Coro, Venezuela S58+114 **104**
Coroata, Brazil Q85-040 **105**
Corocoro, Bolivia S52-171 **104**
Coroico, Bolivia S47-161 **104**
Corrofin, Ireland, Rep. N54+529 **43**
Corona, New S. Wales C10+578 **88**
Coronada, B., Costa Rica T52+090 **101**
Coronation G., N. W. Terr. V40+678 **88**
Coronation I., Antarctica R05-610 **27**
Coronel, Chile S79-370 **103**
Coronel Pringles, Argentina S09-380 **103**
Coronel Suarez, Argentina S11-376 **103**
Coronie, Surinam R69+058 **105**
Coropuna, mt., Peru S76-156 **104**
Corowa, New South Wales C22-360 **109**
Corozal, Belize T81+184 **101**
Corpen Aike, Argentina S56-496 **103**
Corpus Christi & B., Texas U44+278 **94**
Corpus Christi L., Texas U29+282 **94**

Corpus Christi Pass, Texas U43+276 **94**
Corque, Bolivia S46-183 **104**
Corrales, Uruguay R64-314 **103**
Corralitos, Mexico V17+306 **100**
Corregidor, I., Philippines D87+144 **65**
Correze, dep., France M78+453 **54**
Corrib L. Ireland, Rep. N55+534 **43**
Corrientes, Argentina R83-276 **103**
Corrientes, C., Argentina R76-381 **103**
Corrientes, C., Mexico V04+204 **100**
Corrigin, W. Australia E12-322 **110**
Corrimal, New S. Wales B85-344 **109**
Corry, Pennsylvania T28+419 **96**
Corryvreckan, G. of, Scot. N35+561 **41**
Corse, I., France M36+420 **56**
Corsewall Pt., Scotland N31+550 **41**
Corsica. See Corse, I.
Corsicana, Texas U39+322 **95**
Cortes, G. de, Cuba T54+220 **101**
Cortland, New York T07+426 **96**
Cortona, Italy M18+433 **56**
Coruche, Portugal N51+390 **52**
Coruh, R., Turkey K24+407 **74**
Corum, Turkey K61+405 **74**
Corumba, Brazil R75-190 **105**
Corunna. See La Coruña.
Corvallis, Oregon W20+446 **92**
Corwen, Wales N20+530 **38**
Corwin, Alaska Y85+685 **99**
Corydon, Iowa U20+408 **95**
Cosalo, Mexico V09+244 **100**
Coscurita, Spain N15+414 **53**
Coseguina, Vol., Nicaragua T75+130 **101**
Cosenza, Italy L82+393 **57**
Cosquin, Argentina S27-312 **103**
Cossonay, Switzerland M51+466 **45**
Costa Rica, rep.,
  Central America T54+100 **101**
Costermansville. See Bukavu
Costillo Pk., New Mexico U92+368 **94**
Cotabato, Philippines D65+072 **65**
Cotagaita, Bolivia S34-208 **104**
Cotahuasi, Peru S78-152 **104**
Cote Blanche B., Louisiana U10+296 **95**
Cote D'Ivoire. See Ivory Coast
Côte-d'Or, dep., France M60+474 **54**
Côtes-du-Nord, dep., France N18+484 **54**
Cöthen, E. Germany M18+ 517 **48**
Cotonou, Benin M76 + 064 **80**
Cotswold, Hills, England N12+519 **39**
Cottbus, E. Germany M04+518 **48**
Cottica, Surinam R56+038 **105**
Cotulla, Texas U55+284 **94**
Coudersport, Pennsylvania T18+417 **96**
Coudres, I. aux, Quebec S62+474 **91**
Coulagh B., Ireland, Rep. N60+517 **43**
Coulman, I., Antarctica A62-730 **27**
Council Bluffs, Iowa U35+412 **95**
Council Grove, Kansas U39+386 **95**
Coupar-Angus, Scotland N20+565 **41**
Courantyne, R., Guyana, etc. R77+042 **104**
Couronne C., France M60+433 **55**
Courtenay, N. Dakota U51+472 **93**
Courtmacsherry,
  Ireland, Rep. N52+516 **43**
Courtrai, Belgium M70+508 **44**
Court St Etienne, Belgium M62+506 **44**
Couterne, France N02+485 **54**
Couthuin, Belgium M59+505 **44**
Couvin, Belgium M63+501 **44**
Covenas, Colombia T04+094 **104**
Coventry, England N09+524 **37**
Covilhã, Portugal N45+403 **52**
Covington, Kentucky T46+390 **97**
Covington, Tennessee T88+356 **97**
Covington, Virginia T30+378 **97**
Cowal, L., New S. Wales C15-336 **109**
Cowan, L., W. Australia D79-318 **110**
Cowangie, Victoria C51-352 **109**
Cowbridge, Wales N20+514 **38**
Cowdenbeath, Scotland N20+561 **41**
Cowell, S. Australia C79-334 **111**
Cowes, I. of W., England N08+508 **39**
Cowra, New South Wales C07-339 **109**
Coxsackie, New York S83+424 **96**
Cox's Bazar, Bangladesh F78+214 **71**
Coyame, Mexico V01+294 **100**
Coyuca, Mexico U64+183 **100**
Cozumel, I., Mexico T70+204 **100**
Crabbs, Newfoundland R83+482 **90**
Craboon, N.S.W. C03-321 **109**
Cracow. See Krakow
Cradle Mt., Tasmania C24-417 **109**
Craig, Colorado V16+404 **94**
Craigavon, N. Ireland N38+544 **42**
Craig Harbour, N.-W. Terr. T35+760 **89**
Craigue, Ireland, Rep. N42+528 **43**
Craigville, Minnesota U22+479 **93**
Crail, Scotland N16+563 **41**
Craiova, Romania L37+443 **58**
Cranborne, England N11+509 **39**
Cranbrook, Brit. Columbia V65+496 **88**
Crandon, Wisconsin T83+455 **91**
Crane I., Quebec S63+471 **91**
Cranleigh, England N03+511 **39**
Crans, Switzerland M45+463 **45**
Crater Lake National Park,
  Oregon W14+430 **92**
Crateus, Brazil Q64-052 **105**
Crato, Brazil S18-073 **104**
Crato, Brazil Q56-072 **105**
Cravo, Colombia S62+056 **104**
Crawford, Nebraska U80+427 **94**
Crawford, Saskatchewan U22+555 **41**
Crazy Mts., Montana V32+461 **93**
Creag Meagaidh, Scotland N28+569 **40**
Crediton, England N22+508 **38**
Cree L., Saskatchewan V10+578 **88**
Cree R., Saskatchewan V07+584 **88**
Cree R., Scotland N27+550 **41**
Cremona, Italy M30+452 **56**
Cres, I., Yugoslavia M04+448 **56**
Cresco, Iowa U14+434 **95**
Cressy, Victoria C38-381 **109**
Crest, Quebec T24+465 **91**
Creston, Iowa U26+410 **95**
Creswell B., N.-W. Terr. U20+722 **89**
Creswick, Victoria C37-374 **109**
Crete (Kriti), Greece L30+350 **59**
Crete, Nebraska U42+406 **95**

Crete, Sea of, Greece L30+359 **59**
Creuse, dep., France M78+460 **54**
Creusot, le, France M64+468 **54**
Crewe, England N15+531 **37**
Crewkerne, England N17+509 **38**
Criccieth, Wales N25+529 **38**
Crickhowell, Wales N19+519 **38**
Cricklade, England N15+516 **39**
Crieff, Scotland N23+564 **41**
Crimea (Krym), U.S.S.R. K66+450 **60**
Crimmitschau, E. Germany M16+508 **48**
Cripple Creek, Colorado V02+387 **94**
Crisana, Romania L48+468 **58**
Cristobal, Panama T29+093 **101**
Crnagora, Yugoslavia L64+430 **58**
Croagh Patrick, Ireland, Rep. N58+538 **42**
Crockett, Texas U33+313 **95**
Croisic le, France N15+472 **54**
Croker I., N. Terr., Aust. D14-111 **110**
Cromarty, & Firth, Scotland N24+577 **40**
Cromer, England M82+529 **39**
Cromwell, New Zealand A64-449 **112**
Crooked I., Bahamas, The S86+228 **101**
Crookston, Minnesota U40+478 **93**
Crookwell, New S. Wales C03-345 **109**
Croom, Ireland, Rep. N52+525 **43**
Croppa Creek, New S. Wales B88-291 **109**
Cross Fell, England N15+547 **37**
Crosshaven, Ireland, Rep. N50+518 **43**
Crossmolina, Ireland, Rep. N56+541 **42**
Cross Point, Quebec S40+481 **90**
Crotone, Italy L77+391 **57**
Crow Agency, Montana V15+455 **93**
Crowes, Victoria C40-387 **109**
Crowley, Louisiana U13+302 **95**
Crown Prince Olav Ld.,
  Antarctica K25-690 **27**
Crown Princess Martha Ld.,
  Antarctica N30-720 **27**
Crows Nest Pass, Alberta V58+498 **88**
Croydon, England N01+514 **39**
Croydon, Queensland C47-181 **111**
Crozet Is., Indian Ocean J60-463 **77**
Crozier, C., Antarctica A65-770 **27**
Cruden B., Scotland N11+574 **40**
Crumlin, N. Ireland N37+546 **42**
Cruz, Utah V47+388 **92**
Cruz Alta, Argentina S11-330 **103**
Cruz Alta, Brazil R52-286 **103**
Cruz del Eje, Argentina S29-308 **103**
Cruzeiro do Sul, Brazil S76-078 **104**
Cruz Grande, Chile S68-294 **103**
Cruz Grande, Mexico U55+167 **100**
Crystal Brook, S. Australia C71-333 **109**
Crystal Falls, Michigan T80+461 **91**
Crystal Springs, Mississippi U01+320 **97**
Cuamba, Mozambique K50-148 **83**
Cuango, Angola L72-092 **82**
Cuanza, R., Angola M10-092 **82**
Cuareim, Brazil R76-302 **103**
Cuatro Cienegas, Mexico U73+269 **100**
Cuba, New Mexico V12+360 **94**
Cuba, New York T20+423 **91**
Cuba, Portugal N47+382 **52**
Cuba, I., West Indies T59+220 **101**
Cuchi, Angola L78-146 **82**
Cuchillo-Co, Argentina S28-384 **103**
Cuchillo Parado, Mexico U89+294 **100**
Cucumbi, Angola L66-104 **82**
Cucuta, Colombia S75+079 **104**
Cudahy, Wisconsin T77+430 **91**
Cuddalore, India G62+117 **70**
Cuddapah, India G66+144 **70**
Cudgewa, Victoria C13-362 **109**
Cue, W. Australia E12-274 **100**
Cuellar, Spain N26+414 **52**
Cuenca, Ecuador T24-028 **104**
Cuenca, Spain N13+401 **53**
Cuencame. Mexico U83+248 **100**
Cuernavaca, Mexico U55+188 **100**
Cuero, Texas U44+290 **95**
Cuevo, Bolivia S21-204 **104**
Cuglieri, Sardinia M39+402 **57**
Cuiabá, Brazil R80-072 **104**
Cuiaba, Brazil R66-156 **105**
Cuicuina, Nicaragua T57+136 **101**
Cuilcagh, Ireland, Rep. N47+542 **42**
Cuillin Hills, Scotland N38+572 **40**
Cuillin Sd., Scotland N38+571 **40**
Cuiña, P. de, Spain N41+429 **52**
Cuito Cuanavale, Angola L64-152 **84**
Culcairn, New South Wales C18-357 **109**
Culebra, G. de la, Costa Rica T64+108 **101**
Culebra, I., West Indies S32+184 **101**
Culgoa, R., New S. Wales C20-296 **109**
Culgoa, R., Queensland C15-286 **111**
Culiacan, Mexico V15+249 **100**
Cullarin Ra., New S. Wales C03-346 **109**
Cullera, Spain N01+392 **53**
Cullompton, England N22+509 **38**
Cully, Switzerland M50+465 **45**
Culpeper, Virginia T18+384 **97**
Culverden, New Zealand A43-427 **112**
Cumana, Venezuela S24+104 **104**
Cumaria, Peru S84-099 **104**
Cumberland, Brit. Columbia W31+496 **88**
Cumberland, Maryland T22+397 **96**
Cumberland, Virginia T20+375 **97**
Cumberland, Wisconsin U12+456 **93**
Cumberland I., Georgia T39+308 **97**
Cumberland Mts., Tenn., etc. T52+365 **97**
Cumberland Pen., N.-W. Terr. T30+664 **89**
Cumberland Plat., Tenn. T66+351 **97**
Cumberland R., Kentucky, etc. T78+368 **97**
Cumberland Sd., N.-W. Terr. S30+650 **89**
Cumbrae, Great, I., Scotland N30+558 **41**
Cumbria, co., England N18+547 **37**
Cumbrian Mts., England N18+545 **37**
Cumbum, India G65+156 **70**
Cumnock, New S. Wales C07-330 **109**
Cumnock, Scotland N26+554 **41**
Cunene R., Angola M16-172 **84**
Cuneo, Italy M45+444 **56**
Cunnamulla, Queensland C26-280 **111**
Cupar, Scotland N18+563 **41**
Cuprija, Yugoslavia L56+440 **58**
Cura, Venezuela S45+100 **104**
Curaca, Brazil Q59-090 **105**
Curaçoa, I., Caribbean Sea S53+122 **104**
Curaglia, Switzerland M37+467 **45**
Curiapo, Venezuela S07+086 **104**

Curico, *Chile* S67–350 **103**
Curiplaya, *Colombia* S89+003 **104**
Curitiba, *Brazil* R25–256 **103**
Curitibanos, *Brazil* R34–273 **103**
Curlewis, *New South Wales* B88–311 **109**
Curnamona, *S. Australia* C63–316 **109**
Curora, *Mozambique* K42–116 **83**
Currabubula, *New S. Wales* B86–312 **109**
Curraes Novos, *Brazil* Q39–062 **105**
Curralinho, *Brazil* R28–017 **105**
Currane L., *Ireland, Rep.* N61+518 **43**
Curraun Pen., (Corraun),
  Ireland, Rep. N59+539 **42**
Currituck Sd., *N. Carolina* T04+364 **97**
Curtis, I., *Pacific Ocean* Z80–305 **106**
Curua, *Brazil* R52+010 **105**
Curuay, Gde. do, L., *Brazil* R62–022 **105**
Curuca, *Brazil* R17–006 **105**
Curupachi, *Brazil* R76–076 **105**
Curuzú Cuatia, *Argentina* R78-298 **103**
Curwensville, *Pennsylvania* T21+410 **96**
Cury, *Brazil* R63–039 **105**
Cushendall, *N. Ireland* N36+551 **42**
Cushendun, *N. Ireland* N36+551 **42**
Cushing, *Oklahoma* U40+359 **95**
Custer, *S. Dakota* U82+437 **93**
Cut.Bank, *Montana* V44+486 **93**
Cuthbert, *Georgia* T59+318 **97**
Cutra L., *Ireland, Rep.* N53+530 **43**
Cuttack, *India* G24+204 **71**
Cuxhaven, *W. Germany* M38+539 **48**
Cuzco, *Peru* S72–135 **104**
Cyclades, See Kikladhes, Is.
Cygnet, *Tasmania* C18–432 **109**
Cynthiana, *Kentucky* T56+385 **97**
Cyprus, I. and rep., *Medi-*
  terranean Sea K72+350 **76**
Cyrenaica, *Libya* L50+292 **81**
Cyrene. See Shahhat
Czechoslovakia, rep.,
  Central Europe **50-51**
Czersk, *Poland* L72+538 **49**
Czestochowa, *Poland* L65+508 **49**
Dabakala, *Ivory Coast* N26+084 **80**
Dabaro, *Somalia* J68+064 **83**
Dabeiba, *Colombia* T07+070 **104**
Dabhoi, *India* H09+220 **70**
Dabie, *Poland* M02+534 **48**
Dabola, *Guinea* N66+108 **80**
Dabrowa Górnicza, *Poland* L65+504 **49**
Dacca, *Bangladesh* F87+237 **71**
Dadanawa, *Guyana* R88+028 **104**
Dade City, *Florida* T43+284 **97**
Dadri, *India* G82+286 **72**
Dagana, *Senegal* P04+164 **80**
Dagarita, *Somalia* K06+106 **83**
Dagash, *Sudan* K70+190 **81**
Dagda, *Latvia* L15+561 **47**
Dagenham, *England* M89+515 **39**
Dagupan, *Philippines* D88+160 **65**
Dahlak Arch, *Ethiopia* K28+156 **83**
Dahomey, rep., See Benin
Daimiel, *Spain* N22+391 **52**
Daireaux, *Argentina* S11–365 **103**
Dairen, See Luta
Dairut, *Egypt* K86+276 **81**
Daisetsuzan Nat. Park, *Japan* C44+435 **68**
Daishoji, *Japan* C82+363 **68**
Dajarra, *Queensland* C63–218 **111**
Dakar, *Senegal* P14+146 **80**
Dakhla, *Mauritania* P06+ 236 **80**
Dakovica, *Yugoslavia* L58+424 **58**
Dal, *Norway* M22+603 **47**
Dal Alv, *Sweden* L80+602 **47**
Dala, *Angola* L58–112 **82**
Dalan Dszadagad, *Mongolia* F02+437 **64**
Dalat, *Vietnam* E70+ 120 **69**
Dalbandin, *Pakistan* H63+290 **70**
Dalbeattie, *Scotland* N23+549 **41**
Dalbo Sjön, *Sweden* M12+589 **47**
Dalby, *Queensland* B83–270 **111**
Dalby, *Sweden* M12+606 **47**
Dalen, *Netherlands* M49+527 **44**
Dalen, *Norway* M42+595 **47**
Dalgety, *New S. Wales* C07–364 **109**
Dalhart, *Texas* U75+360 **98**
Dalhousie, *India* G84+325 **72**
Dalhousie, *New Brunswick* S38+481 **90**
Dalkeith, *Scotland* N18+559 **41**
Dalkey, *Ireland, Rep.* N36+533 **43**
Dallas, *Oregon* W20+449 **92**
Dallas, *Texas* U41+328 **95**
Dallas, L., *Texas* U42+332 **95**
Dalles, The, *Oregon* W07+456 **92**
Dalmacio Velez, *Argentina* S22–327 **103**
Dalmally, *Scotland* N30+564 **41**
Dalmatia, *Yugoslavia* L82+437 **56**
Dalmatovo, *U.S.S.R.* H73+562 **61**
Dalmau, *India* G54+261 **73**
Dalmellington, *Scotland* N26+553 **41**
Daloa, *Ivory Coast* N38+070 **80**
Dalry, *Scotland* N28+557 **41**
Dalrymple, Mt., *Queensland* C15–206 **111**
Dalton, *England* N19+542 **37**
Dalton, *Ontario* T54+481 **91**
Daltonganj, *India* G35+240 **73**
Dalwhinnie, *Scotland* N25+569 **40**
Daly, *N. Terr., Australia* D22–126 **110**
Daly, R., *N. Terr., Australia* D23–142 **110**
Daly Waters, *N. Terr., Aust.* D10–162 **111**
Dam, *Surinam* R60+046 **105**
Daman, *India* H12+204 **70**
Damanhur, *Egypt* K88+310 **81**
Damar, I., *Indonesia* D38–072 **65**
Damavand, mt., *Iran* J48+360 **75**
Dambe, *Angola* L88–068 **82**
Damghan, *Iran* J34+362 **75**
Damietta, *Egypt* K80+314 **81**
Damiya, *Jordan* K57+321 **76**
Dammam Ad, *Saudi Arabia* J57+265 **75**
Damoh, *India* G63+238 **73**
Dampier Arch., *W. Austr.* E22–204 **110**
Dampier Land, *W. Australia* D73–174 **110**
Dampier Str., *Indonesia* D26–007 **65**
Damqawt, *Yemen, South* J43+166 **75**
Dana, Mt., *California* V85+379 **92**
Danbury, *Connecticut* S81+414 **96**
Danby, *California* V62+347 **92**
Dandenong, *Victoria* C29–380 **109**
Danforth, *Maine* S47+457 **90**
Danger Pt., *Cape Province* L64–348 **84**

Dangra Yum L., *Tibet* G20+310 **71**
Danilov, *U.S.S.R.* K29+582 **60**
Dankaz, *Ethiopia* K44+124 **83**
Danmark Fd., *Greenland* P85+810 **26**
Dannemora, *Sweden* L74+603 **34**
Dannevirke, *New Zealand* A23–400 **112**
Dansville, *New York* T16+426 **96**
Danube (Dunarea, Donau), R.,
  Cent. Europe L70+450 **51**
Danville, *Illinois* T76+401 **95**
Danville, *Kentucky* T59+376 **97**
Danville, *Pennsylvania* T10+410 **96**
Danville, *Virginia* T26+366 **97**
Danzig. See Gdansk
Danzig, G. of, *Poland* L66+546 **49**
Daolatabad, *Afghanistan* H60+364 **75**
Daqq-e-Patargan,
  Iran-Afghanistan H88+341 **75**
Daraban Kalan, *Pakistan* H28+317 **72**
Daraw, *Egypt* K72+240 **81**
Darb, *Saudi Arabia* K16+175 **74**
Darbhanga, *India* G24+262 **73**
Dardanelles, *Turkey* L23+400 **74**
Darende, *Turkey* K45+386 **74**
Dar-es-Salaam, *Tanzania* K34–070 **83**
Dargai, *Pakistan* H19+345 **72**
Dargaon, *India* G33+217 **71**
Dargaville, *New Zealand* A37–359 **112**
Dargo, *Victoria* C16–375 **109**
Darien, *Georgia* T39+344 **97**
Darien, G. of, *Colombia* T10+082 **104**
Dariyah, *Saudi Arabia* J81+247 **74**
Darjeeling, *India* G10+270 **73**
Darling Ra., *W. Australia* E22–314 **110**
Darling, R., *New S. Wales* C44–336 **109**
Darling Downs, *Queensland* C00–276 **111**
Darlington, *England* N09+545 **37**
Darlington, *S. Carolina* T29+343 **97**
Darlington, *Wisconsin* U01+426 **95**
Darlington Point, *N.S.W.* C24–346 **109**
Darlowo, *Poland* L82+544 **49**
Darmstadt, *W. Germany* M38+499 **48**
Daroca, *Spain* N08+411 **53**
Dart, C., *Antarctica* W10–720 **27**
Dart R., *England* N22+505 **38**
Dartmoor, *England* N23+506 **38**
Dartmoor, *Victoria* C53–380 **109**
Dartmouth, *England* N21+503 **38**
Dartmouth, *Nova Scotia* S21+447 **90**
Daru, I., *Papua New Guinea* C41–091 **111**
Darun, *Iran* J58+330 **75**
Daruvar, *Yugoslavia* L77+456 **56**
Darwen, *England* N15+537 **37**
Darwin, *N. Terr., Australia* D24–124 **110**
Darwin, mt., *Chile* S56–548 **103**
Darwin Mt., *Zimbabwe* K80–168 **84**
Daryabad, *India* G51+269 **73**
Daryacheh e Baktegan L.,
  Iran J36+295 **75**
Daryacheh-ye-Namak, *Iran* J50+348 **75**
Daryacheh-ye-Reza'iyeh, *Iran* J88+378 **74**
Dasara, *Bangladesh* G00+239 **73**
Dashibalbar, *Mongolia* E34+495 **64**
Dasht R., *Pakistan* H78+256 **70**
Dasht Ab, *Iran* J21+289 **75**
Dashtiari, *Iran* H82+255 **75**
Daska, *Pakistan* H04+323 **72**
Daspalla, *India* G31+203 **71**
Daspur, *India* G23+220 **73**
Dasuya, *India* G86+318 **72**
Dataganj, *India* G63+280 **73**
Datia, *India* G69+256 **73**
Daudnagar, *India* G33+250 **73**
Daugavgriva, *Latvia* L36+570 **47**
Daugavpils, *Latvia* L21+559 **47**
Daulatabad, *India* G88+200 **70**
Daulat Yar, *Afghanistan* H55+345 **75**
Daule, *Ecuador* T30–018 **104**
Dauletabad, *Iran* J35+361 **75**
Dauphin, *Manitoba* U60+509 **88**
Dauphine, prov., *France* M56+449 **55**
Davao & G., *Philippines* D57+070 **65**
Davenport, *Iowa* U04+415 **95**
Davenport Ra., *N.T., Aust.* D00–209 **111**
Daventry, *England* N07+523 **37**
David, *Panama* T44+085 **101**
David City, *Nebraska* U43+412 **95**
Davignab, *Namibia* L62–276 **84**
Davis Mts., *Texas* U84+308 **94**
Davis Sea, *Antarctica* F60–650 **27**
Davis Str., *Greenland* R80+660 **26**
Davos Dorf, *Switzerland* M31+468 **45**
Davos Platz, *Switzerland* M31+468 **45**
Davy Sd., *Greenland* P40+720 **26**
Dawna R., *Burma* F41+170 **71**
Dawson, *Georgia* T57+318 **97**
Dawson, *Minnesota* U36+449 **93**
Dawson, *New Mexico* V00+366 **94**
Dawson, *N. Dakota* U59+469 **93**
Dawson, *Yukon* X25+643 **88**
Dawson Ra., *Yukon* X22+629 **88**
Dawson, R., *Queensland* C02–255 **111**
Dawson Creek, *B.C.* W02+558 **88**
Dawsonville, *Georgia* T55+344 **97**
Dax, *France* N06+437 **55**
Daylesford, *Victoria* C35–374 **109**
Dayton, *Tennessee* T60+355 **97**
Dayton, *Ohio* T55+398 **91**
Daytona Beach, *Florida* T36+292 **97**
De Aar, *Cape Province* L36–308 **84**
Dead Sea, *Jordan-Israel* K56+314 **76**
Deadwood, *S. Dakota* U82+446 **98**
Deal, *England* M82+512 **39**
Dean, Forest of, *England* N15+518 **38**
Dean Funes, *Argentina* S27–304 **103**
Dease Arm, *N.-W. Terr.* W00+664 **88**
Dease Lake, *Brit. Columbia* W60+580 **88**
Dease R., *Brit. Columbia* W55+592 **88**
Dease Str., *N.-W. Terr.* V20+682 **88**
Death Valley, *California* V72+366 **92**
Deauville, *France* N00+494 **54**
Debar, *Yugoslavia* L57+416 **58**
Debec, *New Brunswick* S46+461 **90**
Debess, *U.S.S.R.* J36+576 **61**
Deblin, *Poland* L49+506 **49**
Debno, *Poland* L92+527 **48**
Debra Markos, *Ethiopia* K42+104 **83**
Debrecen, *Hungary* L51+475 **49**
Decatur, *Alabama* T72+346 **97**
Decatur, *Georgia* T56+338 **97**
Decatur, *Illinois* T84+398 **95**

Decaturville, *Tennessee* T79+355 **97**
Deccan, *India* G80+130 **70**
Deception, I., *South Shetlands* S04–630 **27**
Decín, *Czechoslovakia* M05+508 **48**
Decize, *France* M69+468 **54**
Decorah, *Iowa* U11+412 **95**
Dedeagach. See Alexandroupolis
Dedham, *Massachusetts* S67+423 **96**
Dédougou, *Upper Volta* N20+122 **80**
Dedza, *Malawi* K64–142 **83**
Dee R., *Scotland* N12+571 **40**
Dee R., *Wales* N18+530 **38**
  Deel R., *Ireland, Rep.* N54+526 **43**
Deep Creek L., *Maryland* T26+395 **96**
Deepwater, *New S. Wales* B79–294 **109**
Deer I., *Maine* S52+442 **90**
Deer Lake, *Newfoundland* R74+492 **90**
Deerlijk, *Belgium* M70+508 **44**
Deer Lodge, *Montana* V46+464 **92**
Deer River, *Minnesota* U23+473 **93**
Defferrari, *Argentina* R87–384 **103**
De Funiak Springs, *Florida* T67+307 **97**
Degana, *India* H02+270 **70**
Degerfors, *Sweden* L62+642 **46**
De Gerlache Str., *Antarctica* S20–650 **27**
Degrad, *Brazil* R39+021 **105**
De Grey, R., *W. Australia* E02–204 **110**
Deh Bid, *Iran* J41+306 **75**
Dehra, (Dehra Dun), *India* G71+303 **72**
Dehrud, *Iran* J50+290 **75**
Deim Zubeir, *Sudan* L22+078 **81**
Deinze, *Belgium* M69+510 **44**
Deir Abu Said, *Jordan* K56+325 **76**
Deir 'Ali, *Syria* K52+332 **76**
Deir ez Zor, *Syria* K29+354 **74**
Deir Hafir, *Syria* K44+361 **76**
Deir Shemil, *Syria* K52+352 **76**
Dej, *Romania* L37+471 **49**
Dekalb, *Illinois* T82+419 **95**
De Kalb, *Mississippi* T82+328 **97**
De Kastri, *U.S.S.R.* C55+515 **63**
Dekoven, *Kentucky* T79+376 **97**
Delano Mt., *Utah* V45+385 **98**
Delano Pk., *Utah* V44+384 **94**
Delavan, *Wisconsin* T82+427 **91**
Delaware N.J., etc. T02+418 **91**
Delaware, *Ohio* T49+403 **91**
Delaware, state, *U.S.A.* T03+391 **99**
Delaware B., *Del.-New Jersey* T01+391 **96**
Delaware City, *Delaware* T03+396 **96**
Delaware R., *New York, etc.* T01+405 **96**
Delden, *Netherlands* M50+523 **44**
Delegate, *New S. Wales* C06–370 **109**
Deleitosa, *Spain* N33+396 **52**
De Lemmer, *Netherlands* M56+528 **44**
Delémont, *Switzerland* M46+474 **45**
Delfshaven, *Netherlands* M63+519 **44**
Delft, *Netherlands* M64+520 **44**
Delfzijl, *Netherlands* M48+533 **44**
Delgado C., *Mozambique* K26–108 **83**
Delger, *Mongolia* E56+457 **64**
Delgo, *Sudan* K86+200 **81**
Delhi, *India* G77+286 **72**
Delhi, *New York* T00+423 **96**
Dellenbaugh, Mt., *Arizona* V51+363 **92**
Dellys, *Algeria* M66+366 **80**
Delmenhorst, *W. Germany* M39+530 **48**
Del Norte, *Colorado* V08+376 **94**
Deloraine, *Tasmania* C20–415 **109**
Del Rio, *Texas* U66+294 **94**
Delta, *Colorado* V18+387 **94**
Delta, *Louisiana* U06+329 **97**
Delta, *Missouri* T89+372 **97**
Delta, *Pennsylvania* T08+397 **96**
Delta, *Utah* V46+396 **94**
Delungra, *New S. Wales* B85–296 **109**
Demanda, Sa. de la, *Spain* N18+422 **52**
Demchok, *Tibet* G63+326 **70**
Deming, *New Mexico* V18+323 **94**
Demirji Dagh, *Turkey* L10+391 **74**
Demmin, *E. Germany* M12+539 **48**
Demopolis, *Alabama* T77+325 **97**
Denbigh, *Wales* N20+532 **38**
Denderleeuw, *Belgium* M66+509 **44**
Dendermonde, *Belgium* M65+511 **44**
Dendi, mt., *Ethiopia* K42+086 **83**
Denekamp, *Netherlands* M48+524 **44**
Den Haag. See s' Gravenhage
Denham Ra., *Queensland* C08–260 **111**
Denia, *Spain* M89+388 **53**
Deniliquin, *New S. Wales* C30–356 **109**
Denison, *Iowa* U32+420 **95**
Denison, *Texas* U39+338 **95**
Denizli, *Turkey* L05+377 **74**
Denman, *New S. Wales* B86–324 **109**
Denmark, *S. Carolina* T37+333 **97**
Denmark, kingdom, *W. Eur.* **47**
Denmark Str., *Greenland, etc.* Q00+670 **25**
Den Oever, *Netherlands* M60+529 **44**
Dent Blanche, mt., *Switz.* M44+460 **45**
Denton, *Maryland* T05+389 **91**
Denton, *Texas* U42+332 **95**
D'Entrecasteaux, Is.,
  Papua New Guinea B80–100 **111**
D'Entrecasteaux Pt.,
  W. Australia E24–348 **110**
Denver, *Colorado* V00+397 **94**
Deoband, *India* G74+297 **72**
Deobhog, *India* G44+200 **71**
Deogarh, *India* G32+214 **71**
Deoghar, *India* G12+245 **73**
Deoli, *India* G88+257 **70**
Deoria, *India* G37+265 **73**
De Panne, *Belgium* M74+511 **44**
De Pere, *Wisconsin* T78+445 **91**
Deposit, *New York* T03+421 **91**
Depot Harbor, *Ontario* T31+453 **91**
Dera, *Syria* K53+326 **76**
Dera Bugti, *Pakistan* H35+291 **70**
Dera Ghazi Khan, *Pakistan* H26+301 **72**
Dera Ismail Khan, *Pakistan* H25+318 **72**
Dera Nanak, *India* G89+320 **72**
Derbent, *U.S.S.R.* J71+422 **62**
Derby, *W. Australia* D68–172 **110**
Derby & co., *England* N09+529 **37**
Derecske, *Hungary* L51+474 **49**
Derg L., *Ireland, Rep.* N47+546 **42**
Derg L., *Ireland, Rep.* N50+530 **43**
Derg R., *N. Ireland* N46+547 **42**

De Ridder, *Louisiana* U20+308 **95**
De Rijp, *Netherlands* M61+525 **44**
Dermott, *Arkansas* U07+336 **95**
Derna, (Dernah), *Libya* L44+326 **81**
Dernberg C., *Namibia* L86-278 **84**
Derravaragh L., *Ireland, Rep.* N44+537 **42**
Derryveagh Mts.,
  Ireland, Rep. N49+550 **42**
Derudeb, *Sudan* K54+174 **81**
De Ruyter, *New York* T05+428 **96**
Derventa, *Yugoslavia* L73+450 **56**
Derwent, R., *England* N12+548 **37**
Derwent R., *England* N05+538 **37**
Derwent R., *Tasmania* C22–424 **109**
Derwent Water, *England* N19+546 **37**
Des Arc, *Arkansas* U09+350 **97**
Descalvados, *Brazil* R76–167 **104**
Deschaillons, *Quebec* S72+466 **91**
Deseado, R., *Argentina* S50–468 **103**
Deshambault L., *Sask.* V00+546 **88**
Des Moines & R., *Iowa* U22+416 **95**
Desna, R., *Ukraine* K84+512 **60**
Desolacion, I., *Chile* S84–532 **103**
Desolation C., *Greenland* R25+610 **26**
De Soto, *Missouri* U04+382 **95**
Dessau, *E. Germany* M16+518 **48**
Deta, *Romania* L53+454 **58**
Detroit, *Michigan* T48+424 **91**
Detroit Lakes, *Minnesota* U35+468 **93**
Dett, *Zimbabwe* L18–186 **84**
Deurne, *Netherlands* M55+515 **44**
Deux Rivières, *Ontario* T20+463 **91**
Deux-Sèvres, dep., *France* N03+466 **54**
Déva, *Romania* L43+459 **58**
Dévávanya, *Hungary* L54+471 **49**
Deventer, *Netherlands* M53+523 **44**
Deveron R., *Scotland* N15+577 **40**
Devil's Elbow, *Scotland* N21+569 **41**
Devils Lake, *N. Dakota* U53+481 **93**
Devin, *Bulgaria* L34+417 **58**
Devizes, *England* N12+513 **39**
Devon, co., *England* N22+508 **38**
Devon I., *N.-W. Territories* T60+750 **89**
Devonport, England* N25+504 **38**
Devonport, *New Zealand* A31–368 **112**
Devonport, *Tasmania* C22–412 **109**
De Witt, *Arkansas* U08+343 **97**
Dewsbury, *England* N10+537 **37**
Dexter, *Maine* S56+450 **90**
Dexter, *Missouri* U00+368 **95**
Dezful, *Iran* J70+324 **74**
Dhaba, *Saudi Arabia* K56+274 **74**
Dhahran, *Saudi Arabia* J58+263 **75**
Dhak, *Pakistan* H15+325 **72**
Dhamar, *Yemen* K04+147 **74**
Dhampur, *India* G69+293 **73**
Dhamra, *India* G18+208 **71**
Dhamtari, *India* G50+208 **70**
Dhang Ra., *Nepal* G48+282 **73**
Dhangain, *India* G34+252 **73**
Dhank, *Oman* J23+236 **75**
Dhankuta, *Nepal* G16+270 **73**
Dhariya, *Saudi Arabia* K13+247 **74**
Dharmkot, *India* G88+309 **72**
Dharmsala, *India* G82+322 **72**
Dharwar, *India* H00+156 **70**
Dhaulagiri, mt., *Nepal* G40+287 **73**
Dhiban, *Jordan* K55+315 **76**
Dhidhimotikhon, *Greece* L21+413 **58**
Dhionisiadhes. See Yianisahes Is.
Dholera, *India* H27+222 **70**
Dholpur, *India* G73+267 **73**
Dhond, *India* H01+184 **70**
Dhula, *Yemen, South* J71+150 **74**
Dhulia, *India* H01+209 **70**
Dhurma, *Saudi Arabia* J84+246 **74**
Dhurwai, *India* G66+255 **73**
Dia I., *Crete* L29+354 **59**
Diamante, *Argentina* S04–320 **103**
Diamantina, *Brazil* R69–144 **105**
Diamantina, *Brazil* Q81–182 **105**
Diamantina, R., *Queensland* C53–242 **111**
Diamond, I., *Burma* F64+159 **71**
Diamond Harbour, *India* G10+222 **73**
Dibah, *U.A.E.* J22+257 **75**
Dibai, *U.A.E.* J28+253 **75**
Dibbah, Jebel, *Saudi Arabia* K56+278 **74**
Dibbéla, *Niger* M14+176 **81**
Dibit, *Somalia* J72+060 **83**
Dibrugarh, *India* F60+274 **71**
Dickinson, *N. Dakota* U77+469 **93**
Dickson, *Tennessee* T75+362 **95**
Die, *France* M60+448 **55**
Diefenbaker L., *Saskatchewan* V10+510 **88**
Diego Garcia, I., *Indian Oc.* H35–100 **25**
Diego Suarez, *Madagascar* J64–124 **83**
Dien Bien Phu, *Vietnam* F12+212 **69**
Dieppe, *France* M84+499 **54**
Diest, *Belgium* M60+510 **44**
Dieverbrug, *Netherlands* M52+529 **44**
Dig, *India* G76+274 **72**
Digby, *Nova Scotia* S35+446 **90**
Digby Neck, *Nova Scotia* S37+444 **90**
Dighal, *Yemen, South* J70+146 **74**
Digne, *France* M53+441 **55**
Digoin, *France* M66+465 **54**
Diguel, R., *Irian Jaya,*
  Indon. C60–072 **65**
Dijon, *France* M60+473 **54**
Diksmuide, *Belgium* M73+510 **44**
Dikwa, *Nigeria* M06+120 **81**
Dilam, *Saudi Arabia* J76+240 **74**
Dili, *Timor I., Indonesia* D56–086 **65**
Dillon, *Montana* V46+452 **92**
Dilolo, *Angola* L48–118 **82**
Dilolo, *Zaire* L46–106 **82**
Dimbokro, *Ivory Coast* N28+068 **80**
Dimitrovo (Pernik), *Bulgaria* L42+426 **58**
Dimitrovgrad, *Yugoslavia* L43+431 **58**
Dimla, *Bangladesh* G06+261 **73**
Dimotika. See Dhidhimotikhon.
Dinagat, I., *Philippines* D56+100 **65**
Dinajpur, *Bangladesh* G08+256 **73**
Dinan, *France* N12+485 **54**
Dinanagar, *India* G87+322 **72**
Dinant, *Belgium* M60+503 **44**
Dinapur, *India* G29+256 **73**
Dinar, *Turkey* K89+381 **74**
Dinard, *France* N13+486 **54**

Dinarske Planina, *Yugoslavia* L82+440 **56**
Dinas Mawddwy, *Wales* N22+527 **38**
Dindigul, *India* G72+104 **70**
Dingle & B., *Ireland, Rep.* N62+521 **43**
Dingwall, *Scotland* N27+576 **40**
Dinosaur Nat. Mon., *Colo.* V23+406 **94**
Dinteloord, *Netherlands* M64+516 **44**
Diourbel, *Senegal* P08+146 **80**
Dipalpur, *Pakistan* H08+306 **72**
Dipton, *New Zealand* A69–459 **112**
Dir, *Pakistan* H18+352 **72**
Direction, C., *Queensland* C39–129 **111**
Diredawe, *Ethiopia* K20+094 **83**
Diriamba, *Nicaragua* T66+117 **101**
Dirk Hartogs I., *W. Aust.* E42–258 **110**
Dirksland, *Netherlands* M65+518 **44**
Dirranbandi, *Queensland* C11–284 **111**
Disappointment, C., *Wash.* W24+463 **92**
Disappointment Is.,
    Tuamotu Arch. X38–145 **107**
Disappointment, I., *W. Aust.* D73–234 **110**
Disaster B., *New S. Wales* C00–373 **109**
Discovery B., *Victoria* C54–382 **109**
Disentis, *Switzerland* M37+467 **45**
Disko B., *Greenland* R35+690 **26**
Disko, I., *Greenland* R35+700 **26**
Disna, *Byelorussia* L11+552 **60**
Dison, *Belgium* M55+506 **44**
District of Columbia, *U.S.A.* T12+386 **91**
Diu, *India* H23+208 **70**
Diver, *Ontario* T28+468 **91**
Dividing Range, mts., *Aust.* C10–260 **111**
Diviso, *Colombia* T20+014 **104**
Divrigi, *Turkey* K41+394 **74**
Diwan Chah, *Iran* H85+299 **75**
Diwangiri, *India* F81+268 **71**
Diwaniyah, *Iraq* K01+320 **74**
Dix, *Quebec* T07+482 **91**
Dixmude, *Belgium* M73+510 **44**
Dixon, *Illinois* T87+418 **95**
Dixon, *Kentucky* T76+375 **97**
Dixon Entrance, *B.C.* W75+545 **88**
Diyarbakir, *Turkey* K28+380 **74**
Dizah, *Iran* H76+272 **75**
Djaid, *U.A.E.* J24+254 **75**
Djajapura, *See* Jajapura
Djakarta, *See* Jakarta
Djambi, *See* Jambi
Djawa, *See* Java
Djelfa, *Algeria* M70+346 **80**
Djeneien, *Tunisia* M30+318 **81**
Djerba, I., *Tunisia* M26+338 **81**
Djibouti, *E. Africa* K12+114 **83**
Djidjelh, *Algeria* M54+366 **80**
Djolu, *Zaire* L46+08 **82**
Djougou, *Benin* M80+098 **80**
Djursholm, *Sweden* L72+594 **47**
Dmitriya Lapteva Proliv,
    U.S.S.R. C40+730 **63**
Dnepr R., *Ukraine* K68+470 **60**
Dneprodzerzhinsk, *Ukraine* K62+486 **60**
Dnepropetrovsk, *Ukraine* K60+485 **60**
Dnester (Dniester), R., *Ukr.* L28+489 **60**
Doaktown, *New Brunswick* S37+466 **90**
Dobbyn, *Queensland* C60–198 **111**
Dobele, *Latvia* L40+566 **47**
Doberan, *E. Germany* M19+541 **48**
Dobra, *Czechoslovakia* L50+491 **49**
Dobřany, *Czechoslovakia* M11+497 **48**
Dobrich. *See* Tolbukhin.
Dobruja, *Romania* L10+455 **58**
Dobryanka, *U.S.S.R.* J22+584 **61**
Dobrzyn, *Poland* L66+531 **49**
Doce Leguas, Cayos de las,
    Cuba T25+210 **101**
Doctor Arroyo, *Mexico* U61+238 **100**
Dodecanese, *Greece* L18+360 **59**
Dodge City, *Kansas* U60+378 **95**
Dodgeville, *Wisconsin* U01+430 **95**
Dodman Pt., *England* N29+502 **38**
Dodoma, *Tanzania* K56–062 **83**
Dodson, *Montana* V20+484 **93**
Doel, *Belgium* M64+513 **44**
Doesburg, *Netherlands* M53+520 **44**
Doetinchem, *Netherlands* M52+520 **44**
Dogger Bank, *North Sea* M78+545 **34**
Doha, *Qatar, Arabia* J51+253 **75**
Dohad, *India* H04+228 **70**
Doka, *Saudi Arabia* K23+199 **74**
Dokka, *Yemen* K05+131 **74**
Dokkum, *Netherlands* M54+533 **44**
Dol, *France* N10+485 **54**
Dolbeau, *Quebec* S73+488 **90**
Dolcigno. *See* Ulcinj.
Dôle, *France* M57+471 **54**
Dolent, Mt., *Switzerland* M48+459 **45**
Dolgellau, *Wales* N23+527 **38**
Dollar, *Scotland* N22+562 **41**
Dolo, *Ethiopia* K18+040 **83**
Dolomitiche, Alpi, *Italy* M18+464 **56**
Dolores, *Argentina* R76–364 **103**
Dolores, *Mexico* V35+251 **100**
Dolores, *Spain* N05+381 **53**
Dolphin, C., *Falkland Is.* R84–512 **103**
Dolunnor. *See* Tolun.
Dom, mt., *Irian Jaya,*
    Indon. C78–027 **65**
Domariaganj, *India* G44+272 **73**
Dombås, *Norway* M35+621 **46**
Domburg, *Netherlands* M69+516 **44**
Domel, I., *Burma* F41+115 **71**
Dome Rock Mts., *Arizona* V54+336 **92**
Domfront, *France* N04+486 **54**
Dominica, I., *West Indies* S07+154 **101**
Dominican Rep., *West Indies* S60+190 **101**
Dömitz, *E. Germany* M23+531 **48**
Dom Pedrito, *Brazil* R58–310 **103**
Domuyo, mt., *Argentina* S63–366 **103**
Domvraina, *Greece* L42+383 **59**
Don R., *England* N07+535 **37**
Don, R., *U.S.S.R.* K20+481 **62**
Don R., *Scotland* N13+572 **40**
Donaghadee, *N. Ireland* N33+546 **42**
Donald, *Victoria* C42–364 **109**
Donaldson, *Louisiana* U06+301 **95**
Donau, R., *Central Europe* M14+489 **48**
Donaueschingen, *W. Germany* M39+479 **48**
Don Benito, *Spain* N35+388 **52**
Doncaster, *England* N07+535 **37**
Dondo, *Angola* M04–096 **82**
Donegal & co., *Ireland, Rep.* N49+546 **42**

Donegal B., *Ireland, Rep.* N52+545 **42**
Donegal Pt., *Ireland, Rep.* N58+527 **43**
Donets, R., *U.S.S.R.* K25+480 **61**
Donetsk, *Ukraine* K43+479 **60**
Donga, *Nigeria* M30+076 **81**
Dongara, *W. Australia* E30–290 **110**
Donggala, *Celebes. Indon.* E02–008 **65**
Dong-hoi, *Vietnam* E80+174 **69**
Dongo, *Angola* L86–146 **82**
Dongola, *Sudan* K88+190 **81**
Doniphan, *Missouri* U05+366 **97**
Donji Miholjac, *Yugoslavia* L72+457 **56**
Dønna, *Norway* M15+661 **46**
Don Pia-fai, mt., *Thailand* F22+144 **69**
Doon R. & L., *Scotland* N26+553 **41**
Doorn, *Netherlands* M58+520 **44**
Dora, L., *W. Australia* D72–221 **110**
Doranda, *India* G28+233 **73**
Dorat, le. *France* M83+462 **54**
Dorchester, *England* N15+507 **38**
Dorchester, *New Brunswick* S27+459 **90**
Dorchester, C., *N.-W. Terr.* T20+654 **89**
Dordogne, dep., *France* M85+451 **54**
Dordogne R., *France* N03+450 **55**
Dordrecht, *Netherlands* M62+518 **44**
Dore L., *Saskatchewan* V14+548 **88**
Dore, Mt., *France* M72+454 **54**
Dores, *Brazil* R39–306 **103**
Dori, *Upper Volta* N00+140 **80**
Dorking, *England* N02+512 **39**
Dornie, *Scotland* N33+573 **40**
Dornoch & Firth, *Scotland* N24+579 **40**
Dorotea, *Sweden* L81+643 **46**
Dorrego, *Argentina* S08–387 **103**
Dorrigo, *New S. Wales* B75–304 **109**
Dorset, co., *England* N14+508 **38**
Dorsey, *Montana* V34+464 **93**
Dortmund, *W. Germany* M45+515 **48**
Dos Bahias, C., *Argentina* S33–450 **103**
Doshi, *Afghanistan* H37+356 **75**
Dospat, *Bulgaria* L36+416 **58**
Dosso, *Cameroon* M70+130 **80**
Dossor, *Kazakh* J43+475 **62**
Dothan, *Alabama* T62+312 **97**
Douai, *France* M71+504 **54**
Douala, *Cameroon* M32+040 **81**
Douarnenez, *France* N25+481 **54**
Doubs, dep., *France* M51+471 **54**
Doubtless B., *New Zealand* A39–349 **112**
Doucet, *Quebec* T10+482 **91**
Douglas, *Arizona* V27+313 **94**
Douglas, *Cape Province* L32–290 **84**
Douglas, *Georgia* T47+315 **97**
Douglas, *I. of Man* N27+542 **37**
Douglas, Mt., *Montana* V32+454 **98**
Douglas, *Wyoming* V02+428 **93**
Douglastown, *Quebec* S26+488 **90**
Douglasville, *Georgia* T58+337 **97**
Doullens, *France* M76+502 **54**
Doulus Hd., *Ireland, Rep.* N62+520 **43**
Doume, *Cameroon* M08+044 **81**
Doune, *Scotland* N24+562 **41**
Dounreay, *Scotland* N22+586 **40**
Douro, & R., *Spain-Portugal* N49+411 **52**
Dover, *Delaware* T03+392 **96**
Dover, *England* M82+511 **39**
Dover, *New Hampshire* S65+434 **96**
Dover, *New Jersey* S87+409 **96**
Dover, *Ohio* T39+406 **91**
Dover, *Tasmania* C18–433 **109**
Dover, *Tennessee* T77+365 **97**
Dover, Str.. of,
    England-France M81+505 **54**
Dover Foxcroft, *Maine* S55+452 **90**
Dovrefjell, *Norway* M36+622 **46**
Dow L., *Botswana* L32–214 **84**
Dowa, *Malawi* K66–136 **83**
Down, co., *N. Ireland* M36+543 **42**
Downham Market, *England* M88+526 **39**
Downpatrick, *N. Ireland* N34+543 **42**
Downpatrick Hd.,
    Ireland, Rep. N56+543 **42**
Doyles, *Newfoundland* R85+479 **90**
Doylestown, *Pennsylvania* T01+403 **96**
Drăgăşani, *Romania* L34+446 **58**
Draguignan, *France* M51+436 **55**
Drake, *New S. Wales* B76–289 **109**
Drake Str., *Antarctica* S00–580 **27**
Drakensberg, mts., *S. Africa* L04–270 **84**
Dráma, *Greece* L35+411 **58**
Drammen, *Norway* M28+598 **47**
Dranov I., *Romania* L04+449 **58**
Dras, *Kashmir* G85+344 **72**
Drawsko, *Poland* L85+535 **49**
Drayton, *N. Dakota* U43+486 **93**
Drazinda, *Pakistan* H30+318 **72**
Drem, *Scotland* N16+560 **41**
Drenthe, prov., *Netherlands* M50+528 **44**
Dresden, *E. Germany* M07+511 **48**
Dresden, *Ontario* T44+426 **91**
Dreux, *France* M82+487 **54**
Drimoleague, *Ireland, Rep.* N56+516 **43**
Drin G., *Albania* L63+417 **58**
Drina, R., *Yugoslavia* L66+436 **58**
Drøbak, *Norway* M26+597 **47**
Drogheda & B., *Ireland, Rep.* N38+537 **42**
Droitwich, *England* N13+523 **39**
Drome, dep. & R., *France* M65+447 **55**
Dromod, *Ireland, Rep.* N47+539 **42**
Dromore West, *Ireland, Rep.* N53+542 **42**
Dromore, *N. Ireland* N37+544 **42**
Dromore, *N. Ireland* N45+545 **42**
Drongen, *Belgium* M68+511 **44**
Drum Hills, *Ireland, Rep.* N46+520 **43**
Drumheller, *Alberta* V45+513 **88**
Drummond I., *Michigan* T52+460 **91**
Drummondville, *Quebec* S75+459 **91**
Drumnadrochit, *Scotland* N27+573 **40**
Drumshanbo, *Ireland, Rep.* N48+540 **42**
Drunen, *Netherlands* M59+517 **44**
Druten, *Netherlands* M56+519 **44**
Druz, Jeb. ed, *Syria* K49+326 **76**
Dryden, *Ontario* U15+498 **89**
Drygalski I., *Antarctica* F78–660 **27**
Drymen, *Scotland* N27+561 **41**
Drysdale River, *W. Australia* D49–141 **110**
Dschang, *Cameroon* M30+056 **82**
Dubawnt L., *N.-W. Terr.* U70+638 **88**
Dubbo, *New S. Wales* C08–323 **109**
Dublin, *Georgia* T47+324 **99**
Dublin & co., *Ireland, Rep.* N38+533 **43**

Dublin, *Texas* U50+322 **95**
Dubno, *Ukraine* L26+504 **60**
Du Bois, *Pennsylvania* T23+411 **96**
Dubrovnik, *Yugoslavia* L71+427 **58**
Dubuque, *Iowa* U04+425 **95**
Duchcov, *Czechoslovakia* M08+506 **48**
Duchesne, *Utah* V32+402 **94**
Ducie I., *Pacific Ocean* W26–254 **107**
Duck Is., *Ontario* T48+457 **91**
Dudinka, *U.S.S.R.* G26+693 **62**
Dudley, *England* N13+525 **37**
Duero R., *Spain* N27+416 **52**
Duffel, *Belgium* M61+511 **44**
Dufftown, *Scotland* N19+574 **40**
Dugi Otok, I., *Yugoslavia* M00+440 **56**
Duifken Pt., *Queensland* C50–124 **111**
Duisburg, *W. Germany* M50+515 **48**
Dujana, *India* G80+287 **72**
Duke of Gloucester Grp.,
    Tuamotu Archipelago W80–208 **107**
Duke of York Arch.,
    N.-W. Territories V50+678 **88**
Duk Faiwil, *Sudan* K82+076 **81**
Dulce, G., *Costa Rica* T49+086 **101**
Duluth, *Minnesota* U13+468 **93**
Dulverton, *England* N21+510 **38**
Duma, *Syria* K52+335 **76**
Dumas, *Arkansas* U09+338 **97**
Dumas, *Texas* U71+358 **94**
Dumbarton, *Scotland* N27+559 **41**
Dum-Dum, *India* G09+226 **73**
Dumeir, *Syria* K50+336 **76**
Dumfries, *Scotland* N22+551 **41**
Dumfries & Galloway, reg., *Scot.*
    N26+550 **41**
Dumka, *India* G16+243 **73**
Dumraon, *India* G35+255 **73**
Dunarea (Danube), R., *Cent.*
    Europe L24+441 **51**
Dunbar, *Scotland* N15+560 **41**
Dunblane, *Scotland* N24+562 **41**
Dunboyne, *Ireland, Rep.* N39+534 **43**
Duncan, *Arkansas* U08+346 **97**
Duncan, *Oklahoma* U48+345 **95**
Duncan Pass., *Andaman Is.* F75+112 **71**
Duncannon, *Ireland, Rep.* N41+522 **43**
Duncansby Hd., *Scotland* N18+586 **40**
Dundalk & B., *Ireland, Rep.* N38+540 **42**
Dundas, *Ontario* T30+433 **91**
Dundas, *Tasmania* C27–419 **109**
Dundas Str., *N. Terr., Aust.* D20–110 **110**
Dun Dealgan. *See* Dundalk
Dundee, *Natal* K88–282 **84**
Dundee, *Scotland* N18+565 **41**
Dundee I., *Antarctica* R62–630 **27**
Dundrum & B., *N. Ireland* N35+543 **42**
Dundwa Ra., *Nepal* G46+278 **73**
Dunedin, *New Zealand* A 57–459 **112**
Dunedoo, *New S. Wales* C04–320 **109**
Dunfanaghy, *Ireland, Rep.,* N48+552 **42**
Dunfermline, *Scotland* N21+561 **41**
Dungannon, *N. Ireland* N41+545 **42**
Dungarpur, *India* H08+238 **70**
Dungarven & Harb.,
    Ireland, Rep. N46+521 **43**
Dungbre Ra., *Tibet* G30+350 **71**
Dungeness, *England* M84+509 **39**
Dungiven, *N. Ireland* N41+549 **42**
Dungloe, *Ireland, Rep.* N50+549 **42**
Dungog, *New S. Wales* B80–324 **109**
Dungu, *Zaire* L08+034 **83**
Dunkeld, *Scotland* N22+566 **41**
Dunkerque (Dunkirk), *France* M76+511 **54**
Dunkirk, *New York* T26+425 **96**
Dunkur, *Ethiopia* K54+118 **83**
Dunkwa, *Ghana* N12+060 **80**
Dún Laoghaire, *Ireland, Rep.* N38+532 **43**
Dunlap, *Iowa* U36+420 **95**
Dunlavin, *Ireland, Rep.* N40+530 **43**
Dunleer, *Ireland, Rep.* N38+538 **42**
Dunlop, *Scotland* N27+557 **41**
Dunmanus B., *Ireland, Rep.* N59+516 **43**
Dunmanway, *Ireland, Rep.* N55+517 **43**
Dunmore, *Ireland, Rep.* N52+536 **42**
Dunn, *N. Carolina* T22+353 **97**
Dunnet Hd & B., *Scotland* N20+586 **40**
Dunolly, *Victoria* C38–369 **109**
Dunoon, *Scotland* N30+559 **41**
Duns, *Scotland* N14+558 **41**
Dunstable, *England* N03+519 **39**
Dunvegan & L., *Scotland* N39+574 **40**
Dupulan, *Iran* J56+320 **75**
Du Quain, *Illinois* T86+380 **97**
Duque de York, I., *Chile* T01–506 **103**
Dura, *Jordan* K60+315 **76**
Durango, *Colorado* V17+372 **94**
Durango & state, *Mexico* U88+240 **100**
Durant, *Mississippi* T89+330 **97**
Durant, *Oklahoma* U38+340 **95**
Durazno, *Uruguay* R69–334 **103**
Durazzo. *See* Durrës
Durban, *Natal* K84–298 **84**
Durbe, *Latvia* L52+566 **47**
Durbuy, *Belgium* M57+503 **44**
Durdevac, *Yugoslavia* L78+460 **56**
Durdurch, *Somalia* J68+112 **83**
Dureikish, *Syria* K53+349 **76**
Duren, *W. Germany* M51+508 **48**
Durga Str., *New Guinea* C70–073 **111**
Durham, *N. Carolina* T23+360 **97**
Durham, *Ontario* T35+442 **91**
Durham & co., *England* N09+548 **37**
Durness & Kyle of, *Scotland* N28+586 **40**
Durrës, *Albania* L63+413 **58**
Durrow, *Ireland, Rep.* N44+528 **43**
Dursey I. & Hd., *Ireland, Rep.* N61+516 **43**
Dursley, *England* N14+517 **38**
Duruh, *Iran* H86+322 **75**
Durukhsh, *Iran* J01+331 **75**
D'Urville I., *New Zealand* A37–408 **112**
Dushanbe, *Tadzhik* H37+386 **62**
Dushore, *Pennsylvania* T09+415 **96**
Dusky Sound, *New Zealand* A81–457 **112**
Düsseldorf, *W. Germany* M49+513 **48**
Dusznika, *Netherlands* M60+517 **44**
Duszniki Zdrój, *Poland* L82+508 **49**
Dutch Harb., *Aleutian Is.* Z10+540 **99**
Dutch Guiana. *See* Surinam
Dutton, Mt., *Utah* V44+380 **94**
Duvan, *U.S.S.R.* J12+557 **61**
Duwadami, *Saudi Arabia* K04+248 **74**

Duwwah, *Oman* J07+205 **75**
Dvina, R., *Latvia* L32+568 **47**
Dyatkovo, *U.S.S.R.* K64+535 **60**
Dyce, *Scotland* N13+572 **40**
Dyer, C., *N.-W. Territories* S07+665 **89**
Dyersburg, *Tennessee* T87+360 **97**
Dyfed, co., *Wales* N26+520 **38**
Dyfi R., *Wales* N23+526 **38**
Dyle R., *Belgium* M63+510 **44**
Dyurtyuli, *U.S.S.R.* J31+554 **61**
Dzamyn Ude, *Mongolia* E55+446 **64**
Dzep, *Yugoslavia* L47+427 **58**
Dzerzhinsk, *U.S.S.R.* K09+563 **61**
Dzerzhinsh, *Byelorussia* L17+536 **60**
Dzhagdy Khrebet, *U.S.S.R.* D30+538 **63**
Dzhalal Abad, *Kirgiz.* H12+407 **62**
Dzhalinda, *U.S.S.R.* D67+536 **63**
Dzhambul, *Kazakh.* H21+428 **62**
Dzhetygara, *Kazakh.* H82+524 **62**
Dzhezkazgan, *Kazakh.* H44+480 **62**
Dzhugdzhur Khrebet,
    U.S.S.R. C70+580 **63**
Dzhungarskiy Ala-Tau,
    Kazakh. G60+450 **62**
Dzierzoniow, *Poland* L80+508 **49**
Dzogchen, *China* F36+322 **64**
Eagle, *Alaska* X37+645 **99**
Eagle I., *Ireland, Rep.* N60+543 **42**
Eagle L., *Maine* S56+463 **90**
Eagle Ls., *Maine* S50+471 **90**
Eagle Grove, *Iowa* U24+427 **95**
Eagle Mountain L., *Texas* U45+328 **95**
Eagle Pass, *Texas* U62+287 **94**
Eaglehawk, *Victoria* C35–367 **109**
Eagle River, *Wisconsin* T86+459 **91**
Eagles Nest, *Ireland, Rep.* N58+518 **43**
Ealing, *England* N02+515 **39**
Eardisley, *England* N18+521 **38**
Earith, *England* M89+523 **39**
Earlston, *Scotland* N16+556 **41**
Earlville, *New York* T04+427 **96**
Earn L., *Scotland* N25+564 **41**
Earn, R., *Scotland* N20+564 **41**
Easington, *England* N08+548 **37**
East Anglia, S.E. *England* **39**
East Arlington, *Vermont* S79+431 **91**
East Aurora, *New York* T22+428 **96**
Eastbourne, *England* M88+508 **39**
Eastbourne, *New Zealand* A30–413 **112**
East Dereham, *England* M84+527 **39**
Easter I., *Pacific Ocean* V25–265 **107**
Eastern B., *Maryland* T08+388 **96**
Eastern States, *India* G50+230 **70**
East Grand Forks, *Minnesota* U42+479 **93**
East Kilbride, *Scotland* N25+558 **41**
Eastland, *Texas* U53+324 **95**
East Liverpool, *Ohio* T34+406 **91**
East London, *Cape Province* L12–330 **84**
East Lothian, co., *See* Lothian
Eastmain R., *Quebec* T05+526 **91**
Eastman, *Georgia* T49+322 **97**
Easton, *Maryland* T06+388 **96**
Easton, *Pennsylvania* T02+407 **96**
Eastport, *Maine* S42+449 **90**
East Retford, *England* N06+533 **37**
East St Louis, *Illinois* U01+386 **95**
East Sioux Falls, S. *Dakota* U40+435 **93**
Eastville, *Virginia* T06+373 **96**
Eaton Rapids, *Michigan* T58+425 **91**
Eau Claire, *Wisconsin* U10+448 **93**
Ebbw Vale, *Wales* N19+518 **38**
Eberswalde, *E. Germany* M07+528 **48**
Eboli, *Italy* M00+406 **57**
Ebolowa, *Cameroon* M24+028 **82**
Ebro, R., *Spain* N09+421 **53**
Ecaussines, *Belgium* M65+506 **44**
Ecclefechan, *Scotland* N19+550 **41**
Echallens, *Switzerland* M50+466 **45**
Echo L., *Tasmania* C20–422 **109**
Echo Cliffs, *Arizona* V40+364 **94**
Echt, *Netherlands* M55+511 **44**
Echten, *Netherlands* M52+527 **44**
Echternach, *Luxembourg* M51+498 **48**
Echuca, *Victoria* C31–362 **109**
Eck L., *Scotland* N30+561 **41**
Ecuador, rep., *S. America* **104**
Edam, *Netherlands* M60+525 **44**
Eday, I., *Orkney Is., Scot.* N16+592 **40**
Ed Damer, *Sudan* K66+176 **81**
Ed Damur, *Lebanon* K57+337 **76**
Ed Debba, *Sudan* K86+180 **81**
Eddrachillis B., *Scotland* N31+583 **40**
Ed Dueim, *Sudan* K76+140 **81**
Ede, *Netherlands* M56+521 **44**
Edebäck, *Sweden* M08+601 **47**
Eden, *Maine* S50+444 **90**
Eden, *New South Wales* C01–371 **109**
Eden, *New York* N17+548 **37**
Eden R., *England* **37**
Edenburg, *Orange Free State* L24–296 **84**
Edendale, *New Zealand* A67–463 **112**
Edenderry, *Ireland, Rep.* N42+533 **43**
Edenhope, *Victoria* C52–370 **109**
Edensburg, *Pennsylvania* T23+405 **96**
Edenton, *N. Carolina* T10+361 **97**
Edeowie, *S. Australia* C69–314 **109**
Ederengin Nuru, *Mongolia* F40+434 **64**
Edge Hill, *England* N09+521 **39**
Edgeley, *N. Dakota* U52+464 **93**
Edgemont, *S. Dakota* U83+432 **93**
Edgeøya, I., *Arctic Ocean* L45+780 **62**
Edgerton, *Wisconsin* T84+429 **91**
Edgeworthstown, *Ireland, Rep.* N45+537 **42**
Edhessa, *Greece* L48+408 **59**
Edievale, *New Zealand* A64–458 **112**
Edina, *Missouri* U13+402 **95**
Edinburg, *Texas* U49+264 **94**
Edinburgh, *Scotland* N19+559 **41**
Edirne, *Turkey* L21+417 **74**
Edithburgh, S. *Australia* C74–351 **109**
Edith Cavell, Mt., *Alberta* V78+530 **88**
Edmonton, *Alberta* V52+538 **88**
Edmundston, *New Brunswick* S50+474 **90**
Edremit, *Turkey* L18+397 **74**
Edsele, *Sweden* L81+634 **46**
Edson, *Alberta* V68+538 **88**
Eduni, Mt., *North-West*
    Territories W48+644 **88**
Edward (Amin) L.,
    Zaire-Uganda L02–004 **83**

Edward, R., *New S. Wales* C34–352 **109**
Edwardesabad. *See* Bannu.
Edwards, *New York* T01+443 **91**
Edwards Plat., *Texas* U66+308 **94**
Edwardsville, *Illinois* U00+388 **95**
Eekloo, *Belgium* M69+512 **44**
Efate, I., *Vanuatu* A68-185 **106**
Eferding, *Austria* M06+483 **48**
Effingham, *Illinois* T82+391 **95**
Egadi Is., *Sicily* M17+379 **57**
Egan, *S. Dakota* U40+440 **93**
Egana, *Argentina* R85–369 **103**
Eganville, *Ontario* T13+455 **91**
Eger, *Czechoslovakia. See* Cheb.
Eger, *Hungary* L58+479 **49**
Egersund, *Norway* M54+584 **47**
Egg L., *Quebec* S78+544 **89**
Eggenfelden, *W. Germany* M13+484 **48**
Eghezee, *Belgium* M60+506 **44**
Egin, *Turkey* K39+392 **74**
Eglinton, C., *N.-W. Terr.* S55+707 **89**
Egmont B., *Prince Edward I.* S25+466 **90**
Egmont, Mt., *New Zealand* A35–393 **112**
Egremont, *England* N21+545 **37**
Egridir, *Turkey* K85+378 **74**
Egypt, *N. Africa* L00+250 **81**
Eibergen, *Netherlands* M50+521 **44**
Eichstätt, *Germany* M23+489 **48**
Eidsvoll, *Norway* M22+603 **47**
Eifel, mts., *W. Germany* M50+501 **48**
Eigg I., *Scotland* N37+569 **41**
Eights Coast, *Antarctica* T80–750 **27**
Eighty Mile Beach, *W. Aust.* D95–196 **110**
Eil, *Somalia* J60+078 **83**
Eil L., *Scotland* N31+568 **41**
Eilat, *Israel* K60+296 **76**
Eindhoven, *Netherlands* M57+514 **44**
Eire, *See* Ireland, Rep. of.
Eisden, *Netherlands* M56+508 **44**
Eisenach, *E. Germany* M28+509 **48**
Eisenerz, *Austria* M01+475 **48**
Eisleben, *E. Germany* M21+515 **48**
Ejutla, *Mexico* U40+166 **100**
Ekaterinoslav. *See* Dnepropetrovsk.
Eke, *Belgium* M68+510 **44**
Ekeren, *Belgium* M64+513 **44**
Eketahana, *New Zealand* A26–406 **112**
Ekhinádbes is., *Greece* L54+384 **59**
Ekimchan, *U.S.S.R.* D12+530 **63**
Eksjö, *Sweden* M00+577 **47**
Ekträsk, *Sweden* L61+644 **46**
Ekwan R., *Ontario* T52+537 **89**
El Aaiun, *Morocco* N80+268 **80**
El Abde, *Lebanon* K54+346 **76**
Élafónisi Chan, *Greece* L42+364 **59**
Élafos I., *Greece* L42+365 **59**
El Agheila (Al'Uqaylah)
  Libya L64+302 **81**
El Aguila, *Argentina* S43–363 **103**
El Aina, *Jordan* K55+310 **76**
El Alamein, *Egypt* L07+308 **81**
Elasson, *Greece* L47+399 **59**
Elâzig, *Turkey* K34+386 **74**
Elba, I., *Italy* M28+428 **56**
El Bab, *Syria* K45+364 **76**
El Bahluliye, *Syria* K54+356 **76**
El Banco, *Colombia* S84+090 **104**
El Barco de Valdeorras, *Sp.* N42+424 **52**
Elbasan, *Albania* L60+412 **58**
El Baul, *Venezuela* S50+090 **104**
Elbe R., *Germany* M25+532 **48**
Elbert, Mt., *Colorado* V08+391 **98**
Elbeuf, *France* M83+493 **54**
Elbing. *See* Elblag.
El-Birka, *Saudi Arabia* K27+223 **74**
Elbistan, *Turkey* K47+383 **74**
Elblag, *Poland* L64+542 **49**
El Br'aij, *Syria* K49+343 **76**
Elbrus. mt., *U.S.S.R.* K17+432 **62**
Elburg, *Netherlands* M55+524 **44**
Elburz Mts., *Iran* J56+363 **75**
El Carmen, *Bolivia* S22–145 **104**
El Carmen, *See* Carmen
El Centro, *California* V63+329 **92**
Elche, *Spain* N04+383 **53**
El Chorro, *Argentina* S14–232 **103**
El Cuy, *Argentina* S50–399 **103**
El Dab, *Somalia* J82+088 **83**
El Diwán, *Egypt* K78+224 **81**
El Donfar, *Somalia* J66+104 **83**
Eldora, *Iowa* U18+424 **95**
El Dorado, *Arkansas* U16+332 **95**
El Dorado, *Kansas* U42+378 **95**
El Dorado, *Mexico* V14+242 **100**
El Dorado, *Venezuela* S10+066 **104**
Eldoret, *Kenya* K58+006 **83**
El Djezair (Algiers), *Algeria* M72+366 **55**
El Encanto, *Colombia* S82–012 **104**
Elephant Butte Res., *New*
  Mexico V13+334 **94**
Elephant I., *Antarctica* R60–610 **27**
El Ergh, *Libya* L50+290 **81**
Eleşkirt, *Turkey* K13+399 **74**
Eleuthera I., *Bahamas, The* T10+250 **101**
Elewijt, *Belgium* M63+510 **44**
El Faiyum, *Egypt* K84+294 **81**
El Fasher, *Sudan* L28+136 **81**
El Fuwara, *Saudi Arabia* K15+262 **74**
Elgena, *Ethiopia* K38+170 **83**
El Geneina, *Sudan* L46+134 **81**
El Geteina, *Sudan* K76+146 **81**
Elgg, *Switzerland* M37+475 **45**
El Ghobbe, *Saudi Arabia* K31+239 **74**
Elgin, *Illinois* T80+420 **95**
Elgin, *New Brunswick* S31+458 **90**
Elgin, *Scotland* N20+576 **40**
El Giof. *See* El Jauf.
El Giza, *Egypt* K82+300 **81**
El Golea, *Algeria* M74+306 **80**
Elgon, Mt., *Uganda* K62+012 **83**
El Hamidiya, *Syria* K49+354 **76**
El Hamra, *Syria* K48+353 **76**
El Hamrat, *Syria* K48+345 **76**
El Hasa, *Saudi Arabia* J67+272 **74**
El-Hayath, *Saudi Arabia* K25+261 **74**
El Hijane, *Syria* K51+333 **76**
El Hilla, *Sudan* L16+134 **81**
El Husn, *Jordan* K55+325 **76**
Elie, *Scotland* N17+562 **41**
Elisabethville. *See* Lubumbashi.
Elisavetgrad. *See* Kirovograd.

Elizabeth, *New Jersey* T86+406 **96**
Elizabeth I., *Massachusetts* S65+414 **96**
Elizabeth, *West Virginia* T38+390 **91**
Elizabeth, mt., *Argentina* S59–483 **103**
Elizabeth City, *N. Carolina* T08+363 **97**
Elizabethtown, *Kentucky* T65+377 **97**
Elizondo, *Spain* N09+433 **53**
El Jafr, *Jordan* K53+303 **76**
El Jauf, *Libya* L40+238 **81**
El Judeide, *Syria* K53+336 **76**
Elk Mts., *New Mexico* V18+337 **94**
Elk, *Poland* L46+538 **49**
Elk City, *Oklahoma* U57+354 **95**
El Kerak, *Jordan* K56+312 **76**
El Kharga, *Egypt* K86+254 **81**
Elkhart, *Indiana* T66+417 **91**
Elkhead Mts., *Colorado* V14+408 **94**
Elkhorn, Mt., *Idaho* V45+424 **92**
El Khushniye, *Syria* K55+330 **76**
Elkins, *West Virginia* T29+389 **91**
Elko, *Nevada* V65+408 **92**
Elk Point, *S. Dakota* U40+427 **93**
Elk River, *Minnesota* U22+453 **93**
Elkton, *Maryland* T05+396 **96**
El Lâdhiqīya. *See* Latakia.
El Laghodeh, *Somalia* J66+094 **83**
Ellas, *Greece* L42+385 **59**
Ellef Ringnes I., *N.-W. Terr.* U65+784 **88**
Ellen, Mt., *Utah* V35+382 **94**
Ellenabad, *India* H02+294 **72**
Ellendale, *N. Dakota* U51+460 **93**
Ellensburg, *Washington* W04+470 **92**
Ellerslie, *Prince Edward I.* S23+466 **90**
Ellesmere I., *N.-W. Terr.* T30+780 **88**
Ellesmere, L., *New Zealand* A44–439 **112**
Ellesmere Port, *England* N17+533 **37**
Ellezelles, *Belgium* M68+507 **44**
Ellice Is., *See* Tuvalu
Ellice R., *N.-W. Territories* V05+666 **88**
Ellichpur, *India* G75+212 **70**
Ellicott City, *Maryland* T11+393 **96**
Elliot, *Cape Province* L12–314 **84**
Elliot B., *N.-W. Territories* U35+676 **88**
Elliot Group, *China* D74+393 **66**
Ellon, *Scotland* N12+574 **40**
Ellora, *India* G88+201 **70**
Ellsworth, *Maine* S50+445 **90**
Ellsworth Mts., *Antarctica* U00–770 **27**
Elm, *Switzerland* M35+469 **45**
El Ma'arra, *Syria* K49+360 **76**
Elma Dagh, *Turkey* K72+398 **74**
El Madhiq, *Saudi Arabia* K32+233 **74**
El Mansura, *Egypt* K82+310 **81**
El Mazar, *Jordan* K56+311 **76**
El Mazra'a, *Jordan* K57+313 **76**
El Meget, *Somalia* J80+032 **83**
El Menzil, *Jordan* K54+311 **76**
Elmira, *New York* T11+421 **96**
El Minya, *Egypt* K86+280 **81**
El Molar, *Spain* N22+408 **52**
Elmore, *Victoria* C32–365 **109**
El Muwaqqar, *Jordan* K53+318 **76**
El Obeid, *Sudan* K88+132 **81**
El Odaiya, *Sudan* L10+120 **81**
Elora, *Tennesse* T68+350 **97**
El Oro, *Mexico* V02+259 **100**
El Pardo, *Spain* N24+405 **52**
El Paso, *Illinois* T64+408 **95**
El Paso, *Texas* V09+316 **98**
Elphin, *Ireland, Rep.* N49+538 **42**
Elphinstone I., *Burma* F42+123 **71**
El Pico, *Bolivia* S28–158 **104**
El Pilar, *Venezuela* S18+104 **104**
El Pintado, *Argentina* S08–246 **103**
El Puente del Arzobispo, *Sp.* N31+398 **52**
El Qadmus, *Syria* K53+351 **76**
El Qanawat, *Syria* K50+327 **76**
El Qaryatein, *Syria* K46+342 **76**
El Qathma, *Saudi Arabia* K17+238 **74**
El Qatrana, *Jordan* K54+312 **76**
El Qatrun, *Libya* M02+250 **81**
El Quds esh Sherif. *See* Jerusalem
El Quneitra, *Syria* K55+331 **76**
El Quseir, *Syria* K50+345 **76**
El Quweira, *Jordan* K58+298 **76**
El Reno, *Oklahoma* U48+353 **95**
Elroy, *Wisconsin* U01+437 **91**
El Sadi. *See* Wajir
El Salvador, *Cent. America* T80+135 **101**
Elsenborn, *Belgium* M53+505 **44**
Elsloo, *Netherlands* M55+509 **44**
Elspeet, *Netherlands* M55+523 **44**
Elst, *Netherlands* M55+519 **44**
Elsterwerda, *E. Germany* M09+515 **48**
Eltham, *New Zealand* A34–394 **112**
El Tigre, *Venezuela* S25+089 **104**
El Toro, *Spain* N04+400 **53**
El Transito, *Chile* S61–288 **103**
Eluru, *India* G53+168 **70**
El Valle, *Colombia* T14+062 **104**
Elvas, *Portugal* N43+389 **52**
El Vigia, *Venezuela* S69+086 **104**
Elvira, C., *N.-W. Territories* V12+728 **88**
Ely, *England* M89+524 **37**
Ely, *Minnesota* U12+478 **93**
Ely, *Nevada* V60+393 **92**
Ely, Isle of, *England* M89+525 **37**
Emangulova, *U.S.S.R.* J28+522 **61**
Emba R., *Kazakh* J28+470 **62**
Embarcacion, *Argentina* S25–232 **103**
Embóna, *Greece* L13+362 **59**
Embrun, *France* M51+445 **55**
Emden, *W. Germany* M47+534 **48**
Emerald, *Queensland* C11–232 **111**
Emerald I., *N.-W. Terr.* V58+756 **88**
Emerson, *Manitoba* U42+492 **88**
Emilia-Romagna, reg., *Italy* M26+445 **56**
Eminabad, *Pakistan* H04+321 **72**
Eminence, *Missouri* U08+372 **97**
Emmaste, *Estonia* L44+587 **47**
Emmaville, *New S. Wales* B81–294 **109**
Emmen, *Netherlands* M49+528 **44**
Emmetsburg, *Iowa* U28+431 **95**
Emmons, Mt., *Utah* V32+406 **94**
Emory Pk., *Texas* U80+292 **94**
Empalme, *Mexico* V34+281 **100**
Empedrado, *Argentina* R83–279 **103**
Empire, *Michigan* T66+448 **91**
Emporia, *Kansas* U37+384 **95**
Emporia, *Virginia* T15+367 **97**
Emporium, *Pennsylvania* T20+415 **96**

Emptinne, *Belgium* M59+503 **44**
Ems, *W. Germany* M44+503 **48**
Enard B., *Scotland* N32+581 **40**
Encarnacion, *Paraguay* R65–273 **103**
Encontrados, *Venezuela* S73+091 **104**
Encounter B., *S. Australia* C68–357 **109**
Encruzilhada, *Brazil* R45–305 **103**
Ende, *Flores I., Indonesia* D80–088 **65**
Enderbury I., *Phoenix Is.* Z36–032 **106**
Enderby Ld., *Antarctica* J60–680 **27**
Enderlin, *N. Dakota* U46+466 **93**
Endicott, *New York* T07+421 **96**
Endicott Mts., *Alaska* Y10+674 **99**
Enez, *Turkey* L23+407 **74**
Enez, G. of, *Greece* L25+407 **59**
Enfe, *Lebanon* K55+343 **76**
Enfield, *England* N00+516 **39**
Engano, C., *Philippines* D76+186 **65**
Engelberg, *Switzerland* M40+468 **45**
Engels, *U.S.S.R.* J83+514 **61**
Enggano, I., *Indonesia* F16–054 **65**
Enghien, *Belgium* M66+507 **44**
England, *Great Britain* N12+520 **34**
Englehart, *Ontario* T29+478 **91**
Englewood, *New Jersey* S84+408 **96**
English Chan., *France-Eng.* N12+500 **54**
English R., *Ontario* U25+502 **88**
English Bazar, *India* G11+250 **73**
English Coast, *Antarctica* T00–740 **27**
Enid, *Oklahoma* U48+364 **95**
Enkhuizen, *Netherlands* M58+527 **44**
Enköping, *Sweden* L18+597 **47**
Enna, *Sicily* M04+375 **57**
En Nahud, *Sudan* L10+126 **81**
En Naqura, *Lebanon* K59+331 **76**
En Nebk, *Syria* K50+340 **76**
En Nemara, *Syria* K46+329 **76**
Enngonia, *New S. Wales* C25–294 **109**
Ennis, *Ireland, Rep.* N54+528 **43**
Enniscorthy, *Ireland, Rep.* N39+525 **43**
Enniskillen, *N. Ireland* N46+543 **42**
Ennistimon, *Ireland, Rep.* N56+529 **43**
Enns, *Austria* M03+482 **48**
Enns, R., *Austria* M04+475 **48**
Enontekiö, *Finland* L39+684 **46**
Enriquillo, L.,
  Dominican Rep. S70+186 **101**
Ensanche Colonia Sarmiento,
  Argentina S60–453 **103**
Ensay, *Victoria* C13–374 **109**
Enschede, *Netherlands* M48+522 **44**
Ensenada, *Argentina* R78–348 **103**
Ensenada, *Mexico* V70+317 **100**
Enshih, *China* E63+302 **67**
Entebbe, *Uganda* K76+001 **83**
Enterprise, *Mississippi* T83+322 **95**
Entraygues, *France* M75+446 **55**
Entre Rios, *Brazil* Q48–120 **105**
Entre Rios, *Brazil* Q79–220 **105**
Eolie, Isole, *Italy* M02+387 **57**
Epe, *Netherlands* M54+523 **44**
Epernay, *France* M66+490 **54**
Ephraim, *Utah* V40+394 **94**
Episkopi & B., *Cyprus* K73+346 **76**
Epping & Forest, *England* M89+517 **39**
Epsom, *England* N02+513 **39**
Equatorial Guinea, *W. Afr.* M30+016 **82**
Ercis, *Turkey* K11+390 **74**
Erd, *Hungary* L66+474 **49**
Erebus Gulf, *Antarctica* R75–640 **27**
Erebus Mt., *Antarctica* B30–780 **27**
Eregli, *Turkey* K81+414 **74**
Eregli, *Turkey* K67+375 **74**
Erepecú, L., *Brazil* R69–013 **105**
Eressós, *Greece* L25+391 **59**
Erexim, *Brazil* R43–279 **103**
Erfurt, *E. Germany* M24+510 **48**
Erh Hai, *China* F29+256 **64**
Erhlien, *China* E42+422 **63**
Ericht L., *Scotland* N27+568 **41**
Erie, *Pennsylvania* T31+421 **91**
Erie, L., *U.S.A.-Canada* T40+420 **99**
Ericau, *Ontario* T42+423 **91**
Eriha, *Syria* K50+358 **76**
Erisort L., *Scotland* N38+581 **40**
Eritrea, *Ethiopia* K30+150 **83**
Erlach, *Switzerland* M47+470 **45**
Erlangen, *W. Germany* M24+496 **48**
Erlenbach, *Switzerland* M45+467 **45**
Ermelo, *Netherlands* M56+523 **44**
Ermenek, *Turkey* K73+366 **74**
Ernakulam, *India* G82+100 **70**
Erne L., *N. Ireland* N47+545 **42**
Erne L., Up., *N. Ireland* N45+542 **42**
Ernee, *France* N06+483 **54**
Eromanga, I., *Vanuatu* A65-192 **106**
Erquelinnes, *Belgium* M65+503 **44**
Er Rabba, *Jordan* K56+312 **76**
Er Rahad, *Sudan* K86+128 **81**
Er Ramle, *Syria* K46+357 **76**
Er Rastan, *Syria* K50+349 **76**
Errigal, *Ireland, Rep.* N49+550 **42**
Erris Hd., *Ireland, Rep.* N60+543 **42**
Er Rumman, *Jordan* K55+322 **76**
Erudina, *S. Australia* C64–315 **109**
Erval, *Brazil* R49–319 **103**
Erz Geb., *E. Germany* M12+506 **48**
Erzincan, *Turkey* K34+398 **74**
Erzurum, *Turkey* K22+399 **74**
Erzvilkas, *Lithuania* L44+553 **47**
Esashi, *Japan* C45+450 **68**
Esbjerg, *Denmark* M39+555 **47**
Escada, *Brazil* Q31–082 **105**
Escalante, Isla, *Spain* M71+421 **53**
Escalon, *Mexico* U85+266 **100**
Escanaba & R., *Michigan* T73+458 **91**
Escaut, R., *Belgium* M65+511 **44**
Esch, *Luxembourg* M54+495 **48**
Escholzmatt, *Switzerland* M42+469 **45**
Escudo de Veragua, *Panama* T39+091 **101**
Escuinapa, *Mexico* V04+228 **100**
Escuintla, *Guatemala* U04+142 **100**
Escuminac Pt., *N.B.* S29+471 **90**
Esfahan, *Iran* J50+327 **75**
Eshowe, *Natal* K80–288 **84**
Esk R., *Scotland* N18+559 **41**
Eskdale, *New Zealand* A19–393 **112**
Eske, L., *Ireland, Rep.* N48+547 **42**
Eskilstuna, *Sweden* L81+594 **47**

Eskimo, C., *N.-W. Terr.* U25+610 **89**
Eskisehir, *Turkey* K87+398 **74**
Esla R., *Spain* N35+418 **52**
Eslöv, *Sweden* M10+559 **47**
Esmeralda, I., *Chile* T02–489 **103**
Esmeraldas, *Ecuador* T28+010 **104**
Espalion, *France* M73+445 **55**
Espanola, *Ontario* T40+463 **91**
Esperance, *W. Australia* D79–337 **110**
Esperanza, *Argentina* S06–314 **103**
Espiel, *Spain* N30+382 **52**
Espinho, *Portugal* N52+410 **52**
Espinosa de los Monteros, *Sp.* N21+431 **52**
Espirito Santo, *Brazil* S02–061 **104**
Espirito Santo, *Brazil* Q61–204 **105**
Espiritu Santo, B. del, *Mex.* T74+193 **100**
Espiritu Santo, C., *Argentina* S51–526 **103**
Espiritu Santo, I., *Mexico* V32+244 **100**
Espiritu Santo, I.,
  Vanuatu A76-158 **106**
Esquel, *Argentina* S68–428 **103**
Esquimalt, *Brit. Columbia* W21+484 **88**
Esquina, *Argentina* R87–300 **103**
Es Sa'an, *Syria* K46+353 **76**
Es Safi, *Jordan* K57+310 **76**
Es Salt, *Jordan* K56+320 **76**
Es Samra, *Jordan* K53+322 **76**
Es Sanamein, *Syria* K53+331 **76**
Esse & Alv, *Finland* L41+636 **46**
Essen, *Belgium* M63+515 **44**
Essen, *W. Germany* M48+516 **48**
Essequibo R., *Guyana* R81+068 **104**
Essex, *Ontario* T47+422 **91**
Essex, co., *England* M87+518 **39**
Essex Mt., *Wyoming* V25+419 **98**
Esslingen, *W. Germany* M34+487 **48**
Es Sukhne, *Syria* K37+348 **74**
Es Suweidīya, *Syria* K51+327 **76**
Estabutchie, *Mississippi* T86+314 **97**
Estados, I., de los, *Argentina* S26–548 **103**
Estavayer, *Switzerland* M49+469 **45**
Estcourt, *Natal* L00–290 **84**
Esteli, *Nicaragua* T69+130 **101**
Esternay, *France* M69+487 **54**
Estevan, *Saskatchewan* U79+493 **88**
Estherville, *Iowa* U29+434 **95**
Estin Gol, *China* F26+410 **64**
Estonia, rep., *U.S.S.R.* **47**
Estoril, *Portugal* N56+387 **52**
Estreito, *Brazil* R40–318 **103**
Estremoz, *Portugal* N45+388 **52**
Estrondo, Sa. des, *Brazil* R20–076 **105**
E'Sufeina, *Saudi Arabia* K27+233 **74**
Etah, *India* G68+275 **73**
Etalle, *Belgium* M56+497 **44**
Étampes, *France* M77+484 **54**
Étaples, *France* M80+505 **54**
Etawah, *India* G66+268 **73**
Etawney L., *Manitoba* U47+584 **88**
Eternity Ra., *Antarctica* S20–720 **27**
Ethe, *Belgium* M56+496 **44**
Ethiopia, *E. Africa* **83**
Etivaz, l', *Switzerland* M47+464 **45**
Etive L., *Scotland* N31+565 **41**
Etna, Mt.. *Sicily* M00+378 **57**
Eton, *England* N04+515 **39**
Ettelbrück, *Luxembourg* M53+499 **48**
Etten, *Netherlands* M62+516 **44**
Ettrick, *New Zealand* A63–457 **112**
Ettrick R., *Scotland* N18+555 **41**
Euabalong, *New S. Wales* C21–331 **109**
Euboea. *See* Evvoia, I.
Eucla, *W. Australia* D37–316 **110**
Eudunda, *S. Australia* C66–341 **109**
Eufaula, *Alabama* T61+318 **99**
Eufaula & Res., *Oklahoma* U34+353 **95**
Eugene, *Oregon* W19+441 **96**
Eugmö, *Finland* L43+638 **46**
Eugowra, *New S. Wales* C09–334 **109**
Eumungerie, *New S. Wales* C08–320 **109**
Eunice, *Louisiana* U14+304 **95**
Eupen, *Belgium* M54+506 **44**
Euphrates, R., *Iraq, etc.* J89+315 **74**
Eure, dep., *France* M85+491 **54**
Eureka, *California* W25+408 **92**
Eureka, *Kansas* U38+378 **95**
Eureka, *Nevada* V66+396 **92**
Eureka, *Utah* V41+400 **94**
Eure-et-Loir, dep., *France* M28+484 **54**
Euriowie, *New S. Wales* C50–314 **109**
Euroa, *Victoria* C27–367 **109**
Eursinge, *Netherlands* M51+528 **44**
Euston, *New S. Wales* C44–346 **109**
Eutaw, *Alabama* T77+329 **97**
Eutin, *W. Germany* M26+541 **48**
Eutsuk L., *Brit. Columbia* W40+536 **88**
Evale, *Angola* L86–166 **84**
Evandale, *Tasmania* C17–416 **109**
Evans, L., *Quebec* T12+508 **89**
Evanston, *Illinois* T76+421 **95**
Evanston, *Wyoming* V36+412 **93**
Evansville, *Indiana* T76+380 **97**
Evansville, *Minnesota* U34+461 **93**
Eva Peron, La Plata, *Argent.* R78–349 **103**
Evaux, *France* M75+462 **54**
Eveleth, *Minnesota* U16+472 **93**
Everard, L., *S. Australia* D00–312 **111**
Everest, Mt., *Nepal-Tibet* G18+280 **71**
Everett, *Washington* W12+478 **98**
Evergem, *Belgium* M68+511 **44**
Everglades, The, *Florida* T35+256 **99**
Everglades Nat. Park, *Florida* T36+255 **97**
Evergreen, *Alabama* T72+315 **97**
Evesham & Vale of, *England* N12+521 **39**
Evijärvi, *Finland* L39+634 **46**
Evje, *Norway* M43+586 **47**
Evolène, *Switzerland* M45+461 **45**
Evora, *Portugal* N47+386 **52**
Evreux, *France* M83+490 **54**
Evros, *Greece* L23+413 **58**
Evrykhou, *Cyprus* K73+350 **76**
Évvoia. G. of, *Greece* L40+387 **59**
Évvoia, I., *Greece* L36+386 **59**
Ewarton, *Jamaica* T13+182 **101**
Ewe, L., *Scotland* N34+578 **40**
Exaltacion, *Bolivia* S33–134 **104**
Exe R., *England* N21+507 **38**
Exeter, *England* N21+507 **38**
Exeter, *New Hampshire* S66+430 **96**
Exloo, *Netherlands* M49+529 **44**
Exminster, *England* N21+507 **38**

Exmoor, *England* N21+512 **38**
Exmouth, *England* N20+506 **38**
Exmouth G., *W. Australia* E33-218 **110**
Expedition Ra., *Queensland* C06-242 **111**
Exuma Is., *Bahamas, The* T10+244 **101**
Exuma Sd., *Bahamas, The* T08+244 **101**
Eyasi L., *Tanzania* K60-036 **83**
Eye L., *Quebec* T10+532 **89**
Eyemouth, *Scotland* N12+559 **41**
Eymoutiers, *France* M79+457 **54**
Eyre, *W. Australia* D52-321 **110**
Eyre Cr., *S. Australia* C67-266 **111**
Eyre, L., *S. Australia* C76-282 **111**
Eyre Pen., *S. Australia* C85-334 **111**
Eyrecourt, *Ireland, Rep.* N49+532 **43**
Eyzies, les, *France* M84+449 **55**
Ezcaray, *Spain* N18+423 **52**
Fab, *Somalia* J72+048 **83**
Fåborg, *Denmark* M28+551 **47**
Facatativa, *Columbia* S86+047 **104**
Fada, *Chad* L50+172 **81**
Fadan' Gourma, *Upper Volta* M88+120 **80**
Faddeyevskiy, Ostrov, *Russia* C35+750 **63**
Faenza, *Italy* M19+443 **56**
Faeröerne, *N. Atlantic Ocean* N40+620 **34**
Faeroes. *See* Faeroerne.
Fafa, *Mali* M86+152 **80**
Făgăras, *Romania* L30+458 **58**
Fagarg, *Sudan* L20+118 **81**
Fagerli, *Norway* L83+671 **46**
Fagernes, *Norway* M34+610 **47**
Fagnano, L., *Argentina* S46-546 **103**
Faid, *Saudi Arabia* K14+271 **74**
Faido, *Switzerland* M37+465 **45**
Fai-fo, (Hoi An), *Vietnam* E70+158 **69**
Fair I., *Scotland* N10+595 **40**
Fairbanks, *Alaska* X75+643 **99**
Fairbury, *Illinios* T81+408 **91**
Fairbury, *Nebraska* U43+402 **95**
Fairfield, *Illinois* T80+384 **95**
Fairfield, *Iowa* U12+410 **95**
Fairfield, *Maine* S58+446 **90**
Fairhaven, *Massachusetts* S65+416 **96**
Fair Head, *N. Ireland* N37+552 **42**
Fairlie, *New Zealand* A55-441 **112**
Fairmont, *Minnesota* U27+437 **93**
Fairmont, *West Virginia* T31+395 **91**
Fairview, *Alberta* V82+559 **88**
Fairville, *New Brunswick* S37+453 **90**
Fairweather, Mt., *Alaska* X15+590 **99**
Faith, *S. Dakota* U73+450 **93**
Faizabad, *Afghanistan* H26+371 **75**
Faizabad, *India* G47+267 **73**
Fajr, *Saudi Arabia* K44+289 **74**
Fakfak, *Irian Jaya, Indon.* D17-029 **65**
Fakiya, *Bulgaria* L18+422 **58**
Falam, *Burma* F68+230 **71**
Falama, *Guinea* N52+106 **80**
Fălciu, *Romania* L11+463 **58**
Falcon, Res., *Texas* U56+269 **94**
Falcone, C. of, *Sardinia* M41+410 **57**
Falkenberg, *Sweden* M15+569 **47**
Falkirk, *Scotland* N23+560 **41**
Falkland, *Scotland* N19+562 **41**
Falkland Is., *S. Atlantic Oc.* S00-517 **103**
Falkland Is. Dependencies,
   Antarctica R00-550 **27**
Falknov, *Czechoslovakia* M14+502 **48**
Fallöping, *Sweden* M09+581 **47**
Fall River, *Massachusetts* S67+417 **96**
Falls City, *Nebraska* U34+402 **95**
Falmagne, *Belgium* M61+502 **44**
Falmouth, *Jamaica* T16+185 **101**
Falmouth, *Kentucky* T56+387 **91**
Falmouth & B., *England* N30+501 **38**
False B., *Cape Province* L68-344 **84**
False Point, *India* G19+204 **71**
Falset, *Spain* M85+411 **53**
Falso, C., *Mexico* V30+229 **100**
Falster, I., *Denmark* M18+548 **47**
Faluja, *Israel* K61+316 **76**
Falun, *Sweden* L86+606 **47**
Famagusta & B., *Cyprus* K66+351 **76**
Famatina, *Argentina* S45-290 **103**
Fanad Hd., *Ireland, Rep.* N46+553 **42**
Fannich L., *Scotland* N30+576 **40**
Fanning, I., *Pacific Ocean* Y58+040 **107**
Fanö, I., *Denmark* M39+554 **47**
Fanö Bugt, *Denmark* M41+553 **47**
Fanshawe, C., *N.-W. Terr.* T10+730 **89**
Fanuch, *Iran* J02+266 **75**
Fao, *Iraq* J69+300 **74**
Faradje, *Congo* L02+036 **83**
Farafangana, *Madagascar* J74-230 **83**
Farah, *Afghanistan* H77+324 **75**
Farajja, *Saudi Arabia* J56+218 **75**
Faranah, *Guinea* N64+100 **80**
Faranlep, I., *Caroline Is.* C40+082 **106**
Farasan Is., *Red Sea* K18+168 **74**
Farewell C., *Greenland* Q70+590 **26**
Fargo, *N. Dakota* U41+469 **93**
Faribault, *Minnesota* U20+443 **93**
Faridabad, *India* G76+284 **72**
Faridkot, *India* H02+307 **72**
Faridpur, *India* G83+282 **73**
Faridpur, *Bangladesh* G01+236 **73**
Fariman, *Iran* J02+360 **75**
Farina, *S. Australia* C70-301 **109**
Farmington, *Maine* S61+447 **90**
Farmington, *Missouri* U03+378 **97**
Farmington, *New Mexico* V20+367 **94**
Farmington, *Utah* V42+409 **94**
Farmville, *Virginia* T20+373 **97**
Farnborough, *England* N00+514 **39**
Farne Is., *England* N10+556 **37**
Farnes, *Norway* M43+613 **47**
Farnham, *Quebec* S78+453 **91**
Farnworth, *England* N14+535 **37**
Faro, *Brazil* R71-020 **105**
Faro, *Portugal* N47+370 **52**
Färön, I., *Sweden* L65+579 **47**
Farrukhabad, *India* G63+274 **73**
Farrukhnagar, *India* G79+284 **72**
Farsala, *Greece* L46+393 **59**
Farsi, *Afghanistan* H71+338 **75**
Farsund, *Norway* M49+581 **47**
Farwell, *Michigan* T59+438 **91**
Farwell, *Texas* U78+340 **98**
Fasa, *Iran* J38+289 **75**
Fatahabad, *India* G87+295 **72**

Fatait ibn Kanat,
   Saudi Arabia K10+293 **74**
Fatehabad, *India* G70+271 **73**
Fatehgarh, *India* G62+273 **73**
Fatehpur, *India* H00+280 **72**
Fatehpur, *India* G55+259 **73**
Father L., *Quebec* T02+495 **89**
Fatmomakke, *Sweden* L89+650 **46**
Fatshan, *China* E41+231 **67**
Fatu Hiva, I., *Marquesas Is.* X20-108 **107**
Fawley, *England* N08+508 **39**
Faxaflói, *Iceland* P50+645 **46**
Faxina, *Brazil* R24-238 **105**
Faya. *See* Largeau.
Fayette, *Alabama* T77+337 **95**
Fayette, *Missouri* U16+391 **95**
Fayetteville, *Arkansas* U25+361 **93**
Fayetteville, *N. Carolina* T23+350 **97**
Fayetteville, *Pennsylvania* T14+399 **96**
Fayetteville, *W. Virginia* T37+380 **97**
Fazilka, *India* H06+304 **72**
Fdérik, *Mauritania* N76+226 **80**
Feale R., *Ireland Rep.* N58+525 **43**
Fear, C., *N. Carolina* T16+336 **99**
Featherton, Mt., *Victoria* C17-369 **109**
Fécamp, *France* M87+498 **54**
Fedaracion, *Argentina* R78-309 **103**
Feeagh L., *Ireland, Rep.* N57+539 **42**
Fehmarn, I., *W. Germany* M23+544 **48**
Feifu. *See* Faifo.
Feilding, *New Zealand* A26-400 **112**
Feira de Santana, *Brazil* Q53-124 **105**
Feldbach, *Austria* L85+470 **49**
Feldkirch, *Austria* M33+472 **48**
Felipe Carrillo Puerto, *Mex.* T73+196 **100**
Femund, L., *Norway* M19+623 **46**
Feng chên, *China* E41+405 **66**
Fengshien, *China* E20+346 **66**
Fenghwang, *China* E63+279 **67**
Fengkieh, *China* E63+311 **66**
Fengsiang, *China* E77+343 **66**
Fengyang, *China* E12+328 **66**
Fenit, *Ireland, Rep.* N59+523 **43**
Fenny Stratford, *England* N04+520 **39**
Fens, The, *England* N00+526 **37**
Fenton, *Michigan* T52+428 **91**
Fenyang, *China* E50+373 **66**
Feodosiya & B., *U.S.S.R.* K58+450 **60**
Fergus, *Ontario* T32+437 **91**
Fergus Falls, *Minnesota* U36+463 **93**
Ferguson, *Missouri* U02+387 **97**
Ferguson, *Quebec* S81+478 **91**
Fergusson I., *Papua New Guinea*
   B86-095 **111**
Fermanagh, co., *N. Ireland* N46+543 **42**
Fermoy, *Ireland, Rep.* N50+521 **43**
Fernando Poo I., *See* Macias Nguema
Fernie, *Brit. Columbia* V59+496 **88**
Ferns, *Ireland, Rep.* N39+526 **43**
Ferozepore, *India* H02+309 **72**
Ferrar Gl., *Antarctica* B70-790 **27**
Ferrara, *Italy* M20+448 **56**
Ferrato C., *Sardinia* M32+393 **57**
Ferreira do Zezere, *Portugal* N50+397 **52**
Ferrol del Caudillo, *Spain* N49+434 **52**
Fertile, *Minnesota* U38+476 **93**
Fertö tó, *See* Neusiedler See
Fes, *Morocco* N30+340 **80**
Festus, *Missouri* U02+382 **97**
Fethard, *Ireland, Rep.* N46+524 **43**
Fetlar I., *Scotland* N05+606 **40**
Fez. *See* Fes
Ffestiniog, *Wales* N24+529 **38**
Fiambala, *Argentina* S46-277 **103**
Ficalho, *Portugal* N44+380 **52**
Fichtel Geb., *W. Germany* M18+501 **48**
Fideris, *Switzerland* M31+469 **45**
Fier, *Albania* L63+407 **59**
Fiesch, *Switzerland* M41+444 **45**
Fife, reg., *Scotland* N18+563 **41**
Fife Ness, *Scotland* N15+563 **41**
Figeac, *France* M78+466 **55**
Figline Vald. *Italy* M21+436 **56**
Figueira de Castelo Rodrigo,
   Portugal N42+409 **52**
Figueras, *Spain* M72+423 **53**
Figuig, *Morocco* N08+320 **80**
Fiji Is., *Pacific Ocean* A00-175 **106**
Filakovo, *Czechoslovakia* L61+483 **49**
Filchner Ice Shelf,
   Antarctica R30-790 **27**
Filey, *England* N02+542 **37**
Filiátes, *Greece* L58+396 **59**
Filicudi, I., *Italy* M03+386 **57**
Filipow, *Poland* L44+542 **49**
Filisur, *Switzerland* M32+467 **45**
Fincastle, *Virginia* T29+374 **97**
Findhorn & R., *Scotland* N22+577 **40**
Findlay, *Ohio* T52+410 **91**
Findlay Grp., *N.-W. Terr.* V00+772 **88**
Fingal, *N. Dakota* U47+468 **93**
Fingal, *Tasmania* C13-417 **109**
Finhaut, *Switzerland* M48+461 **45**
Finistère, dep., *France* N24+483 **54**
Finisterre, C., *Spain* N55+428 **52**
Finke, R., *N. Terr., Aust.* D01-255 **111**
Finland, rep., *N. Europe* **46**
Finland, G. of, *N.-W. Europe* **46**
Finlay R., *Brit. Columbia* W25+564 **88**
Finlay Forks, *Brit. Columbia* W23+559 **88**
Finley, *New S. Wales* C28-357 **109**
Finschhafen,
   Papua New Guinea C13-065 **111**
Finspäng, *Sweden* L85+587 **47**
Finsteraarhorn, *Switzerland* M41+465 **45**
Fintona, *N. Ireland* N44+545 **42**
Fionn L., *Scotland* N33+577 **40**
Fionnay, *Switzerland* M46+460 **45**
Fiq, *Syria* K56+328 **76**
Firat, R., *Turkey* K36+397 **74**
Firdaus, *Iran* J11+340 **75**
Firenze, *Italy* M23+438 **56**
Firmat, *Argentina* S09-334 **103**
Firnis, *Turkey* K49+379 **74**
Firozabad, *India* G70+272 **73**
Firozpur Jhirka, *India* G78+277 **72**
Firuzabad, *Iran* J45+288 **75**
Firuze, *Iran* J12+378 **75**
Fish Camp, *Kenya* K56+036 **83**
Fisher Str., *N.-W. Terr.* T50+635 **89**

Fishers I., *New York* S72+412 **96**
Fishbuard & B., *Wales* N30+520 **38**
Fitchburg, *Massachusetts* S71+426 **96**
Fitful Hd., *Scotland* N08+599 **40**
Fitzcarrald, *Peru* S70-117 **104**
Fitzgerald, *Alberta* V40+599 **88**
Fitzgerald, *Tasmania* C21-428 **109**
Fitzpatrick, *Alabama* T65+322 **97**
Fitzroy, *W. Australia* D56-181 **110**
Fitz Roy, C., *N.-W. Terr.* T30+755 **89**
Fitzroy, R., *Queensland* C02-230 **111**
Fitzroy, R., *W. Australia* D63-179 **110**
Fitzwilliam I., *Ontario* T41+455 **91**
Fiume. *See* Rijeka
Fivemiletown, *N. Ireland* N44+544 **42**
Fjälläsen, *Sweden* L59+675 **46**
Flagstaff, *Arizona* V40+35 **94**
Flamborough Hd., *England* N00+542 **37**
Flamingo Tk.,
   Irian Jaya, Indon. C76-057 **65**
Flat, *Alaska* Y48+624 **99**
Flathead, L., *Montana* V55+478 **92**
Flattery, C., *Queensland* C28-150 **111**
Flattery, C., *Washington* W28+479 **98**
Flèche, la, *France* N00+477 **54**
Fleetwood, *England* N18+539 **37**
Flekkefjord, *Norway* M50+583 **47**
Flemington, *New Jersey* S89+405 **96**
Flensburg, *W. Germany* M34+547 **48**
Flers, *France* N03+488 **54**
Fleurance, *France* M86+439 **55**
Fleurier, *Switzerland* M50+469 **45**
Fleuru, *Belgium* M63+505 **44**
Flims, *Switzerland* M34+468 **45**
Flinders I., *S. Australia* D03-335 **111**
Flinders I., *Tasmania* C12-400 **109**
Flinders Ra., *S. Australia* C70-320 **109**
Flinders, R., *Queensland* C52-194 **111**
Flin Flon, *Manitoba* U71+548 **88**
Flint, *Michigan* T52+431 **91**
Flint, *Wales* N19+532 **38**
Flint I., *Pacific Ocean* Y15-105 **107**
Flint R., *Georgia* T57+310 **99**
Flisa, *Norway* M18+606 **47**
Flora, *Illinois* T81+386 **95**
Florac, *France* M69+443 **55**
Floreffe, *Belgium* M61+504 **44**
Florence. *See* Firenze
Florence, *Alabama* T76+348 **97**
Florence, *Arizona* V40+330 **94**
Florence, *Colorado* V02+384 **94**
Florence, *S. Carolina* T29+342 **97**
Florence, *Wisconsin* T80+460 **91**
Florencia, *Argentina* R86-280 **103**
Florencia, *Colombia* T04+017 **104**
Florennes, *Belgium* M62+502 **44**
Florenville, *Belgium* M58+497 **44**
Flores, *Guatemala* T89+170 **100**
Flores, I., *Atlantic Ocean* Q08+394 **80**
Flores I. & Sea, *Indonesia* D80-085 **65**
Floriano, *Brazil* Q78-068 **105**
Floriano Peixoto, *Brazil* S44-092 **104**
Florianopolis, *Brazil* R21-276 **103**
Florida, *Sicily* L89+371 **57**
Florida, state, *U.S.A.* T64+306 **99**
Florida, B., *Florida* T41+250 **99**
Florida, C., *Florida* T31+257 **99**
Florida Mts., *New Mexico* V16+322 **94**
Florida Str., *Bahamas, The* T30+250 **101**
Florida Str., *Florida* T39+244 **99**
Florida City, *Florida* T33+254 **99**
Florida Keys, *Florida* T34+250 **97**
Floridia, *Uruguay* R67-340 **103**
Florina, *Greece* L51+408 **59**
Flöro, *Norway* M61+617 **46**
Flotta, I., *Orkney Is., Scot.* N19+588 **40**
Floydada, *Texas* U68+340 **94**
Flüelen, *Switzerland* M38+469 **45**
Flushing. *See* Vlissingen
Flushing, *New York* S83+407 **96**
Fly, R., *Papua New Guinea* C50-078 **111**
Flying Fish C., *Antarctica* U65-730 **27**
Foča, *Yugoslavia* L67+435 **58**
Focsani, *Romania* L17+456 **58**
Fofa Cahuel, *Argentina* S65-423 **103**
Foggia, *Italy* L87+415 **57**
Fogo I., *Newfoundland* R55+497 **90**
Föhr, I., *W. Germany* M39+547 **48**
Foix, *France* M80+430 **55**
Fokis, *Greece* L46+386 **59**
Folda, Fd., *Norway* M04+676 **46**
Folégandros, I., *Greece* L30+366 **59**
Foleyet, *Ontario* T45+483 **91**
Foligno, *Italy* M14+430 **56**
Folkestone, *England* M83+511 **39**
Folkston, *Georgia* T42+309 **97**
Folkstone, *N. Carolina* T15+345 **97**
Follega, *Netherlands* M56+529 **44**
Fonda, *New York* S86+429 **96**
Fond du Lac, *Minnesota-*
   Wisconsin U09+469 **91**
Fond du Lac, *Saskatchewan* V13+595 **88**
Fond du Lac, *Wisconsin* T81+438 **91**
Fonsagráda, *Spain* N42+431 **52**
Fonseca, G. of, *Honduras* T76+132 **101**
Fontaine, *Belgium* M64+504 **44**
Fontainebleau, *France* M74+484 **54**
Fontana, L., *Argentina* S69-449 **103**
Fontenay le Comte, *France* N05+465 **54**
Foochow, *China* E04+261 **67**
Forbes, *New South Wales* C12+334 **109**
Forbes, Mt., *Alberta* V70+516 **88**
Forcados, *Nigeria* M58+052 **80**
Forcalquier, *France* M56+440 **55**
Førde, *Norway* M55+615 **47**
Fordlandia, *Brazil* R62-038 **105**
Ford Ranges, *Antarctica* X40-770 **27**
Ford's Bridge, *New S. Wales* C27-298 **109**
Fordyce, *Arkansas* U14+338 **95**
Forel, Mt., *Greenland* Q10+670 **26**
Forest, *Ontario* T42+431 **91**
Forestier Pen., *Tasmania* C13-429 **109**
Forfar, *Scotland* N17+566 **41**
Fork, R., N., *Idaho* V42+440 **98**
Forli, *Italy* M18+442 **56**
Forlorn Pt., *Ireland, Rep.* N39+522 **43**
Formby, *England* N16+535 **37**
Formentera I., *Balearic Is.* M81+387 **53**
Formia, *Italy* M08+413 **57**
Formosa, *Argentina* R79-261 **103**
Formosa, *Brazil* R13-156 **105**
Formosa. *See* Taiwan, I.

Formosa Str. *See* Taiwan Hai Hsia
Fornos d'Algôdres, *Portugal* N45+407 **52**
Forres, *Scotland* N22+576 **40**
Forrest, *W. Australia* D41-308 **110**
Forrest, *Victoria* C48-386 **109**
Forrest City, *Arkansas* U04+350 **95**
Forsa, *Sweden* L79+617 **47**
Forsayth, *Queensland* C39-185 **111**
Forsnäs, *Sweden* L68+662 **46**
Forssa, *Finland* L38+608 **47**
Forsyth, *Montana* V10+462 **93**
Fort Albany, *Ontario* T40+525 **89**
Fort Alexander, *Manitoba* U37+504 **88**
Fortaleza, *Amazonas, Brazil* S52-064 **104**
Fortaleza, *Ceara, Brazil* Q52-037 **105**
Fortaleza, state of, *Acre,*
   Brazil S58-100 **104**
Fort Ann, *New York* S80+435 **96**
Fort Archambault, *See* Sarh
Fort Atkinson, *Wisconsin* T83+429 **95**
Fort Augustus, *Scotland* N28+571 **40**
Fort Beaufort, *Cape Province* L20-328 **84**
Fort Bennett, *S. Dakota* U64+447 **93**
Fort Benton, *Montana* V34+478 **93**
Fort Brabant, *N.-W. Terr.* V42+707 **88**
Fort Bragg, *California* W23+395 **92**
Fort Chipewyan, *Alberta* V36+590 **88**
Fort Collins, *Colorado* V00+406 **94**
Fort Coulonge, *Quebec* T11+459 **91**
Fort Crampel, *Central*
   African Republic L64+070 **81**
Ford Dauphin, *Madagascar* J78-250 **83**
Fort Dodge, *Iowa* U25+426 **95**
Fort Edward, *New York* S82+433 **91**
Fortescue, R., *W. Australia* E18-214 **110**
Fort Fairfield, *Maine* S47+467 **90**
Fort Flatters, *Algeria* M50+280 **80**
Fort Fraser, *Brit. Columbia* W28+541 **88**
Fort George, *Scotland* N24+576 **40**
Fort George, R., *Quebec* T20+540 **89**
Fort Gouraud, *See* Fdérik
Fort Grahame, *B.C.* W27+563 **88**
Fort Grey, *New S. Wales* C52-289 **109**
Forth, Firth of, *Scotland* N18+561 **41**
Forth R., *Scotland* N24+561 **41**
Fort Haka, *Burma* F68+226 **71**
Fort Hall, *Kenya* K48-008 **83**
Fort Henrique, *Namibia* M00-174 **84**
Fort Hertz, *Burma* F45+273 **71**
Fort Hill, *See* Chitipa
Fort Howard, *Wisconsin* T78+445 **91**
Fort Hunter, *New York* S85+429 **96**
Fortin Teniente Montania,
   Paraguay S00-220 **103**
Fortin Camacho, *Paraguay* S02-221 **103**
Fortin Lopez, *Paraguay* R89-214 **103**
Fortin Munoz, *Paraguay* S04-235 **103**
Fortin Saavedra, *Paraguay* S00-234 **103**
Fort Jameson, *Zambia* K74-138 **83**
Fort Kent, *Maine* S52+472 **90**
Fort Keogh, *Montana* V05+464 **93**
Fort Lallemand, *Algeria* M52+312 **80**
Fort Lamy, *See* N'Djamena
Fort Laperrine. *See* Tamanrasset
Fort Laramie, *Wyoming* U87+422 **93**
Fort Madison, *Iowa* U08+406 **95**
Fort Maginnis, *Montana* V25+472 **93**
Fort Morgan, *Alabama* T78+303 **97**
Fort Morgan, *Colorado* U83+402 **94**
Fort Munro, *Pakistan* H30+229 **72**
Fort Nelson & R., *B.C.* W17+590 **88**
Fort Ogden, *Florida* T41+271 **97**
Fort Peck, *Montana* V08+480 **93**
Fort Peck Res., *Montana* V16+476 **93**
Fort Pierre, *S. Dakota* U62+443 **93**
Fort Plain, *New York* S88+429 **96**
Fort Polignac, *Algeria* M40+262 **80**
Fort Portal, *Uganda* K88+006 **83**
Fort Randall, *Alaska* Y75+547 **26**
Fort Rice, *N. Dakota* U64+465 **93**
Fortrose, *Scotland* N25+576 **40**
Fort Roseberry, *Zambia* L06-112 **83**
Fort St George. *See* Madras
Fort St John, *B.C.* W07+560 **88**
Fort Sandeman, *Pakistan* H31+314 **72**
Fort Saskatchewan, *Alberta* V48+539 **88**
Fort Scott, *Kansas* U28+378 **95**
Fort Sibut, *Cent. Afr. Rep.* L66+058 **81**
Fort Sill, *Oklahoma* U50+346 **95**
Fort Smith, *Arkansas* U26+353 **95**
Fort Smith, *N.-W. Terr.* V41+600 **88**
Fort Stedman, *Burma* F48+205 **71**
Fort Stockton, *Texas* U76+308 **94**
Fort Sumner, *New Mexico* U85+344 **94**
Fortuna, *California* W25+406 **92**
Fortuna, *Spain* N07+382 **53**
Fortune B., *Newfoundland* R66+471 **90**
Fort Valley, *Georgia* T53+326 **97**
Fort Vermilion, *Alberta* V65+586 **88**
Fort Victoria, *Zimbabwe* K84-202 **84**
Fort Warren, *Wyoming* U89+412 **93**
Fort Wayne, *Indiana* T61+411 **91**
Fort White, *Burma* F67+234 **71**
Fort William, *Scotland* N31+568 **41**
Fort Worth, *Texas* U44+328 **95**
Fort Yates, *N. Dakota* U64+461 **93**
Fort Yukon, *Alaska* X60+663 **99**
Forville, *Belgium* M60+506 **44**
Fosse, *Belgium* M62+504 **44**
Foster, *Victoria* C23-386 **109**
Foster Ls., *Saskatchewan* V03+564 **88**
Fougeres, *France* N07+484 **54**
Foul B., *Egypt* K56+234 **81**
Foul, I., *Burma* F65+182 **71**
Foula, I., *Scotland* N12+602 **34**
Foulness I., *England* M85+516 **39**
Fouly, la, *Switzerland* M47+459 **45**
Foúrnoi, Is., *Greece* L21+376 **59**
Foveaux Strait, *New Zealand* A72-466 **112**
Fowchow. *See* Fowling.
Fowlers B., *S. Australia* D14-320 **110**
Fowling, *China* E76+297 **67**
Fowning, *China* E00+338 **66**
Fowyang, *China* E24+330 **66**
Fox Is., *Aleutian Is.* Z20+530 **99**
Fox R., *Manitoba* U27+556 **88**
Foxe Basin, *N.-W.*
   Territories T20+670 **89**
Foxe Chan., *N.-W.*
   Territories T30+650 **89**
Foxe Pen., *N.-W. Terr.* T10+647 **89**

Foxford, *Ireland, Rep.* N55+540 **42**
Fox River, *Quebec* S26+490 **90**
Foxton, *New Zealand* A28-404 **112**
Foyle L., *N. Ireland* N43+551 **42**
Foyle R., *N. Ireland* N44+550 **42**
Foynes, *Ireland, Rep.* N55+526 **43**
Foz do Acre, *Brazil* S44-088 **104**
Foz do Cunene, *Angola* M18-172 **84**
Foz Embira, *Brazil* S61-074 **104**
Fraire, *Belgium* M63+503 **44**
Framboise, *Nova Scotia* S02+457 **90**
Frameries, *Belgium* M67+504 **44**
Framingham, *Massachusetts* S69+423 **96**
Franca, *Brazil* R15-206 **105**
Francavilla Fontana, *Italy* L75+405 **57**
France, *W. Europe* M78+470 **50**
Frances, *S. Australia* C54-367 **109**
Frances L., *Yukon* W55+610 **88**
Franceville, *Gabon* M04-018 **82**
Franche-Comte, prov., *France* M50+472 **54**
Francistown, *Botswana* L14-214 **84**
Francois L., *British Columbia* W35+541 **88**
Frankfort, *Kansas* U39+397 **95**
Frankfort, *Kentucky* T59+383 **97**
Frankfort, *Michigan* T67+446 **91**
Frankfurt-am-Main, *W. Germany* M38+501 **48**
Frankfurt-an-der-Oder, *E. Germany* M03+523 **48**
Fränkischer Jura, *W. Germany* M21+492 **48**
Franklin, *Louisiana* U08+298 **95**
Franklin, *New Hampshire* S70+434 **96**
Franklin, *New Jersey* S87+411 **96**
Franklin, *N. Carolina* T50+352 **97**
Franklin, *Pennsylvania* T29+414 **96**
Franklin, *Tasmania* C19-432 **111**
Franklin, *Tennessee* T71+358 **97**
Franklin, *Virginia* T12+367 **97**
Franklin, *W. Virginia* T26+386 **97**
Franklin Dist., *N.-W. Terr.* **88-89**
Franklin, I., *Antarctica* A68-760 **27**
Franklin Mts., *N.-W. Territories* W25+656 **88**
Franklin City, *Virginia* T02+380 **97**
Franklin Falls, *N.H.* S70+434 **91**
Frantsa Iosifa Zemyla, *Arctic Ocean* J30+810 **62**
Franz Josef Fd., *Greenland* P85+740 **26**
Franz Josef Land, *See Frantsa Iosifa Zemyla.*
Fraser R., *British Columbia* W13+514 **88**
Fraserburg, *Cape Province* L50-320 **84**
Fraserburgh, *Scotland* N12+577 **40**
Frasertown, *New Zealand* A15-390 **112**
Frasnes, *Belgium* M68+507 **44**
Frater, *Ontario* T57+473 **91**
Frauenfeld, *Switzerland* M37+476 **45**
Fray Bentos, *Uruguay* R80-332 **103**
Fredericia, *Denmark* M31+556 **47**
Frederick, *Maryland* T14+394 **96**
Frederick, *Oklahoma* U54+344 **95**
Frederick, S. *Dakota* U51+458 **93**
Fredericksburg, *Virginia* T15+383 **97**
Fredericktown, *Missouri* U02+375 **95**
Fredericton, *New Brunswick* S40+460 **90**
Frederikshåb, *Greenland* R30+620 **26**
Frederikshavn, *Denmark* M27+575 **47**
Fredonia, *Colombia* T04+060 **104**
Fredonia, *Kansas* U37+376 **95**
Fredonia, *New York* T26+425 **96**
Fredrika, *Sweden* L70+641 **46**
Fredrikstad, *Norway* M24+592 **47**
Freehold, *New Jersey* S85+402 **96**
Freeling, *S. Australia* C67-345 **109**
Freeport, *Illinois* T88+423 **95**
Freeport, *Pennsylvania* T29+407 **96**
Freetown, *Sierra Leone* N80+086 **80**
Fregenal de la Sierra, *Spain* N40+382 **52**
Fréhel, C. *France* N14+487 **54**
Freiberg, *E. Germany* M10+510 **48**
Freiburg, *W. Germany* M43+480 **48**
Freirina, *Chile* S67-284 **103**
Freistadt, *Austria* M03+485 **48**
Freital, *E. Germany* M08+511 **48**
Freixiel, *Portugal* N44+413 **52**
Freixo, *Portugal* N41+411 **52**
Fremantle, *W. Australia* E25-320 **110**
Fremont, *Nebraska* U38+414 **95**
Fremont, *Ohio* T49+414 **91**
Fremont Pk., *Wyoming* V28+432 **93**
Fremont R., *Utah* V35+386 **98**
French I., *Victoria* C28-383 **109**
French R., *Ontario* T32+460 **91**
French Guiana, rep., *S. America* R50+036 **105**
Frenchman R., *Saskatchewan* V20+493 **88**
Frenchman Cap, *Tasmania* C24-423 **109**
Frenchpark, *Ireland, Rep.* N50+539 **42**
French River, *Ontario* T36+459 **91**
French Territory of the Afars and the Issas *See Djibouti*
Fresko, *Ivory Coast* N36+050 **80**
Fresnillo, *Mexico* U77+232 **100**
Fria C., *Namibia* M18-184 **84**
Fresno, *California* V89+368 **92**
Frias, *Spain* N20+428 **52**
Fribourg & canton, *Switz.* M47+468 **45**
Fridtjof Nansen Mt., *Antarctica* A10-850 **27**
Friedland, *E. Germany* M09+536 **48**
Friend, *Nebraska* U44+406 **95**
Friesische Is., Nord., *W. Ger.* M39+546 **47**
Friesische Is., Ost., *W. Germany* M52+538 **48**
Friesland, prov., *Netherlands* M54+531 **44**
Friuli-Venezia Giulia, reg., *Italy* M12+462 **56**
Frobisher B., *N.-W. Terr.* S30+618 **89**
Frobisher L., *Saskatchewan* V20+564 **88**
Fro Havet, *Norway* M35+638 **46**
Frome, *England* N14+512 **38**
Frome, L., *S. Australia* C61-308 **109**
Front Ra., *Colorado* V04+400 **94**
Fronteira, *Portugal* N46+390 **52**
Frontera, *Mexico* U16+186 **100**
Fronteras, *Mexico* V27+310 **100**
Front Royal, *Virginia* T18+389 **96**
Frosinone, *Italy* M10+416 **57**
Frostburg, *Maryland* T24+397 **96**

Frøya, *Norway* M38+637 **46**
Frozen Str., *N.-W. Terr.* T55+658 **89**
Frunze, *Kirgiz.* H02+429 **62**
Frutigen, *Switzerland* M44+466 **45**
Frydek, *Czechoslovakia* L70+497 **49**

Fthiótis, *Greece* L45+388 **59**
Fuchin, *China* D20+474 **64**
Fuchow, *China* E22+280 **67**
Fu-chow, *China* D81+397 **66**
Fuente-Alamo de Murcia, *Sp.* N07+378 **53**
Fuente del Arco, *Spain* N35+382 **52**
Fuentes de Onoro, *Spain* N41+406 **52**
Fuerteventura, I., *Canary Islands* N82+284 **80**
Fuerte, El, *Mexico* V20+268 **100**
Fuerte, R., *Mexico* V22+262 **100**
Fuhsin, *China* D80+421 **66**
Fuji yama (Fuji san), *Japan* C66+354 **68**
Fukien, prov., *China* E12+260 **67**
Fukuei Chiao, *Taiwan* D80 + 255 **64**
Fukui, *Japan* C82+360 **68**
Fukuoka, *Japan* D28+335 **68**
Fukushima, *Japan* C57+377 **68**
Fukuyama, *Japan* C59+415 **68**
Fukuyama, *Japan* D16+345 **68**
Fulda, R., *W. Germany* M33+511 **48**
Fullerton, *Nebraska* U48+414 **95**
Fulton, *Kentucky* T83+365 **97**
Fulton, *Mississippi* T81+343 **97**
Fulton, *Missouri* U12+388 **95**
Fulton, *New York* T07+433 **96**
Fulton Chain Ls., *New York* S89+437 **96**
Funchal, *Madeira I.* P10+326 **80**
Fundão, *Portugal* N45+402 **52**
Fundy, B. of, *N.S.-N.B.* S37+448 **90**
Fünen, *See* Fyn.
Fünfkurchen, *See* Pecs.
Funing, *See* Siapu.
Fure, *Japan* C49+446 **68**
Furg, *Iran* J29+283 **75**
Furneaux Grp., *Tasmania* C13-400 **109**
Furnes, *See* Veurne.
Furqlus, *Syria* K47+346 **76**
Fürth, *W. Germany* M24+494 **48**
Furue, *Japan* D25+314 **68**
Fusagasuga, *Colombia* S86+042 **104**
Fushih, *China* E63+365 **66**
Fushimi, *Japan* C85+350 **68**
Fu-shun, *China* D66+419 **66**
Fusio, *Switzerland* M38+464 **45**
Fuyu, *China* D61+452 **64**
Fyn, *Denmark* M28+553 **47**
Fyne, L., *Scotland* N31+561 **41**
Gabaidu, *Iran* K28-018 **83**
Gabandi, *Iran* J41+272 **75**
Gaberones, *Botswana* L24-246 **84**
Gabès & G. of, *Tunisia* M30+338 **81**
Gabin, *Poland* L62+524 **49**
Gabon, rep., *Cent. Africa* M26-006 **82**
Gabrovo, *Bulgaria* L28+429 **58**
Gach Saran, *Iran* J50+302 **75**
Gadag, *India* G86+155 **70**
Gadsden, *Alabama* T66+340 **97**
Gael Hamkes B., *Greenland* P34+740 **26**
Gaesti, *Romania* L28+447 **58**
Gaeta & G. di, *Italy* M09+412 **57**
Gafsa, *Tunisia* M34+348 **81**
Gagetown, *New Brunswick* S37+457 **90**
Gagnon, *Quebec* S43+516 **89**
Gaibanda, *Bangladesh* G02+253 **73**
Gáidharos, I., *Greece* L18+375 **59**
Gáillac, *France* M78+439 **55**
Gaiman, *Argentina* S34-433 **103**
Gainesboro, *Tennessee* T64+363 **97**
Gainesville, *Alabama* T79+328 **97**
Gainesville, *Florida* T44+296 **97**
Gainesville, *Georgia* T53+342 **97**
Gainesville, *Missouri* U15+366 **97**
Gainsville, *Texas* U42+336 **95**
Gainsborough, *England* N05+534 **37**
Gairdner, L., *S. Australia* C85-316 **111**
Gairloch, *Scotland* N34+577 **40**
Gairlochy, *Scotland* N30+569 **40**
Gala Water, *Scotland* N17+556 **41**
Galag, *Iran* J03+255 **75**
Galangue, *Angola* L82-138 **82**
Galapagos Is., *Pacific Ocean* U00–007 **107**
Galashiels, *Scotland* N17+556 **41**
Galatea, *New Zealand* A20–384 **112**
Galathea B., *Nicobar Is.* F67+066 **71**
Galati, *Romania* L12+454 **58**
Galatz. *See* Galati.
Galax, *Virginia* T36+366 **97**
Galcaio, *Somalia* J76+066 **83**
Galdhøpiggen, mt., *Norway* M40+616 **47**
Galeana, *Mexico* U60+248 **100**
Galeana, *Mexico* V15+301 **100**
Galena, *Illinois* U03+424 **95**
Galesburg, *Illinois* U02+410 **95**
Galeton, *Pennsylvania* T16+417 **96**
Galich, *U.S.S.R.* K16+584 **61**
Galilee, L., *Queensland* C25–222 **111**
Galilee, Sea of. *See* Tiberias L.
Galiuro Mts., *Arizona* V32+326 **94**
Galle, *Sri Lanka* G59+060 **70**
Gallego, *Mexico* V08+298 **94**
Gallegos R., *Argentina* S56–516 **103**
Galley Hd., *Ireland, Rep.* N54+515 **43**
Gallipoli (Gelibolu), *Turkey* L20+408 **59**
Gallipoli, *Italy* L72+401 **57**
Gällivare, *Sweden* L56+670 **46**
Gallo Mts., *New Mexico* V20+341 **94**
Galloway, Mull of, *Scotland* N29+546 **41**
Gallup, *New Mexico* V23+356 **94**
Galong, *New South Wales* C09–346 **109**
Galt, *Ontario* T32+434 **91**
Galty Mts., *Ireland, Rep.* N49+523 **43**
Galtymore, *Ireland, Rep.* N49+524 **43**
Galva, *Illinois* U01+412 **91**
Galveston and B., *Texas* U29+293 **95**
Galvez, *Argentina* S07–320 **103**
Galway (Gaillimh), *Ireland, Rep.* N54+533 **43**
Galway B., *Ireland Rep.* N55+532 **43**
Gambaga, *Ghana* N02+108 **80**
Gambia, The, *W. Africa* P05+130 **80**
Gambia, R., *W. Africa* P00+136 **80**

Gambo, *Newfoundland* R55+488 **90**
Gams, *Switzerland* M33+472 **45**
Gananoque, *Ontario* T07+443 **91**
Gand. *See* Gent
Gandak R., *India* G32+267 **73**
Gandava, *Pakistan* H45+286 **70**
Gander (Airport) & L., *Nfd.* R58+489 **90**
Gandesa, *Spain* M88+411 **53**
Gandia, *Spain* N01+390 **53**
Ganganagar, *India* H07+290 **72**
Gangaw, *Burma* F65+221 **71**
Ganges (Ganga), R., *India* G33+256 **73**
Gangoh, *India* G76+298 **72**
Gangtok, *Sikkim* G08+273 **73**
Ganjam, *India* G29+194 **71**
Ganmam, *New South Wales* C18–348 **109**
Gannat, *France* M71+461 **54**
Gannett Pk., *Wyoming* V28+432 **93**
Gantheame B., *W. Australia* E37–274 **110**
Ganza, *Cent. Afr. Rep.* L44+078 **81**
Gao, *Mali* N00+162 **80**
Gaoual, *Guinea* N80+118 **80**
Gara L., *Ireland, Rep.* N51+539 **42**
Garachine, *Panama* T19+080 **101**
Garah, *New South Wales* C02–290 **109**
Garanhuns, *Brazil* Q38–089 **105**
Garba Tula, *Kenya* K38+004 **83**
Gard, dep., *France* M64+440 **55**
Garda, L. di, *Italy* M26+457 **56**
Gardafui, C., *Somalia* J52+118 **83**
Garden, *Michigan* T69+458 **91**
Garden City, *Kansas* U66+380 **94**
Gardiner, *Maine* S59+442 **90**
Gardiner, *Montana* V35+450 **93**
Gardiner, *Oregon* W24+438 **92**
Gardiners, B. & I., *New York* S73+411 **96**
Gardner I., *Hawaii* Z15 + 250 **106**
Gardula, *Ethiopia* K44+058 **83**
Garelochhead, *Scotland* N29+561 **41**
Garfield, *Utah* V43+408 **94**
Gar Gunsa, *Tibet* G60+321 **70**
Garha, *India* G72+250 **73**
Garhmuktesar, *India* G73+288 **72**
Garhshankar, *India* G82+312 **72**
Garibaldi, *Brazil* R40–293 **103**
Garibaldi Park, *B.C.* W20+500 **88**
Garies, *Cape Province* L72–306 **84**
Gariganus, *Namibia* L72-262 **84**
Garissa, *Kenya* K30–006 **83**
Garland, *Montana* V06+459 **93**
Garm, *Tadzhik* H27+390 **62**
Garmsar, *Iran* J47+353 **75**
Garo Hills, *India* F87+254 **71**
Garonne, R., *France* M83+438 **55**
Garoua, *Cameroon* M10+092 **81**
Garraway, *Liberia* N48+046 **80**
Garrison & Res., *N. Dakota* U69+477 **93**
Garron Pt., *N. Ireland* N36+550 **42**
Garrovillas, *Spain* N39+397 **52**
Garry, L., *N.-W. Territories* U60+659 **88**
Garsen, *Kenya* K30–024 **83**
Garstang, *England* N17+539 **37**
Gartok, *Tibet* G58+318 **70**
Garvagh, *N. Ireland* N40+550 **42**
Gary, *Indiana* T74+416 **91**
Garza, *Argentina* S22–281 **103**
Garzon, *Colombia* T04+021 **104**
Gascogne, G. de, *Fr.-Sp.* N12+437 **55**
Gascogne, prov., *France* M88+435 **55**
Gasconade R., *Missouri* U11+380 **97**
Gascoyne, R., *W. Australia* E16–252 **110**
Gasharbrum, mt., *Kashmir* G80+358 **72**
Gaspé, *Quebec* S27+488 **90**
Gaspé, B. & C., *Quebec* S25+488 **90**
Gaspé Pen., *Quebec* S33+488 **90**
Gaspésia Park, *Quebec* S38+488 **90**
Gasselte, *Netherlands* M49+530 **44**
Gastonia, *N. Carolina* T37+352 **97**
Gastre, *Argentina* S56–421 **103**
Gat (Ghat), *Libya* M30+246 **81**
Gata, *Spain* N39+402 **52**
Gata, C., *Cyprus* K72+345 **76**
Gate City, *Virginia* T45+366 **97**
Gateshead, *England* N09+550 **37**
Gatineau R., *Quebec* T06+460 **91**
Gatooma, *Zimbabwe* L00–184 **84**
Gatun L., *Panama* T29+092 **101**
Gaud-i-Zirreh, *Afghanistan* H80+297 **75**
Gauhati, *India* F79+262 **71**
Gaurihar, *India* G58+253 **73**
Gavdhos, I., *Crete* L36+348 **59**
Gaviao, *Portugal* N48+394 **52**
Gävle, *Sweden* L78+607 **47**
Gävle Bukten, *Sweden* L75+608 **47**
Gawler, *S. Australia* C68–346 **109**
Gawler Ra., *S. Australia* C85–325 **111**
Gaya, *India* G30+248 **73**
Gaya, *Niger* M70+118 **80**
Gayaza, *Uganda* K86–008 **83**
Gaylord, *Michigan* T58+450 **91**
Gaza, *Cent. Afr. Rep.* L88+046 **81**
Gaza, *Egypt* K63+315 **76**
Gazeh Manzil, *Iran* H85+258 **75**
Gazi Antep, *Turkey* K46+371 **74**
Gazik, *Iran* H89+330 **75**
Gdansk, *Poland* L68+544 **49**
Gdynia, *Poland* L69+545 **49**
Gebeit, *Sudan* K50+190 **81**
Gedaref, *Sudan* K56+140 **81**
Gedinne, *Belgium* M60+500 **44**
Geel, *Belgium* M60+512 **44**
Geelong, *Victoria* C34-382 **109**
Geeraardsbergen, *Belgium* M67+508 **44**
Geeveston, *Tasmania* C19–432 **109**
Geh, *Iran* H89+262 **75**
Geikie R., *Saskatchewan* U88+571 **88**
Gela, *Sicily* M04+371 **57**
Gelderland, *Netherlands* M54+521 **44**
Geldrop, *Netherlands* M57+514 **44**
Gelibolu, *Turkey* L20+405 **74**
Gelinden, *Belgium* M58+508 **44**
Gelsenkirchen, *W. Germany* M47 + 516 **48**
Gemas, *Malaysia* F14+026 **69**
Gembloux, *Belgium* M62+506 **44**
Gemena, *Zaire* L60+032 **82**
Gemert, *Netherlands* M56+516 **44**
Gemmenich, *Belgium* M54+507 **44**
Gemmi Pass, *Switzerland* M44+464 **45**
Gemvile, *New South Wales* C43–309 **109**
Genappe, *Belgium* M63+506 **44**
Gendringen, *Netherlands* M52+519 **44**

Genemuiden, *Netherlands* M54+526 **44**
General Acha, *Argentina* S28–374 **103**
General Alvear, *Argentina* S00–360 **103**
General Capdevila, *Argentina* S09–274 **103**
General Grant Nat. Pk., *Cal.* V84+367 **92**
General Guido, *Argentina* R77–366 **103**
General La Madrid, *Argent.* S08–373 **103**
General Lavalle, *Argentina* R72–364 **103**
General MacArthur, *Phil.* D57+115 **65**
General Pico, *Argentina* S23–356 **103**
General Pinto, *Argentina* S12–348 **103**
General Roca, *Argentina* S46–390 **103**
General Viamonte, *Argentina* S06–350 **103**
General Villegas, *Argentina* S18–350 **103**
Geneseo, *New York* T17+428 **96**
Geneva, *Nebraska* U46+405 **95**
Geneva, *New York* T12+428 **96**
Geneva, L. of. *See* Leman, Lac
Genève (Geneva), *Switz.* M53+462 **45**
Genipapo, *Brazil* R04–044 **105**
Genkai Nada, *Japan* D30+337 **68**
Gennargentu, Mte. del, *Sardinia* M34+400 **57**
Gennep, *Netherlands* M54+517 **44**
Genoa. *See* Genova
Genoa, *Victoria* C03–374 **109**
Genova, *Italy* M37+444 **56**
Genova, G. di, *Italy* M36+440 **56**
Gent, *Belgium* M47+349 **45**
Geographe B., *W. Australia* E28–334 **110**
Geographe Chan., *W. Aust.* E38–250 **110**
Georga Zemlya, *Arctic Oc.* J70+805 **62**
George L., *New S. Wales* C04–352 **109**
George L., *New York* S81+436 **96**
George R., *Quebec* S33+580 **89**
Georgetown, *Guyana* R79+066 **104**
Georgetown, *Delaware* T02+387 **91**
Georgetown, *Georgia* T61+319 **97**
George Town, *Gr. Cayman, W.I.* T38+194 **101**
Georgetown, *Kentucky* T57+382 **97**
George Town, *Pinang I., Malaysia* F28 + 054 **69**
Georgetown, *Pr. Edward I.* S15+462 **90**
Georgetown, S. *Carolina* T26+333 **97**
George Town, *Tasmania* C19–411 **109**
Georgetown, *Virginia* T13+389 **96**
Georgia, state, *U.S.A.* T50+330 **99**
Georgian B., *Ontario* T36+455 **91**
Georgian B. Is. Nat. Pk., *Ont.* T30+450 **91**
Georgiyevka, *Kazakh.* G51+493 **62**
Georgiyevsk, *U.S.S.R.* K09+442 **62**
Georgina, R., *Queensland* C71–216 **111**
Gera, *E. Germany* M17+509 **48**
Geraldine, *New Zealand* A53–440 **112**
Geraldton, *W. Australia* E32–286 **110**
Geremoabo, *Brazil* Q50–101 **105**
Gérgal, *Spain* N08+371 **53**
Gerlach, *Nevada* V85+408 **92**
Germania, *Argentina* S12–346 **103**
Germania Land, *Greenland* P30+770 **26**
Germany, E. & W., *Central Europe* **48**
Gerona, *Spain* M73+420 **53**
Gers, dep., *France* M87+437 **55**
Gerze, *Turkey* K58+418 **74**
Getafe, *Spain* N22+403 **52**
Gethsemani, *Quebec* S03+503 **90**
Gettysburg, *Pennsylvania* T14+398 **96**
Gettysburg, S. *Dakota* U60+450 **93**
Getz Ice Shelf, *Antarctica* W10–750 **27**
Gevar, *Turkey* K04+376 **74**
Gevgelija, *Yugoslavia* L45+412 **58**
Ghabaghib, *Syria* K53+332 **76**
Ghadames, *Libya* M32+302 **81**
Ghaghra, R., *India* G42+266 **73**
Ghaida, *Yemen, South* J67+142 **74**
Ghail, *Saudi Arabia* J82+226 **74**
Ghana, *W. Afr.* N10+081 **80**
Gharandal, *Jordan* K59+301 **76**
Ghardaia, *Algeria* M68+322 **80**
Gharian, *Libya* M12+322 **50**
Ghat, *Saudi Arabia* K00+260 **74**
Ghatal, *India* G13+227 **73**
Ghatampur, *India* G59+261 **73**
Ghatghat, *Saudi Arabia* J82+245 **74**
Ghats, Eastern, *India* G56+172 **70**
Ghats, Western, *India* H06+177 **70**
Ghauta, *Saudi Arabia* J79+222 **74**
Ghaziabad, *India* G75+286 **72**
Ghazipur, *India* G38+256 **73**
Ghazir, *Lebanon* K56+340 **76**
Ghazni, *Afghanistan* H39+336 **75**
Georgheni, *Romania* L26+467 **58**
Gherabe, *Saudi Arabia* K27+242 **74**
Ghislenghien, *Belgium* M67+507 **44**
Ghizao, *Afghanistan* H53+335 **75**
Ghobreh, *Oman* J08+230 **75**
Ghorak, *Afghanistan* H59+321 **75**
Ghorian, *Afghanistan* H81+344 **75**
Ghotki, *Pakistan* H34+280 **70**
Giant's Causeway, *N. Ireland* N39+552 **42**
Giaour Dagh, *Turkey* K52+366 **74**
Giarabub, *Libya* L34+296 **81**
Giarre, *Sicily* L89+377 **57**
Gibara, *Cuba* T07+211 **101**
Gibeon, *Namibia* L74-252 **84**
Gibraltar, *Spain* N32+361 **52**
Gibraltar, Str. of, *Spain-Morocco* N33+359 **52**
Gibson Desert, *W. Aust.* D60–237 **110**
Giddings, *Texas* U42+302 **95**
Gien, *France* M74+477 **54**
Giessen, *W. Germany* M38+505 **48**
Gifford, *Scotland* N16+559 **41**
Gifhorn, *W. Germany* M27+525 **48**
Gifu, *Japan* C79+353 **68**
Giganta, La, *Mexico* V39+261 **100**
Gijon, *Spain* N34+435 **52**
Gila Desert, *Arizona* V50+323 **98**
Gila R., *Arizona, etc.* V30+330 **94**
Gilau, *Romania* L40+467 **58**
Gilbert Is., *See* Kiribati
Gilbert, R., *Queensland* C47–172 **111**
Gilbués, *Brazil* Q89–096 **105**
Gilehdar, *Iran* J43+276 **75**
Gilgandra, *New S. Wales* C08–317 **109**
Gilgit & R., *Kashmir* H04+359 **72**
Gilgunnia, *New South Wales* C24–324 **109**
Gill L., *Ireland, Rep.* N50+542 **42**
Gillett, *Arkansas* U09+341 **97**
Gillette, *Wyoming* V03+443 **93**

Gillingham, *England* M87+514 **39**
Gimel, *Switzerland* M52+465 **45**
Ginir, *Ethiopia* K26+070 **83**
Ginzo, *Spain* N46+420 **52**
Gioia, G. di, *Italy* L86+385 **57**
Giornico, *Switzerland* M37+464 **45**
Girardot, *Colombia* S89+042 **104**
Girdle Ness, *Scotland* N12+571 **40**
Giresun, *Turkey* K40+409 **74**
Girga, *Egypt* K78+264 **81**
Giridih, *India* G22+242 **73**
Girilambone, *New S. Wales* C19–312 **109**
Girishk, *Afghanistan* H62+318 **75**
Gironde, dep., *France* N02+448 **55**
Gironde, R., *France* N06+453 **54**
Girvan & R., *Scotland* N29+553 **41**
Gisborne, *New Zealand* A12–387 **112**
Gisors, *France* M79+493 **54**
Giswil, *Switzerland* M41+468 **45**
Gitch, mt., *Ethiopia* K40+132 **83**
Giurgiu, *Romania* L24+439 **58**
Givry, *Belgium* M66+504 **44**
Gizhiga, *U.S.S.R.* B26+621 **63**
Giżycko, *Poland* L49+541 **49**
Gjinokaster, *Albania* L59+401 **59**
Gjoa Haven, *N.-W. Terr.* U43+681 **88**
Gjøvik, *Norway* M26+608 **47**
Glabbeek-Zuurbemde, *Belg.* M60+509 **44**
Glace Bay, *Nova Scotia* S00+462 **90**
Glacier, *British Columbia* V75+511 **88**
Glacier Nat. Park, *Montana* V50+485 **98**
Gladstone, *Michigan* T72+459 **91**
Gladstone, *New S. Wales* B73–310 **109**
Gladstone, *Queensland* B82–217 **111**
Gladstone, *S. Australia* C70–332 **109**
Gladstone, *Tasmania* C13–410 **109**
Gladwin, *Michigan* T57+440 **91**
Glamis, *Scotland* N18+566 **41**
Glamoc, *Yugoslavia* L79+441 **56**
Glamorgan, W. Mid. & S., co., *Wales* N22+517 **38**
Glanaruddery Mts., *Ireland, Rep.* N57+523 **43**
Glärnisch, mt., *Switzerland* M36+470 **45**
Glarus & canton, *Switz.* M36+471 **45**
Glasgow, *Kentucky* T65+370 **97**
Glasgow, *Montana* V10+482 **93**
Glasgow, *Scotland* N26+558 **41**
Glass L., *Scotland* N27+577 **40**
Glassboro, *New Jersey* T00+397 **96**
Glauchau, *E. Germany* M15+508 **48**
Glazov, *U.S.S.R.* J44+582 **61**
Glen, *New Hampshire* S67+441 **91**
Glen Affric, *Scotland* N30+572 **40**
Glenarm, *N. Ireland* N36+550 **42**
Glenburnie, *S. Australia* C54–378 **109**
Glencoe, *Minnesota* U25+448 **93**
Glendale, *Arizona* V44+334 **94**
Glendale, *California* V80+342 **92**
Glencoe, *S. Australia* C57–377 **109**
Glen Coe, *Scotland* N29+567 **41**
Glendive, *Montana* U88+471 **93**
Glendowan Mts., *Ireland, Rep.* N48+550 **42**
Gleneagles, *Scotland* N22+563 **41**
Glenelg, *Scotland* N34+572 **40**
Glenelg, *S. Australia* C69–350 **109**
Glenfinnan, *Scotland* N33+568 **41**
Glengad Hd., *N. Ireland* N43+553 **42**
Glengariff, *Ireland, Rep.* N57+517 **43**
Glen Garry, *Scotland* N30+571 **40**
Glenhope, *New Zealand* A44–416 **112**
Glen Innes, *New S. Wales* B80–298 **109**
Glenluce, *Scotland* N29+549 **41**
Glen Lyon, *Scotland* N26+566 **41**
Glennamaddy, *Ireland, Rep.* N51+536 **42**
Glenreagh, *New S. Wales* B73–300 **109**
Glenrock, *Wyoming* V05+428 **93**
Glenrothes, *Scotland* N19+562 **41**
Glens Falls, *New York* S82+433 **91**
Glen Shee, *Scotland* N20+567 **41**
Glenties, *Ireland, Rep.* N50+548 **42**
Glenville, *West Virginia* T35+389 **91**
Glenwood, *Iowa* U34+410 **95**
Glenwood, *Minnesota* U33+457 **93**
Glenwood Springs, *Colorado* V14+395 **94**
Gletsch, *Switzerland* M40+466 **45**
Glittertind, mt., *Norway* M38+613 **47**
Gliwice, *Poland* L68+503 **49**
Globe, *Arizona* V35+333 **94**
Glogau. *See* Głogów,
Głogów, *Poland* L84+517 **49**
Gloppen, *Norway* M53+618 **46**
Glossop, *England* N12+535 **37**
Gloucester, *Massachusetts* S64+426 **96**
Gloucester, *New Jersey* T01+399 **96**
Gloucester, *New S. Wales* B79–320 **109**
Gloucester, *Virginia* T09+374 **97**
Gloucester & co., *England* N13+519 **39**
Gloversville, *New York* S86+430 **96**
Glukhov, *Ukraine* K66+516 **60**
Glyndebourne, *England* N00+509 **39**
Gmünd, *Austria* M09+469 **48**
Gmünd, *W. Germany* M31+488 **48**
Gmunden, *Austria* M07+479 **48**
Gniew, *Poland* L92+526 **48**
Gniezno, *Poland* L75+525 **49**
Goa, Daman & Diu, *India* H06+155 **70**
Goalpara, *India* F86+261 **71**
Goalundo, *Bangladesh* G01+238 **73**
Gobabis, *Namibia* L66–224 **84**
Gobi, des., *Mongolia, etc.* F00+430 **63**
Gobindpur, *India* G20+238 **73**
Godavari R., *India* G63+186 **70**
Godda, *India* G16+248 **73**
Godech, *Bulgaria* L42+430 **58**
Goderich, *Ontario* T40+437 **91**
Godhra, *India* H07+228 **70**
Gods L., *Manitoba* U35+548 **88**
Gods R., *Manitoba* U20+552 **89**
Godthåb, *Greenland* R32+640 **26**
Goes, *Netherlands* M67+515 **44**
Gogama, *Ontario* T41+476 **91**
Gogebic Ra., *Michigan* T88+467 **91**
Gog Magog Hills, *England* M87+522 **39**
Gohana, *India* G80+291 **72**
Goiânia, *Brazil* R26–166 **105**
Goias, *Brazil* R31–158 **105**
Goil L., *Scotland* N29+561 **41**
Goirle, *Netherlands* M60+515 **44**
Goksun, *Turkey* K51+381 **74**

Golaghat, *India* F66+265 **71**
Golchikha, *U.S.S.R.* G37+718 **62**
Golconda, *Illinois* T81+374 **97**
Golconda, *India* G69+174 **70**
Gołdap, *Poland* L46+543 **49**
Gold Coast. *See* Ghana.
Golden, *Colorado* V02+398 **94**
Golden B., *New Zealand* A42–407 **112**
Golden Lake, *Ontario* T14+455 **91**
Golden Vale, *Ireland, Rep.* N45+525 **43**
Goldfield, *Nevada* V74+379 **92**
Goldsboro, *N. Carolina* T18+354 **97**
Goleniow, *Poland* M01+535 **48**
Gol Gol, *New South Wales* C46–342 **109**
Golmo, *China* F60+362 **64**
Golspie, *Scotland* N24+580 **40**
Goltva, *Ukraine* K67+494 **60**
Gomal Pass, *Pakistan* H29+321 **72**
Gomalcalco, *Mexico* U20+182 **100**
Gombe, *Nigeria* M24+102 **81**
Gomera, I., *Canary Is.* P14+280 **80**
Gómez Farias, *Mexico* U66+248 **100**
Gomez Palacio, *Mexico* U81+256 **100**
Gonaïves, *Haiti* S75+194 **101**
Gonave, I. de la, *Haiti* S78+189 **101**
Gonda, *India* G48+271 **73**
Gondal, *India* H25+220 **70**
Gondo, *Switzerland* M41+462 **45**
Gongka Ling, *China* F26+286 **64**
Gongolgon, *New S. Wales* C19–304 **109**
Gondiądz, *Poland* L43+535 **49**
Gonzales, *Texas* U44+294 **95**
Goodenough I., *Papua New Guinea* B89–094 **111**
Gooderham, *Ontario* T20+449 **91**
Good Hope, *N.-W. Terr.* W52+661 **88**
Good Hope, C. of,
   Cape Province L70–344 **84**
Goodland, *Kansas* U70+392 **94**
Goodooga, *New S. Wales* C16–292 **109**
Goodrich, *Wisconsin* U01+452 **91**
Goodwin Sands, *England* M79+512 **39**
Goole, *England* N05+537 **37**
Goomalling, *W. Australia* E19–312 **110**
Goombalie, *New S. Wales* C28–300 **109**
Goor, *Netherlands* M50+522 **44**
Goose L., *Oregon-California* W03+420 **92**
Goose Bay, *Labrador* S02+534 **89**
Gopalpur, *India* G31+192 **71**
Göppingen, *W. Germany* M32+487 **48**
Gor, *Spain* N18+374 **52**
Gora, *Spain* F36+292 **64**
Gorakhpur, *India* G40+268 **73**
Gordola, *Switzerland* M37+462 **45**
Gordon, *S. Australia* C71–321 **109**
Gordon, *Nebraska* U74+428 **94**
Gordon R., *Tasmania* C26–426 **109**
Gordonsville, *Virginia* T19+381 **97**
Gore, *Ethiopia* K56+080 **83**
Goré, *Chad* L80+078 **81**
Gore, *New Zealand* A66–461 **112**
Gore Bay, *Ontario* T45+459 **91**
Gorebridge, *Scotland* N18+558 **41**
Gorey, *Ireland, Rep.* N38+527 **43**
Gorgan, *Iran* J33+368 **75**
Gorgona, I., *Italy* M31+434 **56**
Gorinchem, *Netherlands* M60+518 **44**
Gorizia, *Italy* M08+460 **56**
Gor'kiy, *U.S.S.R.* K06+564 **61**
Gorlice, *Poland* L54+496 **49**
Gorlitz, *E. Germany* L90+512 **48**
Gorlovka, *Ukraine* K42+484 **60**
Gormanstown, *Tasmania* C26–421 **109**
Gorodets, *U.S.S.R.* K10+567 **61**
Gorodishche, *U.S.S.R.* J86+533 **61**
Gorodnitsa, *Ukraine* L16+508 **60**
Goroke, *Victoria* C51–367 **109**
Gorontalo, *Celebes* D72+006 **65**
Gorrahei, *Ethiopia* K04+066 **83**
Gorsel, *Netherlands* M53+522 **44**
Gort, *Ireland, Rep.* N53+531 **43**
Gorumna I., *Ireland, Rep.* N58+532 **43**
Gorzów Wielkopolski,
   Poland L89+527 **48**
Gosai Than, mt., *Nepal-Tibet* G25+283 **71**
Göschenen, *Switzerland* M38+467 **45**
Gosford, *New South Wales* B83–334 **109**
Goshanak, *Pakistan* H60+264 **70**
Goshen, *New York* S86+413 **96**
Gospić, *Yugoslavia* L88+446 **56**
Gosport, *England* N07+508 **39**
Gossa, *Norway* M49+629 **46**
Gossau, *Switzerland* M34+474 **45**
Gosselies, *Belgium* M63+505 **44**
Gostivar, *Yugoslavia* L54+418 **58**
Göta Älv, *Sweden* M17+581 **47**
Göteborg, *Sweden* M18+577 **47**
Gotha, *E. Germany* M26+510 **48**
Gothenburg. *See* Göteborg,
Gothenburg, *Nebraska* U61+409 **94**
Gotland, I., *Sweden* L68+575 **47**
Goto Retto, *Japan* D36+330 **68**
Gotska Sandon, *Sweden* L65+583 **47**
Göttingen, *W. Germany* M30+515 **48**
Gottwaldov, *Czechoslovakia* L74+492 **49**
Gouda, *Netherlands* M62+520 **44**
Goudswaard, *Netherlands* M65+518 **44**
Gough I., *Atlantic Ocean* N30–414 **85**
Gouin Res., *Quebec* S88+486 **90**
Goulburn, *New South Wales* C02–348 **109**
Goulburn R., *Victoria* C29–362 **109**
Gounarou, *Benin* M74+108 **80**
Goundam, *Mali* N22+164 **80**
Gouré, *Niger* M28+140 **81**
Gournay, *France* M80+495 **54**
Gourock, *Scotland* N29+559 **41**
Gourock Ra., *New S. Wales* C04–358 **109**
Gouverneur, *New York* T03+443 **91**
Gowanda, *New York* T24+424 **91**
Gower, pen., *Wales* N25+516 **38**
Gowna L., *Ireland, Rep.* N45+539 **42**
Goya, *Argentina* R86–292 **103**
Gozo, I. (Malta),
   Mediterranean Sea M04+361 **57**
Graaff Reinet, *Cape Province* L32–324 **84**
Grabow, *Poland* L71+515 **49**
Gračac, *Yugoslavia* L85+443 **56**
Gracefield, *Quebec* T07+461 **91**
Gracias, *Honduras* T82+146 **101**
Gracias a Dios, *Nicaragua* T50+149 **101**

Gradets, *Bulgaria* L21+428 **58**
Grado, *Spain* N37+433 **52**
Grafton, *New South Wales* B73–297 **109**
Grafton, *N. Dakota* U44+484 **93**
Grafton, *W. Virginia* T30+393 **91**
Grafton, Is., *Chile* S80–542 **101**
Grahaju, *Brazil* Q79–068 **105**
Graham, *Texas* U51+331 **95**
Graham Ld. *See* Antarctic Pen. S25–660 **27**
Graham Bell, Os., *Arctic Oc.* H65+811 **62**
Grahamstown, *Cape Province* L20–332 **84**
Grain, *England* M86+514 **39**
Grajewo, *Poland* L45+537 **49**
Grammont. *See* Geeraardsbergen.
Grampian Mts., *Scotland* N26+567 **41**
Grampian, reg., *Scotland* N17+573 **40**
Grampians, mts., *Victoria* C45–372 **109**
Gramsbergen, *Netherlands* M50+526 **44**
Granada, *Nicaragua* T66+120 **101**
Granada, *Spain* N22+372 **52**
Granard, *Ireland, Rep.* N45+538 **43**
Granby, *Quebec* S77+454 **91**
Gran Canaria, I., *Canary Is.* P04+278 **80**
Gran Chaco, *Argentina* S14–270 **103**
Grand Can., *China* E24+375 **64**
Grand I., *Michigan* T70+465 **91**
Grand I., *New York* T24+430 **96**
Grand L., *Louisiana* U08+298 **95**
Grand L., *Louisiana* U16+298 **95**
Grand L., *Maine-N.B.* S45+456 **90**
Grand L., *New Brunswick* S36+460 **90**
Grand L., *Newfoundland* R74+490 **90**
Grand R., *Colorado* V06+400 **94**
Grand R., *Michigan* T61+429 **91**
Grand R., *S. Dakota* U80+456 **98**
Grand Bassa, *Liberia* N60+060 **80**
Grand Bassam, *Ivory Coast* N22+052 **80**
Grand Canyon, *Arizona* V50+356 **98**
Grand Canyon Nat. Park,
   Arizona V45+362 **98**
Grand Cayman, I., *W. I.* T38+193 **101**
Grand Coulee Dam, *Wash.* V84+479 **98**
Grande, B., *Argentina* S50–505 **103**
Grande, Rio, *Brazil* R30–198 **105**
Grande, Sa, *Brazil* Q66–046 **105**
Grande Anse, *N.B.* S31+478 **90**
Grande Comore, I.,
   Comoro Is., Africa K10–116 **83**
Grande de Santiago, R.,
   Mexico U84+212 **100**
Grand Falls, *N.B.* S47+471 **90**
Grand Falls, *Newfoundland* R64+490 **90**
Grand Forks, *B.C.* V81+491 **88**
Grand Forks, *N. Dakota* U42+479 **93**
Grand Haven, *Michigan* T67+431 **91**
Grandin, L., *N.-W. Terr.* V88+640 **88**
Grand Island, *Nebraska* U50+408 **95**
Grand Junction, *Colorado* V22+390 **94**
Grand Junction, *Tennessee* T85+350 **97**
Grand Lahou, *Ivory Coast* N30+052 **80**
Grande Ledge, *Michigan* T58+428 **91**
Grand Manan I., *N.B.* S41+448 **90**
Grand Marais, *Minnesota* U02+477 **91**
Grand Mère, *Quebec* S76+466 **91**
Grand Mesa, *Colorado* V18+391 **94**
Grandola, *Portugal* N51+381 **52**
Grand Piles, *Quebec* S76+467 **91**
Grand Prarie, *Alberta* V84+554 **88**
Grand Rapids, *Michigan* T64+430 **91**
Grand Rapids, *Minnesota* U21+472 **93**
Grandrieu, *Belgium* M65+502 **44**
Grand River, *Quebec* S27+484 **90**
Grandson, *Switzerland* M50+468 **45**
Grand Teton Mt. & Nat. Park,
   Wyoming V35+434 **98**
Grand Tower, *Illinois* T87+376 **97**
Grand Victoria L., *Quebec* T14+476 **91**
Grane, *Norway* M10+656 **46**
Graney L., *Ireland, Rep.* N52+530 **43**
Grangemouth, *Scotland* N22+560 **41**
Granger, *Wyoming* V30+416 **93**
Granite City, *Illinois* U02+387 **95**
Granite Falls, *Minnesota* U33+448 **93**
Granity, *New Zealand* A48–416 **112**
Granja, *Brazil* Q65–031 **105**
Grankulla, *Finland* L32+602 **47**
Granollers, *Spain* M76+416 **53**
Granön, *Sweden* L64+642 **46**
Grant, *U.S.S.R.?* T69+501 **89**
Grant Ra., *Nevada* V63+388 **92**
Grant City, *Missouri* U26+404 **95**
Grantham, *England* N04+529 **37**
Granton, *Scotland* N19+560 **41**
Grantown-on-Spey, *Scotland* N21+573 **40**
Grants, *New Mexico* V17+351 **94**
Grants Pass, *Oregon* W20+425 **92**
Grantsville, *Utah* V45+406 **94**
Granville, *France* M56+452 **55**
Granville, *N. Dakota* U83+487 **93**
Granville, *New S. Wales* B79+434 **96**
Granville, *N. Dakota* U65+483 **93**
Granville L., *Manitoba* U65+562 **88**
Granvin, *Norway* M50+605 **47**
Gras, L., de, *N.-W. Terr.* V35+646 **88**
Grasett, *Ontario* T57+485 **91**
Graskop, *Transvaal* K86–250 **84**
Grasmere, *England* N18+545 **37**
Gräsö, *Sweden* L70+604 **47**
Grassano, *Italy* L82+406 **57**
Grasse, *France* M49+437 **55**
Grassier. *Switzerland* M53+464 **45**
Graubünden, canton, *Switz.* M35+467 **45**
Graus, *Spain* M88+422 **53**
Gravarne, *Sweden* M22+583 **47**
Grave, *Netherlands* M56+518 **44**
Gravelbourg, *Saskatchewan* V09+499 **88**
's Gravenhage, *Netherlands* M64+521 **44**
Gravenhurst, *Ontario* T26+449 **91**
's Gravenzande, *Netherlands* M65+520 **44**
Gravesend, *England* M88+514 **39**
Gravesend, *New S. Wales* B88–296 **109**
Gray, *France* M57+474 **54**
Grayling, *Michigan* T59+447 **91**
Grayville, *Illinois* T78+383 **97**
Graz, *Austria* L87+471 **49**
Great L., *Tasmania* C20–419 **109**
Great Pt., *Massachusetts* S60+414 **96**
Great Australian Bight, *Aust.* D30–336 **110**
Great Barrier Reef, *Aust.* C05–190 **111**
Great Barrington, *Mass.* S80+422 **96**
Great Basin, *Nevada* V75+402 **98**
Great Bear L., *N.-W. Terr.* W00+658 **88**

Great Bend, *Kansas* U53+384 **95**
Great Basket I.,
   Ireland, Rep. N63+521 **43**
Great Dividing Ra., *Aust.* C10–260 **111**
Great Driffield, *England* N03+540 **37**
Great Falls, *Montana* V38+475 **93**
Great Geysir, *Iceland* P31+643 **46**
Great Lake. *See* Tonle Sap
Great Long L., *Quebec* S65+562 **89**
Great Malvern, *England* N14+521 **38**
Great North Mts., *W.Va., etc.* T23+389 **96**
Great Rapids, *Manitoba* U57+534 **88**
Great Salt L., *Utah* V46+412 **92**
Great Salt Lake Des., *Utah* V51+409 **92**
Great Sand Dunes Nat. Mon.,
   Colorado V04+378 **94**
Great Sandy Des., *W. Aust.* D75–202 **110**
Great Sandy I. (Fraser I.),
   Queensland B71–252 **111**
Great Slave L., *N.-W. Terr.* V60+610 **88**
Great Smoky Mts., *Tennessee* T52+356 **97**
Great Smoky Mts. Nat. Park,
   Tennessee T52+357 **97**
Great South B., *New York* S79+406 **96**
Great Torrington, *England* N25+509 **38**
Great Victoria Des.,
   W. Aust. D40–280 **110**
Great Wass I., *Maine* S46+445 **90**
Great Western Tiers,
   Tasmania C22–418 **109**
Great Yarmouth, *England* M80+526 **39**
Grebbestad, *Sweden* M22+587 **47**
Greco, I., *Cyprus* K65+349 **76**
Greece, S. *Europe* L48+380 **51**
Greeley, *Colorado* U88+404 **94**
Green B., *Wisconsin* T77+448 **91**
Green Mts., *Vermont* S77+438 **91**
Green Mts., *Wyoming* V14+424 **93**
Green R., *Kentucky* T73+375 **97**
Green R., *Utah, etc.* V30+386 **94**
Green Bay, *Wisconsin* T78+445 **91**
Greencastle, *Indiana* T10+396 **95**
Greenfield, *Indiana* T65+398 **91**
Greenfield, *Iowa* U26+412 **95**
Greenfield, *Massachusetts* S75+426 **96**
Greenland, *N. America* Q60+700 **26**
Greenland Sea, *Greenland* N50+760 **26**
Greenock, *Scotland* N29+559 **41**
Greenore Pt., *Ireland, Rep.* N38+522 **43**
Greenport, *New York* S74+411 **91**
Green River, *Utah* V31+390 **94**
Green River, *Wyoming* V27+415 **93**
Greensboro, *Georgia* T49+335 **97**
Greensboro, *N. Carolina* T29+361 **97**
Greensburg, *Kansas* U56+376 **95**
Greensburg, *Kentucky* T63+373 **97**
Greensburg, *Pennsylvania* T28+404 **96**
Greenville, *Alabama* T70+318 **97**
Greenville, *Illinois* T86+389 **95**
Greenville, *Kentucky* T73+372 **97**
Greenville, *Liberia* N54+050 **80**
Greenville, *Maine* S58+455 **90**
Greenville, *Michigan* T62+432 **91**
Greenville, *Mississippi* U06+334 **95**
Greenville, *Missouri* U03+372 **95**
Greenville, *N. Carolina* T14+356 **97**
Greenville, *S. Carolina* T45+348 **97**
Greenville, *Tennessee* T47+362 **97**
Greenville, *Texas* U36+332 **95**
Greenwich, *Connecticut* S82+410 **95**
Greenwich, *England* N00+515 **39**
Greenwich, *Rhode Island* S84+418 **96**
Greenwood, *Mississippi* U01+335 **97**
Greenwood, *S. Carolina* T43+342 **97**
Greenwood, *Wisconsin* U04+449 **91**
Greenwood L., *N.Y.-N.J.* S86+412 **96**
Gregory, *S. Dakota* U56+432 **93**
Gregory L., *S. Australia* C66–290 **109**
Gregory Ra., *Queensland* C40–186 **111**
Greifen See, *Switzerland* M38+474 **45**
Greifswald, *E. Germany* M10+541 **48**
Grein, *Austria* M01+483 **48**
Greiz, *E. Germany* M17+506 **48**
Grenada, *Mississippi* T89+338 **97**
Grenada, I., *Windward Is.* S10+121 **101**
Grenadines, Is.,
   Windward Is. S08+127 **101**
Grenchen, *Switzerland* M46+472 **45**
Grenfell, *New South Wales* C11–339 **109**
Grenora, *N. Dakota* U83+487 **93**
Grenoble, *France* M56+452 **55**
Grenville, *Queensland* C41–119 **111**
Gretna, *Louisiana* U08+298 **95**
Gretna, *Virginia* T27+369 **91**
Gretna Green, *Scotland* N18+550 **41**
Grevená, *Greece* L51+401 **59**
Grey Ra., *Qnsld.-N.S.W.* C50–288 **111**
Greybull, *Wyoming* V18+444 **93**
Greycliff, *Montana* V28+457 **93**
Greylock Mt., *Massachusetts* S79+427 **96**
Greymouth, *New Zealand* A52–425 **112**
Greys Butte, mt., *Oregon* V89+429 **92**
Greystones, *Ireland, Rep.* N36+531 **43**
Greytown, *New Zealand* A27–411 **112**
Greytown. *See* San Juan del Norte
Griesalp, *Switzerland* M43+466 **45**
Griffin, *Georgia* T56+332 **97**
Griffith, *New South Wales* C24–343 **109**
Grim C., *Tasmania* C31–407 **109**
Grimsby, *England* N01+535 **37**
Grimstad, *Norway* M38+583 **47**
Grindelwald, *Switzerland* M42+466 **45**
Grindstone, *Michigan* T47+440 **91**
Grinnell, *Iowa* U16+417 **95**
Grinnell Pen., *N.-W. Terr.* U25+766 **88**
Griquatown, *Cape Province* L40–288 **84**
Grïva *Latvia* L21+559 **47**
Grobina, *Latvia* L53+565 **47**
Gröbming, *Austria* M07+474 **48**
Grodno, *Byelorussia* L37+535 **60**
Grodzisk, *Poland* L82+522 **49**
Groenlo, *Netherlands* M50+520 **44**
Groix, I. de, *France* N21+476 **54**
Groningen & prov.,
   Netherlands M50+532 **44**
Grono, *Switzerland* M35+463 **45**
Groote Eylandt,
   N. Terr., Aust C80–140 **111**
Grootfontein, *Namibia* L80–252 **84**
Grootfontein, *Namibia* L70–196 **84**

Groot Natuna, I., *Indonesia* E70+039 **65**
Grossevichi, *U.S.S.R.* C63+479 **63**
Gross Glockner, *Austria* M15+471 **48**
Grosswardein. *See* Oradea
Groton, *New York* T09+426 **96**
Groton, *S. Dakota* U49+455 **93**
Groznyy, *U.S.S.R.* J87+435 **62**
Grudziadz, *Poland* L67+535 **49**
Grues, I. aux, *Quebec* S63+471 **91**
Gruinard B., *Scotland* N33+579 **40**
Grüsch, *Switzerland* M32+470 **45**
Gruyère, Lac de, *Switz.* M47+467 **45**
Gruz, *Yugoslavia* L71+427 **58**
Gruzinskaya (Georgia), rep.,
   U.S.S.R. K10+422 **62**
Grybów, *Poland* L55+496 **49**
Gsteig, *Switzerland* M46+464 **45**
Guabito, Panama T46+096 **101**
Guacanayabo, G. de, *Cuba* T14+206 **101**
Guachipas, *Argentina* S33–256 **103**
Guadalaja, *Spain* N19+406 **52**
Guadalajara, *Mexico* U80+206 **100**
Guadalcanal, *Spain* N35+381 **52**
Guadalcanal, I., *Solomon Is.* B30–095 **106**
Guadalcazar, *Mexico* U62+226 **100**
Guadalquivir, R., *Spain* N30+376 **52**
Guadalupe I., *Mexico* V82+290 **100**
Guadalupe Mts.,
   New Mexico, Texas U00+320 **94**
Guadalupe R., *Texas* U47+296 **98**
Guadalupe-y-Calvo, *Mexico* V11+262 **100**
Guadarrama, *Spain* N25+407 **52**
Guadarrama, Sa. de, *Spain* N24+410 **52**
Guadeloupe, I., *Leeward Is.* S10+162 **101**
Guadiana, R., *Spain* N45+383 **52**
Guadix, *Spain* N19+373 **52**
Guafo & G. de, *Chile* S88–436 **103**
Guaitecas, Is., *Chile* S82–439 **103**
Guajar-a-Mirim, *Brazil* S32–108 **104**
Guajaratuba, *Brazil* S17–050 **104**
Gualeguaychu, *Argentina* R81–330 **103**
Guam, I., *Pacific Ocean* C30+140 **106**
Guamini, *Argentina* S15–370 **103**
Guamo, *Colombia* T00+040 **104**
Guanabacoa, *Cuba* T43+232 **101**
Guanabara, *Brazil* Q82–228 **104**
Guanacevi, *Mexico* V06+259 **100**
Guanahani. *See* San Salvador
Guanajuato, *Mexico* U67+212 **100**
Guanare, *Venezuela* S58+090 **104**
Guanarito, *Venezuela* S54+087 **104**
Guandacol, *Argentina* S52–295 **103**
Guane, *Cuba* T54+223 **101**
Guanica, *Puerto Rico* S41+180 **101**
Guantanamo, *Cuba* T02+202 **101**
Guapi, *Colombia* T17+026 **104**
Guapiles, *Costa Rica* T53+102 **101**
Guapore, *Brazil* R41–289 **103**
Guapore (Rondonia), *Brazil* S31–118 **104**
Guapore, R., *Brazil-Bolivia* S16–128 **104**
Guaqui, *Bolivia* S54–166 **104**
Guarapuava, *Brazil* R40–255 **103**
Guarda, *Portugal* N43+406 **52**
Guasabas, *Mexico* V25+298 **100**
Guasdualito, *Venezuela* S64+072 **104**
Guasipati, *Venezuela* S11+074 **104**
Guatemala, *Guatemala* U03+146 **100**
Guatemala, rep.
   Cent. America U00+154 **100**
Guatrache, *Argentina* S22–378 **103**
Guaviare, R., *Colombia* S56+036 **104**
Guaxupe, *Brazil* R10–212 **105**
Guayabal, *Venezuela* S43+080 **104**
Guayama, *Puerto Rico* S36+181 **101**
Guayaquil, *Ecuador* T29–022 **104**
Guaymas, *Mexico* V35+279 **100**
Guazapares, *Mexico* V15+273 **100**
Guben, *E. Germany* M02+520 **48**
Gubin. *See* Guben
Gudiyatam, *India* G67+130 **70**
Guelma, *Algeria* M46+361 **80**
Guelph, *Ontario* T32+436 **91**
Guemes, *Argentina* S30–246 **103**
Guéret, *France* M79+462 **54**
Guernsey, I., *Channel Is.* N15+495 **54**
Guernsey Res., *Wyoming* U89+424 **93**
Guerrero, *Mexico* V13+284 **100**
Guerrero, *Tamaulipas, Mex.* U56+267 **100**
Guerrero, state, *Mexico* U60+176 **100**
Gugera, *Pakistan* H10+309 **72**
Guiana Highlands, *S. Amer.* R80+028 **104**
Guija, *Mozambique* K74–244 **84**
Guildford, *England* N03+512 **39**
Guildford, *Maine* S56+452 **90**
Guillaumes, *France* M49+441 **55**
Guilo, *Angola* L64–076 **82**
Guimaraes, *Brazil* Q88–020 **105**
Guimarães, *Portugal* N50+414 **52**
Guinea-Bissau, *N.-W. Afr.* P00+120 **80**
Guinea, *West Africa* N60+110 **80**
Guinea, G. of, *N.-W. Africa* M70+030 **82**
Guines, *Cuba* T42+231 **101**
Guingamp, *France* N19+485 **54**
Guiria, *Venezuela* S13+106 **104**
Guise, *France* M68+499 **54**
Guisisil, Vol., *Nicaragua* T67+127 **101**
Gujarat, state, *India* H07+218 **70**
Gujar Khan, *Pakistan* H11+333 **72**
Gujranwala, *Pakistan* H05+321 **72**
Gujrat, *Pakistan* H05+326 **72**
Gulargambone, *N.S.W.* C09–314 **109**
Gulbarga, *India* G78+173 **70**
Gulbene, *Latvia* L20+571 **47**
Gulfport, *Mississippi* T84+304 **95**
Gulgong, *New South Wales* C03–326 **109**
Gulistan, *Pakistan* H50+306 **70**
Gul Koh, *Afghanistan* H42+334 **75**
Gull L., *Quebec* T11+498 **89**
Gullane, *Scotland* N17+560 **41**
Gulpaigan, *Iran* J59+334 **75**
Gulpen, *Netherlands* M55+508 **44**
Gulran, *Afghanistan* H80+351 **75**
Gulu, *Ethiopia* K76+026 **83**
Gum, *Ethiopia* K20+116 **83**
Gummersbach, *W. Germany* M45+510 **48**
Gümüljina, *See* Komotini
Gümüsane, *Turkey* K33+404 **74**
Guna, *India* G76+246 **73**
Gunbad-i-Qabuz, *Iran* J28+373 **75**

Gunbar, *New South Wales* C28–341 **109**
Gunchu, *Japan* D14+338 **68**
Gundagai, *New S. Wales* C12–351 **109**
Gunisao R., *Manitoba* U40+540 **88**
Gunnedah, *New S. Wales* B88–310 **109**
Gunning, *New South Wales* C05–348 **109**
Gunnislake, *England* N25+505 **38**
Gunnison, *Colorado* V12+386 **94**
Gunnison, *Utah* V42+392 **94**
Gunnison R., *Colorado* V14+385 **94**
Guntakal, *India* G75+152 **70**
Guntersville & L., *Alabama* T68+344 **97**
Guntur, *India* G57+164 **70**
Gurais, *Kashmir* H01+346 **72**
Gurdaspur, *India* G87+320 **72**
Gurdon, *Arkansas* U19+338 **95**
Gurgaon, *India* G78+285 **72**
Gurgl, *Austria* M24+469 **48**
Gurha, *India* H20+252 **70**
Gurkha, *Nepal* G32+280 **73**
Gurla Mandhata, mt., *Tibet* G51+304 **70**
Gurnigel, *Switzerland* M45+468 **45**
Gurséy, *Norway* M56+623 **46**
Gurupa, *Brazil* R39–015 **105**
Gurupa, I., *Brazil* R39–010 **105**
Guru Sikhar, *India* H13+247 **70**
Gur'yev, *Kazakh* J50+470 **62**
Gusev, *U.S.S.R.* L47+546 **47**
Gusht, *Iran* H78+277 **75**
Guspini, *Sardinia* M38+396 **57**
Gustav Holm, Kap, *Greenland* Q05+670 **26**
Güstrow, *E. Germany* M17+538 **48**
Guthrie, *Iowa* U27+416 **95**
Guthrie, *Kentucky* T73+367 **97**
Guthrie, *Oklahoma* U44+358 **95**
Guyana, *S. America* R84+050 **104**
Guyenne, prov., *France* M82+446 **55**
Guymon, *Oklahoma* U68+368 **94**
Guyra, *New South Wales* B80–302 **109**
Guzman, *Mexico* U82+196 **100**
Gwa, *Burma* F62+176 **71**
Gwabegar, *New S. Wales* C06–306 **109**
Gwadar, *Pakistan* H76+251 **70**
Gwalior, *India* G71+262 **73**
Gwanda, *Zimbabwe* L06–210 **84**
Gwatar, *Iran* H81+251 **75**
Gweebarra B., *Ireland, Rep.* N51+549 **42**
Gwelo, *Zimbabwe* L02–194 **84**
Gwent, co., *Wales* N18+517 **38**
Gwydir, R., *New S. Wales* B83–304 **109**
Gwyned, co., *Wales* N24+530 **38**
Gyangtse, *Tibet* G03+289 **71**
Gydanski Pol., *U.S.S.R.* G80+700 **62**
Gympie, *Queensland* B74–261 **111**
Györ, *Hungary* L74+477 **49**
Gypsumville, *Manitoba* U51+516 **88**
Gyula, *Hungary* L52+465 **49**
Gzhatsk, *U.S.S.R.* K60+555 **60**
Haacht, *Belgium* M62+510 **44**
Haag, *Switzerland* M33+472 **45**
Haaksbergen, *Netherlands* M49+522 **44**
Haarlem, *Netherlands* M62+524 **44**
Habana, *Cuba* T44+232 **101**
Habban, *Yemen, South* J77+146 **74**
Habbaniyah, *Iraq* K07+334 **74**
Habigang, *Bangladesh* F81+244 **71**
Hachinohe, *Japan* C51+405 **68**
Hadda, *Saudi Arabia* K32+214 **74**
Haddington, *Scotland* N16+560 **41**
Hadera, *Israel* K60+324 **76**
Haderslev, *Denmark* M33+552 **47**
Hadhramaut, *Yemen, South* J76+155 **74**
Hadjin, *Turkey* K53+380 **74**
Haeju, *Korea* D58+380 **64**
Haerhpin, *China* D45+455 **64**
Hafar, *Saudi Arabia* J84+284 **74**
Hafar al Ats, *Saudi Arabia* J80+260 **74**
Haffe. *See* Babenna
Hafnarfjördhur, *Iceland* P41+641 **46**
Hagen, *W. Germany* M45+514 **48**
Hageri, *Estonia* L32+591 **47**
Hagerstown, *Maryland* T16+397 **96**
Hagi, *Japan* D21+344 **68**
Hague, C. de la, *France* N12+497 **54**
Hahnville, *Louisiana* U03+299 **97**
Haibak, *Afghanistan* H42+362 **75**
Hai cheng, *China* D74+409 **66**
Haichow. See Tunghai
Haidar Pasha, *Turkey* L05+410 **74**
Haifa, *Israel* K60+328 **76**
Haig, *W. Australia* D54–309 **110**
Haik'ou, *China* E58+200 **67**
Hail, *Saudi Arabia* K19+275 **74**
Hailar, *China* E02+490 **64**
Haileybury, *Ontario* T28+475 **91**
Hailun, *China* D48+472 **64**
Hailuoto, *Finland* L32+650 **46**
Hainan I., *China* E60+190 **67**
Hainan Str., *China* E60+200 **67**
Hainaut, prov., *Belgium* M66+505 **44**
Haines, *Alaska* X02+594 **88**
Haiphong, *Vietnam* E80+208 **69**
Hair, *Saudi Arabia* J79+244 **74**
Haiten I., *China* E01+256 **67**
Haiti, rep., *West Indies* S74+190 **101**
Hajduböszörmény, *Hungary* L52+477 **49**
Hajima, Jebel, *Saudi Arabia* K44+245 **74**
Hajipur, *India* G28+257 **73**
Hajjar, *China* F72+369 **64**
Hakkâri, *Turkey* K07+376 **74**
Hakodate, *Japan* C55+418 **68**
Hala, *Pakistan* H40+258 **70**
Halacho, *Mexico* U01+204 **100**
Halba, *Lebanon* K54+346 **76**
Halbe, *Saudi Arabia* K11+198 **74**
Halberstadt, *E. Germany* M24+519 **48**
Halden, *Norway* M21+591 **47**
Haleb. *See* Aleppo
Halebiye, *Syria* K31+357 **74**
Halen, *Belgium* M59+509 **44**
Halesworth, *England* M81+524 **39**
Hali, *Saudi Arabia* K20+189 **74**
Halia, *India* G46+248 **73**
Halib, *Saudi Arabia* J31+227 **75**
Haliburton, *Ontario* T21+450 **91**
Halifax, *England* N11+537 **37**
Halifax, *N. Carolina* T16+363 **97**
Halifax & Harb., *N.S.* S22+446 **90**
Halifax B., *Queensland* C18–190 **111**
Halkett C., *Alaska* Y10+708 **99**
Hall, *W. Germany* M32+491 **48**

Hall Is., *Caroline Is.* B76+080 **106**
Hall Ld., *Greenland* R30+810 **26**
Halle, *E. Germany* M18+515 **48**
Halle, *Belgium* M65+507 **44**
Hallein, *Austria* M11+476 **48**
Halley B., *Antarctica* Q15–738 **27**
Halliste, *Estonia* L27+581 **47**
Hällnäss, *Sweden* L62+643 **46**
Hallock, *Minnesota* U42+488 **93**
Hallowell, *Maine* S59+443 **90**
Halls Creek, *W. Australia* D43–181 **110**
Hallstavik, *Sweden* L69+601 **47**
Hallviken, *Sweden* L87+637 **46**
Halmahera, I., *Indonesia* D42+006 **65**
Halmstad, *Sweden* M13+567 **47**
Halsa, *Norway* M41+631 **46**
Hälsingborg, *Sweden* M14+561 **47**
Halstead, *Kansas* U46+360 **95**
Halys, C., *Turkey* K54+417 **74**
Hama, *Syria* K50+351 **76**
Hamada, *Japan* D17+349 **68**
Hamadan, *Iran* J70+348 **74**
Hamaidan, *Saudi Arabia* J37+208 **75**
Hamam, *Saudi Arabia* J86+208 **74**
Hamamatsu, *Japan* C74+347 **68**
Haman, *Iraq* K05+312 **74**
Hamar, *Saudi Arabia* J83+224 **74**
Hamar, *Norway* M23+608 **47**
Hambantota, *Sri Lanka* G53+061 **70**
Hamburg, *W. Germany* M30+536 **48**
Hamburg, *Iowa* U34+406 **95**
Hamburg, *New York* T23+427 **96**
Hamburg, *Pennsylvania* T06+405 **96**
Hamburg, *S. Carolina* T41+335 **97**
Hämeenlinna, *Finland* L33+610 **47**
Hameln, *W. Germany* M34+521 **48**
Hami, *Yemen, South* J61+148 **74**
Hamidiya, *Syria* K54+347 **76**
Hamilton, *Alabama* T78+342 **97**
Hamilton, *New Zealand* A28–378 **112**
Hamilton, *New York* T04+428 **96**
Hamilton, *N. Carolina* T14+359 **97**
Hamilton, *Ohio* T57+394 **91**
Hamilton, *Ontario* T29+433 **91**
Hamilton, *Scotland* N24+558 **41**
Hamilton, *Tasmania* C19–426 **109**
Hamilton, *Victoria* C48–378 **109**
Hamilton, *Washington* W08+480 **88**
Hamilton Inl., *Labrador* R75+543 **89**
Hamilton, L., *Arkansas* U18+344 **95**
Hamilton, L., *Texas* U51+308 **98**
Hamilton R. (Churchill), *Lab.* S10+530 **89**
Hamina, *Finland* L16+605 **47**
Hamirpur, *India* G59+259 **73**
Hamlet, *N. Carolina* T28+349 **97**
Hamley Bridge, *S. Australia* C68–344 **109**
Hamm, *W. Germany* M43+517 **48**
Hamme, *Belgium* M65+511 **44**
Hammerdal, *Sweden* L88+636 **46**
Hammerfest, *Norway* L38+706 **46**
Hammersley Ra., *W. Aust.* E15–220 **110**
Hammond, *Indiana* T75+416 **91**
Hammond, *Louisiana* U02+305 **95**
Hammond, *New Brunswick* S45+474 **90**
Hammond, *S. Australia* C70–325 **109**
Hammonton, *New Jersey* S85+396 **96**
Hamont, *Belgium* M57+512 **44**
Hampden, *New Zealand* A55–453 **112**
Hampden, *N. Dakota* U52+486 **93**
Hampshire, co., *England* N08+510 **39**
Hampton, *Arkansas* U15+335 **97**
Hampton, *Iowa* U18+427 **95**
Hampton, *New Brunswick* S34+455 **90**
Hampton, *New Hampshire* S65+430 **90**
Hampton, *S. Carolina* T37+329 **97**
Hamun-i-Helmand,
   Iran-Afghanistan H82+314 **75**
Hamun-i-Puzak, *Afghanistan* H80+314 **75**
Han, *Belgium* M59+501 **44**
Hanakiya, *Saudi Arabia* K24+253 **74**
Hanau, *W. Germany* M36+501 **48**
Hanchung, *China* E78+331 **66**
Hancock, *Michigan* T81+473 **99**
Hancock, *New York* T02+419 **96**
Handegg, *Switzerland* M40+466 **45**
Handeni, *Tanzania* K42–054 **83**
Hanford, *California* V88+363 **92**
Hanford, *Washington* V87+466 **92**
Hangchow, *China* D89+303 **67**
Hangchow B., *China* D80+306 **66**
Hangu, *Pakistan* H24+335 **72**
Han Kiang, *China* D89+304 **66**
Hankinson, *N. Dakota* U41+461 **93**
Hankö,(Hango), *Finland* L42+599 **47**
Hankow, *China* E04+254 **64**
Hankow (Wuhan), *China* E34+306 **66**
Hanle, *Kashmir* G66+328 **70**
Hanley, *England* N13+530 **37**
Hanmer, *New Zealand* A43–425 **112**
Hanna, *Alberta* V41+514 **88**
Hanna, *Wyoming* V06+414 **93**
Hannibal, *Missouri* U08+396 **95**
Hannover, *W. Germany* M32+524 **48**
Hannut, *Belgium* M60+507 **44**
Hanö-bukten, *Sweden* M02+558 **47**
Hanoi, *Vietnam* E85+210 **69**
Hanover, *Ontario* T36+442 **91**
Hanover, *Pennsylvania* T12+398 **96**
Hanover, *Virginia* T14+377 **97**
Hanover, I., *Chile* S88–510 **103**
Hansi, *India* G84+291 **72**
Hansweert, *Netherlands* M66+515 **44**
Hanumangarh. *See* Bhatnair
Hanyang, *China* E34+305 **67**
Hanyin, *China* E68+329 **66**
Hanza, *Kashmir* H02+364 **72**
Hao, I., *Tuamotu Arch.* X20–190 **107**
Haparanda, *Sweden* L35+658 **46**
Hapora, *Japan* C59+438 **68**
Hapur, *India* G73+287 **72**
Haqal, *Saudi Arabia* K60+292 **74**
Haraiya, *India* G45+268 **73**
Harak, *Saudi Arabia* K48+256 **74**
Harar, *Ethiopia* K18+092 **83**
Hardardera, *Somalia* J74+046 **83**
Hara Usu Nur, *Mongolia* F76+480 **64**
Harbin. See Haerhpin
Harbor Beach, *Michigan* T46+438 **91**
Harbor Spring, *Michigan* T60+455 **91**
Harburg Wilhelmsburg, *Ger.* M30+534 **48**
Harda, *India* G77+223 **70**

Hardanger Fjell, *Norway* M42+609 **47**
Hardanger Fd., *Norway* M54+601 **47**
Hardenberg, *Netherlands* M50+526 **44**
Harderwijk, *Netherlands* M56+523 **44**
Hardin, *Montana* V16+457 **93**
Harding, *Natal* L00–306 **84**
Hardoi, *India* G59+274 **73**
Hardwar, *India* G71+299 **72**
Hardwicke B., *S. Australia* C76–348 **109**
Hardy, Pen., *Chile* S52–555 **103**
Hare B., *Newfoundland* R64+512 **90**
Hare I., *Quebec* S58+479 **91**
Hareidland, *Norway* M54+624 **46**
Hare Indian R., *N.-W. Terr.* W35+663 **88**
Harelbeke, *Belgium* M70+509 **44**
Hargeisa, *Somalia* K06+094 **83**
Hari, R., *Sumatra, Indon* F10–016 **65**
Harihar, *India* G85+146 **70**
Harim, *Syria* K51+362 **76**
Haripur, *Pakistan* H12+340 **72**
Hariq, *Saudi Arabia* J81+237 **74**
Harishpur, *India* G21+201 **71**
Harlan, *Iowa* U32+416 **95**
Harlan, *Kentucky* T47+368 **99**
Harlech, *Wales* N25+529 **38**
Harlem, *Montana* V22+485 **93**
Harlequin Hills, *Nevada* V84+415 **92**
Harlingen, *Netherlands* M57+532 **44**
Harlingen, *Texas* U46+262 **94**
Harlowton, *Montana* V29+464 **93**
Harmanli. *See* Kharmanli
Harnai, *Pakistan* H42+302 **70**
Harney L., *Oregon* V85+432 **92**
Harney Pk., *S. Dakota* U81+438 **93**
Harney Basin, *Oregon* W00+436 **98**
Harnösand, *Sweden* L73+626 **46**
Har Nuur, lake, *Mongolia* F73+480 **63**
Harper, *Liberia* N46+044 **80**
Harran, *Turkey* K35+370 **74**
Harray, L. of, *Orkney, Scot.* N19+590 **40**
Harrington Harbour, *Quebec* R87+505 **90**
Harris, & Sd., of *Scotland* N41+578 **40**
Harrisburg, *Arkansas* U04+355 **95**
Harrisburg, *Illinois* T82+378 **95**
Harrisburg, *Pennsylvania* T12+403 **96**
Harrison, *Arkansas* U18+362 **95**
Harrison, *Michigan* T59+440 **91**
Harrison, C., *Labrador* R67+548 **89**
Harrison L., *Brit. Columbia* W10+498 **88**
Harrisonburg, *Louisiana* U10+318 **97**
Harrisonburg, *Virginia* T23+384 **97**
Harrisonville, *Missouri* U26+386 **95**
Harrisville, *Michigan* T50+447 **91**
Harrodsburg, *Kentucky* T59+378 **97**
Harrogate, *England* N09+540 **37**
Harrow, *England* N02+516 **39**
Hârsova, *Romania* L12+447 **58**
Harspranget, *Sweden* L61+668 **46**
Harstad, *Norway* L81+689 **46**
Hart, *Michigan* T68+437 **91**
Hartford, *Connecticut* S76+418 **96**
Hartland, *New Brunswick* S45+464 **90**
Hartlepool, *England* N07+547 **37**
Hartsville, *Tennessee* T67+364 **97**
Hartville, *Missouri* U18+373 **97**
Harvard, *Illinois* T82+425 **91**
Harvard, Mt., *Colorado* V08+385 **98**
Harvey, *New Brunswick* S42+457 **90**
Harvey, *N. Dakota* U60+478 **93**
Harwell, *England* N08+516 **39**
Harwich, *England* M84+291 **39**
Haryana, state, *India* G84+291 **72**
Harz, mts., *Germany* M27+516 **48**
Hasan Dagh, *Turkey* K66+382 **74**
Hasan Kuli, *Turkmen* J37+378 **62**
Hasanpur, *India* G70+293 **73**
Hasbeya, *Lebanon* K56+334 **76**
Hassan, *India* G83+130 **70**
Hassayampa, *Arizona* V46+334 **98**
Hasselt, *Belgium* M58+509 **44**
Hasselt, *Netherlands* M53+526 **44**
Hastiere, *Belgium* M61+502 **44**
Hastings, *England* M86+509 **39**
Hastings, *Michigan* T62+427 **91**
Hastings, *Minnesota* U16+448 **93**
Hastings, *Nebraska* U50+406 **95**
Hastings, *New Zealand* A19–396 **112**
Hasting's Ra., *New S. Wales* B80–312 **109**
Hateg, *Romania* L42+456 **58**
Hatfield, *England* N06+536 **37**
Hatfield, *New South Wales* C37–339 **109**
Hatha, *Saudi Arabia* K27+228 **74**
Hathras, *India* G71+276 **73**
Ha-tinh, *Vietnam* E85+184 **69**
Hatteras, C., *N. Carolina* T03+352 **97**
Hattiesburg, *Mississippi* T86+312 **95**
Hatton Headline, *N.-W. Terr.* S30+611 **89**
Hatvan, *Hungary* L62+477 **49**
Hat Yai, *Thailand* F27+071 **65**
Haudères, les, *Switzerland* M45+461 **45**
Haugesund, *Norway* M58+594 **47**
Haukipudas, *Finland* L28+652 **46**
Haukivesi, *Finland* L10+622 **46**
Haura, *Yemen, South* J74+139 **74**
Hauraki Gulf, *New Zealand* A30–367 **112**
Haurangi Mts.,
   New Zealand A28–414 **112**
Hauroko, L., *New Zealand* A76–460 **112**
Hausa, *Jordan* K43+299 **76**
Hausstock, mt., *Switzerland* M36+468 **45**
Haut, Isle, *Maine* S52+441 **90**
Hauta, *Yemen, South* J80+135 **74**
Hauta, *Saudi Arabia* J79+236 **74**
Haut Atlas, mts., *Morocco* N50+320 **80**
Haute-Garonne, dep., *France* M81+434 **55**
Haute-Loire, dep., *France* M67+451 **55**
Haute-Marne, dep., *France* M58+482 **54**
Hautes-Alpes, dep., *France* M53+446 **55**
Haute-Saône, dep., *France* M51+477 **54**
Hautes-Pyrénées, dep., *Fr.* M88+431 **55**
Haute Vienne, dep., *France* M85+459 **54**
Haute Volta. *See* Upper Volta
Haut Rhin, dep., *France* M45+479 **54**
Havana. *See* Habana
Havasu L., *Cal.-Ariz.* V56+346 **92**
Havelange, *Belgium* M59+504 **44**
Havelland, *E. Germany* M14+527 **48**
Havelock, *New Brunswick* S32+460 **90**
Havelock I., *Andaman Is.* F72+119 **71**

Havelock North, N.Z. A18-397 112
Haverfordwest, Wales N30+518 38
Haverhill, Massachusetts S67+428 96
Haverstraw, New York S84+412 96
Havre, Belgium M66+505 44
Havre, Montana V28+485 93
Havre de Grace, Maryland T07+396 96
Hawaii I., Hawaii Y30+200 107
Hawaii, state, U.S.A. Y60+250 106
Hawarden, Iowa U38+430 95
Hawea Flat, New Zealand A64-445 112
Hawera, New Zealand A34-396 112
Hawesville, Kentucky T71+379 97
Hawick, Scotland N16+554 41
Hawizeh, Iran J71+315 74
Hawke, C., New S. Wales B76-322 109
Hawker, S. Australia C70-319 109
Hawke's B., New Zealand A16-393 112
Hawkesbury, Ontario S88+456 91
Hawr al Hammar, Iraq J76+308 74
Hawr Saniyah, Iraq J80+320 74
Hay, New South Wales C31-346 109
Hay R., Alberta V72+595 88
Hayes Halvø, Greenland S50+770 26
Hayling I., England N06+508 39
Hayneville, Alabama T70+322 97
Hay-on-Wye, Wales N19+521 38
Hay River, North-West
 Territories V65+606 88
Hays, Kansas U56+388 95
Hayward, Wisconsin U08+460 93
Hazara Highlands, Afghan. H60+339 75
Hazard, Kentucky T49+373 97
Hazaribagh, India G28+240 73
Hazaribagh Ra., India G36+232 73
Hazarjuft, Afghanistan H65+310 75
Hazelton, British Columbia W45+553 88
Hazil, Saudi Arabia K15+299 74
Hazlehurst, Georgia T45+318 97
Hazleton, Pennsylvania T06+410 96
Hazro, Pakistan H15+339 72
Headford, Ireland, Rep. N55+535 43
Healesville, Victoria C27-376 109
Heard I., Indian Ocean H12-520 77
Hearst, Ontario T52+498 89
Heathcote, Victoria C32-369 109
Hebbronville, Texas U52+274 94
Heber, Utah V38+406 94
Heber Springs, Arkansas U12+355 97
Hebrides, Outer, Scotland N42+580 40
Hebron, Jordan K59+315 76
Hebron, Labrador S16+585 89
Hebron, Nebraska U46+401 95
Hebron, N. Dakota U72+469 93
Hecate Str., Brit. Columbia W65+534 88
Hecelchakan, Mexico U01+202 100
Hechingen, W. Germany M36+483 48
Hechtel, Belgium M58+512 44
Hectanooga, Nova Scotia S36+442 90
Hector, Mt., New Zealand A28-409 112
Hede, Sweden M09+624 46
Hedemora, Sweden L84+603 47
Heemstede, Netherlands M62+523 44
Heer, Netherlands M56+508 44
Heerenveen, Netherlands M54+530 44
Heerlen, Netherlands M54+509 44
Heiberg I., N.-W. Terr. U00+782 89
Heide, W. Germany M36+542 48
Heidelberg, W. Germany M38+494 48
Heidelburg, Transvaal L10-266 84
Heiden, Switzerland M33+474 45
Heijen, Netherlands M54+517 44
Heilbronn, W. Germany M35+491 48
Heinola, Finland L23+612 47
Heist, Belgium M71+513 44
Hejaz (Hijaz), Saudi Arabia K40+253 74
Hekla, Mt., Iceland P28+640 46
Helchteren, Belgium M58+511 44
Helder, Den, Netherlands M61+530 44
Helena, Arkansas U04+346 95
Helena, Montana V42+466 93
Helensburgh, Scotland N28+560 41
Helensville, New Zealand A33-367 112
Helgoland, I., W. Germany M43+542 48
Helgoländer, Bucht,
 W. Germany M42+543 48
Hell Gate, British Columbia W34+593 88
Hellin, Spain N10+385 53
Helmand Des., Afghanistan H60+304 75
Helmand R., Afghanistan H70+305 75
Helme, Estonia L25+580 47
Helmond, Netherlands M56+515 44
Helmsdale, Scotland N22+581 40
Helsingfors. See Helsinki
Helsingør, Denmark M15+560 47
Helsinki, Finland L30+602 47
Helston, England N32+501 38
Helvellyn, England N18+545 37
Helvick Hd., Ireland, Rep. N45+520 43
Hemelum, Netherlands M57+529 44
Hemnes, Norway M08+662 46
Hemse, Sweden L70+572 47
Hendaye, France N10+434 55
Henderson, Kentucky T76+378 95
Henderson, Minnesota U24+445 93
Henderson, New York T07+438 91
Henderson, N. Carolina T20+363 97
Henderson, Tennessee T82+354 97
Henderson I., Pacific Ocean W50-246 107
Hendersonville, N. Carolina T45+353 97
Hengchow. See Hengyang
Hengelo, Netherlands M49+523 44
Henghsien, China E64+226 67
Hengshan, China E43+272 67
Hengyang, China E44+270 67
Henjam, I., Iran J25+266 75
Henjareh, Iran J00+282 75
Henley-on-Thames, England N05+515 39
Henlopen, C., New Jersey T00+388 96
Hennebont, France N20+478 54
Henrietta, Texas U49+338 95
Henrietta Maria C., Ontario T44+549 89
Henrique de Carvalho,
 Angola L58-096 82
Henry Mts., Utah V36+380 94
Henryetta, Oklahoma U36+354 95
Henty, New South Wales C18-355 109
Henzada, Burma F58+176 71
Heran, Yemen K13+161 74
Herat, Afghanistan H77+344 75
Herault, dep., France M71+435 55

Herberton, Queensland C28-172 111
Herbertville, New Zealand A21-405 112
Herbertville, Quebec S69+484 90
Herbesthal, Belgium M54+506 44
Herceg Novi, Yugoslavia L69+420 58
Heredia, Costa Rica T54+100 101
Hereford, Texas U74+348 94
Heref. & Worcs., co., England N15+522 38
Hereheretue, I., Pacific Oc. X60-200 107
Herford, W. Germany M38+521 48
Heriot, Germany A64-458 112
Herisau, Switzerland M34+474 45
Herkimer, New York T00+430 96
Herma Ness, Shetland, Scot. N06+608 40
Hermann, Missouri U09+387 95
Hermidale, New S. Wales C20-316 109
Hermil, Lebanon K52+344 76
Hermitage B., Newfoundland R72+475 90
Hermite, Is., Chile S46-560 103
Hermon, Mt. See Sheikh, Jebel esh
Hermosillo, Mexico V36+291 100
Herne, W. Germany M66+507 44
Herne Bay, England M83+514 39
Herning, Denmark M36+561 47
Héron, Belgium M59+506 44
Herowabad, Iran J68+377 74
Herräng, Sweden L68+601 47
Herrera, Argentina S19-285 103
Herrera di Pisuerga, Spain N26+426 52
Herrick, Tasmania C13-411 109
Herrington, Kansas U42+386 95
Hersey, Michigan T63+439 91
Herselt, Belgium M61+511 44
Herstmonceux, England M88+509 39
Hertford, N. Carolina T09+362 97
Hertford & co., England N00+518 39
's Hertogenbosch, Netherl'ds M58+517 44
Herval, Brazil R39-274 103
Hervas, Spain N35+402 52
Hervé, Belgium M56+506 44
Hervey B., Queensland B73-246 111
Hervey Is., Cook Is. Y50-200 106
Herzberg, E. Germany M11+517 48
Herzliya, Israel K61+322 76
Herzogenbuchsee, Switz. M44+472 45
Hesdin, France M78+504 54
Hessen, W. Germany M38+506 48
Heught, Mt., N. Terr., Aust. D23-228 110
Heusden, Netherlands M59+517 44
Hève, C. de la, France M89+495 54
Hexham, England N13+550 37
Heytesbury, England N13+512 39
Heywood, Victoria C50-381 109
Hiakiang, China E67+258 67
Hiawatha, Kansas U34+398 95
Hibbing, Minnesota U18+474 93
Hidalgo, Mexico U59+277 100
Hidalgo, state, Mexico U54+204 100
Hieflau, Austria M02+476 48
Hierro, I., Canary Is. P30+276 80
Highland, reg., Scotland N30+576 40
Highland Park, Illinois T78+422 95
Highmore, S. Dakota U57+445 93
High Point, N. Carolina T30+360 97
Highwood Mts., Montana V32+475 93
Hiimeji, Japan D02+348 68
Hiiumaa, I., Estonia L44+589 47
Hijar, Spain N03+411 53
Hikone, Japan C82+353 68
Hildesheim, W. Germany M30+521 48
Hili, Saudi Arabia J26+244 75
Hillah, al, Iraq K03+325 74
Hill City, Kansas U60+394 95
Hill City, Minnesota U22+470 93
Hillman, Michigan T54+451 91
Hillsboro, Illinois T87+392 95
Hillsboro, N. Carolina T24+362 97
Hillsboro, Texas U42+320 95
Hilsborough, N.B. S28+459 90
Hillsdale, Michigan T58+419 91
Hillston, New South Wales C27-335 109
Hillsville, Virginia T35+368 97
Hilversum, Netherlands M59+522 44
Hilwa, Saudi Arabia J80+233 74
Hilvan, Saudi Arabia K23+222 74
Himachal Pradesh, India G75+320 72
Himalaya Mts., India, etc. G60+300 30
Himanka, Finland L38+641 46
Himare, Albania L62+401 59
Hinckley, Minnesota U18+461 93
Hindeloopen, Netherlands M58+529 44
Hindman, Kentucky T48+373 97
Hindmarsh, L., Victoria C49-360 109
Hindubagh, Pakistan H42+309 70
Hindu Kush, mts.,
 Afghanistan-Pakistan H20+364 70
Hindupur, India G75+139 70
Hingan. See Ankang
Hinganghat, India G66+205 70
Hingham, Montana V33+485 93
Hingho, China E38+410 66
Hinghwa, China E01+329 66
Hinghwa (Putien), China E05+255 67
Hingi, China F00+251 67
Hinglaj, Pakistan H57+255 70
Hingol R., Pakistan H56+250 70
Hingoli, India G76+196 70
Hinnøya, Norway L84+687 46
Hinsdale, Montana V12+484 93
Hinsdale, New Hampshire S75+428 96
Hinton, W. Virginia T35+377 97
Hiro, Japan C40+423 68
Hirosaki, Japan C57+406 68
Hiroshima, Japan D15+344 68
Hisaronu, Turkey K77+416 74
Hisban, Jordan K55+318 76
Hispaniola, I., West Indies S70+190 101
Hissar, India G86+291a72
Hissmofors, Sweden M03+634 46
Hisua, India G27+248 73
Hisya, Syria K49+344 76
Hit, Iraq K14+336 74
Hitra, Norway M38+636 46
Hivaoa, I., Marquesas Is. X24-100 107
Hiwasa, Japan D03+338 68
Hjälmaren, L., Sweden L86+593 47
Hjørring, Denmark M30+575 47
Hkamti, Burma F56+260 71
Hobart, Oklahoma U54+350 95
Hobart, Tasmania C16-430 109
Hobbs, New Mexico U78+326 94

Hoboken, Belgium M64+512 44
Hobro, Denmark M31+566 47
Hochwan, China E82+300 67
Hodal, India G76+279 72
Hodeida, Yemen K12+148 74
Hodgson, Manitoba U46+512 88
Hodmezövásárhely, Hungary L58+464 49
Hoek van Holland,
 Netherlands M65+520 44
Hoyes Bridge, Kenya K58+010 83
Hof, W. Germany M19+503 48
Hofei, China E16+319 66
Hofmeyr, Namibia L70-244 84
Höfn, Iceland P24+648 46
Hohe Tauern, Austria M15+472 48
Hohsien, China E51+244 67
Hoihong, China E59+209 67
Hokianga Harb., N.Z. A39-354 112
Ho-kien-fu, China E23+385 66
Hokitika, New Zealand A54-427 112
Hokkaidō I., Japan C42+430 68
Holbaek, Denmark M20+557 47
Holberg, British Columbia W48+506 88
Holbrook, Arizona V31+348 94
Holbrook, New South Wales C17-358 109
Holdenville, Oklahoma U38+351 95
Holdredge, Nebraska U54+404 95
Holguin, Cuba T08+208 101
Holinkoerh, China E50+404 66
Holland, Michigan T67+428 91
Holland, New York T21+426 96
Holland, Noord, prov., Neth. M61+526 44
Holland, Zuid, prov., Neth. M63+520 44
Holland, Michigan T75+428 91
Hollange, Belgium M56+499 44
Hollidaysburg, Pennsylvania T21+404 96
Hollis, Oklahoma U59+347 95
Hollogne, Belgium M59+507 44
Holly, Colorado U72+381 94
Holly, Michigan T52+428 91
Holly Springs, Mississippi T87+348 95
Hollywood, California V80+341 92
Holmestrand, Norway M28+595 47
Holmsund, Sweden L58+637 46
Holstebro., Denmark M38+563 47
Holstein, Germany M32+539 48
Holsteinsborg, Greenland R40+670 26
Holsworthy, England N26+508 38
Holten, Netherlands M51+523 44
Holton, Kansas U36+394 95
Holwerd, Netherlands M55+534 44
Holy I., England N11+557 37
Holy I., Wales N28+533 38
Holy Cross, Alaska Y60+624 99
Holy Cross, Mt. of the,
 Colorado V09+396 98
Holyhead, Wales N28+533 38
Holyoke, Colorado U74+406 94
Holyoke, Massachusetts S76+422 91
Holywood, N. Ireland N35+546 42
Home B., N.-W. Territories S30+678 89
Homer, Alaska Y10+559 99
Homer, Louisiana U18+328 95
Homer, New York T08+427 91
Homestead, Pennsylvania T29+404 91
Homfray Str., Andaman Is. F72+124 71
Hommelvik, Norway M26+634 46
Homs, Libya M04+326 81
Homs, Syria K50+347 76
Honan. See Loyang
Honan, prov., China E42+340 66
Honda, Columbia S89+052 104
Honda, B., Cuba T49+229 101
Hondo, Mexico U65+277 100
Honduras, rep., C. America T76+150 101
Honduras, C., Honduras T66+160 101
Honduras, G. of, Cent. Amer T70+165 101
Hønefoss, Norway M28+602 47
Honesdale, Pennsylvania T02+415 96
Honfleur, France N00+494 54
Honghai B., China E28+227 67
Hong Kong I., S.-E. Asia E34+223 67
Honiara, I., Solomon Is B30-095 106
Honiton, England N19+508 38
Honolulu, Hawaii Y30+208 107
Honor, Michigan T66+447 91
Honshū, I., Japan C82+353 68
Hood, Mt., Oregon W10+453 92
Hoofdplaat, Netherlands M68+514 44
Hooger Smilde, Netherlands M52+529 44
Hoogeveen, Netherlands M51+527 44
Hoogezand, Netherlands M49+532 44
Hooghalen, Netherlands M51+529 44
Hooghly, India G10+230 73
Hooghly R., India G12+216 73
Hook Hd., Ireland, Rep. N42+521 43
Hookina, S. Australia C71-318 109
Hoopeston, Illinois T76+405 91
Hoorn Den, Netherlands M60+526 44
Hoosick Falls, New York S80+429 91
Hoover Dam, Arizona V57+359 92
Hope, Aransas U21+336 95
Hope, British Columbia W08+494 88
Hopedale, Labrador S03+554 89
Hopeh, prov., China E24+386 66
Hopeland, India G75+139 70
Hopen, I., Barents Sea L30+766 62
Hopes Advance, C., Quebec S56+607 89
Hopetoun, Victoria C46-357 109
Hope Town, Andaman Is. F74+117 71
Hopetown, Cape Province L36-296 84
Hopewell, Virginia T14+372 97
Hopkinsville, Kentucky T75+368 95
Hoppo, China E64+216 67
Hoquiam, Washington W37+470 92
Horaždovice, Czechoslovakia M08+493 48
Horcasitas, Mexico V34+294 100
Horgen, Switzerland M38+473 45
Horka, E. Germany L90+513 48
Hormoz, Iran J31+276 75
Hormuz I., Iran J21+271 75
Hormuz. Str. of,
 Saudi Arabia-Iran J24+266 75
Horn, Austria L86+487 49
Horn, Iceland P44+665 46
Horn, Netherlands M54+516 44
Horn, C., Chile S44-560 103
Horn Mts., N.-W. Terr. V85+617 88
Hornavan, Sweden L74+662 46
Horncastle, England N01+532 37

Hornefors, Sweden L61+637 46
Hornell, New York T16+423 96
Hornopiren, mt., Chile S75-418 103
Hornos, C. de Chile S44-560 103
Hornsby, New South Wales B84-337 109
Hornsea, England N01+539 37
Horonobe, Japan C49+451 68
Horqueta, Paraguay R72-232 103
Horseheads, New York T11+422 96
Horsens, Denmark M31+559 47
Horse Shoe, W. Australia E09-255 110
Horseshoe Res., Arizona V40+340 94
Horsham, England N02+511 39
Horsham, Victoria C47-367 109
Horšovský Tyn, Czech. M13+495 48
Horst, Netherlands M54+515 44
Horten, Norway M27+594 47
Horton, Kansas U34+396 95
Horton, Montana V06+463 93
Horton R., N.-W. Terr. W12+682 88
Hose Ra., Sarawak E38+019 65
Hoshangabad, India G73+227 73
Hoshiarpur, India G83+315 72
Hospel, India G81+153 70
Hospenthal, Switzerland M39+466 45
Hossegor, France N08+437 55
Hoste, I., Chile S56-552 103
Hosur, India G73+128 70
Hotagen, Sweden M05+640 46
Hotseh, China E28+353 66
Hot Springs, N. Carolina T47+359 97
Hot Springs, S. Dakota U81+434 93
Hot Springs Nat. Pk., Ark. U18+346 95
Hotton, Belgium M57+503 44
Houdelaincourt, France M57+485 54
Houffalize, Belgium M55+501 44
Houghton L., Michigan T59+444 91
Houlton, Maine S47+461 90
Houma, Louisiana U04+296 95
Hourn, L., Scotland N34+571 40
Housatonic, R., Conecticut S79+414 96
House Ra., Utah V50+395 94
Houstan, Mississippi T84+339 97
Houston, Missouri U12+374 95
Houston, Texas U32+298 95
Houten, Netherlands M59+520 44
Houtman Abrolhos,
 W. Aust. E42-284 110
Hovd, Mongolia E80+480 64
Hove, England N01+508 39
Hovsgöl Nuur, lake
 Mongolia F25+520 63
Howard, Michigan T63+434 91
Howard, Pennsylvania T16+410 96
Howard, S. Dakota U45+440 93
Howell, Michigan T54+426 91
Howick, Natal L00+294 84
Howland I., Pacific Ocean Z70+005 106
Howley, Newfoundland R72+492 90
Howrah, India G10+226 73
Howth, Ireland, Rep. N36+534 43
Hoy, I. Orkney, Scotland N20+588 40
Hoyes, Spain N41+401 52
Hoyt, New Brunswick S39+456 90
Hoyun, China E42+237 64
Hozat, Turkey K34+393 74
Hrubieszów, Poland L37+508 49
Hsenwi, Burma F42+234 71
Hsiachwan Shan, China E44+216 67
Hsiamen, China E11+244 67
Hsinchu, Taiwan D84+248 67
Hsinking. See Changchun
Hsipaw, Burma F46+226 71
Hsuchang, China E36+340 66
Hsuchow. See Hsuchang
Huachi, Bolivia S44-156 104
Huacho, Peru T16-111 104
Huacrachuco, Peru T12-088 104
Hualgayoo, Peru T22-068 104
Hualienkang, Taiwan D80+240 67
Huambo, Angola L86-128 82
Huanay, Bolivia S48-155 104
Huancabamba, Peru T27-052 104
Huancane, Peru S58-152 104
Huancavelica, Peru T01-126 104
Huancayo, Peru T01-120 104
Huanchaca, Bolivia S40-203 104
Huanchaco, Peru T25-081 104
Huanta, Peru S85-126 104
Huanuco, Peru T08-098 104
Huaras, Peru T16-095 104
Huards, L. aux, Quebec S65+493 90
Huari, Chile S59-200 103
Huariaca, Peru T07-105 104
Huarmey, Peru T19-101 104
Huasco, Chile S67-284 103
Huatusco, Mexico U42+192 100
Huaylas, Peru T17-090 104
Hubli, India G81+153 70
Huchow, China D88+308 66
Hucknall Torkard, England N07+531 37
Huddersfield, England N11+536 37
Hudiksvall, Sweden L77+617 47
Hudson, Maine S53+451 90
Hudson, Wisconsin U16+450 93
Hudson & R., New York S83+423 96
Hudson B., Canada T60+580 89
Hudson R., New York S83+420 91
Hudson Str., Canada S80+620 89
Hudson Falls, New York S81+433 91
Hue, Vietnam E75+165 69
Hueco Mts., New Mex.-Texas V06+320 94
Huedin, Romania L42+469 58
Huehuetenango, Guatemala U08+154 100
Huejutla, Mexico U51+212 100
Huelva, Spain N41+372 52
Huereal Overa, Spain N12+374 53
Huete, Spain N16+402 53
Hughenden, Queensland C35-209 111
Hugo, Oklahoma U33+340 95
Huhehot, China S50+408 66
Huiarau Ra., New Zealand A18-387 112
Hüichŏn, Korea D52+402 64
Huj, Israel K62+315 76
Hukawng Valley, Burma F50+266 71
Hukow, China E23+297 64
Hukuntsi, Botswana L50-240 84
Hula L., Israel K56+331 76
Hulaiba, Iraq J77+301 74
Hulin, China D10+460 64
Hull, England N02+537 37

Hull, *Quebec* T04+455 **91**
Hulst, *Netherlands* M66+513 **44**
Hulun. *See* Hailar
Hulun Chih, *China* E16+448 **64**
Hulutao, *China* D84+407 **64**
Huma, *China* D50+515 **63**
Humacao, *Puerto Rico* S34+183 **101**
Humaita, *Paraguay* R81−271 **103**
Humansdorp, *Cape Province* L32−340 **84**
Humayta, *Brazil* S18−074 **104**
Humber, R., *England* N02+537 **37**
Humbermouth, *Nfd.* R77+490 **90**
Humberside, co., *England* N03+538 **37**
Humboldt, *Iowa* U26+428 **95**
Humboldt, *Saskatchewan* V01+519 **88**
Humboldt, *Tennessee* T84+358 **97**
Humboldt B., *California* W30+408 **98**
Humboldt Glacier, *Greenland* R30+790 **26**
Humboldt R., *Nevada* V80+404 **92**
Hume Res., *New S. Wales* C18−360 **109**
Humenne, *Czechoslovakia* L49+490 **49**
Humphreys, Mt., *Arizona* Y39+354 **94**
Humphreys, Mt., *California* V82+373 **92**
Humphreys, Mt., *Wyoming* V31+443 **93**
Hun, *Libya* L84+292 **81**
Húnaflói, *Iceland* P36+659 **46**
Hunan, prov., *China* E54+266 **67**
Hungary, *Central Europe* L60+470 **51**
Hungchiang, *China* E11+273 **67**
Hungerford, *England* N09+514 **39**
Hungnam, *Korea* D43+400 **64**
Hungtse, *China* E08+332 **66**
Hunsrück, mts., *W. Germany* M46+499 **48**
Hunstanton, *England* M87+529 **39**
Hunter Is., *Tasmania* C31−405 **109**
Hunter Ra., *New S. Wales* C00−330 **109**
Hunter R., *New S. Wales* B82−326 **109**
Huntersville, *W. Virginia* T30+382 **97**
Huntingburg, *Indiana* T72+384 **97**
Huntingdon, *Pennsylvania* T18+405 **96**
Huntingdon and Peterborough, co.
  See Cambridgeshire
Huntington, *New York* S81+408 **96**
Huntington, *Utah* V36+394 **94**
Huntington, *W. Virginia* T45+384 **97**
Huntley, *Montana* V20+458 **93**
Huntly, *New Zealand* A29−376 **112**
Huntly, *Scotland* N17+574 **40**
Huntsville, *Alabama* T69+347 **97**
Huntsville, *Ontario* T25+453 **91**
Huntsville, *Tennessee* T57+364 **97**
Huntsville, *Texas* U32+307 **95**
Hunucma, *Mexico* T89+210 **100**
Hun-yüan-chow, *China* E38+397 **66**
Hunza, *Kashmir* H02+364 **72**
Huon Is., *Pacific Ocean* B10−180 **106**
Huon Pen.,
  Papua New Guinea C20−064 **111**
Huon, R., *Tasmania* C20−431 **109**
Hupeh, prov., *China* E42+315 **66**
Hurd, C., *Ontario* T40+452 **91**
Hurghada, *Egypt* K68+270 **81**
Huron, *S. Dakota* U50+444 **93**
Huron, L., *U.S.A.-Canada* T40+450 **99**
Hurtsboro, *Alabama* T63+323 **97**
Huskvarna, *Sweden* M04+578 **47**
Husum, *W. Germany* M36+545 **48**
Hutchinson, *Kansas* U48+381 **95**
Hutchinson, *Minnesota* U26+450 **93**
Hüttenberg, *Austria* M03+469 **48**
Huttwil, *Switzerland* M43+471 **45**
Huy, *Belgium* M59+505 **44**
Hvar, I., *Yugoslavia* L79+431 **56**
Hwahsien, *China* E40+235 **67**
Hwaian, *China* E04+335 **66**
Hwaijen, *China* E42+399 **66**
Hwaining, *China* E17+305 **67**
Hwaiyang, *China* E30+337 **66**
Hwaiyn. *See* Tsingkiang
Hwangchow. *See* Hwangkang
Hwang-Hai. *See* Yellow Sea
Hwang Ho, R., *China* E24+360 **66**
Hwanghsien, *China* D87+377 **66**
Hwangkang, *China* E30+307 **66**
Hweichow. *See* Sihsien
Hweimin, *China* E15+375 **66**
Hweinan, *China* D53+428 **64**
Hweitseh, *China* F11+264 **67**
Hwohsien, *China* E50+365 **66**
Hyde, *England* N13+535 **37**
Hyden, *Kentucky* T51+372 **97**
Hyden, *W. Australia* E06−322 **110**
Hyde Park, *Vermont* S75+446 **91**
Hyderabad, *India* G69+173 **70**
Hyderabad, *Pakistan* H40+254 **70**
Hyères, *France* M53+431 **55**
Hyères, Is. d', *France* M51+430 **55**
Hyland R., *Yukon* W50+602 **88**
Hyndman Pk., *Idaho* V54+438 **98**
Hyogo, *Japan* D00+347 **68**
Hyrum, *Utah* V42+416 **94**
Hyrynsalmi, *Finland* L08+647 **46**
Hythe, *England* M84+511 **39**
Hythe, *England* N08+509 **39**
Iasi, *Romania* L14+471 **60**
Ibadan, *Nigeria* M66+074 **80**
Ibague, *Colombia* T02+044 **104**
Ibarra, *Ecuador* T18+005 **104**
Ibb, *Yemen* K05+140 **74**
Ibembo, *Zaire* L38+026 **82**
Ibicui, *Brazil* R70−294 **103**
Ibiza, I., *Balearic Is.* M80+390 **53**
Ibresi, *U.S.S.R.* J77+553 **61**
Ibri, *Oman* J22+231 **75**
Ibwe Munyama, *Zambia* L08−162 **84**
Ica, *Peru* T04−140 **104**
Ica, R., *Brazil* S50−028 **104**
Icel, *Turkey* K62+369 **51**
Iceland, I. & rep., *N. Atl. Oc.* **—34**
Ichak, *India* G28+242 **73**
Ichang, *China* E52+307 **66**
Icheng, *China* E46+317 **66**
Ichow. *See* Lini.
Ichun, *China* E33+277 **67**
Idabel, *Oklahoma* U28+338 **95**
Ida Grove, *Iowa* U33+424 **95**
Idah, *Nigeria* M50+072 **80**
Idaho, state, *U.S.A.* V67+444 **98**
Idaho Falls, *Idaho* V42+435 **92**
Ideles, *Algeria* M54+236 **80**
Idfu, *Egypt* K74+250 **81**
Idhra, I., *Greece* L39+374 **59**

Idirtu, *China* F50+374 **64**
Idlib, *Syria* K50+359 **76**
Idutywa, *Cape Province* L10−322 **84**
Ierissós, G. of, *Greece* L36+405 **59**
Ifakara, *Tanzania* K50−082 **83**
Iférouane, *Niger* M48+188 **80**
Ifni, terr., *N.-W. Africa* N64+288 **80**
Igan, *Sarawak* E49+028 **65**
Igarapé, Mirim, *Brazil* R23−020 **105**
Igarka, *U.S.S.R.* G20+675 **62**
Iglesias, *Sardinia* M39+393 **56**
Igli, *Algeria* N12+304 **80**
Igoma, *Tanzania* ' K70−078 **83**
Igra, *U.S.S.R.* J41+574 **61**
Iguaçú & R., *Brazil* R58−256 **103**
Iguala, *Mexico* U56+183 **100**
Iguapé, *Brazil* R16−247 **103**
Iguatu, *Brazil* Q56−064 **105**
Igumira, *Tanzania* K70−068 **83**
Ihosy, *Madagascar* J84−224 **83**
Ihtiman, *Bulgaria* L37+424 **58**
Iida, *Japan* C73+355 **68**
Iisalmi, *Finland* L17+635 **46**
Ijebu-Ode, *Nigeria* M66+068 **80**
IJsselmonde, *Netherlands* M63+519 **44**
IJsselmuiden, *Netherlands* M54+526 **44**
IJsselstein, *Netherlands* M60+520 **44**
IJssel Meer, *Netherlands* M58+527 **44**
IJssel R., *Netherlands* M53+523 **44**
Ijui, *Brazil* R54−284 **103**
Ijzendijke, *Netherlands* M68+513 **44**
Ikaria, I., *Greece* L23+376 **59**
Ikisu, *Tanzania* K66−020 **83**
Ikla, *Estonia* L33+579 **47**
Ikonde, *Tanzania* K88−064 **83**
Ilagan, *Philippines* D79+171 **65**
Ilam, *Nepal* G12+269 **73**
Ilam, *Iran* J82+337 **74**
Ilanz, *Switzerland* M35+468 **45**
Iława, *Poland* L63+536 **49**
Iławka, *Poland* L56+544 **49**
Ile-á-la Crosse, I., *Sask.* V18+554 **88**
Ile-de-France, prov., *France* M75+490 **54**
Ilford, *England* M89+516 **39**
Ilfracombe, *England* N25+512 **38**
Ilhavo, *Portugal* N52+406 **52**
Ilhéus, *Brazil* Q54−148 **105**
Ili, *Kazakh.* G76+438 **62**
Ilia, *Greece* L51+378 **59**
Ilic, *Turkey* K39+394 **74**
Ilich, *Kazakh.* H40+410 **62**
Iligan, *Philippines* D64+080 **65**
Ilimsk, *U.S.S.R.* F08+569 **63**
Iliodhrómia, I., *Greece* L37+392 **59**
Ilion, *New York* T00+430 **96**
Ilkeston, *England* N08+530 **37**
Ilkley, *England* N11+539 **37**
Illapel, *Chile* S67−315 **103**
Ille-et-Vilaine, dep., *France* N11+482 **54**
Illescas, *Spain* N23+401 **52**
Illimani, mt., *Bolivia* S47−166 **104**
Illinois, state, *U.S.A.* U03+398 **99**
Illinois R., *Illinois* U04+398 **95**
Illora, *Spain* N23+373 **52**
Ilmen Oz., *U.S.S.R.* K83+583 **60**
Ilminster, *England* N17+509 **38**
Ilo, *Peru* S68−175 **104**
Iloilo, *Philippines* D75+108 **65**
Ilorin, *Nigeria* M62+084 **80**
Ilpi, *U.S.S.R.* A41+615 **63**
Imabaru, *Japan* D12+340 **68**
Iman, *U.S.S.R.* D07+459 **63**
Imandra, Oz., *U.S.S.R.* K73+675 **62**
Imerimandroso, *Madagascar* J68−176 **83**
Imi, *Ethiopia* K16+064 **83**
Immendingen, *W. Germany* M38+479 **48**
Immingham, *England* N01+536 **37**
Imperatriz, *Brazil* S44−054 **104**
Imperatriz, *Brazil* R14−056 **105**
Imperia, *Italy* M42+439 **56**
Imperial Dam, *Arizona* V57+331 **98**
Imphal, *India* F66+247 **71**
Imroz, I., *Turkey* L26+402 **74**
Imtan, *Syria* K49+324 **76**
Inagua, I. Gt., *Bahamas, The* S80+211 **101**
Inagua, I. Lit., *Bahamas, The* S78+215 **101**
Inarijärvi, *Finland* L18+688 **46**
Inari L., *Finland* L12+690 **46**
Inch, *Ireland, Rep.* N37+527 **43**
Inchkeith, *Scotland* N19+560 **41**
Inchon, *Korea* D50+375 **64**
Incourt, *Belgium* M61+507 **44**
Indaal, L., *Scotland* N38+557 **41**
Indals Älv, *Sweden* L80+629 **46**
Indaw, *Burma* F53+242 **71**
Indawgyi L., *Burma* F52+253 **71**
Independence, *Iowa* U12+425 **95**
Independence, *Kansas* U34+372 **95**
Independence, *Missouri* U26+390 **95**
Independencia, *Argentina* S50−317 **103**
India, rep., *S. Asia* — **70-71**
Indian Des. *See* Thar Des.
Indian L., *New York* S86+437 **96**
Indiana, *Pennsylvania* T25+407 **96**
Indiana, state, *U.S.A.* T72+402 **99**
Indianapolis, *Indiana* T67+398 **91**
Indian Head, *Saskatchewan* U82+505 **88**
Indian House L., *Quebec* S29+562 **89**
Indianola, *Iowa* U22+413 **95**
Indiga, *U.S.S.R.* J67+676 **62**
Indigirka, R., *U.S.S.R.* C30+678 **63**
Indonesia, rep., *S.-E. Asia* E30−050 **65**
Indore, *India* G84+226 **70**
Indre, dep., *France* M80+467 **54**
Indre-et-Loire, dep., *France* M86+472 **54**
Indur. *See* Nizamabad
Indus, R., *Pakistan, etc.* H10+354 **70**
Inebolu, *Turkey* K66+419 **74**
Inez, *Kentucky* T45+378 **97**
Infantes, *Spain* N18+387 **52**
Ingelmunster, *Belgium* M70+509 **44**
Ingersoll, *Ontario* T35+431 **91**
Ingham, *Queensland* C23−188 **111**
Inglefield Inlet, *Greenland* S58+770 **26**
Inglefield Ld., *Greenland* S00+790 **26**
Inglewood, *New Zealand* A34−391 **112**
Inglewood, *Victoria* C37−366 **109**
Ing Luiggi, *Argentina* S27−353 **103**
Ingolstadt, *W. Germany* M22+488 **48**
Ingrid Christensen Coast,
  Antarctica G70−700 **27**

Inhambane, *Mozambique* K58−240 **84**
Ining, *China* G51+440 **62**
Inishark I., *Ireland, Rep* N62+536 **42**
Inishcrone, *Ireland, Rep.* N54+542 **42**
Inishbofin, I., *Ireland. Rep.* N61+536 **42**
Inisheer, I., *Ireland, Rep.* N57+531 **43**
Inishkea I., *Ireland, Rep.* N61+541 **42**
Inishmaan, I., *Ireland, Rep.* N58+531 **43**
Inishmore, I., *Ireland, Rep.* N58+531 **43**
Inishmurray, I., *Ireland Rep.,* N52+544 **42**
Inishowen & Hd.,
  Ireland, Rep. N42+552 **42**
Inishtrahull, *Ireland, Rep.* N43+554 **42**
Inishtrahull Sd., *Ireland, Rep.* N44+554 **42**
Inishturk, I., *Ireland, Rep.* N61+537 **42**
Inklin R., *British Columbia* W75+590 **88**
Inner Sd., *Scotland* N36+574 **40**
Inner Mongolia, *China* F00+410 **64**
Innerleithen, *Scotland* N18+556 **41**
Innertkirchen, *Switzerland* M40+467 **45**
Innisfail, *Queensland* C24−172 **111**
Innsbruck, *Austria* M22+473 **48**
Inny R., *Ireland, Rep.* N47+535 **43**
Inowrocław, *Poland* L71+528 **49**
Inquisivi, *Bolivia* S43−167 **104**
Ins, *Switzerland* M47+470 **45**
In Salah, (Ain Salah) *Alg.* M76+270 **80**
Insar, *U.S.S.R.* K04+538 **61**
Insein, *Burma* F53+168 **71**
In Shan, *China* E72+417 **66**
Insterburg. *See* Chernyakhovsk.
Interlaken, *Switzerland* M43+467 **45**
International Falls, *Minnesota* U20+486 **93**
Interview I., *Andaman Is.* F75+130 **71**
Intragna, *Switzerland* M38+462 **45**
Inutil, B., *Chile* S60−536 **103**
Inveraray, *Scotland* N31+562 **41**
Inverbervie, *Scotland* N14+568 **41**
Invercargill, *New Zealand* A69−464 **112**
Inverell, *New South Wales* B84−288 **109**
Invergordon, *Scotland* N25+577 **40**
Inverkeithing, *Scotland* N20+560 **41**
Inverness, *Nova Scotia* S08+463 **90**
Inverness, *Scotland* N25+575 **40**
Invershin, *Scotland* N26+579 **40**
Inverurie, *Scotland* N14+573 **40**
Investigator Str., *S. Aust.* C75−356 **111**
Inyati, *Zimbabwe* L08−196 **84**
Inza, *U.S.S.R.* J82+538 **61**
Inzer, *U.S.S.R.* J14+542 **61**
Ioannina, *Greece* L55+397 **59**
Iola, *Kansas* U34+379 **95**
Iona, *Nova Scotia* S05+460 **90**
Iona I., *Scotland* N39+563 **41**
Ionia, *Michigan* T60+430 **91**
Ionia, *Montana* V14+453 **93**
Ionian Is., *Greece* L56+387 **59**
Ionian Sea, *Italy, etc.* L72+380 **51**
Ios, I., *Greece* L28+367 **59**
Iowa state, *U.S.A.* U27+418 **99**
Iowa City, *Iowa* U09+416 **95**
Iowa Falls, *Iowa* U20+426 **95**
Ipala, *Mexico* V03+202 **100**
Ipiales, *Colombia* T15+008 **104**
Ipin, *China* F03+287 **67**
Ipiros, *Greece* L55+395 **59**
Ipoh, *Malaysia* F24+046 **69**
Ippy, *Cent. Afr. Rep.* L54+060 **81**
Ipswich, *England* M83+520 **39**
Ipswich, *Queensland* B73−274 **111**
Ipswich, *S. Dakota* U54+454 **93**
Ipu, *Brazil* Q63−043 **105**
Iquique, *Chile* S61−202 **103**
Iquitos, *Peru* S79−038 **104**
Iracoubo, *French Guiana* R49+054 **105**
Iráklia, I., *Greece* L27+368 **59**
Iráklion, *Crete* L29+353 **59**
Iran (Persia), *S.W. Asia* J30+330 **75**
Irapa, *Venezuela* S15+105 **104**
Irapuato, *Mexico* U68+206 **100**
Iraq, rep., *S.-W. Asia* L10+330 **74**
Irazu, Vol., *Costa Rica* T53+102 **101**
Irbid, *Jordan* K55+326 **76**
Irbit, *U.S.S.R.* H72+576 **61**
Irdendyk Mts., *U.S.S.R.* J12+520 **61**
Irgiz, *Kazakh* H83+485 **62**
Irian Jaya, *New Guinea* C60−054 **65**
Iringa, *Tanzania* K56−078 **83**
Irish Sea, *British Isles* N30+536 **34**
Irkutsk, *U.S.S.R.* F04+524 **63**
Iron Mt., *Missouri* U03+375 **97**
Iron City, *Tennessee* T76+350 **97**
Irondale, *Ontario* T21+448 **91**
Iron Knob, *S. Australia* C76−327 **111**
Iron Mountain, *Michigan* T78+458 **91**
Iron River, *Michigan* T82+461 **91**
Iron River, *Wisconsin* U09+465 **93**
Ironton, *Missouri* U04+376 **95**
Ironton, *Ohio* T46+386 **97**
Ironwood, *Michigan* U01+465 **91**
Iroquois, *Ontario* T42+499 **91**
Iroquois Chute, *Quebec* S78+477 **91**
Irrawaddy, *Burma* F60+172 **71**
Irrawaddy, R., *Burma* F54+228 **71**
Irthing R., *England* N17+549 **37**
Irtysh, R., *U.S.S.R.* H35+595 **62**
Irumu, *Zaire* L00+014 **83**
Irvine & R., *Scotland* N28+556 **41**
Irvinestown, *N. Ireland* N46+545 **42**
Isa, Mt., *Queensland* C64−208 **111**
Isabela I., *Galapagos Is.* U10−007 **107**
Isaccea, *Romania* L09+452 **58**
Isafjördhur, *Iceland* P48+661 **46**
Isai Kalat, *Pakistan* H66+269 **70**
Isa Khel, *Pakistan* H42+327 **72**
Isangi, *Zaire* L34+006 **82**
Isari, *Greece* L48+374 **59**
Ischia, I., *Italy* M07+407 **57**
Ise B., *Japan* C80+347 **68**
Iseghem. *See* Izegem
Iselin, *Pennsylvania* T26+406 **96**
Iseltwald, *Switzerland* M42+467 **45**
Isère, dep. & R., *France* M57+452 **55**
Isernia, *Italy* M05+416 **57**
Isha Baidao, *Somalia* K08+030 **83**
Ishan, *China* E68+245 **67**
Ishikari, R., *Japan* C40+435 **68**
Ishim, *U.S.S.R.* H34+562 **62**

Ishimbai, *U.S.S.R.* J23+534 **61**
Ishinomaki B., *Japan* C52+383 **68**
Ishkamish, *Afghanistan* H35+364 **75**
Ishkasham, *Afghanistan* H20+366 **75**
Ishpeming, *Michigan* T76+465 **91**
Ishqanan, *Iran* J38+227 **75**
Isil Kul, *U.S.S.R.* H23+549 **62**
Isiolo, *Kenya* K44+044 **83**
Isisford, *Queensland* C35−241 **111**
Iskenderun, *Turkey* K53+366 **74**
Iskilip, *Turkey* K64+407 **74**
Iskitim, *U.S.S.R.* G40+547 **62**
Iskut R., *British Columbia* W65+568 **88**
Islamabad, *Pakistan* H11+338 **72**
Islampur, *India* G29+249 **73**
Island L., *Manitoba* U25+538 **88**
Island Pond, *Vermont* S71+449 **91**
Islands, B. of, *Newfoundland* R84+493 **90**
Islands, B. of, *New Zealand* A35−353 **112**
Islay I., *Scotland* N37+558 **41**
Isle of Man., *British Is.* N28+542 **37**
Isle of Wight, *England* N08+507 **39**
Isleta, *New Mexico* V11+348 **94**
Isle Verte, *Quebec* S56+480 **90**
Ismailia, *Egypt* K76+306 **81**
Isna, *Egypt* K74+252 **81**
Isoka, *Zambia* K74−104 **83**
Isparta, *Turkey* K87+378 **74**
Israel, rep., *S.-W. Asia* K62+320 **76**
Issoudun, *France* M78+469 **54**
Issyk Kul, Oz., *Kirgiz* G80+424 **62**
Istanbul, *Turkey* L07+411 **74**
Istmina, *Colombia* T11+053 **104**
Istra, *Yugoslavia* M06+452 **56**
Itabaiana, *Brazil* Q31−073 **105**
Itacare, *Brazil* Q54−144 **105**
Itacoatiara, *Brazil* R8J−030 **104**
Itaete, *Brazil* Q67−130 **105**
Itaituba, *Brazil* R64−043 **105**
Itajai, *Brazil* R22−270 **103**
Italy, *Central Europe* M18+440 **50**
Itapecuru-mirim, *Brazil* Q86−033 **105**
Itapemirim, Cachoeiro de,
  Brazil Q67−208 **105**
Itapetininga, *Brazil* R19−235 **105**
Itapura, *Brazil* R39−207 **105**
Itaqui, *Brazil* R70−292 **103**
Itarsi, *India* G72+225 **70**
Itasca, L., *Minnesota* U33+472 **98**
Itauna, *Brazil* Q88−201 **105**
Itéa, *Greece* L46+385 **59**
Ithaca, *Michigan* T58+433 **91**
Ithaca, *New York* T09+424 **96**
Itháci, *See* Ithaka
Ithaka, *Greece* L56+384 **59**
Itiés, *Greece* L50+401 **59**
Itula, *Congo* L12−036 **83**
Iturbe, *Argentina* S32−231 **103**
Ivailovgrad, *Bulgaria* L23+415 **58**
Ivanhoe, *New South Wales* C34−329 **109**
Ivanic Grad, *Yugoslavia* L82+457 **56**
Ivano-Frankovsk, *Ukraine* L34+490 **60**
Ivanovka, *U.S.S.R.* J55+525 **61**
Ivanovo, *U.S.S.R.* K24+570 **60**
Ivdel, *U.S.S.R.* H87+608 **62**
Iviza, I. *See* Ibiza, I.
Ivory Coast, *W. Africa* N40+080 **80**
Iwakuni, *Japan* D17+341 **68**
Iwaniska, *Poland* L52+507 **49**
Ixiamas, *Bolivia* S49−137 **104**
Ixtapa, *Guatemala* U04+139 **100**
Ixtla, *Mexico* U55+186 **100**
Ixtlan de Juarez, *Mexico* U39+174 **100**
Iyang, *China* E16+284 **67**
Iyo Nada, *Japan* D18+336 **68**
Izabal & L., *Guatemala* T85+154 **100**
Izamal, *Mexico* T83+208 **100**
Izegem, *Belgium* M71+509 **44**
Izhevsk, *U.S.S.R.* J40+568 **61**
Izhma R., *U.S.S.R.* J37+650 **62**
Izki, *Oman* J14+229 **75**
Izmail, *Ukraine* L07+454 **60**
Izmir, *Turkey* L17+384 **74**
Izmit, *Turkey* L01+408 **74**
Izra, *Syria* K52+329 **76**
Iztapa, *Guatemala* U04+139 **100**
Izu Pen., *Japan* C66+348 **68**
Izu Shichito, *Japan* C62+343 **68**
Izyum, *Ukraine* K47+492 **60**
Jääski, *U.S.S.R.* L06+610 **47**
Jabalpur, *India* G60+232 **73**
Jabbeke, *Belgium* M72+512 **44**
Jabbul, *Syria* K45+361 **76**
Jablonec, *Czechoslovakia* L89+507 **48**
Jabrin Oasis, *Saudi Arabia* J66+232 **74**
Jaburú, *Brazil* S39−040 **104**
Jaca, *Spain* N03+426 **53**
Jacarezinho, *Brazil* R30−232 **105**
Jachal, *Argentina* S53−303 **103**
Jacitara, *Brazil* S32−019 **104**
Jacksboro, *Tennessee* T55−363 **97**
Jackson, *Kentucky* T50+375 **97**
Jackson, *Louisiana* U07+308 **95**
Jackson, *Michigan* T56+423 **91**
Jackson, *Minnesota* U30+436 **93**
Jackson, *Mississippi* U01+323 **97**
Jackson, *Missouri* T88+374 **97**
Jackson, *N. Carolina* T15+364 **97**
Jackson, *Ohio* T46+391 **97**
Jackson, *Tennessee* T83+356 **97**
Jackson, *Wyoming* V36+434 **93**
Jackson Mts., *Nevada* V81+414 **92**
Jacksonville, *Florida* T40+303 **97**
Jacksonville, *Illinois* U02+398 **95**
Jacksonville, *N. Carolina* T15+348 **97**
Jacksonville, *Texas* U32+320 **95**
Jacmel, *Haiti* S75+183 **101**
Jacobina, *Brazil* Q63−112 **105**
Jacques Cartier, Mt., *Que.* S36+490 **90**
Jacquet River, *N.B.* S36+479 **90**
Jade Mines, *Burma* F53+256 **71**
Jadib, *Yemen, South* J42+166 **75**
Jaén, *Spain* N22+377 **52**
Jafarabad, *India* H22+209 **70**
Jaffa (Yafo), *Israel* K62+320 **76**
Jaffna, *Sri Lanka* G60+097 **70**
Jagadhri, *India* G76+301 **72**
Jagdispur, *India* G33+254 **73**
Jagodina, *Yugoslavia* L53+440 **58**
Jagraon, *India* G87+308 **72**
Jaguarão, *Brazil* R51−324 **103**

Jaguari, *Brazil* R58–295 **103**
Jaguariaira, *Brazil* R28–242 **105**
Jaguaruna, *Brazil* R24–286 **103**
Jahanabad, *India* G30+252 **73**
Jahangirabad, *India* G71+284 **72**
Jahra, *Kuwait* J74+294 **74**
Jahrum, *Iran* J38+284 **75**
Jaicos, *Brazil* Q66–074 **105**
Jaipur, *India* G84+268 **70**
Jaipur, *India* G21+208 **71**
Jais, *India* G51+263 **73**
Jaisalmer, *India* H24+268 **70**
Jajarm, *Iran* J22+370 **75**
Jakarta, *Java, Indonesia* E79+062 **65**
Jäkkvik, *Sweden* L78+663 **46**
Jakobi, *Estonia* L21+592 **47**
Jakobstad. *See* Pietarsaari
Jalalabad, *Afghanistan* H28+345 **72**
Jalalpur, *India* G44+263 **73**
Jalalpur, *Pakistan* H22+295 **72**
Jalalpur, *Pakistan* H04+327 **72**
Jalapa, *Nicaragua* T65+139 **101**
Jalapa Enriquez, *Mexico* U42+195 **100**
Jalasjärvi, *Finland* L43+625 **46**
Jalaun, *India* G64+260 **73**
Jaldak, *Afghanistan* H50+319 **75**
Jalgaon, *India* G86+210 **70**
Jalisco, state, *Mexico* U80+200 **100**
Jalk, *Iran* H74+276 **75**
Jalor, *India* H14+252 **70**
Jalpaiguri, *India* G07+265 **73**
Jaluit, I., *Marshall Is.* A64+060 **106**
Jamaica, I., *West Indies* T14+181 **101**
Jamaja, *Estonia* L48+580 **47**
Jamalabad, *Iran* J73+373 **74**
Jamalpur, *Bangladesh* G00+249 **73**
Jamalpur, *India* G21+253 **73**
Jamberoo, *New S. Wales* B86–346 **109**
Jambi, *Sumatra, Indonesia* F08-016 **65**
Jamdena, I., *See* Yamdena
James B., *Canada* T30+530 **89**
James Ras., *N. Terr., Aust.* D15–241 **110**
James R., *S. Dakota* U50+442 **98**
James R., *Virginia* T20+377 **97**
Jamesburg, *California* W10+364 **92**
James Ross, I., *Antarctica* R75–640 **27**
Jamestown, *New York* T25+421 **91**
Jamestown & Res., *N. Dakota* U52+469 **93**
Jamestown, *S. Australia* C68–332 **109**
James W. Ellsworth Ld.,
  Antarctica U40–770 **27**
Jamiltepec, *Mexico* U47+162 **100**
Jammer Bugt, *Denmark* M36+573 **47**
Jammu & Kashmir H01+327 **72**
Jammu & Kashmir, *India-Pakistan* H00+350 **70**
Jamnagar, *India* H30+224 **70**
Jampur, *Pakistan* H26+296 **72**
Jamrad, *Afghanistan* H42+331 **75**
Jamrao, *Pakistan* H35+255 **70**
Jämsä *Finland* L29+619 **47**
Jamshedpur, *India* G22+228 **73**
Jamui, *India* G22+249 **73**
Jamuna R., *Bangladesh* G02+250 **73**
Jandaq, *Iran* J34+341 **75**
Jandiala, *India* G89+315 **72**
Janesville, *Wisconsin* T84+427 **95**
Jangipur, *India* G11+245 **73**
Jani Khel, *Pakistan* H27+328 **72**
Janjira, *India* H12+184 **70**
Jan Mayen, I., *Arctic Ocean* N55+710 **62**
Janos, *Mexico* V18+310 **100**
Jansath, *India* G73+293 **72**
Jansenville, *Cape Province* L30–330 **84**
Januaria, *Brazil* Q86–154 **105**
Janze, *France* N09+480 **54**
Jaoho, *China* D06+472 **64**
Jaora, *India* G89+236 **70**
Japan & Sea of, *E. Asia* C60+400 **64**
Japen, I., *See* Yapen I.
Japur R., *Brazil* S45+019 **104**
Japvo Mt., *India* F65+256 **71**
Jaragua, *Brazil* R25–265 **103**
Jaragua, *Brazil* R26–157 **105**
Jarales, *New Mexico* V12+346 **94**
Jaramillo, *Argentina* S43–472 **103**
Jarandilla, *Spain* N34+402 **52**
Jardim, *Brazil* Q40–065 **105**
Jardines de la Reina, *Cuba* T24+211 **101**
Jarji, *Nigeria* M46+108 **80**
Jarocin, *Poland* L75+520 **49**
Jaromer, *Czechoslovakia* L85+504 **49**
Jarosław, *Poland* L44+500 **49**
Järpen, *Sweden* M09+634 **46**
Jarrow, *England* N09+550 **37**
Jarvis I., *Pacific Ocean* Y60–002 **106**
Järvsö, *Sweden* L83+617 **47**
Jashpurnagar, *India* G35+229 **73**
Jask, *Iran* J13+257 **75**
Jason I., *Falkland Is.* S07–510 **103**
Jasper, *Florida* T48+305 **97**
Jasper, *Georgia* T57+345 **97**
Jasper, *Texas* U24+310 **95**
Jasper & Park, *Alberta* V80+533 **88**
Jassy. *See* Iasi.
Jastrowie, *Poland* L79+534 **49**
Jaswantnagar, *India* G66+269 **73**
Jaszberény, *Hungary* L60+475 **49**
Jath, *India* G88+170 **70**
Jativa, *Spain* N03+390 **53**
Jatoba, *Brazil* Q50–092 **105**
Jaú, *Brazil* R21–222 **105**
Jauche, *Belgium* M60+507 **44**
Jauf, *Saudi Arabia* K31+299 **74**
Jauhari, *Saudi Arabia* J46+165 **75**
Jauja, *Peru* T02–117 **104**
Jaumave, *Mexico* U57+234 **100**
Jaunjelgava, *Latvia* L44+258 **73**
Jaunpur, *India* G44+258 **73**
Java, I., *Indonesia* E60–073 **65**
Javari, R., *Peru-Brazil* S78–065 **104**
Javier, I., *Chile* S86–471 **103**
Jawa, *Nigeria* M24+128 **81**
Jawalamukhi, *India* G82+318 **72**
Jayapura, *Indonesia* C57+026 **65**
Jazir, *Oman* J20+186 **75**
Jebba, *Nigeria* M62+090 **80**
Jeble, *Syria* K54+354 **76**
Jech Doab, *Pakistan* H14+321 **72**
Jedabya, *Libya* L58+306 **81**
Jedburgh, *Scotland* N15+555 **41**

Jedede, *Saudi Arabia* K29+218 **74**
Jefferson, *Georgia* T51+341 **97**
Jefferson, *Wisconsin* T82+430 **95**
Jefferson, Mt., *Oregon* W11+446 **92**
Jefferson City, *Missouri* U13+386 **95**
Jeffersonville, *Indiana* T64+383 **97**
Jehol. *See* Chêng-têhshih.
Jekabpils, *Latvia* L25+565 **47**
Jelgava, *Latvia* L37+566 **47**
Jelsava, *Czechoslovakia* L59+486 **49**
Jemeppe, *Belgium* M62+505 **44**
Jena, E. *Germany* M21+509 **48**
Jenin, *Jordan* K58+325 **76**
Jenipapo, *Brazil* R84–064 **104**
Jennings, *Louisiana* U16+302 **95**
Jenolan Caves, *New S. Wales* C00–339 **109**
Jeparit, *Victoria* C48–362 **109**
Jeppo, *Finland* L44+634 **46**
Jerablus, *Syria* K42+368 **76**
Jerash, *Jordan* K55+323 **76**
Jeremie, *Haiti* S84+187 **101**
Jerez, *Mexico* U78+228 **100**
Jerez de la Frontera, *Spain* N37+367 **52**
Jeriban, *Somalia* J66+072 **83**
Jericho, *Jordan* K57+319 **76**
Jericho, *Queensland* C24–234 **111**
Jerilderie, *New S. Wales* C26–354 **109**
Jerome, *Arizona* V43+348 **94**
Jerruck, *Pakistan* H40+250 **70**
Jersey, I., *Channel Is.* N13+492 **54**
Jersey City, *New Jersey* S84+407 **96**
Jerseyshore, *Pennsylvania* T14+412 **96**
Jerusalem, *Israel-Jordan* K59+318 **76**
Jervis B., *New South Wales* B86–351 **109**
Jervois Ra., *N. Terr., Aust.* C83–225 **111**
Jesenik, *Czechoslovakia* L77+503 **49**
Jesselton, *Sabah* E24+060 **65**
Jessore, *Bangladesh* G04+231 **73**
Jesup, *Georgia* T41+316 **97**
Jesus I., *Quebec* S81+457 **91**
Jesus Maria, *Argentina* S25–310 **103**
Jesus Maria, *Mexico* V16+282 **100**
Jetalsar, *India* H26+217 **70**
Jeypore, *India* G44+189 **71**
Jezzin, *Lebanon* K57+335 **76**
Jhal, *Pakistan* H45+282 **70**
Jhalrapatan, *India* G82+246 **70**
Jhang Maghiana, *Pakistan* H16+313 **72**
Jhansi, *India* G68+254 **73**
Jhau, *Pakistan* H56+262 **70**
Jhelum, *Pakistan* H08+330 **72**
Jhelum R., *Pakistan* H14+325 **72**
Jhunjhunu, *India* G87+281 **72**
Jiachan, *Tibet* G53+316 **70**
Jianpur, *India* G40+262 **73**
Jibhalanta, *Mongolia* F49+480 **63**
Jicaro, *Nicaragua* T65+138 **101**
Jičin, *Czechoslovakia* L88+505 **49**
Jidd, *Iraq* K32+328 **74**
Jidda, *Saudi Arabia* K35+215 **74**
Jiggitai L., *Tibet* G19+350 **71**
Jihlava, *Czechoslovakia* L87+494 **49**
Jildiah, Jebel, *Saudi Arabia* K15+277 **74**
Jimena de la Frontera, *Spain* N32+365 **52**
Jimenez, *Mexico* U64+290 **100**
Jimenez, *Mexico* V00+270 **100**
Jimma, *Ethiopia* K48+076 **83**
Jim Thorpe, *Pennsylvania* T05+408 **96**
Jind, *India* G82+293 **72**
Jinotega, *Nicaragua* T66+131 **101**
Jipijapa, *Ecuador* T33–012 **104**
Jirgalanta, *Mongolia* F80+480 **63**
Jirm, *Afghanistan* H25+368 **75**
Jisha, *Saudi Arabia* J61+253 **74**
Jisresh Shughur, *Syria* K52+358 **76**
Jiul R., *Romania* L37+441 **58**
Jiza, *Jordan* K54+317 **76**
João Pessoa, *Brazil* Q28–071 **105**
Jodhpur, *India* H12+263 **70**
Joensuu, *Finland* L01+626 **46**
Jofane, *Mozambique* K64–214 **84**
Jogjakarta, *See* Yogyakarta
Johannesburg, *Transvaal* L12–262 **84**
John o' Groats, *Scotland* N18+586 **40**
Johnsonburg, *Pennsylvania* T22+415 **96**
Johnson City, *Tennessee* T44+363 **97**
Johnston I., *Pacific Ocean* Z28+170 **106**
Johnstown, *Ireland, Rep.* N41+534 **43**
Johnstown, *New York* S85+430 **96**
Johnstown, *Pennsylvania* T24+403 **96**
Johore Baharu, *Malaysia* F08+015 **69**
Joinville, *Brazil* R23–263 **103**
Joinville, *France* M59+484 **54**
Joinville I., *Antarctica* R60–630 **27**
Jokkmökk, *Sweden* L61+666 **46**
Jol Plat., *Saudi Arabia* J65+154 **74**
Joliet, *Illinois* T78+415 **95**
Joliette, *Quebec* S81+460 **91**
Jolo, I., *Philippines* D82+059 **65**
Jonava, *Lithuania* L34+551 **47**
Jonesboro, *Arkansas* U04+358 **95**
Jonesboro, *Georgia* T56+335 **97**
Jonesboro, *Illinois* T86+374 **97**
Jonesboro, *Louisiana* U16+322 **97**
Jonesport, *Maine* S46+445 **90**
Joniškis, *Lithuania* L39+562 **47**
Jönköping, *Sweden* M05+558 **47**
Jonquière, *Quebec* S67+484 **90**
Jonuta, *Mexico* U13+180 **100**
Joplin, *Missouri* U27+372 **95**
Jordan, *Minnesota* U22+447 **93**
Jordan, *Montana* V12+473 **93**
Jordan, S.-W. *Asia* K53+310 **74**
Jordan, R., *Israel* K57+323 **76**
Jordan R., *Utah* V42+407 **94**
Jorhat, *India* F65+267 **71**
Jorje Montt, I., *Chile* S88–513 **103**
Jorna da Del Muerto,
  New Mexico V11+330 **94**
Joseph Bonaparte Gulf,
  W. Australia D40–130 **110**
Jostedalsbre Glacier, *Norway* M47+616 **47**
Jotunheimen, *Norway* M42+615 **34**
Joux, L. de, *Switzerland* M52+466 **45**
Jowai, *India* F54+264 **71**
Juan de Fuca Str.,
  U.S.A.-Canada W20+479 **98**
Juan Fernandez I.,
  Pacific Ocean T25–345 **107**
Juan Stuven, I., *Chile* T00–419 **103**
Juárez, *Argentina* R89–376 **103**

Juarez, *Mexico* U01+188 **100**
Juba, *Sudan* K80+050 **81**
Jubba, *Saudi Arabia* K23+280 **74**
Jubbulpore. *See* Jabalpur
Jubeil, *Lebanon* K56+341 **76**
Jubi, C., *Morocco* N78+280 **80**
Jucaro, *Cuba* T23+216 **101**
Juchitan, *Mexico* U31+164 **100**
Judenburg, *Austria* M02+471 **48**
Judique, *Nova Scotia* S09+459 **90**
Judith, *Montana* V28+477 **93**
Judith Pt., *Rhode Island* S67+414 **91**
Juian, *China* D85+278 **67**
Juichow. *See* Kaoan.
Juist, I., *W. Germany* M48+537 **48**
Juiz de Fora, *Brazil* Q80–217 **105**
Jujuy, *Argentina* S32–242 **103**
Jukao, *China* D86+324 **66**
Jukkasjarvi, *Sweden* L52+679 **34**
Julaco, *Bolivia* S46–209 **104**
Julesburg, *Colorado* U74+410 **94**
Juli, *Peru* S57–162 **104**
Juliaca, *Peru* S61–156 **104**
Julianstown, *Ireland, Rep.* N38+537 **42**
Julio de Castilhos, *Brazil* R52–293 **103**
Jullundur, *India* G86+313 **72**
Jumaima, *Iraq* K08+298 **74**
Jumet, *Belgium* M63+504 **44**
Jumilla, *Spain* N08+385 **53**
Jumin, *Iran* J08+345 **75**
Jumla, *Nepal* G47+293 **73**
Jumna (Yamuna), R., *India* G58+260 **73**
Junagarh, *India* H27+216 **70**
Junan, *China* E33+330 **66**
Junction City, *Kansas* U41+390 **95**
Jundiai, *Brazil* R11–232 **105**
Juneau, *Alaska* W86+585 **99**
Junee, *New South Wales* C14–349 **109**
Jungfrau, mt., *Switzerland* M42+465 **45**
Jungfraujoch, *Switzerland* M42+465 **45**
Jungkiang, *China* E68+259 **67**
Junin, *Argentina* S67–400 **103**
Junin, *Argentina* S06–345 **103**
Junin, *Chile* S61–198 **103**
Junin, *Peru* T06–112 **104**
Juning. *See* Junan
Juniper, *New Brunswick* S43+466 **90**
Juniye, (Jounie) *Lebanon* K56+340 **76**
Junsele, *Sweden* L78+637 **46**
Juojarvi, *Finland* L08+628 **46**
Jupia, *Brazil* R39–208 **105**
Juquila, *Mexico* U45+163 **100**
Jura, dep., *France* M54+467 **54**
Jura, mts., *France-Switz.* M54+463 **54**
Jura I. & Sd. of, *Scotland* N35+560 **41**
Jurado, *Colombia* T17+072 **104**
Jurbarkas, *Lithuania* L43+551 **47**
Jurf ed Darawish, *Jordan* K55+307 **76**
Jüri, *Estonia* L30+594 **47**
Juruá, R., *Brazil* S40–045 **104**
Juruena & R., *Brazil* R83–128 **104**
Juruty, *Brazil* R67–020 **105**
Jusiye, *Syria* K50+344 **76**
Jussy, *Switzerland* M52+462 **45**
Justlahuaco, *Mexico* U48+174 **100**
Justo Daract, *Argentina* S31–338 **103**
Jutahy, *Brazil* S42–027 **104**
Juticalpa, *Honduras* T64+146 **101**
Jutland. *See* Jylland
Juuka, *Finland* L05+632 **46**
Juwain, *Afghanistan* H80+316 **75**
Juwara, *Oman* J16+190 **75**
Jylland, *Denmark* M36+562 **47**
Jylland, South, *Denmark* M36+552 **47**
Jyväskylä, *Finland* L26+623 **46**
K2, Mt, *Kashmir* G81+359 **72**
Kabaena, I., *Indonesia* D79–054 **65**
Kabala, *Sierra Leone* N70+096 **80**
Kabale, *Uganda* L00–014 **83**
Kabalega Falls, *Uganda* K80+020 **83**
Kabba, *Nigeria* M54+078 **80**
Kabia, I., *Indonesia* D87–061 **65**
Kabinda, *Zaire* L32–062 **82**
Kabongo, *Zaire* L26–074 **82**
Kabul & R., *Afghanistan* H34+346 **75**
Kabunda, *Zaire* L04–126 **83**
Kabwe, *Zambia* L10–144 **83**
Kačanik, *Yugoslavia* L53+424 **58**
Kachiry, *Kazakh* G84+530 **62**
Kachkar, *U.S.S.R.* H84+544 **61**
Kachuga, *U.S.S.R.* E84+540 **63**
Kadaura, *India* G61+260 **73**
Kadina, *S. Australia* C74–340 **109**
Kadiri, *India* G70+141 **70**
Kadiyevka, *Ukraine* K39+486 **60**
Kadoka, *S. Dakota* U48+438 **93**
Kadom, *U.S.S.R.* K15+546 **61**
Kadugli, *Sudan* L02+110 **81**
Kaduna, *Nigeria* M46+106 **80**
Kadur, *India* G84+136 **70**
Kadyy, *U.S.S.R.* K11+577 **61**
Kadzand, *Netherlands* M70+514 **44**
Kaesong, *Korea* D52+380 **64**
Kaf, *Saudi Arabia* K46+315 **74**
Kafakumba, *Congo* L38–096 **82**
Kafanchan, *Nigeria* M40+096 **80**
Kafia Kingi, *Sudan* L34+092 **81**
Kafra, *Chad* L44+162 **81**
Kafr Behum, *Syria* K50+351 **76**
Kafrun, *Syria* K52+348 **76**
Kagan, *Uzbek* H63+396 **62**
Kagi. *See* Chiai
Kagmar, *Sudan* K88+144 **81**
Kagoshima, *Japan* D27+316 **68**
Kagoshima B., *Japan* D28+311 **68**
Kagul, *Moldavia* L11+459 **60**
Kahafa, *Saudi Arabia* K10+270 **74**
Kahama, *Tanzania* K74–038 **83**
Kahoka, *Missouri* U10+404 **95**
Kahra, *Yemen* J89+141 **74**
Kahror, *Pakistan* H18+296 **72**
Kahta, *Turkey* K38+381 **74**
Kahuta, *Pakistan* H09+336 **72**
Kai-Kep, *Indonesia* D14–058 **65**
Kaiama, *Nigeria* M66+099 **80**
Kaiapoi, *New Zealand* A44–434 **112**
Kai-chow, *China* E30+357 **66**
Kaieteur Fall, *Guyana* R87+052 **104**
Kai fêng, *China* E33+348 **66**
Kaigo, *Sudan* K80+060 **81**
Kaihwa. *See* Wenshan

Kaikoura, *New Zealand* A38–424 **112**
Kaikoura Ra., *New Zealand* A40–421 **112**
Kailas Ra., *India-Tibet* G78+352 **70**
Kaimanawa Mts., *N.Z.* A24–390 **112**
Kaimganj, *India* G64+275 **73**
Kaimur Ra., *India* G48+245 **73**
Kaipara Harb., *New Zealand* A35–364 **112**
Kaira, *India* H13+226 **70**
Kairana, *India* G77+294 **72**
Kairouan, *Tunisia* M30+358 **81**
Kairovo, *U.S.S.R.* J16+558 **61**
Kaisarie. *See* Kayseri
Kaišedorys, *Lithuania* L33+549 **47**
Kaiserslautern, *W. Germany* M43+494 **48**
Kaiser Wilhelm II Ld.,
  Antarctica G00–670 **27**
Kaitangata, *New Zealand* A61–463 **112**
Kaithal, *India* G81+297 **72**
Kai-yuan, *China* D66+427 **66**
Kajaani, *Finland* L13+642 **46**
Kajado, *Kenya* K50–018 **83**
Kajiki, *Japan* D26+317 **68**
Kajuri Kach, *Pakistan* H31+321 **72**
Kakamari, *Uganda* K64+034 **83**
Kakamega, *Kenya* K60+002 **83**
Kakh, *Iran* J08+342 **75**
Kakhovskoye Vdkhr., *Ukr.* K62+471 **60**
Kakia, *Botswana* L40–248 **84**
Kakisa, L., *N.-W. Terr.* V76+607 **88**
Kakori, *India* G55+269 **73**
Kakoyarra, *New S. Wales* C51–317 **109**
Kaksha, *U.S.S.R.* J80+582 **61**
Kalabagh, *Pakistan* H21+330 **72**
Kalabaka, *Greece* L50+397 **59**
Kalabo, *Zambia* L44–150 **84**
Kalabsha, *Egypt* K74+234 **81**
Kalach, *U.S.S.R.* K24+504 **61**
Kaladan, *Burma* F72+211 **71**
Kalahari Des., *Botswana* L40–238 **84**
Kalajoki, *Finland* L36+643 **46**
Kalakan, *U.S.S.R.* E19+552 **63**
Kalakepen, *Sumatra* F43+028 **65**
Kalámai, *Greece* L47+370 **59**
Kalamata. *See* Kalámai.
Kalamazoo, *Michigan* T63+424 **91**
Kalamboa, *Sudan* L30+126 **81**
Kalamos I., *Greece* L55+386 **59**
Kala Nao, *Afghanistan* H71+350 **75**
Kalanaur, *India* G82+289 **72**
Kalangali, *Tanzania* K66–062 **83**
Kalannie, *W. Australia* E18–302 **110**
Kala Sarkari, *Afghanistan* H46+358 **75**
Kalat, *Pakistan* H50+270 **70**
Kalat-i-Ghilzai, *Afghanistan* H49+320 **75**
Kalat-i-Nadiri, *Iran* J01+371 **75**
Kalaw, *Burma* F50+207 **71**
Kale, *Burma* F62+234 **71**
Kalediran, *Turkey* K74+362 **74**
Kalémié *Zaire* L04–060 **83**
Kalewa, *Burma* F64+232 **71**
Kalgan. *See* Changkiakow
Kalgoorlie, *W. Australia* D82–307 **110**
Kalikino, *U.S.S.R.* J35+528 **61**
Kalimnos, I., *Greece* L19+370 **59**
Kalingapatnam, *India* G35+184 **70**
Kalinin, *U.S.S.R.* K56+568 **60**
Kaliningrad, *U.S.S.R.* L57+547 **47**
Kalinino, *U.S.S.R.* E70+599 **63**
Kalispell, *Montana* V56+479 **98**
Kalisz, *Poland* L71+518 **49**
Kaliua, *Tanzania* K80–050 **83**
Kalix Älv, *Sweden* L56+676 **46**
Kalixfors, *Sweden* L59+677 **46**
Kalka, *India* G78+308 **72**
Kalkaska, *Michigan* T61+448 **91**
Kalkfeld, *Namibia* L84-208 **84**
Kalkfontein, *Botswana* L54–222 **84**
Kalkwerk, *Namibia* L76-268 **84**
Kallavesi, *Finland* L14+628 **46**
Kallim, *Chad* L54+128 **81**
Kalloni, *Greece* L23+392 **59**
Kall Sjön, *Sweden* M12+637 **46**
Kalmar, *Sweden* L82+567 **47**
Kalmar Sund, *Sweden* L82+565 **47**
Kalmykovo, *Kazakh* J50+490 **62**
Kalna, *India* G10+232 **73**
Kalocsa, *Hungary* L66+465 **49**
Kalokhorio, *Cyprus* K72+351 **76**
Kalol, *India* H14+234 **70**
Kalpi, *India* G62+261 **73**
Kaltag, *Alaska* Y50+640 **99**
Kaluga, *U.S.S.R.* K52+545 **60**
Kalule, *Zaire* L24–096 **83**
Kalundborg, *Denmark* M23+557 **47**
Kalundu, *Zambia* L02–104 **83**
Kalutara, *Sri Lanka* G61+065 **70**
Kalvariya, *Lithuania* L41+544 **47**
Kalyan, *India* H11+192 **70**
Kalyazin, *U.S.S.R.* K44+572 **60**
Kama, R., *U.S.S.R.* J22+608 **62**
Kamah, *Labrador* S22+590 **89**
Kamaishi, *Japan* C48+393 **64**
Kamalampaka, *Tanzania* K86–056 **83**
Kamalia, *Pakistan* H08+307 **72**
Kaman, *India* G75+276 **72**
Kamaran, I., *Red Sea* K14+154 **74**
Kamasin, *India* G54+255 **73**
Kamassa, *Cameroon* M10+078 **81**
Kamchatka, *U.S.S.R.* B40+560 **63**
Kamen, *U.S.S.R.* G52+538 **62**
Kamenets Podolskiy, *Ukraine* L21+488 **60**
Kamenskoye, *U.S.S.R.* B00+625 **63**
Kamensk Shakhtinski,
  U.S.S.R. K28+483 **61**
Kamensk Ural'skiy, *U.S.S.R.* H79+564 **61**
Kamet, Mt., *India* G71+316 **70**
Kami Iwani, *Japan* D10+351 **68**
Kamina, *Zaire* L30–088 **82**
Kamloops, *Brit. Columbia* W02+462 **56**
Kamnik, *Yugoslavia* M54+462 **56**
Kamouraska, *Quebec* S59+476 **90**
Kampa Dzong, *Tibet* G09+283 **71**
Kampala, *Uganda* K80+003 **83**
Kampen, *Netherlands* M54+526 **44**
Kampot, *Cambodia* F05+106 **69**
Kamptee, *India* G64+212 **70**
Kamsack, *Saskatchewan* U71+513 **88**
Kamyshin, *U.S.S.R.* J88+501 **61**
Kamyshlov, *U.S.S.R.* H74+568 **61**
Kanab, *Utah* V45+370 **94**
Kannauj, *India* G61+270 **73**

Kanawha, R., W. Virginia T38+382 97
Kanayama, Japan C77+356 68
Kanazawa, Japan C80+366 68
Kanchanaburi, Thailand F33+140 69
Kanchipuram, India G61+126 70
Kanchenjunga, mt., Nepal G11+277 73
Kandahar, Afghanistan H56+316 75
Kandalaksha, U.S.S.R. K73+674 62
Kandaya, Latvia L43+570 47
Kandavu, l., Fiji A10-190 106
Kandhla, India G76+293 72
Kandi, India G11+239 73
Kandole, Zaire L38-034 82
Kandos, New South Wales C00-329 109
Kandy, Sri Lanka G57+073 70
Kane, Pennsylvania T23+416 96
Kane Basin, Greenland S60+790 26
Kanev, Ukraine K81+497 60
Kangan, Iran J47+278 75
Kangar, Malaysia F28+064 69
Kangaroo I., S. Australia C76-358 111
Kangāvar, Iran J72+346 74
Kangmar, Kashmir G70+334 70
Kango, Gabon M30+002 82
Kangpao, China E31+418 66
Kangra, India G82+321 72
Kangsa R., Bangladesh F88+250 71
Kanhsien, China E30+259 67
Kani, Burma F61+224 71
Kaniva, Victoria C53-364 109
Kankakee, Illinois T77+411 95
Kankan, Guinea N56+104 80
Kanker, India G50+202 70
Kankesanturai, Sri Lanka G60+098 70
Kan Kiang, China E28+274 64
Kannus, Finland L37+639 46
Kano, Nigeria M38+118 80
Kanpetlet, Burma F67+214 71
Kanpur, India G58+265 73
Kansas, state, U.S.A. U60+387 98
Kansas R., Kansas U36+390 95
Kansas City, Kansas U28+391 95
Kansas City, Missouri U28+390 95
Kansk, U.S.S.R. F55+563 63
Kansu, prov., China E84+350 66
Kantai, India G28+262 73
Kantchari, Upper Volta M82+124 80
Kanturk, Ireland, Rep. N53+522 43
Kanuma, Japan C61+365 68
Kanus, Namibia L68-278 84
Kanyinchaung, Burma F76+210 71
Kaoan, China E27+284 67
Kao-bang, Indo-China E82+227 69
Kaocheng, China E30+349 66
Kaohsiung, Taiwan D88+226 67
Kaolack, Senegal P06+142 80
Kaolan. See Lanchow
Kao Lu-ang, mt., Thailand F32+086 69
Kaomi, China E01+363 66
Kaoyi, China E31+376 66
Kaoyu, China E03+228 66
Kaoyu Hu, China E04+328 66
Kapal, Kazakh G65+452 62
Kapalu, Kashmir G82+352 72
Kapfenberg, Austria L88+473 48
Kapiri Mposhi, Tanzania L06-140 83
Kapiskau R., Ontario T52+526 89
Kapiti I., New Zealand A31-408 112
Kapoeas, R., Borneo E52+001 65
Kapoeta, Sudan K68+048 81
Kaposvár, Hungary L73+464 58
Kapsabet, Kenya K60+002 83
Kapsukas, Lithuania L40+545 47
Kapunda, S. Australia C66-343 109
Kapurthala, India G88+313 72
Kapuskasing, Ontario T46+496 89
Kara, U.S.S.R. H66+692 62
Kara Sea, U.S.S.R. H00+750 62
Kara Bogaz Gol, Turkmen. J40+413 62
Karabuk, Turkey K74+411 74
Karabuta, Iran J73+370 74
Karacabey, Turkey L10+402 74
Karaca Dagh, Turkey K74+394 74
Karachev, U.S.S.R. K60+531 60
Karachi, Pakistan H47+248 70
Karaga, U.S.S.R. B11+592 63
Karaganda, Kazakh H10+500 62
Karaginskiy Os., U.S.S.R. B05+590 63
Karak, Tibet G67+322 70
Kara Kalpakskaya, Uzbek. J12+430 62
Karakelong, I., Indonesia D49+042 65
Karakoram Ra., Kashmir G84+364 72
Karakose, Turkey K12+398 74
Kara Kum, Turkmen J10+393 62
Kara Kum Can., Turkmen H75+370 75
Karaman, Turkey K71+372 74
Karamea, New Zealand A47-412 112
Karamea Bight, N.Z. A50-413 112
Karamsur Pass, Pakistan H08+368 72
Karand, Iran J82+343 74
Karasa, U.S.S.R. J56+547 61
Karasburg, Namibia L66-282 84
Kara Shahr, Sinkiang, China G22+421 62
Karasjok, Norway L27+694 46
Karatina, Kenya K46-004 83
Karatsu, Japan D30+336 68
Karaul, U.S.S.R. G37+701 62
Karauli, India G78+265 73
Karaurgan, Turkey K17+404 74
Kardam, Tibet G54+304 70
Kardhitsa, Greece L48+394 59
Karelskaya A.S.S.R. (Karelia),
rep., U.S.S.R. K80+642 62
Karenni, Burma F45+194 71
Karesuando, Sweden L45+684 46
Karganrud, Iran J66+379 74
Karghalik, Sinkiang, China G75+379 72
Kargil, Kashmir G83+345 72
Kargopol, U.S.S.R. K36+615 60
Karhal, India G66+270 73
Kariba, Dam & L.,
Zam.- Zimb. L06-164 84
Karibib, Namibia L84-218 84
Karikal, India G61+110 70
Karimata, I., Indonesia E67-015 65
Karin, Somalia J86+108 83
Karis, (Karjaa), Finland L38+601 47
Kariz, Iran H85+349 75
Karkaralinsk, U.S.S.R. G87+495 62
Karkkila, Finland L34+605 47
Karla Marksa, Pik, mt., Tad. H16+372 75

Karl-Marx Stadt,
E. Germany M09+508 48
Karlovac, Yugoslavia L87+455 56
Karlovy Vary, Czechoslovakia M13+502 48
Karlsbad. See Karlovy Vary
Karlsborg, Sweden M03+585 47
Karlshamn, Sweden M01+562 47
Karlskrona, Sweden L86+561 47
Karlsruhe, W. Germany M38+490 48
Karlstad, Sweden M09+595 47
Karlukovo, U.S.S.R. B43+688 63
Karmöy, I., Norway M58+593 47
Karnal, India G78+297 72
Karnataka, India G79+123 70
Karnes, Texas U47+289 94
Karnten, prov., Austria M06+467 48
Karona Fall, Guyana R8°+040 104
Karoonda, S. Australia C61-352 109
Karora, Sudan K40+176 83
Karpáthos, I. & Str., Greece L17+356 59
Karperon, Greece L50+400 59
Karroo Great, Cape Province L46-326 84
Kars, Turkey K12+406 74
Karsakpai, Kazakh H50+480 62
Kärsämäki, Finland L25+640 46
Kärsava,.Latvia L14+568 47
Karshi, Uzbek H56+388 62
Karstula, Finland L31+629 46
Karsun, U.S.S.R. J78+542 61
Kartaly, U.S.S.R. H86+530 61
Kartapur, India G87+314 72
Kartse, Kashmir G83+343 72
Karungi, Sweden L37+661 46
Karungu, Kenya K66-010 83
Karunki, Finland L36+661 46
Karur, India G71+112 70
Karvina, Czechoslovakia L69+498 49
Karwar, India H05+149 70
Karymskoye, U.S.S.R. E34+517 63
Kasai R., Zaire L60-034 82
Kasama, Zambia K82-104 83
Kasanga, Tanzania K84-084 83
Kasauli, India G40+099 70
Kasba L., N.-W. Territories U74+604 88
Kasempa, Zambia L26-134 82
Kasenga, Zaire L08-106 83
Kasenga, Zambia L20-158 84
Kasganj, India G68+278 73
Kashan, Iran J53+340 75
Kashgar, China G83+395 62
Kashing,.China D85+308 66
Kashira, U.S.S.R. K40+548 60
Kashiwazaki, Japan C68+374 68
Kashmir, see Jammu and Kashmir
Kashmor, Pakistan H32+283 70
Kasimov, U.S.S.R. K22+549 61
Kasinka, Botswana L34-184 84
Kaskinen, (Kasko) Finland L53+624 46
Kasongo, Zaire L20-044 82
Kásos, I., Greece L19+354 59
Kásós Str., Crete L20+352 59
Kaspichan, Bulgaria L17+433 58
Kassala, Sudan K52+154 83
Kassandra, Greece L39+400 59
Kassel, W. Germany M33+515 48
Kastamonu, Turkey K66+414 74
Kastélli, Crete L38+355 59
Kasterlee, Belgium M60+512 44
Kastoria, Greece L53+405 59
Kastrosikiá, Greece L56+391 59
Kasulu, Tanzania L00-046 83
Kasungu, Malawi K70-132 83
Kasur, Pakistan H03+311 72
Katahdin, Mt., Maine S53+459 90
Katahdin Iron Works, Maine S55+455 90
Katákolon, Greece L52+377 59
Katanga, See Shaba
Katanning, W. Australia E14-336 110
Katav Ivanovsk, U.S.S.R. J11+548 61
Katerini, Greece L45+403 59
Katha, Burma F52+242 71
Kathawachaga, L., N.-W.T. V40+661 88
Katherine, N. Terr., Aust. D16-144 110
Kathmandu, Nepal G28+277 73
Kathua, Kashmir G87+324 72
Katihar, India G14+256 73
Katmai Vol., Alaska T32+580 99
Kato Akhaia, Greece L51+381 59
Káto Nevrokópion, Greece L37+413 58
Katoomba, New S. Wales B88-338 109
Katowice, Poland L66+503 49
Katrine, L., Scotland N27+563 41
Katrineholm, Sweden L83+590 47
Katsina, Nigeria M44+128 80
Kattegat, Sweden-Denmark M24+570 47
Kattowitz. See Katowice
Katwa, India G11+236 236 73
Katwewe, Zaire L10-084 83
Katwijk-aan-Zee, Netherlands M64+522 44
Kauai, I., Hawaii Y58+220 107
Kaufbeuren, W. Germany M26+478 48
Kauhava, Finland L42+631 46
Kaukauna, Wisconsin T80+443 91
Kaunas, Lithuania L36+549 47
Kauriya, India G44+212 71
Kautokeino, Norway L42+689 46
Kavak, Turkey K54+411 74
Kavali, India G60+150 70
Kaválla, India L33+411 58
Kaválla, Greece L34+409 59
Kavkas, Bolshoi & Maly, mts.,
U.S.S.R. K80+415 62
Kawakawa, New Zealand A35-354 112
Kawambwa, Zambia L06-098 83
Kawanoe, Japan D08+340 68
Kawardha, India G53+220 73
Kawasaki, Japan C62+355 68
Kawhia, New Zealand A31-381 112
Kawich Ra., Nevada V71+379 92
Kawkareik, Burma F40+165 71
Kaw Peunan, Thailand F30+097 69
Kaw Samui, Thailand F30+094 69
Kayes, Mali N68+142 80
Kayseri, Turkey K58+387 74
Kaysville, Utah V42+410 94
Kazachye, U.S.S.R. C82+707 63
Kazakhskaya, rep., U.S.S.R. H60+470 62
Kazalinsk, Kazakh H78+457 62
Kazan, U.S.S.R. J66+558 61
Kazanlûk, Bulgaria L28+426 58
Kazérun, Iran J50+296 75

Kazvin, Iran J60+363 74
Kdyne, Czechoslovakia M12+494 48
Kéa (Tziá), I., Greece L34+374 59
Kearney, Nebraska U54+406 95
Keban Maden, Turkey K38+388 74
Ke-bao I., Vietnam E75+212 69
Kecharma, Niger M12+172 81
Kechika R., Brit. Columbia W40+588 88
Kecskemét, Hungary L62+469 49
Kedainiai, Lithuania L36+553 47
Kedgwick, New Brunswick S44+476 90
Kediri, Java, Indonesia E48-079 65
Keele Pk., N.-W. Terr. W60+637 88
Keele R., N.-W. Territories W38+642 88
Keelung (Chilung), Taiwan D80+251 67
Keene, New Hampshire S74+429 96
Keeper Hill, Ireland, Rep. N50+527 43
Keeseville, New York S81+445 91
Keetmanshoop, Namibia L72-266 84
Keewatin, Dist., N.-W. Terr. — 88-89
Keewong, New S. Wales C30-323 109
Kefallinia, Greece L57+382 59
Kegaska, Quebec S07+502 9
Keighley, England N11+539 37
Keila, Estonia L33+593 47
Keita, Chad L42+174 81
Keitele, Finland L22+631 46
Keith, Scotland N18+575 40
Keith, S. Australia C58-361 109
Keith B., N.-W. Territories W10+654 88
Kelamet, Ethiopia K38+160 83
Kelang, Malaysia F22+031 69
Kelcyre, Albania L59+403 59
Kellet, C., N.-W. Terr. W32+718 88
Kelloselkä, Finland L01+670 34
Kells, Ireland, Rep. N41+537 42
Kelme, Lithuania L42+557 47
Kelowna, British Columbia V86+500 88
Kelso, Scotland N15+556 41
Kem, Karelia, U.S.S.R. K62+651 62
Ké Macina, Mali N32+140 80
Kemal Paşa, Turkey L16+383 74
Kemerovo, U.S.S.R. G24+553 62
Kemi, Finland L33+657 46
Kemijärvi Finland L15+667 46
Kemijoki, Finland L28+662 46
Kemmerer, Wyoming V34+418 93
Kemp, L., Texas U55+336 95
Kemp Ld., Antarctica J05-670 27
Kempele, Finland L27+649 46
Kempsey, New South Wales B74-311 109
Kempt L., Quebec S86+475 91
Kempten, W. Germany M28+477 48
Kenai Pen., Alaska Y00+605 99
Kendal, England N16+543 37
Kendall, New York T18+333 96
Kendall, C., N.-W. Terr. T72+640 89
Kendari, Celebes,. D75-038 65
Kendawangan, Borneo E59-024 65
Kenema, Sierra Leone N68+080 80
Ken-tung, Burma B32+212 71
Kenhardt, Cape Province L52-292 84
Kenilworth, England N09+524 37
Kenitra, Morocco N40+344 80
Kenmare, N. Dakota U72+487 93
Kanmare & R., Ireland, Rep. N58+519 43
Kenmore, Scotland N24+566 41
Kennebec, S. Dakota U59+439 93
Kennebec R., Maine S59+443 90
Kennebunk, Maine S63+434 96
Kennet R., England N06+514 39
Kennett, Missouri U01+363 97
Kenogami & L., Quebec S68+483 91
Keno Hill, Yukon X01+643 88
Kenora, Ontario U27+499 88
Kenosha, Wisconsin T77+426 95
Kensington, Prince Edward I. S21+464 90
Kent, New Brunswick S32+466 90
Kent, co., England M86+512 39
Kent I., Maryland T08+389 96
Kent Peninsula, N.-W.
Territories V15+680 88
Kentford, England M87+523 39
Kentucky, state, U.S.A. T70+374 99
Kentucky L., N. Dakota T78+362 95
Kentville, Nova Scotia S27+450 90
Kenya, E. Africa K40+010 83
Kenya, Mt., Kenya K46-004 83
Keokuk, Iowa U08+404 95
Keonjhar, India G26+215 71
Keos (Tzia). See Kea, I.
Kepler Mts., New Zealand A76-454 112
Keppel, I., Falkland Is. S00-512 103
Kerala, state, India G80+100 70
Kerang, Victoria C37-357 109
Kerava, Finland L29+604 47
Kerch, U.S.S.R. K51+454 60
Kerchoual, Mali M88+170 80
Keren, Ethiopia K40+158 83
Kerena, Papua New Guinea C26-081 111
Kerguelen Is., Indian Ocean H30-495 77
Kericho, Kenya K58-004 83
Kerinci, mt., Sumatra F22-016 65
Kerkenbosch. See Zuidwolde
Kerkenna Is., Tunisia M24+346 81
Kerki, Turkmen. H58+377 62
Kérkira & I., Greece L61+396 59
Kerkrade, Netherlands M54+509 44
Kermadec Is., Pacific Ocean Z80-295 106
Kermán, Iran J17+303 75
Kerman Desert, Iran J04+290 75
Kermanshah, Iran J77+343 74
Kerry, co., Ireland, Rep. N58+520 43
Kerry Hd., Ireland, Rep. N60+524 43
Kerzers, Switzerland M47+470 45
Kesagami L., Ontario T30+502 89
Kesariya, India G30+264 73
Kesteren, Netherlands M57+519 44
Kestilä, Finland L22+644 46
Keswick, England N19+546 37
Keszthely, Hungary L76+468 49
Ketapang, Borneo E60-017 65
Ketchikan, Alaska W65+555 99
Ketrzyn, Poland L52+541 49
Kettering, England N04+524 37
Keuka L., New York T13+425 96
Kewanee, Illinois U00+412 95
Kewaunee, Wisconsin T75+445 91
Keweenaw B., Michigan T80+469 91
Keweenaw Pen., Wisconsin T84+466 99

Key L., Ireland, Rep. N50+540 42
Key Harbour, Ontario T34+459 91
Key Largo, Florida T32+251 97
Keyser, W. Virginia T24+395 96
Keysville, Virginia T21+371 97
Key West, Florida T41+246 97
Kezhma, U.S.S.R. F24+590 63
Khabab, Syria K52+330 76
Khabarovsk, U.S.S.R. D00+483 63
Khaburah, Oman J18+240 75
Khadasan, Mongolia F06+478 64
Khadhra, Saudi Arabia K09+285 74
Khadro, Pakistan H37+261 70
Khafs Maqran, Saudi Arabia J83+214 74
Khagaul, India G29+255 73
Khaibar, Saudi Arabia K33+258 74
Khairabad, India G55+274 73
Khairpur, Pakistan H37+275 70
Khairpur, Pakistan H16+296 72
Khaiwan, Yemen K07+165 74
Khalis-ed-Daff, Saudi Arabia K35+220 74
Khalki, I., Greece L14+362 59
Khalkidhki, Greece L40+404 59
Khalkis, Greece L38+385 59
Khal-Mer-Sede, U.S.S.R. G69+675 62
Khalturin, U.S.S.R. J66+586 61
Khaluf, Saudi Arabia J12+204 75
Kham, Iran J25+290 75
Khambat, G. of, H14 + 223 70
Khamiab, Afghanistan H55+374 75
Khamis, Mushait,
Saudi Arabia K10+183 74
Kham-kheut, Laos F03+182 69
Khamr, Yemen K06+161 74
Khanabad, Afghanistan H35+367 75
Khanaqin, Iraq J88+344 74
Khān Baghdādi, Iraq K14+339 74
Khandela, India G87+275 72
Khandwa, India G81+218 70
Khan-ez-Zebib, Jordan K53+315 76
Khanfar, Yemen, South J89 + 133 74
Khangai Shan, Mongolia F50+480 31
Khangarh, Pakistan H23+299 72
Khanh-hoa, Vietnam E66 + 122 69
Khania, Crete L36+355 59
Khaniadhana, India G71+250 73
Khanka Oz., U.S.S.R. D15+449 63
Khanntor, Syria K47+344 76
Khanpur, Pakistan H26+286 72
Khan Sheikhun, Syria K50+354 76
Khan Tengri, Kirgiz. G58+420 62
Khanty Mansiysk, U.S.S.R. H35+610 62
Khanu, Iran J13+280 75
Khan Yunis, Egypt K64+314 76
Kharaghoda, India H19+232 70
Kharan, Pakistan H57+285 70
Kharar, India G13+227 73
Kharkov, Ukraine K53+500 60
Kharmanli, Bulgaria L25+419 58
Kharovsk, U.S.S.R. K29+599 60
Kharsawan, India G25+228 73
Khartaksho, Kashmir G83+349 72
Khartoum, Sudan K74+156 81
Khasab, U.A.E. J23+262 75
Khasfa, Saudi Arabia J35+197 75
Khasi Hills, India F80+254 71
Khaskovo, Bulgaria L27+419 58
Khasmel Girba, Sudan K56+150 81
Khatanga, U.S.S.R. F16+721 63
Khatangsky Guba, U.S.S.R. E50+745 63
Kheralu, India H14+236 70
Kheri, India G55+279 73
Kherlen R., Mongolia E44+480 64
Kherson, Ukraine K74+466 60
Khetri, India G85+280 72
Khilok, U.S.S.R. E56+515 63
Khinis, Turkey K19+394 74
Khinjan, Afghanistan H37+355 75
Khios & I., Greece L24+384 59
Khisfin, Syria K55+329 76
Khiva, Uzbek H86+413 62
Khmel'nitskiy, Ukraine L18+494 60
Khmer, See Cambodia
Kholm, U.S.S.R. K83+572 60
Kholmsk, U.S.S.R. C47+469 63
Không, Laos E84+139 69
Khor, U.S.S.R. D00+479 63
Khóra Sfakion, Crete L35+352 59
Khor Dhahiya, Saudi Arabia J50+189 75
Khor Kalba, Saudi Arabia J22+252 75
Khorramabad, Iran J70+336 74
Khormali, China G04+452 64
Khorramshahr, Iran J70+305 74
Khotan, Sinkiang, China G61+369 62
Khrisoúpolis, Greece L32+410 58
Khrojna, Bulgaria L32+410 58
Khudhfiya, Saudi Arabia J53+190 75
Khujur, Iran J69+358 74
Khumain, Iran J59+338 75
Khungcha, Burma F71+218 71
Khunsar, Iran J58+332 75
Khur, Iran J09+329 75
Khur, Iran J30+338 75
Khurai, India G70+241 73
Khurja, India G73+282 72
Khurma, Saudi Arabia K17+218 74
Khusf, Iran J06+328 75
Khushab, Pakistan H16+323 72
Khushab, Pakistan H16+323 72
Khvalynsk, U.S.S.R. J72+525 61
Khvoy, Iran K00+386 74
Khyber Pass, Pakistan H23+340 72
Kiama, New South Wales B86-347 109
Kiambi, Zaire L20-056 82
Kiambi, Zaire L12-074 83
Kiamichi Mts., Oklahoma U28+346 95
Kian, China E30+271 67
Kiangchow. See Kiangling
Kiangling, China E80+296 67
Kiangpeh, China E80+296 67
Kiangsi, prov., China E24+274 67
Kiangsu, prov., China E00+332 66
Kiangtu. See Yangchow
Kiangyin, China D88+317 66
Kiantajarvi, Finland L05+650 46
Kiao-chow B., China B88+360 66
Kiaohsien, China D89+362 66
Kiating. See Loshan
Kibangula, Zaire L16-048 82
Kibombo, Zaire L24-040 82

Kibondo, *Tanzania* K86–036 **83**
Kicevo, *Yugoslavia* L54+415 **58**
Kichiga, *U.S.S.R.* B09+598 **63**
Kichiginsk, *U.S.S.R.* H82+545 **61**
Kicking Horse Pass, *Alberta* V68+512 **88**
Kidal, *Mali* M82+182 **80**
Kidderminster, *England* N14+524 **37**
Kidnappers, C., *New Zealand* A17–396 **112**
Kidodi, *Tanzania* K48–076 **83**
Kiel, *W. Germany* M29+543 **48**
Kiel (Nord-Ostsee) Kanal.
　W. Germany M35+540 **84**
Kielce, *Poland* L56+510 **49**
Kieldrecht, *Belgium* M65+513 **44**
Kieler Bucht, *W. Germany* M27+545 **48**
Kienchang. See Nancheng
Kiencheng, *China* E62+282 **67**
Kienko, *China* E87+321 **66**
Kienning. See Kienow
Kienow, *China* E09+271 **67**
Kienping, *China* E02+419 **66**
Kienshui, *China* F13+237 **64**
Kienteh, *China* E03+296 **67**
Kiev. See Kiyev
Kiffa, *Mauritania* N68+166 **80**
Kigali, *Rwanda* L00–020 **83**
Kiganga, *Tanzania* K60–078 **83**
Kigoma, *Tanzania* L02–048 **83**
Kihsien, *China* E16+401 **66**
Kii Chan., *Japan* D00+336 **68**
Kijabe, *Kenya* K50–010 **83**
Kikhchik, *U.S.S.R.* B53+535 **63**
Kikinda, *Yugoslavia* L57+458 **58**
Kikkertaksoak I., *Quebec* S27+603 **89**
Kiklådhes, Is., *Greece* L30+370 **59**
Kikori & R., *Papua New Guinea* C35–074 **111**
Kikwit, *Zaire* L66–054 **82**
Kila Drosh, (Drosh), *Pak.* H19+355 **72**
Kilbeggan, *Ireland, Rep.* N45+534 **43**
Kilbourn, *Wisconsin* T89+437 **91**
Kilbrennan Sd., *Scotland* N33+556 **41**
Kilchu, *Korea* D34+410 **64**
Kilcormac, *Ireland, Rep.* N46+532 **43**
Kilcullen, *Ireland, Rep.* N40+531 **43**
Kildare & co., *Ireland, Rep.* N41+532 **43**
Kilfrinnane, *Ireland, Rep.* N51+524 **43**
Kilgarvan, *Ireland, Rep.* N57+519 **43**
Kilian, *China* G73+372 **72**
Kilifi, *Kenya* K30–036 **83**
Kilimanjaro Mt., *Tanzania* K46–030 **83**
Kilindini, *Kenya* K32–040 **83**
Kilkee, *Ireland, Rep.* N58+527 **43**
Kilkeel, *N. Ireland* N36+540 **42**
Kilkenny & co., *Ireland, Rep.* N43+526 **43**
Kilkieran B., *Ireland, Rep.* N58+533 **43**
Kilkis, *Greece* L44+411 **58**
Kilkis, *Greece* L43+409 **59**
Kilkivan, *Queensland* B77–260 **111**
Kill, *Ireland, Rep.* N39+533 **43**
Killala B., *Ireland, Rep.* N55+542 **42**
Killaloe, *Ireland, Rep.* N51+528 **43**
Killarney, *Ireland, Rep.* N57+520 **43**
Killarney, *Ontario* T39+460 **91**
Killary Harb., *Ireland, Rep.* N60+536 **42**
Killashandra, *Ireland, Rep.* N45+540 **42**
Killiecrankie, Pass of,
　Scotland N22+568 **41**
Killimor, *Ireland, Rep.* N50+532 **43**
Killin, *Scotland* N26+565 **41**
Killini, *Greece* L53+379 **59**
Killorglin, *Ireland, Rep.* N59+521 **43**
Killybegs, *Ireland, Rep.* N51+546 **42**
Killyleagh, *N. Ireland* N34+544 **42**
Kilmacthomas, *Ireland, Rep.* N45+522 **43**
Kilmallock, *Ireland, Rep.* N51+524 **43**
Kilmarnock, *Scotland* N27+556 **41**
Kilmore, *Victoria* C30–373 **109**
Kilosa, *Tanzania* K48–068 **83**
Kilrea, *N. Ireland* N39+549 **42**
Kilrush, *Ireland, Rep.* N57+526 **43**
Kilsyth, *Scotland* N24+560 **41**
Kiltamagh, *Ireland, Rep.* N54+538 **42**
Kilwa Kivinje, *Tanzania* K34–088 **83**
Kilwinning, *Scotland* N28+557 **41**
Kima, *Zaire* L18–016 **82**
Kimball, *S. Dakota* U54+437 **93**
Kimberley, *Cape Province* L32–288 **84**
Kimi, *Greece* L35+386 **59**
Kimito, (Kemiö), *Finland* L44+601 **47**
Kimolos, I., *Greece* L33+368 **59**
Kimvula, *Zaire* L84–058 **82**
Kinabulu, mt., *Sabah* E20+062 **65**
Kinbrace, *Scotland* N24+583 **40**
Kincardine, *Ontario* T40+442 **91**
Kincardine, *Scotland* N14+569 **40**
Kincardine-on-Forth, *Scot.* N22+561 **41**
Kinchow Wan, *China* D80+391 **66**
Kincraig, *Scotland* N24+571 **40**
Kindat, *Burma* F63+237 **71**
Kindersley, *Saskatchewan* V22+512 **88**
Kindia, *Guinea* N76+100 **80**
Kindu-Port Empain, *Zaire* L24–030 **82**
Kinel, *U.S.S.R.* J56+532 **61**
Kinel Cherkkassy, *U.S.S.R.* J49+535 **61**
Kineo, *Maine* S58+457 **90**
Kineshma, *U.S.S.R.* K17+575 **61**
King I., *Burma* F40+125 **71**
King I., *Tasmania* C36–400 **111**
King and Queen, *Virginia* T11+376 **97**
King Christian IX Ld.,
　Greenland Q10+680 **26**
King Edward VIII Fall,
　Guyana R88+056 **104**
King Edward VII Land,
　Antarctica Y40–770 **27**
Kingfisher, *Oklahoma* U48+358 **95**
King Frederick VIII Ld.,
　Greenland P40+790 **26**
King Frederick VI Ld.,
　Greenland Q70+630 **26**
Kingfu, *China* F04+284 **64**
King George I.,
　South Shetlands R75–620 **27**
King George Is., *Pacific Oc.* X60–150 **107**
Kidal, *Mali* M82+182 **80**
King George, Mt, *B.C.* V61+504 **88**
King George Sd., *W. Aust.* E10–351 **110**
Kidnappers V Ld., *Antarc.* C00–790 **27**
King George VI Sd., *Antarc.* S50–700 **27**
King George VI Falls,
　Guyana S08+058 **104**

Kingku, *China* F25+236 **64**
King Leopold Ra., *W. Aust.* D60–170 **110**
King Leopold & Queen Astrid
　Coast, *Antarctica* G40–670 **27**
Kingman, *Kansas* U49+376 **95**
Kingmen, *China* E47+310 **66**
Kings Pk., *Utah* V32+407 **94**
Kingsbridge, *England* N23+503 **38**
King's Canyon Nat. Park,
　California V84+371 **92**
Kingsclere, *England* N08+513 **39**
Kingscote, *S. Australia* C74–356 **109**
Kingscourt, *Ireland, Rep.* N41+539 **42**
King's Lynn, *England* M88+528 **39**
King Sound, *W. Australia* D70–166 **110**
Kingsport, *Tennessee* T46+366 **97**
Kingston, *Jamaica* T11+179 **101**
Kingston, *New York* S84+419 **96**
Kingston, *New Zealand* A68–453 **112**
Kingston, *S. Australia* C61–368 **109**
Kingston, *Ontario* T09+443 **91**
Kingston Ra., *California* V71+366 **92**
Kingston-on-Thames, *Eng.* N02+514 **39**
Kingstree, *S. Carolina* T29+336 **97**
Kingswear, *England* N21+503 **38**
Kingtung, *China* F24+243 **64**
Kingushi, *Zaire* L80–052 **82**
Kingussie, *Scotland* N24+571 **40**
King William I., *N.-W. Terr.* U45+684 **88**
King William Ld., *Greenland* P40+750 **26**
Kingwood, *W. Virginia* T28+395 **91**
Kingyang, *China* E74+361 **66**
Kingyüan, See Ishan
Kinhsien, *China* D80+391 **66**
Kinhwa, *China* E02+291 **67**
Kinki, *China* E83+378 **66**
Kinlochewe, *Scotland* N32+576 **40**
Kinlochleven, *Scotland* N30+567 **41**
Kinloch Rannoch, *Scotland* N25+567 **41**
Kinross, *Scotland* N21+562 **41**
Kinsale, *Ireland, Rep.* N51+517 **43**
Kinsale, Old Hd. of, *Ireland,*
　Rep. N51+516 **43**
Kinshasa, *Zaire* L88–044 **82**
Kintap, *Borneo* E29–038 **65**
Kintyre, *Scotland* N34+556 **41**
Kintyre, Mull of, *Scotland* N35+553 **41**
Kinvarra, *Ireland, Rep.* N54+531 **43**
Kinyangiri, *Tanzania* K62–044 **83**
Kiowa, *Kansas* U51+370 **95**
Kiparissia. *Greece* L50+372 **59**
Kiparissia, G. of, *Greece* L52+374 **59**
Kipawa & L., *Quebec* T24+468 **91**
Kipini, *Kenya* K26–026 **83**
Kirá Panayiá, *Greece* see Pélagos, I.
Kirchberg, *Switzerland* M45+471 **45**
Kirensk, *U.S.S.R.* E72+580 **63**
Kirgizskaya, rep., *U.S.S.R.* H10+420 **62**
Kiribati, *Pac. Oc.* A35+007 **106**
Kirin, *China* D50+438 **64**
Kirit, *Somalia* J84+088 **83**
Kiriwina I.,
　Papua New Guinea B84–086 **111**
Kirkagac, *Turkey* L14+390 **74**
Kirkby Lonsdale, *England* N16+542 **37**
Kirkcaldy, *Scotland* N19+561 **41**
Kirkcudbright., *Scot.*, N24+548 **41**
Kirkee, *India* H06+186 **70**
Kirkenes, *Norway* L00+697 **46**
Kirkintilloch, *Scotland* N25+559 **41**
Kirkland Lake, *Ontario* T30+482 **91**
Kirksville, *Missouri* U16+402 **95**
Kirkuk, *Iraq* K04+357 **74**
Kirkwall, *Orkney, Scot.* N18+590 **40**
Kirong Dzong, *Nepal* G28+284 **73**
Kirov, *U.S.S.R.* K64+541 **60**
Kirov, *U.S.S.R.* J62+586 **61**
Kirovgrad, *U.S.S.R.* J01+574 **61**
Kirovograd, *Ukraine* K77+486 **60**
Kirovsk, *U.S.S.R.* K67+675 **62**
Kirriemuir, *Scotland* N18+567 **41**
Kirsanov, *U.S.S.R.* K14+526 **61**
Kirsehir, *Turkey* K65+391 **74**
Kirthar Ra., *Pakistan* H46+270 **70**
Kirun. See Chilung
Kiruna, *Sweden* L58+678 **46**
Kisamba, *Zaire* L36–074 **82**
Kisbér, *Hungary* L72+475 **49**
Kisangani, *Zaire* L28+006 **82**
Kishanganj, *India* G12+261 **73**
Kishangarh, *India* H01+264 **70**
Kishangarh, *India* H27+279 **72**
Kishi, *Nigeria* M66+090 **80**
Kishinev, *Moldavia* L07+470 **60**
Kishtwar, *Kashmir* G85+333 **72**
Kisii, *Kenya* K62–008 **83**
Kisiju, *Tanzania* K34–074 **83**
Kiska, I., *Aleutian Is.* A15+511 **99**
Kiskisink, *Quebec* S73+479 **90**
Kiskunfélégyháza, *Hungary* L61+467 **49**
Kismayu. See Chisimaio
Kispest, *Hungary* L65+475 **49**
Kissaraing I., *Burma* F39+118 **71**
Kissidougou, *Guinea* N60+092 **80**
Kisujszallás, *Hungary* L55+472 **49**
Kisumu, *Kenya* K60–002 **83**
Kisvárda, *Hungary* L48+482 **49**
Kiswe, *Syria* K52+333 **76**
Kita, *Mali* N56+130 **80**
Kitab, *Uzbek.* H48+390 **62**
Kitakyushu, *Japan* D25+338 **68**
Kitchener, *Ontario* T33+434 **91**
Kitchioh, *China* E25+228 **67**
Kitgum, *Uganda* K72+030 **83**
Kithira I., *Greece* L42+363 **59**
Kithirai Chan, *Greece* L42+360 **59**
Kithnos, I., *Greece* L33+374 **59**
Kitima, *Cyprus* K76+348 **76**
Kittanning, *Pennsylvania* T28+408 **96**
Kittatinny Mts., *New Jersey* S89+411 **96**
Kittila, *Finland* L30+676 **46**
Kitui, *Kenya* K42–012 **83**
Kityang, *China* E22+235 **67**
Kitzingen, *W. Germany* M29+497 **48**
Kiuchuan, *China* F38+397 **64**
Kiungchow. See Kiungshan
Kiungchow Str. See Hai Nan
Kiungchow Hai Hsia,
　China E60+202 **67**
Kiungshan, *Hainan I.. China* E57+200 **67**
Kiuruvesi, *Finland* L20+637 **46**

Kivijarvi, *Finland* L29+632 **46**
Kivu L., *Zaire-Rwanda* L06–020 **83**
Kiwai I., *Papua New Guinea* C39–087 **111**
Kiyev, *Ukraine* K87+505 **60**
Kiyma, *Kazakh* H44+518 **62**
Kizel, *U.S.S.R.* J23+592 **62**
Kizil Irmak, *Turkey* K68+400 **74**
Kizil Jilga, *Kashmir* K65+353 **70**
Kizyl Arvat, *Turkmen* J24+390 **62**
Kjerringøy, *Norway* M02+675 **46**
Kladanj, *Yugoslavia* L68+442 **58**
Kladno, *Czechoslovakia* M06+501 **48**
Klagenfurt, *Austria* M04+466 **48**
Klaipeda, *Lithuania* L53+558 **47**
Klamath R., *California* W22+414 **92**
Klamath Falls, *Oregon* W11+422 **92**
Klamath Mts., *California* W18+414 **92**
Klang, See Kelang
Klar Älv, *Sweden* M12+607 **47**
Klerksdorp, *Transvaal* L20–268 **84**
Kleszczele, *Poland* L40+525 **49**
Klimpfjall, *Sweden* M01+650 **46**
Klisura, *Bulgaria* L33+427 **58**
Kliuchi, *U.S.S.R.* J89+526 **61**
Ključ, *Yugoslavia* L79+445 **56**
Klodawa, *Poland* L66+523 **49**
Klofta, *Norway* M23+601 **47**
Klomnice, *Poland* L64+510 **49**
Klondike R., *Yukon* X15+642 **88**
Kloosterzande, *Netherlands* M66+513 **44**
Klosters, *Switzerland* M31+469 **45**
Kluane, L., *Yukon* X22+610 **88**
Klundert, *Netherlands* M63+517 **44**
Knighton, *Wales* N18+523 **38**
Knin, *Yugoslavia* L83+440 **56**
Knob, C., *W. Australia* E05–345 **110**
Knobel, *Arkansas* U04+364 **97**
Knockboy, *Ireland, Rep.* N57+518 **43**
Knockbrack, *Ireland, Rep.* N57+519 **43**
Knockmealdown Mts.,
　Ireland, Rep. N48+522 **43**
Knockower, *Ireland, Rep.* N58+517 **43**
Knokke, *Belgium* M70+513 **44**
Knox, *Pennsylvania* T28+412 **96**
Knox Coast, *Antarctica* F10–660 **27**
Knoxville, *Iowa* U18+412 **95**
Knoxville, *Tennessee* T54+360 **97**
Knysna, *Cape Province* L40–304 **84**
Knyszyn, *Poland* L43+534 **49**
Kobarid, *Yugoslavia* M09+463 **56**
Kōbe, *Japan* C88+348 **68**
København, *Denmark* M14+557 **47**
Koblenz, *W. Germany* M45+504 **48**
Kobrin, *Byelorussia* L34+522 **60**
Kobroör, I., *Indonesia* D02–063 **65**
Kocaeli. See Izmit
Kočane, *Yugoslavia* L46+419 **58**
Kočevje, *Yugoslavia* M01+456 **56**
Kochi, *Japan* D09+335 **68**
Kochiki Retto, *Japan* D32+317 **68**
Kochow. See Mowming
Kodavere, *Estonia* L17+587 **47**
Kodiak & I., *Alaska* Y20+578 **99**
Koeala (Kuala), *Sumatra* F40+034 **65**
Koemai, *Borneo* E50–026 **65**
Koepang (Kupang), *Timor I.,*
　Indonesia D69–102 **65**
Koetai, R., *Borneo* E26+004 **65**
Koffiefontein, *Orange Free*
　State L30–294 **84**
Koforidua, *Ghana* N02+062 **80**
Kofu, *Japan* C68+356 **68**
Kogaluk R., *Quebec* T05+594 **89**
Kohat, *Pakistan* H21+336 **72**
Koh Chang, *Thailand* F16+120 **69**
Kohima, *India* F65+257 **71**
Koh Kong, *Cambodia* F12+113 **69**
Koh Kut, *Thailand* F15+116 **69**
Koh Rong, *Cambodia* F10+107 **69**
Kojnic, *Yugoslavia* L72+439 **58**
Kojonup, *W. Australia* E17–338 **110**
Kokand, *Uzbek* H24+408 **75**
Kokchetav, *Kazakh* H33+533 **62**
Kokhtla Yarva, *Estonia* L15+594 **47**
Kokkola, *Finland* L41+639 **46**
Koko, *Chad* L70+096 **81**
Kokoda,
　Papua New Guinea C13–090 **111**
Kokomo, *Indiana* T67+405 **91**
Koko Nor. See Ching Hai
Kokoshili Ra., *Tibet* G30+357 **71**
Kokpekty, *Kazakh.* G46+488 **62**
Kokstad, *Cape Province* L04–306 **84**
Kokura, *Japan* D25+338 **68**
Kokyar, *Sinkiang, China* G77+374 **72**
Ko-lan-chow, *China* E50+389 **66**
Kolar, *India* G71+132 **70**
Kolari, *Finland* L38+673 **46**
Kolarovgrad, *Bulgaria* L19+433 **58**
Kolberg. See Kołobrzeg,
Kolda, *Senegal* P00+130 **80**
Kolding, *Denmark* M33+555 **47**
Kole, *Zaire* L28+020 **82**
Kolguyev Ostrov, *U.S.S.R.* J65+690 **62**
Kolhapur, *India* H05+168 **70**
Kolin, *Czechoslovakia* L89+500 **48**
Kolkas Rags, *Latvia* L44+577 **47**
Kollick Kenyon Plateau,
　Antarctica V00–770 **27**
Köln, *W. Germany* M48+509 **48**
Kolno, *Poland* L48+534 **49**
Kolo. *Poland* L68+522 **49**
Kolo, *Tanzania* K56–046 **83**
Kolobrzeg, *Poland* L86+542 **49**
Kologriv, *U.S.S.R.* K04+588 **61**
Kolokani, *Mali* N48+134 **80**
Kolomna, *U.S.S.R.* K38+550 **60**
Kolomya, *Ukraine* L30+486 **60**
Kolossia, *Kenya* K56+016 **83**
Kolozsvár, See Cluj
Kolpashevo, *U.S.S.R.* G42+583 **62**
Kolwezi, *Zaire* L26–108 **82**
Kolyma, R., *U.S.S.R.* B60+675 **63**
Kolymskiy, Khrebet, *U.S.S.R.* B30+634 **63**
Komandorskiye Ostr., *U.S.S.R.* A80+550 **63**
Komariya, *Sri Lanka* G49+070 **70**
Komarno, *Czechoslovakia* L71+478 **49**
Komatsu, *Japan* C81+364 **68**
Komi, aut. rep., *U.S.S.R.* J40+650 **62**
Komintern, *U.S.S.R.* K31+477 **61**

Kommunarsk, *Ukraine* U38+485 **60**
Kommunizma, Pk., *Tadzhik.* H17+388 **62**
Komotini, *Greece* L28+410 **58**
Kompong Chan, *Cambodia* E87+120 **69**
Kompong Chnang, *Cambodia* F02+123 **69**
Kompong Som, *Cambodia* F07+111 **69**
Kompong-thom, *Cambodia* F01+127 **69**
Komsomolets Ostrov, *U.S.S.R.* F60+808 **63**
Komsomolsk, *U.S.S.R.* C77+505 **63**
Kondinskoe, *U.S.S.R.* H56+625 **62**
Kondoa, *Tanzania* K56–048 **83**
Kong, *Ivory Coast* N28+092 **80**
Kong Karl's Land, *Arctic Oc.* L05+790 **62**
Kongmoon, *China* E41+226 **67**
Kongor, *Sudan* K82+072 **81**
Kongsberg, *Norway* M32+597 **47**
Kongsmoen, *Norway* M16+648 **46**
Kongsvinger, *Norway* M18+602 **47**
Kongwa, *Tanzania* K52–064 **83**
Königsberg, See Kaliningrad
Konispol, *Albania* L59+397 **59**
Konotop, *Ukraine* K71+513 **60**
Konstantinovka, *Ukraine* K43+485 **60**
Konstantinovsk, *U.S.S.R.* K23+476 **61**
Konstanz, *Switz.* M35+476 **48**
Kontiomaki, *Finland* L11+643 **46**
Konya, *Turkey* K76+380 **74**
Konza, *Kenya* K48–018 **83**
Koondrook, *Victoria* C35–357 **109**
Koonenberry, *New S. Wales* C46–305 **109**
Koorawatha, *New S. Wales* C08–341 **109**
Kootenay Park, *B.C.* V70+506 **88**
Kootwijk, *Netherlands* M55+522 **44**
Koo-wee-rup, *Victoria* C27–382 **109**
Kopeisk, *U.S.S.R.* H80+550 **61**
Kopervik, *Norway* M58+593 **47**
Köping, *Sweden* L84+595 **47**
Kopparberg, *Sweden* M00+599 **47**
Koppigen, *Switzerland* M44+471 **45**
Koprivnica, *Yugoslavia* L79+462 **56**
Kora, *India* G58+261 **73**
Korce, *Albania* L56+407 **59**
Korcheva, *U.S.S.R.* K50+568 **60**
Korcula, I., *Yugoslavia* L78+429 **56**
Korea, N., *Asia* D30+412 **64**
Korea, S., *Asia* D30+368 **64**
Korea Strait, *Asia* D36+393 **64**
Korinthia & Argolis, *Greece* L43+378 **59**
Kórinthos, *Greece* L42+379 **59**
Kórinthos, G. of, *Greece* L44+382 **59**
Koritza. See Korce
Kormakiti, *Cyprus* K72+354 **76**
Kornat, I., *Yugoslavia* L88+438 **56**
Korneuburg, *Austria* L82+484 **49**
Korogwe, *Tanzania* K40–052 **83**
Koroit, *Victoria* C46–383 **109**
Korong Vale, *Victoria* C38–364 **109**
Körös R., *Hungary* L58+468 **58**
Korosten, *Ukraine* L08+510 **60**
Koro Toro, *Chad* L70+160 **81**
Korppoo, *Finland* L50+602 **47**
Korsakov, *U.S.S.R.* C44+466 **63**
Korsnas, *Finland* L53+628 **46**
Korsnes, *Norway* L84+683 **46**
Kortessem, *Belgium* M58+509 **44**
Kortgem, *Netherlands* M67+516 **44**
Korti, *Sudan* K80+180 **81**
Kortrijk (Courtrai), *Belgium* M70+508 **44**
Korumburra, *Victoria* C25–384 **109**
Korwai, *India* G72+241 **73**
Koryakskiy Khrebet, *U.S.S.R.* A60+623 **63**
Korzum, *Turkey* L03+371 **74**
Kos, I., *Greece* L17+368 **59**
Koscierzyna, *Poland* L72+541 **49**
Kosciusko, *Mississippi* T88+330 **95**
Kosciusko, Mt., *N.S.W.* C10–364 **109**
Kosha, *Sudan* K86+206 **81**
Koshchagyl, *Kazakh.* J37+470 **62**
Koshki, *U.S.S.R.* J57+542 **61**
Kosi, *India* G75+277 **72**
Košice, *Czechoslovakia* L52+497 **49**
Kosima, *Kuwait* J73+295 **74**
Koslan, *U.S.S.R.* J66+634 **62**
Köslin, See Koszalin
Koso Gol, *Mongolia* F28+510 **63**
Kosovo Metohija, *Yugoslavia* L54+425 **58**
Kostainica, *Yugoslavia* L81+452 **56**
Kosti, *Sudan* K74+132 **81**
Kostroma, *U.S.S.R.* K24+578 **60**
Koszalin, *Poland* L83+542 **49**
Kota Baharu, *Malaysia* F17+061 **69**
Kotah, *India* G85+252 **70**
Kota Kinabalu, *Sabah* E24+060 **65**
Kotalpur, *India* G14+230 **73**
Kota Tinggi, *Malaysia* F07+018 **69**
Kotcha L., *British Columbia* W08+592 **88**
Kotehandpur,
　Bangladesh G06+234 **73**
Kotel, *Bulgaria* L21+429 **58**
Kotelnich, *U.S.S.R.* J70+584 **61**
Kotelnyy, Ostrov, *U.S.S.R.* C65+754 **63**
Kotido, *Uganda* K66+030 **83**
Kotka, *Finland* L18+605 **47**
Kot Kapura, *India* H01+306 **72**
Kot Kasim, *India* G79+280 **72**
Kotkhai, *India* G74+311 **72**
Kotlas, *U.S.S.R.* J80+612 **62**
Kotli, *Kashmir* H07+335 **72**
Kotonkoro, *Nigeria* M54+110 **80**
Kotri, *Pakistan* H41+253 **70**
Kotturu, *India* G82+148 **70**
Kotzebue Sd., *Alaska* Z00+665 **99**
Kouango, *Cent. Afr. Rep.* L60+050 **81**
Koudougou, *Upper Volta* N13+120 **80**
Koulikoro, *Mali* N46+128 **80**
Kounde, *Cent. Afr. Rep.* M02+060 **81**
Kourou, *French Guiana* R46+052 **105**
Koutiala, *Mali* N32+122 **80**
Kouvola, *Finland* L19+608 **47**
Kovel, *Ukraine* L34+512 **60**
Kovno. See Kaunas
Kovrov, *U.S.S.R.* K22+563 **61**
Kowloon, *China* E35+224 **67**
Koyiu, *China* E45+231 **67**
Koyukuk, R., *Alaska* Y30+655 **99**
Kozan, *Turkey* K55+375 **74**
Kozani, *Greece* L40+403 **59**
Kozhikode. See Calicut
Kra & Isthmus of, *Thailand* F37+104 **69**
Kracheh, *Cambodia* E84+125 **69**
Kragerø, *Norway* M34+588 **47**
Kragujevac, *Yugoslavia* L53+440 **58**

Krakow, *Poland* L60+501 49
Kramatorsk, *Ukraine* K45+487 60
Krammer, *Netherlands* M65+517 44
Kranj, *Yugoslavia* M04+463 56
Kranystaw, *Poland* L41+510 49
Kranz, *U.S.S.R.* L57+549 47
Krapina, *Yugoslavia* L85+462 56
Krasino, *Novaya Zemlya* J35+708 62
Krasnobród, *Poland* L44+505 49
Krasnodar, *U.S.S.R.* K37+451 62
Krasnograd, *Ukraine* K58+494 60
Krasnoufimsk, *U.S.S.R.* J14+566 61
Krasnovisher, *U.S.S.R.* J17+602 62
Krasnovodsk, *Turkmen* J44+401 62
Krasnoyarsk, *U.S.S.R.* F71+562 63
Krasnyi Kholm, *U.S.S.R.* K48+581 60
Krasny Kut, *U.S.S.R.* J78+509 61
Krasnyy Yar, *U.S.S.R.* K02+507 61

Krefeld, *W. Germany* M51+513 48
Kremenchug, *Ukraine* K69+491 60
Kremensk, *U.S.S.R.* K10+497 61
Krems, *Austria* L87+484 49
Kretinga, *Lith.* L53+559 47
Kreuzlingen, *Switzerland* M35+476 45
Kribi, *Cameroon* M30+030 81
Krimml, *Austria* M17+472 48
Krishna, R., *India* G63+166 70
Krishnanagar, *India* G09+234 73
Krishnaraja Res., *India* G81+126 70
Kristiansand, *Norway* M42+581 47
Kristianstad, *Sweden* M05+561 47
Kristiansund, *Norway* M43+631 46
Kristiinankaupunki, *Finland* L52+623 46
Kristinehamn, *Sweden* M05+594 47
Kriti, I., *Greece* L30+350 59
Kriva Palanka, *Yugoslavia* L45+422 58
Krivoy Rog, *Ukraine* K70+478 60
Krizevci, *Yugoslavia* L81+460 56
Krk, I., *Yugoslavia* M02+451 56
Krnov, *Czechoslovakia* L74+501 49
Kroken, *Norway* M04+653 46
Kroměříz, *Czechoslovakia* L76+493 49
Kronoby, *Finland* L42+637 46
Kronshtadt, *U.S.S.R.* L02+600 60
Kroonstad, *Orange Free State* L16−276 84
Kropotkin, *U.S.S.R.* K28+454 62
Krotoszyn, *Poland* L76+517 49
Krško, *Yugoslavia* L87+459 56
Krugersdorp, *Transvaal* L14−262 84
Kruishoutem, *Belgium* M69+509 44
Krunga, *Kenya* K22−018 83
Krung Thep, *Thailand* F27+138 69
Krupnik, *Bulgaria* L40+418 58
Krusevac, *Yugoslavia* L52+436 58
Krustpils, *Latvia* L24+565 47
Krzyz, *Poland* L84+529 49
Ksar el Boukhari, *Algeria* M74+358 80
Kuala, *Sumatra* F44+034 65
Kuala Kangsar, *Malaysia* F25+049 69
Kuala Kerai, *Malaysia* F16+054 65
Kuala Klawang, *Malaysia* F18+030 69
Kuala Lipis, *Malaysia* F17+042 69
Kuala Lumpur, *Malaysia* F20+032 69
Kuandang, *Celebes* D72+008 65
Kuantan, *Malaysia* F10+037 65
Kub, *Namibia* L74-242 84
Kucha, *Sinkiang, China* G43+418 62
Kuching, *Sarawak* E58+016 65
Kuchow. *See* Jungkiang
Kudat, *Sabah* E20+069 65
Kudymkar, *U.S.S.R.* J33+593 62
Kuhak, *Iran* H71+271 75
Kuhak, *Iran* H79+309 75
Kuh Banan, *Iran* J22+315 75
Kuh-e-Bul, *Iran* J55+305 75
Kuh Furgan, *Iran* J22+279 75
Kuh-i-Bul, *Iran* J43+308 75
Kuh-i-Dinar, *Iran* J51+310 75
Kuh-i-Kashigah, *Iran* J28+284 75
Kuhmo, *Finland* L03+641 46
Kuhpayeh, *Iran* J45+327 75
Kuhrud, *Iran* J53+337 75
Kuhsan, *Afghanistan* H82+347 75
Kuibis, *Namibia* L80-268 84
Kuibyshevka, *U.S.S.R.* D39+509 63
Kuikiang, *China* E23+297 67
Kuinre, *Netherlands* M55+528 44
Kukan, *Thailand* F05+146 69
Kukatush, *Ontario* T43+481 91
Kukawa, *Nigeria* M08+128 81
Kukes, *Albania* L58+421 58
Kukong, *China* E41+249 64
Kukong (Shiukwan), *China* E38+248 67
Kulachi, *Pakistan* H27+320 72
Kulaikh, *Saudi Arabia* K25+212 74
Kuldiga, *Latvia* L48+570 47
Kuldja, *Sinkiang, China* G51+440 62
Kulin, *China* E85+281 67
Kulhakangri Mt., *Tibet* F87+280 71
Kulmbach, *W. Germany* M21+501 48
Kulu, *India* G78+319 72
Kulunda, *U.S.S.R.* G67+526 62
Kulwin, *Victoria* C44−350 109
Kumai, *Borneo, Indon.* E50−026 65
Kumamoto, *Japan* D26+328 68
Kumara, *New Zealand* A52−426 112
Kumara, *U.S.S.R.* D48+517 63
Kumasi, *Ghana* N10+068 80
Kumbakonam, *India* G63+110 70
Kumher, *India* G76+273 73
Kumora, *U.S.S.R.* E52+559 63
Kumta, *India* H04+144 70
Kunda, *Estonia* L21+595 47
Kunduz, *Afghanistan* H36+367 75
Kungchang. *See* Lungsi
Kungnung, *India* F70+240 71
Kungrad, *Uzbek* J06+431 62
Kungur, *U.S.S.R.* J19+574 61
Kunhsien, *China* E53+327 66
Kunlun Shan, *China-Tibet* 30-31
Kunming, *China* F14+250 64
Kunsan, *Korea* D50+360 64
Kuopio, *Finland* L14+629 46
Kupa R., *Yugoslavia* M00+455 56
Kupang, *Timor I., Indon.* D69−102 65
Kupishkis, *Lithuania* L30+558 47
Kupyansk, *Ukraine* K45+497 60

Kure, *Japan* D15+342 68
Kure, I., *Hawaii* Z80+288 106
Kureika, *U.S.S.R.* G05+670 62
Kuressare, *Estonia* L45+582 47
Kurgan, *U.S.S.R.* H57+556 62
Kuria Muria Is., *Arabian Sea* J22+175 75
Kurigram, *Bangladesh* G02+258 73
Kurilskiye Ostrova, *U.S.S.R.* C00+458 63
Kurnool, *India* G72+159 70
Kurow, *New Zealand* A57−446 112
Kurram, *Pakistan* H29+339 72
Kurri Kurri, *New S. Wales* B82−328 109
Kursk, *U.S.S.R.* K53+517 60
Kurski Zaliv, *U.S.S.R.* L55+550 47
Kurtalan, *Turkey* K18+384 74
Kuru, *Finland* L37+619 47
Kuruman, *Cape Province* L40−276 84
Kurume, *Japan* D27+332 68
Kurunegala, *Sri Lanka* G58+076 70
Kusa, *U.S.S.R.* J04+553 61
Kusaie, I., *Caroline Is.* B10+053 106
Kushersk, *U.S.S.R.* J30+584 61
Kushiro, *Japan* C33+430 68
Kushk, *Afghanistan* H75+348 75
Kushka, *Turkmen.* H77+352 62
Kushtia, *Bangladesh* G05+239 73
Kushva, *U.S.S.R.* J02+584 61
Kuskokwim B., *Alaska* Y80+590 99
Kusma, *Nepal* G38+282 73
Kustanay, *Kazakh* H70+531 62
Kütahya, *Turkey* L01+393 74
Kutai, R., *Borneo, Indon.* E26+004 65
Kut-al-Hai, *Iraq* J84+322 74
Kutatjane, *Sumatra, Indon.* F44+034 65
Kutch, & Gulf of, *India* H23+232 70
Kutch, Rann of, *India* H30+240 70
Kutchan, *Japan* C56+429 68
Kutin, *Yugoslavia* L80+455 56
Kutno, *Poland* L64+522 49
Kütsing, *China* F07+255 67
Kutu, *Ethiopia* K64+090 83
Kutum, *Sudan* L32+140 81
Kuusamo, *Finland* L05+659 46
Kuusjärvi, *Finland* L07+627 46
Kuwait & state, *The Gulf* J72+294 74
Kuyang, *China* E60+414 66
Kuybyshev, *U.S.S.R.* J58+531 61
Kuybyshev, *U.S.S.R.* G68+559 62
Kuybyshevskoye Vdkhr.,
U.S.S.R. J60+548 61
Kuytan, *U.S.S.R.* F22+544 63
Kuzhbal, *U.S.S.R.* K05+585 61
Kuzino, *U.S.S.R.* J04+571 61
Kuzmin, *Yugoslavia* L64+450 58
Kuznetsk, *U.S.S.R.* J81+530 61
Kuzovatovo, *U.S.S.R.* J75+536 61
Kvaløy, N., *Norway* L65+702 46
Kvaløy, S., *Norway* L68+697 46
Kvarken, *Sweden* L56+634 46
Kvarner, G. of, *Yugoslavia* M05+448 56
Kvarneric, G. of, *Yugoslavia* M01+445 56
Kvesmenes, *Norway* L60+693 46
Kwajalein, Is., *Marshall Is.* A80+088 106
Kwakhanai, *Botswana* L52−218 84
Kwakoegron, *Surinam* R62+051 105
Kwangchang, *China* E23+267 67
Kwangchow, *China* E40+232 67
Kwangchow Wan, *China* E56+210 67
Kwang-nam, *Vietnam* E70+159 69
Kwangnan, *China* F00+241 67
Kwangping. *See* Yungnien
Kwangshun, *China* E82+261 67
Kwangsichuang prov., *China* E72+238 67
Kwangsin. *See* Shangjao
Kwangtung, prov., *China* E36+235 67
Kwania L., *Uganda* K74+016 83
Kwan-tung (Luta) Pen., *Ch.* D86+388 66
Kweichih, *China* E15+307 66
Kweichow. *See* Fengkieh
Kweichow, prov., *China* E84+268 67
Kweihwa. *See* Huhehot
Kweihwa. *See* Tzeyun
Kweilin, *China* E59+254 67
Kweiping, *China* E59+233 67
Kweisui. *See* Huhehot
Kweiteh, *China* F22+360 64
Kweiteh. *See* Shangkiu
Kweiyang, *China* E80+266 67
Kweiyang, *China* E45+258 67
Kwi-chu, *Vietnam* E88+194 69
Kwidzyń, *Poland* L66+538 49
Kwitao, *Burma* F44+257 71
Kwoka, mt., *New Guinea* D15−006 65
Kyabram, *Victoria* C30−363 109
Kyakhta, *U.S.S.R.* E81+504 63
Kyalite Crossing, *N.S.W.* C40−349 109
Kyangin, *Burma* F58+182 71
Kyaring Nor, *China* F46+348 64
Kyaukiaw, *Burma* F72+208 71
Kyaukpyu, *Burma* F69+195 71
Kyaukse, *Burma* F53+215 71
Kybybolite, *S. Australia* C54−369 109
Kyelang, *India* G78+326 72
Kyi R., *Tibet* F80+298 71
Kymi, *Finland* L19+605 47
Kyneton, *Victoria* C33−373 109
Kyoga L., *Uganda* K74+014 83
Kyoto, *Japan* C85+350 68
Kyrenia, *Cyprus* K70+353 76
Kyshtym, *U.S.S.R.* H86+557 61
Kythrea, *Cyprus* K69+352 76
Kyûshû, I., *Japan* D24+330 68
Kyustendil, *Bulgaria* L44+423 58
Kyusyur, *U.S.S.R.* C45+708 63
Kywong, *New South Wales* C20−350 109
Kyzl, *U.S.S.R.* F63+517 63
Kyzyl Kum, *Uzbek, etc.* H70+423 62
Kyzylsk, *U.S.S.R.* J06+526 61
Kzil Orda, *Kazakh* H57+450 62

Laanila, *Finland* L16+684 46
La Argentina, *Argentina* S70−503 103
La Ascención, *Mexico* V18+310 100
La Asunción, *Venezuela* S23+110 104
Laban, *Jordan* K56+309 76
La Banda, *Argentina* S25−277 103
Labang, *Sarawak* E40+033 65
Labe, *Guinea* N74+114 80
Labelle, *Quebec* S89+463 91
Laberge, L., *Yukon* X00+610 88
Labouheyre, *France* N06+442 55
Laboulaye, *Argentina* S20−341 103

Labrador, *Canada* 89
Labrea, *Brazil* S28−072 104
La Brea, *Honduras* T76+134 101
La Brea, *Trinidad* S08+102 104
Labuan, I., *Sabah* E29+054 65
Labuk B., *Sabah* E14+061 65
La Canoa, *Venezuela* S23+086 104
La Carlota, *Argentina* S20−334 103
La Carolina, *Spain* N22+383 52
Laccadive Is., *Lakshadweep* H13+115 70
La Ceiba, *Venezuela* S66+094 104
Lacepede B., *S. Australia* C62−367 109
Lac Frontiere, *Quebec* S60+467 90
Lachen, *Switzerland* M37+472 45
Lachine, *Quebec* S82+455 91
Lachlan R., *New S. Wales* C30−338 109
Lachmangarh, *India* G89+278 72
Lachute, *Quebec* S87+457 91
Lackawanna, *New York* T23+428 96
Lackawaxen, *Pennsylvania* T00+415 96
Lacken Res., *Ireland, Rep.* N39+532 43
La Cocha, *Argentina* S33−278 103
Lacombe, *Alberta* V53+522 88
La Concordia, *El Salvador* T85+134 101
Laconia, *New Hampshire* S69+435 96
La Copelina, *Argentina* S46−372 103
La Coruña, *Spain* N51+433 52
La Crosse, *Wisconsin* U07+438 93
La Cruz, *Columbia* T11+015 104
La Cruz, *Mexico* V01+279 100
Ladakh Ra., *Tibet* G60+322 70
Ladis, *Iran* H82+289 75
Ladoga, L. *See* Ladozhskoye Ozero
La Dorada, *Columbia* S88+055 104
Ladozhskoye Oz., *U.S.S.R.* K84+606 60
Ladwa, *India* G77+300 72
Lady Neunes B., *Antarctica* A70−730 27
Ladysmith, *British Columbia* W23+490 88
Ladysmith, *Natal* L02−288 84
Ladysmith, *Wisconsin* U07+455 93
Lae, *Papua New Guinea* C18−068 111
Laeken, *Belgium* M64+509 44
Laesö, I., *Denmark* M24+573 47
La Esperanza, *Honduras* T81+143 101
La Estrada, *Spain* N51+427 52
Lafayette, *Georgia* T62+347 97
La Fayette, *Indiana* T71+404 91
Lafayette, *Louisiana* U12+302 95
La Florencia, *Argentina* S13−241 103
Lafontaine, *Quebec* S59+471 90
Lagakalaka, *Somalia* J66+060 83
Lagan R., *N. Ireland* N35+546 42
Lages, *Brazil* Q37−056 105
Laggan, *Scotland* N26+570 40
Laggan L., *Scotland* N27+570 40
Laghouat, *Algeria* M72+332 80
Lagonegro, *Italy* L85+401 57
Lagos, *Mexico* U72+214 100
Lagos, *Nigeria* M70+064 80
Lagos, *Portugal* N52+371 52
La Grande, *Oregon* V79+453 92
Lagrange, *Georgia* T60+330 97
Lagrange, *Indiana* T62+416 91
Lagrange, *Kentucky* T62+384 97
La Grange, *W. Australia* D79−186 110
La Granja, *Spain* N24+409 52
La Guaira, *Venezuela* S41+106 104
La Guardia, *Argentina* S33−295 103
La Guardia, *Spain* N53+419 52
Laguna, *Brazil* R23−284 103
Lagunas, *Peru* T04−053 104
Lagunillas, *Bolivia* S22−196 104
Laharpur, *India* G54+276 73
Lahej, *Yemen, South* K00+130 74
Lahijan, *Iran* J60+372 75
Laholm, *Sweden* M12+565 47
Lahore, *Pakistan* H24+316 72
Lahti, *Finland* L26+610 47
Lai, C., *Vietnam* E77+171 69
Laibach. *See* Ljubljana
Lai-chau, *Vietnam* F11+222 69
Laichow. *See* Yehsien
Laigle, *France* M86+488 54
Laila, *Saudi Arabia* J79+223 74
Laingsburg, *Cape Province* L56−330 84
Lairg, *Scotland* N26+580 40
Laishev, *U.S.S.R.* J63+554 61
Laives, *Italy* M22+465 45
Laja, L., *Chile* S68−374 103
Lajao, *Brazil* Q69−192 105
Lajes, *Brazil* R32−278 103
La Japonesa, *Argentina* S39−386 103
La Junquera, *Spain* M73+424 53
La Junta, *Colorado* U81+380 94
Lakatrask, *Sweden* L53+663 46
Lake Andes, *S. Dakota* U52+432 93
Lake Butler, *Florida* T45+300 97
Lake Charles, *Louisiana* U19+302 95
Lake City, *Florida* T46+302 97
Lake City, *Michigan* T61+444 91
Lake District, *England* N19+546 37
Lake Edward, *Quebec* S73+477 91
Lakefield, *Ontario* T20+444 91
Lake Geneva, *Wisconsin* T80+426 91
Lake George, *New York* S82+434 96
Lake Harbour, *N.-W. Terr.* S59+632 89
Lakeland, *Florida* T42+280 97
Lake Majella, *California* W12+365 92
Lake Pleasant, *New York* S86+434 96
Lake Providence, *Louisiana* U07+328 95
Lakes Entrance, *Victoria* C12−378 109
Lakeview, *Minnesota* U12+444 93
Lakeview, *Oregon* W02+422 92
Lakewood, *New Jersey* S85+400 96
Lakewood, *New York* T26+422 96
Lakewood, *Ohio* T40+415 91
Lakhimpur, *India* F65+272 71
Lakhimpur, *India* G55+280 73
Lakki, *Pakistan* H24+325 72
Lakkor Tso, *Tibet* G36+320 71
Lakonia, *Greece* L45+369 59
Lakonia, G. of, *Greece* L44+366 59
Lakota, *Ivory Coast* N34+060 80
Lakota, *N. Dakota* U50+481 93
Lakse Fd., *Norway* L20+705 46
Lakshadweep, *Indian Ocean* H13+115 70
Laktsang, *Tibet* G42+303 71
Lala Musa, *Pakistan* H06+327 72
Lalbagh, *India* G10+242 73
Lalganj, *India* G29+259 73
La Libertad, *Ecuador* T35−022 104

La Libertad, *Guatemala* U01+167 100
La Libertad, *Nicaragua* T61+123 101
La Ligua, *Chile* S67−324 103
Lalin, *Spain* N49+426 52
Lalitpur, *India* G69+247 73
La Maddalena, I., *Sardinia* M34+413 57
La Malbaie, *Quebec* S61+476 91
Lamar, *Colorado* U76+381 94
Lamar, *Missouri* U26+374 95
Lamastre, *France* M63+450 55
Lambach, *Austria* M07+481 48
Lamballe, *France* N15+485 54
Lambay I., *Ireland, Rep.* N36+535 43
Lambayeque, *Peru* T30−066 104
Lambert's Ld., *Greenland* P30+790 26
Lambertville, *New Jersey* T00+403 96
Lámbia, *Greece* L49+379 59
Lamb's Hd., *Ireland, Rep.* N61+517 43
Lamé, *Chad* M02+092 81
Lamego, *Portugal* N47+411 52
Lameroo, *S. Australia* C57−354 109
Lamesa, *Texas* U70+326 94
Lamia, *Greece* L45+389 59
Lamlash, *Scotland* N31+555 41
Lammermuir Hills, *Scotland* N16+559 41
Lamotrek Is., *Caroline Is.* C30+075 106
La Moure, *N. Dakota* U50+464 93
Lampa, *Peru* S80−153 104
Lampedusa, I., *Medit. Sea* M32+355 81
Lampeter, *Wales* N25+521 38
Lamphun, *Thailand* F35+186 69
Lampi, I., *Burma* F41+108 71
Lampton, C., *N.-W. Terr.* W20+710 88
Lamu, *Kenya* K24−024 83
Lamud, *Peru* T17−063 104
Lanark, *Scotland* N23+557 41
Lancashire, co., *England* N16+537 37
Lancaster, *England* N17+540 37
Lancaster, *Missouri* U16+404 95
Lancaster, *New Hampshire* S69+445 91
Lancaster, *New York* T22+429 96
Lancaster, *Pennsylvania* T08+401 96
Lancaster, *S. Carolina* T34+347 97
Lancaster, *Wisconsin* U04+429 91
Lancaster Sd., *N.-W. Terr.* T60+734 89
Lanchow, *China* F07+360 66
Landeck, *Austria* M27+471 48
Landen, *Belgium* M60+508 44
Lander, *Wyoming* V22+429 93
Landerneau, *France* N26+484 54
Landes, dep., *France* N04+440 55
Landfall, I., *Chile* S85−534 103
Landi Khana, *Pakistan* H23+342 72
Landi Kotal, *Pakistan* H23+342 72
Landon, *Sweden* M04+636 46
Landovery, *Wales* N23+520 38
Landsberg, *W. Germany* M25+481 48
Landsberg. *See* Gorzow Wielkopolski
Land's End, *England* N34+500 38
Landshut, *W. Germany* M17+490 48
Landskrona, *Sweden* M13+559 47
Langå, *Denmark* M31+563 47
Langdhas, *Greece* L41+408 59
Langana L., *Ethiopia* K38+076 83
Langchung, *China* E84+315 66
Langeac, *France* M70+451 55
Langeland, I., *Denmark* M26+549 47
Längelmavesi, *Finland* L34+615 47
Langenthal, *Switzerland* M43+472 45
Langholm, *Scotland* N18+552 41
Lang Jökull, *Iceland* P30+646 46
Langkawi, I., *Malaysia* F31+063 69
Langlade, I., *Atlantic Oc.* R68+468 90
Langogne, *France* M67+447 55
Langon, *France* N02+445 55
Langøya, *Norway* M00+687 46
Langport, *England* N17+511 38
Langres, *France* M58+478 54
Langsa, *Sumatra* F42+045 65
Långsele, *Sweden* L78+632 46
Lang-Son, *Vietnam* E79+218 69
Långträsk, *Sweden* L58+654 46
Languedoc, prov., *France* M66+430 55
Lanklaar, *Belgium* M56+510 44
Lankor Tso, *Tibet* G42+325 71
Lannion, *France* N21+488 54
Lansdale, *Pennsylvania* T02+402 96
Lansing, *Michigan* T57+428 91
Lansingburg, *New York* S82+428 91
Lan Tao, *China* E36+223 67
Lanzarote, I., *Canary Is.* N82+290 80
Laoag, *Philippines* D87+182 65
Lao Bao, *Vietnam* E80+165 69
Lao-chang-Ho R., *China* E23+378 66
Lao-Cai, *Vietnam* F07+225 69
Laon, *France* M69+496 54
La Oroya, *Peru* T06−115 104
Laos, *S.-E. Asia* F10+192 69
Lao shan, *China* D86+363 66
Lapalisse, *France* M68+462 54
La Palma, I., *Canary Is.* P30+286 80
La Paragua, *Venezuela* S21+070 104
La Paz, *Argentina* R88−307 103
La Paz, *Argentina* S45−334 103
La Paz, *Bolivia* S49−165 104
La Paz, *Honduras* T76+143 101
La Paz, *Mexico* V32+241 100
Lapchung L., *Tibet* G27+300 71
Lapeer, *Michigan* T50+431 91
La Pelada, *Argentina* S06−309 103
Lapinlahti, *Finland* L16+634 46
Lapithos, *Cyprus* K71+353 76
La Plata, *Argentina* R78+349 103
La Porte, *Indiana* T70+416 95
Laporte, *Pynnsylvania* T09+414 96
La Porte City, *Iowa* U13+424 95
Lapovo, *Yugoslavia* L54+442 58
Lappa Järvi, *Finland* L38+631 46
Lappeenranta, *Finland* L11+610 47
Lappland, *N. Europe* L57+680 46
Lapptrask, *Sweden* L39+660 46
Laprida, *Argentina* S06−378 103
Laptevykh Sea, *U.S.S.R.* D70+750 63
Lăpusul Românesc *Romania* L36+475 49
Lapy, *Poland* L43+530 49
Laqit, *Kuwait* J71+290 74
La Quiaca, *Argentina* S34−222 103
Lar, *Iran* J33+276 75
Larache, *Morocco* N38+350 80
Laragne, *France* M55+443 55

Laramate, *Peru* S89–142 **104**
Laramie, *Wyoming* V04+413 **93**
Laramie Mts., *Wyoming* V06+424 **93**
Laramie Pk., *Wyoming* V02+422 **93**
Larangeiras, *Brazil* S11–132 **104**
La Rasse, *Switzerland* M49+471 **45**
Larbert, *Scotland* N23+560 **41**
Larchwood, *Ontario* T38+466 **91**
Laredo, *Texas* V39+275 **94**
Largeau (Faya), *Chad* L66+180 **81**
Largo, *New Mexico* V17+366 **94**
Largs, *Scotland* N29+558 **41**
Larino, *Italy* M01+418 **57**
La Rioja, *Argentina* S41–294 **103**
Larisa, *Greece* L44+396 **59**
Larkana, *Pakistan* H41+275 **70**
Larnaca & B., *Cyprus* K68+349 **76**
Larne & L., *N. Ireland* N35+549 **42**
Larned, *Kansas* U56+382 **95**
La Robla, *Spain* N34+428 **52**
Laroche, *Belgium* M56+502 **44**
La Rochelle, *France* N07+462 **54**
La Roda, *Spain* N13+392 **53**
Lars Christensen Coast,
  Antarctic H50–680 **27**
Laruns, *France* N03+430 **55**
Larvik, *Norway* M30+590 **47**
Laryak, *U.S.S.R.* G60+612 **62**
La Salle, *Illinois* T84+413 **95**
Las Animas, *Colorado* U80+380 **94**
Las Anod, *Somalia* J76+082 **83**
Las Cejas, *Argentina* S29–269 **103**
Las Coloradas, *Argentina* S64–396 **103**
Las Cruces, *New Mexico* V11+323 **94**
Las Cruces, *New Mexico* V11+325 **98**
La Serena, *Chile* S67–299 **103**
Last Flores, *Argentina* R86–361 **103**
Lasgird, *Iran* J43+353 **75**
Lash, *Afghanistan* H81+316 **75**
Las Heras, *Argentina* S53–465 **103**
Lashio, *Burma* F43+228 **71**
Lashkar, *India* G71+262 **73**
Lasithi, *Crete* L24+350 **59**
Las Khoreh, *Somalia* J70+110 **83**
Las Lajas, *Argentina* S62–385 **103**
Las Lomitas, *Argentina* S03–247 **103**
Las Palmas, *Canary Is.* P04+280 **80**
Las Plumas, *Argentina* S44–436 **103**
Lassen Pk., *California* W09+405 **92**
Lassen Peak Nat. Park, *Cal.* W08+405 **98**
Las Tablas, *Panama* T31+078 **101**
Last Mountain L., *Sask.* V00+510 **88**
Lastovo, I., *Yugoslavia* L79+427 **56**
Las Vacas, *Mexico* U67+295 **100**
Las Vegas, *Nevada* V60+362 **92**
Las Vegas, *New Mexico* V02+356 **94**
Latacunga, *Ecuador* T22–009 **104**
Latakia, *Syria* K55+355 **76**
La Tamba, *Guinea* N60+108 **80**
Laterrière, *Quebec* S67+483 **90**
Latheron, *Scotland* N20+583 **40**
Latrobe, *Pennsylvania* T27+404 **96**
Latrobe, *Tasmania* C22–412 **109**
Latrun, *Jordan* K60+318 **76**
La Tuque, *Quebec* S77+475 **91**
Latvia, rep., *U.S.S.R.* **47**
Lauder, *Scotland* N16+557 **41**
Laufen, *Switzerland* M45+474 **45**
Launceston, *England* N26+506 **38**
Launceston, *Tasmania* C18–414 **109**
Laune R., *Ireland, Rep.* N59+519 **43**
Launggyang, *Burma* F40+260 **71**
La Union, *Chile* S78–403 **103**
La Union, *Mexico* U70+180 **100**
La Union, *El Salvador* T77+134 **101**
La Union, *Spain* N05+377 **53**
Laura, *Queensland* C33–156 **111**
Laura, *S. Australia* C70–331 **109**
La Urbana, *Venezuela* S41+070 **104**
Laurel, *Maryland* T11+391 **96**
Laurel, *Mississippi* T83+316 **95**
Laurel, *Montana* V22+456 **93**
Laurel Hill, *Pennsylvania* T25+402 **96**
Laurens, *S. Carolina* T42+345 **97**
Laurent, *Quebec* S73+471 **91**
Laurentide Mts., *Quebec* S82+465 **90**
Laurentides Park, *Quebec* S68+477 **91**
Lauria, *Italy* L85+400 **57**
Laurie, I., *South Orkneys* Q87+610 **27**
Laurinburg, *N. Carolina* T27+348 **97**
Lausanne, *Switzerland* M50+465 **45**
Lautaro, *Chile* S75–384 **103**
Lautem, *Timor I., Indonesia* D48–084 **65**
Lauzon, *Quebec* S67+468 **91**
Lavacherie, *Belgium* M57+501 **44**
Laval, *France* N05+481 **54**
Laval B., *Quebec* S54+487 **90**
Lavalle, *Argentina* S52–327 **103**
Lavalleja, *Uruguay* R60–340 **103**
Lavamund, *Austria* L90+466 **48**
Lavardac, *France* M88+442 **55**
La Vega, *Dominican Rep.* S63+193 **101**
La Vela, *Venezuela* S57+114 **104**
Laverton, *W. Australia* D75–284 **110**
Laviana, *Spain* N33+432 **52**
Lavina, *Montana* V24+463 **93**
Lavongai, *Bismarck Arch.* B96–030 **106**
Lavos, *Portugal* N53+401 **52**
Lavras, *Brazil* R00–213 **105**
Lavras, *Brazil* R53–308 **103**
Lavras, *Brazil* Q54–068 **105**
Lavrentiya, *U.S.S.R.* Z36+654 **63**
Lávrion, *Greece* L36+377 **59**
Lawk Sawk, *Burma* F48+212 **71**
Lawra, *Ghana* N16+106 **80**
Lawrence, *Kansas* U32+390 **95**
Lawrence, *Massachusetts* S67+427 **96**
Lawrence, *New Zealand* A61–459 **112**
Lawrenceburg, *Tennessee* T75+352 **97**
Lawrenceville, *Illinois* T76+387 **95**
Lawton, *Oklahoma* U50+345 **95**
Laxford L., *Scotland* N31+584 **40**
Laysan I., *Hawaii* Z42+260 **106**
Lazarevac, *Yugoslavia* L59+444 **58**
Lazio, dep., *Italy* M16+420 **57**
Lead, *S. Dakota* U83+444 **93**
Leadhills, *Scotland* N22+554 **41**
Leadville, *Colorado* V08+392 **94**
Leaf R., *Quebec* S65+587 **89**
Leakesville, *Mississippi* T81+311 **97**
Leaksville, *N. Carolina* T28+365 **97**

Leamington, *England* N09+523 **37**
Leamington, *Ontario* T46+421 **91**
Leane L., *Ireland, Rep.* N57+520 **43**
Leatherhead, *England* N03+513 **39**
Leavenworth, *Indiana* T68+382 **97**
Leavenworth, *Kansas* U30+393 **95**
Łeba, *Poland* L74+547 **49**
Lebanon, *Kentucky* T61+375 **97**
Lebanon, *Missouri* U16+377 **95**
Lebanon, *New Hampshire* S74+437 **96**
Lebanon, *Pennsylvania* T09+403 **96**
Lebanon, rep., *W. Asia* K56+340 **74**
Lebesby, *Norway* L18+705 **46**
Lebombo Mts., *S. Africa* K78–250 **84**
Lebork, *Poland* L74+545 **49**
Lebu, *Chile* S82–375 **103**
Lebye, *Lebanon* K52+342 **76**
Lecce, *Italy* L71+404 **57**
Lecco, *Italy* M30+458 **56**
Lectourre, *France* M86+439 **55**
Ledbury, *England* N15+520 **38**
Ledesma, *Argentina* S29–238 **103**
Ledesma, *Spain* N36+411 **52**
Ledo, *India* F55+272 **71**
Lee R., *Ireland, Rep.* N51+519 **43**
Leech Lake, *Minnesota* U28+472 **93**
Leeds, *England* N09+538 **37**
Leende, *Netherlands* M57+513 **44**
Leerbeek, *Belgium* M65+508 **44**
Leerdam, *Netherlands* M59+519 **44**
Leesburg, *Virginia* T15+391 **96**
Leesville, *Louisiana* U20+311 **95**
Leeton, *New South Wales* C21–346 **109**
Leeuwarden, *Netherlands* M55+532 **44**
Leeuwin, C., *W. Australia* E29–340 **110**
Leeward Is., *West Indies* S10+172 **101**
Lefka, *Cyprus* K73+351 **76**
Lefkara, *Cyprus* K70+348 **76**
Lefkoniko, *Cyprus* K67+353 **76**
Lefroy, L., *W. Australia* D80–312 **110**
Legaspi, *Philippines* D68+130 **65**
Legge Pk., *Tasmania* C14–416 **109**
Leghorn, See Livorno.
Legnica, *Poland* L83+512 **49**
Leh, *Kashmir* G74+342 **72**
Le Havre, *France* M89+495 **54**
Lehi, *Utah* V41+404 **94**
Lehututu, *Botswana* L48–240 **84**
Leiah, *Pakistan* H24+310 **72**
Leicester & co., *England* N07+526 **37**
Leichhardt, R., *Queensland* C62–186 **111**
Leiden, *Netherlands* M63+522 **44**
Leigh Creek, *S. Australia* C70–305 **109**
Leighlinbridge, *Ireland, Rep.* N42+527 **43**
Leighton Buzzard, *England* N04+519 **39**
Leignon, *Belgium* M59+503 **44**
Leimuiden, *Netherlands* M62+522 **44**
Leinster, prov., *Ireland, Rep.* N42+530 **43**
Leinster, Mt., *Ireland, Rep.* N41+526 **43**
Leipzig, *E. Germany* M16+514 **48**
Leisele, *Belgium* M74+510 **44**
Leitchfield, *Kentucky* T68+375 **97**
Leith, *Scotland* N19+560 **41**
Leitrim, co., *Ireland, Rep.* N49+543 **42**
Leix (Laois), co., *Ireland,*
  Rep. N44+534 **43**
Leixlip, *Ireland, Rep.* N39+534 **43**
Leiyang, *China* E43+264 **67**
Leka, *Norway* M20+650 **46**
Le Kef, *Tunisia* M38+360 **81**
Leksvik, *Norway* M26+637 **46**
Leland, *Michigan* T64+451 **91**
Leland, *Mississippi* U05+334 **95**
Leleque, *Argentina* S66–424 **103**
Le Maire, Estrecho de, *Arg.* S30–550 **103**
Léman, Lac, *Switzerland* M51+464 **45**
Le Mans, *France* M89+480 **54**
Le Mars, *Iowa* U37+428 **95**
Lemberg. See Lvov.
Lemnos. See Limnos, I.
Lemvethna, *Burma* F59+174 **71**
Lena, R., *U.S.S.R.* D65+692 **63**
Lenina Pk., *Kirgiz.* H13+393 **62**
Leninabad, *Uzbek* H33+403 **62**
Leninakan, *Armyanskaya* K04+408 **62**
Leningrad, *U.S.S.R.* K88+599 **60**
Leninka, *U.S.S.R.* A14+647 **63**
Leninsk, *Turkmen.* H70+390 **62**
Leninsk Kuznetskiy, *U.S.S.R.* G23+545 **62**
Lenk, *Switzerland* M45+465 **45**
Lennox, I., *Chile & Argent.* S42–553 **103**
Lenoir, *N. Carolina* T39+359 **97**
Lens, *France* M73+504 **54**
Lent, *Netherlands* M55+519 **44**
Lentiira, *Finland* L01+644 **46**
Lenvik, *Norway* L71+694 **46**
Lenya, *Burma* F36+115 **71**
Lenz, *Switzerland* M32+467 **45**
Lenzerheide, *Switzerland* M32+467 **45**
Leoben, *Austria* L89+473 **48**
Leola, *S. Dakota* U54+458 **93**
Leominster, *England* N17+522 **38**
Leominster, *Massachusetts* S71+426 **96**
León, *France* N08+439 **55**
León, *Mexico* U70+212 **100**
Leon, *Nicaragua* T72+125 **101**
León, *Spain* N33+426 **52**
León, Monts de, *Spain* N37+426 **52**
Leongatha, *Victoria* C25–384 **109**
Leonidhion, *Greece* L43+372 **59**
Leonora, *W. Australia* D83–286 **110**
Leonteva, *U.S.S.R.* K50+590 **60**
Leopoldsburg, *Belgium* M58+511 **44**
Leopold II L., See Mai-Ndomba L.
Leopoldville. See Kinshasa
Lepepe, *Botswana* L24–234 **84**
Lepontine, Alpi, *Switz.-Italy* M41+463 **45**
Lepreau, *New Brunswick* S39+452 **90**
Lercara Friddi, *Sicily* M08+378 **57**
Lerdo, *Mexico* U82+255 **100**
Lerida, *Spain* M86+416 **53**
Lerma, *Argentina* S34–250 **103**
Lerma, *Spain* N22+420 **51**
Lermoos, *Austria* M25+474 **48**
Léros, I., *Greece* L19+372 **59**
Le Roy, *New York* T18+429 **91**
Lerwick, *Shetland, Scot.* N07+601 **40**
Lesbos. See Lesvos I.
Les Escoumains, *Quebec* S56+483 **90**

Leskovac, L48+430 **58**
Lesotho (Basutoland), *Afr.* L10–294 **84**
Lesozavodsk, *U.S.S.R.* D09+454 **63**
Lesparre, *France* N06+453 **55**
Lesser Slave L., *Alberta* V65+554 **88**
Lessines, *Belgium* M67+507 **44**
Lestijärvi, *Finland* L32+635 **46**
Lesvos, I., *Greece* L22+392 **59**
Leszno, *Poland* L81+518 **49**
Letcher, *S. Dakota* U49+439 **93**
Letchworth, *England* N01+520 **39**
Letea I., *Romania* L04+453 **58**
Lethbridge, *Alberta* V46+497 **88**
Leti Kep., *Indonesia* D42–084 **65**
Letpadan, *Burma* F56+177 **71**
Lette, *New South Wales* C42–344 **109**
Letterfrack, *Ireland, Rep.* N60+535 **43**
Letterkenny, *Ireland, Rep.* N46+550 **42**
Letty Harbour, *N.-W. Terr.* W28+690 **88**
Letur, *Spain* N13+384 **53**
Leucate, *France* M72+429 **55**
Leuchars, *Scotland* N17+564 **41**
Leucite Hills, *Wyoming* V24+418 **93**
Leuk, *Switzerland* M44+463 **45**
Leuser, mt., *Sumatra* F47+038 **65**
Leuven (Louvain), *Belgium* M62+509 **44**
Leuze, *Belgium* M68+506 **44**
Levádhia, *Greece* L43+385 **59**
Levanger, *Norway* M22+638 **46**
Leven, *Scotland* N18+562 **41**
Leven L., *Scotland* N20+562 **41**
Levêque, C., *W. Australia* D72–163 **110**
Levice, *Czechoslovakia* L69+483 **49**
Levick, Mt., *Antarctica* B20–740 **27**
Levin, *New Zealand* A28–406 **112**
Levis, *Quebec* S67+468 **91**
Levitha, I., *Greece* L21+370 **59**
Levkás, I., *Greece* L56+387 **59**
Levoča, *Czechoslovakia* L57+490 **49**
Lewes, *England* N00+509 **39**
Lewes R., *Yukon* X05+616 **88**
Lewis, Butt of, *Scotland* N37+585 **40**
Lewis I., *Scotland* N40+581 **40**
Lewis Ra., *Montana* V52+482 **98**
Lewisburg, *Pennsylvania* T11+410 **91**
Lewisburg, *Tennessee* T73+354 **97**
Lewisburg, *W. Virginia* T33+378 **97**
Lewiston, *Idaho* V72+464 **92**
Lewiston, *Maine* S61+441 **90**
Lewiston, *Michigan* T56+449 **91**
Lewiston, *N. Carolina* T13+362 **97**
Lewistown, *Illinois* U01+404 **91**
Lewistown, *Montana* V27+470 **93**
Lewistown, *Pennsylvania* T16+406 **96**
Lexington, *Georgia* T49+338 **97**
Lexington, *Kentucky* T57+380 **97**
Lexington, *Missouri* U23+392 **95**
Lexington, *Nebraska* U58+408 **95**
Lexington, *N. Carolina* T32+358 **97**
Lexington, *Tennessee* T80+356 **97**
Lexington, *Virginia* T27+377 **97**
Leydsdorp, *Transvaal* K86–240 **84**
Leyte, I., *Philippines* D60+108 **65**
Lezajsk, *Poland* L46+503 **49**
Lha-kang Dzong, *Tibet* F83+281 **71**
Lhasa, *Tibet* F83+296 **71**
Lha-tse Dzong, *Tibet* G14+291 **71**
Lhontse Dzong, *Tibet* F76+284 **71**
Lianchow, See Wuwei
Liangsiang, *China* E22+396 **66**
Liant, C., *Thailand* F26+127 **69**
Liao R., *China* D70+422 **64**
Liaocheng, *China* E24+365 **66**
Liaohsien, *China* E39+370 **66**
Liao-tung, G. of, *China* D86+398 **66**
Liao yang-chow, *China* D71+412 **66**
Liard, *N.-W. Territories* W23+602 **88**
Liard, R., *N.-W. Territories* W23+608 **88**
Liari, *Pakistan* H51+256 **70**
Liberal, *Kansas* U66+370 **94**
Liberdade, *Brazil* S70–072 **104**
Liberec, *Czechoslovakia* L90+508 **48**
Liberia, *Costa Rica* T61+106 **101**
Liberia, rep., *W. Africa* N60+070 **80**
Libertad, *Mexico* V46+298 **100**
Liboi, *Kenya* K24+004 **83**
Libourne, *France* N02+449 **55**
Libreville, *Gabon* M32+004 **82**
Libya, *N. Africa* L60+250 **81**
Licata, *Sicily* M07+371 **57**
Licheng, See Tsinan
Lichfield, *England* N11+527 **37**
Licking R., *Kentucky* T56+387 **97**
Lida, *Byelorussia* L29+539 **60**
Lida-di-Roma, *Italy* M16+417 **57**
Liddel R., *Scot.-Eng.* N17+551 **41**
Liddes, *Switzerland* M47+460 **45**
Liddon G., *N.-W. Terr.* V45+750 **88**
Lidjombo, *Cameroon* L84+026 **82**
Lidköping, *Sweden* M11+585 **47**
Lidzbark, *Poland* L57+541 **49**
Liechtenstein, *Europe* M32+472 **45**
Liège & prov., *Belgium* M57+506 **44**
Liegnitz. See Legnica
Lieksa, *Finland* L00+633 **46**
Lienkong, *China* E23+263 **67**
Lienyunkang, *China* E03+347 **66**
Lienz, *Austria* M14+468 **48**
Liepaja, *Latvia* L54+565 **47**
Lierneux, *Belgium* M55+503 **44**
Lierre, *Belgium* M63+511 **44**
Liers, *Belgium* M57+507 **44**
Liestal, *Switzerland* M44+475 **45**
Lievre, R. du, *Quebec* T03+467 **91**
Lifford, *Ireland, Rep.* N45+548 **42**
Lifu, I., *Loyalty Is.* A75–212 **106**
Ligure, Appennino, *Italy* M36+446 **56**
Liguria, dep. *Italy* M38+445 **56**
Ligurian Sea, *Italy* M39+433 **56**
Lihsien, *China* E50+296 **67**
Likiang, *China* F28+268 **64**
Likimi, *Zaire* L56+028 **82**
Liling, *China* E38+277 **67**
Lilla Edet, *Sweden* M17+581 **47**
Lille, *Belgium* M64+513 **44**
Lille, *France* M71+507 **54**
Lillehammer, *Norway* M27+611 **47**
Lillesand, *Norway* M39+582 **47**
Lillo, *Belgium* M64+513 **44**
Lillo, *Spain* N20+397 **52**

Lillooet, *British Columbia* W11+506 **88**
Lilongwe, *Malawi* K66–140 **83**
Lim Fd., *Denmark* M40+566 **47**
Lima, *Ohio* T55+408 **91**
Lima, *Peru* T12–120 **104**
Limache, *Chile* S68–330 **103**
Limassol, *Cyprus* K72+347 **76**
Limavadv, *N. Ireland* N42+550 **42**
Limay, R., *Argentina* S52–392 **103**
Limay Mahuida, *Argentina* S40–372 **103**
Limbazhi, *Latvia* L32+575 **47**
Limbourg, *Belgium* M54+506 **44**
Limburg, *W. Germany* M42+504 **48**
Limburg, prov. *Belgium* M58+510 **44**
Limchow. See Hoppo.
Limeira, *Brazil* R14–225 **105**
Limerick (Luimneach)
  Ireland, Rep. N52+527 **43**
Limes, *Belgium* M58+496 **44**
Limestone, *Maine* S47+470 **90**
Limmen, *Netherlands* M62+526 **44**
Limmen Bight,
  N. Terr., Australia C86–148 **111**
Limni, *Greece* L40+388 **59**
Limnos, I., *Greece* L29+400 **59**
Limoges, *France* M82+458 **54**
Limon, *Colorado* U83+392 **94**
Limon, *Costa Rica* T48+100 **101**
Limousin, prov., *France* M78+454 **54**
Limoux, *France* M77+431 **55**
Limpopo R.,
  Mozambique etc. K68–250 **84**
Lina, mt., *New Guinea* D07–014 **65**
Linares, *Chile* S70–358 **103**
Linares, *Mexico* U57+248 **100**
Linares, *Spain* N22+381 **52**
Lincheng, *China* E16+349 **66**
Linchwan. See Fuchow
Lincoln, *Argentina* S09–349 **103**
Lincoln, *England* N03+532 **37**
Lincoln, *Illinois* T86+402 **95**
Lincoln, *Maine* S51+454 **90**
Lincoln, *Michigan* T51+447 **91**
Lincoln, *Nebraska* U40+408 **95**
Lincoln, *New Zealand* A45–436 **112**
Lincoln, co., *England* N01+532 **37**
Lincoln Sea, *Arctic Ocean* R35+840 **26**
Lincoln Wolds, *England* N01+534 **37**
Lincolnton, *N. Carolina* T37+355 **97**
Lindau, *W. Germany* M32+475 **48**
Lindesay, Mt., *Queensland* B68–281 **111**
Lindesnes, *Norway* M47+580 **47**
Lindi, *Tanzania* K32–100 **83**
Lindley, *Orange Free State* L12–278 **84**
Lindos, *Greece* L11+361 **59**
Lindsay, *Ontario* T23+444 **91**

Line Is., *Pacific Ocean* Y30+020 **107**
Linfen, *China* E51+360 **66**
Lingchwan, *China* E58+255 **67**
Lingen, *W. Germany* N46+525 **48**
Lingga, I., *Riau Kep.,*
  Indonesia F02–003 **65**
Lingling, *China* E51+263 **67**
Linguere, *Senegal* P00+154 **80**
Lingyun, *China* E81+244 **67**
Linhai, *China* D83+290 **67**
Linhares, *Brazil* Q61–194 **105**
Linho, *China* E75+408 **66**
Linhsien, *China* E45+248 **67**
Lini, *China* E10+351 **66**
Linkiang, *China* D49+416 **64**
Linkiang (Tsingkiang), *China* E27+280 **67**
Linköping, *Sweden* L86+584 **47**
Linkuva, *Lithuania* L36+561 **47**
Linlithgow, *Scotland* N21+550 **41**
Linn, *Missouri* U11+385 **97**
Linnhe, L., *Scotland* N33+566 **41**
Linosa, I., *Medit. Sea* M13+359 **57**
Linping, *China* E33+244 **67**
Lins, *Brazil* R29–218 **103**
Linsi, *China* E11+434 **64**
Lintan, *China* F10+348 **66**
Linth, R., *Switzerland* M36+472 **45**
Linthal, *Switzerland* M36+469 **45**
Linton, *Quebec* S73+473 **91**
Linyu, *China* E01+400 **66**
Linz, *Austria* M04+483 **48**
Lion, G. du, *France* M66+430 **55**
Lion Pt., *N.-W. Territories* W25+727 **88**
Lio Porgyul, *Tibet* G67+320 **70**
Liouesso, *Congo* L86+010 **82**
Lipa, *Yugoslavia* L84+447 **56**
Lipari. & I., *Italy* M01+385 **57**
Lipetsk, *U.S.S.R.* K33+526 **60**
Liping, *China* E66+263 **67**
Lipovets, *Ukraine* L06+492 **60**
Lippstadt, *W. Germany* M40+517 **48**
Lipsoi, I., *Greece* L19+373 **59**
Lira, *Uganda* K74+022 **83**
Lircay, *Peru* S89–130 **104**
Liria, *Spain* N04+396 **53**
Lisala, *Zaire* L50+022 **82**
Lisboa, *Portugal* N55+387 **52**
Lisbon. See Lisboa
Lisburn, *N. Ireland* N36+545 **42**
Lisburne, C. *Alaska* Z00+685 **99**
Liscannor B., *Ireland, Rep.* N57+529 **43**
Lisdoonvarna, *Ireland, Rep.* N56+530 **43**
Lishih, *China* E53+375 **66**
Lishui, *China* E00+285 **67**
Lisianski, I., *Hawaii* Z55+260 **106**
Lisieux, *France* M89+492 **54**
Liskeard, *England* N27+504 **38**
L'Isle, *Switzerland* M52+466 **45**
L'Islet, *Quebec* S62+471 **91**
Lismore, *Ireland, Rep.* N48+521 **43**
Lismore, *New South Wales* B70–286 **111**
Lismore I., *Scotland* N33+565 **41**
Lisnaskea, *N. Ireland* N45+542 **42**
Lissar, *Iran* J66+380 **74**
Listowel, *Ireland, Rep.* N57+524 **43**
Listowel, *Ontario* T36+437 **91**
Lisu, *Ethiopia* K50+100 **83**
Litchfield, *Illinois* T88+392 **95**
Litchfield, *Minnesota* U27+451 **93**
Lith Ai, *Saudi Arabia* K28+202 **74**
Lithgow, *New South Wales* B89–335 **109**
Lithinon, C., *Crete* L32+349 **59**
Lithuania, rep., *U.S.S.R.* **47**

Litoměrice, *Czechoslovakia* M05+505 **48**
Little R., *Missouri* T88+363 **97**
Little Belt Mts., *Montana* V34+468 **93**
Little Current, *Ontario* T42+460 **91**
Little Falls, *Minnesota* U26+460 **93**
Little Falls, *New York* S89+430 **96**
Little Horn Mts., *Arizona* V52+334 **92**
Little River, *Newfoundland* R85+478 **90**
Little River, *New Zealand* A43-437 **112**
Little Rock, *Arkansas* U14+348 **95**
Little Rocky Mts., *Montana* V22+479 **93**
Little Smoky R., *Alberta* V74+546 **88**
Littleton, *Colorado* V00+396 **94**
Littleton, *New Hampshire* S70+443 **91**
Little Valley, *New York* T23+423 **96**
Littoria, *Italy* M13+415 **57**
Liuan, *China* E22+318 **64**
Liuchow, *China* E64+243 **67**
Liupan Shan, *China* E84+356 **66**
Liusvaara, *Karelia* K77+626 **46**
Live Oak, *Florida* T48+303 **97**
Liverpool, *New South Wales* B85-339 **109**
Liverpool, *Nova Scotia* S28+440 **90**
Liverpool & B., *England* N18+534 **37**
Liverpool Coast, *Greenland* P35+710 **26**
Liverpool Plains, *N.S.W.* C00-312 **109**
Liverpool Ra., *New S. Wales* B88-318 **109**
Livingston, *Alabama* T79+326 **97**
Livingston, *Guatemala* T82+158 **100**
Livingston, *Montana* V33+457 **93**
Livingston, *Tennessee* T62+364 **97**
Livingston, *Texas* U30+307 **95**
Livingston, I., *S. Shetlands* S04-630 **27**
Livingstone, *See* Maramba
Livingstonia, *Malawi* K66-108 **83**
Livno, *Yugoslavia* L78+438 **56**
Livny, *U.S.S.R.* K45+524 **60**
Livo Joki, *Finland* L18+655 **46**
Livorno, *Italy* M28+435 **56**
Livramento, *Brazil* R63-308 **103**
Liwa, *Oman* J21+246 **75**
Liwale, *Tanzania* K42-098 **83**
Lizard & Pt., *England* N31+500 **38**
Ljubljana, *Yugoslavia* M03+461 **56**
Ljubuški, *Yugoslavia* L75+432 **56**
Ljungdalen, *Sweden* M13+628 **46**
Ljusdal, *Sweden* L83+618 **47**
Llandaff, *Wales* N19+515 **38**
Llandeilo, *Wales* N24+519 **38**
Llandrindod Wells, *Wales* N20+522 **38**
Llandudno, *Wales* N23+533 **38**
Llanelli, *Wales* N25+517 **38**
Llanerchymedd, *Wales* N26+533 **38**
Llanes, *Spain* N29+434 **52**
Llangollen, *Wales* N19+530 **38**
Llanguihuie, L., *Chile* S76-411 **103**
Llanllyfni, *Wales* N26+530 **38**
Llano Estacado, *New Mex.* U78+340 **94**
Llanrhaiadr, *Wales* N20+528 **38**
Llanrwst, *Wales* N23+531 **38**
Llerena, *Spain* N36+383 **52**
Lleyn Pen., *Wales* N27+529 **38**
Lliamna, L., *Alaska* Y30+595 **99**
Llico, *Chile* S72-347 **103**
Lloydminster, *Saskatchewan* V30+534 **88**
Lluchmayor, *Balearic Is.* M72+395 **53**
Loango, *Congo* M20-046 **82**
Lobbes, *Belgium* M64+504 **44**
Loberia, *Argentina* R83-382 **103**
Lobito, *Angola* M08-124 **82**
Lobos, *Argentina* R86-352 **103**
Lobstick L., *Labrador* S30+540 **89**
Locarno, *Switzerland* M37+462 **45**
Lochalsh, *Ontario* T56+484 **91**
Lochalsh, Kyle of, *Scotland* N34+573 **40**
Lochbuie, *Scotland* N35+564 **41**
Lochcarron, *Scotland* N33+574 **40**
Lochearnhead, *Scotland* N26+564 **41**
Lochem, *Netherlands* M51+522 **44**
Lochgelly, *Scotland* N20+561 **41**
Lochgilphead, *Scotland* N33+560 **41**
Lochgoilhead, *Scotland* N29+562 **41**
Lochinver, *Scotland* N31+582 **40**
Lochmaben, *Scotland* N21+551 **41**
Lochmaddy, *Scotland* N43+576 **40**
Lochnagar, *Scotland* N20+570 **40**
Lochy, L., *Scotland* N29+570 **40**
Lockerbie, *Scotland* N20+551 **41**
Lockhart, *New South Wales* C21-353 **109**
Lock Haven, *Pennsylvania* T15+411 **96**
Lockport, *New York* T22+431 **96**
Locle, le, *Switzerland* M49+471 **45**
Loc Ninh, *Vietnam* E81+118 **65**
Lochristi, *Belgium* M67+511 **44**
Lodeynoye Pole, *U.S.S.R.* K69+608 **60**
Lodhran, *Pakistan* H20+295 **72**
Lodi, *Wisconsin* T87+434 **91**
Lødingen, *Norway* L84+684 **46**
Lodwar, *Kenya* K56+030 **83**
Lodz, *Poland* L63+518 **49**
Loenen, *Netherlands* M54+521 **44**
Loewoek, *Celebes,* D73-010 **65**
Lofer, *Austria* M14+476 **48**
Lofoten, Is., *Norway* M16+680 **46**
Logan, *Montana* V39+459 **93**
Logan, *Utah* V42+418 **94**
Logan, Mt., *Quebec* S40+489 **90**
Logan, Mt., *Yukon* X30+606 **88**
Logansport, *Indiana* T68+408 **95**
Logone R., *Cameroon–Chad* M00+104 **81**
Logrona, *Spain* N15+424 **53**
Lohardaga, *India* G32+234 **73**
Loharu, *India* G85+285 **72**
Loikaw, *Burma* F46+197 **71**
Loir, R., *France* N02+474 **54**
Loire, dep., *France* M67+457 **54**
Loire R., *France* N09+472 **54**
Loire Atlantique, dep., *Fr.* N11+474 **54**
Loiret, dep., *France* M77+479 **54**
Loir-et-Cher, dep., *France* M82+475 **54**
Loja, *Ecuador* T25-040 **104**
Loja, *Spain* N25+372 **52**
Lokeren, *Belgium* M66+511 **44**
Lokka, *Finland* L14+678 **46**
Løkken, *Denmark* M32+574 **47**
Løkken, *Norway* M32+631 **46**
Loko, *Sudan* K84+044 **81**
Lokoja, *Nigeria* N60+078 **80**
Loks I., *N.-W. Territories* S26+620 **89**
Lola, *Angola* M08-144 **82**
Lolland, *Denmark* M20+546 **47**

Lom, *Bulgaria* L41+438 **58**
Loman, *Minnesota* U23+485 **93**
Lomas, *Argentina* R80-348 **103**
Loma Tina, mt., *Dom. Rep.* S64+186 **101**
Lombard, *Montana* V39+461 **93**
Lombardia, dep., *Italy* M30+457 **56**
Lomblen, I., *Indonesia* D70-085 **65**
Lombok, I. & Str., *Indonesia* E24-088 **65**
Lome, *Togo* M84+062 **80**
Lomela, *Zaire* L40-022 **82**
Lomie, *Cameroon* M08+032 **81**
Lommel, *Belgium* M58+512 **44**
Lomond Hills, *Scotland* N20+562 **41**
Lomond L., *Scotland* N28+562 **41**
Łomża, *Poland* L48+532 **49**
Loncoche, *Chile* S77-394 **103**
Loncopue, *Argentina* S64-381 **103**
Londiani, *Kenya* K54-002 **83**
London, *England* N01+515 **39**
London, *Ontario* T37+430 **91**
Londonderry, & co.,
   Northern Ireland N44+550 **42**
Londonderry, C., *W. Aust.* D49-138 **110**
Londonderry, I., *Chile* S64-550 **103**
Long Beach. *S. Carolina* T23+334 **99**
Long I., *Bahamas, The* T01 + 234 **101**
Long I., *New York* S78+408 **96**
Long I., *Nova Scotia* S38+443 **90**
Long L., *Maine* S56+466 **90**
Long L., *Ontario* T70+496 **89**
Long L., *Scotland* N29+562 **41**
Long Ra., *Newfoundland* R74+500 **90**
Longa, *Brazil* Q73-054 **105**
Long Beach, *California* V79+338 **92**
Long Beach, *New Jersey* S85+396 **96**
Long Branch, *New Jersey* S84+403 **96**
Longchamps, *Belgium* M56+500 **44**
Longford, *Tasmania* C18-416 **109**
Longford & co., *Ireland, Rep.* N47+537 **42**
Long Island Sd., *N.Y., etc.* S77+411 **96**
Long Island City, *New York* S84+407 **96**
Long Melford, *England* M86+521 **39**
Longmont, *Colorado* V01+402 **94**
Long Point I., *Ontario* T32+426 **91**
Long Prairie, *Minnesota* U29+460 **93**
Longreach, *Queensland* C35-232 **111**
Longs Pk., *Colorado* V04+402 **94**
Longtown, *England* N18+550 **37**
Longué, *France* N01+474 **54**
Longueuil, *Quebec* S81+456 **91**
Longuyon, *France* M57+494 **54**
Longview, *Texas* U28+324 **95**
Longview, *Washington* W18+461 **92**
Longwy, *France* M55+495 **54**
Long-Xuyen, *Vietnam* E87+104 **69**
Lonneker, *Netherlands* M48+522 **44**
Lons Saunier, *France* M57+467 **54**
Looc, *Philippines* D78+123 **65**
Looe, E. & W., *England* N27+504 **38**
Lookout, C., *N. Carolina* T07+347 **99**
Loolmalasin, mt., *Tanzania* K56-030 **83**
Loop Hd., *Ireland, Rep.* N60+526 **43**
Lopei, *China* D24+476 **64**
Lopez C., *Gabon* M38-006 **82**
Lopik, *Netherlands* M60+520 **44**
Lop Nor, *Sinkiang, China* F88+404 **64**
Lopphavet, *Norway* L54+704 **46**
Lora Hamun, *Pakistan* H61+292 **70**
Lorain, *Ohio* T43+414 **91**
Loralai, *Pakistan* H38+304 **70**
Lorca, *Spain* N10+377 **53**
Lord Howe I., *Pacific Ocean* B35-314 **106**
Lordsburg, *New Mexico* V22+324 **94**
Loreno, *Brazil* R00-226 **105**
Loreto, *Brazil* R02-073 **105**
Loreto, *Mexico* V38+260 **100**
Lorica, *Colombia* T04+092 **104**
Lorient, *France* N20+478 **54**
Lorne, *Victoria* C36-386 **109**
Lorn, Firth of, *Scotland* N34+563 **41**
Lorrach, *W. Germany* M44+476 **48**
Lorraine, prov., *France* M53+487 **54**
Los Andes, *Chile* S64-328 **103**
Los Angeles, *California* V79+341 **92**
Los Angeles, *Chile* S74-375 **103**
Los Blancos, *Argentina* S16-235 **103**
Loshan, *China* F08+296 **67**
Lošinj I., *Yugoslavia* M04+445 **56**
Los Lamentos, *Mexico* V04+305 **100**
Los Menucos, *Argentina* S49-408 **103**
Los Pozos, *Chile* S62-265 **103**
Los Santos, *Panama* T32+080 **101**
Los Santos de Maimona, *Spain* N38+385 **52**
Lossie R., *Scotland* N20+577 **40**
Lossiemouth, *Scotland* N20+577 **40**
Los Teques, *Venezuela* S42+103 **104**
Los Tigres, *Argentina* S16-258 **103**
Los Vilos, *Chile* S69-319 **103**
Lot, dep., *France* M80+446 **55**
Lot, R., *France* M85+445 **55**
Lota, *Chile* S79-371 **103**
Lotbinière, *Quebec* S72+466 **91**
Lot-et-Garonne, dep., *France* M87+443 **55**
Lothian, reg., *Scotland* N18+559 **41**
Lottinga, *Switzerland* M36+465 **45**
Loubet Coast, *Antarctica* S25-680 **27**
Loudeac, *France* N16+482 **54**
Loudima., *Congo* M12-042 **82**
Loudon, *Malawi* K69-122 **83**
Loudon, *Tennessee* T56+357 **97**
Loudun, *France* N00+470 **54**
Louga, *Senegal* P08+154 **80**
Loughborough, *England* N07+528 **37**
Loughborough's I., *Burma* F43+104 **71**
Loughor, *Wales* N24+517 **38**
Loughrea, *Ireland, Rep.* N51+532 **43**
Louhans, *France* M59+466 **54**
Louisa, *Kentucky* T46+381 **97**
Louisburg, *N. Carolina* T20+362 **97**
Louiseville, *Quebec* S78+463 **91**
Louisiade Arch.
   Papua New Guinea B70-110 **111**
Louisiana, state, *U.S.A.* U20+306 **99**
Louis Trichardt, *Transvaal* L00-232 **84**
Louisville, *Colorado* V02+400 **94**
Louisville, *Kentucky* T65+383 **97**
Louisville, *Mississippi* T84+331 **97**
Loule, *Portugal* N48+371 **52**
Loup City, *Nebraska* U54+412 **95**
Lourdes, *France* N01+431 **55**

Lourenço Marques, *See* Maputo
Lourical, *Portugal* N53+401 **52**
Lourinha, *Portugal* N56+392 **52**
Louth, *England* N00+534 **37**
Louth, *New South Wales* C29-306 **109**
Louth & co., *Ireland, Rep.* N39+539 **42**
Louvain, *Belgium* M62+509 **44**
Louveigne, *Belgium* M56+505 **44**
Louviers, *France* M83+492 **54**
Lövanger, *Sweden* L52+643 **46**
Loveland, *Colorado* V00+404 **94**
Lovell, *Wyoming* V21+448 **93**
Loviisa (Lovisa), *Finland* L23+605 **47**
Lovington, *New Mexico* U80+329 **94**
Lövlid, *Sweden* L80+647 **46**
Low, C., *N.-W. Territories* T64+634 **89**
Lowa, *Zaire* L24-014 **82**
Lowell, *Massachusetts* S68+427 **91**
Lowell, *Michigan* T62+429 **91**
Lower Brule, *S. Dakota* U57+441 **93**
Lowestoft, *England* M80+525 **39**
Lowicz, *Poland* L60+521 **49**
Lowland, *N. Carolina* T09+353 **97**
Lowriet, *Belize* T81+182 **101**
Lowville, *New York* T03+438 **91**
Loxton, *S. Australia* C57-345 **109**
Loyalty Is., *Pacific Ocean* A80-210 **106**
Loyang, *China* E45+348 **66**
Loyung, *China* E63+244 **67**
Lozère, dep., *France* M68+444 **55**
Loznica, *Yugoslavia* L65+445 **58**
Luampa, *Zambia* L34-152 **84**
Luan. *See* Changchih
Luanda, *Angola* M10-090 **82**
Luang Prabang, *Laos* F17+198 **69**
Luarca, *Spain* N40+435 **52**
Luashi, *Zaire* L38-110 **82**
Lubaczów, *Poland* L42+501 **49**
Lubana, *Latvia* L20+569 **47**
Lubartow, *Poland* L45+515 **49**
Lubben, *E. Germany* M07+520 **48**
Lubbock, *Texas* U70+336 **94**
Lübeck, *W. Germany* M26+539 **48**
Lubeck, *Victoria* C45-368 **109**
Lübecker B.,
   E. & W. Germany M24+541 **48**
Lubefu, *Zaire* L34-046 **82**
Lubin, *Poland* L82+514 **49**
Lublin, *Poland* L45+512 **49**
Lubliniec, *Poland* L68+507 **49**
Lubnaig, L., *Scotland* N26+563 **41**
Lubumbashi, *Zaire* L14-118 **83**
Luc, le, *France* M52+434 **55**
Lucala, *Angola* L88-094 **82**
Lucan. *Ireland, Rep.* N39+534 **43**
Lucania. *See* Basilicata.
Lucca, *Italy* M27+439 **56**
Lucca, *Jamaica* T19+185 **101**
Luce B., *Scotland* N29+548 **41**
Lucena, *Spain* N27+374 **52**
Lučenec, *Czechoslovakia* L62+483 **49**
Lucera, *Italy* L88+415 **57**
Lucerne. *See* Luzern.
Luch, *U.S.S.R.* K17+570 **61**
Luchow, *China* E88+288 **67**
Luchow (Hofei), *China* E17+319 **66**
Lucinda, *Pennsylvania* T27+413 **96**
Lucindale, *S. Australia* C58-370 **109**
Luckau, *E. Germany* M08+519 **48**
Luckenwalde, *E. Germany* M11+521 **48**
Lucknow, *India* G54+268 **73**
Lucknow, *Ontario* T39+440 **91**
Luçon, *France* N07+465 **54**
Luderitz, *Namibia* L88-266 **84**
Ludhiana, *India* G85+309 **72**
Ludington, *Michigan* T69+440 **91**
Ludlow, *England* N16+524 **38**
Ludvika, *Sweden* L89+601 **47**
Ludwigshafen, *W. Germany* M40+495 **48**
Ludwigslust, *E. Germany* M21+533 **48**
Ludza, *Latvia* L14+565 **47**
Luebo, *Zaire* L52-054 **82**
Luga, *U.S.S.R.* L01+587 **60**
Lugano & L. di, *Switz.* M36+460 **45**
Lugansk, *Ukraine* K34+486 **60**
Lugh Ferrandi, *Somalia* K14+036 **83**
Lugo, *Spain* N45+430 **52**
Lugoj, *Romania* L49+457 **58**
Lugovaia, *Kazakh.* H13+430 **62**
Luhaiya, *Yemen* K14+157 **74**
Luhit R., *India* F54+276 **71**
Luhsien. *See* Luchow.
Luhwang Shan I., *China* D77+297 **67**
Luichow. *See* Hoihong
Luichow Pen., *China* E66+208 **64**
Luime, *Angola* L84-108 **82**
Luitpold Cst., *Antarctica* Q20-770 **27**
Lujan, *Argentina* R85-345 **103**
Lujan, *Argentina* S53-330 **103**
Lujan, *Paraguay* R75-252 **103**
Lukala, *Zaire* M04-056 **82**
Lukavit, *Bulgaria* L35+432 **58**
Lukoyanov, *U.S.S.R.* K03+550 **61**
Lukula, *Zaire* M12-054 **82**
Lule Älv, *Sweden* L18+654 **46**
Lulea, *Sweden* L47+656 **46**
Luluabourg, *Zaire* L46-058 **82**
Lulung, *China* E07+398 **66**
Lumberton, *N. Carolina* T24+346 **97**
Lumbres, *France* M78+507 **54**
Lummen, *Belgium* M59+510 **44**
Lumsden, *New Zealand* A49-457 **112**
Luna, *Arkansas* U06+334 **97**
Lunan B., *Scotland* N15+566 **41**
Lund, *Sweden* M11+557 **47**
Lundy I., *England* N28+512 **38**
Lune, R., *England* N16+542 **37**
Lüneburg, *W. Germany* M28+533 **48**
Lunel, *France* M66+437 **55**
Luneville, *France* M51+486 **54**
Lungan. *See* Pingwu.
Lungki, *China* E13+246 **67**
Lungnan, *China* E24+228 **67**
Lungsi, *China* F03+349 **66**
Lungyen, *China* E18+252 **67**
Luni, *India* H11+260 **70**
Lunino, *U.S.S.R.* J89+536 **61**
Lunz, *Austria* L90+478 **48**
Lupiro, *Tanzania* K50-084 **83**
Lupkow, *Poland* L48+493 **49**

Luputa, *Zaire* L38-072 **82**
Luray, *Virginia* T21+387 **91**
Lurgan, *N. Ireland* N38+544 **42**
Luribay, *Bolivia* S46-170 **104**
Lurøy, *Norway* M13+664 **46**
Lusaka, *Zambia* L10-154 **84**
Lusambo, *Zaire* L40-050 **82**
Lusambo, *Zaire* L44-084 **82**
Lushai Hills, *India* F72+233 **71**
Lushnjë, *Albania* L62+409 **59**
Lushun, *China* D82+388 **66**
Lusk, *Wyoming* U86+427 **93**
Luss, *Scotland* N28+561 **41**
Lut Des., *Iran* J10+310 **30**
Lüta, *China* D80+389 **66**
Luther, *Michigan* T65+441 **91**
Luton, *England* N02+519 **39**
Lutsen, *Minnesota* U04+476 **91**
Lutsk, *Ukraine* L28+508 **60**
Luttre, *Belgium* M64+505 **44**
Luvia, *Finland* L50+613 **47**
Luxembourg, and Grand-duchy of,
   N.-W. Europe M54+497 **48**
Luxembourg, prov., *Belg.* M57+500 **44**
Luxeuil, *France* M52+478 **54**
Luxor, *Egypt* K74+256 **81**
Luzern & canton, *Switz.* M40+471 **45**
Luzon, I., *Philippines* D85+150 **65**
Luzon Str. *Philippines* D75+200 **64**
Luzy, *France* M66+468 **54**
Lvov, *Ukraine* L36+498 **60**
Lwanhsien, *China* E07+397 **66**
Lwan-ping, *China* E13+409 **66**
Lyallpur, *Pakistan* H15+314 **72**
Lybster, *Scotland* N20+583 **40**
Lycksele, *Sweden* L68+646 **46**
Lydavénis, *Lithuania* L41+556 **47**
Lydda, *Israel* K61+320 **76**
Lydenburg, *Transvaal* K88-252 **84**
Lydney, *England* N16+517 **38**
Lyell, Mt., *Brit. Columbia* V72+17 **88**
Lyell, Mt., *California* V85+378 **92**
Lyell Ra., *New Zealand* A46-412 **112**
Lykens, *Pennsylvania* T11+405 **96**
Lyme B., *England* N18+506 **38**
Lyme Regis, *England* N18+507 **38**
Lymington, *England* N09+508 **39**
Lynchburg, *Virginia* T25+374 **97**
Lyndhurst, *S. Australia* C70-303 **109**
Lynn, *Massachusetts* S65+425 **96**
Lynton, *England* N23+512 **38**
Lyon, *France* M61+458 **54**
Lyon, *Montana* V39+448 **93**
Lyonnais, prov., *France* M65+458 **54**
Lyons, *Georgia* T44+322 **97**
Lyons, *Kansas* U49+384 **95**
Lyons, *New York* T12+430 **96**
Lyons, R., *W. Australia* E27-243 **110**
Lys, R., *Belgium, etc.* M69+509 **44**
Lysamis, *Kenya* K42+016 **83**
Łyse, *Poland* L51+534 **49**
Lysekil, *Sweden* M21+583 **47**
Lyss, Switz. M46+471 **45**
Lyster, *Quebec* S69+464 **91**
Lysva, *U.S.S.R.* J31+581 **61**
Lytham St Annes, *England* N18+537 **37**
Lyttelton, *New Zealand* A43-436 **112**
Lytton, *British Columbia* W09+502 **88**
Ma'an, *Jordan* K56+302 **76**
Maarheeze, *Netherlands* M57+513 **44**
Maarianhamina. *See* Mariehamn.
Ma'arret en Numan, *Syria* K50+357 **76**
Maas, R., *Netherlands* M55+518 **44**
Maasbree, *Netherlands* M54+514 **44**
Maaseik, *Belgium* M55+511 **44**
Ma'asir, *Saudi Arabia* K41+307 **74**
Maassluis, *Netherlands* M65+519 **44**
Maastricht, *Belgium* M56+508 **44**
Maatsuyker Is., *Tasmania* C22-436 **109**
Mabote, *Mozambique* K66-222 **84**
Mabrouk, *Mali* N08+194 **80**
Mabuki, *Tanzania* K70-030 **83**
McAdam, *New Brunswick* S44+456 **90**
Macahe, *Brazil* Q71-225 **105**
Macahyba, *Brazil* Q32-059 **105**
McAlester, *Oklahoma* U34+350 **95**
McAlister, mt., *New S. Wales* C02-345 **109**
Macaloje, *Mozambique* K52-120 **83**
Macao (Port.), *China* E38+223 **67**
Macapa, *Brazil* R36+001 **105**
Macás, *Ecuador* T19-024 **104**
Macau, *Brazil* Q40-051 **105**
McCammon, *Idaho* V43+426 **94**
Macclesfield, *England* N18+533 **37**
McClintock Chan., *N.-W. Ter.* U70+714 **88**
McClure, C., *N.-W. Terr.* W08+746 **88**
McClure Str., *N.-W. Terr.* V70+738 **88**
McComb, *Mississippi* U03+312 **97**
McConnellsburg, *Pa.* T18+399 **96**
McCook, *Nebraska* U66+402 **94**
Macdonald, L., *W. Australia* D37-234 **110**
Macdonnel Ranges, *N. Terr., Aust.* D15-232 **110**
McDouall Ra., *N. Terr., Aust.* D00-196 **111**
Macdougall, L., *N.-W. Terr.* U50+660 **88**
Maceio, *Brazil* Q34-095 **105**
Macerata, *Italy* M09+433 **56**
McGill, *Nevada* V59+395 **92**
Macgillycuddy's Reeks,
   Ireland, Rep. N59+520 **43**
McGregor, *Texas* U44+314 **95**
McGregor Ra., *Queensland* C43-268 **111**
Mach, *Pakistan* H48+298 **70**
Machala, *Ecuador* T29-032 **104**
Machareti, *Bolivia* S19-208 **104**
Machias, *Maine* S45+448 **90**
Machias B., *Maine* S44+446 **90**
Machiasport, *Maine* S44+447 **90**
Machicha, *Mozambique* K58-240 **84**
Machilipatnam (Bandar), *India* G52+162 **70**
Machiques, *Venezuela* S75+100 **104**
Machiwara, *India* G83+309 **72**
Machu Picchu, *Peru* S77-128 **104**
Machynlleth, *Wales* N23+528 **38**
Macias Nguema, *Equat - Guinea* M38+036 **80**
Măcin, *Romania* L11+452 **58**
McIntosh, *S. Dakota* U68+459 **93**
Mackay, *Alberta* V40+570 **88**
Mackay, *Queensland* C00-211 **111**
Mackay L., *N.-W. Terr.* V32+640 **88**
Mackay, L., *W. Australia* D37-226 **110**
McKeesport, *Pennsylvania* T29+404 **96**

Mackenna, *Argentina* S27–338 **103**
McKenzie, *Tennessee* T81+361 **97**
Mackenzie B., *Antartica* H05–680 **27**
Mackenzie Dist., *N.-W. Terr.* W00+640 **88**
Mackenzie B., *N.-W. Terr.* X15+688 **88**
Mackenzie Mts., *N.-W. Terr.* W60+642 **88**
Mackenzie R., *N.-W. Terr.* W45+654 **88**
Mackenzie King I., *N.-W. T.* V30+776 **88**
Mackillop, L., *Queensland* C52–262 **111**
Mackinac I. & Str. of, *Mich.* 158+458 **91**
Mackinaw, *Michigan* T59+458 **91**
McKinley, Mt., *Alaska* Y05+628 **99**
Macksville, *New S. Wales* B74–308 **109**
Maclean, *New S. Wales* B71–294 **109**
McLeansboro, *Illinois* T81+381 **97**
Macleay, R., *New S. Wales* B76–308 **109**
Macleod, *Alberta* V50–498 **88**
McLeod R., *N.-W. Terr.* V35+632 **88**
Macloutsi, *Botswana* L10–222 **84**
MacMahon Fort, *Algeria* M80+292 **80**
McMillan, L., *New Mexico* U86+326 **94**
Macmillan Ra., *Yukon* X10+636 **94**
Macmillan R., *Yukon* W85+635 **88**
McMinnville, *Tennessee* T65+357 **97**
McMullen Pk., *Arizona* V24+330 **94**
McMurdo Sd., *Antarctica* A90–770 **27**
McNary, *Arizona* V29+340 **94**
Macomb, *Illinois* U06+404 **95**
Macomer, *Sardinia* M37+402 **57**
Macon, *Georgia* M65+501 **44**
Mâcon, *France* M61+463 **54**
Macon, *Georgia* T52+328 **97**
Macon, *Mississippi* T82+331 **95**
Macon, *Missouri* U15+398 **95**
McPherson, *Kansas* U46+384 **95**
McPherson, *N.-W. Terr.* W89+672 **88**
Macpherson Ra., *Queensland* B75–280 **111**
Macquarie Harb., *Tasmania* C28–423 **109**
Macquarie I., *Pacific Ocean* B35–510 **106**
Macquarie L., *New S. Wales* B81–331 **109**
Macquarie Mt., *N.S.W.* C05–337 **109**
Macquarie, R., *N.S.W.* C15–306 **109**
Macquarie, R., *Tasmania* C17–417 **109**
McRae, *Georgia* T48+320 **97**
Mac-Robertson Ld., *Antarc.* H75–690 **27**
Macroom, *Ireland, Rep.* N54+519 **43**
Macuje, *Colombia* S80+004 **104**
Macusani, *Peru* S62–140 **104**
McVicar Arm, *N.-W. Terr.* V85+652 **88**
Madaba, *Jordan* K55+317 **76**
Madadi, *Chad* L56+182 **81**
Madagascar I., *Indian Oc.* J76–200 **83**
Madahy, *Brazil* Ro6–050 **105**
Madain Salih, *Saudi Arabia* K41+269 **74**
Madan, *Iran* J10+366 **74**
Madaripur, *Bangladesh* F89+232 **71**
Madawaska, *Ontario* T18+455 **91**
Madeira Is., *Atlantic Ocean* P10+326 **80**
Madeira, R., *Brazil* S08–056 **104**
Madeleine, C. de la, *Quebec* S32+493 **90**
Madhepur, *India* G22+262 **73**
Madhipura, *India* G19+259 **73**
Madhopur, *India* G81+260 **70**
Madhopur, *India* G86+323 **72**
Madhubani, *India* G23+264 **73**
Madhupur, *India* G20+243 **73**
Madhya Pradesh, *India* G75+236 **70**
Madinat ash Sh'ab,
  Yemen, South K01 + 127 **74**
Madison, *Georgia* T51+338 **97**
Madison, *Kansas* U37+382 **95**
Madison, *Nebraska* U45+418 **95**
Madison, *New Jersey* S87+407 **96**
Madison, *N. Carolina* T30+364 **97**
Madison, *S. Dakota* U42+440 **93**
Madison, *Wisconsin* T86+430 **95**
Madisonville, *Kentucky* T75+372 **97**
Madoc, *Ontario* T15+445 **91**
Madona, *Latvia* L23+569 **47**
Madras, *India* G58+132 **70**
Madre, Laguna, *Texas* U44+266 **94**
Madre, Sa., *Mexico* V04+250 **100**
Madre, Sierra, *Wyoming* V12+412 **93**
Madre Austral, Lag. de la,
  Mexico U47+246 **100**
Madre de Dios, I., *Chile* T00–502 **103**
Madre de Dios, R., *Peru-Bol.* S54–123 **104**
Madre del Sur, Sa., *Mexico* U65+174 **100**
Madrid, *New Mexico* V08+354 **94**
Madrid, *Spain* N22+404 **52**
Madridejos, *Spain* N21+395 **52**
Madura, I., *Indonesia* G72+100 **70**
Madurai, I., *Indonesia* E40+069 **65**
Maebashi, *Japan* C65+364 **68**
Maeseyck, *Belgium* M55+511 **44**
Maestra, Sa., *Cuba* T10+202 **101**
Mafeking, *Cape Province* L26–260 **84**
Mafia I., *Tanzania* K32–078 **83**
Mafra, *Portugal* N56+390 **52**
Mafraq, *Jordan* K53+324 **76**
Magad Plat. See Jol Plat
Magadan, *U.S.S.R.* B86+595 **63**
Magadi & L., *Kenya* K52–020 **83**
Magadino, *Switzerland* M37+462 **45**
Magallanes. See Punta Arenas
Magallanes, Estrecho de,
  Chile S82–532 **103**
Magangue, *Colombia* S89+092 **104**
Magas, *Iran* H80+271 **75**
Magaz, *Spain* N27+420 **52**
Magburaka, *Sierra Leone* N72+088 **80**
Magdala, *Ethiopia* K34+112 **83**
Magdalen Is., *Quebec* S13+474 **90**
Magdalena, *Bolivia* S25–133 **104**
Magdalena, *Mexico* V35+306 **100**
Magdalena, *New Mexico* V14+342 **94**
Magdalena, B., *Mexico* V42+245 **100**
Magdalena, I., *Chile* S78–447 **103**
Magdalena, R., *Colombia* S88+095 **104**
Magdalena, R., *Mexico* V45+308 **100**
Magdeburg, *E. Germany* M20+521 **48**
Magee I., *N. Ireland* N34+548 **42**
Magellan, Str. of, *Chile* S60–528 **103**
Magerøya, *Norway* L26+709 **46**
Maggia, *Switzerland* M38+462 **45**
Maggiore, L., *Italy* M37+460 **56**
Maghang Tsangpo, R., *Tibet* G35+292 **71**
Maghara, Geb., *Egypt* K70+306 **76**
Magharee Is., *Ireland, Rep.* N60+523 **43**
Maghera, *N. Ireland* N50+548 **42**

Magheratelt, *N. Ireland* N40+548 **42**
Maglaj, *Yugoslavia* L71+446 **58**
Maglie, *Italy* L70+401 **57**
Magnetic Pole, N., *N.-W. T.* U70+760 **88**
Magnitogorsk, *U.S.S.R.* J06+533 **61**
Magnolia, *Alabama* T76+322 **97**
Magnolia, *Arkansas* U19+332 **95**
Magnolia, *Mississippi* U02+311 **95**
Magnolia, *N. Carolina* T20+350 **97**
Magog, *Quebec* S73+453 **91**
Magpie, *Quebec* S27+503 **90**
Magpie L., *Quebec* S28+510 **90**
Maguse L., *N.-W. Terr.* U44+614 **88**
Magwe, *Burma* F60+202 **71**
Mahabad, *Iran* J86+368 **74**
Mahabaleshwar, *India* H07+180 **70**
Mahaban, *India* G73+274 **72**
Mahabharat Ra., *Nepal* G30+274 **73**
Mahaddei Uen, *Somalia* J86+028 **83**
Mahadeo Hills, *India* G72+223 **73**
Mahail, *Saudi Arabia* K17+190 **74**
Mahajamba B. de, *Madag.* J78–154 **83**
Mahajan, *India* H07+287 **72**
Mahalapye, *Botswana* L20–232 **84**
Mahallat, *Iran* J58+339 **75**
Maham, *India* G82+290 **72**
Mahanadi R., *India* G31+206 **71**
Mahanoro, *Madagascar* J68–200 **83**
Mahanoy City,
  Pennsylvania T07+408 **96**
Maharashtra, state, *India* H00+190 **70**
Mahbubnagar, *India* G71+168 **70**
Mahdia, *Tunisia* M24+354 **81**
Mahé, *India.* G87+117 **70**
Mahendragiri, mt., *India* G33+192 **71**
Mahia Pen., *New Zealand* A12–392 **112**
Mahmed-Hussein-magala,
  Iran J55+368 **75**
Mahmudabad, *India* G53+273 **73**
Mahmudabad, *Iran* J47+366 **75**
Mahot I., *Saudi Arabia* J12+205 **75**
Mahunda, *Mozambique* K32–118 **83**
Mahuva, *India* H18+211 **70**
Maibud, *Iran* J35+322 **75**
Maida, *Yemen* K13+163 **74**
Maidan, *Afghanistan* H49+324 **75**
Maidenhead, *England* N04+515 **39**
Maidstone, *England* M87+513 **39**
Maiduguri, *Nigeria* M10+118 **81**
Maienfeld, *Switzerland* M33+470 **45**
Maihar, *India* G55+243 **73**
Maikal Ra., *India* G52+224 **73**
Maikop, *U.S.S.R.* K29+445 **62**
Maimana, *Afghanistan* H60+358 **75**
Mai-Ndombe, L., *Zaire* L70-020 **82**
Main, R., *Germany* M33+498 **48**
Main R., *N. Ireland* N38+547 **42**
Main Barrier Ra., *N.S.W.* C52–31o **109**
Maine, prov., *France* N01+483 **54**
Maine, state, *U.S.A.* S60+450 **99**
Maine, G. of, *Maine, etc.* S54+433 **90**
Maine-et-Loire, dep.,
  France N04+472 **54**
Maing Kaing, *Burma* F58+248 **71**
Maingkwan, *Burma* F50+263 **71**
Mainpuri, *India* G66+272 **73**
Mainstream, *Maine* S57+449 **90**
Mainz, *W. Germany* M40+500 **48**
Maipo, mt., *Argentina* S59–342 **103**
Maipu, *Argentina* R77–368 **103**
Maique R., *Ireland, Rep.* N53+526 **43**
Maison Carrée (El Harrach),
  Algeria M72+366 **80**
Maissin, *Belgium* M59+500 **44**
Mait & I., *Somalia* J78+108 **83**
Maitland, *New South Wales* B81–327 **109**
Maitland, *S. Australia* C74–343 **109**
Maitland, L., *W. Australia* D83–269 **110**
Maiz, *Mexico* U58+224 **100**
Maizura, *Japan* C88+354 **68**
Maja, I., *Indonesia* E63–011 **65**
Majagua, *Colombia* S88+085 **104**
Majitha, *India* H00+317 **72**
Majmaa, *Saudi Arabia* J88+259 **74**
Majorca. See Mallorca
Majunga, *Madagascar* J82–158 **83**
Majuro, Is., *Marshall Is.* A50+065 **106**
Makale, *Ethiopia* K32+134 **83**
Makania, *Tanzania* K44–044 **83**
Makariev, *U.S.S.R.* K07+578 **61**
Makarvey, *U.S.S.R.* J89+561 **61**
Makasar, *Celebes,* see Ujung Pandang
Makassar Str., *Indonesia* E15–032 **65**
Makatea, I., *Tuamotu Arch.* X80–158 **107**
Makedhonia, *Greece* L48+407 **59**
Makemo, I., *Tuamotu Arch.* X54–162 **107**
Makhachkala, *U.S.S.R.* J76+430 **62**
Makhai, *China* F66+381 **64**
Makikihi, *New Zealand* A53–446 **112**
Makindu, *Kenya* K42–024 **83**
Makkinga, *Netherlands* M53+530 **44**
Makla, Jebel el, *Saudi Arabia* K58+286 **74**
Mako, *Hungary* L57+462 **58**
Makongolosi, *Tanzania* K70–084 **83**
Makorako, mt., *N.Z.* A23–391 **112**
Makram, *Saudi Arabia* K32+205 **74**
Makri, *India* G48+198 **70**
Makri, *Turkey* L05+367 **74**
Maksamaa, *Finland* L47+632 **46**
Maku, *Iran* K03+393 **74**
Makum, *India* F57+274 **71**
Makurdi, *Nigeria* M38+078 **80**
Makwiro, *Zimbabwe* K88–178 **84**
Makeyevka, *Ukraine* K42+481 **60**
Mal B., *Ireland, Rep.* N57+528 **43**
Mal B., *Quebec* S25+486 **90**
Mala, *Peru* T10–127 **100**
Malå, *Sweden* L68+652 **46**
Malabang, *Philippines* D65+076 **65**
Malabar Coast, *India* H00+120 **70**
Malabo, *Macias Nguema* M37+038 **80**
Malacca, Str. of,
  Sumatra-Pen-Malaysia F26+025 **65**
Malad City, *Idaho* V44+422 **94**
Maladeta, mt., *Spain* M86+426 **53**
Malaga, *Spain* N26+367 **52**
Malaita, *Solomon Is.* B25–090 **106**
Malakal, *Sudan* K80+094 **81**
Malakand & Pass, *Pakistan* H19+345 **72**
Malang, *Java* E43–080 **65**

Malange, *Angola* L82–096 **82**
Malaren, L., *Sweden* L78+595 **47**
Malargue, *Argentina* S57–355 **103**
Malas, *Ethiopia* K42+164 **83**
Malawi (Nyasaland), *E. Afr.* K66–120 **83**
Malayir, *Iran* J68+343 **74**
Malaysia, *S. E. Asia* **65**
Malazgirt, *Turkey* K13+391 **74**
Malbork, *Poland* L66+540 **49**
Malchow, *E. Germany* M15+535 **48**
Malda, *India* G11+250 **73**
Maldegem, *Belgium* M69+512 **44**
Malden, *Massachusetts* S66+424 **96**
Malden, *Missouri* U00+366 **95**
Malden, I., *Pacific Ocean* Y30–045 **107**
Maldive Is., *Indian Ocean* H10+050 **30**
Maldon, *England* M86+517 **39**
Maldonado, *Uruguay* R60–349 **103**
Maléa, C., *Greece* L41+365 **59**
Malé Karpaty, *Czech.* L77+484 **49**
Malekula, I., *Vanuatu* A73-173 **106**
Máleme, *Crete* L37+355 **59**
Maler Kotla, *India* G85+305 **72**
Malesherbes, *France* M75+483 **54**
Malheur L., *Oregon* V83+433 **92**
Mali, rep., *W. Africa* N00+160 **80**
Malia, *India* H25+230 **70**
Malihabad, *India* G56+269 **73**
Malin Hd., *Ireland, Rep.* N44+554 **42**
Malinau, *Borneo* E20+036 **65**
Malindi, *Kenya* K30–032 **83**
Malines, *Belgium* M61+510 **44**
Malkangiri, *India* G48+185 **71**
Malko Trnovo, *Bulgaria* L15+420 **58**
Mallacoota & Inl., *Victoria* C02–376 **109**
Mallaig, *Scotland* N35+570 **40**
Mállia, G., *Crete* L27+354 **59**
Malloggia, *Switzerland* M32+464 **45**
Mallorca I., *Balearic Is.* M72+395 **53**
Mallow, *Ireland, Rep.* N52+521 **43**
Malmberget, *Sweden* L56+671 **46**
Malmédy, *Belgium* M54+504 **44**
Malmesbury, *England* N13+516 **39**
Malmö, *Sweden* M12+556 **47**
Malmyzh, *U.S.S.R.* J56+565 **61**
Malombe L., *Malawi* K58–146 **83**
Malone, *New York* S86+449 **91**
Malonga, *Zaire* L40–106 **82**
Malpeque B., *P.E.I.* S23+466 **90**
Malta, *Montana* V17+484 **93**
Malta Chan., *Medit. Sea* M02+364 **57**
Malta, I., *Mediterranean Sea* M03+359 **57**
Malters, *Switzerland* M41+470 **45**
Malton, *England* N05+541 **37**
Malung, *Sweden* M08+607 **47**
Malvaglia, *Switzerland* M36+464 **45**
Malvan, *India* H09+161 **70**
Malvern, *Arkansas* U16+344 **95**
Malvern Hills, *England* N14+521 **38**
Malvina, *Quebec* S69+452 **91**
Malvinas, Islas. See Falkland Is.
Mama, *U.S.S.R.* E42+583 **63**
Maman, *Sudan* K50+160 **83**
Mamantel, *Mexico* U07+184 **100**
Mambasa, *Zaire* L06+012 **83**
Mammoth Cave, *Kentucky* T66+372 **97**
Mammoth Cave Nat. Park,
  Kentucky T68+372 **97**
Mamonal, *Colombia* T03+104 **104**
Mamou, *Guinea* N72+104 **80**
Mampoko, *Zaire* L68+008 **82**
Maputo, *Mozambique* K74-260 **84**
Mamu, *Afghanistan* H67+296 **75**
Mamudju, *Celebes,* E07–026 **65**
Man, *Ivory Coast* N46+076 **80**
Man, I. of, *Irish Sea* N27+542 **37**
Manacapuru, *Brazil* S03–033 **104**
Manacor, *Balearic Is.* M71+395 **53**
Manado, *Celebes,* D61+015 **65**
Managua, *Nicaragua* T68+122 **101**
Managua L., *Nicaragua* T68+124 **101**
Manakha, *Yemen* K08+151 **74**
Manama, *Bahrain I.* J57+263 **75**
Mananjary, *Madagascar* J70–214 **83**
Manankoro, *Mali* N44+104 **80**
Manantenina, *Madagascar* J76–244 **83**
Manapouri L., *New Zealand* A75–455 **112**
Manasarowar L., *Tibet* G52+307 **70**
Manasquan, *New Jersey* S85+401 **91**
Manassas, *Virginia* T15+387 **91**
Manaus, *Brazil* S00–030 **104**
Mancelona, *Michigan* T61+449 **91**
Manche, dep., *France* N09+492 **54**
Manchester, *England* N13+535 **37**
Manchester, Greater, co., *Eng.* N14+535 **37**
Manchester, *Iowa* U09+424 **95**
Manchester, *New Hampshire* S69+429 **91**
Manchester, *Tennessee* T67+354 **97**
Manchester, *Virginia* T15+375 **97**
Manchouli, *China* E14+492 **64**
Manchuria, *China* D60+460 **64**
Mancinik, *Turkey* K48+392 **74**
Manda, *Tanzania* K62–106 **83**
Mandal, *Norway* M45+580 **47**
Mandal Gobi, *Mongolia* E83+452 **64**
Mandan, *N. Dakota* U65+468 **93**
Mandarin B., *China* E58+209 **67**
Mander, *Netherlands* M49+524 **44**
Mandera, *Kenya* K20+038 **83**
Mandeville, *Louisiana* U01+304 **97**
Mandi, *India* G78+317 **72**
Mandie, *Mozambique* K68+164 **84**
Mandla, *India* G58+226 **73**
Mandritsara, *Madagascar* J68–158 **83**
Mandvi, *India* H34+228 **70**
Manfred, *New South Wales* C37–334 **109**
Manfredonia, G., di, *Italy* L84+416 **57**
Manfuha, *Saudi Arabia* J79+246 **74**
Mangaia, I., *Cook Is* Y50–220 **107**
Mangaldai, *India* F77+264 **71**
Mangalme, *Chad* L62+122 **81**
Mangalore, *India* H01+129 **70**
Mangareva, I., *Tuamotu
  Archipelago* W88–235 **107**
Mangaweka, *New Zealand* A26–398 **112**
Mangfall Geb., *W. Germany* M18+476 **48**
Manglaralto, *Ecuador* T34–018 **104**
Mangoche, *Malawi* K58–144 **84**
Mangoni, *New Zealand* A39–350 **112**

Mangrol, *India* H30+210 **70**
Mangualde, *Portugal* N47+406 **52**
Mangueria, L. da, *Brazil* R48–332 **103**
Manhatten, *Kansas* U40+392 **95**
Manhay, *Belgium* M56+503 **44**
Manhuassu, *Brazil* Q72–204 **105**
Manicoré, *Brazil* S07–058 **104**
Manifold, C., *Queensland* B85–225 **111**
Manihiki, I., *Pacific Ocean* Y66–105 **106**
Manikarchar, *India* G01+256 **73**
Manikganj. See Dasara
Manikpur, *Bangladesh* F77+218 **71**
Manikuagan R., *Quebec* S52+508 **90**
Manila, *Philippines* D84+146 **65**
Manilla, *New South Wales* B86–307 **109**
Manipur, *India* F65+250 **71**
Manisa, *Turkey* L15+386 **74**
Manistee, *Michigan* T68+443 **91**
Manistee R., *Michigan* T64+445 **91**
Manistique, *Michigan* T68+460 **91**
Manitoba, prov., *Canada* **88**
Manitoba, I., *Manitoba* U52+510 **88**
Manitou Gorge, *Quebec* S57+578 **89**
Manitou Is., *Michigan* T66+451 **91**
Manitoulin I., *Ontario* T42+457 **91**
Manitowaning, *Ontario* T41+457 **91**
Manitowoc, *Wisconsin* T76+442 **9**
Maniwaki, *Quebec* T06+464 **91**
Maniya, *Iraq* K12+308 **74**
Manizales, *Colombia* T03+051 **104**
Manja, *Madagascar* K04–214 **83**
Manjhi, *India* G32+258 **73**
Manjimup, *W. Australia* E23–340 **110**
Manka, *Taiwan* D81+250 **67**
Mankato, *Minnesota* U24+442 **93**
Mankheri, *India* G33+237 **73**
Manlleu, *Spain* M76+420 **53**
Manly, *New South Wales* B83–338 **109**
Manmad, *India* H03+203 **70**
Mannahill, *S. Australia* C60–324 **109**
Mannar, *Sri Lanka* G61+090 **70**
Mannar, G. of, *India* G67+086 **70**
Mannargudi, *India* G64+107 **70**
Mannheim, *W. Germany* M39+495 **48**
Manning, *S. Carolina* T31+337 **97**
Mannum, *S. Australia* C64–349 **109**
Manoa, *Bolivia* S33–097 **104**
Manoel Vieira, *Brazil* S02–104 **104**
Manokwari, *New Guinea* D06–008 **65**
Manono, *Zaire* L16–074 **82**
Manorhamilton, *Ireland, Rep.* N49+543 **42**
Manosque, *France* M55+439 **55**
Manresa, *Spain* M79+417 **53**
Mansehra, *Pakistan* H10+344 **72**
Mansel I., *North-West
  Territories* T30+616 **89**
Mansfield, *England* N07+531 **37**
Mansfield, *Louisiana* U22+320 **95**
Mansfield, *Massachusetts* S67+421 **91**
Mansfield, *Ohio* T45+408 **91**
Mansfield, *Pennsylvania* T13+418 **96**
Mansfield, *Victoria* C24–370 **109**
Mansfield, Mt., *Vermont* S77+446 **91**
Mansi, *Burma* F54+248 **71**
Mansilla de Las Mulas, *Spain* N33+425 **52**
Manta, *Ecuador* T34+009 **104**
Manti, *Utah* V40+392 **94**
Mantilla, *Argentina* R82–288 **103**
Mantova, *Italy* M25+451 **56**
Mantua. See Mantova
Manu, *Peru* S65–123 **104**
Manu'a, I., *Samoa Is.* Z28–150 **106**
Manuel Rodrigue, I., *Chile* S84–528 **103**
Manujan, *Iran* J15+274 **75**
Manus I., *Admiralty Is.* C20–023 **106**
Many, *Louisiana* U21+315 **95**
Manyoni, *Tanzania* K62–058 **83**
Manzala L., *Egypt* K78+312 **81**
Manzanares, *Spain* N20+390 **52**
Manzanillo, *Cuba* T13+204 **101**
Manzanillo, *Mexico* U86+190 **100**
Manzanillo, Pta., *Panama* T27+096 **101**
Mao, *Chad* L88+140 **81**
Mapia Is., *Pacific Ocean* D00+005 **106**
Mapimi, *Mexico* U83+259 **100**
Maping. See Liuchow
Mapire, *Venezuela* S28+076 **104**
Maple Creek, *Saskatchewan* V26+499 **88**
Maqainama, *Saudi Arabia* J67+223 **74**
Maqatin, *Yemen, South* J81 + 135 **74**
Maqna, *Suadi Arabia* K62+284 **74**
Maquela do Zombo, *Angola* L88–062 **82**
Maquinchao, *Argentina* S53–412 **103**
Maquoketa, *Iowa* U04+420 **95**
Mara, *Transvaal* L04+232 **84**
Maraã, *Brazil* S33–019 **104**
Maraba, *Brazil* R24–053 **105**
Maracá, I. de, *Brazil* R32+020 **105**
Maracaibo, *Venezuela* S70+106 **104**
Maracaibo, L. de, *Venezuela* S70+100 **104**
Maracana, *Brazil* R15–008 **105**
Maracassume, *Brazil* R06–020 **105**
Maracay, *Venezuela* S45+103 **104**
Marada, *Libya* L64+290 **81**
Maradi, *Niger* M46+132 **80**
Maragheh, *Iran* J82+374 **74**
Maragogi, *Brazil* Q32–090 **105**
Marakei, I., *Kiribati* A40+025 **106**
Marakwet, *Kenya* K56+010 **83**
Maralinga, S. *Aust.* D20–302 **110**
Maramba, *Zambia* L24–178 **84**
Marand, *Iran* J86+384 **74**
Maranguape, *Brazil* Q52–038 **105**
Marañon R., *Peru* S74–034 **104**
Maras, *Turkey* K48+376 **74**
Marau, *Brazil* Q54–141 **105**
Maravilha, *Brazil* S48–061 **104**
Marazion, *England* N33+501 **38**
Mabella, *Spain* N29+365 **52**
Marble Bar, *W. Australia* E02–211 **110**
Marblehead, *Massachusetts* S65+425 **96**
Marcellino, *Brazil* S44+008 **104**
Marche, *Belgium* M58+502 **44**
Marche, dep., *Italy* M11+433 **56**
Marche, prov. *France* M80+462 **54**
Marchena, *Spain* N32+373 **52**
Marchin, *Belgium* M58+505 **44**
Mar Chiquita, *Argentina* R82–288 **103**
Marcus I., *Pacific Ocean* B70+250 **106**
Marcy, Mt., *New York* S84+441 **91**

Mardan, *Pakistan* H17+342 72
Mar del Plata, *Argentina* R76–379 103
Mardin, *Turkey* K26+373 74
Mare, I., *Loyalty Is.* A70–220 106
Marechal Deodoro, *Brazil* Q34–098 105
Maree I., *Scotland* N33+577 40
Marengo, *Wisconsin* U05+465 91
Margarita, I., *Venezuela* S24+110 104
Margarites, *Crete* L32+354 59
Margate, *England* M82+514 39
Maria I., *Tasmania* C12–427 109
Marianao, *Cuba* T45+230 101
Marianas, Is., *Pacific Ocean* C25+150 106
Marianna, *Arkansas* U05+347 97
Marianna, *Florida* T62+308 97
Marianske Lázně, *Czech.* M14+499 48
Marias, *Montana* V33+479 93
Marias R., *Montana* V48+483 98
Marib, *Yemen* K00+157 74
Maribor, *Yugoslavia* L86+466 56
Maridi, *Sudan* L04+050 81
Marie Byrd Ld., *Antarctica* W60–780 27
Mariefred, *Sweden* L77+592 47
Marie Galante, l., *Leeward Is.* S07+159 101
Mariehamn, *Finland* L60+601 47
Marienbad. *See* Marianske Lázně.
Marienberg, *Netherlands* M51+525 44
Marienbourg, *Belgium* M63+501 44
Marienburg. *See* Malbork
Mariental, *Namibia*, L72–244 84
Marienville, *Pennsylvania* T25+415 96
Mariestad, *Sweden* M07+587 47
Marietta, *Georgia* T57+339 97
Marietta, *Ohio* T39+394 91
Mari Indus, *Pakistan* H20+329 72
Mariiskaya, aut. rep., *U.S.S.R.* J70+564 62
Marina Fall, *Guyana* R88+055 104
Marine City, *Michigan* T45+427 91
Marinette, *Wisconsin* T76+451 91
Marinha Grande, *Portugal* N54+398 52
Marion, *Arkansas* U02+352 97
Marion, *Illinois* T84+377 95
Marion, *Iowa* U10+420 95
Marion, *Indiana* T64+406 91
Marion, *Kentucky* T80+372 97
Marion, *N. Carolina* T42+357 97
Marion, *N. Dakota* U50+466 93
Marion, *Ohio* T49+406 91
Marion, *Virginia* T39+368 97
Marion B., *Tasmania* C12–428 109
Maritsa R., *Bulgaria, etc* L24+419 58
Mariyampole. *See* Kapsukas
Marj, Al., *Libya* L54+324 81
Marjamaa, *Estonia* L33+589 47
Markala, *Mali* N34+140 80
Markapur, *India* G60+157 70
Markelo, *Netherlands* M51+522 44
Marken, I., *Netherlands* M59+524 44
Market Deeping, *England* N02+527 37
Market Drayton, *England* N15+529 37
Market Harborough, *Eng.* N05+525 37
Markethill, *N. Ireland* N39+543 42
Markham, I., *Tibet* G42+350 71
Markham, Mt., *Antartica* B50–830 27
Markovo, *U.S.S.R.* A57+644 63
Marks, *U.S.S.R.* J79+517 61
Markstay, *Ontario* T33+465 91
Marlboro, *Massachusetts* S69+424 96
Marlborough, *Guyana* R82+075 104
Marlborough, *England* N10+514 39
Marlette, *Michigan* T48+433 91
Marlo, *Victoria* C09–378 109
Marmande, *France* M89+445 55
Marmara, Sea of, *Turkey* L10+407 74
Marmaris, *Turkey* L10+369 74
Marne, dep., *France* M64+488 54
Marnoo, *Victoria* C43–367 109
Maroni, R., *Fr. Guiana* R53+029 105
Maroua, *Cameroon* M04+106 81
Marquesas, Is., *Pacific Oc.* X30–100 107
Marquette, *Michigan* T74+465 91
Marquina, *Spain* N15+433 53
Marra, R., *New S. Wales* C17–306 109
Marrakech, *Morocco* N48+316 80
Marrawah, *Tasmania* C32–410 109
Marree, *S. Australia* C72–296 109
Marsabit, *Kenya* K42+022 83
Marsa Hali, *Saudi Arabia* K22+187 74
Marsala, *Sicily* M15+378 57
Marsden, *New South Wales* C14–338 109
Marseille, *France* M58+433 55
Marsh, I., *Louisiana* U12+295 95
Marshall, *Illinois* T76+394 95
Marshall, *Michigan* T60+423 91
Marshall, *Minnesota* U35+445 93
Marshall, *Missouri* U20+391 95
Marshall, *Texas* U26+326 95
Marshall Is., *Pacific Ocean* A60+075 106
Marshall Pass, *Colorado* V08+382 98
Marshalltown, *Iowa* U17+421 95
Marshfield, *Missouri* U18+374 95
Marshfield, *Oregon* W26+434 92
Marshfield, *Wisconsin* U01+447 91
Mars Hill, *Maine* S48+465 90
Marstrand, *Sweden* M20+579 47
Marsum, *Netherlands* M56+532 44
Martaban, *Burma* F45+166 71
Martaban, G. of, *Burma* F50+155 71
Martelange, *Belgium* M56+498 44
Marthas Vineyard, I., *Mass.* S64+412 96
Martigny-Ville, *Switzerland* M48+461 45
Martin, *S. Dakota* U71+432 93
Martin L., *Alabama* T65+328 97
Martina, *Switzerland* M27+469 45
Martinho, *Brazil* R71–059 105
Martinique, I., *Windward Is.* S06+146 101
Martinsburg, *W. Virginia* T18+395 96
Martinsville, *Virginia* T29+367 97
Marton, *New Zealand* A27–401 112
Martos, *Spain* N24+377 52
Martre, Lac la, *N.-W. Terr.* V85+634 88
Maruf, *Afghanistan* H48+315 75
Marugame, *Japan* D07+342 68
Marum, *Netherlands* M52+531 44
Marutea, I., *Tuamotu Arch.* X45–180 107
Marvejols, *France* M71+445 55
Mary, *Turkmen.* H79+375 62
Maryborough, *Queensland* B74–255 111
Maryborough. *See* Portlaoise
Maryborough, *Victoria* C38–371 109
Marydale, *Cape Province* L48–294 84

Maryland, state, *U.S.A.* T10+392 99
Maryport, *England* N21+547 37
Marysville, *California* W10+391 92
Marysville, *New Brunswick* S39+460 90
Maryville, *Kansas* U40+398 95
Maryville, *Missouri* U30+404 95
Mas-afuera, *Pacific Ocean* T35–345 107
Masaka, *Uganda* K80–004 83
Masangena, *Mozambique* K72–216 84
Masara, *Mozambique* K66–182 84
Masasi, *Tanzania* K38–108 83
Masaya, *Nicaragua* T67+120 101
Masbate, I., *Philippines* D70+121 65
Mascara, *Algeria* N00+354 80
Maseru, *Lesotho* L14–292 84
Mashaki, *Afghanistan* H40+333 75
Masharbrum, mt., *Kashmir* G82+356 72
Mashhad, *Iran* J02+363 75
Mashkol, Hamun-i-, *Pak.* H72+281 70
Masi-Manimba, *Zaire* L72–048 82
Masindi, *Uganda* K80+016 83
Masira Chan., *Saudi Arabia* J08+207 75
Masira, G. of, *Saudi Arabia* J10+197 75
Masira I., *Oman* J08+204 75
Masjed Soleymân, *Iran* J63+314 74
Mask L., *Ireland, Rep.* N56+536 42
Masoala C., *Madagascar* J58–160 83
Mason, *Michigan* T57+426 91
Mason City, *Iowa* U19+432 95
Masøy, *Norway* L30+709 46
Massa, *Italy* M29+440 56
Massachusetts, state, *U.S.A.* S80+421 99
Massachusetts B., *Mass.* S63+424 96
Massafra, *Italy* L77+406 57
Massakori, *Chad* L86+130 81
Massapé, *Brazil* Q62–034 105
Massawa, *Ethiopia* K34+156 83
Massena, *New York* S89+449 91
Massénya, *Chad* L82+114 81
Masseube, *France* M87+434 55
Massey, *Ontario* T42+462 91
Massillon, *Ohio* T39+409 91
Masterton, *New Zealand* A26–409 112
Mastuj, *Pakistan* H15+363 72
Mastung, *Pakistan* H49+298 70
Mastura, *Saudi Arabia* K37+231 74
Masulipatnam (Bandar),
   India G52+162 70
Masyaf, *Syria* K52+351 76
Mat, *India* G73+276 72
Mata Amarilla, *Argentina* S68–496 103
Matagalpa, *Nicaragua* T65+130 101
Matagorda, B. & Pen., *Texas* U36+286 94
Matagorda, I., *Texas* U40+282 94
Matakana I., *New Zealand* A23–376 112
Matale, *Sri Lanka* G57+076 70
Matam, *Senegal* N80+156 80
Matamoros, *Mexico* U79+256 100
Matamoros, *Mexico* U45+258 100
Matane, *Quebec* S45+488 90
Matang, *Malaysia* F26+048 69
Matanuska, *Alaska* Y00+614 99
Matanzas, *Cuba* T39+230 101
Matapedia, *Quebec* S42+480 90
Matapedia, L., *Quebec* S45+486 90
Matapozuelos, *Spain* N28+414 52
Matara, *Sri Lanka* G57+060 70
Mataram, *Lombok I., Indon.* E24–085 65
Mataro, *Spain* M75+415 53
Matatiele, *Cape Province* L08–304 84
Mataule, *Brazil* R47+015 105
Mataura, *New Zealand* A66–462 112
Matehuala, *Mexico* U63+236 100
Matera, *Italy* L80+407 57
Mátészalka, *Hungary* L46+479 49
Mateur, *Tunisia* M32+370 81
Matfors, *Sweden* L78+624 46
Mathew Town, *Bahamas, The* S82 + 210 101
Mathura, *India* G74+274 73
Matiara, *India* G16+263 71
Matlock, *England* N09+531 37
Matna, *Sudan* K60+138 81
Matrah, *Oman* J09+236 75
Matruh, *Egypt* L16+312 81
Matsue, *Japan* D12+354 68
Matsumoto, *Japan* C69+362 68
Matsushima, *Japan* C53+384 68
Matsuyama, *Japan* D13+338 68
Mattawa, *Ontario* T22+463 91
Matterhorn, mt., *Switz.-It.* M44+460 45
Matto Grosso, *Brazil* S00–150 104
Mattoon, *Illinois* T80+394 95
Matucana, *Peru* T13+483 91
Matun, *Afghanistan* H30+334 75
Matura, *Brazil* S49–035 104
Maturin, *Venezuela* S19+097 104
Matvaieva, *U.S.S.R.* J13+578 61
Mau, *India* G59+222 73
Mau Aimma, *India* G48+257 73
Maubeuge, *France* M66+503 54
Maubin, *Burma* F56+166 71
Maubourguet, *France* N00+435 55
Maudaha, *India* G59+257 73
Maude, *New South Wales* C34–345 109
Mauele, *Mozambique* K66–244 84
Maues, *Brazil* R73–034 105
Mauganj, *India* G48+246 73
Maugerville, *New Brunswick* S39+459 90
Maui, I., *Hawaii* Y30 + 208 107
Mauleon Licharre, *France* N04+432 55
Maurawan, *India* G55+264 73
Maurice, L., *S. Australia* D24–292 110
Mauritania, rep., *W. Africa* N60+200 80
Mauritius, I., *Indian Ocean* J17–200 77
Maurs, *France* M77+448 55
Mauston, *Wisconsin* U01+438 91
Maumturk Mts., *Ireland, Rep.* N58+535 43
Mawk Mai, *Burma* F43+202 71
Mawson, *Antarctica* H78–680 27
Maxcanu, *Mexico* U00+205 100
Maxton, *N. Carolina* T26+348 97
Maxwelltown, *Scotland* N22+551 41
May, C., *New Jersey* T00+389 96
May, I. of, *Scotland* N15+562 41
Maya, I., *Indonesia* E63-O11 65
Mayaguez, *Puerto Rico* S42+182 101
Mayari, *Cuba* T04+207 101
Mayavaram, *India* G62+112 70
Mayen, *W. Germany* M46+503 48
Mayenne, dep., *France* N05+482 54
Mayersville, *Mississippi* U06+329 97

Mayfield, *Kentucky* T82+367 97
Maymyo, *Burma* F51+220 71
Maynooth, *Ireland, Rep.* N39+534 43
Maynooth, *Ontario* T18+452 91
Mayo, co., *Ireland, Rep.* N56+537 42
Mayoumba, *Gabon* M26–036 82
Mayran, L., *Mexico* U77+258 100
Mays Landing, *New Jersey* S88+394 96
Maysville, *Kentucky* T52+386 97
Mayville, *New York* T22+423 96
Maza, *Argentina* S20–367 103
Mazabuka, *Zambia* L14–158 84
Mazagan (El Jadida), *Morocco* N52+330 80
Mazagão, *Brazil* R39–002 105
Mazamet, *France* M76+435 55
Mazan, *Argentina* S39–288 103
Mazan, *Peru* S78–036 104
Mazapil, *Mexico* U70+247 100
Mazara del Vallo, *Sicily* M14+376 57
Mazaredo, *Argentina* S40–470 103
Mazar-i-Sharif, *Afghanistan* H47+366 75
Mazarron, *Spain* N08+377 53
Mazatenango, *Guatemala* U09+144 100
Mazatlán, *Mexico* V09+232 100
Mazheikyai, *Lithuania* L45+563 47
Mbabane, *Swaziland* K82–264 84
Mbalama, *Mozambique* K38–134 83
Mbale, *Uganda* K66+008 83
Mbandaka, *Zaire* L70+001 82
Mbarangandu, *Tanzania* K50–104 83
Mbarara, *Uganda* K86–006 83
Mbeya, *Tanzania* K70–090 83
Mbozi, *Tanzania* K72–090 83
Mbuji-Mayi, *Zaire* L38–062 82
Mcuburi, *Mozambique* K36–146 83
Mead L., *Nevada, etc.* V57+361 92
Meadville, *Pennsylvania* T31+416 91
Meaford, *Ontario* T33+446 91
Meath, co., *Ireland, Rep.* N39+537 42
Mecatina I. Gt. *Quebec* R83+508 90
Mecatina I. Lit., *Quebec* R86+506 90
Mecca, *Saudi Arabia* K31+214 74
Mechanicville, *New York* S82+429 96
Mechelen, *Belgium* M56+509 44
Mechelen (Malines), *Belg.* M63+510 44
Mecheria, *Algeria* N02+332 80
Mecklenburg, *W. Germany* M18+535 48
Medak, *India* G70+181 70
Medak, *Yugoslavia* L87+444 56
Medan, *Sumatra* F38+036 65
Medanos, *Argentina* S17–389 103
Medellin, *Colombia* T04+061 104
Medemblik, *Netherlands* M59+528 44
Medenine, *Tunisia* M28+334 81
Meder, *Ethiopia* K26+146 83
Medford, *Oregon* W17+423 92
Medford, *Wisconsin* U02+451 91
Medgidia, *Romania* L10+443 58
Media, *Pennsylvania* T02+399 96
Medias, *Romania* L34+461 58
Medicine Bow Ra., *Wyo.-Colo.* V06+408 93
Medicine Hat, *Alberta* V34+500 88
Medina, *Saudi Arabia* K30+246 74
Medina, *New York* T20+432 96
Medina, *N. Dakota* U56+469 93
Medina, *Ohio* T41+411 91
Medinaceli, *Spain* N15+412 53
Medina del Campo, *Spain* N29+413 52
Medina de Rioseco, *Spain* N30+419 52
Medina Sidonia, *Spain* N36+365 52
Médine, *Mali* N68+142 80
Mediterranean Sea, *S. Europe* 50-51
Mednogorsk, *U.S.S.R.* J14+518 61
Medora, *N. Dakota* U81+469 93
Medvezhegorsk, *Karelia* K64+628 62
Medvezhi Osa., *U.S.S.R.* B76+710 63
Medvezhi Yar, *U.S.S.R.* F80+706 63
Medway R., *England* M87+513 39
Meekatharra, *W. Australia* E10–266 110
Meenin. *See* Menin
Meerle, *Belgium* M61+515 44
Meerlo, *Netherlands* M54+515 44
Meersburg, *W. Germany* M35+477 48
Meersen, *Netherlands* M55+509 44
Meerut, *India* G74+290 72
Meeuwen, *Belgium* M57+511 44
Mega, *Ethiopia* K40+040 83
Megalópolis, *Greece* L47+374 59
Megantic, & L., *Quebec* S65+456 91
Mégara, *Greece* L40+380 59
Meghalaya, state, *India* F82+254 71
Megiskan, *Quebec* T13+483 91
Mehar, *Pakistan* H43+272 70
Meherpur, *Bangladesh* G08+238 73
Mehndawal, *India* G41+270 73
Meihsien, *China* E23+244 67
Meiktila, *Burma* F55+208 71
Meiningen, *E. Germany* M28+505 48
Meiringen, *Switzerland* M41+467 45
Meissen, *E. Germany* M09+512 48
Meitene, *Latvia* L38+564 47
Mejillones, *Chile* S62–230 103
Mekatina, *Ontario* T55+471 91
Meknes, *Morocco* N34+340 80
Me-kong, R., *S.-E. Asia* E84+125 69
Melaka, *Malaysia* F17+022 69
Melanesia, *Pacific Oc.* B30–050 106
Melbourne, *Victoria* C30–378 109
Meleuz, *U.S.S.R.* J24+528 61
Melfi, *Italy* L86+410 57
Melfort, *Saskatchewan* U87+531 88
Meligalà, *Greece* L48+372 59
Melilla, *Morocco* N18+352 80
Melipilla, *Chile* S67–336 103
Melitopol, *Ukraine* K58+469 60
Melk, *Austria* L88+483 48
Melle, *France* N01+462 54
Mellier, *Belgium* M57+498 44
Mellingen, *Switzerland* M40+474 45
Melo, *Uruguay* R56–322 103
Melona, *Italy* K59+330 76
Melreux, *Belgium* M57+503 44
Melrose, *Minnesota* U29+457 93
Melrose, *Scotland* N16+556 41
Melton Mowbray, *England* N05+528 37
Melun, *France* M74+485 54
Melut, *Sudan* K76+140 81
Melvich, *Scotland* N24+586 40
Melville, *Saskatchewan* U77+508 88
Melville B., *Greenland* S00+760 26
Melville I., *Queensland* C32–142 111

Melville I., *N. Terr., Aust.* D23–116 110
Melville I., *N.-W. Terr.* V30+756 88
Melville L., *Labrador* R85+538 89
Melville Pen., *N.-W. Terr.* T55+679 89
Melvin L., *N. Ireland-*
  Ireland, Rep. N49+544 42
Memba & B., *Mozambique* K26–142 83
Membij, *Syria* K42+365 76
Memel. *See* Klaipeda
Memphis, *Tennessee* U00+352 97
Memphremagog, L., *Quebec* S74+451 91
Memramcook, *N.B.* S27+460 90
Mena, *Arkansas* U26+346 95
Menai Bridge, *Wales* N25+532 38
Menai Str., *Wales* N26+531 38
Menairi, *Chad* L44+152 81
Ménaka, *Mali* M76+158 80
Menasha, *Wisconsin* T80+442 91
Mendak, *Saudi Arabia* K22+203 74
Mende, *France* M69+445 55
Mendebo Mts., *Ethiopia* K32+068 83
Menderez, R., *Turkey* L08+379 74
Mendip Hills, *England* N16+513 38
Mendocino, C., *California* W27+404 92
Mendota, *Illinois* T85+416 91
Mendota, L., *Wisconsin* T86+431 95
Mendoza, *Argentina* S53–328 103
Mendrisio, *Switzerland* M36+459 45
Menfi, *Sicily* M12+376 57
Menga, *Cameroon* M16+062 81
Meng Chai Nat, *Thailand* F29+152 69
Meng Chumporn, *Thailand* F35+106 69
Meng Fang, *Thailand* F35+198 69
Meng Kalamasai, *Thailand* F09+165 69
Meng Kemmarat, *Thailand* E98+160 69
Meng Krabin, *Thailand* F19+139 69
Meng Kuwi, *Thailand* F31+121 69
Meng Pran Kao, *Thailand* F31+124 69
Meng Pre, *Thailand* F29+182 69
Meng Teun, *Thailand* F35+176 69
Mengtsz, *China* F10+232 64
Meng Uthen, *Thailand* F03+175 69
Menin, *Belgium* M71+508 44
Menindee, *New S. Wales* C45–324 109
Menindee L., *New S. Wales* C46–324 109
Meningie, *S. Australia* C64–357 109
Menjapa, mt., *Borneo* E24+011 65
Menominee & R., *Michigan* T76+451 91
Menomonie, *Wisconsin* U12+448 93
Menorca I., *Balearic Is.* M65+400 53
Mentawai Is., *Indonesia* F40+020 31
Mentok, *Bangka I., Indonesia* E89+020 65
Menton, *France* M45+438 55
Menzelinsk, *U.S.S.R.* J41+557 61
Menzies, *W. Australia* D84–296 110
Meoqui, *Mexico* V03+282 100
Me-ping, R., *Thailand* F30+160 69
Meppel, *Netherlands* M53+527 44
Merabello G., *Crete* L25+352 59
Merano, *Italy* M23+467 56
Merasheen I., *Nfd.* R55+475 90
Merauke, *New Guinea* C57–085 65
Mercara, *India* G85+126 70
Merced, *California* W03+373 92
Mercedaria, mt., *Argentina* S61–320 103
Mercedes, *Argentina* R86–346 103
Mercedes, *Argentina* R79–293 103
Mercedes, *Bolivia* S41–126 104
Mercedes, *Uruguay* R78–333 103
Mercer, *New Zealand* A29–373 112
Mercer, *Pennsylvania* T32+413 91
Merchtem, *Belgium* M65+510 44
Mercy, C., *N.-W. Terr.* S20+650 89
Meredith, *Michigan* T57+442 91
Meredith, C., *Falkland Is.* S04–522 103
Mereg, *Somalia* J76+038 83
Mergentheim, *W. Germany* M32+494 48
Mergui, *Burma* F38+124 71
Mergui Arch., *Burma* F48+116 71
Meribah, *S. Australia* C55–347 109
Merida, *Mexico* T88+209 100
Merida, *Spain* N38+390 52
Merida & Cord. de. *Venez.* S67+084 104
Meriden, *Connecticut* S77+415 96
Meridian, *Mississippi* T82+324 97
Meringur, *Victoria* C52–344 109
Merioneth, co., *see* Gwyned
Merj Uyun, *Lebanon* K57+334 76
Merka, *Somalia* K01+018 83
Merksplas, *Belgium* M61+514 44
Merowe, *Sudan* K80+182 81
Merredin, *W. Australia* E09–314 110
Merrill, *Wisconsin* T88+452 91
Merrimack R., *New Hamp.-*
  Mass. S68+427 96
Merriwa, *New S. Wales* B88–322 109
Merrygoen, *New S. Wales* C05–319 109
Mersey R., *England* N16+534 37
Merseyside, co., *England* N18+534 37
Mersin, *Turkey* K62+369 74
Mersing, *Malaysia* F07+024 65
Mersis, *Somalia* J84+048 83
Mersrags, *Latvia* L41+573 47
Merta, *India* H06+266 70
Merthyr Tydfil, *Wales* N20+518 38
Mertola, *Portugal* N46+376 52
Meru, *Kenya* K44+002 83
Merwe, *Zambia* K82–142 83
Merzig, *W. Germany* M50+494 48
Mesa, *Arizona* V40+334 94
Mesabi Ra., *Minnesota* U20+477 93
Mesagne, *Italy* L73+405 57
Mesará B., *Crete* L32+350 59
Mesa Verde Nat. Park, *Colo.* V22+376 98
Mesen, *Belgium* M73+508 44
Meshghara, *Lebanon* K56+336 76
Meskene, *Syria* K41+360 76
Mesmiye, *Syria* K52+331 76
Mesocco, *Switzerland* M35+464 45
Mesolóngion, *Greece* L51+384 59
Messancy, *Belgium* M55+496 44
Messina, *Sicily* L89+382 57
Messina, *Greece* L49+372 59
Messina, Str. di, *Italy* L87+380 57
Messinia, *Greece* L49+372 59
Messinia, G. of, *Greece* L48+367 59
Mesudiye, *Turkey* K43+405 74
Metan, *Argentina* S30–255 103
Metangula, *Mozambique* K60–128 83
Metaripuá, *Brazil* S40–077 104
Méthana Pen., *Greece* L40+376 59

Methil (Buckhaven & Methil),
  Scotland N18+562 41
Methven, New Zealand A50–436 112
Metis Ls., Quebec S46+483 90
Metis Beach, Quebec S48+487 90
Metkovic, Yugoslavia L74+430 58
Metlakatla, Alaska W65+551 99
Metlika, Yugoslavia L88+456 56
Metropolis, Illinois T83+372 95
Metropolitan, Michigan T77+460 91
Métsovon, Greece L53+398 59
Mettet, Belgium M62+503 44
Mettlen, Switzerland M42+470 45
Mettur Dam, India G74+119 70
Metula, Israel K57+333 76
Metz, France M53+491 54
Meulebeke, Belgium M70+510 44
Meurthe-et-Moselle, dep.,
  France M51+485 54
Meuse, dep., France M57+490 54
Meuse, R., Belgium, etc. M56+490 54
Mexcala & R., Mexico U58+177 100
Mexiana, I., Brazil R27+000 105
Mexicali, Mexico V62+326 100
Mexico, Mexico U55+194 100
Mexico, New York T07+434 96
Mexico, rep. Cent. America 100
Mexico B., New York T08+435 96
Mexico, G. of U00+250 100
Meyadin, Syria K27+350 74
Meyersdale, Pennsylvania T24+398 96
Meymac, France M77+455 54
Mèze, France M68+435 55
Mezen, U.S.S.R. J94+658 62
Mezieres, France M62+497 54
Mezöbereny Békés, Hungary L54+468 49
Mezökövesd, Hungary L57+478 49
Mesötúr, Hungary L56+470 49
Mezquitic, Mexico U82+226 100
Mgori, Tanzania K60–050 83
Mhow, India G85+224 70
Miahuatlan, Mexico U39+165 100
Miajadas, Spain N35+391 52
Miami, Arizona V36+333 94
Miami, Florida T31+257 97
Miami, Oklahoma U30+369 95
Miandowab, Iraq K05+326 74
Miandrivazo, Madagascar J88–196 83
Mianeh, Iran J73+374 74
Miani, India G86+317 72
Miani, Pakistan H11+325 72
Mian Kalai, Pakistan H20+348 72
Mianwali, Pakistan H21+325 72
Miao-tao I., China D86+383 66
Miass, U.S.S.R. J00+558 61
Miastko, Poland L78+540 49
Micay, Colombia T15+029 104
Michailovsk, U.S.S.R. H80+536 61
Micheh, China E59+378 66
Michigan, state, U.S.A. T73+462 99
Michigan, L., U.S.A.-Canada T70+434 99
Michigan City, Indiana T71+417 91
Michipicoten, Ontario T60+482 89
Michipicoten I. & B., Ont. T64+477 91
Michoacan, state, Mexico U72+188 100
Michurinsk, U.S.S.R. K27+529 61
Mickelson, Michigan T59+444 91
Micronesia, Pacific Oc. B30+100 106
Mid Canyon, Montana V41+471 93
Middleboro, Massachusetts S65+419 96
Middelburg, Netherlands M68+515 44
Middelburg, Transvaal L04–258 84
Middelharnis, Netherlands M65+518 44
Middelkerke, Belgium M73+512 44
Middleburg, New York S86+426 91
Middleburg, Pennsylvania T13+408 96
Middlebury, Vermont S79+441 91
Middleham, England N11+543 37
Middlemarch, New Zealand A59–455 112
Middleport, New York T21+431 96
Middlesboro, Kentucky T52+366 97
Middlesbrough, England N07+546 37
Middlesex, Belize T80+172 101
Middleton, Nova Scotia S30+449 90
Middleton-in-Teesdale, Eng. N13+546 37
Middletown, Connecticut S76+416 96
Middletown, Delaware T04+394 91
Middletown, New York S87+414 96
Middletown, Ohio T56+395 91
Middletown, Pennsylvania T11+402 96
Midland, Michigan T55+436 91
Midland, Ontario T29+447 91
Midland, Texas U72+320 94
Midlands, West, co., Eng. N11+525 37
Midleton, Ireland, Rep. N49+519 43
Midlothian, co., see Lothian
Midnapur, India G16+224 73
Midway Is., Hawaii Z60+290 106
Midwest, Wyoming V08+435 93
Midye, Turkey L12+416 74
Miécourt. Switzerland M47+474 45
Miedzyrzec, Poland L44+520 49
Mienning, China F30+239 64
Mienyang, China E40+302 67
Mienyang, China F01+313 66
Mier, Mexico U55+264 100
Mieres, Spain N35+432 52
Mifflintown, Pennsylvania T15+405 96
Migdal Gad, Israel K62+317 76
Mikhaylovgrad, Bulgaria L41+434 58
Mikhaylovka, U.S.S.R. K10+500 61
Mikkeli, Finland L16+617 47
Mikonos, I., Greece L28+375 59
Milaca, Minnesota U22+458 93
Milan, Italy. See Milano
Milan, Missouri U19+402 95
Milan, New Hampshire S67+446 91
Milan, Tennessee T82+364 95
Milang, S. Australia C67–354 109
Milano, Italy M35+455 56
Milas, Turkey L14+373 74
Milazzo, Sicily L89+382 57
Milbank, S. Dakota U40+452 93
Mildenhall, England M87+523 39
Mildura, Victoria C47–342 109
Miléai, Greece L41+393 59
Miles, Queensland C00–267 111
Milesburg, Pennsylvania T17+409 96
Miles City, Montana V05+464 93
Milford, Delaware T02+389 96
Milford, Massachusetts S69+422 96
Milford, Nova Scotia S21+451 90

Milford, Pennsylvania S89+413 96
Milford, Utah V48+384 94
Milford Haven, Wales N30+517 38
Milford Sound, N.Z. A72–447 112
Mili Is., Marshall Islands A44+060 106
Miliana, Algeria M76+362 80
Milk R., Montana V16+486 93
Milkovo, U.S.S.R. B37+549 63
Mill, Netherlands M55+517 44
Mill I., Antarctica F26–650 27
Mill Is., N.-W. Territories T15+642 89
Millau, France M72+441 55
Millbridge, Ontario T16+447 91
Mille Lacs, Minnesota U22+462 93
Miller, S. Dakota U54+446 93
Millerovo, U.S.S.R. K28+489 61
Millersburg, Ohio T41+406 91
Miller's Flat, New Zealand A63–457 112
Mille Vaches, Quebec S55+486 90
Millford, Ireland, Rep. N46+551 42
Millicent, S. Australia C58–376 109
Millinocket, Maine S52+457 90
Millport, Scotland N29+558 41
Millridge, Maine S47+445 90
Millstreet, Ireland, Rep. N54+520 43
Milltown Malbay,
  Ireland. Rep. N56+528 43
Millville, New Jersey T00+394 96
Milne B., Papua New Guinea B86+05 111
Milnor, N. Dakota U45+463 93
Milo, Maine S54+452 90
Milos, I., Greece L33+367 59
Milparinka, New S. Wales C49–294 109
Milton, New Zealand A70–461 112
Milton, Ontario T29+435 91
Milton, Pennsylvania T12+410 96
Milwaukee, Wisconsin T78+430 95
Mimika, New Guinea C82–047 65
Mina al Ahmadi, Kuwait J71+293 74
Minab, Iran J18+271 75
Minaki, Ontario U27+500 88
Minas, Uruguay R62–343 103
Minas de Riotinto, Spain N39+377 52
Minas Novas, Brazil Q76–174 105
Minatitlan, Mexico U27+180 100
Minbu, Burma F60+202 71
Minch Little, Scotland N39+577 40
Minch North, Scotland N36+580 40
Mindanao, I., Philippines D60+074 65
Mindarie, S. Australia C59–349 109
Minden, W. Germany M37+523 48
Minden, Louisiana U20+326 95
Mindoro, I. & Str., Phil. D86+125 65
Mine Hd., Ireland, Rep. N46+520 43
Minehead, England N21+512 38
Mineola, New York S82+407 96
Mineral Ra., Michigan T88+467 91
Mineral Point, Wisconsin U01+429 91
Mineral Wells, Texas U49+328 95
Minga, Zambia K84–144 83
Mingan Is., Quebec S23+502 90
Mingary, S. Australia C55–321 109
Mingin, Burma F63+229 71
Minglanilla, Spain N10+395 53
Mingoyo, Tanzania K32–102 83
Mingshui, China F53+422 64
Minhla, Burma F59+199 71
Minho, Spain-Portugal N49+422 52
Minhow, China E04+261 67
Minicoy, I., Laccadives H11+082 70
Minna, Nigeria M50+096 81
Minneapolis, Minnesota U20+450 93
Minnedosa, Manitoba U60+502 88
Minnesota, state, U.S.A. U36+464 98
Minnesota R., Minn., etc. U36+450 98
Minnik, Syria K48+365 76
Minorca. See Menorca
Minot, N. Dakota U68+483 93
Min Shan, China F12+343 66
Minsk, Byelorussia L15+538 60
Minsk Mazowiecki, Poland L51+522 49
Minto, N. Dakota U44+483 93
Minto Inl., N.-W. Terr. V70+712 88
Minto L., Quebec T02+568 89
Minusinsk, U.S.S.R. F79+537 63
Minya Konka, China F19+295 64
Minyip, Victoria C45–365 109
Mio, Michigan T54+446 91
Miquelon Is.,
  Atlantic Ocean R68+470 90
Mirador, Brazil Q88–063 105
Miraflores, Colombia S78+051 104
Miraj, India H02+169 70
Miramar, Argentina R78–382 103
Mirambeau, France N04+453 55
Miramichie B., N.B. S29+472 90
Miramont, France M87+446 55
Miram Shah, Pakistan H29+330 72
Miranda, Argentina R86–364 103
Miranda, Brazil R69–202 105
Miranda, Nicaragua T57+140 101
Miranda de Ebro, Spain N18+427 52
Miranda do Corvo, Portugal N50+401 52
Miranda do Douro, Portugal N37+415 52
Mirande, France M88+435 55
Mirandela, Portugal N43+415 52
Mirandilla, Spain N37+391 52
Mirdum, Netherlands M57+528 44
Mirebeau, France M89+468 54
Mirim, L., Brazil R48–327 103
Mirjáveh, Iran H81+290 75
Mirnoe, U.S.S.R. G04+623 62
Mirosi, Romania L30+444 58
Mirpur, Kashmir H07+332 72
Mirpur Khas, Pakistan H36+255 70
Mirtoan Sea, Greece L38+368 59
Mirtos, Crete L27+350 59
Mirt Padam, India F58+284 71
Mirzapur, India G44+251 73
Miscou I., New Brunswick S27+480 90
Mishikamau, L., Labrador S25+542 89
Mishrif, Saudi Arabia K01+205 74
Miska, Saudi Arabia K13+249 74
Misoöl, I., New Guinea D30–018 65
Misquah Hills, Minnesota U062+478 91
Misque, Bolivia S32–178 104
Missis, Turkey K56+370 74
Mississippi, state, U.S.A. U00+328 99
Mississippi Delta, Louisiana T70+290 95
Mississippi R., U.S.A. U03+380 99

Mississippi Sd., Mississippi T84+303 95
Missolónghi. See Mesolóngion.
Missoula, Montana V54+469 92
Missouri, state, U.S.A. U20+381 99
Missouri R., U.S.A. U33+408 98
Missouri Valley, Iowa U36+416 95
Mistassini L., Quebec S83+508 89
Mistretta, Sicily M04+379 57
Misurata, (Misrátah), Libya M00+322 81
Mitaka Maria, Uganda K76+001 83
Mitchell, Ontario T37+435 91
Mitchell, Queensland C13–264 111
Mitchell, S. Dakota U48+437 93
Mitchell, Mt., N. Carolina T44–358 97
Mitchell, R., Queensland C47–160 111
Mitchelstown, Ireland, Rep. N50+523 43
Mithankot, Pakistan H28+289 72
Mithi, Pakistan H31+246 70
Mithimna, Greece L23+393 59
Mitho, Vietnam E82+104 69
Mitilini, Lesvos, I., Greece L21+391 59
Mito, Japan C57+364 68
Mitsiz, Gabon M22+008 82
Mittagong, New S. Wales B88–344 109
Mitta Mitta, Victoria C15–365 109
Mittelmark, Germany M10+522 48
Mittelmark, W. Germany M10+522 48
Mitu, Colombia S60+009 104
Mitumba Mts., Zaire L10–016 104
Miyako, Japan C48+397 68
Miyanduab, Iran J83+370 74
Miyazaki, Japan D21+319 68
Mizda, Libya M12+314 81
Mizen Hd., Ireland, Rep. N36+528 43
Mizen Hd., Ireland, Rep. N59+514 43
Mizil, Romania L21+450 58
Mizpah, Montana V01+462 93
Mjölby, Sweden L89+583 47
Mjosa, L., Norway M24+607 47
Mladá Boleslav, Czech. M01+504 48
Mlanje, Mt., See Mulanje Mt.
Mlawa, Poland L58+531 49
Mljet, I., Yugoslavia L75+427 56
Mo, Norway M05+663 46
Moab, Utah V28+386 94
Moama, New South Wales C32–361 109
Mo Ångsåg, Sweden L61+636 46
Moapa, Nevada V59+367 92
Moate, Ireland, Rep. N46+534 43
Moba, Zaire L00+070 82
Mobile & B., Alabama T78+307 97
Mobridge, S. Dakota U63+456 93
Mocajuba, Brazil R26–025 105
Moçambique, Mozambique K26–150 83
Moçâmedes, Angola M16–152 82
Mocha, Yemen K10+133 74
Mocimboa-da-Praia, Mozamb. K28–114 83
Mocksville, N. Carolina T33+358 97
Mocoa, Colombia T10+011 104
Mocorito, Mexico V18+256 100
Moctezuma, Mexico U66+228 100
Moctezuma, Mexico V28+298 100
Modane, France M50+452 55
Modave, Belgium M58+504 44
Modena, Italy M24+446 56
Modesto, California W06+376 92
Modica, Sicily M02+369 57
Modjamboli, Zaire L48+022 82
Mo-duc, Vietnam E66+149 69
Modung, China F50+291 64
Moe, Victoria C22–382 109
Moena, I., Indonesia D75–050 65
Moengo, Surinam R57+056 105
Mofa, Ethiopia K28+106 83
Moffat, Scotland N21+553 41
Mogadiscio (Mogadishu),
  Somalia J88+020 83
Mogador (Essaouira), Mor. N60+314 80
Mogadouro, Portugal N39+414 52
Mogar, Ethiopia K42+080 83
Mogaung, Burma F48+253 71
Mogilev, Byelorussia K88+539 60
Mogilev Podolskiy, Ukraine L13+485 60
Mogocha, U.S.S.R. E02+537 63
Mogochin, U.S.S.R. G39+577 62
Mogok, Burma F51+229 71
Mogollan Mt., New Mexico V22+336 94
Mogollon Mesa, Arizona V34+344 94
Moguer, Spain N41+372 52
Mogur, Ethiopia K28+050 83
Mohacs, Hungary L68+460 58
Mohako, New Zealand A20–391 112
Mohawk, New York T00+430 96
Mohawk R., New York S88+430 96
Moheli I., Comoro Is. K08–124 83
Moher, Cliffs of, Ireland, Rep. N57+530 43
Mohill, Ireland, Rep. N47+539 42
Moho, China D75+534 63
Mohoro, Tanzania K34–082 83
Moia, Sudan L12+050 81
Moine, L. du, Quebec T18+469 91
Moirang, India F67+245 71
Moisaküla, Estonia L29+581 47
Moisie, Quebec S35+503 90
Moissac, France M84+441 55
Mojave, California V79+351 92
Moji, Brazil R09–236 105
Moju & R., Brazil R22–019 105
Mokai, New Zealand A24–385 112
Mokameh, India G24+254 73
Mokolo, Cameroon M08+108 81
Mokpo, Korea D52+348 64
Mokshany, U.S.S.R. K08+534 61
Moldavia, Romania L18+467 58
Moldavia, rep., U.S.S.R. L12+474 60
Molde & R., Norway M47+628 46
Molepolole, Botswana L26–244 84
Môle St Nicolas, Haiti S80+198 101
Molfetta, Italy L80+412 57
Molina, Chile S67–350 103
Molina, Spain N07+381 53
Moline, Illinois U03+414 95
Molino, Florida T74+307 97
Moliro, Zaire K86–084 83
Moll, Belgium M59+512 44
Mollis, Switzerland M35+471 45
Mollosund, Sweden M21+581 47
Molndal, Sweden M18+577 47

Molong, New South Wales C07–331 109
Molotov. See Perm.
Molotovsk (Severodvinsk)
  U.S.S.R. K30+645 62
Molucca Pass., Indonesia D58–007 65
Moluccas, Is., Indonesia D45–012 65
Moma, Mozambique K34–166 83
Mombasa, Kenya K32–040 83
Momchilgrad, Bulgaria L28+415 58
Momeik. See Mong-mit.
Momignies, Belgium M65+500 44
Momotombo, Nicaragua T69+125 101
Mompós. Columbia S87+092 104
Møn. I., Denmark M16+550 47
Monå Fd., Finland L48+635 46
Mona, I., Puerto Rico S48+182 101
Mona Pass., West Indies S50+180 101
Monach, Sd. of, Scotland N45+576 40
Monaco, princip., S. Europe M46+437 55
Monadhliath Mts., Scotland N26+571 40
Monaghan & co.,
  Ireland, Rep. N42+542 42
Monango, N.Dakota U52+462 93
Monar L., Scotland N30+574 40
Monaro Ra., New S. Wales C07–364 109
Monasterace Marina, Italy L81+385 57
Monasterevin, Ireland, Rep. N42+531 43
Monastir, Sardinia M36+394 57
Monastir. See Bitola.
Monastir, Tunisia M24+358 81
Monar L., Scotland N30+574 40
Monbetsu, Japan C40+443 68
Monbuey, Spain N38+420 52
Mönchengladbach, W. Ger. M52+512 45
Monchique, Portugal N51+373 52
Monclova, Mexico U69+269 100
Moncton, New Brunswick S29+461 90
Mondo, Chad L86+138 81
Mondonedo, Spain N44+434 52
Mondovi, Wisconsin U10+446 93
Mondul, Tanzania K52–032 83
Monemvasia, Greece L42+367 59
Monessen, Pennsylvania T30+402 96
Monetny, U.S.S.R. H85+570 61
Monett, Missouri U24+370 95
Moneva, Spain N05+411 53
Monforte, Portugal N45+390 52
Monforte, Spain N45+425 52
Monga, Zaire L42+040 82
Mongalla, Sudan K80+052 81
Monger, L., W. Australia E17–290 110
Möng-Hsu, Burma F40+218 71
Monghyr, India G21+254 73
Mongka, Burma F33+226 71
Möng Kiang, Burma F40+219 71
Mongkol-borey, Cambodia F12+135 69
Möng Kung, Burma F44+216 71
Möng-Kyet, Burma F39+231 71
Mong-mit, Burma F49+231 71
Mongo, Chad L64+122 81
Mongolia, rep., E. Asia F00+450 31
Mongolia, Inner, China F20+404 64
Mongonu, Nigeria M08+126 81
Mongoumba, Cent. Afr. Rep. L70+036 81
Möng-pai, Burma F48+198 71
Möng Pan, Burma F40+203 71
Möng Pawn, Burma F45+208 71
Möng-Sit, Burma F43+205 71
Mongu, Zambia L42–154 84
Moniaive, Scotland N23+552 41
Moniquira, Colombia S82+059 104
Monivea, Ireland Rep. N52+534 43
Monmouth, Illinois U04+409 95
Monmouth, Wales N16+518 38
Monnikendam, Netherlands M60+525 44
Mono L., California V84+380 92
Monomay I. & Pt., Mass. S60+415 96
Monopoli, Italy L76+409 57
Monovar, Spain N05+385 53
Monreal del Campo, Spain N08+408 53
Monroe, Louisiana U13+325 97
Monroe, Michigan T50+419 91
Monroe, N. Carolina T33+350 97
Monroe, Wisconsin T88+426 95
Monroeville, Alabama T74+315 97
Monrovia, Liberia N64+064 80
Mons, Belgium M66+504 44
Monsanto, Portugal N43+401 52
Monsão, Portugal N50+421 52
Monserrato, Sardinia M35+393 57
Monson, Massachusetts S74+422 96
Monster, Netherlands M65+520 44
Mönsterås, Sweden L81+570 47
Mont, Belgium M55+502 44
Montagne Tremblante Park,
  Quebec T00+469 91
Montague, Michigan T68+435 91
Montagu I., S. Sandwich Is. P80–580 27
Montaigu, Belgium M60+510 44
Montalbán, Spain N05+408 53
Montana, state, U.S.A. V38+468 94
Montanchez, Spain N37+393 52
Montargis, France M73+480 54
Montauban, France M82+440 55
Montbard, France M64+476 54
Montblanch, Spain M83+414 53
Montbrison, France M66+456 54
Montclair, New Jersey S85+408 96
Montcornet, France M66+497 54
Mont de Marsan, France N03+439 55
Montdidier, France M75+496 54
Mont Dore, le, France M72+456 54
Monte Alegre, Brazil R54–019 105
Monte Alegre, Brazil R24–189 105
Montebello, Quebec T00+457 91
Monte Carlo, Monaco M46+437 55
Monte Caseros, Argentina R77–302 103
Montecollina, S. Australia C60–294 109
Monte Coman, Argentina S47–346 103
Monte Cristi, Dominican
  Republic S69+199 101
Monte Cristi, Sa. de,
  Dominican Rep. S64+196 101
Montecristo, I., Italy M28+423 56
Montefrio, Spain N24+373 52
Montego Bay, Jamaica T17+186 101
Montélimar, France M62+446 55
Montello, Wisconsin T86+438 91
Montemorelos, Mexico U59+252 100
Montenegro, Yugoslavia L64+426 58
Montereau, France M72+484 54
Monterey, California W11+366 92

Monterey, *Virginia* T27+384 97
Monterey, B. of, *California* W14+367 92
Monteriá, *Colombia* T05+087 104
Monteros, *Argentina* S34–272 103
Monterrey, *Mexico* U61+257 100
Monte San Angelo, *Italy* L84+417 57
Montes Claros, *Brazil* Q82–167 105
Montevideo, *Minnesota* U35+449 93
Montevideo, *Uruguay* R67–349 103
Monte Vista, *Colorado* V08+376 94
Montezuma, *Georgia* T54+324 97
Montfort-sur-Meu, *France* N12+481 54
Montgomery, *Alabama* T68+324 97
Montgomery, *Missouri* U09+390 95
Montgomery, *Wales* N19+526 38
Monthey, *Switzerland* M48+463 45
Monticello, *Arkansas* U10+336 95
Monticello, *Georgia* T52+333 97
Monticello, *Maine* S47+463 90
Monticello, *New York* S88+416 91
Monticello, *Utah* V26+380 94
Montijo, B. de, *Panama* T36+076 101
Montilla, *Spain* N28+375 52
Mont Joli, *Quebec* S49+486 90
Mont Laurier, *Quebec* T03+465 91
Montlucon, *France* M74+464 54
Montmagny, *Quebec* S63+470 90
Montmédy, *France* M58+495 54
Montmirail, *France* M69+489 54
Montmorency, *Quebec* S67+469 91
Montoursville, *Pennsylvania* T12+412 96
Montpelier, *Idaho* V38+423 94
Montpelier, *Vermont* S76+443 91
Montpellier, *France* M67+436 55
Montreal, *Quebec* S82+455 91
Montreal L., *Saskatchewan* V05+542 88
Montrejeau, *France* M87+431 55
Montreuil, *France* M79+505 54
Montreuil Bellay, *France* N01+471 54
Montreux, *Switzerland* M48+464 45
Montrose, *Colorado* V17+384 94
Montrose, *Pennsylvania* T06+418 96
Montrose, *Scotland* N15+567 41
Monts, Pt. des, *Quebec* S44+493 90
Mont-St Jean, *Belgium* M64+507 44
Mont-St-Michel & B., *Fr.* N09+487 54
Montserrat, I., *Leeward Is.* S13+168 101
Monywa, *Burma* F58+220 71
Monza, *Italy* M35+456 56
Monze, *Zambia* L16–162 84
Monzon, *Spain* M89+419 53
Moolawatana, *S. Australia* C62–299 109
Moonbi Ra., *New S. Wales* B84–308 109
Moonta, *S. Australia* C75–341 109
Moora, *W. Australia* E24–306 110
Moorcroft, *Wyoming* V00+443 93
Moore, L., *W. Australia* E15–294 110
Moorefield, *W. Virginia* T24+391 96
Moorfoot Hills, *Scotland* N19+557 41
Moorhead, *Minnesota* U41+469 93
Moorsel, *Belgium* M65+509 44
Moorslede, *Belgium* M72+509 44
Moose L., *Manitoba* U62+540 88
Moose R., *Ontario* T42+505 89
Moosehead L., *Maine* S58+456 90
Moose Jaw, *Saskatchewan* V04+504 88
Moosic, Mts., *Pennsylvania* T03+417 96
Moosomin, *Saskatchewan* U70+501 88
Moosonee, *Ontario* T34+511 89
Mopti, *Mali* N24+142 80
Moquegua, *Peru* S66–172 104
Mora, *Ethiopia* K54+104 83
Mora, *Cameroon* M06+110 81
Mora, *Minnesota* U20+459 93
Mora, *Portugal* N49+389 52
Mora, *Spain* N23+397 52
Mora, *Sweden* M03+610 47
Moradabad, *India* G67+288 73
Mora de Rubielos, *Spain* N05+403 53
Moramanga, *Madagascar* J70-190 83
Morano Calabro, *Italy* L83+399 57
Morar, *India* G70+262 73
Morar L., *Scotland* N34+569 40
Morat. *See* Murten
Moratalla, *Spain* N11+382 53
Morava R., *Yugoslavia* L53+444 58
Moravia, *Czechoslovakia* L75+493 49
Moravska Trebova, *Czech.* L79+498 49
Morawhanna, *Guyana* R88+083 104

Moray Firth, *Scotland* N22+577 40
Morbihan, dep., *France* N18+479 54
Morden, *Manitoba* U50+493 88
Mordialloc, *Victoria* C29–380 109
Mordova, *U.S.S.R.* K22+536 61
Mordovskaia, aut. rep.,
  U.S.S.R. K10+644 62
Morea, *Greece* L46+376 59
Moreau R., *S. Dakota* U72+452 98
Morecambe & B., *England* N17+451 37
Moreda, *Spain* N20+374 52
Moree, *New South Wales* C01–295 109
Moreira, *Brazil* S21–006 104
Morel, *Switzerland* M42+464 45
Morelia, *Mexico* U67+196 100
Morella, *Spain* N01+406 53
Morelos, *Mexico* U65+284 100
Morelos, *Mexico* V13+267 100
Morelos, state, *Mexico* U54+186 100
Morena, *India* G76+261 73
Morena, Sa., *Spain* N24+383 52
Morenci, *Arizona* V26+332 94
Morere, *New Zealand* A13–390 112
Moreton B., *Queensland* B68–267 111
Morez, *France* M54+465 54
Morgan, *S. Australia* C62–340 10
Morgan City, *Louisiana* U07+297 95
Morganton, *N. Carolina* T40+357 97
Morgat, *France* N27+482 54
Morges, *Switzerland* M51+465 45
Morgins, *Switzerland* M49+462 45
Moriana, *India* F64+267 71
Morice L., *Brit. Columbia* W47+540 88
Morinville, *Alberta* V52+540 88
Morioka, *Japan* C53+397 68
Morisset, *New South Wales* B82–332 109
Morlaix, *France* N23+485 54
Mormugao, *India* H07+155 70
Mornington, *Victoria* C29–382 109
Mornington, I., *Chile* T02–498 103
Moro G., *Philippines* D70+069 65

Morobe, *Papua New Guinea* C15–078 111
Morocco, *N.-W. Africa* N30+326 80
Morogoro, *Tanzania* K44–068 83
Morokwen, *Cape Province* L36–262 84
Moron, *Cuba* T22+221 101
Morón, *Venezuela* S49+110 104
Morona, *Ecuador* T15–028 104
Morondava, *Madagascar* K04–204 83
Morón de la Frontera, *Spain* N33+371 52
Morotai, I., *Indonesia* D40+022 65
Moroto, *Uganda* K62+026 83
Morpeth, *England* N10+552 37
Morpeth, *New South Wales* B81–328 109
Morphou & B., *Cyprus* K72+352 76
Morrillton, *Arkansas* U16+352 95
Morrinhos, *Brazil* R25–178 105
Morrinsville, *New Zealand* A27–377 112
Morris, *Illinois* T80+414 95
Morris, *Manitoba* U45+495 88
Morris, *Minnesota* U36+456 93
Morrisburg, *Ontario* T01+449 91
Morris Jesup C., *Arctic Oc.* Q55+840 26
Morrison, *Illinois* U00+418 91
Morristown, *New Jersey* S87+408 96
Morrisville, *New York* T04+430 91
Morro, *Ecuador* T32–026 104
Morrosquillo, G. de, *Colom.* T04+095 104
Mors, *Denmark* M38+568 47
Morshansk, *U.S.S.R.* K19+534 61
Mortagne, *France* M87+485 54
Mortagua, *Portugal* N49+404 52
Mortain, *France* N06+486 54
Mortlake, *Victoria* C43–381 109
Morundah, *New S. Wales* C22–349 109
Moruya, *New S. Wales* B89–360 109
Morven, *New Zealand* A53–448 112
Morven, *Queensland* C18–264 111
Morvi, *India* H24+228 70
Morwell, *Victoria* C22–382 109
Moscow, *Idaho* V72+467 92
Moscow. *See* Moskva
Moselle, dep., *France* M48+489 54
Moselle, R., *France* M53+489 54
Mosera, I. *See* Masira I.
Mosgiel, *New Zealand* A58–458 112
Moshupa, *Botswana* L28–248 84
Mosjøen, *Norway* M11+658 46
Moskenesoya, *Norway* M12+680 46
Moskva, *U.S.S.R.* K45+558 60
Mosquero, *Brazil* R21–012 105
Mosquera, *Colombia* T21+024 104
Mosquito Bank, *Nicaragua* T46+132 101
Moss, *Norway* M26+595 47
Mossamedes, *Angola* M16–152 84
Mossburn, *New Zealand* A70–457 112
Mossel B., *Cape Province* L46–342 84
Mossendio, *Congo* M14+030 82
Mossgiel, *New South Wales* C33–333 109
Mossoro, *Brazil* Q44–052 105
Mossurize, *Mozambique* K72+206 84
Moss Vale, *New S. Wales* B88–346 109
Most, *Czechoslovakia* M08+505 48
Mostar, *Yugoslavia* L73+433 58
Mostardas, *Brazil* R35–310 103
Mosul, *Iraq* K12+365 74
Mota del Marques, *Spain* N31+416 52
Motala, *Sweden* M00+585 47
Motatan, *Venezuela* S63+094 104
Motherwell, *Scotland* N24+558 41
Môtier, *Switzerland* M48+469 45
Môtiers, *Switzerland* M50+469 45
Motihari, *India* G30+266 73
Motôt, *Switzerland* M45+461 45
Motril, *Spain* N08+380 53
Mott, *N. Dakota* U75+464 93
Motueka, *New Zealand* A42–411 112
Motul, *Mexico* T84+211 100
Moturoa, *New Zealand* A36–390 112
Moudala, *Chad* L68+088 81
Moudhros, *Greece* L29+399 59
Moudon, *Switzerland* M49+467 45
Mouila, *Gabon* M24–020 82
Moukden. *See* Shenyang
Moulamein & R., *N.S.W.* C36–351 109
Moulins, *France* M70+466 54
Moulmein, *Burma* F44+164 71
Moulouya R., *Morocco* N22+330 80
Moulton, *Alabama* T74+344 97
Mound City, *Illinois* T85+370 97
Mountain Grove, *Missouri* U14+371 97
Mountain Home, *Arkansas* U15+363 97
Mountain Sheep Bluffs, *Montana*
  V03+473 93
Mountain View, *Arkansas* U13+358 97
Mount Ayr, *Iowa* U26+407 95
Mount Barker, *S. Australia* C67–351 109
Mount Bellew, *Ireland, Rep.*
  N51+535 43
Mount Carmel, *Illinois* T76+384 95
Mount Carmel, *Pennsylvania* T09+408 96
Mount Carroll, *Illinois* U00+421 91
Mount Clemens, *Michigan* T47+426 91
Mount Desert I. (Acadia Nat.
  Park), *Maine* S50+443 90
Mount Drysdale, *N.S.W.* C25–312 109
Mount Forest, *Ontario* T35+440 91
Mount Gambier, *S. Aust.* C55–379 109
Mount Holly, *New Jersey* S89+400 96
Mount Hope, *N.S.W.* C25–329 109
Mount Jewett, *Pennsylvania* T22+417 96
Mount Lofty Ra., *S. Aust.* C66–350 109
Mount Magnet, *W. Aust.* E12–280 110
Mount Manara, *N.S.W.* C36–324 109
Mountmellick, *Ireland, Rep.* N44+531 43
Mount Morgan, *Queensland* C00–237 111
Mount Morris, *New York* T17+427 96
Mount Murray, *Alberta* V39+564 88
Mount Olive, *Mississippi* T88+317 95
Mount Olive, *N. Carolina* T18+352 97
Mount Pleasant, *Iowa* U10+409 95
Mount Pleasant, *Michigan* T59+436 91
Mount Pleasant, *Pa.* T27+402 96
Mount Pleasant, *S. Aust.* C66–348 109
Mount Pleasant, *Tennessee* T75+355 95
Mount Pleasant, *Texas* U43+310 95
Mount Pleasant, *Utah* V40+396 94
Mountrath, *Ireland, Rep.* N45+530 43
Mount Robson Park, *B.C.* W00+530 88
Mounts B., *England* N33+500 38
Mount Sterling, *Kentucky* T54+381 97

Mount Stewart, *P.E.I.* S17+464 90
Mount Union, *Pennsylvania* T18+404 96
Mount Vernon, *Illinois* T84+384 95
Mount Vernon, *Indiana* T77+380 95
Mount Vernon, *Kentucky* T57+374 97
Mount Vernon, *Virginia* T13+387 91
Moura, *Brazil* S10–016 104
Moura, *Portugal* N45+381 52
Mourão, *Portugal* N44+384 52
Mourne Mts., *N. Ireland* N36+542 42
Mourne R., *N. Ireland* N45+548 42
Moussoro, *Chad* L80+136 81
Moutier, *Switzerland* M46+473 45
Moutohora, *New Zealand* A14–383 112
Mowlaik, *Burma* F64+236 71
Mowming, *China* E54+217 67
Mowping, *China* D80+374 66
Moy R., *Ireland, Rep.* N55+541 42
Moyale, *Kenya* K36+034 83
Moyobamba, *Peru* T12–062 104
Mozambique. rep., *E. Africa* K70-200 84
Moehga, *U.S.S.R.* J45+565 61
Mozyr, *Byelorussia* L05+520 60
Mpanda, *Tanzania* K84–064 83
Mporokoso, *Zambia* K88–094 83
Mstislavl,*Byelorussia* K80+541 60
Mtakuja, *Tanzania* K86–072 83
Mtarica, *Mozambique* K48–128 83
Mtito Andei, *Kenya* K40–028 83
Mtoko, *Zimbabwe* K76–174 84
Mtsensk, *U.S.S.R.* K51+533 60
Mu, R., *Burma* F57+228 71
Muaddhdham, el, *Saudi Arabia* K43+278 74
Muang Chaiya, *Thailand* F35+093 69
Muang Chana, *Thailand* F26+070 69
Muang Langsuan, *Thailand* F35+100 69
Muang Nan, *Thailand* F26+188 69
Muang Palien, *Thailand* F32+073 69
Mubarraz, *Saudi Arabia* J62+256 74
Mubende, *Uganda* K82+004 83
Muchinga Mts., *Zambia* K80–116 83
Muckish, *Ireland, Rep.* N48+551 42
Muckros Hd., *Ireland, Rep.* N52+546 42
Mudanya, *Turkey* L07+404 74
Mudawwara, *Jordan* K54+294 76
Muddusjarvi, *Finland* L19+691 46
Mudgee, *New S. Wales* C02–327 109
Mudhnib, *Saudi Arabia* K04+259 74
Mufford C., *Labrador* S13+582 89
Muggendorf, *W. Germany* M23+498 48
Mugia, *Spain* N55+431 52
Mugla, *Turkey* L10+372 74
Muglad, *Sudan* L14+110 81
Muhamdi, *India* G58+279 73
Muhammadabad, *Iran* J05+375 75
Muhammadgarh, *India* G71+237 73
Muharraq, *The Gulf* J56 + 264 75
Mühldorf. *W. Germany* M15+482 48
Mühlehorn, *Switzerland* M35+471 45
Mühlhausen, *E. Germany* M27+512 48
Muhu, *Estonia* L41+586 47
Muhu Väin, *Estonia* L40+588 47
Muinak, *Uzbek.* J06+438 62
Muine Bheag, *Ireland, Rep.* N42+527 43
Mukalla, *Yemen, South* J65+146 74
Mukdahan, *Thailand* F01+164 69
Mukden. *See* Shenyang
Mukhtuya, *U.S.S.R.* E30+607 63
Muktinath, *Nepal* G37+288 73
Muktsar, *India* H03+305 72
Muktui, *Mongolia* E80+492 64
Mula, *Spain* N08+380 53
Mulanje, Mt., *Malawi* K56-156 83
Mulchen, *Chile* S73–377 103
Mulege, *Mexico* V42+268 100
Mulgrave, *Nova Scotia* S08+456 90
Mulheim, *W. Germany* M48+510 48
Mulheim, *W. Germany* M49+515 48
Mulhouse, *France* M46+477 54
Mulki, *India* H01+131 70
Mull Hd., *Orkney, Scot.* N18+594 40
Mull, I., *Scotland* N36+564 41
Mull, Sd. of, *Scotland* N35+565 41
Mullaghareirk Mts., *Ireland, Rep.* N55+523 43
Mullaittivu, *Sri Lanka* G55+093 70
Mullaley, *New South Wales* C01–311 109
Muller Peg., *Borneo* E40+003 65
Mullet L., *Michigan* T57+455 91
Mullewa, *W. Australia* E27–284 110
Müllheim, *Switzerland* M36+476 45
Mullingar, *Ireland, Rep.* N44+535 43
Mullion Creek, *N.S.W.* C05–332 109
Muloorina, *S. Australia* C73–292 109
Mulroy B., *Ireland, Rep.* N46+552 42
Multan, *Pakistan* H21+302 72
Multia, *Finland* L31+624 46
Mumbondo, *Angola* M04–104 82
Mumbwa, *Zambia* L18–150 82
Muna, *Indonesia* D75+050 65
München, *W. Germany* M20+482 48
Muncie, *Indiana* T62+402 91
Mundo Novo, *Brazil* Q63–118 105
Munfordville, *Kentucky* T65+373 97
Mungari, *Mozambique* K68–174 84
Mungindi, *N.S.W.-Qnsld.* C06–289 109
Munich. *See* Munchen
Muniesa, *Spain* N05+410 53
Munising, *Michigan* T70+464 91
Munkfors, *Sweden* M09+599 47
Munnerstadt, *W. Germany* M29+502 48
Munoz Gamero, Pen., *Chile* S80–526 103
Munroe, *Louisiana* U12+324 95
Münster, *W. Germany* M27+466 45
Münster, *Switzerland* M41+465 45
Münster, *Switzerland* M41+472 45
Munster, prov., *Ireland, Rep.* N52+523 43
Muong Attopeu, *Laos* E78+149 69
Muong Borikan, *Laos* F08+186 69
Muong Het, *Laos* F05+208 69
Muong Hiem, *Laos* F10+201 69
Muong Saravan, *Laos* E83+157 69
Muong Sing, *Laos* F23+212 69
Muonio, R., *Swed.-Fin.* L39+677 46
Muonionalusta, *Sweden* L40+679 46
Muotathal, *Switzerland* M37+470 45
Mur, *Yemen* K12+156 74
Murakami, *Japan* C63+382 68
Murat, R., *Turkey* K28+388 74
Murat Dagh, *Turkey* L02+389 74

Murbat, *Oman* J31+171 75
Murça, *Portugal* N45+414 52
Murcheh Khur, *Iran* J52+331 75
Murchison, C., *N.-W. Terr.* S24+636 89
Murchison Falls, *see* Kabalega Falls
Murchison Mts., *N.Z.* A76–452 112
Murchison, R., *W. Aust.* E22–266 110
Murcia, *Spain* N07+380 53
Murdo, *S. Dakota* U65+438 93
Muresul (Maros), R.,
  Romania L54+462 58
Murfreesboro, *Tennessee* T68+358 93
Muri, *Switzerland* M40+473 45
Murias de Paredes, *Spain* N37+429 52
Müritz. See, *E. Germany* M14+534 48
Murjo, mt., *Java* E55–066 65
Murmansk, *U.S.S.R.* K70+690 62
Murmashi, *U.S.S.R.* K70+690 61
Murom, *U.S.S.R.* K18+555 61
Muroran, *Japan* C54+423 68
Muros, *Spain* N54+428 52
Murphy, *N. Carolina* T54+351 97
Murphysboro, *Illinois* T86+378 95
Murray, *Kentucky* T80+366 95
Murray, *Utah* V42+406 98
Murray, R., *N.S.W.*, etc. C39–352 109
Murray Bridge, S. *Australia* C65–352 109
Murray Harbour, *P.E.I.* S15+460 90
Murray River, *P.E.I.* S16+460 90
Murrayville, *Victoria* C53–353 109
Murree, *Pakistan* H10+339 72
Mürren, *Switzerland* M40+466 45
Murrumbidgee, R., *N.S.W.* C35–346 109
Murrumburrah & Harden,
  New South Wales C10–346 109
Murrurundi, *New S. Wales* B85–318 109
Mursan, *India* G72+275 72
Murshidabad, *India* G10+243 73
Mursir, *Oman* J22+249 75
Murten & See, *Switzerland* M47+469 45
Murtoa, *Victoria* C45–367 109
Mururoa I., *Tuamotu Arch.* X10–215 107
Murwara, *India* G57+238 73
Murzuq, *Libya* M06+258 81
Mus, *Turkey* K21+388 74
Musa Kala, *Afghanistan* H61+323 75
Musalamıya, *Saudi Arabia* J65+275 74
Muscat (Masqãt), *Oman* J09+236 75
Muscat & Oman. *See* Oman
Muscatine, *Iowa* U06+414 95
Musemir, *Yemen, South* K02+134 74
Musgrave Harb., *Nfd.* R52+495 90
Musgrave Ra., *New Guinea* C40–063 111
Musgrave Ra., *S. Australia* D20–260 110
Musheramore, *Ireland, Rep.* N54+520 43
Mushie, *Zaire* L78–030 82
Musket Chan., *Mass.* S62+413 96
Muskegon, *Michigan* T68+432 91
Muskegon R., *Michigan* T62+440 91
Muskogee, *Oklahoma* U33+359 95
Muskwaro, L., *Quebec* S06+506 90
Musmar, *Sudan* K56+180 81
Musoma, *Tanzania* K66–016 83
Mussau, I., *Pacific Ocean* C00–020 106
Musselburgh, *Scotland* N18+559 41
Mussidan, *France* M88+450 55
Mussuma, *Angola* L48–142 82
Mustahil, *Ethiopia* K02+052 83
Mustajidda, *Saudi Arabia* K19+266 74
Mustang, *Nepal* G37+291 73
Mustang I., *Texas* U43+276 94
Musters, L., *Argentina* S56–455 103
Muswellbrook, *N.S.W.* B85–323 109
Mut, *Egypt* L06+254 81
Mut, *Turkey* K70+366 74
Mutanda, *Zambia* L22–124 82
Mutano, *Angola* M01–166 84
Mutorai, *U.S.S.R.* F27+615 63
Mutshatsha, *Zaire* L34–056 82
Mutsu B., *Japan* C53+411 68
Mutton I., *Ireland, Rep.* N57+528 43
Mutumbo, *Angola* L76–134 82
Mutupet, *India* G66+104 70
Muwale, *Tanzania* K68–064 83
Muxima, *Angola* M16–092 82
Muy, le, *France* M55+435 55
Muya, *Japan* D02+342 68
Muya, *U.S.S.R.* E24+563 63
Muy Muy, *Nicaragua* T63+127 101
Muzaffarabad, *Kashmir* H09+344 72
Muzaffargarh, *Pakistan* H23+301 72
Muzaffarnagar, *India* G74+294 72
Muzaffarpur, *India* G27+261 73
Muzhi, *U.S.S.R.* H63+655 62
Muzquiz, *Mexico* U69+278 100
Muztagh Ata, *Sinkiang, China* G89+383 72
Mwanza, *Tanzania* K72–026 83
Mweelrea, *Ireland, Rep,* N59+536 42
Mweru, L., *Zaire* L08–090 83
Mwinilunga, *Zambia* L34–120 82
Myanaung, *Burma* F58+82 71
Myall, L., *New S. Wales* B77–325 109
Myadaung, *Burma* F52+238 71
Myaungmya, *Burma* F60+166 71
Myebon, *Burma* F69+201 71
Myenmoletkhat, Mt., *Burma* F37+134 71
Myingyan, *Burma* F57+214 71
Myitkyina, *Burma* F45+254 71
Myjava, *Czechoslovakia* L74+488 49
Mymensingh, *Bangladesh* F87+248 71
Myohaung, *Burma* F53+219 71
Myohaung, *Burma* F71+206 71
Myrdal, *Norway* M47+607 47
Myrtle Creek, *S. Australia* C71–304 109
Myrtleford, *Victoria* C19–366 109
Myslowice, *Poland* L67+502 49
Mysore. *See* Karnataka
Mystic, *S. Dakota* U82+441 93
Mziha, *Tanzania* K44–058 83
Mzimba, *Malawi* K68–120 83
Naaf, *Bangladesh* F75+210 71
Naarden, *Netherlands* M59+523 44
Naas, *Ireland, Rep.* N40+532 43
Nabadwip, *India* G10+234 73
Naband, *Iran* J43+274 75
Nabatiye, *Lebanon* K57+334 76
Nabberu, L., *W. Australia* D87–257 110
Nabha, *India* G83+304 72
Nablus, *Jordan* K59+322 76
Nacaome, *Honduras* T75+136 101
Nachvak L., *Labrador* S21+592 89
Nacimiento. *Mexico* U71+279 100
Nackara, *S. Australia* C65–328 109

Naco, *Arizona* V30+313 **94**
Nacogdoches, *Texas* U28+316 **95**
Nacozari de Garcia, *Mexico* V29+305 **100**
Nadia. *See* Nabadwip
Nadiad, *India* H12+226 **70**
Naerøy, *Norway* M22+648 **46**
Naestved, *Denmark* M20+552 **47**
Nafels, *Switzerland* M36+471 **45**
Naga, *Yemen, D.R.* J64+149 **74**
Naga, *Philippines* D70+136 **65**
Naga Hills, *India* F60+262 **71**
Nagaland, *India* F64+262 **71**
Nagambie, *Victoria* C29–368 **109**
Nagano, *Japan* C71+366 **68**
Nagaoka, *Japan* C67+374 **68**
Nagappattinam, *India* G61+108 **70**
Nagar, *India* G77+321 **72**
Nagar, *Kashmir* H01+362 **72**
Nagar Karnul, *India* G70+164 **70**
Nagar Parkar, *India* H25+243 **70**
Nagasaki, *Japan* D31+327 **68**
Nagaur, *India* H07+270 **70**
Nagda, *India* G87+232 **70**
Nagercoil, *India* G74+083 **70**
Nagha Kalat, *Pakistan* H59+274 **70**
Nagina, *India* G69+295 **73**
Nagoya, *Japan* C78+351 **68**
Nagpur, *India* G65+210 **70**
Nagu, (Nauvo), *Finland* L49+602 **47**
Nagykanizsa, *Hungary* L78+465 **49**
Naha, *Japan* D44+262 **68**
Nahael Niyeu, *Argentina* S39–405 **103**
Nahan, *India* G76+305 **72**
Nahariya, *Israel* K59+330 **76**
Naibandan, *Iran* J15+323 **75**
Naifa, *Saudi Arabia* J53+199 **75**
Naifar, *Iraq* J89+322 **74**
Naihati, *India* G09+229 **73**
Nain, *Labrador* S11+563 **89**
Nain, *Iran* J41+329 **75**
Naini Tal, *India* G63+294 **73**
Nain Sing Ra., *Tibet* G50+326 **70**
Nairn, *Scotland* N23+576 **40**
Nairobi, *Kenya* K52–001 **83**
Naisecho, *Kenya* K48+018 **83**
Naismith, *Montana* V41+484 **93**
Naivasha, & L., *Kenya* K52–008 **83**
Najera, *Spain* N16+424 **53**
Najibabad, *India* G70+296 **73**
Najira, *Saudi Arabia* J70+280 **74**
Nakajo, *Japan* C64+381 **68**
Nakatsu, *Japan* D23+336 **68**
Nakawn Pathom, *Thailand* F30+138 **69**
Nakfa, *Ethiopia* K40+166 **83**
Nakhala, *Saudi Arabia* J53+243 **75**
Nakhaun Phantom, *Thailand* F02+174 **69**
Nakhichevan, *U.S.S.R.* J85+390 **62**
Nakhon Ratchasima, *Thai.* F17+149 **69**
Nakhon Sawan, *Thailand* F30+158 **69**
Nakhon Si Thammarat, *Thai.* F30+084 **69**
Nakina, *Ontario* T70+501 **89**
Nakl Mubarak, *Saudi Arabia* K40+243 **74**
Nakodar, *India* G87+311 **72**
Nakuru, *Kenya* K54–004 **83**
Nalagarh, *India* G79+310 **72**
Nalgonda, *India* G64+170 **70**
Nallamalai Hills, *India* G67+159 **70**
Nalut, *Libya* M24+318 **81**
Namangan, *Uzbek.* H20+412 **62**
Namasagali, *Uganda* K72+010 **83**
Namatail, *Mozambique* K32–158 **83**
Nambala, *Zambia* L18–152 **84**
Nambucca, *New S. Wales* B73–306 **109**
Namcha Barwa, *China* F58+295 **64**
Nam-dinh, *Vietnam* E83+204 **69**
Namhoi. *See* Fatshan
Namib Desert, *Namibia* M04-250 **84**
Namibia, *S. Africa* L76-250 **84**
Namlea, *Buru I., Indonesia* D48–034 **65**
Namling Dzong, *Tibet* G06+296 **71**
Nam Mao R., *Burma* F47+236 **71**
Namoi, *New South Wales* B88–310 **109**
Namonuito, Is., *Caroline Is.* C00+085 **106**
Namorona, *Madagascar* J72–218 **83**
Nampa, *Idaho* V70+436 **92**
Nampula, *Mozambique* K34–152 **83**
Nams Vatn, *Norway* M08+651 **46**
Namsen, R., *Norway* M14+647 **46**
Namsos, *Norway* M21+645 **46**
Namtsy, *U.S.S.R.* D31+627 **63**
Namtu, *Burma* F45+229 **71**
Namur & prov., *Belgium* M61+503 **44**
Namutoni, *Namibia* L78-188 **84**
Namwala, *Zambia* L22–158 **84**
Namyang, *China* E33+252 **67**
Nanaimo, *Brit. Columbia* W34+492 **88**
Nana Kru, *Liberia* N52+048 **80**
Nanan. *See* Tayu
Nanao, *Japan* C78+370 **68**
Nanchang, *China* E24+286 **67**
Nancheng (Hanchung), *China* E78+331 **66**
Nancheng (Kienchang), *China* E20+275 **67**
Nanchung, *China* E83+308 **66**
Nancy, *France* M55+487 **54**
Nanda Devi, mt., *India* G60+304 **70**
Nanded, *India* G75+192 **70**
Nandewar Ra., *N.S.W.* B86–302 **109**
Nanga Parbat, *Kashmir* H03+352 **72**
Nanguar, *Mozambique* K42–124 **83**
Nanjangud, *India* G79+121 **70**
Nankang. *See* Tsingtze
Nanking, *China* E07+320 **66**
Nannine, *W. Australia* E10–268 **110**
Nanning, *China* E70+228 **67**
Nanortalik, *Greenland* Q72+600 **26**
Nanpara, *India* G51+278 **73**
Nanping, *China* E11+267 **67**
Nanripo, *Mozambique* K36–140 **83**
Nan Shan, *China* E74+251 **64**
Nantan, *China* E74+251 **64**
Nantes, *France* N09+472 **54**
Nanticoke, *Pennsylvania* T06+412 **96**
Nantucket, *Massachusetts* S61+413 **91**
Nantucket I., *Massachusetts* S60+412 **96**
Nantucket Sd., *Massachusetts* S62+414 **96**
Nantung, *China* D85+320 **66**
Nantwich, *England* N15+531 **37**
Nanyang, *China* E45+330 **66**
Nanyuki, *Kenya* K48+001 **83**
Naoetsu, *Japan* C70+371 **68**
Napa, *California* W14+383 **92**

Napanee, *Ontario* T12+442 **91**
Napas, *U.S.S.R.* G48+599 **62**
Napier, *New Zealand* A18–395 **112**
Naples. *See* Napoli
Napoleon, *N. Dakota* U58+465 **93**
Napoli, *Italy* M05+409 **57**
Napoli, G. di, *Italy* M07+406 **57**
Naqb Ashtar, *Jordan* K57+300 **76**
Nara, *Mali* N44+152 **80**
Nara, *Japan* C85+347 **68**
Naracoorte, *S. Australia* C56–370 **109**
Naradhan, *New S. Wales* C22–336 **109**
Narativat, *Thailand* F19+064 **69**
Narayanganj, *Bangladesh* F82+236 **71**
Narbada R., *India* G68+230 **73**
Narberth, *Wales* N28+518 **38**
Narbonne, *France* M72+432 **55**
Nares Ld., *Greenland* R25+820 **26**
Nari R., *Pakistan* H43+284 **70**
Narino. *See* Japura
Narken, *Sweden* L44+670 **46**
Narnaul, *India* G85+281 **72**
Narok, *Kenya* K56–012 **83**
Narooma, *New South Wales* B89–363 **109**
Narovchat, *U.S.S.R.* K08+538 **61**
Narowal, *Pakistan* H01+321 **72**
Narrabri, *New South Wales* C01–303 **109**
Narrabri West, *N.S.W.* C02–304 **109**
Narragansett B., *Rhode I.* S69+414 **96**
Narran L. & R., *N.S.W.* C16–296 **109**
Narranderra, *New S. Wales* C21–348 **109**
Narrogin, *W. Australia* E17–328 **110**
Narromine, *New S. Wales* C10–323 **109**
Narsimhgarh, *India* G77+238 **70**
Narsinghpur, *India* G65+229 **73**
Naruta, *Japan* D02+342 **68**
Narva, *Estonia* L11+593 **47**
Narva Laht, *Estonia* L16+596 **47**
Narvik, *Norway* L75+685 **46**
Narwar, *India* G73+257 **73**
Naryan Mar, *U.S.S.R.* J40+677 **62**
Narykary, *U.S.S.R.* H60+634 **62**
Narym, *U.S.S.R.* G50+589 **62**
Naryn, *Kirgiz.* G84+414 **62**
Naseby, *New Zealand* A59–450 **112**
Nashua and R., *N.H.* S69+428 **96**
Nashville, *Arkansas* U22+339 **95**
Nashville, *Illinois* T86+384 **95**
Nashville, *N. Carolina* T18+360 **97**
Nashville, *Tennessee* T71+361 **97**
Nasijarvi, *Finland* L38+616 **47**
Nasia, *Ghana* N04+100 **80**
Nasik, *India* H07+200 **70**
Nasirabad, *India* H01+262 **70**
Naskaupi R., *Labrador* S10+542 **89**
Nassau, *Bahamas,The* T15+250 **101**
Nassau, G. de, *Chile* S46–555 **103**
Nassau, I., *Pacific Ocean* Z03–114 **106**
Nasser, L., *Egypt* K82+216 **81**
Nassjo, *Sweden* M02+577 **47**
Nata, *Panama* T33+084 **101**
Natal, *Brazil* Q31–058 **105**
Natal, *Brazil* S01–068 **104**
Natal, *South Africa* L00–286 **84**
Natal, *Sumatra* F35+006 **65**
Natanes Plat., *Arizona* V26+334 **94**
Natanya, *Israel* K61+323 **76**
Natashquan, *Quebec* S11+502 **90**
Natashquan R., *Quebec* S10+514 **89**
Natchez, *Mississippi* U08+316 **93**
Natimuk, *Victoria* C48–367 **109**
National City, *California* V73+326 **92**
Natividade, *Brazil* R16–115 **105**
Natron L., *Tanzania* K54–024 **83**
Nattavaara, *Sweden* L54+667 **46**
Naturaliste, C., *W. Aust.* E30–334 **110**
Naturawit L., *N.-W. Terr.* U51+635 **88**
Naukhas, *Namibia* L82-236 **84**
Naumburg, *E. Germany* M19+512 **48**
Naumestis, *Lithuania* L43+548 **47**
Naumiestis, *Lithuania* L50+554 **47**
Nauplia. *See* Navplion
Naur, *Jordan* K55+319 **76**
Nauru, I., *Pacific Ocean* A78–003 **106**
Naushahra. *See* Nowshera
Naushahro, *Pakistan* H41+268 **70**
Naushk, *U.S.S.R.* E84+505 **63**
Nauta, *Peru* S81–045 **104**
Nautla, *Mexico* U41+202 **96**
Nauvoo, *Illinois* T86+406 **95**
Nava del Rey, *Spain* N30+414 **52**
Navajo, *Mt., Utah* V36+370 **94**
Navalcarnero, *Spain* N24+403 **52**
Navalmoral, *Spain* N33+399 **52**
Navan, *Ireland, Rep.* N40+537 **42**
Navarino, I., *Chile* S46–550 **103**
Navarre, *Victoria* C48–367 **109**
Navarre, prov., *France* N07+433 **55**
Navojoa, *Mexico* V26+272 **96**
Navplion, *Greece* L43+376 **59**
Navrongo, *Ghana* N06+108 **80**
Navsari, *India* H12+209 **70**
Nawa, *Syria* K54+329 **76**
Nawabganj, *India* G47+269 **73**
Nawabganj, *India* G53+269 **73**
Nawada, *India* G26+249 **73**
Nawah Basoda, *India* G70+236 **73**
Nawahganj, *India* G62+285 **73**
Nawai, *India* G84+264 **70**
Nawalgarh, *India* G88+278 **72**
Naxos, I., *Greece* L27+370 **59**
Nayakhan, *U.S.S.R.* B38+620 **63**
Nayarit, state, *Mexico* V00+220 **96**
Nayarit, Sa. de, *Mexico* U88+226 **96**
Nayoro, *Japan* C44+443 **68**
Nazaré de Mata, *Brazil* Q31–077 **105**
Nazareth, *Belgium* M60+509 **44**
Nazareth, *Israel* K58+327 **76**
Nazas, *Mexico* U85+252 **96**
Nazca, *Peru* S88–148 **104**
Naze, The, *England* M82+519 **39**
Naze, The (Lindesnes), *Nor.* M47+580 **47**
Nazilli, *Turkey* L10+379 **74**
Nazimovo, *U.S.S.R.* F83+595 **63**
Ncheu, *Malawi* K62–148 **83**
Ndala, *Tanzania* K70–046 **83**
Ndeni, I., *Santa Cruz Is.* A82–105 **106**
N'Djamena, *Chad* M00+122 **81**
Ndola, *Zambia* L08–130 **83**
Neagh L., *N. Ireland* N38+546 **42**
Néapolis, *Crete* L26+353 **59**

Near Is., *Aleutian Islands* A40+517 **95**
Neath, *Wales* N23+517 **38**
Nebikon, *Switzerland* M42+472 **45**
Nebit-Dag, *Turkmen.* J36+392 **62**
Nebo Mt., *Utah* V41+398 **94**
Nebraska, state, *U.S.A.* U73+416 **98**
Nebraska City, *Nebraska* U35+406 **95**
Necedah, *Wisconsin* U00+440 **91**
Neckar, R., *W. Germany* M36+492 **48**
Necochea, *Argentina* R83–386 **103**
Nederweert, *Netherlands* M56+513 **44**
Neede, *Netherlands* M50+521 **44**
Needham Market, *England* M84+522 **39**
Needles, *California* V58+348 **92**
Needles, The, *Arizona* V55+345 **92**
Needles, The, *England* N10+507 **39**
Neemuch, *India* H00+245 **70**
Neenah, *Wisconsin* T81+442 **91**
Neerpelt, *Belgium* M57+512 **44**
Nefud Des, *Saudi Arabia* K30+288 **74**
Negaunee, *Michigan* T75+465 **91**
Negocio, *Argentina* S35–418 **103**
Negombo, *Sri Lanka* G61+073 **70**
Negra Pta., *Peru* T36–060 **104**
Negrais, C., *Burma* F65+160 **71**
Negro, R., *Argentina* S30–398 **103**
Negro, R., *Brazil* S20–004 **104**
Negro, R., *Uruguay* R60–324 **103**
Negros, I., *Philippines* D72+100 **65**
Nehavend, *Iran* J71+343 **74**
Nehbandan, *Iran* J00+315 **75**
Neilsville, *Wisconsin* U04+446 **91**
Neisse. *See* Nysa,
Nejd, *Saudi Arabia* K18+256 **74**
Neksø, *Bornholm I., Den.* L89+551 **47**
Nelia Gaari, *New S. Wales* C43–321 **109**
Nelkan, *U.S.S.R.* C84+577 **63**
Nelligen, *New South Wales* B89–356 **109**
Nellore, *India* G60+145 **70**
Nelma, *U.S.S.R.* C65+475 **63**
Nelson, *Brit. Columbia* V73+495 **88**
Nelson, *New Zealand* A40–413 **112**
Nelson, *Victoria* C54–381 **109**
Nelson, C., *Victoria* C51–384 **109**
Nelson Hd., *N.-W. Terr.* W10+710 **88**
Nelson L., *Manitoba* U63+557 **88**
Nelson, Mt., *Brit. Columbia* V68+504 **88**
Nelson R., *Manitoba* U25+562 **88**
Nêma, *Mauritania* N44+166 **80**
Nemecke Pravno, *Czech.* L68+489 **49**
Nemikiachi L., *Quebec* S87+475 **91**
Nemours, (Ghazaouet), *Alg.* N10+350 **80**
Nemours, *France* M74+482 **54**
Nemunas, R., *Lithuania* L40+551 **47**
Nemuro, *Japan* C26+433 **68**
Nemuro B., *Japan* C28+434 **68**
Nen R., *England* N03+526 **37**
Nenagh, *Ireland, Rep.* N49+528 **43**
Nendeln, *Liechtenstein* M33+472 **45**
Neodesha, *Kansas* U35+374 **95**
Neosho, *Missouri* U26+368 **95**
Nepa, *U.S.S.R.* E71+592 **63**
Nepal, *Asia* G50+270 **30**
Nepalganj, *Nepal* G50+280 **73**
Nephi, *Utah* V42+396 **94**
Nephin, *Ireland, Rep.* N56+540 **42**
Nephin Beg, *Ireland, Rep.* N58+540 **43**
Nérac, *France* M88+441 **55**
Nerchinsk, *U.S.S.R.* E19+520 **63**
Nerpio, *Spain* N14+382 **53**
Nerriga, *New South Wales* C00–352 **109**
Nes, *U.S.S.R.* K03+667 **62**
Nesna, *Norway* M12+662 **46**
Nespawa, *Manitoba* U57+503 **88**
Ness L., *Scotland* N27+573 **40**
Ness City, *Kansas* U60+384 **95**
Nesset, *Norway* M42+628 **46**
Nesslau, *Switzerland* M35+472 **45**
Nesthorn, mt., *Switzerland* M42+464 **45**
Nesttun, *Norway* M58+603 **47**
Netherlands, *W. Europe* M54+520 **50**
Nettilling L., *N.-W. Terr.* S65+662 **89**
Nettuno, *Italy* M14+415 **57**
Neubrandenburg,
    E. Germany M10+535 **48**
Neuburg, *W. Germany* M23+487 **48**
Neuchâtel & canton, *Switz.* M48+470 **45**
Neuchâtel, L. de, *Switz.* M49+45
Neufchâtel, *Belgium* M57+498 **44**
Neufchâteau, *France* M56+483 **54**
Neufchâtel, *France* M82+498 **54**
Neufelden, *Austria* M06+485 **48**
Neuhausen, *Switzerland* M38+477 **45**
Neumünster, *W. Germany* M30+541 **48**
Neunkirch, *Switzerland* M39+477 **45**
Neuquen, *Argentina* S49–389 **103**
Neuse R., *N. Carolina* T14+353 **97**
Neusiedler See, *Austria* L79+477 **49**
Neuss, *W. Germany* M50+512 **48**
Neustadt, *W. Germany* M25+541 **48**
Neustettin. *See* Szczecinek
Neustrelitz, *E. Germany* M12+533 **48**
Neu Ulm, *W. Germany* M30+484 **48**
Neuva, I., *Chile & Argent.* S40–552 **103**
Neuva Esperanza, *Bolivia* S28–158 **104**
Neuva Lubeca, *Argentina* S63–446 **103**
Neuve Eglise, *Belgium* M73+508 **44**
Neuveville, *Switzerland* M47+471 **45**
Neuvitas, *Cuba* T14+215 **101**
Nevada, *Iowa* U20+422 **95**
Nevada, *Missouri* U26+378 **95**
Nevada, state, *U.S.A.* V81+395 **98**
Nevada, Sa., *California* W12+411 **98**
Nevada, Sa., *Spain* N20+370 **52**
Nevel, *U.S.S.R.* L00+560 **60**
Nevel'sk, *U.S.S.R.* C48+465 **63**
Nevers, *France* M71+470 **54**
Nevertire, *New South Wales* C14–319 **109**
Nevesinje, *Yugoslavia* L71+433 **58**
Neveyezhkino, *U.S.S.R.* K01+512 **61**
Nevis, I., *Leeward Islands* S15+172 **101**
Nevsehir, *Turkey* K62+386 **74**
Nevyansk, *U.S.S.R.* H89+574 **61**
New Albany, *Indiana* T65+383 **97**
New Albany, *Mississippi* T84+345 **95**
New Amsterdam,
    Guyana R76+061 **105**
Newark, *Delaware* T04+397 **96**
Newark, *England* N05+531 **37**
Newark, *New Jersey* S85+407 **96**

Newark, *Ohio* T45+401 **91**
Newaygo, *Michigan* T65+434 **91**
New Bedford, *Massachusetts* S65+416 **96**
New Bern, *N. Carolina* T12+351 **97**
Newbern, *Tennessee* T86+362 **97**
Newberry, *Michigan* T63+463 **91**
Newberry, *S. Carolina* T40+343 **97**
New Bloomfield, *Pa* T14+404 **96**
New Britain, *Bismarck*
    Archipelago B85–060 **106**
New Britain, *Connecticut* S76+417 **96**
New Brunswick, *New Jersey* S87+405 **96**
New Brunswick, prov.,
    Canada S36+470 **89**
Newburg, *New Brunswick* S45+463 **90**
Newburgh, *New York* S84+414 **96**
Newburgh, *Scotland* N19+563 **41**
Newbury, *England* N08+514 **39**
Newburyport, *Massachusetts* S65+428 **96**
Newby Bridge, *England* N18+543 **37**
New Caledonia, *Pacific Oc.* A85–212 **106**
New Carlisle, *Quebec* S32+480 **90**
Newcastle, *Delaware* T03+397 **91**
Newcastle, *Natal* L00–278 **84**
Newcastle, *New Brunswick* S34+470 **90**
New Castle, *New Jersey* T04+397 **96**
Newcastle, *New South Wales* B80–330 **109**
Newcastle, *N. Ireland* N35+542 **42**
New Castle, *Pennsylvania* T32+411 **91**
Newcastle, *Wyoming* U86+439 **93**
Newcastle Emlyn, *Wales* N27+520 **38**
Newcastle-under-Lyme, *Eng.* N13+530 **37**
Newcastle-upon-Tyne, *Eng.* N10+550 **37**
Newcastle Waters,,
    N.T., Australia D09–173 **111**
Newchwang. *See* Yingkow.
New City, *New York* S84+411 **96**
New Cumberland, *W. Va.* T34+405 **91**
New England Ra., *N.S.W.* B80–306 **109**
Newfane, *Vermont* S76+430 **91**
New Forest, *England* N10+508 **39**
Newfoundland, prov., *Canada* R70+490 **89**
New Galloway, *Scotland* N25+551 **41**
New Georgia, I., *Solomon Is.* B48–080 **105**
New Glasgow, *Nova Scotia* S16+456 **90**
New Guinea, *Pacific Ocean* C60–060 **31**
New Hampshire, state, *U.S.A.* S70+435 **91**
New Hampton, *Iowa* U14+430 **95**
New Haven, *Connecticut* S78+413 **91**
Newhaven, *England* N00+508 **39**
New Haven, *Missouri* U08+386 **97**
New Hebrides, Is., *See* Vanuatu
New Iberia, *Lousiana* U11+300 **95**
New Ireland, *Bismarck Arch.* B75–040 **106**
New Jersey, state, *U.S.A.* S89+404 **99**
New Liskeard, *Ontario* T28+475 **91**
Newe London, *Connecticut* S73+413 **96**
New London, *Wisconsin* T83+445 **91**
New Madrid, *Missouri* T88+366 **95**
Newmarket, *Ireland, Rep.* N54+522 **43**
Newmarket, *England* M88+522 **39**
Newmarket, *Ontario* T27+441 **91**
New Mexico, state, *U.S.A.* V20+344 **98**
Newnes, *New South Wales* B89–332 **109**
Newnham, *England* N16+518 **38**
New Norfolk, *Tasmania* C18–428 **109**
New Orleans, *Louisiana* U00+300 **95**
New Plymouth, *N.Z.* A36–390 **112**
Newport, *Arkansas* U08+356 **97**
Newport, *Ireland, Rep.* N57+539 **42**
Newport, *I. of W., England* N08+507 **39**
Newport, *Kentucky* T57+391 **91**
Newport, *New Hampshire* S73+434 **96**
Newport, *Quebec* S29+483 **90**
Newport, *Rhode Island* S68+435 **96**
Newport, *Vermont* S73+449 **91**
Newport, *Wales* N18+516 **38**
Newport News, *Virginia* T08+370 **97**
Newport-on-Tay, *Scotland* N18+564 **41**
New Providence, I.,
    Bahamas, The T15+250 **101**
Newquay, *England* N30+504 **38**
New Quay, *Wales* N26+522 **38**
New Radnor, *Wales* N19+522 **38**
New Richmond, *Quebec* S35+482 **90**
New Richmond, *Wisconsin* U15+452 **93**
New Rochelle, *New York* S82+409 **96**
New Rockford, *N. Dakota* U59+457 **93**
New Ross, *Ireland, Rep.* N42+524 **43**
Newry & Can.., *N. Ireland* N38+542 **42**
New Salem, *N. Dakota* U68+469 **93**
New Siberian Islands,
    See Novosibirskiye Ostrova
New South Wales, state, *Aust* — **111**
Newton, *Iowa* U18+416 **95**
Newton, *Kansas* U44+381 **95**
Newton, *Massachusetts* S67+424 **96**
Newton, *New Jersey* S89+410 **96**
Newton-Abbot, *England* N22+505 **38**
Newtonmore, *Scotland* N25+571 **40**
Newtown Mount Kennedy,
    Ireland, Rep. N37+531 **43**
Newton-Stewart, *Scotland* N27+550 **41**
Newtown, *Wales* N20+525 **38**
Newtownards, *N. Ireland* N34+546 **42**
Newtown Butler, *N. Ireland* N44+546 **42**
Newtown Hamilton, *N. Ire.* N39+542 **42**
Newtonstewart, *N. Ire.* N44+547 **42**
New Ulm, *Minnesota* U27+443 **91**
New Waterford, *Nova Scotia* S00+463 **90**
New Westminster, *B.C.* W18+492 **88**
New World I., *Nfd.* R59+496 **90**
New York, *New York* S84+408 **91**
New York, state, *U.S.A.* T20+425 **99**
New Zealand, *Australasia* — **112**
Nexö. *See* Neksø.
Neya, *U.S.S.R.* K06+583 **61**
Neyriz, *Iran* J34+296 **75**
Neyshābūr, *Iran* J07+362 **75**
Nezhin, *Ukraine* K79+511 **60**
Ngami, L., *Botswana* L40–210 **84**
Nganglaring Tso, *Tibet* G42+315 **71**
N'Gaoundéré, *Cameroon* M08+074 **81**
Ngapara, *New Zealand* A55–450 **112**
Ngaruawehia, *New Zealand* A29–377 **112**
Ngatik, I., *Caroline Islands* B47+050 **106**
Ngauruhoe, Mt., *N.Z.* A26–391 **112**
Nguni, *Sudan* L14+060 **81**
Ngong, *Kenya* K50–014 **83**
Ngoring Nor, *China* F42+348 **64**
Nguigmi, *Niger* M12+142 **81**

Ngulu, I., *Pacific Ocean* C78+075 **106**
Ngwasi, *Tanzania* K46–086 **83**
Nha-Trang, *Vietnam* E65+123 **69**
Nhill, *Victoria* C50–363 **109**
Niafounke, *Mali* N24+160 **80**
Niagara, *Ontario* T25+433 **91**
Niagara Falls, *New York* T24+431 **91**
Niagara Falls, *Ontario* T24+431 **91**
Niah, *Sarawak* E38+037 **65**
Niamey, *Niger* M78+134 **80**
Nia Nia, *Zaire* L14+014 **83**
Niapa, mt., *Borneo* E15+017 **65**
Nias, I., *Indonesia* F44+011 **65**
Nicaragua, rep., *Cent. Amer.* T62+130 **101**
Nicaragua L., *Nicaragua* T63+116 **101**
Nicastro, *Italy* L82+390 **57**
Nic Doit Soe Pk., *Arizona* V36+364 **94**
Nice, *France* M47+437 **55**
Nicobar Is., *Indian Ocean* F70+085 **71**
Nicolet, *Quebec* S76+462 **91**
Nicoque, *Mozambique* K36–128 **83**
Nicosia, *Cyprus* K70+352 **76**
Nicoya & Pen., *Costa Rica* T62+100 **101**
Nidau, *Switzerland* M47+471 **45**
Nidd R., *England* N10+540 **37**
Nidzica, *Poland* L57+533 **49**
Niedere Tauern, *Austria* M06+473 **48**
Niedersachsen, *W. Germany* M42+528 **48**
Nielle, *Ivory Coast* N34+102 **80**
Niére, *Chad* L50+142 **81**
Nieuw Amsterdam, *Surinam* R60+058 **105**
Nieuwendijk, *Netherlands* M61+518 **44**
Nieuwersluis, *Netherlands* M60+522 **44**
Nieuwkoop *Netherlands* M61+522 **44**
Nieuw Nickerie, *Surinam* R73+058 **105**
Nieuwpoort, *Belgium* M73+511 **44**
Nieuwpoort, *Netherlands* M61+519 **44**
Nieves, *Mexico* U78+240 **100**
Niévre, dep., *France* M68+471 **54**
Nigde, *Turkey* K62+380 **74**
Niger, rep., *W. Africa* M30+156 **81**
Niger R., *W. Africa* N10+150 **80**
Nigeria, *W. Africa* M40+100 **80**
Nighasan, *India* G55+282 **73**
Nigula, *Estonia* L20+595 **47**
Niigata, *Japan* C66+379 **68**
Niihau, I., *Hawaii* Y60+220 **106**
Niitaka Chain, *Taiwan* D84+240 **67**
Nijil, *Jordan* K57+305 **76**
Nijkerk, *Netherlands* M58+522 **44**
Nijmegen, *Netherlands* M55+518 **44**
Nikaria. See Ikaria, I.
Nikiforos, *Greece* L34+412 **58**
Nikki, *Benin* M72+098 **80**
Nikko Nat. Park, *Japan* C64+368 **68**
Nikolayevskiy, *U.S.S.R.* J87+501 **61**
Nikolayev, *Ukraine* K78+470 **60**
Nikolayevsk-na-Amure,
  U.S.S.R. C56+533 **63**
Nikolo Kozelsk, *Ukraine* K71+476 **60**
Nikolskaya Pestrovka, *U.S.S.R.* J84+538 **61**
Nikolsk Berezovka, *U.S.S.R.* J35+561 **61**
Nikopol, *Ukraine* K63+476 **60**
Niksar, *Turkey* K48+407 **74**
Nikšić, *Yugoslavia* L66+428 **58**
Nila, I., *Indonesia* D33–068 **65**
Nile, R., *N. Africa* K72+250 **81**
Niles, *Michigan* T68+418 **91**
Nilgiri, *India* G19+214 **71**
Nilgiri Hills, *India* G81+116 **70**
Nilphamari, *Bangladesh* G07+259 **73**
Nimach, (Neemuch), *India* H00+245 **70**
Nîmes, *France* M64+439 **55**
Nimgiri, Mt., *India* G39+196 **71**
Nimmitabel, *New S. Wales* C05–365 **109**
Nine de Julio, *Argentina* S05–354 **99**
Ninety Mile Beach, *Victoria* C16–382 **109**
Nineveh, *Iraq* K11+366 **74**
Ningan, *China* D33+444 **64**
Ninganpao, *China* E86+373 **66**
Ningerh, *China* F25+231 **64**
Ninghai, *China* D81+293 **67**
Ninghsien, *China* E37+267 **67**
Ninghsien. See Ningpo
Ningiang, *China* E44+283 **67**
Ningkwo. See Suancheng
Ninglingting. See Kinki
Ningpo, *China* D80+298 **67**
Ning-sia. See Yingchwan
Ningteh, *China* E03+267 **67**
Ning-wu-fu, *China* E46+390 **66**
Ning-yüan chow, *China* E80+405 **66**
Ning-yüan-ting, *China* E44+403 **66**
Ninh-binh, *Vietnam* E84+203 **69**
Ninh Hoa, *Vietnam* E66+140 **65**
Ninove, *Belgium* M66+508 **44**
Niobrara R., *Nebraska* U71+424 **98**
Nioet, mt., *Borneo* E60+010 **65**
Nioro, *Mali* N58+152 **80**
Niort, *France* N03+463 **54**
Nios. See los, I.
Nipe, B. de, *Cuba* T04+208 **101**
Nipigon, *Ontario* T80+492 **89**
Nipigon, L., *Ontario* T80+500 **89**
Nipissing, L., *Ontario* T29+462 **91**
Nirmal, *India* G69+191 **70**
Nis, *Yugoslavia* L49+433 **58**
Nisab, *Saudi Arabia* J81+149 **74**
Nisehu, *Kashmir* G65+346 **70**
Nish. See Nis
Nishapur. See Neyshabūr.
Nishio, *Japan* C77+348 **68**
Nisiros, I., *Greece* L17+366 **59**
Nissan, *Solomon Islands* B60–053 **106**
Nissi, *Estonia* L34+591 **47**
Niteroi, *Brazil* Q79–228 **105**
Nith, R., *Scotland* N22+550 **41**
Nitra, *Czechoslovakia* L71+483 **49**
Niue, I. *Cook Islands* Z30–190 **106**
Nivala, *Finland* L30+639 **46**
Nivelles, *Belgium* M64+506 **44**
Nivernais, prov., *France* M68+471 **54**
Nizamabad, *India* G71+187 **70**
Nizampatnam, *India* G55+159 **70**
Nizana, *Israel* K63+309 **76**
Nizhne Chirskaya, *U.S.S.R.* K12+484 **61**
Nizhne Udinsk, *U.S.S.R.* F35+549 **63**
Nizhi Pesha, *U.S.S.R.* J73+668 **62**
Nizhniye Serogozy, *Ukraine* K64+469 **60**
Nizhniy Kresty, *U.S.S.R.* B25+687 **63**
Nizhiy Lomov, *U.S.S.R.* K02+536 **61**

Nizhniy Tagil, *U.S.S.R.* J01+579 **61**
Nizke Tatry, *Czechoslovakia* L63+490 **49**
Njombe, *Tanzania* K60–094 **83**
Nkhota-Kota, *Malawi* K64–130 **84**
N'Kongsamba, *Cameroon* M30+050 **81**
Nmai R., *Burma* F41+264 **71**
Noagarh, *India* G47+204 **71**
Noakhali. See Sudharam
Noanama, *Colombia* T13+047 **104**
Noatak R., *Alaska* Y60+675 **99**
Nochistlan, *Mexico* U44+174 **100**
Noerbø, *Norway* M56+587 **47**
Nogales, *Arizona* V36+313 **94**
Nogaro, *France* N00+438 **55**
Nogent-le-Rotrou. *France* M85+483 **54**
Nogent-sur-Seine, *France* M69+485 **54**
Noginsk, *U.S.S.R.* K40+558 **60**
Nohar, *India* H02+292 **72**
Noirmoutier, I. de, *France* N14+470 **54**
Nokhtuysk, *U.S.S.R.* E11+600 **63**
Nola, *Cent. Afr. Rep.* K84+034 **82**
Nola, *Italy* M03+409 **57**
Nome, *Alaska* Z00+642 **99**
Nomining Ls., *Quebec* T00+465 **91**
Nomoi, Is., *Caroline Islands* B65+060 **106**
Nonacho L., *N.-W. Terr.* V30+614 **88**
Nonancourt, *France* M83+488 **54**
Nong-han, *Thailand* F11+174 **69**
Nong Khai, *Thailand* F13+179 **69**
Nongoma, *Natal* K80–280 **84**
Nong-son, *Vietnam* E72+156 **69**
Nonni, R. (Nun), *China* D64+488 **64**
Nonoava, *Mexico* V10+274 **100**
Nonouti, I., *Kiribati* A35–005 **106**
Nöo, *Estonia* L21+583 **47**
Noojee, *Victoria* C24–379 **109**
Noonthorungee, *N.S.W.* C46–310 **109**
Noordeloos, *Netherlands* M60+519 **44**
Noordwolde, *Netherlands* M53+529 **44**
Nootka I., *Brit. Columbia* W41+498 **88**
Nootongoro, *Tanzania* K62–032 **83**
Nora, *Sweden* M00+595 **47**
Noranda, *Quebec* T25+482 **91**
Nord, dep., *France* M71+505 **54**
Nord Cap (Horn), *Iceland* P44+665 **46**
Norddal, *Norway* M47+623 **46**
Nordenshelda, *Arkh.*, *U.S.S.R.* F55+762 **63**
Nordhausen, *E. Germany* M25+515 **48**
Nordkapp, *Norway* L25+711 **46**
Nordkyn Halvøy, *Norway* L12+709 **46**
Nördlingen, *W. Germany* M27+489 **48**
Nordost Rundingen, *Greenland* N60+810 **26**
Nordreisa, *Norway* L54+698 **46**
Nordrhein-Westfalen, *W. Ger.* M48+518 **48**
Nord Slesvig, *South*
Nordstrand I., *W. Germany* M37+545 **48**
Nordvik, *U.S.S.R.* E53+739 **63**
Nore, *Norway* M36+601 **47**
Nore R., *Ireland, Rep.* N42+523 **43**
Norfolk, *Nebraska* U44+422 **95**
Norfolk, *Virginia* T08+369 **97**
Norfolk, co., *England* M84+527 **39**
Norfolk I., *Pacific Ocean* A72–290 **106**
Norfolk Res., *Arkansas* U14+364 **95**
Norgama, *Pakistan* H50+286 **70**
Norheimsund, *Norway* M53+603 **47**
Norily, *U.S.S.R.* G06+694 **62**
Norman, *N.-W. Territories* W32+649 **88**
Norman, *Oklahoma* U44+352 **95**
Normandie, prov., *France* N00+488 **54**
Normanby I., *Papua New Guinea*
  B84–100 **111**
Normanton, *Queensland* C53–176 **111**
Norman Wells, *N.-W. Terr.* W40+652 **88**
Norquin, *Argentina* S64–377 **103**
Norquinco, *Argentina* S66–418 **103**
Norris, L., *Tennessee* T54+364 **97**
Norris Arm, *Newfoundland* R61+491 **90**
Norristown, *Pennsylvania* T02+402 **96**
Norrköping, *Sweden* L83+586 **47**
Norrsundet, *Sweden* L78+610 **47**
Norrtalje, *Sweden* L68+598 **47**
Norseman, *W. Australia* D80–321 **110**
Norsholm, *Sweden* L84+585 **47**
North C., *Antarctica* A80–700 **27**
North C., *New Zealand* A42–344 **112**
North, C., *Nova Scotia* S02+471 **90**
North Chan., *Ontario* T50+461 **91**
North Chan., *Scot.-N. Ire.* N33+550 **42**
North Downs, *England* M87+513 **39**
North I., *New Zealand* **112**
North Pt., *Prince Edward I.* S24+471 **90**
North Sea, *W. Europe* **34**
North Adams, *Massachusetts* S78+427 **96**
Northallerton, *England* N08+543 **37**
Northam, *W. Australia* E20–316 **110**
Northampton, *Massachusetts* S76+424 **96**
Northampton, *W. Australia* E32–282 **110**
Northampton & co., *Eng.* N05+523 **37**
North Bay, *Ontario* T27+463 **91**
North Bend, *Oregon* W25+434 **96**
North Berwick, *Scotland* N16+560 **41**
North Borneo, *See* Sabah

North Bourke, *N.S.W.* C24–300 **109**
Northbridge, *Massachusetts* S70+422 **96**
North Carolina, state, *U.S.A.* T40+358 **99**
North Creek, *New York* S84+437 **91**
North Dakota, state, *U.S.A.* U78+472 **98**
Northern Circars, *India* G50+165 **70**
Northern Ireland, *Brit. Isles* N40+544 **34**
Northern Territory, *Aust.* **110-111**
Northfield, *Minnesota* U19+445 **93**
North Land. *See* Severnaya Zemlya
North Lisbon, *Wisconsin* U01+439 **91**
North Little Rock, *Arkansas* U13+348 **99**
North Platte, *Nebraska* U64+411 **94**
North Pole, *Arctic Ocean* **26**
North Riding, *see* North Yorkshire
North Ronaldsay, I. & Firth,
  Orkney, Scotland N14+594 **40**
North Shields, *England* N09+550 **37**
North Sydney, *Nova Scotia* S02+462 **90**
North Tonawanday. *N.Y.* T23+430 **96**
North Truchas Pk., *N. Mex.* V04+360 **94**
Northumberland, co., *Eng.* N13+553 **37**
Northumberland, *Pa.* T11+409 **96**

Northumberland Str.,
  New Brunswick, etc. S27+465 **90**
North Vancouver, *B.C.* W19+494 **88**
Northville, *New York* S86+433 **91**
North West C., *W. Aust.* E35–218 **110**
North-West River, *Labrador* S01+537 **89**
North-West Territories, *Can.* **88-89**
Northwich, *England* N19+532 **37**
Northwood, *Iowa* U19+434 **95**
Norton, *Kansas* U60+398 **95**
Norton, *New Brunswick* S34+456 **90**
Norton Sd., *Alaska* Z00+636 **99**
Norwalk, *Connecticut* S81+411 **96**
Norwalk, *Ohio* T46+413 **91**
Norway, *Michigan* T77+458 **91**
Norway, king., *N.-W. Europe* **46-47**
Norwich, *Connecticut* S72+415 **96**
Norwich, *England* M82+526 **39**
Norwich, *New York* T03+425 **96**
Norwood, *Massachusetts* S67+422 **96**
Norwood, *New York* T00+447 **91**
Noshiro, *Japan* C60+402 **68**
Nossegem, *Belgium* M63+509 **44**
Nosy Be. I., *Madagascar* J70–134 **83**
Noto, *Sicily* L89+368 **57**
Noto Pen., *Japan* C80+372 **68**
Notodden, *Norway* M38+595 **47**
Notre Dame B., *Nfd.* R60+497 **90**
Notre Dame Mts., *Quebec* S60+470 **90**
Notre Dame-du-Lac, *Quebec* S53+476 **90**
Nottawasaga B., *Ontario* T32+446 **91**
Nottingham & co., *England* N07+530 **37**
Nottingham I., *N.-W. Terr.* T17+636 **89**
Nouakchott, *Mauritania* P06+180 **80**
Nouchaves, *Angola* L52–108 **82**
Nova Cruz, *Brazil* Q32–064 **105**
Nova Gaia, *Angola* L74–102 **82**
Nova Goa (Panjim),
  Goa, Daman & Diu H07+156 **70**
Nova Lisboa, *See* Huambo
Novara, *Italy* M38+454 **56**
Nova Scotia, prov., *Canada* S20+450 **89**
Nova Venecia, *Brazil* Q63–188 **105**
Novaya Sibir, Ostrov, *U.S.S.R.*
  C10+750 **63**
Novaya Zemlya, *U.S.S.R.* J20+730 **62**
Nova York, *Brazil* Q84–068 **105**
Nové Zámky, *Czech.* L71+480 **49**
Novgorod, *U.S.S.R.* K82+586 **60**
Novi, *Yugoslavia* M01+451 **56**
Novi Pazar, *Bulgaria* L17+434 **58**
Novi Pazar, *Yugoslavia* L57+431 **58**
Novi Sad, *Yugoslavia* L61+453 **58**
Novo Alekseyevka, *Kasakh.* H66+453 **62**
Novocherkassk, *U.S.S.R.* K29+474 **61**
Novokuznetsk, *U.S.S.R.* G17+538 **62**
Novo Mesto, *Yugoslavia* M01+458 **56**
Novomoskovsk, *U.S.S.R.* K43+479 **60**
Novo Moskovsk, *Ukraine* K58+487 **60**
Novo Nikolayevsky, *U.S.S.R.* K13+510 **61**
Novo Redondo, *Angola* M06–114 **82**
Novorossiysk, *U.S.S.R.* K44+448 **62**
Novoshakhtinsk, *U.S.S.R.* K31+477 **61**
Novosibirsk, *U.S.S.R.* G42+550 **62**
Novosibirskiye Ostrova, *U.S.S.R.*
  C60+755 **63**
Novo Troitsk, *U.S.S.R.* J21+545 **61**
Novourgench, *Uzbek* H86+415 **62**
Novska, *Yugoslavia* L78+453 **56**
Novy Jičin, *Czechoslovakia* L72+496 **49**
Novyy Port, *U.S.S.R.* H12+676 **62**
Nowa Wilejka, *Lithuania* L27+547 **47**
Nowendoc, *New S. Wales* B80–316 **109**
Nowgong, *India* F74+263 **71**
Nowinga, *Victoria* C47–346 **109**
Nowra, *New South Wales* B87–349 **109**
Nowshera, *Pakistan* H18+340 **72**
Nowy Sacz, *Poland* L56+496 **49**
Nowy Targ, *Poland* L60+495 **49**
Nowy Tomysl, *Poland* L83+523 **49**
Noya, *Spain* N53+427 **52**
Nozay, *France* N10+476 **54**
Ntungamo, *Uganda* K86–008 **83**
Nuanetsi. *Zimbabwe* K8–214 **84**
Nueces R., *Texas* U48+280 **94**
Nueltin L., *N.-W. Terr.* U56+602 **88**
Nueva Imperial, *Chile* S78–386 **103**
Nuevo, G., *Argentina* S28–426 **103**
Nuevo Laredo, *Mexico* U57+274 **100**
Nuevo Leon, state, *Mexico* U60+262 **100**
Nûgssuaq, Pen., *Greenland* R35+700 **26**
Nuits St Georges, *France* M60+471 **54**
Nukuhiva, I., *Marquesas Is.* X30–100 **107**
Nukuoro, I., *Caroline Is.* B60+040 **106**
Nukus, *Uzbek* J02+424 **62**
Nules, *Spain* N01+398 **53**
Nullagine, *W. Australia* E00–218 **110**
Nullarbor Plain, *W. Aust.* D40–306 **110**
Numato, *Japan* C66+366 **68**
Numazu, *Japan* C67+351 **68**
Numfoor, I., *New Guinea* D01–010 **65**
Numurkah, *Victoria* C27–361 **109**
Nunchia, *Colombia* S74+056 **104**
Nuneaton, *England* N09+525 **37**
Nunivak I., *Alaska* Z15+600 **99**
Nunkiang, *China* D59+490 **64**
Nuoro, *Sardinia* M34+403 **57**
Nuqui, *Colombia* T14+057 **104**
Nurmes, *Finland* L05+636 **46**
Nürnberg, *Germany* M24+494 **48**
Nurpur, *India* G84+323 **72**
Nurri, *Sardinia* M35+397 **57**
Nusaybin, *Turkey* K23+371 **74**
Nushki, *Pakistan* H54+296 **70**
Nutrias, *Venezuela* S56+079 **104**
Nuwara Eliya, *Sri Lanka* G56+070 **70**
Nyada, *Sweden* L72+629 **46**
Nyah, *Victoria* C40–352 **109**
Nyaker, *Sweden* L64+638 **46**
Nyala, *Sudan* L30+120 **81**
Nyalikungu, *Tanzania* K70–026 **83**
Nyandoma, *U.S.S.R.* K29+617 **62**
Nyantákara, *Tanzania* K82–030 **83**
Nyanza, *Rwanda* L00–024 **83**
Nyasa, L., *Malawi* K64–118 **83**
Nyasaland, *See* Malawi
Nyasvipetrovsk, *U.S.S.R.* J03+561 **61**
Nyda, *U.S.S.R.* H11+667 **62**
Nyeri, *Kenya* K48–004 **83**
Nyhammar. *Sweden* M00+603 **47**

Nyiregyhaza, *Hungary* L50+479 **49**
Nykobing, *Denmark* M19+547 **47**
Nykøbing, *Denmark* M37+568 **47**
Nyköping, *Sweden* L78+587 **47**
Nylstroom, *Transvaal* L10–246 **84**
Nyamagee, *New South Wales*
  C22–321 **109**
Nymboida & R., *N.S.W.* B75–299 **109**
Nyngan, *New South Wales* C17–316 **109**
Nyon, *Switzerland* M53+464 **45**
Nyonga, *Tanzania* K78–068 **83**
Nyons, *France* M59+444 **55**
Nysa, *Poland* L76+505 **49**
Nysted, *Denmark* M19+546 **47**
Nyurba, *U.S.S.R.* E10+634 **63**
Nyuya, *U.S.S.R.* E22+606 **63**
Nzega, *Tanzania* K70–042 **83**
Oababatiya, *Israel* K58+324 **76**
Oacoma, *S. Dakota* U56+438 **93**
Oahe Res., *S. Dakota* U62+450 **93**
Oahu, I., *Hawaii* Y45+212 **107**
Oakan, *Japan* C34+434 **68**
Oakbank, *S. Australia* C57–331 **109**
Oakes, *N. Dakota* U48+462 **93**
Oakham, *England* N04+527 **37**
Oakland, *California* W14+378 **92**
Oakland, *Maryland* T26+394 **91**
Oakley, *Kansas* U66+390 **94**
Oakville, *Ontario* T53+476 **91**
Oamaru, *New Zealand* A54–451 **112**
Oates Ld., *Antarctica* B50–700 **27**
Oatlands, *Tasmania* C16–423 **109**
Oaxaca & state, *Mexico* U40+170 **100**
Ob, R., *U.S.S.R.* H55+655 **62**
Obama, *Japan* C85+355 **68**
Oban, *New Zealand* A71–469 **112**
Oban, *Scotland* N33+564 **41**
Obatogamau L., *Quebec* S88+496 **90**
Obbia, *Somalia* J68+054 **83**
Obeh, *Afghanistan* H71+345 **75**
Oberammergau, *W. Germany* M24+476 **48**
Oberhausen, *W. Germany* M49+515 **48**
Oberlin, *Kansas* U63+398 **94**
Oberon, *New South Wales* C01–337 **109**
Oberriet, *Switzerland* M33+473 **45**
Oberwald, *Switzerland* M40+465 **45**
Obi, I., *Indonesia* D44–016 **65**
Obidos, *Brazil* R63–018 **105**
Obidos, *Portugal* N55+394 **52**
Obihiro, *Japan* C40+428 **68**
Obo, *Cent. Afr. Rep.* L20+052 **81**
Oahe Res., *S. Dakota* U62+448 **88**
Obock, *Djibouti* K10+118 **83**
Oborona, *U.S.S.R.* K25+521 **61**
Obrayera, *Nicaragua* T53+143 **101**
Obskaya Guba, *U.S.S.R.* H10+700 **62**
Ocala, *Florida* T43+292 **97**
Ocampo, *Mexico* U57+229 **100**
Ocana, *Colombia* S80+081 **104**
Ocana, *Spain* N21+399 **52**
Occidental, Cord., *Colombia* T10+050 **104**
Ocean I., *Pacific Ocean* A63–012 **106**
Oceana, *W. Virginia* T40+377 **97**
Ocean City, *New Jersey* S87+393 **96**
Ochil Hills, *Scotland* N22+562 **41**
Ocland, *Romania* L28+461 **58**
Ocoa, B. de, *Dominican Rep.* S64+183 **101**
Ocona, *Peru* S78–165 **104**
Oconto, *Wisconsin* T77+449 **91**
Ocos, *Guatemala* U13+145 **100**
Ocotal, *Nicaragua* T68+138 **101**
Ocumare, *Venezuela* S41+101 **104**
Oda, *Ghana* N06+060 **80**
Oda, *Japan* D15+352 **68**
Odaka, *Japan* C54+375 **68**
Odate, *Japan* C57+403 **68**
Odawara, *Japan* C65+352 **68**
Odemira, *Portugal* N52+376 **52**
Odemis, *Turkey* L12+382 **74**
Odense, *Denmark* M28+554 **47**
Oder R., *Germany* M04+527 **48**
Odessa, *Texas* U74+318 **94**
Odessa, *Ukraine* K86+465 **60**
Odienné, *Ivory Coast* N46+096 **80**
Odoorn, *Netherlands* M49+529 **44**
Odorhei, *Romania* L28+463 **58**
Odra R., *Poland* M04+527 **48**
Odzala, *Congo* M02+006 **82**
Oedelem, *Belgium* M70+512 **44**
Oeiras, *Brazil* O73–070 **105**
Oelwein, *Iowa* U11+426 **95**
Oetling, *Argentina* S00–273 **103**
Of, *Turkey* K27+410 **74**
Offaly (Ui Failghe), co.,
  Ireland, Rep. N45+533 **43**
Offenbach, *W. Germany* M38+501 **48**
Ogaki, *Japan* C79+354 **68**
Ogallala, *Nebraska* U70+411 **94**
Ogden, *Utah* V42+412 **94**
Ogdensburg, *New York* T03+447 **91**
Ogilvie, *Yukon* X28+638 **88**
Ogilvie Ra., *Yukon* X00+448 **88**
Ogoja, *Nigeria* M38+068 **80**
Ogoki R., *Ontario* T70+506 **89**
Ogr, *Sudan* L16+120 **81**
Ogulin, *Yugoslavia* L89+452 **56**
Ohakune, *New Zealand* A27–393 **112**
Ohau, L., *New Zealand* A61–442 **112**
Ohey, *Belgium* M59+504 **44**
O'Higgins, mt., *Chile* S80–488 **103**
Ohio, state, *U.S.A.* T53+405 **99**
Ohio R., *U.S.A.* T68+378 **99**
Ohrid, *Yugoslavia* L55+411 **58**
Ohridsko Jezero, *Yugoslavia* L56+410 **58**
Ohura, *New Zealand* A30–389 **112**
Oich L., *Scotland* N29+571 **40**
Oignies, *Belgium* M62+500 **44**
Oil City, *Pennsylvania* T28+414 **96**
Oil Springs, *Ontario* T43+428 **91**
Oirot Tura, *U.S.S.R.* G24+518 **62**
Oirschot, *Netherlands* M58+515 **44**
Oise, dep., *France* M76+494 **54**
Oise, R., *France* M76+490 **54**
Oita, *Japan* D20+332 **68**
Ojinaga, *Mexico* U87+295 **100**
Ojiya, *Japan* C67+373 **68**
Ojocaliente, *Mexico* U73+225 **100**
Ojo de Agua, *Argentina* S23–294 **103**
Ojo del Toro, Pico, *Cuba* T14+200 **101**
Oka R., *U.S.S.R.* K16+558 **61**

Okahandja, Namibia L78-220 84
Okanagan Lake, B.C. W00+499 88
Okanogan R., Washington W00+478 98
Okaukweyo, Namibia L86-190 84
Okavango, R. & Swamp,
  Botswana L40-198 84
Okayama, Japan D06+346 68
Okeechobee, L., Florida T34+269 97
Okehampton, England N24+507 38
Okha, U.S.S.R. C42+537 63
Okhansk, U.S.S.R. J28+576 61
Okhotsk, U.S.S.R. C40+593 63
Okhotsk, Sea of, U.S.S.R. C10+550 63
Okigunto, Japan D12+362 68
Okinawa Gunto, Japan D42+265 68
Oklahoma, state, U.S.A. U54+357 98
Oklahoma City, Oklahoma U45+354 95
Okmulgee, Oklahoma U36+356 95
Okolona, Mississippi T82+342 97
Oktyabrskoy Revolyutsiy, Os.,
  U.S.S.R. F50+790 63
Okućani, Yugoslavia L77+453 56
Okuru, New Zealand A66–439 112
Okushiri I., Japan C63+422 68
Okusi Ambeno, Timor D65-094 110
Olaine, Latvia L36+568 47
Olanchito, Honduras T68+156 101
Öland, I., Sweden L80+567 47
Olary, S. Australia C58–323 109
Olawa, Poland L76+510 49
Olbia, Sardinia M33+409 57
Olcott, New York T22+433 96
Oldcastle, Ireland. Rep. N43+538 42
Oldenburg, W. Germany M25+543 48
Oldenburg, W. Germany M41+532 48
Oldenzaal, Netherlands M48+523 44
Old Forge, Pennsylvania T04+413 96
Oldham, England N13+535 37
Old Orchard, Maine S62+435 90
Old Orchard Beach, Maine S62+435 96
Oldtown, Maine S52+450 90
Olean, New York T21+421 96
Olecko, Poland L45+540 49
Olekminsk, U.S.S.R. D89+603 63
Olenek, U.S.S.R. E45+685 63
Olenek, R., U.S.S.R. D80+727 63
Olenekskiy Zaliv, U.S.S.R. D85+734 63
Oléron, I. d', France N08+460 54
Olga, U.S.S.R. C88+436 63
Olifants Kloof, Botswana L60-222 84
Olimbos. See Olympus.
Oiva de Jerez, Spain N41+383 52
Olivares, Spain N15+397 53
Olivares, Co. de, Argentina S59–303 103
Oliveira, Brazil Q78-122 105
Olivenza, Spain N42+387 52
Olivone, Switzerland M36+465 45
Ollague, Chile S50–212 103
Ollague, mt., Bolivia S49–212 104
Olmedo, Spain N28+413 52
Olney, Illinois T78+387 95
Olomouc, Czechoslovakia L77+496 49
Olot, Spain M75+422 53
Olovyannaya, U.S.S.R. E26+510 63
Olpe, W. Germany M43 + 510 48
Olst, Netherlands M53+523 44
Olsztyn, Poland L57+538 49
Olten, Switzerland M43+473 45
Oltu, Turkey K18+406 74
Oltul R., Romania L33+458 58
Olvera, Spain N31+369 52
Olympia, Greece L50+376 59
Olympia, Washington W17+470 92
Olympic Nat. Park, Wash. W26+476 98
Olympus (Olimbos), mts.,
  Greece L46+400 59
Olympus, Mt., Washington W23+475 98
Olyutorskiy Zaliv, U.S.S.R. A70+600 63
Omagh, N. Ireland N44+546 42
Omaguas, Peru S80–042 104
Omaha, Nebraska U36+412 95
Oman, Arabia J26+238 75
Oman, G. of, Arabia-Iran J10+248 75
Omaruru, Namibia L84-212 84
Ombombo, Namibia M06-186 84
Omdurman, Sudan K76+156 81
Omeo, Victoria C15–371 109
Omer, Michigan T53+440 91
Ometepec, Mexico U50+166 100
Ommen, Netherlands M51+525 44
Omoa, Honduras T79+156 101
Omsk, U.S.S.R. H10+550 62
Omuta, Japan D27+330 68
Omutninsk, U.S.S.R. J46+586 61
Ona, R., U.S.S.R. F50+570 63
Onawa, Iowa U36+420 95
Onaway, Michigan T55+453 91
Onega & R., U.S.S.R. K39+640 62
Onehunga, New Zealand A31–370 112
Oneida, New York T04+431 96
Oneida L., New York T06+432 96
O'Neill, Nebraska U52+424 95
Oneonta, New York T00+425 96
Onezhskoye Oz., U.S.S.R. K60+618 62
Ongole, India G59+156 70
Ongudai, U.S.S.R. G23+508 62
Onich, Scotland N31+567 41
Onipa, Namibia L82-178 84
Onitsha, Nigeria M50+062 80
Onoto, Venezuela S31+098 104
Onotoa, I., Kiribati A30-020 106
Onslow, W. Australia E30–217 110
Onslow B., N. Carolina T12+343 97
Ontario, prov., Canada 89
Ontario, L., U.S.A.-Canada T20+439 99
Onteniente, Spain N00+388 53
Ontiñena, Spain N00+417 53
Oodnadatta, S. Australia C88–273 111
Ooldea, S. Australia D19–305 110
Oostburg, Netherlands M69+513 44
Oostende (Ostende), Belgium M73+512 44
Ooster Schelde, Netherlands M66+516 44
Oosterwolde, Netherlands M52+530 44
Oosthuizen, Netherlands M60+526 44
Oostkamp, Belgium M71+512 44
Oostmalle, Belgium M62+513 44
Oostyoorne, Netherlands M66+519 44
Ootacamund, India G79+114 70
Opala, U.S.S.R. B50+520 63

Opari, Sudan K78+040 81
Opatija, Yugoslavia M04+453 56
Opava, Czechoslovakia L73+499 49
Opelousas, Louisiana U12+304 95
Ophir, Mt., Malaysia F15+024 69
Ophoven, Belgium M55+511 44
Opis, Iraq K04+339 74
Opochka, U.S.S.R. L08+568 60
Opodepe, Mexico V34+300 100
Opole, Poland L73+507 49
Oporto. See Porto
Opotiki, New Zealand A16–380 112
Oppa B., Japan C51+386 68
Oppeln. See Opole
Opunake, New Zealand A37–394 112
Oputo, Mexico V25+300 100
Oqair, Saudi Arabia J59+257 75
Oradea, Romania L48+470 58
Orai, India G63+260 73
Oran, Algeria N04+356 80
Orange, France M61+442 55
Orange, Massachusetts S74+427 96
Orange, New South Wales C05–334 109
Orange Texas U22+301 95
Orange, Virginia T19+382 97
Orange R., S. Africa L70–284 84
Orange City, Iowa U36+430 95
Orangeburg, S. Carolina T35+335 97
Orange Free State, S. Africa L20–284 84
Orangeville, Ontario T31+439 91
Orange Geb., Surinam R60+030 105
Oranmore, Ireland, Rep. N53+533 43
Oras, Philippines D58+121 65
Orăştie, Romania L41+458 58
Oravita, Romania L50+451 58
Oravská Magura, Czech. L65+493 49
Orbe, Switzerland M51+467 45
Orbost, Victoria C09–377 109
Orcera, Spain N16+383 53
Orchha, India G68+253 73
Ord, Mt., W. Australia D60-175 110
Ordenes, Spain N50+431 52
Ord River, W. Australia D37–174 110
Ordu, Turkey K42+409 74
Ordzhonikidze, U.S.S.R. K02 + 430 62
Ordzhonikidzegrad. See Bezhitsa
Örebro, Sweden L89+593 47
Oregon, Illinois T86+419 95
Oregon, state, U.S.A. W15+440 98
Oregon City, Oregon W16+453 92
Öregrund, Sweden L69+603 47
Orekhovo Zuyevo, U.S.S.R. K36 + 558 60
Orel, U.S.S.R. K53+530 60
Orellana, Peru T01–070 104
Orellana, Spain N33+390 52
Orenburg, U.S.S.R. J29 + 517 61
Orense, Spain N47+423 52
Orepuki, New Zealand Q73–463 112
Oresund, Denmark-Sweden M14+560 47
Orgaña, Spain M82+422 53
Orgaz, Spain N23+396 52
Oriental, Cord., Colombia S84+050 104
Oriental, Cord., Peru T04–075 104
Orihuela, Spain N06+381 53
Orillia, Ontario T27+446 91
Orinoco, R., Venezuela S20+083 104
Orissa, state, India G35+210 71
Oristano & G. di, Sardinia M39+399 57
Orivesi, Finland L04+623 46
Oriximiná, Brazil R65-016 105
Orizaba, Mexico U43+188 100
Orizare, Bulgaria L14+427 58
Orkanger, Norway M31+633 46
Orkhon R., Mongolia F08+484 64
Orkney Is., Scotland N18+590 40
Orlando, Florida T38+285 97
Orleanais, prov., France M79+478 54
Orleans, France M79+479 54
Orleans, I. of, Quebec S66+469 91
Orleansville, (El Asnam), Alg. M82+360 80
Orman, Syria K49+325 76
Ormara, Pakistan H62+251 70
Ormondville, New Zealand A22–401 112
Ormskirk, England N18+536 37
Ornach, Pakistan H53+268 70
Orne, dep., France N00+487 54
Örnsköldsvik, Sweden L67+633 46
Orochen, U.S.S.R. D58 + 584 63
Orocue, Colombia S68+046 104
Oroluk, I., Caroline Islands B50+073 106
Oron, U.S.S.R. F70+644 63
Orono, Maine S52+449 90
Oronsay I., Scotland N38+560 41
Orontes, R., Syria K52+356 74
Orosei, & G. di, Sardinia M32+402. 57
Orosi, Vol., Costa Rica T62+110 101
Orroroo, S. Australia C68–328 109
Orsa, Sweden M02+611 47
Orsha, Byelorussia K88+545 60
Orsières, Switzerland M47+460 45
Orsk, U.S.S.R. J08+512 61
Orsova, Romania L45+447 58
Ortegal, C., Spain N47+435 52
Orthez, France N05+435 55
Ortiz, Mexico V03+282 100
Ortiz, Venezuela S43+096 104
Orugueira, Spain N47+434 52
Orulgan, Khrebet, U.S.S.R. D50+677 63
Oruro, Bolivia S43–180 104
Orust, Sweden M20+582 47
Oryekhovo, U.S.S.R. K04+505 61
Osa, U.S.S.R. J27+572 61
Osage, Iowa U16+412 95
Osage City, Kansas U36+386 95
Osaka, Japan C87+347 68
Osakis, Minnesota U31+459 93
Osawatomie, Kansas U30+385 95
Osborne, Kansas U52+394 95
Oscar II Coast, Antarctica S05–640 27
Osceola, Arkansas U00+358 97
Osceola, Iowa U22+410 95
Oschiri, Sardinia M35+407 57
Oscoda, Michigan T50+444 91
Osen, Norway M27+643 46
Osh, Kirgiz H13+405 62
Oshawa, Ontario T23+439 91
O Shima, Japan C64+347 68
Oshkosh, Wisconsin T81+440 91
Oshnoviveh, Iran K00+370 74

Osijek, Yugoslavia L68+455 58
Osilo, Sardinia M36+408 57
Osipenko, U.S.S.R. C81+525 63
Osipovichi, Byelorussia L08 + 533 60
Osire Sud, Namibia L76-212 84
Oskaloosa, Iowa U16+412 95
Oskarshamn, Sweden L81+573 47
Oslo, Norway M25+599 47
Oslo Fd., Norway M26+592 47
Osmanabad, India G83+180 70
Osmancik, Turkey K60+409 74
Osnabrück, W. Germany M42+523 48
Osorno, Chile S79–405 103
Osorno, Spain N26+424 52
Osowiec, Poland L44+535 49
Oss, Netherlands M57+518 44
Ossining, New York S83+412 96
Ostavall, Sweden L87+625 46
Ostende, Belgium M73+512 44
Osterreich, Nieder, prov.,
  Austria L85+486 49
Österreich, Ober, prov.,
  Austria M04+484 48
Ostersund, Sweden M02+632 46
Osthammar, Sweden L70+603 47
Ostrava, Czechoslovakia L70+498 49
Ostroda, Poland L60+537 49
Ostrov, Romania L11+449 58
Ostrov, U.S.S.R. L09+574 60
Ostrovnoe, U.S.S.R. B00+680 63
Ostroleka, Poland L50+531 49
Ostrowiec, Poland L52+509 49
Ostrów Mazowiecka, Poland L49+528 49
Ostuni, Italy L75+407 57
Østvagøy, Norway M02+683 46
Ōsumikaikyō, Japan D24+308 68
Osuna, Spain N30+372 52
Oswego & R., New York T09+434 96
Oswestry, England N18+529 38
Otago Peninsula, N.Z. A52–458 112
Otaki, New Zealand A29–407 112
Otaru & R., Japan C54+432 68
Otasuts, Japan C56+433 68
Otavalo, Ecuador T19+002 104
Otepaa, Estonia L21+580 47
Othris, mts., Greece L45+390 59
Otira, New Zealand A50–428 112
Otis, New Brunswick S43+460 90
Otjiwarongo, Namibia L80-204 84
Otocac, Yugoslavia L89+449 56
Otoineppu, Japan C47+448 68
Otorohanga, New Zealand A28–382 112
Otpor, (Zabaykal'sk), U.S.S.R. E15+497 63
Otranto, Str. of, It.-Albania L66+402 59
Otsego, L., New York S89+428 96
Otsu, Japan C85+350 68
Ottawa, Illinois T83+414 95
Ottawa, Kansas U32+386 95
Ottawa, Ontario T04+454 91
Ottawa Is., N.-W. Terr. T30+596 89
Ottawa R., Quebec, etc. T16+462 91
Otterlo, Netherlands M55+521 44
Otterøy, Norway M49+628 46
Ottignies, Belgium M63+507 44
Otting, W. Germany M14+484 48
Ottumwa, Iowa U14+410 95
Otus, U.S.S.R. K59+450 60
Otway, B., Chile S84–535 103
Otway, C., Victoria C39–389 109
Otwock, Poland L52+521 49
Ötz, Austria M25+472 48
Ötztaler Alpen, Italy M23+470 56
Ouachita Mts., Arkansas, etc. U30+345 99
Ouachita R., Arkansas U23+340 99
Ouagadougou, Upper Volta N08 + 122 80
Ouahigouya, Upper Volta N14 + 134 80
Ouangolodougou, Ivory
  Coast N30+100 80
Ouargla, Algeria M58+316 80
Oubangui R., Congo and Zaire L74+004 82
Ouddorp, Netherlands M66+518 44
Oudekapelle, Belgium M73+510 44
Oudenaarde, Belgium M68+508 44
Oudenbosch, Netherlands M63+516 44
Oudtshoorn, Cape Province L46–336 84
Ouessant, I. d', France N30+484 54
Ouezzane, Morocco N34+348 80
Oughterard, Ireland, Rep. N56+534 43
Ouidah, Benin M78 + 064 80
Oukës, Albania L58+411 58
Oulu, Finland L27+650 46
Oulujärvi, Finland L18+644 46
Oulujoki, Finland L23+648 46
Oum Chalaouba, Chad L58+158 81
Ounasjoki, Finland L32+672 46
Ouricury, Brazil O61–078 105
Ourinhos, Brazil R29–230 105
Ouro Preto, Brazil Q80-204 105
Ouse, R., Norfolk, etc., England
  M88+525 39
Ouse R., Yorks, England N07+539 37
Outardes, R., Quebec S51+490 90
Outardes, R. aux, Quebec S54+500 90
Outjo, Namibia L84-200 84
Outtrim, Victoria C26–385 109
Ouyen, Victoria C46–351 109
Ovalle, Chile S68–306 103
Ovar, Portugal N52+408 52
Over Flakkee I., Netherlands M65+517 44
Overijssel, prov., Netherlands M51+524 44
Overkalix, Sweden L43+663 46
Overmark, Finland L51+626 46
Overpelt, Belgium M58+512 44
Overtornea, Sweden L38+664 46
Oviedo, Spain N35+433 52
Ovruch, Ukraine L07+512 60
Owaka, New Zealand A62–464 112
Owasco L., New York T09+428 96
Owatonna, Minnesota U18+440 93
Owego, New York T08+421 96
Owen, Wisconsin U04+450 91
Owen's I., Burma F39+110 71
Owens L., California V78+364 92
Owensboro, Kentucky T73+378 97
Owen Sound, Ontario T36+446 91
Owen Stanley Ra.,
  Papua New Guinea C14-092 111
Owensville, Indiana T77+383 97
Owenton, Kentucky T59+386 97
Owerri, Nigeria M48+054 80
Owl Creek Mts., Wyoming V25+436 93

Owo, Nigeria M56+072 80
Owosso, Michigan T55+430 91
Owyhee R., Oregon V75+432 92
Ox Mts., Ireland, Rep. N54+541 42
Oxford, Maryland T07+387 91
Oxford, Mississippi T87+344 97
Oxford, New York T04+424 91
Oxford, N. Carolina T21+363 97
Oxford & co., England N08+518 39
Oxley, New South Wales C35–342 109
Oxley's Pk., New S. Wales B88–318 109
Oyapock, R., Brazil, etc. R42+034 105
Oyem, Gabon M20+016 82
Oymyekon, U.S.S.R. C40+630 63
Oyo, Nigeria M66+080 80
Oyster B., Tasmania C11–423 109
Ozark Mts., Ark.-Mo. U20+360 95
Ozark Plat., Missouri, etc. U24+364 99
Ozarks, L. of the, Missouri U18+382 95
Ozd, Hungary L58+482 49
Ozerki, U.S.S.R. J87+520 61
Ozhogino, U.S.S.R. C16+692 63
Ozieri, Sardinia M36+406 57
Ozun, Romania L25+458 58
Paan, Burma F44+170 71
Paan, China F36+299 64
Paarl, Cape Province L66–338 84
Pabianice, Poland L64+517 49
Pabna, Bangladesh G60+240 73
Pacaraima, Sa., Brazil, etc. S18+040 104
Pacasmayo, Peru T27–074 104
Pachbhadra, India H17+260 70
Pachow. See Pachung
Pachuca, Mexico U52+200 100
Pachung, China E80+318 66
Pacific, Missouri U05+385 97
Pacific Ocean 102-103
Paços, Portugal N51+413 52
Padam, Kashmir G79+334 72
Padang, Sumatra F28–009 65
Paderborn, W. Germany M37+517 48
Padilla, Bolivia S26–192 104
Padova, Italy M19+454 56
Padrauna, India G36+269 73
Padre I., Texas U44+268 94
Padstow, England N30+505 38
Padua. See Padova
Paducah, Kentucky T82+370 97
Paducah, Texas U61+340 94
Padul, Spain N22+370 52
Paeroa, New Zealand A26–374 112
Pafuri, Mozambique K82–226 84
Pagai Is., Indonesia F26–030 65
Pagula I., Gulf of Guinea M57+014 82
Pagan, Burma F60+211 71
Pagan, I., Mariana Is. C25+170 106
Pagasai, G. of, Greece L42+392 59
Pago, I., Yugoslavia M00+444 56
Pagong L., Kashmir-Tibet G66+336 70
Pagosa Springs, Colorado V12+372 94
Paharpur, Pakistan H24+321 72
Pahiatua, New Zealand A25–404 112
Pahlavi Dezh, Iran J33+370 75
Pahlevi Bandar-e, Iran J63+375 74
Pahsien, China E21+391 66
Pahsien. See Chungking
Paide, Estonia L26+589 47
Paignton, England N21+504 38
Paiho, China E59+328 66
Päijänne, L., Finland L27+615 47
Pai-Khoi Khrebet, U.S.S.R. H60+675 62
Pailam, India G57+257 73
Pailingmiao, China E56+416 64
Paimpol, France N18+487 54
Painted Des., Arizona V35+360 98
Paintsville, Kentucky T47+378 97
Paisley, Ontario T38+443 91
Paisley, Scotland N26+558 41
Paita, Peru T36–051 104
Pai Tu Hu, China E17+308 66
Paiz do Vinho, Portugal N47+412 52
Pajakumbuh, Sumatra F27–001 65
Pajala, Sweden L40+672 46
Pajares, Spain N34+430 52
Pakakku, Burma F59+213 71
Pakanbaru, Sumatra F22+006 65
Pakaur, India G13+246 73
Pakchan, Burma F37+105 71
Pak-Loi, China E65+214 67
Pakistan, S. Asia H60+280 70
Pak-lay, Laos F21+182 69
Pakpattan, Pakistan H10+303 72
Pakrac, Yugoslavia L77+454 56
Paks, Hungary L67+467 49
Pakse, Laos E85+151 69
Palafrugell, Spain M71+419 53
Palaiokhóra, Crete L38+352 59
Palamau, India G34+239 73
Palamcottah, India G73+087 70
Palamós, Spain M71+418 53
Palamuse, Estonia L20+587 47
Palana, U.S.S.R. B30+590 63
Palanpur, India H15+241 70
Palatka, Florida T40+296 97
Palau Is., Pacific Ocean D02+074 65
Palaw, Burma F38+130 69
Palawan, I., Philippines E10+100 65
Paldiski, Estonia L33+594 47
Palembang, Sumatra F01–030 65
Palena, Chile S78–438 103
Palenque, Mexico U12+174 100
Paleokhorio, Cyprus K71+349 76
Palermo, Argentina S25–246 103
Palermo, N. Dakota U73+483 93
Palermo, Sicily M10+381 57
Palestina, Chile S56–240 103
Palestine, Texas U24+310 95
Palestine, W. Asia K60+320 74
Paletwa, Burma F72+213 71
Palghat, India G79+108 70
Palgrave Pt., Namibia M10-204 84
Palgu Tso, Tibet G26+289 71
Palhiers, France M80+431 55
Palhoca, Brazil R22–278 103
Pali, India H10+257 70
Palime, Togo. M86+068 80
Palisade, Nevada V67+406 92
Paliseul, Belgium M59+499 44
Palizada, Mexico U12+182 100
Palk Str., India G60+100 70
Palkot, India G32+229 73

Palliser B., *New Zealand* A30–415 **112**
Palma, *Balearic Islands* M74+396 **53**
Palma, *Brazil* Q74–212 **105**
Palma, *Brazil* R16–124 **105**
Palma, *Mozambique* K28–110 **83**
Palma, I., *Canary Is* P30+286 **80**
Palmaras, *Brazil* R33–303 **103**
Palmas, *Brazil* R42–265 **103**
Palmas, B., *Mexico* V28+237 **100**
Palmas C., *Liberia* N46+044 **80**
Palmas, G. of, *Sardinia* M39+390 **57**
Palm Beach, *Florida* T30+267 **97**
Palmeira, *Brazil* R50–279 **103**
Palmer Land, *Antarctica* S24–725 **27**
Palmerston, *Ontario* T35+439 **91**
Palmerston I., *Cook Islands* Y80–158 **106**
Palmerston North, *N.Z.* A26–403 **112**
Palmerston South, *N.Z.* A56–454 **112**
Palmira, *Colombia* T08+037 **104**
Palms, *Michigan* T47+436 **91**
Palmyra, *Missouri* U07+398 **95**
Palmyra, *Syria* K41+346 **74**
Palmyra I., *Pacific Ocean* Y72+060 **106**
Palni Hills, *India* G76+104 **70**
Paloh, *Borneo* E64+016 **65**
Paloich, *Sudan* K74+104 **81**
Palo Santo, *Argentina* R86–255 **103**
Palpa, *Nepal* G38+279 **73**
Palu, *Turkey* K30+388 **74**
Palwal, *India* G76+281 **72**
Pambon Chan., *India* G66+092 **70**
Pamekasan, *Indonesia* E39–070 **65**
Pamir, mts., *U.S.S.R.* H15+374 **62**
Pamlico Sd., *N. Carolina* T06+352 **97**
Pampa, *Texas* U66+356 **94**
Pampas, *Peru* S89–122 **104**
Pamplona, *Colombia* S76+076 **104**
Pamplona, *Spain* N10+428 **53**
Panache L., *Ontario* T38+462 **91**
Panagyurishte, *Bulgaria* L35+425 **58**
Panaji, Goa, Daman & Diu H07 + 156 **70**
Panama & rep.,
    Central America T27+090 **101**
Panama Can., *Panama* T28+080 **89**
Panama, G. of, *Panama* T26+080 **101**
Panama City, *Florida* T64+302 **97**
Panarea, I., *Italy* M00+386 **57**
Panat, *Thailand* F23+134 **69**
Panay, I., *Philippines* D75+112 **65**
Pancevo, *Yugoslavia* L56+449 **58**
Panciu, *Romania* L17+459 **58**
Pandan, *Philippines* D77+116 **65**
Pandharpur, *India* G88+177 **70**
Pando, *Uruguay* R66–347 **103**
Paneviys, *Lithuania* L34+558 **47**
Panfilov, *Kazakh.* G59+441 **62**
Panfilovo, *U.S.S.R.* K12+503 **61**
Pangala, *Congo* M02–034 **82**
Pangbourne, *England* N07+515 **39**
Pangkiang, *China* E41+426 **64**
Panguitch, *Utah* V45+378 **94**
Pania Mutombo, *Zaire* L36–054 **82**
Panipat, *India* G78+294 **72**
Panja, *China* F82+400 **64**
Panjim, *See* Panaji
Panjnad R., *Pakistan* H25+290 **72**
Pannerden, *Netherlands* M54+519 **44**
Panruti, *India* G62+118 **70**
Pantanaw, *Burma* F58+169 **71**
Pantar, I., *Indonesia* D66–084 **65**
Pantelleria, I., *Medit. Sea* M18+368 **57**
Pánuco, *Mexico* U67+266 **100**
Pao-an-chow, *China* E29+403 **66**
Paochang, *China* E26+420 **66**
Pão de Assucar, *Brazil* Q45–097 **105**
Pão dos Ferros, *Brazil* Q49–061 **105**
Paoking. *See* Shaoyang
Paola, *Italy* L84+394 **57**
Paola, *Kansas* U30+386 **95**
Paoli, *Indiana* T69+385 **97**
Paoning. *See* Langchung
Paosham, *China* F36+252 **64**
Paoting, *China* E27+389 **66**
Pao-tow, *China* E60+406 **66**
Papakura, *New Zealand* A30–371 **112**
Papantla, *Mexico* U44+205 **100**
Papa Stour I., *Scotland* N10+603 **40**
Papa Westray, I., *Scotland* N17+594 **40**
Papenburg, *W. Germany* M46+531 **48**
Papendrecht, *Netherlands* M62+518 **44**
Paphos, *Cyprus* K76+347 **76**
Paposo, *Chile* S63–250 **103**
Papua, G. of, *Papua New Guinea*
    C30–086 **111**
Papua New Guinea
    Pacific Ocean C60–060 **31**
Papun, *Burma* F45+181 **71**
Pará, *Brazil* R21–014 **105**
Para, R., *Brazil* R20–010 **105**
Paracatu, *Brazil* R11–172 **105**
Paracel Is & Reefs,
    S. China Sea E50+165 **69**
Parachilna, *S. Australia* C70–311 **109**
Parachinar, *Pakistan* H29+339 **72**
Paracin, *Yugoslavia* L52+439 **58**
Paracuro, *Brazil* Q54–034 **105**
Parag, *Iran* H86+255 **75**
Paragould, *Arkansas* U03+361 **99**
Paraguari, *Paraguay* R73–256 **103**
Paraguay, rep., *S. America* --- **103**
Paraguay, R., *Argent.. etc.* R80–267 **103**
Parah, *Afghanistan* H79+342 **75**
Parakes, *Botswana* L48–186 **84**
Parakou, *Benin* M74 + 094 **80**
Paramaribo, *Surinam* R62+057 **105**
Paramonga, *Peru* T17–107 **104**
Paramoshiri, *U.S.S.R.* B55+505 **63**
Paraná, *Argentina* S03–318 **103**
Parana, R., *Argentina* R86–292 **103**
Paranagua, *Brazil* Q80–084 **105**
Paranáiba & R., *Brazil* R37–197 **105**
Parang, *Philippines* D84+059 **65**
Paranga, *Uganda* K72+024 **83**
Parapola I., *Greece* L39+369 **59**
Parattah, *Tasmania* C16–424 **109**
Parbati R., *India* G78+235 **70**
Parbhani, *India* G79+193 **70**
Parchim, *E. Germany* M19+534 **48**
Pardubice, *Czechoslovakia* L84+500 **49**
Parecis, *Brazil* R72–140 **105**

Parecis, Sa. dos, *Brazil* S10–119 **104**
Paren, *U.S.S.R.* B10+624 **63**
Parent, *Quebec* S88+480 **90**
Pareora, *New Zealand* A52–445 **112**
Pariaguan, *Venezuela* S28+088 **104**
Parika, *Guyana* R81+068 **104**
Parinari, *Peru* S87–044 **104**
Paringa. *S. Australia* C55–342 **109**
Parintins, *Brazil* R69–025 **105**
Paris, *France* M76+488 **54**
Paris, *Illinois* T76+396 **95**
Paris, *Kentucky* T55+382 **97**
Paris, *Ontario* T33+432 **91**
Paris, *Tennessee* T80+362 **95**
Paris, *Texas* U34+336 **95**
Parita, B. de, *Panama* T32+081 **101**
Pariz, *Iran* J26+299 **75**
Park Ra., *Colorado* V08+400 **94**
Park Ra., *Wyoming* V14+413 **98**
Parker, *S. Dakota* U42+434 **93**
Parker, C., *N.-W. Terr.* T25+750 **89**
Parker Dam, *Arizona* V55+342 **98**
Parkersburg, *W. Virginia* T39+393 **91**
Parkes, *New South Wales* C11–332 **109**
Park Falls, *Wisconsin* U03+459 **91**
Park Rapids, *Minnesota* U30+469 **93**
Parkston, *S. Dakota* U48+434 **93**
Parma, *Italy* M28+448 **56**
Parmele, *N. Carolina* T13+358 **93**
Parnagua, *Brazil* Q86–103 **105**
Parnahyba, *Brazil* Q71–029 **105**
Parnaiba, R., *Brazil* Q76–037 **105**
Parnu & G., *Estonia* L33+583 **47**
Paro, *Bhutan* G04+274 **73**
Paron, *India* G78+249 **70**
Paroo, R., *New South Wales* C34–300 **109**
Páros, I., *Greece* L29+371 **59**
Parowan, *Utah* V48+388 **94**
Parral, *Chile* S71–361 **103**
Parral, *Mexico* V04+269 **100**
Parramatta, *New S. Wales* B85–338 **109**
Parras, *Mexico* U73+255 **100**
Parrett R., *England* N18+511 **38**
Parry I., *Ontario* T31+453 **91**
Parry Is., *N.-W. Terr.* V30+762 **88**
Parry Sound, *Ontario* T30+454 **91**
Parsa, *India* G30+259 **73**
Parsnip R., *Brit. Columbia* W20+556 **88**
Parsons, *Kansas* U32+374 **95**
Parsons, *W. Virginia* T28+391 **96**
Partabgarh, *India* H01+239 **70**
Partabgarh, *India* G48+259 **73**
Partabpur, *India* G40+234 **73**
Parthenay, *France* N01+466 **54**
Partinico, *Sicily* M11+381 **57**
Partridge L., *Tibet* G20+330 **71**
Partry Mts., *Ireland, Rep.* N57+537 **42**
Pas, The, *Manitoba* U68+540 **88**
Pasadena, *California* V79+341 **92**
Pasargadae, *Iran* J42+302 **75**
Pascagoula, *Mississippi* T81+304 **97**
Pas-de-Calais, dep., *France* M76+505 **54**
Paseagoula & R., *Mississippi* T81+304 **95**
Paskuh, *Iran* H80+276 **75**
Pasley, C., *W. Australia* D69–340 **110**
Pasni, *Pakistan* H70+252 **70**
Paso de Indios, *Argentina* S54–438 **103**
Paso de los Libres, *Argent.* R72–297 **103**
Paso de los Toros, *Uruguay* S39–326 **103**
Paso Limay, *Argentina* S63–405 **103**
Paso Robles, *California* W05+356 **92**
Paspebiac, *Quebec* S31+481 **90**
Pasrur, *Pakistan* H02+322 **72**
Passamaquoddy B., *N.B.* S42+451 **90**
Passau, *W. Germany* M09+486 **48**
Passendale, *Belgium* M72+509 **44**
Passero C., *Sicily* L89+367 **57**
Passaic, *New Jersey* S85+408 **96**
Passo Fundo, *Brazil* R44–281 **103**
Passos, *Brazil* R10–206 **105**
Pasto, *Colombia* T14+012 **104**
Pastrana, *Spain* N18+404 **52**
Pasvik Elv, *Norway* L04+693 **46**
Pásztó, *Hungary* L62+479 **49**
Patagonia, *Argentina* S41–301 **103**
Pátrai, *Brazil* Q43–070 **105**
Patos, L. dos, *Brazil* R40–314 **103**
Patquia, *Argentina* S41–301 **103**
Pátrai, *Greece* L49+383 **59**
Pátrai, G. of, *Greece* L50+383 **59**
Patras. *See* Pátrai
Patrasayar, *India* G15+232 **73**
Patricio Lynch, I., *Chile* T02–485 **103**
Patrocinio, *Brazil* R12–190 **105**
Pattani, *Thailand* F22+068 **69**
Patten, *Maine* S51+460 **90**
Patterson, *Louisiana* U08+297 **97**
Patti, *Sicily* M00+381 **57**
Patutahi, *New Zealand* A12–386 **112**
Patzcuaro, *Mexico* U69+194 **100**
Pau, *France* N02+433 **55**
Pau d'Arco, *Brazil* R26–079 **105**
Paul, L., *N.-W. Territories* V30+651 **88**
Paulista, *Brazil* Q67–082 **105**
Paul's Valley, *Oklahoma* U42+347 **95**
Paungde, *Burma* F57+183 **71**
Pauni, *India* G62+208 **70**
Pautrask, *Sweden* L75+648 **46**
Pavia, *Italy* M35+452 **56**
Pāvilosta, *Latvia* L53+569 **47**
Pavlodar, *Kazakh.* G79+522 **62**
Pavlograd, *Ukraine* K55+486 **60**

Pavlovka, *U.S.S.R.* K10+519 **61**
Pavlovo, *U.S.S.R.* K11+560 **61**
Pavlovsk, *U.S.S.R.* K29+504 **61**
Pavlovski, *U.S.S.R.* K38+558 **60**
Pawnee City, *Nebraska* U37+402 **95**
Paw Paw, *Michigan* T65+422 **91**
Pawtucket, *Rhode Island* S69+419 **96**
Paxoi, I., *Greece* L59+392 **59**
Paxton, *Illinois* T78+405 **95**
Payerne, *Switzerland* M48+468 **45**
Payne L., *Quebec* S75+598 **89**
Payne R., *Quebec* S70+601 **89**
Paynesville, *Minnesota* U29+454 **93**
Payo Obispo. *See* Ciudad Chetumal
Paysandu, *Uruguay* R79–322 **103**
Payson, *Utah* V41+401 **94**
Paz, R., *El Salvador* U00 + 138 **101**
Pazardzhik, *Bulgaria* L34+422 **58**
Pazaung, *Burma* F46+190 **71**
Peace R., *Brit. Columbia* W20+560 **88**
Peace River, *Alberta* V75+560 **88**
Peak, The, *England* N11+534 **37**
Peak Hill, *New S. Wales* C10–328 **109**
Peak Hill, *W. Australia* E08–257 **110**
Peale, Mt., *Utah* V26+384 **94**
Pearce Point, *N.-W. Terr.* W17+690 **88**
Pearl R., *Mississippi* T88+306 **95**
Pearl Harbor, *Hawaii* Y45 + 212 **107**
Pearsall, *Texas* U54+290 **94**
Peary Ld., *Greenland* Q35+830 **26**
Pebane, *Mozambique* K40-168 **83**
Pebble I., *Falkland Islands* R88–512 **103**
Pébo, *Cent. Afr. Rep.* L68+080 **81**
Pec, *Yugoslavia* L58+427 **58**
Pechenga, *U.S.S.R.* K84+696 **62**
Pechora, *U.S.S.R.* J14+648 **62**
Pechora, R., *U.S.S.R.* J47+660 **62**
Pecos, *New Mexico* V04+356 **94**
Pecos, *Texas* U82+314 **94**
Pecos R., *Texas, etc.* U72+310 **94**
Pecs, *Hungary* L71+461 **58**
Pedernales, *Venezuela* S13+098 **104**
Pedhoulas, *Cyprus* K73+350 **76**
Pedregal, *Panama* T44+084 **101**
Pedro Juan Caballero, *Para.* R64–224 **103**
Pedro Luro, *Argentina* S16–396 **103**
Pedrotallagalla, mt., *Sri Lanka* G56+071 **70**
Peebinga, *S. Australia* C54–349 **109**
Peebles, *Scotland* N19+556 **41**
Peekskill, *New York* S83+413 **96**
Peel R., *Yukon* X05+658 **88**
Peenemünde, *E. Germany* M07+541 **48**
Peery L., *New S. Wales* C38–308 **109**
Peetri, *Estonia* L25+589 **47**
Pegasus, & R., *New Zealand* A41–432 **112**
Pega Yoma, *Burma* F55+190 **71**
Pegu, *Burma* F51+173 **71**
Pegunungan Maoke,
    New Guinea C80–038 **65**
Pehan, *China* D52+482 **64**
Pehowa, *India* G80+299 **72**
Pehuajó, *Argentina* S11–357 **103**
Peineta, mt., *Chile* S81–503 **103**
Peiping. *See* Peking
Peipus, L., *See* Chudskoye Oz.
Peixe, *Brazil* R21–120 **105**
Pekan, *Malaysia* F10+036 **69**
Pekin, *Illinois* T88+406 **91**
Peking, *China* E21+400 **66**
Pelagie Is., *Medit. Sea* M13+355 **81**
Pélagos, I., *Greece* L36+393 **59**
Peledui, *U.S.S.R.* E42+597 **63**
Pelée I., *Ontario* T46+418 **91**
Peleng, I., *Indonesia* D70–014 **65**
Peljesac Pen., *Yugoslavia* L76+430 **57**
Pelkosenniemi, *Finland* L15+670 **46**
Pella, *Greece* L48+409 **59**
Pella, *Iowa* U18+414 **95**
Pellegrini, *Argentina* S19–362 **103**
Pellworm I., *W. Germany* M38+545 **48**
Pelly Pt., *N.-W. Terr.* U66+701 **88**
Pelly Ra., *Yukon* W70+612 **88**
Pelly R., *Yukon* W83+618 **88**
Peloncillo Ra., *Arizona* V25+326 **94**
Peloponnisos, *Greece* L48+370 **59**
Pelotas, *Brazil* R45–318 **103**
Pemba Is., *E. Africa* K32–052 **83**
Pembroke, *Ontario* T13+458 **91**
Pembroke, *Wales* N30+517 **38**
Pembroke, C., *Falkland Is.* R76–516 **103**
Pembroke, C., *N.-W. Terr.* T35+635 **89**
Penafiel, *Portugal* N50+412 **52**
Peñafiel, *Spain* N25+413 **52**
Penalva, *Brazil* R00–031 **105**
Penambo Ra., *Sarawak* E30+030 **65**
Peña Negra, Sa. de, *Spain* N37+421 **52**
Penápolis, *Brazil* R30–215 **105**
Peñaranda de Bracamonte,
    Spain N31+409 **52**
Peñarroya, *Spain* N28+383 **52**
Penarth, *Wales* N19+514 **38**
Penas, G. de, *Chile* T00–472 **103**
Pendembu, *Sierra Leone* N64+082 **80**
Pendleton, *Arkansas* U09+340 **97**
Pendleton, *Oregon* V83+457 **92**
Pend Oreille, L., *Idaho* V70+480 **98**
Penedo, *Brazil* Q39–103 **105**
Penedono, *Portugal* N45+410 **52**
Penggaram, *Malaysia* F13 + 019 **69**
Penghu, Is., *China* E23–034 **67**
Penglai, *China* D85+378 **66**
Pengpu, *China* E15+328 **64**
Penguin, *Tasmania* C24–411 **109**
Penhalonga, *Zimbabwe* K74–188 **84**
Peniche, *Portugal* N56+394 **52**
Penicuik, *Scotland* N19+558 **41**
Peñiscola, *Spain* N08+404 **53**
Penn, *N. Dakota* U54+483 **93**
Pennfield, *New Brunswick* S40+451 **90**
Pennine, Alpi, *Switzerland* M46+460 **45**
Pennine Chain, *England* N14+540 **37**
Penns Grove, *New Jersey* T03+397 **96**
Pennsylvania, state, *U.S.A.* T25+408 **99**
Penn Yan, *New York* T12+427 **96**
Penobscot B., *Maine* S54+441 **90**
Penola, *S. Australia* C55–374 **109**
Penong, *S. Australia* D12–318 **109**
Penonome, *Panama* T32+082 **101**
Penrith, *England* N17+547 **37**

Penrith, *New South Wales* B86–338 **109**
Pensacola, *Florida* T73+304 **97**
Penshurst, *Victoria* C46–379 **109**
Pentland Firth, *Scotland* N20+587 **40**
Pentland Hills, *Scotland* N21+558 **41**
Pentwater, *Michigan* T68+438 **91**
Penza, *U.S.S.R.* K00+532 **61**
Penzance, *England* N33+501 **38**
Penzhino, *U.S.S.R.* A71+633 **63**
Penzhinskaya Guba, *U.S.S.R.* B20+610 **63**
Peoria, *Illinois* T88+407 **95**
Peperga, *Netherlands* M54+528 **44**
Pepinster, *Belgium* M55+506 **44**
Peqin, *Albania* L62+411 **58**
Perak, *Malaysia* F28 + 054 **69**
Peralta, *Spain* N11+424 **53**
Perce, *Quebec* S26+485 **90**
Perdido, Mte., *Spain* M87+427 **53**
Pereira, *Colombia* T04+048 **104**
Perelló, *Spain* M86+409 **53**
Perez, *Chile* S60–260 **103**
Pergamno, *Argentina* S04–338 **103**
Perho, *Finland* L33+632 **46**
Peribonca R., *Quebec* S68+510 **90**
Perico, *Argentina* S31–244 **103**
Périgueux, *France* M85+452 **55**
Perija, Sa. de, *Venezuela* S76+100 **104**
Perim I., *Red Sea* K69+127 **74**
Peripery, *Brazil* Q71–042 **105**
Peristéra, I., *Greece* L36+392 **59**
Perlas & Lag. de las, *Nic.* T52+124 **101**
Perlas, Arch. de las, *Pan.* T26+084 **101**
Perm, *U.S.S.R.* J23+580 **61**
Pernambuco (Recife), *Braz.* Q30–080 **105**
Peronne, *France* M72+499 **54**
Péronnes, *Belgium* M65+504 **44**
Perpignan, *France* M73+427 **55**
Perranporth, *England* N31+503 **38**
Perrot I., *Quebec* S84+454 **91**
Perry, *Iowa* U24+418 **95**
Perry, *New York* T18+428 **96**
Perry, *Oklahoma* U44+362 **95**
Perry R., *N.-W. Terr.* U80+666 **88**
Perryville, *Missouri* T89+377 **97**
Persepolis, *Iran* J42+300 **75**
Persia. *See* Iran
Persian Gulf, *See* The Gulf
Perth, *New Brunswick* S46+467 **90**
Perth, *Ontario* T08+449 **91**
Perth, *W. Australia* E25–319 **110**
Perth, *Scotland* N21+564 **41**
Perth Amboy, *New Jersey* S86+405 **96**
Peru, *Indiana* T67+407 **91**
Peru, rep., *S. America* 104
Perufune, *Japan* C40+424 **68**
Perugia, *Italy* M20+431 **56**
Peruíbe, *Brazil* R12–242 **105**
Peruwelz, *Belgium* M68+505 **44**
Pervijze, *Belgium* M73+511 **44**
Pervomaisk, *Ukraine* K85+481 **60**
Perwez, *Belgium* M61+506 **44**
Pesaro, *Italy* M12+439 **56**
Pescadores Is. *See* Penghu Is.
Pescara, *Italy* M05+425 **56**
Peschici, *Italy* L84+419 **57**
Peshawar, *Pakistan* H20+340 **72**
Peshtigo R., *Wisconsin* T80+455 **91**
Pesqueira, *Brazil* Q40–084 **105**
Pestravka, *U.S.S.R.* J60+524 **61**
Petah Tiqva, *Israel* K61+321 **76**
Petalioí, G. of, *Greece* L35+379 **59**
Petalioí, I., *Greece* L34+380 **59**
Pataluma, *California* W16+383 **92**
Peterborough, *England* N03+526 **37**
Peterborough, *Ontario* T20+443 **91**
Peterborough, *S. Australia* C67–329 **109**
Peter I. Øy, *Antarctica* U05–690 **27**
Peterhead, *Scotland* N11+575 **40**
Peterlee, *England* N08+548 **37**
Petermann Fd., *Greenland* S05+810 **26**
Petermann Pk., *Greenland* Q00+730 **26**
Petermann Ra., *W. Aust.* D35–250 **110**
Peter Pond L., *Sask.* V22+558 **88**
Petersburg, *Alaska* W75+568 **99**
Petersburg, *Virginia* T15+372 **97**
Péterupe, *Latvia* L33+573 **47**
Petit Bois I., *Alabama* T80+302 **95**
Petit Francois. *Fr. Guiana* R44+031 **105**
Petit Nord Pen., *Nfd.* R70+509 **90**
Petitot R., *Brit. Columbia* W08+598 **88**
Petitsikapau L., *Labrador* S40+544 **89**
Peto, *Mexico* T82+201 **100**
Petone, *New Zealand* A31–412 **112**
Petoroa, *Chile* S66–321 **103**
Petoskey, *Michigan* T60+454 **91**
Petra, *Jordan* K57+303 **76**
Petra Velikogo Zaliv., *U.S.S.R.* D18+428 **63**
Petrich, *Bulgaria* L41+414 **58**
Petrified Forest Nat. Mon.,
    Arizona V28+348 **94**
Petrinja, *Yugoslavia* L82+454 **56**
Petrodvorets, *U.S.S.R.* L02+598 **60**
Petrolia, *Ontario* T43+429 **91**
Petrolina, *Brazil* Q63–094 **105**
Petropavlovsk, *Kazakh.* H35+549 **62**
Petropavlovsk, *U.S.S.R.* B36+530 **63**
Petropolis, *Brazil* Q80–225 **105**
Petrovac, *Yugoslavia* L51+444 **58**
Petrovsk, *U.S.S.R.* J22+536 **61**
Petrovsk, *U.S.S.R.* E66+513 **63**
Petrovsk, *U.S.S.R.* J88+523 **61**
Petrozavodsk, *U.S.S.R.* K65+618 **62**
Petsamo. *See* Pechenga
Pettigoe, *Ireland, Rep.* N47+545 **42**
Pevas, *Peru* S71–032 **104**
Pewsey, *England* N11+513 **39**
Pézenas, *France* M70+435 **55**
Pforzheim, *W. Germany* M38+489 **48**
Phagwara, *India* G83+312 **72**
Phalodi, *India* H16+270 **70**
Phanom Dang Rae,
    Thailand F16 + 143 **69**
Phan Rang, *Vietnam* E65 + 116 **69**
Phan-Thiet & B. of,
    Vietnam E71+110 **69**
Phaphund, *India* G63+266 **73**
Phatthalung, *Thailand* F29+076 **69**
Phenix City, *Alabama* T60+325 **97**
Phet Buri, *Thailand* F31+132 **69**
Philadelphia, *Pennsylvania* T01+400 **91**
Philip, *S. Dakota* U70+441 **93**
Philippeville, *Belgium* M63+502 **44**

Philippeville & G. of,
(Skikda), *Algeria* M48+366 **80**
Philippi, *W. Virginia* T30+391 **91**
Philippi, L., *Queensland* C66–244 **111**
Philippines, Is., *Pacific Oc.* **65**
Philippopolis. *See* Plovdiv
Philaur, *India* G85+310 **72**
Phillip I., *Victoria* C28–384 **109**
Phillip Edward I., *Ontario* T38+459 **91**
Phillips, *Maine* S62+448 **90**
Phillips, *Wisconsin* U03+457 **91**
Phillipsburg, *Kansas* U56+398 **95**
Phillipsburg, *New Jersey* T01+406 **96**
Philomena, *Alberta* V39+551 **88**
Phitsanulok Muang, *Thailand* F29+170 **69**
Phnom-Penh, *Khmer* F00+115 **69**
Phoenix, *Arizona* V43+334 **94**
Phoenix I., *Phoenix Is.* Z36–040 **106**
Phoenix Is., *Pacific Ocean* Z40–040 **106**
Phoenixville, *Pennsylvania* T03+401 **96**
Pho-mo-chang-thang Tso,
Tibet F87+286 **71**
Phu-dien, *N. Vietnam* E86+190 **69**
Phulji, *Pakistan* H43+270 **70**
Phulpur, *India* G47+255 **73**
Phu-Quoc, I., *Khmer* F06+102 **69**
Phu-yen, *S. Vietnam* E65+134 **69**
Piacenza, *Italy* M32+450 **56**
Pian, R., *New S. Wales* C06–302 **109**
Piangil, *Victoria* C41–351 **109**
Pianosa, I., *Italy* M29+426 **56**
Pias, *Portugal* N45+380 **52**
Piatra Neamt, *Romania* L22+469 **58**
Piazza Armerina, *Sicily* M04+373 **57**
Piazzi, I., *Chile* S84–518 **103**
Pibor Post, *Sudan* K72+068 **81**
Picardie, prov., *France* M78+500 **54**
Piceno. *See* Ascoli.
Pichanal, *Argentina* S26–233 **103**
Picher, *Oklahoma* U30+370 **95**
Pichilemu, *Chile* S71–344 **103**
Pickens, *Mississippi* U00+329 **97**
Pickering, *England* N05+542 **37**
Pickwick L., *Tennessee, etc.* T78+349 **95**
Picola, *Victoria* C29–360 **109**
Picos, *Brazil* Q85–059 **105**
Picton, *New South Wales* B87–342 **109**
Picton, *New Zealand* A36–413 **112**
Picton, *Ontario* T13+440 **91**
Picton, Mt., *Tasmania* C21–432 **109**
Pictou, *Nova Scotia* S15+458 **90**
Pictou I., *Nova Scotia* S17+457 **90**
Picun Leufu, *Argentina* S55–395 **103**
Pidark, *Pakistan* H71+257 **70**
Piedad, La, *Mexico* U73+203 **100**
Piedmont, *Missouri* U05+371 **97**
Piedmont, *Quebec* S84+459 **91**
Piedmont, *S. Carolina* T45+347 **97**
Piedmont, *S. Dakota* U81+442 **93**
Piedrahita, *Spain* N32+405 **52**
Piedras Negras, *Mexico* U63+288 **100**
Piedra Sola, *Uruguay* R67–320 **103**
Pieksämäki, *Finland* L17+623 **46**
Pielinen, *Finland* L04+633 **46**
Pieman R., *Tasmania* C30–417 **109**
Piemonte, dep., *Italy* M44+450 **56**
Pierre, *S. Dakota* U62+444 **93**
Pierreville, *Quebec* S77+461 **91**
Pietarsaari (Jakobstad), *Fin.* L44+637 **46**
Pietermaritzburg, *Natal* K88–296 **84**
Pietersburg, *Transvaal* L04–238 **84**
Piggot, *Arkansas* U02+364 **95**
Pigue, *Argentina* S15–376 **103**
Pihtipudas, *Finland* L26+634 **46**
Pikes Pk., *Colorado* V00+388 **94**
Pikeville, *Kentucky* T45+374 **97**
Pila, *Argentina* R80–360 **103**
Pila, *Poland* L80+532 **49**
Pilao Arcado, *Brazil* Q75–102 **105**
Pilar, *Argentina* S07–314 **103**
Pilar, *Brazil* R28–147 **105**
Pilar, *Paraguay* R80–269 **103**
Pilar, C., *Chile* S88–528 **103**
Pilcaniyeu, *Argentina* S64–410 **103**
Pilibhit, *India* G61+286 **73**
Pillau, *Lithuania* L60+547 **47**
Pilliga, *New South Wales* C07–304 **109**
Pillinger, *Tasmania* C27–424 **109**
Pílos, *Greece* L50+369 **59**
Pilot, The, *New S. Wales* C11–368 **109**
Pilot Knob, *Missouri* U04+374 **97**
Pilsen. *See* Plzen.
Piltene, *Latvia* L50+572 **47**
Pi Mai, *Thailand* F15+152 **69**
Pimentel, *Peru* T29–067 **104**
Pina, *Spain* N03+415 **53**
Pinaki I., *Tuamotu Arch.* X20–195 **107**
Pinaleno Ra., *Arizona* V30+326 **94**
Pinang I., *Malaya* F28+051 **69**
Pinarbasi, *Turkey* K52+387 **74**
Pinar del Rio, *Cuba* T52+224 **101**
Pinckneyville, *Illinois* T87+381 **97**
Pind Dadan Khan, *Pakistan* H12+326 **72**
Pindhos, mts., *Greece* L50+393 **59**
Pindi Gheb, *Pakistan* H16+332 **72**
Pine I., *Florida* T43+266 **97**
Pine Mts., *Kentucky* T52+369 **97**
Pine Bluff, *Arkansas* U12+342 **97**
Pine City, *Minnesota* U18+458 **93**
Pine Creek, *N. Territory,*
Australia D18–138 **110**
Pinedale, *Wyoming* V28+429 **93**
Pinehurst, *N. Carolina* T27+352 **97**
Pineola, *N. Carolina* T42+362 **97**
Pine River, *Minnesota* U26+467 **93**
Pinetown, *Natal* K86–298 **84**
Pineville, *Kentucky* T52+367 **97**
Pineville, *Missouri* U26+366 **95**
Pineville, *W. Virginia* T38+376 **97**
Piney Buttes, *Montana* V12+475 **93**
Ping-chüan-chow, *China* E07+410 **66**
Pingelap, I., *Caroline Is.*
B25+045 **106**
Pingelly, *W. Australia* E18–324 **110**
Pingkiang, *China* E38+285 **67**
Pingliang, *China* E80+354 **66**
Pinglo, *China* E55+246 **67**
Pingrup, *W. Australia* E07–333 **110**
Ping-ting-chow, *China* E39+378 **66**
Pingwu, *China* F02+323 **66**
Pingyang. *See* Linfen.

Pingyüan, *China* E21+371 **66**
Pinhel, *Portugal* N42+408 **52**
Pini, I., *Indonesia* F38+002 **65**
Pinjarra, *W. Australia* E25–326 **110**
Pinnacles, *New South Wales* C52–321 **109**
Pinnaroo, *S. Australia* C55–353 **109**
Pinos, *Mexico* U69+228 **100**
Pinos, I. de, *Cuba* T47+216 **101**
Pinos, Mt., *California* V85+348 **92**
Pinrang, *Celébes,* E02–038 **65**
Pinsk, *Belorussia* L24+521 **60**
Pintados, *Chile* S58–207 **103**
Pinto, *Argentina* S16–292 **103**
Pioneer, Os., *U.S.S.R.* F80+800 **63**
Piotrkow, *Poland* L62+509 **49**
Pipar, *India* H08+264 **70**
Pipestone, *Minnesota* U36+440 **98**
Pipinas, *Argentina* R74–355 **103**
Pipmuacan L., *Quebec* S62+496 **90**
Pippli, *India* G15+216 **71**
Piqua, *Ohio* T56+401 **91**
Piracuruca, *Brazil* Q70–039 **105**
Piraeus. *See* Piraievs.
Piraievs, *Greece* L38+379 **59**
Piramide, mt., *Chile* S81–490 **103**
Piranhas, *Brazil* Q47–095 **105**
Pirapora, *Brazil* R00–173 **105**
Piratini, *Brazil* R49–314 **103**
Piray, *Argentina* R59–266 **103**
Pirgos, *Greece* L45+366 **59**
Pirgos, *Greece* L51+377 **59**
Pirgos, *Crete* L29+350 **59**
Pirin Planina, *Bulgaria-*
Greece L40+415 **58**
Piritu, *Venezuela* S30+101 **104**
Pirmasens, *W. Germany* M45+492 **48**
Pirna, *E. Germany* M06+510 **48**
Pirot, *Yugoslavia* L45+431 **58**
Pir Panjal Ra., *Kashmir* H04+340 **72**
Pisa, *Italy* M28+437 **56**
Pisagua, *Chile* S62–196 **103**
Pisco, *Peru* T08–136 **104**
Pisek, *Czechoslovakia* M05+493 **48**
Pishin, *Pakistan* H48+305 **70**
Pishin, *Iran* H79+261 **75**
Pisticci, *Italy* L80+404 **57**
Pitanguy, *Brazil* Q89–198 **105**
Pitarpunga L., *N.S.W.* C40–344 **109**
Pitcairn I., *Pacific Ocean* W60–254 **107**
Pite Älv, *Sweden* L64+660 **46**
Piteå, *Sweden* L51+653 **46**
Piterka, *U.S.S.R.* J75+506 **61**
Piteşti, *Romania* L31+449 **58**
Pithiviers, *France* M77+482 **54**
Pithoria, *India* G69+241 **73**
Pitlochry, *Scotland* N22+567 **41**
Pitt, Mt., *Oregon* W14+424 **92**
Pitt R., *California* W11+409 **92**
Pittsboro, *N. Carolina* T25+357 **93**
Pittsburg, *Kansas* U28+371 **99**
Pittsburgh, *Pennsylvania* T30+405 **91**
Pittsfield, *Illinois* U05+396 **95**
Pittsfield, *Maine* S56+448 **90**
Pittsfield, *Massachusetts* S79+425 **91**
Pittston, *Pennsylvania* T05+413 **96**
Piua-Petri, *Romania* L13+446 **58**
Piaura, *Peru* T34–052 **104**
Piza, *Latvia* L48+576 **47**
Placentia B., *Newfoundland* R58+468 **90**
Placer Guadalupe, *Mexico* V02+292 **100**
Plainfield, *New Jersey* S87+406 **91**
Plainview, *Nebraska* U49+424 **95**
Plainview, *Texas* U70+342 **94**
Plainwell, *Michigan* T64+425 **91**
Pláka B., *Crete* L34+352 **59**
Plakoti C., *Cyprus* K65+355 **76**
Plana, *Czechoslovakia* M13+498 **48**
Planaltina, *Brazil* R16–156 **105**
Planina, *Yugoslavia* M05+458 **56**
Plant City, *Florida* T43+280 **97**
Plascencia, *Spain* N36+401 **52**
Plaški, *Yugoslavia* L88+450 **56**
Plassen, *Norway* M15+611 **47**
Plaster Rock, *N.B.* S44+470 **90**
Plastun, *U.S.S.R.* C82+446 **63**
Plata, R. de la,
Argent., etc. R70–350 **103**
Platamon. *Greece* L44+400 **59**
Plati, *Greece* L45+405 **59**
Platres, *Cyprus* K73+349 **76**
Platt Nat. Park, *Oklahoma* U42+345 **98**
Platte R., *Nebraska* U60+408 **95**
Platteville, *Wisconsin* U03+428 **95**
Plattsburg, *Missouri* U27+396 **95**
Plattsburg, *New York* S81+447 **91**
Plattsmouth, *Nebraska* U36+410 **95**
Plauen, *E. Germany* M17+505 **48**
Plav, *Yugoslavia* L60+426 **58**
Plavnica, *Yugoslavia* L65+423 **58**
Playas L., *New Mexico* V23+317 **98**
Plaza Huincul, *Argentina* S55–389 **103**
Pleasant B., *Maine* S47+445 **90**
Pleasant Grove, *Utah* V41+404 **94**
Pleasantville, *New Jersey* S87+394 **96**
Pleiku, *S. Vietnam* E72+140 **65**
Plenty, B. of, *New Zealand* A18–378 **112**
Plentywood, *Montana* U88+488 **93**
Plessisville, *Quebec* S70+462 **91**
Plettenberg B., *Cape Prov.* L38–342 **84**
Pleven, *Bulgaria* L33+434 **58**
Pljevlja, *Yugoslavia* L64+434 **58**
Płock, *Poland* L61+525 **49**
Ploiesti, *Romania* L24+449 **58**
Plomarion, *Greece* L22+389 **59**
Plomosa Mts., *Arizona* V53+338 **92**
Plon, *W. Germany* M28+541 **48**
Plonge, Lac la, *Saskatchewan* V13+552 **88**
Plonsk, *Poland* L58+526 **49**
Plovdiv, *Bulgaria* L32+421 **58**
Plumtree, *Rhodesia* L12–206 **84**
Plymouth, *Indiana* T68+414 **91**
Plymouth, *Massachusetts* S64+420 **91**
Plymouth, *New Hampshire* S70+437 **91**
Plymouth, *N. Carolina* T10+359 **97**
Plymouth, *Pennsylvania* T06+413 **96**
Plymouth, *Wisconsin* T78+438 **91**
Plymouth & Sd., *England* N25+504 **38**
Plynlimmon, *Wales* N22+525 **38**
Plzeň, *Czechoslovakia* M10+492 **48**
Poai, *China* E41+352 **66**
Pobedy, Pik, mt., *China, etc.* G60+420 **62**

Pobla de Segur, *Spain* M84+422 **53**
Pocahontas, *Arkansas* U06+362 **95**
Pocahontas, *Virginia* T3¢+373 **97**
Pocatello, *Idaho* V45+428 **94**
Pochinki, *U.S.S.R.* K01+547 **61**
Pochutla, *Mexico* U39+158 **100**
Pocklington, *England* N05+539 **37**
Podkagernaya, *U.S.S.R.* B19+604 **63**
Podkamennaya Tunguska,
U.S.S.R. G00+616 **63**
Podlubovo, *U.S.S.R.* J25+543 **61**
Podolsk, *U.S.S.R.* K45+554 **60**
Pogamasing, *Ontario* T41+469 **91**
Pohai, G. of, *China* E06+385 **66**
Pohai, Str. of, *China* D84+385 **66**
Point L., *N.-W. Territories* V50+652 **88**
Pointe à Pitre, *Leeward Is.* S08+164 **101**
Pointe du Chene, *N.B.* S27+462 **90**
Poitiers, *France* M88+466 **54**
Poitou, prov., *France* N02+465 **54**
Poix, *Belgium* M36+498 **44**
Poix, *France* M78+498 **54**
Pokaakku, I., *Pacific Ocean* A65+140 **106**
Pokaran, *India* H20+268 **70**
Pokataroo, *New S. Wales* C08–296 **109**
Pokemouche, *N.B.* S29+477 **90**
Pokhara, *Nepal* G36+282 **73**
Pokka, *Finland* L26+681 **46**
Pokrovsk, *U.S.S.R.* K14+531 **61**
Pokrovsk, *U.S.S.R.* K36+474 **61**
Pokrovsk. *See* Engels.
Pokrovskoe, *U.S.S.R.* D34+613 **63**
Pola. *See* Pula.
Pola de Siero, *Spain* N34+434 **52**
Poland, rep., *Cent. Europe* L72+520 **51**
Polesk, *U.S.S.R.* L53+548 **47**
Polevskoi, *U.S.S.R.* H89+564 **61**
Polgahawela, *Sri Lanka* G58+074 **70**
Polgar, *Hungary* L53+478 **49**
Poli, *Cameroun* M10+084 **81**
Poliaigos, I., *Greece* L32+368 **59**
Policastro, G. di, *Italy* L86+400 **57**
Poligny, *France* M56+468 **54**
Polillo Is., *Philippines* D78+148 **65**
Pólinos, *See* Poliaigos, I.
Polis, *Cyprus* K75+350 **76**
Pollensa, *Balearic Islands* M71+399 **53**
Polotsk, *Belorussia* L08+555 **60**
Polson, *Montana* V55+477 **92**
Poltava, *Ukraine* K62+496 **60**
Poluostrov Buzachi, *Kazakh.* J50+448 **62**
Pôlva, *Estonia* L18+580 **47**
Polynesia, *Pacific Oc.* Z30–100 **106**
Poman, *Argentina* S37–283 **103**
Pomaro, *Mexico* U75+184 **100**
Pombal, *Brazil* Q47–067 **105**
Pombal, *Portugal* N52+399 **52**
Pombets, *Japan* C38+431 **68**
Pomene, *Mozambique* K56–230 **84**
Pomeroy, *N. Ireland* N41+546 **42**
Pommersche B., *E. Germany* M04+542 **48**
Pomorie, *Bulgaria* L15+426 **58**
Pomorze, *Poland* L72+536 **49**
Pomos Pt., *Cyprus* K75+352 **76**
Pompey's Pillar, *Montana* V17+460 **93**
Ponape, I., *Caroline Islands* B45+070 **106**
Ponca City, *Oklahoma* U42+366 **95**
Ponce, *Puerto Rico* S39+180 **101**
Pondicherry, *India* G61+120 **70**
Pondurawe, *Wales* N23+517 **38**
Pont-Audemer, *France* M87+494 **54**
Pontchartrain, L., *Louisiana* U00+302 **95**
Pont Chateau, *France* N12+474 **54**
Pont d'Ain, *France* M58+461 **54**
Ponte, *Switzerland* M30+466 **45**
Ponte Boa, *Brazil* S36–026 **104**
Ponte da Barca, *Portugal* N51+418 **52**
Ponte de Sôr, *Portugal* N48+392 **52**
Pontefract, *England* N08+537 **37**
Ponte Nova, *Brazil* Q78–204 **105**
Pontevedra, *Spain* N52+424 **52**
Pontiac, *Illinois* T82+409 **91**
Pontiac, *Michigan* T50+427 **91**
Pontianak, *Borneo* E64–002 **65**
Pontivy, *France* N18+481 **54**
Pontoise, *France* M77+491 **54**
Pontotoc, *Mississippi* T84+342 **97**
Pontresina, *Switzerland* M31+465 **45**
Ponts, les, *Switzerland* M50+470 **45**
Pontypool, *Wales* N18+517 **38**
Pontypool, *Ontario* T22+441 **91**
Pontypridd, *Wales* N20+516 **38**
Ponza, I., *Italy* M12+410 **57**
Poole, *England* N12+507 **39**
Poole, Mt., *New S. Wales* C50–297 **109**
Poolewe, *Scotland* N34+578 **40**
Poona, *India* H06+186 **70**
Pooncarie, *New South Wales* C46–334 **109**
Poopelloe, L., *New S. Wales* C36–316 **109**
Poopo, *Bolivia* S42–184 **104**
Poopo, L., *Bolivia* S43–188 **104**
Popa Mt., *Burma* F58+209 **71**
Popakai, *Surinam* R62+032 **105**
Popayan, *Colombia* T09+025 **104**
Poperinge, *Belgium* M74+508 **44**
Poplar, *Montana* V01+481 **93**
Poplar R., *Manitoba* U37+528 **88**
Poplar Bluff, *Missouri* U02+368 **97**
Poplarville, *Mississippi* T87+308 **97**
Popocatepetl, mt., *Mexico* U52+192 **100**
Popovača, *Yugoslavia* L80+456 **56**
Poppel, *Belgium* M60+514 **44**
Porahat, *India* G27+226 **73**
Porbandar, *India* H33+216 **70**
Porcupine R., *Alaska* X40+698 **99**
Poreč, *Yugoslavia* M08+452 **56**
Pori, *Finland* L50+615 **47**
Porjus, *Sweden* L61+670 **46**
Porkhov, *U.S.S.R.* L03+578 **60**
Porkkala, *Finland* L34+600 **47**
Porlamar, *Margarita I.,*
Venezuela S23+109 **104**
Pornic, *France* N13+471 **54**
Poronaysk, *U.S.S.R.* C34+492 **63**
Póros I., *Greece* L39+375 **59**

Poro Tso, *Tibet* G38+310 **71**
Porsanger Fd., *Norway* L28+704 **46**
Porsanger-halvöya, *Norway* L36+700 **46**
Porsgrund, *Norway* M32+591 **47**
Portachuela, *Bolivia* S20–171 **104**
Port Adelaide, *S. Australia* C69–349 **109**
Portadown, *N. Ireland* N39+544 **42**
Portaferry, *N. Ireland* N33+544 **42**
Portage, *Wisconsin* T87+436 **91**
Portage I., *New Brunswick* S30+472 **90**
Portage la Prairie, *Manitoba* U50+500 **88**
Portage River, *N. B.* S30+474 **90**
Portageville, *New York* T18+426 **96**
Portal, *N. Dakota* U75+490 **93**
Portal, *N. Saskatchewan* U76+491 **88**
Port Albert, *Victoria* C20–386 **109**
Portalegre, *Portugal* N45+393 **52**
Portales, *New Mexico* U80+341 **94**
Port Alfred, *Quebec* S65+484 **90**
Port Allen, *Louisiana* U07+304 **97**
Port Antonio, *Jamaica* T69+182 **101**
Portarlington, *Ireland, Rep.* N43+532 **43**
Port Arthur. *See* Lushun
Port Arthur, *Tasmania* C13–432 **109**
Port Arthur, *Texas* U23+299 **95**
Port Augusta, *S. Australia* C74–325 **109**
Port au Port B., *Nfd.* R84+490 **90**
Port au Prince, *Haiti* S73+186 **101**
Port aux Baxques, *Nfd.* R85+476 **90**
Port Blandford, *Nfd.* R55+484 **90**
Port Borden, *Pr. Edward I.* S22+462 **90**
Port Broughton, *South*
Australia C73–336 **109**
Port Campbell, *Victoria* C42–386 **109**
Port Chalmers, *N.Z.* A56–457 **112**
Port Chester, *New York* S81+410 **96**
Port Clinton, *Ohio* T48+415 **91**
Port Cornwallis,
Andaman Islands F72+134 **71**
Port Dalhousie, *Ontario* T26+432 **91**
Port Daniel *Quebec* S29+482 **90**
Port Darwin, *Falkland Is.* R84–518 **103**
Port Davey, *Tasmânia* C24–434 **109**
Port de Paix, *Haiti* S76+199 **101**
Port Dickson, *Malaya* F19+02 **69**
Port Douglas, *Queensland* C28–164 **111**
Port Dover, *Ontario* T31+428 **91**
Portel, *Brazil* R34–019 **105**
Port Elgin, *Ontario* T38+445 **91**
Port Elizabeth, *Cape Prov.* L26–340 **84**
Port Ellen, *Scotland* N37+556 **41**
Port Etienne, *Mauritania* P12+210 **80**
Port Eynon, *Wales* N25+516 **38**
Port Fairy, *Victoria* C47–384 **109**
Port Germein, *S. Australia* C72–330 **109**
Port Gibson, *Mississippi* U06+320 **95**
Port Glasgow, *Scotland* N27+559 **41**
Porglenone, *N. Ireland* N39+549 **42**
Portgordon, *Scotland* N18+577 **40**
Port Harcourt, *Nigeria* M48+048 **80**
Port Hedland, *W. Australia* E08–205 **110**
Porthmadog, *Wales* N25+529 **38**
Port Hope, *Michigan* T46+440 **91**
Port Hope, *Ontario* T20+439 **91**
Port Huron, *Michigan* T45+430 **91**
Portimão, *Portugal* N51+371 **52**
Port Jackson, *New S. Wales* B83–339 **109**
Port Jervis, *New York* S88+414 **96**
Port Joli, *Nova Scotia* S29+439 **90**
Port Kelang, *Malaya* F22+030 **69**
Port Kembla, *New S. Wales* B85-345 **109**
Portland, *Arkansas* U09+332 **97**
Portland, *Maine* S62+437 **90**
Portland, *New South Wales* C00–334 **109**
Portland, *Oregon* W16+455 **92**
Portland, *Victoria* C51–383 **109**
Portland C., *Tasmania* C13–407 407 **109**
Portland Harb. & I., *Eng.* N14+506 **38**
Portland Point, *Jamaica* T13+178 **101**
Portland Prom., *Quebec* T20+590 **89**
Port Lavaca, *Ireland, Rep.* N44+530 **43**
Port Lavaca, *Texas* U40+286 **94**
Portlaw, *Ireland, Rep.* N44+522 **43**
Port Lincoln, *S. Australia* C85–347 **111**
Port Loko, *Sierra Leone* N76+088 **80**
Port Lyautey. *See* Kenitra
Port M'Donnell, *S. Aust.* C56–380 **109**
Port M'Nicoll, *Ontario* T29+448 **91**
Port Macquarie, *N.S.W.* B73–314 **109**
Port Medway, *Nova Scotia* S27+441 **90**
Port Menier, *Anticosti I.,* *Que.* S26+498 **90**
Port Moresby, *Papua New Guinea*
C17–094 **111**
Portnacroish, *Scotland* N32+566 **41**
Port Nelson (abandoned),
Manitoba U18+567 **89**
Portneuf, *Quebec* S71+467 **91**
Port Nolloth, *Cape Province* L78–292 **84**
Port Norris, *New Jersey* T00+392 **91**
Porto, *Portugal* N52+411 **52**
Porto Acre, *Brazil* S46–097 **104**
Porto Alegre, *Brazil* Q57–180 **105**
Porto Alegre, *Brazil* R37–300 **103**
Porto Alegre, *Brazil* Q74–034 **105**
Porto Alexandre, *Angola* M18–158 **84**
Porto Amelia, *Mozambique* K26–130 **83**
Porto Barreirão, *Brazil* R20–126 **105**
Portobelo, *Panama* T28+096 **101**
Porto Botte, *Sardinia* M39+391 **57**
Porto Camargo, *Brazil* R53–234 **105**
Porto Civitanova, *Italy* M08+433 **56**
Porto d'Ascoli, *Italy* M07+429 **56**
Porto de Moz, *Brazil* R42–018 **105**
Porto de Moz, *Portugal* N53+394 **52**
Porto do Jeronymo, *Brazil* R31–186 **105**
Porto Empedocle, *Sicily* M09+373 **57**
Porto Esperanca, *Brazil* R74–197 **105**
Porto Espiridião, *Brazil* R79–158 **104**
Porto Franco, *Brazil* R26–086 **105**
Porto Franco, *Brazil* R13–099 **105**
Porto Franco, *Brazil* R14–064 **105**
Porto Guaira, *Brazil* R55–240 **105**
Port Okha, *India* H36+223 **70**
Portola, *California* W03+398 **92**
Porto Lucena, *Brazil* R60–277 **103**
Porto Mendes, *Brazil* R56–244 **105**
Porto Nacional, *Brazil* R20–108 **105**
Porto Novo, *Benin* M74+064 **80**
Porto Novo, *India* G62+116 **70**

Port Ontario, *New York* T07+435 **96**
Porto Seguro, *Brazil* Q54-163 **105**
Porto Torres, *Sardinia* M40+408 **57**
Porto Vecchio, *Corsica* M35+416 **57**
Porto Velho, *Brazil* S23-088 **104**
Portoviejo, *Ecuador* T32-010 **104**
Port Patrick, *Scotland* N31+548 **41**
Port Pegasus, *New Zealand* A73-472 **112**
Port Phillip B., *Victoria* C31-382 **109**
Port Pirie, *S. Australia* C72-332 **109**
Port Pleasant, *New Jersey* S85+401 **91**
Port Radium, *N.-W. Terr.* V75+659 **88**
Portree, *Scotland* N37+574 **40**
Port Rowan, *Ontario* T33+427 **91**
Port Royal, *Jamaica* T11+179 **101**
Port Royal, *S. Carolina* T34+324 **97**
Portrush, *N. Ireland* N40+552 **42**
Port Safaga, *Egypt* K66+261 **81**
Port Said, *Egypt* K76+312 **81**
Port St John's, *Cape Prov.* L02-318 **84**
Portsalon, *Ireland, Rep.* N46+552 **42**
Port Shepstone, *Natal* K88-308 **84**
Port Simpson, *B.C.* W63+546 **88**
Portsmouth, *England* N07+508 **39**
Portsmouth, *New Hampshire* S65+431 **90**
Portsmouth, *Ohio* T48+387 **91**
Portsmouth, *Virginia* T08+368 **97**
Portsonachan, *Scotland* N31+563 **41**
Portsoy, *Scotland* N16+577 **40**
Port Stanley, *Ontario* T37+427 **91**
Port Stephens, *N.S.W.* B78-328 **109**
Port Sudan, *Sudan* K46+196 **81**
Port Talbot, *Wales* N23+516 **38**
Port Tampa City, *Florida* T45+278 **97**
Port Taufiq, *Egypt* K74+300 **81**
Portugal, *W. Europe* N48+400 **50**
Portugalia, *Angola* L56-074 **82**
Portuguese Guinea. *See* Guinea-Bissau
Portumna, *Ireland, Rep.* N49+531 **43**
Port Vendres, *France* M71+425 **55**
Port Victoria, *Kenya* K66+002 **83**
Port Wakefield, *S. Aust.* C71-342 **109**
Port Washington, *Wisconsin* T77+434 **91**
Port Weller, *Ontario* T25+432 **91**
Porvenir, *Chile* S62-533 **103**
Porvoo, (Borga) *Finland* L26+604 **47**
Posadas, *Argentina* R66-273 **103**
Posadowsky B., *Antarctica* G05-670 **27**
Poschiavo, *Switzerland* M30+463 **56**
Poseh, *China* E81+239 **67**
Posen. *See* Poznan
Poshan, *China* E13+365 **66**
Posht-i-kuh, *Iran* J84+336 **74**
Poso, *Celebes* D86-014 **65**
Poso Danau, *Celebes.* D87-018 **65**
Possession I., *Antarctica* A50-720 **27**
Post, *Texas* U68+332 **94**
Posušje, *Yugoslavia* L76+435 **56**
Potapovo, *U.S.S.R.* G21+687 **62**
Potchefstroom, *Transvaal* L16-266 **84**
Poteau, *Oklahoma* U28+350 **95**
Potemkino, *U.S.S.R.* J84+504 **61**
Potenza, *Italy* L85+407 **57**
Poti, *Gruzinskaya, U.S.S.R.* K20+422 **62**
Potiskum, *Nigeria* M24+116 **81**
Potomac R., *Maryland, etc.* T20+396 **96**
Potosi, *Bolivia* S34-197 **104**
Potosi, *Missouri* U05+379 **97**
Potrerillos, *Chile* S57-265 **103**
Potsdam, *E. Germany* M12+524 **48**
Pottstown, *Pennsylvania* T04+403 **91**
Pottsville, *Pennsylvania* T07+407 **91**
Pouce Coupe, *B.C.* W00+554 **88**
Poughkeepsie, *New York* S83+417 **91**
Pouso Alegre, *Brazil* R72-118 **104**
Pouso Alegre, *Brazil* R06-212 **105**
Povenets, *Karelskaya* K62+628 **62**
Poverty B., *New Zealand* A12-388 **112**
Povoa de Varzim, *Portugal* N53+414 **52**
Povorina, *U.S.S.R.* K16+512 **61**
Povungnituk, *Quebec* T25+602 **89**
Povungnituk R., *Quebec* T05+602 **89**
Powder R., *Montana* V04+453 **98**
Powder River Ra., *Montana* V00+454 **93**
Powderville, *Montana* V01+458 **93**
Powell, L., *Utah* V36+370 **98**
Powell Mts., *Pa.-Va.* T49+366 **97**
Powell Creek, *N.-T. Aust.* D09-179 **111**
Powys, co., *Wales* N23+523 **38**
Poyang, *China* E20+290 **67**
Poyang Hu, *China* E22+290 **67**
Poza de la sal, *Spain* N21+427 **52**
Požarevac, *Yugoslavia* L53+446 **58**
Požega, *Yugoslavia* L74+453 **58**
Poznan, *Poland* L78+524 **49**
Pozo Almonte, *Chile* S58-203 **103**
Pozoblanco, *Spain* N29+384 **52**
Prachim Buri, *Thailand* F22+140 **69**
Prado, *Brazil* Q56-173 **105**
Praga, *Poland* L54+523 **49**
Prague. *See* Praha
Praha, *Czechoslovakia* M04+501 **48**
Praid, *Romania* L29+466 **58**
Prainha, *Brazil* S02-072 **104**
Prairie, *Queensland* C32-209 **111**
Prairie du Chien, *Wisconsin* U06+430 **95**
Prairie du Sac, *Wisconsin* T89+433 **91**
Pratapgarth, *India* G48+259 **73**
Prato, *Italy* M24+439 **56**
Pratt, *Kansas* U53+376 **95**
Pratt City, *Alabama* T71+335 **97**
Pravia, *Spain* N37+434 **52**
Pregolya, R., *U.S.S.R.* L51+546 **47**
Prenay, *Lithuania* L36+546 **47**
Prentice, *Wisconsin* U02+455 **91**
Přerov, *Czechoslovakia* L75+495 **49**
Prescott, *Arizona* V45+345 **92**
Prescott, *Ontario* T03+447 **91**
President R. Sáenz-Pena,
  Argentina S02-266 **103**
Presidente Hermes, *Brazil* S11-113 **104**
Presidente Penna, *Brazil* S11-108 **104**
Prešov, *Czechoslovakia* L53+490 **49**
Prespansko Jezero,
  Albania, etc. L54+409 **59**
Presque Isle, *Maine* S48+466 **90**
Pressburg. *See* Bratislava
Přeštice, *Czechoslovakia* M10+495 **48**
Preston, *England* N16+538 **37**
Preston, *Idaho* V41+421 **94**

Preston, *Minnesota* U13+437 **93**
Prestonpans, *Scotland* N18+560 **41**
Prestonsburg, *Kentucky* T47+377 **97**
Prestwick, *Scotland* N28+555 **41**
Pretoria, *Transvaal* L10-258 **84**
Pretty Boy L., *Maryland* T10+396 **96**
Préveza, *Greece* L56+390 **59**
Pribilof Is. Bering Sea Z30+568 **99**
Příbram. *Czechoslovakia* M06+497 **48**
Price and R., *Utah* V34+396 **94**
Priego, *Spain* N25+374 **52**
Prieska, *Cape Province* L44-296 **84**
Prignitz, *E. Germany* M18+531 **48**
Prijedor, *Yugoslavia* L80+450 **56**
Prijepolje, *Yugoslavia* L62+434 **58**
Prilep, *Yugoslavia* L51+414 **58**
Priluki, *Ukraine* K76+506 **60**
Prim Pt., *Prince Edward I.* S19+461 **90**
Primrose L., *Saskatchewan* V28+549 **88**
Prince Albert, *Cape Province* L48-332 **84**
Prince Albert, *Saskatchewan* V05+534 **88**
Prince Albert Mts., *Antarc.* B25-770 **27**
Prince Albert Park, *Sask.* V00+540 **88**
Prince Albert Pen., *N.-W. T.* V60+718 **88**
Prince Albert Sd., *N.-W. T.* V55+704 **88**
Prince Alfred, C., *N.-W. T.* W29+734 **88**
Prince Charles I., *N.W.T.* T10+672 **89**
Prince Edward I., *Canada* S20+464 **89**
Prince Edward Is., *Indian Oc.* K40-460 **77**
Prince Edwad Pen., *Ont.* T14+440 **91**
Prince George, *B.C.* W17+541 **88**
Prince Harald Ld., *Antarc.* K80-710 **27**
Prince of Wales, C., *Alaska* Z15+653 **99**
Prince of Wales I., *Alaska* W75+556 **99**
Prince of Wales I., *N.-W. T.* V80+600 **88**
Prince of Wales I., *Qnsld.* C47-107 **111**
Prince of Wales Str., *N.-W. T.* V80+724 **88**
Prince Patrick I., *N.-W. T.* W00+756 **88**
Prince Regent Inl., *N.-W. T.* U00+728 **89**
Prince Rupert, *B.C.* W61+543 **88**
Princes Lake, *Ontario* T18+454 **91**
Princess Astrid Ld., *Antarc.* M30-710 **27**
Princess Charlotte B.,
  Queensland C36-142 **111**
Princess Elizabeth Ld.,
  Antartica G70-720 **27**
Princess Ragnhild Ld.,
  Antartica L00-710 **27**
Princess Royal I., *B.C.* W52+530 **88**
Princeton, *Illinois* T87+414 **95**
Princeton, *Indiana* T76+384 **95**
Princeton, *Kentucky* T77+372 **95**
Princeton, *Maine* S46+452 **90**
Princeton, *Wisconsin* T85+438 **91**
Princetown, *England* N24+505 **38**
Princetown, *Pr. Edward I.* S22+465 **90**
Prince William Sd., *Alaska* X70+600 **99**
Principe I., *G. of Guinea* M46+016 **82**
Principe da Beira, *Brazil* S27-124 **104**
Pringles, *Argentina* S23-404 **103**
Prins Karl's Forland,
  Arctic Ocean M25+785 **62**
Prinzapolca, *Nicaragua* T51+134 **101**
Pripyat (Pripet) Marshes,
  Byelorussia L18+520 **60**
Pripyat (Pripet), R.,
  Byelorussia L03+518 **60**
Pristina, *Yugoslavia* L53+427 **58**
Pritzwalk, *E. Germany* M17+532 **48**
Privalnoye, *U.S.S.R.* J83+509 **61**
Prizren, *Yugoslavia* L56+422 **58**
Prizzi, *Sicily* M09+377 **57**
Progreso, *Mexico* 188-212 **100**
Prokop'yevsk, *U.S.S.R.* G20+541 **62**
Prokuplje, *Yugoslavia* L51+433 **58**
Prome, *Burma* F58+188 **71**
Prong, *Ghana* N06+080 **80**
Propria, *Brazil* Q41-103 **105**
Proskurov, *Ukraine* L18+494 **60**
Provence, prov., *France* M54+438 **55**
Providence, *Kentucky* T78+373 **97**
Providence, *N.-W. Terr.* V75+611 **88**
Providence, *Rhode Island* S68+418 **91**
Providence, C., *N.-W. Ter.* V45+736 **88**
Providence I., *Indian Ocean* J50-090 **77**
Provins, *France* M70+485 **54**
Provo, *Utah* V40+402 **94**
Prozor, *Yugoslavia* L74+438 **56**
Prudentopolis, *Brazil* R36-253 **103**
Prudhoe Ld., *Greenland* S45+780 **26**
Prüm, *W. Germany* M51+502 **48**
Prut, R. *U.S.S.R., etc.* L11+468 **58**
Przasnysz, *Poland* L55+530 **49**
Przemysl, *Poland* L43+498 **49**
Przhevalsk, *Kirgiz.* G70+425 **62**
Psará, I., *Greece* L26+386 **59**
Pskov, *U.S.S.R.* L10+578 **60**
Pskovskoye Oz., *U.S.S.R.*
  Estonia L12+580 **60**
Ptuj, *Yugoslavia* L85+464 **56**
Puan, *Argentina* S17-376 **103**
Pucacuro, *Peru* T04-028 **104**
Pucallpa, *Peru* S87-086 **104**
Puchezh, *U.S.S.R.* K11+570 **61**
Puchow. *See* Yungtsi
Puck, *Poland* L69+547 **49**
Pudasjärvi. *Finland* L19+654 **46**
Pudukkottai, *India* G68+104 **70**
Puebla & state, *Mexico* U49+188 **100**
Puebla Bonito, *New Mexico* V17+180 **99**
Puebla de Alcocer, *Spain* N31+390 **52**
Puebla de Sanabria, *Spain* N40+420 **52**
Puebla de Trives, *Spain* N44+425 **52**
Pueblo, *Colorado* U88+383 **94**
Pueblo Hundido, *Chile* S60-263 **103**
Puelches, *Argentina* S35-382 **103**
Puente Caldelas, *Spain* N51+423 **52**
Puentedeume, *Spain* N49+432 **52**
Puerco, R., *Arizona* V28+350 **94**
Puerhken, *Mongolia* F87+460 **63**
Puerto Armuelles, *Panama* T47+084 **101**
Puerto Asis, *Colombia* T09+005 **104**
Puerto Ayacucho, *Venezuela* S46+057 **104**
Puerto Aysen, *Chile* S78-453 **103**
Puerto Barrios, *Guatemala* T80+158 **100**
Puerto Bermudez, *Peru* S89-102 **104**
Puerto Berrio, *Colombia* S87+065 **104**
Puerto Cabello, *Venezuela* S48+105 **104**
Puerto Cabezas, *Nicaragua* T50+140 **101**
Puerto Carreno, *Colombia* S44+063 **104**
Puerto Casado, *Paraguay* R77-223 **103**

Puerto Chicama, *Peru* T27-078 **104**
Puerto Colombia, *Colombia* T00+109 **104**
Puerto Cordoba. *Colombia* S59-014 **104**
Puerto Cortes, *Honduras* T78+157 **101**
Puerto Coyle, *Argentina* S56-508 **103**
Puerto Cumarebo, *Venez.* S56+114 **104**
Puerto de Carrizal, *Chile* S67-281 **103**
Puerto de Chanaral, *Chile* S64-263 **103**
Puerto de Santa Maria, *Spain* N37+366 **52**
Puerto Deseado, *Argentina* S36-476 **103**
Puerto Eten, *Peru* T29-068 **104**
Puerto Harberton, *Argent.* S44-548 **103**
Puerto Heath, *Bolivia* S52-124 **104**
Puerto Ichilo, *Bolivia* S26-170 **104**
Puerto Isabel, *Mexico* V59+317 **100**
Puerto Leguisamo, *Colombia* S88-003 **104**
Puerto Libertad, *El Salvador* T86+134 **101**
Puertollano, *Spain* N25+387 **52**
Puerto Lobos, *Argentina* S31-420 **103**
Puerto Lomas, *Peru* S89-155 **104**
Puerto Madryn, *Argentina* S30-427 **103**
Puerto Maldonado, *Peru* S56-170 **104**
Puerto Mexico, *Mexico* U27+180 **100**
Puerto Montt, *Chile* S78-413 **103**
Puerto Morelos, *Mexico* T70+209 **100**
Puerto Natales, *Chile* S76-516 **103**
Puerto Patillos, *Chile* S61-208 **103**
Puerto Pirámide, *Argentina* S26-426 **103**
Puerto Plata, *Dom. Rep.* S64+198 **101**
Puerto Princesa, *Phil.* E08+097 **65**
Puerto Principe, *Colombia* S85+004 **104**
Puerto Quellen, *Chile* S81-428 **103**
Puerto Quijarro, *Bolivia* R77-178 **104**
Puerto Raso, *Argentina* S32-444 **103**
Puerto Rico, I., *West Indies* S38+183 **101**
Puerto Suarez, *Bolivia* R77-190 **104**
Puerto Sucre, *Bolivia* S32-108 **104**
Puerto Toledo, *Bolivia* S16-175 **104**
Puerto Varas, *Chile* S78-413 **103**
Puerto Victoria, *Peru* T00-098 **104**
Puerto Vulamizar, *Colombia* S75+082 **104**
Puerto Visser, *Argentina* S43-454 **103**
Puerto Wilches, *Colombia* S83+073 **104**
Pueyrredón, L., *Argentina* S71-476 **103**
Pugachev, *U.S.S.R.* J67+520 **61**
Pugal, *India* H14+286 **72**
Puget, *France* M49+440 **55**
Puget Sd.. *Washington* W18+474 **98**
Puglia, dep. *Italy* L80+409 **57**
Pühalepa, *Estonia* L42+589 **47**
Puimro, *Brazil* R58+010 **105**
Pukaki, L., *New Zealand* A59-441 **112**
Pukapaka I., *Tuamotu Arch.* X22-150 **107**
Pukapuka I., *Pacific Ocean* Z06-108 **106**
Pukchong, *Korea* D39+404 **64**
Pukekohe, *New Zealand* A31-372 **112**
Puket, *Thailand* F40+079 **69**
Pukow, *China* E08+321 **66**
Pula, *Yugoslavia* M07+449 **56**
Pulacayo, *Bolivia* S40-204 **104**
Pulap, I., *Caroline Islands* C25+073 **106**
Pulaski, *New York* T07+436 **91**
Pulaski, *Tennessee* T72+352 **97**
Pulaski, *Virginia* T35+371 **97**
Pulicat I.. *India* G59+140 **70**
Pulkkila, *Finland* L25+643 **46**
Pullen I. (Richards I.).
  N.-W. Territories X00+686 **88**
Pullen, *Ontario* T40+494 **89**
Pultneyville, *New York* T13+432 **96**
Puma, *Tanzania* K62-050 **83**
Puna, I., *Ecuador* T31-030 **104**
Punakha, *Bhutan* G01+276 **73**
Punch, *Kashmir* H05+338 **72**
Pundri, *India* G80+298 **72**
Punjab, *India* G84+305 **72**
Puno, *Peru* S60-159 **104**
Punta Alta, *Argentina* S12-388 **103**
Punta Arenas, *Chile* S66-532 **103**
Punta Colorado, *Chile* S66-292 **103**
Punta del Faro, *Sicily* L87+383 **57**
Punta de Pedras, *Brazil* R23-014 **105**
Punta Gorda, *Belize* T83+162 **101**
Puntarenas, *Costa Rica* T58+100 **101**
Punta Salinas, *Venezuela* S61+117 **104**
Punxsutawney. *Pennsylvania* T24+409 **96**
Puolanka, *Finland* L14+649 **46**
Purang Chaka, *Tibet* G47+329 **71**
Purbeck Downs, *England* N15+507 **38**
Purgatoire R., *Colorado* U82+376 **94**
Puri, *India* G24+198 **71**
Purificacion, *Colombia* T00+038 **104**
Purna, *India* G76+192 **70**
Purnea, *India* G15+258 **73**
Purulia, *India* G21+233 **73**
Purus, R., *Brazil, etc.* S32-074 **104**
Purvis, *Mississippi* T86+311 **97**
Purwa, *India* G55+265 **73**
Pusan, *Korea* D36+351 **64**
Pu-san, mt., *Laos* F11+198 **69**
Pushchino, *U.S.S.R.* E62+580 **63**
Pust-i-Badam, *Iran* J27+328 **75**
Putao, *Burma* F43+274 **71**
Putbus, *W. Germany* M09+543 **48**
Putien, *China* E05+255 **67**
Putignano, *Italy* L77+408 **57**
Putnam, *Connecticut* S71+419 **96**
Putnok, *Hungary* L58+483 **49**
Putorana, Gory, *U.S.S.R.* F60+690 **63**
Puttalam, *Sri Lanka* G61+081 **70**
Putte, *Belgium* M64+514 **44**
Putte, *Belgium* M62+511 **44**
Putten, *Netherlands* M56+522 **44**
Putumayo, R., *Colombia, etc.* S88-006 **104**
Putussibau, *Borneo* E42+008 **65**
Puula Vesi, *Finland* L20+617 **47**
Puurs, *Belgium* M64+511 **44**
Puy, le, *France* M67+450 **55**
Puyallup, *Washington* W14+472 **92**
Puy-de-Dôme, dep.. *France* M70+456 **54**
Pwllheli, *Wales* N27+529 **38**
Pyapon, *Burma* F56+162 **71**
Pyatistennoe, *U.S.S.R.* B20+680 **63**
Pyevyek, *U.S.S.R.* A53+698 **63**
Pyhäjärvi, *Finland* L24+636 **46**
Pyhäjärvi, *Finland* L46+610 **47**
Pyhäntä, *Finland* L22+641 **46**
Pyinmana, *Burma* F52+197 **71**
P'ŏngyang, *Korea* D54+393 **64**
Pyramid L., *Nevada* V87+400 **92**

Pyramid Pk., *California* W01+389 **92**
Pyramid Hill, *Victoria* C35-361 **109**
Pyrénées. Mt., *France-Spain* **53**
Pyrénées-Orientales dep.,
  France M76+425 **55**
Pyrzyce, *Poland* M01+531 **48**
Pyu, *Burma* F51+185 **71**
Pyzdry, *Poland* L74+522 **49**
Qafar, *Saudi Arabia* K19+274 **74**
Qaiya, *Saudi Arabia* J88+241 **74**
Qala, *Afghanistan* H14+369 **75**
Qala Mashiz, *Iran* J20+299 **75**
Qal'at al Akhdhar,
  Saudi Arabia K45+281 **74**
Qal'at Dar al Hamra,
  Saudi Arabia K42+275 **74**
Qal'at ed Dab'a, *Jordan* K54+316 **76**
Qal'at el Marqan, *Syria* K54+352 **76**
Qal'at el Mudiq, *Syria* K51+355 **76**
Qal'at Uneiza, *Jordan* K55+305 **76**
Qalqiliya, *Jordan* K60+322 **76**
Qamr B., *Yemen, South* J44+160 **75**
Qara, *Egypt* L20+298 **81**
Qardaha, *Syria* K54+355 **76**
Qartaba, *Lebanon* K55+341 **76**
Qasim, *Saudi Arabia* K21+272 **74**
Qasr Amij, *Iraq* K19+334 **74**
Qasr el Azraq. *Jordan* K49+319 **76**
Qasr e Qand, *Iran* H85+262 **75**
Qasr Haiyaniya,
  Saudi Arabia K14+286 **74**
Qasr ibn Aliya, *Saudi Arabia* K10+291 **74**
Qasr-i-Shirin, *Iran* J86+346 **74**
Qa'taba, *Yemen* K01+139 **74**
Qatana, *Syria* K53+334 **76**
Qatar, *The Gulf* J52+250 **75**
Qatif, *Saudi Arabia* J60+267 **74**
Qayen, *Iran* J05+338 **75**
Qena, *Egypt* K74+262 **81**
Qeshm I., *Iran* J26+267 **75**
Qeys, I., *Iran* J36+265 **75**
Qishn, *Yemen, D.R.* J50+155 **75**
Qishran, I., Saudi Arabia K30+202 **74**
Qizan, *Saudi Arabia* K14+169 **74**
Qom, *Iran* J55+347 **75**
Qotur, *Iran* K04+385 **74**
Qoz Bal 'Air, *Saudi Arabia* K21+192 **74**
Quabbin Res., *Massachusetts* S74+424 **96**
Quadda, *Cent. Afr. Rep.* L46+082 **81**
Quakenbruck, *W. Germany* M42+527 **48**
Quambatook, *Victoria* C39-359 **109**
Quambone, *New S. Wales* C13-309 **109**
Quang Tri, *Vietnam* E77+168 **65**
Quantock Hills, *England* N19+511 **38**
Quarai, *Brazil* R69-304 **103**
Quatre Bras, *Belgium* M63+506 **44**
Qubeiyat, *Lebanon* K52+346 **76**
Quchan, *Iran* J10+371 **75**
Queanbeyan, *New. S. Wales* C04-354 **109**
Quebec, *Quebec* S67+468 **91**
Quebec, prov., *Canada* **89**
Queen Alexandra Ra.,
  Antarctica B20-840 **27**
Queen Anne, *Maryland* T06+388 **96**
Queen Charlotte B.
  Falkland Islands S04-517 **103**
Queen Charlotte Is., *B.C.* W75+530 **88**
Queen Charlotte Is., *B.C.* W50+514 **88**
Queen Charlotte Str., *B.C.* W45+508 **88**
Queen Elizabeth Is., *N.-W.T.* V40+770 **88**
Queen Mary Ld., *Antarctica* F65-670 **27**
Queen Maud G.,
  N.-W. Territories U60+676 **88**
Queen Maud Ld., *Antarc.* L60-720 **27**
Queen Maud Ra., *Antarc.* Y50-870 **27**
Queen's Chan., *N. Terr.,*
  Australia D33-147 **110**
Queenscliff, *Victoria* C32-383 **109**
Queenscliffe, *S. Australia* C74-356 **109**
Queensland, state, *Australia* **111**
Queenstown, *Cape Province* L18-320 **84**
Queenstown, *New Zealand* A68-450 **112**
Queenstown. *See* Cobh
Queenstown, *Tasmania* C27-421 **109**
Queimadas, *Brazil* Q58-110 **105**
Quelimane. *Mozambique* K48-178 **84**
Quemu Quemü, *Argentina* S21-360 **103**
Quequen, *Argentina* R82-385 **103**
Queretaro, *Mexico* U62+206 **100**
Quesnel, *Brit. Columbia* W15+532 **88**
Quesnel L., *Brit. Columbia* W08+528 **88**
Quetta, *Pakistan* H48+302 **70**
Quetzalapa, *Mexico* U49+170 **100**
Quezaltenango, *Guatemala* U09+148 **100**
Quezon City, *Philippines* D83+149 **65**
Quibdo, *Colombia* T10+057 **104**
Quiberon B. de., *France* N18+475 **54**
Quievrain, *Belgium* M68+504 **44**
Quila, *Mexico* V13+245 **100**
Quilca, *Peru* S75-166 **104**
Quilino, *Argentina* S28-301 **103**
Quillabamba, *Peru* S75-128 **104**
Quillan, *France* M77+429 **55**
Quillota, *Chile* S68-328 **103**
Quilon (Kollam), *India* G90+111 **70**
Quilpie, *Queensland* C35-266 **111**
Quimper, *France* N25+480 **54**
Quimperle, *France* N21+479 **54**
Quincy, *Illinois* U08+399 **95**
Quincy, *Massachusetts* S66+423 **91**
Quincy, *Michigan* T59+420 **91**
Quines, *Argentina* S34-321 **103**
Quinnimont, *W. Virginia* T36+378 **97**
Quintana de la Serena, *Sp.* N34+388 **52**
Quintanar de la Orden, *Sp.* N19+396 **52**
Quintana Roo, state, *Mexico* T78+194 **100**
Quipapa, *Brazil* Q36-087 **105**
Quirindi, *New South Wales* B86-316 **109**
Quiriquire, *Venezuela* S18+100 **104**
Quiroga, *Spain* N43+424 **52**
Quissanga, *Mozambique* K28-124 **83**
Quissico, *Mozambique* K62-248 **84**
Quitapa, *Angola* L70-106 **82**
Quito, *Ecuador* T21-002 **104**
Quixada, *Brazil* Q55-050 **105**
Quixeramobim, *Brazil* Q56-052 **105**
Qunsuliye, *Saudi Arabia* K13+221 **74**
Quoich L., *Scotland* N32+571 **40**
Quorn, *S. Australia* C72-323 **109**
Quryat, *Oman* J07+233 **75**
Qus, *Egypt* K74+260 **81**
Qusayar, *Yemen, South* J58+150 **75**

Quseir, *Egypt* K64+260 **81**
Qusuriya, *Saudi Arabia* K03+238 **74**
Quteife, *Syria* K50+337 **76**
Quyon, *Quebec* T08+455 **91**
Raahe, *Finland* L33+646 **46**
Raasay & Sd. of, *Scotland* N37+574 **40**
Rab., I., *Yugoslavia* M02+448 **56**
Raba, *Sumbawa, I., Indon.* E07−085 **65**
Rabat, *Morocco* N42+340 **80**
Rabat Kerim, *Iran* J53+355 **75**
Rabigh, *Saudi Arabia* K36+228 **74**
Rabkob. *See Dharmjaygarh*
Race, C., *Newfoundland* R49+466 **90**
Race, The, *Conn.-New York* S73+412 **96**
Rach-zhia, *Vietnam* E89+100 **69**
Raciborz, *Poland* L71+501 **49**
Racine, *Wisconsin* T77+427 **91**
Rada, *Yemen* K01+146 **74**
Radak Chain, *Marshall Is.* A40+100 **106**
Rădăuţi, *Romania* L24+479 **60**
Radford, *Virginia* T33+371 **97**
Radhanpur, *India* H21+238 **70**
Radhwa, Jebel, *Saudi Arabia* K41+245 **74**
Radnevo, *Bulgaria* L24+423 **58**
Radnor. *See Powys*
Radnor Forest, *Wales* N20+522 **38**
Radom, *Poland* L53+504 **49**
Radomir, *Bulgaria* L42+425 **58**
Radomsko, *Poland* L64+511 **49**
Radstadt, *Austria* M09+474 **48**
Radviliškis, *Lithuania* L39+558 **47**
Radzyn, *Poland* L44+518 **49**
Rae, *N.-W. Territories* V65+633 **88**
Rae Isthmus, *N.-W. Terr.* T70+666 **89**
Rae R., *N.-W. Territories* V70+676 **88**
Rae Bareli, *India* G53+263 **73**
Raeside, L., *W. Australia* D82−290 **110**
Raetihi, *New Zealand* A28−394 **112**
Rafaela, *Argentina* S09−312 **103**
Ragaine, *Lithuania* L48+550 **47**
Ragaz Bad, *Switzerland* M33+470 **45**
Raghugarh, *India* G77+244 **73**
Raghunathpur, *India* G20+235 **73**
Raglan, *New Zealand* A31−378 **112**
Raglan Ra., *New Zealand* A41−420 **112**
Ragunda, *Sweden* L81+631 **46**
Ragusa. *See Dubrovnik*
Ragusa, *Sicily* M02+369 **57**
Rahaeng. *See Tak*
Raheita, *Ethiopia* K12+126 **83**
Rahhyut, *Oman* J40+168 **75**
Raiatea, I., *Society Islands* Y10−168 **107**
Raichur, *India* G76+162 **70**
Raida, *Yemen, South* J74+148 **74**
Raida, *Yemen, South* J57+151 **75**
Raiganj, *India* G11+256 **73**
Raikot, *India* G86+306 **72**
Rainbow, *Victoria* C48−359 **109**
Raingarh, *India* G73+311 **72**
Rainier, Mt., *Washington* W10+468 **92**
Rainy L., *Ontario* U18+488 **89**
Raipur, *India* G50+213 **70**
Raivavae, I., *Austral Is.* X75−245 **107**
Raiwind, *Pakistan* H05+312 **72**
Raja, mt., *Borneo* E44−008 **65**
Rajahmundry, *India* G48+170 **70**
Rajakhera, *India* G71+269 **73**
Rajang, R., *Sarawak* E46+020 **65**
Rajanpur, *Pakistan* H28+291 **72**
Rajapalaiyam, *India* G74+095 **70**
Rajasthan, *India* H10+270 **70**
Rajburi, *Thailand* F32+136 **69**
Rajgarh, *India* G88+286 **72**
Rajkot, *India* H25+222 **70**
Rajmahal, *India* G13+250 **73**
Rajmahal Hills, *India* G24+245 **73**
Rajpura, *India* G80+305 **72**
Rajshahi, *Bangladesh* G08+243 **73**
Rajura, *India* G64+197 **70**
Rakahanga, I., *Pacific Oc.* Y66−100 **106**
Rakaposhi, mt., *Kashmir* H03+361 **72**
Raka Tsangpo, R., *Tibet* G20+296 **71**
Rakvere, *Estonia* L22+593 **47**
Raleigh, *New South Wales* B73−305 **109**
Raleigh, *N. Carolina* T22+356 **99**
Raleigh B., *N. Carolina* T06+348 **97**
Ralik Chain, *Marshall Is.* A70+080 **106**
Ram, *Jordan* K57+296 **76**
Rama, *Ethiopia* K30+124 **83**
Rama, *Israel* K58+329 **76**
Ramadi, *Iraq* K10+334 **74**
Ramallah, *Jordan* K59+319 **76**
Ramallo, *Argentina* S00−335 **103**
Ramanthapuran, *India* G67+094 **70**
Rambouillet, *France* N79+487 **54**
Ramee, *Burma* F66+192 **71**
Ramgarh, *India* H00+281 **72**
Ramgarh, *India* G54+228 **73**
Ramgarh, *India* G26+236 **73**
Ram Hormuz, *Iran* J63+312 **74**
Ramishk, *Iran* J06+269 **75**
Ramkola, *India* G42+236 **73**
Ramle, *Israel* K61+319 **76**
Ramnagar, *India* G57+226 **73**
Ramnagar, *Kashmir* G88+328 **72**
Ramnagar, *Pakistan* H07+323 **72**
Râmnicul Sărat, *Romania* L18+454 **58**
Râmnicu Valcea, *Romania* L34+451 **58**
Ramore, *Ontario* T32+484 **91**
Ramoutsa, *Botswana* L26−248 **84**
Rampart House, *Yukon* X35+671 **88**
Rampur, *India* G33+210 **71**
Rampur, *India* G74+315 **72**
Rampur, *India* G66+288 **73**
Ramsay, *Ontario* T44+454 **91**
Ramsbottom, *England* N14+537 **37**
Ramsele, *Sweden* L81+635 **46**
Ramsey, *Isle of Man* N26+543 **37**
Ramsey I., *Wales* N32+519 **38**
Ramsgate, *England* M82+513 **39**
Ramsgate, *Tasmania* C19−435 **109**
Ramsjö, *Sweden* L86+621 **47**
Ramskapelle, *Belgium* M73+511 **44**
Ramtha, *Jordan* K54+326 **76**
Ramtok, *India* G63+215 **70**
Rana, Fd., *Norway* M12+662 **46**
Ranaghat, *India* G09+231 **73**

Rancagua, *Chile* S65−341 **103**
Rance, *Belgium* M64+501 **44**
Ranchi, *India* G28+234 **73**
Ranchito, *Mexico* U71+233 **100**
Rand, *New South Wales* C21−356 **109**
Randalstown, *N. Ireland* N38+547 **42**
Randazzo, *Sicily* M00+379 **57**
Randers, *Denmark* M30+564 **47**
Randolph, *Vermont* S76+439 **91**
Random I., *Newfoundland* R52+481 **90**
Randsfjord, *Norway* M27+603 **47**
Ranenburg, *U.S.S.R.* K30+532 **61**
Ranfurly, *New Zealand* A59−451 **112**
Rangamati, *Bangladesh* F77+227 **71**
Rangeley, *Maine* S64+450 **90**
Rangeley Ls., *Maine* S65+449 **90**
Rangemore, *New S. Wales* C34−354 **109**
Ranger, *Texas* U52+322 **98**
Rangiora, *New Zealand* A44−433 **112**
Rangitaiki, R., *New Zealand* A20−385 **112**
Rangitikei, R., *New Zealand* A27−401 **112**
Rangitoto Ra., *New Zealand* A26−385 **112**
Rangoon & R., *Burma* F53+168 **71**
Rangpur, *Bangladesh* G04+257 **73**
Rania, *India* H01+295 **72**
Ranibennur, *India* G86+147 **70**
Raniganj, *India* G12+259 **73**
Raniganj, *India* G17+236 **73**
Ranikhet, *India* G63+296 **73**
Rankin Inl., *N.-W. Terr.* U15+632 **89**
Rankins Springs, *N.S.W.* C22−339 **109**
Rannoch, L., *Scotland* N26+567 **41**
Rannoch Moor, *Scotland* N28+566 **41**
Ranong, *Thailand* F39+100 **65**
Rantauparapat, *Sumatra* F31+021 **65**
Rantekombola, mt., *Celebes.* E00−034 **65**
Rantsila, *Finland* L26+645 **46**
Ranua, *Finland* L21+659 **46**
Rapa, I., *Austral Islands* X65−275 **107**
Rapadama, *Upper Volta* N06+122 **80**
Raphoe, *Ireland, Rep.* N45+549 **42**
Rapid City, *S. Dakota* U80+441 **93**
Rapla, *Estonia* L31+590 **47**
Rappahannock R., *Virginia* T10+381 **97**
Rapperswil, *Switzerland* M37+472 **45**
Raqqa, *Syria* K36+359 **74**
Rarotonga, I., *Cook Islands* Y60−210 **106**
Ras al Had, *Oman* J01+225 **75**
Ras al Khaymah, *U.A.E.* J24+259 **75**
Rashad, *Sudan* K84+118 **81**
Rashadiya, *Jordan* K56+307 **76**
Rasheiye, *Lebanon* K55+335 **76**
Rashin, *Korea* D28+420 **64**
Rashm, *Iran* J34+352 **75**
Rasht, *Iran* J62+373 **74**
Raška, *Yugoslavia* L56+433 **58**
Ras Lanuf, *Libya* L67+304 **81**
Rason, L., *W. Australia* D64−286 **110**
Rasova, *Romania* L12+442 **58**
Rasskazovo, *U.S.S.R.* K19+526 **61**
Ratangarh, *India* H02+280 **72**
Rat Buri, *Thailand* F32+136 **69**
Rathdrum, *Ireland, Rep.* N37+529 **43**
Rathfriland, *N. Ireland* N37+542 **42**
Ratheale, *Ireland, Rep.* N54+525 **43**
Rathlin I., *N. Ireland* N37+553 **42**
Rathnew, *Ireland, Rep.* N36+530 **43**
Ratibor. *See Raciborz.*
Ratnagiri, *India* H10+170 **70**
Raton, *New Mexico* U87+369 **94**
Rattlesnake Ra., *Wyoming* V14+428 **93**
Rattray Hd., *Scotland* N11+576 **40**
Rättvik, *Sweden* L89+609 **47**
Rauch, *Argentina* R85−367 **103**
Raudha, *Yemen* K05+155 **74**
Raukumara Ra., *N.Z.* A12−380 **112**
Rauma, *Finland* L51+611 **47**
Rautavaara, *Finland* L10+635 **46**
Rautio, *Finland* L35+641 **46**
Rauwaq, Jebel er, *Syria* K48+341 **74**
Ravar, *Iran* J20+314 **75**
Ravenna, *Italy* M17+444 **56**
Ravi R., *Pakistan* H03+317 **72**
Rawaidha, *Saudi Arabia* K02+239 **74**
Rawalpindi, *Pakistan* H11+336 **72**
Rawandiz, *Iraq* K30+367 **74**
Rawatsar, *India* H04+292 **72**
Rawene, *New Zealand* A39−354 **112**
Rawlinna, *W. Australia* D58−309 **110**
Rawlins, *Wyoming* V14+418 **93**
Rawson, *Argentina* S31−433 **103**
Ray, C., *Newfoundland* R86+476 **90**
Rayadrug, *India* G79+148 **70**
Raymond, *Alberta* V47+495 **88**
Raymondville, *Texas* U46+266 **94**
Rayon, *Mexico* U58+218 **100**
Rayon, *Mexico* V34+296 **100**
Rays Hill, *Pennsylvania* T20+398 **96**
Razelm L., *Romania* L06+448 **58**
Razgrad, *Bulgaria* L21+435 **58**
Razmak, *Pakistan* H31+327 **72**
Ré, I. de, *France* N08+462 **54**
Reading, *England* N06+514 **39**
Reading, *Pennsylvania* T05+404 **91**
Real, Cord., *Bolivia* S50−162 **104**
Real, Cord, *Ecuador, etc.* T24−020 **104**
Real Castillo, *Mexico* V67+320 **100**
Realico, *Argentina* S25−351 **103**
Realp, *Switzerland* M39+466 **45**
Reata, *Mexico* U67+262 **100**
Rebun, I., *Japan* C54+454 **68**
Recalde, *Argentina* S07−365 **103**
Recherche Arch., *W. Aust.* D73−346 **110**
Rechna Doab, *Pakistan* H15+310 **72**
Recht, *Belgium* M54+503 **44**
Recife, *Brazil* Q30−080 **105**
Reconquista, *Argentina* R88−291 **103**
Recreio, *Brazil* R77−080 **105**
Red Des., *Wyoming* V18+420 **93**
Red L., *Minnesota* U30+480 **93**
Red R., *Louisiana, etc.* U12+313 **95**
Red R., *Minn. Man.* U42+479 **88**
Red R. *See Song-koi.*
Red Sea, *Africa-Arabia* K50+200 **30**
Redbank, *New Jersey* S85+403 **96**
Red Bluff Res., *New Mex.-Texas* U84+320 **94**
Redby, *Minnesota* U29+479 **93**
Red Cliffs, *Victoria* C47−344 **109**

Red Deer, *Alberta* V53+520 **88**
Red Deer R., *Alberta* V38+510 **88**
Redding, *California* W14+406 **92**
Redditch, *England* N12+523 **37**
Redempção, *Brazil* R65−106 **105**
Redfield, *Arkansas* U13+344 **97**
Redfield, *S. Dakota* U55+449 **93**
Red Hill, *S. Australia* C71−336 **109**
Red Hill, *Victoria* C30−384 **109**
Red Indian L., *Nfd.* R70+488 **90**
Redlands, *California* V73+341 **92**
Red Lodge, *Montana* V26+452 **93**
Red Oak, *Iowa* U31+410 **95**
Redon, *France* N13+477 **54**
Redondeta, *Spain* N51+422 **52**
Red Pine, *New Brunswick* S34+474 **90**
Redruth, *England* N31+502 **38**
Redruth, *Michigan* T79+466 **91**
Red Salt L., *Tibet* G18+338 **71**
Red Wing, *Minnesota* U15+446 **93**
Redwood Falls, *Minnesota* U31+445 **93**
Ree L., *Ireland, Rep.* N48+535 **43**
Reed City, *Michigan* T63+439 **91**
Reedsburg, *Wisconsin* U00+435 **91**
Reefton, *New Zealand* A49−421 **112**
Reelfoot, L., *Tennessee* T86+364 **95**
Refresco, *Chile* S59−254 **103**
Regensburg, *Germany* M17+490 **48**
Reggan, *Algeria* M88+264 **80**
Reggio, *Italy* L86+381 **57**
Reggio nell'Emilia, *Italy* M26+447 **56**
Reghin, *Romania* L32+468 **58**
Regina, *Saskatchewan* U87+504 **88**
Registro do Araguaia, *Brazil* R41−157 **105**
Regua, *Portugal* N47+412 **52**
Rehoboth, *Namibia* L78−232 **84**
Rehovo, *Israel* K61+319 **76**
Reichenbach, *E. Germany* M16+506 **48**
Reidsville, *N. Carolina* T28+364 **97**
Reigate, *England* N01+512 **39**
Reigi, *Estonia* L45+589 **47**
Reims, *France* M66+493 **54**
Reina Adelaide, Arch. de la, *Chile* T00−522 **103**
Reindeer L., *Saskatchewan* U75+570 **88**
Reinosa, *Spain* N25+430 **52**
Reitan, *Norway* M22+629 **46**
Reitz, *Orange Free State* L10−278 **84**
Rekinniki, *U.S.S.R.* B07+608 **63**
Relizane, (Ighil-Izane), *Alg.* M86+356 **80**
Remanso, *Brazil* Q73−096 **105**
Remarkable, Mt., *S. Aust.* C71−328 **109**
Rembang, *Java* E52−067 **65**
Remedios, *Cuba* T27+225 **101**
Remedios, *Panama* T40+083 **101**
Remiremont, *France* M51+480 **54**
Remoulins, *France* M63+440 **55**
Remscheid, *W. Germany* M47+512 **48**
Remüs, *Switzerland* M28+468 **45**
Rena, *Norway* M22+611 **47**
Renaix, *Belgium* M68+507 **44**
Renca, *Argentina* S32−327 **103**
Rendsburg, *Germany* M32+543 **48**
Renfrew, *Ontario* T10+455 **91**
Renfrew, *Scotland* N26+559 **41**
Rengat, *Sumatra* F14−006 **65**
Reni, *India* H00+287 **72**
Renigunta, *India* G63+138 **70**
Renk, *Sudan* K72+118 **81**
Renkum, *Netherlands* M56+520 **44**
Renmark, *S. Australia* C56−342 **109**
Rennell, I., *Solomon Islands* B29−120 **106**
Rennes, *France* N10+481 **54**
Reno, *Nevada* V89+395 **92**
Renovo, *Pennsylvania* T16+413 **91**
Rensselaer, *New York* S82+426 **91**
Renswoude, *Netherlands* M57+521 **44**
Renville, *Minnesota* U32+448 **93**
Reo, *Flores I., Indonesia* D87−083 **65**
Réole la, *France* N00+445 **55**
Repartição, *Brazil* R67−048 **105**
Republic Dominican, *W.I.* S64+190 **101**
Republican R., *Nebraska* U54+400 **95**
Repulse B., *N.-W. Terr.* T66+662 **89**
Repulse B., *Queensland* C05−206 **111**
Requena, *Peru* S81−049 **104**
Requena, *Spain* N07+395 **53**
Resita, *Romania* L49+453 **58**
Resistencia, *Argentina* R84−274 **103**
Resolution, *New Zealand* A80−457 **112**
Resolution, *N.-W. Terr.* V52+609 **88**
Resolution I., *N.-W. Terr.* S30+614 **89**
Rethel, *France* M64+495 **54**
Réthimnon, *Crete* L33+354 **59**
Retie, *Belgium* M61+513 **44**
Réunion I., *Indian Ocean* J30−210 **77**
Reusel, *Netherlands* M59+514 **44**
Reutlingen, *W. Germany* M35+485 **48**
Reutte, *Austria* M26+475 **48**
Revda, *U.S.S.R.* J00+568 **61**
Revel. *See Tallinn*
Revelstoke, *B.C.* V79+509 **88**
Revilla Gigedo Is., *Mexico* V42+190 **100**
Revivum, *Israel* K61+310 **76**
Rewa, *India* G52+245 **73**
Rewari, *India* G80+282 **72**
Rey, I. del, *Panama* T25+084 **101**
Reydharfjord, *Iceland* N81+650 **46**
Reyes, *Mexico* U74+196 **100**
Reykjavik, *Iceland* P41+641 **46**
Reynosa, *Mexico* U50+260 **100**
Reza'iyeh, *Iran* K00+376 **74**
Rêžekne, *Latvia* L16+565 **47**
Rhatikon, mts., *Switzerland-Austria* M32+470 **45**
Rhayader, *Wales* N21+523 **38**
Rheden, *Netherlands* M54+520 **44**
Rhein R., *Germany, etc.* M46+506 **48**
Rheine, *W. Germany* M46+523 **48**
Rheinland-Pfalz, *W. Germany* M48+502 **48**
Rhenen, *Netherlands* M57+520 **44**
Rheydt, *W. Germany* M51+512 **48**
Rhine, *N.-W. Europe* M50+510 **50**
Rhinelander, *Wisconsin* T87+457 **91**
Rhode I., *Rhode Island* S68+415 **96**
Rhode Island, state, *U.S.A.* S70+416 **99**
Rhodes. *See Rodhos, I.*
Rhodesia, N. *See Zambia*
Rhodesia, *See Zimbabwe*
Rhon Geb., *W. Germany* M30+504 **48**
Rhondda, *Wales* N21+516 **38**

Rhône, dep., *France* M62+459 **54**
Rhône, R., *France, etc.* M62+445 **55**
Rhyl, *Wales* N21+533 **38**
Riaño, *Spain* N30+430 **52**
Riau, Kep., arch., *Indon.* F04+004 **65**
Riaza, *Spain* N21+413 **52**
Ribabesella, *Spain* N30+434 **52**
Ribadeo, *Spain* N42+433 **52**
Ribble R., *England* N14+539 **37**
Ribe, *Denmark* M38+553 **47**
Ribeirão Preto, *Brazil* R17−212 **105**
Ribera, *Sicily* M11+375 **57**
Riberalta, *Bolivia* S36−110 **104**
Riccall, *England* N06+538 **37**
Riccarton, *New Zealand* A44−435 **112**
Rice Lake, *Wisconsin* U10+455 **93**
Richards C., *Arctic Ocean* T30+830 **26**
Richardson Mts., *N.Z.* A68−448 **112**
Richardton, *N. Dakota* U74+469 **93**
Richey, *Montana* U89+477 **93**
Richfield, *Utah* V43+388 **92**
Richibucto, *New Brunswick* S29+467 **90**
Richland, *Missouri* U14+379 **97**
Richland, *Washington* V86+463 **92**
Richland Center, *Wisconsin* U02+433 **91**
Richmond, *California* W15+379 **92**
Richmond, *Cape Province* L38−314 **84**
Richmond, *England* N10+544 **37**
Richmond, *England* N02+514 **39**
Richmond, *Indiana* T59+399 **91**
Richmond, *Kentucky* T56+378 **97**
Richmond, *Maine* S59+441 **90**
Richmond, *New South Wales* B86−336 **109**
Richmond, *New York* S85+406 **91**
Richmond, *New Zealand* A41−413 **112**
Richmond, *Quebec* S73+457 **91**
Richmond, *Queensland* C41−208 **111**
Richmond, *Utah* V41+419 **94**
Richmond, *Virginia* T15+375 **97**
Richmond R., *New S. Wales* B70−289 **109**
Richwood, *Minnesota* U35+469 **93**
Richwood, *W. Virginia* T33+382 **97**
Rickmansworth, *England* N03+516 **39**
Ricla, *Spain* N09+415 **53**
Riddes, *Switzerland* M47+462 **45**
Ridgetown, *Ontario* T41+425 **91**
Ridgway, *Pennsylvania* T22+414 **91**
Ridi, *Nepal* G39+280 **73**
Riding Mount Park, Man. U60+506 **88**
Ridout, *Ontario* T48+476 **91**
Riesa, *E. Germany* M10+513 **48**
Rietavas, *Lithuania* L48+557 **47**
Rieti, *Italy* M13+424 **56**
Rifle, *Colorado* V17+395 **94**
Riga, *Latvia* L35+569 **47**
Riga, G. of *Latvia* L36+577 **47**
Rigan, *Iran* J06+286 **75**
Rigmati, *Iran* J11+276 **75**
Rignasco, *Switzerland* M38+463 **45**
Rigolet, *Labrador* R80+542 **89**
Rihand Dam, *India* G43+241 **73**
Rijeka, *Yugoslavia* M04+453 **56**
Rijswijk, *Netherlands* M64+521 **44**
Rimatara, I., *Austral Is.* Y20−230 **107**
Rimini, *Italy* M15+440 **56**
Rimouski, *Quebec* S51+484 **90**
Rincon, *Cuba* T44+230 **101**
Rincon, *New Mexico* V12+326 **98**
Rindal, *Norway* M35+631 **46**
Rineanna, *Ireland, Rep.* N53+527 **43**
Ringarooma B., *Tasmania* C14−408 **109**
Ringelspitz, mt., *Switz.* M34+469 **45**
Ringkøbing, *Denmark* M40+561 **47**
Ringvassøy, I., *Norway* L66+700 **46**
Ringwood, *Victoria* C29−378 **109**
Rinihue, *Chile* S75−397 **103**
Riobamba, *Ecuador* T22−018 **104**
Rio Branco, *Brazil* R27−251 **103**
Rio Branco, *Brazil* S48−100 **104**
Rio Branco, R., *Brazil* S09+015 **104**
Rio Branco, *Uruguay* R51−325 **103**
Rio Bueno, *Chile* S78−404 **103**
Rio Chico, *Argentina* S52−498 **103**
Rio Chico, *Venezuela* S35+103 **104**
Rio Colorado, *Argentina* S25−389 **103**
Rio Conchos, *Mexico* V00+292 **94**
Rio Cuarto, *Argentina* S26−332 **103**
Rio de Janeiro, *Brazil* Q80−229 **105**
Rio de Oro, *Colombia* S80+084 **104**
Rio-de-Oro, *Morocco* N80+250 **80**
Rio Fenix, *Argentina* S66−464 **103**
Rio Florido, *Mexico* V01+265 **100**
Rio Gallegos & R., *Argent.* S56+516 **103**
Rio Grande, *Argentina* S47−538 **103**
Rio Grande, *Brazil* R43−320 **103**
Rio Grande, *Mexico, etc.* U48+300 **94**
Rio Grande City, *Texas* U53+264 **94**
Rio Grande del Norte, *Mexico-U.S.A.* V02+308 **100**
Rio Hacha, *Colombia* S77+115 **104**
Rio Hondo, *Argentina* S29−275 **103**
Rio Muerto, *Argentina* S10−262 **103**
Rio Mulato, *Bolivia* S41−196 **104**
Rio Muni, *W. Africa* M30+016 **82**
Rio Negro, *Brazil* R29−261 **103**
Rionero in Vulture, *Italy* L86+409 **57**
Rio Pardo, *Brazil* R53−203 **105**
Rio Verde, *Brazil* R35−178 **105**
Rio Verde, *Ecuador* T26+010 **104**
Rio Verde, *Mexico* U60+220 **100**
Rioz, *France* M54+475 **54**
Riozinho, *Brazil* S41−094 **104**
Ripats, *Sweden* L56+669 **46**
Ripley, *California* V59+335 **92**
Ripley, *England* N09+531 **37**
Ripley, *Mississippi* T84+347 **97**
Ripley, *New York* T28+422 **96**
Ripley, *Tennessee* T88+360 **97**
Ripley, *W. Virginia* T40+388 **91**
Ripon, *England* N09+541 **37**
Ripon, *Quebec* T01+459 **91**
Ripon, *Wisconsin* T83+439 **91**
Risafe, *Syria* K37+357 **74**
Risalpur, *Pakistan* H18+341 **72**
Risbäck, *Sweden* L59+673 **46**
Rishiri, I., *Japan* C53+452 **68**
Rishon-le-Zion, *Israel* K61+320 **76**
Risør, *Norway* M34+587 **47**
Ristijarvi, *Finland* L10+645 **46**
Risut, *Oman* J36+170 **75**
Ritchie's Arch., *Andaman Is.* F70+122 **71**

Rivadavia, *Argentina* S18–241 **103**
Rivas, *Nicaragua* T65+115 **101**
Rivera, *Argentina* S20–371 **103**
Rivera, *Uruguay* R64–310 **103**
Riverhead, *New York* S76+409 **91**
Rivero, I., *Chile* S86–456 **103**
Riversdale, *New Zealand* A67–459 **112**
Riverside, *California* V74+340 **92**
Riverside Mt., *California* V57+340 **92**
Riverton, *New Zealand* A71–463 **112**
Riverton, *S. Australia* C67–342 **109**
Riverton, *Wyoming* V20+430 **93**
Riviera di Levante, *Italy* M34+440 **54**
Riviera di Ponente, *Italy* M42+438 **54**
Rivière à Pièrre, *Quebec* S73+470 **91**
Rivière du Loup, *Quebec* S57+479 **90**
Riyadh (Ar Riyàd),
  Saudi Arabia J80+246 **74**
Riyaq, *Lebanon* K54+339 **76**
Rizaiyeh. *See* Rezà'iveh
Rize, *Turkey* K25+413 **74**
Rizokarpaso, *Cyprus* K64+356 **76**
Rizzuto C., *Italy* L77+389 **57**
Roa, *Spain* N24+417 **52**
Roanne, *France* M66+461 **54**
Roanoke, *Alabama* T62+332 **97**
Roanoke, *Virginia* T30+373 **97**
Roanoke R., *N. Carolina* T18+366 **97**
Roaringwater B.,
  Ireland, Rep. N57+515 **43**
Roatan I., *Honduras* T69+164 **101**
Robat Thana, *Pakistan* H84+298 **70**
Robbins I., *Tasmania* C30–407 **109**
Robe, *S. Australia* C62–372 **109**
Robe, Mt., *New S. Wales* C53–316 **109**
Robe R., *Ireland, Rep.* N55+536 **42**
Roberts, *Montana* V25+454 **93**
Robertsfors, *Sweden* L55+642 **46**
Robertsganj, *India* G41+247 **73**
Robertsport, *Liberia* N68+068 **80**
Robertstown, *Ireland, Rep.* N41+532 **43**
Robertstown, *S. Australia* C66–340 **109**
Roberval, *Quebec* S73+485 **90**
Robeson Ch., *Arctic Ocean* S00+820 **26**
Robinson, *Illinois* T76+390 **95**
Robinson Crusoe, I., *Chile* T25–335 **107**
Robinson's, *Newfoundland* R83+483 **90**
Robinvale, *Victoria* C43–345 **109**
Robore, *Bolivia* R87–183 **104**
Robson, Mt., *B.C.* V84+533 **88**
Robstown, *Texas* U46+278 **94**
Roca, la, *Spain* N40+391 **52**
Rocha, *Uruguay* R55–344 **103**
Rochdale, *England* N13+536 **37**
Rochefort, *Belgium* M59+502 **44**
Rochefort, *France* N06+459 **54**
Rochester, *England* M87+514 **39**
Rochester, *Michigan* T49+427 **91**
Rochester, *Minnesota* U15+441 **93**
Rochester, *New Hampshire* S66+433 **91**
Rochester, *New York* T16+432 **91**
Rochester, *Victoria* C32–364 **109**
Roche-sur-Yon, la, *France* N09+467 **54**
Rock Pt., *New Zealand* A47–409 **112**
Rock, The, *New S. Wales* C18–353 **109**
Rockall, I., *Atlantic Ocean* N82+575 **34**
Rockefeller Plateau, *Antarc.* X40–800 **27**
Rockford, *Alabama* T68+329 **97**
Rockford, *Illinois* T85+423 **91**
Rockhampton, *Queensland* B86–232 **111**
Rock Hill, *S. Carolina* T36+349 **97**
Rockingham, *N. Carolina* T29+349 **97**
Rock Island, *Illinois* U04+415 **91**
Rockland, *Maine* S55+441 **90**
Rockland, *Massachusetts* S65+421 **96**
Rockland, *Ontario* T02+455 **91**
Rockport, *Indiana* T72+379 **97**
Rockport, *Missouri* U34+404 **95**
Rock Springs, *Wyoming* V26+416 **93**
Rockstone, *Guyana* R81+058 **104**
Rockville, *Maryland* T13+391 **96**
Rockwell City, *Iowa* U28+424 **95**
Rockwood, *Tennessee* T58+358 **97**
Rocky Mts., *N. America* V30+550 **88**
Rockyford, *Colorado* U82+381 **94**
Rocky Mount, *N. Carolina* T16+360 **97**
Rockymount, *Virginia* T29+370 **97**
Rocky Mt. Nat. Park, *Colo.* V09+406 **98**
Rocroi, *France* M63+499 **54**
Rødby, *Denmark* M22+547 **47**
Rodez, *France* M75+443 **55**
Rodhopi, *Greece* L28+412 **58**
Rodhos, *Greece* L12+362 **59**
Rodhos, I., *Greece* L14+364 **59**
Rodkhan, *Pakistan* H64+261 **70**
Rodney, *Mississippi* U07+319 **97**
Rodopi Planina, *Bulg.-Greece* L36+415 **59**
Rodosto. *See* Tekirdag
Rodriguez, I., *Indian Ocean* H70–195 **77**
Roe R., *N. Ireland* N42+551 **42**
Roebourne, *W. Australia* E17–208 **110**
Roermond, *Netherlands* M54+512 **44**
Roesbrugge, *Belgium* M74+509 **44**
Roeselare, *Belgium* M71+509 **44**
Roes Welcome Sound,
  N.-W. Territories T70+650 **89**
Roeulx, *Belgium* M65+505 **44**
Rogachev, *Byelorussia* L00+531 **60**
Rogers City, *Michigan* T53+455 **91**
Rogersville, *New Brunswick* S33+468 **90**
Rogersville, *Tennessee* T48+364 **97**
Rogliano, *Corsica* M33+374 **55**
Rohri, *Pakistan* H36+276 **70**
Rohtak, *India* G80+289 **72**
Roi Et, *Thailand* F08+161 **69**
Roisin, *Belgium* M68+503 **44**
Rojas, *Argentina* S04–342 **103**
Rokishkis, *Lithuania* L25+560 **47**
Rolde, *Netherlands* M50+530 **44**
Rolla, *Missouri* U11+380 **97**
Rolle, *Switzerland* M52+465 **45**
Rolvsøya, *Norway* L36+709 **46**
Roma, *Queensland* C07–265 **111**
Roma, *Sweden* L69+575 **47**
Roma, *Italy* M15+419 **57**
Romang I., *Indonesia* D46–077 **65**
Romaine, *Quebec* S04+502 **90**
Romaine R., *Quebec* S21+514 **90**
Roman, *Romania* L19+469 **58**
Romania, *S.-E. Eur.* L24+460 **51**
Romans, *France* M60+451 **55**

Romanshorn, *Switzerland* M34+476 **45**
Romanzof, C., *Alaska* Z10+618 **99**
Rome, *Georgia* T61+342 **97**
Rome, *New York* T03+432 **91**
Rome. *See* Roma.
Romerèe, *Belgium* M62+501 **44**
Romford, *England* M89+516 **39**
Romney, *W. Virginia* T23+393 **91**
Romney Marsh, *England* M85+511 **39**
Romny, *Ukraine* K69+508 **60**
Rømø. I., *Denmark* M39+551 **47**
Romodanovo, *U.S.S.R.* J88+544 **61**
Romont, *Switzerland* M48+467 **45**
Romsdalshorn, *Norway* M43+625 **46**
Romsey, *England* N09+510 **39**
Ron, *Vietnam* E81+178 **69**
Ronda, *Kashmir* G89+355 **72**
Rondà, *Spain* N31+367 **52**
Rondeau, *Ontario* T42+423 **91**
Rondonia, state, *Brazil* S31–118 **104**
Ronge Lac la, *Sask.* V00+552 **88**
Rønne, *Bornholm, I., Den.* M01+551 **47**
Ronneby, *Sweden* L88+562 **47**
Ronne Entrance, *Antarctica* T00–720 **27**
Ronne Ice Shelf, *Antarctica* S00–770 **27**
Ronse, *Belgium* M68+507 **44**
Roosendaal, *Netherlands* M63+515 **44**
Roosevelt, I., *Antarctica* Y65–800 **27**
Roosevelt Res., *Arizona* V33+340 **98**
Rooseveltown, *New York* S88+450 **91**
Roosky, *Ireland, Rep.* N47+538 **42**
Roper, R., *N. Terr., Aust.* D00–154 **111**
Roquefort, *France* N02+440 **55**
Rora Hd., *Orkney* N21+589 **40**
Rori, *India* G89+297 **72**
Røros, *Norway* M21+626 **46**
Rorschach, *Switzerland* M33+475 **45**
Røs Vatn, *Norway* M06+658 **46**
Rosa, la, *Switzerland* M30+464 **45**
Rosa, Monte, *Switz.-Italy* M43+459 **45**
Rosablanche, mt., *Switz.* M46+461 **45**
Rosarinho, *Brazil* R85–036 **104**
Rosario, *Argentina* S04–329 **103**
Rosario, *Brazil* Q86–029 **105**
Rosario, *Chile* S60–243 **103**
Rosario, *Mexico* V03+263 **100**
Rosario, *Mexico* V64+301 **100**
Rosario, *Mexico* V05+229 **100**
Rosario de la Frontera,
  Argentina S30–258 **103**
Rosario Oeste, *Brazil* R68–148 **105**
Rosario Tala, *Argentina* R85–323 **103**
Rosas, *Spain* M71+423 **53**
Rosas, G. of, *Spain* M70+422 **53**
Roscommon, *Michigan* T58+445 **91**
Roscommon & co.,
  Ireland, Rep. N49+536 **42**
Roscrea, *Ireland, Rep.* N47+529 **43**
Rose, i., *Samoa* Z18–150 **106**
Roseau, *Minnesota* U34+488 **93**
Rosebery, *Tasmania* C27–418 **109**
Rosebud, *S. Dakota* U65+432 **93**
Roseburg, *Oregon* W20+432 **92**
Rosedale, *Mississippi* U06+338 **97**
Roseires, *Sudan* K64+118 **81**
Rosenheim, *W.Germany* M17+478 **48**
Rosetown, *Saskatchewan* V16+514 **88**
Rosetta (Rashid), *Egypt* K88+314 **81**
Rosier, C., *Quebec* S25+489 **90**
Rosignano Marittamo, *Italy* M27+433 **56**
Rosignol, *Guyana* R76+063 **104**
Roslavl, *U.S.S.R.* K73+540 **60**
Rosport, *Luxembourg* M51+498 **44**
Ross, *England* N16+519 **38**
Ross, *New Zealand* A55–429 **112**
Ross, *Tasmania* C15–420 **109**
Ross Ice Shelf, *Antarctica* Z80–810 **27**
Ross, I., *Antarctica* A70–770 **27**
Ross I., *Burma* F42+122 **71**
Ross R., *Yukon* W70+618 **88**
Ross Sea, *Antarctica* Z30–750 **27**
Rossa, *Switzerland* M34+445 **45**
Ross & Cromarty, co., *See* Highland
Rossano, *Italy* L80+396 **57**
Rosscarberry, *Ireland, Rep.* N54+516 **43**
Rosseau L., *Ontario* T28+452 **91**
Rossel I., *Papua New Guinea* B66–114 **111**
Rossignol, *Belgium* M57+497 **44**
Rossignol L., *Nova Scotia* S31+442 **90**
Rossland, *British Columbia* V78+492 **88**
Rosslare Harb, *Ireland, Rep.* N38+523 **43**
Rosslyn, *Virginia* T13+389 **96**
Rosta, *Norway* L61+690 **46**
Rosthern, *Saskatchewan* V09+529 **88**
Rostock, *E. Germany* M18+541 **48**
Rostov, *U.S.S.R.* K32+472 **61**
Rostov, *U.S.S.R.* K34+572 **60**
Roswell, *New Mexico* U87+334 **94**
Rosyth, *Scotland* N21+560 **41**
Rota, I., *Mariana Islands* C27+148 **106**
Rothenburg, *Germany* M29+494 **48**
Rotherham, *England* N08+534 **37**
Rothesay, *Scotland* N30+558 **41**
Roti, I., *Indonesia* D72–108 **65**
Roto, *New South Wales* C27–331 **109**
Rotorua, *New Zealand* A22–381 **112**
Rotterdam, *Netherlands* M63+519 **44**
Rotuma, I., *Fiji* A17–130 **106**
Roubaix, *France* M71+507 **54**
Rouen, *France* M84+495 **54**
Rôuge, *Estonia* L18+577 **47**
Roulers, *Belgium* M71+509 **44**
Round Mt., *New S. Wales* B77–304 **109**
Roundup, *Montana* V22+464 **93**
Roura, *Fr. Guiana* R44+046 **105**
Rous, Pen., *Chile* S55–555 **103**
Rousay I., *Orkney, Scotland* N18+592 **40**
Rouse's Point, *New York* S80+450 **91**
Rousseau, *S. Dakota* U61+443 **93**
Roussillon, prov., *France* M74+427 **55**
Rouveen, *Netherlands* M53+526 **44**
Rouyn, *Quebec* T25+482 **91**
Rovaniemi, *Finland* L26+665 **46**
Roveredo, *Switzerland* M35+462 **45**
Rovigo, *Italy* M19+451 **56**
Rovinari, *Romania* L41+449 **58**
Rovno, *Ukraine* L22+506 **60**
Rowena, *New South Wales* C07–298 **109**
Roxburgh, *New Zealand* A64–457 **112**
Roxburgh, *Scotland* N15+556 **41**
Roxbury, *New York* S87+423 **96**
Royal Canal, *Ireland, Rep.* N38-534 **43**

Royale, I., *Michigan* T84+480 **91**
Royan, *France* N06+456 **54**
Rozet, *Wyoming* V02+443 **93**
Rožňava. *Czechoslovakia* L57+485 **49**
Rtishchevo, *U.S.S.R.* K07+523 **61**
Ruabon, *Wales* N18+530 **37**
Ruahine Ra., *New Zealand* A24–400 **112**
Ruapehu, Mt., *New Zealand* A26–393 **112**
Rubtsovsk, *U.S.S.R.* G53+513 **62**
Ruby, *Alaska* Y30+645 **99**
Rucava, *Latvia* L53+561 **47**
Rudauli, *India* G49+267 **73**
Rudbar, *Afghanistan* H74+301 **75**
Ruddervoorde, *Belgium* M71+511 **44**
Rudkøbing. *Denmark* M26+549 **47**
Rudnaya Pristan, *U.S.S.R.* C84+442 **63**
Rudok, *Tibet* G62+334 **70**
Rudolf L., *Kenya* K54+034 **83**
Rueiba, *Sudan* L08+156 **81**
Ruel, *Ontario* T39+472 **91**
Ruffec, *France* M89+460 **54**
Rufino, *Argentina* S16–342 **103**
Rugby, *England* N08+524 **37**
Rugby, *N. Dakota* U60+484 **93**
Rugeley, *England* N12+528 **37**
Rügen, I., *E. Germany* M10+544 **48**
Rui Khaf, *Iran* H89+346 **75**
Rūjiena, *Latvia* L28+579 **47**
Ruk, *Pakistan* H38+278 **70**
Rukumkot, *Nepal* G44+286 **73**
Rukwa L., *Tanzania* K76–080 **83**
Rumania. *See* Romania.
Rum, I., *Scotland* N38+570 **40**
Rumbek, *Sudan* L02+068 **81**
Rumburk, *Czechoslovakia* M03+509 **48**
Rumegies, *France* M70+505 **44**
Rumford Falls, *Maine* S63+445 **90**
Rumigny, *France* M66+498 **44**
Rumillies, *Belgium* M69+506 **44**
Rum Jungle, *N. Terr., Aust.* D24–123 **110**
Rumoi, *Japan* C50+439 **68**
Rumuruti, *Kenya* K50+002 **83**
Runanga, *New Zealand* A52–424 **112**
Runcorn, *England* N16+533 **37**
Rungwa, *Tanzania* K68–070 **83**
Rungwe Mt., *Tanzania* K66–092 **83**
Rupar, *India* G81+309 **72**
Rupbas, *India* G75+270 **73**
Rupert, *Idaho* V54+426 **94**
Rurrenabaque, *Bolivia* S45–145 **104**
Rururtu I., *Tubuai Islands* X60–250 **107**
Rusape, *Zimbabwe* K78–186 **84**
Ruse (Ruschuk), *Bulgaria* L24+438 **58**
Ruseifa, *Jordan* K54+320 **76**
Rusele, *Sweden* L72+648 **46**
Rushworth, *Victoria* C30–366 **109**
Rusne, R., *Lithuania* L51+552 **47**
Russas, *Brazil* Q48–049 **105**
Russel, C., *N.-W. Terr.* V75+753 **88**
Russelkonda, *India* G32+200 **71**
Russell, *Kansas* U54+388 **95**
Russell, *New Zealand* A35–353 **112**
Russell Pt., *N.-W. Terr.* V62+729 **88**
Russellville, *Alabama* T76+345 **95**
Russellville, *Kentucky* T72+368 **97**
Russian Soc. Federated Soviet
  Reps. (Russia), *U.S.S.R.* **62-63**
Russkoye Ustye, *U.S.S.R.* C07+713 **63**
Russo, *Switzerland* M38+462 **45**
Rustak, *Afghanistan* H31+371 **75**
Rustburg, *Virginia* T25+372 **97**
Ruston. *Louisiana* U16+326 **95**
Rutba, *Iraq* K29+329 **74**
Rutherfordton, *N. Carolina* T42+353 **97**
Ruthi, *Switzerland* M33+473 **45**
Ruthin, *Wales* N20+531 **38**
Rutland, *Vermont* S78+436 **91**
Rutland, co., *See* Leicester & co.
Rutland I., *Andaman Is.* F74+114 **71**
Ruurlo, *Netherlands* M51+521 **44**
Ruvuma R., *Mozambique* K30–108 **83**
Ruwenzori, Mts., *Uganda* L00+004 **83**
Ružomberok, *Czechoslovakia* L64+491 **49**
Rwanda, *Central Africa* L00-025 **83**
Ryan, L., *Scotland* N30+550 **41**
Ryazan, *U.S.S.R.* K32+546 **60**
Ryazhsk, *U.S.S.R.* K30+537 **60**
Rybachiy, Pol., *U.S.S.R.* K75+694 **62**
Rybinsk, *U.S.S.R.* K37+580 **60**
Rybinskoye Res., *U.S.S.R.* K40+586 **60**
Rybnoe, *U.S.S.R.* E85+729 **63**
Ryde, *I. of W., England* N07+507 **39**
Rye, *England* M86+510 **39**
Rye Patch Res., *Nevada* V80+406 **92**
Rylstone, *New South Wales* C00-328 **109**
Rymarov, *Czechoslovakia* L77+499 **49**
Rypin, *Poland* L64+531 **49**
Ryukyu Retto, *Japan* D50+250 **64**
Rzeszów, *Poland* L48+501 **49**
Rzhev, *U.S.S.R.* K64+563 **60**
Saalfeld, *E. Germany* M22+506 **48**
Saanen, *Switzerland* M46+465 **45**
Saarbrücken, *W. Germany* M48+492 **48**
Saaremaa, I., *Estonia* L44+584 **47**
Saariselkä, *Finland* L12+682 **46**
Saarland, *W. Germany* M46+493 **48**
Saarlouis, *W. Germany* M50+493 **48**
Saas Grund, *Switzerland* M42+461 **45**
Saavedra, *Argentina* S15-378 **103**
Saavedra, *Chile* S80-387 **99**
Saba, *(N. Borneo), Borneo* **65**
Sabac, *Yugoslavia* L62+448 **58**
Sabah (N. Borneo), *Borneo* **65**
Sabalgarh, *India* G78+262 **70**
Sabana, Arch. de, *Cuba* T30+232 **101**
Sabanalarga, *Colombia* T00+106 **104**
Sabancuy, *Mexico* U06+190 **100**
Sab Biyar, *Syria* K44+338 **76**
Sabile, *Latvia* L44+570 **47**
Sabiñanigo, *Spain* N03+425 **53**
Sabine and L., *Texas* U23+296 **95**
Sabine R., *Texas* U23+296 **95**
Sabine Mt., *Antarctica* A65–720 **27**
Sable, *France* N02+478 **54**
Sable, C., *Florida* T37+252 **99**
Sable, C., *Nova Scotia* S33+435 **90**
Sable I., *Nova Scotia* S08+437 **90**
Sables d'Olonne, les, *France* N10+465 **54**
Sabrina Coast, *Antarctica* E45–660 **27**
Sabzawar (Shindand), *Afghan.* H77+334 **75**
Sabzawar, *Iran* J14+362 **75**

Sacandaga Res. & R.,
  New York S85+431 **96**
Sac City, *Iowa* U30+424 **95**
Sacedon, *Spain* N17+405 **53**
Sachigo R., *Ontario* U05+546 **89**
Sachsen-Anhalt, *W. Germany* M22+520 **48**
Sackets Harbor, *New York* T07+439 **91**
Sackville, *New Brunswick* S26+459 **90**
Saco, *Maine* S63+435 **90**
Saco, *Montana* V14+485 **93**
Sacramento, *Brazil* R14–199 **105**
Sacramento, *California* W09+385 **92**
Sacramento Mts., *New Mex.* V03+332 **94**
Sacramento R., *California* W12+392 **92**
Sada, *Yemen* K07+169 **74**
Sádaba, *Spain* N07+423 **53**
Sadabad, *India* G72+274 **73**
Sada Bandeira, *Angola* M08–148 **82**
Sadad, *Syria* K48+343 **76**
Saddleback Mt., *Maine* S63+449 **90**
Sadhaura, *India* G77+304 **72**
Sadij. *Iran* J07+257 **75**
Sadiya, *India* F56+278 **71**
Sa'diya, Jebel, *Saudi Arabia* K29+207 **74**
Sadmarda, *Afghanistan* H47+356 **75**
Sado, I., *Japan* C70+380 **68**
Sadra, *India* H13+233 **70**
Saduan, *Saudi Arabia* K11+192 **74**
Saeki, *Japan* D19+330 **68**
Safad, (Zefat), *Israel* K57+330 **76**
Safed Koh Ra., *Afghan.-Pak.* H26+340 **72**
Saffuriya, *Israel* K58+327 **76**
Safi, *Morocco* N56+320 **80**
Safidabeh, *Iran* H87+308 **75**
Safif, *Saudi Arabia* J53+214 **75**
Safita, *Syria* K53+348 **76**
Safranbolu, *Turkey* K73+412 **74**
Saga, *Japan* D28+332 **68**
Sagaing, *Burma* F54+218 **71**
Sagami B., *Japan* C64+352 **68**
Sagar, *India* G67+238 **73**
Sagar I., *India* G10+217 **73**
Sagata, *Ethiopia* K60+058 **83**
Sagauli, *India* G31+267 **73**
Sage Plains, *Oregon* W06+437 **92**
Saginaw, *Michigan* T54+435 **91**
Saginaw B., *Michigan* T52+440 **91**
Sagone, G. de, *Corsica* M39+421 **56**
Sagres, *Portugal* N53+370 **52**
Sagua la Grande, *Cuba* T30+228 **101**
Saguenay R., *Quebec* S64+483 **90**
Sagunto, *Spain* N01+397 **53**
Saham, *Oman* J19+242 **75**
Sahambavany. *Madagascar* J60-142 **83**
Sahand, mt., *Iran* J82+376 **74**
Sahara Desert. *Africa* **80-81**
Saharanpur, *India* G74+297 **72**
Saharien Atlas Mts., *Algeria* M80+334 **80**
Sahaswan, *India* G67+281 **73**
Sahiadriparvat Ra., *India* G85+206 **70**
Sahibganj, *India* G14+252 **73**
Sahiwal, *Pakistan* H11+307 **72**
Sahuajo, *Mexico* U76+200 **100**
Sahuaripa, *Mexico* V24+288 **100**
Sahugun, *Spain* N30+423 **52**
Sahun, *Yemen, South* J72+141 **74**
Sahy, *Czechoslovakia* L66+481 **49**
Sahyadri Mts., *India* H03+150 **70**
Saibai, I., *Papua New Guinea* C44-095 **111**
Saida. *See* Sidon
Saidabad, *Iran* J26+295 **75**
Saidapet, *India* G58+130 **70**
Said Bundas, *Sudan* L32+084 **81**
Saidpur, *India* G41+256 **73**
Saidu, *Pakistan* H16+348 **70**
Saignelégier, *Switzerland* M48+473 **45**
Saigon, *Vietnam* E80+108 **69**
Saihut. *Yemen. South* J53+153 **75**
Sailana, *India* H00+235 **70**
Saimaa Kanal, *Fin.-U.S.S.R.* L10+610 **47**
Saimaa, L., *Finland* L12+613 **47**
St Abb's Hd., *Scotland* N13+559 **41**
St Affrique, *France* M73+440 **55**
St Agatha, *Maine* S50+472 **90**
St Agreve, *France* M64+450 **55**
St Albans, *England* N02+517 **39**
St Albans, *Vermont* S79+448 **91**
St Amour, *France* M58+464 **54**
St Andre, *Quebec* S58+477 **90**
St André C., *Madagascar* K04-164 **83**
St Andrews, *New Brunswick* S42+451 **90**
St Andrews, *New Zealand* A53-445 **112**
St Andrews, *Scotland* N17+563 **41**
Ste Anne, *Quebec* S60+474 **90**
Ste Anne de Beaupré, *Quebec* S66+470 **91**
Ste Anne de la Pérage, *Que.* S73+466 **91**
Ste Anne des Monts, *Quebec* S39+491 **90**
St Anns Bay, *Jamaica* T13+185 **101**
St Anthonis, *Netherlands* M55+516 **44**
St Anthony, *Idaho* V41+440 **98**
St Antönien, *Switzerland* M31+470 **45**
St Arnaud, *Victoria* C41-367 **109**
St Asaph, *Wales* N21+532 **38**
St Augustin, C. de,
  Madagascar K10-238 **83**
St Augustine, *Florida* T38+299 **97**
St Austell & B., *England* N29+503 **38**
Ste Barbara, *Venezuela* S22+096 **104**
St Barthélemy, I. *Leeward Is.* S17+179 **101**
St Béat, *France* M86+429 **55**
St Bečej, *Yugoslavia* L60+456 **58**
St Bernard Pass, Gd.,
  Switzerland-Italy M46+457 **56**
St Boniface, *Manitoba* U40+500 **88**
St Bride's B., *Wales* N32+518 **38**
St Brieuc, *France* N17+485 **54**
St Calais, *France* M86+480 **54**
St Catherines, *Ontario* T25+432 **91**
Ste Cécile. *Quebec* S66+457 **91**
St Chamond. *France* M63+455 **54**
St Charles, *Michigan* T55+433 **91**
St Charles, C., *Labrador* R64+524 **89**
St Chély d'Apcher, *France* M70+448 **55**
St Christopher, I. (St Kitts),
  Leeward Islands S16+153 **101**
St Clair, *Michigan* T45+429 **91**
St Clair, L., *Mich.-Ont.* T46+425 **91**
St Clair L., *Tasmania* C23-421 **109**
St Cloud, *Minnesota* U25+456 **93**
St Croix, *Switzerland* M51+468 **45**
St Croix, R., *Wisconsin* U16+457 **99**

St Davids & Hd., *Wales* N32+519 **38**
St Denis, *France* M76+489 **54**
St di Nova Siri, *Italy* L80+402 **57**
St Dizier, *France* M60+486 **54**
St Elias Mt., *Alaska* X40+604 **99**
St Elias Ra., *Yukon* X30+602 **88**
Saintes, *France* N04+457 **54**
St Étienne, *France* M64+454 **54**
St Eustatius, I., *Leeward Is.* S17+175 **101**
St Fabien, *Quebec* S53+483 **90**
St Fargeau, *France* M72+477 **54**
St Felicien, *Quebec* S74+486 **90**
Saintfield, *N. Ireland* N35+545 **42**
St Filipsland, *Netherlands* M65+516 **44**
St Fillans, *Scotland* N25+564 **41**
St Finans B., *Ireland, Rep.* N58+518 **43**
St Florent & G. de, *Corsica* M35+428 **56**
St Florentin, *France* M68+480 **54**
St Flour, *France* M72+450 **55**
St Francis, *Maine* S54+472 **90**
St Francis B., *Namibia* M02-252 **84**
St Francis, L., *Quebec* S67+459 **91**
St Francis, L., *Quebec* S86+452 **91**
St Francis R., *Arkansas* U03+358 **97**
St Francis R., *Quebec* S64+459 **91**
St Fulgent, *France* N07+469 **54**
St Gabriel de Brandon, *Que.* S80+463 **91**
St Gallen & canton, *Switz.* M34+464 **45**
St Gaudens, *France* M86+431 **55**
St Gédéon, *Quebec* S70+485 **90**
St George, *New Brunswick* S41+452 **90**
St George Hd., *N.S.W.* B86-352 **109**
St George I., *Bering Sea* Z29+564 **99**
St Georges, *Fr. Guiana* R41+037 **105**
St George's B., *Nfd.* R86+483 **90**
St George's Chan., *Ire.-Wales* N34+520 **38**
St Georges de Beauce, *Que.* S64+461 **90**
St Gérard, *Belgium* M62+502 **44**
St Germain, *France* M77+488 **54**
St German, *Puerto Rico* S42+181 **101**
St Gheorghe I., *Romania* L03+450 **58**
St Ghislain, *Belgium* M67+504 **44**
St Gilgen, *Austria* M10+477 **48**
St Gilles, *France* M64+437 **55**
St Gillis, *Belgium* M65+510 **44**
St Gillis-Waas, *Belgium* M65+512 **44**
St Gingolph, *Switzerland* M49+464 **45**
St Girons, *France* M83+430 **55**
St Gotthard, pass, *Switz.* M38+466 **45**
St Guenolé, *France* N26+478 **54**
St Helena, *Atlantic Ocean* N36-158 **85**
St Helena B., *Cape Province* L72-328 **84**
St Helens, *England* N17+535 **37**
St Helens, Mt., *Washington* W12+461 **92**
St Hilaire, *New Brunswick* S51+473 **90**
St Hubert, *Belgium* M58+500 **44**
St Hyacinthe, *Quebec* S78+457 **91**
St Ignace, *Michigan* T59+459 **91**
St Imier, *Switzerland* M48+472 **45**
St Irénée. *Quebec* S63+473 **91**
St Ives, *England* N01+524 **37**
St Ives & B., *England* N33+502 **38**
St Jacques, *New Brunswick* S51+475 **90**
St James, *Minnesota* U28+440 **93**
St James, C., *B.C.* W67+518 **88**
St Jan, *Belgium* M73+509 **44**
St Jean, *France* M52+453 **54**
St Jean. *Quebec* S79+453 **91**
St Jean d'Angély, *France* N03+459 **54**
St Jean de Luz, *France* N10+434 **55**
St Jérôme. *Quebec* S84+458 **91**
St Joachim, *Quebec* S65+471 **91**
St John, *New Brunswick* S36+453 **90**
St John, West, *N.B.* S37+452 **90**
St John B., *Newfoundland* R76+509 **90**
St John, L., *Quebec* S72+486 **90**
St John, Mt., *Quebec* S22+504 **90**
St Johns, *Arizona* V27+345 **94**
St John's, Michigan* T57+430 **91**
St Johns, *Newfoundland* R46+475 **90**
St John's Pt., *Ireland, Rep.* N51+546 **42**
St John's Pt., *N. Ireland* N34+542 **42**
St Johns R., *Florida* T39+300 **97**
St Johnsbury, *Vermont* S72+445 **91**
St Joseph, *Louisiana* U07+319 **97**
St Joseph, *Michigan* T68+422 **91**
St Joseph, *Missouri* U30+398 **95**
St Joseph, *Quebec* S65+463 **90**
St Joseph I., *Ontario* T54+462 **91**
St Joseph I., *Texas* V42+280 **94**
St Joseph L., *Ontario* U02+510 **89**
Ste Justine, *Quebec* S62+464 **91**
St Kilda, Is., *Scotland* N51+578 **40**
St Kitts, I., *West Indies* S16+173 **101**
St Laurent, *Fr. Guiana* R55+054 **105**
St Lawrence, *Queensland* C03-222 **111**
St Lawrence, G. of, *Canada* S12+486 **90**
St Lawrence I., *Alaska* Z30+632 **99**
St Lawrence, R., *Quebec* S62+474 **89**
St Lawrence Seaway,
  N. America T01+448 **91**
St Leger, *Belgium* M56+496 **44**
St Léonard, *France* M81+458 **54**
St Leonard, *New Brunswick* S47+472 **90**
St Leonards, *England* M87+509 **39**
St Lewis, C., *Labrador* R64+528 **89**
St Lin, *Quebec* S83+458 **91**
St Lô, *France* N06+491 **54**
St Louis, *Mauritania* P10+160 **80**
St Louis, *Michigan* T58+434 **91**
St Louis, *Missouri* U02+386 **97**
St Louis, L., *Quebec* S83+454 **91**
St Louis de Kent, *N.B.* S30+467 **90**
St Lucia C., *Natal* K74-284 **84**
St Lucia, I., *Windward Is.* S05+140 **101**
St Lucia L., *Natal* K76-280 **84**
St Luke's I.. *Burma* F41+102 **71**
St Maartensdijk, *Netherlands* M66+515 **44**
St Magnus B., *Scotland* N09+604 **40**
St Maixent, *France* N01+464 **54**
St Malo & Gulf, *France* N12+487 **54**
St Marc, *Haiti* S76+192 **101**
St Mard, *Belgium* M57+496 **44**
Ste Marie C., *Madagascar* J88-256 **83**
Ste Marie I., *Madagascar* J60-170 **83**
St Marks, *Florida* T55+302 **97**
St Martin, I., *Leeward Is.* S18+181 **101**
St Martins, *New Brunswick* S33+454 **90**
St Mary B., *Nova Scotia* S37+442 **90**
St Mary Is., *India* H03+135 **70**

St Mary's, *Ontario* T37+433 **91**
St Marys, *Pennsylvania* T22+414 **96**
St Marys, *Tasmania* C11-416 **109**
St Mary's B., *Newfoundland* R53+467 **90**
St Mary's L., *Scotland* N19+555 **41**
St Mary's Pk., *S. Australia* C65-315 **111**
St Matthew I.. *Alaska* Z45+603 **99**
St Matthew's I., *Burma* F41+100 **71**
St Maurice, *Switzerland* M48+462 **45**
St Maurice R., *Quebec* S77+475 **91**
St Mazimin, *France* M55+435 **55**
St Meen, *France* N13+482 **54**
St Michael, *Alaska* Y70+631 **99**
St Michaels, *Maryland* T05+389 **91**
St Moritz, *Switzerland* M31+465 **45**
St Nazaire, *France* N15+473 **54**
St Neots, *England* N02+522 **37**
St Nicolaasga, *Netherlands* M56+529 **44**
St Nicolas. *See* St Niklaas
St Niklaas, *Belgium* M65+512 **44**
St Niklau, *Switzerland* M43+462 **45**
St Odilienberg, *Netherlands* M54+512 **44**
St Omer, *France* M77+508 **54**
Saintonge, prov.. *France* N02+454 **54**
St Paul, *Minnesota* U19+450 **93**
St Paul I., *Bering Sea* Z32+570 **99**
St Paul, I., *Indian Ocean* G76-386 **77**
St Paul de Fenouillet, *France* M75+428 **55**
St Peter, *Minnesota* U24+443 **93**
St Peter, *Prince Edward I.* S15+464 **90**
St Peter, L., *Quebec* S78+461 **91**
St Petersburg, *Florida* T46+278 **97**
St Petersburg, *Pennsylvania* T28+412 **96**
St Pierre. *Martinique, W.I.* S06+147 **101**
St Pierre. I., *Quebec* S64+469 **91**
St Pierre. I., *Atlantic Ocean* R67+468 **90**
St Pol, *France* M76+504 **54**
St Polten, *Austria* L87+482 **49**
St Pons, *France* M73+435 **55**
St Pourçain, *France* M70+463 **54**
St Quentin, *France* M70+499 **54**
St Raymond, *Quebec* S71+469 **91**
St Rémi d'Amherst. *Quebec* S89+461 **91**
St Roch, *Quebec* S61+473 **90**
St Sébastien C., *Madagascar* J68-124 **83**
St Sernin-sur-Rance, *France* M75+439 **55**
St Servan, *France* N12+486 **54**
St Sever, *France* N03+438 **55**
St Simeon, *Quebec* S59+478 **91**
St Simon, *Quebec* S54+482 **90**
St Stephen, *New Brunswick* S44+452 **90**
St Thecle, *Quebec* S75+469 **91**
Ste Thérèse, L.. *N.-W. Terr.* W07+646 **88**
St Thomas, *Ontario* T37+428 **91**
St Thomas, I., *Virgin Is.* S30+184 **101**
St Tronde. *See* St Truiden
St Tropez, *France* M50+433 **55**
St Truiden, *Belgium* M59+508 **44**
St Valery, *France* M80+502 **54**
St Valery-en-Caux, *France* M86+499 **54**
St Veit, *Austria* M04+468 **48**
St Vincent, *Windward Is.* S07+132 **101**
St Vincent C., *Madagascar* K10-220 **83**
St Vincent, G., *S. Australia* C72-346 **109**
St Vith, *Belgium* M53+503 **44**
St Xavier, *Montana* V16+454 **93**
Saipan, I., *Mariana Is.* C25+152 **106**
Saiping, *China* E36+326 **64**
Saiun, *Yemen, South* J66 + 160 **74**
Saivomuotka, *Sweden* L41+681 **46**
Saiyidwala, *Pakistan* H09+311 **72**
Saka Dzong, *Tibet* G28+295 **71**
Sakai, *Japan* C87+346 **68**
Sakaka, *Saudi Arabia* K29+299 **74**
Sakakawea, L., *N. Dakota* U74+476 **93**
Sakania, *Zaire* L08-128 **83**
Sakaria, R., *Turkey* K86+400 **74**
Sakata, *Japan* C61+389 **68**
Sakesar, *Pakistan* H17+324 **72**
Sakha, *Saudi Arabia* K08+232 **74**
Sakhalin, *U.S.S.R.* C40+510 **63**
Sakhalinskiy Zaliv, *U.S.S.R.* C55+539 **63**
Saki, *U.S.S.R.* K68+451 **60**
Šakiai, *Lithuania* L42+549 **47**
Sakishima Gunto, *Japan* D66+244 **68**
Sakr, *Yemen, D.R.* J48+156 **75**
Sakti, *India* G42+220 **73**
Säkylä, *Finland* L46+610 **47**
Sala. *Czechoslovakia* L73+482 **49**
Sala, *Sweden* L80+599 **47**
Salatsgriva, *Latvia* L34+578 **47**
Salada, L., *Mexico* V63+322 **100**
Salado, R., *Argentina* S14-292 **103**
Salado, R., *Texas* U58+270 **94**
Salaga, *Ghana* N04+086 **80**
Salahiye, *Syria* K26+348 **74**
Salala, *Oman* J35+171 **75**
Salama, *Guatemala* U02+151 **100**
Salamanca, *Mexico* U67+206 **100**
Salamanca, *New York* T22+422 **91**
Salamanca, *Spain* N34+409 **52**
Salamaua, *Papua New Guinea* C18-072 **111**
Salamina, *Colombia* T03+054 **104**
Salamis & I.. *Greece* L39+379 **59**
Salangen, *Norway* L74+690 **46**
Salas, *Spain* N38+434 **52**
Salas de los Infantes, *Spain* N19+420 **52**
Salaverry, *Peru* T24-083 **104**
Sala-y-Gomez I., *Pacific Oc.* V00-258 **107**
Salbris, *France* M78+474 **54**
Saldana, *Spain* N29+425 **52**
Saldus, *Latvia* L45+567 **47**
Sale, *Victoria* C18-381 **109**
Salekhard, *U.S.S.R.* H51+664 **62**
Salem, *Illinois* T84+386 **95**
Salem, *India* G71+118 **70**
Salem, *Massachusetts* S65+425 **91**
Salem, *Missouri* U10+376 **97**
Salem, *New Jersey* T03+396 **91**
Salem, *Oregon* W18+449 **92**
Salem, *Virginia* T31+373 **97**
Salemi, *Sicily* M13+378 **57**
Sälen, *Sweden* M11+612 **47**
Salerno, *Italy* M02+407 **57**
Salerno, G. di, *Italy* M02+405 **57**
Salford, *England* N14+535 **37**
Salida, *Colorado* U66+384 **94**
Salina, *Kansas* U46+388 **95**
Salina, *Malawi* K64-136 **83**
Salina, *Utah* V41+390 **94**
Salina, I., *Italy* M01+386 **57**

Salina Cruz, *Mexico* U32+162 **100**
Salinas, *California* W10+366 **92**
Salinas, *Ecuador* T35-022 **104**
Salinas, *Mexico* U70+226 **100**
Salinas, *Mexico* U61+259 **100**
Salinas Pk., *New Mexico* V09+334 **94**
Salinas R., *California* W09+364 **92**
Saline R.. *Kansas* U58+391 **98**
Salinitas, *Chile* S60-250 **103**
Salinópolis. *Brazil* R15-007 **105**
Salisbury, *England* N11+511 **39**
Salisbury, *Maryland* T03+385 **99**
Salisbury, *New Brunswick* S30+460 **90**
Salisbury, *N. Carolina* T33+356 **97**
Salisbury, *Zimbabwe* K84-178 **84**
Salisbury, *S. Australia* C68-348 **109**
Salisbury I., *N.-W. Terr.* T12+639 **89**
Salisbury L., *Uganda* K66+016 **83**
Salisbury Plain, *England* N11+512 **39**
Salkhad, *Syria* K50+325 **76**
Salyan, *Nepal* G47+284 **73**
Salmon R., *Idaho* V62+452 **92**
Salmon River Mts., *Idaho* V58+444 **92**
Salo, *Finland* L41+604 **47**
Salon, *France* M60+436 **55**
Salon, *India* G51+260 **73**
Salonica. *See* Thessaloniki
Salonta, *Romania* L50+469 **58**
Salop, co., *England* N16+544 **37**
Salqin, *Syria* K51+361 **76**
Salsette I., *India* H13+192 **70**
Salt Fd., *Norway* M06+672 **46**
Salt L., *Utah* V46+392 **94**
Salt L., *W. Australia* E37-240 **110**
Salt Ls., *W. Australia* D40-290 **110**
Salt Ra., *Pakistan* H18+326 **70**
Salt R., *Arizona* V34+338 **94**
Salta, *Argentina* S33+248 **103**
Saltash, *England* N25+504 **38**
Saltcoats, *Scotland* N29+556 **41**
Saltdal, *Norway* L87+671 **46**
Saltee, Is., *Ireland, Rep.* N40+521 **43**
Saltillo, *Mexico* U65+255 **100**
Salt Lake City, *Utah* V42+408 **94**
Salto, *Argentina* S02-343 **103**
Salto, *Uruguay* R78-314 **103**
Salto Grande, *Brazil* Q60-160 **105**
Salton Sea, *California* V66+334 **92**
Salt Plains Res., *Oklahoma* U50+368 **95**
Saltrou, *Haiti* S71+183 **101**
Salt Sulphur Springs, *W.Va.* T34+376 **97**
Saltville, *Virginia* T41+369 **97**
Saluda, *Virginia* T09+377 **97**
Salûm & G. of, *Egypt* L30+316 **81**
Salur, *India* G40+186 **71**
Salut, Is. du, *Fr. Guiana* R46+054 **105**
Saluzzo, *Italy* M45+446 **56**
Salvador (Bahia), *Brazil* Q51-130 **105**
Salvador, L., *Louisiana* U01+296 **95**
Salvador, El, rep., *Cent Amer.* T84+136 **101**
Salvaterra, *Portugal* N53+390 **52**
Salvatierra, *Mexico* U65+202 **100**
Salzburg, *Austria* M12+478 **48**
Salzwedel, *E. Germany* M23+528 **48**
Samahala, *Botswana* L38-196 **84**
Samalut, *Egypt* K86+282 **81**
Samana & B., *Dom. Rep.* S56+192 **101**
Samar, I., *Philippines* D60+117 **65**
Samarai, *Papua New Guinea* B87-107 **111**
Samarinda, *Borneo* E17-006 **65**
Samarkand, *Uzbek.* H48+395 **62**
Samarra Balad, *Iraq* K06+342 **74**
Samastipur, *India* G25+259 **73**
Samawa, *Iraq* J89+312 **74**
Sambalpur, *India* G35+214 **71**
Sambeek, *Netherlands* M54+516 **44**
Sambhal, *India* G69+285 **73**
Sambhar, *India* G88+268 **70**
Sambor, *Ukraine* L40+496 **60**
Samborombón, B., *Argent.* R70-359 **103**
Sambre, R., *Belgium* M64+504 **44**
Same, *Japan* C51+405 **68**
Samedan, *Switzerland* M31+465 **45**
Sami, *Pakistan* H70+260 **70**
Samira, *Saudi Arabia* K17+264 **74**
Sam Ka, *Burma* F48+202 **71**
Sam-nua, *Laos* F05+204 **69**
Samoa Is., *Pacific Ocean* Z40-150 **106**
Samokov, *Bulgaria* L39+423 **58**
Samorogan, *Upper Volta* N30+114 **80**
Samos, I., *Greece* L19+337 **59**
Samothrace. *See* Samothraki I.
Samothráki I., *Greece* L27+405 **59**
Sampacho, *Argentina* S28-334 **103**
Sampit, *Borneo* E41-028 **65**
Samrée, *Belgium* M56+502 **44**
Samsat, *Turkey* K39+376 **74**
Samshui, *China* E42+232 **67**
Samsø I., *Denmark* M26+558 **47**
Samsu, *Korea* D42+413 **64**
Samsun, *Turkey* K52+414 **74**
Samthar, *India* G67+258 **73**
Samuie Str., *Thailand* F30+092 **69**
San, *Mali* N28+130 **80**
San'a, *Yemen* K05+154 **74**
Sanam, Jebel, *Iraq* J75+301 **74**
Sanandaj, *Iran* J77+354 **74**
San Andres Mts., *New Mex.* V08+330 **94**
San Angelo, *Texas* U61+313 **98**
San Antioco, I., *Sardinia* M40+390 **57**
San Antonio, *Chile* S56-233 **103**
San Antonio, *Mexico* V08+330 **100**
San Antonio, *Texas* U51+294 **95**
San Antonio, C.. *Argentina* R70-366 **103**
San Antonio, C., *Cuba* T59+218 **101**
San Antonio Pk., *New Mex.* V06+368 **94**
San Antonio R. & B., *Texas* U44+286 **94**
San Antonio Oeste, *Argent.* S30-408 **103**
San Bartolomeu de Nessines,
  Portugal N50+372 **52**
San Benedetto del Tronto, *It.* M07+430 **56**
San Benito, *Mexico* U14+147 **100**
San Benito, *Texas* U46+261 **94**
San Benito Is., *Mexico* V64+282 **100**
San Bernardino, *California* V74+341 **92**
San Bernardino Ra., *Cal.* V66+340 **92**
San Blas, *Argentina* S14-405 **103**
San Blas, *Mexico* V02+215 **100**

San Blas, *Mexico* V22+262 **100**
San Blas, C., *Florida* T62+297 **99**
San Blas, G. de, *Panama* T23+096 **101**
San Borja, *Mexico* V52+288 **100**
Sanborn, *N. Dakota* U49+469 **93**
San Carlos, *Argentina* S35-260 **103**
San Carlos, *Argentina* S55-337 **103**
San Carlos, *Argentina* S31-312 **103**
San Carlos, *Chile* S71-363 **103**
San Carlos, *Mexico* U53+244 **100**
San Carlos, *Nicaragua* T58+111 **101**
San Carlos,
  Amazonas, Venez. S42+019 **104**
San Carlos, *Cojedes, Venez.* S52+097 **104**
San Carlos, L. *Arizona* V32+332 **94**
San Carlos de Bariloche,
  Argentina S68-411 **103**
San Carlos del Zulia, *Venz.* S70+090 **104**
Sanchez, *Dominican Rep.* S58+192 **101**
San Clemente, *Spain* N15+394 **53**
San Cosme, *Paraguay* R68-272 **103**
San Cristobal, *Argentina* S07-303 **103**
San Cristobal, *Mexico* U15+168 **100**
San Cristobal, *Venezuela* S73+078 **104**
San Cristobal I., *Galapagos Is.* U00-007 **107**
San Cristobal, I., *Solomon Is.* B20-110 **106**
Sancti Spiritus, *Cuba* T27+218 **101**
Sand, *Norway* M52+595. **47**
Sandakan, *Sabah* E11+059 **65**
Sanday I. & Sd., *Orkney, Scot.* N15+592 **40**
Sandbach, *England* N14+532 **37**
Sandefjord, *Norway* M29+591 **47**
Sandefjord B., *Antarctica* G80-700 **27**
Sanders, *Arizona* V26+352 **94**
Sandgate, *England* M83+511 **39**
Sandgate, *Queensland* B72-272 **111**
Sandhornøy, *Norway* M06+671 **46**
Sandia, *Peru* S57-143 **104**
San Diego, *California* V73+327 **92**
San Diego, *Texas* U50+277 **94**
San Diego, C., *Argentina* S31-547 **99**
San Diego de Cabrutica,
  Venezuela S28+084 **104**
Sandikli, *Turkey* K88+384 **74**
Sandila, *India* G56+259 **73**
San Dimas, *Mexico* V04+241 **100**
Sandnes, *Norway* M56+589 **47**
Sandoa, *Zaire* L44-098 **82**
San Domingos, *Portugal* N45+377 **52**
Sandoway, *Burma* F63+185 **71**
Sandown, *I. of Wight, Eng.* N07+507 **39**
Sandpoint, *Idaho* V70+480 **98**
Sandringham, *England* M87+528 **39**
Sandstone, *Minnesota* U17+461 **93**
Sandstone, *W. Australia* E05-279 **110**
Sandträsk, *Sweden* L52+661 **46**
Sandusky, *Michigan* T47+434 **91**
Sandusky, *Ohio* T46+414 **91**
Sandvig, *Bornholm, I., Den.* M01+553 **47**
Sandwich, *England* M82+513 **39**
Sandwich, *Ontario* T48+423 **91**
Sandy C., *Queensland* B70-246 **111**
Sandy L., *Manitoba* U68+598 **88**
Sandy L., *Ontario* U18+531 **89**
San Esteban de Formaz,
  Spain N19+415 **52**
San Felipe, *Chile* S65-327 **103**
San Felipe, *Guatemala* U10+146 **100**
San Felipe, *Mexico* U01+179 **100**
San Felipe, *Mexico* U67+215 **100**
San Felipe, *Venezuela* S52+104 **104**
San Feliu de Guixals, *Spain* M72+418 **53**
San Feliu de Llobregat, *Sp.* M78+414 **53**
San Félix, *Venezuela* S16+083 **104**
San Felix I., *Pacific Ocean* U05-250 **107**
San Fernando, *Chile* S66-344 **103**
San Fernando, *Mexico* U49+248 **100**
San Fernando, *Mexico* V63+300 **100**
San Fernando, *Philippines* D88+166 **65**
San Fernando, *Trinidad* S08+103 **104**
San Fernando de Apure,
  Venezuela S45+077 **104**
San Fernando de Atabapo,
  Venezuela S47+040 **104**
Sanford, *Florida* T38+288 **97**
Sanford, *Maine* S65+435 **90**
Sanford, *N. Carolina* T25+355 **97**
Sanford, Mt., *Alaska* X60+620 **99**
San Francisco, *Argentina* S13-314 **103**
San Francisco, *California* W15+378 **92**
San Francisco Mts., *Arizona* V42+354 **94**
San Francisco Pk., *Arizona* V40+355 **98**
Sanga, *Angola* L88-114 **82**
Sangareddipet, *India* G71+176 **70**
Sanger, *N. Dakota* U66+472 **93**
Sanggau, *Borneo* E56+002 **65**
Sangihe Kep., *Indonesia* D58+027 **65**
San Giovanni in Fiore, *Italy* L80+393 **57**
Sangkulirang, *Borneo* E12+010 **65**
Sangla Hill, *Pakistan* H09+316 **72**
Sangre de Cristo Mts., *Colo.-
  New Mexico* V01+370 **94**
Sangre Grande Town,
  Trinidad S06+106 **104**
Sangrur, *India* G85+302 **72**
Sangwin, *Liberia* N56+054 **80**
San Ignacio, *Bolivia* S33-150 **104**
San Ignacio, *Bolivia* S05-162 **104**
San Ignacio, *Mexico* V07+241 **100**
San Ignacio, *Mexico* V48+271 **100**
San Ignacio, *Paraguay* R72-269 **103**
Sanish, *N. Dakota* U75+480 **93**
San Javier, *Argentina* S00-305 **103**
San Javier, *Chile* S70-356 **103**
São João, *Portugal* N44+412 **52**
San Joaquin, *Bolivia* S29-132 **104**
San Jorge, G. de, *Argentina* S40-460 **103**
San Jorge, *Bolivia* S04-176 **104**
San José, *California* W12+373 **92**
San José, *Colombia* S71+025 **104**
San José, *Costa Rica* T54+099 **101**
San José, *Guatemala* U05+139 **100**
San José, *Uruguay* R70-342 **103**
San José, G., *Argentina* S26-422 **103**
San José, I., *Mexico* V34+250 **100**
San José Carpizo, *Mexico* U03+194 **100**
San José de Amacuro, *Venez.* S03+085 **104**
San José de Feliciano, *Argent.* R83-303 **103**
San José del Cabo, *Mexico* V28+230 **100**
San José da Ocune, *Colombia* S61+041 **104**
San Juan, *Bolivia* R88-177 **104**
San Juan, *Puerto Rico* S36+185 **101**

San Juan, *Venezuela* S50+111 **104**
San Juan & R., *Argentina* S51–316 **103**
San Juan, C., *Argentina* S22–548 **103**
San Juan Mts., *Colorado* V12+374 **94**
San Juan, R., *Mexico* U32+181 **100**
San Juan, R., *Nicaragua* T54+108 **101**
San Juan R., *Utah, etc.* V30+372 **94**
San Juan de Camarones,
  Mexico V06+250 **100**
San Juan de Guadalupe,
  Mexico U77+245 **100**
San Juan del Norte, *Nic.* T52+110 **101**
San Juan de los Lagos, *Mex.* U73+213 **100**
San Juan del Rio, *Mexico* U59+204 **100**
San Juan del Sur, *Niçaragua* T65+114 **101**
San Juan Sabinas, *Mexico* U68+278 **100**
San Julian, *Argentina* S47–493 **103**
San Justo, *Argentina* S03–307 **103**
Sankuri Post, *Kenya* K32–004 **83**
San Lazaro, C., *Mexico* V43+247 **100**
San Leandro, *California* W13+377 **92**
San Lorenzo, *Argentina* S04–327 **103**
San Lorenzo, *Ecuador* T23+013 **104**
San Lorenzo, *Honduras* T74+134 **101**
San Lorenzo, *Mexico* V35+306 **100**
San Lorenzo, *Peru* S56–115 **104**
San Lorenzo Is., *Mexico* V46+286 **100**
San Lorenzo del Escorial, *Sp.* N25+406 **52**
Sanlucar la Mayor, *Spain* N37+374 **52**
San Lucas, *Bolivia* S31–200 **104**
San Lucas, C., *Mexico* V29+229 **100**
San Luis, *Argentina* R81–276 **103**
San Luis, *Argentina* S39–332 **103**
San Luis, *Cuba* T02+203 **101**
San Luis de la Paz, *Mexico* U61+212 **100**
San Luis Obispo, *California* W04+353 **92**
San Luis Potosi & state,
  Mexico U65+222 **100**
Sanluri, *Sardinia* M37+396 **57**
San Marcos, *Colombia* T01+086 **104**
San Marino, rep., *Italy* M15+441 **56**
San Martin, *Argentina* S64–440 **103**
San Martin, *Colombia* S82+038 **104**
San Martin, L., *Chile-Argent.* S76–489 **103**
San Martin de los Andes,
  Argentina S68–402 **103**
San Martin de Valdeiglesais,
  Spain N26+403 **52**
San Martinho, *Portugal* N55+395 **52**
San Mateo, *Florida* T39+296 **97**
San Mateo, *Spain* M89+404 **53**
San Mateo Pk., *New Mexico* V15+339 **94**
San Matias, *Bolivia* R79–164 **104**
San Matias, G., *Argentina* S26–414 **103**
San Maura. *See* Levkás I.
San Miguel, *Bolivia* S05–166 **104**
San Miguel, *Mexico* U65+209 **100**
San Miguel, *Peru* S83–130 **104**
San Miguel, *El Salvador* T79+135 **101**
San Miguel. *See* Rey, I. del
San Miguel, B. de, *Panama* T19+084 **101**
San Miguel I., *California* W02+341 **92**
San Miguel, R., *Bolivia* S20–160 **104**
San Miguel de Tucuman,
  Argentina S32–268 **103**
San Nicolás, *Argentina* S01–334 **103**
Sano Nocera, *Italy* M02+407 **57**
San Pablo, *Bolivia* S40–216 **104**
San Pablo, C., *Argentina* S40–543 **103**
San Pedro, *Argentina* R87–338 **103**
San Pedro, *Bolivia* S37–181 **104**
San Pedro, *Belize* T78+180 **101**
San Pedro, *California* V80+337 **92**
San Pedro, *Ivory Coast* N40+048 **80**
San Pedro, *Mexico* U78+259 **100**
San Pedro, *Paraguay* R72–240 **103**
San Pedro Chan, *California* V87+336 **92**
San Pedro R., *Arizona* V32+326 **94**
San Pedro de Arimena,
  Colombia S70+044 **104**
San Pedro del Gallo, *Mexico* U87+256 **100**
San Pedro del Lloc, *Peru* T26–076 **104**
San Pedro de Macoris,
  Dominican Rep. S56+186 **101**
San Pedro do Sul, *Portugal* N48+407 **52**
San Pedro Soloma, *Guat.* U08+157 **100**
San Pedro Sula, *Honduras* T78+155 **101**
San Pietro I., *Sardinia* M40+392 **56**
San Quintin & B., *Mexico* V66+304 **100**
San Rafael, *Argentina* S50–346 **103**
San Rafael, *California* W15+379 **92**
San Rafael, *New Mexico* V18+352 **98**
San Ramon, *Mexico* V66+308 **100**
San Ramon, *Peru* T01–111 **104**
San Remo, *Italy* M43+438 **56**
San Roque, *Argentina* R82–286 **103**
San Salvador, *Angola* M04–062 **82**
San Salvador, *Bahamas, The* S88 + 240 **101**
San Salvador, *El Salvador* T86 + 137 **101**
Sansanne Mango, *Togo* M86+104 **80**
San Sebastian, *Spain* N12+433 **53**
San Sebastian & B. de,
  Argentina S51–533 **103**
San Severo, *Italy* L88+417 **57**
Sans Souci, *Ontario* T29+451 **91**
Santa, *Peru* T22–090 **104**
Santa Ana, *Bolivia* S34–138 **104**
Santa Ana, *Bolivia* R82–186 **104**
Santa Ana, *California* V77+337 **92**
Santa Ana, *Ecuador* T32–012 **104**
Santa Ana, *Mexico* V35+305 **100**
Santa Ana, *Peru* S77–129 **104**
Santa Ana, *El Salvador* T87 + 140 **101**
Santa Anna (Bananal), I. de,
  Brazil R32–114 **105**
Santa Antonio da Gloria,
  Brazil Q50–093 **105**
Santa Barbara, *California* V88+344 **92**
Santa Barbara, *Honduras* T80+149 **101**
Santa Barbara Chan., *Cal.* W06+343 **92**
Santa Barbara Is., *California* W00+340 **98**
Santa Barbara de Samana,
  Dominican Rep. S56+192 **101**
Santa Carolina, *Brazil* S44–077 **104**
Santa Catalina, *Chile* S58–252 **103**
Santa Catalina I., *California* V80+334 **92**
Santa Catalina, I., *Mexico* V34+257 **100**
Santa Catalina, mt., *Mexico* V63+309 **100**
Santa Catalina Ra., *Arizona* V34+324 **94**
Santa Catarina, *Mexico* V28+231 **100**
Santa Catarina, I., *Brazil* R21–276 **103**
Santa Clara, *Brazil* S58–024 **104**

Santa Clara, *Cuba* T30+224 **101**
Santa Clara, Sa., *Mexico* V54+273 **100**
Santa Coloma de Farnes, *Sp.* M74+418 **53**
Santa Cruz, *Argentina* S52–500 **103**
Santa Cruz, *Bolivia* S20–177 **104**
Santa Cruz, *Brazil* Q61–200 **105**
Santa Cruz, *Brazil* S75–059 **104**
Santa Cruz, *California* W12+370 **92**
Santa Cruz, *Chile* S68–346 **103**
Santa Cruz, *Mexico* V02+258 **100**
Santa Cruz, *Mexico* V34+312 **100**
Santa Cruz, *Nicaragua* T66+134 **101**
Santa Cruz, *Peru* T05–056 **104**
Santa Cruz, *Philippines* D81+140 **65**
Santa Cruz Chan. & I., *Cal.* V89+340 **92**
Santa Cruz Is., *Pacific Ocean* A80–112 **106**
Santa Cruz, I., *West Indies* S28+178 **101**
Santa Cruz, R., *Argentina* S66–502 **103**
Santa Cruz de Bravo, *Mex.* T76+196 **100**
Santa Cruz de la Zarza, *Sp.* N20+400 **52**
Santa Cruz del Sur, *Cuba* T19+208 **101**
Santa Cruz de Tenerife,
  Canary Is. P08+284 **80**
Santa Elena, *Ecuador* T35–023 **104**
Santa Eufemia, G. di, *Italy* L84+389 **57**
Santa Fé, *Argentina* S05–316 **103**
Santa Fé, *Cuba* T46+217 **101**
Santa Fé, *New Mexico* V06+356 **94**
Santa Helena, *Brazil* R56–249 **103**
Santa Helena, *Brazil* R02–024 **105**
Santai, *China* F00+311 **66**
Santa Innes, B., *Mexico* V41+269 **100**
Santa Isabel, *Argentina* S41–362 **103**
Santa Isabel. *See* Macias Nguema
Santalnes, I., *Chile* S76–539 **103**
Santa Lucia, *Cuba* T06+210 **101**
Santa Luzia, *Brazil* R18–162 **105**
Santa Margarita, I., *Mexico* V41+244 **100**
Santa Maria, *Argentina* S36–266 **103**
Santa Maria, *Brazil* R52–297 **103**
Santa Maria, *California* W03+349 **92**
Santa Maria, I., *Atlantic Oc.* P61+372 **80**
Santa Maria, I., *Chile* S81–370 **103**
Santa Maria, mt., *Argentina* S56–362 **103**
Santa Maria del Rio, *Mex.* U64+218 **100**
Santa Maria di Leuea C., *It.* L70+398 **57**
Santa Maria la Real de Nieva,
  Spain N26+411 **52**
Santa Maria Nova, *Brazil* R28–092 **105**
Santa Marta, *Colombia* S85+112 **104**
Santa Monica, *California* V81+341 **92**
Santa Monica B., *California* V88+338 **92**
Santander, *Colombia* T08+030 **104**
Santander, *Spain* N23+434 **52**
Santa Paula, *California* V84+342 **92**
Santa Philomena, *Brazil* R04–091 **105**
Santa Quiteria, *Brazil* Q76–034 **105**
Santarem, *Brazil* Q55–137 **105**
Santarem, *Portugal* N52+392 **52**
Santa Rita, *Venezuela* S68+104
Santa Rosa, *Argentina* S31–323 **103**
Santa Rosa, *Argentina* S49–331 **103**
Santa Rosa, *Bolivia* S07–170 **104**
Santa Rosa, *Brazil* R57–278 **103**
Santa Rosa, *California* W16+384 **92**
Santa Rosa, *Honduras* T84+147 **101**
Santa Rosa, *New Mexico* U88+348 **94**
Santa Rosa, *Uruguay* R76–303 **103**
Santa Rosa I., *California* W01+340 **92**
Santa Rosa de Toay, *Argent.* S25–365 **103**
Santa Rosalia, *Mexico* V44+272 **100**
Santa Vitoria do Palmar,
  Brazil R50–336 **103**
Santerem, *Brazil* R58–024 **105**
Santiago, *Brazil* R59–291 **103**
Santiago, *Chile* S64–334 **103**
Santiago, *Mexico* V28+236 **100**
Santiago, *Mexico* V01+217 **100**
Santiago, *Panama* T35+081 **101**
Santiago, *Dominican Rep.* S64+194 **101**
Santiago de Compostela, *Sp.* N51+429 **52**
Santiago, Cerro, *Panama* T40+087 **101**
Santiago, Sa. de, *Bolivia* S00–183 **104**
Santiago de Cuba, *Cuba* T05+201 **101**
Santiago del Estero, *Argent.* S26–278 **103**
Santiago Papasquiaro, *Mex.* V02+248 **100**
Santilland, *Spain* N24+433 **52**
Santipur, *India* G08+232 **73**
Santis, mt., *Switzerland* M34+472 **45**
Santo Angelo, *Brazil* R56–283 **103**
Santo Antonio, *Brazil* S24–089 **104**
Santo Antonio, *Brazil* S21–124 **104**
Santo Antonio, *Brazil* R43–009 **105**
Santo Antonio do Zaire,
  Angola M16–064 **82**
Santo Corazon, *Bolivia* R82–179 **104**
Santo Domingo, *Cuba* T31+226 **101**
Santo Domingo,
  Domin. Rep. S59+186 **101**
Santo Domingo, *Mexico* V65+307 **100**
San Tomé, *Venezuela* S24+091 **104**
Santorini, *See* Thira, I.
Santos, *Brazil* R08–238 **105**
Santo Thome, *Argentina* R67–285 **103**
Santo Tomas, *Mexico* V68+315 **100**
Santo Tomas, *Peru* S74–144 **104**
Santvliet, *Belgium* M64+513 **44**
San Urbano, *Argentina* S09–336 **103**
San Vicente, *El Salvador* T82 + 136 **101**
San Vito C., *Italy* L77+404 **57**
São Anna do Livramento,
  Brazil R63–309 **103**
São Antonio de Balsas,
  Brazil R06–076 **105**
São Antonio do Ica, *Brazil* S48–031 **104**
São Benedicto, *Brazil* S10–002 **104**
São Bento do Norte, *Brazil* Q36–051 **105**
São Borja, *Brazil* R66–287 **103**
São Carlos, *Brazil* R17–221 **105**
São Christovão, *Brazil* Q44–110 **105**
São Domingos, *Brazil* R07–135 **105**
São Domingos, *Brazil* R17–016 **105**
São Felippe, *Brazil* S59–065 **104**
São Felippe, *Brazil* S44+004 **104**
São Felix, *Brazil* R44–065 **105**
São Francisco, *Brazil* Q58–038 **105**
São Francisco, *Brazil* Q77–063 **105**
São Francisco, *Brazil* Q89–160 **105**
São Francisco, *Brazil* R56–046 **105**
São Francisco do Sul & I. de,
  Brazil R22–263 **103**

São Francisco. R., *Brazil* Q56–089 **105**
Sao Hill, *Tanzania* K60–084 **83**
São Jeronimo, *Brazil* R36–237 **105**
São Jeronymo, *Brazil* R40–299 **103**
São Joao da Barra, *Brazil* Q66–216 **105**
São Joao da Boa Vista, *Brazil* R11–218 **105**
São Joao del Rei, *Brazil* Q85–210 **105**
São João do Araguaya, *Brazil* R22–053 **105**
São João do Piauhy, *Brazil* Q74–084 **105**
São Joaquim, *Brazil* S44 000 **104**
São Joaquin, *Brazil* R66–048 **105**
São José, *Brazil* R42–320 **103**
São José, *Brazil* R22–276 **103**
São José, *Brazil* S38–003 **104**
São José do Duro, *Brazil* R08–113 **105**
São José do Mipibu, *Brazil* Q31–061 **105**
São José dos Martyrios,
  Brazil R20–063 **105**
São Jose do Rio Prêto, *Brazil* R26–207 **105**
São Jose dos Mattoes, *Brazil* Q79–054 **105**
São José do Tocantins, *Brazil* R21–144 **105**
São Lourenço & R., *Brazil* R61–165 **105**
São Luis, *Brazil* Q86–026 **105**
São Luis, I. de, *Brazil* Q86–025 **105**
São Luiz do Caceres, *Brazil* R76–162 **105**
São Luiz Gonzaga, *Brazil* R60–283 **103**
São Marcello, *Brazil* R01–110 **105**
São Mateus do Sul, *Brazil* R32–260 **103**
São Matheus,. *Brazil* Q59–188 **105** .
São Miguel, *Brazil* R14–016 **105**
São Miguel, I., *Atlantic Oc.* P64+380 **80**
Saona, I. *Dominican Rep.* S52+182 **101**
Saône, R., *France* M60+463 **54**
Saône-et-Loire, dep., *France* M61+466 **54**
Sao Paulo, *Brazil* R10–234 **105**
Sao Paulo de Olivenca, *Brazil* S53-035 **104**
São Raymundo Nonato,
  Brazil Q76–090 **105**
São Sebastião & I. da, *Brazil* R02–238 **105**
São Simão, *Brazil* R15–214 **105**
São Thomé I., *G. of Guinea* M50+002 **82**
São Vicente, *Brazil* R09–238 **105**
São Vicente, *Brazil* R19–058 **105**
Sapaya, *Ecuador* T24+008 **104**
Sapiéntza I., *Greece* L50+367 **59**
Saposoa, *Peru* T10–070 **104**
Sapporo, *Japan* C52+430 **68**
Sapri, *Italy* L86+400 **57**
Sapulpa, *Oklahoma* U37+360 **95**
Saqqez, *Iran* J82+363 **74**
Saragossa (Zaragoza), *Spain* N05+416 **53**
Saraikela, *India* G24+227 **73**
Sarajevo, *Yugoslavia* L70+438 **58**
Sarala, *U.S.S.R.* G04+550 **62**
Saranac Lake, *New York* S85+444 **91**
Saranda, *India* G28+222 **73**
Sarandi del Yi, *Uruguay* R64–333 **103**
Sarangarh, *India* G41+215 **71**
Saranovo, *Bulgaria* L35+422 **58**
Saransk, *U.S.S.R.* J89+542 **61**
Sarapul, *U.S.S.R.* J38+565 **61**
Sarasota, *Florida* T45+273 **97**
Saratoga, *Wyoming* V11+415 **93**
Saratoga L., *New York* S82+430 **96**
Saratoga Springs, *New York* S82+431 **91**
Saratov, *U.S.S.R.* J84+515 **61**
Saratsi-ting, *China* E53+407 **66**
Sarawak, *Borneo* E54+013 **65**
Sarbaz, *Iran* H82+266 **75**
Sárbogárd, *Hungary* L68+469 **49**
Sarco, *Chile* S69–288 **103**
Sardarshahr, *India* H03+285 **103**
Sardasht, *Iran* J87+361 **74**
Sardegna, I., *Italy* M36+400 **57**
Sardhana, *India* F34+291 **72**
Sardinia. *See* Sardegna.
Sardis, *Mississippi* T89+344 **97**
Sardis Res., *Mississippi* T88+345 **95**
Sardoal, *Portugal* N49+396 **52**
Sareks Nat. Park, *Sweden* L76+673 **46**
Sargans, *Switzerland* M33+471 **45**
Sarh, *Chad* L70+092 **81**
Sari, *Iran* J42+366 **75**
Sarikamis, *Turkey* K15+404 **74**
Sarina, *Queensland* C04–215 **111**
Sariñena, *Spain* N01+418 **53**
Sar-i-Pul, *Afghanistan* H54+361 **75**
Sar-i-Pul, *Iran* J85+345 **74**
Sarir, *Libya* L46+276 **81**
Sark, I., *Channel Islands* N14+494 **54**
Sarkad, *Hungary* L52+468 **49**
Sarlat, *France* M83+449 **55**
Sarles, *N. Dakota* U54+490 **93**
Sarmi, *New Guinea* C68–019 **65**
Sarmiento, mt., *Chile* S65–545 **103**
Sarna, *Sweden* M11+617 **47**
Sarnen, *Switzerland* M40+469 **45**
Sarnia, *Ontario* T44+430 **91**
Saronic G., *Greece* L38+376 **59**
Saronno, *Italy* M35+456 **56**
Sarpsborg, *Norway* M23+593 **47**
Sarpul, *Iran* J58+371 **75**
Sarrebourg, *France* M48+487 **54**
Sarreguemines, *France* M48+491 **54**
Sarre Union, *France* M47+489 **54**
Sarria, *Spain* N44+428 **52**
Sart, *Belgium* M54+505 **44**
Sartene, *Corsica* M36+416 **57**
Sarthe R. & dep., *France* M89+480 **54**
Sarufutsu, *Japan* C48+452 **68**
Sarur, *Saudi Arabia* J12+233 **75**
Saruru, *Japan* C40+421 **68**
Sarvar, *Hungary* L79+472 **49**
Sasa Baneh, *Ethiopia* K08+078 **83**
Sasaram, *India* G35+249 **73**
Sasawara, *Tanzania* K48–116 **83**
Sasebo, *Japan* D32+331 **68**
Saskatchewan, prov., *Canada*
Saskatchewan R., *Sask.* V30+509 **88**
Saskatchewan R. S., *Sask.* V20+530 **88**
Saskatoon, *Saskatchewan* V19+518 **88**
Saskylakh, *U.S.S.R.* E36+720 **63**
Sasmaka, *Latvia* L44+573 **47**
Sasovo, *U.S.S.R.* K18+543 **61**
Sassandra & R., *Ivory Coast* N36+050 **80**
Sassari, *Sardinia* M39+407 **57**
Sassnitz, *E. Germany* M08+545 **48**
Sastre, *Argentina* S11–318 **103**
Sas-van-Gent, *Netherlands* M67+512 **44**
Satadougou, *Mali* N68+126 **80**
Satara, *India* H05+178 **70**

São Francisco. R., *Brazil* Q56–089 **105**
Säter, *Sweden* L86+603 **47**
Satevo, *Mexico* V06+279 **100**
Satins, *France* M55+470 **54**
Satka, *U.S.S.R.* J06+550 **61**
Satkhira, *Bangladesh* G05+227 **73**
Satoraljaujhely, *Hungary* L50+484 **49**
Satpura Ra., *India* H05+217 **70**
Satul, *Thailand* F30+066 **69**
Satu Mare, *Romania* L43+478 **49**
Sauda, *Norway* M52+597 **47**
Saudi Arabia, *S.-W. Asia* **74**
Saugeen Pen., *Ontario* T38+451 **91**
Saugerties, *New York* S84+421 **91**
Sauk Center, *Minnesota* U30+457 **93**
Sauk Rapids, *Minnesota* U25+456 **93**
Saulieu, *France* M65+473 **54**
Sault Ste Marie, *Michigan* T56+465 **91**
Sault Ste Marie, *Ontario* T56+465 **91**
Saumur, *France* N01+473 **54**
Saunders, I., *S. Sandwich Is.* P80–570 **27**
Sauqira B., *Oman* J16+185 **75**
Saurashtra, *India* H25+220 **70**
Sava, R., *Yugoslavia* L61+447 **58**
Savai'i, I., *Samoa Islands* Z45–140 **106**
Savalan, mt., *Iran* J73+383 **74**
Savanna, *Illinois* U01+421 **91**
Savannah, *Georgia* T37+321 **97**
Savannah, *Missouri* U30+399 **95**
Savannah R., *Georgia-S. Car.* T46+340 **97**
Savannakhet, *Laos* F02+166 **69**
Savanna la Mar, *Jamaica* T19+183 **101**
Savantvadi, *India* H07+160 **70**
Savanur, *India* G87+150 **70**
Save, *Benin* M76 + 080 **80**
Save R., *Mozambique* K60-210 **84**
Saveh, *Iran* J58+352 **75**
Savenay, *France* N12+473 **54**
Savoie, dep., *France* M49+455 **54**
Savoie, prov., *France* M53+457 **54**
Savona, *Italy* M39+443 **56**
Savonlinna, *Finland* L07+619 **46**
Savu Sea, *Indonesia* D80–096 **65**
Savukoski, *Finland* L11+673 **46**
Sawa, *Yemen, South* J74 + 159 **74**
Sawatch Mts., *Colorado* V10+388 **94**
Sawel, *N. Ireland* N42+548 **42**
Saxmundham, *England* M81+522 **39**
Saxnäs, *Sweden* L88+649 **46**
Saxton, *Pennsylvania* T20+402 **96**
Saya, *Syria* K54+351 **76**
Sayan, *Peru* T13–110 **104**
Sayan, Vostochnya, *U.S.S.R.* F30+525 **63**
Sayan, Zapadnyy, *U.S.S.R.* F60+535 **63**
Sayre, *Oklahoma* U56+354 **95**
Sayre, *Pennsylvania* T09+420 **96**
Sayula, *Mexico* U82+198 **100**
Scafell Pike, *England* N19+544 **37**
Scalea, *Italy* L85+398 **57**
Scanteia, *Romania* L15+470 **58**
Scapa Flow, *Orkney, Scot.* N18+589 **40**
Scarba, I., *Scotland* N34+562 **41**
Scarboro, *Maine* S62+436 **90**
Scarborough, *England* N02+543 **37**
Scariff I., *Ireland, Rep.* N62+517 **43**
Scârisoara, *Romania* L43+465 **58**
Scatari I., *Nova Scotia* R88+460 **90**
Schafer, *N. Dakota* U79+478 **93**
Schaffhausen & canton,
  Switzerland M38+477 **45**
Schelde, Ooster & Wester,
  Netherlands M66+515 **44**
Schenectady, *New York* S83+428 **91**
Scheveningen, *Netherlands* M64+521 **44**
Schiedam, *Netherlands* M64+519 **44**
Schiermonnikoog I,
  Netherlands M53+535 **44**
Schiphol, *Netherlands* M61+523 **44**
Schleins, *Switzerland* M27+469 **45**
Schleswig, *W. Germany* M33+545 **48**
Schleswig-Holstein,
  Germany M33+540 **48**
Schneidemühl. *See* Piła.
Schoharie, *New York* S86+427 **96**
Schönbuhl, *Switzerland* M45+470 **45**
Schonebeck, *E. Germany* M20+520 **48**
Schongau, *W. Germany* M25+478 **48**
Schoonhoven, *Netherlands* M61+519 **44**
Schötz, *Switzerland* M42+472 **45**
Schouten, I., *Tasmania* C11–424 **109**
Schouwen I., *Netherlands* M67+517 **44**
Schuchinsk, *Kazakh* H28+530 **62**
Schull, *Ireland, Rep.* N57+515 **43**
Schuls, *Switzerland* M28+468 **45**
Schüpfheim, *Switzerland* M42+470 **45**
Schuyler, *Nebraska* U42+414 **95**
Schwabach, *W. Germany* M24+493 **48**
Schwägalp, *Switzerland* M34+473 **45**
Schwandorf, *W. Germany* M17+493 **48**
Schwaner, Peg., *Borneo* E46–011 **65**
Schwarzhorn, mt., *Switz.* M43+462 **45**
Schwarzwald, *W. Germany* M38+486 **48**
Schwedt, *E. Germany* M04+531 **48**
Schweidnitz. *See* Swidnica
Schweinfurt, *W. Germany* M29+501 **48**
Schwerin, *E. Germany* M22+536 **48**
Schwyz & canton, *Switz.* M38+470 **45**
Sciacca, *Sicily* M12+375 **57**
Scilly, Is. of, *England* N38+500 **38**
Scituate, *Massachusetts* S64+422 **96**
Scobey, *Montana* V02+488 **93**
Scone, *New South Wales* B85–320 **109**
Scone, *Scotland* N20+564 **41**
Scoresby, C., *N.-W. Terr.* U20+714 **89**
Scoresby Ld., *Greenland* P85+730 **26**
Scoresby Sd., *Greenland* P38+700 **26**
Scotia, *Ontario* T26+455 **91**
Scotia Sea, *Antarctica* R90–580 **27**
Scotland, *Great Britain* N24+560 **34**
Scotland, *S. Dakota* U46+431 **93**
Scott, C., *Brit. Columbia* W51+507 **88**
Scott Inl., *N.-W. Territories* S65+710 **89**
Scott I., *Antarctica* A02–670 **27**
Scott, Mt., *Oregon* W12+432 **98**
Scott City, *Kansas* U66+384 **94**
Scottsbluff, *Nebraska* U82+416 **98**
Scottsdale, *Tasmania* C16–412 **109**
Scourie, *Scotland* N31+584 **40**
Scranton,·*Pennsylvania* T04+414 **91**
Scridain, L., *Scotland* N37+563 **41**
Scugog L., *Ontario* T23+442 **91**
Scunthorpe, *England* N04+536 **37**

Scutari (Shkodër), *Albania* L63+421 **58**
Scutari (Uskudar), *Turkey* L06+411 **74**
Seaford, *Delaware* T04+386 **91**
Seahorse Pt., *N.-W. Terr.* T30+641 **89**
Sea Isle City, *New Jersey* S88+392 **91**
Scal R., *Manitoba* U40+590 **88**
Sea Lake, *Victoria* C43–356 **109**
Sea Lion Is., *Falkland Is.* R84–524 **103**
Searcy, *Arkansas* U10+352 **95**
Seattle, *Washington* W14+476 **92**
Sebago L., *Maine* S63+439 **90**
Sebastián Vizcaino B. de,
  Mexico V58+282 **100**
Sebenico. *See* Sibenik
Sebewaing, *Michigan* T50+437 **91**
Sebha, (Sabhah), *Libya* M04+270 **81**
Sebin Karahisar, *Turkey* K40+403 **74**
Sebree, *Kentucky* T75+376 **97**
Sečovce, *Czechoslovakia* L50+487 **49**
Secretary I., *New Zealand* A78–452 **112**
Secunderabad, *India* G68+175 **70**
Seda, *Lithuania* L47+561 **47**
Sedalia, *Missouri* U20+389 **99**
Sedan, *France* M60+497 **54**
Sedan, *S. Australia* C64–346 **109**
Sedano, *Spain* N23+427 **52**
Sedbergh. *England* N15+543 **37**
Seddon, *New Zealand* A35–417 **112**
Seddonville, *New Zealand* A48–415 **112**
Sedhiou, *Senegal* P04+128 **80**
Sedom, *Israel* K57+311 **76**
Sedrun, *Switzerland* M37+467 **45**
Seeheim, *Namibia* L72-270 **84**
Seelisberg, *Switzerland* M38+470 **45**
Sées, *France* M89+486 **54**
Seewis, *Switzerland* M32+470 **45**
Sefrou, *Morocco* N30+340 **80**
Sefton, *New Zealand* A41–432 **112**
Sefton, Mt., *New Zealand* A59–437 **112**
Segorbe, *Spain* N03+398 **53**
Ségou, *Mali* N38+132 **80**
Segovia, *Spain* N25+409 **52**
Segovia, R., *Nicaragua* 154+147 **101**
Seguela, *Ivory Coast* N42+080 **80**
Sehkukeh, *Iran* H81+307 **75**
Sehwan, *Pakistan* H43+264 **70**
Seibo, *Dominican Rep.* S54+190 **101**
Seiland, *Norway* L40+704 **46**
Seine, R., *France* M87+495 **54**
Seine-et-Marne, dep., *France* M73+487 **54**
Seine-et-Oise, dep., *France* M79+488 **54**
Seine-Maritime, dep., *Fr.* M86+497 **54**
Seitler, *U.S.S.R.* K61+454 **60**
Seiyala, *Egypt* K74+226 **81**
Sejal, *Colombia* S48+026 **104**
Sekenke, *Tanzania* K66–044 **83**
Seki, *Japan* C78+354 **68**
Sekieshan I., *China* D76+303 **67**
Sekondi, *Ghana* N10+050 **80**
Sektyakh, *U.S.S.R.* D60+700 **63**
Selby, *England* N06+538 **37**
Selby, *S. Dakota* U60+454 **93**
Selemiya, *Syria* K48+350 **76**
Selenga, R., *Mong.-U.S.S.R.* E80+515 **63**
Selima Oasis, *Sudan* L04+212 **81**
Selinsgrove, *Pennsylvania* T11+408 **96**
Selkirk, *Manitoba* U42+502 **88**
Selkirk, *Yukon* X14+631 **88**
Selkirk, *Scotland* N17+555 **41**
Selkirk Mts., *Brit. Columbia* V70+500 **88**
Selle, Sa. de la, *Haiti* S72+184 **101**
Selles, *France* M81+473 **54**
Selma, *Alabama* T72+324 **97**
Selma, *N. Carolina* T20+355 **97**
Selous Mt., *Yukon* W68+634 **88**
Selva, *Argentina* S13–297 **103**
Selwyn, *Queensland* C56–215 **111**
Selwyn Ra., *Queensland* C60–214 **111**
Selwyn Ra., *Yukon* W60+634 **88**
Selzaete, *Belgium* M67+512 **44**
Sem, *Norway* M28+593 **47**
Semarang, *Java* E58–070 **65**
Seminoe Res., *Wyoming* V11+420 **93**
Semipalatinsk, *Kazakh* G59+505 **62**
Semnan, *Iran* J40+356 **75**
Senador Pompeu, *Brazil* Q56–055 **105**
Senatobia, *Mississippi* U00+346 **97**
Sendai, *Japan* C53+383 **68**
Seneca L., *New York* T11+427 **91**
Seneca Falls, *New York* T11+429 **96**
Sénégal, rep., *W. Africa* P00+146 **80**
Sénégal, R., *W. Africa* N80+150 **80**
Senev, *Michigan* T66+463 **91**
Senga Hill, *Zambia* K82–094 **83**
Sengilei, *U.S.S.R.* J67+540 **61**
Senise, *Italy* L82+402 **57**
Senj, *Yugoslavia* M01+450 **56**
Senja, *Norway* L76+693 **46**
Senna Madureira, *Brazil* S53–092 **104**
Senneterre, *Quebec* T14+484 **91**
Sens, *France* M70+482 **54**
Senta, *Yugoslavia* L59+459 **58**
Sentinel Ra., *Antarctica* T80–770 **27**
Seondha, *India* G67+262 **73**
Seoni, *India* G63+221 **73**
Seoni-Malwa, *India* G75+225 **73**
Seoul (Sôul), *Korea* D48+377 **64**
Separation Pt., *New Zealand* A42–407 **112**
Seperior, *Nebraska* U48+400 **95**
Sepólno, *Poland* L74+535 **49**
Sepulveda, *Spain* N22+413 **52**
Sequeros, *Spain* N36+405 **52**
Sequoia Nat. Park., *Cal.* V83+365 **92**
Serai, *Syria* K54+358 **76**
Serakhs, *Turkmen* H83+365 **62**
Serampore, *India* G10+228 **73**
Serbia, *Yugoslavia* L52+430 **58**
Serdeles, *Libya* M26+258 **81**
Serdobol, *Karelia* K86+617 **46**
Serdobsk, *U.S.S.R.* K04+525 **61**
Serengeti Nat. Pk., *Tanzania* K60–020 **83**
Sergach, *U.S.S.R.* J88+556 **61**
Sergiyevsk, *U.S.S.R.* J53+540 **61**
Serifos, I., *Greece* L33+372 **59**
Sermata, I., *Indonesia* D36–085 **65**
Serov, *U.S.S.R.* H88+599 **62**
Serowe, *Botswana* L20–224 **84**
Serpa, *Portugal* N45+379 **52**
Serpins, *Portugal* N49+402 **52**
Serpukhov, *U.S.S.R.* K46+549 **60**

Sèrrai, *Greece* L39+411 **58**
Serra San Bruno, *Italy* L82+386 **57**
Serrezuela, *Argentina* S32–306 **103**
Sertã, *Portugal* N49+398 **52**
Sertig, *Switzerland* M31+467 **45**
Sérvia, *Greece* L48+401 **59**
Serviceton, *Victoria* C54–364 **109**
Sesheke, *Zambia* L30–174 **84**
Sete, *France* M68+434 **55**
Sete Lagoas, *Brazil* Q85–194 **105**
Setif, *Algeria* M58+360 **80**
Setubal, *Portugal* N53+385 **52**
Seul, Lac, *Ontario* U15+502 **89**
Sevan, Oz., *Armyan, U.S.S.R.* K00+403 **62**
Sevastopol, *U.S.S.R.* K68+446 **60**
Sevelen, *Switzerland* M33+471 **45**
Seven Islands (Sept-Îles),
  Quebec S38+503 **90**
Sevenoaks, *England* M89+513 **39**
Severac-le-Château, *France* M72+443 **55**
Severn, *Cape Province* L42–268 **84**
Severn, *Ontario* T77+558 **89**
Severn R., *England* N15+526 **37**
Severn, R., *Ontario* T88+543 **89**
Severnaya Dvina, *U.S.S.R.* K10+628 **62**
Severnaya Zemlya, *U.S.S.R.* F50+800 **63**
Sevier L., *Utah* V49+390 **92**
Sevier R., *Utah* V44+394 **94**
Sevilla, *Spain* N36+374 **52**
Seville. *See* Sevilla
Seward, *Alaska* X86+602 **99**
Seward Pen., *Alaska* Y80+651 **99**
Seybaplaya, *Mexico* U04+196 **100**
Seychelles, Is., *Indian Ocean* J30–050 **77**
Seydhisfjördhur, *Iceland* N84+653 **46**
Seymchan, *U.S.S.R.* B76+630 **63**
Seymour, *Indiana* T66+390 **91**
Seymour, *Victoria* C29–370 **109**
Seyne, *France* M51+444 **55**
Sezanne, *France* M68+487 **54**
Sfakiá. *See* Khóra Sfakion.
Stântu Gheorghe. *Romania* L25+459 **58**
Sfax, *Tunisia* M26+348 **81**
Sfira, *Syria* K46+361 **76**
Sgurr Mor., *Scotland* N30+577 **40**
Shaam, *U.A.E.* J23+260 **75**
Shaba, *Zaire* L50+100 **82**
Shadegan, *Iran* J68+306 **75**
Shadrinsk, *U.S.S.R.* H69+560 **61**
Shaduela, *Ethiopia* K18+134 **83**
Shadwan, I., *Egypt* K66+274 **81**
Shafa Amr, *Israel* K59+328 **76**
Shaftesbury, *England* N13+510 **39**
Shahabad, *India* G79+302 **72**
Shahabad, *India* G60+276 **73**
Shah Abdul Azim, *Iran* J52+356 **75**
Shahba, *Syria* K50+328 **76**
Shahbandar, *Pakistan* H43+241 **70**
Shah Dad, *Iran* J14+306 **75**
Shahdadkot, *Pakistan* H42+278 **70**
Shahdadpur, *Pakistan* H38+268 **70**
Shahdara, *India* G76+287 **72**
Shadheri, *Pakistan* H12+337 **72**
Shahdol, *India* G51+230 **73**
Shahganj, *India* G44+260 **73**
Shahi, *Iran* J43+365 **75**
Shahin, *Iran* J81+367 **74**
Shahjahanpur, *India* G61+278 **73**
Shahjui, *Afghanistan* H44+325 **75**
Shahpur, *Pakistan* H15+323 **72**
Shàhpūr, *Iran* K02+382 **74**
Shahpura, *India* H01+257 **70**
Shah Rakht, *Iran* J00+338 **75**
Shahr-i-Babak, *Iran* J30+320 **75**
Shahriza, *Iran* J49+320 **75**
Shahr-i-Zabul, *Iran* H81+310 **75**
Shahrud, *Iran* J30+364 **75**
Shahsien, *China* E14+264 **67**
Shaiba, *Saudi Arabia* K12+280 **74**
Shajara, *Saudi Arabia* J84+223 **74**
Shakhty, *U.S.S.R.* K28+476 **61**
Shakopee, *Minnesota* U21+448 **93**
Shakubetsueki, *Japan* C37+428 **68**
Shala L., *Ethiopia* K38+074 **83**
Shalasha, *Sudan* L20+106 **81**
Shamil, *Iran* J20+274 **75**
Shammar, Jebel, *Saudi Arabia* K24+277 **74**
Shamokin, *Pennsylvania* T10+408 **91**
Shanghai, *China* D81+312 **66**
Shangjao, *China* E12+285 **67**
Shangkiu, *China* E26+345 **66**
Shangtung Pen., *China* D86+370 **64**
Shangyiu, *China* E32+260 **67**
Shan-hai-kwan. *See* Linyu.
Shansien, *China* E53+347 **66**
Shanklin, I. of W., *England* N07+506 **39**
Shanna, *Saudi Arabia* J54+190 **75**
Shannon, *New Zealand* A27–405 **112**
Shannon, I., *Greenland* P25+750 **26**
Shannon, R. & Airport,
  Ireland, Rep. N52+527 **43**
Shansi, *China* E48+380 **66**
Shantarskiye Os., *U.S.S.R.* C73+550 **63**
Shantung, prov., *China* E12+360 **66**
Shaohing, *China* D86+300 **67**
Shaowu, *China* E15+273 **67**
Shaoyang, *China* E51+272 **67**
Shap, *England* N16+545 **37**
Shapinsay, I., *Orkney Is., Scot.* N17+590 **40**
Shaqa, *Qatar, Saudi Arabia* K25+198 **74**
Shaqiq, *Saudi Arabia* J51+257 **75**
Shaqra, *Saudi Arabia* J89+252 **74**
Sharakpur, *Pakistan* H05+315 **72**
Sharjah, *U.A.E.* J72+254 **75**
Shark B., *W. Australia* E40–254 **110**
Sharon, *Pennsylvania* T33+413 **91**
Sharqi, Jeb, esh, *Leb.-Syria* K52+340 **76**
Sharr, Jebel el, *Saudi Arabia* K55+276 **74**
Sharya, *U.S.S.R.* J87+584 **61**
Shasi, *China* E46+302 **67**
Shasta, *California* W15+407 **92**
Shasta, Mt., *California* W13+415 **92**
Shasta Res., *California* W12+408 **92**
Shatra, *Iraq* J84+314 **74**
Shatt-al-Arab, *Iraq* J73+307 **74**
Shaubek, *Jordan* K57+305 **76**
Shawano, *Wisconsin* T82+448 **91**
Shawinigan Falls, *Quebec* S77+465 **91**
Shawnee, *Oklahoma* U42+353 **95**
Shawneetown, *Illinois* T79+377 **97**
Shchors, *Ukraine* K78+518 **60**

Sheboygan, *Wisconsin* T76+438 **91**
Shediac, *New Brunswick* S27+462 **90**
Sheelin L., *Ireland, Rep.* N44+538 **42**
Sheenjik R., *Alaska* X55+673 **80**
Sheep Haven, *Ireland, Rep.* N48+552 **42**
Sheep's Hd., *Ireland, Rep.* N59+515 **43**
Sheerness, *England* M85+514 **39**
Sheffield, *Alabama* T76+348 **97**
Sheffield, *England* N09+534 **37**
Sheffield, *New Zealand* A48–434 **112**
Sheffield, *Tasmania* C22–414 **109**
Sheikh, Jeb. esh, *Syria* K55+334 **76**
Sheikh 'Abd er Rahman. *See* Arka.
Sheikh Miskin, *Syria* K53+328 **76**
Sheikh 'Othman, *Yemen, South* K00+129 **74**
Sheik Seraq, *Syria* K46+330 **76**
Shekha, *Yemen, South* J64+151 **74**
Shekhupura, *Pakistan* H05+317 **72**
Sheklung, *China* E36+231 **67**
Shelburne, *Nova Scotia* S32+438 **90**
Shelburne, *Ontario* T31+441 **91**
Shelby, *Michigan* T68+436 **91**
Shelby, *Montana* V41+485 **93**
Shelby, *N. Carolina* T38+352 **97**
Shelbyville, *Illinois* T84+394 **95**
Shelbyville, *Kentucky* T61+382 **97**
Shelbyville, *Tennessee* T69+356 **97**
Sheldon, *Iowa* U35+412 **95**
Shelikhova Zaliv, *U.S.S.R.* B45+600 **63**
Shellharbour, *New South Wales* B85–346 **109**
Shelter I., *New York* S74+411 **96**
Shenandoah, *Iowa* U32+408 **95**
Shenandoah, *Pennsylvania* T07+409 **91**
Shenandoah R., *Virginia* T18+392 **96**
Shenandoah Junct., *W. Va.* T17+394 **96**
Shenandoah Nat. Park, *Va.* T20+384 **97**
Shenchow. *See* Yuanling.
Shendam, *Nigeria* M34+088 **81**
Shendi, *Sudan* K70+166 **81**
Shèngın, *Albania* L63+418 **58**
Shenkursk, *U.S.S.R.* K12+623 **62**
Shensi, prov., *China* E66+350 **66**
Shenyang, *China* D70+418 **66**
Sheopur, *India* G80+256 **70**
Shepetovka, *Ukraine* L17+502 **60**
Shepparton, *Victoria* C27+364 **109**
Sheppey, I. of, *England* M85+514 **39**
Sherada, *Ethiopia* K52+072 **83**
Sherard Osborn Fd.,
  Greenland R30+820 **26**
Sherbro I., *Sierra Leone* N76+078 **80**
Sherbrooke, *Quebec* S72+454 **91**
Sheridan, *Wyoming* V12+448 **93**
Sheridan, Mt., *Wyoming* V34+443 **93**
Sherman, *Texas* U40+336 **95**
Sherpur, *Bangladesh* G03+246 **73**
Sherridon, *Manitoba* U66+551 **88**
Shetland (Zetland), *Scotland* N06+604 **40**
Shevaroy Hills, *India* G68+119 **70**
Sheyenne, *N. Dakota* U55+479 **93**
Shiant Is. & Sd. of, *Scotland* N38+579 **40**
Shibam, *Yemen, South* J68+159 **74**
Shibarghan, *Afghanistan* H55+366 **75**
Shibata, *Japan* C64+379 **68**
Shibin el Kom, *Egypt* K84+306 **81**
Shickshock Mts., *Quebec* S44+488 **90**
Shiel, L., *Scotland* N34+568 **41**
Shieldaig, *Scotland* N34+575 **40**
Shigatse, *Tibet* G07+293 **71**
Shihnan. *See* Enshih.
Shih Pao Shan, *China* E64+294 **64**
Shihshow, *China* E45+296 **67**
Shihtao, *China* D76+369 **66**
Shihtsien, *China* E70+275 **67**
Shikarpur, *Pakistan* H38+278 **70**
Shikohabad, *India* G68+271 **73**
Shikoku, I., *Japan* D06+340 **68**
Shilka & R., *U.S.S.R.* E23+519 **63**
Shillelagh, *Ireland, Rep.* N39+527 **43**
Shillong, *India* F79+255 **71**
Shiloh, *Tennessee* T80+350 **97**
Shilongol, *China* E24+434 **64**
Shimoga, *India* G86+140 **70**
Shimoni, *Kenya* K34–046 **83**
Shimonoseki, *Japan* D29+324 **68**
Shimoshima, *Japan* D29+324 **68**
Shimshal & Pass, *Kashmir* G88+364 **72**
Shin, L., *Scotland* N27+581 **40**
Shinas, *Oman* J22+247 **75**
Shinghar, *Pakistan* H31+317 **72**
Shingu, *Japan* C84+337 **68**
Shinjo. *Japan* C58+388 **68**
Shinshar, *Syria* K49+346 **76**
Shinyanga, *Tanzania* K70–036 **83**
Shipets, *Japan* C29+436 **68**
Shippigan, *New Brunswick* S28+477 **90**
Shippigan I., *New Brunswick* S28+478 **90**
Shiraishi, *Japan* C56+380 **68**
Shiraz, *Iran* J45+296 **75**
Shireza, *Pakistan* H56+277 **70**
Shirley, *Montana* V04+466 **93**
Shirley Mts., *Wyoming* V09+422 **93**
Shirokaya, *U.S.S.R.* B47+619 **63**
Shisur, *Saudi Arabia* J39+182 **75**
Shiuhing. *See* Koyiu.
Shiukwan, *China* E38+248 **67**
Shivpuri, *India* G74+254 **73**
Shizugawa, *Japan* C51+387 **68**
Shizuoka, *Japan* C69+350 **68**
Shklov. *U.S.S.R.* K88+542 **60**
Shkoder, *Albania* L63+421 **58**
Shoal Harbour,
  Newfoundland R54+482 **90**
Shoalhaven R., *N.S.W.* B86–348 **109**
Shoeburyness, *England* M85+515 **39**
Shoka, *Taiwan* D86+241 **67**
Sholapur, *India* G84+176 **70**
Shonai. *See* Tsuruoka.
Shorkot, *Pakistan* H17+308 **72**
Short, *Missouri* U06+368 **97**
Short Mts., *W. Virginia* T22+392 **96**
Short Pine Hills, *S. Dakota* U80+453 **93**
Shoshone Falls, *Idaho* V57+424 **97**
Shoshone Mts., *Wyoming* V28+442 **93**
Shoshone Res., *Wyoming* V25+442 **98**
Shovo Tso, *Tibet* G40+313 **71**
Shreveport, *Louisiana* U22+325 **95**
Shrewsbury, *England* N17+537 **37**
Shropshire (Salop), *See* Salop
Shtora, *Lebanon* K55+338 **76**
Shubuta, *Mississippi* T82+318 **97**
Shuikow, *China* E07+263 **67**

Shujabad, *Pakistan* H22+299 **72**
Shumagin Is., *Alaska* Y60+549 **99**
Shumaisa, *Saudi Arabia* J87+249 **74**
Shumen, *Bulgaria* L19+433 **58**
Shumerlya, *U.S.S.R.* J81+555 **61**
Shunking. *See* Nanchung.
Shunteh. *See* Singtai.
Shuqra, *Yemen, South* J86+134 **74**
Shurab, *Iran* J21+338 **75**
Shurma, *Saudi Arabia* K18+232 **74**
Shuru Tso, *Tibet* G22+302 **71**
Shushal, *Kashmir* G68+335 **70**
Shushtar, *Iran* J67+321 **74**
Shusp, *Iran* J00+317 **75**
Shuttleton, *New S. Wales* C24–322 **109**
Shuya, *U.S.S.R.* K21+568 **61**
Shuyang, *China* E07+342 **66**
Shwebo, *Burma* F56+225 **71**
Shwedaung, *Burma* F59+186 **71**
Shwegyin, *Burma* F48+180 **71**
Siam. *See* Thailand.
Siam, G. of, *Thailand, etc.* F20+110 **69**
Sian, *China* E66+342 **66**
Siangtan, *China* E43+279 **67**
Siangyang, *China* E47+320 **66**
Siangyin, *China* E42+286 **67**
Siao Hingan Ling, *China* D42+488 **64**
Siapu, *China* E00+269 **67**
Siargao, I., *Philippines* D54+100 **65**
Siaton, *Philippines* D72+091 **65**
Siauliai, *Lithuania* L40+559 **47**
Sib, *Oman* J11+237 **75**
Sibenik, *Yugoslavia* L85+437 **56**
Siberut, I., *Indonesia* F36–014 **65**
Sibi, *Pakistan* H42+296 **70**
Sibiu, *Romania* L35+458 **58**
Sibolga, *Sumatra* F37+018 **65**
Sibsagar, *India* F61+270 **71**
Sibu, *Sarawak* E49+022 **65**
Sicasica, *Bolivia* S46–174 **104**
Sichang, *China* F16+278 **64**
Sicie C., *France* M55+430 **55**
Sicilia, I., *Italy* M06+380 **57**
Sicilian Channel,
  Mediterranean Sea M18+373 **57**
Sicily. *See* Sicilia, I.
Sicuani, *Peru* S67–143 **104**
Sid, *Yugoslavia* L65+452 **58**
Sidaka, *Iraq* K02+369 **74**
Sideby (Siippy), *Finland* L52+621 **47**
Siderno Marina, *Italy* L82+383 **57**
Sidhout, *India* G66+145 **70**
Sidi Barrani, *Egypt* L24+316 **81**
Sidi Beben, *Libya* L70+306 **81**
Sidi-bel-Abbes, *Algeria* N04+352 **80**
Sidi Ifni. *Ifni. N.-W. Africa* N69+288 **80**
Sidlaw Hills, *Scotland* N19+565 **41**
Sidnaw, *Michigan* T82+465 **91**
Sidney, *Montana* U86+477 **93**
Sidney, *Nebraska* U78+412 **94**
Sidney, *New York* T02+423 **91**
Sidon (Saida), *Lebanon* K58+336 **76**
Sidra, Gulf of, *Libya* L70+316 **81**
Siedlce, *Poland* L47+522 **49**
Siegen, *W. Germany* M42+509 **48**
Siem-Reap, *Cambodia* F06+133 **69**
Siena, *Italy* M26+433 **56**
Sieradz, *Poland* L68+516 **49**
Sierra Colorada, *Argentina* S46–406 **103**
Sierra Grande, *Argentina* S32–414 **103**
Sierra Leone, *W. Africa* N70+088 **80**
Sierra Mojada, *Mexico* U82+273 **100**
Sierra Rosaria, *Argentina* S48–427 **103**
Sifnos, I., *Greece* L32+370 **59**
Sigean, *France* M72+430 **55**
Sighet, *Romania* L37+479 **49**
Sighisoara, *Romania* L31+462 **58**
Siglufjördhur, *Iceland* P23+662 **46**
Sigmaringen. *W. Germany* M35+481 **48**
Sigourney, *Iowa* U14+412 **95**
Sigsig, *Ecuador* T23–030 **104**
Sigüenza, *Spain* N16+411 **53**
Siguiri, *Guinea* N56+114 **80**
Sigulda, *Latvia, U.S.S.R.* L31+572 **47**
Sihl See, *Switzerland* M37+471 **45**
Sihsien, *China* E09+288 **67**
Siilinjärvi, *Finland* L14+630 **46**
Sikandarabad, *India* G74+285 **72**
Sikandra Rao, *India* G70+277 **73**
Sikar, *India* G89+275 **72**
Sikasso, *Mali* N34+112 **80**
Si Kiang, R., *China* E54+232 **64**
Siking. *See* Sian
Sikinos, I., *Greece* L29+367 **59**
Sikkim, *India* G09+275 **73**
Sila, La., *Italy* L81+392 **57**
Silailrsk, *U.S.S.R.* J14+523 **61**
Silao, *Mexico* U69+209 **100**
Silchar, *India* F73+248 **71**
Silenen, *Switzerland* M38+468 **45**
Silenrieux, *Belgium* M64+502 **44**
Silesia, *Montana* V23+455 **93**
Silgarhi, *Nepal* G54+293 **73**
Silifke, *Turkey* K67+364 **74**
Silistra, *Bulgaria* L16+441 **58**
Siljan, L., *Sweden* M02+609 **47**
Silkeborg, *Denmark* M33+561 **47**
Silloth, *England* N20+549 **37**
Sils, *Switzerland* M31+464 **45**
Silvaplana, *Switzerland* M31+465 **45**
Silva Porto, *Angola* L78–124 **82**
Silver L., *Oregon* W06+431 **92**
Silver City, *New Mexico* V20+328 **94**
Silverton, *Colorado* V17+378 **94**
Silverton, *New S. Wales* C53–320 **109**
Silves, *Brazil* R80–027 **104**
Silves, *Portugal* N50+372 **52**
Silvretta, mts.,
  Austria-Switzerland M30+469 **48**
Simand, L., *Quebec* T22+477 **91**
Simcoe, *Ontario* T32+429 **91**
Simcoe, L., *Ontario* T26+444 **91**
Simeulue, I., *Indonesia* F54+025 **65**
Simferopol, *U.S.S.R.* K66+450 **60**
Simi, I., *Greece* L13+366 **59**
Simla, *India* G77+310 **72**
Simleul Silvaniei, *Romania* L43+472 **49**
Simo, *Finland* L31+657 **46**
Simola, *Finland* L11+609 **47**
Simon, L., *Quebec* T01+460 **91**
Simpelveld, *Netherlands* M54+508 **44**

Simplon and Pass, *Switzerland* M42+462 45
Simpson, Fort, *N.-W. Terr.* W11+614 88
Simpson, C., *Alaska* Y25+709 88
Simpson Des., *Australia* C80-254 111
Simpson, I., *Chile* S83-459 103
Simuna, *Estonia* L22+590 47
Sinai, pen., *Egypt* K70+290 81
Sinaloa, state, *Mexico* V12+250 100
Sinaloa & R., *Mexico* V20+260 100
Sinamaica, *Venezuela* S71+110 104
Sinbo, *Burma* F48+247 71
Sinchang, *China* D84+295 67
Sin-chow, *China* E43+385 66
Sind, *Pakistan* H40+255 70
Sindel, *Bulgaria* L15+431 58
Sindhuli Garhi, *Nepal* G25+272 73
Sind Sagar Doab, *Pakistan* H21+311 72
Sines, *Portugal* N53+379 52
Singa, *Sudan* K66+132 81
Singapore & Str., *S. Asia* F07+012 69
Singaraja, *Bali I., Indon.* E29-081 65
Singen, *W. Germany* M38+477 48
Singhbhum, *India* G27+224 73
Singida, *Tanzania* K62-046 83
Singitic G., *Greece* L36+402 59
Singkawang, *Borneo* E66+010 65
Singkep, I.,
  Riouw Arch., Indon. F04-006 65
Singleton, *New South Wales* B83-326 109
Singora. *See Songkhla*
Singsingsia, *China* F58+418 64
Singtai, *China* E33+371 66
Sinho, *China* E28+375 66
Sinhsien, *China* E44+384 64
Sinhwa, *China* E52+277 67
Sining, *China* F18+363 64
Siniscola, *Sardinia* M32+406 57
Sinj, *Yugoslavia* L80+437 56
Sinjar, & Jebel, *Iraq* K18+364 74
Sinjil, *Israel* K58+320 76
Sinkiang, *China* G30+400 30
Sin-min-fu, *China* D74+420 66
Sinnamary, *Fr. Guiana* R47+053 105
Sinning, *China* E55+266 67
Sinoe L., *Romania* L06+446 58
Sinoia, *Zimbabwe* K88-172 84
Sinop, *Turkey* K58+420 74
Sinton, *Texas* U44+280 94
Sintra, *Portugal* N56+388 52
Sinuiju, *N. Korea* D64+401 64
Sinyang, *China* E35+322 66
Sion, *Switzerland* M46+462 45
Sioux City, *Iowa* U38+426 95
Sioux Falls, *S. Dakota* U40+435 93
Sioux Lookout, *Ontario* U11+502 89
Siparia, *Trinidad* S09+102 104
Sipolilo, *Zimbabwe* K86-166 84
Sipora, I., *Indonesia* F32-022 65
Siquisique, *Venezuela* S58+106 104
Sira, *India* G78+138 70
Sira. *See Siros, I.*
Siracusa, *Sicily* M88+371 57
Sirajganj, *Bangladesh* G01+245 73
Sir Douglas, Mt., *Alberta* V60+505 88
Sir Edward Pellew Group,
  N. Territory, Australia C77-157 111
Siretul, R., *Romania* L18+462 58
Sirhind, *India* G81+306 72
Siri, *Ethiopia* K36+080 83
Sirjan, *Iran* J28+296 75
Sirna, I., *Greece* L20+363 59
Sironcha, *India* G60+188 70
Sironj, *India* G74+241 73
Siros, I., *Greece* L30+374 59
Sirsa, *India* H00+295 72
Sirsi, *India* G68+286 73
Sirsi, *India* H00+146 70
Sirte (Surt), *Libya* L80+312 81
Sisak, *Yugoslavia* L82+454 56
Sisaket, *Thailand* F04+150 69
Sisal, *Mexico* U00+211 100
Sisi, *Botswana* L16-218 84
Sisopon, *Cambodia* F12+136 69
Sister I., E., *Tasmania* C13-397 109
Sister I., W., *Tasmania* C14-397 109
Sisteron, *France* M54+442 55
Sitamarhi, *India* G27+266 73
Sitamau, *India* G87+240 70
Sitapur, *India* G56+275 73
Sitara, *Saudi Arabia* J83+227 74
Sithonia, *Greece* L37+401 59
Sitia, *Crete* L23+352 59
Sitka, *Alaska* X04+569 99
Sitpur, *Pakistan* H25+292 72
Sittang, *Burma* F49+174 71
Sittang, R., *Burma* F51+192 71
Sittard, *Netherlands* M55+510 44
Sitten. *See Sion*
Sivand, *Iran* J42+301 75
Sivas, *Turkey* K48+398 74
Siverek, *Turkey* K34+378 74
Sivrihisar, *Turkey* K81+395 74
Sivry, *Belgium* M65+502 44
Siwa, *Egypt* L28+292 81
Siwalik Hills, *India* G73+304 70
Siwan, *India* G34+262 73
Sixmilebridge, *Ireland, Rep.* N53+527 43
Sixteen, *Montana* V36+462 93
Sjælland, *Denmark* M18+556 47
Sjötorp, *Sweden* M06+588 47
Skadarsko Jezero, *Yugosl.-Alb.* L64+422 58
Skagafjord, *Iceland* P28+660 46
Skagen, *Denmark* M26+577 47
Skagerrak, *Norway-Denmark* M42+573 47
Skagway, *Alaska* X00+592 99
Skaneateles, L., *New York* T08+428 96
Skara, *Sweden* M09+584 47
Skarnes, *Norway* M20+602 47
Skardu, *Kashmir* G86+353 72
Skeena R., *Brit. Columbia* W52+546 88
Skegness, *England* M88+531 37
Skellefte Alv, *Sweden* L66+654 46
Skellefteå, *Sweden* L54+647 46
Skiathos, I., *Greece* L39+392 59
Skibbereen, *Ireland, Rep.* N56+515 43
Skiddaw, mt., *England* N19+546 37
Skien, *Norway* M32+592 47
Skierniewice, *Poland* L59+520 49
Skiftet Kihti, *Finland* L54+600 47
Skipton, *England* N12+540 37
Skiros, I., *Greece* L32+389 59
Skive, *Denmark* M36+566 47

Skofja Loka, *Yugoslavia* M04+462 56
Skópelos, I., *Greece* L36+391 59
Skopin, *U.S.S.R.* K33+538 60
Skopje, *Yugoslavia* L51+420 58
Skövde, *Sweden* M07+584 47
Skovorodino, *U.S.S.R.* D67+540 63
Skowhegan, *Maine* S58+448 90
Skradin, *Yugoslavia* L85+438 56
Skrunda, *Latvia* L48+567 47
Skudenshamn, *Norway* M58+592 47
Skuodas, *Lithuania* L51+562 47
Skye, I., *Scotland* N38+574 40
Slagelse, *Denmark* M22+554 47
Slamet, mt., *Java* E66-072 65
Slammannon, *New S. Wales* C38-320 109
Slane, *Ireland, Rep.* N39+537 42
Slaney R., *Ireland, Rep.* N39+524 43
Slapin, L., *Scotland* N36+571 /40
Slatina, *Yugoslavia* L74+457 /58
Slatina, *Romania* L34+444 58
Slatington, *Pennsylvania* T03+407 96
Slave R., *N.-W. Territories* V48+604 88
Slåveni, *Romania* L33+441 58
Slavgorod, *U.S.S.R.* G70+532 62
Slavonia, *Yugoslavia* L72+454 58
Slavonski Brod, *Yugoslavia* L72+452 56
Slavyansk, *Ukraine* K44+488 60
Slea Hd., *Ireland, Rep.* N63+521 43
Sleaford, *England* N02+530 37
Sleat, Sd. of, *Scotland* N35+571 40
Sleepers, The, *N.-W. Terr.* T36+572 89
Sleydinge, *Belgium* M68+511 44
Slide Mt., *New York* S86+420 91
Sliedrecht, *Netherlands* M61+518 44
Slievanea, *Ireland, Rep.* N61+522 43
Slieve Anierin, *Ireland, Rep.* N48+541 42
Slieve Aughty, Mts.,
  Ireland, Rep. N51+531 43
Slieve Bernagh, *Ireland, Rep.* N51+528 43
Slieve Bloom Mts.,
  Ireland, Rep. N45+530 43
Slieve Car, *Ireland, Rep.* N58+541 42
Slieve Donard, *N. Ireland* N35+542 42
Slievefelim Mts., *Ireland, Rep.* N50+527 43
Slieve Gamph Mts.,
  Ireland, Rep. N54+541 42
Slieve League, *Ireland, Rep.* N52+546 42
Slieve Mish, mts., *Ireland, Rep.* N59+522 43
Slieve Miskish, *Ireland, Rep.* N60+516 43
Slievemore, *Ireland, Rep.* N60+540 42
Slievenakilla, *Ireland, Rep.* N48+542 42
Slievenamon, *Ireland, Rep.* N45+524 43
Slieve Snaght, *Ireland, Rep.* N44+552 42
Slieve Tooey, *Ireland, Rep.* N52+548 42
Sligo & co., *Ireland, Rep.* N51+542 42
Sligo B., *Ireland, Rep.* N53+543 42
Slite, *Sweden* L67+577 47
Sliven, *Bulgaria* L22+427 58
Slobodskoy, *U.S.S.R.* J58+587 61
Sloka, *Latvia* L38+569 47
Slonim, *Byelorussia* L28+530 60
Sloten, *Netherlands* M56+529 44
Slough, *England* N04+515 39
Slovakia, *Czechoslovakia* L60+485 49
Slovenija, *Yugoslavia* M00+459 56
Slovensko, *Czechoslovakia* L60+488 49
Sluis, *Netherlands* M70+513 44
Sluiskil, *Netherlands* M67+513 44
Slunj, *Yugoslavia* L86+451 56
Slussfors, *Sweden* L82+655 46
Slutsk, *Byelorussia* L15+530 60
Slyne Hd., *Ireland, Rep.* N61+534 43
Slyudyanka, *U.S.S.R.* F08+516 63
Smerwick Harb., *Ireland, Rep* N62+522 43
Smethport, *Pennsylvania* T21+418 96
Smilde, *Netherlands* M51+530 44
Smiltene, *Latvia* L25+574 47
Smith, *Alberta* V54+551 88
Smith B., *N.-W. Territories* T20+770 89
Smith B., Gt. Bear L.,
  N.-W.Territories W15+661 88
Smith I., *Quebec* T24+606 89
Smith I., *South Shetlands* S12-630 27
Smithers, *British Columbia* W42+548 88
Smithfield, *N. Carolina* T20+355 97
Smithfield, *Virginia* T11+370 97
Smithfield, *Utah* V41+418 94
Smithland, *Kentucky* T80+371 97
Smiths Falls, *Ontario* T06+449 91
Smithton, *Tasmania* C29-409 109
Smoky R., *Alberta* V78+552 88
Smoky Hill R., *Kansas* U65+388 98
Smøla, *Norway* M42+634 46
Smolensk, *U.S.S.R.* K78+548 60
Smoothstone L., *Sask.* V13+542 88
Smyrna. *See Izmir*
Snaefell, *Isle of Man* N27+543 37
Snake, R. & Canyon,
  Washington, etc. V83+464 92
Snake R., *Yukon* W77+657 88
Snares Is., *New Zealand* A81-481 112
Snåsa, *Norway* M16+642 46
Snåsa Vatn, *Norway* M18+642 46
Sneek, *Netherlands* M56+530 44
Sneen, *Ireland, Rep.* N59+518 43
Snizort, L., *Scotland* N39+576 40
Snøhetta, mt., *Norway* M34+623 46
Snow Flake, *Arizona* V31+345 94
Snow Lake, *Martoba* U60+548 88
Snow Pk., *Wyoming* V09+414 98
Snowdon, mt., *Wales* N24+530 38
Snowtown, *S. Australia* C71-338 109
Snow Water L., *Nevada* V60+406 94
Snowy Mts., *Vict.-N.S.W.* C12-366 109
Snowy R., *Victoria* C11-386 109
Snyder, *Texas* U66+326 94
Soanzano, *Italy* L80+403 57
Soazza, *Switzerland* M35+463 45
Sobakin, *U.S.S.R.* J71+538 61
Soboko, *Cent. Afr. Rep.* L30+068 81
Sobrado, *Brazil* R49-055 105
Sobral, *Brazil* Q62-037 105
Sobrance, *Czechoslovakia* L47+487 49
Sobraon, *India* H00+311 72
Sochi, *U.S.S.R.* K34+438 62
Social Circle, *Georgia* T52+336 97
Society Is., *Pacific Ocean* Q20-150 107
Socorro, *Colombia* S80+064 104
Socorro, *New Mexico* V12+341 94
Socorro I., *Mexico* V36+188 100
Socotra, I., *Indian Ocean* J36+124 83

Soc-trang, *Vietnam* E84+096 69
Sodankylä, *Finland* L20+674 46
Soda Springs, *Idaho* V40+426 94
Söderfors, *Sweden* L77+604 47
Söderhamn, *Sweden* L78+613 47
Söderköping, *Sweden* L82+585 47
Södertälje, *Sweden* L74+592 47
Sodiri, *Sudan* L06+142 81
Sodus, *New York* T12+432 96
Sodus Pt., *New York* T12+432 96
Soela (Sulu) Eiln, *Indonesia* D58-018 65
Soemba (Sumba), I., *Indon.* E00-100 65
Soembawa (Sumbawa), I.,
  Indonesia E10-088 65
Soerabaja, *See Surabaya*
Soest, *W. Germany* M41+516 48
Soest, *Netherlands* M58+522 44
Sofala, *Mozambique* K62-202 84
Sofala, *New South Wales* C02-331 109
Sofiya (Sofia), *Bulgaria* L40+427 58
Sogamosa, *Colombia* S77+057 104
Sogndal, *Norway* M52+583 47
Sogne Fd., *Norway* M54+611 47
Söğut, *Turkey* K89+401 74
Sohag, *Egypt* K80+266 81
Sohagpur, *India* G51+233 73
Sohan R., *Pakistan* H16+330 72
Sohawal, *India* G55+246 73
Soheb, *Yemen, South* J79+139 74
Sohna, *India* G77+283 72
Soignies, *Belgium* M66+506 506 44
Soissons, *France* M70+494 54
Soke, *England* N02+526 37
Soke, *Turkey* L16+378 74
Sok Gomba, *Tibet* F68+320 64
Sok Karmalinsk, *U.S.S.R.* J45+541 61
Sokki, *Chad* L68+112 81
Soko, *U.S.S.R.* K29+594 60
Sokol, *U.S.S.R.* K29+594 60
Sokota, *Ethiopia* K36+126 83
Sokoto, *Nigeria* M58+128 80
Sola Consilina, *Italy* L87+404 57
Solai, *Kenya* K52+001 83
Solbad Hall, *Austria* M21+473 48
Soledad, *Venezuela* S21+082 104
Soledade, *Brazil* S55-066 104
Solent, The, *England* N08+508 39
Solenzara, *Corsica* M34+418 57
Sol Iletsk, *U.S.S.R.* J29+511 61
Solimoes (Amazonas), R.,
  Brazil S40-020 104
Solingen, *W. Germany* M48+512 48
Sollefteå, *Sweden* L76+632 46
Solok, *Sumatra* F25-007 65
Solomon Is., *Pacific Ocean* B30-060 106
Solomon R., *Kansas* U59+396 98
Solon, *India* G77+309 72
Solothurn & canton, *Switz.* M45+472 45
Solsona, *Spain* M81+420 53
Solstad, *Norway* M17+651 46
Soltau, *W. Germany* M31+530 48
Solund, I., *Norway* M60+611 47
Solway, *Minnesota* U31+475 93
Solway Firth, *Eng.-Scot.* N22+548 37
Solwezi, *Zambia* L22-122 82
Soma, *Turkey* L14+392 74
Somalia, *E. Africa* K00+050 83
Sombor, *Yugoslavia* L66+458 58
Sombreiro Chan., *Nicobar Is.* F70+076 71
Sombrerete, *Mexico* U81+238 100
Sombrero, I., *Leeward Is.* S21+187 101
Somcuta Mare, *Romania* L39+475 49
Someren, *Netherlands* M56+514 44
Somerset, *Kentucky* T58+371 97
Somerset, *Pennsylvania* T24+400 91
Somerset, *Queensland* C45-108 111
Somerset, co., *England* N18+510 38
Somerset I., *N.-W. Terr.* U20+730 89
Somerset Res., *Vermont* S77+430 96
Somerville, *New Jersey* S88+405 96
Somerville, *Tennessee* T86+353 97
Somme, *Belgium* M58+503 44
Somme, dep., *France* M76+500 54
Somme, R., *France* M79+502 54
Sommieres, *France* M66+438 55
Somoto, *Nicaragua* T70+136 101
Somovit, *Bulgaria* L31+437 58
Somzee, *Belgium* M63+503 44
Son R., *India* G32+253 73
Sonamukhi, *India* G16+232 73
Sonbarsa, *India* G18+253 73
Sönderborg, *Denmark* M31+549 47
Sonepat, *India* G78+290 72
Song-Cau, *Vietnam* E65+135 69
Songea, *Tanzania* K56-108 83
Songkhla, *Thailand* F27+071 69
Song-koi, R., *Vietnam* F10+229 69
Sonhat, *India* G45+235 73
Sonkajärvi, *Finland* L15+637 46
Sonkovo, *U.S.S.R.* K47+578 60
Sonmiani, *Pakistan* H50+258 70
Sonneberg, *E. Germany* M23+503 48
Sonogno, *Switzerland* M37+463 45
Sonora, state & R., *Mexico* V38+288 100
Sonoyta, *Mexico* V47+319 100
Sonpur, *India* G36+208 71
Sonpur, *India* G29+257 73
Sonson, *Colombia* T01+057 104
Soochow, *China* D86+313 66
Soping. *See Yuyu*
Sopley, *England* N11+508 39
Soppero, *Sweden* L50+681 46
Sopron, *Hungary* L80+476 56
Sopur, *Kashmir* H03+343 72
Sora, *Italy* M08+417 57
Sorata, *Bolivia* S52-158 104
Sorbas, *Spain* N11+371 53
Sorell, *Tasmania* C15-428 109
Sörenberg, *Switzerland* M42+468 45
Sörfold, *Norway* L87+675 46
Sorgono, *Sardinia* M35+400 57
Soria, *Spain* N15+418 53
Soriano, *Uruguay* R80-336 103
Sornico, *Switzerland* M38+464 45
Sorocaba, *Brazil* R15-234 105
Soroki, *Moldavia* L10+482 60
Sorol, I., *Caroline Is.* C55+075 106
Soromesis, *Botswana* L46-194 84
Soron, *India* G67+279 73

Sorong, *New Guinea* D22-008 65
Sororoca, *Brazil* S09+008 104
Soroti, *Uganda* K68+016 83
Sørøya I., *Norway* L44+705 46
Sorrento, *Italy* M04+406 57
Sorsele, *Sweden* L75+655 46
Sortavala, *Karelia* K86+617 46
Sosnovka, *U.S.S.R.* K21+532 61
Sosnovo Ozerskoye, *U.S.S.R.* E50+526 63
Sosnowiec, *Poland* L66+504 49
Sosva, *U.S.S.R.* H80+592 62
Soto la Marina, *Mexico* U49+237 100
Sotra, I., *Norway* M60+603 47
Sotuta, *Mexico* T83+205 100
Souanke, *Congo* M06+020 82
Soudan, *N. Terr. Aust.* C77-200 111
Souflion, *Greece* L23+411 58
Souillac, *France* M81+449 55
Soul. *See Seoul*
Soure, *Brazil* R21-007 105
Soure, *Portugal* N52+401 52
Souris, *Manitoba* U62+497 88
Souris, *Prince Edward I.* S13+464 90
Sousse, *Tunisia* M26+358 81
Souterraine, la, *France* M81+462 54
South Africa, rep., *Africa* L30-280 84
South Downs, *England* N04+507 39
South I., *New Zealand* 112
Southampton, *England* N08+509 39
Southampton, *New York* S74+409 91
Southampton, *Ontario* T38+445 91
Southampton, C., *N.-W. Terr.* T52+618 89
Southampton I., *N.-W. Terr.* T60+646 89
South Australia, state, *Aust.* 110-111
South Bend, *Indiana* T68+417 91
South Bend, *Washington* W23+467 92
Southbridge, *Massachusetts* S72+422 96
Southbridge, *New Zealand* A46-438 112
South Boston, *Virginia* T24+367 97
South Carolina, state, *U.S.A.* T40+341 99
South China Sea, *Asia* E60+100 31
South Dakota, state, *U.S.A.* U78+448 98
South-East C., *Tasmania* C19-436 109
South-East C., *Victoria* C22-390 109
Southend-on-Sea, *England* M86+515 39
Southern Alps, *New Zealand* A60-436 112
Southern Cross, *W. Australia* E04-311 110
South Foreland, *England* M83+511 39
South Georgia, I., *Atlant. Oc.* Q40-540 27
South Hadley Falls, *Mass.* S76+422 96
South Haven, *Michigan* T68+424 91
South Indian L., *Manitoba* U52+568 88
South Jacksonville, *Florida* T40+303 97
South Milwaukee, *Wisconsin* T77+430 91
South Nahanni R.,
  N.-W. Territories W40+616 88
South Orkneys, Is., *Atlantic*
  Ocean R00-610 27
South Paris, *Maine* S63+443 90
South Pittsburg, *Tennessee* T64+350 97
South Polar Plateau., *Antarc.* B30-870 27
South Pole, *Antarctica* 27
Southport, *England* N18+536 37
Southport, *Prince Edward I.* S18+463 90
Southport, *Queensland* B70-279 111
South River, *New Jersey* S87+404 96
South Ronaldsay I., *Scot.* N18+588 40
South Sandwich. Is., *Atl. Oc.* P80-570 27
South Shetland Is., *Antarc.* S00-630 27
South Shields, *England* N08+550 37
South-West C., *Tasmania* C23-435 109
South-West Africa, *See* Namibia
South Yemen, *Asia* J80+150 74
South Yorkshire, co., *Eng.* N08+535 37
Souza, *Brazil* Q49-067 105
Souzel, *Brazil* R44-024 105
Souzel, *Portugal* N46+389 52
Sovetsk, *U.S.S.R.* L48+551 47
Sovetsk, *U.S.S.R.* J66+576 61
Sovetskaya Gavan, *U.S.S.R.* C57+488 63
Soy, *Kenya* K58+008 83
Soya & B., *Japan* C50+454 68
Soya Misaki, *Japan* C49+455 68
Soyopa, *Mexico* V26+290 100
Spa, *Belgium* M55+505 44
Spain, *W. Europe* N24+400 50
Spalato. *See Split*
Spalding, *England* N01+528 37
Spalding, *S. Australia* C68-334 109
Spandau. *W. Berlin* M11+525 48
Spanish, *Ontario* T44+462 91
Spanish Fork. *Utah* V40+401 94
Spanish Town, *Jamaica* T12+180 101
Sparks, *Nevada* V89+395 92
Sparta, *Illinois* T88+382 95
Sparta, *N. Carolina* T37+365 97
Sparta, *Wisconsin* U05+439 91
Sparta (Sparti), *Greece* L46+371 59
Spartanburg, *S. Carolina* T42+350 97
Spartivento C., *Italy* L83+379 57
Spask, *U.S.S.R.* J64+550 61
Spask, *U.S.S.R.* K11+538 61
Spassk, *U.S.S.R.* D13+447 63
Spencer, *Iowa* U30+432 95
Spencer, *S. Dakota* U46+437 93
Spencer G., *S. Australia* C78-340 111
Spenser Mts., *New Zealand* A44-420 112
Sperrin Mts., *N. Ireland* N42+548 42
Spetsai I., *Greece* L41+372 59
Spey, R., *Scotland* N19+576 40
Speyer, *W. Germany* M39+493 48
Spezand, *Pakistan* H48+299 70
Spezia, La, *Italy* M31+441 56
Sphinx, *Montana* V36+452 93
Spilsby, *England* M89+532 37
Spinazzola, *Italy* L83+410 57
Spiringen, *Switzerland* M38+469 45
Spirit Lake, *Iowa* U30+434 95
Spitsbergen, *Arctic Ocean* L40+800 62
Spitsbergen, Vest, *Arctic*
  Ocean L80+790 62
Spittal, *Austria* M09+468 48
Split, *Yugoslavia* L81+435 56
Split L., *Manitoba* U38+560 88
Splügen, *Switzerland* M34+466 45
Splügen Pass, *Switzerland-Italy*
  M30+465 45
Spofford, *Texas* U62+292 94
Spokane, *Washington* V75+476 92
Spoleto, *Italy* M14+428 56
Spontin, *Belgium* M60+503 44
Sporadhes, *Aegean Sea* L18+370 59

Sporadhes, Voriai, *Aegean Sea* L32+392 **59**
Spotsylvania, *Virginia* T16+382 **97**
Spree R., *E. Germany* M06+523 **48**
Spremberg, *E. Germany* M04+516 **48**
Sprimont, *Belgium* M56+505 **44**
Springbok, *Cape Province* L72–296 **84**
Spring City, *Tennessee* T59+356 **97**
Springdale, *Arkansas* U24+362 **93**
Springdale, *Montana* V32+457 **93**
Springer, *New Mexico* U88+364 **94**
Springerville, *Arizona* V26+342 **94**
Springfield, *Colorado* U76+374 **94**
Springfield, *Georgia* T38+323 **97**
Springfield, *Illinois* T88+398 **91**
Springfield, *Massachusetts* S75+421 **91**
Springfield, *Missouri* U20+372 **95**
Springfield, *Ohio* T53+399 **91**
Springfield, *Vermont* S75+433 **96**
Springfontein, *Orange Free State* L26–304 **84**
Springhill, *Nova Scotia* S24+456 **90**
Spring Hope, *N. Carolina* T19+360 **97**
Springlands, *Guyana* R73+058 **105**
Spring Place, *Georgia* T59+348 **97**
Springsure, *Queensland* C12–239 **111**
Springville, *New York* T22+425 **91**
Springville, *Utah* V40+402 **94**
Spruce Brook, *Newfoundland* R79+488 **90**
Spruce Knob, *W. Virginia* T28+387 **96**
Spruga, *Switzerland* M39+462 **45**
Squillace, G. di, *Italy* L78+387 **57**
Srbija (Serbia), *Yugoslavia* L58+435 **58**
Srebrenica, *Yugoslavia* L65+441 **58**
Sredinnyy Khrebet, *U.S.S.R.* B30+570 **63**
Sredne Kamchatsk, *U.S.S.R.* B31+555 **63**
Sredne Kolyma, *U.S.S.R.* B80+670 **63**
Sredne Vilyuysk, *U.S.S.R.* D70+639 **63**
Srem, *Poland* L78+521 **49**
Srepok, R., *Cambodia* E78+136 **65**
Sretensk, *U.S.S.R.* E12+524 **63**
Srikakulam, *India* G36+183 **71**
Sri Lanka, *S. Asia* G55+076 **70**
Sri Madhopur, *India* G86+274 **72**
Srinagar, *Kashmir* H01+341 **72**
Srirangapatnam, *India* G79+124 **70**
Srivilliputtur, *India* G74+095 **70**
Srnetica, *Yugoslavia* L81+445 **56**
Sroda, *Poland* L76+522 **49**
Stackpool, *Ontario* T41+479 **91**
Stack's Mts., *Ireland, Rep.* N57+523 **43**
Stadacona, *Quebec* S73+474 **91**
Staden, *Belgium* M72+510 **44**
Staffa, I., *Scotland* N38+564 **41**
Stafford, *Arizona* V28+328 **94**
Stafford, *England* N13+528 **37**
Stafford, *Kansas* U52+379 **95**
Stafford, *Virginia* T15+384 **97**
Stafford, co., *England* N12+529 **37**
Staines, *England* N03+514 **39**
Stambaugh, *Michigan* T81+461 **91**
Stamford, *Connecticut* S81+411 **91**
Stamford, *England* N03+526 **37**
Stamprooi, *Netherlands* M56+512 **44**
Stanberry, *Missouri* U28+403 **95**
Stanchik, *U.S.S.R.* B89+710 **63**
Standerton, *Transvaal* L04–270 **84**
Standish, *Michigan* T54+439 **91**
Stange, *Norway* M23+607 **47**
Stanislav, *Ukraine* L34+490 **49**
Stanley, *Falkland Is.* R78–516 **99**
Stanley, *Tasmania* C28–408 **109**
Stanley Falls, *See* Boyoma Falls
Stanleyville. *See* Kisangani L28+006 **82**
Stann Creek, *Belize* T80+170 **101**
Stanovoy Khrebet, *U.S.S.R.* D60+557 **63**
Stans, *Switzerland* M40+470 **45**
Stansmore Ra., *W. Australia* D45–214 **110**
Stanthorpe, *Queensland* B78–285 **111**
Stanton, *Michigan* T61+433 **91**
Stanton, *N. Dakota* U69+473 **93**
Staphorst, *Netherlands* M53+526 **44**
Staples, *Minnesota* U29+463 **93**
Stara Planina, *Bulgaria* L30+427 **59**
Staraya Russa, *U.S.S.R.* K80+580 **60**
Stara Zagora, *Bulgaria* L26+424 **58**
Starbuck, I., *Pacific Ocean* Y32–055 **107**
Star City, *Arkansas* U11+340 **97**
Stargard, *Poland* L90+533 **48**
Starkville, *Mississippi* T84+334 **95**
Starkweather, *N. Dakota* U53+485 **93**
Starobel'sk, *Ukraine* K36+492 **60**
Starodub, *U.S.S.R.* K73+526 **60**
Starogard, *Poland* L69+540 **49**
Staro Konstantinov, *Ukraine* L16+498 **60**
Staryy Oskol, *U.S.S.R.* K43+512 **60**
Staten I., *Argentina. See* Estados, I. de los
Staten I., *New York* S85+406 **96**
Statesville, *N. Carolina* T35+357 **97**
Stattlandet, *Norway* M58+622 **46**
Staunton, *Virginia* T25+382 **97**
Stavanger, *Norway* M56+590 **47**
Stavelot, *Belgium* M54+504 **44**
Stavenisse, *Netherlands* M66+516 **44**
Stavern, *Norway* M30+590 **47**
Staveren, *Netherlands* M58+529 **44**
Stavropol, *U.S.S.R.* K20+450 **62**
Stawell, *Victoria* C43–371 **109**
Steckborn, *Switzerland* M36+477 **45**
Steele, *N. Dakota* U60+469 **93**
Steelton, *Pennsylvania* T11+402 **96**
Steelville, *Missouri* U08+380 **95**
Steenbergen, *Netherlands* M64+516 **44**
Steensel, *Netherlands* M58+514 **44**
Steenwijk, *Netherlands* M53+528 **44**
Stefanie L., *Ethiopia* K48+046 **83**
Steiermark, prov., *Austria* M00+472 **48**
Stein, *Switzerland* M37+477 **45**
Steinkjer, *Norway* M21+640 **46**
Stekene, *Belgium* M66+512 **44**
Stellarton, *Nova Scotia* S16+456 **90**
Stenay, *France* M59+495 **54**
Stendal, *E. Germany* M19+526 **48**
Stenness, L. of, *Orkney, Scot.* N19+590 **40**
Stenträsk, *Sweden* L61+663 **46**
Stephenson, *Michigan* T76+454 **91**
Stephenville, *Newfoundland* R81+485 **90**
Stepnoy, *U.S.S.R.* K05+465 **62**
Stepnyak, *Kazakh.* H25+531 **62**
Sterea, *Greece* L48+387 **59**
Sterling, *Colorado* U79+406 **94**
Sterling, *Illinois* T88+418 **95**

Sterlitamak, *U.S.S.R.* J24+536 **61**
Šternberk, *Czechoslovakia* L77+497 **49**
Sterrebeek, *Belgium* M63+509 **44**
Stettin. *See* Szczecin
Stettler, *Alberta* V45+520 **88**
Steubenville, *Ohio* T34+404 **91**
Stevens Point, *Wisconsin* T88+445 **91**
Stewart, *Brit. Columbia* W60+557 **88**
Stewart River, *Yukon* X26+636 **88**
Stewart, I., *Chile* S68–548 **103**
Stewart Is., *New Zealand* A73–470 **112**
Stewart R., *Yukon* X05+640 **88**
Stewart Sd., *Andaman Is.* F72+130 **71**
Steyr, *Austria* M04+480 **48**
Stia, *Italy* M20+438 **56**
Stikine R., *Brit. Columbia* W70+568 **88**
Stillwater, *Minnesota* U17+451 **93**
Stillwater, *Oklahoma* U42+362 **95**
Stimlje, *Yugoslavia* L54+424 **58**
Štip, *Yugoslavia* L47+417 **58**
Stirling, *Scotland* N24+561 **41**
Stirling Ra., *W. Australia* E10–342 **110**
Stjernøya, *Norway* L44+703 **46**
Stockholm, *Sweden* L72+594 **47**
Stockinbingal, *New South Wales* C13–346 **109**
Stockport, *England* N13+534 **37**
Stockton, *California* W08+379 **92**
Stockton, *Kansas* U56+394 **95**
Stockton, *New South Wales* B80–329 **109**
Stockton-on-Tees, *England* N08+546 **37**
Stoer, Pt. of, *Scotland* N32+583 **40**
Stoke-on-Trent, *England* N13+530 **37**
Stolbovaya, *U.S.S.R.* B69+645 **63**
Stolp. *See* Słupsk
Ston, *Yugoslavia* L74+428 **56**
Stonehaven, *Scotland* N13+569 **40**
Stony L., *Ontario* T19+445 **91**
Stony Crossing, *New South Wales* C39–351 **109**
Stony Stratford, *England* N06+520 **39**
Stor Sjön, *Sweden* M04+633 **46**
Stora Lulevatten, *Sweden* L64+672 **46**
Stora Sjöfallets Nat. Park, *Sweden* L74+676 **46**
Storavan, *Sweden* L70+657 **46**
Stord, I., *Norway* M58+598 **47**
Støren, *Norway* M28+631 **46**
Storforshei, *Norway* M03+664 **46**
Storlien, *Sweden* M17+634 **46**
Storm B., *Tasmania* C15–432 **109**
Storm Lake, *Iowa* U31+426 **95**
Storman, *Sweden* L77+650 **46**
Storvik, *Sweden* L82+606 **47**
Stour, R., *England* M84+520 **39**
Stourbridge, *England* N13+525 **37**
Stourport, *England* N14+524 **37**
Stowmarket, *England* M84+522 **39**
Strabane, *N. Ireland* N45+548 **42**
Strachan, *Quebec* T00+480 **91**
Strachan I., *Papua N. Guin.,* C47-090 **111**
Stradbally, *Ireland, Rep.* N43+530 **43**
Strahan, *Tasmania* C28–422 **109**
Stralsund, *E. Germany* M12+543 **48**
Strand, *Norway* M54+590 **47**
Stranda, *Norway* M48+623 **46**
Strangford, *N. Ireland* N33+544 **42**
Strangford L., *N. Ireland* N33+545 **42**
Strangways Springs, *South Australia* C80–289 **111**
Stranorlar, *Ireland, Rep.* N46+548 **42**
Stranraer, *Scotland* N30+549 **41**
Strasbourg, *France* M43+485 **54**
Strasburg, *Virginia* T20+390 **96**
Strässa, *Sweden* L89+598 **47**
Stratford, *Connecticut* S78+412 **96**
Stratford, *Michigan* T60+445 **91**
Stratford, *New Zealand* A34–393 **112**
Stratford, *Ontario* T36+434 **91**
Stratford, *Victoria* C18–379 **109**
Stratford-upon-Avon, *England* N10+522 **37**
Strathalbyn, *S. Australia* C67–352 **109**
Strathclyde, reg., *Scotland* N32+558 **41**
Strathcona Park, *B.C.* W35+498 **88**
Strathpeffer, *Scotland* N27+576 **40**
Strathroy, *Ontario* T40+430 **91**
Strathy Pt., *Scotland* N24+586 **40**
Strathyre, *Scotland* N26+563 **41**
Straubing, *W. Germany* M15+489 **48**
Strba, *Czech.* L60+491 **49**
Streaky B., *S. Australia* D05–324 **111**
Streator, *Illinois* T83+411 **95**
Strelka, *U.S.S.R.* B79+618 **63**
Strelka, *U.S.S.R.* F14+617 **63**
Strelka, *U.S.S.R.* F70+581 **63**
Strencis, *Latvia* L26+576 **47**
Stribro, *Czechoslovakia* M12+497 **48**
Strijbeek, *Netherlands* M61+515 **44**
Strijen, *Netherlands* M63+517 **44**
Strimón, G. of, *Greece* L36+406 **59**
Strokestown, *Ireland, Rep.* N48+538 **42**
Strōma, I., *Scotland* N19+586 **40**
Stromboli, I., *Italy* L89+388 **57**
Stromeferry, *Scotland* N33+573 **40**
Stromness, *Orkney, Scot.* N20+590 **40**
Strömsberg, *Sweden* L75+604 **47**
Strömsbruk, *Sweden* L76+619 **47**
Strömstad, *Sweden* M23+590 **47**
Strömsund, *Sweden* L86+639 **46**
Ströms Vattudäl, *Sweden* M04+644 **46**
Strömtorp, *Sweden* M03+593 **47**
Strongoli, *Italy* L78+393 **57**
Stronsay I., & Firth, *Scot.* N15+591 **40**
Stroud, *England* N13+517 **39**
Stroudsburg, *Pennsylvania* T01+410 **96**
Struga, *Yugoslavia* L56+412 **58**
Strule, R., *N. Ireland* N44+547 **42**
Struma, R.. *Bulgaria-Greece* L42+418 **58**
Strumica, *Yugoslavia* L44+414 **58**
Stryy, *Ukraine* L37+493 **60**
Strzelecki Pk., *Tasmania* C13–402 **109**
Strzelin, *Poland* L78+508 **49**
Stuart, *Florida* T32+272 **97**
Stuart, *Virginia* T32+366 **97**
Stuart Ra., *S. Australia* D05–290 **111**
Stuart Highway, *N.T., Aust.* D06–186 **111**
Stugun, *Sweden* L86+632 **46**
Stung-Treng, *Cambodia* E84+135 **69**
Sturgeon Bay, *Wisconsin* T75+449 **91**
Sturgeon Falls, *Ontario* T30+464 **91**

Sturgis, *S. Dakota* U82+444 **93**
Sturt Des., *S. Australia, etc.* C54–282 **111**
Sturt, Mt., *New S. Wales* C50–296 **109**
Stuttgart, *Arkansas* U10+345 **97**
Stuttgart, *W. Germany* M35+488 **48**
Suakin, *Sudan* K46+196 **81**
Suancheng, *China* E07+309 **66**
Süan-hwa, *China* E29+406 **66**
Suaqui, *Mexico* V27+286 **100**
Subeimanieh, *Iran* J54+358 **75**
Subh, Jebel, *Saudi Arabia* K36+237 **74**
Subotica, *Yugoslavia* L62+461 **58**
Sucha, *Poland* L62+498 **49**
Suchan, *U.S.S.R.* D11+430 **63**
Süchow (Tungshan), *China* E15+343 **66**
Sucre, *Bolivia* S32–192 **104**
Sudan, rep. *Africa* — **81**
Sudbury, *England* M86+520 **39**
Sudbury, *Ontario* T36+465 **91**
Suddie, *Guyana* R81+070 **104**
Sudety, mts., *Czech., etc.* L84+507 **49**
Sudharam, *Bangladesh* F83+228 **71**
Suez, *Egypt* K74+300 **81**
Suez Canal, *Egypt* K75+310 **81**
Suez, Gulf of, *Egypt* K72+286 **81**
Suffolk, *Virginia* T09+367 **97**
Suffolk, co., *England* M84+523 **39**
Suggsville, *Alabama* T76+316 **97**
Suhl, *E. Germany* M26+506 **48**
Sufu. *See* Ipin
Suihwa, *China* D47+466 **64**
Suining, *China* E12+339 **66**
Suipacha, *Bolivia* S33–215 **104**
Suir R., *Ireland, Rep.* N43+523 **43**
Suiteh, *China* E59+374 **66**
Sujangarh, *India* H02+277 **72**
Sujanpur, *India* G86+323 **72**
Sujanpur, *India* G81+318 **72**
Sujica, *Yugoslavia* L77+438 **56**
Sukarnapura. *See* Djajapura
Sukarno, Pk. *See* Puntjak Djaja.
Sukhumi, *Gruzinskaya* K25+430 **62**
Sukkur, *Pakistan* H37+276 **70**
Suklek B., *Labrador* S20+588 **89**
Sukow, *China* E45+375 **66**
Sukumo, *Japan* D13+330 **68**
Sulaiman Ra., *Pakistan* H30+310 **70**
Sulaimiya, *Saudi Arabia* J57+242 **74**
Sulaiyil, *Saudi Arabia* J87+204 **74**
Sulaymānīva. *Iraq* J87+356 **74**
Sulecin, *Poland* L87+521 **49**
Sulgen, *Switzerland* M35+475 **45**
Sulina, *Romania* L02+451 **58**
Sulitelma, mt., *Norway* L82+671 **46**
Sullana, *Peru* T34–049 **104**
Sullivan, *Illinois* T82+396 **95**
Sullivan, *Indiana* T74+390 **95**
Sullivan, *Missouri* U07+382 **97**
Sulmona, *Italy* M07+419 **57**
Sulphur Springs, *Texas* U34+332 **95**
Sultan Bulak, *Iran* J65+358 **74**
Sultan Dagh, *Turkey* K84+383 **74**
Sultan Hamud, *Kenya* K46–020 **83**
Sultaniyeh, *Iran* J67+365 **74**
Sultanpur, *India* G47+262 **73**
Sultanpur, *India* H00+312 **72**
Sulu Arch., *Philippines* D82+055 **65**
Sulu Kep., *Indonesia* D58–018 **65**
Sulu Sea, *Philippines* E00+081 **65**
Sumagawa, *Japan* C48+434 **68**
Sumatra. I.. *Indonesia* F30+005 **65**
Sumba. I.. *Indonesia* E00–100 **65**
Sumbawa, I., *Indonesia* E10–088 **65**
Sumbur, *Mongolia* E68+465 **64**
Sumburgh Hd., *Scotland* N08+599 **40**
Sümeg. *Hungary* L77+470 **49**
Sumiswald, *Switzerland* M44+470 **45**
Summerside, *Pr. Edward I.* S22+464 **90**
Summit, *S. Dakota* U42+453 **93**
Sumperk, *Czechoslovakia* L79+500 **49**
Sumprabum, *Burma* F44+266 **71**
Sumter, *S. Carolina* T32+339 **97**
Sumy, *Ukraine* K61+509 **60**
Suna, *Tanzania* K62–056 **83**
Sunapee, *New Hampshire* S72+434 **96**
Sunart L., *Scotland* N34+567 **41**
Sunbury, *Pennsylvania* T11+409 **91**
Suncho Corral, *Argentina* S21–279 **103**
Sunchow. *See* Kweiping
Suncook, *New Hampshire* S69+431 **91**
Sunda Str., *Indonesia* F00–064 **65**
Sundance, *Wyoming* U86+444 **93**
Sundargarh, *India* G35+221 **73**
Sunderland, *England* N08+549 **37**
Sundridge, *Ontario* T27+458 **91**
Sundsvall, *Sweden* L76+624 **46**
Sungari Res., *China* D50+430 **64**
Sungari R., *China* D60+456 **64**
Sungkiang, *China* D81+311 **66**
Sunndal, *Norway* M38+627 **46**
Sunnyside, *Utah* V32+395 **94**
Suntar, *U.S.S.R.* E14+622 **63**
Sunyani, *Ghana* N14+074 **80**
Suonnejoki, *Finland* L17+625 **46**
Supaul, *India* G20+261 **73**
Superior, *Wisconsin* U12+467 **93**
Superior L., *U.S.A.-Canada* T80+475 **99**
Supiori, I., *New Guinea, Indonesia* C87–006 **65**
Suq ash Shuyukh, *Iraq* J81+309 **74**
Sur, *Oman* J03+226 **75**
Sur (Tyre), *Lebanon* K59+333 **76**
Sura R., *U.S.S.R.* J81+551 **61**
Surab, *Pakistan* H52+283 **70**
Surabaya, *Java* E43–072 **65**
Surajgarh, *India* G85+283 **72**
Surakarta, *Java* E55–075 **65**
Suran, *Syria* K49+353 **76**
Surapur, *India* G79+166 **70**
Surat, *India* H12+211 **70**
Suratgarh, *India* H06+293 **72**
Surat. Thani, *Thailand* F34+091 **69**
Surendranagar, *India* H20+227 **70**
Surgères, *France* N05+461 **54**
Surgut, *U.S.S.R.* G70+613 **62**
Suri, *India* G15+239 **73**
Surigao Str., *Philippines* D60+092 **65**
Surin, *Thailand* E99+148 **69**
Surinam (Dutch Guiana) *S. America* R70+040 **105**

Suriname, R., *Surinam* R63+042 **105**
Suriya, *Yemen, South* J84+135 **74**
Surling, Mt., *Vietnam* E73+115 **69**
Surrey, co., *England* N03+513 **39**
Sursee, *Switzerland* M44+472 **45**
Sursk, *Ukraine* K61+484 **60**
Süs (Susch), *Switzerland* M30+468 **45**
Susa, *Iran* J70+323 **74**
Susak, *Yugoslavia* M03+447 **56**
Susquehanna R., *Pa., etc.* T08+398 **91**
Sussex, *New Brunswick* S33+457 **90**
Sussex, E. & W., co., *England* N01+510 **39**
Susteren, *Netherlands* M55+511 **44**
Sutherland, *Cape Province* L56–324 **84**
Sutherland, co., *See* Highland
Suting. *See* Tahsien.
Sutlej R., *Pakistan* H12+302 **72**
Sutsien, *China* E10+339 **66**
Sutton, *Ontario* T26+443 **91**
Suure Jaani, *Estonia* L27+585 **47**
Suvasesi, *Finland* L11+626 **46**
Suvorov, I., *Pacific Ocean* Y80–138 **106**
Suwair, *Saudi Arabia* K28+301 **74**
Suwałki, *Poland* L43+541 **49**
Suwayh, *Oman* J02+222 **75**
Suwayq, *Oman* J15+239 **75**
Suweilih, *Jordan* K55+320 **76**
Suwo Nada, *Japan* D21+338 **68**
Svalbard, *Arctic Ocean* L60+790 **62**
Svanstein, *Sweden* L37+666 **46**
Svappavaara, *Sweden* L54+677 **46**
Svørholt-halvøya, *Norway* L24+704 **46**
Svartenhuk Pen., *Greenland* R38+720 **26**
Svartisen, *Norway* M06+666 **46**
Svartvik, *Sweden* L76+623 **46**
Švekšna. *Lithuania* L50+556 **47**
Svendborg, *Denmark* M26+551 **47**
Sventoji, *Lithuania* L53+560 **47**
Sverdlovsk, *U.S.S.R.* H86+568 **61**
Sverdrup Is., *N.-W. Terr.* U30+778 **88**
Sverdrup, Os., *U.S.S.R.* G64+745 **62**
Svishtov, *Bulgaria* L28+436 **58**
Svitavy. *Czechoslovakia* L80+497 **49**
Svobodny, *U.S.S.R.* D41+514 **63**
Svolvaer, *Norway* M02+682 **46**
Swabi, *Pakistan* H15+341 **72**
Swakopmund, *Namibia* M02-226 **84**
Swale R., *England* N09+543 **37**
Swan, R., *W. Australia* E22–314 **110**
Swan Hill, *Victoria* C39–354 **109**
Swan Reach, *S. Australia* C62–346 **109**
Swan River, *Manitoba* U66+524 **88**
Swansea, *Tasmania* C12–422 **109**
Swansea & B., *Wales* N24+516 **38**
Swanton, *Vermont* S79+449 **91**
Swarzewo, *Poland* L70+547 **49**
Swastika, *Ontario* T31+481 **91**
Swat & R., *Pakistan* H15+350 **72**
Swaziland, *S. Africa* K80–264 **84**
Sweden, *N.-W. Europe* **46–47**
Sweet Grass Hills, *Montana* V37+489 **93**
Sweetwater, *Texas* U62+324 **94**
Swellendam, *Cape Province* L58–340 **84**
Swidnica, *Poland* L81+509 **49**
Swidwin, *Poland* L67+503 **49**
Swift Current, *Saskatchewan* V17+502 **88**
Swilly L., *Ireland, Rep.* N45+552 **42**
Swinburne, C., *N.-W. Terr.* U54+710 **88**
Swindon, *England* N11+515 **39**
Swinemünde. *See* Swinioujscie
Swinford, *Ireland, Rep.* N54+539 **42**
Swinoujscie, *Poland* M04+539 **48**
Switzerland, *Central Europe* M42+470 **50**
Swords, *Ireland, Rep.* N37+534 **43**
Syasstroy, *U.S.S.R.* K75+602 **60**
Sybil Pt., *Ireland, Rep.* N63+522 **43**
Sycamore, *Illinois* T82+420 **91**
Sydney, *New South Wales* B83–339 **109**
Sydney, *Nova Scotia* S01+461 **90**
Sydney Mines, *Nova Scotia* S01+463 **90**
Syeti Vrach, *Bulgaria* L40+416 **58**
Syktyvkar, *U.S.S.R.* J56+616 **62**
Sylhet, *Bangladesh* F78+250 **71**
Sylt, I., *W. Germany* M40+549 **48**
Sylte, *Norway* M46+623 **46**
Syracuse, *Kansas* U70+380 **94**
Syracuse, *New York* T06+430 **96**
Syracuse, *Sicily* M88+371 **57**
Syr Darya, *Kazakh.* H50+440 **62**
Syria, *W. Asia* K40+350 **74**
Syrian Des., *Iraq, etc.* K30+323 **74**
Sysert, *U.S.S.R.* H86+566 **61**
Syurkum, *U.S.S.R.* C57+500 **63**
Syzran, *U.S.S.R.* J68+532 **68**
Szarvas, *Hungary* L56+469 **49**
Szczecin, *Poland* M03+534 **48**
Szczecinek, *Poland* L80+537 **49**
Szczecinski Zalew, *E. Germany-Poland* M04+537 **48**
Szczytno, *Poland* L54+536 **49**
Szechwan, prov., *China* E84+308 **66**
Szeged, *Hungary* L59+463 **58**
Székesféhervar, *Hungary* L69+472 **49**
Szekszard, *Hungary* L68+463 **58**
Szemao, *China* F23+227 **64**
Szenan, *China* E69+279 **67**
Szengen, *China* E72+235 **67**
Szentes, *Hungary* L58+467 **49**
Szolnok, *Hungary* L59+472 **49**
Szombathely, *Hungary* L80+472 **56**
Szreńsk, *Poland* L59+530 **49**
Szrotawa, *Poland* L87+516 **49**
Taba, *Saudi Arabia* K16+269 **74**
Tabab, *Saudi Arabia* K15+187 **74**
Tabala, *Saudi Arabia* K15+197 **74**
Tabas, *Iran* J19+337 **75**
Tabasara, Sierra de, *Panama* T36+086 **101**
Tabasco, state, *Mexico* U20+180 **100**
Tabas Sunnikhane, *Iran* H89+327 **75**
Tabatinga, *Brazil* R22–216 **105**
Tabatinga, *Brazil* S60–045 **104**
Tabelbala, *Algeria* N20+292 **80**
Table B., *Mt., Cape Prov.* L69–339 **84**
Taboieiro, *Brazil* R81–052 **104**
Tábor, *Czechoslovakia* M02+494 **48**
Tabora, *Tanzania* K74–050 **83**
Tabriz, *Iran* J82+381 **74**
Tabu, *Ivory Coast* N44+046 **80**
Tabuk, *Saudi Arabia* K28+285 **74**
Tabut, *Yemen South* J47+159 **75**
Tacambaro. *Mexico* U67+190 **100**

Tache, L., *N.-W. Territories* W03+642 **88**
Tacloban, *Philippines* D60+111 **65**
Tacna, *Peru* S62–180 **104**
Taco, *Argentina* S20–256 **103**
Tacoma, *Washington* W15+473 **92**
Taconic Mts., *N.Y.-Mass.* S80+425 **96**
Tacuarembo, *Uruguay* R66–317 **103**
Tadcaster, *England* N08+539 **37**
Tadjoura & G. of, *Djibouti* K12+116 **83**
Tadoussac, *Quebec* S58+481 **90**
Tadzhikskaya, rep., *U.S.S.R.* H30+390 **62**
Taegu, *Korea* D38+358 **64**
Taejŏn, *Korea* D44+363 **64**
Taf R., *Wales* N27+518 **38**
Tafalla, *Spain* N10+425 **53**
Taff R., *Wales* N20+515 **38**
Tafila, *Jordan* K56+309 **76**
Taft, *Iran* J34+318 **75**
Taftville, *Connecticut* S72+415 **96**
Taganrog & G., *U.S.S.R.* K36+473 **61**
Taga Zong, *Bhutan* G00+270 **71**
Tagish, *Yukon* W86+602 **88**
Tagula, I., *Papua New Guinea* B70–115 **111**
Tagus, *N. Dakota* U72+484 **93**
Tagus. *See* Tajo R.
Tahakopa, *New Zealand* A63+465 **112**
Tahat Mt., *Algeria* M56+230 **80**
Tahcheng, *China* G42+467 **62**
Ta Hingan Ling, *China* D84+480 **64**
Tahiti, I., *Society Islands* X82–180 **107**
Tahoe, L., *California* W00+391 **92**
Tahora, *New Zealand* A31–390 **112**
Tahoua, *Niger* M58+148 **80**
Tahsien, *China* E75+313 **66**
Tahta, *Egypt* K82+268 **81**
Tahuna, *Indonesia* D58+037 **65**
Tai-an, *China* E17+362 **66**
Taichow. *See* Linhai.
Taichung, *Taiwan* D86+242 **67**
Taieri, R., *New Zealand* A58–456 **112**
Taïf, *Saudi Arabia* K28+211 **74**
Tai-hang-shan, *China* E36+370 **66**
Taihape, *New Zealand* A25–396 **112**
Taihsien, *China* E00+325 **66**
Taihsien, *China* E43+391 **66**
Tai Hu, *China* D88+312 **66**
Taiku, *China* E46+374 **66**
Tailem Bend, *S. Australia* C63–353 **109**
Taima, *Saudi Arabia* K36+277 **74**
Tainan, *Taiwan* D88+230 **67**
Taipale, *Finland* L04+627 **46**
Taipei, *Taiwan* D82+250 **67**
Taiping. *See* Tsungtso.
Taiping, *Malaysia* F26+049 **69**
Taiping. *See* Tangtu.
Taipingchwan, *China* D72+444 **64**
Taipinghs. *See* Wanyuan.
Taira, *Japan* C54+371 **68**
Tairadate Str., *Japan* C56+411 **68**
Taishan I., *China* D77+303 **67**
Taishet, *U.S.S.R.* F41+560 **63**
Taishun, *China* E01+275 **67**
Taitao, Pen. de *Chile* S88–462 **103**
Taiwan, I., *China* D84+240 **67**
Taiwan Hai Hsai, *China* E06+240 **67**
Taiwara, *Afghanistan* H63+335 **75**
Taiyetos, mts., *Greece* L46+370 **59**
Taiyiba, *Jordan* K57+303 **76**
Taiyuan, *China* E45+378 **66**
Ta'izz, *Yemen* K06+136 **74**
Tajan, *Borneo* E59–001 **65**
Tajo, R., *Spain-Portugal* N44+397 **52**
Tajrish, *Iran* J52+358 **75**
Tajumulco, mt., *Guatemala* U11+151 **100**
Tak, *Thailand* F35+169 **69**
Takada, *Japan* C70+371 **68**
Takahashi, *Japan* D08+348 **68**
Takaka, *New Zealand* A43–409 **112**
Takao. *See* Kaohsiung.
Takaoka, *Japan* C78+368 **68**
Takapuna, *New Zealand* A31–368 **112**
Takasaki, *Japan* C66+363 **68**
Takaungu, *Kenya* K30–038 **83**
Takayama, *Japan* C76+362 **68**
Takefu, *Japan* C83+358 **68**
Takhta Bazar, *Turkmen* H74+360 **62**
Takht-i-Sulaiman, *Pakistan* H30+316 **72**
Takingeun, *Sumatra* F49+047 **65**
Takla L., *British Columbia* W35+554 **88**
Takla Makan, des., *Sinkiang, China* G40+380 **30**
Takoradi, *Ghana* N12+050 **80**
Ta-ku, *China* E14+389 **66**
Takuapa, *Thailand* F40+088 **69**
Talagang, *Pakistan* H15+329 **72**
Talaimanar, *Sri Lanka* G62+091 **70**
Talasski Ala Tau, *Kirgiz.* H20+423 **62**
Talar Ra., *Pakistan* H64+254 **70**
Talara, *Peru* T38–045 **104**
Talavera de la Reina, *Spain* N29+399 **52**
Talca, *Chile* S70–354 **103**
Talcahuano, *Chile* S79–367 **103**
Tali, *China* E61+348 **66**
Tali, *China* F30+257 **64**
Taliabu, I., *Indonesia* D60–018 **65**
Taliwang, *Sumbawa I., Indonesia* E19–088 **65**
Talladega, *Alabama* T67+334 **97**
Tallahassee, *Florida* T56+304 **97**
Tallangatta, *Victoria* C16–362 **109**
Tallata-Mafara, *Nigeria* M54+124 **80**
Tallinn, *Estonia* L31+595 **47**
Tallow, *Ireland, Rep.* N48+521 **43**
Tallulah, *Louisiana* U07+324 **95**
Tallulah Falls, *Georgia* T50+347 **97**
Talmenka, *U.S.S.R.* G39+538 **62**
Talou Shan, *China* E82+280 **64**
Talsi, *Latvia* L45+572 **47**
Taltal, *Chile* S63–254 **103**
Tamale, *Ghana* N04+094 **80**
Tamanrasset, *Algeria* M58+226 **80**
Tamaqua, *Pennsylvania* T06+408 **96**
Tamar R., *England* N25+505 **38**
Tamar R., *Tasmania* C19–412 **109**
Tamarite de Litera, *Spain* M87+419 **53**
Tamási, *Hungary* L71+467 **49**
Tamatave, *Madagascar* J64–182 **83**
Tamaulipas, state, *Mexico* U53+235 **100**
Tamaya, *Chile* S69–305 **103**
Tamba, *Zimbabwe* L02–214 **84**
Tambach, *Kenya* K56+006 **83**

Tambacounda, *Senegal* N82+138 **80**
Tambo de Mora, *Peru* T07–135 **104**
Tambohorano, *Madagascar* K06–176 **83**
Tamboril, *Brazil* Q63–048 **105**
Tambov, *U.S.S.R.* K22+527 **61**
Tambura, *Sudan* L14+056 **81**
Tame, *Colombia* S71+066 **104**
Tamel Aiken, *Argentina* S66–482 **103**
Tamiahua & L., *Mexico* U46+212 **100**
Tamil Nadu, state, *India* G70+114 **70**
Tamins, *Switzerland* M33+468 **45**
Tamluk, *India* G12+223 **73**
Tammisaari (Ekenäs), *Finland* L39+600 **47**
Tammu, *Burma* F54+242 **71**
Tampa, *Florida* T45+280 **97**
Tampa B., *Florida* T46+278 **99**
Tampere, *Finland* L37+615 **47**
Tampico, *Mexico* U48+222 **100**
Tamra, *Saudi Arabia* J88+204 **74**
Tamsalu, *Estonia* L23+591 **47**
Tamtsak Bulak, *Mongolia* E13+470 **64**
Tamworth, *England* N10+526 **37**
Tamworth, *New S. Wales* B85–311 **109**
Tana Fd., *Norway* L10+707 **46**
Tana, I., *Vanuatu* A65–195 **106**
Tana L., *Ethiopia* K46+118 **83**
Tana, R., *Norway* L23+698 **46**
Tanabe, *Japan* C88+338 **68**
Tanabu, *Japan* C52+413 **68**
Tanaga I., *Aleutian Is.* Z80+512 **99**
Tanah Merah, *Malaysia* F17+057 **69**
Tanahmerah, *New Guinea* C60–062 **65**
Tanami, *N. Terr., Australia* D32–200 **110**
Tanana, *Alaska* Y10+652 **99**
Tanana, R., *Alaska* X60+635 **99**
Tananarive (Antananarivo), *Madagascar* J76–190 **83**
Tancanhuitz, *Mexico* U54+216 **100**
Tancheng, *China* E09+346 **66**
Tanda, *India* G44+266 **73**
Tanda Urmar, *India* G86+316 **72**
Tandil, *Argentina* R85–372 **103**
Tandou L., *New S. Wales* C47–326 **109**
Taneatua, *New Zealand* A18–380 **112**
Tanega Shima, *Japan* D24+306 **68**
Tanen-taung-gyi Mts., *Thailand-Burma* F42+191 **69**
Tanga, *Tanzania* K36–050 **83**
Tanganyika. *See* Tanzania
Tanganyika, L., *E. Cent. Afr.* L00–050 **83**
Tangen, *Norway* M22+606 **47**
Tangermünde, *E. Germany* M18+526 **48**
Tangier, (Tanger), *Morocco* N34+356 **80**
Tang-shan, *China* E11+396 **66**
Tangshan, *China* E21+344 **66**
Tangtu, *China* E09+316 **66**
Tangui, *U.S.S.R.* F24+555 **63**
Tanimbar Kep., *Indon.* D22–074 **65**
Tanjungpandan, *Billiton I., Indonesia* E74–027 **65**
Tanjungperiuk, *Java, Indon.* E78+060 **65**
Tanjungredeb, *Borneo* E16+021 **65**
Tanjungselor, *Borneo* E16+028 **65**
Tank, *Pakistan* H27+322 **72**
Tankapirtti, *Finland* L16+682 **46**
Tankse, *Kashmir* G70+340 **70**
Tännäs, *Sweden* M14+625 **46**
Tanta, *Egypt* K84+308 **81**
Tantung, *China* D63+401 **66**
Tanuf, *Oman* J17+230 **75**
Tanzania, *E. Africa* K60–050 **83**
Tao, *Burma* F71+228 **71**
Taoan, *China* D73+454 **64**
Taochow. *See* Lintan
Taofu, *China* F23+310 **64**
Taormina, *Sicily* L88+378 **57**
Taos, *New Mexico* V04+364 **94**
Tapa, *Estonia* L24+592 **47**
Tapachula, *Mexico* U13+149 **100**
Tapah, *Malaysia* F22+042 **69**
Tapajos, R., *Brazil* R63–040 **105**
Tapalque, *Argentina* S00–362 **103**
Tapan, *Sumatra* F24–021 **65**
Tapanui, *New Zealand* A64–459 **112**
Tapa Shan, *China* E67+320 **66**
Tapauá, *Brazil* S26–057 **104**
Tapera do Retiro, *Brazil* S11–099 **104**
Taplang Dzong, *Nepal* G14+274 **73**
Tappahannock, *Virginia* T11+381 **97**
Tapti R., *India* G78+216 **70**
Tapuaenuku, mt., *N.Z.* A38–420 **112**
Taqa, *Oman* J33+171 **75**
Taquanalsinho, *Brazil* R80–092 **104**
Taquara, *Brazil* R35–297 **103**
Taquaretinga, *Brazil* Q36–079 **105**
Tara, *U.S.S.R.* H05+567 **62**
Tarabulus esh Sham (Tripoli), *Lebanon* K55+344 **76**
Taradale, *New Zealand* A18–395 **112**
Tarago, *New South Wales* C02–351 **109**
Tarahumare, Sa., *Mexico* V16+280 **100**
Tarakan, *Borneo* E14+034 **65**
Tarakli, *Turkey* K87+404 **74**
Taralga, *New South Wales* C01–344 **109**
Tarana, *New South Wales* C01–336 **109**
Taranaki Bight, N., *N.Z.* A36–388 **112**
Taranaki Bight, S., *N.Z.* A38–397 **112**
Tarancón, *Spain* N18+400 **52**
Taranto, *Italy* L76+404 **57**
Taranto, G. di, *Italy* L77+400 **57**
Tarapoto, *Peru* T08–065 **104**
Taraqua, *Brazil* S49–002 **104**
Tararua Ra., *New Zealand* A28–409 **112**
Tarascon, *France* M80+428 **55**
Tarasp, *Switzerland* M28+468 **45**
Tarata, *Peru* S61–177 **104**
Tarauaca, *Brazil* S31+648 **63**
Tarawa, I., *Kiribati* A40+020 **106**
Tarawera, *New Zealand* A20–390 **112**
Tarazona, *Spain* N10+419 **53**
Tarazona de la Mancha, *Sp.* N12+392 **53**
Tarbagatai Khrebet, *Kazakh.* G40+470 **62**
Tarbat Ness, *Scotland* N23+579 **40**
Tarbert, *Ireland, Rep.* N56+526 **43**
Tarbert, *Scotland* N32+558 **41**
Tarbert, *Scotland* N41+579 **40**
Tarbes, *France* N00+432 **55**
Tarboro, *N. Carolina* T15+359 **97**
Tarchan, *Tibet* G52+310 **70**
Tarcoola, *S. Australia* D02–307 **111**
Tarcoon, *New South Wales* C20–303 **109**
Tarcutta, *New South Wales* C14–353 **109**

Taree, *New South Wales* B76–320 **109**
Tärendö, *Sweden* L44+672 **46**
Târgovişte, *Romania* L27+449 **58**
Târgu Mures, *Romania* L33+466 **58**
Târgul Ocna, *Romania* L20+463 **58**
Tarija, *Bolivia* S29–214 **104**
Tarim, Basin R., *Sinkiang* G30+400 **30**
Tarlac, *Philippines* D87+156 **65**
Tarma, *Peru* T05–114 **104**
Tarn, dep. & R., *France* M77+438 **55**
Tärna, *Sweden* L88+657 **46**
Tarn-et-Garonne, dep., *Fr.* M81+442 **55**
Tarnobrzeg, *Poland* L50+506 **49** ·
Tarnów, *Poland* L54+500 **49**
Tarnowskie Gory, *Poland* L67+505 **49**
Tarn Taran, *India* H00+314 **72**
Taroudant, *Morocco* N54+304 **80**
Tarragona, *Spain* M82+411 **53**
Tarran Hills, *New S. Wales* C23–326 **109**
Tarrega, *Spain* M83+416 **53**
Tarsale, *U.S.S.R.* G70+648 **62**
Tarso Muri, mt., *Libya* L68+212 **81**
Tarsus, *Turkey* K61+370 **74**
Tartagal, *Argentina* S22–227 **103**
Tartas, *France* N05+438 **55**
Tartna Point, *New S. Wales* C45–330 **109**
Tartu, *Estonia* L19+583 **47**
Tartus, *Syria* K55+349 **76**
Tarum, *Iran* J26+281 **75**
Taseevo, *U.S.S.R.* F61+573 **63**
Taseko Ls., *Brit. Columbia* W22+514 **88**
Tashi Bhup Tso, *Tibet* G30+322 **71**
Tashihto, *China* F82+438 **64**
Tashkent, *Uzbek.* H34+415 **62**
Tashkurghan, *Afghanistan* H43+367 **75**
Tash Kurghan, *China* G88+377 **72**
Tashmalik, *China* G86+392 **72**
Tasil, *Syria* K54+328 **76**
Taskan, *U.S.S.R.* B89+630 **63**
Tasköprü, *Turkey* K62+416 **74**
Tasman B., *New Zealand* A40–410 **112**
Tasman, Mt., *New Zealand* A58–435 **112**
Tasman Mts., *New Zealand* A45–410 **112**
Tasman Pen., *Tasmania* C13–431 **109**
Tasmania I. & state, *Aust.* C20–420 **111**
Tassgong, *Bhutan* T80+272 **71**
Tata, *Hungary* L70+478 **49**
Tatakoto, *Tuamotu Arch* X20–175 **107**
Tatarsk, *U.S.S.R.* G84+552 **62**
Tatarskaya, aut. rep., *U.S.S.R.* J60+553 **62**
Tatarskiy Proliv, *U.S.S.R.* C50+500 **63**
Tathlina, L., *N.-W. Terr.* V75+604 **88**
Tating, *China* E86+271 **67**
Tatinnai L., *N.-W. Terr.* U47+606 **88**
Tatnam C., *Manitoba* U05+578 **89**
Tatong, *Victoria* C24–367 **109**
Tatranská Lomnica, *Czech.* L59+491 **49**
Tatry, mts., *Poland-Czech.* L60+493 **49**
Tatta, *Pakistan* H43+247 **70**
Tatu R., *China* F22+320 **64**
Tatuhy, *Brazil* R16–232 **105**
Ta-tung, *China* E41+401 **66**
Tatung Ho, *China* F14+370 **64**
Tauapeçaçú, *Brazil* S06–025 **104**
Taubate, *Brazil* R03–230 **105**
Tauha, *Brazil* Q62–060 **105**
Taumarunui, *New Zealand* A28–388 **112**
Taumgdwingyi, *Burma* F56+200 **71**
Taunggyi, *Burma* F48+209 **71**
Taungup, *Burma* F64+189 **71**
Taunton, *England* N18+510 **38**
Taunton, *Massachusetts* S67+419 **91**
Taunus, mts., *W. Germany* M40+503 **48**
Taupo & L., *New Zealand* A24–387 **112**
Tauranga & Harb., *N.Z.* A23–377 **112**
Tauste, *Spain* N07+419 **53**
Tauysk, *U.S.S.R.* C03+598 **63**
Tavda, *U.S.S.R.* H57+581 **62**
Taverne, *Switzerland* M36+461 **45**
Tavistock, *England* N25+505 **38**
Tavolara, I., *Sardinia* M32+409 **57**
Tavoy & R., *Burma* F41+140 **71**
Tavoy I., *Burma* F40+130 **71**
Tavsanli, *Turkey* L03+396 **74**
Tawang, *India* F78+276 **71**
Tawas City, *Michigan* T51+443 **91**
Tawau, *Sabah* E12+043 **65**
Tawitawi, I., *Philippines* E00+052 **65**
Taxco, *Mexico* U57+184 **100**
Tay, Firth of & R., *Scotland* N19+564 **41**
Tay, L., *Scotland* N25+565 **41**
Tayga, *U.S.S.R.* G27+558 **62**
Taylor, Mt., *New Mexico* V18+352 **94**
Taylorsville, *Alabama* T69+345 **97**
Taylorsville, *N. Carolina* T37+359 **97**
Tayport, *Scotland* N17+564 **41**
Tayside, reg., *Scotland* N23+567 **41** ·
Taytay, *Philippines* E04+108 **65**
Tayü, *China* E34+255 **67**
Tayung, *China* E57+292 **67**
Taza, *Morocco* N24+342 **80**
Tazewell, *Virginia* T39+371 **97**
Tazovskaya G., *U.S.S.R.* G85+692 **62**
Tbilisi, *Gruzinskaya, U.S.S.R.* K01+418 **62**
Tchad. *See* Chad
Tchaouróu, *Benin* M76+088 **80**
Tczew, *Poland* L67+541 **49**
Te Anau, L., *New Zealand* A73–452 **112**
Teano Ra., *W. Australia* E10–245 **110**
Teapa, *Mexico* U18+174 **100**
Te Aroha, *New Zealand* A26–376 **112**
Te Awamutu, *New Zealand* A28–380 **112**
Teboursouk, *Tunisia* M34+364 **81**
Tebyulyakh, *U.S.S.R.* C31+648 **63**
Tecamachalco, *Mexico* U46+188 **100**
Tecka & R., *Argentina* S65–434 **103**
Tecolutla, *Mexico* U43+205 **100**
Tecoripe, *Mexico* V18+290 **100**
Tecpan, *Mexico* U62+172 **100**
Tecuniseh, *Michigan* T54+420 **91**
Tedzhen, *Turkmen.* H87+373 **62**
Tegerhi, *Libya* M04+240 **81**
Tegucigalpa, *Honduras* T72+141 **101**
Teheruak L., *N.-W. Terr.* U72+663 **88**
Tehpao, *China* E83+233 **67**
Tehran, *Iran* J52+357 **75**
Tehri, *India* G69+304 **70**
Tehsien, *China* E22+375 **66**
Tehuacan, *Mexico* U44+185 **100**

Tehucan, *Mexico* U44+185 **100**
Tehuantepec, *Mexico* U32+164 **100**
Tehuantepec, G. of, *Mexico* U30+158 **100**
Tehauntepec, Isth. of, *Mex.,* U28+172 **100**
Teian. *See* Anlu
Teifi, R., *Wales* N26+520 **38**
Teign, R., *England* N22+506 **38**
Teignmouth, *England* N21+505 **38**
Teith, R., *Scotland* N24+561 **41**
Tekapo, L., *New Zealand* A57–439 **112**
Te Karaka, *New Zealand* A13–384 **112**
Tekari, *India* G31+250 **73**
Tekirdag, *Turkey* L15+410 **74**
Te Kuiti, *New Zealand* A29–383 **112**
Tela, *Honduras* T75+158 **101**
Tel-Aviv-Yafo, *Israel* K62+321 **76**
Telegraph Creek, *B.C.* W67+581 **88**
Telichie, *S. Australia* C61–317 **109**
Telkalakh, *Syria* K52+347 **76**
Tel Kochek, *Syria* K17+370 **74**
Tell Bise, *Syria* K49+348 **76**
Tell Ejine, *Syria* K48+358 **76**
Tell el Milh, *Israel* K60+312 **76**
Tellicherry, *India* G87+118 **70**
Teloloapan, *Mexico* U60+182 **100**
Tel Or, *Israel* K56+326 **76**
Telpos-iz, *U.S.S.R.* J05+637 **62**
Telsen, *Argentina* S41–424 **103**
Tel'shvay, *Lithuania* L46+560 **47**
Telukbetung, *Sumatra, Indon.* E89–054 **65**
Teluk Cenarawasih, *New Guinea* D00-024 **65**
Tembeling, *Malaysia* F16+040 **69**
Temblador, *Venezuela* S17+090 **104**
Teme R., *England* N15+523 **37**
Temesvar. *See* Timisoara
Temir, *Kazakh.* J18+491 **62**
Temir Tau, *U.S.S.R.* G16+532 **62**
Temiscouata, L., *Quebec* S53+476 **90**
Temma, *Tasmania* C31–413 **109**
Temnikov, *U.S.S.R.* K10+546 **61**
Temora, *New South Wales* C15–345 **109**
Temosachic, *Mexico* V15+288 **100**
Tempe, *Arizona* V41+334 **94**
Tempio, *Sardinia* M35+409 **57**
Temple, *Texas* U44+310 **95**
Templemore, *Ireland, Rep.* N47+528 **43**
Temse, *Belgium* M65+511 **44**
Temta, *U.S.S.R.* J84+575 **61**
Temuco, *Chile* S76–386 **103**
Temuka, *New Zealand* A52–440 **112**
Tenanzingo, *Mexico* U57+189 **100**
Tenasique, *Mexico* U09+174 **100**
Tenasserim, *Burma* F36+120 **71**
Tenasserim R., *Burma* F37+136 **71**
Tenby, *Wales* N28+517 **38**
Ten Degree Chan., *Andaman Islands* F75+098 **71**
Tenerife, I., *Canary Is.* P10+282 **80**
Ténès, *Algeria* M84+362 **80**
Tengchow. *See* Penglai
Tengiz, Oz., *Kazakh.* H35+504 **62**
Tennant's Creek, *N. Territory, Australia* D05–195 **111**
Tennessee, state, *U.S.A.* T80+357 **99**
Tennessee Pass, *Colorado* V07+394 **98**
Tennessee R., *Kentucky, etc.* T79+368 **97**
Tenterfield, *New S. Wales* B78–290 **109**
Ten Thousand Is., *Florida* T37+256 **99**
Ten Thousand Smokes, Val. of, *Alaska* Y35+578 **99**
Teocaltiche, *Mexico* U77+215 **100**
Teocuitatlan, *Mexico* U80+200 **100**
Téophilo Otoni, *Brazil* Q69–178 **105**
Tepatitlan, *Mexico* U77+208 **100**
Tepehuanes, *Mexico* V05+254 **100**
Tepelene, *Albania* L60+403 **59**
Tepic, *Mexico* U89+215 **100**
Teramo, *Italy* M08+426 **56**
Terang, *Victoria* C43–383 **109**
Ter Apel, *Netherlands* M48+529 **44**
Terban, *Jebel, Saudi Arabia* K18+197 **74**
Terborg, *Netherlands* M52+519 **44**
Terenceville, *Newfoundland* R58+477 **90**
Teresina, *Brazil* Q77–050 **105**
Teressa I., *Nicobar Is* F71+083 **71**
Terewah L., *New South Wales* C16–296 **109**
Terezin, *Czechoslovakia* M05+505 **48**
Teri, *Pakistan* H23+332 **72**
Teri Nam Tso, *Tibet* G26+310 **71**
Termez, *Uzbek.* H47+370 **62**
Termini Imerese, *Sicily* M08+380 **57**
Termoli, *Italy* M00+420 **57**
Termonde, *Belgium* M65+510 **44**
Ternate, *Halmahera I.* D46+008 **65**
Terneuzen, *Netherlands* M67+513 **44**
Terni, *Italy* M14+426 **56**
Ternopol, *Ukraine* L27+496 **60**
Terowie, *S. Australia* C67–331 **109**
Terpeniya, Zal, *U.S.S.R.* C40+485 **63**
Terracina, *Italy* M10+413 **57**
Terralba, *Sardinia* M38+397 **57**
Terra Nova, *Newfoundland* R55+485 **90**
Terra Santa, *Brazil* R69–019 **105**
Terrazas, *Mexico* V17+303 **100**
Terrebonne B., *Louisiana* U04+292 **95**
Terre Haute, *Indiana* T74+395 **91**
Terrel, *Texas* U38+327 **95**
Terrel, Mt., *Utah* V40+386 **94**
Terror Mt., *Antarctica* B30–790 **27**
Terry, *Montana* V02+468 **93**
Terschelling I., *Netherlands* M58+534 **44**
Teruel, *Spain* N07+404 **53**
Tervola, *Finland* L31+661 **46**
Tervuren, *Belgium* M63+508 **44**
Teshekpuk, L., *Alaska* Y20+705 **88**
Tesin, *Mongolia* F44+492 **64**
Tesio, *Japan* C50+459 **68**
Teslin, *Yukon* W76+602 **88**
Teslin L., *Yukon* W75+600 **88**
Teslin R., *Yukon* W84+609 **88**
Tessaoua, *Niger* M40+134 **80**
Tessenderlo, *Belgium* M59+511 **44**
Tete, *Mozambique* K68-162 **84**
Teton Ra., *Wyoming* V36+436 **93**
Tetouan (Tetuan), *Morocco* N32+356 **80**
Tetyukhe, *U.S.S.R. See* Rudnaya Pristan
Tetyushi, *U.S.S.R.* J67+549 **61**
Teulada, *Sardinia* M37+390 **57**
Teulada C., *Sardinia* M38+389 **57**
Teutoburger Wald, *W. Germany* M41+521 **48**

Tevere. See Tiber
Teviot, R., Scotland N15+555 41
Tevriz, U.S.S.R. H16+573 62
Te Waewae B., N.Z. A76–463 112
Texarkana, Arkansas U24+334 95
Texas, state, U.S.A. U67+318 98
Texcoco, Mexico U53+195 100
Texel I., Netherlands M61+531 44
Texoma, L., Oklahoma U40+340 95
Tezpur, India F73+266 71
Thachap Kangri, Tibet G46+334 70
Thadiq, Saudi Arabia J86+252 74
Thailand, S.-E. Asia F30+160 69
Thakhek, Laos F01+174 69
Thal, Pakistan H26+334 72
Thale Sap, L., Thailand F28+075 69
Thalkirch, Switzerland M34+466 45
Thames, New Zealand A27–372 112
Thames, Firth of, N.Z. A28–370 112
Thames R., Connecticut S73+414 96
Thamès, England N00+515 39
Thana, India H12+194 70
Thanesar, India G79+299 72
Thanh-hoa, Vietnam E86+198 69
Thanjavur, India G65+108 70
Thann, France M47+478 54
Thar Des., India H27+257 70
Tharrawaddy, Burma F55+176 71
Tharsis, Spain N42+376 52
Thásos I., Greece L32+407 59
Thásos Str., Greece L32+408 59
Thatcher, Arizona V28+328 94
Thaton, Burma F46+169 71
Thaungdut, Burma F62+244 71
Thayer, Missouri U10+365 97
Thayetmyo, Burma F59+193 71
Thazi, Burma F53+208 71
The Gulf, Arabia, etc. 74-75
Thelon R., N.-W. Territories U84+645 88
Theodore, Queensland B89–250 111
Theodore Roosevelt L., Ariz. V37+337 94
Thérmai, G. of, Greece L43+402 59
Thérmiá. See Kithnos, I.
Thermopolis, Wyoming V19+437 93
Thesprotia, Greece L58+395 59
Thessalia, Greece L46+395 59
Thessaloniki, Greece L42+406 59
Thetford, England M85+524 39
Thetford Mines, Quebec S67+461 91
Theux, Belgium M55+505 44
Thibodaux, Louisiana U04+298 95
Thief River Falls, Minnesota U38+482 93
Thielsen, Mt., Oregon W12+432 92
Thielt, Belgium M70+510 44
Thies, Senegal P12+148 80
Thimbu, Bhutan G06+275 73
Thingvalla vatn, Iceland P37+642 46
Thio, Ethiopia K24+146 83
Thionville, France M53+494 54
Thíra, I., Greece L27+364 59
Thirsk, England N08+542 37
Thirtyone Mile L., Quebec T05+461 91
Thisted, Denmark M38+570 47
Thistilfjord, Iceland P02+663 46
Thityabin, Burma F56+233 71
Thiviers, France M84+455 54
Thjórsá, R., Iceland P23+645 46
Thok Jalung, Tibet G51+323 70
Tholen & I., Netherlands M65+515 44
Thomaston, Georgia T56+329 97
Thomastown, Ireland, Rep. N43+525 43
Thomasville, Georgia T54+308 97
Thompsonville, Connecticut S76+420 96
Thomson Ville, Michigan T65+445 91
Thongwa, Burma F51+167 71
Thorn. See Torun
Thornhill, Scotland N23+552 41
Thórshavn, Faeroe Is. N41+618 34
Thórshöfn, Iceland P01+662 46
Thouars, France N01+469 54
Thourout. See Torhout
Thousand Isles, New York T06+443 91
Thousand Lake Mt., Utah V39+384 94
Thraki, Dhitiki, Greece L24+412 58
Three Hummock I., Tasmania C30+404 109
Three Kings Is., N.Z. A47–341 112
Three Points C., Ghana N14+048 80
Three Rivers, Michigan T64+420 91
Three Rivers (Trois Rivières),
  Quebec S76+464 89
Throssel Ra., W. Australia D80–220 110
Thueyts, France M65+447 55
Thuin, Belgium M64+503 44
Thule, Greenland S58+760 26
Thule I. South Sandwich Is. P80–590 27
Thumail, Iraq K13+331 74
Thun, Switzerland M44+468 45
Thunder B., Michigan T50+450 91
Thunder Bay, Ontario T86+486 89
Thuner See, Switzerland M44+467 45
Thur, R., Switzerland M37+476 45
Thurgau, canton, Switz. M36+476 45
Thüringen, W. Germany M24+507 48
Thüringer Wald, E. Germany M24+505 48
Thurles, Ireland, Rep. N47+527 43
Thurloo Downs, N.S.W. C40–293 109
Thursday I., Queensland C47–105 111
Thurso & R., Scotland N21+586 40
Thusis, Switzerland M33+467 45
Tia, New South Wales B80–312 109
Tiaret, Algeria M82+354 80
Tiassale, Ivory Coast N30+060 80
Tibati, Cameroon M16+064 81
Tiber (Tevere), R., Italy M15+420 57
Tiberias & L., Israel K56+328 76
Tibet, China G30+325 30
Tibnin, Lebanon K58+332 76
Tibooburra, New S. Wales C48–293 109
Tiburón, Haiti S86+184 101
Tiburon I., Mexico V45+289 100
Ticino, canton, Switzerland M38+463 45
Ticonderoga, New York S80+439 91
Ticul, Mexico T87+204 100
Tidjikja, Mauritania N70+184 80
Tidworth, England N10+512 39
Tiebissou, Ivory Coast N30+072 80
Tiefencastel, Switzerland M32+467 45
Tieh-ling, China D67+423 66
Tiel, Netherlands M57+519 44
Tielt, Belgium M70+510 44
Tien Chih, China F14+246 64
Tien-chwang-tai, China D78+409 66

Tienen (Tirlemont), Belgium M61+508 44
Tienpaoshan, China E15+419 66
Tiensha Pass, China E79+341 66
Tien Shan, Central Asia G70+430 30
Tienshui, China E84+344 66
Tientsin (Tienching), China E17+391 66
Tiermas, Spain N06+426 53
Tierra del Fuego,
  Chile-Argentina S50–540 103
Tiffin, Ohio T49+411 91
Tifton, Georgia T51+314 97
Tiganesti, Romania L23+447 58
Tighina. See Bendery.
Tighnabruaich, Scotland N31+559 41
Tigil, U.S.S.R. B37+577 63
Tignish, Prince Edward I. S24+470 90
Tigris, R., Iraq J86+325 74
Tihwa, China G14+437 62
Tijuana, Mexico V74+324 100
Tikhvin, U.S.S.R. K70+596 60
Tikrit, Iraq K08+346 74
Tiksi, U.S.S.R. D36+716 63
Tilburg, Netherlands M60+516 44
Tilbury, England M88+514 39
Tilcara, Argentina S32–236 103
Tilichiki, U.S.S.R. A83+605 63
Tilamook, Oregon W23+454 92
Tillangchong I., Nicobar Is. F68+085 71
Tillsonburg, Ontario T34+429 91
Tilos, I., Greece L16+364 59
Tilpa, New South Wales C33–310 109
Tilsit. See Sovetsk.
Timanski Kryazh, U.S.S.R. J60+650 62
Timaru, New Zealand A52–444 112
Timbalier B., Louisiana U02+292 95
Timber Lake, S. Dakota U66+454 93
Timboon, Victoria C42–385 109
Timbuktu. See Tombouctou.
Timiskaming, Quebec T25+467 91
Timisoara, Romania L53+458 58
Timmins, Ontario T38+485 91
Timor, I. & Sea, Indonesia D60–100 65
Timote, Argentina S14–354 103
Tinaca Pt., Philippines D58+056 65
Tinahely, Ireland, Rep. N39+528 43
Tindouf, Algeria N46+274 80
Tineo, Spain N39+433 52
Tingchow. See Changting.
Tingha, New South Wales B83–300 109
Tinghsien, China E29+385 66
Tingnan, China E31+246 67
Tingo Maria, Peru T05–091 104
Tingri Dzong, Tibet G20+285 71
Tinian, I., Mariana Is. C26+140 106
Tinkhannock, Pennsylvania T06+415 96
Tinnevelly. See Tirunelveli.
Tinogasta, Argentina S46–281 103
Tinos, I., Greece L29+376 59
Tinsukia, India F57+274 71
Tintigny, Belgium M57+497 44
Tintina, Argentina S16–270 103
Tintinara, S. Australia C59–358 109
Tinwald, New Zealand A49–439 112
Tioman, Pulau, I., Malaysia F05+028 69
Tionesta, Pennsylvania T27+415 96
Tipperary & co., Ireland, Rep. N49+525 43
Tipton, Iowa U14+418 95
Tiracumba, Sa. de, Brazil R10–036 105
Tiran, I., Saudi Arabia K63+280 74
Tirana. See Tiranë.
Tiranë, Albania L62+413 58
Tiraspol, Moldavia L02+468 60
Tire, Turkey L14+380 74
Tireboli, Turkey K37+409 74
Tiree, I., Scotland N41+565 41
Tirgu Jiu, Romania L40+450 58
Tirich Mir, Pakistan H19+363 72
Tirlemont, Belgium M60+508 44
Tirlyanski, U.S.S.R. J08+542 61
Tírnavos, Greece L46+397 59
Tirol, Austria M22+471 48
Tiruchirapalli, India G68+107 70
Tiruchendur, India G71+084 70
Tiru Kona Malai. See Trincomalee.
Tirunelveli, India G73+088 70
Tirupati, India G64+136 70
Tiruvannamalai, India G65+123 70
Tisiye, Syria K51+324 76
Tissa, Nigeria M28+074 81
Tisza (Tisa), R., Hungary-
  Yugoslavia L56+475 51
Titalyah, Bangladesh G09+265 73
Titicaca, L., Bolivia-Peru S56–158 104
Titisee, W. Germany M41+479 48
Titograd, Yugoslavia L65+424 58
Titovo Uzice, Yugoslavia L61+439 58
Titu, Romania L27+447 58
Titusville, Pennsylvania T28+417 91
Tiwi, Oman J04+228 75
Tixkokob, Mexico T85+210 100
Tixtla, Mexico U55+176 100
Tizimin, Mexico T77+211 100
Tizi Ouzou, Algeria M66+366 80
Tjalang, See Calang
Tjilatjap, See Cilacap
Tjirebon, See Cirebon
Tjörn, I., Sweden M20+580 47
Tlacotalpan, Mexico U34+186 100
Tlaltenango, Mexico U80+218 100
Tlapa, Mexico U51+176 100
Tlaxcala & state, Mexico U50+193 100
Tlaxiaco, Mexico U46+173 100
Tlemcen, Algeria N08+350 80
Tméssa, Libya L86+264 81
Toay, Argentina S26+368 103
Toba, Japan D79+345 68
Tobago, I., Trinidad S04+112 101
Toba Meer, Sumatra F37+026 65
Tobarro, Spain N10+386 53
Tobel, Switzerland M36+475 45
Tobelo, Halmahera I., Indon. D42+016 65
Tobermory, Ontario T40+452 91
Tobermory, Scotland N36+566 41
Toboali, Bangka I., Indonesia E81–030 65
Toboli, Celebes, D89–008 65
Tobolsk, U.S.S.R. H39+581 62
Tobruq (Tobruk), Libya L36+320 81
Toccoa, Georgia T50+346 97
Toco, Chile S58–220 103
Tocopilla, Chile S62–220 103
Tocumwal, New S. Wales C28–359 109

Tocuyo, Venezuela S59+098 104
Todenyang, Kenya K54+044 83
Todmorden, England N13+537 37
Todos Santos, Mexico V31+235 100
Todos Santos, B., Mexico V71+317 100
Toe Hd., Ireland, Rep. N55+515 43
Togarakaikyo, Japan D28+301 68
Toghraqbulaq, China F68+404 64
Togo, rep., W. Africa M88+080 80
To Huping Tso, Tibet G41+342 71
Tojo, Japan D11+348 68
Tokanga, U.S.S.R. K33+680 62
Tokanui, New Zealand A66–465 112
Tokar, Sudan K44+182 83
Tokara Retto, Japan D32+296 68
Tokat, Turkey K50+403 74
Tokatidake, Japan C42+434 68
Tokelau Is., Pacific Ocean Z45–090 106
Tokmak, Kirgiz. G88+429 62
Tokomaru, New Zealand A10–382 112
Tokoto, China E53+403 66
Tokushima, Japan D03+341 68
Tokuyama, Japan D19+340 68
Tōkyō & B., Japan C62+357 68
Tolaga Bay, New Zealand A10–384 112
Tolbukhin, Bulgaria L13+435 58
Toledo, Chile S63–273 103
Toledo, Ohio T51+417 91
Toledo, Spain N24+399 52
Toledo, Mtes. de, Spain N26+397 52
Tolo, G. of, Celebes, D76–022 65
Tolsta Hd., Scotland N37+583 40
Toluca, Mexico U58+193 100
Toluca, Montana V17+457 93
Tolun, China E22+423 66
Tölz, Bad, Germany M21+478 48
Tomah, Wisconsin U03+440 91
Tomahawk, Wisconsin T88+455 91
Tomar, Portugal N51+396 52
Tomari, U.S.S.R. C46+477 63
Tomaszów Mazowiecki, Pol. L60+515 49
Tomatin, Scotland N24+573 40
Tomatumari, Guyana R84+053 104
Tombigbee R., Alabama T77+135 99
Tombouctou, Mali N18+168 80
Tome, Chile S78–366 103
Tomiko, Ontario T27+466 91
Tomini, G. of, Celebes, D86–004 65
Tomintoul, Scotland N20+572 40
Tomkinson Ra., Australia D38–260 110
Tommot, U.S.S.R. D51+590 63
Tomsk, U.S.S.R. G30+563 62
Tom's River, New Jersey S85+399 91
Tonala, Mexico U22+158 100
Tonate, French Guiana R44+049 105
Tonawanda, New York T23+430 96
Tonbridge, England M88+512 39
Tønder, Denmark M37+549 47
Tondi, India G66+098 70
Tonga, Sudan K84+094 81
Tonga, Is., Pacific Ocean Z60–220 106
Tongala, Victoria C31–363 109
Tongeren, Belgium M57+508 44
Tongeren, Madagascar K04–236 83
Tongoy, Chile S69–304 103
Tongres. See Tongeren.
Tongue & Kyle of, Scotland N26+585 40
Tongue R., Montana V08+454 98
Tonichi, Mexico V25+288 100
Tonk, India G85+262 70
Tonkin, Vietnam F00+214 69
Tongking, G. of, S.E. Asia E70+204 69
Tonkhil, Mongolia F68+464 64
Tonkova, U.S.S.R. G00+607 62
Tonle Sap, Cambodia F06+129 69
Tonneins, France M88+444 55
Tonnerre, France M66+478 54
Tonopah, Nevada V73+382 92
Tønsberg, Norway M27+593 47
Tooele, Utah V44+405 92
Toowoomba, Queensland B78–274 111
Top Oz., Karelskaya K80+657 62
Topeka, Kansas U34+390 95
Topolčany, Czechoslovakia L71+486 49
Torez, Ukraine K40+480 61
Torhout (Thourout), Belg. M71+511 44
Tori, India G31+237 73
Toriñana, C., Spain N56+430 52
Torino, Italy M44+451 56
Torit, Sudan K74+044 81
Torma, Estonia L19+588 47
Torne Trask, Sweden L66+684 46
Torneträsk, Sweden L62+682 46
Tornio, Finland L35+659 46
Tornionjoki, Sweden L48+676 46
Tornquist, Argentina S13-382 103
Törökszentmiklós, Hungary L58+472 49
Toroni, G. of, Greece L38+401 59
Toronto, New South Wales B81-330 109
Toronto, Ontario T26+437 91
Toronto, S. Dakota U40+446 93
Tororo, Uganda K64+006 83
Toros Dağlari, Turkey K80+370 74
Torquay, England N21+505 38
Torre Annunziata, Italy M03+408 57
Torreblanca, Spain M89+402 53
Torre del Greco, Italy M04+408 57
Torrelaguna, Spain N21+408 52
Torrelapaja, Spain N12+415 53
Torrelavega, Spain N24+433 52
Torrens, L., S. Australia C74-310 109
Torrente, Spain N03+394 53
Torreon, Mexico V34+287 100
Torres, Mexico V34+287 100
Torres Is., Pacific Ocean A80-140 106
Torres Novas, Portugal N51+395 52
Torres Vedras, Portugal N55+391 52
Torrevieja, Spain N04+380 53
Torridon, L., Scotland N34+576 40
Torrijos, Spain N28+400 52
Torrington, Connecticut S79+418 96
Torrington, Wyoming U86+421 93
Torrowangee, New S. Wales C51-314 109
Torrox, Spain N24+367 52
Torsby, Sweden M12+602 47
Tortola, I., Virgin Is. S28+185 101
Tortorici, Sicily M09+380 57
Tortosa, Spain M87+407 53
Tortosa, Spain N24+367 52
Tortue, I., Haiti S76+201 101

Tortuga I., Mexico V42+274 100
Torun, Poland L68+531 49
Tory, I. Ireland, Rep. N49+552 42
Torzhok, U.S.S.R. K61+571 60
Tosa B., Japan D08+334 68
Toscana, dep., Italy M23+434 56
Tosco-Emiliano, Appinnino,
  mts., Italy M26+444 56
Tossa, Spain M73+417 53
Tostado, Argentina S11–292 103
Totana, Spain N15+378 53
Totling, Tibet G61+314 70
Totma, U.S.S.R. K14+600 62
Totnes, England N22+504 38
Totonicapam, Guatemala U08+150 100
Totskoye, U.S.S.R. J43+525 61
Tottenham, New S. Wales C16–322 109
Tottori, Japan D05+355 68
Touba, Ivory Coast N46+084 80
Toubkal, mt., Morocco N48+310 80
Touggourt, Algeria M84+328 80
Toul, France M55+487 54
Toulon, France M82+436 55
Toulouse, France M82+436 55
Toungoo, Burma F51+190 71
Touquet, le, France M80+505 54
Touraine, prov., France M86+471 54
Tourane (Da Nang), Vietnam E71+161 69
Tourbis, L., Quebec S85+473 91
Tourcoing, France M71+507 54
Tour-du-Pin, la, France M58+456 54
Tournai, Belgium M70+506 44
Tournon, France M61+451 55
Tournus, France M61+465 54
Tours, France M86+474 54
Touws River, Cape Province L58–334 84
Towamba, New South Wales C02–371 109
Towanda, Pennsylvania T09+417 96
Towari, Celebes D81–046 65
Towcester, England N06+521 39
Tower City, N. Dakota U46+469 93
Townsend, Montana V39+463 93
Townsend, Mt., N.S.W. C10–364 109
Townsville, Queensland C19–193 111
Towoeti Danau, Celebes, D82–028 65
Towson, Maryland T09+394 96
Towy R., Wales N25+519 38
Toyah L., Texas U81+313 94
Toyama & B., Japan C76+367 68
Tozeur, Tunisia M42+338 81
Trabzon, Turkey K33+410 74
Tracadie, New Brunswick S30+475 90
Tracy, Minnesota U34+442 93
Tradom, Tibet G36+303 71
Traer, Iowa U14+422 95
Trahiry, Brazil Q56–033 105
Trahynas, Brazil R22–144 105
Traiguen, Chile S76–382 103
Traiguen, I., Chile S83–455 103
Trail, British Columbia V76+493 88
Tralee & B., Ireland, Rep. N58+523 43
Tramore, Ireland, Rep. N43+522 43
Tranas. Sweden M00+581 47
Trancas, Argentina S32–263 103
Trancoso, Portugal N44+408 52
Trang, Thailand F33+076 69
Trangan, I., Indonesia D04–067 65
Trangie, New South Wales C12–321 109
Tranquebar, India G61+111 70
Tranqueira, Brazil Q82–082 105
Transcona, Manitoba U42+500 88
Transilvania, Romania L32+465 58
Transvaal, S. Africa L00–250 84
Transylvanian Alps,
  Romania L42+450 58
Trapani, Sicily M15+380 57
Traralgon, Victoria C21–382 109
Trasimeno, L., Italy M17+431 56
Trasparga, Spain N47+431 52
Traunstein, W. Germany M14+478 48
Travancore, India G80+090 70
Travellers L., New S. Wales C47–333 109
Traverse B., Michigan T63+451 91
Traversay Is., Atlantic Ocean P85–560 27
Traverse City, Michigan T64+448 91
Travis, L., Texas U48+304 95
Trawbreaga B., Ireland, Rep. N44+553 42
Trěvič. Czechoslovakia L85+492 49
Trebinje, Yugoslavia L70+427 58
Trebizond. See Trabzon
Tree River Post, N.-W. Terr. V47+672 88
Tregaron, Wales N24+522 38
Treig, L., Scotland N28+568 41
Treinta-y-Tres, Uruguay R57–332 103
Trelew, Argentina S32–432 103
Trelleborg, Sweden M11+554 47
Tremadoc B., Wales N26+528 38
Tremblant, Mt., Quebec S87+463 91
Tremiti Is., Italy L87+420 56
Tremont, Maine S50+443 90
Tremp, Spain M85+422 53
Trencin, Czechoslovakia L72+489 49
Trenel, Argentina S26–355 103
Trenque Lauquen, Argentina S17–359 103
Trent. See Trento
Trent Canal, Ontario T24+445 91
Trent, R., England N04+530 37
Trentino-Alto Adige, reg.,
  Italy M22+465 56
Trento, Italy M23+461 56
Trenton, Georgia T63+348 97
Trenton, Michigan T49+422 91
Trenton, Missouri U20+401 95
Trenton, New Jersey S89+402 96
Trenton, Ontario T16+442 91
Trenton, Tennessee T84+360 97
Tréport, le, France M82+501 54
Tres Arroyos, Argentina S02–384 103
Tres Lomas, Argentina S17–364 103
Tres Marias, Is., Mexico V10+215 100
Tres Montes, Pen., Chile T02–469 103
Tres Virgenes, Las, Mexico V46+274 100
Treves. See Trier
Trevino, Mexico U68+260 100
Treviso, Italy M17+457 56
Trevna, Bulgaria L27+428 58
Triabunna, Tasmania C13–425 109
Triana, Spain N36+374 52
Tricase, Italy L70+399 57
Trichinopoly. See Tiruchirapalli
Trichur, India G82+106 70
Trida, New South Wales C30–330 109

Trier, *W. Germany* M50+497 **48**
Trieste, *Italy* M07+457 **56**
Trikeri Str., *Greece* L41+390 **59**
Trikkala, *Greece* L50+396 **59**
Trikomo, *Cyprus* K67+353 **76**
Trim, *Ireland, Rep.* N41+536 **43**
Trincomalee, *Sri Lanka* G53+086 **70**
Trinidad, *Bolivia* S28–148 **104**
Trinidad, *Colorado* U87+372 **94**
Trinidad, *Cuba* T29+218 **97**
Trinidad, *Uruguay* R72–336 **103**
Trinidad, I., *Argentina* S12–392 **103**
Trinidad I., *Atlantic Ocean* P87–203 **85**
Trinidad I., *West Indies* S07+105 **104**
Trinity & B., *Newfoundland* R50+482 **90**
Trinity, *Texas* U32+310 **95**
Trinity Pen, *Antarctica* R75–640 **27**
Trinity R., *Texas* U30+312 **95**
Trionto C., *Italy* L78+396 **57**
Tripoli (Tarabulus), *Libya* M10+328 **81**
Tripoli, *Lebanon* K55+345 **76**
Tripolis, *Greece* L46+375 **59**
Tripolitania, *Libya* M00+300 **81**
Tripura, *India* F80+240 **71**
Tristan da Cunha, *Atlantic Oc.* N76–372 **85**
Triunfo, *Mexico* V31+239 **100**
Trivandrum, *India* G79+085 **70**
Trmbesh, *Bulgaria* L27+434 **58**
Trn, *Bulgaria* L44+428 **58**
Trnava, *Czechoslovakia* L75+484 **49**
Trobriand Is.,
  Papua New Guinea B84–086 **111**
Trogir, *Yugoslavia* L82+435 **56**
Trios Pistoles, *Quebec* S55+481 **90**
Trois Ponts, *Belgium* M55+504 **44**
Trois Rivières, *Quebec* S76+464 **91**
Troitsk, *U.S.S.R.* H81+540 **61**
Troitsk, *U.S.S.R.* K07+541 **61**
Troitsko Pechorsk, *U.S.S.R.* J23+629 **62**
Trollhättan, *Sweden* M16+583 **47**
Trollheimen, *Norway* M36+629 **46**
Tromen, mt., *Argentina* S60–371 **103**
Tromsø, *Norway* L66+697 **46**
Trondheim & Fd., *Norway* M28+635 **46**
Troödos, *Cyprus* K73+349 **76**
Troon, *Scotland* N28+555 **41**
Tropea, *Italy* L85+387 **57**
Troppau. *See Opava*
Trosa, *Sweden* L75+589 **47**
Trossachs, *Scotland* N26+562 **41**
Trout Lake, *Michigan* T60+462 **91**
Trowbridge, *England* N13+513 **39**
Troy, *New York* S82+427 **91**
Troy, *Turkey* L22+400 **74**
Troyes, *France* M66+483 **54**
Truba, *Saudi Arabia* K11+283 **74**
Truer Ra., *Northern
  Territory, Australia* D21–222 **110**
Trujillo, *Honduras* T66+158 **101**
Trujillo, *Peru* T24–082 **104**
Trujillo, *Spain* N35+395 **52**
Trujillo, *Venezuela* S62+093 **104**
Truk, I., *Caroline Is.* B82+070 **106**
Truksum, *Tibet* G40+300 **71**
Trumbull, *Mt., Arizona* V50+364 **92**
Trundle, *New South Wales* C15–329 **109**
Truns, *Switzerland* M36+467 **45**
Truro, *England* N30+502 **38**
Truro, *Nova Scotia* S19+454 **90**
Truro, *S. Australia* C65–344 **109**
Truskmore, *Ireland, Rep.* N50+544 **42**
Trutnov, *Czechoslovakia* L85+506 **49**
Trzebnica, *Poland* L78+514 **49**
Tržič, *Yugoslavia* M04+464 **56**
Tsabong, *Botswana* L46–262 **84**
Tsagan Olom, *Mongolia* F50+467 **64**
Tsahura, *Yemen, South* J70+148 **74**
Tsangbe, *Bhutan* G05+271 **73**
Tsanghsien. *See Wuchow*
Tsangwu, *China* E51+235 **67**
Tsaochow. *See Hotseh*
Tsaokiang, *China* E28+376 **66**
Tsaritsyn. *See Volgograd*
Tsavo Nat. Park, *Kenya* K40–028 **83**
Tschenstochau. *See Czestochowa*
Tschiertschen, *Switzerland* M32+468 **45**
Tseelim, *Israel* K63+313 **76**
Tsehchow. *See Tsincheng*
Tselinograd, *Kazakh* H21+512 **52**
Tsemah, *Israel* K56+327 **76**
Tsengshing, *China* E37+233 **67**
Tses, *Namibia* L56–064 **82**
Tshikapa, *Zaire* L56–064 **82**
Tsho Mirari L., *Kashmir* G70+329 **72**
Tsimlyanskoye Vdkhr.,
  U.S.S.R. K12+470 **61**
Tsinan, *China* E17+367 **66**
Tsincheng, *China* E43+353 **66**
Tsinchow. *See Tienshui*
Tsing-chow, *China* E29+381 **66**
Tsingchow. *See Yitu*
Tsing Hai *See Ching Hai*
Tsingkiang, *China* 27+280 **67**
Tsingkiang, *China* E06+336 **66**
Tsingkow, *China* E05+348 **66**
Tsingtao, *China* D88+361 **66**
Tsingtze (Singtze), *China* E23+294 **67**
Tsingyüan. *See Paoting*
Tsingyün, *China* E42+237 **67**
Tsining, *China* E20+354 **64**
Tsinkiang, *China* E09+249 **67**
Tsinsien, *China* E22+284 **67**
Tsinyang, *China* E42+351 **66**
Tsitsihar, *China* D66+474 **64**
Tsivilsk, *U.S.S.R.* J71+558 **61**
Tsivory, *Madagascar* J84–242 **83**
Tskhinvali, *Gruzinskaya* K07+425 **62**
Tso-motre-tung, L., *Tibet* G10+284 **71**
Tsu, *Japan* C81+347 **68**
Tsugaru Str., *Japan* C54+416 **68**
Tsugitaka, mt., *Taiwan* D82+248 **64**
Tsungfa, *China* E38+236 **67**
Tsungming, *China* D81+316 **66**
Tsungtso, *China* E76+224 **64**
Tsunhwa, *China* E12+403 **66**
Tsunyi, *China* E79+277 **67**
Tsuruga, *Japan* C83+356 **68**
Tsuruoka, *Japan* C61+387 **68**
Tsuyama, *Japan* D06+350 **68**
Tsuyung, *China* F20+250 **64**
Tua, *Portugal* N45+412 **52**
Tua, *Zaire* L80–036 **82**

Tuakau, *New Zealand* A30–373 **112**
Tuam, *Ireland, Rep.* N53+535 **43**
Tuamarina, *New Zealand* A36–414 **112**
Tuamotu Arch., *Pacific Oc.* X30–200 **107**
Tuao, *Philippines* D82+178 **65**
Tuapse, *U.S.S.R.* K36+441 **62**
Tuatapere, *New Zealand* A74–461 **112**
Tubai, I., *Society Islands* Y10–160 **107**
Tubarão, *Brazil* R24–285 **103**
Tubas, *Jordan* K58+323 **76**
Tubbercurry, *Ireland, Rep.* N52+540 **42**
Tubingen, *W. Germany* M36+485 **48**
Tubize, *Belgium* M65+507 **44**
Tubuai, I., *Austral Islands* X88–210 **107**
Tubutama, *Mexico* V39+308 **100**
Tucacas, *Venezuela* S49+108 **104**
Tuckernuck I., *Massachusetts* S61+413 **96**
Tuckerton, *New Jersey* S86+396 **91**
Tucson, *Arizona* V36+322 **94**
Tucson Ra., *Arizona* V37+324 **94**
Tucumcari, *New Mexico* U42+352 **94**
Tucunare, *Brazil* R63–051 **105**
Tucupita, *Venezuela* S12+090 **104**
Tucurui, *Brazil* R26–038 **105**
Tudela, *Spain* N10+421 **53**
Tufi, *Papua New Guinea* C04–092 **111**
Tug, *Turkey* K16+385 **74**
Tuguegarao, *Philippines* D80+176 **65**
Tugur, *U.S.S.R.* C79+537 **63**
Tukums, *Latvia* L41+569 **47**
Tula, *Mexico* U55+200 **100**
Tula, *Mexico* U58+230 **100**
Tula, *U.S.S.R.* K44+542 **60**
Tulan, *China* F38+369 **64**
Tulancingo, *Mexico* U50+201 **100**
Tularosa, *New Mexico* V06+330 **94**
Tularosa Basin, *New Mexico* V09+329 **94**
Tulcan, *Ecuador* T16+008 **104**
Tulcea, *Romania* L07+452 **58**
Tulchin, *Ukraine* L07+487 **60**
Tulear, *Madagascar* K08–234 **83**
Tuli, *Zimbabwe* L04–220 **84**
Tulkarm, *Jordan* K60+323 **76**
Tullahoma, *Tennessee* T68+353 **97**
Tullamore, *Ireland, Rep.* N45+533 **43**
Tullamore, *New S. Wales* C15–327 **109**
Tulle, *France* M79+453 **55**
Tullow, *Ireland, Rep.* N40+528 **43**
Tulsa, *Oklahoma* U36+362 **95**
Tulsk, *Ireland, Rep.* N49+538 **43**
Tulu, *Ethiopia* K22+072 **83**
Tulua, *Colombia* T08+041 **104**
Tulun, *U.S.S.R.* F27+545 **63**
Tunaco & Rado de,
  Colombia T22+017 **104**
Tumany, *U.S.S.R.* B55+611 **63**
Tumbarumba, *N.S.W.* C12–358 **109**
Tumbes, *Peru* T33–035 **104**
Tumit-Guna, *China* E55+414 **66**
Tumkur, *India* G77+132 **70**
Tumlong, *India* G08+274 **73**
Tummel, R., *Scotland* N24+567 **41**
Tummo, *Libya* M06+224 **81**
Tump, *Pakistan* H76+260 **70**
Tumu, *Ghana* N12+108 **80**
Tumucumaque, Sa., *Brazil* R52+018 **105**
Tumupasa, *Bolivia* S48–142 **104**
Tumut & R., *New S. Wales* C11–354 **109**
Tunas de Zaza, *Cuba* T28+216 **101**
Tunbridge Wells, *England* M88+511 **39**
Tuncurry, *New South Wales* B76–321 **109**
Tundla, *India* G72+272 **70**
Tundubai, *Sudan* L44+146 **81**
Tunduru, *Tanzania* K46–112 **83**
Tüngan, *China* E53+264 **67**
Tungchang. *See Liaocheng*
Tungchow. *See Tali*
Tungchwan. *See Hweitseh*
Tungchwan. *See Santai*
Tunghai, *China* E04+346 **66**
Tungho, *China* D38+460 **64**
Tunghsien, *China* E20+398 **66**
Tunghwa, *China* D56+416 **64**
Tungjen, *China* E65+277 **67**
Tungkun, *China* E37+230 **67**
Tungkwan, *China* E59+346 **66**
Tungkwan, *China* E65+350 **66**
Tungliao, *China* D76+436 **64**
Tungshan. *See Suchow*
Tungtai, *China* D87+329 **66**
Tung Ting Hu, *China* E45+290 **67**
Tunguska, R., *U.S.S.R.* F30+640 **63**
Tunhwang, *China* F61+402 **64**
Tuni, *India* G44+173 **71**
Tunica, *Mississippi* U02+347 **97**
Tunis, *Tunisia* M30+368 **81**
Tunisia, *N. Africa* M30+350 **81**
Tunja, *Colombia* S81+056 **104**
Tunnsjø, *Norway* M10+647 **46**
Tunuyan & R., *Argentina* S55–335 **103**
Tuoy Khaya, *U.S.S.R.* E51+622 **63**
Tuparoa, *New Zealand* A10–379 **112**
Tupelo, *Mississippi* T82+343 **97**
Tupilco, *Mexico* U20+184 **100**
Tupinambaranas, I., *Brazil* R80–034 **104**
Tupiza, *Bolivia* S34–213 **104**
Tupper Lake, *New York* S87+442 **91**
Tuquarussu, *Brazil* R20–102 **105**
Tuquerres, *Colombia* T15+010 **104**
Tura, *India* F89+255 **71**
Tura, *U.S.S.R.* F30+641 **63**
Turaba, *Saudi Arabia* K20+208 **74**
Turakom, *Laos* F15+184 **69**
Turbat-i-Heideri, *Iran* J06+353 **75**
Turbat-i-Jam, *Iran* H86+353 **75**
Turbo, *Colombia* T10+081 **104**
Turda, *Romania* L37+466 **58**
Tureia I., *Tuamotu Arch.* X20–208 **107**
Turfan, *Sinkiang, China* G02+429 **64**
Turgay, *Kazakh* H69+499 **62**
Turgutlu, *Turkey* L14+385 **74**
Türi, *Estonia* L27+588 **47**
Turiaçu, *Brazil* R02–018 **105**
Turiamo, *Venezuela* S46+105 **104**
Turin. *See Torino*
Turkestan, *Kazakh, etc.* H40+432 **62**
Turkey, rep., *Europe-Asia* K78+390 **51**
Turkmenskaya, rep., *U.S.S.R.* H40+405 **62**
Turks Is., *Bahamas, The* S67+214 **101**
Turku, *Finland* L47+604 **47**
Turneffe Is., *Belize* T77+174 **101**
Turnhout, *Belgium* M60+513 **44**

Türnoovo, *Bulgaria* L27+430 **58**
Turnu Severin, *Romania* L44+446 **58**
Turquino, Pico de, *Cuba* T10+200 **101**
Turr, *Ethiopia* K08+064 **83**
Turrialba, *Costa Rica* T52+100 **101**
Turshiz, *Iran* J10+352 **75**
Turtkul, *Uzbek.* H84+415 **62**
Turtle Mts., *N. Dakota* U61+490 **93**
Turukta, *U.S.S.R.* E30+610 **63**
Turukhansk, *U.S.S.R.* G11+657 **62**
Turun, *Iran* J20+355 **75**
Turut, *Iran* J29+355 **75**
Turzovka, *Czechoslovakia* L68+494 **49**
Tus, *Iran* J03+366 **75**
Tuscaloosa, *Alabama* T76+332 **97**
Tuscarora Mts., *Pa.* T17+402 **96**
Tuscola, *Illinois* T80+398 **91**
Tuscumbia, *Alabama* T76+347 **97**
Tuscumbia, *Missouri* U15+383 **97**
Tuticorin, *India* G71+090 **70**
Tuttlingen, *W. Germany* M37+479 **48**
Tutuila, I., *Samoa* Z33–150 **106**
Tuvalu, *Pacific Ocean* A15-090 **106**
Tuwairifa, *Saudi Arabia* J62+216 **74**
Tuweiq, Jeb. el, *Jordan* K46+295 **76**
Tuxpan, *Mexico* U44+210 **100**
Tuxpan, *Mexico* V01+218 **100**
Tuxtepec, *Mexico* U37+181 **100**
Tuxtla & Vol. de, *Mexico* U31+185 **100**
Tuxtla Gutierrez, *Mexico* U18+168 **100**
Tuy, *Spain* N52+421 **52**
Tuyen-Quang, *Vietnam* E89+217 **69**
Tuy-hoa, *Vietnam* E64+131 **69**
Tuyun, *China* E75+263 **67**
Tuz Gölu, *Turkey* K70+386 **74**
Tuzla, *Yugoslavia* L68+446 **58**
Tvärän, *Sweden* L54+656 **46**
Tvurditsa, *Bulgaria* L26+427 **58**
Twante, *Burma* F54+166 **71**
Tweed, *Ontario* T14+445 **91**
Tweed, R., *Scotland* N13+557 **41**
Tweedsmuir Hills, *Scotland* N20+554 **41**
Tweedsmuir Park, *B.C.* W35+534 **88**
Twelve Pins, *Ireland, Rep.* N59+535 **43**
Twenty-five de Mayo, *Argent.* S46–380 **103**
Twenty-five de Mayo, *Argent.* S01–354 **103**
Twin Buttes, *Montana* V02+486 **93**
Twin Falls, *Idaho* V57+425 **92**
Twofold B., *New S. Wales* C00–370 **109**
Two Harbors, *Minnesota* U10+470 **93**
Two Mountains, L. of, *Que* S86+455 **91**
Two Rivers, *Wisconsin* T76+442 **91**
Tyler, *Texas* U31+322 **98**
Tygda, *U.S.S.R.* D52+532 **63**
Tyler, *Texas* U32+324 **95**
Tyndinski, *U.S.S.R.* D61+553 **63**
Tyndall, Mt., *New Zealand* A55–433 **112**
Tyne & Wear, co., *England* N09+550 **37**
Tynemouth, *England* N08+550 **37**
Tynset, *Norway* M25+623 **46**
Tyr (Sour), *Lebanon* K59+330 **76**
Tyrone, *Pennsylvania* T19+407 **96**
Tyrone, co., *N. Ireland* N43+546 **42**
Tyrrell, L., *Victoria* C43+354 **109**
Tyrrhenian Sea, *Italy* M18+400 **57**
Tyumen, *U.S.S.R.* H57+572 **62**
Tywyn, *Wales* N24+526 **38**
Tzechung, *China* E33+364 **66**
Tzeya Ho, *China* E26+380 **64**
Tzeyung, *China* E18+356 **66**
Tzeyun, *China* E82+256 **67**
Uani, *Nicaragua* T58+138 **101**
Uau el Chebir, *Libya* L78+252 **81**
Uaupés & R., *Brazil* S42–001 **104**
Uba, *Brazil* R18–197 **105**
Ubait, *Saudi Arabia* K33+285 **74**
Ubari, *Libya* M14+266 **81**
Uberaba, *Brazil* R18–197 **105**
Uberlandia, *Brazil* R20–190 **105**
Überlingen, *W. Germany* M35+477 **48**
Ubon Muang, *Thailand* F01+153 **69**
Ubsa Nor, *Mongolia* F73+503 **63**
Ucayali, R., *Peru* S88–060 **104**
Uch, *Pakistan* H23+293 **72**
Uchiza, *Peru* T08–084 **104**
Uckfield, *England* M89+510 **39**
Udain, *Yemen* K06+141 **74**
Udaipur, *India* H07+246 **70**
Uddevalla, *Sweden* M19+584 **47**
Udd Jaur, *Sweden* L73+660 **46**
Uden, *Netherlands* M56+517 **44**
Udine, *Italy* M11+461 **56**
Udong, *Cambodia* F01+117 **69**
Udon Thani, *Thailand* F13+175 **69**
Udskaya Guba, *U.S.S.R.* C85+550 **63**
Udzha, *U.S.S.R.* E19+717 **63**
Uelen, *U.S.S.R.* Z30+660 **63**
Ueno, *Japan* C82+348 **68**
Ufa, *U.S.S.R.* J24+547 **61**
Uganda, *E. Africa* K70+010 **83**
Ugwashi-Uku, *Nigeria* M50+062 **82**
Uherske Hradistě, *Czech.* L75+491 **49**
Ui Failghe. *See Offaly*
Uist, North, I., *Scotland* N43+576 **40**
Uist, South, I., *Scotland* N43+573 **40**
Uitenhage, *Cape Province* L28–338 **84**
Uitgeest, *Netherlands* M62+525 **44**
Ujhani, *India* G66+280 **73**
Ujjain, *India* G85+230 **70**
Ujpest, *Hungary* L45+476 **49**
Ujung Pandang, *Celebes* E03-052 **65**
Ukermark (Uckermark),
  E. Germany M08+532 **48**
Ukhta, *Karelskaya* K85+652 **62**
Ukiah, *California* W20+391 **92**
Ukmerge, *Lithuania* L31+553 **47**
Ukraine, rep., *U.S.S.R.* L00+490 **60**
Ulaanbaatar, *Mongolia* E79+479 **64**
Ulangom, *Mongolia* F77+500 **63**
Ulan Ude, *U.S.S.R.* E74+520 **63**
Ulcinj, *Yugoslavia* L65+419 **58**
Ulithi, I., *Pacific Ocean* C60+100 **106**
Ulladulla, *New S. Wales* B87–354 **109**
Ullapool, *Scotland* N31+579 **40**
Ullared, *Sweden* M14+571 **47**
Ulldecona, *Spain* M87+406 **53**
Ullswater, L., *England* N18+546 **37**
Ullung Do, *Sea of Japan* D25+376 **68**
Ulm, *W. Germany* M30+484 **48**
Ulmarra, *New South Wales* B72–296 **109**

Ulster, prov.,
  Ireland, Rep.-N. Ire. N48+548 **42**
Ulster Canal,
  Ireland, Rep.-N. Ire. N42+542 **42**
Ultima, *Victoria* C41–355 **109**
Ulua, *Honduras* T76+158 **101**
Ulukisla, *Turkey* K63+376 **74**
Ulva, I., *Scotland* N37+565 **41**
Ulverston, *England* N19+542 **37**
Ulverstone, *Tasmania* C23–412 **109**
Ulyanovsk, *U.S.S.R.* J70+544 **61**
Ülzen, *W. Germany* M27+530 **48**
Uman, *Ukraine* K88+488 **60**
Umanak Fd., *Greenland* R35+710 **26**
Umarkot, *Pakistan* H31+253 **70**
Umbria, reg., *Italy* M15+429 **56**
Umea, *Sweden* L58+638 **46**
Umm Ar Rusays, *Oman* J07+205 **75**
Umm el Qulban, *Saudi Arabia* K20+279 **74**
Umm Kuteira, *Sudan* L30+146 **81**
Umm Lej, *Saudi Arabia* K46+250 **74**
Umm Qasr, *Iraq* J73+300 **74**
Umm Ruwaba, *Sudan* K84+128 **81**
Umnak I., *Aleutian Is.* Z20+529 **99**
Umtali, *Zimbabwe* K74–188 **84**
Umtata, *Cape Province* L08–318 **84**
Umvuma, *Zimbabwe* K86–194 **84**
Una, *India* G82+315 **72**
Una R., *Yugoslavia* L80+452 **56**
Unadilla, *New York* T02+423 **96**
Unalakleet, *Alaska* Y65+637 **99**
Unalaska, *Aleutian Is.* Z10+535 **99**
Uncastillo, *Spain* N06+424 **53**
Uncia, *Bolivia* S39–185 **104**
Uncompahgre Plat., *Colorado* V20+385 **94**
Underbool, *Victoria* C49–352 **109**
Undur Khan, *Mongolia* E57+474 **64**
Ungarie, *New South Wales* C18–336 **109**
Ungava B., *Quebec* S45+594 **89**
União, *Brazil* Q77–045 **105**
União, *Brazil* S69–096 **104**
União da Victoria, *Brazil* R36–262 **103**
União Marara, *Brazil* S11–008 **104**
Uniejów, *Poland* L67+520 **49**
Unimak I., *Aleutian Is.* Y85+544 **99**
Unini, *Peru* S84–106 **104**
Union, *Argentina* S35–352 **103**
Union, *Argentina* S50–292 **103**
Union, *Missouri* U06+384 **97**
Union, *S. Carolina* T40+347 **97**
Union City, *Tennessee* T85+364 **97**
Union of Soviet Socialist Republics,
  (U.S.S.R.). *Europe-Asia* 30-31
Uniontown, *Kentucky* T77+378 **97**
Uniontown, *Pennsylvania* T29+396 **96**
Unionville, *Missouri* U18+405 **95**
Unionville, *Nevada* V80+404 **92**
United Arab Emirates,
  S.-W. Asia J35+240 **75**
United Kingdom of Gt. Britain
  & N. Ire., *N.-W. Europe* **34**
United States of America
  (U.S.A.) **98-99**
United States Ra. *N.-W. Terr.* T30+810 **26**
Unnao, *India* G57+265 **73**
Unst, I., *Scotland* N05+607 **40**
Unterwalden, canton, *Switz.* M41+469 **45**
Unzha, *U.S.S.R.* K06+580 **61**
Uozu, *Japan* C75+368 **68**
Upata, *Venezuela* S15+081 **104**
Upemba L., *Zaire* L22–086 **82**
Upernivik, *Greenland* R40+730 **26**
Upington, *Cape Province* L52–284 **84**
Upolu, I., *Samoa* Z40–140 **106**
Upper Marlboro, *Maryland* T10+388 **96**
Upper Sandusky, *Ohio* T50+408 **91**
Upper Seal L., *Quebec* S84+558 **89**
Upper Volta, rep., *W. Afr.* N15+130 **80**
Uppsala, *Sweden* L74+599 **47**
Ur, *Iraq* J85+310 **74**
Uracoa, *Venezuela* S14+091 **104**
Urakawa, *Japan* C43+422 **68**
Ural R., *U.S.S.R.* J54+508 **62**
Uralla, *New South Wales* B82–306 **109**
Uralsk, *U.S.S.R.* J52+513 **62**
Uralskiye Khrebet, *U.S.S.R.* J10+535 **62**
Urana, *New South Wales* C23–354 **109**
Uranium City, *Saskatchewan* V20+598 **88**
Urapunga, *N. Terr., Aust.* D03–147 **110**
Ura Tyube, *U.S.S.R.* H36+400 **62**
Urawa, *Japan* C62+358 **68**
Urbakh, *U.S.S.R.* J78+512 **61**
Urbino, *Peru* S70–137 **104**
Urda, *U.S.S.R.* J75+488 **62**
Urdzhar, *U.S.S.R.* G70+520 **62**
Ure R., *England* N11+543 **37**
Ures, *Mexico* V32+292 **100**
Urfa, *Turkey* K37+372 **74**
Urgun, *Afghanistan* H35+329 **75**
Uri, canton, *Switzerland* M38+468 **45**
Uribe, *Colombia* S85+031 **104**
Uribia, *Colombia* S73+116 **104**
Urisino, *New South Wales* C38–297 **109**
Urnasch, *Switzerland* M34+473 **45**
Urtazymsk, *U.S.S.R.* J07+520 **61**
Urtuin, *Mongolia* E26+462 **64**
Uruapan, *Mexico* U72+194 **100**
Urubamba & R., *Peru* S74–134 **104**
Urucará, *Brazil* R76–024 **105**
Urucu, *Brazil* Q64–177 **105**
Urucui, *Brazil* Q87–072 **105**
Uruguaiana, *Brazil* R72–297 **103**
Uruguay, rep., *S. America* **103**
Uruguay, R., *Uruguay, etc.* R81–334 **103**
Urumchi, *Sinkiang, China* G14+437 **62**
Urumes Surhra, *Syria* K48+361 **76**
Urussanga, *Brazil* R26–286 **103**
Urville, Tg. d', *New Guinea* C73–015 **65**
Uryupinsk, *U.S.S.R.* K18+508 **61**
Urzhum, *U.S.S.R.* J60+571 **61**
Urziceni, *Romania* L20+446 **58**
Usak, *Turkey* L04+387 **74**
Usakos, *Namibia* L86–220 **84**
Usborne, mt., *Falkland Is.* R84–516 **103**
Usedom, *E. Germany* M06+540 **48**
Ushant I. *See Quessant, I. d'*
Ushirombo, *Tanzania* K78–034 **83**
Ush Tobe, *U.S.S.R.* G69+455 **62**
Ushuaia, *Argentina* S50–548 **103**
Usk, *Wales* N17+517 **38**
Usk, R., *Wales* N19+518 **38**
Uska, *India* G41+272 **73**

Uskedal, *Norway* M55+599 **47**
Uskudar, *Turkey* L06+411 **74**
Usole, Siberskoye, *U.S.S.R.* F09+528 **63**
Uspenskiy, *U.S.S.R.* H13+488 **62**
Usquil, *Peru* T21–079 **104**
Ussel, *France* M76+456 **54**
Ussuri, R., *U.S.S.R.* D08+465 **63**
Ussuriysk, *U.S.S.R.* D18+437 **63**
Ust Aldan, *U.S.S.R.* D35+635 **63**
Ust Amginskoye, *U.S.S.R.* D01+628 **63**
Ust Apuka, *U.S.S.R.* A61+605 **63**
Ust Belaya, *U.S.S.R.* A40+652 **63**
Ust' Bolsheretsk, *U.S.S.R.* B52+527 **63**
Ust' Chaun, *U.S.S.R.* A57+688 **63**
Uster, *Switzerland* M38+473 **45**
Usti nad Labem, *Czech.* M05+507 **48**
Ust Ishim, *U.S.S.R.* H25+575 **62**
Ust Kamenogorsk, *Kazakh.* G45+500 **62**
Ust Khayryuzovo, *U.S.S.R.* B49+570 **63**
Ust Kut, *U.S.S.R.* E85+570 **63**
Ust Maya, *U.S.S.R.* D02+604 **63**
Ust' Nera, *U.S.S.R.* C31+644 **63**
Ust Sopochnoye, *U.S.S.R.* B55+560 **63**
Ust Tsilma, *U.S.S.R.* J48+654 **62**
Ust Uda, *U.S.S.R.* F10+543 **63**
Ust Urt, plat., *U.S.S.R.* J30+440 **62**
Ust Usa, *U.S.S.R.* J18+660 **62**
Ust Ukoye, *U.S.S.R.* H66+543 **61**
Ust Yenisei Port, *U.S.S.R.* G34+698 **62**
Ustyuzhna, *U.S.S.R.* K52+588 **60**
Usumacinta, R., *Mexico* U08+168 **100**
Usumbura (Bujumbura), *Burma* L04–034 **83**
Utah, state, *U.S.A.* V45+391 **98**
Utah L., *Utah* V41+402 **92**
Utajarvi, *Finland* L22+647 **46**
Utena, *U.S.S.R.* L27+555 **47**
Utete, *Tanzania* K38–080 **83**
Uthal, *Pakistan* H50+257 **70**
Utiarity, *Brazil* R80–131 **104**
Utica, *New York* T01+431 **91**
Utiel, *Spain* N07+396 **53**
Utikuma L., *Alberta* V63+557 **88**
Utraula, *India* G46+273 **73**
Utrecht, *Natal* K88–276 **84**
Utrecht & prov., *Netherlands* M59+521 **44**
Utrera, *Spain* N35+372 **52**
Utsjoki, *Finland* L18+699 **46**
Utsunomiya, *Japan* C60+366 **68**
Uttar Pradesh, *India* G65+280 **70**
Uttaradit, *Thailand* F30+176 **69**
Uusikaarlepyy, *Finland* L45+635 **46**
Uusikaupunki, *Finland* L51+608 **47**
Uvac, *Yugoslavia* L63+436 **58**
Uvat, *U.S.S.R.* H38+591 **62**
Uvéa. I., *Loyalty Islands* A78–205 **106**
Uvira, *Zaire* L06–034 **83**
Uvs Nuur, lake, *Mongolia* F73+503 **63**
Uxbridge, *Massachusetts* S70+421 **96**
Uxbridge, *Ontario* T25+441 **91**
Uxmal, *Mexico* T89+204 **100**
Uyu Chaung R., *Burma* F55+252 **71**
Uyuni, *Bolivia* S41–205 **104**
Uzbekskaya, rep., *U.S.S.R.* H60+400 **62**
Uzdin, *Yugoslavia* L56+452 **58**
Uzgen, *U.S.S.R.* H10+406 **62**
Uzhgorod, *U.S.S.R.* L46+486 **60**
Uzyansk, *U.S.S.R.* J12+536 **61**
Vaal R., *S. Africa* L30–282 **84**
Vaalwater, *Transvaal* L10–242 **84**
Vaasä, *Finland* L50+631 **46**
Vac, *Hungary* L65+478 **49**
Vache, I. La, *Haiti* S82+181 **101**
Vadsø, *Norway* L02+701 **46**
Vaduz, *Liechtenstein* M33+471 **45**
Værøy, *Norway* M14+677 **46**
Vags Fd., *Norway* L78+690 **46**
Vah, R., *Czechoslovakia* L73+485 **49**
Vaila, I., *Scotland* N09+602 **40**
Vairowal, *India* G89+314 **72**
Valais, canton, *Switzerland* M47+462 **45**
Val Brillant, *Quebec* S45+485 **90**
Valcheta, *Argentina* S37–407 **103**
Valday, *U.S.S.R.* K69+579 **60**
Valday Hills, *U.S.S.R.* K72+576 **60**
Valdepeñas, *Spain* N21+388 **52**
Valderredible, *Spain* N24+428 **52**
Valderrobres, *Spain* M89+409 **53**
Valdez, *Alaska* X70+610 **99**
Valdez, Pen., *Argentina* S24–422 **103**
Valdivia, *Chile* S80–398 **103**
Valdosta, *Georgia* T50+308 **97**
Valea-lui-Mihai, *Romania* L47+475 **49**
Valença, *Brazil* Q71–066 **105**
Valençay, *France* M81+471 **54**
Valence, *France* M61+450 **55**
Valencia, *Spain* N02+395 **53**
Valencia, *Venezuela* S48+102 **104**
Valencia, Gulf of, *Spain* N87+394 **53**
Valencia de Alcantara, *Spain* N43+394 **52**
Valencia de Don Juan, *Spain* N33+423 **52**
Valenciennes, *France* M69+503 **54**
Valeni de Munte. *Romania* L24+452 **58**
Valencia I., *Ireland, Rep.* N62+519 **43**
Valentin, mt., *Chile* S80–465 **103**
Valentine, *Nebraska* U64+428 **94**
Valera, *Venezuela* S63+093 **104**
Valga, *U.S.S.R.* L24+578 **47**
Valjala, *U.S.S.R.* L43+584 **47**
Valjevo, *Yugoslavia* L61+443 **58**
Valkeakoshi, *Finland* L35+612 **47**
Valkenburg, *Netherlands* M55+509 **44**
Valladolid, *Mexico* T77+205 **100**
Valladolid, *Spain* N44+418 **52**
Valldemosa, *Balearic Is.* M74+397 **53**
Valle-D'Aosta, reg., *Italy* M47+457 **58**
Valle de La Pascua, *Venez.* S36+092 **104**
Valle de Santiago, *Mexico* U68+203 **100**
Valledupar, *Colombia* S79+104 **104**
Vallejo, *California* W13+381 **92**
Vallenar, *Chile* S65–284 **103**
Valletta, *Malta* M03+359 **57**
Valley City, *N. Dakota* U48+469 **93**
Valleyfield, *Quebec* S85+453 **91**
Vallgrund, *Finland* L52+632 **46**
Vallorbe, *Switzerland* M52+467 **45**
Valmaseda, *Spain* N19+432 **52**
Valmiera, *U.S.S.R.* L27+575 **47**
Valona. *See* Vlone
Valona I., *Albania* L63+404 **59**
Valoria la Buena, *Spain* L63+418 **52**
Valparaiso, *Chile* S70–330 **103**

Valparaiso, *Indiana* T72+414 **95**
Valparaiso, *Mexico* U81+228 **100**
Vals Platz, *Switzerland* M35+466 **45**
Valtimo, *Finland* L07+637 **46**
Valverde de Jucar. *Spain* N14+397 **53**
Valverde del Caming, *Spain* N40+376 **52**
Van & Gölu, *Turkey* K10+385 **74**
Vana Vändra, *Estonia* L30+587 **47**
Van Buren, *Arkansas* U26+354 **99**
Van Buren, *Maine* S48+471 **90**
Van Buren, *Missouri* U06+370 **97**
Vanceboro, *Maine* S45+455 **90**
Vancouver, *Brit. Columbia* W19+493 **88**
Vancouver, *Washington* W16+456 **92**
Vancouver I., *Brit. Columbia* W34+500 **88**
Vancouver, Mt., *Yukon* X26+605 **88**
Vandalia, *Illinois* T85+389 **95**
Van Diemen. C.. *N.T., Aust.* D27–111 **110**
Van Diemen G.;
  N. Territory, Australia D18–119 **110**
Vanegas, *Mexico* U66+239 **100**
Vänern. L., *Sweden* M12+589 **47**
Vänersborg. *Sweden* M16+584 **47**
Vangaindrano, *Madagascar* J74–234 **83**
Van Horn Mts., *Texas* V00+308 **94**
Vankarem, *U.S.S.R.* Z66+678 **63**
Vanndale, *Arkansas* U05+353 **97**
Vannes, *France* N17+477 **54**
Vannøy, *Norway* L60+701 **46**
Vanovara, *U.S.S.R.* F15+604 **63**
Vanrhynsdorp, *South Africa* L68–316 **84**
Vanuatu, *Pac. Oc.* A70–170 **106**
Vanua Levu, I., *Fiji* A04–170 **106**
Var, dep., *France* M52+435 **55**
Varanasi, *India* G42+254 **73**
Varanger-halvøya, *Norway* L00+700 **46**
Varanger Halvøy, *Norway* L06+704 **46**
Varaždin, *Yugoslavia* L82+463 **56**
Varberg, *Sweden* M16+571 **47**
Vardar R., *Greece, etc.* L46+414 **58**
Vardø, *Norway* K84+703 **46**
Vares, C. de, *Spain* N46+435 **52**
Varese, *Italy* M38+458 **56**
Varkaus, *Finland* L13+623 **46**
Varna, *Bulgaria* L12+432 **58**
Varnavin, *U.S.S.R.* K00+574 **61**
Värtsilä, *Finland* K86+622 **46**
Vasht, *Iran* H83+282 **75**
Vasknarva, *U.S.S.R.* L14+590 **47**
Vassar, *Michigan* T51+434 **91**
Vastanfors, *Sweden* L85+600 **47**
Västerås, *Sweden* L81+597 **47**
Väster Dal Älv. *Sweden* M10+611 **47**
Västervik, *Sweden* L80+578 **47**
Vasvar, *Hungary* L78+471 **49**
Vatican City (Citta del
  Vaticano), *Italy* M15+417 **57**
Vaticano C.. *Italy* L85+387 **57**
Vatna Jökull, *Iceland* P12+645 **46**
Vatomandry, *Madagascar* J66–194 **83**
Vättern, L., *Sweden* M04+580 **47**
Vättis, *Switzerland* M33+469 **45**
Vaucluse, dep., *France* M59+440 **55**
Vaud, canton, *Switzerland* M51+466 **45**
Vaughn, *New Mexico* V00+348 **94**
Vaxjö. *Sweden* M01+569 **47**
Vaygach. Ostrov. *U.S.S.R.* J00+700 **62**
Vechel, *Netherlands* M55+516 **44**
Vedia, *Argentina* S10–344 **103**
Vedrin, *Belgium* M61+505 **44**
Veere, *Netherlands* M68+516 **44**
Vega & Fd., *Norway* M18+656 **46**
Vegornitis, L., *Greece* L49+407 **59**
Vegreville, *Alberta* V43+536 **88**
Vejle, *Denmark* M33+557 **47**
Vela, *Argentina* R88–374 **103**
Velaines, *Belgium* M69+507 **44**
Velebit Planina, *Yugoslavia* L88+445 **56**
Veles, *Yugoslavia* L49+417 **58**
Velestinon, *Greece* L43+394 **59**
Velez Rubio, *Spain* N12+377 **53**
Veliki Ustyug, *U.S.S.R.* J83+609 **62**
Velikiye Luki, *U.S.S.R.* K87+564 **60**
Velizh, *U.S.S.R.* K83+556 **60**
Velletri, *Italy* M13+417 **57**
Vellore, *India* G66+129 **70**
Velp, *Netherlands* M54+520 **44**
Velsen, *Netherlands* M62+525 **44**
Velsk, *U.S.S.R.* K17+611 **60**
Venado, *Mexico* U66+230 **100**
Venado Tuerto, *Argentina* L12–337 **103**
Vendee, dep., *France* N10+467 **54**
Vendôme, *France* M84+478 **54**
Venendaal, *Netherlands* M57+520 **44**
Veneto, reg., *Italy* M16+454 **56**
Venezia, & G. di, *Italy* M16+454 **56**
Venezuela, rep., *S. America* **104**
Venezuela, G. de, *Venezuela* S66+115 **104**
Vengurla, *India* H08+159 **70**
Venice. *See* Venezia
Venlo, *Netherlands* M53+514 **44**
Vennacher, L., *Scotland* N26+562 **41**
Venraij, *Netherlands* M54+515 **44**
Ventotene, I., *Italy* M04+408 **57**
Ventspils, *U.S.S.R.* L50+574 **47**
Ventura, *California* V86+343 **92**
Venus B.. *Australia* C26–388 **109**
Vera, *Argentina* S02–294 **103**
Vera, *Spain* N11+372 **53**
Veracuz and state, *Mexico* U37+191 **100**
Veramin, *Iran* J49+354 **75**
Veraval, *India* H28+209 **70**
Verbania, *Switzerland* M39+460 **45**
Vercelli, *Italy* M39+453 **56**
Verde, C., *See* Vert, C.
Verde R., *Arizona* V40+338 **94**
Verdun, *France* M58+491 **54**
Verdun, *Quebec* S85+455 **91**
Vereshchagino, *U.S.S.R.* G15+641 **62**
Vereshchagino, *U.S.S.R.* J31+581 **61**
Vereya. *U.S.S.R.* K54+553 **61**
Verga C., *Guinea* N88+104 **80**
Vergara, *Uruguay* R53–329 **103**
Vergennes, *Vermont* S79+441 **91**
Verin, *Spain* N44+419 **52**
Verkhne Imbatskoe, *U.S.S.R.* G12+632 **62**
Verkhne Uralsk, *U.S.S.R.* J06+538 **61**
Verkhne Vilyuysk, *U.S.S.R.* D88+633 **63**
Verkhoturye, *U.S.S.R.* H67+589 **62**
Verkhoyansk, *U.S.S.R.* D09+672 **63**
Verkhoyanskiy Khr., *U.S.S.R.* D30+650 **63**
Vermilion, *S. Dakota* U42+428 **93**

Vermilion B., *Louisiana* U12+296 **95**
Vermont, state, *U.S.A.* S80+437 **99**
Vernal, *Utah* V28+404 **94**
Verneuil, *France* M86+487 **54**
Vernon, *British Columbia* V85+503 **88**
Veroia, *Greece* L47+405 **59**
Verona, *Italy* M24+454 **56**
Vernon, *Texas* U55+342 **95**
Verrieres, les, *Switzerland* M51+469 **45**
Versailles, *France* M77+488 **54**
Versailles, *Kentucky* T59+381 **97**
Versam, *Switzerland* M34+468 **45**
Vert, C., *Senegal* P16+148 **80**
Verte, I., *Quebec* S57+480 **90**
Vertrijk, *Belgium* M61+508 **44**
Verviers, *Belgium* M55+506 **44**
Vervins, *France* M66+498 **54**
Vesanto, *Finland* L21+629 **46**
Vesoul, *France* M53+476 **54**
Vessem, *Netherlands* M58+514 **44**
Vest Fd., *Norway* M06+678 **46**
Vesta, *Costa Rica* T48+097 **101**
Vesterålen. Is., *Norway* M00+693 **46**
Vest Vägøy, *Norway* M06+682 **46**
Vesyegonsk, *U.S.S.R.* K47+587 **60**
Veszprem, *Hungary* L73+471 **49**
Vetluga, *U.S.S.R.* J85+579 **61**
Vetluga, R., *U.S.S.R.* J89+573 **62**
Veurne, *Belgium* M74+511 **44**
Vevey, *Switzerland* M49+465 **45**
Vex, *Switzerland* M46+462 **45**
Viacha, *Bolivia* S50–166 **104**
Viana, *Brazil* Q88–031 **105**
Viborg, *Denmark* M34+564 **47**
Vibo Valentia, *Italy* L83+387 **57**
Vicente de la Barquera, S.,
  Spain N26+434 **52**
Vicenza, *Italy* M21+455 **56**
Vich, *Spain* M76+419 **53**
Vichuquen, *Chile* S72–348 **103**
Vichy, *France* M69+461 **54**
Vicksburg, *Mississippi* U06+324 **97**
Vicosa, *Brazil* Q66–036 **105**
Victor Harbour, *S. Australia* C69–356 **109**
Victoria, *Argentina* S01–325 **103**
Victoria, *British Columbia* W20+485 **88**
Victoria, *Hong Kong* E34+220 **64**
Victoria, *Texas* U42+288 **94**
Victoria, state, *Australia* — **111**
Victoria Falls, *Zimbabwe* L24–178 **84**
Victoria I., *N.-W. Territories* V30+710 **88**
Victoria L., *New S. Wales* C52–340 **109**
Victoria L., *Uganda, etc.* K70–010 **83**
Victoria Ld., *Antarctica* B30–740 **27**
Victoria Mt., *Burma* F67+214 **71**
Victoria, Mt.,
  Papua New Guinea C17–088 **111**
Victoria, R., *N.Terr., Aust.* D26–154 **110**
Victoria do Mearim, *Brazil* Q87–034 **105**
Victoria Point, *Burma* F39+100 **71**
Victoria River Downs
  N. Territory, Australia D14–162 **110**
Victoriaville, *Quebec* S72+461 **91**
Victoria West, *South Africa* L42–314 **84**
Victorica, *Argentina* S32–361 **103**
Vicuna, *Chile* S64–300 **103**
Vidago, *Portugal* N45+417 **52**
Vidin, *Bulgaria* L43+440 **58**
Viedma, *Argentina* S18–407 **103**
Viedma, L., *Argentina* S74–496 **103**
Vienna (Wien), *Austria* L82+482 **49**
Vienne, *France* M61+455 **54**
Vienne, dep., *France* M88+465 **54**
Vienne R., *France* M87+471 **54**
Vientiane, *Laos* F15+180 **69**
Vieques, I. de, *West Indies* S32+182 **101**
Vierlingsbeek, *Netherlands* M54+516 **44**
Vierwaldstatter See, *Switz.* M39+470 **45**
Vierzon Ville, *France* M78+472 **54**
Vietnam *S.E.Asia* E70+195 **69**

Vigan, *Philippines* D87+176 **65**
Vigan, le, *France* M68+440 **55**
Vigia, *Brazil* R19–008 **105**
Vigia Chico, *Mexico* T74+197 **100**
Vigo & R., *Spain* N52+422 **52**
Vigrestad, *Norway* M56+585 **47**
Vihanti, *Finland* L30+645 **46**
Vijayanagar, *India* G80+154 **70**
Vijayavada, *India* G56+165 **70**
Vijosë R., *Albania* L62+406 **59**
Vikaviskis, *U.S.S.R.* L42+546 **47**
Vikna, *Norway* M24+649 **46**
Vila Arriage, *Angola* M10–146 **82**
Vila de Cangombe, *Angola* L60–144 **82**
Vila de João Belo, *Mozamb.* K68-252 **84**
Vila Lugela, *Mozambique* K48-170 **84**
Vila Luso, *Angola* L60-120 **82**
Vila Machado, *Mozambique* K64-194 **84**
Vila Manica, *Mozambique* K72-190 **84**
Vilanculos, *Mozambique* K58-220 **84**
Vilani, *U.S.S.R.* L18+566 **47**
Vila Nova de Famalicão,
  Portugal N51+414 **52**
Vila Nova de Gerveira, *Port.* N52+419 **52**
Vila Pereira de Eça, *Angola* L86–172 **84**
Vila Pery, *Mozambique* K70–194 **84**
Vila Real, *Portugal* N47+413 **52**
Vilar Formoso, *Portugal* N41+406 **52**
Vila Serpa Pinto, *Angola* N80–146 **82**
Vila Velha de Rodao, *Port.* N46+397 **52**
Vila Verissimo, *Angola* L56–082 **82**
Vila Viçosa, *Portugal* N44+388 **52**
Vilcheka, Os., *Arctic Ocean* H85+807 **62**
Vilhelmina, *Sweden* M06+646 **46**
Vilhena, *Brazil* S01–126 **104**
Viljandi, *U.S.S.R.* L26+584 **47**
Villa Angela, *Argentina* S04–275 **103**
Villa Bella, *Bolivia* S32–105 **104**
Villa Bens, *Morocco* N81 + 274 **80**
Villa Bittencourt, *Brazil* S56–015 **104**
Villablino, *Spain* N38+430 **52**
Villacañas, *Spain* N20+396 **52**
Villacarriedo, *Spain* N22+432 **52**
Villach, *Austria* M07+465 **48**
Villa Cisneros, *See* Dakhla
Villa Constitucion, *Argentina* S02–332 **103**
Villa del Rosario, *Paraguay* R73–245 **103**
Villa de Rosario, *Argentina* S22–316 **103**
Villa Dolores, *Argentina* S31–319 **103**
Villafranca, *Spain* N41+426 **52**
Villafranca del Cid, *Spain* N02+404 **53**

Villafranca del Panadés. *Sp.* M80+413 **53**
Villaguay, *Argentina* R84–319 **103**
Villa Guillermina, *Argentina* R87–282 **103**
Villa Hermosa, *Mexico* U18+179 **100**
Villa Hidalgo, *Mexico* U87+261 **100**
Villa Iris, *Argentina* S20–382 **103**
Villa Jordão, *Brazil* S73–095 **104**
Villajoyosa, *Spain* N01+385 **53**
Villalba, *Spain* N46+432 **52**
Villaldama, *Mexico* U62+264 **100**
Villalón de Campos, *Spain* N30+421 **52**
Villalonga, *Argentina* S16–400 **103**
Villalpando, *Spain* N33+419 **52**
Villa Maria, *Argentina* S20–324 **103**
Villa Mercedes, *Argentina* S33–336 **103**
Villa Montes, *Bolivia* S21–212 **104**
Villa Murtinho, *Brazil* S32–104 **104**
Villanueva de Cordoba, *Sp.* N28+383 **52**
Villa Nova, *Brazil* R77–068 **105**
Villa Nova, *Brazil* Q39–104 **105**
Villanova, *Greece* L11+364 **59**
Villa Novo, *Brazil* R41–012 **105**
Villanueva-de-la-Serena, *Sp.* N35+390 **52**
Villanueva-y Geltrú, *Spain* M81+413 **53**
Villaodrid, *Spain* N43+433 **52**
Villaputzu, *Sardinia* M33+395 **57**
Villarcayo, *Spain* N21+429 **52**
Villareal, *Spain* N01+399 **53**
Villarrica, *Chile* S74–392 **103**
Villarrica, *Paraguay* R68–257 **103**
Villarrobledo, *Spain* N16+393 **53**
Villa Sanjurjo, *Morocco* N28+352 **80**
Villavicencio, *Colombia* S76+040 **104**
Villaviciosa, *Spain* N32+435 **52**
Villa Viejo, *Colombia* T02+030 **104**
Villazon, *Bolivia* S34–220 **104**
Villefort, *France* M67+444 **55**
Villefranche-de-Rouergue,
  France M78+443 **55**
Ville Marie, *Quebec* T27+473 **91**
Villena, *Spain* N05+386 **53**
Villeneuve-sur-Lot, *France* M86+444 **55**
Villeurbanne, *France* M61+458 **54**
Villingen, *W. Germany* M39+481 **48**
Villisca, *Iowa* U30+409 **95**
Villo-Duca-Abruzzi, *Somalia* J86+026 **83**
Villupuram, *India* G62+121 **70**
Vilnius (Vilna), *Lithuania* L28+546 **47**
Vilvoorde, *Belgium* M63+509 **44**
Vilyui, R., *U.S.S.R.* E30+670 **63**
Vimioso, *Portugal* N39+417 **52**
Vimperk, *Czechoslovakia* M08+490 **48**
Viña del Mar, *Chile* S70–330 **103**
Vinai Haven I., *Maine* S53+441 **90**
Vinaroz, *Spain* M87+405 **53**
Vincennes, *Indiana* T75+386 **95**
Vinchiaturo, *Italy* M02+415 **57**
Vindel Alv, *Sweden* L70+651 **46**
Vindhya Ra., *India* G80+222 **70**
Vineland, *New Jersey* T00+395 **96**
Vineyard Sd., *Massachusetts* S64+414 **96**
Vinh, *Vietnam* E86 + 187 **69**
Vinh Loi, *Vietnam* E85 + 093 **69**
Vinita, *Oklahoma* U32+366 **95**
Vinkovci, *Yugoslavia* L67+453 **58**
Vinnitsa, *Ukraine* L10+492 **60**
Vintes, *Ecuador* T28–015 **104**
Vinton, *Iowa* U12+422 **95**
Viransehir. *Turkey* K31+374 **74**
Virden, *Manitoba* U65+498 **88**
Virgin Is., *West Indies* S28+185 **101**
Virginia, *Ireland, Rep.* N42+538 **42**
Virginia, *Minnesota* U15+475 **93**
Virginia, state, *U.S.A.* T27+374 **99**
Virginia City, *Montana* V42+452 **93**
Virginia Falls, *N.-W. Terr.* W32+616 **88**
Viroqua, *Wisconsin* U05+436 **91**
Virovitica, *Yugoslavia* L76+458 **58**
Virpazar, *Yugoslavia* L65+423 **58**
Virtasalmi, *Finland* L15+621 **46**
Virton, *Belgium* M57+496 **44**
Virtsu, *Estonia* L39+586 **47**
Viru, *Peru* T22–084 **104**
Vis, I., *Yugoslavia* L83+430 **56**
Visalia, *California* V86+363 **92**
Visby, *Gotland, Sweden* L70+577 **47**
Viscount Melville Sd.,
  N.-W. Territories V30+732 **88**
Visé. *Belgium* M56+507 **44**
Viseu, *Portugal* N47+407 **52**
Vishakhapatnam, *India* G40+177 **71**
Viški, *Latvia* L19+561 **47**
Viso, Mte., *Italy* M48+447 **56**
Visoko, *Yugoslavia* L71+440 **82**
Visp, *Switzerland* M43+463 **45**
Vista Alegre, *Brazil* S06+017 **104**
Vistula (Wisla), R., *Poland* L50+515 **49**
Vitebsk, *Byelorussia* K89+551 **60**
Viterbo, *Italy* M17+424 **56**
Vitigudino, *Spain* N38+410 **52**
Viti Levu, I., *Fiji* A10–177 **106**
Vitim, R., *U.S.S.R.* E40+590 **63**
Vitoria, *Brazil* Q62–203 **105**
Vitoria, *Spain* N16+429 **53**
Vitry-le-François, *France* M62+487 **54**
Vitteaux, *France* M63+474 **54**
Vittoria, *Sicily* M03+369 **57**
Viver, *Spain* N04+399 **53**
Vivero, *Spain* N45+434 **52**
Vivi, *U.S.S.R.* F41+640 **63**
Vivonne & B., *S. Australia* C77–359 **109**
Vivorata, *Argentina* R76–378 **103**
Vizeu, *Brazil* R07–012 **105**
Vizianagram, *India* G39+181 **71**
Vizirul Romania L14+449 **58**
Vizovice, *Czechoslovakia* L73+492 **49**
Vizzini, *Sicily* M02+372 **57**
Vlaanderen, Oost, *Belgium* M68+509 **44**
Vlaanderen, West, *Belgium* M72+510 **44**
Vlaardingen, *Netherlands* M64+519 **44**
Vladimir, *U.S.S.R.* K28+561 **60**
Vladimirovka, *U.S.S.R.* J83+484 **61**
Vladivostok, *U.S.S.R.* D18+430 **63**
Vlieland I., *Netherlands* M60+533 **44**
Vlissingen, *Netherlands* M69+514 **44**
Vlone, *Albania* L63+405 **59**
Vltava R., *Czechoslovakia* M03+504 **48**
Voghera, *Italy* M36+450 **56**
Vohemar, *Madagascar* J60–134 **83**
Vöhma, *Estonia* L27+586 **47**
Voi, *Kenya* K38–034 **83**

Voiotia, *Greece* L39+382 **59**
Voiron, *France* M57+452 **54**
Voitsberg, *Austria* L89+470 **48**
Voiviis, L., *Greece* L43+395 **59**
Vojvodina, *Yugoslavia* L60+454 **58**
Volcano B., *Japan* C56+424 **68**
Volga, R., *U.S.S.R.* J85+477 **62**
Volgograd, *U.S.S.R.* K04+487 **61**
Volissos, *Greece* L24+385 **59**
Volkhov, R., *U.S.S.R.* K78+596 **60**
Volochanka, *U.S.S.R.* F64+710 **63**
Volochisk, *Ukraine* L23+495 **60**
Vologda, *U.S.S.R.* K32+592 **60**
Volokolamsk, *U.S.S.R.* K54+561 **60**
Volozhin, *Byelorussia* L22+541 **60**
Volsk, *U.S.S.R.* K60+595 **60**
Volsk, *U.S.S.R.* J75+521 **61**
Volta R., *Ghana* M88+060 **80**
Voltveti, *Estonia* L30+582 **47**
Vonêche, *Belgium* M60+501 **44**
Voorburg, *Netherlands* M64+521 **44**
Voorschoten, *Netherlands* M63+521 **44**
Voorst, *Netherlands* M53+522 **44**
Voorthuizen, *Netherlands* M56+522 **44**
Vopnafjordhur, *Iceland* N88+658 **46**
Vorab, mt., *Switzerland* M35+469 **45**
Vorarlberg, *Austria* M31+472 **48**
Vorauen, *Switzerland* M36+470 **45**
Vorkuta, *U.S.S.R.* H67+674 **62**
Vormsi, I., *Estonia* L40+590 **47**
Voronezh, *U.S.S.R.* K35+517 **60**
Voroshilovgrad, *Ukraine* K34+486 **60**
Vosges, dep. & mts., *France* M50+482 **54**
Voss, *Norway* M51+606 **47**
Vostock I., *Pacific Ocean* Y15–100 **107**
Votkinsk, *U.S.S.R.* J36+570 **61**
Voulijoki, *Finland* L18+642 **46**
Vouvry, *Switzerland* M49+463 **45**
Vouziers, *France* M62+493 **54**
Voxna, *Sweden* L86+613 **47**
Voyampolka, *U.S.S.R.* B33+584 **63**
Voznesensk *U.S.S.R.* K82+475 **60**
Vrancv, *Czechoslovakia* L50+489 **49**
Vrangelya, Ostrov, I., *U.S.S.R.* A00+718 **63**
Vranje, *Yugoslavia* L49+425 **58**
Vratsa, *Bulgaria* L39+432 **58**
Vrbitsa, *Bulgaria* L20+430 **58**
Vrchovina Českomoravska.
  Czechoslovakia L84+495 **49**
Vredefort, *O.F.S.* L16–270 **84**
Vrin, *Switzerland* M36+467 **45**
Vrindaban, *India* G73+276 **73**
Vroomshoop, *Netherlands* M51+524 **44**
Vršac, *Yugoslavia* L52+451 **58**
Vrútky, *Czechoslovakia* L67+491 **49**
Vryburg, *Cape Province* L32–270 **84**
Vučitrn, *Yugoslavia* L54+428 **58**
Vukovar, *Yugoslavia* L66+454 **58**
Vulcan, *Missouri* U04+374 **97**
Vulcano, I., *Italy* M00+384 **57**
Vulpera, *Switzerland* M28+468 **45**
Vyatka (Kirov), *U.S.S.R.* J62+586 **61**
Vyatka, R., *U.S.S.R.* J65+577 **62**
Vyazemski, *U.S.S.R.* D01+475 **63**
Vyazma, *U.S.S.R.* K63+551 **60**
Vyazniki, *U.S.S.R.* K17+563 **61**
Vyborg, *U.S.S.R.* L07+606 **60**
Vyrnwy, L., *Wales* N21+528 **38**
Vyrtsyarv Oz., *Estonia* L24+583 **47**
Vyru, *Estonia* L18+578 **47**
Vyshniy Volochek, *U.S.S.R.* K63+576 **60**
Vyskov, *Czechoslovakia* L78+493 **49**
Vytegra, *U.S.S.R.* K52+610 **60**
Wa, *Ghana* N14+102 **80**
Waalwijk, *Netherlands* M60+517 **44**
Wabash R., *Indiana* T76+392 **95**
Wabiskaw R., *Alberta* V55+568 **88**
Waboose Dam, *Ontario* T78+506 **89**
Wabos, *Ontario* T55+468 **91**
Wabra, *Saudi Arabia* J56+274 **74**
Wabuda, I.,
  Papua New Guinea C38–084 **111**
Waco, *Texas* U43+315 **95**
Wad, *Pakistan* H51+272 **70**
Waddamana, *Tasmania* C20–421 **109**
Wadden Zee, *Netherlands* M57+533 **44**
Waddington Mt., *B.C.* W33+513 **88**
Wadebridge, *England* N29+505 **38**
Wadena, *Minnesota* U31+464 **93**
Wadesboro, *N. Carolina* T31+350 **97**
Wad Hamid, *Sudan* K74+166 **81**
Wadi-es-Sir, *Jordan* K55+320 **76**
Wadi Gemal I., *Egypt* K60+246 **81**
Wadi Halfa, *Sudan* K82+216 **81**
Wadi Musa, *Jordan* K57+303 **76**
Wadi Medani, *Sudan* K70+144 **81**
Wafi, *Saudi Arabia* K07+249 **74**
Wageningen, *Netherlands* M56+520 **44**
Wager B., *N.-W. Territories* U00+654 **89**
Wagga Wagga, *N.S.W.* C16–351 **109**
Wagin, *W. Australia* E15–332 **110**
Wagoner, *Oklahoma* U34+360 **95**
Wahabis, *Saudi Arabia* K20+243 **74**
Wahla, *Saudi Arabia* K20+180 **74**
Wahoo, *Nebraska* U40+412 **95**
Waiau, *New Zealand* A41–426 **112**
Waichow. See Waiyeung
Waigeo, I., *New Guinea* D26–002 **65**
Waiheke I., *New Zealand* A29–368 **112**
Waihi, *New Zealand* A25+374 **112**
Waikaia, *New Zealand* A67–457 **112**
Waikare Moana, *N.Z.* A17–387 **112**
Waikari, *New Zealand* A44–429 **112**
Waikato, R., *New Zealand* A25–382 **112**
Waikerie, *S. Australia* C60–342 **109**
Waikouaiti, *New Zealand* A55–456 **112**
Waimakariri, R., *N.Z.* A46–434 **112**
Waimate, *New Zealand* A54–447 **112**
Waimes, *Belgium* M53+504 **44**
Wainfleet, *England* M89+531 **37**
Wainganga R., *India* G61+212 **70**
Waingapu, *Sumba I., Indon.* D89–096 **65**
Wainwright, *Alaska* Y60+705 **99**
Waipara, *New Zealand* A41–430 **112**
Waipawa, *New Zealand* A20–399 **112**
Waipukurau, *New Zealand* A20–400 **112**
Wairarapa, L., *New Zealand* A28–412 **112**
Wairau, R., *New Zealand* A40–416 **112**

Wairio, *New Zealand* A72–458 **112**
Wairoa, *New Zealand* A16–391 **112**
Wais, *Iran* J66+315 **74**
Waitara, *New Zealand* A34–390 **112**
Waitomo, *New Zealand* A29–383 **112**
Waiuku, *New Zealand* A32–372 **112**
Waiyeung, *China* E33+231 **67**
Wajir, *Kenya* K30+016 **83**
Wakamatsu, *Japan* C60+375 **68**
Wakasa B., *Japan* C86+357 **68**
Wakatipu, L., *N.Z.* A68–451 **112**
Wakayama, *Japan* C89+342 **68**
Wakba, *Jordan* K54+303 **74**
Wake I., *Pacific Ocean* A80+192 **106**
Wakefield, *England* N09+537 **37**
Wakonichi L., *Quebec* S84+501 **90**
Wakrah, *Qatar, Arabia* J51+252 **75**
Waksa, *Iraq* K07+308 **74**
Wakuan Hu, *China* E18+324 **66**
Walachia, *Romania* L24+448 **58**
Walbrzych, *Poland* L82+508 **49**
Walcha, *New South Wales* B81–310 **109**
Walcheren I., *Netherlands* M69+515 **44**
Wald, *Switzerland* M37+473 **45**
Waldia, *Ethiopia* K32+118 **83**
Waldoboro, *Maine* S56+441 **90**
Waldport, *Oregon* W24+444 **92**
Walen See, *Switzerland* M35+471 **45**
Walenstadt, *Switzerland* M34+471 **45**
Wales, *Great Britain* N20+524 **34**
Walgett, *New South Wales* C11–300 **109**
Walgreen Coast, *Antarctica* U50–720 **27**
Walhalla, S. *Carolina* T48+347 **97**
Walhalla, *Victoria* C21–379 **109**
Walker, *Minnesota* U28+471 **93**
Walker, L., *Nevada* V82+388 **92**
Walker's Ra., *Oregon* W10+434 **92**
Walkerton, *Ontario* T37+441 **91**
Walkerville, *Ontario* T48+424 **91**
Wallace, *Idaho* V65+475 **92**
Wallaceburg, *Ontario* T43+426 **91**
Wallal, *Western Australia* D85–198 **110**
Wallaroo, *S. Australia* C75–340 **109**
Wallasey, *England* N18+534 **37**
Wallaston, Mt.,
  N. Territory, Australia D15–166 **110**
Walla Walla, *New S. Wales* C19–358 **109**
Walla-Walla, *Washington* V80+461 **92**
Wallenpaupack, L., *Pa.* T01+414 **96**
Wallingford, *England* N07+516 **39**
Wallis L., *New South Wales* B76–322 **109**
Wallowa Mts., *Oregon* V74+452 **92**
Walney I., *England* N20+541 **37**
Walnut Cove, *N. Carolina* T31+363 **97**
Walsall, *England* N12+526 **37**
Walsenburg, *Colorado* U88+376 **94**
Walsoorden, *Netherlands* M66+514 **44**
Walterboro, *S. Carolina* T34+329 **97**
Waltham, *England* M87+518 **39**
Waltham, *Massachusetts* S67+424 **96**
Waltham, *Quebec* T12+459 **91**
Walton, *New York* T01+422 **96**
Walvis Bay, *Namibia* M02–230 **84**
Walwale, *Ghana* N04+104 **80**
Wamba, *Zaire* L12+020 **83**
Wamel, *Netherlands* M57+519 **44**
Wampsville, *New York* T04+430 **91**
Wana, *Pakistan* H33+323 **72**
Wanaaring, *New S. Wales* C35–297 **109**
Wanaka & L., *New Zealand* A65–445 **112**
Wanbi, *S. Australia* C58–348 **109**
Wandiwash, *India* G62+126 **70**
Wandre, *Belgium* M56+507 **44**
Wandsbek, *W. Germany* M30+536 **48**
Wan Fou Shan, *China* E32+292 **67**
Wanganella, *New S. Wales* C31–352 **109**
Wanganui & R., *N.Z.* A30–399 **112**
Wangaratta, *Victoria* C22–364 **109**
Wangyehmiao, *China* D77+460 **64**
Wanhsien, *China* E70+308 **66**
Wankie, *Zimbabwe* L28–184 **84**
Wanping, *China* E21+398 **66**
Wantage, *England* N08+516 **39**
Wanyuan, *China* E70+321 **66**
Wapeelo, *Iowa* U08+412 **95**
Wappapello Res., *Missouri* U02+370 **95**
Wapheton, *N. Dakota* U40+462 **98**
Wapiti R., *Alberta* V87+548 **88**
Warandab, *Ethiopia* K06+070 **83**
Warangal, *India* G62+180 **70**
Waratah, *Tasmania* C27–415 **109**
Waratah B., *Victoria* C24–388 **109**
Warburton, *Victoria* C26–378 **109**
Wardair, *Ethiopia* J89+068 **83**
Wardha & R., *India* G68+208 **70**
Ware, *England* N00+518 **39**
Waremme, *Belgium* M58+507 **44**
Warialda, *New South Wales* B86–296 **109**
Warka, *Poland* L53+518 **49**
Warmbad, *Namibia* L66–284 **84**
Warmbaths, *Transvaal* L10–250 **84**
Warm Springs, *Virginia* T28+380 **97**
Warnemünde, *E. Germany* M17+542 **48**
Warner L., *Oregon* V89+423 **92**
Warneton, *Belgium* M72+507 **44**
Warora, *India* G65+203 **70**
Warracknabeal, *Victoira* C45–363 **109**
Warragul, *Victoria* C25–382 **109**
Warrego, R., *New S. Wales* C28–296 **109**
Warren, *Arkansas* U13+336 **97**
Warren, *Illinois* U00+425 **91**
Warren, *Minnesota* U40+482 **93**
Warren, *New South Wales* C13–318 **109**
Warren, *Ohio* T35+413 **91**
Warren, *Pennsylvania* T25+418 **96**
Warrenpoint, *N. Ireland* N37+541 **42**
Warrensburg, *Missouri* U22+388 **95**
Warrenton, *Virginia* T17+387 **96**
Wellington, I, *Chile* T00–495 **103**
Warrenton, *Virginia* T17+387 **96**
Warri, *Nigeria* M56+056 **80**
Warrington, *England* N16+534 **37**
Warrnambool, *Victoria* C45–384 **109**
Warroad, *Minnesota* U32+489 **93**
Warroh, *Ethiopia* K12+086 **83**
Warrumbungle Ra., *N.S.W.* C03–313 **109**
Warsaw, *Indiana* T65+412 **91**
Warsaw, *New York* T19+427 **96**
Warsaw, *N. Carolina* T19+350 **97**
Warsaw. See Warszawa
Warszawa, *Poland* L54+523 **49**
Warta, *Poland* L68+517 **49**

Warta R., *Poland* L71+524 **49**
Wartburg, *Tennessee* T57+361 **97**
Warwick, *Queensland* B78–280 **111**
Warwick, *Rhode Island* S68+417 **96**
Warwick & co., *England* N09+524 **37**
Wasatch Mts., *Utah* V36+400 **94**
Waseca, *Minnesota* U20+440 **93**
Wasen, *Switzerland* M43+471 **45**
Wash, The, *England* M88+530 **37**
Washington,
  District of Columbia T12+389 **91**
Washington, *Indiana* T72+386 **95**
Washington, *Iowa* U10+413 **95**
Washington, *Missouri* U07+386 **97**
Washington, *New Jersey* T00+407 **96**
Washington, *N. Carolina* T12+355 **97**
Washington, *Ohio* T51+396 **91**
Washington, *Pennsylvania* T32+402 **91**
Washington, *Virginia* T19+387 **96**
Washington, state, *U.S.A.* W12+475 **98**
Washington I., *Pacific Ocean* Y60+048 **106**
Washington Ld., *Greenland* S00+800 **26**
Washington, Mt., *N.H.* S67+443 **91**
Washir, *Afghanistan* H66+321 **75**
Washuk, *Pakistan* H61+277 **70**
Wasmes, *Belgium* M67+504 **44**
Wassen, *Switzerland* M38+467 **45**
Wataroa, *New Zealand* A58–433 **112**
Watchet, *England* N20+512 **38**
Waterbury, *Connecticut* S78+415 **96**
Waterford, *New Brunswick* S32+457 **90**
Waterford (Port Láirge),
  Ireland, Rep. N43+522 **43**
Waterford Harb., *Ireland, Rep.* N42+522 **43**
Waterloo, *Belgium* M64+507 **44**
Waterloo, *Illinois* U01+384 **97**
Waterloo, *Iowa* U14+425 **95**
Waterloo, *Ontario* T33+435 **91**
Waterloo, *Quebec* S75+454 **91**
Watertown, *New York* T06+440 **91**
Watertown, *S. Dakota* U43+449 **93**
Watertown, *Wisconsin* T82+432 **91**
Waterville, *Maine* S58+446 **90**
Watervliet, *New York* S82+428 **96**
Waterways, *Alberta* V38+564 **88**
Watford, *England* N03+517 **39**
Watford City, *N. Dakota* U80+479 **93**
Watkins Glen, *New York* T12+424 **96**
Watlings I., *Bahamas, The* S88 + 240 **101**
Watonga, *Oklahoma* U51+358 **95**
Watou, *Belgium* M74+508 **44**
Watrous, *Saskatchewan* V02+513 **88**
Watsa, *Zaire* L02+028 **83**
Watseka, *Illinois* T76+408 **95**
Watson, *Utah* V24+398 **94**
Watsonville, *California* W11+369 **92**
Watt, *New Brunswick* S43+454 **90**
Watts Bar L., *Tennessee* T58+355 **97**
Wattsville, *Alabama* T67+336 **97**
Wau, *Papua New Guinea* C20–074 **111**
Wau, *Sudan* L12+078 **81**
Wauchope, *New South Wales* B74–315 **109**
Wauchula, *Florida* T41+276 **97**
Waukaringa, *S. Australia* C64–323 **109**
Waukegan, *Illinois* T77+424 **95**
Waukesha, *Wisconsin* T78+430 **95**
Waupaca, *Wisconsin* T85+444 **91**
Waupun, *Wisconsin* T82+436 **91**
Waurika, *Oklahoma* U48+342 **95**
Wausau, *Wisconsin* T88+450 **91**
Wautoma, *Wisconsin* T86+442 **91**
Wauwatosa, *Wisconsin* T79+431 **91**
Wave Hill, *N. Terr., Aust.* D24–175 **110**
Waveney, R., *England* M81+525 **39**
Waverley, *New Zealand* A30–399 **112**
Waverly, *New York* T09+420 **96**
Waverly, *Ohio* T48+392 **91**
Wavre, *Belgium* M62+507 **44**
Waxahachie, *Texas* U41+324 **95**
Waycross, *Georgia* T44+312 **97**
Wayland, *Ontario* T53+480 **91**
Wayne, *W. Virginia* 145+382 **97**
Waynesboro, *Georgia* T42+330 **97**
Waynesboro, *Pennsylvania* T16+398 **96**
Waynesville, *N. Carolina* T48+355 **97**
Waynoka, *Oklahoma* U54+366 **95**
Wazirabad, *Pakistan* H05+324 **72**
Weald, The, *England* M89+511 **39**
Wear, R., *England* N10+548 **37**
Weatherford, *Texas* U46+328 **95**
Weatherly, *Pennsylvania* T06+402 **96**
Weaver, R., *England* N16+532 **37**
Webb City, *Missouri* U26+372 **95**
Webbwood, *Ontario* T41+463 **91**
Webster, *S. Dakota* U45+453 **93**
Webster City, *Iowa* U22+425 **95**
Webster Springs, *W. Virginia* T33+385 **97**
Wechelderzande, *Belgium* M61+513 **44**
Weda B., *Halmahera, Indon.* D40+002 **65**
Weddell I., *Falkland Islands* S06–518 **103**
Weddell Sea, *Antarctica* Q00–700 **27**
Wedderburn, *Victoria* C39–364 **109**
Wedgeport, *Nova Scotia* S36+437 **90**
Wednesbury, *England* V12+526 **37**
Weed, *California* W14+414 **92**
Weedon, *Quebec* S68+458 **91**
Weedsport, *New York* T09+430 **96**
Weeping Water, *Nebraska* U37+408 **95**
Weert, *Netherlands* M56+512 **44**
Weesen, *Switzerland* M35+471 **45**
Weesp, *Netherlands* M60+523 **44**
Wee Waa, *New S. Wales* C04–302 **109**
Weichang, *China* E11+418 **66**
Weiden, *W. Germany* M17+496 **48**
Weifang, *China* E06+367 **66**
Wei-hai, *China* D78+374 **66**
Wei Ho, R., *China* E76+342 **64**
Weihwei. See Chihsien
Weilmoringle, *New S. Wales* C19–292 **109**
Weimar, *E. Germany* M22+509 **48**
Weipa, *Queensland* C48–130 **111**
Weinfelden, *Switzerland* M35+476 **45**
Weiser, *Idaho* V72+442 **92**
Wei Shan Hu, *China* E18+350 **66**
Weissenfels, *E. Germany* M18+512 **48**
Weisshorn, mt., *Switzerland* M44+461 **45**
Weissmies, mt., *Switzerland* M42+461 **45**
Weisstannen, *Switzerland* M34+470 **45**
Wejh, *Saudi Arabia* K51+263 **74**
Welch, *W. Virginia* T38+375 **97**

Weldon, *N. Carolina* T16+364 **97**
Welford, *Queensland* C38–251 **111**
Welland, *Ontario* T25+430 **91**
Welland, R., *England* N03+527 **37**
Wellesley Is., *Queensland* C63–164 **111**
Wellin, *Belgium* M59+501 **44**
Wellingborough, *England* N04+523 **37**
Wellington, *Kansas* U42+372 **95**
Wellington, *New S. Wales* C06–326 **109**
Wellington, *New Zealand* A31–413 **112**
Wellington, *S. Australia* C64–354 **109**
Wellington, I., *Chile* T00–495 **103**
Wellington L., *Victoria* C16–380 **109**
Wells, *Norfolk, England* M85+530 **39**
Wells, *Somerset, England* N16+512 **38**
Wells, *Nevada* V60+411 **92**
Wellsboro, *Pennsylvania* T14+418 **96**
Wellsville, *Missouri* U10+390 **95**
Wellsville, *New York* T18+421 **96**
Wels, *Austria* M06+482 **48**
Welsford, *New Brunswick* S38+455 **90**
Welshpool, *Wales* N19+526 **38**
Welwyn Garden City, *Eng.* N01+518 **39**
Wema, *Zaire* L50–006 **82**
Wembo Niama, *Zaire* L32–042 **82**
Wemyss Bay, *Scotland* N29+559 **41**
Wenatchee, *Washington* W02+474 **92**
Wenchow, *China* D86+280 **67**
Wenshan, *China* F04+236 **67**
Wensi, *China* E53+353 **66**
Wentworth, *New S. Wales* C48–341 **109**
Weobley, *England* N17+522 **38**
Wernhout, *Netherlands* M62+514 **44**
Werribee, *Victoria* C32–379 **109**
Werris Creek, *New S. Wales* B86–313 **109**
Wervershoof, *Netherlands* M59+527 **44**
Wervik, *Belgium* M72+508 **44**
Wesel, *W. Germany* M50+517 **48**
Wesenberg, *E. Germany* M12+532 **48**
Weser, R., *W. Germany* M36+526 **48**
Wessel Is., *N. Terr., Aust.* C81–112 **111**
Wesson, *Mississippi* U02+317 **97**
West B., *Louisiana* T75+291 **95**
West Allis, *Wisconsin* T79+431 **91**
West Barra, *Scotland* N08+601 **40**
West Bay City, *Michigan* T54+436 **91**
West Bend, *Wisconsin* T79+435 **91**
West Bengal, *India* G15+224 **71**
West Branch, *Michigan* T55+443 **91**
West Bromwich, *England* N12+525 **37**
Westbrook, *Maine* S62+437 **90**
Westbury, *Tasmania* C19–415 **109**
Westby, *New South Wales* C16–355 **109**
West Calder, *Scotland* N21+559 **41**
West Chester, *Pennsylvania* T04+399 **96**
Westerly, *Rhode Island* S71+413 **96**
Westende, *Belgium* M73+512 **44**
Western Australia, state, *Aust.* **110**
Western Samoa, *Samoa* Z60–150 **10**
Wester Schelde, *Netherlands* M67+514 **44**
Westfalen, *W. Germany* M42+518 **48**
Westfield, *Massachusetts* S76+421 **91**
Westfield, *New Brunswick* S38+454 **90**
Westfield, *New York* T28+420 **96**
Westfield, *Pennsylvania* T16+419 **96**
West Frankfort, *Illinois* T84+379 **95**
West Hartlepool, *England* N07+547 **37**
West Indies, *Caribbean Sea* S70+200 **85**
West Irian (Irian Barat), See Irian Jaya
West Linton, *Scotland* N20+557 **41**
West Lothian, co., See Lothian
Westmeath, co., *Ireland, Rep.* N45+535 **43**
Westminster, *Maryland* T12+396 **96**
Westmorland, co., See Cumbria
West Nicholson, *Zimbabwe* L04–212 **84**
Weston, *Sabah* E26+053 **65**
Weston, *West Virginia* T33+390 **91**
Weston-super-Mare, *England* N18+513 **38**
Westplains, *Missouri* U12+368 **95**
West Point, *Arkansas* U10+352 **97**
West Point, *Georgia* T61+329 **97**
West Point, *Mississippi* T82+336 **95**
Westpoint, *Nebraska* U40+418 **95**
West Point, *New York* S84+413 **96**
West Point, *Virginia* T11+375 **97**
Westport, *Ireland, Rep.* N57+538 **42**
Westport, *New Zealand* A50–417 **112**
Westport, *Ontario* T09+447 **91**
Westray I, & Firth, *Scot.* N18+593 **40**
West Riding, See West Yorkshire
West Union, *Iowa* U12+430 **95**
West Virginia, state, *U.S.A.* T40+384 **99**
Westwoud, *Netherlands* M59+527 **44**
West Yorkshire, *Eng.* N10+537 **37**
Wetar, I. & Str., *Indonesia* D52–080 **65**
Wetaskiwin, *Alberta* V50+532 **88**
Wetterhorn, mt., *Switzerland* M41+466 **45**
Wetumpka, *Alabama* T67+326 **97**
Wewoka, *Oklahoma* U40+352 **95**
Wexford & co., *Ireland, Rep.* N39+523 **43**
Wexford B. & Harb., *Ireland, Rep.* N37+523 **43**
Wey, R., *England* N03+514 **39**
Weybridge, *England* N03+514 **39**
Weyburn, *Saskatchewan* U83+497 **88**
Weymont, *Quebec* S83+479 **91**
Weymouth, *England* N15+506 **38**
Weymouth, *Nova Scotia* S36+444 **90**
Whakataki, *New Zealand* A22–408 **112**
Whakatane, *New Zealand* A18–380 **112**
Whale R., *Quebec* S44+574 **89**
Whale, R., Gt., *Quebec* T15+551 **89**
Whale, R., Lit., *Quebec* T08+555 **89**
Whales, B. of, *Antarctica* Z00–790 **27**
Whalsay, I., *Scotland* N06+604 **40**
Whangarei, *New Zealand* A34–358 **112**
Wharanui, *New Zealand* A35–419 **112**
Wharfe, R., *England* N09+539 **37**
Wharton, *Texas* U35+293 **95**
Wheatland, *Wyoming* V00+420 **93**
Wheatland Res., *Wyoming* V04+418 **93**
Wheaton, *Minnesota* U39+458 **93**
Wheeler Dam & L., *Alabama* T73+348 **97**
Wheeler Pk., *Nevada* V56+391 **92**
Wheeling, *W. Virginia* T34+401 **91**
Whetstone Buttes, *N. Dakota* U77+462 **93**
Whitbourne, *Newfoundland* R51+474 **90**
Whitburn, *England* N04+545 **37**
Whitby, *Ontario* T24+439 **91**
Whitchurch, *Salop, Eng.* N16+530 **37**
Whitchurch, *Hants, Eng.* N08+512 **39**

White B., *Newfoundland* R68+500 **90**
White L., *Louisiana* U14+298 **95**
White Mts., *New Hampshire* S68+443 **91**
White R., *Arkansas* U12+360 **95**
White R., *Indiana* T74+385 **97**
White R., *S. Dakota* U73+439 **98**
White R., *Utah, etc.* V24+400 **94**
White R., *Yukon* X32+632 **88**
White Cliffs, *New S. Wales* C42-309 **109**
White Earth, *N. Dakota* U77+484 **93**
Whitefish, *Montana* V58+483 **98**
Whitefish B., *Michigan* T59+469 **91**
Whitehall, *Michigan* T68+434 **91**
Whitehall, *New York* S80+435 **91**
Whitehaven, *England* N21+545 **37**
Whitehorse, *Yukon* X00+606 **88**
White Horse Hills, *England* N10+515 **39**
White Mark, *Tasmania* C13-401 **109**
White Pass, *Brit. Columbia* W88+596 **88**
White Plains, *New York* S83+410 **96**
White River, *Ontario* T61+488 **89**
White River, *S. Dakota* U65+435 **93**
White River Junction,
  Vermont S74+434 **99**
White Russia (Byelorussia)
  rep., *U.S.S.R.* L12+536 **60**
White Sulphur Springs,
  Montana V36+465 **93**
White Volta, R., *Ghana* N06+088 **80**
Whitfield, *Victoria* C22-368 **109**
Whiting, *New Jersey* S86+399 **91**
Whitley Bay, *England* N09+551 **37**
Whitney, *Ontario* T19+455 **91**
Whitney, Mt., *California* V80+366 **92**
Whittier, *California* V78+339 **92**
Whittlesea, *Victoria* C29-375 **109**
Whitton, *New South Wales* C23-345 **109**
Wholdaia L., *N.-W. Terr.* U86+604 **88**
Whyalla, *S. Australia* C75-330 **109**
Wiarton, *Ontario* T37+447 **91**
Wichita, *Kansas* U44+377 **95**
Wichita Falls & R., *Texas* U50+338 **95**
Wichita Mts., *Oklahoma* U54+347 **95**
Wick, *Scotland* N19+584 **40**
Wickliffe, *Missouri* T86+370 **95**
Wicklow & co., *Ireland, Rep.* N36+530 **43**
Wicklow Hd., *Ireland, Rep.* N36+530 **43**
Wicklow Mts., *Ireland, Rep.* N39+530 **43**
Widnes, *England* N16+534 **37**
Wielbark, *Poland* L54+534 **49**
Wielen, *Poland* L83+528 **49**
Wieliczka, *Poland* L60+500 **49**
Wielun, *Poland* L69+512 **49**
Wien, *Austria* L82+482 **49**
Wiener Neustadt, *Austria* L83+478 **49**
Wierzbnik, *Poland* L53+511 **49**
Wiesbaden, *W. Germany* M41+501 **48**
Wiesen, *Switzerland* M32+467 **45**
Wigan, *England* N16+536 **37**
Wight, I. of, *England* N08+507 **39**
Wigton, *England* N19+548 **37**
Wigtown, *Scotland* N27+549 **41**
Wigtown B., *Scotland* N25+548 **41**
Wijhe, *Netherlands* M53+524 **44**
Wijk, *Netherlands* M56+508 **44**
Wijk, *Netherlands* M58+520 **44**
Wil, *Switzerland* M36+475 **45**
Wilcannia, *New S. Wales* C41-316 **109**
Wildhorn, mt., *Switzerland* M46+464 **45**
Wildstrubel, mt., *Switzerland* M45+464 **45**
Wildwood, *Florida* T42+288 **97**
Wildwood, *New Jersey* S89+390 **91**
Wilhelmshaven, *W. Germany* M41+535 **48**
Wilkes Ld., *Antarctica* E20-690 **27**
Wilkes Barre, *Pennsylvania* T05+412 **96**
Wilkesboro, *N. Carolina* T37+362 **97**
Wilkin's Str., *Antarctica* S80-710 **27**
Wilkolaz, *Poland* L46+510 **49**
Willamette R., *Oregon* W19+449 **92**
Willcox, *Arizona* V29+323 **94**
Willemsdorp, *Netherlands* M62+517 **44**
Willemstad, *Curaçao I.* S53+121 **104**
Willemstad, *Netherlands* M63+517 **44**
William, Mt., *Victoria* C44-374 **109**
Williams, *Arizona* V43+352 **94**
Williams Pt., *North-West
  Territories* V68+688 **88**
Williamsburg, *Kentucky* T55+368 **97**
Williamsburg, *Virginia* T10+372 **97**
Williamsport, *Indiana* T74+403 **95**
Williamsport, *Pennsylvania* T13+413 **96**
Williamston, *N. Carolina* T13+358 **97**
Williamsville, *Missouri* U03+370 **97**
Willimantie, *Connecticut* S73+417 **96**
Williston, *Cape Province* L54-314 **84**
Williston, *N. Dakota* U82+481 **93**
Willmar, *Minnesota* U30+451 **93**
Willochra, *S. Australia* C71-322 **109**
Willow L., *N.-W. Territories* W07+620 **88**
Willow Creek, *Montana* V40+458 **93**
Willow Lake R., *N.-W. Terr.* W15+620 **88**
Willowmore, *Cape Province* L38-332 **84**
Willow Springs, *Missouri* U12+370 **95**
Wills Mt., *Pennsylvania* T22+399 **96**
Wilmette, *Illinois* T77+422 **91**
Wilmington, *California* V80+338 **92**
Wilmington, *Delaware* T03+397 **96**
Wilmington, *N. Carolina* T18+342 **97**
Wilmington, *S. Australia* C72-326 **109**
Wilnis, *Netherlands* M61+522 **44**
Wilno, *Ontario* T15+455 **91**
Wilson, *N. Carolina* T18+357 **97**
Wilson's Prom., *Victoria* C22-388 **109**
Wilsonville, *Alabama* T69+332 **97**
Willunga, *S. Australia* C69-353 **109**
Wiltshire (Wilts), co., *Eng.* N11+514 **39**
Wiluna, *W. Australia* D88-266 **110**
Wimbledon, *N. Dakota* U51+472 **93**
Wimmera, R., *Victoria* C47-368 **109**
Winburg, *Orange Free State* L18-286 **84**
Winchendon, *Massachusetts* S72+427 **91**
Winchester, *England* N08+511 **39**
Winchester, *Kentucky* T55+380 **97**
Winchester, *Ontario* T02+451 **91**
Winchester, *Tennessee* T69+352 **97**
Winchester, *Virginia* T19+392 **96**
Wind R., *Yukon* X00+654 **88**
Wind Cave Nat. Pk., *S. Dak.* U82+434 **93**
Windermere & L., *England* N18+544 **37**
Windhoek, *Namibia* L78-226 **84**
Windom, *Minnesota* U31+439 **93**

Wind River Pk. & Mts.,
  Wyoming V25+424 **98**
Windsor, *Colorado* V00+405 **94**
Windsor, *Connecticut* S76+419 **96**
Windsor, *England* N04+515 **39**
Windsor, *Missouri* U21+386 **95**
Windsor, *N. Carolina* T12+361 **97**
Windsor, *New South Wales* B86-337 **109**
Windsor, *Nova Scotia* S25+450 **90**
Windsor, *Ontario* T48+423 **91**
Windsor, *Quebec* S72+456 **91**
Windsor, *Vermont* S75+435 **91**
Windward Is., *West Indies* S06+138 **101**
Windward Pass., *West Indies* S84+200 **101**
Winfield, *Kansas* U42+372 **95**
Winfield, *W. Virginia* T41+385 **97**
Wingen, *New South Wales* B85-319 **109**
Wingene, *Belgium* M70+510 **44**
Wingham, *New South Wales* B77-319 **109**
Wingham, *Ontario* T38+439 **91**
Winisk R., *Ontario* T70+548 **89**
Winnebago, *Minnesota* U25+438 **93**
Winnebago L., *Wisconsin* T81+440 **91**
Winnemucca, *Nevada* V76+410 **92**
Winnemucca L., *Nevada* V86+400 **92**
Winner, *S. Dakota* U42+434 **93**
Winnett, *Montana* V20+470 **93**
Winnfield, *Louisiana* U16+319 **97**
Winnipeg, *Manitoba* U43+499 **88**
Winnipeg, L., *Manitoba* U45+526 **88**
Winnipegosis, *Manitoba* U60+514 **88**
Winnipegosis, L., *Manitoba* U60+530 **88**
Winnipesaukee, L., *N.H.* S68+436 **91**
Winnsboro, *S. Carolina* T37+344 **97**
Winona, *Minnesota* U10+441 **93**
Winscale, *England* N21+544 **37**
Winschoten, *Netherlands* M48+533 **44**
Winslow, *Arizona* V34+350 **94**
Winsted, *Connecticut* S78+419 **96**
Winston Salem, *N. Carolina* T32+361 **97**
Winter Ra., *Oregon* W09+430 **92**
Winterhaven, *California* V58+327 **92**
Winter Haven, *Florida* T39+281 **97**
Winterport, *Maine* S53+446 **90**
Winterset, *Iowa* U24+413 **95**
Winterswijk, *Netherlands* M49+520 **44**
Winterthur, *Switzerland* M38+475 **45**
Winton, *New Zealand* A69-462 **112**
Winton, *Queensland* C41-222 **111**
Wirksworth, *England* N09+531 **37**
Wirrabara, *S. Australia* C71-330 **109**
Wirral Pen., *England* N18+533 **37**
Wirrega, *S. Australia* C56-362 **109**
Wirt, *Minnesota* U23+478 **93**
Wisbech, *England* M89+527 **37**
Wisconsin, state, *U.S.A.* U07+447 **99**
Wisconsin R., *Wisconsin* T89+452 **91**
Wisconsin Rapids, *Wisconsin* T89+444 **91**
Wise, *Virginia* T46+370 **97**
Wishaw, *Scotland* N23+558 **41**
Wishek, *N. Dakota* U58+462 **93**
Wisla (Vistula), R., *Poland* L51+517 **49**
Wismar, *E. Germany* M22+539 **48**
Witham, R., *England* N02+532 **37**
Withlacoochee B., *Florida* T57+290 **99**
Witputs, *Namibia* L80-276 **84**
Witry, *Belgium* M56+498 **44**
Witten, *W. Germany* M46+515 **48**
Wittenberg, *E. Germany* M14+519 **48**
Wittenberge, *E. Germany* M19+530 **48**
Wittenoon, *Western Aust.* E09-213 **110**
Wittingen, *W. Germany* M26+527 **48**
Wittlich, *W. Germany* M15+532 **48**
Wittstock, *E. Germany* M15+532 **48**
Wivenhoe, *England* M84+518 **39**
Wloclawek, *Poland* L66+526 **49**
Wodonga, *Victoria* C19-361 **109**
Woerden, *Netherlands* M61+521 **44**
Wognum, *Netherlands* M57+526 **44**
Wohlen, *Switzerland* M40+473 **45**
Wokam, I., *Indonesia* D03-058 **65**
Wolbrom, *Poland* L61+504 **49**
Woleai, I., *Caroline Islands* C40+065 **106**
Wolfe I., *Ontario* T08+442 **91**
Wolfeboro, *New Hampshire* S67+436 **91**
Wolfe City, *Texas* U36+332 **95**
Wolf Point, *Montana* V04+481 **93**
Wolfsberg, *Austria* M01+468 **48**
Wolfville, *Nova Scotia* S26+450 **90**
Wolgast, *E. Germany* M08+540 **48**
Wolhusen, *Switzerland* M42+471 **45**
Wollaston, *England* N04+522 **39**
Wollaston Foreland,
  Greenland P28+740 **26**
Wollaston, Is., *Chile* S44-557 **103**
Wollaston L., *Saskatchewan* U80+584 **88**
Wollongong, *New S. Wales* B85-344 **109**
Wolseley, *S. Australia* C54-364 **109**
Wolstenholme, C., *Quebec* T15+621 **89**
Wolvega, *Netherlands* M54+529 **44**
Wolverhampton, *England* N13+526 **37**
Wolvertem, *Belgium* M64+509 **44**
Wolverton, *England* N05+521 **39**
Woman River, *Ontario* T46+475 **91**
Wonoka, *S. Australia* C70-317 **109**
Wonthaggi, *Victoria* C27-386 **109**
Wood R., *Saskatchewan* V12+500 **88**
Woodbridge, *England* M82+521 **39**
Wood Buffalo Park, *Alberta* V50+594 **88**
Woodburn, *New South Wales* B70-290 **109**
Woodbury, *New Jersey* T01+398 **96**
Woodford, *Newfoundland* R49+474 **90**
Woodlark I., *Papua New Guinea*
  B74+093 **111**
Woodroffe, Mt., *S. Australia* D23-264 **110**
Woods, L., *N. Terr., Aust.* D10-179 **110**
Woods, L. of the, *Ontario* U09+345 **68**
Woods Hole, *Massachusetts* S64+415 **96**
Woodside, *Utah* V32+392 **94**
Woodside, *Victoria* C19-385 **109**
Woodstock, *Illinois* T80+424 **95**
Woodstock, *New Brunswick* S45+461 **90**
Woodstock, *Ontario* T35+432 **91**
Woodstock, *Vermont* S75+436 **96**
Woodstock, *Virginia* T21+388 **96**
Woodsville, *New Hampshire* S72+441 **91**
Woodville, *New Zealand* A24-403 **112**
Woodward, *Oklahoma* U57+364 **95**
Wooler, *England* N12+555 **37**
Wooltana, *S. Australia* C64-305 **109**
Woolwich, *England* N00+515 **39**
Woomera, *S. Australia* C82-312 **111**

Woonsocket, *Rhode Island* S69+420 **96**
Woonsocket, *S. Dakota* U50+441 **93**
Worcester, *Cape Province* L64-338 **84**
Worcester, *England* N13+522 **37**
Worcester, *Massachusetts* S71+423 **91**
Worcester, co., *See* Hereford & Worcs.
Workington, *England* N21+546 **37**
Worksop, *England* N07+533 **37**
Workum, *Netherlands* M57+530 **44**
Worland, *Wyoming* V18+440 **93**
Worms, *W. Germany* M40+496 **48**
Worthing, *England* N02+508 **39**
Worthington, *Minnesota* U32+436 **93**
Worthington, *Ontario* T39+464 **91**
Wotho, I., *Marshall Islands* A85+100 **106**
Woudenberg, *Netherlands* M57+521 **44**
Woudrichem, *Netherlands* M60+518 **44**
Wounta, *Nicaragua* T51+135 **101**
Wour, *Chad* L86+212 **81**
Wouw, *Netherlands* M64+515 **44**
Wowoni, I., *Indonesia* D72-041 **65**
Wrangel I. *See* Vrangelya, Ostrov
Wrangell, *Alaska* W70+564 **99**
Wrangell, Mt., *Alaska* X62+616 **99**
Wrath C., *Scotland* N30+586 **40**
Wray, *Colorado* U74+400 **94**
Wrexham, *Wales* N18+530 **38**
Wright, Mt., *New S. Wales* C46-312 **109**
Wrightsville, *Georgia* T46+327 **97**
Wrightsville Beach, *N.
  Carolina* T17+342 **97**
Wrigley, *N.-W. Territories* W25+637 **88**
Wroclaw, *Poland* L78+511 **49**
Wroxham, *England* M82+527 **39**
Wuchang, *China* D46+449 **64**
Wuchang, *China* D34+305 **67**
Wuchow (Tsangwu), *China* E51+235 **67**
Wuchwan, *China* E51+411 **66**
Wudam, *Saudi Arabia* J15+238 **75**
Wuhan, *China* E32+304 **66**
Wuhing. *See* Soochow
Wuhsien. *See* Soochow
Wuhu, *China* E09+314 **66**
Wukang, *China* E56+268 **67**
Wukari, *Nigeria* M32+078 **81**
Wukiang, *China* E25+380 **66**
Wu Kiang, R., *China* E72+280 **64**
Wuntho, *Burma* F55+239 **71**
Wuppertal, *W. Germany* M47+513 **48**
Wurttemberg, *W. Germany* M36+485 **48**
Wurzburg, *W. Germany* M30+498 **48**
Wurzen, *E. Germany* M14+514 **48**
Wushih, *Hainan Island* E62+192 **64**
Wusiang, *China* E42+368 **66**
Wusih, *China* D88+316 **66**
Wusin, *China* E00+318 **66**
Wutai, *China* E14+377 **66**
Wutsin, *China* E00+318 **66**
Wuustwezel, *Belgium* M63+514 **44**
Wuwei, *China* F14+379 **66**
Wu Yi Shan, *China* E21+270 **67**
Wuyüan, *China* E70+411 **66**
Wuyuon, *China* D32+490 **64**
Wyalong, West, *New S. Wales* C17-339 **109**
Wyandotte, *Michigan* L49+422 **91**
Wyandra Res., *New South
  Wales* C06-339 **109**
Wye, R., *England-Wales* N16+520 **38**
Wyk, *W. Germany* M39+547 **48**
Wymondham, *England* M83+526 **39**
Wyndham, *New Zealand* A66-463 **112**
Wyndham, *W. Australia* D41-154 **110**
Wynne, *Arkansas* U05+352 **95**
Wynyard, *Tasmania* C26-410 **109**
Wyoming, state, *U.S.A.* V26+436 **98**
Wyong, *New South Wales* B82-333 **109**
Wyoming Pk., *Wyoming* V34+426 **93**
Wysokie Mazowieckie, *Poland* L45+529 **49**
Wyszkow, *Poland* L51+526 **49**
Wytheville, *Virginia* T37+369 **97**
Xanthi, *Greece* L31+412 **58**
Xanxere, *Brazil* R45-268 **103**
Xapuri, *Brazil* S52-107 **104**
Xenia, *Montana* V31+486 **93**
Xeró, *See* Peristera I.
Xibury, *Brazil* S43-053 **104**
Xilokastron, *Greece* L44+381 **59**
Xingu, *Brazil* S55-082 **104**
Yaan, *China* F11+300 **64**
Yaapeet, *Victoria* C48-358 **109**
Yaate, *Lebanon* K53+340 **76**
Yablonovy Khrebet Mts.,
  U.S.S.R. E50+510 **63**
Yabrud, *Syria* K50+339 **76**
Yackandandah, *Victoria* C17-362 **109**
Yacuiba, *Bolivia* S22-218 **104**
Yagvilidno, *U.S.S.R.* J21+558 **61**
Yakhtul, *Yemen* K10+135 **74**
Yakima, *Washington* W03+466 **92**
Yako, *Volta* N14+128 **80**
Yakoma, *Zaire* L46+038 **82**
Yaku Kaikyo, *Japan* D25+303 **68**
Yaku Shima, *Japan* D27+303 **68**
Yakutsk, *U.S.S.R.* D31+621 **63**
Yale, *British Columbia* W08+496 **88**
Yale, *Michigan* T47+432 **91**
Yalgoo, *W. Australia* E20-282 **110**
Yalinga, *Cent. Afr. Rep.* L40+065 **81**
Yallourn, *Victoria* C22-381 **109**
Yalogo, *Cent. Afr. Rep.* L78+054 **81**
Yalpunga, *New S. Wales* C48-289 **109**
Yalta, *U.S.S.R.* K64+446 **60**
Yalu, *China* D77+483 **64**
Yalu R., *China, etc.* D60+407 **64**
Yalung R., *China* F28+314 **64**
Yalutorovsk, *U.S.S.R.* H53+568 **62**
Yamada, *Japan* C79+345 **68**
Yamagata, *Japan* C58+382 **68**
Yamaguchi, *Japan* D21+342 **68**
Yamal, Pol., *U.S.S.R.* H30+715 **62**
Yamba, *New South Wales* B70-294 **109**
Yambol, *Bulgaria* L21+425 **58**
Yamdena I., *Indonesia* D22+077 **65**
Yamdok Tso, *Tibet* F85+290 **71**
Yamethin, *Burma* F52+204 **71**
Yampol, *U.S.S.R.* L10+483 **60**
Yampol, *U.S.S.R.* L23+499 **60**
Yamsk, *U.S.S.R.* B66+593 **63**
Yamuna R., *India* G58+260 **73**
Yanac, *Victoria* C51-361 **109**
Yanam, *India* G47+168 **71**
Yanaoca, *Peru* S69-143 **104**

Yancannia, *New S. Wales* C44-303 **109**
Yanco, *New South Wales* C22-346 **109**
Yanda, R., *New South Wales* C25-310 **109**
Yandoon, *Burma* F56+170 **71**
Yangchow, *China* E04+323 **66**
Yangihissar, *Sinkiang, China* G83+389 **72**
Yang-kao, *China* E38+404 **66**
Yangku. *See* Taiyuan
Yangtze Kiang, R., *China* E70+308 **66**
Yangyuan, *China* E34+401 **66**
Yankton, *S. Dakota* U44+429 **93**
Yannina. *See* Ioannina
Yantabulla, *New S. Wales* C30-294 **109**
Yaoundé, *Cameroon* M20+038 **81**
Yap, I., *Pacific Ocean* C70+093 **106**
Yapen I., *Irian Jaya, Indon.* C82+018 **65**
Yaraka, *Queensland* C36-248 **111**
Yarda, *Chad* L66+184 **81**
Yare R., *England* M81+526 **39**
Yarensk, *U.S.S.R.* J65+623 **62**
Yarim, *Yemen* K04+145 **74**
Yarkand, *Sinkiang, China* G77+384 **72**
Yarmouth, *I. of Wight, Eng.* N09+507 **39**
Yarmouth, *Maine* S61+438 **90**
Yarmouth, *Nova Scotia* S37+438 **90**
Yarmouth, Great, *England* M80+526 **39**
Yaroslavl, *U.S.S.R.* K30+576 **60**
Yarram, *Victoria* C20-385 **109**
Yarrawonga, *Victoria* C24-360 **109**
Yarrow, R., *Scotland* N18+555 **41**
Yartsevo, *U.S.S.R.* G00+602 **63**
Yarumal, *Colombia* T03+070 **104**
Yarylgach, *U.S.S.R.* K73+456 **60**
Yasanyama, *Zaire* L53+042 **81**
Yasin, *Kashmir* H10+364 **72**
Yasothon, *Thailand* F04+158 **65**
Yass & R., *New S. Wales* C07-348 **109**
Yatakala, *Niger* M88+146 **80**
Yathkyed L., *N.-W. Terr.* U35+630 **88**
Yatsushiro, *Japan* D26+325 **68**
Yatta, *Jordan* K59+314 **76**
Yatung, *Tibet* G06+274 **71**
Yauca, *Peru* S87-157 **104**
Yautepec, *Mexico* U54+188 **100**
Yavarete, *Colombia* S54-002 **104**
Yawata, *Japan* D25+388 **68**
Yazd, *Iran* J33+319 **75**
Yazdan, *Iran* H85+337 **75**
Yazoo City, *Mississippi* U02+328 **95**
Ybbs, *Austria* M00+482 **48**
Ye, *Burma* F43+153 **71**
Yea, *Victoria* C27-372 **109**
Yecla, *Spain* N07+386 **53**
Yecora, *Mexico* V22+288 **100**
Yéfira, *Greece* L44+407 **59**
Yefremov, *U.S.S.R.* K42+532 **60**
Yegros, *Paraguay* R68-265 **103**
Yehcheng. *See* Karghalik
Yehkiatsi, *China* E24+318 **64**
Yehpaishow, *China* E01+413 **66**
Yehsien, *China* E00+372 **66**
Yelabuga, *U.S.S.R.* J47+558 **61**
Yelan, *U.S.S.R.* K08+509 **61**
Yelatma, *U.S.S.R.* K20+550 **61**
Yeldyak, *U.S.S.R.* J20+556 **61**
Yelets, *U.S.S.R.* K39+526 **60**
Yelizarovo, *U.S.S.R.* H45+615 **62**
Yell, I. & Sd., *Scotland* N07+606 **40**
Yellandu, *India* G59+177 **70**
Yellow Mt., *New S. Wales* C19-327 **109**
Yellow R. *See* Hwang Ho
Yellow Sea, *China* D78+350 **66**
Yellowhead Pass, *Alberta* V80+532 **88**
Yellowstone L., *Wyoming* V32+440 **98**
Yellowstone Nat. Pk., *Wyo.* V34+447 **93**
Yellowstone R., *Montana, etc.* U86+473 **93**
Yellowtail Res., *Montana* V20+450 **93**
Yemanzhelinka, *U.S.S.R.* H82+548 **61**
Yemen, *Asia* K10+173 **74**
Yemen, South *Asia* J80+150 **74**
Yenakiyevo, *Ukraine* K41+482 **60**
Yenan (Fushih), *China* E63+366 **66**
Yenangyaung, *Burma* F60+204 **71**
Yenbo, *Saudi Arabia* K42+242 **74**
Yencheng, *China* D89+333 **66**
Yenchih, *China* F50+420 **64**
Yenchow. *See* Tzeyang
Yenda, *New South Wales* C23-343 **109**
Yenisei, R., *U.S.S.R.* G20+680 **62**
Yeniseysk, *U.S.S.R.* F78+583 **63**
Yeniseyskiy Zaliv, *U.S.S.R.* G60+724 **62**
Yenki, *China* D32+428 **64**
Yenki (Kara Shahr), *China* G22+421 **62**
Yenping. *See* Nanping
Yentai, *China* D82+375 **66**
Yeoval, *New South Wales* C08-328 **109**
Yeovil, *England* N16+510 **38**
Yeper, *Belgium* M73+508 **44**
Yeráki, *Greece* L44+370 **59**
Yerbogachen, *U.S.S.R.* E73+614 **63**
Yerevan, *Armyanskaya, U.S.S.R.* K03+402 **62**
Yeropol, *U.S.S.R.* A66+651 **63**
Yeshbum, *Yemen, South* J79+145 **74**
Yessei, *U.S.S.R.* F17+683 **63**
Yeste, *Spain* N14+384 **53**
Yesud ha Ma'ala, *Israel* K56+331 **76**
Yetman, *New South Wales* B86-289 **109**
Ye-u, *Burma* F57+228 **71**
Yeu, I. d', *France* N14+467 **54**
Yeungkong, *China* E48+217 **64**
Yevsyeevo, *U.S.S.R.* B69+673 **63**
Yeysk, *U.S.S.R.* K40+465 **62**
Yezd-i-Khast, *Iran* J47+316 **75**
Yhu, *Paraguay* R66-250 **103**
Yi, R., *Uruguay* R71-333 **103**
Yianisadhes Is., *Crete* L22+354 **59**
Yiannitsá, *Greece* L46+407 **59**
Yibna, *Israel* K62+319 **76**
Yidha, *Greece* L45+406 **59**
Yihsien, *China* E26+394 **66**
Yingchisa. *See* Yangihissar
Yingchow. *See* Fowyang
Yingchwan, *China* E82+385 **66**
Yinghsien, *China* E41+395 **66**
Yingkow, *China* D77+407 **66**
Yingtak, *China* E40+242 **67**
Yinkanie, *S. Australia* C58-343 **109**
Yioúra, I., *Greece* L32+376 **59**

Yithion, *Greece* L45+368 **59**
Yitu, *China* E09+367 **66**
Yiyang, *China* E46+287 **67**
Yocalla, *Bolivia* S36–192 **104**
Yochow. *See Yoyang*
Yogovsk, *U.S.S.R.* J22+576 **61**
Yogyakarta, *Java* E58+079 **65**
Yoho Park, *Brit. Columbia* V70+512 **88**
Yokkaichi, *Japan* C80+350 **68**
Yoko, *Cameroon* M16+056 **81**
Yokohama, *Japan* C62+354 **68**
Yokosuku, *Japan* C62+352 **68**
Yokote, *Japan* C57+393 **68**
Yola, *Nigeria* M16+092 **81**
Yonago, *Japan* D10+354 **68**
Yone Zawa, *Japan* C59+379 **68**
Yonkers, *New York* S83+409 **96**
Yonne, dep., *France* M69+478 **54**
York, *England* N07+539 **37**
York, *Nebraska* U46+408 **95**
York, *Pennsylvania* T11+400 **96**
York, *W. Australia* E19–319 **110**
York C., *Greenland* S50+760 **26**
York, C., *Queensland* C45–108 **111**
York R., *Virginia* T10+374 **97**
York Sd., *W. Australia* D58–150 **110**
Yorke Pen., *S. Australia* C74–346 **109**
Yorketown, *S. Australia* C75–350 **109**
York Factory, *Manitoba* U16+567 **89**
Yorkshire, North, co., *Eng.* N08+542 **37**
Yorkshire Moors, *England* N05+544 **37**
Yorkshire Wolds, *England* N03+540 **37**
Yorkton, *Saskatchewan* U75+511 **88**
Yorktown, *Virginia* T09+372 **97**
York Village, *Maine* S64+432 **90**
Yoro, *Honduras* T71+150 **101**
Yosemite Nat. Park. *Cal.* V88+379 **92**
Yoshkar Ola, *U.S.S.R.* J72+568 **61**
Youghal & Harb., *Ireland, Rep.* N47+519 **43**
Youghiogheny River Res.,
  Penn. etc. T27+397 **96**
Youkadouma, *Cameroon* M00+036 **81**
Young, *New South Wales* C10+343 **109**
Younghusband Pen., *S. Aust.* C64–360 **109**
Youngstown, *Ohio* T34+411 **91**
Yount Pk., *Wyoming* V30+440 **93**
Yoyang, *China* E40+294 **67**
Yozgat, *Turkey* K62+398 **74**
Ypres (Yeper), *Belgium* M73+508 **44**
Ypsilanti, *Michigan* T52+423 **91**
Yreka, *California* W16+417 **92**
Ysabel, I., *Solomon Islands* B35–080 **106**
Yssingeaux, *France* M65+451 **55**
Ystad, *Sweden* M07+555 **47**
Ytterhogdal, *Sweden* M01+622 **46**
Yüanchow. *See Chihkiang*
Yüanchow. *See Ichun*
Yüanling, *China* E58+285 **67**
Yubalia, *S. Australia* C58–336 **109**
Yubi C., *Morocco* N78+280 **80**
Yucamani, mt., *Peru* S60–170 **104**
Yucatan, state, *Mexico* T84+208 **100**
Yucatan Chan., *Mex.-Cuba* T66+216 **101**
Yugoslavia (Jugoslavia),
  Cent. Europe L70+440 **51**
Yuhsien, *China* E32+398 **66**
Yuhwan, *China* D82+282 **67**
Yukhnov, *U.S.S.R.* K59+548 **60**

Yukon Terr., *Canada* W80+610 **88**
Yukon, R., *Alaska* Y60+626 **99**
Yulin, *China* E62+383 **66**
Yuma, *Arizona* V58+329 **98**
Yuma, *Colorado* U76+401 **94**
Yumen, *China* F50+410 **63**
Yungchow. *See Lingling*
Yungera, *Victoria* C41–348 **109**
Yungfu, *China* E60+250 **67**
Yungki. *See Kirin*
Yungkia. *See Wenchow*
Yungnien, *China* E31+368 **66**
Yungning (Nanning), *China* E70+228 **67**
Yungning, *China* F25+277 **64**
Yungping. *See Lulung*
Yungshun, *China* E61+290 **67**
Yungsin, *China* E33+270 **67**
Yungsui, *China* E63+286 **67**
Yungtsi, *China* E59+349 **66**
Yunhsien, *China* E54+329 **66**
Yunsi, *China* E57+331 **66**
Yunta, *S. Australia* C63–326 **109**
Yurievets, *U.S.S.R.* K11+574 **61**
Yurimaguas, *Peru* T07–059 **104**
Yurlovka, *U.S.S.R.* J79+536 **61**
Yurmysh, *U.S.S.R.* H70+572 **61**
Yushu, *China* F50+332 **64**
Yütze, *China* E44+377 **66**
Yuyang, *China* E67+288 **67**
Yuyu, *China* E46+402 **66**
Yverdon, *Switzerland* M50+468 **45**
Ywathit, *Burma* F45+192 **71**
Zaachila, *Mexico* U41+168 **100**
Zaandam, *Netherlands* M61+524 **44**
Zabid, *Yemen* K11+141 **74**
Zabrze, *Poland* L67+504 **49**
Zacapa, *Guatemala* T88+149 **100**
Zacapoaxtla, *Mexico* U46+198 **100**
Zacatecas & state, *Mexico* U76+228 **100**
Zadar, *Yugoslavia* L89+441 **56**
Zadonsk, *U.S.S.R.* K36+524 **60**
Zafarabad, *Iran* J75+390 **74**
Zafarwal, *Pakistan* H01+323 **72**
Zafra, *Spain* N38+384 **52**
Zagazig, *Egypt* K80+306 **81**
Zagreb, *Yugoslavia* L84+458 **56**
Zahedan, *Iran* H84+295 **75**
Zahle, *Lebanon* K46+329 **76**
Zahran, *Saudi Arabia* K06+174 **74**
Zaidiya, *Yemen* K12+152 **74**
Zainsk, *U.S.S.R.* J47+553 **61**
Zaire, rep., *Cent. Africa* L50–050 **82**
Zaisan, *Kazakh.* G30+474 **62**
Zaječar, *Yugoslavia* L46+439 **58**
Zakho, *Iraq* K13+373 **74**
Zakin, *Afghanistan* H81+326 **75**
Zakinthos, I., *Greece* L56+378 **59**
Zakroczyn, *Poland* L55+498 **49**
Zákros, *Crete* L22+351 **59**
Zalău. *Romania* L42+472 **49**
Zalew Wiślany, *Poland* L62+544 **49**
Zalma, *Missouri* U01+370 **97**
Zambia, *Africa* L30–150 **84**
Zambezi R., *S.-E. Africa* K52–186 **84**
Zamboanga, *Philippines* D77+070 **65**
Zamora, *Ecuador* T22–042 **104**
Zamora de Hadalgo, *Mex.* U74+199 **100**
Zamora, *Spain* N34+415 **52**
Zandberg, *Netherlands* M48+529 **44**

Zandvoort, *Netherlands* M63+524 **44**
Zanesville, *Ohio* T42+399 **91**
Zangla, *Kashmir* G78+336 **72**
Zanjan, *Iran* J69+367 **74**
Zante. *See Zakinthos I.*
Zanzibar & I., *E. Africa* K34–062 **83**
Zapala, *Argentina* S61–388 **103**
Zapallar, *Argentina* R87–265 **103**
Zapata Pen., *Cuba* T40+223 **101**
Zaporozhye, *Ukraine* K59+479 **60**
Zara. *See Zadar*
Zaragoza, *Colombia* S89+074 **104**
Zaragoza, *Mexico* U57+241 **100**
Zaragoza, *Spain* N05+416 **53**
Zaragozo, *Mexico* U81+260 **100**
Zaraguro, *Ecuador* T25–036 **104**
Zarand, *Iran* J20+308 **75**
Zarasai, *Lithuania* L22+558 **47**
Zarauz, *Spain* N13+433 **53**
Zaraza, *Venezuela* S32+094 **104**
Zaria, *Nigeria* M44+110 **80**
Zarki, *Poland* L64+507 **49**
Zarnûqa, *Saudi Arabia* J61+250 **74**
Zarqa, *Jordan* K53+321 **76**
Zaruma, *Ecuador* T28–038 **104**
Zarzis, *Tunisia* M35+335 **81**
Zatec, *Czechoslovakia* M09+503 **48**
Zavitinsk, *U.S.S.R.* D33+500 **63**
Zawiercie, *Poland* L63+505 **49**
Zaysan, Oz., *Kazakh* G35+480 **62**
Zbaszyn, *Poland* L84+522 **49**
Zdunska Wola, *Poland* L66+516 **49**
Zealand, *New Brunswick* S41+461 **90**
Zealand. *See Sjaelland*
Zebak, *Afghanistan* H21+364 **75**
Zebdani, *Syria* K53+337 **76**
Zebid Qadhima, *Saudi Arabia* K35+224 **74**
Zeebrugge, *Belgium* M71+513 **44**
Zeehan, *Tasmania* C28–419 **109**
Zeeland, prov., *Netherlands* M67+515 **44**
Zeerust, *Transvaal* L24–256 **84**
Zegharta, *Lebanon* K55+344 **76**
Zeila, *Somalia* K10+112 **83**
Zeist, *Netherlands* M58+521 **44**
Zeitz, *E. Germany* M17+510 **48**
Zelaf, *Syria* K46+329 **76**
Zele, *Belgium* M66+511 **44**
Železná Ruda, *Czech.* M11+491 **48**
Zella, *Libya* L76+284 **81**
Zelman, *U.S.S.R.* J84+507 **61**
Zemio, *Cent. Afr. Rep.* L30+050 **81**
Zemun, *Yugoslavia* L57+448 **58**
Zenica, *Yugoslavia* L73+442 **58**
Zepce, *Yugoslavia* L72+445 **58**
Zermatt, *Switzerland* M43+460 **45**
Zernez, *Switzerland* M29+467 **45**
Zetland (Shetland), *Scot.* N07+604 **40**
Zevenbergen, *Netherlands* M62+516 **44**
Zeya, *U.S.S.R.* D47+537 **63**
Zeyma, *Saudi Arabia* K29+217 **74**
Zgierz, *Poland* L63+519 **49**
Zgorzelec. *See Görlitz.*
Zhdanov, *Ukraine* K44+471 **60**
Zhigansk, *U.S.S.R.* D70+667 **63**
Zhitomir, *Ukraine* L08+504 **60**
Zhmerinka, *Ukraine* L10+490 **60**
Ziarat, *Pakistan* H43+304 **70**
Ziba. *See Dhaba.*
Zidani Most, *Yugoslavia* L89+461 **56**

Ziemupe, *Latvia* L53+568 **47**
Zierikzee, *Netherlands* M66+516 **44**
Zijpe, *Netherlands* M66+517 **44**
Zikhron Ya'aqoy, *Israel* K60+325 **76**
Zile, *Turkey* K54+402 **74**
Zilfi, *Saudi Arabia* K02+262 **74**
Zilina, *Czechoslovakia* L67+492 **49**
Zima, *U.S.S.R.* F18+540 **63**
Zimapan, *Mexico* U56+207 **100**
Zimbabwe, *S.E. Africa* L00–200 **84**
Zinder, *Niger* M36+138 **81**
Zingst, pen., *E. Germany* M14+544 **48**
Zion Nat. Park, *Utah* V48+374 **92**
Zira, *India* H00+310 **72**
Ziraquira, *Colombia* S84+050 **104**
Zirc, *Hungary* L73+473 **49**
Zitacuaro, *Mexico* U63+193 **100**
Zittau, *E. Germany* M01+509 **48**
Zizers, *Switzerland* M32+469 **45**
Zlatoust, *U.S.S.R.* J02+551 **61**
Zmeinogorsk, *U.S.S.R.* G47+511 **62**
Znin, *Poland* L74+528 **49**
Znojmo, *Czechoslovakia* L84+489 **49**
Zoar, *Labrador* S19+558 **89**
Zofingen, *Switzerland* M42+473 **45**
Zoisa, *Tanzania* K50–058 **83**
Zolder, *Belgium* M58+510 **44**
Zollino, *Italy* L71+402 **57**
Zolotoye, *U.S.S.R.* J85+508 **61**
Zomba, *Malawi* K58–154 **83**
Zonguldak, *Turkey* K78+416 **74**
Zorita, *Spain* N34+393 **52**
Zoute, Het, *Belgium* M70+514 **44**
Zoutkamp, *Netherlands* M52+533 **44**
Zrenjanin, *Yugoslavia* L58+454 **58**
Zuara, *Libya* M18+328 **81**
Zuevka, *U.S.S.R.* J55+585 **61**
Zug & canton, *Switzerland* M39+472 **45**
Zuger See, *Switzerland* M39+471 **45**
Zuhab, *Iran* J85+347 **74**
Zuid Beijerland, *Netherlands* M64+518 **44**
Zuider Zee. *See IJsselmeer*
Zuidland, *Netherlands* M65+518 **44**
Zuid Natoena Eiln., *Indon.* E66+028 **65**
Zuidwolde, *Netherlands* M51+527 **44**
Zuila, *Libya* L88+262 **81**
Zukur, Jab., *Yemen* K13+140 **74**
Zula, *Ethiopia* K32+152 **83**
Zulfikar, *Afghanistan* H82+356 **75**
Zumbo, *Mozambique* K88–156 **84**
Zumpango, *Mexico* U54+198 **100**
Zundert, *Netherlands* M62+515 **44**
Zungeru, *Nigeria* M54+098 **80**
Zuni, Mt., *New Mexico* V18+352 **94**
Zürich & canton. *Switz.* M39+474 **45**
Zürich See, *Switzerland* M38+472 **45**
Zurzach, *Switzerland* M40+476 **45**
Zutphen, *Netherlands* M53+522 **44**
Zwai L., *Ethiopia* K38+078 **83**
Zwartsluis, *Netherlands* M54+526 **44**
Zweelo, *Netherlands* M50+528 **44**
Zweibrucken, *W. Germany* M47+493 **48**
Zweisimmen, *Switzerland* M46+466 **45**
Zwickau, *E. Germany* M15+507 **48**
Zwoleń, *Poland* L51+513 **49**
Zwolle, *Netherlands* M53+525 **44**
Zyrardów. *Poland* L57+521 **49**
Zyryanka, *U.S.S.R.* B85+645 **63**
Zyryanovsk, *Kazakh.* G35+498 **62**
Zyyi, *Cyprus* K70+347 **76**